A Concise Restatement of DONATIVE TRANSFERS and TRUSTS

Edited and Compiled by

THOMAS P. GALLANIS

Allan D. Vestal Chair in Law and Associate Dean for Research
The University of Iowa College of Law

A·L·I·

WEST ACADEMIC PUBLISHING

Printed in the United States of America.

ISBN: 978-0-314-25284-5

DIRECTOR'S FOREWORD

The American Law Institute's Concise Restatements provide a useful service to the profession. They condense multi-volume texts spanning thousands of pages into a single volume in a compact, convenient, and readily accessible format that is designed specifically for law students as an adjunct to their casebook and for others seeking an authoritative overview of a field. Concise Restatements are a wonderful way to introduce law students to the ALI's work and to have them focus on the role the Restatements of the Law play in our legal system. Our hope is that they will then be more sophisticated users of our work throughout their career.

The ALI has already completed three Concise Restatements. A Concise Restatement of Torts is in its third edition; originally compiled in 2000 by Professor Kenneth S. Abraham of the University of Virginia School of Law, it was revised and updated in 2010 and again in 2013 by Professor Ellen M. Bublick of the University of Arizona James E. Rogers College of Law. The second, A Concise Restatement of Property, was compiled in 2001 by Professor Lance Liebman of Columbia Law School, then the ALI Director. And the third, A Concise Restatement of the Law Governing Lawyers, was compiled in 2007 by Professor Vincent R. Johnson of St. Mary's University School of Law and Professor Susan Saab Fortney of Texas Tech University School of Law.

We are now launching the fourth project in this series: A Concise Restatement of Donative Transfers and Trusts, which combines portions of the Restatement Third of Property (Wills and Other Donative Transfers), completed in 2011, and the Restatement Third of Trusts, completed in 2012. For this undertaking, the ALI is very thankful to its Editor, Professor Thomas P. Gallanis of the University of Iowa College of Law, who served as an Associate Reporter on the latter project.

RICHARD L. REVESZ
Director
The American Law Institute

April 2017

DIRECTOR'S FOREWORD

[illegible]

EDITOR'S FOREWORD

The Restatements of Property and Trusts have greatly influenced the law of trusts and estates.

The Restatement Third of Property (Wills and Other Donative Transfers) was completed in 2011. Its principal drafters were its Reporter, Professor Lawrence W. Waggoner of the University of Michigan, and its Associate Reporter, Professor John H. Langbein of Yale University.

The Restatement Third of Trusts was completed in 2012. Its principal drafters were its Reporter, Professor Edward C. Halbach, Jr., of the University of California at Berkeley, and a team of Associate Reporters: in alphabetical order, Professors Thomas P. Gallanis of the University of Iowa, William M. McGovern of the University of California at Los Angeles, Jeffrey N. Pennell of Emory University, and Randall W. Roth of the University of Hawai'i.

Together, the Restatement Third of Property (Wills and Other Donative Transfers) and the Restatement Third of Trusts consist of seven volumes and more than 3,500 pages. This one-volume compilation contains the most important parts of these Restatements, but some editing choices had to be made. This book follows the editing conventions of A Concise Restatement of Torts, Third Edition (Bublick ed. 2013): deletions are noted by ellipses (three dots for deletions internal to a sentence and four dots for others); however, the deletion of an entire lettered Comment or an entire Illustration is not noted, because the Comment lettering and Illustration numbering are sufficient to alert readers to these deletions. Cross-references to now-superseded Restatement sections have been updated, where possible, by including the corresponding current Restatement reference in brackets.

For assistance in preparing this volume, I am delighted to thank my administrative assistant, Amanda Bibb, and my student research assistants: Matthew Blumenreich, Daniel McGrath, and Brian Page.

THOMAS P. GALLANIS
Iowa City, Iowa

April 2017

ABOUT THE AMERICAN LAW INSTITUTE

The American Law Institute was founded in 1923 following a study conducted by a group of prominent American judges, lawyers, and teachers known as "The Committee on the Establishment of a Permanent Organization for the Improvement of the Law."

The Committee reported that the two chief defects in American law—its uncertainty and its complexity—had produced a "general dissatisfaction with the administration of justice."

According to the Committee, the law's uncertainty stemmed in part from a lack of agreement on fundamental principles of the common law, while the law's complexity was attributed to the numerous variations within different jurisdictions of the United States.

The Committee recommended that a lawyers' organization be formed to improve the law and its administration. This led to the creation of ALI. The Institute's mission, as set out in its charter, is to "to promote the clarification and simplification of the law and its better adaptation to social needs, to secure the better administration of justice, and to encourage and carry on scholarly and scientific legal work."

ALI's incorporators included Chief Justice and former President William Howard Taft, future Chief Justice Charles Evans Hughes, and former Secretary of State Elihu Root. Judges Benjamin N. Cardozo and Learned Hand were among its early leaders.

The Institute's founding Committee recommended that the first undertaking should address uncertainty in the law through a restatement of basic legal subjects that would tell judges and lawyers what the law was. The formulation of such a restatement thus became ALI's first endeavor.

Between 1923 and 1944, Restatements of the Law were developed for Agency, Conflict of Laws, Contracts, Judgments, Property, Restitution, Security, Torts, and Trusts. In 1952, the Institute started the Restatement Second—works that covered subjects not included in the first Restatement, as well as new editions of the original Restatements that updated them and reflected new analyses and concepts. A third series of Restatements was inaugurated in 1987, and work on that series continues today. For some subjects, a Restatement Fourth has been launched.

The Institute also engages in the study of legal areas thought to need reform; the resulting recommendations for change in the law usually are published as Principles of the Law. Other Institute projects have resulted in the development of model statutory formulations, including the Model Penal Code and, in collaboration with the Uniform Law Commission, the Uniform Commercial Code.

The ALI's working method is to choose for each project one or more experts as "Reporters" and to subject each of their successive drafts to detailed review by a diverse group of "Advisers," designated by the Institute's Director based on their knowledge and experience, and by a special consultative group of interested Institute members. After appropriate revision, a draft is next submitted for review to the Institute's Council, a governing body of some 60 members drawn from the various branches of the legal profession, and then, as a "Tentative Draft," to the membership as a whole at the Institute's Annual Meeting, during which time it is also made generally available for public comment and review. When the project in its entirety has been approved by both the Council and the membership, the final, official text is prepared for publication.

The Institute's membership includes judges, practitioners, and law teachers from all areas of the United States as well as many foreign countries, selected on the basis of professional achievement and demonstrated interest in the improvement of the law. Ex officio members include the Chief Justice and Associate Justices of the Supreme Court of the United States, the Attorney General and the Solicitor General of the United States, the chief judges of the federal courts of appeals and the highest courts of the states, law school deans, and the presidents of the American Bar Association, state bar associations, and other prominent legal organizations.

SUMMARY OF CONTENTS

CONCISE RESTATEMENT OF WILLS AND OTHER DONATIVE TRANSFERS

CONCISE RESTATEMENT OF TRUSTS

SUMMARY OF CONTENTS

TABLE OF CONTENTS

CONCISE RESTATEMENT OF WILLS AND OTHER DONATIVE TRANSFERS

A Concise Restatement of DONATIVE TRANSFERS and TRUSTS

CONCISE RESTATEMENT OF WILLS AND OTHER DONATIVE TRANSFERS

INTRODUCTION

This Restatement presents a comprehensive treatment of the American law of wills, will substitutes, intestacy, gifts, present and future interests, and other matters generally considered to be within the topic, including the construction of donative documents. The coverage includes subjects treated in the Restatement of Property and the Restatement Second of Property (Donative Transfers), as well as subjects not previously covered in those Restatements.

Donative transfers are at the core of family estate planning. Family estate planning, however, calls for the application and utilization of many fields of law, fields such as federal and state tax law and corporate, partnership, contract, agency, and domestic relations law. The treatment of the law of donative transfers proceeds with these and other relevant fields in background. This Restatement covers the rules pertaining to the gratuitous disposition of family property and could, in tandem with the Restatement of Trusts, be labeled the Restatement of Family Property Law.

The organizing principle of the American law of donative transfers is freedom of disposition. Property owners have the nearly unrestricted right to dispose of their property as they please, either during life or at death. They may transfer property in trust or not in trust, may give the transferee outright or limited ownership, may divide the ownership into present and future interests, and may create powers that give the transferor, the transferee, or another the ability to affect the transfer in various ways.

Throughout this Restatement, references are made to the Original and to the Revised Uniform Probate Code (UPC or Code). The Original UPC was promulgated in 1969 by the National Conference of Commissioners on Uniform State Laws (Uniform Law Commission). Minor amendments were made to the 1969 version over the next two decades. The Uniform Law Commission undertook a major overhaul of Article VI of the Code in 1989 and of Article II in 1990. Article VI covers nonprobate transfers on death, and Article II covers intestacy, wills, and other donative transfers. A few minor amendments to the 1989–1990 version have been made in the years following 1990. The 1989–1990 period marks the division between the Original and the Revised UPC. References to the Original UPC are to the Code as promulgated in 1969 and as amended up to the 1989–1990 period. References to the Revised UPC are to the Code as it currently exists, i.e., as revised in 1989 and 1990 and as later amended.

This Restatement begins, in Division I, with probate transfers (transfers at death by will or intestacy). It then moves, in Division II, to nonprobate transfers (outright gifts and will substitutes). Division III covers a variety of protective doctrines, such as the requirement that a donor have capacity to make a donative transfer and be free from fraud and undue influence. Also covered among the protective doctrines are the spouse's forced share and related matters. Division IV concerns the construction, reformation, and modification of donative documents. Divisions V and VI turn, respectively, to class gifts and powers of appointment. Division VII covers present and future interests. Division VIII, the final portion, deals with social restrictions on the freedom of disposition, including the Rule Against Perpetuities.

DIVISION I

PROBATE TRANSFERS (WILLS AND INTESTACY)

Introductory Note: Division I addresses donative transfers taking place at death by testacy or intestacy. These transfers are commonly called probate transfers. Property that a decedent owns at death and that his or her estate acquires after death is generally used first to pay family, exempt property, and homestead allowances, claims against the decedent's estate, expenses of administration, and taxes levied against the estate. What is left is the decedent's net probate estate. Subject to overriding claims and rights provided by applicable law, such as the right of the decedent's surviving spouse to take an elective share or to elect other marital rights, the decedent's net probate estate passes to the decedent's devisees under the decedent's will or, in default of a valid will, to the decedent's heirs by intestacy.

Division I is organized into five chapters. Chapter 1 covers definitions and basic principles. Chapter 2 covers intestacy. Chapter 3 covers the execution of wills. Chapter 4 covers the revocation of wills, the revival of revoked wills, and the doctrine of ineffective revocation (generally known in the case law as dependent relative revocation). Chapter 5 addresses various topics concerning changes that can take place between the time that the testator executes a will and the time of death—ademption by extinction, ademption by satisfaction, antilapse statutes, and related matters.

CHAPTER 1

DEFINITIONS AND BASIC PRINCIPLES

§ 1.1. Probate Estate

§ 1.2. Requirement of Surviving the Decedent

§ 1.3. Noncitizens

Introductory Note: Chapter 1 is preliminary to the remaining chapters on probate transfers. The material in Chapter 1 is relevant to probate transfers in general, i.e., whether the transfer occurs by testacy or intestacy.

Chapter 1 contains three sections. Section 1.1 defines the probate estate. Probate transfers affect only the probate estate. Section 1.2 covers the requirement of surviving the decedent. Donative transfers cannot be made to deceased persons. Because probate transfers take place at the decedent's death, they cannot be made to persons who fail to survive the decedent. Section 1.3 reverses the archaic rule that a person who is not a citizen cannot transmit or receive property by devise or descent.

§ 1.1. Probate Estate

(a) A decedent's "probate estate" is the estate subject to administration under applicable laws relating to decedents' estates. The probate estate consists of property owned by the decedent at death and property acquired by the decedent's estate at or after the decedent's death.

(b) The "net probate estate" is the probate estate after deduction for family, exempt property, and homestead allowances, claims against the estate (including funeral expenses and expenses of administration), and taxes for which the estate is liable. Subject to overriding claims and rights provided by applicable law, such as the right of the decedent's surviving spouse to take an elective share or to elect other marital rights, the decedent's net probate estate passes to the decedent's heirs or devisees by intestate or testate succession.

Comment:

a. *Terminology.* As used in this Restatement, the term *probate estate* or *probate property* refers to assets subject to administration under applicable laws relating to decedents' estates, unless the context indicates that the term "probate" refers to the procedure of "probating" (proving) a decedent's will. To be subject to administration, the property must be owned by the decedent at death or acquired by the decedent's estate at or after the decedent's death. Property owned at death or acquired at or after death is commonly called probate property. . . . .

This Restatement uses the term *heirs* to refer to the persons who succeed to a decedent's net probate estate by intestate succession, and uses the term *devisees* to refer to the persons who succeed to a decedent's net probate estate by testate succession. . . . .

b. *Property owned at death.* In most cases, the major component of a decedent's probate estate consists of property that the decedent owned at death. . . . .

Property in which the decedent owned an interest immediately before death is not included in the probate estate if the decedent's interest expires upon death, although . . . such property might be part of the decedent's gross estate for federal estate tax purposes and might be subject to the spouse's elective share. Thus, property in which the decedent was a joint tenant or had a life estate is not included in the decedent's probate estate. . . . .

c. *Property acquired after death.* A decedent's probate estate may sometimes contain property that was acquired by the decedent's estate after the decedent's death. Such property includes property to which the decedent had a right at death, such as income derived from property that the decedent owned at death or payments under contracts that the decedent entered into before death. The estate may also include property acquired after death to which the decedent had no right at death, such as an employee bonus awarded after death. . . . .

d. *Property acquired at the instant of death.* A difficult question is whether property acquired at the instant of death is owned by the decedent *at* death or acquired by the decedent's estate *after* death. Although this question is relevant to certain questions of federal estate taxation, it is immaterial to the question of whether such property is part of the decedent's probate estate. Whichever category in which it properly belongs, it is probate property. . . . .

e. *Net probate estate.* The probate estate is liable for the payment of claims allowed against the estate (including funeral expenses and expenses of administration), taxes for which the estate is liable, and family, exempt property, and homestead allowances. The net probate estate is the probate estate reduced by these claims, taxes, and allowances. Subject to other overriding claims and rights provided by applicable law, such as the right of the decedent's surviving spouse to take an elective share or to elect other marital rights, the decedent's net probate estate passes to the decedent's heirs by intestate succession or to the decedent's devisees by testate succession. See Comment *a* for a discussion of the terms "heirs" and "devisees" as used in this Restatement.

f. *Abatement of devises and intestate shares to pay claims.* This Restatement adheres to the definition of "claims" in the Uniform Probate Code. As defined in UPC § 1–201(6), the term "claims," in respect to estates of decedents, includes liabilities of the decedent, whether arising in contract, tort, or otherwise, and liabilities of the estate arising at or after the death of the decedent, including funeral expenses and expenses of administration. The term does not include estate or inheritance taxes.

The decedent's creditors are entitled, within the time limits imposed by the controlling state law, to have their claims satisfied out of the decedent's probate estate. The decedent's creditors may also be entitled to have their claims satisfied out of the decedent's will substitutes, to the extent provided by applicable law. See, e.g., UPC § 6–215 . . . .

Claimants must assert their claims within a reasonable time after death or their claims will be unenforceable against the estate. Typically, statutory law specifies the time allowed creditors to assert their claims.

g. *Taxes.* Liability for the decedent's income taxes for the year of death and for the estate's income taxes falls on the decedent's probate estate, as do any other taxes owed by the decedent at death, such as federal gift taxes, local real estate taxes, and any other taxes incurred by the estate.

Probate transfers and certain nonprobate transfers are both subject to the federal estate tax. There are two views concerning liability for estate taxes. Under one view, liability falls entirely on the probate estate, except to the extent that state or federal law, or the decedent's will, provide otherwise. This Restatement rejects this view, and adopts the other view. The view adopted in this Restatement is that, unless the decedent's will provides otherwise, liability for estate taxes is "equitably apportioned," meaning that a proportionate part of the estate tax burden is placed on nonprobate assets that are includible in the taxable estate. . . .

h. Family allowance. Family allowance provisions vary from state to state. The Uniform Probate Code family allowance is designed to provide the surviving spouse and minor dependent children a reasonable allowance out of the estate for their maintenance during the period of administration. The decedent's personal representative may determine the family allowance in a lump sum not exceeding $18,000 (in excess of liens) or in periodic installments not exceeding $1,500 a month for one year. Amounts exceeding these amounts may be ordered by the court.

The UPC's family allowance has priority over all claims except the homestead allowance (see Comment *j*). The family allowance is not charged against any benefit or share passing to the spouse or children by intestate succession, by elective share, or by will, unless the will provides otherwise.

i. Exempt property. The UPC's exempt property allowance protects certain property such as household furniture, automobiles, furnishings, appliances, and personal effects from the claims of creditors. The protection is limited in value. The value cap in the Revised UPC is $10,000, but that figure could be changed in the future in response to inflation. The exempt property allowance has priority over all claims. It is not chargeable against any benefit or share passing to the spouse or children by intestate succession, by elective share, or by will, unless the will provides otherwise.

j. Homestead. The homestead allowance is a uniquely American contribution to laws giving a decedent's dependent survivors limited protection in the family home. The original homestead provisions commonly granted the surviving spouse and minor children the right to occupy the decedent's dwelling house as long as they wished to do so. The laws seem to have originated in 1839 in the Republic of Texas. English law is the source of a different idea. The widow had a right, called the widow's quarantine, to "tarry in the chief house of her husband for forty days," 4 James Kent, Commentaries on American Law 61 (1st ed. 1830), and there are early American decisions recognizing this as a part of the common law. Some American legislation has extended this right for a year.

By contrast, the more prevalent variety of American homestead legislation, though framed primarily in terms of exempting the homestead from the claims of the owner's creditors during life, commonly grants a decedent's spouse or minor children a right of occupancy in certain real estate of the decedent that may continue for much longer periods. These homestead statutes vary markedly in the amount and scope of protection given to family survivors. For example, though homestead rights are typically subject to ceilings of rather low value, in a few states the ceiling is high or there is no ceiling at all.

The UPC's homestead allowance is unique, in that it provides for a lump-sum amount instead of a right of occupancy. The shift to a money substitute protects all surviving spouses and minor children, regardless of whether the decedent owned real estate or merely leased it (or owned a mobile home not classified as real estate). Even though the UPC's homestead allowance does not grant the surviving spouse a right of occupancy, the spouse has a money substitute that might be used to acquire such an interest if the spouse desires. With the cooperation of the personal representative, a spouse's right to money from an estate can readily be converted into an interest in real estate—as a distribution in kind to the spouse, as a sale or lease of land to the spouse, or as some combination of the two. See UPC § 3–906. In this connection, it may be noted that under the UPC, the spouse has priority either to serve as the personal representative or to choose who serves, unless a probated will nominates someone else who qualifies and accepts the appointment. See UPC § 3–203.

§ 1.2. Requirement of Surviving the Decedent

An individual who fails to survive the decedent cannot take as an heir or a devisee.

Comment:

a. *Requirement of survival at common law.* A donative transfer cannot be made to a deceased person. Because probate transfers take place at the decedent's death, they cannot be made to an individual who fails to survive the decedent.

At common law, the requirement of survival implicit in a probate transfer is satisfied if the heir or devisee survives the decedent by only an instant. Administration of the common law rule became troublesome in the early decades of the 20th century, as vehicular accidents claiming the lives of both driver and passenger started to occur more frequently. Too often, proving which of the two survived became difficult if not impossible. A series of uniform acts has attempted not only to alleviate the problem of proof but also to provide for an intent-effecting result in cases of simultaneous or near-simultaneous deaths (see Comments *b*, *c*, and *d*).

It is important to note that these uniform acts adhere to the principle of this section that an individual who fails to survive the decedent cannot take as an heir or a devisee. By their terms, the uniform acts simply provide easier-to-administer rules for determining which of two decedents survived the other, or for treating one as surviving the other.

b. *Treatment of "simultaneous deaths" under the Original Uniform Simultaneous Death Act.* The Uniform Simultaneous Death Act (Original USDA), promulgated in 1940 and amended in small detail in 1953, provides that when there is no sufficient evidence that two individuals died otherwise than simultaneously, each decedent's property is distributed as if that person survived the other. In such cases, the legislation prevents property from passing from one estate to another estate. By doing so, the legislation achieves two purposes. First, it assures that each decedent's property passes to that person's relatives rather than through the other decedent's estate to the other person's relatives. Second, by not passing the property through two estates, the legislation avoids the expenses that would arise from double administration. . . .

c. *Treatment of near-simultaneous deaths under the Original Uniform Probate Code.* By providing that each decedent's property passes to that person's relatives and by preventing double administrative costs, the Original USDA reached a sensible result. The shortcoming of the Original USDA was that it limited its result to instances in which there was no sufficient evidence that two decedents died otherwise than simultaneously. Experience under the Original USDA suggested that instances of near-simultaneous deaths—in which one decedent did survive the other but by an insubstantial period of time—should receive the same treatment.

To respond to the problem of near-simultaneous deaths, the Original UPC instituted a 120-hour requirement of survival. For purposes of testacy, intestacy, and homestead and exempt property allowances, a person who fails to survive the decedent by 120 hours is deemed to have predeceased the decedent. This bright-line test eliminates most of the litigation that arose under the Original USDA about whether the devisee, heir, or other taker survived the decedent. The rule also better serves the decedent's intention by limiting the devolution of property to beneficiaries who can derive a personal benefit from the property, rather than a rule that would allow the property to pass to the estates of beneficiaries who cannot personally benefit, and from there to their heirs or devisees. . . . .

d. Revised Uniform Probate Code and Revised Uniform Simultaneous Death Act. The Revised Uniform Probate Code continued the 120-hour requirement of survival, but added a clear-and-convincing evidence standard of proof. Under the Revised UPC, a person who cannot be established by clear and convincing evidence to have survived the decedent by 120 hours is deemed to have predeceased the decedent. By resolving doubtful questions of survival by 120 hours in favor of nonsurvival, the clear-and-convincing-evidence standard of proof is designed to further the decedent's presumed intention of passing property only to persons who can personally benefit from it. . . . .

The Uniform Simultaneous Death Act (Revised USDA) was revised in 1991 and 1993 to incorporate the Revised UPC approach.

Under both the Revised UPC and the Revised USDA, the 120-hour requirement of survival applies not only to probate transfers, but also to certain nonprobate transfers taking effect at death, such as life insurance and joint tenancies. With respect to any probate or nonprobate transfer effected by a donative document, such as a will, or with respect to a joint tenancy whether created by a donative transfer or not, the 120-hour requirement of survival is a rule of construction that yields to a finding of a contrary intent and is subject to certain other specified exceptions. Under the Revised USDA, but not under the Revised UPC, the contrary intent must appear in the governing instrument. . . . .

e. Judicial approach. The underlying policy of the Revised USDA is to resolve close cases in favor of non-survival because that outcome usually better serves the decedent's intent. This policy commends itself in applying the common-law requirement of survival and in cases of ambiguity under earlier legislative regimes. The policy should at the very least be implemented by requiring proof of survival by clear and convincing evidence, unless there is a contrary intent or a tax advantage in treating the other decedent as the survivor, or unless that approach is contrary to an applicable statute.

f. Determination of the time of death. On the rules for determining the time of death, see the Uniform Determination of Death Act and UPC § 1–107 . . . .

g. Validity and construction of a testamentary disposition to the "estate" or to the "executor" of a deceased person. Although an individual who fails to survive the decedent cannot take as a devisee, a devise to the "estate" or to the "executor" of a deceased person is valid.

The meaning of a devise to the "estate" or to the "executor" of a deceased person is a question of construction, of carrying out the presumed intent of the *testator*. The testator's presumed intent in making such a devise is to pass the property to the *beneficiaries* of the previous decedent's estate. Ordinarily, this presumed intent is better served by passing the devised property directly to the beneficiaries of the previous decedent's estate as if the previous decedent died immediately after the testator, rather than adding the devised property to the previous decedent's probate estate, which might necessitate reopening the previous decedent's estate (and in some cases, reopening the estates of other decedents, until the devised property finally trickles down to living persons).

If the previous decedent died intestate, the devised property passes directly to the persons who would have been the previous decedent's heirs if the previous decedent died immediately after the testator's death. If the previous decedent died testate, the devised property passes directly to the devisees of the previous decedent's will as if the previous decedent died immediately after the testator's death, subject to the possible application of an antilapse statute (see § 5.5). . . . .

§ 1.3. Noncitizens

Except as otherwise provided by applicable statute, the fact that an individual, or an individual through whom he or she claims, is not or was not a citizen of the United States does not disqualify the individual from acquiring or transmitting property through testate or intestate succession.

Comment:

a. Purpose. This provision, codified in many states and in the Original and Revised Uniform Probate Code, eliminates the archaic rule that a noncitizen cannot acquire or transmit land by descent or devise, a rule based on the feudal notions of a tenant's obligations to the King. Although there never was a corresponding rule as to personalty, this section applies to both and implements the basic premise that distinctions between real and personal property should be abolished.

b. Statutory restrictions. The rule of this section applies except as otherwise provided by an applicable statute. . . . .

CHAPTER 2

INTESTACY

Introductory Note: This chapter discusses intestate succession. Intestate succession is controlled by statute. A statute of intestacy operates as a default regime for a person who dies intestate or partially intestate.

§ 2.1. General Principles and Definitions

(a) A decedent who dies without a valid will dies intestate. A decedent who dies with a valid will that does not dispose of all of the decedent's net probate estate dies partially intestate.

(b) The decedent's intestate estate, consisting of that part of the decedent's net probate estate that is not disposed of by a valid will, passes at the decedent's death to the decedent's heirs as provided by statute.

Comment:

a. Introduction. A decedent who dies without a valid will dies *intestate*. A decedent who dies with a valid will that does not dispose of all of the decedent's net probate estate dies *partially intestate*. A decedent who dies intestate or partially intestate is sometimes called *the intestate* or *the intestate decedent.*

The decedent's intestate estate consists of that part of the decedent's net probate estate (see § 1.1(b)) that is not disposed of by a valid will. The intestate estate passes at the decedent's death to the decedent's *heirs* as provided by statute.

b. Historical note—origins of modern intestacy law. The American statutes on intestate succession derive in part from two sources in English law: the common-law canons of descent, which determined inheritance of land, and the English Statute of Distribution, 1670, 22 Car. 2, c. 10, which governed succession to personal property.

The separate treatment of land and personal property in the English law of intestate succession gave rise to a special terminology. Inheritance of land was called "descent." The word "inheritance" was reserved for intestate succession to *land.* Those who took land on intestacy were called "heirs." Succession to *personal property* was often called "distribution" because title to personal property passed to the personal representative, who made distribution to those entitled after paying debts and other charges against the estate. As a consequence, statutes on intestate succession were (and often still are) called "statutes of descent and distribution." Those who took personalty on intestacy were called "distributees" or "next of kin."

Although the rules for intestate succession to real and personal property have major points of difference in a few American jurisdictions, and minor ones in some others, the trend has been to eliminate such differences. Today, in well over two-thirds of the states, there is a single system of inheritance for both real and personal property.

With the modern tendency to eliminate differences between succession to real and personal property, the old terminology is disappearing. Lawyers now often use the words "inheritance," "heirs," and "next of kin" without regard to the character of the property.

One difference remains in most states, however. In accordance with the traditions of English intestacy law, title to and the right of possession of land pass directly to the heirs, whereas title to and the right of possession of personal property pass to the administrator, a fiduciary who is now often encompassed under the title "personal representative." The same distinction appears in the law of wills. Title to and possession of land disposed of by will vest in the devisee, whereas title to and possession of personal property pass to the personal representative, the executor where the will names an executor. Where there is legislation on the point, however, title to both real and personal property usually passes directly to the heirs or devisees, subject to a right of possession in the personal representative for purposes of properly administering the estate. See, e.g., UPC §§ 3–101, –709.

c. Historical note—intestacy as a default regime. Intestate succession is a default regime, which operates in the absence of a valid will.

Intestacy has not always served as default law. It originated as mandatory law. Property was forced to pass by intestacy because there was then no power to make a will. The power to dispose of *personal* property by will was recognized early. The ecclesiastical courts asserted jurisdiction over succession to personal property on death, and encouraged bequests for religious and charitable purposes, as well as for the decedent's family. During the Anglo-Saxon period, testamentary disposition of *land* was possible, but recognition ceased within about a century after the Norman Conquest. The devise of land by will "stood condemned," Maitland wrote, "because it is a death-bed gift, wrung from a man in his agony. In the interest of honesty, in the interest of the lay state, a boundary must be maintained against ecclesiastical greed and the other-worldliness of dying men." 2 Frederick Pollock & Frederic W. Maitland, History of English Law 328 (2d ed. 1898). By contrast, the church courts never gained jurisdiction over succession to land, and the Crown courts were not concerned with seeing that a landowner atoned for his wrongs by devoting a portion of his property to pious objects.

By the English Statute of Wills of 1540, 34 & 35 Hen. 8, c. 5, § 14, men (but not women) were granted some power to dispose of their land by will, in effect beginning the process of transforming intestacy from a rule of mandatory law into a default rule. It was not until the 19th century that the power of testation was granted to women by the Married Women's Property Acts.

d. When heirship is determined. Heirship is determined at the decedent's death. The decedent's death is when intestate property passes by intestacy to the decedent's heirs. Before the decedent's death, a potential heir has no property interest but merely an "expectancy" (an inchoate interest) in the decedent's intestate estate. A person who fails to survive the decedent, or fails to survive the decedent by some statutorily required period of time such as 120 hours, cannot be an heir. See § 1.2. A child in gestation at the decedent's death is considered to be in being at the decedent's death if the child is subsequently born viable. Revised UPC § 2–108 provides that a child "in gestation at a particular time is treated as living at that time if the individual lives 120 hours or more after birth." Although the traditional view is that a child who is conceived and born after the decedent's death cannot be an heir, this proposition is open to reexamination in the case of a child produced from genetic material of the *decedent* by assisted reproductive technology, so long as the child is born within a reasonable time after the decedent's death in circumstances indicating that the decedent would have approved of the child's right to inherit. See § 2.5, Comment *l*.

Before the decedent's death, a person who would be an heir if the decedent died immediately is an *heir apparent*. In older terminology, a distinction was drawn between an "heir apparent" and an "heir presumptive." The distinction is of little use and is not preserved in this Restatement. An "heir apparent" was a person who could not be displaced as an heir by the birth, marriage, or adoption of a nearer relative; for example, a child would be an heir apparent. An "heir presumptive" was a person who could be displaced as an heir by the birth, marriage, or adoption of a nearer relative; for example, a parent of an unmarried, childless person would be an heir presumptive of the unmarried, childless person if the parent could be displaced as an heir should the unmarried, childless person marry or have or adopt a child.

A relative who would be an heir if a nearer relative or a number of nearer relatives fail to survive the decedent is not an heir apparent.

e. Partial intestacy. Partial intestacy arises when the decedent's last will does not dispose of his or her entire net probate estate. The commonest example occurs when a will does not contain a residuary clause. In the absence of a residuary clause, the decedent's residuary estate passes by intestacy to the decedent's heirs at the decedent's death.

Partial intestacy can also occur if the decedent's will contains a residuary clause that does not dispose of the decedent's entire residuary estate. A residuary clause might only dispose of a portion of the decedent's residuary estate, such as a clause that provides "I devise one-half of my residuary estate to. . . ." The other half of the decedent's residuary estate would pass by intestacy to the decedent's heirs at the decedent's death. . . . .

§ 2.2. Intestate Share of Surviving Spouse

An intestate decedent's surviving spouse takes a share of the intestate estate as provided by statute. The exact share differs among the states. Not infrequently, the spouse takes the entire intestate estate if the decedent leaves no surviving descendants or parents and, in some states, if the decedent also leaves no other specified relative such as a descendant of a parent. Older statutes tend to reduce the spouse's share to a fraction such as one-half or one-third when the decedent leaves a surviving descendant or another specified relative. Under the Revised Uniform Probate Code, the surviving spouse takes either the entire intestate estate or a specified lump sum plus a specified percentage of the excess, if any, depending on what other relatives survive the decedent.

Comment:

a. Revised Uniform Probate Code. The Revised UPC grants the surviving spouse the entire intestate estate when the decedent is not survived by descendants or parents. It provides that the surviving spouse also receives the entire intestate estate if the decedent is survived by descendants—if they are also descendants of the surviving spouse and if the surviving spouse has no descendants who are not the decedent's descendants.

If the decedent has children by a prior marriage, the Revised UPC grants the surviving spouse the first $100,000 plus 50 percent of any remaining balance of the intestate estate. If only the surviving spouse has children by a prior marriage, the Revised UPC grants the surviving spouse the first $150,000 plus 50 percent of any remaining balance of the intestate estate. Distribution date values are used in satisfying the lump-sum portion of the spouse's share, treating the lump-sum portion as the equivalent of a pecuniary devise.

b. Original Uniform Probate Code. As originally promulgated in 1969, the UPC granted the decedent's surviving spouse the entire intestate estate if the decedent left neither surviving issue nor surviving parents. If the decedent left surviving issue (all of whom were also issue of the surviving spouse), or if the decedent left a surviving parent, the spouse's share was the first $50,000 plus one-half of the remaining balance of the intestate estate. If the decedent were survived by a child (or descendants of a deceased child) who was not the surviving spouse's child, the spouse's share was one-half of the intestate estate.

c. Nonuniform Probate Code Law. Under non-UPC law, the surviving spouse usually inherits the entire intestate estate if the decedent leaves no surviving descendants or parents. If the decedent does leave descendants, the intestate estate may be divided between the spouse and the descendants. If the decedent leaves no descendants but does leave a parent or parents, the intestate estate may be divided between the spouse and the parent or parents.

Non-UPC law commonly entitles the decedent's surviving spouse to one-third of the intestate estate if the decedent is survived by children (or descendants of deceased children), with the remaining two-thirds passing to the decedent's descendants. Other variations exist. Some non-UPC statutes award half each to the surviving spouse and the descendants. Elsewhere the spouse receives half if one descendant survives but a third if more than one descendant survives; the remaining half or two-thirds goes to the descendants. Most pre-UPC statutes drew no distinction between the decedent's descendants who are also descendants of the decedent's spouse and any descendants who are not.

If the decedent is not survived by children (or descendants of deceased children), but is survived by one or both parents, the spouse's share under non-UPC statutes is often one-half, with the other half going to the decedent's parent or parents. Other variations exist. In a few states, the spouse shares the intestate estate with the decedent's siblings if both parents have predeceased. Other states have unique systems for allocating the intestate estate between the spouse and parents. Some non-UPC law gives the entire intestate estate to the surviving spouse and nothing to the decedent's parents.

d. Community property. In community-property states, the surviving spouse's share of the decedent's separate property and the decedent's half of the couple's community property may differ. The Original and Revised Uniform Probate Code have a special section for community-property states. Both versions provide that the surviving spouse takes all of the decedent's half of the community-property but takes the same share of the decedent's separate property as the spouse would take in a non-community-property state (as described in Comments *b* and *c*). See Revised UPC § 2–102A; Original UPC § 2–102A.

e. *Putative spouse.* Unless precluded by applicable statute, a *putative spouse* is treated as a legal spouse for purposes of intestacy. A putative spouse is a person who cohabited with the decedent in the good-faith but mistaken belief that he or she was married to the decedent. The strongest evidence of a claimant's good-faith belief that he or she was married to the decedent is proof the they participated in a marriage ceremony. Because neither the Original nor the Revised UPC explicitly denies rights to putative spouses, a putative-spouse doctrine is compatible with the UPC. A putative-spouse doctrine is expressly adopted in the Uniform Marriage and Divorce Act (1983).

Conferring the status of "spouse" on a putative spouse is straightforward if the putative spouse is the only person claiming to be the decedent's surviving spouse. That person takes the share that a legal spouse would take. The problem becomes more complicated if there are multiple claimants, e.g., if the intestate decedent is survived by both a putative spouse and a legal spouse, or by two or more putative spouses. If there are multiple claimants, the court should exercise its power of equitable apportionment to divide the intestate estate among the claimants as appropriate in the circumstances. A starting point for apportionment would be to strike a ratio according to the length of time that each claimant cohabited with the decedent. Under this approach, for example, if one claimant cohabited with the decedent for 15 years and the other claimant cohabited with the decedent for five years, the starting point would be to award the first claimant three-fourths of the spouse's share and the latter one-fourth. Other factors, however, may also be considered in arriving at the final division, such as the needs of each claimant and the number of the decedent's joint children with each claimant and their needs.

f. *Common-law spouse.* A common-law spouse is a spouse for purposes of intestate succession in states recognizing common-law marriage.

g. *Domestic partner.* A developing question is the right of the domestic partner of an unmarried intestate decedent to be treated as a surviving spouse for purposes of intestacy or otherwise to be entitled to an intestate share. . . . .

§ 2.3. Intestate Share of Surviving Descendants

(a) An intestate decedent's surviving descendants take the entire intestate estate if the decedent leaves no surviving spouse, and they take any portion of the intestate estate not passing to the surviving spouse if the decedent leaves a surviving spouse.

(b) The decedent's surviving descendants take by representation. There are several systems of representation.

Comment:

a. *Parentelic system.* In design, the intestacy statutes initially utilize the *parentelic system* for determining heirs other than the surviving spouse (see, e.g., Revised UPC § 2–103), though only a few states prescribe that system indefinitely. The parentelic system is based on a preference for persons who are in the nearest parentela to the intestate decedent. A parentela consists of an ancestor and that ancestor's surviving descendants. The parentelic system provides that the first parentela (the decedent's own surviving descendants, sometimes referred to as *lineal* descendants or *direct* descendants) have first priority and inherit first. If no member of that parentela survives the decedent, the second parentela (the decedent's parents and their descendants) inherit next. If no member of that parentela survives the decedent, the third parentela (the decedent's grandparents and their descendants) inherit next; and so on. Under this system, for example, the grandson of the decedent's sister (who is a descendant of the decedent's parents) takes in preference to an uncle (who is a descendant of the decedent's grandparents). The parentelic system was utilized by the canons of descent and to a lesser degree by the Statute of Distribution.

This section of the Restatement is concerned with the first parentela—the intestate decedent's descendants.

b. Share of descendants. In the absence of a surviving spouse, the law of all states awards the entire intestate estate to the decedent's descendants. Some statutes use the term *descendants,* while other statutes use the term *issue.* The two terms are synonymous—each term denotes a multiple-generation class that includes all generational levels down the decedent's descending line.

When a decedent dies leaving a surviving spouse and one or more surviving descendants, the decedent's descendants take the portion of the intestate estate not passing to the surviving spouse. See § 2.2. Under some non-UPC statutes, and under UPC law in estates of modest size, the spouse may receive the entire estate to the exclusion of the decedent's descendants. Under other non-UPC statutes, and under UPC law in larger estates, the spouse and descendants share the estate.

c. Representation in general. The decedent's descendants take *by representation.* The idea of taking by representation is traceable to the English canons of descent, which governed the succession to real estate. The canons provided that lineal descendants should represent their deceased ancestors in inheritance. Representation was also used in the English Statute of Distribution, which governed succession to personalty.

A principal feature of representation is that the estate is divided among the living descendants who are nearest to the decedent in each descending line. A descendant who has a living ancestor who is also a descendant of the decedent is not an eligible taker.

If all of the decedent's children survive the decedent, or if the only children who predecease the decedent leave no descendants who survive the decedent, each surviving child takes an equal share. The spouses of descendants do not share in the decedent's estate.

Charts are used in the following illustrations to depict the facts at the intestate's death. Brackets around a person's name indicate that the person is then deceased (or treated as deceased). See § 1.2.

Illustration:

1. G, a widow, had three children, A, B, and C. G died intestate, survived by A, B, and C. In chart form, the facts at G's death are as follows:

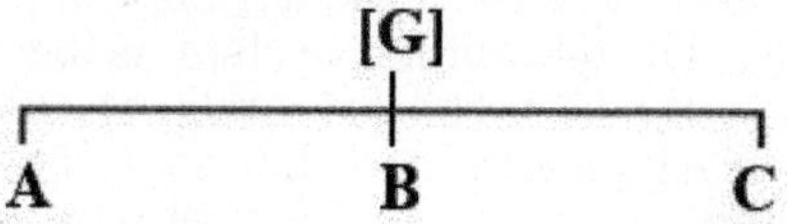

A takes one-third, B takes one-third, and C takes one-third.

Because of steadily increasing longevity . . . , three-generation families are quite common and four-generation families are not unusual. Many people live long enough to have grown grandchildren and young great-grandchildren A system of representation is invoked whenever there is an unusual order of deaths, i.e., whenever one or more of the decedent's *children* predeceases the decedent *and* leaves descendants who survive the decedent. The probability of an unusual order of deaths is increased by the fact that under many intestacy statutes, especially those modeled on the Original or Revised UPC, the surviving spouse often takes the entire intestate estate to the exclusion of the decedent's descendants (see § 2.2, Comments *a* and *b*), thus deferring the descendants' inheritance until the surviving spouse dies. The greater longevity of many surviving spouses increases the possibility that the spouse will outlive one or more of the children.

Illustration:

3. G, a widow, had four children, A, B, C, and D. G died intestate, survived by A, B, and C. D predeceased G. D left a spouse and two children, X and Y, who survived G. In chart form, the facts at G's death are as follows:

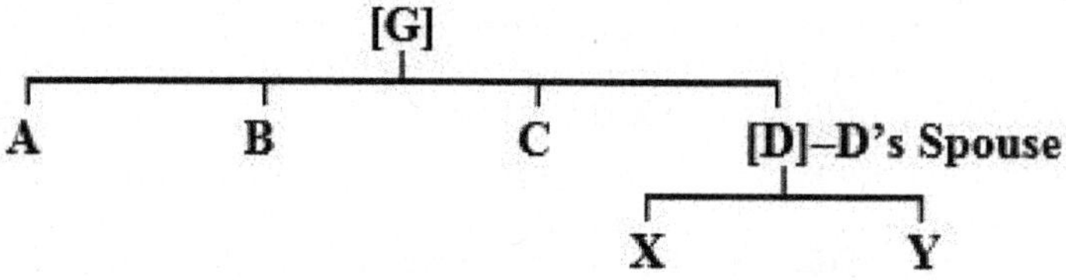

Regardless of the system of representation employed in applicable state law, A takes one-fourth, B takes one-fourth, C takes one-fourth, and X and Y take one-eighth each as D's representative.

There are several systems of representation. The various systems are strict per stirpes (Comment *d*), per capita with representation (modified per stirpes) (Comment *e*), Original UPC system (Comment *f*), and Revised UPC system (per capita at each generation) (Comment *g*). In Illustration 3, all of the systems reach the same result. The various systems only reach different results in more complex—and more exceptional—situations.

d. Strict per stirpes. The term *per stirpes* does not have a universally accepted meaning. This Restatement uses the term *strict per stirpes* to refer to how per stirpes is usually defined. The strict per-stirpes system is faithful to the idea of representation: Each grandchild or more remote descendant takes not only as a representative of his or her deceased parent, but has the right to share with his or her siblings or siblings' descendants the same portion of the decedent's estate as that descendant's parent would have taken if that parent had survived the decedent. The strict per-stirpes system was used by the common law under the canons of descent for land. See 2 William Blackstone, Commentaries *218 (1765–69).

The mechanics for determining shares under the strict per-stirpes system involve three steps:

Step One: Divide the estate into primary shares at the generation nearest to the decedent (i.e., at the children generation). This primary-share generation is often described by the courts as the generation at which the "stocks" or "roots" are determined. The number of primary shares is equal to the number of children alive at the decedent's death plus the number of children who predeceased the decedent leaving descendants who survived the decedent. If any child is deceased and has left no living descendants, that child is disregarded in determining the number of primary shares. The number of primary shares is determined at the children generation even when no child survives the decedent.

Step Two: Allocate the primary shares. One share goes to each living child, if any. One share also goes to the descendants of each deceased child with living descendants, if any.

Step Three: Divide and subdivide each primary share allocated to the living descendants of a deceased child. Each of the primary shares is divided and subdivided among the deceased child's descendants in the same manner as if the deceased child and other younger-generation descendants who have died were the decedent.

Illustration:

4. G, a widower, had three children, A, B, and C. G died intestate. A, B, and C predeceased G. A left two children, X and Y, who survived G. B left one child, Z, who survived G. C left three children, U, V, and W, who survived G. In chart form, the facts at G's death are as follows:

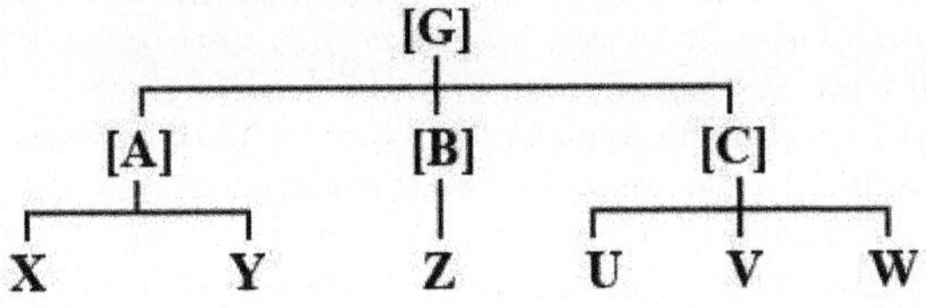

Under the strict per-stirpes system, G's estate is divided equally among the children's families, i.e., into three shares. The one-third share for A's family is then divided into two sub-shares, giving each of A's two children, X and Y, one-sixth of G's estate. The one-third share for B's family passes to B's child, Z. The one-third share for C's family is divided into three sub-shares, giving each of C's three children, U, V, and W, a one-ninth share of G's estate.

e. Per-capita-with-representation (modified per stirpes). With the exception of the first step, the mechanics of this system are identical to the strict per-stirpes system. *Step One* in this system is to divide the estate into primary shares at the generation nearest to the decedent *that contains at least one living member*. Thus, if *all* of the decedent's children are deceased, but at least one grandchild is alive, as in Illustration 4, the primary shares are determined at the grandchildren generation rather than at the children generation. In a strict sense, then, the grandchildren take in their own right, *per capita* (i.e., in equal shares), and not as representatives of the decedent's deceased children.

If, however, one of the grandchildren in Illustration 4 had also predeceased G, leaving living descendants, the descendants of that deceased grandchild would take in a representative capacity. Hence, the system is called "per capita *with representation*," a term that really means per capita at the nearest generation with a living member, with descendants of deceased members of that generation taking by representation.

Since the second and third steps in this system and in the strict per-stirpes system are the same, this system is sometimes called *modified per stirpes*. A few courts have employed this system when operating under the statutory term "per stirpes."

f. Original Uniform Probate Code system. As originally promulgated in 1969, the UPC adopted a variation of the per-capita-with-representation system. The Original UPC meant to codify *Step One* of the per-capita-with-representation system and to fix the primary-share generation at the nearest generation to the decedent containing at least one living member.

The Original UPC departed from the per-capita-with-representation system at *Step Three*. Under the Original UPC, each share allocated to the descendants of a deceased member of the primary-share generation is divided and subdivided "in the same manner." The meaning of the phrase "in the same manner" is that each share allocated to the descendants of a deceased member of the primary-share generation is divided as if the deceased member of the primary-share generation were the decedent with respect to his or her primary share. Thus, the primary share is subdivided at the nearest generation to the deceased descendant containing at least one living member. A useful way of describing the Original UPC's system is that it is per capita with per capita representation.

The Original UPC system differs from the per-capita-with-representation system described in Comment *e*. The per-capita-with-representation system is in reality *per capita with per stirpes representation*. *Step Three* of that system divides and subdivides each of the primary shares as under *Step Three* of the per-stirpes system. The primary shares are divided and subdivided at the nearest generation to the deceased descendant regardless of whether that generation contains any living member. Illustration 5 illustrates the difference between the two systems.

Illustration:

5. G, a widow, had three children, A, B, and C. G died intestate, survived by B and C. A predeceased G. A had two children, X and Y. Both X and Y also predeceased G. X had two children, M and N, who survived G. Y had one child, P, who survived G.

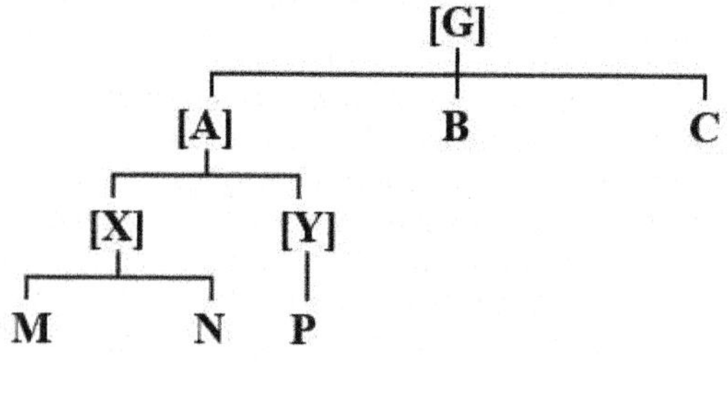

Under the Original UPC system, B takes one-third and C takes one-third. A's one-third primary share is divided equally among M, N, and P, giving each a one-ninth share. Under the per-capita-with-representation system, however, A's primary share would be subdivided at the deceased grandchildren generation, giving M and N a one-twelfth share each and giving P a one-sixth share.

g. Per-capita-at-each-generation system (Revised Uniform Probate Code). As revised in 1990, the UPC further refined the system of representation, adopting the per-capita-at-each-generation system. The original version of the UPC neither assured equality among the children's families nor equality among members of the same generation whose parents had predeceased the decedent. The revised version assures equality among members of the same generation whose parents predeceased them. The revised system is illustrated in Illustration 6 below.

Illustration:

6. G, a widow, had three children, A, B, and C. G died intestate, survived by A. B and C predeceased G. B had one child, Z. C had three children, U, V, and W.

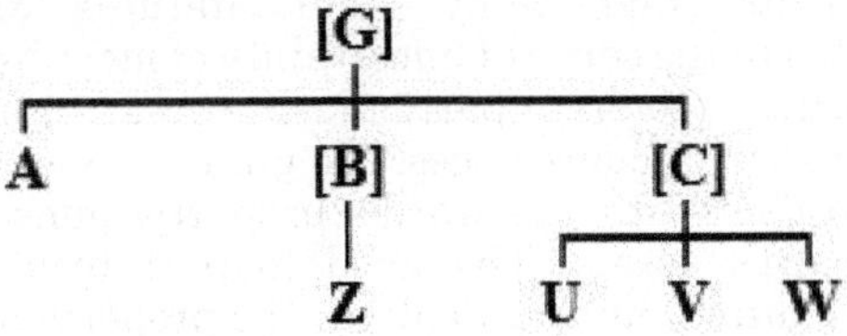

Both the original and revised versions of the UPC give a one-third share to A. However, under the original version, the four grandchildren would not receive equal shares. Z would represent B and would get a full one-third share. The other three would represent C and take a one-ninth share each. Under the revised version, however, equality among the four grandchildren is achieved. The revised version achieves equality by the device of treating the four grandchildren as representing both B and C. This representational system treats B and C as if they were one person who had four children, giving each grandchild an equal share.

The mechanics for determining shares under the per-capita-at-each-generation system require three steps:

Step One: Divide the estate into primary shares at the nearest generation to the decedent that contains at least one living member. The number of primary shares is the number of living persons in that generation plus the number of deceased persons in that generation who have living descendants.

Step Two: Allocate one primary share to each living member of the primary-share generation.

Step Three: Combine the remaining primary shares, if any, into a single share and treat the descendants already allocated a share and their descendants as though they had predeceased the decedent. Then distribute that single share among the decedent's descendants in accordance with Step One.

This system consistently results in "horizontal equality," (i.e., equality among members of the same generation) as distinguished from the "vertical equality" (i.e., equality among children's families) consistently accomplished by the per-stirpes system.

h. *Guardianship.* If a decedent leaves an heir who is a minor or is otherwise legally incapacitated, a guardian or conservator may have to be appointed to receive and manage the intestate assets passing to the minor or incapacitated heir. A surviving parent is the natural guardian of his or her minor child, but only of the child's person. A court appointment may be necessary to give the parent authority over the child's property. If there is no parent, a court may have to appoint someone to take responsibility for the heir's custody and care, a guardian of the person. A guardian may be responsible for the minor's or incapacitated heir's person or property or both, but often the appointment is unclear about the extent of the guardian's responsibility. It is generally assumed that a court-appointed guardian has authority for both the person and the property of a ward unless the terms of the appointment provide otherwise. If there are multiple children, separate guardianships may have to be issued for each child, even if the same person is appointed guardian for each child.

The guardian does not have title to the ward's property. Rather, the guardian is custodian of the property with limited powers. These powers are defined by statute, and many older statutes define those powers inadequately, both in the sense of uncertainty of meaning and failure to grant certain important powers, particularly concerning investment and distributions. In such circumstances, the guardian may have to obtain court authorization to deal with the ward's property, generating expenses that diminish the ward's assets. The need to post bond and to file judicial accountings, if required, further depletes the property available to the ward.

Several states have enacted conservatorship or guardianship statutes that ameliorate some of these problems. (The term "conservator" replaces the term "guardian of the estate" often used in earlier parlance.) The UPC, for example, grants the conservator the type of title to the protected property that a trustee would have and grants powers, duties, and liabilities comparable to those of a trustee. Relaxing the extensive judicial supervision that characterizes traditional property guardianships, the UPC specifically grants substantial management powers to the conservator, exercisable without court order. These powers include the power to lease, sell, mortgage, or exchange assets; to borrow money; to pay creditor claims; to invest (subject to the same requirements applicable to trustees); and to distribute income and principal for the child's support, education, care, or benefit. See UPC § 5–423. . . . . The UPC's guardianship and related provisions are also promulgated as a free-standing uniform law called the Uniform Guardianship and Protective Proceedings Act. . . . .

§ 2.4. Intestate Share of Surviving Ancestors and Collateral Relatives

(a) If an intestate decedent leaves no surviving spouse and no surviving descendant, nearly all intestacy statutes grant the intestate estate to the second parentela (the decedent's surviving parents or, if deceased, to the parent's surviving descendants) and if no member of the second parentela survives the decedent, to the third parentela (the decedent's grandparents or, if deceased, to the grandparent's surviving descendants).

(b) If no member of the second or third parentela survives the decedent, the intestacy statutes diverge, but most follow one of two

patterns. Either the intestate estate escheats to the state or the intestate estate passes per capita to the decedent's nearest kindred as determined by the civil-law method, with the relatives having the nearer common ancestor taking exclusively under some statutes. Under statutes of the latter sort, the estate escheats to the state only if the decedent leaves no surviving kindred.

Comment:

a. Ancestors and collaterals. Apart from the intestate decedent's own descendants, his or her blood relatives are either ancestors or collaterals. A collateral relative is descended from an ancestor of the decedent. A collateral relative of the whole blood is descended from a pair of the decedent's ancestors. A collateral relative of the half blood is descended from one of the decedent's ancestors, but not from a pair of them. The status of collateral relatives of the half blood is discussed in Comment *f*. Under § 2.5, an adopted child is treated as a child of his or her adoptive parents or parent and may in certain circumstances continue to be treated as a child of his or her genetic parents.

A collateral relative is not simply a descendant of an ancestor, however, because that category may include the descendants or ancestors of the decedent. The decedent's daughter is not only a descendant of the decedent, but also of the decedent's parents. Each of the decedent's parents is not only an ancestor of the decedent, but also a descendant of one set of the decedent's grandparents. Thus, the strict meaning of a collateral relative is a relative who is a descendant of an ancestor, excluding, however, the decedent's own descendants and ancestors. Examples of collateral relatives are: brothers, sisters, nephews, and nieces (descended from the decedent's parents); and aunts, uncles, and cousins (descended from the decedent's maternal or paternal grandparents).

b. Parentelic system—second and more remote parentela. As noted in § 2.3, Comment *a*, most intestacy statutes utilize the *parentelic system* for determining heirs other than the surviving spouse. When there is no surviving spouse and no surviving member of the first parentela (the decedent's own descendants), the second parentela (the decedent's parents and their descendants) inherit next; and so on.

c. Parents. The decedent's parents and their descendants inherit to the exclusion of more remote ancestors and their descendants. The decedent's parents and their descendants inherit, however, only if the decedent leaves no surviving descendants of his or her own. Under the Revised UPC, parents of decedents with large estates inherit if the decedent leaves a surviving spouse but no descendants. The parents take one-fourth of that part of the intestate estate, if any, that is in excess of $200,000.

Non-UPC law often gives the parents a much larger share. Often the parents will be granted half and the spouse half when the decedent leaves a surviving spouse but no descendants. The Original UPC gives the parents half of that part of the estate, if any, that exceeds $50,000.

If the decedent leaves neither a surviving spouse nor surviving descendants, the decedent's parents inherit to the exclusion of the decedent's surviving siblings or their descendants under most intestacy statutes. This rule applies under both the original and revised versions of the UPC. In a few states, under various formulas, the decedent's parents, brothers, and sisters share in the estate. Under one version, the decedent's parents, brothers, and sisters take equal shares; if only one parent survives, that parent takes a double share; if a brother or sister is deceased, the surviving descendants of that brother or sister take the deceased sibling's share, by representation.

d. Ancestral property. At common law, land returned to the branch of the family from which the decedent inherited it. See 2 William Blackstone, Commentaries *220 (1st ed. 1765–69). Some type of ancestral-property rule—usually restricted to land, but not always—still persists in a few states. When the rule is followed, it sometimes applies only to the estates of unmarried minors or of surviving spouses.

Neither the Original nor the Revised UPC contains an ancestral-property rule. The rationale is that any benefits of the rule are outweighed by the administrative costs, which include tracing and accounting for accretions.

e. Descendants of parents. If neither of the decedent's parents survives, the descendants of the decedent's parents inherit by representation. The system of representation employed in the jurisdiction will most likely be the same system employed in the jurisdiction for representation among the decedent's own descendants. The Revised UPC applies the per-capita-at-each-generation system. See § 2.3, Comment *g*.

f. Relatives of the half blood. A relative of the half blood is a collateral relative who shares one common ancestor with the decedent. If, for example, the decedent's mother or father has children from a prior marriage, those children will be the decedent's half brothers or half sisters. Descendants of the decedent's half brothers or half sisters are also related to the decedent by the half blood. Today, relatives of the half blood are generally—though not universally—treated the same as relatives of the whole blood. The principle of equal treatment is codified in some states and in the Original and Revised UPC.

g. Relatives by affinity. Blood or adopted relatives of the decedent's spouse, such as the spouse's parents, siblings, or descendants of siblings, and spouses of the decedent's blood or adopted relatives, such as daughters-in-law and sons-in-law, are relatives by affinity. The intestacy statutes, including the UPC, exclude them from inheriting.

h. Third parentela. If there is no surviving member of the first or second parentela, the UPC and most non-UPC statutes go to the third parentela. Under the Original and Revised UPC, the estate is first divided into paternal and maternal halves (if there is at least one grandparent or descendant of a grandparent in each half). If the surviving grandparents or descendants of a grandparent are all on one side, that side takes the whole. If both of the grandparents on one side predeceased the decedent, that half is a separate parentela for purposes of representation among the descendants of the grandparents who head up that half.

i. Inheritance beyond the third parentela: unlimited inheritance by distant relatives versus limiting inheritance to close relatives. If no member of the third or of a nearer parentela survives the decedent, the question arises whether relatives beyond the third parentela should be entitled to inherit or whether the estate should escheat to the state, thus excluding more remote relatives from inheriting.

A number of states follow a rule of *unlimited inheritance.* (See Comment *j* for the method by which this rule is implemented.) The rule of unlimited inheritance means that an intestate estate escheats to the state only if the decedent leaves no surviving relatives, no matter how distant the relationship. Both the English canons of descent and the Statute of

Distribution provided for inheritance by any blood relative. Through the first half of the 20th century, many American intestacy laws followed these ancient English models.

Giving distant relatives inheritance rights makes probate administration more complex. As relatives become more remote from the decedent, difficulties in the proof of heirship increase. Furthermore, these difficulties complicate the administration of testate estates, when probate law requires these relatives to be identified and located so that they might have the opportunity to contest wills offered for probate. The more distant the decedent's relatives, the more likely they are to be persons with whom the decedent had no personal or social ties.

England abandoned the rule of unlimited inheritance in 1925 . . . .

Both the original and revised versions of the UPC abandon the rule of unlimited inheritance, and provide that if no member of the third or of a nearer parentela survives the decedent, the intestate estate escheats to the state.

j. Implementing a rule of unlimited inheritance; determining degrees of kinship. The parentelic system of going, step by step, up the ladder of ancestral seniority can theoretically continue forever, but very few states do that. Nearly all states reach a stopping point. Many intestacy statutes utilize the parentelic system through the second parentela (parents and their descendants) or through the third parentela (grandparents and their descendants), but not beyond. A few states continue the parentelic system through the fourth parentela (great-grandparents and their descendants) before stopping. Wherever such statutes set the stopping point, they usually provide that if no member of any of the specified parentela survives the decedent, the estate passes to the decedent's "nearest kindred" or "next of kin." The statutes frequently add the phrases "in equal degree" or "without representation" or both.

Such statutory provisions make it necessary to determine degrees of kinship between the decedent and those claiming a share of the estate. Under the "nearest kindred" part of the statute, the relatives in the *lowest* degree of kinship, being the decedent's nearest living relatives, share the estate equally. This type of distribution is *nonrepresentational*. In other words, it might be described as "per capita without representation." Each relative must take, if at all, in his or her own right and not as a representative of a deceased ancestor. Each heir takes an equal share, because all the relatives who are entitled to participate in the estate will be in the same degree.

In its primary sense, each degree reflects a difference of one generation. Thus, a parent of the decedent is related to the decedent in the first degree, a grandparent is in the second degree, and so on. The determination of the degree relationship is somewhat more complicated when it comes to collateral relatives, as discussed below.

k. Determining degrees of kinship under the civil-law method. As to collateral relatives, the method for computing degrees of kinship used in American law goes back to the interpretation by the English judges of the Statute of Distribution of 1670. The Statute of Distribution provided for distribution of personal property to "next of kindred in equal degree" in the event the decedent left no descendants.

The English judges followed the civil-law method of computing degrees of kinship. This method consists of counting generations under the following formula: count the number of generations (1) up from the decedent to the decedent's ancestor who is also an ancestor of the collateral relative and (2) down from that common ancestor to the collateral relative. The total of these two figures constitutes the degree of kinship for each collateral relative. See 4 Richard Burn, Ecclesiastical Law 538–43 (9th ed. 1842). Under the civil-law method, a sister or brother is related to the decedent in the second degree, a niece or nephew is related in the third degree, and an aunt or uncle is also related in the third degree. Many American statutes explicitly provide that degrees shall be computed according to the method of the civil law. When the statute is silent on the point, most courts have used this method.

The table below shows the degree of relationship to the decedent under the civil-law method of persons in the fourth and fifth parentela.

Degree of Relationship to the Decedent Under the Civil-Law Method	***Fourth Parentela***	***Fifth Parentela***
3	Great Grandparents	
4	Great Uncles/Aunts	Great-Great Grandparents
5	First Cousins Once Removed	Great-Grand Uncles/Aunts
6	Second Cousins	First Cousins Twice Removed
7	Second Cousins Once Removed	Second Cousins Once Removed
8	Second Cousins Twice Removed	Third Cousins
9	Second Cousins Thrice Removed	Third Cousins Once Removed

l. The modified civil-law method. Under a fairly widespread statutory modification of the civil-law method, when two or more collateral relatives in equal degree claim through different common ancestors, those claiming through the ancestor nearest to the decedent take to the exclusion of the others.

Illustration:

1. G died intestate, without leaving a surviving spouse or anyone in the first, second, or third parentela. G's surviving relatives were his third cousins, A and B, his second cousin twice removed, C, and his second cousin thrice removed, D. A, B, and C would be G's nearest kindred under the civil-law method. They are all related to G in the eighth degree. D is related to G in the ninth degree and does not take. If the modified civil-law method were followed, G's nearest kindred would be C, his second cousin twice removed, because her common ancestor (G's great-grandparents) are closer than the common ancestor of his third cousins (G's great-great grandparents).

§ 2.5. Parent and Child Relationship

For purposes of intestate succession by, from, or through an individual:

(1) An individual is the child of his or her genetic parents, whether or not they are married to each other, except as otherwise provided in paragraph (2) or (5) or as other facts and circumstances warrant a different result.

(2) An adopted individual is a child of his or her adoptive parent or parents.

(A) If the adoption removes the child from the families of both of the genetic parents, the child is not a child of either genetic parent.

(B) If the adoption is by a relative of either genetic parent, or by the spouse or surviving spouse of such a relative, the individual remains a child of both genetic parents.

(C) If the adoption is by a stepparent, the adopted stepchild is not only a child of the adoptive stepparent but is also a child of the genetic parent who is married to the stepparent. Under several intestacy statutes, including the Uniform Probate Code, the adopted stepchild is also a child of the other genetic parent for purposes of inheritance from and through that parent, but not for purposes of inheritance from or through the child.

(3) A stepchild who is not adopted by his or her stepparent is not the stepparent's child.

(4) A foster child is not a child of his or her foster parent or parents.

(5) A parent who has refused to acknowledge or has abandoned his or her child, or a person whose parental rights have been terminated, is barred from inheriting from or through the child.

Comment:

a. *Child's relationship to genetic parents; nonmarital children.* A nonmarital child is just as much a child of his or her genetic parents as a marital child. Thus, except as circumstances warrant a different result, a child is the child of his or her genetic parents, whether or not they are married to each other. Exceptions to this rule include, in certain circumstances, a child who is adopted out of the family or who results from assisted reproductive technologies. See Comments *e* and *l*.

b. *Proving parentage.* Paternity may be established by any reliable scientific method, including DNA analysis.

c. *Presumption of paternity.* A child born to a married woman is presumptively the genetic child of the woman's husband. The particulars of the presumption, such as who has standing to bring a suit to rebut the presumption and whether or not there is a time limit for bringing a such a suit, depend on applicable law. . . . .

d. *Adopted child's relationship to adoptive parent or parents.* An adopted child is treated as a child of his or her adoptive parent or parents. Most intestacy statutes, including the Original and Revised UPC, treat an adopted child as a full member of the child's adoptive family.

Illustration:

1. C and D adopted X. X's genetic parents were A and B. X is a descendant of C and D for inheritance purposes. If C, or any of C's relatives from whom C would potentially inherit, die intestate, X would

be treated as C's child. X would also be treated as D's child if D, or any of D's relatives from whom D would potentially inherit, dies intestate.

e. Adoption that removes child from the families of both of the genetic parents; child's relationship to genetic parents. Despite the general principle that an individual is a child of his or her genetic parents (see Comment *a*), the opposite rule applies when the child has been adopted by strangers. Because the adoption removes the child from the families of both of the genetic parents, such a child is treated as not being a child of either genetic parent. Most statutes, including the Original and Revised UPC, establish the general principle that adopted children are *exclusively* members of their adopting families for inheritance purposes. Such an adoption breaks the ties to the child's genetic families. The adopting family becomes the child's replacement family.

Illustration:

2. A and B were the genetic parents of X. Upon birth, X was relinquished to an agency for placement. The agency placed X for adoption by C and D, a married couple who were unrelated and unknown to A and B. C and D adopted X. The adoption removed X from the families of A and B. X is not treated as the child of A or B, and does not inherit from or through either of them. Nor do the relatives of either A or B inherit from or through X.

f. Effect of adoption by a maternal or a paternal relative on child's relationship to nonadopting side. Most intestacy statutes fail to address the relationship of an adopted child to his or her nonadopting genetic family in the case of an adoption by a maternal or a paternal relative. To the extent that the statutory language permits, a child who is adopted by a maternal or a paternal relative of either genetic parent, or by the spouse or surviving spouse of such a relative, remains a child of both genetic parents. See, however, Comment *i* for the rule that prevents an adopted child from inheriting double shares in both adoptive and genetic capacities.

Illustration:

3. F and M, a married couple with one child, X, were killed in an airplane crash. After the deaths of F and M, M's sister, A, and A's husband, B, adopted X. F's father, PGF, a widower, then died intestate. Unless precluded by clear statutory language, X should be treated as PGF's grandchild (F's child).

g. Post-death adoption that does not remove child from genetic families. When someone with ties to the genetic family or families adopts a child after the death of the child's genetic parent, even if the adopting parent is not a relative of either genetic parent or a spouse or surviving spouse of such a relative (see Comment *f*), the child continues to be the child of both genetic parents for purposes of intestacy. Once a child has taken root in a family, an adoption after the death of one or both genetic parents is likely to be by someone chosen or approved of by the genetic family, such as a person named as guardian of the child in a deceased parent's will. In such a case, the child does not become estranged from the genetic family. Subsection (2)(A) of this section should not be interpreted as severing inheritance rights by, from, or through the genetic parents. Such an adoption has not "removed" the child from the families of both genetic parents, as that term is used in that subsection. Such a child continues to be a child of both genetic parents, as well as a child of the adopting parents. California implements this policy in § 6451 of the California Probate Code by providing that an adoption occurring "after the death of either of the natural parents" does not "sever[ ] the relationship of parent and child between an adopted person and a natural parent of the adopted person" if "the natural parent and the adopted person lived together at any time as parent and child, or the natural parent was married to or cohabiting with the other natural parent at the time the person was conceived and died before the person's birth." . . . .

Illustration:

4. F and M, a married couple with a four-year-old child, X, were involved in an automobile accident that killed F and severely injured M. M's injuries were permanent and caused her to be bedridden and under constant care for the rest of her life. Neither M's parents nor F's father (F's mother had died before the accident) nor any other relative was in a position to take custody of X. M consented to X being adopted by her close friends, A and B, a married couple approximately of the same ages as M. After the adoption became final, F's father and M's parents continued to have close contact with X, often visiting each other and sharing some holidays together. A and B often brought X to M's bedside for visits. F's father, PGF, a widower, then died intestate. Unless precluded by clear statutory language, X should be treated as PGF's grandchild (F's child).The result would be the same if both F and M were killed in the accident, their wills appointed A and B the guardians of the person of X, and A and B subsequently successfully petitioned to adopt X.

h. Adopted stepchildren. When a stepparent adopts his or her stepchild, the child is treated as a child of the adoptive stepparent and of the child's genetic parent who is married to the stepparent. Under many intestacy statutes, including the Uniform Probate Code, an adopted stepchild is also a child of his or her other genetic parent (the noncustodial genetic parent) for purposes of inheritance from and through that genetic parent, but not for purposes of inheritance from or through the child. Some non-UPC statutes distinguish between post-divorce and post-death stepparent adoptions, providing that even for purposes of inheritance from and through the noncustodial genetic parent, the ties to that parent and that parent's genetic family are cut in the case of a post-divorce stepparent adoption but continue in the case of a post-death stepparent adoption.

Illustration:

5. A and B were married and had two children, X and Y. A died, and B married C. C adopted X and Y. X and Y would be treated as B's children and as C's children for all purposes of inheritance. X and Y would be treated as A's children for purposes of inheritance from and through A but not for purposes of inheritance from or through X or Y. Thus, if A's father, G, died intestate, survived by X and Y and by G's daughter (A's sister), S, G's heirs would be S, X, and Y. S would take half and X and Y would take one-fourth each. This was a post-death stepparent adoption. Under the law of several states, including the UPC, C's adoption of X and Y would not break G's ties with X and Y, and they would inherit from him.

i. No double shares. A child who is adopted by a genetic relative cannot inherit from an intestate decedent in both a genetic and an adoptive capacity.

Illustration:

7. F and M, a married couple, had two children, X and Y. M died. After M's death, F married M's sister, A, who adopted X but did not adopt Y because Y was then a self-supporting adult living independently. A died. Then MGM (X's grandmother, the genetic mother of M and A) died intestate. Although, under the UPC and some non-UPC statutes, X is a child of her predeceased mother (M) as well as a child of her adoptive mother/genetic aunt (A), X cannot inherit from MGM in both capacities. MGM is not treated as if she had three grandchildren, X being counted twice and Y being counted once. MGM has only two grandchildren, X and Y. X can only take a single share, based on the share that gives her the larger amount. In this case, both shares give her the same amount—a half share, with Y taking the other half.

j. Stepchildren and foster children. A stepchild or a foster child is generally not treated as a child of his or her stepparent or foster parent or parents.

Illustration:

8. A and B were married with one child, X. A and B got divorced and B was awarded custody of X. B married C. C did not adopt X. X would not be treated as C's child because C never adopted X. X is C's stepchild. X would be treated as B's child. X is B's genetic child. X would be treated as A's child. X is A's genetic child. Had C adopted X, X would be treated as C's child and would still be treated as B's child. Under the UPC and some non-UPC statutes, X would also still be treated as A's child. See Comment *h*.

In one state, California, a stepchild or a foster child (and his or her descendants) is entitled to inherit from and through his or her stepparent or foster parent if "the relationship of parent and child" began "during the person's minority and continued throughout the parties' joint lifetimes" and if "it is established by clear and convincing evidence that the foster parent or stepparent would have adopted the person but for a legal barrier." Had C in Illustration 8 sought to adopt X but was prevented from doing so because A refused to consent, X would be treated as C's child under the California statute.

Under the law of a few states, a stepchild inherits from or through the stepparent if the intestate decedent leaves no surviving spouse and no adopted or genetic relatives. . . . .

k. "Equitable adoption" of foster children. A foster child who has not been formally or legally adopted by his or her foster parents may nevertheless obtain inheritance rights under a doctrine called "equitable adoption." Courts also refer to this doctrine as "virtual adoption," "de facto adoption," or "adoption by estoppel." Courts in over half the states have recognized such a doctrine, but courts in at least eight states have rejected it. The strongest factual situation presented for applying the doctrine is when the foster parents had expressly contracted to adopt the child, but failed to complete the adoption procedures. Even if the child cannot prove an express contract, however, courts have found an implied contract under certain circumstances, or have concluded that a child is equitably adopted if the child can prove that he or she bore a relationship to the foster parents that was identical to that of an adopted child.

l. Children produced by assisted reproductive technologies. The development of a great variety of reproductive technologies . . . raises the question of how to treat a child who is produced by some such means. In general, such a child should be treated as part of the family of the parent or parents who treat the child as their own and raise the child, one or both of whom might not be the child's genetic parent. . . . .

One reproductive technology that does not raise any legal issue is artificial insemination of a wife with the semen of her husband, a procedure referred to as *artificial insemination husband (AIH)*. A child conceived by this method is the genetic child of both husband and wife.

As noted in § 2.1, Comment *d*, the traditional view is that a child who is conceived and born after the decedent's death cannot be an heir. This proposition, however, is open to reexamination with respect to a child produced from genetic material of the decedent by assisted reproductive technology. Most statutory codifications, including enactments of the Original or Revised Uniform Probate Code, are not inconsistent with such a reexamination because they do not preclude inheritance by a child conceived after the decedent's death. They merely provide that a child who is in gestation at the decedent's death is treated as then living. . . . .

This Restatement takes the position that, to inherit from the decedent, a child produced from genetic material of the decedent by assisted reproductive technology must be born within a reasonable time after the decedent's death in circumstances indicating that the decedent would have approved of the child's right to inherit. A clear case would be that of a child produced by artificial insemination of the decedent's widow with his frozen sperm. If the AIH procedure occurs after the husband's death, and if the child is born within a reasonable time after the husband's death, the child should be treated as the husband's child for purposes of inheritance *from* the husband. Once conceived, such a child is the husband's and wife's child for all purposes of inheritance by, from, or through an intestate decedent who dies thereafter.

m. Barring inheritance by parent (and parent's relatives) if parent has refused to acknowledge or has abandoned the child, or a person whose parental rights have been terminated. A parent who has refused to acknowledge or has abandoned his or her child, or a person whose parental rights have been terminated, should be barred from inheriting from or through the child. (A person whose parental rights have been terminated is no longer the child's legal parent, but a former parent.) The parent's ancestors and collateral relatives should also be barred from inheriting through the parent from the child. If, however, an ancestor or a collateral relative, or a spouse of such a relative, contributed to the support or care of the child, or maintained a familial relationship with the child, that line is not barred.

Illustration:

9. F and M had a child, X. F and M were not married and did not live together. F did not acknowledge X as his child, and refused to contribute toward X's support. F is barred from inheriting from or through X. So are F's ancestors and collateral relatives. If, however, F's parents (or either of them) or any other ancestor or collateral relative of F, or spouse of such a relative, contributed to the support or care of the child, or maintained a familial relationship with the child, F's ancestors and collateral relatives are not barred from inheriting from or through X.

§ 2.6. Advancements

An inter vivos gift made by an intestate decedent to an individual who, at the decedent's death, is an heir is treated as an advancement against the heir's intestate share if the decedent indicated in a contemporaneous writing, or if the heir acknowledged in writing, that the gift was so to operate.

Comment:

a. Historical note. An advancement is an inter vivos gift that reduces the donee's share of the donor's intestate estate. The original purpose of the doctrine was to implement the decedent's presumed intent to equalize the amounts inherited by his or her children. By taking into account lifetime gifts, the doctrine achieved a more equal sharing by the children of their parent's wealth when the parent died without a will.

Most American jurisdictions originally modeled their advancements statute on the English Statute of Distribution of 1670, which provided only the manner of accounting for these lifetime gifts. The English courts treated all gifts made by the decedent during life as advancements, except gifts of small sums or gifts made for the purpose of maintenance or in satisfaction of the decedent's support obligation. Proof of whether a gift fell within one of the exceptions to the rule rested on objective evidence of the nature or purpose of the gift.

At first, American statutes also made no attempt to define an advancement or to provide guidelines on the type of transfers to be treated as advancements. Unlike their English counterparts, however, the American courts generally refused to adopt any categoric tests to identify advancements. Instead, they interpreted the advancements statutes as authorizing an inquiry to determine if the decedent's specific intent was to make an advancement rather than an absolute gift.

b. Comprehensive codification. Gradually, over time, the doctrine of advancements came to be codified more comprehensively. Two features are commonly found in comprehensive advancements statutes that differ from the doctrine at common law. First, the recipient of an advancement need not be a child of the donor. The scope of permissible recipients ranges from any descendant to any ancestor or collateral relative, or, as under the Uniform Probate Code, any person who turns out to be an heir, including the decedent's surviving spouse. Second, most statutes require written evidence of an intent that the gift be an advancement. Under the UPC, a gift is an advancement only if the donor declares in a contemporaneous writing or the donee acknowledges in writing that the gift is an advancement. Because most inter vivos transfers today are intended to be absolute gifts or are carefully integrated into a total estate plan, this Restatement adheres to the UPC rule.

c. Writing. The decedent's contemporaneous writing or the heir's written acknowledgment need not specifically state that the gift is an advancement. Any indication that the gift is to be taken into account in computing the division and distribution of the decedent's intestate estate is sufficient, no matter how expressed.

The donor of a gift cannot transform a previous, unqualified gift into an advancement by a subsequent change of mind. To safeguard against giving effect to a subsequent change of mind, this section, supported by a substantial body of uniform and nonuniform legislation (see Statutory Note), requires the decedent's writing to be a contemporaneous writing. No such requirement applies to an heir's written acknowledgment, however.

d. *Valuation.* Property advanced is valued as of the time the heir came into possession or enjoyment of the property or as of the time of the decedent's death, whichever first occurs, except that a gift of a life insurance policy on the decedent's life is the value of the proceeds at the decedent's death, reduced by any loans outstanding.

e. *Donee must turn out to be an heir.* The donee must be an heir at the decedent's death. The donee need not be an heir apparent at the time of the gift. For example, if the decedent, G, made an inter vivos gift intended to be an advancement to a grandchild at a time when the decedent's child who is the grandchild's parent is alive, the grandchild would not then be an heir apparent. See § 2.1, Comment *d.* Nevertheless, if G's intent that the gift be an advancement is contained in a written declaration or acknowledgment, the gift is regarded as an advancement if G's child (who is the grandchild's parent) predeceases G, making the grandchild an heir.

f. *Gift need not be an outright gift.* To be an advancement, the inter vivos donative transfer need not be an outright or present gift. It can be a will substitute, such as the designation of the donee as the beneficiary of the decedent's life-insurance policy or the beneficiary of the remainder interest in a revocable inter vivos trust.

g. *Computation of shares—hotchpot method.* The traditional method of taking an advancement into account in distributing the decedent's intestate estate is the hotchpot method. The hotchpot method is illustrated by the following example.

Illustration:

1. G died intestate, survived by his wife (W) and his three children (A, B, and C) by a prior marriage. G's probate estate is valued at $190,000. During his lifetime, G had advanced A $50,000 and B $10,000. G memorialized both gifts in a writing declaring his intent that they be advancements. The case is governed by the Uniform Probate Code. The first step in the hotchpot method is to add the value of the advancements to the value of G's probate estate. This combined figure is called the hotchpot estate. In this case, G's hotchpot estate preliminarily comes to $250,000 ($190,000 + $50,000 + $10,000). W's intestate share of a $250,000 estate under the UPC is $175,000 ($100,000 + ½ of $150,000). The remaining $75,000 is divided equally among A, B, and C, or $25,000 each. This calculation reveals that A has received an advancement greater than the share to which he is entitled; A can retain the $50,000 advancement, but is not entitled to any additional amount. A and A's $50,000 advancement are therefore disregarded and the process is begun over. Once A and A's $50,000 advancement are disregarded, G's revised hotchpot estate is $200,000 ($190,000 + $10,000). W's intestate share is $150,000 ($100,000 + ½ of $100,000). The remaining $50,000 is divided equally between B and C, or $25,000 each. From G's intestate estate, B receives $15,000 (B already having received $10,000 of his ultimate $25,000 share as an advancement); and C receives $25,000. The final division of G's probate estate is $150,000 to W, zero to A, $15,000 to B, and $25,000 to C.

h. *Effect if donee predeceases the decedent; donee's descendants not chargeable.* If the recipient of the property fails to survive the decedent, the gift is not taken into account in computing the division and distribution of the decedent's intestate estate, unless the decedent's contemporaneous writing provides otherwise. The basis for this rule, which is codified in the UPC, is that the heir must have received the advanced property in order to be charged with the advancement.

Illustration:

2. During her lifetime, G had advanced $10,000 to her son, A. G died intestate, leaving a probate estate of $50,000. G was survived by her daughter, B, and by A's child, X. A predeceased G. G's advancement to A is disregarded under the Uniform Probate Code. G's $50,000 intestate estate is divided into two equal shares, half ($25,000) going to B and the other half ($25,000) going to A's child, X. If A had survived G, the advancement to A would be taken into account in the division of G's intestate estate. Under the hotchpot method, illustrated above, G's hotchpot estate would be $60,000 (probate estate of $50,000 plus advancement to A of $10,000). A would take half of this $60,000 amount, or $30,000, but would be charged with already having received $10,000 of it. Consequently, A would take only a 2/5 share ($20,000) of G's intestate estate, and B would take the remaining 3/5 share ($30,000). A could not use a disclaimer to give his child, X, a larger share than A was entitled to. The effect of a disclaimer by A would be that the disclaimant's "interest" would devolve to A's descendants as if the disclaimant had predeceased the decedent. The "interest" that A disclaimed would be a right to a 2/5 share of G's estate, not a ½ share. Consequently, A's 2/5 share ($20,000) would pass to A's child, X.

i. *Partially intestate estates.* The doctrine of advancements applies to the intestate portion of a partially intestate estate as well as to a totally intestate estate.

j. *Releases and assignments.* A presumptive heir (or devisee) can *release* an expectancy interest to the decedent or *assign* an expectancy interest to a third person. A contract to release or assign an expectancy interest is only enforceable in equity and only if the heir (or devisee) receives fair consideration. If a releasor or assignor predeceases the decedent, the right of the descendants of a releasor but not of an assignor are cut off by the ancestor's action.

k. *Cross-reference.* For the testacy counterpart of the doctrine of advancements, see § 5.4 (ademption by satisfaction).

§ 2.7. Negative Wills

A decedent's will may expressly exclude or limit the right of an individual or class to succeed to property of the decedent passing by intestate succession.

Comment:

a. *Scope.* This section authorizes the decedent, by will, to exclude or limit the right of an individual or class to share in the decedent's intestate estate, in effect disinheriting that individual or class. A group or class of relatives to be disinherited can refer to a limited class of relatives (such as "my brothers and sisters") or to "all of my relatives" (or "all my heirs"). The class to be disinherited need not be limited to a group constituting some but not all of the testator's heirs. If the testator disinherits all heirs, the intestate estate escheats to the state.

By specifically authorizing negative wills, this section reverses the common-law rule, which defeats a testator's intent for no sufficient reason.

b. Construction. Whether or not in a specific case the decedent's will has excluded or limited the right of an individual or class to take a share of the decedent's intestate estate is a question of construction. A clear case would be one in which the decedent's will expressly states that an individual is to receive none of the decedent's estate. Examples would be testamentary language such as "my brother, Hector, is not to receive any of my property" or "Brother Hector is disinherited."

Another unproblematic case would be one in which the will states that an individual is to receive only a nominal devise, such as "I devise $50 to my brother, Hector, *and no more*." Without the phrase "and no more," the provision would not prevent Hector from taking his intestate share in addition to the $50 devise.

An individual need not be identified by name to be excluded. Thus, if brother Hector is the decedent's only brother, Hector could be identified by a term such as "my brother."

c. Effect. If a decedent expressly excludes or limits the right of an individual or class to take by intestate succession, the share of the decedent's intestate estate to which the disinherited individual or class would have succeeded passes as if that individual or class had disclaimed the intestate share. Thus, if the decedent's will provides that brother Hector is to receive $50 and no more, Hector is entitled to the $50 devise (because Hector is not treated as having predeceased the decedent for purposes of testate succession), but the portion of the decedent's intestate estate to which Hector would have succeeded passes as if Hector had disclaimed his intestate share. The consequence of a disclaimer by Hector of his intestate share is that Hector's intestate share passes to Hector's descendants by representation.

Illustration:

1. G died partially intestate. G is survived by brother Hector, Hector's three children (X, Y, and Z), and the child (V) of a deceased sister. G's will excluded Hector from sharing in G's intestate estate. V takes half of G's intestate estate. X, Y, and Z split the other half, i.e., they take 1/6 each. Had Hector not been excluded by G's will, the share to which Hector would have succeeded would have been ½. That half, not the whole of G's intestate estate, is what passes to Hector's descendants by representation as if Hector had disclaimed his intestate share. Note that if brother Hector had actually predeceased G, or was treated as if he predeceased G by reason of not surviving G by a required period such as 120 hours (e.g., under UPC § 2–104), then no consequence flows from Hector's disinheritance: V, X, Y, and Z would each take 1/4 of G's intestate estate.

CHAPTER 3

EXECUTION OF WILLS

Introductory Note: Chapter 2 covered the rules of intestacy, which operate in default of a valid will. Chapter 3 addresses the execution of wills and related matters. Chapter 3 is divided into two parts. Part A covers the formalities for executing a will and Part B covers a variety of related doctrines, such as the doctrines of republication by codicil, incorporation by reference, and independent significance.

Part A. Execution Formalities

§ 3.1. Attested Wills

A will is validly executed if it is in writing and is signed by the testator and by a specified number of attesting witnesses under procedures provided by applicable law.

Comment:

a. Definition of will; when operative. A *will* is a donative document that transfers property at death, amends, supplements, or revokes a prior will, appoints an executor, nominates a guardian, exercises a testamentary power of appointment, or excludes or limits the right of an individual or class to succeed to property of the decedent passing by intestate succession. The term "will" includes a codicil. A codicil is simply a will that amends or supplements a prior will.

A will does not become operative until the testator's death to transfer property, appoint an executor, nominate a guardian, exercise a testamentary power of appointment, or exclude or limit the right of an individual or class to succeed to property of the decedent passing by intestate succession. A will does operate upon execution, however, to revoke or amend a prior will. See Chapter 4.

b. Testate estate. The *testate estate* of a decedent is that part of the decedent's net probate estate (see § 1.1(b)) that passes to the decedent's devisees under a valid will.

c. Testator. A *testator* is a person who dies with a valid will. A testator is said to have died "testate," as opposed to a person who dies without a valid will, who is said to have died "intestate." Older usage distinguished between the "testator" (if a man) and the "testatrix" (if a woman), but with the increasing disuse of needlessly gendered terms, the distinction has been widely discarded. This Restatement refers to a person who dies with a valid will as the "testator."

d. Devise and devisee. A *devise* is a disposition of property, real or personal, in a will. A *devisee* is a person who is named in a will to receive real or personal property. A devisee takes by testate succession, as opposed to an heir of an intestate who takes by intestate succession.

In older usage, the terms "devise" and "devisee" were reserved for dispositions of *land* by will. A disposition of *personal property* was a "legacy" or "bequest," and the recipient was a "legatee." Today these words are commonly used interchangeably. The Uniform Probate Code defines the word "devise" as "a testamentary disposition of real or personal property." This Restatement adheres to the newer usage and refers to testamentary dispositions of land or personal property as "devises" and the recipients as "devisees."

e. Choice of law. Most probate codes, including the Original and Revised Uniform Probate Code, contain a choice-of-law provision. . . . . The UPC provides that a will is validly executed if it was executed in compliance with the law at the time of execution of the place where the will was executed, or of the law where at the time of execution or at the time of death the testator was domiciled, had a place of abode, or was a national. The policy underlying such legislation is to promote the validation of wills by maximizing the number of jurisdictions with whose law an instrument may be found to comply. This policy commends itself as a principle of decisional law in a state that does not have such choice-of-law legislation.

f. Statutory formalities for attested wills. Executing a valid will requires the testator to manifest an intent to make a will (Comment *g*) and to comply with specified statutory formalities. The main statutory formalities for attested wills have been in force for centuries. They are writing, signature, and attestation. The will must be: (1) in writing; (2) signed by the testator; and (3) signed by a specified number of attesting witnesses in accordance with procedures provided by applicable law. The procedures provided by applicable law, especially the details regarding signature and attestation, vary considerably from state to state.

Before the adoption of the Original Uniform Probate Code in 1969, American statutes were—and still are in many non-UPC states—largely copied from one or the other (or, in some cases, partly from both) of two English statutes: the Statute of Frauds of 1677 and the Wills Act of 1837.

> *Statute of Frauds*, 1677, 29 Car. 2, c. 3. § 5. [A]ll devises and bequests of any lands . . . shall be in writing and signed by the party so devising the same or by some other person in his presence and by his express directions and shall be attested and subscribed in the presence of the said devisor by three or four credible witnesses or else they shall be utterly void and of none effect.
>
> *Wills Act*, 1837, 7 Wm. 4 & 1 Vict. c. 26. § 9. [N]o will shall be valid unless it shall be in writing and executed in manner hereinafter mentioned; (that is to say,) it shall be signed at the foot or end thereof by the testator, or by some other person in his

presence and by his direction; and such signature shall be made or acknowledged by the testator in the presence of two or more witnesses present at the same time, and such witnesses shall attest and subscribe the will in the presence of the testator, but no form of attestation shall be necessary.

The later English statute, the Wills Act of 1837, increased rather than decreased the statutory formalities. Prior to the promulgation of the Original Uniform Probate Code, most American states had opted for a statute modeled on the lower-formality Statute of Frauds. The Original UPC lowered the formalities still further in order to "validate the will whenever possible." Original UPC General Comment to Art. II, Part 5. The Original UPC required only that a will be in writing, signed by the testator, and signed by two persons who witnessed either the testator's act of signing or the testator's acknowledgment of either the signature or the will. As revised in 1990, the UPC essentially carries forward the set of formalities of the Original UPC.

Revised Uniform Probate Code § 2–502. Execution; Witnessed Wills;. . . .

(a) [An attested] will must be:

in writing;

signed by the testator or in the testator's name by some other individual in the testator's conscious presence and by the testator's direction; and

signed by at least two individuals, each of whom signed within a reasonable time after he [or she] witnessed either the signing of the will as described in paragraph (2) or the testator's acknowledgment of that signature or acknowledgment of the will.

A court should never impose formal requirements beyond those in the statute.

g. Testamentary intent. To be a will, the document must be executed by the decedent with testamentary intent, i.e., the decedent must intend the document to be a will or to become operative at the decedent's death. Whether the decedent executed a document with testamentary intent is a question of fact on which evidence of intention may be considered. A clear, unambiguous expression of testamentary intent in the document raises a strong (but not irrebuttable) presumption that the document was executed with testamentary intent. The presumption is rebuttable only by clear and convincing evidence. . . . .

In the absence of a clear expression of testamentary intent in the document, testamentary intent can be inferred from the document or established by extrinsic evidence. See § 3.2, Comment *c*.

h. Publication requirement. A few non-UPC statutes require the testator to "publish" the will to the attesting witnesses. The English Wills Act of 1837 did not impose such a requirement, nor did the English Statute of Frauds of 1677, nor does the Uniform Probate Code.

To satisfy the publication requirement, when imposed by applicable law, the testator must signify to the attesting witnesses that the document is the testator's will. Ideally, the testator makes an explicit statement to the witnesses, such as "This is my will," but any signification, including the testator's silent acquiescence in someone else's statement to the witnesses that the document is the testator's will, satisfies the publication requirement.

The publication requirement does not require the testator to inform the attesting witnesses of the contents of the will, but only that the document that they are signing as attesting witnesses is the testator's will.

i. *The writing requirement.* All the statutes, including the original and revised versions of the Uniform Probate Code, require a will to be in writing. The requirement of a writing does not require that the will be written on sheets of paper, but it does require a medium that allows the markings to be detected. A will, for example, scratched in the paint on the fender of a car would be in writing, but one "written" by waving a finger in the air would not be.

j. *Testator's signature.* All the statutes, including the Uniform Probate Code, require the testator to sign the will. To be a signature, the testator must write his or her name with the intent of adopting the document as his or her own. A signature provides evidence of finality, and serves to distinguish the final will from a preliminary draft, an incomplete document, or scribbled thoughts about how the will might take shape in the future. The testator's handwritten name in freestanding form at the end of the document unquestionably satisfies the signature requirement. The testator's handwritten name in freestanding form at any other place on the document raises an inference that the testator "signed" the document.

A person's name written in his or her own handwriting is not necessarily a signature. If the testator's name is not written in freestanding form, then there should be other evidence that the testator adopted the document as his or her will in order to count the handwritten name as a signature. See Comment *k*.

Ideally, the testator "signs" the will by writing out his or her name in full. Signature by mark or cross is sufficient, however. So also is signature by term of relationship (such as "Dad," "Mom," or "Auntie"), abbreviation, nickname, a pet name, a first name, a last name, initials, or pseudonym, or even by fingerprint or seal. The name need not be spelled correctly. It need not be legible. It may be made with the assistance of another, who guides the testator's hand. The crucial requirement is that it must be done with intent of adopting the document as the testator's will.

Most statutes, including the Original and Revised UPC, allow another person to sign the testator's name if it is done in the presence and at the direction of the testator. See Comment *n*. A further requirement, sometimes imposed by non-UPC statutes, is that a person who signs for the testator must also sign his or her own name and sometimes also give his or her address; a few of these statutes provide that the failure to comply does not invalidate the will.

k. *Location of testator's signature.* Neither the UPC nor the non-UPC statutes that are derived from the English Statute of Frauds specify a place where the testator's signature must be located. A recurring problem under these statutes is the case in which the only place where the testator's handwritten name appears is in the exordium, that is, in a clause at the beginning of the will stating that "I, [name of testator], do make, publish, and declare this to be my last will and testament." Since the testator's name is not in freestanding form, the handwritten name should not be counted as a signature unless there is evidence that the person adopted the document as his or her will. See Comment *j*. . . . .

l. *The sign-at-end requirement.* The English Wills Act of 1837 required the testator to sign "at the foot or end" of the will. See Comment *f*.

In this country, a small number of states require the testator's signature to be at the end of the will. A difficulty that recurs under these statutes arises when there is a provision or set of provisions that appears on the will below the testator's signature. The inference is that these provisions were added after the testator signed the document. Depending on the facts and circumstances, these provisions might be given effect under the harmless-error doctrine (see § 3.3), but if not, their existence does not invalidate the will and prevent the provisions appearing above the testator's signature from being given effect.

m. The sign-first requirement. Because the act of signing by the witnesses is the final act of authentication, the testator must ordinarily sign the will before the witnesses sign. If, however, the testator and the witnesses sign as part of a single (or continuous) transaction, the exact order of signing is not critical.

Under the UPC and under non-UPC statutes modeled on the English Statute of Frauds, the witnesses need not see the testator sign nor see the testator's signature. If the testator's signature appears above the witnesses' signatures, that raises an inference that the testator signed first.

Non-UPC statutes modeled on the English Wills Act commonly require that the testator's signature "be made or acknowledged by the testator in the presence of" the witnesses. Under this more restrictive statutory formulation, the testator must either sign the will or acknowledge his or her signature in the presence of the witnesses.

n. Signature by another. The testator need not sign the will himself or herself. The statutes allow someone else to sign the testator's name for the testator, if the testator directed the other person to sign the testator's name and if the other person acted in the testator's presence. In determining whether the person signed in the testator's presence, this Restatement adopts and the UPC codifies the conscious-presence test and rejects the line-of-vision test (see Comment *p*). . . . .

o. Number and competency of attesting witnesses. Nearly all states require two attesting witnesses. At one time, a substantial minority of states required three attesting witnesses, but the number of states requiring three attesting witnesses has dwindled. See Statutory Note.

The English Statute of Frauds of 1677 required the witnesses to be "credible." In this country, most non-UPC statutes require the witnesses to be either "credible" or "competent." Today in almost all states the conviction of a crime no longer renders a person an incompetent witness to a will. Mental incompetency, whether from mental deficiency, extreme intoxication, or the influence of drugs, remains a ground of disqualification as a witness. A few states specifically provide by statute a minimum age, such as 18, for attesting witnesses. More commonly, however, no age is specified in the statute. If no age is specified in the statute, a minor is a valid witness, unless the minor was not old enough to observe, remember, and relate the facts occurring at the execution ceremony.

Interested witnesses—disqualified at common law. The Statute of Frauds of 1677 was construed to disqualify a witness who was a devisee under the will and, therefore, presumed interested in sustaining the will. At that time, a person who was a party or had an interest in the outcome of litigation was disqualified from testifying as a witness because of that interest. In construing the Statute of Frauds, the courts carried over this incapacity of the testimonial witness to the attesting witness. The result was that a will wholly failed if a necessary attesting witness was also a devisee.

Purging statutes. After a time, it came to be thought in England that the invalidity of the entire will was unnecessarily harsh on the other devisees. To remedy the situation, a statute—commonly referred to as a *purging statute*—was passed in 1752, providing that the disposition to the attesting witness should be void, but the witness should "be admitted as a witness to the execution of such will." 25 Geo. 2, c. 6, § 1. By eliminating the witness's interest, the witness was rendered "credible" and the will was saved.

In this country, as indicated above, most non-UPC statutes require attesting witnesses to be either "credible" or "competent." The witness must qualify at the time of execution, hence a subsequent change in status does not remedy the disqualification. The devise of a beneficial interest is usually regarded as disqualifying the witness, unless there is a purging statute similar to the English statute of 1752. Almost all non-UPC states have purging-type legislation. Most American purging statutes provide a partial exception for a devisee who is also an heir of the testator or a devisee under the testator's prior will. Under this exception, an heir or devisee forfeits only that portion of his or her devise that exceeds the amount that he or she would have taken by intestacy or under a prior will if the will in question were invalid. . . . .

Supernumerary witnesses. If an interested witness is a supernumerary witness, the witness takes his or her full devise because the will was witnessed by a sufficient number of disinterested witnesses. . . . .

Spouse of a witness. The common-law disqualification of a witness who had an interest in the outcome of litigation extended also to the witness's spouse. This rule was applied in England to hold that the spouse of a devisee was not a credible witness to a will. Moreover, the 1752 purging statute did not save the will, since it only applied to the attesting witness. The situation was adjusted in the English Wills Act of 1837 by invalidating a devise to the spouse of an attesting witness as well as to the witness, thus allowing the purging statute to save the will. See 7 Wm. 4 & 1 Vict., c. 26, § 15.

In this country, the spouse of a devisee is not an "interested" witness unless the purging statute expressly voids all or a portion of a devise to a devisee if his or her spouse serves as an attesting witness.

Uniform Probate Code—interest of attesting witness does not disqualify the witness. The Original Uniform Probate Code materially altered the treatment of interested witnesses. Under the UPC, an interested witness is neither disqualified as an attesting witness nor forfeits any portion of his or her devise. Close to 40 percent of the states now follow this rule. The rule is continued without substantive amendment in the UPC as revised in 1990. The main rationale for not disqualifying an interested witness is to prevent unjust results for home-made wills in which family members innocently serve as witnesses. A devise to an interested witness remains a suspicious circumstance, which is relevant to a claim of fraud or undue influence. See [Division III] of this Restatement on Protective Doctrines.

p. Signing "in the presence of" another. Non-UPC statutes commonly require the witnesses to sign the will "in the presence of" the testator. Signing by the witnesses outside of the presence of the testator, followed by an acknowledgment of the signature in the testator's presence, is generally not permitted.

Statutes modeled on the English Wills Act of 1837 commonly impose additional signing-in-the-presence-of requirements. The statutes require that the *testator* sign (or acknowledge his or her signature) "in the presence of" the *witnesses* and that the *witnesses* sign "in the presence of" *each other*. There are two interpretations of the presence requirement, the line-of-vision test and the conscious-presence test.

Line-of-vision test. Under the *line-of-vision test,* the witnesses must sign within the testator's "line of vision." It is not necessary for the testator to have watched the witnesses sign, as long as the testator could have watched them sign. Even under the line-of-vision test, an exception is made for a blind testator; the witnesses need only sign in the testator's conscious presence. The line-of-vision test is disapproved in this Restatement.

Conscious-presence test. This Restatement adopts the *conscious-presence test,* which recognizes that a person can sense the presence or actions of another without seeing the other person. If the testator and the witnesses are near enough to be able to sense each other's presence, typically by being within earshot of one another, so that the testator knows what is occurring, the presence requirement is satisfied.

Uniform Probate Code. Instead of codifying the conscious-presence test, both the Original and the Revised Uniform Probate Code dispense with the "presence" requirement. The "presence" requirement is retained only for cases in which the testator directs someone else to sign on his or her behalf. The Original Code required that person to sign the testator's name "in the testator's presence." The revised version requires the person to sign the testator's name "in the testator's *conscious* presence." (Emphasis added). See Comment *n*.

The UPC does not require the *witnesses* to sign in the presence of the testator or in the presence of each other. It requires the witnesses to "witness" the testator's act of signing the will or "witness" the testator's act of acknowledging either the signature or the will. The witnessing requirement means that the witnesses must observe the act. The requirement would not be satisfied by showing simply that the act took place in their line of vision.

The UPC's abrogation of the requirement that the witnesses sign in the testator's presence raises a question about whether there is any time limit on when the witnesses must sign the will after they have witnessed the testator's signature or acknowledgment of the signature or of the will. The Original Code left this question open, but as revised in 1990, the Code requires the witnesses to sign within a reasonable time after they witnessed one of the required acts.

q. *Attestation clauses.* An attestation clause is located immediately below the testator's signature and above the signature of the attesting witnesses. An illustrative attestation clause provides:

The foregoing instrument, consisting of ________ typewritten pages, including this page, was signed, published and declared by the above named testator to be his/her last will, in the presence of us; we, in his/her presence, at his/her request, and in the presence of each other, have hereunto subscribed our names as witnesses; and we declare that at the time of the execution of this instrument the testator, according to our best knowledge and belief, was of sound mind and under no constraint.

Dated at ______________, ________, this ________ day of ________, ________.

______________________	______________________
Witness	Address
______________________	______________________
Witness	Address

Although no state requires that a will contain an attestation clause, the use of one is desirable because it raises a rebuttable presumption of the truth of the recitals.

r. *Self-proved wills.* Several statutes, including the Uniform Probate Code, provide that a will may be self-proved. A self-proved will is a will for which the testator and the witnesses have executed an affidavit before a notary public or similar officer detailing the procedures followed in the execution of the testator's will. The effect of a self-proved will varies among jurisdictions. In some jurisdictions a self-proved will conclusively establishes that all formalities have been met. The Original and Revised UPC provision conclusively presumes that all the signature requirements imposed by its wills statute have been met and creates a rebuttable presumption that all other requirements for a valid will have been met. A self-proved will also serves to eliminate the need for having the witnesses testify upon the filing of the will to prove its authenticity.

A signature affixed to a self-proving affidavit is treated as a signature affixed to the will, if so treating it is necessary to establish the will's due execution. . . . .

s. *Conditional wills.* A will may be made conditional by clear language indicating that the will is to take effect only if some particular event happens. Recitals of inducement are not conditions. Thus, merely stating the purpose of making the will, such as stating that "I am making this will because I am about to go on a trip," does not make a will conditional.

§ 3.2. Holographic Wills

Statutes in many states provide that a will, though unwitnessed, is validly executed if it is written in the testator's handwriting and signed by the testator, and, under some statutes, dated in the testator's handwriting.

Comment:

a. Statutory formalities for holographic wills. Holographic wills are authorized by statute in over half of the states. Holographic will formality has evolved through three phases:

> *Typical first-generation holographic-will statute.* "A holographic will is one that is entirely written, dated, and signed by the hand of the testator. It is subject to no other form, and need not be witnessed."
>
> *Second-generation holographic-will statute—Original Uniform Probate Code.* "A will which does not comply with [the requirements for an attested will] is valid as a holographic will, whether or not witnessed, if the signature and the material provisions are in the handwriting of the testator."
>
> *Third-generation holographic-will statute—Revised Uniform Probate Code.* "A will that does not comply with [the requirements for an attested will] is valid as a holographic will, whether or not witnessed, if the signature and material portions of the document are in the testator's handwriting."

The holographic-will statutes entail a significant reduction in formality by comparison with the requirements for attested wills (see § 3.1). The holographic-will statutes allow the testator to dispense with attestation entirely. Handwriting substitutes for attestation in holographic testation. Although handwriting provides superior evidence of genuineness, handwriting does not serve the protective and cautionary policies, nor does it serve the evidentiary values associated with having attesting witnesses observe and participate in executing the will. Accordingly, the legislature's decision to recognize holographic testation represents a determination to accept a lower level of formality. (Regarding the purposes of formalities, see § 3.3, Comments *a* and *b*.)

b. Extent of handwritten portion. The essential characteristic of the first-generation holographic-will statute (Comment *a*) is that it requires a holographic will to be *entirely* written, signed, and dated in the testator's handwriting. In cases in which nonholographic matter appears in the document, two theories have emerged in the case law to validate the affected will in some circumstances—the intent theory and the surplusage theory. Both theories recognize that words or marks on a sheet of paper that are not in the testator's handwriting do not necessarily disqualify the handwritten portion as a holographic will. Under the intent theory, words or marks not intended by the testator to be part of the will need not be in the testator's handwriting. Under the surplusage theory, the portions of the document in the testator's handwriting are given effect as a holographic will if they make sense as a will standing alone, without regard to the portions of the document not in the testator's handwriting. This Restatement adopts the surplusage theory. A jurisdiction committed to the intent theory should adopt a presumption that any portion that is surplusage—any portion not essential for the handwritten provisions to make sense as a will—was not intended by the testator to be part of the will. Because the main achievement of the handwriting requirement is superior evidence of genuineness, any portion of the will sufficient to generate an analyzable handwriting sample achieves the main purpose of the handwriting requirement for holographic testation. . . . .

Because the main purpose of requiring a holographic will to be handwritten is to provide a more substantial handwriting sample than the testator's signature alone supplies, the document need not be *entirely* handwritten to fulfill the purpose. Neither the Original nor the Revised Uniform Probate Code requires a holographic will to be entirely written in the handwriting of the testator. The UPC authorizes a holographic will that is composed of handwritten and nonhandwritten portions. The nonhandwritten portion is part of the holographic will. In addition, neither the Original nor Revised UPC requires a holographic will to be dated. Both do require that the testator sign the will. The Original UPC requires the "material provisions" to be in the handwriting of the testator and the Revised UPC requires the "material portions" of the document to be in the handwriting of the testator. The purpose of changing from "material provisions" to "material portions" was to leave no doubt about the validity of a will in which immaterial parts of a dispositive provision—such as "I give, devise, and bequeath"—are not in the testator's handwriting. The material portion of a dispositive provision—which must be in the testator's handwriting under the Revised UPC—are the words identifying the property and the devisee. Even under the Original UPC, the surplusage theory should be applied to disregard immaterial nonhandwritten portions of a dispositive provision. . . . .

A holographic will is not invalid because it is written in a foreign language.

c. *Testamentary intent—holographic wills.* Holographic wills as well as attested wills must be executed with testamentary intent. See § 3.1, Comment *g*. Testamentary intent need not be shown from the face of the will, but can be established by extrinsic evidence. Extrinsic evidence can also be used to establish the meaning of a holographic will. . . . .

In holographic-will cases, it may be important to identify what constitutes extrinsic evidence. Under a first-generation holographic-will statute, the nonholographic material on a preprinted will form is extrinsic evidence that can be used to establish testamentary intent as well as the meaning of the holographic material. Under the second- or third-generation holographic-will statutes, however, the nonholographic material on a preprinted will form is part of the holographic will, not extrinsic evidence. . . . .

d. *Signature requirement.* All holographic-will statutes require the testator to sign the will. The signature requirement for holographic wills is the same as that for attested wills, see § 3.1, Comment *j*, except that holographic-will statutes usually do not authorize someone else to sign the will on the testator's behalf. A few holographic-will statutes (but not the UPC) require the testator's signature to appear at the end of the document. See § 3.1, Comment *l*.

e. *Date.* Some holographic-will statutes (but not the UPC) require that the will be dated in the testator's handwriting. The date need not be accurate. The fact that more than one date appears on the document in the testator's handwriting does not invalidate the will. The date can be rendered in various styles, such as May 11, 1996, May 12, '96, 5/12/96, 5-12-96, 5.12.96. If numbers only are used, the fact that either of the first two numbers is 12 or below—such as 5/12/96—does not invalidate the will. Although the first number "5" might refer to the day of the month, and the second number "12" to the month, customary usage in the United States is that the first number refers to the month and the second number refers to the day of the month. An inference therefore arises that 5/12/96 refers to May 12, 1996, not to December 5, 1996.

f. Handwritten alteration of a holographic will. After the testator signs a holographic will, the testator may validly make a handwritten alteration of the will without re-signing the document.

g. Handwritten alteration of an attested will. In a jurisdiction that permits holographic wills, the testator may validly make a handwritten alteration of a previously executed attested will if he or she signs the alteration and, if the statute so requires, dates it. The handwritten alteration is treated as a holographic codicil. The codicil is valid under any holographic-will statute because it is entirely written, signed, and (if required) dated in the testator's handwriting. The nonhandwritten portions of the original, attested will constitute extrinsic evidence, however, that can be considered in determining testamentary intent and the meaning of the handwritten codicil.

Illustration:

9. *Handwritten alteration of attested will.* As originally executed, G's attested will devised $10,000 to her brother, A; $20,000 to her brother, B; and $15,000 to her brother, C. After G's death, G's will was found with "$10,000" crossed out and the figure "$12,000" written in above it, with "$20,000" crossed out and the figure "$3,000" written in above it, and with "$15,000" crossed out and the figure "$7,500" written in above it. All the alterations were in G's handwriting. G also initialed and dated each of the alterations in her handwriting. The handwritten alterations are valid as a holographic codicil to G's attested will. . . . . Dating the alterations is not essential, unless the holographic-will statute requires holographic wills to be dated. Standing alone, the handwriting neither expresses testamentary intent nor has any intelligible meaning. The handwriting merely says "$12,000," "$3,000," and "$7,500," followed by G's initials and a date. The terms of the attested will, however, constitute extrinsic evidence that can be considered in determining testamentary intent and the meaning of the holographic codicil. . . . . The terms of the attested will provide the context that demonstrates that the handwritten codicil was written and signed with testamentary intent. They also show that the $12,000 was to go to A, the $3,000 was to go to B, and the $7,500 was to go to C.

h. Nuncupative wills. Statutes in a number of states allow personal property (often subject to a ceiling on value), and in a few instances real property, to pass under nuncupative or oral wills. "Soldiers in active military service" and "mariners or sailors at sea" traditionally have been excused from the more rigorous testamentary formalities. See Statute of Frauds, 1677, 29 Car. 2, c. 3, §§ 19–21, 23; Wills Act, 1837, 7 Wm. 4 & 1 Vict., c. 26, § 11. Some states allow a person in his or her "last illness"—"one so violent that the testator has not the time, opportunity, or means to make a written will in legal form"—to make an oral will, provided certain requirements are met. The testator must: (1) be dying and know it; (2) express orally the intent to make an oral will; and (3) call upon "competent" witnesses (usually at least two) to witness that the spoken words are his or her last will. The witnesses must put into writing their testimony within a prescribed time after the act and, generally, the nuncupative act must take place within the testator's home, unless he or she was "surprised" by the "last illness" while on a journey.

§ 3.3. Excusing Harmless Errors

A harmless error in executing a will may be excused if the proponent establishes by clear and convincing evidence that the decedent adopted the document as his or her will.

Comment:

a. *Purpose of the statutory formalities.* The purpose of the statutory formalities described in § 3.1 (Attested Wills) and § 3.2 (Holographic Wills) is to determine whether the decedent adopted the document as his or her will. The formalities are meant to facilitate this intent-serving purpose, not to be ends in themselves.

Four discrete functions have been attributed to the formalities—the evidentiary, cautionary, protective, and channeling functions. The evidentiary function requires solid evidence of the existence and content of the decedent's directions. The cautionary function requires some indication that the decedent arrived at these directions with adequate awareness. The protective function attempts to assure that the contents and the execution of the will were the product of the decedent's free choice. The channeling function is meant to facilitate a substantial degree of standardization in the organization, language, and content of most wills, so that they can be prepared and administered in a fairly routine manner.

b. *Excusing harmless errors.* As noted in Comment *a*, the purpose of the statutory formalities is to determine whether the decedent adopted the document as his or her will. Modern authority is moving away from insistence on strict compliance with statutory formalities, recognizing that the statutory formalities are not ends in themselves but rather the means of determining whether their underlying purpose has been met. A will that fails to comply with one or another of the statutory formalities, and hence would be invalid if held to a standard of strict compliance with the formalities, may constitute just as reliable an expression of intention as a will executed in strict compliance.

This Restatement, supported by the Restatement Second, Property (Donative Transfers) § 33.1, Comment *g*, and by the Revised UPC . . ., is aligned with this modern trend. This Restatement adopts the position that a harmless error in executing a will may be excused if the proponent establishes by clear and convincing evidence that the decedent adopted the document as his or her will.

The trend toward excusing harmless errors is based on a growing acceptance of the broader principle that mistake, whether in execution or in expression, should not be allowed to defeat intention nor to work unjust enrichment. The movement to cure well-proved mistakes in expression is reflected in [Chapters 10, 11, and 12] of this Restatement, on Construction, Reformation, and Modification of Donative Documents.

The question in each case is whether a defect in execution was harmless in relation to the purpose of the statutory formalities, not in relation to each individual statutory formality scrutinized in isolation. Examining each formality in isolation could simply result in an inquiry as technical and non-purposive as the strict-compliance approach. The purposive question is whether the evidence regarding the overall conduct of the testator establishes, in a clear and convincing manner, that the testator adopted the document as his or her will.

In applying this standard to particular cases, a hierarchy of sorts has been found to emerge among the formalities. The requirement of a writing is so fundamental to the purpose of the execution formalities that it cannot be excused as harmless under the principle of this Restatement. Only a harmless error in executing a *document* can be excused under this Restatement.

Among the defects in execution that can be excused, the lack of a signature is the hardest to excuse. An unsigned will raises a serious but not insuperable doubt about whether the testator adopted the document as his or her will. A particularly attractive case for excusing the lack of the testator's signature is a crossed will case, in which, by mistake, a wife signs her husband's will and the husband signs his wife's will. Because attestation makes a more modest contribution to the purpose of the formalities, defects in compliance with attestation procedures are more easily excused.

Illustrations:

1. *Letter of instructions; draft prepared in accordance with instructions.* G sent a signed letter to his attorney giving directions for the preparation of his will. G died while the will was being prepared. Neither the letter nor the draft prepared by his attorney can be given effect because G never adopted either document as his will.

2. *Incomplete signature.* G neglected to make a will until she was near death. After giving instructions for the preparation of her will, she had the draft brought to her bedside. Witnesses were present as the will execution began. G had written several letters of her name but had not completed writing her signature when she suddenly fell back and died. Shortly after G's death, the witnesses signed the document. G's failure to complete her signature is a harmless error that may be excused because her act of partially signing the document in these circumstances constitutes clear and convincing evidence that G adopted the document as her will.

3. *Attestation defect—witness failed to sign.* H and W, husband and wife, arrived at their attorney's office to execute their wills, which had been prepared in accordance with their instructions. Two legal secretaries, who were to act as attesting witnesses, were present when H signed his will and when W signed her will. Both witnesses then signed H's will in H's presence. One of the witnesses signed W's will in W's presence, but for some unexplained reason, the other witness neglected to sign. The failure to obtain the signature of one of the witnesses is a harmless error that may be excused because the evidence establishes by clear and convincing evidence that W adopted the document as her will.

4. *Attestation defect—witness signed outside testator's presence.* G was ill in bed and unable to come to his attorney's office. G's attorney, who had drafted G's will in accordance with G's directions, arranged to go to G's house to conduct the execution ceremony. As G's attorney looked on, G signed the will. G's attorney had expected two neighbors to attend and act as attesting witnesses, but the neighbors never showed up. G's attorney then signed the will as one of the attesting witnesses, took the will back to her office and showed the document to one of her law partners, informing the partner that the document was G's will and that G had requested that the law partner witness the will as an attesting witness. The law partner then telephoned G and inquired as to whether the instrument presented was his will. After G verified that

it was, the law partner, in the presence of the drafting attorney, signed the document as an attesting witness. The drafting attorney's law partner testified that he knew G's voice. The failure of the drafting attorney's law partner to sign in the presence of the testator (or in a UPC jurisdiction, the failure to sign after witnessing the testator's act of signing or of acknowledging his signature or his will), is a harmless error that may be excused because the evidence establishes by clear and convincing evidence that G adopted the document as his will.

c. Scope of harmless-error rule. The harmless-error rule established in this section applies not only to defective execution but also to the validity of attempts to revoke a will or to revive a revoked will, topics covered in Chapter 4.

Part B. Related Doctrines

§ 3.4. Republication by Codicil

A will is treated as if it were executed when its most recent codicil was executed, whether or not the codicil expressly republishes the prior will, unless the effect of so treating it would be inconsistent with the testator's intent.

Comment:

a. Historical background. A codicil is a document that amends or supplements a prior will. See § 3.1, Comment *a.*

Execution of a codicil is usually thought to have the effect of *re-executing* the will that it amends or supplements. This idea of republication by codicil apparently originated as a device to subvert the rule that a will could not dispose of land acquired after the will was executed.

From an early time, a will could bequeath after-acquired personal property, but it was not until the Wills Act of 1837 that English law permitted a will to operate on after-acquired land. The church courts had jurisdiction over wills of personal property and borrowed from Roman law the concept that a will could dispose of after-acquired chattels. Some power to devise land arose under the Statute of Wills of 1540, which enabled any person who should "have" certain land to dispose of it "by last will and testament . . . ." This language was soon construed as allowing disposition only of land owned by the testator when executing the will.

The Wills Act of 1837 reversed the old rule regarding after-acquired land, permitting disposition by will of "all real estate and all personal estate which [the testator] shall be entitled to, either at law or in equity, at the time of [the testator's] death." In the United States, the rule restricting the disposition of after-acquired land has been everywhere eliminated, in most states by statute. See, e.g., Unif. Prob. Code § 2–602 (1990).

b. Intent-effecting doctrine. The doctrine of republication by codicil is to be applied unless the effect would be inconsistent with the testator's intent. That a codicil contains a provision expressly republishing the prior will does not require the doctrine to be applied. The doctrine is still inapplicable if the effect of applying it would be inconsistent with the testator's intent.

Illustrations:

1. G's will, executed on June 15, 1989, devised $15,000 to "the person who will be identified in a letter that will be found in my effects." On August 18, 1994, G executed a codicil to his will changing personal

representatives. After G's death in 1995, his will and codicil were found in a desk drawer along with a letter dated July 2, 1993, stating that the $15,000 devise was to go to his "friend, Shannon." Although the letter was not in existence when the will was originally executed, the doctrine of republication by codicil treats the will as having been executed on August 18, 1994. Consequently, the requirement for incorporating the July 2, 1993, letter into the will that the letter must have been in existence when the will was executed (see § 3.6) is satisfied.

3. G's will, executed three years before his death, created a testamentary trust for his surviving spouse, and made equal monetary devises to each of his two children, A and B. Four months before his death, and after his third child, C, was born, G executed a codicil to his will that altered the marital-deduction trust in order to take advantage of a change in tax law. The codicil expressly republished his prior will. Applicable law contains a pretermitted-heir statute that gives a share of the estate to a child who is born after the will is executed. The doctrine of republication by codicil is not applied because application of the doctrine would prevent G's third child, C, from taking a share of his estate under the pretermitted-heir statute.

§ 3.5. Integration of Multiple Pages or Writings Into a Single Will

To be treated as part of a will, a page or other writing must be present when the will is executed and must be intended to be part of the will.

Comment:

a. Introduction. A will, whether on a single page or on multiple pages or composed of other kinds of writings, is a single document that needs to be executed only once. Each page or writing that makes up a will need not be independently executed. What is required is that the pages or other writings that were intended to be part of the will were all present at the time of execution. Pages or other writings that were present at the time of execution but not intended to be part of the will are not part of the will.

b. Physical connection. Quite commonly, all pages of a will are stapled or otherwise fastened together at the time of execution. This is not a requirement, however. In fact, no physical connection, not even by devices such as paper clips, is required.

Physical connection does, however, support an inference that the physically connected pages or other writings were present at the time of execution and that they were intended to be part of the will. See Comment *d.*

c. Internal coherence. Even if the pages or other writings are not physically connected, internal coherence of the provisions raises an inference that the pages or other writings were present at the time of execution and that they were intended to be part of the will. See Comment *d.*

Internal coherence is present if the pages or other writings appear to be part of a single document. This inference can arise, for example, if the sentences from one page to the next appear to be a continuum, or if the pages or provisions appear to be a continuum or are numbered sequentially.

d. Extrinsic evidence. Whether or not the pages or other writings offered as a single will were present at the time of execution and were intended to be part of the will is a question of fact upon which extrinsic evidence is admissible. Consequently, extrinsic evidence is admissible to counter the inference raised by physical connection or internal coherence. Extrinsic evidence is also admissible to establish that the pages or other writings were present at the time of execution and were intended to be part of the will, even if there was no physical connection or internal coherence.

e. Writings on other than sheets of paper. A will must be in writing, save for the highly unusual and restricted case of the nuncupative will (§ 3.2, Comment *h*). See § 3.1, Comment *i*, for the proposition that any writing on a medium that allows the markings to be detected is sufficient. Examples of writings on other than sheets of paper include writings on envelopes, business cards, and pay stubs, and even words scratched on an automobile fender. Consequently, a will can be composed of writings on other than sheets of paper, or composed of a combination of sheets of paper and other kinds of writings.

Because due execution does not require the testator's signature or the signature of the witnesses to appear on a page containing provisions of the will, nor on the same page, a will can be composed of writings containing dispositive or other provisions and writings containing signatures. Thus, a will can consist of sheets of paper containing dispositive or other provisions that are inside an envelope on the outside of which are the signature of one or more of the testator and the witnesses. Moreover, if the envelope is sealed, the physical connection provided by sealing the envelope with the pages inside supports an inference that the sheets inside and the envelope were present at the time of execution and were intended by the testator to be part of the will.

§ 3.6. Incorporation by Reference

A writing that is not valid as a will but is in existence when a will is executed may be incorporated by reference into the will if the will manifests an intent to incorporate the writing and the writing to be incorporated is identified with reasonable certainty.

Comment:

a. Requirements. There are three requirements for incorporating a writing into a will by reference: The writing to be incorporated must be in existence when the will is executed; the will must manifest an intent to incorporate the writing; and the writing to be incorporated must be identified with reasonable certainty. If these requirements are satisfied, the writing is incorporated into the will by reference, even though the writing is not itself valid as a will.

An additional requirement sometimes imposed at common law was that the will must *refer* to the writing as one that was in existence when the will was executed. Because this requirement has proved to be intent-defeating, this Restatement does not adopt it as a requirement. The requirement was also deliberately omitted from the Uniform Probate Code codification of the doctrine.

Incorporation by reference differs from the doctrine of integration, covered in § 3.5. A writing that is integrated into the will must be present when the will was executed, and therefore by definition must exist when the will was executed. A writing to be incorporated by reference must also exist, but need not be present, when the will was executed.

Only writings can be incorporated by reference. Oral statements cannot be incorporated by reference. An oral instruction to a devisee regarding the use of a devise for the benefit of another might, however, be given effect as a secret trust. See Restatement Second, Trusts § 55; Restatement Third, Trusts § 18, Comment *b*, Illustrations 1 and 2.

b. *Writing in existence when will executed.* Only a writing that was in existence when the will was executed may be incorporated into the will by reference. A writing that came into existence after the will was executed cannot be incorporated by reference, although such a writing might be given effect by statutory authority (see § 3.9), under the doctrine of independent significance (see § 3.7), or as a secret trust (see Restatement Second, Trusts § 55; Restatement Third, Trusts § 18, Comment *b*, Illustration 3).

For purposes of incorporation by reference, the date when a will is considered to be executed is the date when the last codicil to the will was executed, unless (as is unlikely) so treating it would be inconsistent with the testator's intent. See § 3.4.

Whether or not a writing was in existence when the will was executed is a question of fact on which extrinsic evidence is admissible. A writing that is dated on or before the day that the will was executed is presumed to have been in existence when the will was executed. If the will refers to a writing as existing when the will was executed, a writing that fits the will's description but is undated is presumed to have been in existence when the will was executed. On the other hand, if the will clearly refers to a writing as one that does not currently exist but will be prepared in the future, the writing cannot be incorporated by reference. A mere statement that a writing will be found with my important papers is not, however, a statement that the writing does not currently exist.

Illustration:

1. G's will, executed on June 15, 1989, devised $15,000 to "the person who will be identified in a letter that will be found in my effects." On August 18, 1994, G executed a codicil to his will changing personal representatives. After G's death in 1995, his will and codicil were found in a desk drawer along with a letter dated August 18, 1994, stating that the $15,000 devise was to go to his friend, Shannon. Although the letter was not in existence when the will was originally executed, the doctrine of republication by codicil (see § 3.4) treats the will as having been executed on August 18, 1994. Consequently, the requirement for incorporating the August 18, 1994, letter into the will that the letter must have been in existence when the will was executed is satisfied. Had G not executed a codicil on or after August 18, 1994, the August 18, 1994 letter could not have been incorporated by reference because it was not in existence when the will was executed.

c. *Manifestation of intent to incorporate.* In order for a will to incorporate a writing by reference, the will must manifest an intent to incorporate the writing. This requirement is liberally construed. Any manifestation of intent to incorporate is sufficient, and thus, explicit language such as "I incorporate the following writing by reference" is not necessary.

d. *Incorporating defectively executed will.* A validly executed codicil to a defectively executed will manifests an intent to incorporate the will into the codicil, giving effect to the provisions in the will. The use of an asterisk or words such as "See next page" or "See below" can manifest an intent to incorporate by reference a writing attached to the will or written below the signature of the witnesses.

e. Identification of writing to be incorporated. In order for a will to incorporate a writing by reference, the writing to be incorporated must be identified with reasonable certainty. In order to satisfy this requirement, the will must contain a description that is sufficient to identify the writing and there must be an existing writing that reasonably corresponds to the description. This requirement is liberally construed. The description need not be so precise that it leaves absolutely no doubt about the identity of the incorporated writing. A general description will do, such as "the will of my spouse" or "a letter that will be found among my important papers." The only requirement is that the trier of fact must be reasonably satisfied that the writing is the one referred to.

f. Writing need not be in testator's handwriting to be incorporated into holographic will. A holographic will can incorporate a writing not in the testator's handwriting. Such an incorporation does not affect the holographic character of the will.

g. Pour-over devise validated by incorporation by reference. For the use of the doctrine of incorporation by reference in validating a pour-over devise, see § 3.8, Comment *c*.

h. Effect of incorporation by reference. A writing that is incorporated into a will by reference is treated as part of the will for purposes of distribution, construction, and administration of the estate, if required, but it is not a physical part of the will and need not be offered for probate nor be made part of the public record.

§ 3.7. Independent Significance

The meaning of a dispositive or other provision in a will may be supplied or affected by an external circumstance referred to in the will, unless the external circumstance has no significance apart from its effect upon the will.

Comment:

a. Rationale. The doctrine of independent significance is universally accepted. Under the doctrine, a provision in a will may validly refer to an external circumstance having significance apart from its effect upon the will. The term "external circumstance" includes any fact, act, or event existing or occurring outside the four corners of the will. An external circumstance has independent significance if it is one that would naturally occur or be done for some reason other than the effect it would have on the testamentary disposition, notwithstanding that it might occur or be done, or did occur or was done, for the purpose of affecting the testamentary disposition. The rationale for the doctrine is that the independent significance of the external circumstance—its lifetime or nontestamentary character—substitutes for attestation even though the circumstance itself is not attested. The circumstance may occur or come into existence before or after the execution of the will or before or after the testator's death.

The statutory formalities for executing a will (see § 3.1) make the doctrine a necessary feature of wills law. Were it not for the doctrine, routine provisions such as class gifts and residuary clauses could fail on the ground that the devisees or property covered were not identified in an attested writing. Both class gifts and residuary clauses can be affected by post-execution events of independent significance—the birth, death, or adoption of children, the acquisition or disposal of property—that determine the devisees and the property covered.

b. *Act of devisee or of third party.* An act of a devisee or of a third party can have independent significance. The act of having or adopting a child is an example, giving validity to a devise in the form of a class gift to the "children" of a designated person. The execution or revocation of another person's will is an external event having independent significance. A more exotic illustration of a devise validated by the doctrine of independent significance would be one "to the person who wins the gold medal in women's tennis singles at the first Olympic Games to be held after my death."

c. *Act of testator.* An act of the testator can have independent significance. The act of acquiring or disposing of property is an example. A devise of "the car I will own at my death" or a devise of "the balance on hand in my checking account at my death" is valid because the testator's act of buying a car or of depositing and withdrawing money has independent significance.

A devise of "the contents of my safe-deposit box" is valid because the testator's act of placing items in or removing them from the safe-deposit box is regarded as having independent significance.

d. *Conditions.* The condition in conditional devises often refers to acts having independent significance. For example, a devise "to A if A survives me, but if not, to B if B survives me" is valid because the condition upon which the identity of the person who takes the devised property depends is an event or events having independent significance.

e. *Unattested writing; exercise of power of appointment.* A devise to the persons named or of the property identified in an unattested writing to be prepared by the testator in the future has no independent significance, and is invalid unless authorized by statute (see § 3.9) or unless enforceable as a secret trust (see Restatement Second, Trusts § 55 (1959); Restatement Third, Trusts § 18, Comment *b*, Illustration 3).

The exercise or nonexercise of a power of appointment by a third person is valid, but not on the theory that the exercise has independent significance. It is valid on the theory that the exercise relates back and becomes part of the testator's will, even if the writing exercising the power is not executed in accordance with the statutory formalities for wills.

f. *Pour-over devise validated by independent significance.* For the use of the doctrine of independent significance in validating a pour-over devise, see § 3.8, Comment *d*.

§ 3.8. Pour-Over Devises

(a) A "pour-over" devise is a provision in a will that (i) adds property to an inter vivos trust or (ii) funds a trust that was not funded during the testator's lifetime but whose terms are in a trust instrument that was executed during the testator's lifetime.

(b) A pour-over devise may be validated by statute, by incorporation by reference, or by independent significance.

Comment:

a. *Introduction.* A "pour-over" devise is a provision in the testator's will that (i) adds property to an inter vivos trust (the *receptacle* trust) or (ii) funds a trust that was not funded during the testator's lifetime but whose terms are in a trust instrument that was executed during the testator's lifetime (the *unfunded* trust). The receptacle trust or unfunded trust instrument need not be established by or prepared for the testator as settlor, but can be established by or prepared for another. Unless validated by statute, by incorporation by reference (see § 3.6), or by independent significance (see § 3.7), a pour-over devise is invalid because the beneficial devisees are not identified in a document executed in compliance with the statutory formalities for a valid will. (Invalidity of a pour-over devise does not invalidate the receptacle trust.)

b. Pour-over devise validated by statute. Nearly all states have enacted legislation validating pour-over devises in specified circumstances. The Original Uniform Testamentary Additions to Trusts Act (Original UTATA) was promulgated in 1960. A revised version (Revised UTATA) was promulgated in 1991.

Under Original UTATA, a devise to the trustee of an inter vivos trust was valid "if the trust is identified in the testator's will and its terms are set forth in a written instrument (other than a will) executed before or concurrently with the execution of the testator's will or in the valid last will of a person who has predeceased the testator (regardless of the existence, size, or character of the corpus of the trust)." The devise is "not invalid because the trust is amendable or revocable, or both, or because the trust was amended after the execution of the will or after the death of the testator."

Under Revised UTATA, a devise to the trustee of an inter vivos trust is valid "if the trust is identified in the testator's will and its terms are set forth in a written instrument, other than a will, executed before, concurrently with, or after the execution of the testator's will or in another individual's will if that other individual has predeceased the testator, regardless of the existence, size, or character of the corpus of the trust." The trust itself need not be established during the testator's lifetime, but can be established *by* the pour-over devise. (A trust is not established by executing a trust document; a trust is only established by transferring property to the trust. See Restatement Second, Trusts §§ 31–32; Restatement Third, Trusts § 2; see also id. § 41.) The pour-over devise is not invalid because the trust is amendable or revocable, or because the trust was amended after the execution of the will or the testator's death.

c. Pour-over devise validated by incorporation by reference. Of the common-law bases for validating pour-over devises, the doctrine of incorporation by reference (see § 3.6) is less satisfactory than independent significance (see Comment *d*). Incorporation by reference should be utilized only if no other theory is available. Prior to the widespread enactment of statutes validating pour-over devises, the doctrine of incorporation by reference was initially the only theory for validating such devises, but it applied in limited circumstances. In order for that doctrine to be applicable, the inter vivos trust instrument had to be in existence when the will was executed. If this requirement was met, some courts would still only incorporate the terms of an *irrevocable* trust. Other courts would incorporate the terms of a revocable and amendable trust, but not if the trust had been amended *after* the will was executed. Because the post-execution amendment could not be incorporated, the court was left with the choice of incorporating only the terms of the original trust or invalidating the devise altogether. The usual choice was to invalidate the devise altogether because incorporating the original terms of the trust, ignoring the amendment, would be intent defeating.

d. Pour-over devise validated by independent significance. The other common-law doctrine for validating a pour-over devise is the doctrine of independent significance (see § 3.7). Independent significance provides a validating basis that is more satisfactory than incorporation by reference. Under independent significance, the trust instrument does not have to be in existence when the will is executed, and post-execution amendments to the trust are given effect. The only requirement under the doctrine of independent significance is that the inter vivos trust must be more than nominally funded in order to give the trust document and any subsequent amendments independent significance.

Illustration:

1. G's lawyer prepared a revocable and amendable inter vivos trust document and a will that devised the residue of G's estate to the trustee of the inter vivos trust, providing that the residue should "be added to and become part of the trust and be managed in accordance with the provisions of the trust as they exist at my death." When G came into the lawyer's office to execute both documents, G decided to make a small change in the provisions of the inter vivos trust. G went ahead and executed the will. G's lawyer made the requested changes in the trust, and G came back the next day and executed the trust. Subsequently, G funded the trust with $100,000 of publicly traded securities. Later still, G amended the dispositive provisions of the trust. Although applicable law includes the original version of UTATA, the pour-over devise is not validated by that statute because the trust document did not come into existence in final form until after the will was executed. See Comment *b*. (Note that the devise would have been validated by Revised UTATA.) A pour-over devise not validated by UTATA is not necessarily invalid. The common-law doctrines can still be invoked to validate it. In this case, the doctrine of incorporation by reference would not succeed because the trust document and the subsequent amendment were not in existence when the will was executed. The doctrine of independent significance, however, works to validate the devise because the post-execution creation of the trust and subsequent amendment have independent significance, in that they control the disposition of the securities that became the corpus of the inter vivos trust.

e. Single trust. Unless the testator's will clearly manifests a contrary intent, the property covered by a pour-over devise is added to and becomes part of the receptacle inter vivos trust. It does not create a separate testamentary trust with terms identical to the terms of the inter vivos trust.

Although, in theory, it might appear that a pour-over devise validated only by incorporation by reference would create a testamentary trust with terms identical to those of the inter vivos trust, that is not the position adopted in this Restatement. Even if the only doctrine validating a pour-over devise is the doctrine of incorporation by reference, the pour-over devise merely adds property to the previously established receptacle inter vivos trust. Even when the pour-over devise supplies the initial funding of and thus creates the trust, the trust it creates is an inter vivos trust, unless the testator's will clearly manifests a contrary intent. [Cf.] Restatement Third, Trusts § 19, Comment *i*.

f. Pour-up transfers to testamentary trusts. Transfers to testamentary trusts from arrangements such as inter vivos trusts, life insurance or pension beneficiary designations, or another person's will, are sometimes called *pour-up transfers*. Pour-up transfers are valid. They do not raise the question addressed in this section because the terms of the receptacle trust (the testamentary trust) satisfy the Statute of Wills. See Restatement Third, Trusts § 19, Comment *a*.

§ 3.9. Testamentary Disposition by Unattested Writing

When permitted by statute, a will may devise property as provided in a separate unattested writing even though the writing has no independent significance and does not satisfy the requirements for incorporation by reference.

Comment:

a. Introduction. Unless authorized by statute, or validated by the doctrine of incorporation by reference, a separate unattested writing having no independent significance cannot control the testamentary disposition of property. A number of states, however, have enacted the Original or Revised version of § 2–513 of the Uniform Probate Code . . ., which authorizes such a disposition under specified circumstances.

b. Original Uniform Probate Code. Under § 2–513 of the Original Uniform Probate Code, a will may devise certain types of property by a "written statement or list" having no independent significance without satisfying the requirements for incorporating the writing into the will by reference. In order for the unattested writing to be effective, the will itself must "refer to" the writing; the reference in the will may be to a writing "to be in existence at the time of the testator's death." The type of property that may be devised in this fashion is limited to "items of tangible personal property not otherwise specifically disposed of by the will, other than money, evidence of indebtedness, documents of title, and securities, and property used in trade or business." The separate unattested writing must be either handwritten or signed by the testator, must "describe the items and the devisees with reasonable certainty," may be prepared before or after the will was executed, and may be "altered by the testator" after it was prepared.

c. Revised Uniform Probate Code. As revised in 1990, the Uniform Probate Code modified § 2–513 in two significant respects. The revision expands the type of property that may be disposed of by this method, permitting "tangible personal property not otherwise specifically disposed of by the will, other than money" to be disposed of by an unattested writing. The revised version also requires that the separate unattested writing be signed by the testator; it does not allow an unsigned handwritten document to control the disposition of property. The Official Commentary notes that the drafters were concerned that the lack of signature suggests that the testator lacked the requisite testamentary intent. The Official Commentary also notes, however, the possibility that the harmless-error rule of § 2–503 (see § 3.3) might apply and allow an unsigned document to be effective if a proponent proves by clear and convincing evidence that the testator adopted the document as his or her will or as a codicil to his or her will.

d. Property described with reasonable certainty. Both the original and revised versions of § 2–513 require that the separate unattested writing "describe the items [to be disposed of] with reasonable certainty." This does not mean, however, that each item of property covered must be separately itemized. The Official Commentary states that a general statement such as "all my tangible personal property other than money" or "all my tangible personal property located in my office" would normally be sufficient.

e. Property not otherwise specifically disposed of by the will. One of the limitations appearing in both the original and revised versions of § 2–513 is that the separate unattested writing cannot dispose of items of property that are otherwise specifically disposed of in the will itself. The Official Commentary to the revised version, however, notes that the will may state that the "written statement or list takes precedence over any contrary devise in the will."

Illustrations:

1. G's will devised her antique desk to her granddaughter, A. It also contained the following clause:

> I might leave a written statement or list disposing of items of tangible personal property. If I do and if my written statement or list is found and is identified as such by my Personal Representative no later than 30 days after the probate of this will, then my written statement or list is to be given effect to the extent authorized by law and is to take precedence over any contrary devise or devises of the same item or items of property in this will.

After G's death, G's personal representative discovered the will in the top drawer of G's antique desk. G's personal representative also discovered in the same drawer a typed piece of paper signed by G that says: "Antique desk to granddaughter, B." Applicable law contains the revised version of § 2–513 of the Uniform Probate Code. The antique desk goes to B, not to A.

2. The facts are the same as in Illustration 1, except that the clause in G's will did not state that the list "is to take precedence over any contrary devise or devises of the same item or items of property in this will," or words to that effect. The antique desk goes to A, not to B, because the antique desk was otherwise specifically disposed of by G's will.

CHAPTER 4

REVOCATION OF WILLS

Introductory Note: This chapter addresses the revocation of wills, revival of revoked wills, and the doctrine of ineffective revocation (widely known in the case law as the doctrine of dependent relative revocation).

§ 4.1. Revocation of Wills

(a) A testator may revoke his or her will in whole or in part by subsequent will or by revocatory act.

(b) The dissolution of the testator's marriage is a change in circumstance that presumptively revokes any provision in the testator's will in favor of his or her former spouse. Neither marriage nor marriage followed by birth of issue is a change in circumstance that revokes a will or any part of a will.

General Comment:

a. Introduction. From the time of execution, a will is inherently revocable throughout the testator's remaining lifetime. A will need not contain a clause expressly reserving the right to revoke in order for it to be revocable.

Revocation of wills is governed by statutory law in all American jurisdictions. The testator may revoke his or her will or a part of it by: (1) executing a subsequent will that expressly revokes the will or specified part or that revokes the will or part by inconsistency; or (2) performing a revocatory act on the will with intent to revoke. To revoke a will or part of a will by subsequent will or by act, the testator must have the requisite testamentary capacity and must be free from fraud, duress, or undue influence. (Testamentary capacity, fraud, duress, and undue influence are covered in subsequent chapters of this Restatement.) Provisions in a will favoring the testator's former spouse, and under the Revised Uniform Probate Code, favoring relatives of the former spouse, are also revoked by dissolution of the testator's marriage.

A revocation takes effect when the subsequent will is executed, the act is performed, or the marriage is dissolved. A will that is revoked is inoperative unless it is revived (see § 4.2) or the revocation is ineffective (see § 4.3).

The harmless-error rule of § 3.3 applies to questions of compliance with the requirements for revocation. See § 3.3, Comment *c*.

Comment on Subsection (a)—Revocation by Subsequent Will:

b. Revocation by subsequent will. Revocation by subsequent will can occur by express revocation or by inconsistency. In order for revocation by subsequent will to be effective, the subsequent will must itself be validly executed. See §§ 3.1, 3.2. If there is a defect in execution, the defect may be excused under the harmless-error rule. See § 3.3. As provided in § 3.1, Comment *a*, the term "will" includes a codicil and also includes a document that serves only to revoke an earlier will. A holographic will can revoke a formal, attested will.

c. Express revocation. All revocation statutes authorize express revocation. Professionally drafted wills routinely contain a revocation clause. Express revocation results from a revocation clause, such as one providing that "this will revokes all previous wills and codicils made by me." A clause providing that "this will revokes all previous wills made by me" is effective to revoke all previous wills *and codicils*, since the term "will" includes "codicil." See § 3.1, Comment *a*.

Partial revocation by subsequent will is uniformly authorized. A codicil to a will might add a provision to the will, but it might also revoke a provision or amend a provision by deleting specified words and substituting others.

d. Revocation by inconsistency. Revocation statutes provide that, in the absence of an express revocation, an earlier will is revoked by an "inconsistent" subsequent will. "Revocation by inconsistency," sometimes called "implied revocation," occurs when a testator executes a will that does not include an express revocation clause. Such a will is typically drafted without the aid of an attorney. When a testator dies with two (or more) wills and the later will does not expressly revoke the earlier will, the question is whether the testator intended the later will to replace the earlier will in whole or in part or merely to supplement the earlier will.

If the later will makes a complete disposition of the testator's estate, it is presumed that the testator intended the later will to replace the earlier will. Clear and convincing evidence is required to rebut this presumption. Unless the presumption is rebutted by clear and convincing evidence, the earlier will is revoked and only the later will is operative on the testator's death. This presumption is adopted in Restatement Second, Property (Donative Transfers) § 33.2, Comment *b*, and is codified in the Revised UPC. If the later will purports to make a complete disposition of the testator's estate, but fails to do so because, for example, the residuary devisee predeceases the testator (and no antilapse statute applies), the case is governed by the doctrine of ineffective revocation. See § 4.3.

If the later will does not make a complete disposition of the testator's estate, it is presumed that the testator intended the later will to supplement rather than replace the earlier will. If this presumption is not rebutted by clear and convincing evidence, the later will revokes the earlier will only to the extent that the later will is inconsistent with the earlier will. Each will is fully operative on the testator's death to the extent that they are not inconsistent. This presumption is adopted in Restatement Second, Property (Donative Transfers) § 33.2, Comment *b*, and is codified in the Revised UPC.

If the earlier will and the later will are both operative under the above rules, and if both wills contain a cash devise to the same devisee, the testator's intent controls whether the devisee takes the sum of the two amounts or only the amount in the later will. This is a question of construction on which all evidence of intention may be considered. See [Chapters 10, 11, and 12] of this Restatement, on Construction, Reformation, and Modification of Donative Documents. The same constructional problem is presented when the earlier will devises a specified number of shares in a corporation and a second will devises the same or a different number of shares in the same corporation to the same devisee.

Comment on Subsection (a)—Revocation by Revocatory Act:

e. Revocation by revocatory act. In addition to authorizing revocation of a will by subsequent will, statutory law in all states also authorizes revocation of a will by an unattested act. Although the act is unattested, the by-product is that the decedent's estate passes by intestacy or under an earlier will. Passing property by intestacy does not require a validly executed writing, whereas when property passes under an earlier will it passes under a validly executed writing.

To revoke a will by act, the testator must perform a revocatory act on the will with the intent to revoke. Alternatively, someone else must perform a revocatory act on the will in the testator's presence and at the testator's direction. Revocatory acts include burning, tearing, canceling, obliterating, and destroying. The Revised UPC revocation provision provides in relevant part:

> *§ 2–507. Revocation by Writing or by Act.* A will or any part thereof is revoked . . . by performing a revocatory act on the will, if the testator performed the act with the intent and for the purpose of revoking the will or part or if another individual performed the act in the testator's conscious presence and by the testator's direction. For purposes of this paragraph, "revocatory act on the will" includes burning, tearing, canceling, obliterating, or destroying the will or any part of it. A burning, tearing, or canceling is a "revocatory act on the will," whether or not the burn, tear, or cancellation touched any of the words on the will.

f. Revocatory act on will; duplicate wills. The revocatory act must be performed on the will. Performing the act on another document or on an unexecuted copy of the will is insufficient. If, however, the act was performed on the wrong document due to wrongdoing or mistake, a constructive trust may be imposed on the devisees of the will in favor of the persons who would have taken had the will been revoked. Alternatively, if the intent to revoke is proved by clear and convincing evidence, the failure to perform the act on the will, accompanied by performance of the act on a copy that the testator mistakes for the will, may be excused as a harmless error. See § 3.3.

If the testator executed more than one copy of the same will, each duplicate is considered to be the testator's will. The will is revoked if the testator, with intent to revoke, performs a revocatory act on one of the duplicates. The testator need not perform a revocatory act on all the duplicates.

g. Sufficiency of the act. The revocatory acts commonly specified in the statutes are burning, tearing, canceling, obliterating, and destroying. The revocatory act must be performed on the will (Comment *f*), but it need not touch the words on the will. The act need not be one so severe that it intrinsically demonstrates an intent to revoke. An insignificant act, such as a small tear or burn is sufficient, as long as the evidence establishes that the testator performed the act with the intent to revoke. See, however, Comment *h* concerning situations in which the testator changes his or her mind in midstream and does not complete the revocatory act to the full extent originally intended.

Among the prescribed methods of revoking by act, much of the litigation has concerned cancellation, particularly words of cancellation. Cancellation encompasses acts such as crossing out or marking through the will or part of it or writing words on the will such as "canceled" or "null and void." Some courts have required words of cancellation to touch the words on the will, in order to distinguish between a revocation by cancellation and a revocation by subsequent will. These courts put words of cancellation into the category of revocation by subsequent will when the words of cancellation do not touch the words on the will, thus requiring the words to be executed in accordance with the statutory formalities for wills. Although it is understandable that a distinction must be drawn between revocation by words of cancellation and revocation by subsequent will, a better distinction—and the distinction adopted in this Restatement and codified in the UPC as revised in 1990 (see Comment *e*)—is between words written on the will and words written on another document. Words written on another document cannot serve as a revocation by cancellation. Words written on the will, whether they touch the words on the will or not, can be a revocation by cancellation. . . . .

h. *Abandonment of intention before completion of the act.* As noted in Comment *g*, a small tear or burn can be a sufficient revocatory act. If, however, the testator intended to perform a more extensive revocatory act, but changed his or her mind and abandoned the effort, there is no revocation. . . . .

i. *Partial revocation by act.* A revocatory act may be intended to affect only part of the will. Most revocation statutes, including the Original and Revised UPC, specifically authorize partial revocation by act. The UPC is illustrative in providing that "[a] will *or any part thereof* is revoked . . . by performing a revocatory act on the will. . . ." (Emphasis added.) A few nonuniform statutes speak of revocation of "a will or any clause thereof." A few revocation statutes, however, do not specifically authorize partial revocation by act, and under these statutes the practice has not generally been permitted. The unavoidable byproduct of revoking a devise, at least if it is a preresiduary devise, is usually to pass the revoked devise to the residuary devisee. Although the residuary devisee was named in an attested writing, the act of adding property to that devise by an unattested act having no independent significance has been troublesome to some courts. Consequently, partial revocation by act has not generally been permitted unless authorized by statute.

Even when partial revocation by act is authorized by statute, there still remains a measure of resistance to the practice. Although these statutes are held to permit revocation by act of a complete devise, it has sometimes been held that a partial revocation by act is ineffective if its purpose and effect would be to rearrange the shares within a single devise or otherwise to rewrite the terms of the will by deleting selected words.

This Restatement disapproves any distinction between revocation of a complete devise and rearranging shares within a single devise or otherwise rewriting the terms of the will by deleting selected words. It is a classic example of a distinction without a difference. It is not supported by the language of the statutes specifically authorizing the revocation by act of "a will or any part thereof." In authorizing revocation of a will "or *any* part thereof" by act, the legislature has not limited the authorization to revocation of a complete devise. The legislature not only granted broad approval of deleting words but of the natural consequence of doing so—giving effect to the will as if the deleted words were not present. . . . .

j. *Presumption if lost or mutilated will traced to testator's possession.* If a will is traced to the testator's possession and cannot be found after death, there are three plausible explanations for its absence: The testator destroyed it with the intent to revoke; the will was accidentally destroyed or lost; or the will was wrongfully destroyed or suppressed by someone dissatisfied with its terms. Of these plausible explanations, the law presumes that the testator destroyed the will with intent to revoke it.

If a will is traced to the testator's possession and it is found after death with a revocatory act performed on it, there are two plausible explanations for its condition: The testator performed the act with the intent to revoke or the act occurred accidentally. It seems less likely, though still possible, that someone dissatisfied with the terms of the will performed a revocatory act on it and left it where it could be found. Of the plausible explanations for the condition of the will, the law presumes that the testator performed the act on the will with intent to revoke it.

The presumption that the testator destroyed the will or performed some other revocatory act on it with intent to revoke is rebuttable. Because of the other plausible explanations for a will's absence or condition, the presumption is not such a strong one that clear and convincing evidence is required to rebut it. Moreover, the presumption regarding a mutilated will must be tempered when the act is a blemish that could easily have occurred accidentally, such as a small tear across a corner or a singe mark that could have been caused by a dropped cigarette ash. Although insignificant acts such as these are technically sufficient as revocatory acts (see Comment *g*), they must be shown to have been done by the testator with the intent to revoke.

k. Probate of unrevoked lost or destroyed wills. If a will cannot be located after death, but the trier of fact finds that it was not revoked, the will is entitled to probate if its due execution and contents can be proved. Commonly in such cases, the will is proved by evidence of a law-office or other copy, or from the drafter's notes and recollection. If its full contents cannot be proved, the will is entitled to probate to the extent that its contents can be proved.

l. Act performed by another. Even if the testator did not perform a revocatory act on the will with intent to revoke, the will is still revoked by act if the testator directed another to perform the act and if the other person performed the act in the testator's presence. In determining whether the revocatory act was performed in the testator's presence, this Restatement, supported by the Revised UPC § 2–507, adopts the conscious-presence test and rejects the line-of-vision test. See also § 3.1, Comment *p*. . . . .

m. Revocation of codicil by act—effect on will. The revocation by act of a codicil to a will does not revoke the will, but the revocation is presumed to revive portions of the will that the codicil revoked. See § 4.2, Comment *g*.

n. Revocation of will by act—effect on codicil. The revocation of a will by act does not revoke a codicil to the will. If the codicil depends on the revoked will for its meaning, however, the codicil may have no effect as a matter of construction. . . . .

Comment on Subsection (b)—Revocation by Dissolution of the Marriage:

o. Revocation because of dissolution of the marriage. The dissolution of the testator's marriage, including divorce or annulment, is a change in circumstance that presumptively revokes any provision in the testator's will in favor of his or her former spouse. The term "provision in the testator's will in favor of his or her former spouse" not only encompasses a dispositive provision in favor of the former spouse, but also a provision nominating the former spouse to act in any fiduciary or representative capacity (such as personal representative, executor, trustee, conservator, agent, or guardian), a provision conferring a general or nongeneral power of appointment on the former spouse, and other provision of similar import.

The presumption is rebuttable. The Revised UPC provides that the presumption is rebutted if it is provided otherwise in the express terms of the will, a court order, or a contract relating to the division of the marital estate made between the testator and the former spouse before or after the marriage, divorce, or annulment.

Most revocation statutes, including the Original UPC, limit the scope of the revocation to provisions in favor of the *former spouse*. Under Revised UPC § 2–804, dissolution of the testator's marriage also revokes any provision in the testator's will in favor of a relative of the former spouse who, after the dissolution, is no longer related to the testator by blood, adoption, or affinity.

The revoked provisions pass as if the former spouse—and, under the Revised UPC, relatives of the former spouse—predeceased the testator. (The mechanism used in the Revised UPC is to give effect to any revoked provision as if the former spouse or relative of the former spouse disclaimed.)

Illustration:

12. *Effect of divorce.* H and W had no children by their marriage to each other, but each had adult children by a former marriage. During their marriage to each other, H executed a will devising all of his property to W if W survived him. H's will contained an alternative devise providing that if W failed to survive him, one-half of his property should go to his children and one-half to W's children. (W also executed a will, which contained reciprocal provisions.) H and W were subsequently divorced. H died soon after the divorce, survived by W, H's children, and W's children. The devise in H's will to W is revoked and passes as if W predeceased him. Under the Revised UPC, the alternative devise to W's children is also revoked and passes as if W's children had predeceased him. H's estate would therefore pass entirely to his children. See § 5.5, Comment *o*. If the controlling revocation statute provides only that the devise to W is revoked, the court should effectuate the purpose of the statute by extending its terms to revoke the devise to W's children. The rationale for extending the statute is that the H would not want his estate to be divided between his and W's children. A factor bearing on H's intent is that the divorce dissolved any agreement between him and W that the survivor would split his or her estate between the two sets of children. After the divorce, W no longer had any obligation, legal or otherwise, to split her estate between the two sets of children.

At an earlier time, statutes in a large number of states provided for revocation by operation of law in cases of "subsequent changes in the conditions or circumstances of the testator." These broadly worded "change-in-circumstances" statutes were widely construed to revoke provisions in a predivorce will in favor of the decedent's former spouse in the case of divorce coupled with a property settlement. In the vast majority of states, the broadly worded "change-in-circumstances" statutes have been replaced by the more specific statutory provision described above, revoking predivorce provisions upon dissolution of the marriage alone.

p. Application to will substitutes. The principles of Comment *o* also apply to a donative transfer in the form of a will substitute, such as a revocable trust or a life-insurance-beneficiary designation. On the application of these principles to a revocable trust, see Restatement Third, Trusts § 25, Comment *c* and Illustration 11. Any revocable provision in favor of the former spouse or relative of the former spouse in a will substitute is revoked upon dissolution of the marriage. The principles of Comment *o* also apply to a joint tenancy, effecting a severance of the joint tenancy and transforming the interests of the former spouses into an equal tenancy in common.

q. *No revocation upon marriage or marriage plus birth of issue.* Marriage or marriage plus birth of issue is not a change in circumstance that revokes a will or any part of a will. At common law, premarital wills of women were revoked upon marriage and premarital wills of men were revoked upon marriage and birth of issue. The wills were revoked as soon as the operative event or events occurred. At one time in the United States, the common-law approach was codified in many states, except that most of the statutes made no distinction between men and women. More than half the states had statutes that revoked a premarital will upon marriage alone or upon marriage and birth of issue. Only a few states presently have marriage-revocation statutes. . . . . Because modern probate codes invoke other means of protecting the testator's new spouse and children against unintended disinheritance, marriage or marriage plus birth of issue should no longer be treated as a change of circumstance that revokes a premarital will.

r. *Homicide.* The felonious and intentional killing of the decedent is sometimes described as an event that "revokes" any provision in the testator's will in favor of the killer. In this Restatement, a person who criminally causes the death of another forfeits any right to take as an heir, a devisee, or a beneficiary of a will substitute of the victim. The governing principle is the supervening public policy that prevents a wrongdoer from profiting from the wrong, and not revocation by the testator. This topic is covered in [Chapter 8] of this Restatement on Protection Against Wrongdoing.

§ 4.2. Revival of Revoked Wills

(a) A will that was revoked by a later will is revived if the testator: (i) reexecuted the previously revoked will; (ii) executed a codicil indicating an intent to revive the previously revoked will; (iii) revoked the revoking will by act intending to revive the previously revoked will; or (iv) revoked the revoking will by another, later will whose terms indicate an intent to revive the previously revoked will.

(b) A will that was revoked by act is revived if the testator: (i) reexecuted the will; (ii) executed a codicil indicating an intent to revive the previously revoked will; or (iii) performed an act on the will that clearly and convincingly demonstrates an intent to reverse the revocation.

(c) A testamentary provision that was revoked by dissolution of the testator's marriage is revived if: (i) the testator remarried the former spouse, reexecuted the will, or executed a codicil indicating an intent to revive the previously revoked provision; or (ii) the dissolution of the marriage is nullified.

General Comment:

a. *Meaning of "revival."* "Revival" is the term used in the law to refer to the process of reinstating or revalidating a previously revoked will. The harmless-error rule of § 3.3 applies to questions of compliance with the requirements for revival. See § 3.3, Comment *c*.

Comment on Subsection (a)—Revival of a Will That Was Revoked by a Later Will:

b. *Scope.* Subsection (a) addresses the question of revival of a will that was revoked by a later will. In the following discussion, the will that was revoked by the later will is sometimes referred to as Will No. 1 or as the previously revoked will, and the later will that revoked Will No. 1 is referred to as Will No. 2 or as the revoking will. A will that was revoked by a later will is revived if the testator: (i) reexecuted the previously revoked will; (ii) executed a codicil indicating an intent to revive the previously revoked will; (iii) revoked the revoking will by act intending to revive the previously revoked will; or (iv) revoked the revoking will by another, later will whose terms indicate that the testator intended to revive the previously revoked will.

Subsection (a) differentiates between situations in which the testator revoked the revoking will and those in which the testator did not revoke the revoking will. If the testator did not revoke the revoking will, there are only two methods of reviving the previously revoked will: reexecuting it or executing a codicil indicating an intent to revive the previously revoked will (Comment *c*). If the testator revoked the revoking will, either of these methods—reexecution or codicil—is still recognized. But the previously revoked will is also revived if the testator revoked the revoking will *by act* intending to revive the previously revoked will (Comments *d* through *g*) or revoked the revoking will *by a later will* whose terms indicate an intent to revive the previously revoked will (Comment *h*).

c. *Revival by reexecuting the previously revoked will or by executing a codicil indicating an intent to revive the previously revoked will.* If a testator reexecutes a will (Will No. 1) that was revoked by a later will (Will No. 2), or executes a codicil indicating an intent to revive the previously revoked will (Will No. 1), the previously revoked will is revived and becomes the testator's latest will. If the previously revoked will was revived by codicil, the doctrine of republication by codicil presumptively treats the previously revoked will as having been executed on the date of execution of the codicil that revived it. See § 3.4.

The English Wills Act of 1837 adopted the rule that reexecution and revival by codicil were the *only* methods of reviving a previously revoked will. A small number of American states maintains this rule by statute. In these states, the third method of reviving a previously revoked will adopted in this Restatement and in many American states—revoking the later will intending to revive the previously revoked will—is not available.

Revival that occurs either by reexecution or by codicil does not require statutory authority. For revival to occur either by reexecution or by codicil, the earlier will must be *validly* reexecuted or the codicil must be *validly* executed. Thus, at the time of reexecution or execution, the testator must have possessed the necessary capacity to make a will, must have been free of fraud, duress, and undue influence, and must have complied with the statutory formalities for a valid will. On the latter, see §§ 3.1, 3.2, and 3.3. Whether a codicil indicates an intent to revive the previously revoked will is a question of construction, of determining the testator's intent. On that question, see [Chapters 10, 11, and 12] of this Restatement, on Construction, Reformation, and Modification of Donative Documents.

Revival by reexecution or by codicil need not be connected to a revocation of Will No. 2. If the testator did not revoke Will No. 2, the effect of reviving

Will No. 1 and making it the testator's latest will might be to revoke Will No. 2 by subsequent will. On that question, see § 4.1. . . .

d. Revival by revoking the revoking will by act: historical note—English law. Revival of a will that was revoked by a later will not only occurs as a consequence of reexecuting the earlier will or executing a codicil indicating an intent to revive the earlier will. Revival can also occur as a consequence of revoking the later will by act.

In England, prior to the Wills Act of 1837, the effect of revoking the later will was not controlled by statute. Indeed, English law then had no statutory provision on revival at all. Although the Statute of Frauds of 1677 provided for revocation by later will or by act to the document, that statute was silent on the question of revival. Two rules emerged in the English case law on the effect of revoking the later will, one from the ecclesiastical courts, which had jurisdiction over succession to personal property, the other from the common-law courts, which had jurisdiction when an issue of title to freehold land was raised. Under the ecclesiastical rule, the question of revival depended on the testator's intent. If, in revoking the later will, the testator intended to revive the earlier one, the earlier one was revived. If the testator's intent was not to revive the earlier will, it was not revived.

Under the common-law rule, however, the testator's intent was not important. At common law, the earlier will became the testator's valid will automatically, not because it was revived but because it was treated as if it had never been revoked. A later will, at common law, could not revoke an earlier will upon execution. It could only revoke the earlier will if the later will remained valid at the testator's death. If a testator revoked a later will, the earlier will never became revoked and remained valid.

As noted in Comment *c*, the English Wills Act of 1837 adopted the rule that the only methods of reviving a previously revoked will are by reexecution or by codicil, thus abrogating the common-law and ecclesiastical rules. This is known as the "anti-revival" rule.

e. Revival by revoking the revoking will by act: American law. In the United States, revival by revoking a later will is covered by statute in most states. These legislative initiatives exhibit a move toward the ecclesiastical rule, under which revival turns on the testator's intent, although a few statutes still follow the anti-revival position of the English Wills Act, requiring either a reexecution of the previously revoked will or the execution of a codicil showing an intent to revive it.

Under the original and revised version of the Uniform Probate Code, revival occurs if "it is evident from the circumstances of the revocation of the subsequent will or from the testator's contemporary or subsequent declarations that the testator intended the previous will to take effect as executed." See Comment *f*.

Under another formulation, once widely adopted but now replaced by the UPC in many states, revival of the earlier will occurs if "it appears by the terms of such revocation [of the later will] that it was [the testator's] intent to revive and give effect to the first will" or if "after such revocation the [testator] shall duly republish his first will." Much of the case law under this statutory formulation adopts an unnecessarily restrictive interpretation, holding that revival requires an *attested writing* indicating an intent to revive the earlier will. In effect, this restricts the phrase "appears by the terms of such revocation" to cases in which the testator revoked the subsequent will *in writing*. This interpretation nearly precludes revival in cases in which the testator revokes the subsequent will *by act*, since the only way that the "terms of" a revocation by act (other than a cancellation) can state an "intention to revive and give effect to the first will" is by *oral* declaration. This interpretation treats the word "republished" as requiring a validly executed codicil. Consequently, despite the more liberal language of this statutory formulation, some decisions interpreted it as requiring the same elements as the English Wills Act—either reexecution of the earlier will or execution of a codicil indicating an intent to revive. A more permissive interpretation of this statutory language would come closer to the position adopted in this Restatement. The phrase "by the terms of such revocation [of the later will]" could be interpreted as allowing extrinsic evidence of the testator's intention, and the phrase "republishes the revoked will" could be interpreted as occurring not only by executing a codicil but also by the testator orally declaring to the attesting witnesses of the previously revoked will that he or she intends the earlier will to be revived. These interpretations would bring practice under this statutory formulation more into line with the position of this Restatement.

In the small number of states in which revival is not covered by statute, there appears to be a preference for the English ecclesiastical rule. In a few states, no decisions exist on the question.

Consequently, the majority of American jurisdictions follow a rule, either by statute or by case law, that is consistent with this section, under which the question of revival depends on the testator's intent. Even the "anti-revival" rule of the English Wills Act is consistent with the policy of this section in the sense that revival purportedly depends on the testator's intent. The English anti-revival rule departs from this section, however, in that it requires the testator's intent to be expressed by an attested act—either by reexecuting the earlier will or by executing a codicil declaring an intent to revive.

f. Revival by revoking the revoking will by act: intent to revive the earlier will. The position of this Restatement is that, if permitted by the controlling statutory provision or if no statutory provision exists, the revocation by act of a will that revoked an earlier will revives the earlier will if it is proved that the testator intended to revive the earlier will. As noted in Comment *e*, the original and revised versions of the UPC are completely consistent with this proposition. Under the UPC, revival occurs if "it is evident from the circumstances of the revocation of the subsequent will or from the testator's contemporary or subsequent declarations that the testator intended the previous will to take effect as executed." In effect, this formulation means that if a testator revokes a will that revoked an earlier will, the earlier will is revived if it is proved that the testator intended to revive the earlier will.

The testator's intent to revive the earlier will can be shown by direct or circumstantial evidence. Direct evidence would include the testator's oral declarations that the earlier will is to be effective. Circumstantial evidence would include the fact that the earlier will is found in the testator's important papers. . . . .

An intent to revive a former will is ineffective if it was the product of a mistake in inducement. The burden of proof is on the party claiming that it was the product of a mistake in inducement. . . . .

g. Revival by revoking an amending codicil by act. A situation in which Will No. 2 completely revokes Will No. 1 is to be distinguished from a situation in which No. 2 is a codicil that merely amends (partly revokes) No.

1. As discussed in Comment *f*, if the testator revokes No. 2 in the former situation, No. 1 is revived if it is proved that the testator's intent was to revive No. 1. In the latter situation, however, if the testator revokes No. 2, the intent to revive the revoked parts of No. 1 is presumed. This presumption reflects the understanding that a person revoking an amending document ordinarily thinks that he or she has revoked the amendments, leaving the original document unamended. This presumption is codified in the Revised UPC § 2–507.

h. *Revival by revoking the revoking will by a later will.* If the testator revokes the revoking will by another, later will, the earlier will is revived if the terms of the later will indicate an intent to revive the earlier will.

Comment on Subsection (b)—Revival of a Will That Was Revoked by Act:

i. *Reviving a will revoked by act.* Subsection (b) addresses the question of revival of a will that was revoked by act. Such a will is revived if the testator: (i) reexecuted the will; (ii) executed a codicil indicating an intent to revive the previously revoked will; or (iii) performed an act on the will that clearly and convincingly demonstrates an intent to reverse the revocation. A clear-and-convincing-evidence standard of proof is imposed for revival by performing an act demonstrating an intent to reverse the revocation because of the limited experience with revival in such cases. As experience grows, the standard of proof might be reduced to the regular standard of a preponderance of the evidence.

Reexecution of a will that was revoked by act is not always possible, nor is it always possible to perform an act on the will that demonstrates an intent to reverse the revocation. A will, for example, that was burned up, torn up and thrown away, or otherwise destroyed cannot be reexecuted, nor can an act be performed on the will that demonstrates an intent to reverse the revocation. However, a will might be revoked by act by marking "X's" through it, or by writing words such as "this will is void" in the margin. In cases such as these, the will can be reexecuted, and an act can be performed on the will that clearly and convincingly demonstrates an intent to reverse the revocation. Revocation by tearing up the will and keeping the pieces is also a situation in which it is possible to perform an act on the will that demonstrates an intent to reverse the revocation.

If an act has been performed on the will, it is presumed that the testator performed the act if the will is traced to the testator's possession and found in his or her effects after death. The presumption is rebuttable. See § 4.1, Comment *j*. . . . .

Comment on Subsection (c)—Revival of a Provision That Was Revoked by Dissolution of Marriage:

j. *Reviving a testamentary provision revoked by dissolution of marriage.* Subsection (c) addresses the question of revival of a provision of a will that was revoked by dissolution of the testator's marriage. Such a provision is revived if: (i) the testator remarried the former spouse, reexecuted the will, or executed a codicil indicating an intent to revive the previously revoked provision; or (ii) the dissolution of the marriage is nullified. This rule applies to a provision in favor of the testator's former spouse or in favor of a relative of the testator's former spouse that was revoked by dissolution of the testator's marriage. See § 4.1(b) and Comment *o*. For purposes of subsection (c) and this Comment, the term "dissolution of the testator's marriage" covers divorce and annulment.

§ 4.3. Ineffective Revocation (Dependent Relative Revocation)

(a) A partial or complete revocation of a will is presumptively ineffective if the testator made the revocation:

(1) in connection with an attempt to achieve a dispositive objective that fails under applicable law, or

(2) because of a false assumption of law, or because of a false belief about an objective fact, that is either recited in the revoking instrument or established by clear and convincing evidence.

(b) The presumption established in subsection (a) is rebutted if allowing the revocation to remain in effect would be more consistent with the testator's probable intention.

Comment:

a. Rationale and historical note. This section deals with a doctrine known in the case law as dependent relative revocation. This doctrine treats a revocation as presumptively ineffective in specified circumstances. The presumption is rebutted if allowing the revocation to remain in effect would be more consistent with the testator's probable intention. The circumstances in which a revocation is presumptively ineffective are that the testator made the revocation (1) in connection with an attempt to achieve a dispositive objective that fails under applicable law or (2) because of a false assumption of law, or because of a false belief about an objective fact, that is either recited in the revoking instrument or established by clear and convincing evidence. The doctrine is more aptly called the *doctrine of ineffective revocation*, the term used in this Restatement.

The doctrine of ineffective revocation is most frequently applied in cases in which a revocation was made in connection with an attempt to achieve a dispositive objective that fails under applicable law. Application of the doctrine in these cases seldom produces the precise result that the donor wanted, but rather an outcome that comes closer to the donor's dispositive objective than allowing the revocation to remain in effect. The long-term trend of the modern law of donative transfers is towards giving effect to the donor's dispositive objective, through, for example, a greater willingness to consider extrinsic evidence (see § 10.2 this Restatement), the harmless-error rule (see § 3.3), and the more permissive revival rule (see § 4.2). As this trend continues, the occasions for applying the doctrine of ineffective revocation will become ever fewer. Still, when the donor's dispositive objective fails under applicable law, or when the revocation was made because of a false assumption of law or a false belief about an objective fact, the doctrine will continue to be needed to prevent severe injustice.

The doctrine of ineffective revocation originated in equity in the early part of the 18th century as a means of rectifying certain types of mistake. The doctrine applied initially if the testator, in revoking his or her will, acted under a mistake of law or fact. For example, if a testator revoked a later will, mistakenly thinking that the effect would be to revive an earlier will, equity treated the revocation of the later will as ineffective. Over time, the doctrine came to be explained more commonly as a doctrine of conditional revocation and less commonly as rectification of a mistake. The attempted revival example would be described as one in which the testator revoked the later will on condition that the earlier will was revived. Because the condition was not satisfied, the revocation of the later will was ineffective.

This Restatement treats the doctrine of ineffective revocation as one of independent integrity, grounded neither in a conditional-revocation analysis nor exclusively in a mistake analysis. Under this Restatement, the doctrine of ineffective revocation applies (1) if the testator revokes a will in whole or in part in connection with an attempt to achieve a dispositive objective that fails under applicable law or (2) if the testator revokes a will in whole or in part because of a false assumption of law, or a false belief about an objective fact, when that false assumption or belief is recited in the revoking instrument or is established by clear and convincing evidence.

The conditional-revocation theory is thoroughly unsatisfactory as a basis of the doctrine. The notion that the testator actually intended to make the revocation conditional is a fiction (but see Comment *j*). The mistake theory is unsatisfactory as an exclusive basis of the doctrine. Equity only grants relief for mistake if the actor was laboring under an erroneous belief *at the time of the act* (see Restatement of Restitution §§ 6 and 7 [Restatement Third, Restitution and Unjust Enrichment § 5). This restriction makes the mistake theory too limiting, and the doctrine of ineffective revocation has properly been extended to cases in which the testator was not mistaken when he or she revoked (see Comments *c* and *e*).

A revocation to which this section applies is only presumptively ineffective, not automatically ineffective. The revocation is still given effect when the court determines that the testator, if given the choice, would probably have preferred the revocation to remain in effect rather than to have it set aside. This is a question of fact, to be determined on the basis of relevant evidence. When the revocation was made in connection with a failed attempt to achieve a dispositive objective, an always relevant and often decisive factor on the question of probable intention is whether the outcome of treating the revocation as ineffective comes closer to the testator's failed dispositive objective than the outcome of allowing the revocation to remain in effect. If the outcome of allowing the revocation to remain in effect comes closer to the testator's failed dispositive objective, this tends to rebut the presumption. Consequently, if, from this comparison or from other relevant evidence, it is established that the testator's probable intention would have been for the revocation to stand, the presumption is rebutted and the revocation remains in effect. Otherwise, the presumption prevails and the revocation is nullified on the theory that, had the testator known that revoking the will would not facilitate intention, the testator would not have formed an intent to revoke. Under this doctrine, then, if the presumption is not rebutted, the will is valid and effective because it was never revoked.

The doctrine of ineffective revocation is to be distinguished from revival of a formerly revoked will, the topic covered by § 4.2. Under the revival doctrine, an effectively revoked will is rendered valid and effective because it has been reinstated by subsequent conduct showing an intent to revive it, not because the revocation was ineffective.

Most situations in which a revocation is presumptively ineffective arise in one of the factual patterns treated in the Comments below. Comments *b* through *g* address situations in which a testator revokes a will in whole or in part in connection with an attempt to achieve a dispositive objective that fails under applicable law. The term "dispositive objective" includes changes in administrative provisions of a donative document as well as changes in distributive shares, since administrative provisions aid in implementing donative intent. The failed dispositive objective need not be contained in another will. It can be contained in a donative document other than a will or in the testator's understanding of the pattern of disposition under intestacy.

Comments *h* and *i* address situations in which the testator revokes a will in whole or in part because of a false assumption of law, or a false belief about an objective fact.

b. Revocation to revive an earlier will. A revocation is presumptively ineffective if a testator, in a failed effort to revive an earlier will, revokes a later will by revocatory act. In such a case, the testator's dispositive objective that failed is the pattern of distribution contained in the earlier will. In order to show that the testator revoked the later will intending to revive the earlier will, the testator's intent to revive the earlier will must be established under § 4.2. Under § 4.2, establishing such an intent would be sufficient to revive the earlier will, making the doctrine of ineffective revocation inapplicable. However, in those few jurisdictions in which a showing of an intent to revive the earlier will is insufficient under applicable revival law, the revocation of the later will is presumptively ineffective under the doctrine of ineffective revocation. The presumption is rebutted if it is shown that allowing the revocation to remain in effect would be more consistent with the testator's probable intention. Always relevant to probable intention is a comparison of the pattern of distribution under intestacy with the pattern of distribution under the later will to see which comes closer to the testator's failed dispositive objective. If the pattern of distribution under intestacy more closely approximates the pattern of distribution under the earlier will than the pattern of distribution under the later will, this evidence points strongly toward rebutting the presumption and enforcing the revocation.

Illustrations:

1. G, a widower, had two adult children, A and B. G's relationship with A was strained. G executed a will (Will No. 1) devising 25 percent of his estate to A and 75 percent to B. Later, G's relationship with A improved, and G executed a new will (Will No. 2) that devised 40 percent of his estate to A and 60 percent to B. Later still, G's relationship with A deteriorated, and G destroyed Will No. 2, intending to revive Will No. 1. The applicable revival statute, however, requires G either to reexecute Will No. 1 or to execute a codicil declaring an intent to revive Will No. 1. Because G did neither, Will No. 1 was not revived. G's revocation of Will No. 2 was made in connection with an attempt to achieve a dispositive objective that is not given effect under the applicable revival statute—to make Will No. 1 his operative will. Consequently, under the doctrine of ineffective revocation, the revocation of Will No. 2 is ineffective unless G's probable intention would be to allow the revocation to remain in effect. An important factor bearing on this question is whether the pattern of distribution under intestacy more closely approximates G's failed dispositive objective (the pattern of distribution under Will No. 1) than the pattern of distribution under Will No. 2. If the revocation of Will No. 2 is allowed to remain in effect, causing G to die intestate, A and B would divide G's estate equally, but if Will No. 2 is treated as not revoked, A receives 40 percent and B receives 60 percent. If no other evidence is introduced on the question of probable intention, the revocation of Will No. 2 is ineffective because the pattern of distribution under Will No. 2 (40 percent to A, 60 percent to B) comes closer to G's failed dispositive objective (25 percent to A, 75 percent to B) than the pattern of distribution under intestacy (50 percent to A, 50 percent to B). Consequently, Will No. 2 is not revoked. Note that G's revocation of Will No. 2, which occurred in an attempt to achieve a dispositive objective that fails under applicable law, was also based on a mistake of law. G mistakenly thought that revoking

Will No. 2 would serve to revive Will No. 1. G's revocation of Will No. 2 was manifestly not based, however, on a conditional intent to revoke Will No. 2. A person who actually intended to effect a conditional revocation of a document would not completely destroy that document.

2. The facts are the same as those in Illustration 1, except that Will No. 2 devised 55 percent of G's estate to A and 45 percent to B. If no other evidence is introduced on the question of probable intention, the revocation of Will No. 2 remains in effect because the pattern of distribution under intestacy (50 percent to A, 50 percent to B) comes closer to G's failed dispositive objective (25 percent to A, 75 percent to B) than Will No. 2 (55 percent to A, 45 percent to B). In consequence, G has died intestate.

c. Revocation intending to make a replacement will. A revocation is presumptively ineffective if a testator, failing in an attempt to replace one will (the first will) with another will (the replacement will), revokes the first will by revocatory act. In such a case, the failed dispositive objective that the testator intended to achieve in connection with revoking the first will is the pattern of distribution contained in the replacement will. If the testator initiated steps toward executing a replacement will that are sufficient to make the dispositive plan that he or she wanted to achieve provable, it is presumed that the testator's revocation of the first will was made in connection with an intent to replace it with the replacement will. After death, the only evidence available may be the ineffectively executed replacement will, and sometimes but not necessarily the revoked first will. Consequently, the doctrine of ineffective revocation would be too restricted if it required evidence of the time of revocation and of a contemporaneous intent to make a replacement will. There need not be affirmative proof of the time of revocation or that, at the time of revocation, the testator intended to replace the first will with a replacement will.

In order for the doctrine of ineffective revocation to apply to this situation, the testator's dispositive objective must be provable. Otherwise, there is no objective benchmark from which to gauge whether the testator's probable intention would be to have the revocation stand or fall. In cases coming under Comment *b*, where the testator revoked a later will intending to revive a former one, the pattern of distribution of the former will serves as the benchmark. In cases coming under this Comment, where the testator revoked the first will in connection with an intention to make a replacement will, the pattern of distribution of the replacement will serves as the benchmark.

If the testator's replacement will is validly executed under applicable law (see §§ 3.1, 3.2, and 3.3), resort to the doctrine of ineffective revocation is inappropriate. If, however, applicable law does not validate the replacement will, the revocation of the first will is presumptively ineffective. The presumption is rebutted if it is shown that allowing the revocation to remain in effect would be more consistent with the testator's probable intention. Always relevant to probable intention is a comparison of the pattern of distribution under intestacy with the pattern of distribution under the first will to see which more closely approximates the testator's failed dispositive objective. Evidence that the pattern of distribution under intestacy more closely approximates the pattern of distribution under the replacement will than the pattern of distribution under the first will points strongly toward rebutting the presumption and enforcing the revocation. . . . .

If the testator never had a plan to make a replacement will, the doctrine of ineffective revocation is inapplicable. Similarly, if the testator intended to make a replacement will but never took steps to complete the plan, the doctrine cannot be applied. The testator's uncompleted plan to make a replacement will provides no benchmark against which to gauge whether the testator's probable intention would be to have the revocation stand or fall. The revocation stands. . . . .

d. Ineffective alterations. A testator sometimes attempts to alter a will by marking it up—by crossing out attested language and inserting unattested substitute language. The purpose is usually to alter the disposition of property or the designation of persons. Under the harmless-error rule of § 3.3 (and Revised Uniform Probate Code § 2–503), such an alteration will be validated if the proponent proves by clear and convincing evidence that the testator intended the alteration to constitute part of his or her will. Apart from the harmless-error rule, a testator may, in handwriting, effectively alter a holographic will without re-signing it (and without re-dating it, if applicable law requires holographic wills to be dated). See § 3.2, Comment *f*. A testator may, in handwriting, effectively alter an attested will if applicable law recognizes holographic wills and if the alteration is signed (and, if required by the statute, dated). See § 3.2, Comment *g*. The doctrine of ineffective revocation is inapplicable in these cases because the testator's intent as expressed in the altered document can be fully carried out.

At the other extreme, partial revocation by act is not recognized in some jurisdictions. If, under applicable law, neither the act of crossing out attested language nor of inserting unattested substitute language is recognized as valid, the will is given effect as originally written. The doctrine of ineffective revocation has no room to operate in this situation because the attempted partial revocation is ineffective.

In many jurisdictions, however, at least for nonholographic wills, one but not the other of the two acts is effective. The act of crossing out attested language is effective as a partial revocation, but the act of inserting unattested language is ineffective because not executed in accordance with the statutory formalities for wills. These are the cases in which the doctrine of ineffective revocation can come into operation. Because the partial revocation was made in connection with an attempt to achieve a dispositive objective that fails under applicable law, the partial revocation is presumptively ineffective unless allowing it to remain in effect would be more consistent with the testator's probable intention.

The following discussion assumes that applicable law gives effect to partial revocation by act but does not give effect to unattested insertions. If the testator, in an attempt to change devisees (or fiduciaries or others), has crossed out the name of one person and written in the name of another person, many factors may bear on probable intention. In these cases, it is important to identify who would take the revoked devise if the revocation remains in effect. If the person who would take the revoked devise is the person whom the testator attempted to substitute, the testator would probably want the revocation to remain in effect. The testator might also prefer the revocation to remain in effect if the persons who would take the revoked devise are closely related to the intended devisee, such as the intended devisee's children. See § 11.3(c)(3) and Comment *j* thereto of this Restatement, recognizing a constructional preference for the construction that favors close family members.

Also tending to indicate that the testator would probably want the revocation to remain in effect would be evidence that the testator's relationship with the original devisee had deteriorated, so that his or her dominant motive in revoking was to deprive the original devisee of the property. See Illustration 11. On the other hand, if the testator had not become hostile to the original devisee, but merely decided to give the property to someone more preferable (or to someone more preferable to the original devisee, such as the devisee's child), this would tend to support the presumption that the testator would probably want the revocation to be ineffective. . . . . As always, all relevant evidence may be considered in determining the testator's probable intention.

If the testator, in an attempt to change amounts, crossed out one amount and wrote in a different amount, an important factor bearing on probable intention is whether the testator attempted to increase or decrease the original amount. Perhaps the easiest case for the application of the doctrine of ineffective revocation is one in which the testator attempted to increase the original amount. In this type of case, the testator would probably want the revocation to be ineffective. Indeed, the testator would probably think it odd for the law to characterize his or her intent as *revocatory*. Rather than trying to revoke the original devise, the testator tried to add to it.

If the testator attempted to decrease the original amount, an instructive question is whether the reduction is more or less than 50 percent of the original amount. A reduction of more than 50 percent of the original amount would tend to rebut the presumption and suggest that the testator would probably want the revocation to remain in effect. A reduction of less than 50 percent of the original amount would tend to support the presumption and suggest that the testator would probably want the revocation to be ineffective. In both cases, however, other relevant evidence may also be considered in determining the testator's probable intention. In some cases the testator's attempt to decrease the original amount is accompanied by an attempt to increase the amount to another devisee or other devisees by a comparable amount.

Furthermore, when the testator marks up a will in a variety of ways—raising some amounts, lowering some amounts, changing one or more persons—each attempted but ineffective alteration can be treated as part of a whole or be treated separately, whichever approach would produce a final result that comes closer to the testator's intention. That is, ineffective alterations within a single will need not be treated alike. If it would further intent, the presumption that a partial revocation is ineffective can be found rebutted for some but not for other ineffective alterations.

Illustrations:

7. As originally executed, G's attested will devised $10,000 to her brother, A; $20,000 to her brother, B; and $15,000 to her brother, C. After G's death, G's will was found with "$10,000" crossed out and the figure "$12,000" written in above it, with "$20,000" crossed out and the figure "$3,000" written in above it, and with "$15,000" crossed out and the figure "$7,500" written in above it. All the alterations were in G's handwriting. G's revocation of the $10,000 devise was made in connection with an attempt to increase the amount to $12,000, G's revocation of the $20,000 devise was made in connection with an attempt to decrease the amount to $3,000, and G's revocation of the $15,000 devise was made in connection with an attempt to decrease the amount to $7,500. Assume that applicable law does not allow G's dispositive

objectives to be given effect because the writings directing that the devised amounts be $12,000, $3,000, and $7,500 were not executed in accordance with the statute of wills. . . . The revocations of the $10,000, $20,000, and $15,000 devises are presumptively ineffective. With respect to the devise to A, G's failed dispositive objective was actually to increase it, not to revoke it. (Had G pursued her objective by merely writing in "plus $2,000" above the "$10,000," the added words would not be given effect but the original $10,000 devise would not be affected.) Consequently, treating the revocation of the $10,000 devise as ineffective carries out G's intention better than allowing the revocation to remain in effect. With respect to the devise to B, the fact that the attempted reduction is more than 50 percent of the original amount suggests that allowing the revocation of the $20,000 devise to remain in effect carries out G's intention better than treating the revocation as ineffective. Unless other evidence shows that G's probable intention would be to have the revocation be ineffective, the revocation of B's devise remains in effect. With respect to the devise to C, the fact that the attempted reduction is exactly 50 percent of the original amount means that comparing the outcome of allowing the revocation to remain in effect with the outcome of treating the revocation as ineffective does not rebut the presumption. Unless other evidence rebuts the presumption, the revocation is ineffective.

11. As originally executed, G's attested will devised the residue of her estate to her live-in companion, A. Subsequently, G and A separated. Some years later, G began living with B. G adopted B's infant son, X. G and B raised X to adulthood. At G's death, G and B were unmarried but still living together. After G's death, G's will was found with her important documents. In the residuary clause, the name of A was crossed out and, in G's handwriting, the name of B was written in above it. Both A and B survived G. Were G to die intestate, her sole heir would be her adopted son, X. G revoked her residuary devise to A in connection with a failed attempt to devise her residuary estate to B. G's dispositive objective was to give nothing to A and the residue of her estate to B. Under the doctrine of ineffective revocation, the revocation of the devise to A is presumptively ineffective. The presumption is rebutted if allowing the revocation to remain in effect would be more consistent with G's probable intention. If the revocation is ineffective, A will take the residue of G's estate, but if the revocation remains in effect, A will take nothing and X, now an adult, will take the residue of G's estate by intestacy. Because G would probably prefer to have her residuary estate pass to her adopted son (who is also B's son) than to have it pass to A, the outcome of allowing the revocation to remain in effect comes closer to G's failed dispositive objective than treating the revocation as ineffective. Hence it would be more consistent with G's probable intention to allow the revocation to remain in effect and allow the residuary estate to pass to X by intestacy.

12. As originally executed, G's attested will devised the residue of his estate to his live-in companion, A. Subsequently, G and A separated. Some years later, G began living with B. Later, G and B separated, and G went back to living with A. At G's death, G and A were unmarried but still living together. After G's death, G's will was found with his important documents. In the residuary clause, the name of A was crossed out and, in G's handwriting, the name of B was written in above it. The name of B was also crossed out and, in G's handwriting, the name of A was written in above it. Both A and B survived G. Were G to die

intestate, his heirs would be his brothers and sisters. G revoked his residuary devise to A in connection with a failed attempt to devise his residuary estate to B. G's dispositive objective was to give nothing to A and the residue of his estate to B. Subsequently, however, G's dispositive objective was to give nothing to B and the residue of his estate to A. By crossing out the name of B and writing in A's name, G canceled the revocation of the devise to A, thus reviving it. See § 4.2, Comment *i*, Illustration 10, where the possibility of applying the harmless-error rule of § 3.3 is also discussed. Should either the theory of revival or harmless error not be available in the jurisdiction, an alternative theory is to apply the doctrine of ineffective revocation. Under that alternative theory, the revocation of the devise to A would be presumptively ineffective. The presumption is rebutted if allowing the revocation to remain in effect would be more consistent with G's probable intention. In considering this question, it would be unreasonable to ignore G's latest dispositive objective (to devise the residue to A, not B), even though G's dispositive objective when he revoked was to devise the residue to B, not A. If the revocation of A's devise is ineffective, A will take the residue of G's estate, but if the revocation remains in effect, A will take nothing and G's brothers and sisters will take the residue of G's estate by intestacy. Because the outcome of treating the revocation as ineffective achieves G's latest dispositive objective, the revocation is ineffective and G's residuary estate passes to A under the terms of the will as originally executed.

e. Express revocation by subsequent will. The doctrine of ineffective revocation may be applied when a later will that expressly revoked an earlier will contains one or more dispositive provisions that fail under applicable law. The revocation of the earlier will is presumptively ineffective to the extent necessary to give effect to the dispositive provision in the earlier will that the failed dispositive provision in the later will replaced.

Illustration:

16. G executed a will devising specific property to X, residue to Y. Subsequently, G executed a second will that expressly revoked all former wills, devised the same specific property to X, and devised the residue to Y and Z. X's husband was an attesting witness to the second will. Applicable law provides that a devise is invalid if the devisee or the spouse of the devisee is an attesting witness. Under the doctrine of ineffective revocation, the revocation of the devise to X in the first will is ineffective. By treating the revocation of the devise to X as ineffective, G's dispositive objective is fully carried out.

In some cases, the doctrine of ineffective revocation may be applied in a manner that avoids failure of the dispositive provision in the later will by, for example, rendering ineffective the revocation of a saving clause in the earlier will.

Illustration:

18. G executed a will devising $400,000 in trust, providing for the income to go to his children for the life of the survivor, then for the corpus to go to his grandchildren who live to age 25. A perpetuity saving clause in the will required the trust to terminate no later than 21 years after the death of the survivor of G's descendants living at G's death. Subsequently, G executed a second will, expressly revoking all prior wills. The second will made some changes in certain specific and

pecuniary devises in the prior will, repeated the $400,000 devise creating the trust, but omitted the perpetuity saving clause. Under the common-law Rule Against Perpetuities, which applies in the jurisdiction, the future interest in the $400,000 trust to G's grandchildren who live to age 25 is invalid. Under the doctrine of ineffective revocation, the revocation of the perpetuity saving clause in the first will is ineffective. By treating the revocation of the perpetuity saving clause as ineffective, G's dispositive objective is fully carried out.

f. Revocation by implication or by inconsistency. The doctrine of ineffective revocation may be applied when a later will that revoked an earlier will by implication contains one or more dispositive provisions that fail under applicable law. The revocation of the earlier will is presumptively ineffective in whole or in part. Thus, Illustrations 14 through 18 would be resolved in the same way if the second will in each Illustration did not contain an express revocation clause but did, under § 4.1, revoke the earlier will by implication.

The doctrine may also be applied when a dispositive provision in a later codicil revokes a dispositive provision of an earlier will by inconsistency, and the inconsistent dispositive provision fails under applicable law.

g. Revocation to die intestate. A revocation is presumptively ineffective if a testator revokes a will mistakenly thinking that the pattern of distribution under intestacy carries out his or her intention. In this situation, the testator's dispositive objective will ordinarily not be proved by written evidence. If not, the testator's expectation of the pattern of distribution under intestacy must be proved by clear and convincing evidence. The expected pattern must also differ from the actual distributive pattern under intestacy. If the pattern of distribution under the will comes closer to the expected pattern of distribution than the actual pattern of distribution under intestacy, the revocation is ineffective, unless other evidence establishes that the testator's probable intention would be to allow the revocation to remain in effect.

The principle of this Comment is applicable to a partial as well as to a complete revocation of a will. A partial revocation is presumptively ineffective if the revoked part passes by intestacy, as, for example, when a testator revokes the residuary clause mistakenly thinking that the pattern of distribution under intestacy carries out his or her intention.

h. Revocation caused by a false assumption of law recited in revoking instrument or established by clear and convincing evidence. Although most mistake-of-law cases involve an attempt to achieve a dispositive objective that is provable but fails, the category is not restricted to such situations. If a testator revokes a will in whole or in part because of a false assumption of law, even though the revocation was not made in connection with an attempt to achieve a dispositive objective that fails under applicable law, the revocation is presumptively ineffective if the false assumption was recited in the revoking instrument or is established by clear and convincing evidence. Compare § 12.1, Comment *i* of . . . this Restatement (authorizing reformation of a will in case of a mistake in the inducement proved by clear and convincing evidence).

Illustrations:

19. After executing a will devising land to a church, G executed a codicil stating that he was revoking the devise to the church because the church was an unincorporated association and devises to such

associations are invalid. Actually, the law of the jurisdiction allows unincorporated associations to take title to land, by construing the devise as one in trust with the officers of the association as trustees and the members as beneficiaries. G's revocation of the devise to the church is presumptively ineffective.

20. After executing a will devising land to a church, G crossed out the devise. After G's death, it is established by clear and convincing evidence that G crossed out the church's devise because G believed that the devise would be invalid. G thought that the church, being an unincorporated association, could not take title to land. Actually, the law of the jurisdiction allows unincorporated associations to take title to land by treating such associations as quasi-corporate entities. G's revocation of the devise to the church is presumptively ineffective.

i. Revocation caused by a false belief about an objective fact recited in revoking instrument or established by clear and convincing evidence. If a testator revokes a will in whole or in part because of a false belief about an objective fact, even though the revocation was not made in connection with an attempt to achieve a dispositive objective that fails under applicable law, the revocation is presumptively ineffective if the false belief was recited in the terms of the revoking instrument or is established by clear and convincing evidence. Compare § 12.1, Comment *i*, of . . . this Restatement (authorizing reformation of a will in case of a mistake in the inducement proved by clear and convincing evidence).

Illustrations:

21. G, having been informed that her favorite nephew, N, a soldier, had been killed in combat, wrote across a $10,000 devise to him in her will the words "Canceled because N died in combat." Shortly after G's death, N, who had not been killed in combat but had been taken prisoner of war, was released. Because G revoked the devise to him based on a mistake of fact, the revocation is ineffective unless allowing the revocation to remain effective would be more consistent with G's probable intention. Consequently, unless overcome by other evidence, the revocation is ineffective and G's devise to N takes effect.

23. The same facts as in Illustration[ ] 21 . . ., except that G's revocation of N's $10,000 devise did not recite the reason for the revocation. Extrinsic evidence establishes by clear and convincing evidence that G revoked the devise because she thought N had died in combat. The result is the same as in Illustration[ ] 21 . . . .

In order for the doctrine of ineffective revocation to apply, the false belief must be about an *objective* fact. The doctrine does not apply, for example, if a testator revokes a will in whole or in part because of a belief that a devisee does not love him or her, no matter how much the devisee claims that he or she really did love the testator. If, however, a revocation is the product of an insane delusion or fraud, the revocation would be ineffective for that reason, quite apart from the principle of this section.

The doctrine of ineffective revocation does not apply when a testator purports to base a revocation on a fact that is peculiarly within the testator's knowledge, even though the cited "fact" turns out to be false. If the testator recites a reason for revoking that he or she must have known to be false, the testator is considered to have made the recital as a pretext to disguise an intention to revoke in any event. The mistaken fact asserted in the recital did not induce the revocation.

Illustration:

24. G's will contains a $10,000 devise to his niece, N. G executed a codicil stating that he revoked the devise to N because G had made substantial gifts to N. Although N can establish that G did not give her substantial gifts, the revocation stands. Because whether or not G made substantial gifts to N is a fact peculiarly within G's knowledge, the revocation of N's devise was not based on a mistake of fact. Note, however, that if G had actually taken steps to make substantial gifts to N, but unbeknownst to G, the attempted gifts failed due to an external cause, the doctrine could be applied. For example, if G gave money to a third party to give to N, but the third party absconded with the money, the doctrine could be applied to render the revocation ineffective.

j. Conditional revocation. Although the conditional-revocation theory is not adopted as the rationale for the doctrine of ineffective revocation (see Comment *a*), a testator can make a conditional revocation of a will. For example, if a testator executes a codicil stating that "I revoke my will on condition that [stating the condition]," or words to that effect, the revocation is conditional, and the revocation is ineffective if the condition is not satisfied.

k. Application of doctrine to donative documents other than wills. Although the typical application of the doctrine of ineffective revocation is to revocation of a will, the doctrine is applicable, in appropriate situations, to the revocation in whole or in part of any donative document. The doctrine is not restricted to revocation of wills. Also, as noted in Comment *a*, if a testator revokes a will in connection with an attempt to achieve a donative objective that fails under applicable law, the failed donative objective need not be contained in another will but can be contained in a donative document other than a will or, as described in Comment *g*, in the testator's understanding of the pattern of distribution under intestacy.

CHAPTER 5

POST-EXECUTION EVENTS AFFECTING WILLS

Introductory Note: There will always be some interval between the execution of a will and the testator's death. The interval is sometimes long, sometimes short. Older wills, sometimes called "stale" wills, are just as valid as "fresher" ones, but have the potential to do mischief if they are out of date.

Many of the issues addressed in this chapter could—and should—be avoided by foresight and careful drafting. The doctrines addressed in this chapter operate as default rules. They apply because, and only to the extent that, the testator and the testator's attorney failed to address the issue explicitly in a will provision.

§ 5.1. Classification of Devises

Devises are classified as specific, general, demonstrative, or residuary:

(1) A *specific devise* is a testamentary disposition of a specifically identified asset.

(2) A *general devise* is a testamentary disposition, usually of a specified amount of money or quantity of property, that is payable from the general assets of the estate.

(3) A *demonstrative devise* is a testamentary disposition, usually of a specified amount of money or quantity of property, that is primarily payable from a designated source, but is secondarily payable from the general assets of the estate to the extent that the primary source is insufficient.

(4) A *residuary devise* is a testamentary disposition of property of the testator's net probate estate not disposed by a specific, general, or demonstrative devise.

Comment:

a. *Classification.* Devises are traditionally divided into four classes—specific, general, demonstrative, and residuary. Some of the doctrines addressed in this chapter only apply to a devise of a certain class or apply differently to different classes.

As used in this Restatement, the term *devise* refers to a testamentary disposition of either real or personal property. See § 3.1, Comment *d*.

b. *Specific devises.* A *specific devise* is a testamentary disposition of a specifically identified asset. The dispositive language describing the asset can range in degree of specificity. Examples can range from a devise of "my desk" to a devise of "the desk in my study," from a devise of "my ruby ring" to a devise of "the ruby ring that I inherited from Aunt Bertha," from a devise of "my cabin" to a devise of "my cabin on Lake Tahoe," from a devise of "my house" to a devise of "my house at 312 Franklin Avenue," or from a devise of "my car" to a devise of "my Buick" or a devise of "my 1998 Buick Riviera."

A specific devise need not refer to property owned by the testator at the time of execution of the will. A devise can be specific even if it refers to property owned or to be owned at death, such as a devise of "the house I own and am residing in at my death" or of "the car I own at death."

A devise is also specific if it relates to a fractional or percentile share of a specifically identified asset, for example, a devise of "fifty percent of the balance on hand in my checking account at my death" or of "two-thirds of the X-Y-Z Mutual Fund shares owned by me at my death."

c. *General devises.* A *general devise* is a testamentary disposition, usually of a specified amount of money or quantity of property, that is payable from the general assets of the estate. Examples include a devise of "$100,000," of "1,000 shares of X-Y-Z Corporation," or of "500 ounces of gold bullion." If the estate does not own the specified quantity of property, for example if the estate does not own 1,000 shares of X-Y-Z Corporation or 500 ounces of gold bullion, the personal representative may have to purchase it for the devisee.

A species of a general devise is a devise of a specified amount of money. A devise of a specified amount of money is also sometimes called a *pecuniary devise.* A pecuniary devise can state a sum of money or state a formula from which a sum of money is derived. A pecuniary amount derived by formula is often used in tax clauses, such as a devise of "the smallest pecuniary amount that, if allowed as a federal estate tax marital deduction, would result in the least possible federal estate tax being payable by reason of my death," or a devise of "the largest pecuniary amount, if any, that will not increase the federal estate taxes payable by reason of my death."

Although a general devise usually takes the form of a devise of a specified amount of money or quantity of property, the category is not so limited. Any devise that is payable out of the general assets of the estate is a general devise. For example, a devise of "all of my property" or of "all of my personal property" is a general devise, as is a devise of "one-half of my estate."

d. *Demonstrative devises.* A *demonstrative devise* is a testamentary disposition, usually of a specified amount of money or quantity of property, that is primarily payable from a designated source, but is secondarily payable from the general assets of the estate to the extent that the primary source is insufficient. Examples include a devise of "$5,000 out of my bank account," or of "$10,000 from the proceeds of the sale of my X-Y-Z bonds." If, however, the devise indicates that it is to be paid *only* from a designated source (for example, a devise of "$5,000 out of my bank account if that much money is on hand at my death"), the devise is specific, not demonstrative. Demonstrative devises are less frequently used than the other types.

e. *Residuary devises.* A *residuary devise* is a testamentary disposition of property of the testator's net probate estate not disposed by a specific, general, or demonstrative devise. The residuary devise is usually the last dispositive provision of the will, and often takes the form of devising "all of the rest, residue, and remainder of my estate." A residuary devise can divide the residuary estate among more than one person on a fractional or a percentage basis.

f. Nonresiduary or preresiduary devises. Sometimes a statute or a governing instrument refers to a "nonresiduary" or to a "preresiduary" devise or clause. These terms refer to all devises that are not a residuary devise.

g. Construction. The category into which a particular devise falls is a question of construction, on which the testator's overall purpose is relevant. Thus, if it serves the testator's purposes, a devise might be classified one way for purposes of one rule but another way for purposes of another rule.

On construction generally, see [Chapters 10, 11, and 12] of this Restatement, on Construction, Reformation, and Modification of Donative Documents.

§ 5.2. Failure ("Ademption") of Specific Devises by Extinction

(a) If specifically devised property, in its original or in a changed form, is in the testator's estate at death, the devisee is entitled to the specifically devised property.

(b) If specifically devised property is not in the testator's estate at death, the devisee is entitled to any proceeds remaining unpaid at death of (i) any sale, (ii) any condemnation award, or (iii) any insurance on or other recovery for damage to or loss of the property.

(c) Subject to subsection (b), if specifically devised property is not in the testator's estate at death, the specific devise fails unless failure of the devise would be inconsistent with the testator's intent.

Comment:

a. Entitlement of specific devisee. If specifically devised property is in the testator's estate at death, the devisee is entitled to the specifically devised property, whether that property is in its original or in a changed form. If the specifically devised property is in a changed form, the devisee takes the property in its changed form. For an explanation of the change-in-form principle, see Comment *d*.

b. Historical note—"identity" versus "intent" theory of ademption. The common law developed two conflicting theories of ademption, the "identity" theory and the "intent" theory. Under the "identity" theory, which predominates in the case law, a specific devise completely fails—i.e., the devisee is entitled to nothing—if the specifically devised property is not in the testator's estate at death. Like any doctrine that treats the testator's intent as irrelevant, the identity theory sometimes operates to defeat intent, sometimes not, but then only by coincidence. Under the "intent" theory, however, the testator's intent is central to the inquiry. Under that theory, the devise fails unless the evidence establishes that failure would be inconsistent with the testator's intent (see Comments *g* and *h*). This section adopts the "intent" theory of ademption.

Although the testator's intent is nominally irrelevant under the identity theory, it is well documented in the case law that courts purportedly following the identity theory frequently manipulate doctrine to effectuate intent anyway. By adopting the intent theory, this Restatement prefers the more candid analysis of the problem.

c. Specific devise. The doctrine of ademption by extinction only applies to specific devises. For the definition of a specific devise, see § 5.1. For purposes of ademption, it is well established that there is a presumption against classifying a devise as specific. (For purposes of abatement, the presumption runs the other way, in order to protect the devise from bearing a proportionate part of claims against the estate. See § 1.1, Comment *f.*)

To rebut the presumption against classifying a devise as specific, the language creating the devise must unambiguously be in the form of a specific devise. For example, a devise of a specific number of shares of stock (e.g., "1,000 shares of X-Y-Z Corporation stock") is ordinarily classified as general, not specific, even if the testator owned that exact number of shares when executing the will. In order for the devise to be classified as specific, the language would ordinarily have to contain additional language indicating the particular shares (e.g., "*my* 1,000 shares of X-Y-Z Corporation stock").

When it turns out that the named source for payment of a devise is not in the testator's estate at death or is insufficient to cover payment in full, the presumption against classifying a devise as specific usually results in classifying the devise as demonstrative, unless the language affirmatively states that the devisee's claim is limited to that source.

d. Change in form. Even though a specifically devised asset is not in the testator's estate in its original form, the specific devise does not fail if the asset is in the testator's estate in a changed form. By well-established authority, the change-in-form principle applies if the change in form is insubstantial. It is not possible to give a comprehensive list of what types of post-execution transactions amount to a mere change in form and what types do not. It is clear, however, that if the testator gives the property to the devisee or to another, the change-in-form principle cannot operate because the testator has received nothing in return for the gift. The testator's estate owns no product into which the subject of the original devise was changed.

It is also clear that if the testator sells the property, and holds the cash proceeds of the sale at death, those cash proceeds do not amount to the specifically devised asset in a changed form, whether tracing is possible or not. The reason is that the change into cash is too substantial a change to be treated as the same asset though in a changed form. Cash is the opposite of something specific, because the holder of cash has nearly infinite options to spend or invest it.

A mere change in location or custodial institution is usually treated as a change in form. For example, if the testator's will devises her "bank account in the X-Bank," and the testator later switches her account to the Y-Bank, the change in financial institution would be a mere change in form. Another example would be a devise of "my Picasso print hanging on the wall in the living room," where sometime after executing the will the testator moved the print to a wall in the master bedroom, or put the print in storage.

The fact that the testator did not initiate a change makes the application of the change-in-form principle more likely. For example, if the testator's will made a specific devise of certain financial assets such as certain stock, the change-in-form principle would apply to the securities of another organization acquired as a result of a merger, consolidation, reorganization, or other distribution by the original organization or by any successor, related, or acquiring organization. See also § 5.3 (Effect of Stock Splits, Stock Dividends, and Other Distributions on Devises of a Specified Number of Securities). The principle would not, however, apply to any cash that the testator received in place of the original securities.

Illustration:

1. *Stock in merged corporation.* G's will devised "my 1,000 shares of X-Y-Z Corporation stock." After executing her will, X-Y-Z Corporation merged with M-N-O Corporation to become M-X Corporation. All shareholders of X-Y-Z Corporation received a certain amount of cash and three shares of M-X stock for every share of X-Y-Z Corporation stock owned. At death, as a result of the merger, G owned 3,000 shares of M-X Corporation stock. The devisee is entitled to G's 3,000 shares of M-X because they represent the original 1,000 shares of X-Y-Z in a changed form. The devisee is not, however, entitled to any of the cash received when the two corporations merged. (The result in this case would be the same under the principle of § 5.3, even if the devise were general. . . . .)

The most difficult question under the change-in-form principle arises if the testator replaced the specifically devised property with property of like kind and function. Although the case law has traditionally resisted extending the change-in-form principle to replacement property, the Revised UPC § 2–606 provides that the devisee of a specific devise is entitled to "real or tangible personal property owned by the testator at death which the testator acquired as a replacement for specifically devised real or tangible personal property." This position commends itself to decisional law in appropriate cases, i.e., those in which the result appears to be consistent with the testator's intent.

Illustration:

2. *Replacement car.* G's will devised to X "my Chevrolet." After she executed her will, she sold (or traded in) her Chevrolet and bought a newer model Dodge; later, she sold (or traded in) the Dodge and bought a newer model Mercury. She owned the Mercury when she died. Unless other evidence indicates a contrary intent, the change-in-form principle applies, entitling X to the Mercury. If G had sold her Chevrolet (or any of the replacement cars) and used the proceeds to buy shares in a mutual fund, which she owned at death, the change-in-form principle would not award the shares in the mutual fund to X. If G owned an automobile at death as a replacement for her Chevrolet, however, the fact that it was bought with funds other than the proceeds of the sale of the Chevrolet or of any replacement car would not prevent the change-in-form principle from applying.

e. Time of construction; generic language. When the language describing specifically devised property is generic, the devisee is entitled to any property that the language describes, even though that is not the property that the testator owned and that the language described when the will was executed. For example, if the testator's will devises "my house" or "my car," the devisee is entitled to the house or car that the testator owns at death, even though that is not the house or car that the testator owned when executing the will. Cf. § 3.7 (Independent Significance).

The same analysis applies to a specific devise of securities. Suppose, for example, that the testator's will devised "my 1,000 shares of X-Y-Z Corporation stock." The testator later sold (or otherwise disposed of) those securities, and then later purchased (or otherwise acquired) securities that met the description in the will. If, at death, the testator owned 1,000 or more shares of X-Y-Z Corporation stock, the devisee is entitled to 1,000 of those shares, even though they are not the same shares that the testator owned when executing the will. If, at death, the testator owned less than 1,000 shares, the devisee is entitled to all the shares that the testator owned. The devisee is also entitled to have the difference made up from any X-Y-Z shares that are in the estate in a changed form and is additionally entitled to any amounts as otherwise provided in this section. See also § 5.3 (Effect of Stock Splits, Stock Dividends, and Other Distributions on Devises of a Specified Number of Securities).

A devise of securities that does not specify a number of shares, but devises "all" (or a specified fraction or percentage) of the testator's shares of a certain stock covers all (or the specified fraction or percentage) of shares of that stock that the testator owns at death, regardless of how those shares were acquired.

Illustration:

3. *Additional shares.* G's will devised "all of my shares of X-Y-Z Corporation stock." When G executed her will, she owned 1,000 shares of X-Y-Z Corporation stock. After executing her will, G purchased another 200 shares. After she purchased the additional shares, X-Y-Z Corporation split its stock 2-for-1. At death, G owned 2,400 shares of X-Y-Z Corporation stock. The devisee is entitled to all 2,400 shares owned by G at her death.

Courts often give an incorrect rationale for these results. To avoid ademption, courts often say that a will is construed *as if* it were executed immediately before death. This is sometimes called the "time-of-death" construction. As made clear in § 10.2, Comment *g*, of . . . this Restatement, however, a will is construed in light of the testator's intention *at the time of execution*, which refers to the time of actual execution, not to a fictitious time of execution. The correct rationale is that the testator's use of such generic language evidences an intent to devise whatever property the language describes that the testator owns at death.

f. Unpaid proceeds at death. Under the Uniform Probate Code, the devisee of a specific devise is entitled to: (1) any balance of the purchase price, together with any security agreement, owing from a purchaser to the testator at death by reason of sale of the property; (2) any amount of a condemnation award for the taking of the property unpaid at death; (3) any proceeds unpaid at death on fire or casualty insurance on or other recovery for injury to the property; or (4) property owned by the testator at death and acquired as a result of foreclosure, or obtained in lieu of foreclosure, of the security interest for a specifically devised obligation. These provisions commend themselves to adoption by decisional law.

g. Failure inconsistent with testator's intent; disposition by a guardian, conservator, or agent. At some point in life, a testator might become incapacitated, and his or her financial affairs taken over by a representative such as a guardian, conservator, or agent under a durable power of attorney. If, during a testator's incapacity, the testator's representative sells or mortgages specifically devised property, failure of the devise is presumptively inconsistent with the testator's intent. Unless the presumption is rebutted, the specific devise does not fail. Rather, the specific devisee is entitled to a general pecuniary devise equal to the net sale price or amount of the unpaid loan. Similarly, if while the testator is incapacitated, specifically devised property is condemned or damaged, and if the representative collects a condemnation award, insurance proceeds, or recovery for the injury, the specific devisee is presumptively entitled to a general pecuniary devise equal to the amount of the condemnation award, insurance proceeds, or recovery. There need not be an adjudication of incapacity in order for these rules to apply. Any disposition by an agent under a durable power is presumed to be for a testator who is incapacitated. An adjudication that the testator's incapacity has ceased obviates these rules, however, if the testator survives the adjudication by a period of time sufficient to afford the testator a reasonable opportunity to learn what happened and to change the will.

These rules also apply if the testator's representative disposes of a specifically devised asset by gift to a third party. In case of such a disposition by gift, the devisee is presumptively entitled to a general pecuniary devise of the date-of-death value of the specific asset. If the specific asset no longer exists or cannot be located, the date-of-death value is to be estimated.

The presumption that failure of the devise would be inconsistent with the testator's intent is rebutted if the gift is by an agent under a durable power and the durable power specifically authorized the agent to make a gift of the specifically devised asset. The presumption is similarly rebutted if the gift is approved by a court order and the court, in authorizing the gift, examined the will and determined that the gift was not inconsistent with the testator's intent. UPC § 5–427 authorizes the court and conservator to examine the testator's will.

h. Failure inconsistent with testator's intent. As explained in Comment *b*, this Restatement adopts the intent theory of ademption and rejects the identity theory. If a specifically devised asset is not in the testator's estate at death, in its original or a changed form, and if none of the other rules of this section avoid ademption, ademption still does not occur if failure of the devise would be inconsistent with the testator's intent. Except for those cases covered by Comment *g*, the party opposing ademption bears the burden of proof on the issue of intent.

If the testator's will expressly conditions the specific devise on owning the property at death, ademption cannot be avoided because ademption cannot be inconsistent with the testator's intent. In the absence of such an express condition, the testator's manifested plan of distribution can raise an inference that ademption would or would not be inconsistent with the testator's intent. On determining intent from a will as a whole, see § 10.2, Comment *b*, of . . . this Restatement. A feature that raises a strong inference that ademption would be inconsistent with the testator's intent arises from the use of equalizing devises, thus exhibiting a plan that would be upset if one of the devises were to fail.

If it is determined that ademption would be inconsistent with the testator's intent, the specific devisee is entitled to a general pecuniary devise of the date-of-death value of the specific asset. If the specific asset no longer exists or cannot be located, the date-of-death value is to be estimated. . . . .

i. Application of this section to will substitutes. The principles of this section also apply to a will substitute, such as a revocable trust, that contains the equivalent of a specific devise.

§ 5.3. Effect of Stock Splits, Stock Dividends, and Other Distributions on Devises of a Specified Number of Securities

A devise of a specified number of securities carries with it any additional securities acquired by the testator after executing the will to the extent that the post-execution acquisitions resulted from the testator's ownership of the described securities.

Comment:

a. Historical and scope note. The rule of this section has historically been restricted to specific devises of securities. Recent case and statutory law has moved away from using classification of the devise as the determining factor for applying the rule of this section. This section aligns itself with the current trend. Under this section, the classification is irrelevant. The rule of this section applies to any devise of a specified number of securities, whether the devise is specific, general, or otherwise. Thus it is irrelevant whether the devise refers to "*my* [number] of shares of X-Y-Z Corporation stock," to "[number] of *my* shares of X-Y-Z Corporation stock," or simply to "[number] shares of X-Y-Z Corporation stock." The rationale for this rule is that a testator, in devising a specified number of securities, ordinarily intends to give to the devisee the economic equivalent of that number of securities at the testator's death.

b. Post-execution acquisitions; scope of coverage. The additional securities that the testator acquires and that pass to the devisee under this section can be securities of the same organization acquired by reason of action initiated by the organization or by any successor, related, or acquiring organization; or securities of another organization acquired as a result of a merger, consolidation, reorganization, or other distribution by the organization or by any successor, related, or acquiring organization. Also covered are securities of the same organization acquired as a result of a plan of dividend reinvestment in which the testator enrolled. See Comment *c*.

This section only applies to additional securities that are acquired as the result of the testator's ownership of the described securities. Any post-execution purchases of additional securities are not covered, nor are any securities acquired by exercise of purchase options. The rule of this section does not apply to cash distributions occurring before death with respect to a described security.

Illustrations:

1. *Stock split.* G's will devised "1,000 shares of X-Y-Z Corporation stock." After executing her will, X-Y-Z Corporation split its stock 2-for-1. At death, as a result of the stock split, G owned 2,000 shares of X-Y-Z Corporation stock. Whether or not G's devise is specific or general, the devisee is entitled to G's 2,000 shares of X-Y-Z. The devisee is not, however, entitled to any cash dividends paid to G before death on the original or additional X-Y-Z shares.

2. *Stock dividend.* G's will devised "1,000 shares of X-Y-Z Corporation stock." After executing her will, X-Y-Z Corporation declared and paid a stock dividend of two shares of stock for every 100 shares owned. At death, as a result of the stock dividend, G owned 1,020 shares of X-Y-Z Corporation stock. Whether or not G's devise is specific or general, the devisee is entitled to G's 1,020 shares of X-Y-Z. The devisee is not, however, entitled to any cash dividends paid to G before death on the original or additional X-Y-Z shares.

4. *Stock in merged corporation.* G's will devised "1,000 shares of X-Y-Z Corporation stock." After executing her will, X-Y-Z Corporation merged with M-N-O Corporation to become M-X Corporation. All shareholders of X-Y-Z Corporation received a certain amount of cash and three shares of M-X stock for every share of X-Y-Z Corporation stock owned. At death, as a result of the merger, G owned 3,000 shares of M-X Corporation stock. Whether or not G's devise is specific . . . or general,

the devisee is entitled to G's 3,000 shares of M-X. The devisee is not, however, entitled to any of the cash received when the two corporations merged or to any cash dividends paid to G before death on the X-Y-Z or M-X shares.

5. *Subsequent purchase.* G's will devised "1,000 shares of X-Y-Z Corporation stock." After executing her will, G purchased 500 more shares of X-Y-Z Corporation stock. At death, as a result of the purchase, G owned 1,500 shares of X-Y-Z Corporation stock. The devisee is only entitled to 1,000 shares of X-Y-Z. The devisee is not entitled to the additional 500 shares that G purchased. Nor is the devisee entitled to any cash dividends paid to G before death on the original or on the additional shares.

The rule of this section—that a devise of a specified number of securities carries with it any additional securities acquired by the testator after executing the will to the extent that the post-execution acquisitions resulted from the testator's ownership of the described securities—applies to a case in which the testator owned the exact number or more of the described securities when executing the will, but later sold (or otherwise disposed of) those securities, and then later purchased (or otherwise acquired) securities that meet the description in the will, following which additional securities are acquired as a result of the testator's ownership of the later-acquired securities. The rule of this section also applies whether or not the testator owned the exact number or more of the described securities when executing the will. The rule applies to a case in which the testator later purchased (or otherwise acquired) such securities.

Although this section is expressed in terms of additional securities acquired through, for example, a stock split, the same principle applies to a reverse stock split. If, for example, in Illustration 1, X-Y-Z Corporation had split its stock 1-for-2, so that at death, as a result of the reverse stock split, G owned 500 shares of X-Y-Z Corporation stock, the devisee would be entitled to G's 500 shares of X-Y-Z.

c. Dividend reinvestment programs. The rule of this section applies to additional shares acquired under any dividend reinvestment program in which the testator enrolled. This is the rule adopted in Revised UPC § 2-606(a)(3). Although these additional shares are not the death-time economic equivalent of the specified number of shares, the testator's action in enrolling in the dividend reinvestment program ties those additional shares to the original shares, thus raising an inference that the testator's intent was to pass those additional shares to the devisee rather than to the residuary takers. The inference, of course, may be overcome by evidence indicating a contrary intent. . . . .

d. Post-death acquisitions. The rule of this section applies to pre-death and post-death stock splits, stock dividends, and other distributions regarding devises of a specified number of securities. The rule of this section is well established for post-death stock splits, stock dividends, and other distributions if the devise of securities is specific. General devises, however, do not generally carry with them post-death stock splits, stock dividends, and other distributions but instead bear interest if not paid within a certain period after death. If the rule concerning interest is restricted to general *pecuniary* devises, as it is under the Uniform Probate Code, the rule of this section poses no conflict with that rule. In other states, however, the rule of this section should still apply to post-death stock splits, stock dividends, and other distributions on the rationale that, for purposes of this rule, any devise of securities is treated as a specific devise.

Devises of property other than securities also pose questions of whether the devisee is entitled to post-death accessions and accretions. . . . .

e. *Rule of construction.* The rule of this section is a rule of construction that yields to a contrary intent. For example, if in Illustration 2, the will had devised "1,000 shares of X-Y-Z stock, but not any additional shares acquired by reason of stock dividends," the testator's intent would be controlling and the devisee would only be entitled to 1,000 shares.

f. *Cross-reference.* This section applies to devises of a specified number of securities. A devise of a specified number of securities is to be distinguished from a devise of "my shares of X-Y-Z Corporation stock," of "all of my shares of X-Y-Z Corporation stock," or of "[a specified fraction or percentage] of my shares of X-Y-Z Corporation stock." Under § 5.2, Comments *d* and *e*, such a devise would be construed as referring to all (or the specified fraction or percentage) of the shares of X-Y-Z Corporation stock owned by the testator at death, including those in a changed form and also including additional shares purchased by the testator, as well as additional shares acquired due to stock splits, stock dividends, and other distributions.

§ 5.4. Ademption By Satisfaction

An inter vivos gift made by a testator to a devisee or to a member of the devisee's family adeems the devise by satisfaction, in whole or in part, if the testator indicated in a contemporaneous writing, or if the devisee acknowledged in writing, that the gift was so to operate.

Comment:

a. *Nature of ademption by satisfaction.* The doctrine of ademption by satisfaction is an intent-effecting doctrine. It recognizes that a testator, after executing a will, might decide to benefit a devisee by gift rather than by devise. Ideally, the testator would effect that intent by making the gift *and* revoking the devise, or if the gift was only intended to substitute for the devise in part, by making the gift and partially revoking the devise. The doctrine of ademption by satisfaction operates when the testator neglected to revoke or partly revoke the devise. The doctrine operates in effect to revoke or partly revoke the devise by preventing the devisee from receiving a double benefit against the testator's wishes, once by receiving the gift and again by receiving the devise.

b. *Written evidence that gift was to satisfy devise.* Most gifts are made without strings attached, and not intended to satisfy a devise. Consequently, this section, supported by statutory law, including the Uniform Probate Code, provides that, in order for a gift to satisfy a devise in whole or in part, the testator must acknowledge in a contemporaneous writing or the devisee must acknowledge in writing that the gift was so to operate. The required evidence of intent can take different forms: (i) a statement in the will itself providing for deduction of the gift or any future gifts, (ii) a written statement of the testator in a contemporaneous writing indicating that the gift is in full or partial satisfaction of the devise, or (iii) a written statement of the devisee acknowledging that the gift is in full or partial satisfaction of the devise. The Uniform Probate Code requires that the written evidence of intent take one of these three forms.

c. Application to devises of land. Historically, the doctrine of satisfaction was not applicable to devises of land. This rule was based on purely technical grounds . . . and defeated intent. The rule is not followed in this Restatement nor by modern statutory law.

d. Gifts of different property. A devise can be satisfied in whole or in part by a gift of different property. The gift need not be of the devised property nor of the same type of property. Moreover, to be a gift in satisfaction, the gift need not be an outright gift; it can be in the form of a will substitute, such as designating the devisee as the beneficiary of the testator's life insurance policy or the beneficiary of the remainder interest in a revocable inter vivos trust.

e. Application to specific devises. A gift can satisfy a specific devise. If the testator gives the devised property to the devisee, the doctrine of ademption by extinction (see § 5.2) potentially applies. If the testator makes a gift of different property, however, the doctrine of ademption by satisfaction is potentially applicable.

f. Gift to member of devisee's family. A gift can satisfy a devise even though the gift is not made to the devisee, as long as there is written evidence of intention (see Comment *b*).

Illustration:

1. *Gifts to devisee and devise's spouse.* G's will made a $20,000 devise to his adult child, A. G was a widower. Shortly before his death, G in consultation with his accountant decided to take advantage of the $10,000 annual gift-tax exclusion and sent a check for $10,000 to A and another check for $10,000 to A's spouse, B. The checks were accompanied by a letter from G explaining that the gifts were made for tax purposes and were in lieu of the $20,000 devise to A. The $20,000 devise is fully satisfied by the gifts to A and B.

g. Partial or complete satisfaction. A gift can operate as a partial or a complete satisfaction of a devise, depending on what the written declaration or acknowledgment provides. If the written declaration or acknowledgment provides that the gift completely satisfies the devise, that is controlling regardless of the value of the gift. If the written declaration or acknowledgment provides that the gift satisfies a certain fraction or percentage of the devise, or a certain amount of the devise, that is controlling regardless of the value of the gift. If the written declaration or acknowledgment provides that the value of the gift is to be deducted from the value of the devise, the time of valuation of the gift specified in the declaration or acknowledgment is controlling. Otherwise, for purposes of partial satisfaction, the gift is valued when the devisee came into possession or enjoyment of the property or at the testator's death, whichever occurs first.

h. Effect if devisee fails to survive the testator. If the devisee fails to survive the testator, a gift in full or partial satisfaction of the devise reduces or eliminates the devise, as appropriate, for purposes of applying an antilapse statute, unless the testator's contemporaneous writing provides otherwise.

i. Cross-reference. For the intestacy counterpart of the doctrine of ademption by satisfaction, see § 2.6 (Advancements).

§ 5.5. Antilapse Statutes

Antilapse statutes typically provide, as a rebuttable rule of construction, that devises to certain relatives who predecease the

testator pass to specified substitute takers, usually the descendants of the predeceased devisee who survive the testator.

Comment:

a. Circumstances in which antilapse statutes operate; lapsed devises. Because testamentary transfers take place at the testator's death, not when the will was executed, they cannot be made to individuals who fail to survive the testator. The doctrine of lapse, explained more fully in § 1.2, is that a devise to a devisee who fails to survive the testator lapses, i.e., it fails. The devise does not pass to the deceased devisee's estate.

A distinction is sometimes drawn between *lapsed* devises and *void* devises. A lapsed devise is one to a devisee who was alive when the will was executed but who failed to survive the testator. A void devise is one to a devisee who was dead when the will was executed. The distinction is of no consequence in modern law, and is not perpetuated in this Restatement. Both types are subsumed herein under the term "lapsed devises."

A devise to an individual lapses if the devisee fails to survive the testator, but a devise in the form of a class gift only lapses if *all* of the class members fail to survive the testator. Because the devisee who failed to survive the testator in the following Illustrations did not leave any descendants who survived the testator, these Illustrations do not raise any question of the application of an antilapse statute.

Illustrations:

1. *Devise to an individual who predeceases the testator.* G's will devised "$15,000 to A." A predeceased G without leaving any descendants who survived G. A's devise lapses.

2. *Devise to a class; no class member survives the testator.* G's will devised "$15,000 to A's children." A had three children, X, Y, and Z. X, Y, and Z predeceased G without leaving any descendants who survived G. The devise to A's children lapses.

3. *Devise to a class; one class member survives the testator.* G's will devised "$15,000 to A's children." A had three children, X, Y, and Z. X and Y predeceased G without leaving any descendants who survived G, but Z survived G. The devise to A's children does not lapse. The share that X and Y would have taken had they survived G goes to Z, who takes the entire $15,000.

b. General operation of modern antilapse statutes. Modern antilapse statutes do not reverse the lapse rule. To do so, they would have to provide that a devise to a devisee who fails to survive the testator passes to the deceased devisee's estate. Instead, they provide that the property that the devisee would have taken had he or she survived the testator passes to specified substitute takers, typically the descendants of the deceased devisee who survive the testator.

c. Protected devisees. Very few antilapse statutes apply to all devisees who fail to survive the testator. Most extend their protection only to specified relatives, not including the testator's spouse. The prevailing pattern, including the pattern under section 2–603 of the Revised Uniform Probate Code, is to extend antilapse protection to grandparents and descendants of grandparents. In line with modern trends, the Revised UPC also extends antilapse protection to stepchildren. To the extent possible, non-UPC statutes should be construed to cover stepchildren.

d. Substitute takers. The substitute takers under most antilapse statutes are the deceased devisee's descendants who survive the testator. To be treated as surviving the testator, sections 2–702 and 2–603 of the Uniform Probate Code require the devisee's descendants to survive the testator by 120 hours. They take the property to which the devisee would have been entitled had the devisee survived the testator by 120 hours. These descendants take by representation.

e. Application. Antilapse statutes apply to all types of devises—specific, general, demonstrative, and residuary. For the statute to operate, the devise must be to a member of the protected class who leaves one or more descendants who survive the testator. Antilapse statutes do not apply to devises to persons who are outside the protected class nor to devises to members of the protected class who leave no descendants surviving the testator.

f. Contrary intent. Antilapse statutes establish a strong rule of construction, designed to carry out presumed intention. They are based on the constructional preference against disinheriting a line of descent, which in turn implements the constructional preference for preserving equality among different lines of descent. See § 11.3(c)(3) and Comments *b* and *d* of . . . this Restatement. Comment *d* states:

> A rule of construction based on one or more strong constructional preferences is especially difficult to rebut. For example, because the rule of construction reflected in antilapse statutes derives from the strong constructional preference against disinheriting a line of descent, antilapse statutes are especially difficult to rebut.

Consequently, these statutes should be given the widest possible sphere of operation and should be defeated only when the trier of fact determines that the testator wanted to disinherit the line of descent headed by the deceased devisee. Many antilapse statutes recognize a contrary intent only if it is expressed in the will. Other statutes, including the Revised Uniform Probate Code § 2–601, allow extrinsic evidence on the question of contrary intent.

g. Contrary intent; alternative devise. An alternative devise indicates a contrary intent, and hence overrides an antilapse statute, if the alternative devisee survives the testator and is otherwise entitled to take (i.e., is not prevented from taking because of an unsatisfied condition). The devise goes to that alternative devisee rather than to the primary devisee's descendants under the antilapse statute. If the alternative devise is in the form of a class gift, at least one class member but not necessarily all class members must survive and be otherwise entitled to take.

Illustrations:

4. *Alternative devise to individual who is entitled to take.* G's will devised "$15,000 to A, but if A does not survive me, to B." A predeceased G, leaving a descendant who survived G. B survived G. Although A is within the class of protected devisees under the applicable antilapse statute, A's $15,000 devise passes to B, the alternative devisee, and not to A's descendant under the antilapse statute.

5. *Alternative devise to class; one class member is entitled to take.* G's will devised "$15,000 to A, but if A does not survive me, to B's children." A predeceased G, leaving a descendant who survived G. B had three children, X, Y, and Z, but only X survived G. Neither Y nor Z left

any descendants who survived G. Although A is within the class of protected devisees under the applicable antilapse statute, A's $15,000 devise passes to X as the only class member of the alternative devise who survived G, and not to A's descendant under the antilapse statute.

A residuary clause does not constitute an alternative devise with respect to a preresiduary devise unless the will specifically provides that, upon lapse or failure, the preresiduary devise, or preresiduary devises in general, pass under the residuary clause.

Illustrations:

6. *Residuary clause that does not create an alternative devise.* G's will devised "$10,000 to my daughter, A" and devised "the rest, residue, and remainder of my estate" to a named charity. A predeceased G, leaving a child, X, who survived G. A's $10,000 devise passes to X under the antilapse statute, not to the charity under the residuary clause. The residuary clause does not create an alternative devise because neither it nor any other language in the will specifically provides that A's $10,000 devise or lapsed or failed devises in general pass under the residuary clause.

7. *Residuary clause that creates an alternative devise.* Same facts as in Illustration 6, except that G's residuary clause devised "the rest, residue, and remainder of my estate, including all failed and lapsed devises," to a named charity. The named charity still exists and is in operation at G's death. A's $10,000 devise passes to the charity under the residuary clause, not to X under the antilapse statute. The residuary clause expressly creates an alternative devise in favor of the charity and that alternative devisee is entitled to take under the will.

A devise to a devisee's "estate" if the devisee predeceases the testator constitutes an alternative devise. For the construction of such an alternative devise, see § 1.1, Comment *c*, Illustration 19; § 1.2, Comment *g*.

h. Contrary intent; survival language. An often litigated question is whether language requiring the devisee to survive the testator, without more, constitutes a sufficient expression of a contrary intent to defeat the antilapse statute. The majority view is that such language signifies a contrary intent. Because such a survival provision is often boiler-plate form-book language, the testator may not understand that such language could disinherit the line of descent headed by the deceased devisee. When the testator is older than the devisee and hence does not expect the devisee to die first, or if the devisee was childless when the will was executed, it seems especially unlikely that a provision requiring the devisee to survive the testator was intended to disinherit the devisee's descendants.

A linguistic argument sometimes employed by courts adopting the view that words of survival automatically express a contrary intent is that, when words of survival are used, there is nothing upon which the antilapse statute can operate; the devise itself, it is said, is eliminated by the devisee's having predeceased the testator. The language of most antilapse statutes, including Revised UPC § 2–603, nullifies this argument by providing that the deceased devisee's descendants take the property to which the devisee would have been entitled had the devisee survived the testator.

Not infrequently, when there is an alternative devise (see Comment *g*), survival language is attached to the primary devise but not to the alternative devise. The survival language attached to the primary devise does not bar application of the antilapse statute if the alternative devisee fails to survive the testator or is otherwise not entitled to take. If both the primary and the alternative devisees fail to survive the testator, and both leave descendants who survive the testator, the devised property presumptively passes to the descendants of the primary devisee rather than to the descendants of the alternative or secondary devisee. Because the testator preferred the primary devisee over the secondary devisee, it is rebuttably presumed that the testator would prefer the primary devisee's descendants over the secondary devisee's descendants (Illustration 8). This presumption is rebutted, however, if giving the devise to the alternative devisee's descendants would better preserve equality among different lines of descent or would otherwise be more consistent with the testator's manifested plan of distribution (Illustration 9).

Illustrations:

8. *Both primary and secondary devisees predecease the testator; both leave surviving descendants.* G's will devised "my diamond ring to A, but if A does not survive me, to B" and devised "my diamond studded watch to B, but if B does not survive me, to A." A predeceased G, leaving a descendant who survived G. B also predeceased G, leaving a descendant who survived G. Both A and B are within the class of devisees protected by the applicable antilapse statute. Under the antilapse statute, the diamond ring passes to A's descendant, not to B's descendant, and the diamond studded watch passes to B's descendant, not to A's descendant. To do otherwise would be inconsistent with the testator's manifested plan of distribution.

9. *Primary devisee and one of two secondary devisees predecease the testator; both leave surviving descendants.* G's will devised "$50,000 to my child, A, if he is living at my death; if not, to A's children, X and Y." A and Y predeceased G. A's child, X, and Y's children, M and N, survived G. Under the antilapse statute, $25,000 (half of the $50,000 devise) clearly passes to X. Although presumptively the other half would pass to the descendants of A, the primary devisee, rather than to the descendants of Y, the secondary devisee, the presumption is rebutted in this case in order to preserve equality among different lines of descent. Thus, the share that Y would have taken had Y survived G passes solely to Y's descendants, not to A's descendants (which would give half of that half to X and the other half of that half to Y's children). Therefore, the final distribution under the antilapse statute would be that $25,000 (half of the $50,000 devise) passes to X and $25,000 (the other half) is divided equally between Y's children, M and N. The same result would be reached if the alternative devise were in the form of a class gift ("if not, to A's children").

Even if there is no alternative devise, the courts should be cautious in automatically concluding that survival language manifests a deliberate decision by the testator to disinherit the line of descent headed by a deceased devisee. As indicated in Comment *e*, antilapse statutes are based on the constructional preference against disinheriting a line of descent. As explained in § 11.3, Comment *j*, of . . . this Restatement, that constructional preference

> is strongest when applied to direct descendants of the donor (sometimes called *lineal* descendants). The preference is less strong, but still forceful, when applied to descendants of the donor's ancestors (sometimes called *collateral* descendants), and becomes somewhat weaker the farther removed the ancestor is [from] the donor.

Thus, the trier of fact should be especially reluctant to find that survival language manifests a contrary intent in cases in which the deceased devisee is one of the testator's children, or other direct descendant, and the effect of refusing to apply the antilapse statute would be to disinherit one or more grandchildren or great-grandchildren.

i. Contrary intent; clear, direct, unmistakable statement. The clearest way of stating a contrary intent is to do so directly, in language that is understandable to the testator, language that leaves no doubt that the testator considered the possibility of the devisee failing to survive the testator and decided against substituting the devisee's descendants. Language such as "and not to [the devisee's] descendants if [the devisee] fails to survive me" is an unmistakable expression of a contrary intent. If the language occurs in a will drafted by an attorney, the client has the opportunity to approve or disapprove of the result. A blanket provision stating that if any devisee fails to survive the testator, the devised property is "not to pass to the devisee's descendants" is equally clear.

j. Application to class gifts. Antilapse statutes apply to class gifts to single-generation classes, whether or not the language of the statute explicitly covers class gifts. Antilapse statutes do not, however, apply to class gifts to multiple-generation classes, such as gifts to "issue," "descendants," "heirs of the body," "heirs," "next of kin," "relatives," or "family," because these types of class gifts already pass the shares of deceased class members to their surviving descendants without statutory intervention.

The property devised to a single-generation class is divided among the class members who survive the testator, if any, and the descendants of deceased class members who survive the testator, if any. Each surviving class member takes the share that he or she would have taken had the deceased class members also survived the testator. Each deceased class member's surviving descendants take by representation the share that the deceased class member would have taken had the deceased class member survived the testator. A class member who fails to survive the testator and leaves no descendants who survive the testator is disregarded.

Illustrations:

10. *One class member survives the testator; two predecease, one with and one without surviving descendants.* G's will devised "$15,000" "to my children." G had three children, A, B, and C. A predeceased G, leaving two children, X and Y, who survived G. B predeceased G without leaving any descendants who survived G. C survived G. As the only surviving class member, C takes one-half ($7,500). Under the applicable antilapse statute, X and Y divide the one-half share that A would have taken had A survived G ($3,750 each).

11. *All classes members predecease the testator; some but not all leave surviving descendants.* G's will devised "$15,000" "to my children." G had three children, A, B, and C. A predeceased G, leaving two children, X and Y, who survived G. B predeceased G without leaving any descendants who survived G. C predeceased G, leaving one child, Z, who survived G. Under the applicable antilapse statute, X and Y divide the one-half share that A would have taken had A survived G ($3,750 each), and Z takes the one-half share that C would have taken had C survived G ($7,500).

k. Application to alternative devises. Antilapse statutes apply to alternative devises as well as to primary devises.

Illustrations:

12. *Alternative devise to an individual.* G's will devised "$15,000 to A, but if A does not survive me, to B." A predeceased G without leaving any descendants who survived G. B predeceased G leaving a descendant who survived G. B is within the class of protected devisees under the applicable antilapse statute. The $15,000 devise passes to B's descendant under the antilapse statute.

13. *Alternative devise to a class.* G's will devised "$15,000 to A, but if A does not survive me, to B's children." A predeceased G without leaving any descendants who survived G. B had three children, X, Y, and Z, but only X survived G. X, Y, and Z are within the class of protected devisees under the applicable antilapse statute. Both Y and Z left descendants who survived G. As the only surviving class member, X takes one-third ($5,000). Under the applicable antilapse statute, Y's descendants divide by representation the one-third share that Y would have taken had Y survived G ($5,000), and Z's descendants divide by representation the one-third share that Z would have taken had Z survived G ($5,000).

l. *Application to powers of appointment.* If the testator's will exercises a power of appointment in favor of an appointee who predeceases the testator, the antilapse statute should be applied even if the language of the statute does not expressly cover appointments. In the absence of express language in the statute, the appointee should be treated as a devisee. See Restatement Second, Property (Donative Transfers) § 18.6 [Restatement Third, Property (Wills and Other Donative Transfers § 19.12]. Section 2–603 of the Revised Uniform Probate Code expressly applies to appointments.

m. *Application to void devises.* Antilapse statutes apply to void as well as to lapsed devises. As indicated in Comment *a*, this Restatement treats both types of devises as "lapsed devises."

n. *Failed preresiduary devises pass to residue.* Unless an antilapse statute applies, a preresiduary devise (i.e., a specific, general, or demonstrative devise) that fails for any reason becomes part of the residue.

Illustration:

14. *Failed preresiduary devise.* G's will devised "$10,000 to A," "$15,000 to B, but if B does not survive me, to C," and "all the rest, residue, and remainder of my estate to X, Y, and Z." A, B, and X predeceased G, none leaving any descendants who survived G. C, Y, and Z survived G. A's $10,000 devise lapses and falls to the residue. B's $15,000 devise goes to C as the alternative devisee. The residue, which includes A's $10,000 devise, passes equally to Y and Z.

o. *Lapse in the residue; rejection of the no-residue-of-a-residue rule.* For the purpose of determining what happens to the share of a residuary devisee who fails to survive the testator, a residuary clause that devises the residue to two or more persons is treated as if it created a class gift, even if the devise is not in the form of a class gift. The contrary rule, sometimes called the *no-residue-of-a-residue rule,* is not followed in modern statutory law, including the Uniform Probate Code, nor in this Restatement. Thus, if an antilapse statute does not apply, the share of a residuary devisee that fails for any reason passes to the other residuary devisee, or, if more than one, to the other residuary devisees in proportion to the interest of each in the remaining part of the residue. A residuary devise lapses and passes to intestacy only if an antilapse statute does not apply and no residuary devisee survives the testator.

Illustrations:

15. *Residuary [devise] to three individuals; one survives; two predecease, one with and the other without surviving descendants.* G's will devised the "rest, residue, and remainder of my estate to A, B, and C." A survived G. B predeceased G, leaving descendants who survived G. C predeceased G without leaving descendants who survived G. A, B, and C are within the class of protected devisees under the applicable antilapse statute. Half of the residue passes to A and half passes under the applicable antilapse statute to B's descendants.

18. *Residuary [devise] to three individuals; all predecease without surviving descendants.* G's will devised the "rest, residue, and remainder of my estate to A, B, and C." A, B, and C predeceased G, none leaving any descendants who survived G. The residue passes by intestacy to G's heirs.

The no-residue-of-a-residue rule is rejected for all situations in which a devise to a residuary devisee fails, regardless of the reason for the failure. . . . .

p. Application to revocable trusts and other will substitutes. The beneficiary's interest in will substitutes other than revocable trusts is ordinarily subject to an express condition of survival of the donor. The remainder interest in a revocable inter vivos trust is presumptively subject to a condition of survival of the settlor. If the condition of survival is not express, it is implied. See Restatement Second, Property (Donative Transfers) § 34.6, Comment *b*, Illustration 3 [Restatement Third, Property (Wills and Other Donative Transfers) § 26.1, Comment *e*]. Antilapse statutes, however, apply by analogy to revocable trusts and other will substitutes. See Restatement Second, Property (Donative Transfers) § 27.1, Comment *e*; § 27.2, Comment *f*; § 34.6, Comment *b* [Restatement Third, Property (Wills and Other Donative Transfers) § 7.2, Comment *f*]; Restatement Third, Trusts § 25, Comment *e*; Revised Uniform Probate Code § 2–706. Thus, unless there is a contrary intent, if the beneficiary of a revocable trust or other will substitute who is in the class of relatives covered by the applicable antilapse statute (see Comment *c*) predeceases the settlor or donor, leaving descendants who survive the settlor or donor, the beneficiary's descendants take the beneficiary's interest (unless that interest was limited to the life of the predeceased beneficiary). Revised UPC § 2–707 goes farther, and establishes an antilapse-type rule for future interests in trusts, whether revocable or irrevocable. Under this provision, the descendants of a beneficiary of a future interest who fails to survive the distribution date (the time when the future interest is to take effect in possession or enjoyment) take in place of the deceased beneficiary.

DIVISION II

NONPROBATE TRANSFERS (GIFTS AND WILL SUBSTITUTES)

Introductory Note: Division II addresses donative transfers taking place during life, as opposed to donative transfers taking place at death, which is the subject of Division I. Donative transfers taking place during life can be outright gifts or will substitutes, hence the term *nonprobate* transfers.

Division II contains two chapters: Chapter 6 covers gifts and Chapter 7 covers will substitutes.

CHAPTER 6

GIFTS

Introductory Note: This chapter covers gifts of property. Section 6.1 sets forth requirements that are applicable to all gifts of property. The next two sections address gifts of personal property (§ 6.2) and gifts of land (§ 6.3).

§ 6.1. Requirements Applicable to All Gifts of Property

(a) To make a gift of property, the donor must transfer an ownership interest to the donee without consideration and with donative intent.

(b) Acceptance by the donee is required for a gift to become complete. Acceptance is presumed, subject to the donee's right to refuse or disclaim.

Comment:

a. *Scope.* This Chapter addresses gifts of an ownership interest in property. As used in this Chapter, the term "property" includes land and personal property and any interest therein. Most gifts transfer full ownership—absolute ownership (if personal property) or ownership in fee simple absolute (if land). It is also possible to transfer less than full ownership, as in the case of a gift of a life estate or a remainder interest, in trust or not. The creation of a trust, however, is within the province of the Restatement of Trusts. See Restatement Third, Trusts §§ 10–26.

This Chapter does not cover gifts of services. A homeowner who, free of charge, helps a neighbor paint a room, or a lawyer who, free of charge, prepares a will for a relative, has made a gift of services. Although such services have a fair market value, they are not gifts of an ownership interest in property. Contrast Comment *k*, which concerns the forgiveness of an indebtedness as constituting a gift of property.

Nor does this Chapter cover the gratuitous bailment of a chattel, under which an owner transfers possession but not an ownership interest to another. Under a gratuitous bailment, the bailor can reclaim the chattel from the bailee on demand. The loan of a car to a son or daughter to use while in college would constitute a gratuitous bailment. For the distinction between a bailment and a trust, see Restatement Third, Trusts § 5, Comment *f*.

b. *Donative intent.* To be a gift, a transfer must be made with donative intent. The requirement of donative intent is the essence of a gift.

Donative intent is to be distinguished from donative motive. The motive for making a gift is a complex matter and does not determine whether or not a gift was intended. The relevant criterion is intent to transfer an ownership interest gratuitously, as opposed to engaging in an exchange transaction or making an involuntary transfer.

c. *Effective transfer.* A gift only occurs if the donor makes an effective transfer of an ownership interest. The transfer of personal property, necessary to perfect a gift, may be made by delivery of the property or by inter vivos donative document. See § 6.2. The transfer of land, necessary to perfect a gift, must be evidenced in a writing that is executed in compliance with the formalities required by the applicable statute of frauds. See § 6.3.

In order to make an effective transfer of an ownership interest, the donor must own the property being transferred, have an intent to make the transfer, and satisfy any applicable formalities for making a transfer.

The donor cannot transfer to the donee a greater ownership interest in the property than the donor owns. If the donor purports to give the donee a greater ownership interest than the donor owns, the donee will receive whatever interest that the donor could have given the donee in the subject matter of the gift. . . . .

In determining whether the donor was the owner of the property, substance controls over form. For example, if the donor purchases property and has the seller transfer ownership to the donee, the donor has made a gift of the purchased property to the donee. The transaction is treated as if the donor purchased the property in the donor's own name and then gave the property to the donee. Such a transaction is treated under the federal gift tax as an "indirect" gift. See Treas. Reg. § 25.2511–1(c)(1), –1(h)(2).

d. *Voluntary transfer.* To be a gift, the transfer must be voluntary. An involuntary transfer—a transfer in satisfaction of a legal obligation—is not a gift. The term legal obligation includes not only a debt or other obligation arising from an enforceable contract, but also an obligation imposed by court judgment, a duty of support imposed by law, and any other obligation imposed by law. Because a parent is obliged to support a minor child, the parent is not making a gift when providing food, clothing, and shelter for the parent's minor child.

A transfer in satisfaction of someone else's legal obligation, however, may be a gift. Thus, A's gratuitous payment of B's debt would be a gift from A to B, assuming that the payment met the other requirements for a gift.

e. *Without consideration.* To be a gift, the transfer must be made without consideration. However, as discussed in Comments *g* and *h*, a transfer for an inadequate consideration or one that is conditioned on the recipient paying an obligation of the donor can be a gift in part.

f. *Present transfer.* To make a gift, the donor must make a present transfer. The donor cannot make a present transfer of property that the donor does not own or that does not exist. The donor also cannot make a future transfer of property that the donor does own, although the donor can make a present transfer of a future interest in owned property.

The common-law doctrine of *estoppel by deed* is consistent with the requirement that the donor can only make a present transfer of property that the donor owns. Under the doctrine of estoppel by deed, a purported transfer of land that the transferor does not own becomes enforceable and takes place automatically if the land is later acquired, but only if the deed represents to the grantee that title of a specified quality is being conveyed, which most warranty deeds but few quitclaim deeds do. Under this doctrine, the transfer takes place when the property is acquired, not upon execution of the deed.

The common-law doctrine of *equitable election* is also consistent with the requirement that the donor can only make a present transfer of property that the donor owns. Suppose that G, the owner of a diamond ring worth $15,000, transfers the ring to X and purports to transfer a ruby necklace worth $12,000 that X owns to Y. The doctrine of equitable election treats G as transferring the ring to X on condition that X transfer X's necklace to Y. If X accepts the ring, obligating himself or herself to transfer the necklace to Y, G has made a gift to Y of the necklace, making the transaction a form of indirect gift described in Comment *c*. In effect, G bought X's necklace and then gave it to Y. G may also have made a gift to X of $3000. See Comment *g*.

g. *Part-gift, part-sale.* A transfer intended to be for less than an adequate consideration is called a part-gift, part-sale. The gift portion, for which the donor received no consideration, is the value of the property transferred reduced by the value of what the donor received in exchange. If, however, the sale price is the result of arm's-length bargaining without donative intent, no gift arises. The buyer simply made a good bargain.

h. *Net gift.* A donor who makes a taxable gift has primary liability for paying the federal gift tax. The donor, however, may condition the gift on the donee's promise to pay the gift tax, in which case the promise constitutes consideration to the donor and reduces the amount of the gift. Such a gift, conditioned upon the donee's payment of the gift tax, is referred to as a "net gift."

i. *Donee's acceptance presumed.* Acceptance by the donee is required for a gift to become complete. A gift is ordinarily beneficial to the donee and for that reason acceptance is presumed, subject to the donee's right to refuse or disclaim under an applicable disclaimer statute or, in the absence of an applicable disclaimer statute, within a reasonable time after learning of the gift.

j. *Effect of valid restraint on alienation.* A purported gift of an interest that is subject to a valid restraint on alienation is ineffective because the donor lacks the power to make the purported gift. The validity of restraints on alienation is covered in a later Division. See also Restatement Second, Trusts §§ 152–157; Restatement Third, Trusts §§ 57–60; Unif. Trust Code §§ 501–507.

k. *Forgiveness of indebtedness.* The forgiveness of an indebtedness is a gift of property if made without consideration and with donative intent. If the debtor is a natural object of the creditor's bounty, allowing the statute of limitations to run on a debt is presumed to have been made with donative intent. The family context of such a transaction creates the presumption of a gift. . . . .

l. *Gift by incapacitated donor's conservator or agent.* A gift made by an incapacitated person's lawfully appointed conservator (sometimes called guardian of property) or agent under a durable power of attorney, if authorized, is attributed to the incapacitated person. See §§ 8.1, 8.2.

m. *Gift as an advancement or gift in satisfaction.* A gift may be an advancement on the donee's intestate share or a gift in satisfaction of a devise in the donor's will. See § 2.6 on advancements and § 5.4 on ademption by satisfaction.

n. *Protective doctrines.* Various protective doctrines may invalidate a donative transfer, such as rules invalidating (i) a donative transfer by a mentally incapacitated donor, (ii) a transfer procured by undue influence, or (iii) a transfer in derogation of the surviving spouse's right to an elective share at the donor's death. These doctrines are considered in . . . Chapters 8 and 9.

o. *Mistake in inter vivos gifts.* If a donor makes a mistake in perfecting an inter vivos gift, there may be a remedy in the law of restitution and unjust enrichment. See Restatement Third, Restitution and Unjust Enrichment § 11, which provides:

§ 11. *Mistake in Gifts Inter Vivos*

(1) A [donor who transfers something more than or different from the intended gift, or whose gift is made to someone other than the intended donee,] has a claim in restitution as necessary to prevent the unintended enrichment of the recipient.

(2) A donor whose gift is induced by invalidating mistake has a claim in restitution as necessary to prevent the unintended enrichment of the recipient.

(3) If a [donor] attempts to make a gift and dies or becomes incapacitated in the belief that the gift has been perfected, and as a result of mistake the attempted gift

(a) is wholly or partly ineffective;

(b) transfers something other than the property intended; or

(c) transfers property to someone other than the intended donee;

the intended donee has a claim in restitution as necessary to prevent the unjust enrichment of the unintended recipient [or of the donor's successors, as the case may be].

See also § 6.2, Comment *z*; § 6.3, Comment *p*; § 8.1, Comment *i*; Restatement Third, Trusts § 16.

p. *Donative promises.* A statement by the donor that he or she will give property to the donee sometime in the future generally is not enforceable. Such a transaction is normally analyzed under contract doctrine as being unenforceable because it lacks consideration. The donee may, however, be entitled to a remedy if the promise induced the donee to take action to the donee's detriment. See Restatement Second, Contracts § 90. . . .

An enforceable promise to leave property by will must also be supported by consideration and, under UPC § 2–514, "may be established only by (i) provisions of a will stating material provisions of the contract, (ii) an express reference in a will to a contract and extrinsic evidence proving the terms of the contract, or (iii) a writing signed by the decedent evidencing the contract." The UPC also provides that the execution of a joint will or mutual wills does not create a presumption of a contract not to revoke the will or wills.

§ 6.2. Gifts of Personal Property

The transfer of personal property, necessary to perfect a gift, may be made

(1) by delivering the property to the donee or

(2) by inter vivos donative document.

Comment on Paragraph (1)—Perfecting Gift of Personal Property by Delivering the Property to the Donee:

a. *Donative intent.* In order for a delivery of personal property to effect a gift, the requirements for making a gift set forth in § 6.1 must be satisfied, notably the requirement of donative intent. When the owner of an item of personal property delivers it to another, the purpose of the delivery is not self-evident. There can be many reasons for delivering an item of personal property to another, even for doing so without consideration. The purpose of the delivery might, for example, simply be to make the deliveree the owner's agent or bailee. Thus, delivery is an ambiguous act. Delivery only constitutes a gift if it is done with donative intent to transfer an ownership interest. See § 6.1, Comment *b*.

Just as an ambiguity in the terms of a donative document justifies the use of extrinsic evidence to clarify the ambiguity (see § 11.2), the ambiguity inherent in the act of delivery justifies the use of extrinsic evidence to establish whether or not the delivery was done with donative intent. All relevant evidence on this question may be considered, including the owner's statements and circumstances, the relationship between the owner and deliveree, the circumstances of the delivery, and the value of the delivered property and its relationship to the owner's overall wealth.

If the evidence establishes that the owner intended to make a gift, and if the other requirements for making a gift are satisfied (see § 6.1), the delivery constitutes a gift, whether the delivery is to the intended donee or to a third person for the intended donee. . . . .

b. *Delivery.* When done with donative intent, delivery fulfills the requirement of a present transfer in the law of gifts (see § 6.1, Comment *d*). Delivery impresses on the donor that the donor is parting with dominion and control and constitutes an event that supplies objective evidence of this parting. The "wrench" of delivery impresses on the donor that he or she has engaged in an act of finality. Once the property has been delivered with donative intent, the donor has no right to have the property returned.

c. *Physical delivery.* The conventional method of making a gift of tangible personal property is by physical delivery. (But see Comment *i*, on tangible personal property for which there is a title-registration system.) Physical delivery occurs when the donor hands the property over to the donee. One advantage of physical delivery is that it makes the gift self-executing. By putting the donee in possession of the property, physical delivery usually obviates the need for the donee to seek judicial enforcement of the gift.

Physical delivery is not always feasible, on account of the nature or location of the property. In such a case, delivery may take one of two other forms: constructive or symbolic. This Restatement, however, rejects the rule that only physical delivery will suffice if the nature or location of the property makes physical delivery possible. Even if physical delivery is feasible, constructive or symbolic delivery is sufficient. Constructive delivery and symbolic delivery are treated in Comments *f*, *g*, and *h*.

d. *Delivery unnecessary when property in the possession of the donee.* When the subject of an intended gift is already in the possession of the donee, the donor is not required to retrieve the property in order to redeliver it to the donee. The donor need only manifest intent that the property belongs to the donee. . . . .

e. *Delivery when property in the common possession of the donor and donee.* Delivery becomes problematic when the subject of a purported gift is in the common possession of the donor and donee, such as when the donor and donee reside in the same household and the subject of the purported gift is located in that household. In such a case, the purported gift may be established by proof (i) that the donor notified the donee that the property belongs to the donee and (ii) that subsequent conduct of the donor and donee was consistent with the donee's ownership of the property. . . . .

f. *Household goods and furnishings of married couple; other marital gifts.* Regardless of which spouse wrote the check, signed the credit- or debit-card slip, or paid cash for the purchase of household goods and furnishings, or which spouse's funds were used to pay for their purchase, such goods are presumed to be owned by a married couple in joint tenancy with the right of survivorship, or in tenancy by the entireties in states recognizing that form of ownership in personal property.

Other marital gifts, however, are normally owned individually by the donee. Birthday, anniversary, or holiday gifts from one spouse to the other are owned by the donee spouse. In community-property states, a gift from one spouse to the other is owned by the donee spouse as separate property, even if the donor spouse paid for the gift out of community funds.

g. *Constructive or symbolic delivery.* Constructive or symbolic delivery is a substitute for physical delivery. Courts frequently do not distinguish between the two. In fact, no legal consequence turns on the distinction, because either type of delivery is effective to perfect a gift of personal property. The traditional understanding is that a delivery is constructive if the donor gives the donee the means of obtaining possession or control of the subject of the gift, for example by giving the donee the key to the place where the property is located.

The traditional understanding of symbolic delivery is that it is one in which the donor gives the donee an object or item that symbolizes the subject of the gift. The classic example of a symbolic delivery is delivery of an inter vivos donative document to the donee. (Gifts of personal property having substantial value are frequently made by inter vivos donative document rather than by physical delivery. This Restatement treats gifts made by document as a separate means of effecting a gift of personal property. See Comments *p* through *x*.) . . . .

h. *Symbolic delivery of intangible personal property.* Another recurrent example of symbolic delivery occurs with respect to a gift of intangible personal property. A donor may make a gift of intangible personal property by delivering the instrument evidencing the claim that constitutes the intangible personal property. Such instruments include bonds, shares of stock, insurance policies, and bank passbooks.

If the instrument provides that a transfer of the claim can be made only in a specified manner, the preferred method of making a gift of such property is to follow the specified procedure. If the specified procedure is not followed, however, delivery of the instrument with donative intent constitutes a gift as between the donor and the donee. The attempted restriction on transfer is for the protection of the one against whom the claim can be asserted. The fact that the donor did not follow the specified procedure for making the transfer may, however, cast doubt on donative intent. Consequently, the donee must establish donative intent by clear and convincing evidence. If the donee carries that burden of proof, the donee may require the donor or the donor's successors to do whatever is necessary to have the transfer recognized by the one against whom the claim may be asserted. . . . .

i. Tangible personal property subject to registered title. Controlling federal or state law requires registration of the title to certain items of personal property, such as automobiles, boats, or airplanes. The delivery of that type of personal property to an intended donee, or to a third person for the intended donee, with donative intent is effective as between the donor and the donee to place the ownership of the personal property in the donee. The adverse consequences of the failure to register the personal property in the name of the donee depend on the terms of the registration law. The donor's failure to follow the specified procedure for making the transfer casts doubt on the claim of donative intent. Consequently, the donee must establish donative intent by clear and convincing evidence. If the donee carries that burden of proof, the donee may require the donor or the donor's successors to do whatever is necessary to have the title properly registered in the donee's name. . . . .

j. Gift by donor's agent. The donor may give a power of attorney to another person to make gifts of the donor's personal property. See § 6.1, Comment *l*. In such a case, the agent (attorney-in-fact) may make a delivery of the personal property that is the subject matter of the gift to the same extent as the donor. If the power given to the agent is a durable power of attorney (i.e., one that is not revoked by the donor's incapacity), the agent can make a delivery of the subject matter of the gift even though the donor could not make a delivery because of his or her incapacity. Whether a durable power of attorney authorizes an agent to make gifts on behalf of an incapacitated principal is a question of construction of the power of attorney. On this question, see § 8.1, Comment *k*.

k. Delivery to a third person for the donee. Delivery may be made to a third person for the intended donee. If the delivery is made with intent to make a present transfer to the donee (see § 6.1, Comment *f*), the gift is completed when the delivery is made to the third person. In the absence of additional language or circumstances that indicate otherwise, the delivery of the personal property to a third person "for" the intended donee is presumed to be the equivalent of delivery to the intended donee. In these circumstances, the third person is treated as the donee's agent. . . . .

l. Wedding presents. A wedding present is implicitly conditional on the wedding taking place.

Illustration:

13. A and B were engaged to be married, the date of the anticipated marriage was announced, and invitations to the wedding were mailed to various people by the bride's parents. Wedding presents arrived at the bride's house prior to the wedding date. The conclusion is justified that the wedding gifts were made on the condition that they be returned to the donors if the marriage did not take place. If the marriage does not take place, the donors have a right to have the wedding presents returned.

If the marriage does take place, a further question is whether a present is to the bride, to the groom, or to both jointly. Unless the nature of the subject matter of the gift makes it peculiarly usable by one but not the other, the gift is presumed to be to the bride and groom jointly in equal undivided shares. Normally, the donor of a wedding present does not manifest any intention regarding the form of concurrent ownership. In the absence of additional language or circumstances that indicate otherwise, the donees take the gift as joint tenants with right of survivorship or as tenants by the entirety if that form of ownership is recognized by local law. (Taking as tenants by the entirety is possible because a wedding present does not become complete until after the wedding, even if the gift was delivered before the wedding; for the same reason, the gift could be community property in a community-property state.)

This Comment applies equally to gifts to couples who are planning to be united in a same-sex civil union or a same-sex commitment or similar ceremony, except that the couple cannot take the gifts in tenancy by the entirety or as community property.

m. *Engagement rings.* This Restatement takes the position that a gift of an engagement ring in contemplation of marriage is implicitly conditioned on the wedding taking place. The donor of such a gift has the right to have the ring returned if the marriage is canceled, regardless of whether there was fault in terminating the engagement or who formally broke the engagement. This Comment applies equally to a ring given in contemplation of being united in a same-sex civil union or a same-sex commitment or similar ceremony.

There are two competing rules, both rejected in this Restatement. One is called the fault rule. Under that rule, the donor's right to have the ring returned depends on which party was at fault in breaking the engagement. This rule is rejected for essentially the same reasons that have led to the adoption of no-fault divorce. A fault rule would inevitably invite acrimony and encourage each party to blame the other. The concept of fault is itself subject to varying definitions. In a particular case, fault may not exist or may only be slight.

The other rule rejected in this Restatement is sometimes called the modified no-fault rule. Under that rule, the donor's right to have the ring returned depends on which party formally broke the engagement. Because the person who breaks the engagement may not have caused the underlying deterioration in the relationship, the modified no-fault rule can result in substantial injustice.

Illustration:

14. A and B become engaged to marry. A gives B an engagement ring. B renews an intimate relationship with a previous boyfriend. A finds out about it and breaks the engagement. Regardless of who was at fault or who formally broke the engagement, A has the right to have the ring returned. Under the rejected fault rule, A would presumably have a right to have the ring returned. Under the rejected modified no-fault rule, A would have no right to have the ring returned because A broke the engagement.

n. *Gifts by check.* A donor who has decided to give a sum of money to a donee may do so by delivery of cash or of a check. The delivery of cash, if the delivery otherwise satisfies the requirements of § 6.1, constitutes a completed gift upon delivery. The delivery of a certified check, a cashier's check, or a similar instrument (such as a teller's check bought from the issuer) that puts the amount of the check beyond the donor's dominion and control also constitutes a completed gift upon delivery.

The delivery of an uncertified personal check to a noncharitable donee, however, does not ordinarily constitute a completed gift. Delivery does not serve to transfer the donor's funds in the hands of the drawee bank, nor does delivery of the check obligate the donor to make the payment. The gift becomes complete when the funds are transferred or the donor becomes obligated to make the payment. This occurs when the check is accepted, certified, or paid by the drawee bank or when the payee or a subsequent holder negotiates the check to a holder in due course.

Under Uniform Commercial Code (U.C.C.) § 4–403, the donor has a right to stop payment of a check. If the donor does not stop payment and is alive and has mental capacity when the check is accepted, certified, or paid by the drawee bank or when the donee or a subsequent holder negotiates the check to a holder in due course, the gift is effective. If the timing of the gift is important for federal gift-tax purposes, the effective date of the gift relates back to the time when the check was deposited by the donee.

If the donor dies or becomes mentally incapacitated before the check is accepted, certified, or paid by the drawee bank or before the donee or a subsequent holder negotiates the check to a holder in due course, the gift is ordinarily ineffective. To be sure, U.C.C. § 4–405 provides that the donor's death or incapacity does not "revoke[ ] the authority to accept, pay, collect, or account until the bank knows of the fact of death or of an adjudication of incompetence and has reasonable opportunity to act on it," and also provides that "[e]ven with knowledge, a bank may for 10 days after the date of death pay or certify checks drawn on or before that date unless ordered to stop payment by a person claiming an interest in the account." The Official Comment, however, indicates that these provisions are for the protection of the bank and not determinative of the ownership of the funds. Thus, U.C.C. § 4–405 does not undercut the proposition that the gift of a check is ordinarily ineffective if the donor dies or becomes mentally incapacitated before the check is accepted, certified, or paid by the drawee bank or before the donee or a subsequent holder negotiates the check to a holder in due course. The donee, however, may be entitled to a remedy in the law of restitution and unjust enrichment. See Comment *z*, which refers to § 6.1, Comment *o*. In addition, under Comment *yy*, the gift may be perfected on the basis of donative intent alone if the donor's intent to make an irrevocable gift when delivering the check is established by clear and convincing evidence.

If the check is to a charity, the gift may become complete upon the delivery of the check. Under Restatement Second, Contracts § 90, charitable pledges are enforceable even though not supported by consideration. The relation-back doctrine applies for tax purposes to render the gift complete upon the delivery of the check.

o. *Gifts of less than full ownership by delivery.* As noted in § 6.1, Comment *a*, most gifts transfer full ownership, particularly gifts of personal property that are perfected by delivery. It is also possible to perfect a gift of less than full ownership by delivery, as in the case of a gift of a life estate or a remainder interest. The question in such a case is one of determining what the donor's intent was when making the delivery. In modern practice, however, the preferred method of making a gift of less than full ownership is by inter vivos donative document, not by delivery.

Comment on Paragraph (2)—Perfecting Gift of Personal Property by Inter Vivos Donative Document:

p. *Scope.* An effective transfer of personal property, necessary to perfect a gift of such property, may be made by inter vivos donative document. Such a document is often called a deed of gift. If a gift is made by inter vivos donative document, physical delivery of the item of personal property to the donee is not necessary. In order for a gift of personal property to be made by inter vivos donative document, the general requirements for making a gift set forth in § 6.1 must be satisfied.

q. *Inter vivos donative document.* An inter vivos donative document is a writing that is signed by the donor that (1) identifies the donor and donee; (2) describes the subject matter of the gift; and (3) specifies the nature of the interest given.

r. *Writing.* The terms of an inter vivos donative document must be in writing. The requirement of a writing is satisfied if the text is inscribed on a tangible medium or is stored in an electronic or other medium and is retrievable in perceivable form.

s. *Signature.* An inter vivos donative document must be signed by the donor. If the text is inscribed on a tangible medium, the requirement of a signature is satisfied if the writing contains the donor's signature someplace on the document. The normal place for the donor's signature is at the end of the document, but such placement is not essential for the document to be signed by the donor. For example, a document in the donor's handwriting that provides, "I, Henry Jones, hereby give to Mary Smith my 10 shares of X stock," is signed by Henry Jones.

If the text is stored in an electronic or other medium and is retrievable in perceivable form, an electronic signature satisfies the signature requirement. An electronic signature is a sound, symbol, or process attached to or logically associated with the writing and executed or adopted by the donor with the intent to sign the writing.

t. *Identification of donor and donee, subject matter of the gift, and nature of interest given.* The identity of the donor and the donee, the subject matter of the gift, and the nature of the interest given must be ascertainable from the terms of the document of transfer as construed in accordance with Division IV on Construction, Reformation, and Modification of Donative Documents (Chapters 10, 11, and 12).

An inter vivos donative document may transfer any type of personal property, whether tangible or intangible, including contract rights such as those embodied in a life-insurance policy, shares of stock, a bond, or a promissory note.

The interest transferred to the donee may be the donor's entire interest in all or in a divided or undivided share of the gift property, or may be a limited interest, such as a life estate. The interest given may be a present interest or a future interest. The donor may retain a reversionary interest in the property. The document of transfer may create concurrent interests in the donor and donee or concurrent interests in several donees. The document of transfer may create a present interest in the donor with a future interest in the donee that may be revocable by the donor or irrevocable by the donor. The interest given the donee may be legal or equitable. . . . .

u. *Present transfer.* The mere preparation of a donative document does not effect a present transfer necessary to perfect a gift. Such a writing becomes effective when the donor manifests the intention that the document is to be operative to make a present transfer. See § 6.1, Comment *f.*

The delivery of the document by the donor to the donee is an act manifesting that the donor intends the document to be presently operative, unless there is evidence that the delivery was made for some other purpose. If, for example, the purpose of the delivery was to allow the donee or the donee's representative to inspect the document to see if any portion of it should be rephrased, the delivery would lack its normal significance.

Delivery of an inter vivos donative document occurs when the donor puts the document beyond retrieval.

Illustrations:

19. G mails a letter to her son S. The letter signed by G states: "This is to let you know that you now own the painting that hangs in my living room. You can pick it up at your convenience." This letter is an inter vivos donative document, effective when mailed.

20. G owns 100 shares of stock in X Company. The stock certificate contains a blank form allowing the owner to make transfer instructions to the corporation's transfer agent. G fills in the blank spaces, naming G's son S as transferee, signs his own name, and mails the stock certificate to S. The stock certificate is an inter vivos donative document, effective when mailed.

21. G purchased 20 state lottery tickets for the multi-million-dollar drawing that was to take place that evening. After purchasing the tickets, but before the drawing, G sent a message by electronic mail (e-mail) to his son and daughter stating: "Today I bought 20 tickets for the X-State lottery drawing tonight. I hereby give each of you a ¼ ownership interest in those tickets. Your mother and I retain a ½ ownership interest in those tickets. Dad." The e-mail is an inter vivos donative document, effective when sent. The same result would be reached if G's message was sent to his son and daughter by telefax.

A delivery of the document by the donor to someone other than the donee is a manifestation that the document is presently operative, unless the circumstances indicate otherwise. The third-person recipient of the document may be the donor's agent to carry out the donor's instructions regarding the delivery of the document, in which case the document is not operative until the delivery is made in accordance with these instructions. A delivery of the document may be made to a third person under circumstances that put the document beyond retrieval by the donor, in which case the document is legally operative at the time of delivery to the third person.

A manifestation that the document is to be presently operative may be made without delivery of the document to anyone, if the outward and visible acts of the donor evidence an intent to make a present transfer.

Comment Applicable to Both Paragraphs (1) and (2)—Gifts of Personal Property by Delivery or by Donative Document:

v. Gift limited by donor's ownership interest. As noted in § 6.1, Comment c, the donor cannot transfer to the donee a greater beneficial interest in the property than the donor owns. If the donor purports to give the donee a greater interest than the donor owns, the donee will only receive the interest that the donor could have given. . . . .

w. Right to possession of subject matter of gift. A gift confers ownership of the transferred interest on the donee, which ordinarily gives the donee the right to possession of the property. . . . .

Although a gift confers ownership of the transferred interest on the donee, which ordinarily gives the donee the right to possession of the property, if the specified beneficial interest is a future interest, the property will be in the possession of someone other than the donee (unless the gift is to the owner of the possessory interest). If the gift gives the donee a present beneficial interest in the subject matter of the gift, the transfer of that interest occurs even though the possession remains unchanged.

x. Construction, reformation, and modification of donative documents. The doctrines set forth in Division IV (Chapters 10, 11, and 12) for the construction, reformation, and modification of donative documents fully apply to inter vivos donative documents effecting a gift of personal property, as well as to all other donative documents.

y. Acceptance by donee. A gift of personal property is not complete until it is accepted by the donee. Acceptance is ordinarily presumed. See § 6.1(b) and § 6.1, Comment *i*.

yy. Perfecting a gift on the basis of donative intent alone. The question addressed in this Comment is whether a gift of personal property can be perfected on the basis of donative intent alone. An oral declaration of trust of personal property is recognized as valid without delivery of anything or notice by the donor to the intended donee (see Restatement Third, Trusts § 20; Restatement Second, Trusts § 17(a)). Section 407 of the Uniform Trust Code (UTC) and some case law requires that such a trust be established by clear and convincing evidence. Section 3.3 of this Restatement excuses noncompliance with the formalities for execution of a will if there is clear and convincing evidence of testamentary intent. By analogy to those authorities, this Restatement adopts the position that a gift of personal property can be perfected on the basis of donative intent alone if the donor's intent to make a gift is established by clear and convincing evidence.

Illustration:

25. The facts are the same as those in Illustration 21, except that G sent his e-mail message only to his daughter, and added a sentence to the message stating, "Please tell your brother." The conclusion is justified that G's intent to make a gift to his son is established by clear and convincing evidence and thus that G made a gift to his son of an undivided ¼ ownership interest in the lottery tickets.

z. Mistakes in inter vivos gifts of personal property. If a donor makes a mistake in perfecting an inter vivos gift of personal property, such as if the donor is induced by mistake to make the gift or if the donor transfers more than or different property than intended or attempts to make a gift and dies or becomes mentally incapacitated in the belief that the gift has been perfected, there may be a remedy in the law of restitution and unjust enrichment. See § 6.1, Comment *o*.

Comment on Gifts Causa Mortis:

zz. Gift causa mortis. If the donor of a gift of personal property was in apprehension of imminent death when making the gift, the gift is presumed to be revocable. Such a gift is referred to as a gift causa mortis. Failure to revoke within a reasonable time after the donor is no longer in apprehension of imminent death causes the donor's right of revocation to lapse.

The gift causa mortis resembles a testamentary disposition but differs in that the intended donee acquires conditional ownership and present enjoyment in the subject matter of the gift during the donor's lifetime. It thus differs both from the will and from the common will substitutes discussed in Chapter 7, under which the donor retains beneficial enjoyment of the property until death.

The distinctive requirement for a gift causa mortis is that the gift be made by the donor in apprehension of imminent death. The donor must fear death from a specific cause within the near future. The mere fact that a person is advanced in age and might soon die does not mean that the donor is in apprehension of imminent death.

Illustration:

26. G is going to the hospital to have a major operation that she reasonably fears may be fatal. Just before going to the hospital, G hands a box containing jewelry to her daughter saying, "I want you to have the contents of this box." The gift is a gift causa mortis and is revocable by G.

Although some authority has held that the donor's recovery from the apprehended peril automatically revokes a gift causa mortis, this view has led to difficulties. This Restatement adheres to the position adopted in Restatement Second, Property (Donative Transfers) § 31.3 that the donor's failure to revoke within a reasonable time after abatement of the donor's apprehension of imminent death terminates the right of revocation.

Illustration:

28. G is going to the hospital to have a major operation that G fears may be fatal. Just before going to the hospital, G hands a box containing jewelry to her daughter, D, saying, "I want you to have the contents of this box." The gift is a gift causa mortis. The operation is performed successfully and full recovery is expected. A month later, while convalescing at home, G dies of a heart attack that had no relationship to the operation. Although G recovered from that which caused the apprehension of imminent death, G did not revoke the gift before her death. Consequently, D is entitled to keep the box of jewelry even though the gift was revocable at the time of G's death.

If the donor of a gift causa mortis, while still in apprehension of imminent death, reacquires possession of the property from the person to whom it was delivered, that action is inconsistent with an intention that the gift remain in effect and is treated as revoking the gift.

A gift causa mortis may be revoked by words or acts of the donor while the donor is still in apprehension of imminent death. . . . .

Although gifts causa mortis have traditionally been limited to gifts of personal property by delivery, this Restatement adheres to the position adopted in Restatement Second, Property § 32.2, Comment *d*, that a gift of personal property made by inter vivos donative document may also be the subject of a gift causa mortis. A gift of personal property by inter vivos document is presumed to be an absolute gift and not a gift causa mortis, even if the donor was in apprehension of imminent death at the time of the gift.

Whether the gift is perfected by delivery or by donative document, language or circumstances indicating that a gift is not revocable by the donor rebut the presumption of gift causa mortis. If the donor over the past years has made annual gifts to various donees to obtain a tax advantage, as for example to take advantage of the annual gift-tax exclusion, and gifts are made that follow that pattern at a time when the donor is in apprehension of imminent death, the conclusion is justified that the gifts are not gifts causa mortis. Similarly, if prior to the donor's death a gift-tax return is prepared and signed by the donor, this would ordinarily evidence intent to make an outright gift rather than a gift causa mortis.

§ 6.3. Gifts of Land

The transfer of land, necessary to perfect a gift, must be evidenced in a writing that is executed in compliance with the formalities required by the applicable statute of frauds.

General Comment:

a. Scope. A gift of land (other than a lease for a specified term, usually not exceeding one year) must be evidenced in a writing that is executed in compliance with the formalities required by the applicable statute of frauds. Such a writing is referred to as a deed. The applicable statute of frauds is that of the jurisdiction where the land is located. The statute of frauds does not apply to a gift of personal property.

b. Historical note. The English Statute of Frauds of 1677, 29 Charles II, c.3, § 1 (An Act for Prevention of Frauds and Perjuries), from which the various state statutes of frauds are derived, established the requirement that a transfer of an interest in land must be evidenced by an instrument in writing. Originally, the law required that transfers of freehold interests in land take place by a feoffment, i.e., a ceremonial physical transfer between the transacting parties, taking place on the land. No instrument in writing was required, and none could render the ceremony unnecessary. In time, the feoffment became disused and was replaced by the common recovery, a collusive lawsuit that allowed transfer by writing in the form of a spurious lawsuit, manipulating the Common Pleas court rolls to have the effect of written transfer. Then came the Statute of Uses (1536), under which the transfer of title to land to another could be made by a document (the bargain and sale or the covenant to stand seized), creating an equitable estate that the Statute of Uses transformed into a legal estate. Documentary transfer, unaccompanied by any ceremony of physical delivery of the land, became permissible. The Statute of Frauds provided, in relevant part, that no freehold interest "shall at any time hereafter be assigned, transferred, granted, or surrendered, unless it be by deed or note in writing, signed by the party or parties so assigning, granting, or surrendering the same, or their agents, thereunto lawfully authorised by writing, or by Act and operation of Law." By insisting that no freehold could be transferred except as evidenced by an instrument in writing signed by the transferor, the Statute of Frauds made documentary transfer compulsory.

c. Requirement of a writing. Although different versions of the statute of frauds have been adopted in the various states, certain core requirements exist. The writing must satisfy the requirements for an inter vivos donative document described in § 6.2, Comments *q* through *t*. Specifically, there must be a writing that is signed by the donor and that identifies the donor and donee, describes the subject matter of the gift, and specifies the nature of the interest given.

d. Present transfer. The mere preparation of a deed does not effect a present transfer necessary to perfect a gift of land. A deed becomes effective when the donor manifests the intention that the deed is to be operative to make a present transfer. See § 6.1, Comment *f*.

As noted in § 6.2, Comment *u*, the delivery of the deed by the donor to the donee is an act manifesting the donor's intention that the deed is to be presently operative, unless there is evidence that the delivery was made for some other purpose, as, for example, to allow the donee or the donee's representative to inspect the document to see if any portion of it should be revised. Delivery of the deed occurs when the donor puts the document beyond retrieval.

A manifestation that the deed is to be presently operative may be made without delivery of the deed to anyone, if the outward and visible acts of the donor evidence an intent to make a present transfer. Recording the deed under the recording statute presumptively constitutes a manifestation of intent that the deed is to be presently operative. See Comment *e.*

e. *Recording statutes; effect of recordation.* All states have a recording statute for recording transfers of land. Donative transfers as well as sales of land can be recorded. Although recordation of the deed is not necessary to perfect a gift of land, unless a statute expressly so requires, recording the deed presumptively constitutes a manifestation that the deed is to be presently operative.

In order to record a deed, statutory provisions in some states require that the document of transfer be signed, sealed, attested, and acknowledged. Recordation of a recordable document protects the donee's rights as against a bona fide purchaser for value (BFP) because recordation gives a BFP constructive notice of the prior transfer to the donee. Recordation of a document that is not recordable does not give such constructive notice, but it may be seen by one examining the record and thereby give actual notice of the donee's rights under the document. Recording statutes differ among the states in type and detail.

f. *Gift limited by donor's ownership interest.* As provided in § 6.1, Comment *c*, the donor cannot transfer to the donee a greater beneficial interest in the property than the donor owns. If the donor purports to give the donee a greater interest than the donor owns, the donee will only receive the interest that the donor could have given. . . . .

g. *Specified beneficial interest.* The interest transferred to the donee may be the donor's entire interest in all or in a divided or undivided share of the gift property, or may be a limited interest, such as a life estate. The interest given may be a present interest or a future interest. The donor may retain a reversionary interest in the property. The deed may create concurrent interests in the donor and donee or concurrent interests in several donees. The deed may create a present interest in the donor with a future interest in the donee that may be revocable by the donor or irrevocable by the donor. The interest given the donee may be legal or equitable.

h. *Right to possession.* A deed ordinarily confers on the donee the right to possession of the property. If the specified interest described in the deed is a future interest, however, the property will be in the possession of someone other than the donee (unless the gift is to the owner of the possessory interest).

If, under all the facts and circumstances, the deed was intended to make a present transfer of ownership (see § 6.1, Comment *f*), the transfer of that interest occurs even though the possession remains unchanged. . . . .

i. *Acceptance by donee.* A gift of land is not complete until it is accepted by the donee. Acceptance is ordinarily presumed. See § 6.1(b) and § 6.1, Comment *i.*

j. *Inter vivos trust of land—requirement of a writing.* On the requirement that an inter vivos trust of land be expressed in writing, see Restatement Third, Trusts §§ 22–24.

k. Oral lease for a fixed or computable period of time. The statutes of frauds allow, generally speaking, oral leases of land if the initial period of the lease, measured from its making, does not exceed the specified period in the statute. In most jurisdictions, the period specified in the statute is for leases that do not exceed one year.

An oral lease for a fixed or computable period of time is invalid if the period measured from the commencement of the lease exceeds the period specified in the Statute of Frauds. See Restatement Second, Property (Landlord and Tenant) § 2.1, Comment *c*. . . . .

l. Periodic tenancy. An oral lease rent free of a periodic tenancy, with the initial period being less than the specified period in the Statute of Frauds, is valid. The rule pertains even though the tenancy may continue from period to period and eventually exceed the period specified in the Statute. See Restatement Second, Property (Landlord and Tenant) § 2.1, Comment *d*.

m. Tenancy at will. An oral tenancy at will rent free is one that is terminable at the will of either party. If this tenancy is terminable from its inception at the will of either party without advance notice, the parties have not specified any fixed or computable period that exceeds the period specified in the Statute of Frauds. See Restatement Second, Property (Landlord and Tenant) § 2.1, Comment *e*.

n. Condominiums and cooperatives. The owner of a condominium has an interest in land, and a gift of the condominium requires the use of an inter vivos donative document. The owner of a cooperative, by contrast, owns stock in the cooperative, which stock carries with it the right to a lease of some specified area of land. A gift of a cooperative may be accomplished by either an inter vivos donative document or by delivering the stock with the manifested intention that the donee is to own the stock (see § 6.2). If the bylaws of the cooperative require some form of approval before the transfer of the stock in the cooperative entitles a stockholder to a lease of an apartment, the gift is nevertheless complete upon delivery of the stock or deed.

o. Construction, reformation, and modification of donative documents. The doctrines set forth in Division IV (Chapters 10, 11, and 12) for the construction, reformation, and modification of donative documents apply to inter vivos donative documents effecting a gift of land, as well as to all other donative documents.

p. Mistakes in inter vivos gifts of land. If a donor makes a mistake in perfecting an inter vivos gift of land, such as the case in which the donor is induced by mistake to make the gift or the donor transfers more than or different property than intended or attempts to make a gift and dies or becomes mentally incapacitated in the belief that the gift has been perfected, there may be a remedy in the law of restitution and unjust enrichment. See § 6.1, Comment *o*.

CHAPTER 7

WILL SUBSTITUTES

Introductory Note: Chapter 7 addresses will substitutes. Like a gift (see Chapter 6), a will substitute is a nonprobate transfer. A will substitute differs from an outright gift, however, in that it passes to the donee a right to future possession or enjoyment that shifts to the donee at the donor's death. Section 7.1 defines will substitutes and provides that they are valid. Section 7.2 addresses the extent to which will doctrines are applicable to will substitutes.

§ 7.1. Will Substitute—Definition and Validity

(a) A will substitute is an arrangement respecting property or contract rights that is established during the donor's life, under which (1) the right to possession or enjoyment of the property or to a contractual payment shifts outside of probate to the donee at the donor's death; and (2) substantial lifetime rights of dominion, control, possession, or enjoyment are retained by the donor.

(b) To be valid, a will substitute need not be executed in compliance with the statutory formalities required for a will.

Comment:

a. *Scope and rationale.* Because outright gifts and irrevocable trusts do not serve the function of a will, they are not wills and need not be executed in compliance with the statutory formalities required for wills. A will substitute, however, does serve the function of a will. This section makes clear that a will substitute need not be executed in compliance with the statutory formalities required for a will.

A will substitute serves the function of a will because it is an arrangement respecting property or contract rights that is established during the donor's life under which (1) the right to possession or enjoyment of the property or to a contractual payment shifts outside of probate to the donee at the donor's death; and (2) substantial lifetime rights of dominion, control, possession, or enjoyment are retained by the donor. (The term "control" includes rights to revoke the arrangement or to alter the designation of the death-time beneficiary.) Common property or contractual arrangements that are used as will substitutes include revocable inter vivos trusts, life insurance, pension and employee-benefit accounts, multiple-party accounts with banks and other financial intermediaries, payable- or transfer-on-death arrangements, joint ownership with right of survivorship, and annuities with death benefits.

The term "will substitute" presupposes that the arrangement under which the right to possession or enjoyment of the property or to a contractual payment shifts outside of probate to the donee at the donor's death is donative in nature. Arrangements such as life insurance or joint tenancies that are established pursuant to a business or commercial transaction are beyond the scope of this section, although the proposition stated in subsection (b) that such arrangements need not be executed in compliance with the statutory formalities required for a will applies *a fortiori* to the business or commercial context.

To be valid, a will substitute need not be executed in compliance with the statutory formalities for a will because a will substitute is not a will. A will transfers ownership of probate property at death. See § 3.1, Comment *a*. Property subject to a will substitute is not probate property at death because it is then treated as no longer owned by the donor. . . . .

The traditional explanation for why a will substitute is not a will is that a will substitute transfers ownership during life—it effects a *present* transfer of a *nonpossessory future* interest or contract right, the time of possession or enjoyment being postponed until the donor's death. Anglo-American law recognizes that a nonpossessory future interest is an ownership interest even though it is subject to a power or other conditions that might not be permanently resolved until the interest takes effect in possession or enjoyment. Likewise, a contract right can be conferred on another even though the contract right is a right to possession or enjoyment of money or other property some time in the future and is subject to a power or other conditions that might not be permanently resolved until the contract right becomes enforceable.

A related distinction between a will and a will substitute is that a will can pass property that the testator acquires after the will is executed. See § 3.1, Comment *a*. A will substitute, being an inter vivos transfer, relates to property or contract rights that the donor owns when establishing the arrangement or adds to the arrangement later. See § 6.1, Comment *c*.

An arrangement respecting either property or contract rights can be used as a will substitute. An arrangement respecting property is one under which the donor's property is segregated from other property. An example of such an arrangement is a trust. An arrangement respecting contract rights is one under which a financial intermediary incurs a contractual obligation to make a certain payment but is not required to segregate any property for that particular payment. An example of such an arrangement is a life-insurance contract.

As noted above, the traditional explanation for why will substitutes are not wills is the present-transfer theory. A will substitute need not be executed in compliance with the statutory formalities required for a will because a will substitute effects a present transfer of a nonpossessory future interest or contract right, the time of possession or enjoyment being postponed until the donor's death. An alternative explanation is that will substitutes need not be characterized as effecting a present transfer to escape characterization as a will. Rather, the donor is free to transfer wealth on death either in the probate system or in the nonprobate system or in both. When using the nonprobate system, the donor uses its forms, which typically arise from the commercial practice of financial intermediaries. When using the state-operated transfer system of probate administration, the donor uses the forms appropriate to that system (for testation) or allows that system to operate by default (in the case of intestacy). The statute of wills does not require wealth transfers on death to occur by probate; the statute merely requires that probate transfers comply with the statute's formalities. Because the statute of wills does not govern nonprobate transfers, wealth holders may use these alternative wealth-transfer systems on death by means of will substitutes.

b. Revocable inter vivos trusts. A revocable inter vivos trust is not a will and hence does not have to be executed in accordance with the formalities of a will. When created, the revocable inter vivos trust transfers a future interest to the remainder beneficiary of the trust. The fact that the interest of the remainder beneficiary is subject to the settlor's power to revoke or amend the trust, or is subject to a condition of survival of the settlor (see § 5.5, Comment *p*), and may be subject to other conditions, does not transform the inter vivos trust into a will. . . . .

c. *Life insurance.* A life-insurance policy is a third-party beneficiary contract. The insured enters into a contract with the insurer under which the insurer, in exchange for the insured's premium payment(s), obligates itself to pay an amount equal to the proceeds of the policy on the insured's death to the insured's designated beneficiary. The death benefit may be payable in the form of a lump-sum payment, an annuity for the surviving beneficiary, or some other form. When used as a will substitute, the beneficiary designation in the policy makes a present donative transfer of a contract right to collect the proceeds of the policy on the insured's death. Although the life-insurance contract pays out at death, the beneficiary designation—when made—is treated as conferring a contract right on the beneficiary. Although life-insurance policies commonly reserve to the owner the right to change the beneficiary and require the beneficiary to survive the insured, the beneficiary designation is valid without being executed in compliance with the statutory formalities required for a will. The proceeds pass to the beneficiary outside of probate. . . . .

d. *Pension and employee-benefit accounts.* Pension and employee-benefit accounts that have a death benefit take a variety of forms, ranging from defined-benefit pension plans to defined-contribution plans, such as 401(k)s, 401(a)s, 403(b)s, 457(b)s, profit-sharing plans, Keogh or SEP plans for the self-employed, Individual Retirement Accounts (IRAs), and many others. Although the right to possession or enjoyment of the property or a contractual payment shifts outside of probate to the death-beneficiary at the employee's death, and the employee retains substantial rights for life, such as the right to designate or change the death-beneficiary, the beneficiary designations in these accounts are valid without being executed in compliance with the statutory formalities required for a will.

Federal law in the pension area creates mandatory spousal shares (qualified joint and retirement survivor annuities, qualified preretirement annuities) limiting the amount or portion that is subject to gratuitous transfer in a variety of these accounts. See ERISA § 205(a), 29 U.S.C. § 1055(a).

e. *Joint tenancy and other forms of undivided ownership with right of survivorship.* Joint tenancy with right of survivorship is a form of undivided ownership that is often used as a will substitute. In most states, two or more persons, related or unrelated, may hold land or personal property in joint tenancy with right of survivorship. Married couples may have other options. In some states, married couples may hold land or personal property as tenants by the entirety. In some states, married couples may hold land or personal property as community property with right of survivorship.

Although some features of these forms of undivided ownership differ, including their tax consequences, one common feature causes them to be frequently used as will substitutes—the right of survivorship. On the death of a co-owner, property held in joint tenancy with right of survivorship passes outside of probate to the surviving joint tenant or joint tenants. On the death of a spouse, property held as tenants by the entirety or as community property with the right of survivorship passes outside of probate to the decedent's surviving spouse.

To be valid, a deed creating a joint tenancy, tenancy by the entirety, or community property with right of survivorship need not be executed in compliance with the statutory formalities required for a will.

f. *Multiple-party accounts.* The account registration of a multiple-party account with a bank or other financial intermediary is valid without being executed in accordance with the statutory formalities required for the execution of a will. If the account has a survivorship or pay-on-death feature, the balance on hand in the account at death passes outside of probate to the survivor.

Not all multiple-party accounts are established with donative intent to provide for a survivorship feature. For example, a nonsurvivorship agency account, as authorized by Revised Uniform Probate Code § 6–205, is not a will substitute. The balance on hand at the death of the depositor does not pass to the agent, but instead passes as an asset of the depositor's probate estate. . . . .

An account with a financial intermediary such as a stock brokerage firm or an investment company may be created in the name of the donor (the one who supplies the financial assets in the account) and the donee, with right of survivorship. The terms of the arrangement regarding the respective rights of the donor and the donee while both are alive depend on the terms of the agreement. The account application or registration need not be executed in accordance with the statutory requirements for the execution of a will.

g. *Payable-on-death arrangements.* There are several types of payable-on-death arrangements. One is a POD bank account that is carried in the name of the depositor (the donor) and is "payable on the death of the depositor to" the designated beneficiary. Another is a government bond that is taken in the name of the purchaser (the donor), payable on the death of the purchaser to another person (the donee). Still another is a security that is registered in the name of the owner "transfer on death" to a designated beneficiary. An example of such registration is "John Jones TOD Martha Jones." Such registration is authorized by the Uniform TOD Security Registration Act (1989), which is incorporated into the Revised Uniform Probate Code §§ 6–301 to –311 and has been enacted in nearly all states.

The beneficiary designation in a POD or a TOD arrangement is valid without being executed in accordance with the statutory formalities required for a will. . . . .

h. *Annuity with a death benefit.* Insurance companies offer for sale a variety of annuity contracts. If the annuity contract has a death benefit, the death benefit may be payable in the form of a lump-sum payment, an annuity for the surviving beneficiary, or some other form. An annuity with a death benefit is a property or contractual arrangement established during life. The fact that the owner may have lifetime dominion, control, possession, or enjoyment of the property or contract does not transform the donor's designation of the death-benefit beneficiary or any subsequent change of beneficiary into a will. The beneficiary designation need not be executed in compliance with the statutory formalities for a will.

i. *Totten trusts.* A Totten trust (also called a tentative trust or bank-account trust) presumptively arises when a person makes a deposit in an account with a bank or a similar financial institution in the depositor's own name "as trustee" or "in trust" for another. The Institute's position on Totten trusts, set forth in Restatement Third, Trusts § 26, is that such trusts are valid without being executed in compliance with the formalities required for a will and that, unless revoked, the balance on hand at the depositor's death passes outside probate to the beneficiary.

j. *Other will substitutes.* The common will substitutes identified and discussed in the preceding Comments are not intended to constitute an exhaustive list. Rather, the principle endorsed in the Restatement is that no arrangement respecting property or contract rights established during life is rendered testamentary merely because (i) the right to possession or enjoyment of the property or a contractual payment shifts outside of probate to the donee at the donor's death and (ii) substantial lifetime rights of dominion, control, possession, or enjoyment are retained by the donor.

§ 7.2. Application of Will Doctrines to Will Substitutes

Although a will substitute need not be executed in compliance with the statutory formalities required for a will, such an arrangement is, to the extent appropriate, subject to substantive restrictions on testation and to rules of construction and other rules applicable to testamentary dispositions.

Comment:

a. *Rationale.* A will substitute is valid without being executed in compliance with the statutory formalities for a will. Will substitutes are not wills. A will transfers ownership at death, but a will substitute effects a present transfer of a property interest or a contract right. See § 7.1.

Although the validity of a will substitute does not depend on its being executed in compliance with the statutory formalities required for a will, a will substitute serves the function of a will. It shifts the right to possession or enjoyment to the donee at the donor's death. In this sense, a will substitute is in reality a nonprobate will. A will substitute is therefore, to the extent appropriate, subject to substantive restrictions on testation and to rules of construction and other rules applicable to testamentary dispositions. Substantive restrictions on testation constitute important policies restricting disposition of property after the owner's death that should not be avoidable simply by changing the form of the death-time transfer. By contrast, rules of construction and other interpretative devices aid in determining and giving effect to the donor's intention or probable intention and hence should apply generally to donative documents.

A will substitute is subject to rules of construction only to the extent appropriate. For example, Comment *f* points out that the principles of § 5.2 on failure ("ademption") of specific devises by extinction also apply to a will substitute, such as a revocable trust, but only for a will substitute that contains the equivalent of a specific devise.

Historically, some of the rules of construction were formulated only for wills because wills then constituted the principal means of transmitting property at death. Some rules of construction were placed in the probate code, which led the legislature to draft them as rules applicable to wills. As will substitutes have proliferated and become alternative means of passing property at death, legislatures and courts have sometimes been slow to expand the scope of these rules to transactions to which they should be fully applicable in policy. This Restatement (along with the Restatement Third, Trusts, the Revised Uniform Probate Code, and the Uniform Trust Code) moves toward the policy of unifying the law of wills and will substitutes. This section draws together doctrines from other Chapters that implement this policy, presented in the order in which they appear in this Restatement.

b. Claims and statutory allowances. As noted in § 1.1, Comments *e* and *f*, the decedent's probate estate is liable for the payment of claims allowed against the estate (including funeral expenses and expenses of administration), taxes for which the estate is liable, and family, exempt property, and homestead allowances. The decedent's creditors and the decedent's surviving spouse and children claiming statutory allowances may also be entitled to have their claims satisfied out of the decedent's will substitutes of various types, to the extent provided by applicable law. See, e.g., Uniform Trust Code § 505; UPC § 6–102 (Revised 1998); Uniform TOD Security Registration Act § 9 (Revised UPC § 6–309) (Revised 1998); Restatement Third, Trusts § 25, Comment *e*.

c. The 120-hour requirement of survival. The Original Uniform Probate Code introduced a rule of construction that devisees must survive the decedent by 120 hours or more, but the terms of the statute applied only to transfers by will. See Original UPC § 2–601; see also § 2–104 (similar rule for intestacy). The Revised Uniform Simultaneous Death Act and the Revised Uniform Probate Code expanded the 120-hour requirement of survival to all donative documents (wills and inter vivos donative documents, including will substitutes) that require the donee to survive the donor. . . . . As noted in § 1.2, Comment *e*, the underlying policy of the Revised USDA is to resolve close cases in favor of non-survival because that outcome usually better serves the donor's intent. This policy commends itself in applying the common-law requirement of survival and in cases of ambiguity under earlier legislative regimes. In the sphere of will substitutes, this policy should at minimum be implemented by requiring proof of survival by clear and convincing evidence, unless there is a contrary intent or a tax advantage in treating the other decedent as the survivor, or unless that approach is contrary to an applicable statute.

d. Harmless-error rule. The harmless-error rule of § 3.3 applies to the creation, revocation, or amendment of a will substitute, including the designation or change of the beneficiary.

e. Revocation or amendment of a will substitute by later will. A revocable trust may be revoked or amended by a later will. See Restatement Third, Trusts § 63, Comment *h*; Uniform Trust Code § 602(c). At least one state has by statute authorized the revocation by a later will of will substitutes except real-property joint tenancies, life insurance, retirement plans, and a few other will substitutes. A few judicial decisions have upheld the effort to revoke certain will substitutes by a later will. . . . . It is generally agreed that Totten trusts may be revoked by will (see Restatement Third, Trusts § 26, Comment *c*), but under Revised UPC § 6–213(b) POD accounts, including Totten trusts, cannot be changed by will.

Insurance contracts, multiple-party accounts, pension accounts, and other will substitutes commonly require the account owner to follow a particular procedure for altering or amending the beneficiary designation, such as completing a form supplied by the financial intermediary or other payor. Such a term governs as a matter of the contract between the account owner and the financial intermediary or payor. It sometimes happens that the account owner misunderstands this requirement and attempts to revoke the beneficiary designation by will. The courts are divided about whether to enforce the account term, thereby defeating the account owner's later contrary expression of donative intent.

In such cases, when the financial intermediary or other payor has paid the beneficiary of record on the account in good faith before learning of the later inconsistent designation in the will, the account term is effective to protect the financial intermediary or payor from liability to the beneficiary designated in the will. In such circumstances, that intended beneficiary is remitted to an action in restitution against the account-designated beneficiary who received the payment. See Restatement of Restitution § 126 [Restatement Third, Restitution and Unjust Enrichment §§ 47–48].

When the financial intermediary or payor receives notice of the inconsistent beneficiary designation contained in the subsequent will before paying the beneficiary of record on the account, the financial intermediary or payor should pay the proceeds as directed under the will, notwithstanding the failure of the account owner to comply with the account term specifying account-specific procedures for revocation or alteration. If the financial intermediary or payor is uncertain about the priority or effectiveness of the attempted revocation or alteration by will, the financial intermediary or payor may discharge its responsibilities by interpleading and/or paying the proceeds into court.

When a designation by will supersedes a designation contained in the instrument of account, the proceeds remain separate from probate property and pass in accordance with the provisions of the nonprobate account, unless the language of the later will expresses an intent that the account proceeds are to become part of the probate estate.

The principles set forth in this Comment also apply to circumstances in which the account owner attempts to modify the beneficiary designation by a subsequent instrument other than a validly executed will. Because such an instrument does not comply with the formalities required for a will to assure that the document represents the owner's donative intent (see § 3.1), the proponent of such an instrument bears the burden of proving by clear and convincing evidence that the instrument reflects the account owner's donative intent. See § 3.3; see also § 7.2, Comment *d*.

The party alleging revocation bears the burden of proving that an asserted revocation actually referred to the will substitute in question. Thus, a mere residuary clause in a later will or a comparable provision in a later revocable inter vivos trust does not revoke an earlier beneficiary designation in a will substitute.

f. *Will doctrines applicable to post-execution events.* The principles of § 4.1(b) on revocation caused by the dissolution of marriage fully apply to revocable will substitutes. See § 4.1, Comment *p*. See also Revised UPC § 2–804.

The principles of § 5.2 on failure ("ademption") of specific devises by extinction also apply to a will substitute, such as a revocable trust, that contains the equivalent of a specific devise. See § 5.2, Comment *i*.

With the exception of a joint tenancy and a multiple-party account with a survivorship feature (other than an account with a POD designation), the principles of § 5.5 on antilapse doctrines apply to a will substitute that requires the donee to survive the donor. See § 5.5, Comment *p*. See also Revised UPC § 2–706.

g. *Protective doctrines.* The protective doctrines set forth in Chapter 8 (Invalidity Due to the Donor's Incapacity or Another's Wrongdoing) fully apply to will substitutes. The protective doctrines set forth in Chapter 9

(Protections Against Disinheritance) are applicable to will substitutes on a selective basis, as provided in Chapter 9.

h. Construction, reformation, and modification of donative documents. The doctrines set forth in Division IV (Chapters 10, 11, and 12) for the construction, reformation, and modification of donative documents fully apply to will substitutes as well as to other donative documents.

i. Rules of construction applicable to class gifts. In some states, the probate code contains rules of construction applicable to class gifts in wills. The rules of construction applicable to class gifts set forth in Division V of this Restatement are fully applicable to a class gift in a will substitute or any other donative document.

j. Social restrictions on freedom of disposition. The principles set forth in Division VIII regarding social restrictions on the freedom of disposition apply to will substitutes on a selective basis, as provided in Division VIII.

k. State and federal law. The rules covered under this section apply as a matter of state law to will substitutes governed by state law. These rules inform the federal common law of will substitutes under the Employee Retirement Income Security Act (ERISA) or other federal law.

DIVISION III
PROTECTIVE DOCTRINES

Introductory Note: This Division addresses various protective doctrines. Chapter 8 deals with invalidity arising from the donor's incapacity or another's wrongdoing. The protective doctrines covered in this chapter apply to all donative transfers, including gifts, trusts, will substitutes, and testamentary transfers.

Chapter 9 addresses protection of the donor's surviving spouse against intentional disinheritance and protection of the donor's spouse and children or descendants against unintentional disinheritance. The protective doctrines covered in this chapter apply only to testamentary transfers.

CHAPTER 8

INVALIDITY DUE TO THE DONOR'S INCAPACITY OR ANOTHER'S WRONGDOING

Introductory Note: This chapter is divided into three parts. Part A covers the capacity necessary to make a donative transfer. Part A contains sections on mental capacity and on minority. To make a gift, the donor must have donative intent (see § 6.1, Comment *b*), and to make a will, the testator must have testamentary intent (see § 3.1, Comment *g*). The law protects a person who lacks mental capacity or is a minor by not recognizing the validity of any donative or testamentary intent formed by such a person.

Part B deals with wrongdoing by others. Part B contains two sections. Section 8.3 addresses invalidity due to undue influence, duress, or fraud, and § 8.4 discusses invalidity due to homicide under the slayer rule.

Part C addresses the validity and effect of no-contest clauses.

Part A. Donor's Capacity

§ 8.1. Requirement of Mental Capacity

(a) A person must have mental capacity in order to make or revoke a donative transfer.

(b) If the donative transfer is in the form of a will, a revocable will substitute, or a revocable gift, the testator or donor must be capable of knowing and understanding in a general way the nature and extent of his or her property, the natural objects of his or her bounty, and the disposition that he or she is making of that property, and must also be capable of relating these elements to one another and forming an orderly desire regarding the disposition of the property.

(c) If the donative transfer is in the form of an irrevocable gift, the donor must have the mental capacity necessary to make or revoke a will and must also be capable of understanding the effect that the gift may have on the future financial security of the donor and of anyone who may be dependent on the donor.

Comment:

a. *Scope.* This section addresses the mental capacity required in order to make or revoke a donative transfer. Comments *n, o, p, q,* and *r* also cover some subsidiary but related matters, such as the capacity to receive a donative transfer and to serve in a fiduciary capacity. This section applies to all donative transfers, whether inter vivos or testamentary.

b. *Rationale.* The law of donative transfers is premised upon implementing the donor's intent. The law requires that the donor have the mental capacity to form such an intent. Moreover, the requirement that the donor must have mental capacity in order to make or revoke a will, will substitute, or gift serves a protective function. In order to make a gift, the donor must be able to formulate a legally effective donative intent (see § 6.1, Comment *b*), and in order to make a will, the testator must be able to formulate a legally effective testamentary intent (see § 3.1, Comment *g*). The law protects a person who lacks mental capacity by providing that such a person is incapable of effectively formulating the requisite donative or testamentary intent.

c. *Standard for mental capacity to make or revoke a will.* To have mental capacity to make a will, the law requires the testator to be "of sound mind." To be "of sound mind," the testator must, when executing a will, be capable of knowing and understanding in a general way the nature and extent of his or her property, the natural objects of his or her bounty, and the disposition that he or she is making of that property, and must also be capable of relating these elements to one another and forming an orderly desire regarding the disposition of the property.

The natural objects of a testator's bounty include the testator's closest family members, who are not limited to blood or adoptive relatives or to those who would take by intestacy. For example, a testator's stepchildren are natural objects of the testator's bounty, even though stepchildren do not ordinarily take by intestacy (see § 2.5, Comment *j*). Relatives by affinity do not take by intestacy but could be counted as natural objects of a testator's bounty in the case in which the testator was close to them. To have testamentary capacity, the testator need not know the identity or location of remote relatives who are beyond his or her immediate family circle.

The natural objects of the testator's bounty might include nontraditional as well as traditional family members. For example, a testator's domestic partner as defined in § 6.03 of the [American Law Institute's] Principles of the Law of Family Dissolution: Analysis and Recommendations is a natural object of the testator's bounty. So also is the testator's unmarried partner under any other relationship entitling the donor's unmarried partner to intestacy rights under applicable law, such as a civil-union relationship under the law of Vermont (or under a similar law of another state) or a relationship based on the partners' signed reciprocal beneficiary designation under the law of Hawaii (or under a similar law of another state).

The requirement that the testator must, when executing a will, be capable of knowing and understanding in a general way the natural objects of his or her bounty does not suggest that a testator must devise his or her property to those persons or devise it to them in the shares embodied in the intestacy statutes. Indeed, one of the common reasons for making a will is to create a dispositive plan that does not track the pattern of distribution in intestacy. A will that favors persons who are not close family members or a will that favors family members disproportionately to their relationship to the testator is not evidence that the testator did not know and understand in a general way the natural objects of his or her bounty.

Although many statutes of wills do not expressly say that a testator must be "of sound mind" to revoke a will, the same requirement of mental capacity applies. To revoke a will by revocatory act, the testator must have intent to revoke (see § 4.1, Comment *e*). An intent to revoke is only recognized if the testator has mental capacity when performing the revocatory act. To revoke a will by subsequent will, the testator must have capacity to make a will when executing the will that revokes the prior will.

A purported will or revocation of a will by a person who lacks the mental capacity to make a will is void. (See § 3.1, Comment *a*, for the definition of the term "will.") Because a testamentary power of appointment can only be exercised in a valid will, a person who lacks the mental capacity to make a will lacks the capacity to exercise a testamentary power of appointment.

d. Standard for mental capacity to make an irrevocable gift. Because an irrevocable gift depletes financial resources that the donor may yet need, the standard for mental capacity to make an irrevocable gift is higher than that for making a will. To have mental capacity to make an irrevocable inter vivos gift, the donor must have the mental capacity necessary to make or revoke a will and must also be capable of understanding the effect that the gift may have on the future financial security of the donor and of anyone who may be dependent on the donor. See Restatement Third, Trusts § 11, Comment *c*.

For purposes of this section and Comment, the term "gift" includes an inter vivos donative transfer of any kind, in trust or not, and also includes an exercise of a presently exercisable power of appointment.

e. Standard for mental capacity to make, revoke, or amend a revocable will substitute. The capacity requirement applicable to wills (see Comment *c*) applies to those will substitutes that are revocable and that serve to pass property to others at death while not depriving the owner of the benefit of the property during life. To the extent revocable, such will substitutes include inter vivos trusts and also include beneficiary designations in insurance policies, pension accounts, annuity contracts, securities registered in transfer on death (TOD) form, payable on death (POD) accounts, Totten Trusts, and joint-and-survivor bank and brokerage accounts. See § 7.1. Cf. Restatement Third, Trusts § 11, Comment *b*.

f. Burden of proof. The party contesting the validity of a donative transfer has the burden of persuasion in establishing that the donor lacked mental capacity to make the transfer. Section 3–407 of the Uniform Probate Code captures the prevailing view on the burden of proof and the view adopted in this Restatement:

> UPC Section 3–407. *[Formal Testacy Proceedings; Burdens in Contested Cases.]* . . . Contestants of a will have the burden of establishing lack of testamentary intent or capacity, undue influence, fraud, duress, mistake or revocation. Parties have the ultimate burden of persuasion as to matters with respect to which they have the initial burden of proof.

g. Effect of purported gift by person who lacks mental capacity to make a gift. A purported gift by a person who lacks the mental capacity to make a gift is voidable, not void. See Restatement Third, Restitution and Unjust Enrichment § 16. The principal consequence of treating such a purported gift as voidable rather than void relates to third-party rights (see Comment *j*).

Another consequence is that, in the unlikely event that the purported donor regains capacity, the purported donor may either disaffirm or ratify the gift. Such a disaffirmance or ratification amounts to a deferred, legally effective expression or rejection of donative intent. The failure to disaffirm within a reasonable time after regaining capacity constitutes ratification of the gift. If the purported donor dies without regaining capacity, the person who would succeed to the subject matter of the purported gift if it were disaffirmed may either disaffirm or ratify the gift. That person's failure to disaffirm within a reasonable time after the mentally incapacitated person's death constitutes a ratification of the gift. See Restatement Third, Trusts § 11, Comment *e*.

h. *Effect of adjudication of mental incapacity.* An adjudication of mental incapacity to manage property, which is usually accompanied by the appointment of an unlimited, full, or plenary conservator (called a guardian of the property in some states), raises a rebuttable presumption that the protected person lacks the capacity to make an irrevocable gift. A purported gift by such a person is void, not voidable, if the protected person lacks the capacity necessary for making an irrevocable gift at the time of the purported gift.

An adjudication of mental incapacity to manage property does not conclusively establish that the protected person subsequently lacked capacity to make, revoke, or amend a will or a revocable will substitute. Such an adjudication does, however, raise a rebuttable presumption that the protected person lacked the requisite capacity, shifting the burden of proof to the proponent to show that the protected person possessed the requisite capacity when taking the action in question.

i. *Mistakes in inter vivos gifts.* If a donor makes a mistake in perfecting an inter vivos gift or establishing a will substitute but believes that the gift has been perfected and subsequently becomes mentally incapacitated, there may be a remedy in the law of restitution and unjust enrichment. See § 6.1, Comment *o;* § 6.2, Comment *z;* § 6.3, Comment *p*.

j. *Third-party rights.* The distinction between void and voidable transfers is relevant principally to cases in which the immediate donee has subsequently transferred the property to a bona fide purchaser. If the initial transfer was voidable, a bona fide purchaser from the transferee takes good title. If the initial transfer was void, a bona fide purchaser from the transferee obtains no title. See Restatement Third, Restitution and Unjust Enrichment § 16, Comment *d*.

k. *Donative transfer by conservator.* If a conservator (called a guardian of the property in some states) of a mentally incapacitated person is appointed by a court, the actions of the conservator or guardian are subject to the supervision of the court. The court may authorize the conservator to make inter vivos donative transfers of the protected person's property that would be reasonable from a tax or estate-planning standpoint. Under § 5–427 of the Revised Uniform Probate Code (§ 427 of the Uniform Guardianship and Protective Proceedings Act), under certain conditions "a conservator for a protected person other than a minor may make gifts that the protected person might have been expected to make, in amounts that do not exceed in the aggregate for any calendar year 20 percent of the income of the estate in that year." . . . .

Courts have doubted that they have the power to authorize the conservator or guardian to make, amend, or revoke a will for the protected person unless a statute expressly authorizes that power. Such a power is now expressly authorized in § 5–411 of the Revised Uniform Probate Code (§ 411 of the Uniform Guardianship and Protective Proceedings Act). By contrast, the Original Uniform Probate Code § 5–407(b)(3) had expressly precluded the court from authorizing the execution of a will by the conservator for a protected person. . . . .

l. Donative transfer by agent under durable power of attorney. A person who is mentally competent may execute a durable power of attorney. A durable power of attorney continues to be effective after the principal becomes mentally incapacitated. The agent (attorney-in-fact) may make inter vivos donative transfers of the mentally incapacitated person's property to the extent allowed by the terms of the power of attorney. A power of attorney that does not expressly authorize the agent to make inter vivos donative transfers but does authorize the agent to perform any act that the principal might do if competent is ambiguous. In accordance with §§ 10.2 and 11.2, relevant extrinsic evidence may be considered in determining whether the power authorizes the agent to make such transfers. Among the extrinsic evidence that may be considered in resolving the ambiguity are the principal's history of making inter vivos donative transfers and the principal's relationships with the persons to whom those transfers were made. Unless authorized by statute, however, the power of attorney may not empower the agent to make a will for the mentally incapacitated person.

A durable power of attorney is not revoked by the death of the principal with respect to an agent who, without actual knowledge of the principal's death, acts in good faith under the power. Any action taken in good faith by an attorney-in-fact without knowledge of the principal's death binds the principal's successors in interest, unless the action so taken was otherwise invalid or unenforceable or a third party with whom the agent is dealing has actual knowledge of the principal's death. See Restatement Third, Agency § 3.11, Comment *b*. . . . .

m. Lucid interval. A person who is mentally incapacitated part of the time but who has lucid intervals during which he or she meets the standard for mental capacity (see Comments *c*, *d*, and *e*) can, in the absence of an adjudication or statute that has contrary effect, make a valid will or a valid inter vivos donative transfer, provided such will or transfer is made during a lucid interval.

Illustration:

6. G's daughter D contests the will of her father on the ground of mental incapacity. G had suffered from schizophrenia and had been in and out of mental hospitals for 20 years. G was on medication when executing the will. The will is valid if G, when executing the will, was experiencing a lucid interval during which he satisfied the standard for mental capacity for executing a will as set forth in Comment *c*.

n. Capacity to receive a donative transfer. Mental incapacity does not deprive a person from having capacity to acquire ownership of property by donative transfer. Thus, a mentally incapacitated person may receive property by will, intestate succession, or gift. A mentally incapacitated person may receive a donative transfer outright, in trust, or under a custodianship. A guardian or conservator may have to be appointed to administer property received by a mentally incapacitated person outright. On the power of a guardian or conservator to make a donative transfer for the ward, see Comment *h*. On guardianship in general, see § 2.3, Comment *h*.

o. Capacity to serve as a fiduciary. Although a mentally incapacitated person has capacity to take and hold property in trust or otherwise, a person who lacks mental capacity to contract or make a conveyance (see Restatement Second, Contracts §§ 12 to 15) cannot serve in a fiduciary capacity because such a person cannot properly fulfill the duties of a fiduciary. If a person who assumed a fiduciary office while mentally competent subsequently becomes mentally incapacitated, the person is subject to removal from the fiduciary office.

p. *Capacity to execute a power of attorney or serve as agent for another.* A person who lacks mental capacity to contract or make a conveyance (see Restatement Second, Contracts § 15) cannot execute a power of attorney that authorizes another to contract or make a conveyance on his or her behalf. Similarly, a person who lacks mental capacity to contract or make a conveyance cannot serve as agent for another because such a person cannot perform the functions of an agent. If a person who became an agent while mentally competent subsequently becomes mentally incapacitated, the person loses authority to continue serving as agent.

q. *Capacity to execute an advance health-care directive or serve as agent or surrogate under the Uniform Health-Care Decisions Act.* Under the Uniform Health-Care Decisions Act, an adult or emancipated minor may give an individual instruction (defined as "an individual's direction concerning a health-care decision for the individual"), execute a written power of attorney for health care (defined as "the designation of an agent to make health-care decisions for the individual granting the power"), or designate any individual to act as surrogate (defined as "an individual, other than a patient's agent or guardian, authorized under this [Act] to make a health-care decision for the patient"). See Unif. Health-Care Decisions Act §§ 1, 2, 5. Sections 2 and 5 of the Act make it clear that an adult or emancipated minor must have "capacity" to give an individual instruction, execute a written power of attorney for health care, or designate any individual to act as surrogate. For this purpose, "capacity" is defined in § 1 as "an individual's ability to understand the significant benefits, risks, and alternatives to proposed health care and to make and communicate a health-care decision." An individual who lacks capacity as so defined cannot serve as agent or surrogate to make health-care decisions for another or otherwise represent another in health-care matters.

r. *Capacity to witness a will.* On the capacity required in order to serve as a witness to a will, see § 3.1, Comment *o*.

s. *Insane delusion.* An insane delusion is a belief that is so against the evidence and reason that it must be the product of derangement. A belief resulting from a process of reasoning from existing facts is not an insane delusion, even though the reasoning is imperfect or the conclusion illogical. Mere eccentricity does not constitute an insane delusion.

A person who suffers from an insane delusion is not necessarily deprived of capacity to make a donative transfer. A particular donative transfer is invalid, however, to the extent that it was the product of an insane delusion.

§ 8.2. Incapacity Due to Minority

(a) A minor does not have capacity to make a will. A purported will made by a minor is void.

(b) A minor does not have capacity to make a gift. A purported gift made by a minor is voidable, not void. Before reaching majority, the minor may disaffirm the gift. After reaching majority, the minor may either disaffirm or ratify the gift. The failure to disaffirm within

a reasonable time after reaching majority constitutes a ratification of the gift.

(c) For purposes of this section, a "minor" is a person who has not reached the age of majority or the age of capacity for the purpose in question and who is not emancipated. The age of majority is 18, unless an applicable statute provides otherwise.

Comment:

a. *Scope.* This section addresses a minor's capacity to make a donative transfer. Comments *e, f, g,* and *h* address related matters, such as capacity to receive a donative transfer and to serve in a fiduciary capacity. This section and its Comments do not address other matters affected by minority, such as a minor's capacity to enter into a contract (see Restatement Second, Contracts § 14), sue or be sued, enter into marriage, vote, purchase liquor, or obtain a driver's license. Nor does it address family-law matters such as parental control or parental support.

This section applies to all donative transfers, whether inter vivos or testamentary.

b. *Age of majority.* A minor is a person who has not yet reached the age of majority or the age of capacity for the purpose in question. At common law, the age of majority was 21. Today, for most purposes in most states, statutes have lowered the age of majority to 18. The position of this Restatement is that the age of majority is 18, unless an applicable statute provides otherwise.

The age of majority is an uneven matter in many states. Although some states have a general statute specifying the age of majority for all purposes, many states do not. Instead, state statutes define adulthood or the age of capacity for purposes of that statute, and the age of adulthood or capacity is not necessarily the same in each particular statute.

Unless otherwise noted, the term "minor" as used in this section and commentary refers to a minor who is not emancipated. (An emancipated minor is treated as an adult for many purposes. See Comment *i.*)

c. *Capacity to make a will.* A minor does not have capacity to make a will. A purported will made by a minor is void. Since a minor lacks the capacity to make a will, a minor lacks the capacity to exercise a testamentary power of appointment.

In implementing this principle, the will statutes seldom use the term "minor." Instead, they state that a person must have reached a specified age, usually age 18, to make a valid will. The UPC, for example, provides that "[a]n individual 18 or more years of age who is of sound mind may make a will." Revised UPC § 2–501; Original UPC § 2–501 (similarly worded).

d. *Capacity to make a gift.* In the absence of a statute specifying a general age of majority for all purposes or for the specific purpose of making a gift, the age required to enter into a contract controls the age of majority for making a gift in a particular state.

Although a minor does not have capacity to make a gift, a purported gift by a minor is voidable, not void. Before reaching majority, the minor may disaffirm the gift. After reaching majority, the minor may either disaffirm or ratify the gift. The failure to disaffirm within a reasonable time after reaching majority constitutes ratification of the gift. If the minor dies before reaching majority, the person who would succeed to the subject matter of the purported gift if it were disaffirmed may either disaffirm or ratify the gift. That person's failure to disaffirm within a reasonable time after the minor's death constitutes a ratification of the gift.

For purposes of this section and Comment, the term "gift" includes an inter vivos donative transfer of any kind, in trust or not, and also includes an exercise of a presently exercisable power of appointment.

e. Capacity to receive a donative transfer. A minor has capacity to acquire ownership of property by donative transfer. Thus, a minor may receive property by will, intestate succession, or gift. A minor may receive a donative transfer outright, in trust, or under a custodianship. A guardian may have to be appointed to manage property received by a minor outright. On guardianship, see § 2.3, Comment *h*.

f. Capacity to serve as a fiduciary or agent. Although a minor has capacity to take and hold property in trust, a minor cannot serve as trustee. Being able only to enter into voidable contracts or make voidable conveyances (see Restatement Second, Contracts §§ 12–15), a minor cannot properly administer a trust. Thus, a court should ordinarily remove a minor trustee and appoint a substitute trustee to serve, at least until the minor comes of age. See Restatement Second, Trusts §§ 91, 109 [Restatement Third, Trusts § 32, Comment *c*].

A minor does not have the capacity to serve as personal representative of an estate under the Uniform Probate Code. See UPC § 3–203(f)(1).

A minor cannot be a custodian under the Uniform Transfers to Minors Act or a custodial trustee under the Uniform Custodial Trust Act. See Unif. Transfers to Minors Act § 9 ("adult" defined as "an individual who has attained the age of 21 years"); Unif. Custodial Trust Act §§ 5, 18 ("adult" defined as "an individual who is at least 18 years of age").

A minor is not expressly prohibited from being a guardian or a conservator for a minor or incapacitated person under the Uniform Guardianship and Protective Proceeding Act. See Unif. Guardianship and Protective Proceeding Act §§ 201, 202, 301, 302, 309, 413. Section 413 provides that, in appointing a conservator, the court shall consider persons "otherwise qualified" in a specified order of priority. Since the duty of a conservator is to manage the assets of the protected person (see id. § 418), the requirement that the appointee be "otherwise qualified" should be interpreted to preclude the appointment of a minor as conservator.

Although the Uniform Durable Power of Attorney Act does not expressly prohibit a minor from executing or from being designated as an agent under a durable power of attorney, the purpose of a durable power is that it not be affected if the principal subsequently becomes incapacitated. See Unif. Durable Power of Attorney Act § 1. By implication, a person who is incapacitated by reason of minority lacks capacity to execute a durable power and also lacks capacity to serve as an agent under a durable power.

g. Capacity to execute an advance health-care directive. Under the Uniform Health-Care Decisions Act, an adult or emancipated minor may give an individual instruction (defined as "an individual's direction concerning a health-care decision for the individual"), execute a written power of attorney for health care (defined as "the designation of an agent to make health-care decisions for the individual granting the power"), or designate any individual to act as surrogate (defined as "an individual, other than a patient's agent or guardian, authorized under this [Act] to make a health-care decision for the patient"). See Unif. Health-Care Decisions Act §§ 1, 2, 5 (the Act does not define the term "adult" or "emancipated minor").

If no agent or guardian has been appointed or if the appointed agent or guardian is not reasonably available, and if the adult or emancipated minor has not designated a surrogate, "any member of the following classes of the patient's family who is reasonably available, in descending order of priority, may act as surrogate: (1) the spouse, unless legally separated; (2) an adult child; (3) a parent; or (4) an adult brother or sister." Unif. Health-Care Decisions Act § 5.

h. Capacity to witness a will. A minor is not usually disqualified from serving as an attesting witness to a will, although a few states specifically provide by statute a minimum age, such as 18, for attesting witnesses. More commonly, however, no age is specified in the statute. If no age is specified in the statute, a minor is a valid witness, unless the minor was not old enough to observe, remember, and relate the facts occurring at the execution ceremony. See § 3.1, Comment *o*.

i. Emancipated minor. An emancipated minor is treated as an adult for many purposes. An emancipated minor has capacity to acquire ownership of property by donative transfer. If, under state law, an emancipated minor has capacity to enter into contracts and make conveyances, such a minor can serve in various fiduciary capacities.

The law regarding emancipation is not uniform throughout the United States nor well-developed in many states. A comprehensive California statute provides that an emancipated minor is a person under the age of majority who is or has been married, who is on active duty with the armed forces of the United States, or for whom a judicial declaration of emancipation has been issued. See Cal. Fam. Code § 7002. A judicial declaration of emancipation may be issued if the minor is at least 14 years of age; the minor willingly lives separate and apart from the minor's parents or guardian with the consent or acquiescence of the minor's parents or guardian; the minor is managing his or her own financial affairs; and the source of the minor's income is not derived from any activity declared to be a crime by the laws of this state or the laws of the United States. See Cal. Fam. Code § 7120.

The California statute provides, insofar as relevant to the field of donative transfers, that an emancipated minor is considered an adult for the purposes of the minor's capacity to consent to medical, dental, or psychiatric care, without parental consent, knowledge, or liability; give a delegation of power; make or revoke a will; make a gift, outright or in trust; convey or release contingent or expectant interests in property, including marital property rights and any right of survivorship incident to joint tenancy, and consent to a transfer, encumbrance, or gift of marital property; exercise or release the minor's powers as donee of a power of appointment unless the creating instrument otherwise provides; create for the minor's own benefit or for the benefit of others a revocable or irrevocable trust; revoke a revocable trust; elect to take under or against a will; renounce or disclaim any interest acquired by testate or intestate succession or by inter vivos transfer, including exercise of the right to surrender the right to revoke a revocable trust; and make certain elections pertaining to community property. See Cal. Fam. Code § 7050.

Part B. Protection Against Wrongdoing

§ 8.3. Undue Influence, Duress, or Fraud

(a) A donative transfer is invalid to the extent that it was procured by undue influence, duress, or fraud.

(b) A donative transfer is procured by undue influence if the wrongdoer exerted such influence over the donor that it overcame the donor's free will and caused the donor to make a donative transfer that the donor would not otherwise have made.

(c) A donative transfer is procured by duress if the wrongdoer threatened to perform or did perform a wrongful act that coerced the donor into making a donative transfer that the donor would not otherwise have made.

(d) A donative transfer is procured by fraud if the wrongdoer knowingly or recklessly made a false representation to the donor about a material fact that was intended to and did lead the donor to make a donative transfer that the donor would not otherwise have made.

General Comment:

a. Scope. This section applies to all donative transfers, whether inter vivos or testamentary.

References in this section to the term "donative transfer" include not only the initial making of a donative transfer but also the revocation or amendment of a donative transfer that was previously made.

b. Burden of proof. The burden of establishing undue influence, duress, or fraud (referred to herein as the "wrong") is on the party contesting the validity of a donative transfer. In some circumstances, the contestant's case may be aided by a presumption of invalidity. See Comment *f*.

c. The wrongdoer. Typically, the wrongdoer procures a donative transfer for himself or herself. Sometimes, however, the wrongdoer procures the donative transfer for the benefit of another, such as a member of the wrongdoer's family. In such a case, the donative transfer is invalid whether or not the beneficiary of the wrong acquiesced in the wrong or even knew that the wrong was committed.

d. Effect of undue influence, duress, or fraud. Ordinarily, only the donative transfer that was procured by undue influence, duress, or fraud is invalid. Thus, if a devise in a will was procured by one of these wrongful acts, only that devise, not the entire will, is ordinarily invalid. The court may, however, hold the entire will invalid if it determines that complete invalidity would better carry out the testator's intent.

Illustrations:

1. G's will devised $100,000 to X and devised the residue of his estate to Y. X was found to have exerted undue influence on G. The $100,000 devise is invalid and passes to Y under the residuary clause in G's will.

2. G's first will devised $100,000 to a named charity and devised the residue of her estate to Y. Subsequently, G executed a second will that devised $25,000 to the named charity, $175,000 to X, and the residue of her estate to Y. X was found to have exerted undue influence

on G with respect to the second will. If only the $175,000 devise to X were held invalid, the $175,000 would pass to Y under the residuary clause and the named charity would only receive $25,000. The court would be justified in holding that the second will is invalid in its entirety, allowing G's estate to pass under G's first will.

Comment on Subsection (b)—Undue Influence:

e. Undue influence. The doctrine of undue influence protects against overreaching by a wrongdoer seeking to take unfair advantage of a donor who is susceptible to such wrongdoing on account of the donor's age, inexperience, dependence, physical or mental weakness, or other factor. A donative transfer is procured by undue influence if the influence exerted over the donor overcame the donor's free will and caused the donor to make a donative transfer that the donor would not otherwise have made. The alleged wrongdoer need not be present when the donative document was executed in order to exert undue influence. Direct evidence of the wrongdoer's conduct and the donor's subservience is rarely available to establish the actual exertion of undue influence. The contestant's case must usually be based on circumstantial evidence, and in certain cases, is aided by a presumption of undue influence. See Comment *f*.

In the absence of direct evidence of undue influence, circumstantial evidence is sufficient to raise an inference of undue influence if the contestant proves that (1) the donor was susceptible to undue influence, (2) the alleged wrongdoer had an opportunity to exert undue influence, (3) the alleged wrongdoer had a disposition to exert undue influence, and (4) there was a result appearing to be the effect of the undue influence.

f. Presumption of undue influence. A presumption of undue influence arises if the alleged wrongdoer was in a confidential relationship with the donor and there were suspicious circumstances surrounding the preparation, formulation, or execution of the donative transfer, whether the transfer was by gift, trust, will, will substitute, or a donative transfer of any other type. The effect of the presumption is to shift to the proponent the burden of going forward with the evidence, not the burden of persuasion. The presumption justifies a judgment for the contestant as a matter of law only if the proponent does not come forward with evidence to rebut the presumption. See Comment *g* for what constitutes a confidential relationship, and see Comment *h* for what constitutes suspicious circumstances surrounding the preparation, formulation, or execution of the donative transfer.

The presumption is strengthened if the beneficiary of the alleged wrongdoing was not a natural object of the testator's bounty (for discussion of the term "natural object of the testator's bounty," see § 8.1, Comment *c*). Because generous donative transfers to the donor's spouse or surviving spouse are not unnatural, such transfers are rarely the result of undue influence. Under § 8.1, Comment *c*, a testator's domestic partner as defined in § 6.03 of the [American Law Institute's] Principles of the Law of Family Dissolution: Analysis and Recommendations is as much a natural object of the testator's bounty as a donor's spouse. So also is the donor's unmarried partner under any other relationship entitling that person to intestacy rights under applicable law, such as a civil-union relationship or a relationship based on the partners' signed reciprocal beneficiary designation. A testator's decision to leave a substantial devise or even the bulk or all of his or her estate to his or her unmarried partner is not a basis for invalidating a will on the ground of undue influence. A dispositive plan favoring either spouse or partner is not considered unnatural. Thus, to invalidate such a plan on the ground of undue influence requires strong evidence that the will was not the result of the testator's free and independent judgment.

A will or other donative transfer that favors persons who are in a confidential relationship but who are not natural objects of a testator's bounty is not necessarily unnatural when considered in the light of all the surrounding circumstances. For example, when all the circumstances are considered, it might be natural for someone to make a relatively small donative transfer to a hired caregiver.

Some courts have held that in the case of an irrevocable inter vivos donative transfer, a presumption of undue influence arises merely from the existence of a confidential relationship with the donor. This Restatement rejects this position in favor of the position adopted by other courts that such a presumption only arises if, in addition to the confidential relationship, there are suspicious circumstances surrounding the preparation, formulation, or execution of the donative transfer.

g. Confidential relationship—fiduciary, reliant, or dominant-subservient. Traditionally, the single term "confidential relationship" has been used to describe a relationship that gives rise to a presumption of undue influence if coupled with suspicious circumstances. When examined more closely, the term "confidential relationship" embraces three sometimes distinct relationships—fiduciary, reliant, or dominant-subservient. For purposes of clarity, this Restatement refers to these relationships separately, although any one of them can be called "confidential" and give rise to a presumption of undue influence.

A fiduciary relationship is one in which the confidential relationship arises from a settled category of fiduciary obligation. Some fiduciary relationships are between the donor and a hired professional. For example, an attorney is in a fiduciary relationship with his or her client, an institutional trustee is in a fiduciary relationship with the beneficiaries of the trust, and an institutional guardian or conservator is in a fiduciary relationship with his or her ward or protected person. Other fiduciary relationships are not necessarily between the donor and a hired professional. For example, an agent under a power of attorney is in a fiduciary relationship with his or her principal, but the donor's agent under a power of attorney frequently is a close family member or trusted friend who receives no fee for acting as agent. So also an individual trustee, guardian, or conservator might be a close family member or a trusted friend who might not receive a fee for acting in that capacity.

Whether a reliant relationship exists is a question of fact. The contestant must establish that there was a relationship based on special trust and confidence, for example, that the donor was accustomed to be guided by the judgment or advice of the alleged wrongdoer or was justified in placing confidence in the belief that the alleged wrongdoer would act in the interest of the donor. Examples might include the relationship between a financial adviser and customer or between a doctor and patient.

Whether a dominant-subservient relationship exists is a question of fact. The contestant must establish that the donor was subservient to the alleged wrongdoer's dominant influence. Such a relationship might exist between a hired caregiver and an ill or feeble donor or between an adult child and an ill or feeble parent.

In a particular case, these three relationships might overlap. That is, the alleged wrongdoer might be in a fiduciary, reliant, and dominant-subservient relationship with the donor. In another case, however, the relationships might not overlap. For example, an ill or feeble donor might be suspicious of the motives of a hired caregiver, but still be in a subservient relationship with that person, feeling that "I must do what he or she says."

h. Suspicious circumstances. The existence of a confidential relationship is not sufficient to raise a presumption of undue influence. There must also be suspicious circumstances surrounding the preparation, execution, or formulation of the donative transfer. Suspicious circumstances raise an inference of an abuse of the confidential relationship between the alleged wrongdoer and the donor.

In evaluating whether suspicious circumstances are present, all relevant factors may be considered, including: (1) the extent to which the donor was in a weakened condition, physically, mentally, or both, and therefore susceptible to undue influence; (2) the extent to which the alleged wrongdoer participated in the preparation or procurement of the will or will substitute; (3) whether the donor received independent advice from an attorney or from other competent and disinterested advisors in preparing the will or will substitute; (4) whether the will or will substitute was prepared in secrecy or in haste; (5) whether the donor's attitude toward others had changed by reason of his or her relationship with the alleged wrongdoer; (6) whether there is a decided discrepancy between a new and previous wills or will substitutes of the donor; (7) whether there was a continuity of purpose running through former wills or will substitutes indicating a settled intent in the disposition of his or her property; and (8) whether the disposition of the property is such that a reasonable person would regard it as unnatural, unjust, or unfair, for example, whether the disposition abruptly and without apparent reason disinherited a faithful and deserving family member.

Illustration:

3. G, an elderly and enfeebled widower, transferred a substantial portion of his assets into a revocable trust prepared by his attorney, X. Under the terms of the trust, G was to receive the income for life, and at his death, the corpus was to be paid to X. X, as G's attorney, was in a confidential relationship with G. There were suspicious circumstances surrounding the preparation, formulation, or execution of the revocable trust because X drafted the revocable trust and X was not a natural object of G's bounty. These factors justify shifting the burden of proof to X to come forward with evidence that G was free from undue influence when he executed the revocable trust.

A testator's decision to leave a substantial devise or even the bulk or all of his or her estate to voluntary caregivers—relatives or other persons voluntarily caring for the testator—is not a basis for invalidating a will, in the absence of suspicious circumstances tending to show that the will was not the testator's free and independent decision.

Illustration:

5. G, a widow, became seriously ill and could not take care of everyday physical needs such as bathing and dressing. G had a daughter, A, whom she had not seen for 25 years. When contacted about her mother's illness, she refused to help. G's sister, X, and her husband, Y, took G into their house and cared for her during the last year-and-a-half of her life. Two months before her death, G requested Y, who was an attorney, to prepare a will for her that would devise all of her estate to her sister, X (Y's wife). Y told G that he could not prepare the will, but

that he would find another attorney for her. Y put G into contact with an attorney in another firm who specialized in trusts and estates. The attorney met with G privately and subsequently prepared a will for G that devised her estate to X. Although it could be concluded that X was in a confidential relationship with G, the second element necessary to shift the burden of proof—suspicious circumstances surrounding the formulation of the will—is lacking. Although Y put G in touch with the drafting attorney, Y's behavior was appropriate in the circumstances and does not establish a suspicious circumstance, nor is the disposition of G's property in the will unnatural. Indeed, it is natural to disinherit a child who refused to help a parent when ill and in need and to prefer instead a relative who did provide the needed care.

Comment on Subsection (c)—Duress:

i. Duress. A donative transfer is procured by duress if the wrongdoer threatened to perform or did perform a wrongful act that coerced the donor into making a donative transfer that the donor would not otherwise have made. An act is wrongful if it is criminal or one that the wrongdoer had no right to do. See Restatement Second, Contracts §§ 174–176. Although an act or a threat to do an act that the wrongdoer had a right to do does not constitute duress, such a threat or act can constitute undue influence, for example, a threat to abandon an ill testator.

Comment on Subsection (d)—Fraud:

j. Fraud. A donative transfer is procured by fraud if the wrongdoer knowingly or recklessly made a false representation to the donor about a material fact that was intended to and did lead the donor to make a donative transfer that the donor would not otherwise have made.

Failure to disclose a material fact does not constitute fraud unless the alleged wrongdoer was in a confidential relationship with the donor.

Illustration:

6. G's doctor agreed to provide support for G for his remaining life in return for G's promise to execute a will devising his entire estate to the doctor. The doctor knew but failed to disclose to G that G only had a short time to live. Because G's doctor was in a confidential relationship with G, the doctor's failure to disclose a material fact constitutes fraud. G's will devising his entire estate to the doctor is invalid.

k. Innocent or negligent misrepresentation. An innocent or negligent misrepresentation is not fraud. To constitute fraud, the wrongdoer must knowingly or recklessly make a false representation about a material fact. An innocent or negligent misrepresentation regarding a material fact can, however, lead the donor to make a donative transfer that the donor would not otherwise have made. In such a case, the donative transfer has been induced by mistake, and should be remedied accordingly. See § 6.1, Comment *o*; § 6.2, Comment *z*; § 6.3, Comment *p*; § 12.1 and Comments *f* and *i*.

l. Remedy for wrongful interference in law of restitution and unjust enrichment. Although a donative transfer that is procured by a wrongful act such as undue influence, duress, or fraud is invalid, other forms of wrongdoing have effects that cannot be remedied simply by invalidating a transfer. For example, wrongdoing that prevents the making of a will or other donative transfer, or that prevents a revocation or modification of a will or other donative transfer, gives rise to a claim in restitution for the purpose of preventing unjust enrichment, as measured in light of the donor's frustrated intentions. See Restatement of Restitution § 184, Comments *f* and *i* [Restatement Third, Restitution and Unjust Enrichment §§ 46, 55]. An appropriate remedy in such cases is typically the imposition of a constructive trust.

Illustration:

10. G, who was ill in bed, desired to revoke his will. He asked his nephew, N, to get his will from his desk, bring it back to the bedroom, and tear it up. N left the room and returned with an envelope in his hand, which he told G contained the will. In G's presence and at his direction, N tore the envelope up and threw the pieces into a waste basket. After G's death, it was discovered that G's will had not been torn up. Although G had the intent to revoke, the will was not revoked because no physical act had been performed on the document. See § 4.1, Comments *g* and *l*. The harmless-error rule might apply to give effect to the revocation. See § 4.1, Comment *a*; § 3.3, Comment *c*. If not, a constructive trust is imposed on the devisees of G's will in favor of those who would have succeeded to G's estate if the will had been revoked.

m. Remedy in tort for intentional interference with a gift or an inheritance. One who by fraud, duress, or other tortious means intentionally prevents another from receiving from a third person an inheritance or gift that he or she would otherwise have received is subject to liability to the other for loss of the inheritance or gift. See Restatement Second, Torts § 774B.

n. Cross-reference—Lawyer drafting donative document benefiting lawyer. The position of the Institute on the ethical considerations of a lawyer preparing a donative document that benefits the lawyer is set forth in Restatement Third, The Law Governing Lawyers § 127, as follows:

§ 127. A Client Gift to a Lawyer

(1) A lawyer may not prepare any instrument effecting any gift from a client to the lawyer, including a testamentary gift, unless the lawyer is a relative or other natural object of the client's generosity and the gift is not significantly disproportionate to those given other donees similarly related to the donor.

(2) A lawyer may not accept a gift from a client, including a testamentary gift, unless:

(a) the lawyer is a relative or other natural object of the client's generosity;

(b) the value conferred by the client and the benefit to the lawyer are insubstantial in amount; or

(c) the client, before making the gift, has received independent advice or has been encouraged, and given a reasonable opportunity, to seek such advice.

o. Forgery. Although not specifically addressed in the black letter of this section, forgery is another wrong that is a ground of contest. If the donor's signature on a donative document was forged, the document is not valid because the document was not signed by the donor. See § 3.1, Comment *j*; § 6.3, Comment *c*. If what purports to be the testator's handwriting on a holographic will was forged, the holographic will is not valid because the handwritten portion of the document was not in the testator's handwriting. See § 3.2, Comment *b*. Like the other grounds of contest, the burden of establishing the wrong (the forgery, in this case) is on the party contesting the validity of the donative transfer. See Comment *b*.

Note, however, that the testator's signature on a will would not be regarded as forged if the testator directed another person to sign the testator's name and if the other person acted in the testator's presence. See § 3.1, Comment *n*.

§ 8.4. Homicide—the Slayer Rule

(a) A slayer is denied any right to benefit from the wrong. For purposes of this section, a slayer is a person who, without legal excuse or justification, is responsible for the felonious and intentional killing of another.

(b) Whether or not a person is a slayer is determined in a civil proceeding under the preponderance of the evidence standard rather than beyond a reasonable doubt. For purposes of the civil proceeding, however, a final judgment of conviction for the felonious and intentional killing of the decedent in a criminal proceeding conclusively establishes the convicted person as the decedent's slayer.

Comment:

a. *Slayer rule.* The principle of this section is that a person who, without legal excuse or justification, is responsible for the felonious and intentional killing of the decedent (referred to herein as the "slayer") is denied any right to benefit from the wrong. This principle, known as the *slayer rule*, is a rule of the civil or private law, not a rule of criminal law.

The slayer rule occupies an important but limited place in the law. The slayer rule is not punitive, that being the function of the criminal law. Nor is it compensatory, that being the function of tort law in an action for wrongful death (see Comment *q*). Thus, the slayer rule does not cause the killer to forfeit any of his or her own property (see Comment *o*), but prevents the killer from benefiting from the wrong that he or she has committed.

b. *Rationale.* The rationale for the slayer rule is the prevention of unjust enrichment, in accord with the maxim that a wrongdoer cannot profit from his or her wrong. Any enrichment accruing to a slayer from the wrong is unjust and is not allowed. The slayer's motive in committing the wrong is irrelevant. Application of the slayer rule does not depend on a showing that the motive for the slaying was to obtain a financial benefit.

c. *Scope of the slayer rule.* The slayer rule is not limited to cases in which the property would have gone to another if the slayer had not committed the wrong. The rule also applies to cases in which the property probably would have gone to the slayer eventually.

The slayer rule is not limited to donative transfers from the victim. By interfering with the order of deaths, a slaying causes the victim to die before he or she would have died in the natural course of events. Accordingly, the slayer is not allowed to benefit from the victim's premature death whether or not the victim was the donor. For example, if the remainder beneficiary of a trust is responsible for the felonious and intentional killing of the income beneficiary, the slayer is denied the right to immediate possession of the corpus. . . .

d. Conviction in criminal proceeding establishes convicted person as slayer. The question of whether a person is responsible for the felonious and intentional killing of the decedent is determined in a civil proceeding under the preponderance of the evidence standard. The criminal law standard of proof of beyond a reasonable doubt is inapplicable because the slayer's life or liberty is not at risk in the civil proceeding.

Because a final conviction in the criminal proceeding satisfied the higher standard of proof, a final judgment of conviction establishing criminal responsibility for the felonious and intentional killing of the decedent, such as a conviction for murder, conclusively establishes the convicted person as the decedent's slayer for purposes of the civil proceeding. There is no need to retry the matter under a lower standard of proof in the civil proceeding. See Restatement Second, Judgments § 85(2)(a). A judgment of conviction is considered final after all right of appeal has been exhausted. A prisoner's right to petition for habeas corpus does not mean that a judgment of conviction has not become final, however, for otherwise a judgment of conviction might never become final.

e. Final judgment of conviction in criminal proceeding not necessary. The absence of a final judgment of conviction establishing a person as a slayer for purposes of this section (see Comment *d*) does not preclude the court in a civil proceeding from determining that a person is responsible for the felonious and intentional killing of the decedent. Whether or not a person is responsible for the felonious and intentional killing of the decedent is determined in a civil proceeding under the preponderance of the evidence standard rather than beyond a reasonable doubt. Thus, an acquittal in a criminal proceeding or a conviction that has not become final does not prevent the civil proceeding from going forward under the preponderance of the evidence standard. Nor does a conviction or a guilty or a no-contest plea to a lesser offense. The slayer rule may apply even though the wrongdoer was never tried in a criminal proceeding. The wrongdoer might not have been tried in a criminal proceeding for a variety of reasons, including the prosecutor's decision not to file charges, a grand jury's decision not to indict, or the wrongdoer's absence or immunity from prosecution, such as in the not uncommon situation in which the wrongdoer commits suicide after killing the victim.

f. Felonious and intentional killing. If the alleged wrongdoer was convicted of a crime in a criminal proceeding, the question in the civil proceeding is whether the conviction conclusively establishes the convicted person as a slayer for purposes of the slayer rule. See Comment *d*. In the absence of such a conviction, the question in the civil proceeding is whether the person is responsible for the felonious and intentional killing of another, without legal excuse or justification. The terms "felonious" and "intentional" should be defined in light of the public policy to which the slayer rule is directed—to prevent the wrongdoer from profiting from the wrong.

The term "felonious" refers to criminal offenses that are felonies. The Model Penal Code § 1.04(2) provides that "[a] crime is a felony if it is so designated in this Code or if persons convicted thereof may be sentenced [to death or] to imprisonment for a term that, apart from an extended term, is in excess of one year."

An offense punishable by death is a felony. An offense punishable by a term of imprisonment for more than one year is classified as a felony in the federal criminal-justice system and in the criminal-justice system of about half of the states. An offense punishable by imprisonment in a state penitentiary (as opposed to a fine or incarceration in a jail) is classified as a felony in most of the remaining states. The two definitions tend to converge because an offense punishable in a state penitentiary is almost always an offense punishable by a term of imprisonment for more than one year.

The term "felonious" refers to the offense, not to whether the alleged offender is prosecutable for a felony in a criminal proceeding. For example, in the case of a murder-suicide, the alleged offender who committed suicide is not prosecutable in a criminal proceeding for the felony. Another example is that of a juvenile who in some states is not prosecutable for a felony. The question in such cases is not whether the alleged offender is prosecutable but whether the offense is a felony.

The killing must not only be felonious but must also be intentional. A person is responsible for the "intentional" killing of another if the person acted with an intent to kill. The intent to kill need not be premeditated. The term "intentional" is not confined to consequences that the actor has the purpose of producing, but includes consequences that the actor knows to a substantial certainty will ensue from the actor's conduct. See Restatement Third, Torts: [Liability for Physical and Emotional Harm] § 1.

The slayer rule does not apply if the killing was reckless, accidental, or negligent. A killing is reckless when the actor knows of the risk of harm created by the conduct or knows facts that make that risk obvious to a reasonable person in that situation, and the precaution that would eliminate or reduce the risk involves burdens that are so slight relative to the magnitude of the risk as to render the failure to adopt the precaution a demonstration of indifference to the risk. See Restatement Third, Torts: [Liability for Physical and Emotional Harm] § 2. A killing is negligent when the actor does not exercise reasonable care under all the circumstances. See Restatement Third, Torts: [Liability for Physical and Emotional Harm] § 3; Model Penal Code § 2.02(2)(d).

g. Principal, accomplice, co-conspirator, or accessory before the fact. To be responsible for the felonious and intentional killing of another, the wrongdoer need not be a principal in the first or second degree. An accomplice, co-conspirator, or accessory before the fact can share responsibility for the felonious and intentional killing of another.

h. Without legal excuse or justification. A person is not a slayer for purposes of this section if the person acted with legal excuse or justification. Thus, all the defenses available in a criminal proceeding, including self defense and incapacity due to mental illness or infancy, are also available under the slayer rule in the civil proceeding.

i. Statutory coverage. When the slayer rule is codified, as it is in most states . . ., it prevents the slayer from succeeding to the property or other benefit as provided by the statute. The slayer rule as enunciated in this section applies in the absence of a more specific statute. If a statute covers some but not all of the situations in which a killer stands to benefit from the wrong as provided in this section, the slayer rule as enunciated in this section applies to the situations not covered by the statute.

j. Denial of statutory benefits arising from victim's death. The victim's slayer is denied all statutory benefits with respect to the victim's estate, including any intestate share, elective share, omitted spouse's or child's share, homestead allowance, exempt property, and family allowance. For purposes of these statutory rules, the victim's intestate estate passes and is administered as if the slayer predeceased the victim.

k. *Benefits under victim's donative documents.* The slayer is denied any revocable disposition or appointment of property made by the victim to the slayer in a donative document. The slayer is also denied any revocable provision in the victim's donative document conferring a general or a nongeneral power of appointment on the slayer and also any revocable nomination by the victim of the slayer to serve in any fiduciary or any representative capacity, including as personal representative, executor, trustee, or agent.

Provisions of the victim's donative documents are given effect as if the slayer predeceased the victim, triggering application of antilapse doctrines in appropriate cases. See §§ 5.5; 7.2, Comment *f.* In the case of a denied nomination in a fiduciary or representative capacity, provisions of the victim's donative documents are given effect as if the slayer predeceased the victim, but without application of antilapse doctrines. . . . .

l. *Joint tenancy and tenancy by the entirety.* If the slayer and victim owned property in joint tenancy with the right of survivorship or in tenancy by the entirety, the slayer cannot succeed to the victim's fractional share by survivorship. The Institute substantially reaffirms the view that was adopted in the Restatement of Restitution § 188 [Restatement Third, Restitution and Unjust Enrichment § 45], under which the slayer retains only the right to half of the income from the property for life. The position of the Institute is that, except where a different result is dictated by statute, the decision to treat a felonious killing as effecting a severance of a joint tenancy or a tenancy by the entirety requires an equitable justification. Such a justification may be present, for example, when the predominant consequence of a judicially-decreed severance is to adjust the rights of innocent parties. By contrast, if the predominant consequence of a judicially-decreed severance would be to benefit the slayer at the expense of the estate of the victim, treating the slayer as having accomplished by felony what the slayer did not accomplish lawfully, a decree giving homicide the effect of severance is presumptively inappropriate. The question whether there may be circumstances in which this presumption may be rebutted is deferred to Restatement Third, Restitution and Unjust Enrichment.

m. *Other wrongful acquisition of property.* As noted in Comment *b*, the slayer rule is not limited to forfeiture of donative transfers from the victim. The felonious and intentional killing of the decedent interferes with the order of deaths, causing the victim to die before he or she would have died in the natural course of events. The slayer is not allowed to profit from the victim's premature death whether or not the victim was the donor.

Illustrations:

6. *Indefeasibly vested remainder beneficiary kills life tenant.* K had an indefeasibly vested remainder in an irrevocable trust created by G. K killed the income beneficiary, V. Because K forfeits any right to benefit from his wrong, K is not entitled to the full value of the corpus. V's estate is entitled to an amount equal to the present value of the income interest for V's remaining life expectancy. K receives the remaining corpus, which is the present value of the remainder interest determined actuarially. See Restatement of Restitution § 188, Comment *c* [Restatement Third, Restitution and Unjust Enrichment § 45, Comment *g*].

7. *Contingent remainder beneficiary kills life tenant.* The facts are the same as those in Illustration 6, except that K's remainder was contingent on survival of V, with an alternative contingent remainder to

C if K fails to survive V. As in Illustration 6, V's estate is entitled to an amount equal to the present value of the income interest for V's remaining life expectancy. Unlike the result in Illustration 6, however, K is not entitled to the remaining corpus. K's interference with the order of deaths causes the uncertainty whether K would have survived V to be resolved against K. C is therefore entitled to the remaining corpus. The same result would be reached if C's remainder was also contingent on surviving V. See Restatement of Restitution § 188, Comment *c* [Restatement Third, Restitution and Unjust Enrichment § 45, Comment *g*].

n. *Mercy killing—assisted suicide.* The question of whether the slayer rule applies in cases of mercy killing and assisted suicide has not yet come before the courts, though it has been discussed in the scholarly literature. The question is whether the killer's benign motive, and the victim's request and participation where present, undercut the application of the principle of preventing unjust enrichment that otherwise requires application of the slayer rule.

o. *Slayer's own property not forfeited.* The slayer rule does not cause the forfeiture of any of the slayer's own property.

Illustrations:

8. *Tenant in common kills other tenant in common.* K and V owned property in tenancy in common. K feloniously and intentionally killed V. K does not forfeit her undivided half interest in the tenancy in common property.

10. *Life tenant kills remainder beneficiary.* K was the income beneficiary of an irrevocable trust. Upon K's death, the remainder was to go to V. K feloniously and intentionally killed V. K does not forfeit her income interest.

The principle that the slayer rule does not cause the forfeiture of any of the slayer's own property applies to property that the victim irrevocably gave to the slayer before the killing. Thus, if V irrevocably gave $10,000 to K and if K later feloniously and intentionally killed V, K does not forfeit the $10,000 gift. . . . .

Although the slayer rule does not cause the forfeiture of any of the slayer's own property, the slayer might be liable in a wrongful-death action. See Comment *q*.

p. *Principle of this section broadly applicable.* The slayer rule is a principle directed to the prevention of unjust enrichment. It applies even though the precise situation in which a slayer stands to benefit from his or her wrong is not specifically addressed in the Comments and Illustrations.

q. *Wrongful death.* To be contrasted with the slayer rule of this section is the possibility that the slayer may be liable in a wrongful-death proceeding. See Restatement Second, Torts § 925.

Part C. No-Contest Clauses

§ 8.5. No-Contest Clauses

A provision in a donative document purporting to rescind a donative transfer to, or a fiduciary appointment of, any person who institutes a proceeding challenging the validity of all or part of the

donative document is enforceable unless probable cause existed for instituting the proceeding.

Comment:

a. *Scope.* A no-contest clause, also called an *in terrorem* clause, is enforceable unless probable cause existed for instituting the proceeding. A no-contest clause typically provides for the rescission of any benefit to a devisee, beneficiary, or donee who challenges the validity of the document, or of a term of the document.

This section only addresses the validity of a no-contest clause that pertains to proceedings that challenge the validity of a donative document (or a portion of such a document). A clause that purports to prohibit beneficiaries from enforcing fiduciary duties owed to the beneficiaries by trustees or other fiduciaries does not fall within the scope of this section. Although sometimes couched as a no-contest clause, such a measure functions as an exculpation clause and is governed by the standards applying to such clauses. See, e.g., Restatement Second, Trusts § 222 [Restatement Third, Trusts § 96]; Uniform Trust Code § 1008.

Grounds of contest include the grounds addressed in this Chapter—incapacity (§§ 8.1 and 8.2) and undue influence, duress, fraud, or forgery (§ 8.3)—as well as other grounds leading to the invalidity of the document or any of its provisions. See Comment *d.*

b. *Rationale.* The starting point for analyzing the validity of no-contest clauses is the policy in favor of the freedom of disposition. The donor's intention—expressed in this case in the no-contest clause—is given effect to the maximum extent allowed by law. See § 10.1. A no-contest clause may serve several worthwhile purposes. Such a clause may deter unwarranted challenges to the donor's intent by a disappointed person seeking to gain unjustified enrichment at the expense of others. The clause may prevent costly litigation that would deplete the estate or besmirch the reputation of the donor when the donor is no longer alive to provide a defense. Such a clause may also discourage a contest directed toward coercing a settlement—the so-called strike suit.

Against the benefits of a no-contest clause is the concern that the jurisdiction of the court to determine the validity of a donative transfer not be defeated. A purported donative transfer by a donor who lacked the capacity to make the transfer, or a transfer that was procured by wrongdoing, should be invalid. This Restatement, therefore, supported by Restatement Second, Property (Donative Transfers) § 9.1, the Uniform Probate Code § 3–905, and the majority of decisions and statutes, provides that a no-contest clause is valid and enforceable unless the challenge was based on probable cause.

Under that standard, the persons restrained by the no-contest clause retain the right to litigate, and if the litigation is successful, the no-contest clause fails along with the challenged transfer. If a beneficiary litigates unsuccessfully and then seeks to claim under the donative transfer, the beneficiary suffers the penalty imposed by the transferor for such conduct unless that beneficiary can establish that there was probable cause for instituting the proceeding. When the contestant establishes that there was probable cause for instituting the proceeding, it would be a contravention of public policy to enforce the no-contest clause.

c. *Probable cause.* Probable cause exists when, at the time of instituting the proceeding, there was evidence that would lead a reasonable person, properly informed and advised, to conclude that there was a substantial likelihood that the challenge would be successful. A factor that bears on the existence of probable cause is whether the beneficiary relied upon the advice of independent legal counsel sought in good faith after a full disclosure of the facts. The mere fact that the person mounting the challenge was represented by counsel is not controlling, however, since the institution of a legal proceeding challenging a donative transfer normally involves representation by legal counsel.

Where a statute prohibits the suppression of a document that appears to be the will of a decedent, a no-contest clause in another will is inapplicable to any person who presents another potential will to the probate court. . . . .

d. Construction of no-contest clauses. No-contest clauses are construed narrowly, consistent with their terms. The institution of a proceeding to contest a will or other donative transfer, or to challenge a particular provision, upon any of the grounds within the scope of the no-contest clause, normally violates the clause. In the absence of specific language to the contrary, the clause should be construed to be violated regardless of whether the action is subsequently withdrawn immediately after its institution, prior to a hearing, at the trial, or at any time thereafter. The mere filing of a paper that is intended solely to procure time to ascertain the facts upon which the decision to institute a proceeding must rest should not be construed to constitute the institution of an action to contest or to challenge. . . . .

A suit to construe, reform, or modify the language of a donative document is not a contest of the document and hence is not a violation of a no-contest clause, unless the construction, reformation, or modification advocated by the person bringing the suit would invalidate the donative document or any of its provisions . . . . A proceeding brought by a beneficiary for the purpose of resolving an ambiguity, or for reforming or modifying the document, valid under all possible constructions or valid under the construction advocated by the beneficiary, is not a contest as that term is used in this section. In such a case, the beneficiary is seeking merely to determine and to protect the donor's intention and is not seeking to circumvent it . . . .

e. Indirect contests or challenges. A restraint otherwise valid under the rule stated in this section is violated, not only by a direct contest or challenge instituted by the beneficiary and alleging any of the grounds within the scope of the restraint, but also by voluntary conduct of the beneficiary that amounts to an indirect contest or challenge. For example, such a restraint is violated when the person restrained voluntarily instigates or aids another person in that person's attempt to contest the will or other donative document or any of its provisions. Such aid may consist of sharing the expenses of the proceeding. Such aid may involve the beneficiary entering into an agreement with the person instituting the proceeding whereby the beneficiary is assured, in return for assistance at the trial, that he or she will receive the property transferred to him or her in the donative document, even if it is overthrown . . . or the particular provision stricken from it.

f. Actions in a representative capacity. A beneficiary may be acting, not only on his or her own behalf, but as a representative of some other person interested in the estate of the transferor, in the capacity of guardian, committee, executor, administrator, or otherwise. Where a person in a representative capacity institutes a proceeding contesting the donative document or any of its provisions, the failure of that contest or challenge should have no effect on his or her own gift, unless the representative status is being used as a means of presenting personal views. A representative action is analogous to instigating a contest or challenge by another person.

A contest of a will or other donative document or any of its provisions, initiated and conducted by a guardian of an infant, or by a committee or a conservator of an incapacitated person on behalf of the ward, should not constitute a breach of a provision against contest or challenge that will affect the interest of the infant or ward.

g. Conduct of someone other than the beneficiary. The interest of one beneficiary is not affected when the conduct that triggers the no-contest clause is that of another person, unless the donative document so provides. For example, a transferor may provide for the rescission of a gift to a grandchild in the event that the disinherited parent of the grandchild institutes proceedings either to contest the donative document or to challenge any of its provisions. A restraint against such contest or challenge, however, will not be construed to have this breadth of application unless the language and circumstances of the dispositive document clearly reveal that the transferor intended that result. Similarly, unless the language and circumstances of the dispositive document clearly indicate a contrary intention, a restraint is not construed to operate against the beneficiary when a contest or challenge is instigated by a person who will receive the transferred property in the event of a violation of the restraint, or is brought primarily for the purpose of causing the property to devolve upon the subsequent taker . . . .

h. Effect of the absence of a gift over. If the restraint does not contain a gift over on its violation, the person whose interest is rescinded is barred from taking the rescinded interest under the residuary clause or by intestacy. Cf. § 2.7 (Negative Wills). The absence of a gift over upon instituting proceedings has no effect. If, however, the language and circumstances of the transfer are ambiguous in regard to the presence or absence of a restraint, the absence of a gift over is a relevant factor indicating that the language was not intended to create a restraint against contest or against challenging particular provisions of the donative document.

i. Donative transfers other than wills. This section applies to no-contest clauses in all donative documents, not only in wills. No-contest clauses have traditionally appeared more frequently in wills than in other donative documents. With the increase in the use of revocable inter vivos trusts as will substitutes, no-contest clauses and clauses restraining challenges of particular provisions in those trusts serve the same purpose as do such clauses in wills, and the same test applies to determine the validity of those clauses in the two comparable situations.

CHAPTER 9

PROTECTIONS AGAINST DISINHERITANCE

Introductory Note: The protections against disinheritance covered in this chapter arise upon death and divide into two categories—protections against *intentional* disinheritance and protections against *unintentional* disinheritance. This chapter deals with law that is entirely statutory.

Part A. Protections Against Intentional Disinheritance

Introductory Note: Part A of this chapter covers the elective share of the surviving spouse. In states having the community-property regime of marital property, no provision is made for the surviving spouse to take an elective share because each spouse acquires an undivided ownership interest in half of the property that the couple acquired during the marriage other than by gift, devise, or inheritance. The elective share of the surviving spouse is therefore a feature of non-community-property states. Some community-property states do recognize elective-share-type rights in so-called quasi-community property, however, which is property acquired in a non-community-property state that would have been community property had it been acquired in a community-property state.

§ 9.1. Surviving Spouse's Elective Share—Non-Community-Property States Other Than Those That Have Adopted a Revised Uniform Probate Code-Type Statute

(a) In nearly all of the non-community-property states, the decedent's surviving spouse is entitled to elect a share of the decedent's property. The exact share differs among the states. The predominant share in the states that have not adopted a Revised Uniform Probate Code-type statute is one-third.

(b) In a state whose statute subjects the decedent's probate estate and specified nonprobate assets to the elective share, the

elective-share fraction is applied to the sum of the value of the probate estate and the value of the specified nonprobate assets.

(c) In a state whose statute subjects the decedent's "estate" to the elective share, the elective share is applied to the value of the decedent's estate which, for purposes of calculating the elective share, includes (i) the value of the decedent's probate estate, (ii) the value of property owned or owned in substance by the decedent immediately before death that passed outside of probate at the decedent's death to donees other than the surviving spouse, and (iii) the value of irrevocable gifts to donees other than the surviving spouse made by the decedent in anticipation of imminent death.

Comment:

a. *Scope.* This section addresses the right of a surviving spouse to elect a share of the decedent's estate in the non-community-property states that have not adopted the Revised Uniform Probate Code. The elective share of the Revised UPC is covered in § 9.2. The elective share is sometimes called the *forced share*, the *statutory share*, or the *nonbarrable share*.

b. *Purpose and theory of the elective share.* The purpose of the elective share is to grant the decedent's surviving spouse an appropriate protection against being disinherited. The prevailing view of marriage is that it is an economic partnership, which imports a goal of equalizing the marital assets. The community-property system implements this theory of marriage during the marriage. Under the community-property system, each spouse owns an undivided half interest in the marital estate, defined as property acquired during the marriage other than by gift, devise, or inheritance. Neither property acquired before the marriage nor property acquired during the marriage by gift, devise, or inheritance is counted in the community (or marital estate), and so remains separate property. The community-property states do not have elective-share statutes, because the marital assets have already been equalized through the ownership rights that attached during the marriage.

Another recognition of the partnership theory of marriage occurs in divorce law, through the widely adopted equitable-distribution regimes. The specifics of the equitable-distribution regimes vary from state to state regarding the property that is subject to equitable distribution, the factors to be considered, and the amount of discretion granted to the courts in dividing up that property. Despite the differences, equitable distribution echoes community property at divorce by implementing the partnership theory. See [the American Law Institute's] Principles of the Law of Family Dissolution: Analysis and Recommendations § 4.09, Comment *b*; Restatement Second, Property (Donative Transfers) § 34.1(1) and Comments *b*, *c*, and *d*.

Apart from the elective share adopted in the Revised Uniform Probate Code (see § 9.2), elective-share law has not based the elective share on the partnership theory of marriage. Instead, elective-share law in non-Revised-UPC jurisdictions is still shaped by its antecedents in the common-law concepts of dower and curtesy.

c. *Common-law antecedents of elective-share law—Historical note on dower and curtesy.* At early common law, the decedent's surviving spouse was a distributee of personal property under the English Statute of Distribution, but was not an heir to land under the common-law canons of descent. The widow, instead, was entitled to dower and the widower, if the marriage produced issue, was entitled to curtesy.

Dower gave a surviving widow a life estate in one-third of the inheritable freehold land that her husband held during the marriage. Curtesy gave a surviving widower a life estate in all the inheritable freehold land that his wife held at any time during coverture. The estate in curtesy arose upon birth of issue.

Dower and curtesy have largely been abolished in the United States and replaced by a statutory elective share that accrues to the surviving spouse upon the deceased spouse's death.

d. Non-Revised-UPC elective share. Although dower and curtesy have largely been abolished in the United States and replaced by elective-share statutes, elective-share law (other than the elective share of the Revised UPC) is heavily influenced by its common-law antecedents, in that it typically grants a surviving spouse a right to elect one-third of the deceased spouse's estate. Unlike its common-law antecedents, however, the elective share usually applies to personalty as well as land, and the gender of the surviving spouse is now irrelevant. The elective share is a full ownership interest, not merely a life estate.

In order to take the elective share under many non-UPC statutes, but not under the UPC, the surviving spouse must renounce the deceased spouse's will and take the elective share instead. Under the Original (and Revised) UPC, the surviving spouse does not renounce the will in order to take the elective share. Instead, any transfer to the surviving spouse by will, intestacy, or will substitute counts toward satisfying the elective share.

Comment on Subsection (b)—the Elective Share in States Whose Statutes Subject the Decedent's Probate Estate and Specified Nonprobate Assets to the Elective Share:

e. Augmented estate of the Original UPC. The elective-share statutes of some states, mostly those statutes modeled on the Original Uniform Probate Code, provide that the decedent's probate estate and specified nonprobate assets are subject to the spouse's elective share. Under the Original UPC, the surviving spouse is entitled to elect a one-third share of the decedent's "augmented estate." The decedent's net probate estate is augmented by including:

(1) the value of specified nonprobate transfers of the decedent during the marriage that benefit donees other than the surviving spouse (see Comment *j*) and (ii) gifts by the decedent during the marriage to a donee within two years of death to the extent that the aggregate gifts to any one donee in either of the years exceed $3000; and

(2) value of property owned by the surviving spouse at the decedent's death and property transferred by the spouse during the marriage that would have been included in the spouse's augmented estate under paragraph (1) if the spouse had predeceased the decedent, to the extent that the owned or transferred property was derived from the decedent by means other than testate or intestate succession without a full consideration in money or money's worth. Property owned by the surviving spouse at the decedent's death or previously transferred by the surviving spouse is presumed to have been derived from the decedent, except to the extent that the surviving spouse establishes that it was derived from another source.

f. The decedent's nonprobate transfers included in the augmented estate. The Original UPC includes in the augmented estate the following nonprobate transfers of the decedent during the marriage: (i) any transfer under which the decedent retained at the time of death the possession or enjoyment of, or right to income from, the property; (ii) any transfer to the extent that the decedent retained at the time of death a power, either alone or in conjunction with any other person, to revoke or to consume, invade, or dispose of the principal for the decedent's own benefit; (iii) any transfer whereby property is held at the decedent's death by the decedent and another with right of survivorship; and (iv) any transfer made to a donee within two years of death to the extent that the aggregate transfers to any one donee in either of the years exceed $3000. Specifically excluded from the augmented estate are any transfers made with the written consent or joinder of the surviving spouse, any life insurance, accident insurance, joint annuity, or pension payable to a person other than the surviving spouse, and any transfers for which the decedent received adequate and full consideration in money or money's worth.

g. Liability for satisfying the elective share. In satisfying the elective share of the Original UPC, the statute requires that the value of property that passes or passed to the surviving spouse, or would have passed but was renounced, be used first. Remaining property is so applied that liability for the unsatisfied balance is equitably apportioned among the recipients of the augmented estate in proportion to the value of their interests therein.

h. Incapacitated surviving spouse. If the surviving spouse is a "protected person" as defined in the Original UPC, the election may be exercised only by order of court after finding that exercise is necessary to provide support for the surviving spouse during his or her probable life expectancy.

Comment on Subsection (c)—the Elective Share in States Whose Statutes Subject the Decedent's "Estate" to the Elective Share:

i. Protection against disinheritance by nonprobate transfers. Non-UPC forced-share statutes ordinarily grant the decedent's surviving spouse an elective share of one-third of the decedent's "estate."

An elective or forced share that only applies to the decedent's probate estate is ineffective, because such a regime invites evasion by means of will substitute or end-of-life gifts. If the surviving spouse is to be protected from disinheritance by will, the surviving spouse must also be protected from disinheritance by those means.

Consequently, for purposes of calculating the amount of the elective share, the following are counted as part of the decedent's "estate": (i) the value of property owned or owned in substance by the decedent immediately before death that passed outside of probate at the decedent's death to donees other than the surviving spouse and (ii) the value of irrevocable gifts to donees made by the decedent in anticipation of imminent death.

j. Property owned or owned in substance immediately before death. Although property owned or owned in substance by the decedent immediately before death that passed outside of probate at the decedent's death is not part of the decedent's probate estate (see §§ 1.1 and 7.1), such property is owned in substance by the decedent through various powers or rights, such as the power to revoke, withdraw, invade, or sever, or to appoint the decedent or the decedent's estate as beneficiary. Consequently, for purposes of calculating the amount of the elective share, the value of property owned or owned in substance by the decedent immediately before death that passed outside of probate at the decedent's death to donees other than the surviving spouse is counted as part of the decedent's "estate." The decedent's motive in creating, exercising, or not exercising any of these powers is irrelevant.

The property to be counted as part of the decedent's estate for purposes of calculating the forced share includes property that the decedent owned in substance immediately before death and passed outside of probate at the decedent's death to someone other than the surviving spouse. It is irrelevant whether the decedent acquired substantive ownership of the property before or after the marriage by gift or otherwise from someone else. The objective is to equate property owned in substance with probate property, which includes property that the decedent acquired before or after the marriage by gift or otherwise from someone else.

k. Irrevocable gifts in anticipation of imminent death. Although property given away by the decedent in anticipation of imminent death is neither part of the decedent's probate estate (see § 1.1) nor owned in substance by the decedent immediately before death, the value of an irrevocable gift made in anticipation of imminent death to donees other than the surviving spouse is counted as part of the decedent's "estate" for purposes of calculating the spouse's forced share. Otherwise, the forced share would be open to easy evasion by death-bed or near death-bed gifts.

Any irrevocable transfer, if made in anticipation of imminent death, can fall within this principle. The transfer need not be an outright gift. It can be an irrevocable transfer, such as one in trust with a retained life estate. Or, it can be an irrevocable relinquishment or assignment of a power, right, or item of property that, had it been retained, would have caused the value of the property to be included in the decedent's "estate" under § 9.1(c)(ii) as property owned or owned in substance by the decedent immediately before death that would have passed outside of probate at the decedent's death to beneficiaries other than the surviving spouse. See Comment *j*.

l. Liability for satisfying the elective share. In determining how liability for satisfying the elective share is apportioned, primary consideration should be given to retaining the decedent's dispositive plan to the extent possible and allocating the liability as the decedent would probably have done had the decedent addressed the question. The dispositive plan is ascertained by looking at all relevant probate and nonprobate transfers by the decedent.

In ascertaining the method that the decedent would have adopted for reducing transfers to others to satisfy the rights of the surviving spouse, attention should be paid to the constructional preferences identified in § 11.3(c)(3). The preference for descendants over collaterals supports satisfying the spouse's claim from property given to persons others than relatives, then gifts to relatives other than descendants. The preference for manifested intent supports using intestate property before reaching residuary gifts under the decedent's will and will substitutes, and using residuary gifts under the will and will substitutes before reaching specific gifts.

§ 9.2. Surviving Spouse's Elective Share Under the Revised Uniform Probate Code

(a) Under the Revised Uniform Probate Code, the decedent's surviving spouse is entitled to an elective-share amount calculated by applying a specified percentage to the augmented estate. The percentage increases with the length of the marriage until it reaches

a maximum of 50 percent, which is the percentage applicable to a marriage that has lasted 15 years or longer.

(b) The augmented estate consists of the sum of four components:

(1) the value of the decedent's net probate estate;

(2) the value of the decedent's nonprobate transfers to persons other than the surviving spouse;

(3) the value of the decedent's nonprobate transfers to the surviving spouse; and

(4) the value of the surviving spouse's net assets at the decedent's death, plus the surviving spouse's nonprobate transfers to others.

(c) In satisfying the elective-share amount, the decedent's probate and nonprobate transfers to the surviving spouse and the marital portion of the surviving spouse's assets are applied first. If these amounts equal or exceed the elective-share amount, the surviving spouse is not entitled to any additional amount. If the elective-share amount is not satisfied from these items, the decedent's probate and nonprobate transfers to others are proportionately liable to satisfy the balance.

Comment:

a. Purpose and theory of the elective share. For the prevailing view of marriage as an economic partnership, see § 9.1, Comment *b*.

b. Principal feature of the Revised UPC. The principal feature of the Revised UPC elective share that distinguishes it from other elective-share statutes (as described in § 9.1) is that it seeks to implement the economic-partnership theory of marriage by equalizing marital assets at death. With the exception of the Revised UPC elective share, elective-share law has not based the elective share unambiguously on the partnership theory of marriage. Instead, non-Revised UPC elective-share law is still influenced by its antecedent in the common-law concepts of dower and curtesy. See § 9.1.

The partnership theory of marriage suggests that, if the surviving spouse so elects, the marital assets should be equalized. In order to achieve that objective, the Revised UPC statute constructs a system that separates the marital assets from the nonmarital assets for both the decedent spouse and the surviving spouse. In order to achieve the objective of assuring that the surviving spouse obtains a fully equal share of the marital assets, marital assets of both spouses that were placed in certain will substitute or other nonprobate transfer form are counted as part of the augmented estate.

The elective share separates the marital from the nonmarital assets by means of a mechanically determined approximation system rather than by post-death classification on an asset-by-asset basis (which would sometimes require complicated and costly tracing to source).

c. The "elective-share percentage." The approximation system for separating the marital from the nonmarital assets is implemented by the following schedule, under which the elective-share percentage is adjusted to the length of the marriage:

If the decedent and the spouse were married to each other:	***The elective-share percentage is:***
Less than 1 year	Supplemental Amount Only.
1 year but less than 2 years	3% of the augmented estate
2 years but less than 3 years	6% of the augmented estate
3 years but less than 4 years	9% of the augmented estate
4 years but less than 5 years	12% of the augmented estate
5 years but less than 6 years	15% of the augmented estate
6 years but less than 7 years	18% of the augmented estate
7 years but less than 8 years	21% of the augmented estate
8 years but less than 9 years	24% of the augmented estate
9 years but less than 10 years	27% of the augmented estate
10 years but less than 11 years	30% of the augmented estate
11 years but less than 12 years	34% of the augmented estate
12 years but less than 13 years	38% of the augmented estate
13 years but less than 14 years	42% of the augmented estate
14 years but less than 15 years	46% of the augmented estate
15 years or more	50% of the augmented estate.

This schedule is designed to separate (by approximation, hence arbitrarily) the couple's marital and nonmarital assets. Each of the percentages is intended to represent 50 percent of the couple's marital assets. For example, to say that the elective-share percentage is 15 percent in a marriage that lasted five but less than six years means that the system deems 30 percent of the couple's assets to be marital assets, and deems 70 percent of their assets to be nonmarital assets that are not subject to equalization. By utilizing percentages based upon duration of the marriage, the system spares difficult factual determinations about the characterization of property as "marital" or "nonmarital."

d. The augmented estate. The elective-share percentage is applied to the value of the augmented estate. The augmented estate is composed of the sum of four components: the value of the decedent's net probate estate; the value of the decedent's nonprobate transfers to persons other than the surviving spouse (see Comment *e*); the value of the decedent's nonprobate transfers to the surviving spouse; and the value of the surviving spouse's net assets at the decedent's death, together with the surviving spouse's nonprobate transfers to others.

e. The decedent's nonprobate transfers to persons other than the surviving spouse. The statute divides the decedent's nonprobate transfers to persons other than the surviving spouse into three broad categories:

(1) *Property owned or owned in substance by the decedent immediately before death:* This category includes property (such as a revocable trust) over which the decedent alone, immediately before death, held a presently exercisable general power of appointment; the decedent's fractional interest in property held by the decedent in joint tenancy with the right of survivorship; the decedent's ownership interest in property or accounts held in POD, TOD, or co-ownership registration with the right of survivorship; and proceeds of insurance, including accidental death benefits, on the life of the decedent, if the decedent owned the insurance policy immediately before death.

(2) *Property transferred by the decedent in specified forms to someone other than the surviving spouse during the marriage:* This category includes property transferred into an irrevocable trust with a retained right to income or any transfer in which the decedent created a power over income or property, exercisable by the decedent alone or in conjunction with any other person, or exercisable by a nonadverse party, to or for the benefit of the decedent, creditors of the decedent, the decedent's estate, or creditors of the decedent's estate.

(3) *Property transferred by the decedent in specified forms within two years of death:* This category includes property over which the decedent irrevocably relinquished or assigned a power, right, or item of property that, had it been retained, would have caused the value of the property to be included in the augmented estate or property that the decedent irrevocably transferred to another to the extent the aggregate transfers to any one donee in either of the two years exceeded $10,000.

f. The "elective-share amount." Applying the elective-share percentage to the augmented estate yields the "elective-share amount." This is the amount to which the surviving spouse is ultimately entitled, but because of the system by which this amount is satisfied (see Comment *h*), the spouse is not necessarily entitled to take this amount from the decedent's estate or transferees.

g. The supplemental elective-share amount. The Revised UPC also provides for a supplemental elective-share amount, a special feature for small estates that is designed to bring the surviving spouse's assets at least up to $50,000 or as close to that figure as the value of the assets permits. This feature is based on a support theory, not on the partnership theory of marriage. For an illustration of this feature of the Revised UPC, see Illustration 3.

h. Satisfying the elective-share amount. In satisfying the elective-share amount, the decedent's probate and nonprobate transfers to the surviving spouse and the marital portion of the surviving spouse's assets are applied first. If these amounts equal or exceed the elective-share amount, the surviving spouse is not entitled to any additional amount. If the elective-share amount is not satisfied from these items, the decedent's probate and nonprobate transfers to others are proportionately liable to satisfy the balance.

Illustrations:

1. *Marriage of 15 Years or Longer.* A and B were married to each other more than 15 years. A died, survived by B. A's will left nothing to

B, and A made no nonprobate transfers to B. A made one nonprobate transfer to others (a revocable inter vivos trust) worth $100,000.

Components of the Augmented Estate	**Title-Based Ownership Values**	***Marital Portion = 100%***
A's net probate estate	$300,000	*$300,000*
A's nonprobate transfers to others	$100,000	*$100,000*
A's nonprobate transfers to B	0	*0*
B's assets and nonprobate transfers to others	$200,000	*$200,000*
Augmented Estate	$600,000	*$600,000*

The elective-share percentage for a 15-year or longer marriage is 50 percent. This means that B's elective-share amount is $300,000 (50% of $600,000). All of B's assets ($200,000) count first toward satisfying the elective-share amount. A's net probate estate and nonprobate transfers to others are liable for the unsatisfied balance of $100,000, which is the amount needed to bring B's own $200,000 up to $300,000. If B had died first, survived by A, A would not be entitled to take any amount from B's estate because A already owned more than 50 percent of the marital assets.

2. *Shorter Than 15-Year Marriage.* A and B were married to each other more than five but less than six years. A died, survived by B. A's will left nothing to B, and A made no nonprobate transfers to B. A made one nonprobate transfer to others (a revocable inter vivos trust) worth $100,000.

Components of the Augmented Estate	Title-Based Ownership Values	*Marital Portion = 30%*
A's net probate estate	$300,000	*$90,000*
A's nonprobate transfers to others	$100,000	*$30,000*
A's nonprobate transfers to B	0	*0*
B's assets and nonprobate transfers to others	$200,000	*$60,000*
Augmented Estate	$600,000	*$180,000*

The elective-share percentage for a five-year marriage is 15 percent. This means that B's elective-share amount is $90,000 (15% of $600,000). To say that A's entitlement is $90,000 presupposes (by approximation) that $180,000 of their $600,000 are marital assets—assets subject to equalization. Hence, B's entitlement is half of that amount, or $90,000. Exempted from equalization is the other $420,000 of their combined assets, some of which would have been A's nonmarital or exempted property and the rest of which would have been B's nonmarital or exempted property. The system applies the same ratio to the asset mix of each spouse as it does to the couple's combined assets. To say that the elective-share percentage is 15 percent means that the combined assets are treated as being in a 30/70 ratio (30% marital, subject to equalization; 70% nonmarital, exempted from equalization). This same ratio, in turn, governs the approximation of each spouse's mix of marital and nonmarital property. Consequently, the system attributes 30 percent of A's $400,000 ($120,000) to marital property and the other 70 percent ($280,000) to nonmarital property. The system does the same for B's $200,000, i.e., it treats 30 percent ($60,000) as marital property and 70 percent ($140,000) as nonmarital property. Accordingly, B is treated as already owning $60,000 of the $180,000 of marital property. Sixty thousand dollars of B's $90,000 elective-share amount comes from B's own assets. A's net probate estate and nonprobate transfers to others are liable for the unsatisfied balance of $30,000. (Because $120,000 of A's assets are attributed to marital property, removing $30,000 of those $120,000 from A and adding that $30,000 to B's $60,000 in marital assets equalizes the aggregate $180,000 marital assets in a 50/50 split—$90,000 for A and $90,000 for B.)

If B Had Died First: If B had died first, survived by A, A would not be entitled to take any amount from B's estate because A already owned more than 50 percent of the marital assets.

3. *Supplemental elective-share amount*. After A's death in Illustration 1, B married C. Five years later, B died, survived by C. B's will left nothing to C, and B made no nonprobate transfers.

Components of the Augmented Estate	Values
B's net probate estate	$90,000
B's nonprobate transfers to others	0
B's nonprobate transfers to C	0
C's assets and nonprobate transfers to others	$10,000
Augmented Estate	$100,000

The first step is to calculate the elective-share amount that is payable from B's net probate estate. This amount is $12,000, which, when added to C's $10,000 in assets, totals $22,000. C is therefore entitled to a supplemental elective-share amount of $28,000, which is the amount necessary to bring C's $10,000 in assets and C's right to an elective share of $12,000 up to $50,000.

i. Exclusions from the augmented estate. Any transfer that was supported by adequate and full consideration in money or money's worth as well as any transfer that was made with the written consent or joinder of the surviving spouse is excluded from the augmented estate.

j. Incapacitated surviving spouse. If the surviving spouse is incapacitated, the portion of the elective-share amount payable from the decedent's net probate estate and nonprobate transfers to others is placed into a statutory support trust for the surviving spouse. Because the surviving spouse is not entitled to all the income for life, the statutory support trust does not qualify for the federal estate tax marital deduction. However, none of the decedent's voluntary transfers to the surviving spouse is forced into the statutory trust. These are the amounts that are payable to the surviving spouse by testate or intestate succession or by nonprobate transfer to the surviving spouse, which count first toward satisfying the elective-share amount. Consequently, if the decedent spouse established a marital-deduction trust for the surviving spouse, or made any other probate or nonprobate transfer to the surviving spouse that qualifies for the marital deduction, those transfers remain undisturbed, and hence retain their marital-deduction qualification.

k. Protection of payors and other third parties. A payor or other third party is protected from liability if payment or distribution is made before receiving written notice of an intent to take the elective share.

§ 9.3. Before-Tax Treatment of an Election

The amount of the elective share is calculated by applying the elective-share fraction or percentage to the estate or augmented estate without reduction by the amount of any tax liability imposed on (i) the decedent's estate by an applicable estate or similar transfer tax or (ii) the recipients of property from a decedent's estate by an applicable inheritance or similar tax.

Comment:

a. *Scope.* This section applies to all elective-share regimes, regardless of form. See §§ 9.1, 9.2.

b. *Estate or similar transfer tax imposed on the decedent's estate.* In calculating the amount of the elective share, the elective-share fraction or percentage is applied to the estate or augmented estate without reduction by the amount of any tax liability imposed on the decedent's estate by an applicable estate or similar transfer tax.

Once the amount of the elective share is calculated, the next question is whether any of the estate tax is to be apportioned to the elective share. The apportionment rules provide that any estate or similar transfer tax imposed on the decedent's estate is to be apportioned only among the recipients of taxable transfers. To the extent that the elective share is not taxable, by virtue of qualifying for a deduction, exemption, credit, or similar provision, no part of the estate tax is to be apportioned to the elective share. Under the current federal estate tax, the elective share is typically not taxable because it qualifies for the federal estate tax marital deduction.

c. *Inheritance or similar tax imposed on the recipients of property from a decedent.* In calculating the amount of the elective share, the elective-share fraction or percentage is applied to the estate or augmented estate without reduction by the amount of any tax liability imposed on the recipients of property from a decedent's estate by an applicable inheritance or similar tax. Such a tax is charged against each recipient's share. The amount of the surviving spouse's elective share is not affected by the tax imposed on other recipients.

Once the amount of the elective share is calculated, the elective share is treated as a transfer from the decedent to the decedent's surviving spouse, and is taxed accordingly. The elective share is entitled to any deduction, exemption, credit, or similar provision that applies to such a transfer under the applicable inheritance-tax system. State inheritance-tax systems typically provide that a transfer to the decedent's surviving spouse is wholly or partly exempt from liability for such tax.

§ 9.4. Premarital or Marital Agreement

(a) The elective share and other statutory rights accruing to a surviving spouse may be waived, wholly or partially, or otherwise altered, before or during marriage, by a written agreement that was signed by both parties. An agreement that was entered into before marriage is a premarital agreement. An agreement that was entered into during marriage is a marital agreement. Consideration is not necessary to the enforcement of a premarital or a marital agreement.

(b) For a premarital or a marital agreement to be enforceable against the surviving spouse, the enforcing party must show that the surviving spouse's consent was informed and was not obtained by undue influence or duress.

(c) A rebuttable presumption arises that the requirements of subsection (b) are satisfied, shifting the burden of proof to the surviving spouse to show that his or her consent was not informed or was obtained by undue influence or duress, if the enforcing party shows that:

(1) before the agreement's execution, (i) the surviving spouse knew, at least approximately, the decedent's assets and asset values, income, and liabilities; or (ii) the decedent or his or her representative provided in timely fashion to the surviving spouse a written statement accurately disclosing the decedent's significant assets and asset values, income, and liabilities; and either

(2) the surviving spouse was represented by independent legal counsel; or

(3) if the surviving spouse was not represented by independent legal counsel, (i) the decedent or the decedent's representative advised the surviving spouse, in timely fashion, to obtain independent legal counsel, and if the surviving spouse was needy, offered to pay for the costs of the surviving spouse's representation; and (ii) the agreement stated, in language easily understandable by an adult of ordinary intelligence with no legal training, the nature of any rights or claims otherwise arising at death that were altered by the agreement, and the nature of that alteration.

Comment:

a. Scope. This section applies to both premarital and marital agreements dealing with the elective share and other spousal statutory rights arising on death. For the Institute's position on the enforceability of premarital and marital agreements dealing with dissolution of marriage during life, see Chapter 7 of the [American Law Institute's] Principles of the Law of Family Dissolution: Analysis and Recommendations.

A premarital agreement is one that was entered into before marriage. A marital agreement is one that was entered into during marriage.

This section deals with a premarital or a marital agreement that waives or otherwise alters the surviving spouse's right to an elective share and other spousal statutory rights arising on death. Although both parties to the agreement were living when the agreement was executed, the enforceability of the agreement arises after the decedent's death, hence this section and commentary refer to the parties as the decedent and the surviving spouse, even when referring to the time when the agreement was negotiated and executed.

b. Rationale. Elective-share systems and other statutory rights arising on death protect against unilateral disinheritance of a spouse but do not interfere with genuinely consensual arrangements that waive or reduce such spousal rights. Although protective in purpose, elective-share law is default law, which the parties may alter or abrogate. The parties may decline to have an economic partnership of the kind characteristic of most first marriages. It is particularly common, for example, for two previously married older persons contemplating marriage to wish to ensure that on the first spouse's death, all or most of the decedent's property will go to the decedent's children rather than to the surviving spouse (and ultimately, perhaps, to the surviving spouse's children). Freedom to make an enforceable agreement of this character not only facilitates the marriage of such a couple, but may also improve the quality of the marriage, smoothing the spouses' relationship to their respective children by providing assurance that the new marriage will not interfere with the children's expectations.

While there are good reasons to respect such contracts, the relationship between parties contracting in anticipation of marriage, or in the midst of an ongoing marriage, requires legal standards different from ordinary commercial settings. A party negotiating a commercial contract can engage in arms-length dealings to maximize partisan advantage. Parties to a premarital or a marital agreement are in a relationship of trust and confidence. Entering into or operating within a marriage, an individual may have expectations about his or her partner that may impair the capacity for self-protective judgment, or the inclination to exercise it. The law reasonably requires greater assurance that the parties understand and appreciate the consequences of such a premarital or a marital agreement.

c. *Writing.* To be enforceable, an agreement covered by this section must be in writing. On what constitutes a writing, see § 6.2, Comment *r*.

d. *Signature of both parties; unilateral waiver.* Unless a statute allows a unilateral waiver, an agreement covered by this section is only enforceable if it is signed by both parties. Under the Original and the Revised Uniform Probate Code, a unilateral waiver signed only by the surviving spouse is enforceable. See Revised UPC § 2–213; Original UPC § 2–204. On what constitutes a signature, see § 6.2, Comment *s*.

e. *Agreement enforceable without consideration.* Both a premarital and a marital agreement are enforceable without consideration, but otherwise such agreements are subject to general principles of contract law. See Comment *k*.

f. *Burden of proof.* Because the parties to a premarital or a marital agreement are in a relationship of trust and confidence, subsection (b) places the burden of proof on the enforcing party (the party seeking to enforce the agreement against a surviving spouse who claims the elective share or other statutory rights in violation of the agreement). Accord, Principles of the Law of Family Dissolution: Analysis and Recommendations § 7.04(2). The enforcing party must show that the surviving spouse's consent was informed and was not obtained by undue influence or duress. The burden of proof shifts to the surviving spouse to show the opposite, however, if the rebuttable presumption established in subsection (c) of this section applies. See Comments *g*, *h*, *i*, and *j*.

g. *Presumption that surviving spouse's consent was informed and was not obtained by undue influence or duress.* If the enforcing party shows the existence of the circumstances described in subsection (c) of this section, the enforcing party benefits from a rebuttable presumption that the requirements of subsection (b) of this section are satisfied, shifting the burden of proof to the surviving spouse.

The rebuttable presumption minimizes the risk of the agreement being found defective in circumstances in which, before the agreement's execution, the surviving spouse knew the decedent's financial situation, understood what legal rights or claims he or she might have as the decedent's surviving spouse, understood how the proposed agreement intended to alter those rights, and had (or had a reasonable opportunity to have) independent legal representation in negotiating the agreement. The rebuttable presumption is thus designed to increase the predictability and enforceability of premarital and marital agreements by facilitating planning that minimizes the risk of the agreement being found defective.

h. *Knowledge of the decedent's financial situation.* The surviving spouse must be shown to have had knowledge of the decedent's financial situation when the agreement was executed in order for the rebuttable presumption provided in subsection (c) to arise. Such knowledge is crucial to understanding the agreement's significance, as the assets are themselves the subject of the agreement.

To have the benefit of the rebuttable presumption under subsection (c), the enforcing party must show that, before the agreement's execution, (i) the surviving spouse knew, at least approximately, the decedent's assets and asset values, income, and liabilities; or (ii) the decedent or his or her representative provided in timely fashion to the surviving spouse a written statement accurately disclosing the decedent's significant assets and asset values, income, and liabilities. In circumstances in which the decedent's property consisted importantly of assets for which an immediately ascertainable market price is not available, such as close-corporation shares or interests in real estate, the duty to disclose asset values requires the decedent to supply suitable appraisals.

If the parties to the agreement were married or lived together for many years and commingled their finances, or had been business partners, they may have had knowledge of each other's financial situation before the contract negotiations were begun, and such a showing will satisfy the requirements of subsection (c)(1) of this section. In the more typical case in which the parties did not have such knowledge, written disclosure in connection with the agreement is required.

i. Representation by independent legal counsel. Showing that the surviving spouse had knowledge of the decedent's financial situation when the agreement was executed is essential but not sufficient to give rise to the rebuttable presumption provided in subsection (c) of this section.

The surviving spouse must also have understood what legal rights or claims that he or she might have as the decedent's surviving spouse and understood how the proposed agreement intended to alter those rights. Under subsection (c)(2) of this section, that requirement can be satisfied by showing that the surviving spouse was represented by independent legal counsel. An independent counsel can be expected to provide advice that is customized to the client's particular situation, explain the legal rights that would accrue to the client as surviving spouse, and negotiate the terms of the agreement on behalf of the client.

j. Reasonable opportunity to obtain independent legal counsel and clear explanation of the import of the agreement. If the surviving spouse was not represented by independent legal counsel, the enforcing party can obtain the benefit of the rebuttable presumption by making two further showings. First, the enforcing party must show that the surviving spouse had a reasonable opportunity to obtain independent legal counsel in a timely fashion. That is, the enforcing party must show that the decedent or the decedent's representative advised the surviving spouse, in timely fashion, to obtain independent legal counsel; and if the surviving spouse was needy, offered to pay for the costs of the surviving spouse's representation.

The enforcing party must also show that the agreement stated, in language easily understandable by an adult of ordinary intelligence with no legal training, the nature of any rights or claims otherwise arising at death that were altered by the agreement, and the nature of that alteration.

To qualify under subsection (c)(3) of this section, the language must be explicit, concrete, and reasonably complete, but need not address every detail of the agreement's legal significance. For example, the language need not ordinarily explain the tax consequences of the agreement's provisions (although such an explanation would be necessary if tax planning was a primary purpose of the agreement and the tax impact on the surviving spouse is both significant and adverse).

k. Unconscionability. In accordance with general principles of contract law, a premarital or a marital agreement is unenforceable if it was unconscionable when it was executed. The question is to be decided by the court in the light of all the material facts. See Restatement Second, Contracts § 208, Comment *f*; Principles of the Law of Family Dissolution: Analysis and Recommendations § 7.01, Comment *e*. Among the material facts that are to be considered is the amount that the agreement provides for the surviving spouse. That amount may be considered in relation to the decedent's financial condition when the agreement was executed or in relation to the portion of the decedent's estate granted to the surviving spouse by the elective-share statute and other spousal statutory rights arising on death. Also to be considered is the financial and family situation of both parties when the agreement was executed. For example, in the case of a late-in-life second marriage, where both parties were financially secure and each party had children by a prior marriage, an agreement that completely waived each party's right to an elective share and other spousal rights arising on the other's death would not be unconscionable when executed.

Part B. Protections Against Unintentional Disinheritance

§ 9.5. Protection of Surviving Spouse Against Unintentional Disinheritance by a Premarital Will

(a) Under the Original or Revised Uniform Probate Code, the testator's surviving spouse is entitled to a specified share of the testator's estate if the testator's will was executed before the marriage, unless:

(1) the will or other evidence indicates that the will was made in contemplation of the marriage;

(2) the will expresses the intention that it be effective notwithstanding any subsequent marriage; or

(3) the testator provided for the spouse by transfer outside the will and the intent that the transfer be in lieu of a testamentary provision is shown by the testator's statements or is reasonably inferred from the amount of the transfer or other evidence.

(b) Under the Original Uniform Probate Code, the surviving spouse's share is the share that the spouse would have received if the testator had died intestate, but the spouse is only entitled to that share if the premarital will fails to provide for the surviving spouse. In satisfying the spouse's share, the devises made by the premarital will abate according to the rules of abatement for the payment of claims (see § 1.1, Comment *f*).

(c) Under the Revised Uniform Probate Code, the surviving spouse's share is the share that the spouse would have received if the testator had died intestate as to that portion of the testator's estate, if any, that is not devised to the testator's children of a prior marriage or their descendants (or that does not pass to such descendants under an antilapse or other statute). Any devise in the

premarital will to the surviving spouse counts toward satisfying the spouse's entitlement.

Comment:

a. Source. The statutory provision protecting the testator's surviving spouse from unintentional disinheritance by a will executed before the marriage (a premarital will) originated in the Original Uniform Probate Code and was refined in the Revised Uniform Probate Code.

b. Premarital will. The statutes described in this section apply only to a premarital will, i.e., a will executed before the testator's marriage to the surviving spouse. If the testator and the surviving spouse were married to each other more than once, a premarital will is a will executed by the testator at any time when they were not married to one another. Thus, a will executed during a previous marriage to the surviving spouse is not a premarital will. However, a will executed during a previous marriage to a spouse other than the surviving spouse is a premarital will.

Comment on Subsection (a):

c. Protection against unintentional disinheritance. The statutes described in this section protect the testator's surviving spouse against unintentional disinheritance resulting from a premarital will. The earlier approach to the problem took the form of the common-law doctrines revoking a premarital will, doctrines that are obsolete and are disapproved in this Restatement. See Comment *i*. As elective-share statutes came to replace dower and curtesy (see § 9.1, Comment *c*), the elective share was initially thought to provide sufficient protection against disinheritance by a premarital will. The Original UPC provided an omitted-spouse provision in addition to the elective share. The purpose was both to reduce the frequency of elections under the elective share and to provide a share for the surviving spouse more related to the amount that the testator would probably have wanted the spouse to have, had the testator addressed the need to update the premarital will to take account of the marriage.

d. Exceptions. Because the protection afforded by these statutes only relates to unintentional disinheritance, the statutes do not apply if (1) the will or other evidence indicates that the will was made in contemplation of the marriage; (2) the will expresses the intention that it be effective notwithstanding any subsequent marriage; or (3) the testator provided for the spouse by transfer outside the will and the intent that the transfer be in lieu of a testamentary provision is shown by the testator's statements or is reasonably inferred from the amount of the transfer or other evidence. The proponent of the will bears the burden of proof on these exceptions.

The Revised UPC expressly incorporates all three exceptions. Although the Original UPC expressly incorporates only the second and third of these exceptions, the position of this Restatement, supported by case law, is that the first exception—that the will or other evidence indicates that the will was made in contemplation of the marriage—also applies to enactments of the Original UPC. A premarital will that was made in contemplation of the marriage is presumed to express the testator's intentions regarding the share that he or she wants the devisee to take after the marriage in his or her capacity as spouse. In order to be executed in contemplation of the marriage, the will must be executed when the testator and the prospective spouse had marriage plans. Merely being romantically involved is not sufficient to establish that the will was executed in contemplation of the marriage.

In determining whether the third exception applies—whether the testator provided for the spouse by transfer outside the will with the intent that the transfer be in lieu of a testamentary provision—the court may consider all relevant evidence. The transfers outside the will can be in any form including outright gifts and will substitutes, and can be made before as well as after the marriage. The amount of the transfer may be considered in isolation or in relation to the portion of the testator's estate granted by the statute or in relation to the testator's total estate.

Comment on Subsection (b)—the Original UPC Omitted Spouse Provision:

e. Premarital will must "fail to provide" for the surviving spouse. The omitted-spouse's share under the Original UPC is the surviving spouse's intestate share—the share that the survivor would have received had the testator died intestate. In order for the survivor to be entitled to this intestate share, the testator's premarital will must "fail to provide" for the surviving spouse.

Most premarital wills devise nothing to the later-to-be spouse. On occasion, however, principally in the case of a will executed some time before a later-in-life second marriage, a testator executes a will that makes a devise to the later-to-be spouse, usually in the capacity of "friend." The express requirement that the premarital will must "fail to provide" for the surviving spouse might suggest that the spouse would not be entitled to an omitted-spouse's share in such a case because the will makes some provision for the spouse. Nearly all courts recognize that such an interpretation of the statute defeats its purpose by not taking into account the changed circumstances that the marriage represents. Some of these courts have held that, despite a devise in the premarital will to the later-to-be spouse, the surviving spouse is entitled to an omitted-spouse's share if the premarital will was not executed in contemplation of the marriage. These courts have also held that, when a premarital will contains a devise to the later-to-be spouse, the spouse bears the burden of proving that the will was *not* executed in contemplation of the marriage. Other courts have placed on the surviving spouse the burden of establishing that the premarital will was not executed in contemplation of the marriage and also the burden of establishing that the devise in the premarital will was of an amount or value that could not reasonably represent the testator's effort to provide by will for the surviving spouse in the capacity of "spouse."

This Restatement adopts the interpretation that the surviving spouse is entitled to an omitted-spouse's share unless the premarital will containing a devise to the later-to-be spouse was executed in contemplation of the marriage. The burden of proving that the will was executed in contemplation of the marriage is on the party opposing the spouse's entitlement.

f. Satisfying the omitted-spouse's intestate share. In satisfying the omitted-spouse's intestate share, the Original UPC provides that devises made by the premarital will abate according to the ordinary rules of abatement for the payment of claims (see § 1.1, Comment *f*). Under these rules, shares of heirs and devisees abate in the following order: (1) intestate shares; (2) residuary devises; (3) general devises; (4) specific devises. The shares of heirs and devisees abate proportionately within each class.

The use of the ordinary rules of abatement creates a problem when the premarital will devises property to the later-to-be spouse. If the will was not made in contemplation of the marriage, the spouse is entitled to an omitted-spouse's share. If the devise to the later-to-be spouse was a general or specific devise, the spouse may be allowed to keep the devise and also take an omitted-spouse's share, payment of which is borne by the residue of the estate. . . . .

Comment on Subsection (c)—the Revised UPC Entitlement Provision:

g. Spouse's intestate share in the portion of testator's net probate estate that does not pass to testator's children of a prior marriage or their descendants. The Revised UPC provision protecting the spouse against unintentional disinheritance is not strictly an "omitted" spouse statute. Application of the Revised UPC does not depend upon the premarital will "failing" to provide for the surviving spouse. If the premarital will makes a devise to the later-to-be spouse, the value of that devise simply counts toward satisfying the share to which the spouse is entitled (the spouse's guaranteed share). See Comment *h*.

The spouse's guaranteed share under the Revised UPC is not the spouse's intestate share in the testator's entire net probate estate, as it is under the Original UPC. Rather, it is the spouse's intestate share in the testator's net probate estate reduced by any portion that is devised to the testator's children of a prior marriage or their descendants (or that passes to such descendants under an antilapse or other statute). (The actual statutory language is more precise, limiting the spouse's guaranteed share to the intestate share in "that portion of the testator's [net probate] estate, if any, that neither is devised to a child of the testator who was born before the testator married the surviving spouse and who is not a child of the surviving spouse nor is devised to a descendant of such a child or passes under Sections 2–603 [the antilapse statute] or 2–604 [failure of testamentary provision] to such a child or to a descendant of such a child." . . . .) The purpose of the change was to adjust the statute to the different situation of a premarital will affecting a first marriage and a premarital will affecting a later-in-life second marriage, where one or both spouses are likely to be widowed with assets and children from the prior marriages.

h. Satisfying the spouse's guaranteed share. Under the Revised UPC, any devise in the premarital will to the surviving spouse counts toward satisfying the spouse's guaranteed share. If the premarital will does not make a devise to the later-to-be spouse or makes a devise of a lesser value than the spouse's guaranteed share, other devises—except devises passing to the testator's children by a previous marriage or their descendants—abate to make up any deficiency according to the rules of abatement for the payment of claims. See Comment *f*. If the premarital will makes a devise to the later-to-be spouse of an equal or greater value than the spouse's guaranteed share, the spouse is not entitled to any extra amount.

Illustrations:

2. *Premarital will to a first marriage.* When in his late 20s, A executed a will devising his entire estate to his brothers and sisters. Later, A married B. Three years later, A died in an airplane crash. A was survived by B and by his brothers and sisters. B is entitled to her intestate share in A's entire net probate estate. Under the Revised UPC, that intestate share is the entire estate. See § 2.2, Comment *a*.

4. *Premarital will not containing a devise to the testator's later-to-be spouse; later-in-life second marriage.* H and W enjoyed a long and happy marriage, which produced two children, A and B. W died at age

70, survived by H, age 68. W's will devised her entire estate to H if he survived her; if not, to A and B in equal shares. H's will, executed at the same time, devised his entire estate to W if she survived him; if not, to A and B in equal shares. Some few years after W's death, H remarried. He never thought to change his will after the marriage; he assumed that W having predeceased him, his property would be divided equally between A and B. (His new wife, W-2, was financially well off.) A few months after his second marriage, H suffered a heart attack and died. H was survived by his second wife, W-2, and by A and B. H's net estate was valued at $150,000. W-2 takes nothing under the Revised UPC omitted-spouse provision. Since H devised everything to A and B, children of the former marriage, nothing is left to which W-2 is entitled as an intestate share.

i. *Marriage or marriage followed by birth of issue does not revoke premarital will.* Neither marriage nor marriage followed by birth of issue revokes a premarital will or any part of a premarital will. See § 4.1(b) and Comment *q*.

§ 9.6. Protection of Child or Descendant Against Unintentional Disinheritance

(a) A child of the testator, or under some statutes a descendant of the testator, who was not provided for in the testator's will may be entitled to a specified share of the testator's estate as provided by statute. Most of the statutes, including the Original and Revised Uniform Probate Code, only protect a child who was born or adopted after the will was executed.

(b) A child of the testator who was not provided for in the testator's will because the testator thought that the child was dead may be entitled to a specified share of the testator's estate as provided by statute.

(c) The omitted child or descendant is entitled to the specified share unless a contrary intent or other statutory exception is established.

Comment:

a. *Scope.* The statutes that protect a child or a descendant of a child from unintentional disinheritance are sometimes called *omitted-child* statutes or *pretermitted-heir* statutes.

b. *Omitted afterborn or after-adopted child under the Original Uniform Probate Code.* The Original UPC provides that if a testator's will fails to provide for a child born or adopted after the execution of the will, the omitted child receives an intestate share—the share in the net probate estate equal in value to that which the child would have received if the testator had died intestate.

The omitted afterborn or after-adopted child receives this share unless (1) it appears from the will that the omission was intentional; (2) when the will was executed the testator had one or more children and devised substantially all the estate to the other parent of the omitted child; or (3) the testator provided for the child by transfer outside the will, and the intent that the transfer be in lieu of a testamentary provision is shown by statements of the testator or from the amount of the transfer or other evidence.

In satisfying a child's intestate share, devises abate as provided under the ordinary rules of abatement for the payment of claims (see § 1.1, Comment *f*).

c. Omitted afterborn or after-adopted child under the Revised Uniform Probate Code. The Revised UPC provides that if a testator's will fails to provide for a child born or adopted after the execution of the will, the omitted afterborn or after-adopted child receives a share in the net probate estate that depends on whether or not the testator had children living when the will was executed and, if so, whether the will made a devise to any of the then-living children.

If the testator had no child living when the will was executed, an omitted afterborn or after-adopted child receives an intestate share, unless the will devised all or substantially all of the estate to the other parent of the omitted child and that other parent survives the testator and is entitled to take under the will. In satisfying the child's intestate share, devises abate as provided under the ordinary rules of abatement for the payment of claims (see § 1.1, Comment *f*).

If the testator had one or more children living when the will was executed, and the will made a devise to one or more of the then-living children, an omitted afterborn or after-adopted child is entitled to share in the portion of the testator's estate devised to the testator's then-living children as if the child had been given an equal share of that portion of the estate. To the extent feasible, the interest granted an omitted afterborn or after-adopted child is to be of the same character, whether equitable or legal, present or future, as that devised to the testator's then-living children. Devises to the testator's then-living children abate ratably. In abating the devises of the then-living children, the court is directed to preserve to the maximum extent possible the character of the testamentary plan adopted by the testator.

Illustrations:

1. When G executed her will, she had two living children, A and B. Her will devised $7500 to each child. After G executed her will, she had another child, C. C is entitled to $5000. Two thousand five hundred dollars (1/3 of $7,500) of C's entitlement comes from A's $7500 devise (reducing it to $5000) and $2500 (1/3 of $7500) comes from B's $7500 devise (reducing it to $5000).

2. The facts are the same as in Illustration 1, except that G's will devised $10,000 to A and $5000 to B. C is entitled to $5000. Three thousand three hundred thirty-three dollars (1/3 of $10,000) of C's entitlement comes from A's $10,000 devise (reducing it to $6667) and $1667 (1/3 of $5000) comes from B's $5000 devise (reducing it to $3333).

An omitted afterborn or after-adopted child is entitled to a share under the Revised UPC unless (1) it appears from the will that the omission was intentional or (2) the testator provided for the omitted afterborn or after-adopted child by transfer outside the will and the intent that the transfer be in lieu of a testamentary provision is shown by the testator's statements or is reasonably inferred from the amount of the transfer or other evidence. The party who is claiming that one of the exceptions applies has the burden of persuasion on the elements of that exception.

The Revised UPC does not grant a share to an afterborn or after-adopted child if the testator had one or more children living when the will was executed, but the will did not make a devise to any of the then-living children.

d. Nonuniform omitted-child statutes. The nonuniform omitted-child statutes vary widely. Although most statutes only grant an intestate share to an omitted child if the child was born or adopted after the execution of the testator's will, some grant an intestate share to any omitted child or descendant, or in some cases descendants of a deceased child. Others grant an intestate share to any omitted afterborn child but only if the testator had one or more children living when the will was executed. Still others grant an intestate share to any omitted afterborn child but only if the testator had one or more children living when the will was executed and one or more of the living children were provided for in the will. Still others grant an intestate share to any omitted afterborn child but only if the testator had no child living when the will was executed. . . . .

Any nonuniform statute that refers to a child or descendant born before or after a specified time includes a child who is adopted before or after the specified time.

e. Republication by codicil. Under the doctrine of republication by codicil, a will is treated as if it were executed when its most recent codicil was executed, whether or not the codicil expressly republishes the prior will. The doctrine is not applied, however, if the effect of its application would be inconsistent with the testator's intent, as would usually be the case if its application would bar a share to an afterborn or after-adopted child under an omitted-child statute. See § 3.4.

Illustration:

3. G's will, executed three years before his death, created a testamentary trust for his surviving spouse, and made equal monetary devises to each of his two children, A and B. Four months before his death, and after his third child, C, was born, G executed a codicil to his will that altered the marital-deduction trust in order to take advantage of a change in tax law. The codicil expressly republished his prior will. Applicable law contains an omitted-child statute that gives a share of the estate to a child who is born after the will is executed. The doctrine of republication by codicil is not applied because application of the doctrine would prevent G's third child, C, from taking a share of his net probate estate under the pretermitted-heir statute.

f. Class gift. A class gift, by nature, includes afterborn or after-adopted members of the specified class, because class terms permit increase of class members. If the testator's will contains a class gift in favor of his or her children or descendants, any child who is born or adopted after the execution of the will is provided for in the will, and thus does not receive an additional share under an omitted-child statute.

g. Disclaimer by child. A child who disclaims a share under a will or other donative document cannot then claim an omitted-child's share. For example, if an afterborn or after-adopted child who is provided for by class gift (see Comment *f*) files a disclaimer, the disclaimer does not allow the child to invoke the omitted-child statute, which if applicable might give the child a greater share. The disclaimer causes the child to be treated as if the child had predeceased the testator, and, if the disclaimant had descendants, an applicable antilapse statute should give the disclaimed interest to the child's descendants as substitute takers (see § 5.5).

h. Pour-over devise. If the testator's will contains a pour-over devise (see § 3.8), a child who is a beneficiary of the trust into which the devise pours over is not entitled to an omitted-child's share.

Illustration:

4. When G executed her will, she and her husband had one child, A. G's will devised $10,000 to A and the residue of her estate to a revocable inter vivos trust. The trust provides that on G's death, the income is to be paid to G's husband for life, and at the husband's death, the principal of the trust is to be paid to G's descendants then living, by representation. After G executed her will, she and her husband had a second child, B. Because B is a beneficiary of the class that is to receive the principal of the trust when the husband dies, B is not entitled to an omitted-child's share.

i. Contrary intent. Omitted-child statutes protect the testator's children and sometimes descendants, usually those born or adopted after the will is executed, from *unintentional* disinheritance. Consequently, such statutes yield to a contrary intent. The statutes themselves usually specify how and what must be proved to establish a contrary intent. Comments *b* and *c* describe the provisions of the Original and Revised Uniform Probate Code. The nonuniform statutes vary widely on how a contrary intent is established. . . . . Unless the applicable omitted-child's statute provides otherwise, extrinsic evidence of intent may be considered in determining whether an omission was intentional. See § 10.2.

j. Child omitted because believed dead. Both the Original and Revised UPC and some nonuniform statutes provide that a living child who is omitted from the testator's will solely because the testator believed that the child was dead receives an intestate share.

DIVISION IV

CONSTRUCTION, REFORMATION, AND MODIFICATION OF DONATIVE DOCUMENTS

Scope of Division IV. Division IV addresses the process of giving meaning and effect to a donative document. This is largely a matter of determining the donor's intention and of construing, reforming, or modifying the document to give effect to that intention to the maximum extent possible.

The discussion throughout this Division assumes that the donative document is valid, that is, that the donor executed the document in accordance with any applicable law regarding formalities, intended to make the transfer, possessed the necessary capacity to make the transfer, and was free of fraud, duress, and undue influence. See Divisions I and II on Formalities and Division III on Protective Doctrines.

As noted, this Division addresses the process of giving meaning and effect to a donative document. A document of transfer such as a will or a trust is normally donative in its entirety.

Some documents, such as life-insurance policies and employee-benefit plans, also make donative transfers, but in the context of bargained-for arrangements. The rules for determining the meaning of donative documents set forth in this Division apply to the donative provisions of these documents, typically the beneficiary designations, even though these documents as a whole are not entirely donative in character. The "donative document" in such a case is the donative provision or provisions of the larger document.

In some instances, a transfer made in a will, trust, beneficiary designation, or similar document is made pursuant to a contract, such as a premarital or postmarital agreement, a divorce settlement, or a will contract. Regarding the application of this Division to dispositive provisions required by contract, see § 10.1, Comment *e*.

CHAPTER 10

GENERAL PRINCIPLES

Introductory Note: Chapter 10 presents general principles to be used in establishing the donor's intention and giving effect to that intention. Chapter 11 addresses the constructional processes for resolving ambiguities. Chapter 12 addresses measures for reforming or modifying unambiguous language in a donative document in accordance with the donor's intention.

§ 10.1. Donor's Intention Determines the Meaning of a Donative Document and Is Given Effect to the Maximum Extent Allowed by Law

The controlling consideration in determining the meaning of a donative document is the donor's intention. The donor's intention is given effect to the maximum extent allowed by law.

Comment:

a. *Rationale.* The organizing principle of the American law of donative transfers is freedom of disposition. Property owners have the nearly unrestricted right to dispose of their property as they please. This section implements this fundamental principle by stating two well-accepted propositions: (1) that the controlling consideration in determining the meaning of a donative document is the donor's intention; and (2) that the donor's intention is given effect to the maximum extent allowed by law.

b. *Meaning of a donative document.* This section distinguishes between meaning and effect. In this Restatement, apart from exceptional cases in which reformation or modification is warranted (see Chapter 12), the word "construction" is used to designate the final product of the process of determining the meaning of a donative document (see Chapter 11).

The controlling consideration in determining the meaning of a donative document is the donor's intention. The controlling consideration in determining whether the donor's intention is given effect is whether the donor's intention is allowed by law. Note, however, that various constructional preferences, such as the constructional preferences for the construction that is more in accord with public policy than other plausible constructions and for the construction that is more legally effective than other plausible constructions (see § 11.3), bear on meaning and may lead to constructions that avoid conflict with overriding rules of law. Note also that, in some situations, a donative document may be modified to achieve the donor's tax objectives. See § 12.2.

c. *Effect of a donative document.* Unless disallowed by law, the donor's intention not only determines the meaning but also the effect of a donative document.

American law does not grant courts any general authority to question the wisdom, fairness, or reasonableness of the donor's decisions about how to allocate his or her property. The main function of the law in this field is to facilitate rather than regulate. The law serves this function by establishing rules under which sufficiently reliable determinations can be made regarding the content of the donor's intention.

American law curtails freedom of disposition only to the extent that the donor attempts to make a disposition or achieve a purpose that is prohibited or restricted by an overriding rule of law. The term "rule of law" is used in a broad sense to include rules and principles derived from the U.S. Constitution, a state constitution, or public policy; rules and principles set forth in federal or state legislation or in municipal ordinances; rules and principles of the common law and of equity; and rules and principles contained in governmental regulations. A rule of law is an overriding rule of law if it is applicable and prohibits or restricts the disposition or purpose that the donor intends.

Among the rules of law that prohibit or restrict freedom of disposition in certain instances are those relating to spousal rights; creditors' rights; unreasonable restraints on alienation or marriage; provisions promoting separation or divorce; impermissible racial or other categoric restrictions; provisions encouraging illegal activity; and the rules against perpetuities and accumulations. The foregoing list is illustrative, not exhaustive.

d. Scope. Division IV addresses the processes of determining the donor's intention and of giving effect to that intention by construction, reformation, or modification. Other Divisions address the overriding rules of law that prohibit or restrict the effect to be given to the donor's intention.

e. Contractual transfers. In some instances, one or more transfers made in wills, trusts, beneficiary designations, or similar documents are made pursuant to a contract, such as a premarital or a marital agreement (see § 9.4), a divorce settlement, or a will contract. Although these transfers are not donative transfers, and although the transferor is not a donor, various rules stated in this Division, such as the rules regarding the use of extrinsic evidence and the use of constructional preferences in resolving ambiguities, can help determine the meaning and effect of contractual transfers of this type. Consequently, the rules set forth in this Division may be appropriately adapted to such cases. See § 11.2, Comments *g* and *m*; § 11.3, Comment *l*; and § 12.1, Comment *n*.

§ 10.2. Permissible Evidence for Determining Donor's Intention

In seeking to determine the donor's intention, all relevant evidence, whether direct or circumstantial, may be considered, including the text of the donative document and relevant extrinsic evidence.

Comment:

a. Scope note. This section outlines the types of evidence that may be considered in seeking to determine the donor's intention. Subsequent Chapters in this and other Divisions supply additional detail and illustrate the use of various types of evidence in proceedings for construction, reformation, or modification of a donative document.

The donor's intention is sometimes referred to in this Restatement as the donor's *actual* intention, in order to contrast it with the intention that is *attributed* to the donor by an applicable constructional preference or rule of construction. See § 11.3.

b. Reading donative document as an entirety. The text of a donative document must be read in its entirety. Each portion, whether it be a word, phrase, clause, sentence, paragraph, article, or some other portion, is connected to a whole. The donor is presumed to intend that the various portions complement or modify each other. The case may arise, for instance, in which two portions, read in isolation, appear contradictory. But, when construction of the document as a consistent whole would be facilitated by reading one portion as modifying the other or reading both as mutually modifying each other, that construction prevails.

Illustration:

1. G, owning a parcel of land in fee simple absolute, executes and delivers a deed that contains a clause conveying the land "to A and her heirs." A later clause provides that "if A dies without descendants surviving her, the land goes to B and his heirs." Taken in isolation, the conveyance "to A and her heirs" would give A a fee simple absolute, an estate that is inconsistent with the later clause giving the land to B if A dies without descendants surviving her. When read as a whole, however, this deed contains no repugnancy but creates a defeasible fee simple in A and a contingent future interest in B that takes effect in possession if A dies without descendants surviving her.

The meaning of various words or phrases in a donative document can be controlled by definitions of those words or phrases contained in the document. In the absence of a controlling definition, the meaning of various words or phrases may be deduced from the use of those terms elsewhere in the document.

The necessity for reading the donative document as a whole does not, however, justify the so-called plain-meaning rule, which relies solely on the document's text and excludes extrinsic evidence. The plain-meaning rule is archaic because it unduly stresses a supposed ordinary meaning of the words employed. This rule has long been discredited, and is disapproved here, because the text of a document is so colored by the circumstances surrounding its formulation that evidence regarding the donor's intention is always relevant. See § 12.1, Comment *d*.

c. Historical note on use of terms "admissible" and "inadmissible." Courts often say that extrinsic evidence is "admissible" or "inadmissible" in determining the meaning of donative documents. When courts say this, they are using the terms in a specialized sense. "Admissibility" of extrinsic evidence as an aid in construing a donative document is a matter of substantive law, not the law of evidence. To avoid confusion with the general law of evidence, this Restatement uses the expression "may be considered" rather than the term "admissible" when characterizing extrinsic evidence that may properly be taken into account in determining the donor's intention.

d. Surrounding circumstances. Extrinsic evidence of the circumstances surrounding the execution of the donative document that might bear on the donor's intention, directly or circumstantially, may always be considered. Examples include evidence of the donor's occupation, property at the time of execution of the document, and relationships with family members and with other persons, including the designated or apparently designated donees. Because a donor formulates his or her intention largely based upon what the donor knows or believes concerning the persons whom he or she includes or excludes as donees, evidence regarding this knowledge or belief can help in the construction of a donative document. Thus, when the fact tends to illuminate the meaning of the text employed, it is proper to show, for example, that a donor knew or believed a particular person to be incapacitated, dead, wealthy, in need of funds, friendly, unfriendly, or related by blood to the donor or to other affected persons.

e. Surrounding circumstances—skill of drafter. A significant element of the surrounding circumstances may be whether the drafter of the document was a layperson (usually the donor) or a person experienced in the use of legal or other specialized terminology (usually the donor's lawyer). A donative document drafted by a layperson is to be construed to have the meaning that a lay drafter would have intended. Thus, under the doctrine of personal usage (see § 11.2(b)(3)), the drafter's lack of familiarity with financial terminology would be a factor supporting a construction of a disposition of "all my stocks and bonds" to include not only the assets that are technically stocks and bonds but also certain warrants that the donor customarily spoke of as "bonds." Thus, also, especially in a will containing no other dispositive provisions, the drafter's lack of familiarity with legal terminology might support construing a devise of "all my personal property" to include interests in land owned by the donor; or might support construing a devise of "all my money" to include all the donor's assets.

Conversely, when the drafter is a legal professional or other person experienced in the use of legal terminology, words and phrases are presumed to bear their customary legal connotations. Indeed, the forms that professional drafters use for their clients commonly embody the contributions of many hands accumulated across the years. In such a case, the donor adopts the language of others rather than crafting his or her own. One of the things that the donor is free to do with the freedom of disposition that the law allows is to delegate the drafting of the donative document. In such a case, the court properly attributes the language of the document to the donor, as the expression of his or her intention. However, it must always be borne in mind that the donor's intention controls the meaning of the document. Although a donor utilized a drafting agent, and although the drafting agent, if a lawyer, usually will have expressed the donor's intention completely and accurately, the meaning of the document produced by that agent is controlled by the donor's intention. Extrinsic evidence, where relevant, may always be considered on the question of the donor's objectives and the extent to which the drafting agent ascertained and reflected those objectives.

f. Direct evidence of intention. Direct as well as circumstantial evidence relevant to the donor's intention may be considered. Direct evidence relevant to the donor's intention includes documents and testimony evidencing the donor's intention; the donor's own declarations of intention, written or oral; contents of the drafting agent's files; and written or oral statements made to the donor by the drafting agent or another concerning the contents or effect of the document, to the extent that the donor acquiesced, silently or expressly, in the other person's statements. A donor's declarations of intention are found in such utterances as the donor's oral statements or conversations, letters, memoranda, and written or oral statements instructing the drafting agent regarding the preparation of the donative document.

g. Extrinsic evidence—time to which evidence relates. Although the primary focus is on the donor's intention at the time of execution of the donative document, post-execution events can sometimes be relevant in determining the donor's intention. Post-execution statements of the donor, for example, can relate to the donor's intention at the time of execution. In addition, if the donative document was ambiguous when executed, the donor might not have recognized the ambiguity at the time of execution and hence might not then have formed an intention on the question. Similarly, if the donative document was not ambiguous when executed, but became ambiguous because of post-execution events, the donor might not then have anticipated these events and might not then have formed an intention on the question. A subsequent event giving rise to an ambiguity might focus the donor's mind on the application of the document regarding that subsequent event. Consequently, post-execution indications of intention may properly be considered in resolving an ambiguity if they shed light on the donor's intention at the time of execution or on what the donor's intention would probably then have been had the ambiguity been recognized or the subsequent event been anticipated. As with any other circumstance bearing on the donor's intention, the probative force of post-execution indications of intention must be weighed by the trier of fact.

It must always be kept in mind that, if the donor formed an intention at the time of execution, even if the donative document is amendable, the donor is not permitted to amend the document by later changing his or her mind without complying with the requirements for making such an amendment. For example, a testator who executed a will devising $10,000 to A is not later permitted to increase or decrease the amount of A's devise by oral declarations; the testator must execute a codicil or a new will to accomplish that purpose. . . . .

Illustration:

2. G executed a will devising "my diamond ring" to her niece, A. When G executed this will and when G died, she owned two diamond rings, one of which she customarily wore on her finger and the other of which she had placed in her safety-deposit box. At a family gathering after executing her will, G held up her hand and told several family members that A was going to receive this ring when she, G, died. This evidence may be considered in seeking to establish which ring G intended to devise to A.

h. Rules of evidence. The principle of this section—that all relevant evidence may be considered in seeking to determine the donor's intention—is a rule of substantive law and is subject to the rules of evidence, such as the hearsay rule, the attorney-client privilege, and the competency rules (including the so-called dead-man's act). To the extent appropriate, the rules of evidence should be construed to allow direct evidence of the donor's intention, whether the evidence concerns utterances or events occurring before or after execution of the donative document.

Documentary evidence and oral and written testimony concerning the donor's declarations of intention should be held admissible under exceptions to the hearsay rule. Declarations of intention made before execution of the donative document should be held admissible under the exception for statements expressing an intent to do an act. Declarations of intention made after execution of the donative document should be held admissible under (1) a special exception for post-execution statements with respect to a donative document; (2) the exception for evidence indicating a state of mind (the donor's post-execution declarations asserting his or her belief that he or she executed a donative document of certain contents or effect); or (3) the exception for circumstantial evidence indicating a state of mind (the donor's post-execution statements indirectly and circumstantially indicating a belief that he or she executed a donative document of certain contents or effect).

The attorney-client privilege does not apply to communications that are relevant to the donor's intention. See Restatement Third, The Law Governing Lawyers § 81 ("The attorney-client privilege does not apply to a communication from or to a decedent relevant to an issue between parties who claim an interest through the same deceased client, either by testate or intestate succession or by an inter vivos transaction."). Thus, the privilege does not preclude the use of documentary evidence in the hands of the donor's attorney, nor does it bar the use of the attorney's oral or written testimony. The purpose of the attorney-client privilege is to protect the client from disclosure of communications between the client and attorney. See id. § 68, Comment *c*. To the extent that the privilege continues after the death of the client in actions against the estate (see id. § 77, Comment *c*), a proceeding to resolve an ambiguity in a donative document is not viewed as an adverse proceeding against the estate, but a contest between two or more different constructions of the document. The privilege is not available in this setting because invoking it would not protect the client or his or her estate but rather a claimant to that estate. The client's interest is best protected by admission of all relevant evidence that will assist in determining his or her intention.

If the donor is dead at the time of the lawsuit, evidence of the donor's declarations of intention should be admissible notwithstanding that a dead-man act is in force in the jurisdiction. Dead-man acts generally bar testimony by the survivor of a "transaction" with the decedent, when offered against the decedent's estate. In many jurisdictions, it has been held that the concept of "transaction" in such statutes contemplates exchange transactions, as opposed to donative transfers. To the extent the statutory language permits, dead-man acts should be construed not to interfere with the introduction of documentary evidence or testimony by a witness regarding the donor's statements about the content of his or her will or other donative document, even if the documentary evidence or the testimony stems from a witness who is a devisee, beneficiary, nominee, or appointee or claims to be a devisee, beneficiary, nominee, or appointee of the donative provision in question.

i. Standard of proof—ambiguous and unambiguous documents. This section is only concerned with the types of evidence that may be considered in seeking to determine the donor's intention, not with the standard of proof necessary to establish that intention. The standard of proof to be applied depends on whether the document is ambiguous or unambiguous.

A document that is unambiguous is entitled to a strong (but not irrebuttable) presumption of correctness, that is, to a strong presumption that it accurately expresses the donor's intention. An unambiguous document may be reformed, but to do so takes a showing *by clear and convincing evidence* that the donor's intention differed from the terms of the document. See § 12.1.

An ambiguous document is not entitled to a presumption of correctness because the ambiguity establishes that the document does not adequately express the donor's intention. Consequently, in a construction suit to resolve ambiguities for which there is no applicable constructional preference or rule of construction, the donor's intention need only be established by a *preponderance of the evidence*. If the ambiguity is presumptively resolved by a constructional preference or a rule of construction, the standard of proof ordinarily required to overcome the constructional preference or rule of construction is preponderance of the evidence. By statute or case law, however, clear and convincing evidence may be required to overcome some rules of construction. See Chapter 11.

CHAPTER 11

RESOLVING AMBIGUITIES

Introductory Note: Chapter 11 applies the general principles of §§ 10.1 and 10.2 to the problem of resolving ambiguities. The term "ambiguity" is defined in § 11.1.

Section 11.2 addresses ambiguities for which there is no applicable rule of construction and for which no applicable constructional preference is contrary to the evidence of the donor's intention. Consequently, this section does not address ambiguities that require weighing evidence of the donor's intention against a contrary constructional preference or rule of construction, but does use a few Illustrations in which the evidence of the donor's intention accords with an applicable constructional preference.

Section 11.3 identifies a set of constructional preferences. If a constructional preference applies to an ambiguity, the ambiguity is resolved by the constructional preference, unless evidence establishes that the donor had a different intention.

§ 11.1. Ambiguity Defined

An ambiguity in a donative document is an uncertainty in meaning that is revealed by the text or by extrinsic evidence other than direct evidence of intention contradicting the plain meaning of the text.

Comment:

a. Scope note. This section defines an ambiguity in a donative document as an uncertainty in meaning that is revealed by the text or by extrinsic evidence other than direct evidence of intention contradicting the plain meaning of the text. An uncertainty in meaning shows that the document contains an inadequate expression of the donor's intention. Ambiguities often but not necessarily arise in situations in which two or more constructions of the document are plausible.

Certain types of ambiguity arise recurrently. These are ambiguous descriptions, mistaken inclusions or omissions, and cases in which the donor's customary usage of terms differs from the ordinary meaning of terms used in the document. Each of these types is treated in § 11.2.

When the text of a donative document is ambiguous, the donor's intention is not always ascertainable from the text alone. Although it is customary to distinguish between latent and patent ambiguities, no legal consequences attach to the distinction. The terms are used for descriptive purposes only. A patent ambiguity is an ambiguity that appears from the text alone (Comment *b*) and a latent ambiguity is one that is revealed by extrinsic evidence other than direct evidence of intention contradicting the plain meaning of the text (Comment *c*).

b. *Patent ambiguity.* A patent ambiguity is an ambiguity that is apparent from the text of the donative document. A patent ambiguity can arise in a variety of settings, for example, in a case in which two portions of a document conflict with one another (the ambiguity can sometimes be resolved by reading the document as an entirety: see § 10.2, Comment *b*); or in a case in which it is unclear to which portion of a document a provision applies . . .; or in a case in which a word is used that has more than one dictionary meaning, such as whether a devise of "my money" only refers to the testator's cash on hand or also includes checking, savings, or money-market accounts, mutual funds, stocks and bonds, even land. Another typical instance of patent ambiguity arises where the text of a donative document reveals that language has been, or appears to have been, included or omitted by mistake. This type of patent ambiguity is treated in § 11.2(b)(2) and Comments *n* through *q*.

c. *Latent ambiguity.* A latent ambiguity is an ambiguity that is not apparent merely from reading the text of the donative document but becomes apparent from extrinsic evidence. Language in a will, for example, that devises property "to my cousin John," contains a latent ambiguity if evidence extrinsic to the document reveals that the testator had no cousin named John when he executed his will but did then have a nephew named John and a cousin named James. As this example shows, extrinsic evidence must be considered in deciding whether a latent ambiguity exists. Such evidence includes information relating to the circumstances surrounding the execution of the document (see § 10.2, Comment *d*). If the donative document is a will, information relating to the testator's circumstances at death must also be considered in order to determine the property available for distribution and the persons who are living at the testator's death or who survive the testator by a prescribed period of time.

Note that *direct evidence of intention contradicting the plain meaning of the text* does not establish a latent ambiguity. If the testator in the above example had a cousin named John when he executed his will, the devise "to my cousin John" would not be rendered ambiguous by evidence that the testator directed his lawyer to designate the testator's cousin James as the devisee and that the lawyer's secretary typed in John's name by mistake. Compare § 12.1, however, for the possibility of reforming the will if the testator's intention to designate his cousin James as the devisee rather than his cousin John can be shown by clear and convincing evidence.

Although latent ambiguities can arise in a variety of settings, ambiguous description is the prototype. See § 11.2(b)(1) and Comments *h* through *m*. Another instance of latent ambiguity arises when the donor's personal usage differs from the ordinary meaning of a term used in the text. See § 11.2(b)(3) and Comments *r* through *u*.

d. *Resolving ambiguities.* In resolving ambiguities, there is a difference in procedure between ambiguities to which no rule of construction or constructional preference applies (§ 11.2) and ambiguities to which a rule of construction or a constructional preference applies (§ 11.3).

§ 11.2. Resolving Ambiguities in Accordance with the Donor's Intention

(a) An ambiguity to which no rule of construction or constructional preference applies is resolved by construing the text of the donative document in accordance with the donor's intention,

to the extent that the donor's intention is established by a preponderance of the evidence.

(b) Ambiguities to which no rule of construction or constructional preference applies include those arising when:

(1) the text or extrinsic evidence (other than direct evidence contradicting the plain meaning of the text) reveals a mistaken description of persons or property.

(2) the text reveals an apparent mistaken inclusion or omission.

(3) extrinsic evidence (other than direct evidence contradicting the plain meaning of the text) reveals that the donor's personal usage differs from the ordinary meaning of a term used in the text.

Comment on Subsection (a):

a. Scope note. This section sets forth the general principle for resolving ambiguities in accordance with the donor's intention, to the extent that the donor's intention is established by a preponderance of the evidence. The types of evidence from which the donor's intention can be established are set forth in § 10.2.

.... When a constructional preference merely reinforces evidence of intention that is sufficient by itself to establish the donor's intention, . . ., it is appropriate to say that the ambiguity is resolved in accordance with the donor's actual as opposed to attributed intention.

b. Rationale. Because the primary objective of construction is to give effect to the donor's intention, extrinsic evidence relevant to the donor's intention may be considered along with the text of the document in seeking to determine the donor's intention. To the extent that the donor's intention is established from the types of evidence described in § 10.2, the text is construed in accordance with that intention. Because an ambiguous document is not entitled to a presumption of correctness (see § 10.2, Comment *i*), the donor's intention need only be established by a preponderance of the evidence. To the extent that the donor's intention is not established by a preponderance of the evidence, techniques of construction may be applied to give effect to intention to the extent possible. See Comments *c*, *f*, *k*, and *q*.

c. Techniques of construction. In resolving ambiguities in wills, but not in other donative documents, courts often say that the only remedy available is to delete erroneous portions of the document so that the remaining language declares or can be construed as declaring the testator's intention. The deletion of the erroneous portions of a document is sometimes called the doctrine of *falsa demonstratio non nocet*, which means that mere erroneous description does not vitiate. . . . . The technique of deleting but not adding language is meant to avoid violating the Statute of Wills, which requires the will to be executed in accordance with certain formalities. See § 3.1.

On the question of initial execution, however, modern authority is moving away from insistence on strict compliance with the statutory formalities for wills. Section 3.3 adopts a harmless-error rule, under which a harmless error in executing a will may be excused if the proponent establishes by clear and convincing evidence that the decedent adopted the document as his or her will. See also Restatement Second, Property (Donative

Transfers) § 33.1, Comment *g*; Revised Uniform Probate Code § 2–503. Under the Revised UPC, a document or writing on a document that was not executed in compliance with the statutory formalities is treated as if it had been properly executed "if the proponent of the document or writing establishes by clear and convincing evidence that the decedent intended the document or writing to constitute . . . the decedent's will . . . ."

The trend away from insisting on strict compliance with statutory formalities is based on a growing acceptance of the broader principle that mistake, whether in execution or in expression, should not be allowed to defeat intention and work unjust enrichment. A broader principle, therefore, underlies the movement to excuse defective execution and the subject of this and the next Chapter of the Restatement, curing defective expression.

Well before the trend toward excusing execution defects commenced, some courts were taking a candid approach to techniques of construction, rejecting the deletion-only approach and forthrightly acknowledging that the evidence may require words in a will to be changed, transposed, or supplied, as well as deleted. Deleting language that was executed in compliance with the statutory formalities is already changing the text to make it accord with intention. The line between deleting and changing, transposing, or supplying words is artificial and difficult to defend. This Restatement takes the position that construction need not be limited to deleting words for the purpose of maneuvering what remains of the text into what is known to be the donor's intention. The text of the document should be construed in a straightforward manner in accordance with the donor's intention as proved by the evidence.

The important point is not the way the remedy is crafted, but the familiar basis for effecting the remedy. In the case of an ambiguity in a will or other donative document, the correcting remedy is justified because the text does not adequately express the donor's intention. Once an ambiguity is revealed, it is well accepted that extrinsic evidence may be considered in resolving the ambiguity. When the donor's intention is then proved by a preponderance of the evidence, the final step, correcting the mistaken expression, should follow as a matter of remedy, and should not be unnecessarily hindered by an artificial line between deleting and adding.

d. Extrinsic evidence. Once an ambiguity, patent or latent, is established, direct as well as circumstantial evidence of the donor's intention may be considered in resolving the ambiguity in accordance with the donor's intention. See § 10.2, Comment *h*. As noted in Comment *a*, the donor's intention need only be established by a preponderance of the evidence. . . . .

e. Construction by fiduciary or other payor. In resolving an ambiguity in a donative document, the construction placed on the document by the fiduciary (or other payor) is not entitled to a presumption of correctness in litigation. The court resolves the matter de novo. The position is different, however, if the donative document grants the fiduciary (or other payor) authority to resolve questions of construction and provides that the fiduciary's decision shall be binding on all interested parties. In such cases, the clause does not make the fiduciary's decision controlling but does entitle it to a strong presumption of correctness that is to be set aside only if it is arbitrary or made in bad faith. On the analogous question of reviewing a fiduciary's decisions regarding the exercise of discretionary distributive powers, see Restatement Third, Trusts § 50.

f. Construction where ambiguity not resolved by the evidence. In rare cases of ambiguity, the evidence does not fully establish the donor's intention. In the absence of an applicable constructional preference or rule of construction (see § 11.3), the document, in such cases, may be construed to carry out the donor's intention to the extent possible. See Comments *k* and *q* for further discussion and illustration of this principle.

g. *Contractual transfers.* As noted in § 10.1, Comment *e*, one or more transfers made in wills, trusts, beneficiary designations, or similar documents are sometimes made pursuant to a contract, such as a premarital or a marital agreement (see § 9.4), a divorce settlement, or a will contract. Although these transfers are not donative transfers and the transferor is not a donor, this section and various other rules stated in this Division can help determine the meaning and effect of contractual transfers of this type.

The obligatory character of such transfers can complicate this process, however. Either the contract (for example, a will contract) or the document of transfer that purports to implement the contract (here, the will), or both, can be ambiguous. Resolving ambiguities in the contract is governed by the law of contracts, as reflected in the Restatement Second of Contracts or its successor, but this Division of the Restatement Third of Property, appropriately adapted to the situation, can be helpful in resolving ambiguities in the implementing document of transfer. If, for example, the transferor's contractual obligation as set forth in the contract is clear and unambiguous, but the implementing document contains an ambiguity, extrinsic evidence of the transferor's intention may be considered in seeking to resolve the ambiguity. Note, however, that § 11.3 promulgates a constructional preference for resolving ambiguities in accordance with the transferor's contractual obligations. This constructional preference would resolve the ambiguity in the implementing document, in the absence of persuasive evidence that the transferor intended to breach the contractual obligation. For further discussion and illustrations of the application of this Division to contractual transfers, see Comment *m*; § 11.3, Comment *l*; and § 12.1, Comment *n*.

Comment on Subsection (b)(1):

h. *Ambiguous description of persons or property.* As noted in § 11.1, Comments *a* and *b*, a type of ambiguity that arises recurrently is an ambiguous description of property or persons.

i. *Ambiguous description of property.* Ambiguities in text describing donated property can arise in a variety of settings. An ambiguity arises, for example, if extrinsic evidence shows (1) that the language does not precisely fit any property that the donor owned when the donative document was executed . . .; or (2) that the language, precisely or imprecisely, fits more than one item of property that the donor then owned . . . .

Note, however, that a latent ambiguity does not necessarily arise simply because the donor did not own a described item of property when the document was executed. There would be no latent ambiguity, for example, if the language contemplates application to property that the donor will own at a later time, such as in a devise of "the automobile that I own at death." Compare Comment *l*.

j. *Ambiguous description of a person.* Latent ambiguities regarding the description of a person can arise in a variety of settings, for example, if extrinsic evidence shows (1) that the language does not precisely fit any person who existed when the donative document was executed . . .; (2) that the language does not precisely fit any person whom the donor then knew or knew of, even though the language does precisely fit a then-existing person . . .; or (3) the language, precisely or imprecisely, fits more than one person whom the donor then knew or knew of . . . . In some cases, a constructional preference or a rule of construction applies to an ambiguous description of a person. Among the constructional preferences that might apply are those favoring family members over non-family members and close family members over more remote family members, as well as the constructional preference for the construction that does not disinherit a line of descent. See § 11.3, Comment *j*.

The fact that the donor did not know or know of a described person when the document was executed does not necessarily give rise to a latent ambiguity, however, if the language contemplates application to persons who come into existence or acquire a contemplated status after the document is executed. Language creating a class gift or identifying persons by the use of terms of relationship, for example, commonly contemplates, or is presumed by rules of construction to contemplate, the inclusion of afterborn and after-adopted persons. See Division V on class gifts.

In ambiguous-description-of-property cases, evidence of objective facts, such as evidence that the donor did not own the described property or owned more than one item of the described property, usually suffices to prove that the text ambiguously describes the intended property. So also in some cases involving ambiguous description of a person, . . . evidence of objective facts, such as evidence pertaining to the status of spouse, usually suffices to prove that the text ambiguously describes the intended person. Ambiguous description cases are not, however, confined to such cases. Ambiguity in a description can also be shown by subjective evidence.

A misdescription of a person can also arise from a patent ambiguity. For example, if a donative document names the same person twice as beneficiary of the same or different pecuniary amounts, extrinsic evidence may be considered to show that one of the provisions was intended for someone else. Such a misdescription, if established by a preponderance of the evidence, can be remedied by construction. . . . .

k. Construction where ambiguity not resolved by the evidence. As noted in Comment *b*, in rare cases of ambiguity, the evidence does not adequately establish the donor's intention by a preponderance of the evidence. If a constructional preference or a rule of construction applies to the ambiguity, the ambiguity is resolved by the constructional preference or rule of construction. See § 11.3. In the absence of an applicable constructional preference or rule of construction, the ambiguous provision need not always fail. Rather than allow the provision to fail, the document may in some cases be construed to carry out that part of the donor's intention that is known. This approach is supported by the constructional preference for the construction that renders the document more effective than other plausible constructions. See § 11.3. . . . .

Only if the text and extrinsic evidence shed so little light on the donor's intention that it is not possible to know enough about it to carry out any part of it should a provision fail for uncertainty. See Comment *q* for further discussion and illustration of this principle.

l. Distinguishable cases. To be distinguished from the type of latent ambiguity treated in this subsection are cases that raise the question of equitable election or ademption by extinction. A question of equitable election may arise in a case in which a testator devised unowned property to one devisee and owned property to a devisee who owns the unowned, devised property. See § 6.1, Comment *f*. A question of ademption by extinction may arise in a case in which a testator did own the described property when executing the will but no longer owned it at death. See § 5.2.

m. Contractual transfers. As noted in § 10.1, Comment *e*, and § 11.2, Comment *g*, a transfer made in a will, trust, beneficiary designation, or similar document is occasionally made pursuant to a contract, such as a premarital or a marital agreement (see § 9.4), a divorce settlement, or a will contract. As discussed in § 11.2, Comment *g*, if the transferor's contractual obligation is unambiguous, but the document implementing the transfer contains an ambiguity, extrinsic evidence of the transferor's intent may be considered in seeking to resolve the ambiguity. However, because of the constructional preference for the construction that accords with the transferor's contractual obligations (§ 11.3), the ambiguity in the implementing document would be so resolved, unless there is a finding of a different intention. Suppose, however, that both the contract and the implementing document of transfer contain an identical or closely similar ambiguity. Assuming no persuasive evidence that the transferor intended to breach the contractual obligation, the ambiguity in the implementing document of transfer would be resolved by consulting evidence that would be used to resolve the parallel ambiguity in the contract. This evidence would ordinarily include evidence relating to the intention of the promisee as well as the intention of the transferor-promisor. See, e.g., Restatement Second, Contracts §§ 200–230. . . . .

Comment on Subsection (b)(2):

n. Text reveals an apparent mistaken inclusion or omission. As noted in § 11.1, Comments *a* and *b*, a patent ambiguity arises if the *text of the document* reveals that language was apparently included or omitted by mistake. *Extrinsic evidence* of a mistaken inclusion or omission cannot establish an ambiguity. For example, a document is not shown to be ambiguous by a contention that a power to revoke was mistakenly omitted from an inter vivos trust. Efforts to establish through extrinsic evidence that language was mistakenly included in or omitted from a donative document are covered by § 12.1 on reformation.

The primary objective of construction is to give effect to the donor's intention. When the text of a donative document reveals on its face that language was apparently mistakenly included or omitted, the document contains a patent ambiguity. In such cases, the text of the document and extrinsic evidence may be considered in seeking to determine the donor's intention, i.e., in seeking to determine whether language was or was not mistakenly included or omitted, and if so, the content of the mistakenly included or omitted language. To the extent that the donor's intention is established by a preponderance of the evidence from the types of evidence described in § 10.2, the text is construed in accordance with that intention.

o. Deriving mistakenly included or omitted language by implication from text of the document. In some cases, the court can derive the mistakenly included or omitted language by implication from the text of the donative document. Deriving mistakenly omitted language from the text of the document is supported by the constructional preference for the construction that renders the document more effective than other plausible constructions. See § 11.3. When the donative document repeats portions of the text, and the context indicates that the duplication was accidental or otherwise unintentional, an inference arises that the text was intended to be included only once . . . . In some cases of mistaken omission, the exact language appears in the text itself and needs only to be inserted at the place from which that language was omitted . . . . The exact language need not be found in the text, however, in order for the mistakenly omitted language to be derived from the text of the document . . . .

If the text yields an inference of the donor's intention, that inference is not necessarily conclusive. Extrinsic evidence may also be considered to support or contradict the inference. If no extrinsic evidence is introduced on the question, the inference establishes the donor's intention. If extrinsic evidence is introduced on the question, that evidence along with the inference derived from the text must be weighed in determining the donor's intention. Once the donor's intention is established by a preponderance of the evidence from the types of evidence described in § 10.2, the donative document is construed in accordance with that intention.

p. Mistakenly included or omitted language established by extrinsic evidence. In some cases, the mistakenly included or omitted language cannot be inferred from the text of the donative document. In such a case, extrinsic evidence may be considered to establish the content of the mistakenly included or omitted language. . . . .

q. Construction where ambiguity not resolved by the evidence. As noted in Comment *f*, the evidence in rare cases of ambiguity does not establish the donor's intention by a preponderance of the evidence. The document, in such cases, may be construed to carry out the donor's intention to the extent possible. See also Comment *k*.

Only if the text and extrinsic evidence shed so little light on the donor's intention that it is not possible to know enough about it to carry out any part of it should a provision fail for uncertainty. . . . .

Comment on Subsection (b)(3):

r. Personal usage. As noted in § 11.1, Comments *a* and *c*, a latent ambiguity arises if the donor's personal usage differs from the ordinary meaning of a term used in the text. The ordinary meaning of a term is the sense in which it is used in common discourse or, if the term is a legal term, the accustomed sense in which it is used in law.

The donor's personal usage is the donor's habitual usage of a term in an idiosyncratic manner; the donor's habitual usage of a term in a manner used in the donor's profession, business, religion, or academic discipline, or in some other organization, group, or other segment of society of which the donor is a member or with which the donor is familiar; or, under Comment *s*, the usage adopted for purposes of the donative document. Personal usage does not, however, embrace *direct extrinsic evidence of intention contradicting the plain meaning of the text.* If a testator who had a cousin John and a nephew John executed a will devising property "to my cousin John," evidence that the testator directed her lawyer to designate her nephew John as the devisee and that the lawyer's secretary typed in "cousin" by mistake would not establish an ambiguity based on personal usage. The devise would, however, be rendered ambiguous on the basis of personal usage by evidence that the testator habitually referred to her nephew John as her cousin John.

The primary objective of construction is to give effect to the donor's intention. When the donor's personal usage differs from the ordinary meaning of a term used in the text, the document contains a latent ambiguity. In such cases, the types of evidence described in § 10.2 may be considered in seeking to establish the donor's intention by a preponderance of the evidence, i.e., in seeking to determine whether the donor intended the term to be defined in accordance with its ordinary meaning or in accordance with his or her personal usage of the term.

s. *Establishing donor's usage from the donative document.* The donor's usage of terms in a donative document can be established by other portions of the document. The most straightforward application of this principle arises in the case in which the donative document contains its own set of definitions. If, for example, the term "descendants" is defined to mean children and grandchildren, but not more remote descendants, that definition controls the meaning of the term "descendants" wherever that term appears in the document, even though the ordinary meaning of "descendants" includes descendants of any degree. See § 10.2, Comment *b*.

A less straightforward, but nevertheless appropriate, application of this principle arises when a word or phrase is used consistently throughout the donative document. See § 10.2, Comment *b*. If, for example, a donative document consistently uses the term "person" to mean only natural persons and in a fashion that excludes juristic persons such as corporations, an inference arises that the term "person" is confined to natural persons wherever that term appears.

t. *Establishing donor's usage from extrinsic evidence.* When extrinsic evidence reveals a discrepancy between the donor's personal usage of a term in a donative document and the ordinary meaning of the term, there is a latent ambiguity regarding which meaning the donor intended. For example, evidence may show that the donor customarily referred to a particular person by a name other than that person's proper name or nickname . . . or that the donor customarily referred to a particular person or persons by some term of relationship that was inaccurate . . . . Notice that the extrinsic evidence used to establish the donor's personal usage, and hence a latent ambiguity, does not violate § 11.1, Comment *c*, because such evidence does not involve direct evidence of intention contradicting the plain meaning of the text.

The donor's personal usage of a term can serve two functions. When there is a discrepancy between the donor's personal usage and the ordinary meaning of a term, the personal usage reveals an ambiguity. The extrinsic evidence of the donor's personal usage also constitutes circumstantial (but not direct) evidence that the donor intended the term to be defined in accordance with his or her personal usage. Thus, in the absence of other evidence that the donor intended to adopt the ordinary meaning of a term, the term in question would be construed in accordance with the donor's personal usage. If other evidence is introduced on the question, that evidence is considered along with the personal-usage evidence in seeking to determine the donor's intention. Once the donor's intention is established by a preponderance of the evidence, the document is construed in accordance with that intention. . . . .

When the term in question is a legal term appearing in a document drafted by a legal professional, the inference arises that the term was intended to be defined in accordance with its legal meaning, even when there is evidence that the donor had a contrary personal usage. See § 10.2, Comment *e*. The evidence of professional usage tends to overcome the personal-usage evidence. Thus, the legal term would ordinarily be construed in accordance with its legal meaning. If there is other evidence on the question, however, that evidence is considered in seeking to determine the donor's intention. . . . .

u. *Personal-usage evidence as resolving other ambiguities.* Personal-usage evidence can have a bearing on cases involving ambiguities that arise for reasons other than a discrepancy between ordinary meaning and personal usage . . . .

§ 11.3. Rules of Construction and Constructional Preferences

(a) An ambiguity to which a rule of construction applies is resolved by the rule of construction, unless evidence establishes that the donor had a different intention.

(b) In the absence of an applicable rule of construction, an ambiguity to which a constructional preference applies is resolved by the constructional preference, unless evidence establishes that the donor had a different intention. If conflicting constructional preferences apply, the constructional preference that is most persuasive in the circumstances prevails unless evidence establishes that the donor had a different intention.

(c) The foundational constructional preference is for the construction that is more in accord with common intention than other plausible constructions. Constructional preferences derived from the preference for common intention include the constructional preferences for:

(1) the construction that is more in accord with the donor's general dispositive plan than other plausible constructions.

(2) the construction that renders the document more effective than other plausible constructions, including the construction that favors completeness of disposition and the construction that avoids illegality.

(3) the construction that favors family members over non-family members, the construction that favors close family members over more remote family members, and the construction that does not disinherit a line of descent.

(4) the construction that gives more favorable tax consequences than other plausible constructions.

(5) the construction that accords with the transferor's contractual obligations.

(6) the construction that is more in accord with public policy than other plausible constructions.

Comment on Subsections (a) and (b):

a. *Rationale.* As defined in § 11.1, a donative document is ambiguous if the text or extrinsic evidence (other than direct evidence of intention contradicting the plain meaning of the text) reveals an uncertainty in the meaning of the document. Rules of construction and constructional preferences assist in resolving many types of ambiguities, but they do not constitute evidence of the donor's *actual* intention. They are devices that *attribute* intention to *individual* donors in particular circumstances on the basis of *common* intention.

The donor's intention controls the meaning of a donative document to the extent that the donor's intention is sufficiently established. In case of a conflict between the intention of an individual donor and a rule of construction or a constructional preference, the donor's intention, when sufficiently established, is controlling. Because rules of construction and constructional preferences are merely presumptive, they are rebuttable upon a finding of different intention. If there is no finding of a different intention, however, the meaning of the ambiguous portion of the document is controlled by the rule of construction or constructional preference. Rules of construction and constructional preferences therefore operate as special-purpose presumptions in the law of donative transfers.

Rules of construction and constructional preferences do not assist in resolving all types of ambiguities. Rules of construction and constructional preferences cannot supply that which must be supplied by extrinsic evidence. Thus, for example, if a donative document is ambiguous because its text reveals that language was mistakenly omitted, the ambiguity may be resolved by extrinsic evidence showing the content of the omitted language (see § 11.2, Comments *p* and *q*), but not by a rule of construction or constructional preference, unless the mistakenly omitted language appears elsewhere in the donative document or can be inferred from the document (see § 11.2, Comment *o*).

b. Constructional preferences distinguished from rules of construction. Constructional preferences are general in nature. They provide general guidance for construing a wide variety of ambiguities in donative documents. Because of their generality, more than one constructional preference can apply to a particular ambiguity. Usually, the overlapping constructional preferences point to the same result, but not always; they sometimes conflict.

Rules of construction are specific in nature. They provide guidance for resolving specific situations or construing specific terms. Rules of construction are derived from one or more constructional preferences. For example, the rule of construction embodied in the antilapse statutes is derived from the constructional preference for avoiding disinheritance of a line of descent. The rule of construction that presumes an intent to include adopted children in class gifts is derived from the constructional preferences for the construction that carries out common intention and for the construction that accords with public policy. Because rules of construction, in contrast to constructional preferences, address relatively delimited problems, rules of construction ought not to overlap or conflict with one another within the law of a given jurisdiction.

Once a constructional preference or a set of overlapping constructional preferences have crystallized into a rule of construction, the rule of construction becomes the exclusive source of attributed intention for resolving ambiguities to which it applies, displacing the antecedent constructional preferences. To the extent that antecedent constructional preferences conflicted with one another when applied to the type of ambiguity at issue, the conflict is resolved by adopting the rule of construction. The rule of construction is based upon the constructional preference or preferences deemed to carry the most weight for that situation. Thus, an ambiguity to which a rule of construction applies is resolved by considering only the rule of construction together with evidence of the donor's intention. Antecedent constructional preferences are no longer considered.

c. "Construction" versus "interpretation." As noted in § 10.1, Comment *b*, this Restatement uses the word "construction" to designate the final product of the process of determining the meaning of a donative document (apart from exceptional cases in which reformation or modification is warranted (see Chapter 12)). Textwriters and courts sometimes state that there are two distinct processes involved in determining the meaning of a donative document. Under this conception, "interpretation" refers to the process of searching for the donor's actual intention by looking to the text of the document and extrinsic evidence. "Construction" refers to the process of attributing intention from constructional preferences and rules of construction. The process of interpretation is sometimes thought to occur first, followed by construction only when interpretation fails.

Interpretation and construction are not completely distinct processes, however, nor are they applied sequentially. Interpretation and construction are part of a single process. Distinguishing between actual and attributed intention is useful in determining which governs if the two conflict. Actual intention, when sufficiently established, always overcomes attributed intention. The key notion, however, is "when sufficiently established." Although constructional preferences and rules of construction are sometimes referred to as "default rules," this does not mean that they only govern in default of evidence of actual intention. The term, properly understood, means that they govern in default of sufficiently persuasive evidence of contrary actual intention.

In deciding whether actual intention is sufficiently established to overcome attributed intention, the process of construction requires all factors to be brought to bear simultaneously and conflicting factors to be considered against each other. This is a single process. Take, for example, a case in which there is an applicable constructional preference or rule of construction. It would misdescribe the process to say that the constructional preference or rule of construction ought to be consulted only if there is *no* evidence of actual intention. Rather, the constructional preference or rule of construction is considered together with any evidence of actual intention. Evidence of actual intention may itself consist of conflicting elements, some supporting the constructional preference or rule of construction and some contradicting it.

d. Considering a constructional preference or a rule of construction with evidence of actual intention. Because the primary objective of construction is to give effect to actual intention, to the extent that actual intention can be established, constructional preferences and rules of construction yield when a different intention is found. In determining whether the donor's actual intention overcomes a constructional preference or rule of construction, both the text of the document read as an entirety and extrinsic evidence of the donor's intention may be considered, as described in § 10.2, unless consideration of extrinsic evidence is precluded by statute (see below). Extrinsic evidence and inferences derived from the text of the document tending to support as well as tending to overcome a constructional preference or a rule of construction must be considered as part of a single process. The single nature of this process is described in Comment *c*.

Sometimes a codified rule of construction provides that it prevails unless the donative document, another specified document, or one of a list of specified documents expressly provides otherwise. Since constructional preferences are seldom codified, it is uncommon to find a similar statutory provision regarding a constructional preference. Nevertheless, if a statute provides that a particular constructional preference or rule of construction can only be rebutted by an express statement in a document, extrinsic evidence may not be considered to support, rebut, or contradict the constructional preference or rule of construction. If, however, the elements prescribed in § 12.1 are satisfied, the appropriate document can be reformed to insert language into its text expressly stating an intention contrary to the constructional preference or rule of construction. See § 12.1, Comment *k*.

Some constructional preferences and rules of construction have more force and are therefore more difficult to rebut than others. Because constructional preferences are general in nature, two or more constructional preferences might apply in a given case and point to the same result or to differing results. If such overlapping constructional preferences lead to the same result, they reinforce each other and are more difficult to rebut. If they lead to differing results, they tend to neutralize each other unless the trier of fact determines that one is more weighty than the other in the particular case. The ambiguity in such a case is resolved by considering each of the constructional preferences together with evidence of the donor's intention to determine which resolution of the ambiguity is the most persuasive in the circumstances.

A rule of construction based on one or more strong constructional preferences is especially difficult to rebut. For example, because the rule of construction reflected in antilapse statutes derives from the strong constructional preference against disinheriting a line of descent, antilapse statutes are especially difficult to rebut. See § 5.5, Comments *f*, *g*, *h*, and *i*.

e. *Implications for judicial administration*. Rules of construction and constructional preferences straddle the law/fact line. Accordingly, some disputes about the construction of donative documents will be tried to juries in some jurisdictions. Under the law of procedure, historic distinctions among types of transfer remain important in ascertaining whether a jury demand is permissible under the law of the particular jurisdiction. Thus, disputes about the meaning of trust instruments are normally treated as arising in equity, where the judge alone determines fact. Some American jurisdictions follow English practice in treating the construction of wills as a jury-free appendage of equity, others process such disputes to juries.

Where a jury demand is permissible, the familiar techniques for allocating functions between judge and jury pertain. In a case in which there is no evidence on a disputed matter, or in which the evidence is manifestly lopsided, summary-disposition techniques such as summary judgment and directed verdict will vest responsibility for decision with the judge. Thus, for example, in a lapse case to which the antilapse statute would apply unless contrary evidence overcomes the statute, and in which there is no evidence or virtually no evidence that the donor formed such a contrary intent, the judge would apply the antilapse statute as a matter of law without the participation of the jury. By contrast, in a case in which there is conflicting evidence on the matter, the judge would instruct the jury on the presumption effected by the antilapse statute, and leave the jury to determine whether the evidence overcame it.

Rules of construction and constructional preferences are generalized intuitions about donors' intentions. When relevant, a rule of construction or a constructional preference assists the trier of fact in ascertaining the particular donor's intention in circumstances in which evidence of actual intention is inadequate or altogether missing. Accordingly, in a case tried to a jury, the jury needs to be apprised of the rule of construction or constructional preference, for which purpose the judge employs the usual techniques of jury instruction in response to motions of counsel.

Comment on Subsection (c):

f. *Scope note*. This section discusses the process of considering a rule of construction together with evidence of the donor's intention. Various rules of construction are set forth throughout this Restatement at locations appropriate to the subject matter of the rule of construction. For example, the rules of construction on whether and in what circumstances adopted children or nonmarital children are presumptively included in class gifts are set forth in Division V on class gifts.

This section collects a number of significant constructional preferences, but it does not purport to present an exhaustive list of them. Other constructional preferences, whether recognized in the current case law or developed in the future, may be applied as the court deems appropriate.

g. Constructional preference for the construction that accords with common intention; derivatives. The foundational constructional preference is for the construction that is more in accord with common intention than other plausible constructions. In the absence of evidence that establishes by a preponderance of the evidence that the particular donor's intention differs from common intention, ambiguities are resolved to the extent possible by construing the document to accord with common intention.

From this foundational constructional preference, several subsidiary constructional preferences are derived. These derivative constructional preferences, which are not listed in any order of priority, are the constructional preferences for: (1) the construction that is more in accord with the donor's general dispositive plan than other plausible constructions; (2) the construction that renders the document more effective than other plausible constructions, including the construction that favors completeness of disposition and the construction that avoids illegality; (3) the construction that favors family members over non-family members, the construction that favors close family members over more remote family members, and the construction that does not disinherit a line of descent; (4) the construction that gives more favorable tax consequences than other plausible constructions; (5) the construction that accords with the transferor's contractual obligations; and (6) the construction that is more in accord with public policy than other plausible constructions.

h. Constructional preference for construction that accords with general dispositive plan. One of the strongest derivatives of the constructional preference for the construction that accords with common intention is the constructional preference for the construction that accords with the donor's general dispositive plan. In application, this constructional preference favors the construction that produces an overall result that is more consistent with the donor's general dispositive plan than might be produced by an attempt to resolve the ambiguity by a narrow examination of punctuation or of isolated words, phrases, sentences, or other portions of the document. In the case of a will, this may require comparing the pattern of distribution produced by each plausible construction (including identifying those who would take under a partial intestacy) to determine which construction seems to yield the pattern of distribution coming closest to the decedent's overall intention.

i. Constructional preference for construction that renders document as effective as possible. All other things being equal, most donors would want their donative documents to be as effective as possible. This constructional preference underlies two more specific constructional preferences for resolving ambiguities: one favoring completeness of disposition, the other favoring avoidance of invalidity. The preference for completeness of disposition supports resolving an ambiguity, in the case of a will, in a manner that makes a complete disposition of the donor's assets and all interests in those assets or, in the case of a donative document other than a will, of all interests in the property covered by the document. . . . . The preference for avoiding invalidity supports resolving an ambiguity to avoid an invalidity such as might otherwise be caused by a violation of the common-law Rule Against Perpetuities in the minority of states still following that rule. (Matters concerning perpetuities are covered in Division VIII.)

In a particular case, the constructional preference for the construction rendering the document as effective as possible may come into conflict with the constructional preference for the construction that accords as closely as possible to the donor's general dispositive plan (Comment *c*). In such a case, the constructional preference for the construction that accords as closely as possible to the donor's general dispositive plan generally takes precedence. For example, the constructional preference for completeness of disposition may argue for avoiding an intestacy, but an intestacy or partial intestacy might result in an overall pattern of distribution that is more consistent with the donor's overall plan of distribution. If so, in the absence of factors or circumstances pointing the other way, the preferred construction is the one that is more consistent with the donor's overall plan of distribution.

j. Constructional preferences for the construction that favors family members over non-family members, the construction that favors close family members over more remote family members, and the construction that does not disinherit a line of descent. The constructional preferences for the construction that favors family members over non-family members, the construction that favors close family members over more remote family members, and the construction that does not disinherit a line of descent are strong derivatives of the foundational constructional preference for the construction that accords with common intention.

For purposes of the constructional preference for the construction that favors family members over non-family members, a relative by blood, adoption, or marriage is considered to be a family member. . . . . So also are nontraditional family members, such as the donor's domestic partner as defined in § 6.03 of the [American Law Institute's] Principles of the Law of Family Dissolution: Analysis and Recommendations. See § 2.2, Comment *g*; § 8.1, Comment *c*.

For purposes of the constructional preference for the construction that favors close family members over more remote family members, the donor's close family members are those identified in § 8.1, Comment *c*, as the natural objects of the donor's bounty. In addition, relatives who share a nearer common ancestor than other relatives are closer family members . . ., and, within the line of descent from the same common ancestor, relatives who are in the nearer generation to the common ancestor are closer family members. For example, a niece is a closer family member than a first cousin because the niece shares a nearer common ancestor (the parent of the donor, as opposed to the grandparent of the donor). A brother is a closer family member than a nephew because, although they share the same common ancestor (the parent of the donor), the brother is only one generation removed from that common ancestor, whereas the nephew is two generations removed from that common ancestor. Whole-blood relatives are not treated as closer family members than half-blood relatives.

The constructional preference against disinheriting a line of descent is strongest when applied to direct descendants of the donor (sometimes called *lineal* descendants). The preference is less strong, but still forceful, when applied to descendants of the donor's ancestors (sometimes called *collateral* descendants), and becomes somewhat weaker the farther removed the ancestor is from the donor. . . . .

k. Constructional preference for favorable tax consequences. Most donors would prefer that their dispositions receive as favorable a tax treatment as is consistent with their general dispositive plan. Consequently, a proper derivative of the foundational constructional preference for the construction that accords with common intention is a constructional preference for favorable tax consequences. . . . .

l. Constructional preference for construction that accords with the transferor's contractual obligations. Most transferors intend to abide by their contractual obligations. Thus, if a transfer made in a will, trust, beneficiary designation, or similar document is made pursuant to a contract, such as a premarital or a marital agreement (see § 9.4), a divorce settlement, or a will contract, an ambiguity in the implementing document of transfer is resolved in accordance with the construction that accords with the transferor's contractual obligation, in the absence of persuasive evidence that the transferor intended to breach the contract. . . . .

m. Constructional preference for construction that is more in accord with public policy than other plausible constructions. As a general matter, most donors intend to be law-abiding and hence would prefer that their donative dispositions not violate public policy. This constructional preference can have many subsidiary applications. For example, public policy, as evidenced by decisions of the U.S. Supreme Court and of other federal and state courts, is hostile to categoric exclusion of nonmarital children from class gifts. Consequently, an appropriate application of this constructional preference would be one that favors resolving ambiguities in class gifts against blanket exclusion of nonmarital children.

Similarly, a provision in a donative document that is ambiguous because it might plausibly be construed either to impose or not to impose a discriminatory restriction deemed to be against public policy, such as one promoting racial injustice, should, unless overcome by evidence of a different intention, be construed against imposing such a restriction.

Public policy favors alienability of property, and hence disfavors restrictions on alienability. Consequently, ambiguities in donative documents affecting alienability should, unless overcome by evidence of a different intention, be resolved in favor of the construction that does not curtail alienability or curtails it less than other plausible constructions.

This constructional preference is not to be confused with rules that sometimes disregard or defeat the donor's intention on the basis of public policy. Like the other constructional preferences, the preference for congruence with public policy only assists in resolving ambiguities, and would be overcome by evidence of a different intention. If, on the basis of the evidence, the donor's intention is found to prefer a result that is inconsistent with public policy, the donor's intention controls the meaning, though not necessarily the effect, of the donative document. Whether the donor's intention can be given effect is addressed in other parts of this Restatement. See § 10.1, Comment *c*.

CHAPTER 12

REFORMING AND MODIFYING DONATIVE DOCUMENTS

Introductory Note: Chapter 11 addressed measures for carrying out the donor's intention regarding donative documents that contain an ambiguity. Chapter 12 addresses measures that are available to carry out the donor's intention regarding donative documents that are unambiguous. Two topics are covered: reformation of donative documents to correct mistakes and modification of donative documents to achieve the donor's tax objectives.

§ 12.1. Reforming Donative Documents to Correct Mistakes

A donative document, though unambiguous, may be reformed to conform the text to the donor's intention if it is established by clear and convincing evidence (1) that a mistake of fact or law, whether in expression or inducement, affected specific terms of the document; and (2) what the donor's intention was. In determining whether these elements have been established by clear and convincing evidence, direct evidence of intention contradicting the plain meaning of the text as well as other evidence of intention may be considered.

Comment:

a. Scope note. This section only addresses reformation as a method of correcting mistakes in donative documents. It does not address the full range of equitable remedies for correcting mistakes in donative transfers. For example, this section does not address situations such as those in which a donor makes a mistake in perfecting an inter vivos gift (see § 6.1, Comment *o*) or in which a donor is entitled to restitution or rescission in equity because the donor was induced by a mistake of fact or law to make a gift that the donor would not have made if the donor had known the truth. Nor does this section address denial of probate or partial denial of probate as a possible remedy for correcting mistakes in wills in appropriate circumstances.

b. Rationale. When a donative document is unambiguous, evidence suggesting that the terms of the document vary from intention is inherently suspect but possibly correct. The law deals with situations of inherently suspicious but possibly correct evidence in either of two ways. One is to exclude the evidence altogether, in effect denying a remedy in cases in which the evidence is genuine and persuasive. The other is to consider the evidence, but guard against giving effect to fraudulent or mistaken evidence by imposing an above-normal standard of proof. In choosing between exclusion and high-safeguard allowance of extrinsic evidence, this Restatement adopts the latter. Only high-safeguard allowance of extrinsic evidence achieves the primary objective of giving effect to the donor's intention. To this end, the full range of direct and circumstantial evidence relevant to the donor's intention described in § 10.2 may be considered in a reformation action.

Equity rests the rationale for reformation on two related grounds: giving effect to the donor's intention and preventing unjust enrichment. The claim of an unintended taker is an unjust claim. Using the equitable remedy of reformation to correct a mistake is necessary to prevent unjustly enriching the mistaken beneficiary at the expense of the intended beneficiary.

c. Historical background. The reformation doctrine for donative documents other than wills is well established. Equity has long recognized that deeds of gift, inter vivos trusts, life-insurance contracts, and other donative documents can be reformed if it is established by clear and convincing evidence: (1) that a mistake of fact or law, whether in expression or inducement, affected specific terms of the document; and (2) what the donor's intention was. Reformation of these documents is granted, on an adequate showing of proof, even after the death of the donor.

This section unifies the law of wills and will substitutes by applying to wills the standards that govern other donative documents. Until recently, courts have not allowed reformation of wills. The denial of a reformation remedy for wills was predicated on observance of the Statute of Wills, which requires that wills be executed in accordance with certain formalities. See § 3.1. Reforming a will, it was feared, would often require inserting language that was not executed in accordance with the statutory formalities. Section 11.2, however, authorizes inserting language to resolve *ambiguities* in accordance with the donor's intention. As noted in § 11.2, Comment *c*, modern authority is moving away from insistence on strict compliance with the statutory formalities on the question of initial execution of wills. Section 3.3 adopts the position that a harmless error in executing a will may be excused "if the proponent establishes by clear and convincing evidence that the decedent adopted the document as his or her will." See also Restatement Second, Property (Donative Transfers) § 33.1, Comment *g*. The Revised Uniform Probate Code § 2–503 also adopts a harmless-error rule. Under the Revised UPC, a document or writing on a document that was not executed in compliance with the statutory formalities is treated as if it had been properly executed "if the proponent of the document or writing establishes by clear and convincing evidence that the decedent intended the document or writing to constitute . . . the decedent's will . . . ."

The trend away from insisting on strict compliance with statutory formalities is based on a growing acceptance of the broader principle that mistake, whether in execution or in expression, should not be allowed to defeat intention. A common principle underlies the principle of this section, which authorizes reformation of unambiguous donative documents (including wills) to correct mistakes, and the movement (1) to excuse defective execution under § 3.3 and (2) to authorize insertion of language to resolve ambiguities in donative documents under § 11.2.

The important difference between § 11.2 and this section is the burden of proof. Ambiguity shows that the donative document contains an inadequate expression of the donor's intention. Here, because there is no ambiguity, clear and convincing evidence is required to establish that the document does not adequately express intention.

Recent cases and statutes have begun to recognize that wills can be reformed. The Uniform Trust Code § 415 provides that testamentary as well as inter vivos trusts can be reformed "if it is proved by clear and convincing evidence that both the settlor's intent and the terms of the trust were affected by a mistake of fact or law, whether in expression or inducement." Restatement Second, Property (Donative Transfers) § 34.7, Comment *d*, also accepted the proposition that wills as well as other donative documents can be reformed to correct mistakes, stating:

> The general law of mistake, under which a mistake may be significant enough to justify the conclusion that the donative transfer should be set aside or reformed, is incorporated herein by reference and made applicable to both wills and other donative documents of transfer.

This section extends the conventional reformation remedy for inter vivos donative documents to wills, hence to all donative documents.

d. Plain-meaning rule disapproved. The so-called plain-meaning rule is disapproved to the extent that that rule purports to exclude extrinsic evidence of the donor's intention. The plain meaning, Wigmore noted, "is simply the meaning of the people who did *not* write the document." The objective of the plain-meaning rule, to prevent giving effect to mistaken or fraudulent testimony, is sufficiently served by subjecting extrinsic evidence that contradicts what appears to be the plain meaning of the text to a higher than normal standard of proof, the clear-and-convincing-evidence standard.

e. Standard of proof—clear and convincing evidence. There are two standards of proof for civil cases—preponderance of the evidence and clear and convincing evidence. This section imposes the clear-and-convincing-evidence standard of proof. Reformation is permissible only if the elements stated in this section are established by clear and convincing evidence.

The normal standard of proof in civil cases is preponderance of the evidence. Under that standard, the evidence must establish a probability that an assertion is true, i.e., that it is more probable than not that the assertion is true. A higher degree of probability is required under the clear-and-convincing-evidence standard. Although this higher standard of proof defies quantification, it is generally agreed that it requires an assertion to be established by a high degree of probability, though not to an absolute or moral certainty or beyond a reasonable doubt.

The standard of proof serves various functions. It alerts potential plaintiffs to the strength of evidence required in order to prevail, instructs the trier of fact regarding the level of confidence needed to find for the plaintiff, and allocates the risk of an erroneous factual determination.

The higher standard of proof under this section imposes a heightened sense of responsibility upon the trier of fact. When the case is tried before a judge, the judge should respond by rendering a thorough, reasoned set of findings that deal with the relevant contested facts. A collateral benefit of requiring clear and convincing proof is that an appellate court will rightly feel free to scrutinize the trial court's work more closely than in the typical preponderance-of-the-evidence review. As a practical matter, this greater scrutiny pressures the trial judge to do an especially careful job.

Absolute certainty about the truth of assertions of fact can seldom be established. Because a determination of fact is based on probability, not certainty, there is always a risk of error. An erroneous factual determination can result in a judgment for the plaintiff when the truth, were it known, would warrant a judgment for the defendant, and vice versa. The higher standard of proof under this section imposes a greater risk of an erroneous factual determination on the party seeking reformation than on the party opposing reformation. Tilting the risk of an erroneous factual determination in this fashion is appropriate because the party seeking reformation is seeking to establish that a donative document does not reflect the donor's intention. This tilt also deters a potential plaintiff from bringing a reformation suit on the basis of insubstantial evidence.

f. Nature of reformation and constructive trust. The grounds stated in this section, if established by clear and convincing evidence, support an order of reformation and, if necessary, other equitable relief such as the imposition of a constructive trust. An order of reformation alters the text of a donative document so that it expresses the intention it was intended to express. Thus, unless otherwise stated, a judicial order of reformation relates back and operates to alter the text as of the date of execution rather than as of the date of the order or any other post-execution date.

If property was previously distributed under the mistaken terms of the document, the court may impose a constructive trust or take other remedial steps in addition to issuing an order of reformation. A constructive trust is an equitable remedy that can be used to require property in the hands of an unintended recipient to be transferred to the intended beneficiary. Thus, the court imposes the constructive trust in favor of the intended beneficiary. Unless otherwise stated, the constructive trust imposed under this section presupposes that the order of reformation relates back and operates to alter the text as of the date of the donor's execution of the document.

g. Grounds for reformation. In order to support the equitable remedy of reformation, the extrinsic evidence must establish, by clear and convincing evidence, (1) that a mistake of fact or law affected the expression, inclusion, or omission of specific terms of the document, and (2) what the donor's actual intention was in a case of mistake in expression or what the donor's actual intention would have been in a case of mistake in the inducement. A petition for reformation can be brought under this section by any interested person, before or after the donor's death.

h. Limitations on the scope of reformation. Reformation is a rule governing mistakes in the content of a donative document, in a case in which the donative document does not say what the transferor meant it to say. Accordingly, reformation is not available to correct a failure to prepare and execute a document . . . . Nor is reformation available to modify a document in order to give effect to the donor's post-execution change of mind . . . or to compensate for other changes in circumstances . . . .

i. Mistake in expression or inducement. If proved by clear and convincing evidence, a mistake justifies an equitable remedy, whether the mistake is one of expression or inducement. A mistake of expression arises when a donative document includes a term that misstates the donor's intention (Illustration 4), fails to include a term that was intended to be included (Illustration 5), or includes a term that was not intended to be included (Illustration 6). A mistake in the inducement arises when a donative document includes a term that was intended to be included or fails to include a term that was not intended to be included, but the intention to include or not to include the term was the product of a mistake of fact or law (Illustrations 7 and 8).

Illustrations:

4. G's will devised "$1,000 to A." Extrinsic evidence, including the testimony and files of the drafting attorney, shows that there was a mistake in transcription and that G's intention was to devise $10,000 to

A. If this evidence satisfies the clear-and-convincing-evidence standard of proof, the will is reformed to substitute "$10,000" for "$1,000."

5. G created an inter vivos trust. The trust document did not contain a clause reserving to G a power to revoke the trust. Controlling law provides that a trust is irrevocable in the absence of an expressly retained power to revoke. After G signed the document, G's financial condition changed and G sought to revoke the trust. Extrinsic evidence shows that G intended to create a revocable trust and so instructed her attorney; and shows that G's attorney mistakenly failed to include the revocation clause. If this evidence satisfies the clear-and-convincing-evidence standard of proof, the trust document is reformed to insert the mistakenly omitted power to revoke.

6. G's will devised "$1,000 to A." Extrinsic evidence, including the testimony and files of the drafting attorney, shows that there was a mistake in transcription and that G's intention was not to devise any property to A. Although earlier drafts of G's will contained the devise to A, there is evidence that G had instructed his attorney to delete the devise in the final draft and that, by mistake, G's attorney failed to carry out G's instructions. If this evidence satisfies the clear-and-convincing-evidence standard of proof, the will is reformed to delete the devise to A.

7. G created an inter vivos trust. The trust document did not contain a clause reserving to G a power to revoke the trust. Controlling law provides that a trust is irrevocable in the absence of an expressly retained power to revoke. After G signed the document, G's financial condition changed and G sought to revoke the trust. Extrinsic evidence shows that G intended to create a revocable trust and did not understand the need for a revocation clause. If this evidence satisfies the clear-and-convincing-evidence standard of proof, the trust document is reformed to insert a power to revoke.

8. G created an inter vivos trust of the bulk of his assets. The trust document did not contain a clause reserving to G a power to revoke the trust. Controlling law provides that a trust is irrevocable in the absence of an expressly retained power to revoke. After G signed the document, G sought to revoke the trust. Extrinsic evidence shows that G established the trust when he was in line for a high-level position in the federal government. From the press reports he had read, he mistakenly believed that he had to place all of his assets into an irrevocable trust in order to comply with federal policies on public-service conflicts of interest. G liquidated much of his property, and placed the bulk of his assets into the irrevocable trust. Subsequently, G learned that federal policies did not require him to transfer his assets to an irrevocable trust. If this evidence satisfies the clear-and-convincing-evidence standard of proof, the trust document is reformed to insert a power to revoke.

j. Particularity of proof. In order to support an order of reformation or the imposition of a constructive trust, the petitioner must prove, by clear and convincing evidence, both (1) that a mistake of fact or law affected specific terms of the document, and (2) what the donor's true intention was. Both elements must be proved with particularity. For example, a claim that "if only my aunt had known how much I loved her, she would have left me more" lacks sufficient particularity to support a petition for remedy. Proof that the donor instructed his or her attorney to "give me an estate plan that incurs the lowest possible tax liability" lacks sufficient particularity to support a reformation remedy.

Notice, however, that the requirement of particularity does not require proof that the donor personally made the mistake nor proof that the donor formulated the exact language needed to carry out his or her intention. A remedy will lie if a mistake of the donor's advisor or drafting agent has affected specific terms of the document by failing properly to formulate the language necessary to carry out the donor's intention. Suppose, for example, that the petitioner proves by clear and convincing evidence that the testator instructed his lawyer to draft a will that devised certain property to child C. A remedy will lie if the lawyer drafted a will that misdescribed the intended property or the intended devisee. The petitioner need not prove that the testator formulated the exact language necessary to carry out his intention, which the testator's lawyer mistakenly failed to include. The testator properly relies upon the lawyer to draft the language necessary to carry out his intention.

k. Statutory rules of construction. Just as the requirement of particularity discussed in Comment *j* does not require the petitioner to prove that the donor formulated the exact language necessary to carry out intention, neither does the petitioner need to prove that the donor expressly intended to overcome a statutory rule of construction. Statutes often provide that a particular rule of construction prevails unless the donative document, another specified document, or one of a list of specified documents expressly provides otherwise. See § 11.3. Such rules of construction purport to govern when the document is silent. If the elements of this section are satisfied by clear and convincing evidence, however, a petition for reformation can be sustained to insert language into the document that rebuts the rule of construction. Suppose, for example, that the petitioner proves by clear and convincing evidence that the donor instructed his or her lawyer to draft a will that devised certain property to child, A, but not to A's children if A predeceased the donor leaving children who survived the donor. A remedy will lie if the lawyer drafted a will that failed to include language necessary to defeat the applicable antilapse statute. As reformed under this section, the donor's will defeats the antilapse statute because it includes language expressly contradicting that statutory rule of construction. As stated in Comment *j*, the petitioner need not prove that the donor formulated the exact language necessary to carry out his or her intention and that the donor's lawyer, by mistake, failed to include the donor's language; the donor properly relies upon the lawyer to draft the language necessary to carry out his or her intention.

l. Donor's signature after having read document does not bar remedy. Proof that the donor read the document or had the opportunity to read the document before signing it does not preclude an order of reformation or the imposition of a constructive trust. The English Law Reform Committee, in recommending the adoption of a reformation doctrine for wills, stated well the rationale for this position:

> We have also considered whether any special significance ought to be given to cases in which the will has been read over to the testator, perhaps with explanation, and expressly approved by him before execution. In our view it should not. Some testators are inattentive, some find it difficult to understand what their solicitors say and do not like to confess it, and some make little or no attempt to understand. As long as they are assured that the words used carry out their instructions, they are content. Others may follow

> every word with meticulous attention. It is impossible to generalise, and our view is that reading over is one of the many factors to which the court should pay attention, but that it should have no conclusive effect.

Law Reform Committee, Nineteenth Report: Interpretation of Wills, Cmnd. No. 5301, at 12 (1973).

m. Defenses: change of position by recipient; bona fide purchaser; laches; etc. All defenses generally available in equity to a suit to reform a donative document or to impose a constructive trust upon the recipient of property distributed under a donative document are available under this section. For example, a reformation order is ineffective and the imposition of a constructive trust does not lie against a person regarding property that he or she received without giving value therefor if, after receiving the property and without knowledge of the circumstances justifying reformation under this section, the recipient changed position in a way that makes it inequitable to require the recipient to return that property or its value. See Restatement of Restitution §§ 69, 142 [Restatement Third, Restitution and Unjust Enrichment § 65]. See also Restatement Second, Trusts §§ 292, 333 [Restatement Third, Trusts §§ 12, 62, 108]; Restatement Second, Contracts § 155 and Comment *f*.

A reformation order is ineffective and the imposition of a constructive trust does not lie against a person regarding property that he or she has received if the recipient gave value therefor without knowledge of the circumstances justifying reformation under this section. See Restatement of Restitution §§ 13, 123, 141, 173, 174 [Restatement Third, Restitution and Unjust Enrichment §§ 66–69]. See also Restatement Second, Trusts §§ 283–320 [Restatement Third, Trusts § 108]; Restatement Second, Contracts § 155 and Comment *f*.

A person otherwise entitled to reformation or to a constructive trust is barred from recovery if the complainant has failed to bring, or, having brought, has failed to prosecute a suit for so long a time and under such circumstances that it would be inequitable to permit the complainant to prosecute the suit. A cause of action may also be barred by lapse of time because of an applicable statute of limitations. See Restatement of Restitution § 148 [Restatement Third, Restitution and Unjust Enrichment § 70].

n. Contractual transfers. If a will, trust, beneficiary designation, or similar document is made pursuant to a contract, such as a premarital or a marital agreement (see § 9.4), a divorce settlement, or a will contract, ambiguities in the implementing document of transfer are presumptively resolved in accordance with the transferor's contractual obligation. See § 11.2, Comments *g* and *m*; § 11.3, Comment *l*. If, however, the implementing document of transfer is unambiguous and clearly deviates from the transferor's contractual obligation, the remedy would normally lie in a breach-of-contract action against the transferor or the transferor's estate. On the other hand, if clear and convincing evidence establishes that the deviation was the product of mistake, the rule of this section supplies an alternative means of curing the breach by reforming the document of transfer to accord with the contract.

§ 12.2. Modifying Donative Documents to Achieve Donor's Tax Objectives

A donative document may be modified, in a manner that does not violate the donor's probable intention, to achieve the donor's tax objectives.

Comment:

a. *Scope note.* This section authorizes modification of a donative document to achieve the donor's tax objectives, to the extent that the proposed modification does not violate the donor's probable intention. The term modification rather than reformation is used in this section to distinguish the situation covered here from the situation, covered by § 12.1, in which the donative document fails to express the donor's original, particularized intention.

b. *Rationale.* This section is based on probable intention (see Comment *f*). The rationale for modifying a donative document is that the donor would have desired the modification to be made if he or she had realized that the desired tax objectives would not be achieved. A similar rationale underlies the cy pres doctrine for charitable trusts, the deviation doctrine for private trusts, and the special-purpose reformation doctrine for curing perpetuity violations.

c. *Establishing the donor's tax objectives.* Modification under this section requires that the donor's tax objectives be established by a preponderance of the evidence. The donor's tax objectives can be established by the express terms of the donative document, by inference from the donative document, or by extrinsic evidence. See § 10.2. The donor's tax objectives can be specific, such as an objective to qualify a disposition for the federal estate tax charitable deduction; or general, such as an objective to minimize taxes.

d. *Achieving the donor's tax objectives.* Achieving the donor's tax objectives by modifying a donative document is straightforward if the donor's tax objectives concern state taxes, unless controlling state law expressly disallows the governing effect of the modification for state tax purposes.

Achieving the donor's tax objectives is more complicated if the donor's tax objectives concern federal taxes, as they often do. Federal law controls the federal tax consequences of a transaction. From time to time, however, federal law expressly recognizes specified modifications of a donative document as controlling for certain federal tax purposes. Current examples of federal statutory recognition include modifying split-interest charitable trusts in certain cases to qualify the value of the charitable interest for the federal income, gift, or estate tax charitable deduction, modifying trusts for noncitizen spouses in order to qualify them as qualified domestic trusts, and dividing trusts for purposes of the federal generation-skipping transfer tax. The primary purpose of this section is to authorize any modification that is clearly effective under federal law if the donor's tax objectives relate to federal taxes, or that is clearly effective under state law if the donor's tax objectives relate to state taxes, subject to the requirement in either case that the modification not violate the donor's probable intention.

When federal tax law is unclear regarding the tax consequences of a proposed modification, modification to achieve the donor's federal tax objectives is more problematic. Courts should be cautious in granting a requested order of modification in such circumstances. In addition to requiring that the modification not violate the donor's probable intention (see Comment *f*), the proponent of modification bears the burden of showing a reasonable prospect that the proposed modification will be effective for federal tax purposes.

e. Failure to achieve tax objectives need not be related to post-execution change in tax law. Although failure to achieve the donor's tax objectives is often due to a change in the tax law occurring after the document was executed, this section is not restricted to that situation. Federal law sometimes accepts modification in situations in which the tax law did not change after execution. It would be too restrictive, therefore, to limit this section to post-execution changes in tax law.

f. Modification not to violate the donor's probable intention. To be authorized under this section, the proposed modification must not violate the donor's probable intention. In many cases, this requirement is easily satisfied. The modification necessary to achieve the donor's tax objectives may consist merely of an order to divide a trust into two or more trusts, leaving the combined interests of each beneficiary unaffected. Indeed, for some tax purposes, federal law may accept a modification only if it does not change the quality, value, or timing of the interests of the beneficiaries.

In other situations, the modification necessary to achieve the donor's tax objectives may require an alteration of beneficial interests. Such an alteration is acceptable so long as it does not violate the donor's probable intention. In determining the donor's probable intention, the donor's non-tax as well as tax objectives are to be considered. The greater the proposed alteration, the more rigorous the court should be in measuring the requested modification against the donor's probable intention. One measure of the donor's probable intention is the donor's general dispositive plan. Even if it is questionable whether the modification would be consistent with the donor's general dispositive plan, however, the court can still find that it does not violate the donor's probable intention if the detrimentally affected beneficiaries consent to the proposed modification. Such consent makes it more likely that the donor would have approved of the modification, whether or not the modification alters the donor's general dispositive plan.

g. Time when modification becomes effective. Unlike a court-ordered reformation under § 12.1, a court-ordered modification under this section does not necessarily relate back to the date of execution. This is because modification, unlike reformation (see § 12.1), does not give effect to original, particularized intention but to probable intention—to what the donor's intention would probably have been had the donor known that his or her objectives could not be achieved under the donative document as formulated. Under this section, a court-ordered modification takes effect whenever necessary to achieve the purpose for which the modification is ordered.

DIVISION V
CLASS GIFTS

Scope of Division V. Division V addresses a variety of features that are unique to class gifts. A class gift is a disposition to beneficiaries who are described by a group label and are intended to take as members of a group. Despite the word "gift," a disposition creating a class gift need not take the form of an inter vivos gift, but can be created in a donative transfer of any type.

Class gifts are used extensively in estate-planning practice, especially multiple-generation class gifts, such as gifts to "issue" or "descendants." A class gift to "issue" or "descendants" serves a dual purpose. It automatically includes beneficiaries who enter the class later, and it substitutes the descendants of a beneficiary whose death or other event causes the beneficiary to be excluded from the class. See §§ 14.4, 15.3. This ability to adjust to later events makes such a class gift useful in both wills and trusts. It also makes such a class gift useful in life-insurance and pension-plan beneficiary designations, but unfortunately some insurance companies and plan administrators have been reluctant to accept class-gift designations, preferring instead that the beneficiaries be individually designated by name and Social Security number.

There are four chapters in this Division. Chapter 13 serves as an introduction to class gifts. It defines a class gift and distinguishes a class gift from a disposition to specific beneficiaries who are intended to take as individuals.

Chapter 14 addresses the presumptive meaning of various terms of relationship commonly used in class gifts. It discusses questions of status, that is, who qualifies as a class member.

Chapter 15, titled "Increase and Decrease in Class Membership," focuses on the time when the beneficiaries are determined with finality. This chapter explores in more detail a feature of class gifts: the ability to fluctuate in the number and identity of the ultimate takers. This topic includes what are commonly referred to as the class-closing rules.

Chapter 16 addresses class gifts to heirs. It fills out the meaning of a class gift to heirs and repudiates the Rule in Shelley's Case and the Doctrine of Worthier Title.

Import of the word "presumption" in this Division. Every section in this Division except §§ 13.2(b), 15.2, 16.2, and 16.3 promulgates a rule of construction. A rule of construction is not a mandatory rule of law, but is rebutted if the language or circumstances establish that the transferor had a different intention. As stated in § 11.3, Comment *a*, rules of construction "operate as special-purpose presumptions in the law of donative transfers." The presumption or presumptive meaning embodied in a rule of construction imposes the burden of persuasion on the party seeking to establish a different intention, not merely the burden of going forward with evidence in rebuttal of the presumption.

Use of the terms "beneficiary" and "share." In this section, and in this Division, the terms "beneficiary" and "share" are used in two senses. In the case of a disposition that has become operative, the term "beneficiary" refers to someone who has a property interest or contract right. In the case of a disposition that has yet to become operative, such as a disposition in the will of a living testator, the term "beneficiary" refers to someone who only has a potential property interest. The term "share" can refer either to a beneficiary's fixed share or potential share.

CHAPTER 13

GENERAL CHARACTERISTICS OF A CLASS GIFT

Introductory Note: Chapter 13 is an introductory chapter to Division V on class gifts. The chapter has two sections. Section 13.1 defines a class gift and specifies the terms of a disposition that presumptively create a class gift. Section 13.2 distinguishes a class gift from a disposition to beneficiaries whose identities and shares are fixed and specifies the terms of a disposition that presumptively create a disposition to beneficiaries whose identities and shares are fixed.

§ 13.1. Class Gift Defined; How Created

(a) A class gift is a disposition to beneficiaries who take as members of a group. Taking as members of a group means that the identities and shares of the beneficiaries are subject to fluctuation.

(b) A disposition is presumed to create a class gift if the terms of the disposition identify the beneficiaries only by a term of relationship or other group label. The presumption is rebutted if the language or circumstances establish that the transferor intended the identities and shares of the beneficiaries to be fixed.

Comment:

a. *Scope.* Subsection (a) defines a class gift. Subsection (b) identifies the terminology that presumptively creates a class gift.

b. *Question of intent.* Whether or not a disposition creates a class gift is a question of the transferor's intent. The question is whether, in the circumstances of the particular case, the transferor, by using a term of relationship or other group label to describe the beneficiaries, intended them to take as members of a group or intended them to take as individuals whose shares and identities are fixed and inflexible. As noted in the Restatement of Property § 279, Comment *a*: "The intention of the conveyor that there be the possibility of fluctuation in the number of takers is the factor which differentiates a class gift from a gift to individuals singly." For general principles to be used in determining the transferor's intent, see Division IV (Chapters 10, 11, and 12).

The terms of the disposition may raise a rebuttable presumption regarding whether a disposition creates a class gift. A disposition presumptively creates a class gift when its terms identify the beneficiaries only by a term of relationship or other group label (see Comment *g*). The disposition presumptively creates a gift to beneficiaries whose identities and shares are fixed when the terms of the disposition identify the beneficiaries by name or by a term of relationship or other group label and by name or number (see § 13.2). Because of the flexibility of a class gift, as compared with the inflexibility of a gift to individuals whose shares and identities are fixed, the presumption favoring class-gift classification is not easily rebutted.

c. Term of relationship or other group label. A term of relationship or other group label is one that identifies the beneficiaries by a common characteristic. A term of relationship is one that refers to a family relationship, such as "children," "grandchildren," "brothers," "sisters," "brothers and sisters," "nieces," "nephews," "nieces and nephews," "issue," or "descendants." A group label is one that is defined by statute, such as "heirs" or "next of kin," or any other group label, such as "the members of the X-Y-Z Investment Club, of which I am currently a member, as constituted on the date of my death." (For the division of the property among the class members in such a class, see § 14.2, Comment *j*.)

d. Taking as members of a group. To create a class gift, the transferor must intend that the beneficiaries take as members of a group. Taking as members of a group means that the identities and shares of the beneficiaries are subject to fluctuation by the addition of new members, by the subtraction of existing members, or by both (see Comments *h* and *j*).

Although the beneficiaries of a class gift take as members of a group, there need not be more than one group member, or indeed any group member, in existence when the donative document was executed in order for the disposition to create a class gift. Taking as members of a group merely means that it is possible for more than one beneficiary to take.

e. Class gift can be created in a donative transfer of any type. A class gift can be created in a will, a trust, a will substitute, a deed of gift, a beneficiary designation in a life-insurance policy or a pension plan, or in a donative transfer of any other type. The word "gift" is somewhat of a misnomer, because the creation of a class gift is not limited to a disposition in the form of an inter vivos gift.

f. Present or future interest. A class gift may take the form of a present interest or a future interest. A present interest in favor of a class is often called an "immediate class gift." A future interest in favor of a class is often called a "postponed class gift."

g. Disposition identifying the beneficiaries only by term of relationship or other group label. When the terms of the disposition identify the beneficiaries only by a term of relationship (such as "my children," "my grandchildren," or "my descendants"), the disposition presumptively creates a class gift, because the terms of the disposition indicate that the beneficiaries are to take as members of a group. The presumption is rebutted if evidence establishes that the transferor intended specific beneficiaries whose identities and shares are fixed.

A disposition that uses a term of relationship or other group label but expressly excludes one or more persons (such as "to my nephews and nieces except X and Y" or "to A's issue not including those who are adopted") also presumptively creates a class gift, but those who are excluded cannot be beneficiaries of the class gift.

h. Membership of the group subject to fluctuation by increase, decrease, or both. Taking as members of a group means that the membership of the group is subject to fluctuation by increase (i.e., by the addition of new members), by decrease (i.e., by the subtraction of existing members), or by both. In the case of an inter vivos transfer, the time from which the membership of the group can fluctuate by increase, decrease, or both is marked from the time that the transfer becomes effective. In the case of a will, the time from which the membership of the group can fluctuate by increase, decrease, or both is marked from the time that the will was executed. See Restatement of Property § 279, Comment *d*.

Increase in the membership of the group occurs when a new member is added due to birth, adoption, marriage, or some other reason. When a new member is added to the group, the potential shares of existing members of the group abate proportionally.

Decrease in the membership of the group occurs when an existing member is subtracted on account of death, divorce, disqualification, or some other reason. When someone is subtracted from the group, the potential shares of the remaining members of the group are proportionally enlarged. In effect, a class gift that is subject to decrease contains an implied gift over to the other members of the group.

The membership of the group need not be subject to both increase and decrease, but can be subject to only one. A class gift that is subject to decrease, but not increase, is created in a disposition to beneficiaries who cannot increase physiologically. An example is a devise in a will "to my brother's children" in a case in which the testator's brother was deceased at the time that the will was executed and there was then no possibility of a child being produced posthumously by assisted reproduction. In this example, the devise creates a class gift even though the testator's brother cannot have any more children.

i. Shares to be determined on a fractional basis. Taking as members of a group means that the ultimate share of each beneficiary is determined on a fractional basis. Consequently, even when a new member is added or an existing member is subtracted, the final takers divide the property on the appropriate fractional basis. See §§ 14.2, 14.4. The aggregate value of the class gift is not affected by the number of final takers. Upon distribution, the class-gift property is divided among the then-entitled beneficiaries on a fractional basis, no matter their number. A disposition of $100,000 "to my nieces and nephews" is divided five ways if, upon distribution, it turns out that there are five nieces and nephews, but is divided three ways if it turns out that there are three.

j. Class closing: when ability to increase or decrease ceases. At some point, a class closes, i.e., the ability of the membership to increase and decrease comes to an end, and the ultimate takers are determined. At the latest, a class closes when a class member is entitled to distribution. For discussion of this topic, see Chapter 15. For application of the class-closing rules to specific-sum class gifts, see Comment *l* and § 15.1, Comment *l*. See also § 15.2, Comment *f*.

k. Single-generation and multiple-generation class gifts. Class gifts can generally be divided into two types: single-generation class gifts and multiple-generation class gifts. A single-generation class gift is limited to one generation, such as "children," "grandchildren," "brothers," "sisters," "brothers and sisters," "nieces," "nephews," or "nieces and nephews." A multiple-generation class gift, such as a class gift to "issue" or "descendants," potentially includes beneficiaries in more than one generation. A class gift to "heirs," "next of kin," or "family" is also a multiple-generation class gift; such class gifts are covered in Chapter 16.

l. Specific-sum "class gifts." A disposition of a fixed sum or amount to each member is a hybrid. Such a disposition shares one of the characteristics of a class gift—it is subject to open to admit new members. Such a gift, however, lacks one of the characteristics of an ordinary class gift, because the beneficiaries do not divide the property on a fractional basis.

Illustration:

1. Grantor died, leaving a will that devised "$10,000 to each of my grandchildren." When Grantor executed his will, he had two grandchildren, X and Y. Thereafter, but before his death, another grandchild, Z, was born. Had Z not been born, the aggregate amount of the gift would have been $20,000. Z's birth increases the aggregate amount of the gift to $30,000. X, Y, and Z are each entitled to $10,000.

Because a specific-sum class gift is a hybrid, such a gift is treated as a class gift for some but not all purposes. For example, although a specific-sum class gift is subject to open, the time during which it is subject to open may be more limited than for an ordinary class gift (see § 15.1, Comment *l*) and the exclusion of a class member has a different effect than it does for an ordinary class gift (see § 15.2, Comment *f*).

m. Application of antilapse statutes to class gifts created in wills. An antilapse statute applies to a will-created single-generation class gift, whether or not the language of the statute explicitly covers class gifts. An antilapse statute is not needed and does not apply to a will-created multiple-generation class gift, because that type of class gift automatically substitutes the surviving descendants of a group member who fails to survive the testator. See § 5.5, Comments *a* and *j*.

§ 13.2. Class Gift Distinguished from Disposition to Beneficiaries Whose Identities and Shares Are Fixed; How Created

(a) A disposition does not create a class gift if the identities and shares of the beneficiaries are fixed.

(b) In determining whether a disposition is to beneficiaries whose identities and shares are fixed, the following rules apply:

(1) If the terms of a disposition expressly fix the identities and shares of the beneficiaries, the disposition is to beneficiaries whose identities and shares are fixed.

(2) If the terms of a disposition identify the beneficiaries (i) by their names or (ii) by a term of relationship or other group label and either by name or number or by name and number, the disposition is presumed to be to beneficiaries whose identities and shares are fixed. The presumption is rebutted if the language or circumstances establish that the transferor intended the beneficiaries to take as a class, i.e., as members of a group.

Comment:

a. Scope and rationale. A disposition to beneficiaries whose identities and shares are fixed does not create a class gift. Such a disposition is sometimes referred to as a disposition to beneficiaries taking as individuals. As provided in § 13.1, the distinguishing characteristic of a class gift is that the beneficiaries are intended to take as a group whose membership and shares are not fixed but are subject to fluctuation.

In a case in which the identities and shares of the beneficiaries are fixed, the consequences are twofold: no one can be added as a beneficiary and no beneficiary's share can be increased if another beneficiary cannot take, for example, because that other beneficiary fails to satisfy a requirement of survival.

Even if a disposition does not create a class gift, there are alternative theories, addressed in Comments *e* through *h*, under which the gift can have one of the features of a class gift. Comment *e* addresses the Uniform Probate Code section under which an afterborn or after-adopted child of the testator can be added as a beneficiary, and Comments *f*, *g*, and *h* address cases in which a beneficiary's share can be increased if another beneficiary cannot take.

b. Disposition expressly fixing the identities and shares of the beneficiaries. When the terms of a disposition expressly fix both the identities and the shares of the beneficiaries (such as "half to X and half to Y" or "50% to X, 30% to Y, and 20% to Z"), the disposition does not create a class gift. In cases such as these, the terms of the disposition are clear and unambiguous, and can only be altered by reformation (see § 12.1, which is codified in Uniform Probate Code § 2–805 and, for trusts, in Uniform Trust Code § 415) or, in the case of a residuary disposition, by the rejection of the no-residue-of-a-residue rule (see Comment *g*). See also Comment *h* for the proposition that a disposition of this type can be construed to contain an implied gift over if the circumstances establish that such a construction better carries out the transferor's intent.

Unfortunately, many life-insurance and pension beneficiary-designation forms force the insured or employee to fix the identities and shares of the beneficiaries expressly. The forms typically do not permit class gifts but require identifying the beneficiaries by name, Social Security number, and relationship to the insured, and also require designating the percentage of the proceeds to be allocated to each named beneficiary. The forms also typically provide for an express gift over to the other beneficiaries if one or more fail to survive the insured, thus precluding the application of an antilapse-type statute such as Uniform Probate Code § 2–706. See Comment *f*.

c. Disposition identifying the beneficiaries only by name; disposition identifying the beneficiaries by a term of relationship or other group label and either by name or number or by name and number. If a disposition identifies the beneficiaries only by name, without any reference to a term of relationship or other group label, the disposition is presumed not to create a class gift. For example, in a disposition "to X and Y," the disposition presumptively fixes the identities and shares of the beneficiaries, i.e., half to X and half to Y. The presumption arises regardless of whether X and Y are related or unrelated, but when the named individuals form a natural class or bear the same relationship to one another (e.g., if X and Y are the transferor's grandchildren), the presumption is more easily rebutted. See Comment *d(2)* and Illustration 13.

Unless the presumption is rebutted, Comment *a* makes it clear that two consequences result. First, no one else can be added as a beneficiary. If, for example, X and Y are the transferor's only grandchildren, no after-born and after-adopted grandchild can be added as a beneficiary. Second, X and Y are beneficiaries only of half; neither is a beneficiary of the other half. If, for example, X but not Y fails to satisfy a requirement of survival and no antilapse statute applies, the half share that X would have taken does not pass to Y (unless Y happens to be the residuary beneficiary).

Similarly, if a disposition identifies the beneficiaries by a term of relationship or other group label and either by name or number, or if a disposition identifies the beneficiaries by a term of relationship or other group label and both by name and number, the disposition presumptively does not create a class gift. For example, in a disposition "to my grandchildren, X and Y" or "to my two grandchildren," or "to my two grandchildren, X and Y," the disposition presumptively fixes the identities and shares of the beneficiaries, i.e., half to X and half to Y. Unless the presumption is rebutted, Comment *a* makes it clear that two consequences result. First, no after-born and after-adopted grandchild can be added as a beneficiary. Second, X and Y are beneficiaries only of half; neither is a beneficiary of the other half. If, for example, X but not Y fails to satisfy a requirement of survival and no antilapse statute applies, the half share that X would have taken does not pass to Y (unless Y happens to be the residuary beneficiary).

The presumption in these cases is rebutted if the language or circumstances establish that the transferor intended the beneficiaries to take as members of a group and, in the cases in which the beneficiaries are named or numbered, intended the naming or numbering to be merely secondary or incidental to that purpose. On rebutting the presumption, see Comment *d*.

Illustrations:

1. Grantor died, leaving a will that devised her shares in X-Y-Z mutual fund "to my children, A and B." When Grantor executed her will, she had two children, A and B. Later, Grantor had another child, C, who survived Grantor. The disposition presumptively does not create a class gift, but a disposition of half to A and half to B. Unless the presumption is rebutted, C does not participate in the devise, unless an omitted-child statute gives C a share in the devised property (see Comment *e*). Even if an omitted-child statute does not give C a share in the devised property, such a statute will likely give C a share in Grantor's estate.

3. Grantor died, leaving a will that devised $200,000 "to my two children." When Grantor executed his will, he had two children, A and B. Later, Grantor had another child, C, who survived Grantor. Because Grantor had two children when he executed his will, the reference to "my two children" is presumed to refer to A and B as individuals, not to "my children" taking as members of a group. The disposition presumptively does not create a class gift, but a disposition of half to A and half to B. Unless the presumption is rebutted, C does not participate in the devise, unless an omitted-child statute gives C a share in the devised property (see Comment *e*). Even if an omitted-child statute does not give C a share in the devised property, such a statute will likely give C a share in Grantor's estate.

d. Rebutting the presumption. As noted in Comment *c*, the presumption against class-gift classification is rebutted if the language or circumstances establish that the transferor intended the beneficiaries to take as members of a group. This question is best understood as a question of the transferor's intent. For the type of evidence that is permissible for establishing the transferor's intent, see § 10.2. An important factor in determining the transferor's intent is the transferor's overall dispositive plan. See § 11.3. If the transferor's overall dispositive plan would be better served by classifying the gift as a class gift, the presumption is rebutted.

How strong is the presumption against class-gift classification and how easily can it be rebutted? Because of the inflexibility of a gift to individuals whose shares and identities are fixed, as compared with the flexibility of a class gift, the presumption against class-gift classification is not strong. Whether or not the presumption is rebutted depends on the facts and circumstances of each individual case. As noted in the Restatement of Property § 280, Comment *f*, "[m]any factors tend to establish . . . a contrary intent. . . ." See Comment *d(3)*.

d(1). Presumption rebutted by the dispositive language. Following are Illustrations in which the dispositive language rebuts the presumption against class-gift classification.

Illustrations:

7. Grantor died, leaving a will that devised $100,000 "to A's children X and Y and to any other child of A who may hereafter be born or adopted." A predeceased Grantor. Before Grantor's death, A had one additional child, Z. Grantor was survived by X, Y, and Z. The terms of the disposition indicate that Grantor contemplated the children of A as members of a group, thus creating a class gift. Consequently, X, Y, and Z share the property equally.

8. Grantor died, leaving a will that devised $100,000 "to all my nieces and nephews, namely A, B, C, D, and E." After Grantor executed her will, but before she died, two additional nieces (P and Q) and one nephew (R) were born. The word "all" in the terms of the disposition creates an ambiguity. In the absence of evidence resolving the ambiguity, the ambiguity is resolved by the constructional preference for the construction for equality among the lines of descent. See § 11.3. Under that constructional preference, Grantor's overall dispositive plan is better served by classifying Grantor's disposition as creating a class gift. Consequently, all of Grantor's nieces and nephews would share in the devise, including the three who were born after she executed her will.

d(2). Presumption rebutted by the circumstances. As noted in Comment *d*, the inflexibility of a gift to individuals whose shares and identities are fixed, as compared with the flexibility of a class gift, means that the presumption against class-gift classification is not strong. Also as noted in Comment *d*, an important factor in determining the transferor's intent is the transferor's overall dispositive plan. If the transferor's overall dispositive plan would be better served by classifying the gift as a class gift, the presumption is rebutted. Following are Illustrations in which the transferor's overall dispositive plan rebuts the presumption against class-gift classification.

Illustrations:

10. Grantor died, leaving a will that devised $100,000 to "my children A and B and the children of my deceased son C, namely X and Y." X predeceased Grantor. Because X died without issue, the antilapse statute does not apply (see § 5.5). The disposition manifests an intent for equality of distribution among Grantor's descending lines. The disposition to the children of C is therefore construed to create a class gift, causing the one-sixth share that X would have taken to pass to Y. If A had also predeceased Grantor without issue, the one-third share that A would have taken would be divided equally between B and Y.

13. Grantor died, leaving a will that devised her vacation cabin on Lake Michigan "to A and B." When Grantor executed her will, she had two children, A and B. Later, after Grantor executed her will, Grantor

had another child, C, who survived Grantor. Although Grantor's disposition does not identify A and B as her children, A and B form a natural class, because they bear the same relationship to one another and to Grantor. Because Grantor's disposition manifests an intent to pass her vacation cabin to her children, the presumption against class-gift classification is rebutted, and the cabin passes to A, B, and C. Even if the presumption against a class gift were not rebutted, an omitted-child statute might give C a share in the devised property (see Comment *e*).

d(3). Factors listed in the Restatement of Property that tend to establish a contrary intent. The Restatement of Property § 281 lists factors that tend to establish a contrary intent. This Restatement adopts that list and incorporates by reference that section of the Restatement of Property, including its Comments and Illustrations. . . . .

e. Omitted-child statute of Uniform Probate Code. Even if a disposition does not create a class gift, the omitted-child statute of the Uniform Probate Code (UPC) provides that if a testator's will fails to provide for a child born or adopted after the execution of the will, if the testator had one or more children living when the will was executed, and if the will made a devise to one or more of the then-living children, an omitted afterborn or after-adopted child is entitled to share in the portion of the testator's estate devised to the testator's then-living children as if the child had been given an equal share of that portion of the estate. See § 9.6, Comment *c*.

Illustration:

16. When Grantor executed her will, she had two living children, A and B. Grantor died, leaving a will that devised $90,000 "to my children, A and B." After Grantor executed her will, she had another child, C. Grantor's devise is presumed not to have created a class gift, because the takers are named. Nevertheless, even if it is determined that the presumption is not rebutted, so that the devise does not create a class gift, the UPC provides that C is entitled to 1/3 of the $90,000 as if the devise had created a class gift. Even if the applicable omitted-child statute does not give C a share in the devised property, such a statute will likely give C a share in Grantor's estate.

An omitted afterborn or after-adopted child is entitled to a share under the UPC unless (1) it appears from the will that the omission was intentional or (2) the testator provided for the omitted afterborn or after-adopted child by transfer outside the will and the intent that the transfer be in lieu of a testamentary provision is shown by the testator's statements or is reasonably inferred from the amount of the transfer or other evidence. The party who is claiming that one of the exceptions applies has the burden of persuasion on the elements of that exception.

f. Express gift over. A disposition that does not create a class gift may contain an express gift over of the share of any beneficiary whose interest fails. The express gift over may be to the other beneficiary or beneficiaries or to another beneficiary or beneficiaries. An express gift over defeats the possible application of an antilapse statute, as long as at least one alternative beneficiary is entitled to take. See § 5.5, Comment *g*.

Illustration:

17. Grantor died, leaving a will that devised $90,000 "to my children, A, B, and C or, if any predecease me, to those who survive me." A predeceased Grantor, leaving a child, X, who survived Grantor. B and

C survived Grantor. Although Grantor's devise presumptively did not create a class gift, A's share passes to B and C because of the express gift over "to those who survive me." X does not take A's share under an antilapse statute because the express gift over establishes a contrary intent and thus defeats such a statute. The $90,000 is divided equally between B and C.

g. Implied gift over to the other beneficiary or beneficiaries—residuary disposition. A residuary disposition to two or more beneficiaries is treated as if it contained a gift over to the other beneficiary or beneficiaries, even if the disposition is not in the form of a class gift. See § 5.5, Comment *o*, which rejects the no-residue-of-a-residue rule, following UPC § 2–604. Although an express gift over can defeat the possible application of an antilapse statute, an implied gift over does not do so. Consequently, the substitute gift provided by the antilapse statute, if the statute is applicable, overrides the implied gift over, and the share that a predeceased residuary beneficiary would have taken passes under the statute to the substitute takers (typically the predeceased beneficiary's surviving descendants).

If the antilapse statute does not apply for any reason, such as because the predeceased beneficiary is not a protected beneficiary (see § 5.5, Comment *c*) or because a protected beneficiary did not leave any descendant who could be substituted (see § 5.5, Comment *d*), the implied gift over takes effect, and the failed share of the residuary beneficiary passes to the surviving residuary beneficiary or beneficiaries in proportion to the interest of each in the remaining part of the residue. A residuary disposition fails only if the antilapse statute does not apply and no residuary beneficiary or descendant of a residuary beneficiary is entitled to take. For purposes of this rule, a residuary disposition in a will is a testamentary disposition of the testator's net probate estate not disposed by a specific, general, or demonstrative devise (see § 5.1(4)), and includes a devise of the testator's entire estate. For illustrations, see § 5.5, Comment *o*. The principle of this Comment is not restricted to a residuary clause in a will but applies to a residuary clause in any donative document, including a revocable inter vivos trust.

Illustration:

18. Grantor died, leaving a will that devised "the rest, residue, and remainder of my estate to my children, A, B, and C." A predeceased Grantor, leaving a child, X, who survived Grantor. B predeceased Grantor without leaving any surviving descendant. C survived Grantor. The share that A would have taken passes under the applicable antilapse statute to X. Although Grantor's devise presumptively did not create a class gift, half of the share that B would have taken goes to X (as A's substitute taker under the antilapse statute) and half to C. The result is that Grantor's estate is divided equally between X and C. The same result would be reached if Grantor's will had devised "all of my estate to my children, A, B, and C," because, for purposes of Comment *f*, a residuary disposition includes a devise of the testator's entire estate.

h. Implied gift over to the other beneficiary or beneficiaries—nonresiduary disposition. The rule as promulgated in the Restatement of Property § 280 and adopted in the case law is that there is no implied gift over to the other beneficiary or beneficiaries unless the disposition creates a class gift. This Restatement offers a different approach. The only question in Illustration[ ] . . . 10 . . . is what happens to the lapsed share of a beneficiary who predeceased the testator. Assume, for the sake of argument, that the court in those and similar cases was unwilling to conclude that the disposition creates a class gift. The court in a case such as these should consider the narrower approach of finding an implied gift over. The question of whether or not to find an implied gift over is best understood as a question of the transferor's overall plan of distribution. See § 11.3. An implied gift over should be found if the transferor's overall plan of distribution would be better served if the lapsed share passed to the other devisees rather than to the residue. . . .

Under subsection (b)(1) and Comment *b*, a disposition that expressly fixes the identities and shares of the beneficiaries (such as "half to X and half to Y" or "50% to X, 30% to Y, and 20% to Z") does not create a class gift. However, even a disposition of this type can be construed to contain an implied gift over if the circumstances establish that such a construction better carries out the transferor's intent.

Illustration:

19. Grantor died, leaving a will that devised her vacation cabin in Sun Valley, Idaho, "half to my daughter B and half to my son C" and devised the residue of her estate to X charity. B predeceased Grantor without leaving any descendants who survived Grantor. C survived Grantor. When Grantor executed her will, Grantor had three children, A, B, and C. It could reasonably be concluded that Grantor's reason for not using a class gift "to my children" was to exclude A. If so, it could also be reasonably concluded that there is an implied gift over as between B and C, so that B's share does not lapse and pass to X charity under Grantor's residuary clause but goes over to C. Although an express gift over can defeat the antilapse statute (see Comment *f*), an implied gift over does not do so.

CHAPTER 14

PRESUMPTIVE MEANING OF CLASS-GIFT TERMS OF RELATIONSHIP

Introductory Note: This chapter sets forth rules of construction that attribute presumptive meaning to terms of relationship that are commonly used as group labels in class gifts—terms such as "children," "grandchildren," "brothers," "sisters," "nephews," "nieces," "cousins," "issue," and "descendants." A rule of construction controls the meaning of such a term unless the language or circumstances establish that the transferor had a different intention. See § 11.3. The burden of proof is on the party who would attribute to the transferor an intent that is different from that attributed by the rule of construction. See § 10.2 for the use of extrinsic and other evidence that may be considered in determining the transferor's intention.

Although the focus of this chapter is on the presumptive meaning of terms of relationship for class-gift purposes, the same presumptive meaning applies by analogy to these terms in a donative disposition that is not in class-gift form but nevertheless uses a term of relationship to identify the beneficiaries. An example would be a remainder interest "to my deceased sister's children," in a case in which the remainder interest is not subject to a condition of survival.

This chapter is divided into three parts. Part A addresses single-generation terms of relationship. Part B treats multiple-generation terms of relationship (other than heirs or next of kin, which are covered in Chapter 16). Part C deals with questions of status.

Part A. Single-Generation Class Gifts

§ 14.1. Class Gift to "Children" and Other Single-Generation Classes

Unless the language or circumstances establish that the transferor had a different intention, terms of relationship in a single-generation class gift mean only the members of the specified generation and do not include children or more remote descendants of living or deceased members of that generation. For example:

(1) the term "children" means descendants in the first generation and does not include grandchildren or more remote descendants.

(2) the term "grandchildren" means descendants in the second generation and does not include great-grandchildren or more remote descendants.

(3) the term "brothers and sisters" means the other children of either or both parents and does not include the children of brothers and sisters or more remote descendants.

(4) the term "nieces and nephews" means the children of brothers and sisters and does not include the children of the nieces and nephews or more remote descendants.

(5) the term "cousins" means the children of uncles and aunts and does not include the cousin's children or more remote descendants.

Comment:

a. *Scope.* The rule of this section is that, unless the language or circumstances establish that the transferor had a different intention, terms of relationship that refer to relatives in a single generation (such as "children") mean only the members of the specified generation and do not include children or more remote descendants of living or deceased members of that generation. Comment *g* discusses situations in which the language or circumstances establish that the transferor did intend the word "children" to include grandchildren and more remote descendants.

The rule of this section must be read in conjunction with Part C of this Chapter, which deals with the status of adopted children (§§ 14.5, 14.6), nonmarital children (§ 14.7), children of assisted reproduction (§§ 14.8 and 14.9), and relatives by marriage (§ 14.10).

This section must also be read in conjunction with Chapter 15, which deals with the exclusion of members of the first generation who are born or adopted after the class closes or who fail to satisfy a requirement of survival or some other requirement.

Although the focus of this section is on the presumptive meaning of single-generation terms of relationship for class-gift purposes, the same presumptive meaning applies by analogy to these terms in a donative disposition that is not in class-gift form but nevertheless uses a term of relationship to identify the beneficiaries. An example would be a remainder interest "to my deceased sister's children," in a case in which the remainder interest is not subject to a condition of survival.

b. Rationale. In ordinary usage, the term "children" means descendants in the first generation and does not include grandchildren or more remote descendants. The same ordinary usage applies to other single-generation terms of relationship, such as "grandchildren," "brothers and sisters," "nieces and nephews," and "cousins." The rule of this section presupposes that, when these or any other single-generation terms of relationship are used, the transferor intended their normal usage.

c. Transferee of class member need not be a member of class. A class member who has a transmissible present or future interest can transfer that interest to a non-class member. The child's transferee does not take as a class member but as a transferee of a class member, taking the share that the class member would have taken but for the transfer.

d. Substitute takers under antilapse statute need not be members of class. As provided in § 5.5, Comments *a* and *j*, and in § 13.1, Comment *m*, antilapse statutes apply to class gifts to single-generation classes such as gifts to "children." The substitute takers do not take as class members but as statutory substitutes for deceased class members.

e. Implied gift to "children" of a designated person. The rule of this section is applicable to an implied gift to "children" to the same extent as an express gift to "children." An implied gift to "children" may arise in the case of a gift by Grantor "to my daughter D for life and if D dies without children surviving her, to my son S." The implication of a gift to D's children who survive her is based on the gap in the language of the disposition that would arise if D leaves children surviving her. The fact that there is a gift over to Grantor's son if D dies without children surviving her justifies the inference that D's children are to take if there are any who survive D. Additional language or circumstances could lead to the conclusion that the implied gift in this situation is to D's "issue," a class-gift term that does not exclude grandchildren or more remote issue (see § 14.3). For further discussion of gaps in dispositions and how they are filled, see Division VII.

f. Gift to the "heirs" construed as gift to "children." When a gift is made to the "heirs" of a designated person, additional language or circumstances may show that the transferor used the word "heirs" to mean "children." In such a case, the rule of this section is applicable. See § 16.1, Comment *m*.

g. Construing "children" to mean "issue." Because the rule of this section is a rule of construction, it yields to a finding that additional language or circumstances establish that the transferor had a different intention. The cases in which it is justified to construe "children" to mean "issue" (or, as some courts put it, "children" includes grandchildren and more remote descendants) generally involve an ambiguity. An ambiguity is defined in § 11.1 as an "uncertainty in meaning that is revealed by the text or by extrinsic evidence other than direct evidence of intention contradicting the plain meaning of the text." In the case of an ambiguity, and in the absence of compelling evidence to the contrary, the constructional preference for the construction that does not disinherit a line of descent (§ 11.3(c)(3)) is a factor that supports construing "children" to mean "issue."

The Comments below address the more frequently encountered circumstances that justify such construction: where "children" is coupled with words of representation (Comment *g(1)*), where "children" and "issue" (or "children" and "descendants") are used interchangeably (Comment *g(2)*), where the disposition would fail unless "children" is construed to mean "issue" (Comment *g(3)*), and where to do so is more consistent with the transferor's overall dispositive plan (Comment *g(4)*). These cases often involve postponed class gifts to "children," because in many cases the applicable antilapse statute works to substitute the descendants of single-generation class members who predecease the testator, yielding the same result in effect. See Comment *d*. . . . .

g(1). Construing "children" to mean "issue" when "children" is coupled with language of representation. A disposition that couples the term "children" with a direction that distribution be representational (such as "per stirpes" or "by right of representation") is internally inconsistent and hence ambiguous. See § 11.1, Comment *b*. A representational form of distribution suggests the continual substitution of descendants for deceased children until the distribution date. See § 15.3. The constructional preference for the construction that does not disinherit a line of descent (§ 11.3(c)(3)) further justifies construing the term "children" to mean "issue," in the absence of compelling evidence to the contrary. . . . .

g(2). Construing "children" to mean "issue" when "children" and "issue" are used interchangeably. The use of the term "children" and "issue" (or "descendants") interchangeably is ambiguous, thus invoking the constructional preference for the construction that does not disinherit a line of descent (§ 11.3(c)(3)). In such a case, in the absence of compelling evidence to the contrary, the term "children" is construed to mean "issue." . . . .

g(3). Construing "children" to mean "issue" when gift to "children" would otherwise be ineffective. Construing a gift to "children" as meaning "issue" is justified when the gift would otherwise be ineffective. In such a case, the constructional preference for completeness of disposition (which the courts sometimes refer to as a presumption against intestacy or lapse) (§ 11.3(c)(2)) is reinforced by the constructional preference for the construction that does not disinherit a line of descent in support of construing "children" to mean "issue" (§ 11.3(c)(3)).

Illustration:

3. Grantor died, leaving a will that devised the residue of his estate in trust, directing the trustee to pay the income to LT for life, then to distribute the trust principal to LT's then-living "children." LT had two children, C1 and C2, both of whom survived Grantor. Both C1 and C2 predeceased LT. C1 left no children, but C2 left a child, GC, who survived LT. Because the future interest to LT's children would otherwise be ineffective, the word "children" is construed to mean "issue." The trust principal goes to GC.

g(4). Construing "children" to mean "issue" to effectuate overall dispositive plan. Construing "children" to mean "issue" is justified when to do so is more consistent with the transferor's overall dispositive plan. Cases falling within this category often involve an overall dispositive plan that indicates an intent to benefit equally two or more groups or descending lines, and such indicated intent cannot be accomplished unless "children" is construed to mean "issue."

Illustration:

5. Grantor died, leaving a will that devised the residue of her estate in trust, directing the trustee to divide the income equally among Grantor's "children." The trust was to terminate on the death of Grantor's last living child. Upon termination, the trust principal was to be distributed to "the descendants of my children." After Grantor's death, one of Grantor's two children, C1, died, survived by his daughter, GD. Grantor's other child, C2, was still living. In the absence of

compelling evidence that Grantor had a different intention, the word "children" is construed to include grandchildren and more remote descendants, so that C1's share of income goes to GD rather than to C2. This construction is justified because the terms of the trust make no express provision regarding the disposition of the share of income previously received by a deceased child and because the trust principal on termination of the trust is to be distributed to the descendants of Grantor's children. See Restatement Third, Trusts § 49, Comment *c*.

h. *Reformation.* If it is established by clear and convincing evidence that, by mistake, the word "children" was used rather than "issue," the error can be corrected by reformation. See § 12.1.

i. *Children of earlier or later marriages.* An ambiguity may arise in a gift to "children" if the designated parent has children by an earlier or a later marriage, either before or after the donative document was executed. All relevant evidence may be considered in resolving the ambiguity (§ 11.1).

The fact that the designated parent has children by more than one marriage does not always create an ambiguity. For example, a class gift "to my children" is not ambiguous and includes all of the transferor's children. A class gift "to my children born to my wife Winona" only includes the transferor's children with his wife Winona, and does not include any other children of the transferor. . . . .

j. *Gift to "sons" or "daughters."* By analogy to the rule of this section, a gift "to the sons" of a designated person or "to the daughters" of a designated person excludes grandsons and granddaughters in the absence of additional language and circumstances indicating a different intention.

k. *Stepchildren.* Unless the language or circumstances establish that the transferor had a different intention, stepchildren are not included in a class gift to "children." See § 14.10 (Relative by Marriage). An adopted stepchild, however, is a presumptive member of the class. See § 14.5 (Adopted Child as Child of Adopting Parent).

l. *Single-generation class gifts other than class gifts to "children."* Single-generation class gifts (other than class gifts to "children") include class gifts to "grandchildren," "brothers and sisters," "nephews and nieces," "cousins," or similar single-generation class-gift terms. Unless the language or circumstances establish that the transferor had a different intention, the class members are those so designated and do not include the children or more remote descendants of class members.

The presumptive meaning of a single-generation class gift to a class other than children is linked to the presumptive meaning of "children" promulgated in this section. The presumptive meaning of "child" is a descendant of the designated person in the first generation. A "grandchild," therefore, is a "child" of a "child" of the designated person, and a "great-grandchild" is a "child" of a "grandchild" of the designated person.

Although the presumptive meaning of a single-generation class designation other than one to children is that the single-generation class term does not include the children or more remote descendants of class members, the principles of Comments *g*, *g(1)*, *g(2)*, *g(3)*, and *g(4)* apply to all single-generation class gifts, not only to class gifts to children. Thus, the language or circumstances may establish that children or more remote descendants of class members are to take in place of deceased class members.

m. Class gift to "brothers and sisters." The "brothers and sisters" of a designated person are the "children of either or both of the parents of the designated person, exclusive of the designated person." Although a child of one but not the other of the parents of the designated person is a relative of the halfblood, relatives of the halfblood are presumptively treated the same as those of the whole blood in determining who is included in the presumptive meaning of a class gift. The language of a disposition that would establish a contrary intent would include language such as "to my brothers and sisters of the whole blood." Circumstances that would establish a contrary intent might include cases in which there was little or no relationship with the half-blood relative. . . . .

n. Class gift to "cousins." A class gift to "cousins" is construed as a gift to first cousins, not a gift to all cousins. A gift to all cousins would be void for indefiniteness. Consequently, the "cousins" of a designated person are the "children" of the designated person's uncles and aunts. The uncles and aunts of the designated person are the "children" of the designated person's grandparents, exclusive of the designated person's parents.

§ 14.2. Single-Generation Class Gifts—How Property Divided

Unless the language or circumstances establish that the transferor had a different intention, the property that is the subject of a single-generation class gift is divided equally among the eligible class members.

Comment:

a. Rationale. In the case of a single-generation class gift, the transferor's presumptive intent is that each member of the class is to share equally in the subject matter of the gift. This type of distribution is sometimes described as a per capita distribution.

Although the focus of this section is on single-generation class gifts, the rule of this section applies by analogy to a donative disposition that is not in class-gift form but nevertheless uses a single-generation term of relationship to identify the beneficiaries. An example would be a remainder interest "to my deceased sister's children," in a case in which the remainder interest is not subject to a condition of survival.

b. Class identified by relationship to a designated person. The characteristic single-generation class gift is one that is identified by the relationship of the class to a designated person. The designated person often is but need not be named. Examples abound, but the following will suffice to illustrate this straightforward proposition: a class gift to "my children," to "my brothers and sisters," to "my sister's grandchildren," to "A's children," to "B's nieces and nephews," "to C's uncles and aunts." The presumptive meaning of these and similar dispositions is that each eligible class member takes an equal share.

c. Ambiguity in class identified by relationship to another class. The rule of this section applies to a single-generation class that is identified by the relationship of the class to a class. Thus, for example, a class gift to the "children of my children" is the equivalent of a class gift to "my grandchildren," a class gift to the "children of my brothers and sisters" is the equivalent of a class gift to "my nephews and nieces," and a class gift to "my children's grandchildren" is the equivalent of a class gift to "my great-grandchildren." The presumptive meaning of these and similar dispositions is that each eligible class member takes an equal share.

d. Ambiguity in class identified by relationship to two or more designated persons. The rule of this section applies to a single-generation class that is identified by the relationship of the class to two or more designated persons. Thus, for example, in a class gift "to the children of A and B," the transferor has created a single class, and the presumptive construction is that each eligible class member takes an equal share, as opposed to half being divided equally among the children of A and the other half being divided equally among the children of B. The presumption is stronger if the class members are in the same relationship to the transferor, as for example if A and B were the transferor's children, so that the "children of A and B" are the transferor's grandchildren.

e. Multiple classes. A disposition to multiple classes raises a different question. If a disposition is made to "the children of my daughter A and the children of my son B," the transferor has described the transferor's grandchildren but has divided them into two classes. The presumptive meaning of such a disposition is that the property is to be divided into halves, one being divided equally among the children of A and the other being divided equally among the children of B. The other alternative, dividing the property equally among the children of A and B as a single class, is unlikely to have been the transferor's intent, because such an outcome could have been more simply and conventionally achieved by saying "equally among the children of A and B" or, if A and B are the transferor's only children, "equally among my grandchildren."

Similarly, a disposition to "the children of my daughters and the children of my sons" would be divided into halves, one being divided equally among the children of the daughters and the other being divided equally among the children of the sons. . . . .

The presumption that the transferor intended separate classes is stronger if the different classes take at different times.

Illustration:

3. Grantor created a trust, directing the trustee to pay the income to A and B for their respective lives, with the trust principal on the death of each to go to the children of the one so dying. In the absence of language or circumstances indicating a different intent, half of the trust principal is divided equally among the children of A at A's death and half is divided equally among the children of B at B's death.

f. Ambiguity created by disposition to a parent and the parent's children (or issue)—the Rule in Wild's Case repudiated. A disposition to a named individual and his or her "children" (or "issue"), or a similar class-gift term, is ambiguous. Wild's Case, 6 Coke 16b (K.B. 1599), promulgated what has come to be known as the Rule in Wild's Case. The rule applied only to a devise of land, and provided that if the parent had no children at the date of the devise, the parent would take a fee tail estate, but if the parent then had children, the parent and the children would take concurrently as joint tenants. Whatever justification there may have been at the time of *Wild's Case* for such a rule of construction, there is no justification for the rule today. The rule was repudiated in the Restatement Second of Property (Donative Transfers) § 28.3 and is repudiated in this Restatement.

Today, the presumptive meaning of a disposition to a named individual and his or her "children" or "issue," or a similar class-gift term, is that it creates successive rather than concurrent enjoyment. Hence, the presumptive meaning of a disposition "to A and his children" or "to A and her issue" is that A takes a life interest and A's children or issue take the future interest. If the future interest is to A's "children," the division of the future interest is covered by this section (§ 14.2), and if the future interest is to A's "issue," the division of the future interest is covered by § 14.4.

f(1). Contrary intent—tenancy in common. The presumptive meaning of a disposition to a named individual and his or her children or issue "as tenants in common" is that the beneficiaries take concurrently, not successively. The problem is presented, however, whether the parent's share as a tenant in common is an undivided half interest or an undivided interest equal to the undivided interest of each class member. In the absence of additional language or circumstances that indicate otherwise, the parent takes an undivided half interest because the transferor is presumed not to equate the ancestor with his or her descendants.

f(2). Contrary intent—joint tenancy. If a disposition is made to a named individual and his or her "children" or "issue" in the manner that would create a valid joint tenancy under the applicable local law, and if local law continues to follow the common-law unities of time, title, interest, and possession, the undivided shares of the beneficiaries must be the same. If, however, applicable local law does not follow the common-law unities of time, title, interest, and possession, the parent takes an undivided one-half interest and the children or issue take equal undivided interests in the other half.

f(3). Future interest. The rule of Comment *f* applies to a disposition that creates a future interest in the named individual and his or her "children" or "issue."

f(4). Contrary intent—transfer in trust. The case of a transfer in trust raises different questions. If the benefits under the trust are in income, it is common for the settlor to intend concurrent enjoyment of the income by a parent and his or her children as income beneficiaries of a trust. Spreading the income among family members may also have an income-tax advantage. Hence, the rule of Comment *f* is not applicable to a gift of an income interest under a trust to a named individual and his or her "children" or his or her "issue." The beneficiaries enjoy the income interest concurrently, in the absence of additional language or circumstances that indicate otherwise.

If, however, the named individual and his or her children or issue take a future interest in the principal of the trust, the rule of Comment *f* applies, in the absence of additional language or circumstances that indicate otherwise. See Comment *f(3).*

g. Ambiguity created by disposition to designated individual (other than the parent of the class) and class. A disposition to one or more designated individuals (other than the parent of the class) and one or more classes is ambiguous. The ambiguity is whether each individual and each class take an equal share, or whether the individuals are treated as part of the class and divide the property on a per capita basis. In a disposition "to A and the children of B," does A take half and B's children take the other half, or is A treated as a member of an artificial class with B's children? Unless the language or circumstances establish a different intention, A takes half and B's children take the other half, each child taking an equal share in the children's half.

The resolution is not changed if the disposition is "to A and the children of B as tenants in common." If the disposition is "to A and the children of B as joint tenants," however, the resolution is changed if local law continues to adhere to the common-law unities of time, title, interest, and possession. These unities require that the undivided shares of the beneficiaries must be the same.

h. Single-generation class gift construed as multiple-generation class gift. The concept that the facts and circumstances may justify construing "children" to mean "issue" extends to other single-generation class gifts. See § 14.1, Comment *g(1)* (construing "children" to mean "issue" when "children" is coupled with language of representation); Comment *g(2)* (construing "children" to mean "issue" when "children" and "issue" are used interchangeably); Comment *g(3)* (construing "children" to mean "issue" when gift to "children" would otherwise be ineffective); and Comment *g(4)* (construing "children" to mean "issue" to effectuate overall dispositive plan).

For example, a class gift to the "children" of a designated person coupled with words of representation (such as "per stirpes" or "by right of representation") is internally inconsistent and hence ambiguous. As provided in § 14.1, Comment *g(1)*, a representational form of distribution suggests the continual substitution of descendants for deceased children until the distribution date. This, together with the constructional preference for the construction that does not disinherit a line of descent (§ 11.3(c)(3)), justifies construing the term "children" to mean "issue," in the absence of compelling evidence to the contrary. Thus, the eligible children take equal shares, with the issue of a deceased child dividing by representation the share that the deceased child would have taken. . . . .

An additional ambiguity is raised if the single-generation class is more than one generation removed from the designated person. If, for example, a gift is made to the "grandchildren" or to the "nieces and nephews" of a designated person "per stirpes," the described class members might stem from different children or different siblings of the designated person. In such case, the words "per stirpes" suggest an initial division of the property into shares at the generation above the generation of the class members, with one share going to the children of each child or of each sibling. In this situation, as in the situation covered in the preceding paragraph, the words "per stirpes" also cause the share of a deceased class member to be divided by representation among his or her descendants.

Illustration:

4. Grantor's will created a trust, directing the trustee to pay the income "to my wife W for life, then to distribute the trust principal to the grandchildren of my brother B, on a per stirpes basis." B has five grandchildren: GC1 and GC2 are children of B's son, and GC3, GC4, and GC5 are children of B's daughter. All five grandchildren survived W. The conclusion is justified that the words "on a per stirpes basis" require the division of the trust principal into two shares, one share for the children of B's son, and one share for the children of B's daughter. The one-half allocated to the children of B's son is divided per capita between GC1 and GC2. The one-half allocated to the children of B's daughter is divided per capita among GC3, GC4, and GC5.

i. Transferee or successor. The transferees or successors of a class member take the share that the class member would have taken.

j. Nontraditional class. A class gift to nonrelatives, such as a class gift "to the members of the X-Y-Z Investment Club, of which I am currently a member," is treated as a single-generation class gift for purposes of division of the property, even though the members of the class might be in different generations. Unless the language or circumstances establish that the transferor had a different intention, the property is divided equally among the eligible class members.

Any other nontraditional class gift is treated similarly. For example, a gift to "my spouse, H, my sister, S, and my sister's children, X and Y, taking as a class and not as individuals" is treated as a single-generation class gift for purposes of division of the property, even though the takers are in different generations. Unless the language or circumstances establish that the transferor had a different intention, the property is divided equally among the eligible class members.

For consideration of when such a class gift closes to future entrants, see § 15.1, Comment *d*.

Part B. Multiple-Generation Class Gifts (Other Than Class Gifts to Heirs or Next of Kin)

§ 14.3. Class Gift to "Issue" or "Descendants"

Unless the language or circumstances establish that the transferor had a different intention, the term "issue" or "descendants" means the designated ancestor's descendants of the first and more remote generations.

Comment:

a. Scope. The terms "issue" and "descendants" have the same meaning. The rule of this section is that when used as a term of relationship in a class gift, either term presumptively means a succession of generations down from the designated ancestor. The term "children" refers to the first generation down from the designated ancestor. Each succeeding generation down from the designated ancestor is made up of the "children" of the prior generation. Hence, the presumptive meaning of the word "children" as developed in § 14.1 must be applied at each generational level to determine the beneficiaries who constitute the class of "issue" or "descendants."

The rule of this section must be read in conjunction with Part C of this Chapter dealing with questions of status. Part C covers the status of adopted children (§§ 14.5, 14.6), nonmarital children (§ 14.7), children of assisted reproduction (§§ 14.8 and 14.9), and relatives by marriage (§ 14.10). This section must also be read in conjunction with Chapter 15, which deals with the exclusion of descendants who are born or adopted after the class closes or who fail to satisfy a requirement of survival or some other requirement.

b. Representational distribution. As developed more fully in § 14.4, the beneficiaries of a class gift to "issue" or "descendants" take by representation. A principal feature of representation is that the property is divided among the living descendants who are nearest to the designated ancestor in each descending line. A descendant who has a living ancestor who is also a descendant of the designated ancestor is not an eligible taker.

c. Language or circumstances indicating an intent to narrow presumptive meaning of "issue" or "descendants." Language or circumstances may indicate an intent to exclude some persons who would otherwise be included in the presumptive meaning of a class gift to "issue" or "descendants." A disposition to "female issue of A" or to "issue of A by his wife W" would narrow the possible takers under the disposition.

d. Language or circumstances indicating an intent to expand the presumptive meaning of "issue" or "descendants." A transferor may intend to expand the presumptive meaning of a class gift to "issue" or "descendants" of a designated person to include persons who would be excluded from a gift to "children" under §§ 14.1 and 14.5 to 14.9. For example, an intent might be manifested to include "stepchildren" or to include children adopted out who would otherwise be excluded.

e. Presumptive meaning of "heirs of the body." The terms "heirs of the body," "bodily heirs," "heirs by blood," "blood heirs" or a similar term mean issue or descendants who would take under the applicable statute of intestacy. Unlike a class gift to "heirs" or "next of kin," these terms exclude the surviving spouse and relatives other than direct descendants. See Part C regarding questions such as whether adopted children are included in such terms.

§ 14.4. Multiple-Generation Class Gifts—How Property Divided

Unless the language or circumstances establish that the transferor had a different intention, the property that is the subject of a multiple-generation class gift, other than one to heirs or next of kin, is divided among the eligible takers by representation.

Comment:

a. Historical note—class gift to "issue" or "descendants." The multiple-generation class gift addressed in this section is one to "issue" or "descendants." (A class gift to heirs or next of kin is also a multiple-generation class gift; that type of class gift is addressed in Chapter 16.) The terms "issue" and "descendants" are synonymous, and include descendants of every degree of relationship to the designated ancestor. The early English rule favored a per capita distribution among all descendants. In the United States, the former English rule has long been replaced by one favoring distribution on a representational basis. The difference not only involves what shares each descendant takes, but which descendants take. In a per capita form of distribution, all descendants take, and take equally. In a representational form of distribution, only the living descendants who are nearest to the designated ancestor in each descending line take. Consequently, a descendant with a living ancestor who is also a descendant of the designated ancestor does not take. See § 2.3, Comment *c*.

b. Class identified by relationship to a designated person. The typical class gift to issue or descendants is identified by the relationship of the class to a designated person. Examples include a class gift to "my issue," to "my sister's descendants," and to "A's issue." In these and similar cases, each eligible class member presumptively takes by representation.

c. Form of representation. The terms of a class gift to "issue" or "descendants" often specify a form of representation, such as "per stirpes." Such a specification controls. For the definition of "per stirpes" for purposes of intestate succession, see § 2.3, Comment *d*. It is assumed that the transferor who employs that term in a donative document intends that meaning, in the absence of language or circumstances indicating that the transferor had a different intent.

If the donative document does not specify a form of representation, the property is divided in accordance with the form of representation adopted in the intestacy law of the domicile of the designated ancestor. Regarding the various systems of representation for purposes of intestacy, see § 2.3, Comments *d*, *e*, *f*, and *g*.

Illustration:

1. Grantor transfers property by will "to my wife W for life, then to my issue." Grantor has three children, C1, C2, and C3, on the date he executes his will. C3 dies before Grantor, leaving two children, GC1 and GC2. Grantor dies. W dies. Grantor's descendants living on W's death are C1 and three children of C1; C2 and four children of C2; and GC1 and GC2 the children of the deceased C3. In the absence of additional language or circumstances that indicate otherwise, the rule of this section applies. Under all systems of representation, the distribution to Grantor's issue is one-third to C1, one-third to C2, one-sixth to GC1, and one-sixth to GC2.

d. Contrary intent—distribution to be made per capita. The transferor may direct that the distribution to the issue of the designated person is to be made on a per capita basis. The historical meaning of a per capita distribution as applied to a multiple-generation class is that all the beneficiaries are to receive equal shares, without regard to generation and without an implied requirement of survival to the date of distribution. Today, however, the preferred construction of a per capita disposition to a multiple-generation class is that it invokes the system of representation known as per capita with representation, as described in § 2.3, Comment *e*.

Illustration:

3. Grantor transfers property by will to Trustee to hold in trust. Trustee is directed "to pay the income to Grantor's son S for life, then to distribute the trust property to S's issue on a per capita basis." S has three children, C1, C2, and C3. C1 has two children, GC1 and GC2; C2 has three children, GC3, GC4, and GC5; and C3 has four children, GC6, GC7, GC8, and GC9. Grantor dies. S dies, survived by all of the children and grandchildren. Under the archaic construction, the trust property would pass to C1, C2, C3, GC1, GC2, GC3, GC4, GC5, GC6, GC7, GC8, and GC9, each receiving 1/12th of the trust property. Under the preferred construction adopted in this Restatement, the trust property passes to C1, C2, and C3, each receiving 1/3.

e. Ambiguity in class identified by relationship to a class or to two or more designated persons. A multiple-generation class that is identified by the relationship of the class to a class is ambiguous. The ambiguity is resolved differently from the resolution regarding a single-generation class gift that is identified by the relationship of the class to a class. Although a class gift to the "children of my children" is presumptively treated as the equivalent of a class gift to "my grandchildren," so that the grandchildren take per capita (see § 14.2, Comment *c*), the ambiguity in a class gift to the "issue of my children" is resolved by presumptively treating the disposition as creating multiple classes, one for the issue of each child.

Similarly, a class gift to the "issue of A and B" or a class gift to the "issue of A and the issue of B" is ambiguous. In the absence of language or circumstances indicating that the transferor had a different intention, the ambiguity is resolved by presumptively treating the disposition as creating multiple classes, half going to the issue of A and half going to the issue of B.

f. Ambiguity created by disposition to a parent and the parent's issue (or children)—the Rule in Wild's Case repudiated. The Rule in Wild's Case is repudiated. See § 14.2, Comment *f*. In a disposition (other than one in trust) "to A and his or her issue," A takes a life interest and A's issue take the future interest, in the absence of additional language or circumstances indicating that the transferor had a different intention.

g. Ambiguity created by disposition to designated individual (other than the parent of the class) and class. A disposition to one or more designated individuals (other than the parent of the class) and one or more classes is ambiguous. The ambiguity is resolved by presumptively treating the disposition as granting each individual and each class an equal share. Thus, in a disposition "to A and the issue of B," A takes half and B's issue take the other half, unless the language or circumstances establish a different intention.

The resolution is not changed if the disposition is "to A and the issue of B as tenants in common." If the disposition is "to A and the issue of B as joint tenants," however, the resolution is changed if local law continues to follow the common-law unities of time, title, interest, and possession. These unities require that the undivided shares of the beneficiaries must be the same. If, however, applicable local law does not follow the common-law unities of time, title, interest, and possession, A takes an undivided one-half interest and the issue of B take undivided interests in the other half.

h. Ambiguity created by phrase "in equal shares per stirpes." The phrase "in equal shares per stirpes" is to be avoided in drafting because the phrase is internally inconsistent: Those who take "per stirpes" do not take equally. The ambiguity is resolved by construing the phrase "in equal shares per stirpes" as meaning that the initial shares are equal but those equal shares are distributed on a stirpital basis.

Part C. Questions of Status

Introductory Note: Part C deals with resolving questions of status, such as whether an adopted child, a nonmarital child, a child of assisted reproduction, or a child related to the transferor by marriage is presumptively treated as a "child" of a specified person for class-gift purposes. These sections are phrased in this manner in order to link the sections in Part C to the definition of "child" in § 14.1, which in turn links to single-generation and multiple-generation class gifts as covered in Parts A and B. For example, if the question is whether an adopted child is included in a class gift to the transferor's "grandchildren," the answer is that the adopted child is included if under § 14.5 or § 14.6 the adopted child is treated as a "child" of the transferor's child.

Although the focus of Part C is on resolving questions of status for class-gift purposes, the same rules apply by analogy to these questions in donative dispositions that are not in class-gift form but nevertheless use a term of relationship to identify the beneficiaries. An example would be a remainder interest "to my deceased sister's children," in a case in which the remainder interest is not subject to a condition of survival.

§ 14.5. Adopted Child as Child of Adopting Parent

Unless the language or circumstances establish that the transferor had a different intention, an adopted child is treated as follows for class-gift purposes:

(1) In construing a class gift created by the adopting parent, the adopted child is a child of the adopting parent.

(2) In construing a class gift created by someone other than the adopting parent, the adopted child is treated as a child of the adopting parent, but only if:

(A) the adoption took place before the child reached the age of majority; or

(B) the adopting parent:

(i) functioned as a parent of the child before the child reached the age of majority; or

(ii) was the child's stepparent or foster parent.

Comment:

a. Scope. This section addresses an adopted child's status for class-gift purposes as a child of the adopting parent.

Although the focus of this section is on an adopted child's status for class-gift purposes, the rule of this section applies by analogy to a donative disposition that is not in class-gift form but nevertheless uses a term of relationship to identify the beneficiaries. An example would be a remainder interest "to my deceased sister's children," in a case in which the remainder interest is not subject to a condition of survival.

b. Class gift created by the adopting parent. In construing a class gift created by an adopting parent, the adopted child is presumptively treated as a child of that adopting parent, even if the adopted child was adopted after reaching the age of majority, the adopted child was not a stepchild or a foster child, and the adopting parent did not function as a parent of the adopted child before the adoption. The rationale of this rule is that transferor-adopting parent can dispose of his or her own property in any way he or she wishes.

Illustration:

1. When Grantor was 50 years old, he created an irrevocable inter vivos trust, directing the trustee to pay the income to Grantor's mother M for life and, on M's death, to distribute the trust property "to Grantor's children who survive M." Grantor has two genetic children. When Grantor is 60 years old, he decides he would like to have his wife share in the distribution of the trust property on M's death. The applicable adoption laws allow adult adoptions, even adoption of a spouse. Grantor adopts his wife, who is 40 years old at the time of the adoption. M dies, survived by Grantor's two genetic children and Grantor's adopted wife. Grantor's adopted wife is entitled to share in the trust property on the same basis as Grantor's two genetic children. The same result would be reached if Grantor adopted his domestic partner or lover.

c. Class gift created by someone other than the adopting parent. In construing a class gift created by someone other than the adopting parent, the adopted child is treated as a child of the adopting parent only if: (i) the adoption took place before the child reached the age of majority; or (ii) the adopting parent functioned as a parent of the child before the child reached the age of majority or was the child's stepparent or foster parent. The purpose is to prevent someone other than the transferor from engaging in a manipulative adoption—such as adopting an adult (a spouse, for example, or a domestic partner) to make that person a beneficiary under a class gift created by someone else. The transferor has in effect given the donee authority, similar to the authority given an agent, to determine the donee's "children" or "issue." But the transferor's use of the term "children" or "issue" implies an intent to include only adoptees with whom the adopter had developed an actual parent-child relationship.

d. Class gift created by someone other than the adopting parent—paragraph (2)(A): adoption took place before the child reached the age of majority. If the adoption took place before the child reached the age of majority, the adopted child is presumptively treated for class-gift purposes as the child of the adopting parent because it is assumed that the contemplated parent-child relationship developed between the adopting parent and the adopted child.

Illustration:

3. Grantor's will devises property in trust, directing the trustee to pay the income to Grantor's daughter LT for life and, on LT's death, to distribute the trust property "to LT's children." LT and her husband H have one natural-born child, C1. LT and H adopt a seven-year-old child, C2, who was then in foster care. (LT and H were not the child's foster parents.) From the date of the adoption forward, LT and his wife functioned as parents to C2. C2 is presumptively treated as a child of LT for purposes of the class gift "to LT's children."

Although it would be rare that an adoption will be in process when the child reaches the age of majority . . . such an adoption is treated as occurring before the child reaches that age for purposes of the rule of this section.

e. Class gift created by someone other than the adopting parent—paragraph (2)(B)(i): adopting parent functioned as a parent of the child before the child reached the age of majority. If the adoption took place after the adopted child reached the age of majority, the rule of this section requires proof that the adopting parent functioned as a parent of the adopted child before the child reached the age of majority. When the adopting parent did not function as a parent of the adopted child before the child reached the age of majority (and when the adopted child is not the adopting parent's stepchild or foster child), the type of parent–child relationship between the adopting parent and the child as presumably contemplated by the transferor never developed.

Functioning as a parent of the adopted child before the child reached the age of majority requires behaving toward the child in a manner consistent with being the child's parent and performing functions that are customarily performed by a parent, such as fulfilling parental responsibilities toward the child, recognizing or holding out the child as the individual's child, materially participating in the child's upbringing, and residing with the child in the same household as regular members of that household. For a list of factors that also bear on this determination, see [the American Law Institute's] Principles of the Law of Family Dissolution: Analysis and Recommendations § 2.03(3), (4), (5), and (6) . . . . Insubstantial conduct, such as an occasional gift or social contact, is insufficient.

Illustrations:

4. Grantor's will devises property in trust, directing the trustee to pay the income to Grantor's son LT for life and, on LT's death, to distribute the trust property "to LT's children." Some years after Grantor's death, LT's wife's sister and her husband are killed in an accident. LT's wife's sister and her husband had a child, X, who survived and was under the age of majority. LT and his wife took X into their

home and functioned as X's parents. After X reached the age of majority, LT and his wife decide to adopt X. LT's adopted child is presumptively treated as a child of LT for purposes of the class gift "to LT's children."

6. Grantor's will devises property in trust, directing the trustee to pay the income to Grantor's son LT for life and, on LT's death, to distribute the trust property "to LT's children." When LT is 60 years old, he decides he would like to have his wife share in the distribution of the trust property on his death. He adopts his wife, who is 40 years old at the time of the adoption. LT's adopted wife is not presumptively treated as LT's child for purposes of the class gift "to LT's children." The same result would be reached if LT adopted his adult domestic partner or lover or any other adult to whom LT never functioned as a parent before the adoptee reached the age of majority.

f. Class gift created by someone other than the adopting parent—paragraph (2)(B)(ii): adopting parent was the child's stepparent or foster parent. If the adopting parent adopted a stepchild, before or after the child reached the age of majority, the child is presumptively treated for class-gift purposes as a child of the adopting parent. Since such an adoption is not a manipulative adoption, the transferor would presumably approve of treating the adopted stepchild for class-gift purposes as the child of the adopting parent. In such a case, it is not necessary that the adopting stepparent functioned as a parent of the stepchild before the child reached the age of majority.

Illustration:

7. Grantor's will devises property in trust, directing the trustee to pay the income to Grantor's daughter LT for life and, on LT's death, to distribute the trust property "to LT's children." Some years after Grantor's death, LT and her husband divorce. LT marries a man who had previously been married and had a child by that previous marriage. After the child reached the age of majority, LT adopts her stepchild. LT's adopted stepchild is presumptively treated as a child of LT for purposes of the class gift "to LT's children." It makes no difference whether the stepchild was or was not beyond the age of majority when LT married the child's father.

If the adopting parent adopted a foster child, before or after the child reached the age of majority, the child is presumptively treated for class-gift purposes as a child of the adopting parent. The transferor would presumably approve of treating an adopted foster child for class-gift purposes as the child of the adopting foster parent, even if the adoption took place after the child reached the age of majority.

Illustration:

8. Grantor's will devises property in trust, directing the trustee to pay the income to Grantor's son LT for life and, on LT's death, to distribute the trust property "to LT's children." Some years after Grantor's death, LT and his wife W took in a series of foster children for brief periods. One foster child, however, remained with LT and his wife beyond the time when the child reached the age of majority. After the child reached the age of majority, LT and his wife decided to adopt the foster child. LT's adopted foster child is presumptively treated as a child of LT for purposes of the class gift "to LT's children."

g. Stranger-to-adoption doctrine disapproved. Although the rule of this section distinguishes between a transferor and a nontransferor adoption, the rule is not a confirmation of the "stranger-to-the-adoption doctrine." The stranger-to-the-adoption doctrine, under which an adoptee adopted by a nontransferor, even a child adopted as an infant, was not treated as part of the adopting family, has largely been abrogated in the case and statutory law, and is disapproved in this Restatement.

h. *Equitable adoption.* Although a foster child has not been formally or legally adopted by his or her foster parent or parents, a foster child who has been equitably adopted under the doctrine of equitable adoption described in § 2.5, Comment *k*, is an adopted child for purposes of the rule of this section.

i. *No double shares.* A child who is adopted by a genetic relative cannot take as a class member in both a genetic and an adopting capacity. For a similar rule regarding intestacy, see § 2.5, Comment *i*.

§ 14.6. Adopted Child as Child of Genetic Parent

Unless the language or circumstances establish that the transferor had a different intention, an adopted child is not treated for class-gift purposes as a child of either genetic parent, except that:

(1) If the adoption is by the spouse or domestic partner of either genetic parent, the child remains a child of both genetic parents.

(2) If the adoption is by a relative of either genetic parent, or by the spouse or surviving spouse or domestic partner or surviving domestic partner of such a relative, the child remains a child of both genetic parents.

(3) If the adoption occurs after the death or incapacity of either genetic parent and:

(A) if the adoption is by someone nominated by a genetic parent to be the child's guardian, the child remains a child of both genetic parents.

(B) if the adoption is not by someone who was nominated by a genetic parent to be the child's guardian, the child remains a child of a genetic parent from whom or from whose family the child does not subsequently become estranged.

Comment:

a. *Scope.* This section addresses an adopted child's status for class-gift purposes as a child of the child's genetic parent or parents.

Although the focus of this section is on an adopted child's status for class-gift purposes, the rule of this section applies by analogy to a donative disposition that is not in class-gift form but nevertheless uses a term of relationship to identify the beneficiaries. An example would be a remainder interest "to my deceased sister's children," in a case in which the remainder interest is not subject to a condition of survival.

b. *Adopted child's relationship to genetic parents.* Except as provided in paragraphs (1), (2), and (3) (see Comments *c*, *d*, and *e*), an adopted child is presumptively not a child of his or her genetic parents for class-gift purposes. When the adoption removes the child from the broader family circle of both of the genetic parents, as would normally be the case when the child has been adopted by strangers, the adoption breaks the ties to the child's genetic families. Because the adopting family becomes the child's replacement family, the transferor presumptively would not want the child to be treated as a child of the genetic parents for class-gift purposes, whether the transferor was the child's genetic parent or someone else.

Illustration:

1. A and B were the genetic parents of X. Upon birth, X was relinquished to an agency for placement. By prearrangement, the agency placed X for adoption by C and D, a married couple who were unrelated and unknown to A and B. C and D adopted X. Unless the facts or circumstances establish that the transferor had a different intention, X is not treated as the child of A or B for class-gift purposes.

c. Adoption by spouse or domestic partner of genetic parent. For class-gift purposes, a child adopted by the spouse or the domestic partner of a genetic parent presumptively is a child of the adopting parent and also remains a child of both genetic parents.

Illustration:

2. Grantor's will devises property in trust, directing the trustee to pay the income in equal shares "to Grantor's grandchildren living on each income payment date until no grandchild of Grantor is living or until 21 years after the death of the surviving grandchild of Grantor living on Grantor's death, whichever first occurs, at which time the trust property is to be distributed to Grantor's issue then living, or if no issue of Grantor is then living, the trust property is to be distributed to the X charity." When Grantor's will was executed, Grantor had two children, a son S and a daughter D. S had one child at the time of Grantor's death, and D had two children. S's wife W had a child by a previous marriage, a stepchild of S, who has been raised in S's home. After Grantor's death, S adopts his stepchild. Unless the facts or circumstances establish that the transferor had a different intention, the adopted child is treated as a child of S for class-gift purposes. The same result would obtain if W was S's domestic partner instead of S's wife.

d. Adoption by a maternal or a paternal relative or by the spouse or surviving spouse or domestic partner or surviving domestic partner of such a relative. For class-gift purposes, a child who is adopted by a maternal or a paternal relative of either genetic parent, or by the spouse or surviving spouse or domestic partner or surviving domestic partner of such a relative, presumptively remains a child of both genetic parents.

Illustration:

3. F and M, a married couple with one child, X, were killed in an airplane crash. After the deaths of F and M, M's sister, A, and A's husband, B, adopted X. Unless the facts or circumstances establish that the transferor had a different intention, X is also treated as a child of F and M for class-gift purposes.

e. Post-death or post-incapacity adoption. If the adoption occurs after the death or incapacity of either genetic parent, and if the adoption is by someone nominated by a genetic parent to be the child's guardian, the child remains a child of both genetic parents. If the adoption is not by someone who was nominated by a genetic parent to be the child's guardian, the child remains a child of a genetic parent from whom or from whose family the child does not subsequently become estranged. Once a child has taken root in a family, an adoption after the death or incapacity of one or both genetic parents is likely to be by someone chosen or approved of by the genetic family, such as a person named as guardian of the child in a deceased parent's will. In such a case, the child does not become estranged from the genetic family. For class-gift purposes, therefore, the child remains a child of both genetic parents if the adoption is by someone nominated by a genetic parent to be the child's guardian; and the child remains a child of a genetic parent from whom or from whose family the child does not subsequently become estranged if the adoption is by someone nominated by a genetic parent to be the child's guardian.

Illustration:

4. F and M, a married couple with a four-year-old child, X, were involved in an automobile accident that killed F and severely injured M. M's injuries were permanent and caused her to be bedridden and under constant care for the rest of her life. Neither M's parents nor F's father (F's mother had died before the accident) nor any other relative was in a position to take custody of X. M consented to X being adopted by her close friends, A and B, a married couple approximately of the same age as M. After the adoption became final, F's father and M's parents continued to have close contact with X, often visiting X and sharing holidays with X. A and B often brought X to M's bedside for visits. Unless the facts or circumstances establish that the transferor had a different intention, X is treated as a child of F and M for class-gift purposes. The result would be the same if both F and M were killed in the accident, their wills appointed A and B the guardians of the person of X, and A and B subsequently successfully petitioned to adopt X.

f. *No double shares.* A child who is adopted by a genetic relative cannot take as a class member in both a genetic and an adopting capacity. For a similar rule regarding intestacy, see § 2.5, Comment *i*.

§ 14.7. Child of Parents Not Married to Each Other

Unless the language or circumstances establish that the transferor had a different intention, a child of parents not married to each other (a nonmarital child) is treated as follows for class-gift purposes:

(1) In construing a class gift created by the child's genetic parent, the nonmarital child is a child of the genetic parent.

(2) In construing a class gift created by someone other than the child's genetic parent, the nonmarital child is a child of the genetic parent, but only if:

(A) any of the following functioned as a parent of the child before the child reached the age of majority: (i) the genetic parent; (ii) the genetic parent's grandparent or a descendant of the genetic parent's grandparent; or (iii) the spouse, surviving spouse, domestic partner, or surviving domestic partner of any of the foregoing; or

(B) the genetic parent intended to function as a parent of the child before the child reached the age of majority, but an event, such as death or incapacity, intervened to prevent the genetic parent from functioning in that capacity.

Comment:

a. Scope and rationale. This section addresses the status for class-gift purposes of a child of parents who are not married to each other (a nonmarital child).

Although the focus of this section is on a nonmarital child's status for class-gift purposes, the rule of this section applies by analogy to a donative disposition that is not in class-gift form but nevertheless uses a term of relationship to identify the beneficiaries. An example would be a remainder interest "to my deceased sister's children," in a case in which the remainder interest is not subject to a condition of survival.

Historically, a child born out of wedlock was treated as "filius nullius," the child of no one (literally, the son of no one). A nonmarital child was not treated as a child of the genetic parent for class-gift purposes. The attitude of society has now shifted, and the case and statutory law have followed suit.

The rule of this section distinguishes between class gifts created by a transferor who is a genetic parent of the nonmarital child and class gifts created by someone else. A genetic parent is an individual whose sperm or eggs were used to conceive a child. The transferor's nonmarital child is presumptively treated as a child of the transferor for class-gift purposes. The nonmarital child of someone other than the transferor is treated as a child of the child's genetic parent, but only if the genetic parent or the genetic parent's parent, grandparent, uncle, aunt, brother, sister, niece, or nephew, or the spouse, surviving spouse, domestic partner, or surviving domestic partner of any of the foregoing, functioned as a parent of the child before the child reached the age of majority or an event, such as death or incapacity, intervened to prevent the genetic parent from functioning in that capacity.

b. Nonmarital child who is adopted. The status of a nonmarital child who is adopted is determined under §§ 14.5 and 14.6.

c. Transferor's nonmarital child. For class-gift purposes, the transferor's nonmarital child is presumptively treated as a child of the transferor. If the genetic parent of a nonmarital child creates a class gift in favor of his or her "children" or "issue," the nonmarital child is presumptively treated as a child of the transferor and thus included in the class.

d. Nontransferor's nonmarital child. This Restatement adopts an agency concept with respect to a nontransferor's nonmarital child. Under this concept, the transferor is presumed to view the genetic parent or the genetic parent's family as the transferor's agent. The transferor has in effect ceded authority to the genetic parent to determine who is a member of the transferor's family. If the genetic parent, or the genetic parent's grandparent or a descendant of the genetic parent's grandparent, or the spouse, surviving spouse, domestic partner, or surviving domestic partner of any of the foregoing, functioned as a parent of the child before the child reached the age of majority, the transferor is presumed to have wanted the child to be treated as a child of the genetic parent for class-gift purposes. For the criteria used in determining whether a person functioned as a parent of a child, see § 14.5, Comment *e*. Merely obeying a child-support order, however, does not satisfy this requirement. Involuntarily providing support is inconsistent with functioning as a parent of the child.

Illustration:

1. Grantor died, leaving a will that devised the residue of her estate in trust, directing the trustee to pay income to the testator's

daughter, LT, for life. On LT's death, Grantor directed the trustee to distribute the trust principal to LT's children. LT was the mother of two children, C1 and C2. C1 was born out of wedlock. LT raised C1 as a single parent. Subsequently, LT married H and had a second child, C2, with H. For purposes of the class gift to "LT's children" created by Grantor, C1 is presumptively treated as a child of LT because LT functioned as a parent of C1 before C1 reached the age of majority. For class-gift purposes, C1 is not treated as a child of the stepfather H unless H adopts C1.

If the genetic parent intended to function as a parent of the child but an event, such as death or incapacity, intervened to prevent the genetic parent from functioning in that capacity, the child is presumptively treated for class-gift purposes as a child of the genetic parent.

Illustration:

4. Grantor died, leaving a will that devised the residue of her estate in trust, directing the trustee to pay income to the testator's son, LT, for life. On LT's death, Grantor directed the trustee to distribute the trust principal to LT's children. LT's domestic partner was pregnant with LT's child. LT and his domestic partner looked forward to the birth of their child, had bought a crib and decorated what was to be the baby's room in their apartment, and planned to get married after the child was born. On his way to work, LT was killed when a truck crashed into his car. LT's domestic partner subsequently gave birth to their child. LT's nonmarital child is presumptively treated as his child for purposes of the class gift "to LT's children."

e. *Contrary intent.* The presumption established by this section is rebutted if the language or circumstances establish that the transferor had a different intention. Language indicating an intent to exclude nonmarital children would include, for example, language restricting the class gift to "children born in wedlock."

§ 14.8. Child of Assisted Reproduction: Non-Surrogacy

Unless the language or circumstances establish that the transferor had a different intention, a child of assisted reproduction whose birth mother is not acting as a surrogate for an intended parent or parents is treated for class-gift purposes as a child of:

(1) the child's birth mother; and

(2) another person, if any, who consented to assisted reproduction by the birth mother with intent to be treated as the child's other parent. Consent to assisted reproduction by the birth mother with intent to be treated as the child's other parent is established if the person:

(A) signed a writing or other record, before or after the child's birth, exhibiting intent, in light of all the facts and circumstances, to be treated as the child's other parent; or

(B) in the absence of a signed writing or other record that satisfies paragraph (2)(A):

(i) functioned as the child's other parent within a reasonable time after the child's birth;

(ii) intended to function as the child's other parent within a reasonable time after the child's birth but was prevented from doing so by an event such as death or incapacity; or

(iii) intended to be treated as the other parent of a posthumously conceived child, but only if that intent is established by clear and convincing evidence.

Comment:

a. *Scope.* This section provides rules of construction for determining, for class-gift purposes, who is a parent of a child of assisted reproduction when the birth mother is not acting as a surrogate for an intended parent or parents. Section 14.9 provides rules of construction for cases in which the birth mother is acting as a surrogate for an intended parent or parents.

Although the focus of this section is on the status of a child of assisted reproduction for class-gift purposes when the birth mother is not acting as a surrogate for an intended parent or parents, the rule of this section applies by analogy to a donative disposition that is not in class-gift form but nevertheless uses a term of relationship to identify the beneficiaries. An example would be a remainder interest "to my deceased sister's children," in a case in which the remainder interest is not subject to a condition of survival.

Rules of construction apply unless the language or circumstances establish that the transferor had a different intention. See § 11.3.

Assisted-reproduction technologies (often referred to as "ART") encompass methods of causing pregnancy other than by sexual intercourse. These methods currently include intrauterine insemination (previously and sometimes currently called artificial insemination), donation of eggs, donation of embryos, in vitro fertilization and transfer of embryos, and intracytoplasmic sperm injection. See Comment *b*.

b. *Brief primer on assisted-reproductive technologies—internal and external fertilization.* There are currently two main types of assisted-reproductive technologies, although variations of these two procedures are practiced and being continually refined. The two types are internal and external fertilization. Internal fertilization occurs inside the uterus of the woman who is to become pregnant (the birth mother). External fertilization occurs in a laboratory procedure outside the uterus and is followed by implantation of the fertilized egg (embryo) into the uterus of the woman who is to become pregnant.

Internal fertilization includes artificial insemination (AI) and gamete intrafallopian transfer (GIFT). AI is a procedure whereby a man's sperm is injected directly into the uterus of the woman who is to become pregnant. GIFT is a procedure whereby a woman's eggs (oocytes) are retrieved from her ovaries and mixed with sperm, but not actively fertilized. The mixed sperm and eggs are subsequently injected into the woman who is to become pregnant and placed where they would be in natural fertilization.

External fertilization is commonly referred to as in vitro fertilization (IVF) or sometimes in vitro fertilization-embryo transfer (IVF-ET). IVF is a procedure whereby a woman's eggs are retrieved from her ovaries and fertilized with a man's sperm in a laboratory procedure outside the uterus to produce embryos; the embryos are subsequently placed in the uterus of a woman to produce a pregnancy. In this Restatement, the term "IVF" is not limited to the case in which the woman who donates the eggs is to become pregnant. In some lexicons, the term is so limited and the term "egg donation" is used to refer to cases in which the egg donor and the birth mother are different women. In this Restatement, the term "IVF" is used to refer to both types of cases.

Although it is hard to imagine that methods of assisted reproduction other than variants of internal or external fertilization will be developed in the future, they might be. For class-gift purposes, a child produced by any such new method should be treated in a manner that is consistent with the principles of this section.

c. *Child of assisted reproduction is automatically treated for class-gift purposes as child of the child's non-surrogacy birth mother.* In the non-surrogacy situation, the birth mother is a woman who has voluntarily become pregnant by means of assisted-reproduction technology. It therefore seems appropriate to conclude that her purpose was to have *her* child. Regardless of whether she is the child's genetic mother (i.e., whether or not the egg that was fertilized was her egg or the egg of a third-party donor), her action in undergoing the procedure automatically establishes that the child is her child for class-gift purposes. This position is consistent with Uniform Probate Code (UPC) §§ 2–705(b); 2–120(c) and the Uniform Parentage Act § 201(a) (2002).

If, subsequent to the child's birth, the birth mother gives the child up for adoption and the child is adopted, a parent-child relationship is established between the child and the child's adoptive parent or parents (see § 14.5; accord UPC § 2–118) and the parent-child relationship with the birth mother is usually severed (see § 14.6; accord UPC § 2–119).

d. *Genetic relationship not necessarily controlling.* When a woman becomes pregnant by means of assisted reproduction, the child's genetic lineage is not necessarily controlling for class-gift purposes. A person who signed a writing or other record exhibiting intent to be treated as the other parent of the child, who functioned as the other parent of the child, or who intended to function as the other parent of the child but was prevented from doing so by an event such as death or incapacity, might or might not be a genetic parent of the child. A reference in the donative document to "lawful children" or children "born in wedlock" does not manifest a different intention.

e. *Signed writing or other record exhibiting intent to be treated as the other parent of the child.* Unless the language or circumstances establish that the transferor had a different intention, a child of assisted reproduction is treated for class-gift purposes as a child of a person who signed a writing or other record, before or after the child's birth, exhibiting intent, in light of all the facts and circumstances, to be treated as the other parent of the child. A writing or other record consenting to the use of a person's sperm or eggs by the birth mother or authorizing the birth mother to make decisions regarding the disposition of the person's deposited sperm or eggs exhibits the requisite intent. Such a writing or other record is often made by filling out and signing a form provided by a fertility clinic at the time the person makes a sperm or eggs deposit and is controlling unless consent is withdrawn before the placement of eggs, sperm, or embryos.

f. *Functioned as the other parent of the child.* In the absence of a writing or other record exhibiting intent to be treated as the other parent of the child, such intent can be shown by actually functioning as the other parent of the child. Such behavior demonstrates intent to be treated as the other parent of the child and for the child to be treated as a child of that person for class-gift purposes. For the criteria used in determining whether a person functioned as a parent of a child, see § 14.5, Comment *e*.

g. Intended to function as or be treated as the other parent of the child. If an event such as death or incapacity prevents a person from functioning as the other parent of the child, evidence establishing that the person intended to do so is sufficient to treat the child as a child of that person for class-gift purposes. Alternatively, a posthumously conceived child is treated as a child of a person who intended to be treated as the other parent of the posthumously conceived child, if such intent is exhibited in a signed writing or other record or is otherwise established by clear and convincing evidence. On posthumous conception, see Comment *k*.

h. Birth mother is married. If the birth mother is married and if she and her spouse are not separated and no divorce or annulment proceedings are pending, it is presumed that the birth mother's spouse functioned as a parent of the child or intended to do so. Accord UPC §§ 2–705(b), 2–120(h). The same presumption is extended to partners in a domestic partnership (see Comment *i*), where the partners are not separated and the partnership has not been terminated and is not in the process of being terminated.

In the case of an opposite-sex marriage in which the married birth mother was artificially inseminated, the sperm that is injected sometimes comes from the husband and sometimes from a third party. If the husband's sperm is used, the procedure is known as *homologous artificial insemination* or *artificial insemination husband (AIH)*. A child produced by AIH is the genetic child of the husband and the wife and is so treated for class-gift purposes, assuming that the husband functioned as the other parent of the child. In the case of an opposite-sex or a same-sex marriage in which the sperm of a third party is used, the procedure is known as *heterologous artificial insemination* or *artificial insemination donor (AID)*. A child produced by AID is the genetic child of the sperm donor and the married birth mother. For class-gift purposes, however, such a child is treated as the child of the birth mother's spouse, assuming that the birth mother's spouse functioned as a parent of the child. The child is not treated as the child of the sperm donor.

In the case of an opposite-sex marriage in which the married birth mother became pregnant by in vitro fertilization, the man's sperm sometimes comes from the husband and sometimes from a third party, and the woman's eggs sometime come from the wife and sometime from a third party. A child produced from the husband's sperm and the wife's eggs is the genetic child of the husband and the wife and is so treated for class-gift purposes, assuming that the husband functioned as the other parent of the child. In the case of an opposite-sex or a same-sex marriage in which the sperm or eggs come from a third-party donor, with the embryo being placed in the uterus of the married birth mother to produce a pregnancy, the child is the genetic child of the sperm and egg donors. For class-gift purposes, however, the child is treated as the child of the birth mother and the birth mother's spouse, assuming that the birth mother's spouse functioned as the other parent of the child. The child is not treated as the child of a third-party sperm or egg donor.

Illustrations:

1. Grantor died, leaving a will that devised property in trust, directing the trustee to pay the income to Grantor's daughter D for life and, on D's death, to distribute the trust property "to D's issue per stirpes." When Grantor executed his will and at Grantor's death, D was married to H1. D had two children that were conceived by her by sexual

intercourse with H1. After Grantor's death, D and H1 were divorced and D married H2. D and H2 were unable to have a child by sexual intercourse and decided to have a child by assisted reproduction. The procedure was successful, D became pregnant, and she gave birth to her third child. Since D was not acting as a surrogate mother, the child is her child for purposes of the class gift to "D's issue." See Comment *c*. Grantor's knowledge that D had two children without using assisted reproduction and therefore might not have contemplated that she would have a child by this means is not a basis for concluding that Grantor would have intended to exclude the child produced by artificial insemination.

2. Grantor died, leaving a will that devised property in trust, directing the trustee "to pay the income to Grantor's son S for life and, on S's death, to distribute the trust property to S's issue per stirpes." When Grantor executed his will and when Grantor died, S was married to W. S and W had two children conceived by sexual intercourse. After Grantor's death, S became infertile. W and S wanted another child, and arrangements were made to have her artificially inseminated with the sperm of another man whose identity was not revealed to either W or S. W and S were not separated and no divorce or annulment proceedings were pending. Although S did not sign a record or other writing exhibiting intent to be treated as the parent of the child, when a child is produced for a married person who is not separated from his or her spouse and no divorce or annulment proceedings are pending, it is presumed that S intended to function as a parent of the child. The circumstances of the assisted reproduction corroborate S's intent. The procedure was successful, W became pregnant, and she gave birth to her third child. S functioned as a parent to the child by bringing the child up in his home and raising the child. The person whose sperm was used was not aware of where or when it was used. The child thus produced by W is presumptively treated as S's child for purposes of the class gift "to S's issue." The fact that the child produced by artificial insemination is not S's genetic child is not a factor indicating that Grantor had a contrary intent, since S intended to and did function as a parent of the child.

i. Unmarried but partnered birth mother. If the birth mother is not married but is partnered with another, the child is the child of the birth mother's partner under the same rules applicable to the spouse of a married birth mother under Comment *g*. For purposes of this Restatement, an unmarried partnership includes persons who qualify as domestic partners under § 6.03 of the [American Law Institute's] Principles of the Law of Family Dissolution: Analysis and Recommendations. The term also includes unmarried partners under any other relationship entitling the partners to intestacy or other spousal-equivalent rights under applicable law, such as a civil union or domestic-partner relationship under the laws of various states.

If one or both unmarried partners adopt a child of assisted reproduction, then the child is classified as an adopted child with respect to the adopting parent or parents, and the child's status is determined under § 14.5.

j. Unmarried and unpartnered birth mother. If the birth mother is an unmarried and unpartnered woman who desires to have a child by assisted reproduction, using the sperm of a third-party sperm donor, then, unless the language or circumstances establish that the transferor had a different intention, the child is the child of the birth mother and not of the sperm donor.

If the unmarried and unpartnered birth mother subsequently marries or enters into an unmarried partnership with another, the child is not treated under this Section as the child of the new spouse or partner. A subsequent spouse or partner functions more as a stepparent of the child, not as a parent of the child. Under § 14.5, however, the child would be treated as the adopted child of the new spouse or partner if that spouse or partner adopts the child.

k. Posthumous conception. As its name implies, posthumous conception occurs when the birth mother conceives a child by assisted reproduction after the decedent's death. For class-gift purposes, the child is the child of the birth mother. See Comment *c*. The question for class-gift purposes is whether the decedent is treated as the other parent of the child. Under paragraph (2)(A), the decedent is treated as the other parent of the child if the decedent signed a writing or other record that, in light of all the facts and circumstances, exhibited the decedent's intent to be treated as the child's other parent. Accord UPC §§ 2–705(b), 2–120(f)(1). The writing or other record need not expressly refer to post-death conception. Some consent forms merely provide that the decedent consents to the procedure or consents to the procedure with intent to "be a parent" of the child, but do not specifically provide that if assisted reproduction were to occur after death, the decedent would "be a parent" of the child.

In a case in which the decedent gave no consent in writing or other record, the child is nevertheless treated for class-gift purposes under paragraph (2)(B)(ii) as the child of the decedent if the decedent intended to function as the child's other parent within a reasonable time after the child's birth but was prevented from doing so by an event such as death or incapacity (accord UPC §§ 2–705(b), 2–120(f)(2)(B)); or under paragraph (2)(b)(iii) if the decedent intended to be treated as the other parent of the child, but only if that intent is established by clear and convincing evidence (accord UPC §§ 2–705(b), 2–120(f)(2)(C)). The burden of proof is on the party claiming that the decedent intended to be treated as the child's other parent.

In one case, however, the burden of proof is shifted to the party claiming that the decedent did not intend to be treated as the child's other parent. That is the case in which the decedent deposited sperm before his death and the birth mother is the decedent's surviving spouse or domestic partner. In that case, there is a presumption that the deceased spouse or partner consented to be treated as the child's other parent.

k(1). Post-death sperm retrieval. Cases of post-death sperm retrieval (sometimes called sperm harvesting)—cases in which the deceased husband or male partner did not deposit sperm before his death but his widow or surviving female partner had his sperm harvested after his death—raise different issues. These cases make it possible for a widow or surviving female partner, unilaterally and without any previous discussion with her deceased husband or male partner, to have his sperm harvested so that she could become pregnant with "his" child without his prior approval in order to gain unjustified control of class-gift rights for the child from him and possibly from one or more of his relatives. In such a case, therefore, the burden of proof that the deceased husband or male partner consented to be treated as the child's father remains on his widow or surviving female partner, even if at his death no divorce proceeding was pending or the partnership was not dissolved or in the process of being dissolved. That burden would be satisfied if the deceased husband or partner signed a writing or other record expressly consenting to be treated as the child's father in case of post-death retrieval. In the absence of such a writing or other record, the widow or surviving partner has the burden of proof to establish by clear and convincing evidence that the decedent consented to post-death retrieval with intent to be treated as the child's father.

l. *Dissolution of marriage or domestic partnership or withdrawal of consent.* The UPC addresses the problem of dissolution of marriage by providing that "[i]f a married couple is divorced before placement of eggs, sperm, or embryos, a child resulting from the assisted reproduction is not a child of the birth mother's former spouse, unless the former spouse consented in a record that if assisted reproduction were to occur after divorce, the child would be treated as the former spouse's child." UPC § 2–120(i). This Restatement adopts that rule for class-gift purposes, and extends the rule to dissolution of a domestic partnership.

The UPC addresses withdrawal of consent by providing that "[i]f, in a record, an individual withdraws consent to assisted reproduction before placement of eggs, sperm, or embryos, a child resulting from the assisted reproduction is not a child of that individual, unless the individual subsequently [signed a writing or other record that, in light of all the facts and circumstances, exhibited the decedent's intent to be treated as the child's other parent or functioned as the child's other parent no later than two years after the child's birth]." UPC § 2–120(j). This Restatement adopts that rule for class-gift purposes, but substitutes "a reasonable time" for "two years" and extends the rule to dissolution of a domestic partnership.

If, after dissolution, the intended parent remarries or enters into a new domestic partnership, the child is not treated under this Section as the child of the new spouse or domestic partner. A new spouse or domestic partner functions more as a stepparent of the child, not as a parent of the child. Under § 14.5, however, the child would be treated as the adopted child of the new spouse or domestic partner if that spouse or partner adopts the child.

m. *Contrary intent.* For purposes of determining whether the language or circumstances indicate that the transferor had a different intention, a provision in a governing instrument relating to the inclusion or exclusion of a child of parents who are not married to each other does not apply to a child of assisted reproduction, unless of course the provision specifically refers to a child of assisted reproduction as a nonmarital child. Technically, for example, a posthumously conceived child born to a decedent's surviving widow could be considered a nonmarital child. A provision in a will, trust, or other governing instrument that relates to the inclusion or exclusion of a nonmarital child, or to the inclusion or exclusion of a nonmarital child under specific circumstances, would not have been inserted with a child of assisted reproduction in mind. Unless that type of provision specifically refers to a child of assisted reproduction, such a provision does not state a contrary intention to the rule of construction contained in this section.

n. *Third-party donor.* A third-party donor of sperm or eggs that are used for assisted reproduction has no parent-child relationship with the child.

o. *Class-closing rules.* For application of the class-closing rules to children of assisted reproduction, see § 15.1, Comment *j*.

§ 14.9. Child of Assisted Reproduction: Surrogacy

Unless the language or circumstances establish that the transferor had a different intention, a child of assisted reproduction whose birth mother is acting under a surrogacy agreement for an intended parent or parents is treated for class-gift purposes as a child of an intended parent who functioned as a parent of the child

within a reasonable time after the child's birth. The child is not a child of the surrogate unless a court order designates her as the child's mother or she is the child's genetic mother and no intended parent functioned as a parent of the child within a reasonable time after the child's birth.

Comment:

a. Scope. This section provides rules of construction for determining, for class-gift purposes, who is a parent of a child of assisted reproduction when the birth mother is acting under a surrogacy agreement for an intended parent or parents. Section 14.8 provides rules of construction for cases in which the birth mother is not acting as a surrogate for an intended parent or parents. Although the focus of this section is on the status of a child of assisted reproduction for class-gift purposes when the birth mother is acting under a surrogacy agreement for an intended parent or parents, the rule of this section applies by analogy to a donative disposition that is not in class-gift form but nevertheless uses a term of relationship to identify the beneficiaries. An example would be a remainder interest "to my deceased sister's children," in a case in which the remainder interest is not subject to a condition of survival.

b. Surrogacy agreement. A surrogacy agreement, called a gestational agreement in the Uniform Probate Code (UPC), is an agreement between a female surrogate and an intended parent or parents. The surrogate, called the gestational carrier in the UPC, agrees to become pregnant by assisted reproduction, carry the child to birth, and turn the child over to the intended parent or parents, who will then function as the parent or parents of the child. The child, called the gestational child in the UPC, is called the surrogacy child in this Restatement.

c. Genetic relationship with intended parent or parents irrelevant. In some cases of assisted reproduction by a surrogate, the sperm or eggs or both come from the intended parents and in other cases the sperm or eggs or both come from third-party donors. For purposes of the rule of construction in this section, it makes no difference whether an intended parent has a genetic relationship with the surrogacy child. Accord UPC §§ 2–705(b); 2–121.

d. Enforceability or legality of surrogacy agreement or arrangement irrelevant. In some states, surrogacy agreements are unenforceable or illegal. For class-gift purposes, however, the enforceability or legality of the surrogacy agreement or arrangement is irrelevant. Voluntary performance of an illegal or unenforceable agreement still produces a child who is entitled to be treated as someone's child. Because this section only deals with class gifts, the question cannot arise unless a child is actually born. The only question is who has a parent-child relationship with the child. Disregarding the enforceability or legality of the surrogacy agreement has the added advantage of avoiding conflict-of-laws questions that might otherwise arise because of the mobility of society. For example, a child might be born as a result of a surrogacy agreement that was valid under the law applicable when the contract was entered into but the intended parents or parent moved and later died in a state in which surrogacy contracts are illegal (or vice versa). It would be unacceptable for the law to hold that a child who grew up in the household of the intended parents or parent is not a child of the intended parents or parent simply because the surrogacy agreement was illegal.

e. Merely entering into a surrogacy agreement not sufficient to establish a parent-child relationship. Merely entering into a surrogacy agreement is not sufficient to establish a parent-child relationship with the intended parent or parents. An intended parent must also function as a parent of the surrogacy child within a reasonable time after the child's birth. The UPC §§ 2–705(b), 2–121(d)(2)(A) provides that the intended parent must function as a parent of the child within two years after the child's birth, which seems an appropriate period for a court to adopt as a reasonable time. If there are two intended parents, but only one functions as a parent of the child within a reasonable time after the child's birth, the child is a child of the intended parent who functioned in that capacity and, except as provided in Comment *f* or *g*, not of the intended parent who did not function in that capacity.

f. *Death of an intended parent while surrogate is pregnant.* In a limited set of circumstances, an intended parent who died while the surrogate was pregnant can still have a parent-child relationship with the surrogacy child for class-gift purposes. There are three situations in which the parent-child relationship can arise. First is the case in which there were two intended parents and the other intended parent functioned as a parent of the child within a reasonable time after the child's birth. Second is the case in which there were two intended parents, the other intended parent also died while the surrogate was pregnant, and a relative of either decedent or the spouse or surviving spouse of a relative of either decedent functioned as a parent of the child within a reasonable time after the child's birth. Third is the case in which there was no other intended parent and a relative of or the spouse or surviving spouse of a relative of the decedent functioned as a parent of the child within a reasonable time after the child's birth. In each of these cases, the decedent has a parent-child relationship with the child. Accord UPC §§ 2–705, 2–121(d)(2).

g. *Surrogacy agreement entered into after death or incapacity.* In a limited set of circumstances, a parent-child relationship can be established between a surrogacy child and a decedent whose sperm or eggs were used after the decedent's death to conceive a child under a surrogacy agreement entered into after the decedent's death. The requirement is that the decedent must have intended to be treated as the parent of the child. The decedent's intent may be shown by a writing or other record signed by the decedent that considering all the facts and circumstances exhibits the decedent's intent or by other facts and circumstances that establish the decedent's intent by clear and convincing evidence. The same rule is extended to a surrogacy agreement entered into after incapacity. Accord UPC §§ 2–705(b), 2–121(e).

h. *Presumption: Surrogacy agreement after spouse's or domestic partner's death or incapacity.* Unless there is clear and convincing evidence of a contrary intent, a decedent is deemed to have intended to be treated as the parent of a surrogacy child for purposes of Comment *g* if the decedent, before death, deposited the sperm or eggs that were used to conceive the child, when the decedent deposited the sperm or eggs, the decedent was married and no divorce proceeding was pending, and the decedent's spouse or surviving spouse functioned as a parent of the child within a reasonable time after the child's birth. The same rule is extended to a surrogacy agreement entered into after incapacity. Accord UPC §§ 2–705(b), 2–121(f) (substituting a two-year period for a reasonable-time period). Under this Restatement, the same presumption is extended to partners in a domestic partnership, where the partners are not separated and the partnership has not been terminated and is not in the process of being terminated.

h(1). *Post-death sperm or egg retrieval.* Cases of post-death sperm or egg retrieval (sometimes called sperm or egg harvesting)—cases in which the deceased spouse or deceased partner did not deposit sperm or eggs before death but the decedent's surviving spouse or surviving partner had the decedent's sperm or eggs harvested after his or her death and then entered into a surrogacy agreement—raise different issues. These cases make it possible for a surviving spouse or partner, unilaterally and without any previous discussion with the deceased spouse or partner, to have the decedent's sperm or eggs harvested so that the surviving spouse or partner could engage a surrogate in order to have the resulting child be treated as the decedent's child without the decedent's prior approval in order to gain unjustified control of class-gift rights for the child from the decedent and possibly from one or more of the decedent's relatives. In such a case, therefore, the burden of proof that the decedent consented to be treated as the child's other parent remains on the surviving spouse or partner even if at the decedent's death no divorce proceeding was pending or the partnership was not terminated and is not in the process of being terminated. That burden would be satisfied if the decedent signed a writing or other record expressly consenting to be treated as the child's other parent in case of post-death retrieval. In the absence of such a writing or other record, the surviving spouse or partner has the burden of proof to establish by clear and convincing evidence that the decedent consented to post-death retrieval with intent to be treated as the child's other parent. In order for the child to be treated as the decedent's child, the surviving spouse or partner must also function as a parent of the child within a reasonable time after the child's birth.

i. Contrary intent. For purposes of determining whether the language or circumstances indicate that the transferor had a different intention, a provision in a governing instrument relating to the inclusion or exclusion of a child of parents who are not married to each other does not apply to a surrogacy child, unless the provision specifically refers to a surrogacy child as a nonmarital child. Technically, for example, a posthumously conceived surrogacy child born to a decedent's surviving widow could be considered a nonmarital child. A provision in a will, trust, or other governing instrument that relates to the inclusion or exclusion of a nonmarital child, or to the inclusion or exclusion of a nonmarital child under specific circumstances, would not have been inserted with a surrogacy child in mind. Unless that type of provision specifically refers to a surrogacy child, such a provision does not state a contrary intention to the rule of construction contained in this section.

j. Surrogate. Although the surrogate is the birth mother, the surrogacy agreement assumes or might state explicitly that she never intended to have, and under this Restatement almost never has, a parent-child relationship with the child. The intent of the agreement was that upon or shortly after birth she would turn the child over to the intended parents or parent, who would then raise the child as their, her, or his own. Under this Restatement, a child who is born under a surrogacy agreement is almost never treated for class-gift purposes as a child of the surrogate. The only situation in which the surrogate would have a parent-child relationship with the child would be one in which a court order designates her as the child's mother or one in which she is the child's genetic mother and no intended parent functioned as a parent of the child within a reasonable time after the child's birth. Current practice discourages surrogacy arrangements in which the surrogate has a genetic relationship with the child, such as would be the case if the surrogate becomes pregnant by artificial insemination but would not be the case if she becomes pregnant by in vitro fertilization using the eggs of a female intended parent or of a third-party donor. Accord UPC §§ 2–705(b), 2–121(c).

k. *Third-party donor.* A third-party donor of sperm or eggs that are used for assisted reproduction has no parent-child relationship with a surrogacy child.

l. *Class-closing rules.* For application of the class-closing rules to surrogacy children, see § 15.1, Comment *j*.

§ 14.10. Relative by Marriage

Unless the language or circumstances establish that the transferor had a different intention, a term of relationship in a class gift does not include relatives by marriage.

Comment:

a. *Rationale.* A class gift that does not specifically include or exclude relatives by marriage (sometimes referred to as "relatives by affinity") is ambiguous. In the case law, the question raised most frequently is whether a class gift to "children" or "issue" includes unadopted stepchildren or on whether a class gift to collateral relatives such as "nieces and nephews" includes the children of a brother-in-law or sister-in-law. The question can also arise with respect to other terms of relationship, such as whether a class gift to "brothers and sisters" includes brothers-in-law and sisters-in-law, or whether a class gift to "uncles and aunts" includes the husband or wife of a blood or adopting uncle or aunt.

The traditional rule of construction is that a term of family relationship does not include relatives by marriage, unless the language or circumstances establish that the transferor had a different intention. That rule was adopted in the Restatement Second of Property (Donative Transfers) § 25.6 and is reaffirmed here. A relative by marriage lacks a blood or adoptive relationship to the designated person.

Although the focus of this section is on the status of relatives by marriage for class-gift purposes, the rule of this section applies by analogy to a donative disposition that is not in class-gift form but nevertheless uses a term of relationship to identify the beneficiaries.

b. *Contrary intent—otherwise empty class.* The rule of this section is a rule of construction and therefore yields to a finding of a different intention, as indicated by the language or circumstances of the particular case. A circumstance that frequently justifies overcoming the presumption against the inclusion of relatives by marriage is one in which, looking at the facts existing when the donative document was executed, the class was then and foreseeably would be empty unless the transferor intended to include relatives by marriage.

Illustration:

2. Grantor died, leaving a will that devised property in trust, directing the trustee to pay the income to Grantor's wife W for life, and on her death, to distribute the trust property to "my grandchildren." W had children by a prior marriage who were Grantor's stepchildren. Grantor never had any children of his own and he never adopted his stepchildren. It is reasonable to conclude that under these circumstances Grantor meant the children of his stepchildren when his will gave the future interest under the trust to Grantor's "grandchildren."

c. Contrary intent—reciprocal wills; ancestor participates in raising child other than a stepchild. Circumstances that may justify overcoming the presumption against the inclusion of relatives by marriage are not limited to cases in which the class would otherwise be empty. Other circumstances include reciprocal wills (Illustration 4) and cases in which an ancestor participates in raising a relative by marriage other than a stepchild (Illustration 5).

Illustrations:

4. Grantor died, leaving a will that devised her entire estate "to my husband if he survives me, but if not, to my nieces and nephews." Grantor's husband H predeceased her. H's will devised his entire estate "to my wife if she survives me, but if not, to my nieces and nephews." Both Grantor and H had nieces and nephews. In these circumstances, "my nieces and nephews" is construed to include Grantor's nieces and nephews by marriage.

5. *Ancestor participated in raising relative by marriage other than a stepchild.* Grantor's will devised property in trust, directing the trustee to pay the income in equal shares "to my nieces and nephews living on each income payment date until the death of the last survivor of my nieces and nephews, at which time the trust shall terminate and the trust property shall be distributed to the X charity." Grantor's wife W was deceased when Grantor executed his will. W had one brother who predeceased her. Grantor and W took the brother's children, the wife's nieces and nephews, into their home and raised them. Grantor had one sister who predeceased him, and Grantor and W were close to her children, Grantor's nieces and nephews. Under these circumstances, the conclusion is justified that the disposition "to my nieces and nephews" includes the children of W's brother as well as the children of Grantor's sister.

The language of the disposition may also establish a contrary intent.

Illustration:

6. Grantor died, leaving a will that devised half of his estate to his wife W and half to "my children." Grantor had one child by a prior marriage, and W had two children by a prior marriage. Grantor did not adopt his stepchildren. Grantor's relationship with his stepchildren was close, and he participated in raising them. The use of the plural "children" is a factor indicating that Grantor intended to include his stepchildren in the class gift to his children.

d. Contrary intent established on the basis of personal usage. Extrinsic evidence that the donor habitually referred to his or her relatives by marriage as his or her relatives would constitute evidence of a contrary intent. For example, a class gift to the donor's "nieces and nephews" could be construed as referring to nieces and nephews by marriage if the donor habitually referred to them as "my nieces and nephews." See § 11.2, Comment *r*. Such evidence would be especially strong if the class gift would be otherwise empty. See Comment *b*.

CHAPTER 15

INCREASE AND DECREASE IN CLASS MEMBERSHIP

Introductory Note: As discussed in § 13.1, the principal features of a class gift (other than a class gift to heirs) are: (1) the membership of the class is typically not static, but is subject to fluctuation by increase or decrease until the time when a class member is entitled to distribution; and (2) upon distribution, the property is divided among the then-entitled class members on a fractional basis.

This chapter addresses these two features of a class gift (other than one to heirs): increase and decrease in class membership. At some point, the ability of a class to increase comes to an end, and the ultimate takers are determined. Part A addresses the rules for determining when the ability of a class to increase comes to an end. These are the so-called class-closing rules, the rules that determine when a class closes to future-born or future-adopted members. Part B addresses decrease in class membership brought about through the failure of a class member to satisfy a condition of survival or some other condition.

Part A. Increase in Class Membership

Introductory Note: Increase in a class occurs when a new member is added to the class on account of birth, adoption, marriage, or for some other reason. A class gift that is subject to increase is said to be "subject to open" or, under older terminology, "subject to partial divestment." When a new member is added to a class, the shares of existing class members abate proportionally. See § 13.1, Comment *h*.

Part A addresses the rules for determining when the ability to increase comes to an end. Of course, the ability of a class to increase is ended when it is no longer physiologically capable of increasing. Under the so-called class-closing rules, however, a class can be closed to future entrants earlier.

Whether the class gift is to an immediate or a postponed class (see § 13.1, Comment *f*), the class-closing rules are based on a single principle. A class that has not yet closed physiologically closes when a beneficiary of the class gift is entitled to distribution of his or her share. Since the beneficiaries of a class gift take on a fractional basis (see § 13.1, Comment *i*), the time of distribution even for one beneficiary of the class gift requires the determination of that beneficiary's share. The numerator of the fraction for each then-entitled beneficiary is one, but the denominator cannot be known unless the maximum membership of the class is fixed at that point.

§ 15.1. When Class Closes—Rule of Convenience

Unless the language or circumstances establish that the transferor had a different intention, a class gift that has not yet closed physiologically closes to future entrants on the distribution date if a beneficiary of the class gift is then entitled to distribution.

Comment:

a. Scope. This section addresses the class-closing rules for a class gift that has not yet closed physiologically. In this section, the "beneficiary of a class gift" not only includes a class member but also includes a substitute for, a transferee of, or a successor to a class member.

b. Distribution date. As used in this Restatement, the term "distribution date" with respect to a class gift refers to the time when an immediate or a postponed class gift is to take effect in possession or enjoyment. The distribution date for an immediate class gift taking effect on the death of the testator is the time of death of the testator, not the beginning or end of the calendar day of the testator's death and not when the testator's estate is actually distributed. The distribution date for a postponed class gift taking effect in possession or enjoyment on the death of the income beneficiary is the time of death of the income beneficiary, not the beginning or end of the calendar day of the income beneficiary's death and not when the principal of the trust is actually distributed.

c. Physiological closing. A class closes physiologically when events that can cause a class to increase become physiologically impossible, events such as births or adoptions. The physiological closing of a class is traditionally based on the assumption that death terminates the possibility of having children. Thus, a class gift in the transferor's will to the transferor's children physiologically closes upon the transferor's death, and a class gift to the transferor's grandchildren physiologically closes upon the death of the transferor's last living child. A class member who is in gestation or in the process of being adopted when the class closes is regarded as in being on the closing date. See Comments *h* and *i*.

Frozen sperm, ova, and embryos, however, make it possible to have children by assisted reproduction after death. See § 14.8, Comment *k*. The treatment of a child produced posthumously by assisted reproduction is considered in Comment *j*.

In the vast majority of cases, no frozen sperm, ova, or embryos capable of producing a post-death child exist, and the traditional assumption about the parent's death marking the physiological closing of the class prevails.

Death also terminates the possibility of getting married. A class gift to "my sons-in-law and daughters-in-law" closes physiologically at the death of the transferor's last living child.

d. Class closing under the rule of convenience. The rule of this section is a rule of construction known as the *rule of convenience*. Under that rule, a class gift that has not yet closed physiologically closes to future entrants on the distribution date if at least one beneficiary of the class gift is then entitled to distribution, unless the language or circumstances establish that the transferor had a different intention. The rule of convenience applies both to single-generation and to multiple-generation class gifts.

In the case of an immediate class gift in a will (see Comment *e*), the class closes at the testator's death because that time is treated as the distribution date. In the case of a postponed class gift in the principal of a trust payable at the death of the income beneficiary (see Comment *f*), the class closes at the income beneficiary's death because that time is treated as the distribution date. See Comment *b*. Although the actual distribution of the property never takes place when the testator or the income beneficiary dies, and is necessarily delayed for administrative reasons, the rule of convenience treats the time of death in both cases as the time when the class closes. By treating the time of death as the time when the class closes, the rule of convenience contributes certainty and eliminates the possibility of manipulation that would arise if the time of closing were delayed until the time of actual distribution.

In the case of an immediate class gift in a will or a postponed class gift in the principal of a trust payable at the death of the income beneficiary, all of the devised property or all of the principal of the trust is typically distributed to all beneficiaries of the class gift then entitled. In some cases, however, the class-gift property is not all distributed at one time, but the payments are spread out sequentially over time. These special cases are addressed in separate Comments below. See Comments *m*, *n*, *p*, and *q*. Regardless of how the payments are structured, the rule of convenience closes the class when one beneficiary of the class gift is entitled to distribution. When one beneficiary of the class gift becomes entitled to distribution, the transferor, it is presumed, would want that beneficiary to take possession of his or her share absolutely, and not to have that share be subject to partial divestment later. Taking an interest that is subject to partial divestment upon the birth or adoption of additional class members would render the property less useful to the class member and less marketable. Moreover, were the interest in personal property, some device such as the posting of security to protect the interests of unborn or unadopted members of the class would be needed. This presumption about the transferor's intention is rebutted if the language or circumstances establish that the transferor had a different intention. If the presumption is not rebutted, the only way to achieve the transferor's objective is to close the class when one beneficiary of the class gift is entitled to distribution. At that point, both the numerator and the denominator of the fraction must be fixed.

Once a class has been closed by the rule of convenience, persons not yet in being are not entitled to participate in the class gift, even though they otherwise fit the class label. New entrants come into a class only if they come into being while the class is still open. See Comments *h*, *i*, and *j*.

Although the rule of convenience closes a class before the class would close physiologically, the rule as applied to single-generation class gifts seldom has the effect of eliminating the interests of actual after-conceived or after-adopted children. For example, suppose a devise "to the children of my brother B," where B survives the testator and is therefore deemed capable of fathering or adopting more children. If, at the testator's death, B is 65 years old, the probability that B will father or adopt another child is remote in most cases. Closing the class at the testator's death in such a case benefits the existing class members without harming after-conceived or after-adopted class members, because there will be none.

e. *Immediate class gifts created by will*. Immediate class gifts are typically created by will. As indicated, the rule of convenience comes into operation only if the class has not closed physiologically by the time of distribution, which in the case of a will is deemed to be the testator's death, not when the administration of the estate is completed. In the absence of the possibility of a child produced posthumously by assisted reproduction (see Comment *j*), an immediate testamentary devise to the children of the testator does not require premature closing. Similarly, a devise to the children of a person other than the testator does not close prematurely if the person predeceases the time of distribution. If the person is still living at the time of distribution, however, an application of the rule of convenience is necessary. When at least one beneficiary of the class gift is in being, an immediate gift closes at the testator's death.

Illustration:

1. Grantor died, leaving a will that devised the residue of his estate "to my grandchildren." When Grantor executed his will, his only son A had a child (X). Subsequently, but before Grantor's death, a second child (Y) was born. Grantor was survived by his son A and by his two grandchildren, X and Y. No other grandchildren were in being at Grantor's death. Under the rule of convenience, the class remains open until Grantor's death but closes at that time, even though A is still alive and is therefore deemed to be capable of having more children. X and Y each take an undivided interest in half of the property absolutely. Their interests are not subject to partial divestment in favor of any later born or later adopted child of A. If, at Grantor's death, A's wife was pregnant, and Grantor's third grandchild (Z) was born viable, Z would be considered to have been "in being" at Grantor's death, and consequently Z would participate in the class gift. X, Y, and Z would each take an undivided one-third possessory interest in the property in fee simple absolute. If A's child was not born viable, the child would not be considered in being at Grantor's death and the child would be excluded from the class.

The rule of convenience also applies to a class gift to nonrelatives, a class gift such as a devise in a will "to the members of the X-Y-Z Investment Club, of which I am currently a member." Such a class closes to future entrants at the testator's death, so that anyone joining the investment club after the testator's death is excluded from the class. For treatment of this type of class gift, see also § 13.1, Comment *c*, § 14.2, Comment *j*.

f. Postponed class gift taking effect on the termination of the preceding interest. The typical postponed class gift takes effect on the termination of a preceding life estate or a lifetime income interest in a trust. As indicated, the rule of convenience comes into operation only if the class has not closed physiologically by the time of distribution, which in the case of such a postponed class gift is deemed to be the life tenant's or the lifetime beneficiary's death. In the absence of sperm or ova capable of producing a post-death child, a postponed class gift to the children of the life beneficiary does not require premature closing. If the parent of the class is still living at the time of distribution, however, an application of the rule of convenience is necessary. When at least one beneficiary of the class gift is in being, a postponed class gift taking effect on the termination of a preceding interest closes on the death of the life tenant or life beneficiary.

Illustration:

5. Grantor died, leaving a will that devised the residue of her estate in trust, directing the trustee to pay the income "to A for life, and at A's death, to distribute the trust principal to B's children." Grantor was survived by A, B, and B's child (X). A second child (Y) was born to B

during A's lifetime. B's third child (Z) was born after A's death. B survived A. The class closes at A's death. X and Y are members of the class. Z is excluded from the class.

g. Contrary intent—language "before or after." The rule of this section is a rule of construction. Any language in the donative document that is inconsistent with the rule of this section is controlling. Language directing that the property is to go to class members "born before or after" the time when the rule of this section would otherwise close the class indicates a contrary intent. Giving effect to "before or after" language presents an administrative problem, however. In the case, for example, of a testamentary disposition "to my grandchildren whether born or adopted before or after my death," what distribution is to be made to the members of the class who are alive and ready to take on the death of the testator, and what is to be done to assure that appropriate shares will be available for after-conceived and after-adopted class members?

If the subject matter is land, the class members ready to take would normally be entitled to enjoyment in possession of undivided interests in the land. The undivided interests of each total the entire interest in the land, but are subject to partial divestment by birth or adoption of new class members. The holders of the undivided interests in the land do not have to account to after-conceived and after-adopted class members for benefits received by them from the enjoyment of the possession of the land before any partial divestment.

If the subject matter is personal property, the class members ready to take should be entitled to immediate enjoyment of the property, but with the imposition of adequate safeguards to assure that the shares of any after-conceived and after-adopted class members will be forthcoming. This can be done by placing the property in trust to be managed for their benefit and the benefit of any after-conceived and after-adopted children until the class can no longer increase. The existing class members from time to time will receive all the current benefits from the management of the property in the trust with no obligation to account for such benefits to after-conceived and after-adopted class members.

Instead of using a trust, the property may be delivered to the class members who are ready to take, subject to partial divestment by birth or adoption of new class members. The class members ready to take may be required to provide bond that the property or its value will be forthcoming in sufficient amount to make up the shares of any after-conceived and after-adopted class members. In this situation as well, there is no obligation to account for the benefits received by the existing class members from the enjoyment of the property in possession before a partial divestment occurs.

h. Child in gestation. For class-gift purposes, a child is regarded as in being during the period of gestation. Consequently, a child in gestation when a class closes is not excluded from the class gift if the child is born viable. The Uniform Probate Code (UPC) requires the child to live 120 hours or more after birth. See UPC § 2–108. . . . .

i. Adoption in process. By analogy to a child in gestation, a child who is in the process of being adopted is regarded for class-gift purposes as an adopted child during the period the adoption is in process. Consequently, that child is not excluded from the class gift if the adoption is concluded within a reasonable time.

j. Child produced posthumously by assisted reproduction. In cases in which the distribution date is the deceased parent's death, a child produced posthumously by assisted reproduction is treated as in being at the decedent's death for purposes of the class-closing rules, if the child was born or in utero within a reasonable time after the decedent's death. See Illustration[ ] 7 . . . . Determining whether birth or pregnancy occurred within a reasonable time after the decedent's death requires a balancing of the interest in final settlement of trusts and estates and allowing the surviving spouse or domestic partner time to grieve before making a decision whether to go forward with an assisted-reproduction procedure, and how soon after death an attempt was made to produce a pregnancy through assisted reproduction, whether successful or not. For a comparable rule regarding the right of the child to take by intestacy from the decedent, see § 2.5, Comment *l*. The UPC provides that a child who is conceived after the decedent's death is treated as in being at the decedent's death if the child is in utero not later than 36 months after the decedent's death or born not later than 45 months after the decedent's death (UPC §§ 2–120(k) and 2–121(h)), which seem appropriate periods for a court to adopt as reasonable times.

In cases in which the distribution date arises after the deceased parent's death, a child produced posthumously by assisted reproduction is in being on the date when the child is in utero for purposes of the class-closing rules, just as is any other child. See Illustration 10.

Illustrations:

7. Grantor, a member of the armed forces, executed a military will shortly before being deployed to a war zone. Grantor died, leaving a will that devised "90 percent of my estate to my wife W and 10 percent of my estate to my children." Grantor also left frozen sperm at a sperm bank in case he should be killed in action. Grantor consented to be the parent of the child within the meaning of § 14.8, Comment *k*. Grantor was killed in action. After H's death, W decided to become artificially inseminated with his frozen sperm so she could have his child. If the child so produced is born or in utero within a reasonable time after Grantor's death, the child is treated as in being at Grantor's death and is included in the class under the rule of convenience.

10. Grantor created a revocable inter vivos trust shortly before her death. The trustee was directed to pay the income to Grantor for life, then "to pay the income to the children of my son S commencing upon each child's twenty-first birthday, and at the death of S's last surviving child, to pay the principal of the trust to X charity." When Grantor died, S, had an infant daughter with his wife W. Shortly after being diagnosed with leukemia, S feared that he would be rendered infertile by the disease or by the treatment for the disease, so he left frozen sperm at a sperm bank. S consented to be the parent of the child within the meaning of § 14.8, Comment *k*. After Grantor's death, S died, and S's widow W decided to become artificially inseminated with his frozen sperm so that she could have a second child by him. Upon reaching 21, S's second child is entitled to receive half of the income.

k. Empty class. The rule of convenience provides that an immediate class gift created by will closes at the testator's death and that a postponed class gift taking effect at the termination of a preceding interest (such as a life estate or an income interest for life) closes at the termination of the preceding interest. If the class is then empty, however, i.e., there is no beneficiary of the class gift then alive or in being, does the class nevertheless close on the distribution date? The traditional rule is that, unless the language or circumstances establish a different intent, the class remains open until it closes physiologically, despite the administrative inconvenience in doing so. It is assumed that the transferor would choose this option in preference to the other two options: (i) have the class gift fail entirely, or (ii) give all of the property to the first class member who is born or adopted after the testator's death or after the termination of the preceding interest. In many cases, however, the circumstances may establish that the transferor would prefer to have the class gift fail entirely. This would be the case if the circumstances indicate that it is improbable that there will be any after-conceived or after-adopted class members because of the age or physical condition of the prospective parent.

Illustration:

11. Grantor died, leaving a will that devised the residue of his estate "to my grandchildren." At Grantor's death, his only child S, a son, was still alive, but S had no living children and none was then in gestation. If S was then 22 years old, the rule of convenience would not close the class at Grantor's death, but would keep it open as long as it is possible for a child of S to come into being, despite the administrative costs in doing so. All after-conceived and after-adopted grandchildren, if any, are entitled to participate. If, however, S was then 62 years old, the class would close at Grantor's death, resulting in the failure of the class gift and causing the residue of Grantor's estate to pass to Grantor's heirs by intestacy.

l. *Empty specific-sum class gift.* As noted in § 13.1, Comment *l*, a specific-sum class gift is a hybrid. As such, this type of class gift is not governed by the ordinary rules applicable to class gifts generally. A specific-sum class gift closes when the gift becomes effective, whether or not any class member is then alive or in being. If no class member is then alive or in being, the class gift fails. The alternative of keeping the class open until it closes physiologically is rejected because doing so would delay the distribution of a substantial portion, if not all of, the testator's estate.

m. *Class gift distributable as each class member reaches a specified age.* A class gift that is distributable to each member of the class who reaches a specified age closes when the first class member reaches that age. Class members then in being are not excluded but will take their respective shares if they fulfill the specified age contingency. The shares of those who are not excluded by the closing of the class, but whose gifts fail because they fail to satisfy the age contingency, go to enlarge the shares of those class members who satisfy the age contingency.

Illustrations:

13. Grantor's will bequeathed $90,000 to be divided equally among those of Grantor's grandchildren who reach the age of 21. (This type of bequest is conventionally left in trust, and provides for discretionary payment to the grandchildren or perhaps for the accumulation of the income until distribution.) If one of Grantor's grandchildren reached 21 before Grantor's death, the class would close when Grantor died. If none of Grantor's grandchildren reached 21 before Grantor's death, the class would close when the first grandchild reached 21. If X were the first grandchild to reach 21, and there were two other grandchildren (Y and Z) then alive, X would be entitled to one-third and the other two-thirds would be held by the trustee, who would distribute

half of the remaining property to Y when Y reaches 21 and all of the remaining property to Z when Z subsequently reaches 21. The rule of convenience excludes from the class any grandchild born or adopted after X reached 21.

n. Immediate class gift subject to complete divestment. If an immediate class gift is subject to complete divestment, the ownership interests of the existing class members are already subject to divestment. There is no added "inconvenience" (of the type that the rule of convenience was designed to avoid) in requiring each existing class member's interest to be subject to *partial* divestment as well. Consequently, the class closes at the earlier of the divesting condition happening or failing to happen, but not before.

Illustration:

15. Grantor died, leaving a will that devised land "to my grandchildren, but if any grandchild should die before attaining 21, his or her share to go to my then surviving grandchildren." Grantor was survived by children and grandchildren. All of the grandchildren were under 21. Additional grandchildren were born after G's death. G's devise creates both a primary class gift and a series of gift-over class gifts. The primary class—"to my grandchildren, but if . . ."—does not close at Grantor's death because this class gift is subject to complete divestment. Because it is subject to complete divestment, there is no "inconvenience" in requiring it also to be subject to partial divestment. Thus the class remains open at Grantor's death, and closes at the earlier of a grandchild reaching 21 or dying under 21. There are two possible class-closing times because either event triggers a distribution. The primary class must close when a grandchild reaches 21, if that happens first, because that is when it is necessary to determine the fractional portion to distribute to that grandchild. The primary class must close when a grandchild dies under 21, if that happens first, because that is when it is necessary to determine the fractional portion to distribute to the gift-over class—the grandchildren then surviving. None of the gift-over classes—the share of any grandchild who dies under 21 "to my then surviving grandchildren"—closes at Grantor's death because none of these classes is then entitled to distribution. Each of these gift-over classes close whenever a grandchild (a member of the primary class) dies under 21, giving rise to a right of distribution of that grandchild's share. To illustrate: Suppose that after Grantor's death GC-1 dies at age 17; GC-1's share goes over to the grandchildren then living. Suppose that five years later, GC-2 dies at age 20; GC-2's share goes over to the grandchildren then living (including any grandchild who was born or adopted after GC-1's death). Each gift-over class is treated as a separate class gift and closes only when distribution to that class occurs. If, however, the disposition had said that any share of a grandchild dying under 21 is to be added to the shares of the other grandchildren, then the class would not close upon one dying under 21.

o. Class gift distributable when youngest member of class reaches a specified age. A class gift that is distributable when the youngest member of the class reaches a specified age is ambiguous. There are two plausible constructions. One is that the class closes when no living class member is under the specified age. The other is that the class closes when the youngest member of the class whenever born reaches that age. The former construction is preferred unless the facts and circumstances make it likely that another class member will subsequently be born or adopted.

Illustration:

16. Grantor devised property in trust, income to Grantor's grandchildren, trust principal to be equally divided among Grantor's grandchildren when the youngest grandchild attains 21. Grantor was survived by her son, A, then age 30, who was married and had two children, X (age 8) and Y (age 6). After Grantor's death, Y reached 21. A was still living and married to the same wife. No further grandchildren had been born or were in gestation on Y's 21st birthday. The class closed when Y reached 21 because Y was the youngest grandchild then living.

p. *Periodic income or other payments.* An income interest payable to class members from time to time living constitutes a series of successive postponed class gifts. Each of these classes closes on its distribution date.

Illustration:

18. Grantor died, leaving a will that devised property in trust, directing the trustee to pay the income in equal shares to Grantor's grandchildren until the death of Grantor's last living grandchild, then to pay the trust principal to X charity. When Grantor died, grandchild V and grandchild X were living. Subsequently, grandchild Y was conceived and born, then grandchild Z. V and X each start out receiving one-half of the income, but this prevails only until Y is born. When Y is born, V, X, and Y each receive one-third of the income until Z is born. When Z is born, each grandchild receives one-quarter of the income. The rule of convenience operates to give the living grandchildren absolute ownership in distributed income. It is neither inconvenient nor consistent with donative intent to exclude after-conceived grandchildren with regard to future income.

If a child is in gestation on an income-payment date, or is then in the process of being adopted, allowing that child to share in the income payment would place a serious burden on the trustee to investigate to determine whether a share of the income payment has to be set aside for such possible additions to the class membership. Consequently, in the absence of additional language or circumstances that indicate the transferor intends to place such burden on the trustee, the class member in gestation, or in the process of being adopted, is excluded from sharing in income payable before birth or adoption.

A legal life interest in favor of a described class is sufficiently similar to an income interest in favor of a class under a trust to justify similar treatment in regard to the closing of the class. Each life tenant in possession holds a life estate subject to partial divestment in favor of additional class members.

A trust that calls for periodic annuity payments to be made to class members from time to time living constitutes a series of successive class gifts. Each of these classes closes on the payment date.

A trust that calls for income payments to be made to the class on a regular basis and, in addition, provides for mandatory payments of some portion of the trust principal to be made to the class from time to time on a schedule that does not correspond to the scheduled income payments, for example, distribution of trust principal to each class member at age 25, 30, and 35, requires special treatment. Each required payment of income would be treated as discussed above, but any required distribution of trust principal would not exclude a class member in gestation, or in the process of being adopted, on the date the mandatory distribution of trust principal is to be made, in the absence of additional language or circumstances that indicate otherwise.

q. Discretionary distributions. A trust may be discretionary in various ways. The trustee may have discretion to make distributions of income or principal to those members of a class that the trustee selects. The trustee may have complete discretion regarding when to make distributions. Or, the trustee may be required to make distributions at specified times but may have discretion to select the class members who will be entitled to each distribution. A class member in gestation, or in the process of being adopted, when the trustee makes the selection is eligible to be selected.

Illustration:

19. Grantor died, leaving a will that devised property in trust, authorizing the trustee "to distribute such amount or amounts of income, from time to time, to such one or more of the grandchildren of Grantor, as Trustee shall in Trustee's discretion determine." The trust is to terminate on the death of the survivor of Grantor's grandchildren living on Grantor's death, at which time the trust property is to be distributed "to Grantor's issue then living on a per stirpes basis, and if no issue of Grantor is then living, the trust property is to be distributed to the X charity." When Trustee selects a date for a distribution of income to selected grandchildren of Grantor, the class closes to after-conceived and after-adopted grandchildren on that date with respect to that distribution of trust property, but the class is not closed to after-conceived and after-adopted grandchildren with respect to later distributions of income. A child in gestation or in the process of being adopted on the selected date is eligible to receive a distribution.

Part B. Decrease in Class Membership

Introductory Note: Decrease in a class occurs because a class member fails to satisfy a requirement of survival or some other requirement. Section 15.2 addresses the situation in which the law imposes a requirement of surviving the time when the donative document takes effect as a dispositive instrument. In the case of a class gift created by will, a class member who fails to survive the testator is excluded from the class. Sections 15.3 through 15.4 address cases in which the requirement of survival is imposed privately, either expressly in or by implication from the donative document.

§ 15.2. Class Member Who Is Deceased When Donative Document Takes Effect

A class member who is deceased when the donative document takes effect as a dispositive instrument is excluded from the class.

Comment:

a. Rationale and scope. A donative transfer cannot be made to a person who is deceased because a decedent lacks juridical personality. Because this rule is mandatory, not a rule of construction, language in the donative document expressly requiring survival is surplusage. The requirement of survival derives from the law, not from the document. Consequently, a class member who dies before the donative document takes effect as a dispositive instrument is excluded from the class. Although the transferor cannot override the rule of this section, he or she can create an express gift over to a substitute taker, even to the "estate" or "executor" of a predeceased class member (for the preferred construction of such a gift over, see § 1.2, Comment *g*). An antilapse statute in many cases also provides for a gift over to a substitute taker (see Comment *c*).

The rule of this section applies whether the class member died before or after the donative document was executed. The rule also applies to single-generation and multiple-generation class gifts.

The rule of this section applies to a class member who is treated as if the beneficiary is deceased when the donative document takes effect as a dispositive instrument. See, e.g., UPC § 2–702.

b. *Wills.* A will takes effect as a dispositive instrument at the testator's death, not when the will was executed. See § 3.1, Comment *a*. Hence all devisees in a will, including the beneficiaries of a class gift, must survive the testator. See § 1.2, Comment *e*; § 5.5, Comment *a*. A class member who fails to survive the testator is excluded from the class. Unless an antilapse statute applies (see Comment *c*; § 5.5, Comment *j*), unless there is an effective express gift over of a deceased class member's share, or unless the class gift is a specific-sum class gift (see Comment *f*), the failure of a class member to survive the testator enlarges the shares of the class members who survive the testator. See § 13.1, Comment *h*. A class gift that has closed physiologically at the testator's death (see § 15.1, Comment *c*) lapses if none of the class members and no substitute for a class member survive the testator. . . .

c. *Antilapse statutes.* Antilapse statutes apply to class gifts to single-generation classes, whether or not the language of the statute explicitly covers class gifts. Antilapse statutes do not, however, apply to class gifts to multiple-generation classes, such as gifts to "issue," "descendants," "heirs of the body," "heirs," "next of kin," "relatives," or "family," because these types of class gifts already pass the shares of deceased class members to their surviving descendants without statutory intervention.

Under a typical antilapse statute, the property devised to a single-generation class is divided among the class members who survive the testator, if any, and the descendants of deceased class members who survive the testator, if any. Each surviving class member takes the share that he or she would have taken had the deceased class members also survived the testator. Each deceased class member's surviving descendants take by representation the share that the deceased class member would have taken had the deceased class member survived the testator. A class member who fails to survive the testator and leaves no descendants who survive the testator is disregarded.

Illustration:

3. Grantor died, leaving a will that devised $15,000 "to my children." Grantor had three children, A, B, and C. A predeceased Grantor, leaving two children, X and Y, who survived Grantor. B predeceased Grantor without leaving any descendants who survived Grantor. C survived Grantor. As the only surviving class member, C takes one-half ($7500). Under the applicable antilapse statute, X and Y divide the one-half share that A would have taken had A survived Grantor ($3750 each). If Grantor's devise had been "to my issue, by representation," the result would have been the same but without the application of the antilapse statute. If Grantor's devise had been "to my children, the share of any deceased child to go to that child's descendants by representation," the result would have been the same but without the application of the antilapse statute.

d. Revocable trusts and other will substitutes. Revocable trusts and other will substitutes are treated as wills for purposes of requiring survival of the transferor and applying the applicable antilapse statute. See § 5.5, Comment *p*; § 7.2, Comment *f*. If the donative document in Illustration[ ] . . . 3 . . . had not been a will, but a revocable trust with the income payable to Grantor for life, the result would have been the same . . . .

e. Deeds. A deed is effective as a dispositive instrument when the transferor manifests the intention that the deed is to be operative as a present transfer, such as by delivery. See § 6.2, Comment *u*; § 6.3, Comment *d*. . . .

f. Specific-sum class gift. In the case of a specific-sum class gift (see § 13.1, Comment *l*), the exclusion of a class member does not enlarge the shares of the other class members. The disposition of the specified amount that the excluded class member would have taken lapses.

Illustration:

6. Grantor died, leaving a will that devised "$10,000 to each of my children, and the residue of my estate to X charity." When Grantor executed his will, he had three children, C1, C2, and C3. C1 predeceased Grantor without leaving any descendants who survived Grantor. The $10,000 that C1 would have taken had C1 survived Grantor does not go to enlarge the shares of C2 and C3, but instead passes under the residuary clause. C2 and C3 still take $10,000 each under the specific-sum class gift, and no more. If C1 had left one or more descendants who survived Grantor, those descendants would be substituted for C1 under most antilapse statutes (see Comment *c* and § 5.5) and would divide C1's $10,000 by representation.

§ 15.3. Postponed Class Gift—Beneficiary of Multiple-Generation Class Gift Fails to Survive Distribution Date

Unless the language or circumstances establish that the transferor had a different intention, a beneficiary of a postponed multiple-generation class gift who fails to survive the distribution date is excluded from the class.

Comment:

a. Distribution date. For the definition of the "distribution date" as used in this Restatement, see § 15.1, Comment *b*.

b. Scope and rationale. This section applies to a class member who has survived the effective date of the document (see § 15.2) but has failed to survive the distribution date, and thus cannot benefit personally from his or her share as a class member.

This section applies to postponed multiple-generation class gifts to issue or descendants. It does not apply to postponed class gifts to heirs or next of kin. For the rule of construction applicable to class gifts to heirs or next of kin, see § 16.1.

A future interest to issue or descendants is presumptively divided by representation. See § 14.3. The rule of construction of this section is based on the nature of a representational form of distribution. Under that form of distribution, the property is divided among the living descendants who are nearest to the designated ancestor in each descending line. A descendant who has a living ancestor who is also a descendant of the designated ancestor is not an eligible taker. Consequently, a continuing process of substitution is inherent in a representational form of distribution. A descendant who dies before the distribution date with issue is replaced in the class by his or her issue who survive the distribution date. A descendant who dies without issue before the distribution date is not replaced, because that descending line has died out. The share of a descendant who dies without issue before the distribution date is shifted to the other descending lines that still have living issue on the distribution date. To give maximum effect to this process, it continues until the distribution date. This process is the basis for implying a condition of surviving the distribution date. Accordingly, a class member who fails to survive the distribution date is excluded from the class.

The rule of construction of this section is also supported by the strong constructional preference, set forth in § 11.3(c)(3), favoring the construction that does not disinherit a line of descent having one or more living members on the distribution date and excluding a line of descent that then has no living member.

Illustration:

1. Grantor created a revocable inter vivos trust, directing the trustee to pay the income to Grantor for life, then to pay the income to Grantor's daughter LT for life, then to distribute the trust principal of the trust "to LT's issue." LT had three children, C1, C2, and C3. C1 survived LT. C2 predeceased LT, leaving issue who survived LT. C3 predeceased LT. C3 had one child, GC, who also predeceased LT. GC had no issue. Half of the principal of the trust passes to C1. The other half passes to C2's issue who survived LT, to be divided among them by representation. C3's line is excluded because it has no living member on the distribution date.

c. "Children" construed to mean "issue." As provided in § 14.1, Comments *g*, *g(1)*, *g(2)*, *g(3)*, and *g(4)*, the word "children" is sometimes construed to mean "issue." If so, and if the class gift is a postponed class gift, the rule of this section applies. See § 15.4, Comment *h*.

d. Heirs of the body. As provided in § 14.3, Comment *e*, the term "heirs of the body" means issue or descendants who would take under the applicable statute of intestacy. Consequently, the rule of this section applies to a postponed class gift to the heirs of the body of a designated ancestor.

e. Express condition of survival. If a condition of surviving the distribution date is stated expressly and unambiguously, this language of the disposition supports the rule of this section. In Illustration 1, for example, if the trust had provided that the future interest in trust principal was to go "to LT's issue who survive LT, by representation," the unambiguous requirement of survival of LT would support the rule of this section.

f. Express condition of survival—construction if ambiguous. An express condition of survival is sometimes stated ambiguously. If the trust in Illustration 1 had provided that the principal of the trust was to go "to LT's surviving issue," the question is whether LT's issue must survive LT or Grantor or the creation of the trust. Unless the language or circumstances establish that the transferor had a different intention, the ambiguity is resolved by construing the word "surviving" as relating to the distribution date—LT's death in this case.

g. Contrary intent. The rule of this section is a rule of construction that yields if the language or circumstances establish that the transferor had a different intention. Because under § 14.4, Comment *d*, the preferred construction of a per capita disposition to a multiple-generation class is that it invokes the system of representation known as per capita with representation, as described in § 2.3, Comment *e*, language specifying that the distribution is to be made per capita does not express a different intention.

Language expressly requiring survival of an event occurring before the distribution date does not express a different intention.

Illustration:

2. Grantor's will created a trust, directing the trustee to pay the income to Grantor's son LT for life, then to distribute the principal of the trust "to LT's issue per capita." At Grantor's death, LT had three children, C1, C2, and C3. C1 survived LT. C2 predeceased LT, leaving two children who survived LT. C3 predeceased LT. C3 had one child, who also predeceased LT without issue. Half of the trust principal goes to C1 and half goes to C2's two children who survived LT.

§ 15.4. Postponed Class Gift—Beneficiary of Single-Generation Class Gift Fails to Survive Distribution Date

Unless the language or circumstances establish that the transferor had a different intention, or unless an applicable statute provides otherwise, a beneficiary of a postponed single-generation class gift who fails to survive the distribution date or any other future time or event is not excluded from the class. The deceased class member's share passes through his or her estate.

Comment:

a. Distribution date. For the definition of "distribution date" as used in this Restatement, see § 15.1, Comment *b*.

b. Scope. This section applies to a class member who has survived the effective date of the document (see § 15.2) but has failed to survive the distribution date or any other future time or event, and thus cannot personally enjoy his or her share as a class member.

c. Rationale of the rule of this section—traditional doctrine. The traditional rule of construction with respect to a single-generation class gift is that a condition of survival of the distribution date or of any other future time or event is not implied. Accordingly, the share of a deceased class member passes through his or her estate. Section 15.4 adheres to the traditional rule, because it is the rule best suited within the confines of the common-law tradition to approximate the likely preference of the transferor, supported by the constructional preference for the construction that does not disinherit a line of descent (see § 11.3(c)(3)). A rule better suited to the transferor's purposes would not only recognize an implied condition of survival, but also an implied substitute gift to the descendants of a deceased class member who survive the distribution date. The traditional technique of the common law, however, is to effectuate intent by construction, and not by the creation of substitutionary shares not expressed by the transferor. There are judicial decisions in which the court found an implied gift on the basis of the facts and circumstances of an individual case. For example, in the case of a disposition "to A for life, and if A dies without issue, to B," courts have found an implied gift to A's issue if A dies with issue. But courts have not presumed to create a substitute gift in all cases, as the antilapse statutes have been able to command.

d. Historical rationale no longer convincing. The traditional rule had its origin in the constructional preference for vested interests and its corollary, the constructional preference for vesting at the earliest possible moment. Although the origin of the preference for early vesting is somewhat obscure, it is generally thought to be based on the desire to avoid the now-defunct rule of destructibility of contingent remainders and the once overly harsh but now widely liberalized or abolished Rule Against Perpetuities. Neither the constructional preference for vested interests nor for vesting at the earliest possible time is endorsed in this Restatement. See § 11.3.

e. Modern rationale—"trickle-down" theory. The strongest justification for the rule of this section is "that it enables the deceased class member to pass his share to his issue, thereby keeping the benefits of the gift equal among the descendant lines." Restatement Second, Property (Donative Transfers) § 27.3, Comment *a*. This is sometimes known as the "trickle-down" theory. Under this theory, the share of a deceased class member will descend through the class member's estate and, when the trust is dissolved at some later time, might end up benefiting the deceased class member's descendants. The traditional rule produces the best chance within the common-law tradition of protecting a descending line that has one or more living members on the distribution date.

It would probably be within the traditional technique of the common law to construe single-generation class gifts as presumptively being subject to an implied condition of survival of the distribution date, as is already done with respect to multiple-generation class gifts (see § 15.3). By itself, however, an implied condition of survival of the distribution date would make it impossible for the trickle-down theory to work. Unless a court is willing to couple a survival requirement with a blanket presumption creating a substitute gift to the descendants of a deceased class member, merely implying a condition of survival of the distribution date in all cases would extinguish the possibility of benefit to the deceased class member's descendants. Another possible approach would be to restrict the rule of construction against implying a condition of survival to instances in which the deceased beneficiary left descendants who survived the distribution date. That approach, while recommended to courts for adoption, is not adopted in this Restatement because of lack of judicial or legislative authority.

The principal weakness of the traditional rule is this: although the share of a deceased class member might end up in the hands of the deceased class member's descendants, it might not. The deceased class member might die without issue. The deceased class member might die intestate, in which case there might be multiple heirs, one or more of whom also predecease the distribution date. On the distribution date, the deceased class member's share can easily pass to complete strangers. To be sure, a class member who survives the distribution date can also pass his or her share to complete strangers, but at least the class member who survives the distribution date has the right to enjoy his or her share personally.

Another weakness of the traditional rule is the administrative cost of identifying the owner or owners of the interest on the distribution date. Identifying the current owners requires tracing the nonpossessory future interest through the estate of any class member who died before the distribution date and perhaps tracing fractional shares of the interest through the estates of the class member's successors in interest if any of them have also died before the distribution date.

Consequently, the traditional rule is a crude and costly means of protecting the deceased class member's descendants from disinheritance, but probably is the only means of doing so within the traditional technique of the common law.

The traditional rule applies equally to cases in which the future interest is not subject to any other conditions, as in Illustration 1, and to cases in which the future interest is subject to an express condition other than a condition of survival, as in Illustration 2.

Illustrations:

1. Grantor created a revocable inter vivos trust, directing the trustee to pay the income to Grantor for life, then to pay the income to Grantor's daughter LT for life, then to distribute the principal of the trust "to LT's children." LT had three children, C1, C2, and C3. C1 survived LT. C2 predeceased LT, leaving descendants who survived LT. C3 predeceased LT. C3 had one child, GC, who also predeceased LT. GC had no descendants. Under the rule against implied conditions of survival, one-third of the trust principal goes to C1, one-third goes to C2's estate, and the remaining one-third goes to C3's estate. C2's share might trickle down to C2's descendants. C3's share cannot trickle down to C3's descendants because there are none. C3's line has no living members on the distribution date.

2. Grantor died, leaving a will that devised property in trust, directing the trustee to pay the income to Grantor's daughter LT for life, and at her death to pay the principal of the trust "to LT's children who survive her, but if LT leaves no children surviving her, to my other children." Grantor was survived by LT and by three other children, C1, C2, and C3. LT died without children. C1 survived LT. C2 and C3 predeceased LT. C2 left descendants who survived LT, but C3 left no surviving descendants. One-third of the trust principal goes to C1, one-third goes to the estate of C2 (and hence might end up in the hands of C2's descendants), and one-third goes to the estate of C3 (even though C3 left no surviving descendants). It is irrelevant that the class gift "to my other children" was conditioned on LT dying without children surviving her.

f. Contrary intent—express condition of survival. The rule of this section is a rule of construction that yields if the language or circumstances establish that the transferor had a different intention. If a condition of surviving the distribution date is stated expressly and unambiguously, the language of the disposition expresses an intent contrary to the rule of this section. In Illustrations 1 and 2, for example, if the trusts had provided that the principal of the trust was to go "to LT's children who survive LT," the entire principal of both trusts would pass to C1. C2's descendants would end up with nothing. See Comment *h*, however for the possibility of avoiding such an inequality among the descending lines by construing the word "children" to mean "issue." Such a construction, which is permissible whether there is or is not an express condition of survival, would cause half of the trust principal in both cases to pass to C1 and half to C2's descendants by representation.

g. Express condition of survival—construction if ambiguous. An express condition of survival is sometimes stated ambiguously. If the trusts in Illustrations 1 and 2 had provided that the principal of the trust was to go "to LT's surviving children," it would be unclear to what event the word "surviving" relates. The word "surviving" might relate to surviving LT or to surviving Grantor. Unless the language or circumstances establish that the transferor had a different intention, the ambiguity is resolved by construing the word "surviving" as referring to the distribution date (LT's death) because that is the more natural meaning of the language. Under this construction, the entire principal of both trusts would pass to C1. C2's descendants would end up with nothing. See Comment *h*, however, for the possibility of avoiding such an inequality among the descending lines by construing the word "children" to mean "issue." Such a construction would cause half of the trust principal in both cases to pass to C1 and half to C2's descendants by representation. Another possible but less satisfactory means of avoiding an inequality among the descending lines would be to construe the word "surviving" as relating to G's death, thus allowing the trickle-down theory to operate at least with respect to C2's descending line.

h. "Children" construed to mean "issue." As provided in § 14.1, Comment *g*, the language or circumstances often justify construing the word "children" to mean "issue." See § 14.1, Comment *g(1)* (construing "children" to mean "issue" when "children" is coupled with language of representation), Comment *g(2)* (construing "children" to mean "issue" when "children" and "issue" are used interchangeably), Comment *g(3)* (construing "children" to mean "issue" when gift to "children" would otherwise be ineffective), and Comment *g(4)* (construing "children" to mean "issue" to effectuate overall dispositive plan). If "children" is construed to mean "issue," and if the class gift is a postponed class gift, the rule of § 15.3 applies. See § 15.3, Comment *c*. The great advantage of a class gift to issue (or descendants) is that it includes a descending line that has not died out by the distribution date and excludes a descending line that has died out by the distribution date, without risk of diversion, thus fulfilling the constructional preference for the construction that does not disinherit a line of descent. See § 11.3(c)(3). In Illustrations 1 and 2, such a construction would cause half of the trust principal to pass to C1 and half to C2's descendants by representation.

The concept of construing a single-generation class as a multiple-generation class is not limited to construing "children" to mean "issue," but extends to other single-generation class gifts. If the language or circumstances so justify, a class gift, for example, to "grandchildren" or to "nieces and nephews" may be construed to include issue of a deceased class member. See § 14.1, Comment *l*.

i. Antilapse-type statutes. A few states have enacted legislation that extends antilapse-type coverage to postponed single-generation class gifts. Most of these statutes are based on § 2–707 of the Uniform Probate Code (UPC), which only applies to future interests created in a trust. These statutes provide a more direct and efficient means of protecting equality among different lines of descent than the rule of this section. Under UPC § 2–707, a beneficiary of a single-generation class gift who fails to survive the distribution date is excluded from the class, but the beneficiary's descendants who survive the distribution date, if any, take by representation in the beneficiary's place. To prevent the statute from being intent-defeating, the substitution of descendants only applies if the trust document fails to create an alternative future interest that is entitled to take effect in possession or enjoyment or if the evidence establishes that the settlor had a contrary intention (a clause expressing a contrary intention would be one that provided that "if any class member predeceases the distribution date, the class member's share is not to pass to the deceased class member's descendants"). In effect, this provision applies the antilapse statute applicable to wills and will substitutes (see § 5.5) as if the transferor were a testator who died on the distribution date. Section 2–706 of the UPC applies the same approach to beneficiary designations under life-insurance policies and similar arrangements.

UPC § 2–707 self-adjusts to different situations by including all lines with living descendants at the distribution date and excluding all lines without living descendants at the distribution date. In Illustrations 1 and 2, UPC § 2–707 would pass half of the trust principal to C1 and half to C2's descendants who survived the distribution date. No part of the trust principal in either case would pass down C3's descending line, because that descending line had died out by the distribution date. No part of the trust principal would pass through the estate of a predeceased class member or the estates of a predeceased class member's successors in interest.

The Restatement Second of Property (Donative Transfers) endorsed the approach of such statutes by stating that "it would be a better overall result to provide a substitute taker for the deceased class member and avoid involvement of the class member's share in his or her estate." Restatement Second, Property (Donative Transfers) § 27.3, Comment *b*. The Restatement Second also took the position that "[t]he policy of these statutes commends itself to decisional law." Restatement Second, Property (Donative Transfers) § 27.3, Comment *i*. A court that is willing to adopt this antilapse-type approach judicially should prefer it to the rule of this section. . . .

CHAPTER 16

CLASS GIFTS TO HEIRS

Introductory Note: This chapter addresses the special case of class gifts to heirs. Section 16.1 outlines the presumptive meaning of such class gifts. Sections 16.2 and 16.3 repudiate two archaic common-law rules relating to class gifts to heirs: the Rule in Shelley's Case and the Doctrine of Worthier Title. These rules served feudal purposes but are now intent-defeating and lack any sound basis in public policy. Both rules have been abolished in England.

§ 16.1. Class Gift to "Heirs"—Presumptive Meaning

Unless the language or circumstances establish that the transferor had a different intention, the term "heirs" (or a like term), in a class gift to the "heirs" (or to a class described by a like term) of a designated person, means the persons who would succeed to the designated person's intestate estate if the designated person died intestate on the distribution date owning only the subject matter of the gift.

Comment:

a. *Scope.* This section addresses the presumptive meaning of the term "heirs" or a like term, when used in a class gift as a "word of purchase," not as a "word of limitation." *Words of purchase* and *words of limitation* are terms of art carried over from the parlance of English common law. Words of purchase operate to designate a class of beneficiaries. Words of limitation operate to designate the extent of a beneficiary's interest. At one time in England, a disposition "to A" gave A only a life estate. To give A a fee simple absolute, the disposition had to say "to A and his (or her) heirs."

Today, words of limitation are not necessary to give the transferee a fee simple absolute. Sometimes the phrase "and his (or her) heirs" is used nevertheless, normally without legal effect. The use of the term "heirs" in this sense is outside the scope of this section. The subject of this section is the use of "heirs" or a like term as a word of purchase, such as in a disposition "to A for life, remainder to A's heirs." Such a disposition gives A a life estate and gives A's heirs the remainder interest.

b. *Like term.* This section applies to class gifts to "heirs" or to a class described by a like term. A like term has similar import to the term "heirs." Like terms include "heirs at law," "next of kin," "statutory distributees," "representatives," "family," and "relatives." In order to avoid invalidity of a class gift to "family" or "relatives" on the ground of indefiniteness, these terms are construed to mean "heirs." The term "heirs of the body" is not a like term. See § 14.3, Comment *e*.

c. *Rationale.* This section provides that, unless the language or circumstances establish that the transferor had a different intention, a designated person's "heirs" are determined as if the designated person died intestate on the distribution date owning only the subject matter of the gift, regardless of whether the designated person is then alive or died earlier.

If the designated person is still alive, the benefit of this construction is that the property can be distributed presently. This construction avoids delaying distribution until the designated person dies at some later time. The rationale is the same as that underlying the class-closing rules. See § 15.1.

If the designated person died before the distribution date, the benefit of this construction is that the property is distributed directly to the person's closest family members then living. This construction avoids reopening the estates of any heirs who were living at the designated person's death but who died before the distribution date, and it spares having to identify and trace their successors in interest, who might or might not be family members. This rationale is the same as that underlying the construction of a devise to the "estate" or "executor" of a deceased person (see § 1.2, Comment *g*) and the rule of construction adopted in § 15.3.

d. Distribution date. As used in this Restatement, the term "distribution date" refers to the time when an interest is to take effect in possession or enjoyment. The distribution date for an immediate class gift created by will takes effect in possession or enjoyment on the death of the testator, not the beginning or end of the calendar day of the testator's death and not when the property is actually distributed. The distribution date for a postponed class gift taking effect in possession or enjoyment on the death of an income beneficiary is the time of death of the income beneficiary, not the beginning or end of the calendar day of the income beneficiary's death and not when the principal of the trust is actually distributed.

e. Immediate class gifts. In the case of an immediate class gift, the distribution date is the time when the donative document takes effect as a dispositive instrument. A will takes effect as a dispositive instrument at the testator's death, not when the will was executed.

Except for a devise to the testator's heirs, the designated person is likely to survive the effective date of the donative document or to have died earlier. The designated person is unlikely to have died exactly when the donative document became effective as a dispositive instrument, though that event is remotely possible.

Illustrations:

1. Grantor died, leaving a will that devised property "to my heirs." Grantor's heirs are determined at Grantor's death.

2. Grantor died, leaving a will that devised property "to A's heirs." A survived Grantor. If A died when Grantor died, A's heirs would be A's two children, C1 and C2. Unless the language or circumstances establish that Grantor had a different intention, A's heirs are determined as if A died when Grantor died. The property is distributed half to C1 and half to C2.

f. Postponed class gifts. In the case of a postponed class gift, the distribution date is the time when the postponed class gift takes effect in possession or enjoyment. See § 15.3, Comment *a*, and § 15.4, Comment *a*.

In most cases of a postponed class gift, the death of the designated person will be the distribution date, because most postponed class gifts to heirs are to the heirs of the life tenant or the lifetime income beneficiary of a trust.

Illustrations:

4. Grantor died, leaving a will that devised property "to LT for life, remainder to LT's heirs." LT's heirs are determined at LT's death, which is the distribution date.

5. Grantor died, leaving a will that devised property "to LT for life, remainder to A's heirs." A survived both Grantor and LT. Unless the language or circumstances establish that Grantor had a different intention, A's heirs are determined as if A died when LT died.

g. Applicable intestacy statute; choice of law. The designated person's heirs are the persons who would succeed to the designated person's intestate estate if the designated person died intestate on the distribution date owning only the subject matter of the gift. The applicable statute is the one that would then be applied by the jurisdiction whose law, including its rules regarding choice of law, would apply in determining the intestate successors.

Between the execution of the donative document and the distribution date, many circumstances relevant to the determination of the ultimate takers may change. The applicable intestacy law may be amended, the designated person may change domiciles, and the nature of the property and its location may change. If the transfer is in trust, the trustee may replace the inception property with other property, including land in different jurisdictions. In determining the designated person's heirs, the facts and law as they exist on the distribution date are controlling.

If on the distribution date the subject matter of the gift is land, the applicable intestacy law is determined by the law of the jurisdiction in which the land is located, including its rules regarding choice of law. If on the distribution date the subject matter of the gift is personal property, the applicable intestacy law is determined by the law of the designated person's domicile, or domicile at death if the designated person predeceased the distribution date, including its rules regarding choice of law. If on the distribution date the subject matter of the gift consists of both land and personal property and the land is located in a jurisdiction other than the designated person's domicile, both jurisdictions' intestacy laws will apply. Also, if there is land in more than one jurisdiction, the intestacy law of each situs will apply.

h. Surviving spouse. If the designated person predeceased the distribution date, and if the designated person's surviving spouse is living but is remarried on the distribution date, the surviving spouse is not an heir of the designated person. The surviving spouse is not an heir because his or her remarriage removes his or her status as the spouse of the deceased designated person. In determining the heirs of the designated person, the remarried surviving spouse is treated as if he or she predeceased the distribution date.

i. Escheat. If on the distribution date the designated person has no living heirs, his or her intestate estate escheats to the state.

j. Ambiguity created by disposition to the heirs of more than one person. A class gift to the heirs of more than one person is ambiguous. The ambiguity is whether the heirs are treated as a single class or as a set of separate classes. The ambiguity is resolved by treating each set of heirs as a separate class, each set taking an equal share. Thus, in a disposition "to the heirs of A and B," or "to the heirs of A and the heirs of B," half of the property goes to the heirs of A (determined as if A died on the distribution date) and half to the heirs of B (determined as if B died on the distribution date). This resolution is consistent with the resolution of the ambiguity contained in a disposition to the issue of more than one person (see § 14.4, Comment *e*).

Illustration:

9. Grantor died, leaving a will that devised property in trust, directing the trustee to "pay the income to my issue from time to time living until the death of my last living child, and then to distribute the trust principal to the heirs of my children." Grantor was survived by her four children, C1, C2, C3, and C4. C1 died 10 years after Grantor's death, C2 died 15 years after Grantor's death, C3 died 20 years after Grantor's death, and C4 died 25 years after Grantor's death. Unless the language or circumstances establish that Grantor had a different intention, upon the death of C4, one-fourth of the property is distributed to C1's heirs determined as if C1 died when C4 died, one-fourth is distributed to C2's heirs determined as if C2 died when C4 died, one-fourth is distributed to C3's heirs determined as if C3 died when C4 died, and the remaining one-fourth is distributed to C4's heirs determined at C4's death.

k. Ambiguity created by dispositions to one or more designated persons and the heirs of one or more designated persons. A disposition to one or more designated persons and the heirs of one or more persons is ambiguous. The ambiguity is whether each individual and each class take an equal share or whether the individuals are treated as part of the class and divide the property on a per capita basis. The ambiguity is resolved by giving each individual and each class an equal share. In a disposition "to A and the heirs of B," A takes half and the heirs of B take the other half. This resolution is consistent with the resolution of the ambiguity contained in a disposition to one or more persons and the issue of one or more persons (see § 14.4, Comment *g*).

Illustration:

10. Grantor died, leaving a will that devised property to A for life, remainder to B and the heirs of A. B survived A. Unless the language or circumstances establish that Grantor had a different intention, B takes half and A's heirs take the other half.

l. Contrary intent. The rule of this section is a rule of construction. Language in the donative document that is inconsistent with the rule of this section is controlling. For example, suppose a testator's will devised property "to A for life, remainder to my heirs determined at the time of my death." Such a direction is controlling to the extent it is inconsistent with the rule of this section. Or, suppose a testator's will devised property "to A for life, remainder to A's heirs determined under the law of State X." Such a direction is controlling to the extent it is inconsistent with the rule of this section.

m. Contrary intent—heirs determined to mean children. When a gift is made to the "heirs" of a designated person, additional language or circumstances may establish that the transferor used the word "heirs" to mean "children." In such a case, the rule of § 14.1 is applicable. See § 14.1, Comment *f*.

n. Contrary intent—exclusion of an heir. An exclusion of a person or class from a class gift to heirs is controlling. In applying the rule of this section, the excluded person or class is deemed to have predeceased the distribution date. Cf. § 2.7. In a devise "to my heirs other than my son S," for example, the testator's heirs are determined under the rule of this section as if S predeceased the testator. Similarly, in a devise "to my heirs other than my daughter D and her issue," the testator's heirs are determined under the rule of this section as if D and D's issue predeceased the testator.

§ 16.2. Rule in Shelley's Case Not Recognized

The Rule in Shelley's Case is not recognized as part of American law. A remainder interest in favor of the life tenant's heirs (or the heirs of the body of the life tenant) passes to the life tenant's heirs (or the heirs of the body of the life tenant), not to the life tenant.

Comment:

a. Historical statement of the Rule in Shelley's Case. The Rule in Shelley's Case provided that a remainder interest in land in favor of the life tenant's heirs (or the heirs of the body of the life tenant) passed to the life tenant if the remainder was of the same quality as that of the life estate. The Rule in Shelley's Case was a rule of law, not a rule of construction, hence it was intent-defeating rather than intent-effecting.

The name of the rule derives from Wolfe v. Shelley, 1 Co.Rep. 93b, 76 Eng. Rep. 206 (K.B. 1581), although the rule itself was recognized in the early part of the 14th century. See Provost of Beverley's Case, Y.B. 40 Edw. IV., Hil. No. 18 (C.P. 1366); Abel's Case, Y.B. 18 Edw. II 577, 135 Eng. Rep. 381 (C.P. 1324). Because remainder interests were probably not recognized as valid future interests until the latter part of the 13th century (after the Statute De Donis, 1285), and contingent remainders were not fully recognized until much later, the Rule may at first have been intent-effecting rather than intent-defeating. Although the point was not finally settled until Perrin v. Blake, 1 Wm.Bl. 672, 96 Eng. Rep. 392 (1769), Lord Coke's classic statement of the Rule (in his argument for the defendant in Wolfe v. Shelley) described it as a rule of law. Crafting the Rule as a rule of law had favorable revenue effects for the king and the mesne lords, as the court explained in the Provost of Beverley's Case. Forcing the remainder to go to the life tenant meant that the land would pass to the life tenant's heirs by descent rather than by purchase. The feudal dues to the lord pertained only when land descended on the owner's death.

b. Nonrecognition of the Rule in Shelley's Case. The Rule in Shelley's Case is not recognized as part of American law. A remainder interest in favor of the life tenant's heirs or the heirs of the life tenant's body passes to the life tenant's heirs or the heirs of the life tenant's body, not to the life tenant. The Restatement Second of Property (Donative Transfers) § 30.1(3) stated that the Rule should be abolished by judicial decision to the extent it has not been abolished by statute. More recently, the Restatement Third, Trusts § 49, Comment *a(1)*, provides that the Rule in Shelley's Case is not recognized.

The original rationale for the Rule in Shelley's Case has long since disappeared. The Rule is intent-defeating, provokes litigation, and cannot be justified as an instrument of social policy. Although in a few cases the Rule may have the effect of making a parcel of land more alienable, the Rule applies too narrowly to be justified on that basis, since it affects only contingent remainders in the heirs (or heirs of the body) of the life tenant.

The Rule in Shelley's Case developed subrules that are not relevant now that the rule is repudiated, and they are not reproduced here. These subrules are preserved in prior Restatements. See Restatement Second, Property (Donative Transfers) § 30.1; Restatement of Property § 312.

§ 16.3. Doctrine of Worthier Title Not Recognized

The doctrine of worthier title is not recognized as part of American law, neither as a rule of law nor as a rule of construction. An inter vivos transfer purporting to create a future interest in the transferor's heirs or next of kin creates a future interest in the transferor's heirs or next of kin, not a reversionary interest in the transferor.

Comment:

a. Historical statement of the doctrine of worthier title. The doctrine of worthier title was originally a mandatory rule of law providing that a purported transfer by a living person of a future interest to his or her heirs (effective in possession at the transferor's death) was a nullity, leaving the transferor with a reversionary interest. This rule was established as part of the English feudal law. As a mandatory rule of law, the doctrine was understood to be an intent-defeating measure that was justified by then-existing feudal policy. There was a preference for title by descent rather than by purchase. The overlord was entitled to the valuable incidents of relief (an inheritance tax) when an heir inherited land, and, with respect to many types of land ownership, the overlord was entitled also to the valuable incidents of wardship and marriage when an inheriting heir was a minor or a woman. These incidents were preserved if, in an inter vivos transfer by Grantor of a future interest "to my heirs," typically reserving a life estate in Grantor, the purported transfer to Grantor's heirs was deemed a nullity. By this construction, the heirs acquired their interests by descent from Grantor at Grantor's death, rather than by purchase. In the early stages of development, the rule was a rule of law applicable only to transfers of land.

Judge Cardozo's decision in the case of Doctor v. Hughes, 122 N.E. 221 (N.Y. 1919), recast the American version of the doctrine as a rule of construction, which provided that when a transferor, by an inter vivos transfer, purported to create a future interest in the transferor's own heirs, the transferor was presumed to intend to retain a reversion rather than confer a future interest on his or her heirs. Noting that the doctrine had been a mandatory rule of law in England and that it had been abolished there by the Inheritance Act, 1833, 3 & 4 Wm. IV, c. 106, § 3, Judge Cardozo wrote:

> But in the absence of modifying statute, the rule persists to-day, at least as a rule of construction, if not as one of [law]. . . . We do not say that the ancient rule survives as an absolute prohibition limiting the power of a grantor. . . . There may be times, therefore, when a reference to the heirs of the grantor will be regarded as the gift of a remainder, and will vest title in the heirs presumptive as upon a gift to the heirs of others. . . . But at least the ancient rule survives to this extent, that to transform into a remainder what would ordinarily be a reversion, the intention to work the transformation must be clearly expressed.

From this time forward, the courts in New York and many other states applied the worthier-title doctrine as a rule of construction, though some states continued to apply the doctrine as a mandatory rule of law.

In shifting the doctrine to a rule of construction, Judge Cardozo may have desired to soften the old rule of law by allowing it to yield to the grantor's contrary intention. But shifting a mandatory rule of law to a rule of construction is not a natural evolutionary step in legal development. Rules of law and rules of construction stem from entirely different premises. Rules of law are intent-defeating; rules of construction are intent-effecting. Defeating intention is only justified to vindicate goals of public policy. The function of a rule of law is to prohibit individual choice deemed unduly harmful to society. See § 10.1. Rules of construction, on the other hand, operate in areas in which society as a whole is indifferent to the result. The only public-policy goal that rules of construction vindicate is giving effect to private intention in areas of societal indifference. Rules of construction seek to facilitate this intent-effecting goal by providing a presumptive meaning—one designed to accord with common intention—to words that have failed to express the actual intention of the parties clearly. See § 11.3.

When the policy basis of a rule of law disappears, as it has with respect to the worthier-title doctrine, the normal course is for the legislature to abrogate the rule (as Parliament did in 1833) or for the courts to attempt to limit its mischief, or ultimately to abrogate the rule. Shifting the worthier-title doctrine from a rule of law to one of construction is not a normal step in the evolutionary process of law, and it has done more harm than good.

This rule of construction presumes that when a grantor says "then to my heirs," the grantor meant "reversion in myself." The presumption is rebutted, though, if the grantor says "then to my heirs, really." This supposed rule of construction disregards the core principle of construction: instead of taking unclear language and presumptively attributing common meaning to it (the normal function of a rule of construction), it takes clear language and presumptively attributes abnormal meaning to it.

The shift to a rule of construction expanded rather than contracted the scope of the doctrine. Because of its feudal origins, the common-law rule applied only to land. As a rule of construction, there is less basis for limiting the rule, and it has been applied to both land and personalty. That expansion is quite serious, since most modern future interests are created in trusts of personal property.

As a rule of construction, the doctrine invites litigation and promotes unpredictability. This might not have occurred to the degree it did in New York and elsewhere had the courts insisted on adhering to Judge Cardozo's statement that the doctrine could be rebutted only by a clear expression of a contrary intent. But cases after Doctor v. Hughes reduced the presumption to a regular one under which the contrary intent could be shown from the instrument as a whole or from surrounding circumstances. The court in one New York case stated that "the presumption which exists from the use of the common-law doctrine as a rule of construction has lost much of its force since Doctor v. Hughes. . . . Evidence of intent need not be overwhelming in order to allow the remainder to stand." Matter of Burchell, 87 N.E.2d 293 (N.Y. 1949).

b. Nonrecognition of the doctrine of worthier title. This Restatement provides that the doctrine of worthier title is not recognized as part of American law, neither as a rule of law nor as a rule of construction. The original rationale for the worthier-title doctrine has long since disappeared, the doctrine is intent-defeating, can produce unexpected adverse tax consequences, and has no justification in public policy. A transferor who actually wants to retain a reversionary interest can do so by simple language to that effect.

The Restatement Third, Trusts § 49, Comment *a(1)*, provides that the doctrine of worthier title is not recognized, and the Uniform Probate Code (UPC) § 2–710 provides that the doctrine is abolished both as a rule of law and as a rule of construction.

c. Testamentary branch of the doctrine of worthier title not recognized. The above discussion relates to the inter vivos branch of the doctrine of worthier title. At one time, there was also a testamentary branch of the doctrine. Under the testamentary branch, a devise to the heirs of the testator was a nullity if the interest created in their favor was identical to that which such heirs would have taken by descent if there had been no devise to them. No such rule existed as to bequests of personalty. This rule originated under the feudal system to preserve the feudal incidents of relief, wardship, and marriage, which arose only if the new tenant of land acquired an interest by descent from the former tenant, rather than by purchase under the terms of a devise.

The testamentary branch of the doctrine was not recognized as part of American law in the Restatement Second of Property (Donative Transfers) § 30.2(2), and remains not recognized under this Restatement. Accordingly, a devise to the testator's heirs is valid and effective as a devise to the testator's heirs.

DIVISION VI
POWERS OF APPOINTMENT

Scope of Division VI. Division VI addresses powers of appointment.

Historical development. In the history of English law, powers of appointment were primarily the outgrowth of efforts to circumvent the rule that many of the most important types of interests in land could not be devised. Despite this rule, which was not firmly abrogated until the second half of the 17th century, it became possible for an owner to achieve the practical equivalent of a devise by granting the property in the owner's lifetime upon uses to be appointed by the owner's will. The exercise of the power was effective, although a devise would have been void.

Modern use of powers of appointment. The modern use of powers of appointment is not to circumvent any rule of law, but to serve worthy family and tax purposes. Powers of appointment are used routinely in modern estate-planning practice. They are created in trusts to build flexibility into the estate plan and to achieve or avoid certain tax consequences.

Relationship to Division V. Division VI is related to Division V on class gifts, for the permissible appointees and the appointees of a power of appointment are often expressed in class-gift terms.

CHAPTER 17

INTRODUCTION TO POWERS OF APPOINTMENT: TERMINOLOGY AND DEFINITIONS

Introductory Note: Chapter 17 introduces the topic of powers of appointment. Part A contains definitions of the various terms that are central to the law of powers of appointment. Section 17.1 defines a power of appointment. Section 17.2 addresses the terminology associated with a power of appointment. The relevant terms are "appointive property," "donor," "donee," "permissible appointees," "appointees," and "takers in default."

Part B divides powers of appointment into their various categories. Section 17.3 distinguishes between a general power of appointment and a nongeneral power of appointment. Section 17.4 distinguishes between a presently exercisable power of appointment and a power that is exercisable only on some future date. Section 17.5 distinguishes between an exclusionary and a nonexclusionary power (traditionally called an exclusive and a nonexclusive power).

Part A. Definitions

§ 17.1. Power of Appointment Defined

A power of appointment is a power that enables the donee of the power to designate recipients of beneficial ownership interests in or powers of appointment over the appointive property.

Comment:

a. Terminology. The terms associated with a power of appointment are defined in § 17.2. Those terms are "donor," "donee," "permissible appointees," "appointee," "taker in default of appointment," and "appointive property." In brief, the "donor" is the person who created or reserved the power. The "donee" is the person on whom the power was conferred or in whom the power was reserved. The "permissible appointees" are the persons to whom an appointment is authorized. An "appointee" is a person to whom an appointment has been made. A "taker in default of appointment" is a person who takes part or all of the appointive property to the extent that the power has not been effectively exercised. The "appointive property" is the property or property interest that is subject to a power of appointment.

b. Power of appointment not transferable. The donee of a power of appointment cannot transfer the power to another. If the donee dies without exercising the power, the power lapses (expires). The power does not pass through the donee's estate to the donee's successors in interest.

Although the donee cannot transfer the donee's power of appointment to another, the donee can exercise the power by conferring on an appointee another power of appointment over the appointive property. See § 19.13, Comments *f* and *g*; § 19.14, Comment *e*.

c. Power of appointment distinguished from beneficial ownership. The beneficial owner of an interest in property ordinarily has the power to transfer ownership interests in or confer powers of appointment over that property to or on others by probate or nonprobate transfer. Regarding probate transfers, see Division I (Chapters 1 through 5). Regarding nonprobate transfers, see Division II (Chapters 6 and 7).

By contrast, a power of appointment traditionally confers the authority to designate recipients of beneficial ownership interests in or powers of appointment over property that the donee does not own. . . . .

Although a power of appointment traditionally confers authority on someone who is not the beneficial owner of the appointive property, . . . a power of appointment can be (and often is) reserved by the former owner of the appointive property. The term "donor-donee" is sometimes used herein to refer to such a person.

d. Power of appointment over remainder interest. A power to designate the beneficial recipient of a remainder interest is a power of appointment. The appointive property is the remainder interest. . . . .

e. Power of revocation, amendment, or withdrawal. In modern law, as reflected in this Restatement and in the Restatement Third of Trusts, a power to revoke or amend a trust or a power to withdraw principal from a trust is recognized as a power of appointment over the principal of the trust, whether the power is reserved by the transferor or conferred on another. See Restatement Third, Trusts § 56, Comment *b*. Regarding whether the settlor of a trust has impliedly retained a power to revoke or amend the trust, see Restatement Third, Trusts § 63, Comment *c*. A power to withdraw principal from a trust is sometimes called a power of invasion.

A power to withdraw income from a trust is recognized as a power of appointment over the income of the trust, whether the power is reserved by the transferor or conferred on another.

Regarding the treatment of a power to withdraw income or principal that is subject to an ascertainable standard, see § 17.4(c).

f. Power to direct trustee to distribute income or principal to another. A power to direct a trustee to distribute income to another is a power of appointment over income, even if the donee of the power is an income beneficiary of the trust. A power to direct a trustee to distribute principal to another is a power of appointment over principal, even if the donee of the power is an income or remainder beneficiary of the trust. Also, by implication, a power of revocation or withdrawal of principal (see Comment *e*) is a power to direct a trustee to distribute principal to another, because such a power permits the donee not only to withdraw principal for himself or herself but also to direct the trustee to distribute principal to another. Similarly, a power to withdraw income from a trust permits the donee not only to withdraw income for himself or herself but also to direct the trustee to distribute income to another.

If the donee of a power to direct a trustee to distribute income or principal to another is the income beneficiary of the trust, the donee's power is effective despite any spendthrift restraint on the donee's income or remainder interest. See Restatement Third, Trusts § 58, Comment *b(1)*.

If the donee of a power to direct a trustee to distribute income or principal to another is the income or remainder beneficiary of the trust, the donee's power is a power appendant (see § 17.3, Comment *g*), to the extent that the power overlaps the donee's owned income or remainder interest. An exercise of such a power may therefore be treated for some purposes (such as gift tax or fraudulent-transfer law) as a transfer of the owned income or remainder interest and an exercise of a power of appointment over the other interests in the principal of the trust. . . . .

g. Fiduciary distributive powers. A fiduciary distributive power is a power of appointment (a nongeneral power), but it is not a discretionary power of appointment. In the case of a discretionary power of appointment, which is the principal subject of this Division, the donee may exercise the power arbitrarily as long as the exercise is within the scope of the power. See Chapter 19. In the case of a fiduciary distributive power, the fiduciary's exercise is subject to fiduciary obligations as provided in the Restatement Third of Trusts. See Restatement Third, Trusts § 86; see also id. § 50, Comment *a*. Because the exercise of a fiduciary distributive power is subject to fiduciary obligations, this Restatement, except as otherwise provided herein (for example, see below), defers to the Restatement Third of Trusts for the law governing the exercise of a fiduciary distributive power.

Fiduciary distributive powers include a trustee's power to distribute principal to or for the benefit of an income beneficiary, or for some other person, or to pay income or principal to a designated beneficiary, or to distribute income or principal among a defined group of beneficiaries. Unlike a discretionary power of appointment, a fiduciary distributive power does not lapse upon the termination of the fiduciary's appointment (by death, resignation, or otherwise), but survives in a successor fiduciary. Nevertheless, a fiduciary distributive power, like a discretionary power of appointment, cannot be validly exercised in favor of or for the benefit of someone who is not a permissible appointee (see § 19.14, Comment *f*) and is subject to the Rule Against Perpetuities under the same rules applicable to a trust or other donative disposition of property created by the exercise of a discretionary nongeneral power of appointment (see § 27.1, Comment *j(3)*).

h. Management powers. A power over management of property, sometimes called an administrative power, is not a power of appointment. For example, a power of sale coupled with a power to invest the proceeds of the sale, as commonly held by a trustee of a trust, is not a power of appointment, but is an administrative power. A power of sale merely authorizes the power holder to substitute money for the property sold, but does not authorize the holder of the power of sale to alter the beneficial interests in the substituted property.

i. Power of appointment distinguished from a power to designate or replace trustee or other fiduciary. A power to designate or replace a trustee or other fiduciary is not a power of appointment. A power to designate or replace a trustee or other fiduciary involves property management and is a power to designate only the nonbeneficial holder of property.

j. Power of appointment distinguished from a power of attorney. A power of attorney is not a power of appointment. A power of attorney creates a relationship of principal and agent between the one who gives the power (the principal) and the one who holds the power (the agent or attorney-in-fact). Restatement Third of Agency § 1.04(7) defines a power of attorney as "an instrument that states an agent's authority," and the Uniform Power of Attorney Act § 102 defines a power of attorney as "a writing or other record, evidenced by the record to be a power of attorney, in which a principal grants authority to an agent." A power of appointment does not create an agency relationship between the donor and the donee of the power.

k. "Imperative power." In this Restatement, unless otherwise indicated, the term "power of appointment" refers to a power of appointment regarding which the donee of the power is under no duty to exercise the power.

Sometimes the terms "imperative power," "mandatory power," or "power in trust" are used to refer to a nongeneral power in which there is an implied gift in default of appointment to the permissible appointees of the power. See § 19.23. The terms "imperative power," "mandatory power," or "power in trust" are misleading and are not used in this Restatement to refer to a power in which there is such an implied gift in default. Likewise, the Restatement Third of Trusts, in §§ 45 and 46, does not use the term "imperative power," "mandatory power," or "power in trust" in referring to a power of selection that the trustee is under a duty to exercise.

l. Authority to create additional powers of appointment over the appointive property. On the authority of the donee of a power of appointment to create one or more additional powers of appointment over the appointive property, see §§ 17.2, Comment *c*; 19.13; 19.14.

§ 17.2. Terminology Associated with a Power of Appointment

(a) "Donor." The "donor" ("creator") is the person who created or reserved the power of appointment. Before creating the power, the donor was either the owner of the appointive property or the donee of a power of appointment with respect to the appointive property.

(b) "Donee." The "donee" ("power holder") is the person on whom the power of appointment was conferred or in whom the power was reserved. If the donor reserved the power in himself or herself, the donor is also the donee, and the term "Donor-Donee" is sometimes used to refer to such a person.

(c) "Permissible Appointees." The "permissible appointees" ("objects") are the persons to whom an appointment is authorized.

(d) "Impermissible Appointee." An impermissible appointee ("nonobject") is anyone who is not a permissible appointee.

(e) "Appointee." An "appointee" is a person to whom an appointment has been made.

(f) "Taker in default of appointment." A "taker in default of appointment" ("taker-in-default") is a person who takes part or all of the appointive property to the extent that the power is not effectively exercised. The clause that identifies the taker- or takers-in-default is called the gift-in-default clause. The gift-in-default

clause often identifies the takers-in-default as a class (i.e., a class gift).

(g) "Appointive property." The "appointive property" is the property or property interest that is subject to a power of appointment.

Comment:

a. Parties. The creation of a power of appointment requires that there be a donor, a donee, permissible appointees, and appointive property. The other parties are not necessary to the creation of a power of appointment. If the donee is authorized to appoint to anyone, there will not be impermissible appointees. Because the donee is under no duty to exercise a power of appointment, there might not be an appointee. The donor is not required to designate a taker in default of appointment, although failure to do so is unwise.

Illustration:

1. Donor transferred property in trust, directing the trustee to pay the income to Donee for life, then to pay the principal to those of Donee's descendants as Donee shall by will appoint; in default of appointment, to the X charity. Donee subsequently died, leaving a will that exercised her power of appointment in favor of her adult child, C. Donor is the donor of the power (the creator). Donee is the donee of the power (the power holder). Donee's descendants are the permissible appointees of the power (objects). Upon Donee's death, C becomes the appointee. Before Donee's death, the X charity was the taker-in-default, but Donee's appointment to C terminated that interest.

b. Reserved power. In the case of a reserved power, the same person is both the donor and the donee.

c. Power created by exercise of power. On the authority of the donee to create one or more additional powers over the appointive property, see §§ 19.13; 19.14. If a donee exercises a power by creating another power, the donee of the first power is the donor of the second power, and the donee of the second power is an appointee of the first power.

d. Unborn donee. A power can be conferred on an unborn donee. A power conferred on an unborn donee arises on the donee's birth. Under the Rule Against Perpetuities as adopted in this Restatement, however, a power cannot be conferred on a donee, born or unborn, who is more than two generations younger than the transferor. See § 27.1, Comment *d(2)*. For purposes of this rule, the donor is the transferor. If the power was created by the exercise of a power (see Comment *c*), the transferor is, with one exception, the donor of the first power. The exception is the case in which the first donee's power was a general power presently exercisable. In that case, the transferor is the donee of the first power (who is also the donor of the second power). See § 27.1, Comments *j*, *j(1)*, *j(2)*, and *j(3)*.

e. Designated donee deceased. A power cannot be conferred on an individual who is deceased at the effective date of the disposition purporting to create the power. See § 19.11.

f. Permissible appointee. The permissible appointees of a power of appointment may be narrowly defined (for example, "to such of the donee's descendants as the donee shall select"), broadly defined (for example, "to such persons as the donee shall select, except the donee, the donee's estate, the donee's creditors, or the creditors of the donee's estate"), or unlimited (for example, "to such persons as the donee shall select").

A permissible appointee of a power of appointment does not have a property interest that he or she can transfer to another in order to make the transferee a permissible appointee of the power. Were it otherwise, a permissible appointee could transform an impermissible appointee into a permissible appointee, exceeding the intended scope of the power and thereby violating the donor's intention.

g. *Appointee.* An appointee is a person to whom an appointment has been made. An appointment cannot be validly made to an impermissible appointee of the power.

h. *Taker-in-default-of-appointment.* A taker-in-default-of-appointment (often called the "taker-in-default") has a property interest that can be transferred to another. If a taker-in-default transfers the interest to another, the transferee becomes a taker-in-default.

i. *Power cannot be transferred.* Although the donee of a power of appointment cannot transfer the power to another (see § 17.1, Comment *b*), the donee can (as noted in Comment *c*) exercise a power by creating another power in another donee.

j. *Appointive property.* The appointive property is the property or property interest subject to the power. If the power is over the property itself, as opposed to a specified interest in the property, the appointive property is sometimes referred to as the appointive asset(s). If the power is over a specified interest, such as a remainder interest, the appointive property is sometimes referred to as the appointive interest.

Part B. Categories of Powers of Appointment

Introductory Note: Powers of appointment are divided into different categories, depending on who are the permissible appointees (general versus nongeneral power), when and by what type of document the power can be exercised (presently exercisable versus testamentary versus postponed), and by whether a permissible appointee must receive a share of the appointive assets (exclusionary versus nonexclusionary power).

In determining which type of power is created, the general principle of construction is that a power is presumed to fall into the category that gives the donee the maximum discretionary authority, except to the extent that the language creating the power specifically restricts the donee's authority. Thus, for example, a power is general unless the language specifies that the donee cannot exercise the power in favor of the donee, the donee's estate, or the creditors of either. A power is presently exercisable unless the language specifies that the power can only be exercised at some later time or in some document such as a will that only takes effect at some later time. A power is exclusionary unless the language specifies that a permissible appointee must receive a certain amount or portion of the appointive assets if the power is exercised.

§ 17.3. General Power; Nongeneral Power

(a) A power of appointment is general to the extent that the power is exercisable in favor of the donee, the donee's estate, or the creditors of either, regardless of whether the power is also exercisable in favor of others.

(b) A power of appointment that is not general is a nongeneral power.

Comment:

a. General power of appointment. A general power of appointment enables the donee to exercise the power in favor of the donee, the donee's estate, or the creditors of either, regardless of whether the power is also exercisable in favor of others. Language creating a power of appointment is construed as creating a general power unless the language expressly prohibits exercise in favor of the donee, the donee's estate, and the creditors of either.

b. Historical note: nongeneral power of appointment. The Restatement of Property § 320 divided powers of appointment into two categories: general powers and special powers. Restatement Second, Property (Donative Transfers) § 11.4 divided powers into general powers and nongeneral powers.

In the Restatement, a special power was defined as one that can be exercised "only in favor of persons, not including the donee, who constitute a group not unreasonably large." Thus, the Restatement classified a power to appoint to anyone in the world except the donee, the donee's creditors, the donee's estate, or the creditors of the donee's estate as a hybrid, observing that such powers are so rare that it would not be useful to state the rules applicable to them. See Restatement of Property § 320, Comment *a*.

By the time that the Restatement Second was promulgated, such powers had become "fairly common," because the tax laws treated them as nontaxable. In the Restatement Second, a nongeneral power was defined as any power that is not a general power. Thus, the Restatement Second's category of nongeneral power encompassed a power to appoint among a defined and limited class of permissible appointees and a power to appoint to anyone in the world except the donee, the donee's creditors, the donee's estate, or the creditors of the donee's estate. The Restatement Second noted, however, that "some legal consequences may be different with respect to a non-general power of appointment that has practically unlimited [permissible appointees] and one that has objects restricted to a defined limited class of persons." Restatement Second, Property (Donative Transfers) § 11.4, Comment *b*. Among the legal consequences that differ are whether a nongeneral power is exclusionary or nonexclusionary (see § 17.5) or whether in certain cases there is an implied gift in default to the permissible appointees of a nongeneral power (see § 19.23).

This Restatement continues the approach of the Restatement Second by recognizing the same categories—general and nongeneral powers—and by defining them the same way.

Illustrations:

1. Donor transferred property in trust, directing the trustee to pay the income "to Donee for life, remainder in principal to such person or persons as Donee shall appoint; in default of appointment, remainder to X." Donee's power is a general power because Donor did not forbid Donee from exercising the power in Donee's own favor.

2. Donor transferred property in trust, directing the trustee to pay the income "to Donee for life, remainder in principal to such of Donee's descendants as Donee shall by will appoint; in default of appointment, remainder to X." Donee's power is a nongeneral power, because Donee is authorized to appoint only among her own

descendants, a group that does not include Donee or Donee's creditors. This power would be classified as a *special* power under the nomenclature of the Restatement of Property, because the permissible appointees are reasonable in number.

c. Power of revocation, amendment, or withdrawal. A power to revoke, amend, or withdraw is a power of appointment (§ 17.1, Comment *e*). Such a power is a general power because it is exercisable in favor of the donee of the power.

d. Effect of fiduciary exercising authority to change nongeneral power to general power and vice versa. If the settlor of a trust empowers the trustee or a trust protector to change a donee's general power into a nongeneral power or to change a donee's nongeneral power into a general power, the donee's power is either general or nongeneral depending on the scope of the donee's power at any particular time.

Illustration:

4. Donor transferred property in trust, directing the trustee to pay the income "to Donee (Donor's daughter) for life, remainder in principal to such of Donee's descendants as Donee shall by will appoint." The terms of the trust provide that the trustee can at any time and from time to time expand the class of permissible appointees of Donee's power to include the creditors of Donee's estate or, having done so, to remove the creditors of Donee's estate from the class of permissible appointees. When the trust was created, Donee's power was a nongeneral power. Later, the trustee exercises the authority to add Donee's estate creditors as permissible appointees. As a result, Donee's nongeneral power becomes a general power. Later still, the trustee exercises the authority to remove Donee's estate creditors as permissible appointees. Donee's general power has now become a nongeneral power.

e. Joint power with nonadverse party or with adverse party. If a power of appointment can be exercised in favor of the donee, the donee's estate, or the creditors of either, the power is a general power even if the donee can only exercise the power with the joinder of a nonadverse party. If the power can only be exercised with the joinder of an adverse party, however, the power is not a general power. An adverse party is a person who has a substantial beneficial interest in the trust or other property arrangement that would be adversely affected by the exercise or nonexercise of the power in favor of the donee, the donee's estate, or the creditors of either; a nonadverse party is a person who does not have such an interest.

Illustration:

5. Donor transferred property in trust, directing the trustee to pay the income "to Donee for life, remainder in principal to such person or persons as Donee, with the joinder of X, shall appoint; in default of appointment, remainder to X." Donee's power is not a general power because X is an adverse party.

f. Collateral power; power in gross. In traditional terminology, a power of appointment is "collateral" if the donee has no owned interest in the appointive assets. A power of appointment is "in gross" if the donee has an owned interest in the appointive assets separate from the donee's power of appointment, such as when the income beneficiary of a trust has a power of appointment over the remainder interest. The terms *collateral power* and *power in gross* are descriptive only, and carry no legal consequences.

g. Power appendant. In traditional terminology, a power of appointment is appendant to the extent that the donee owns the appointive property. Any purported exercise of a power appendant in favor of another carries with it the donee's owned property or property interest, either as a transfer of the owned property or property interest or as the subject of the exercise of the power of appointment. Conversely, any purported transfer of the owned property or property interest terminates the power over that property or property interest.

Illustration:

7. Donor conveyed real property "to such persons as Donee-Owner shall appoint, and until and in default of appointment, to Donee-Owner and her heirs." If Donee-Owner executes an instrument purporting to exercise the power, the instrument is also construed as a conveyance of Donee-Owner's owned interest, and Donee-Owner thereafter has no ownership interest in the appointed property. If Donee-Owner executes and delivers a deed conveying the property or an interest therein to another, the instrument is also construed as an exercise of the power, and Donee-Owner thereafter has no power to divest the grantee's property interest by a purported exercise of Donee-Owner's power.

§ 17.4. Power Presently Exercisable; Testamentary Power; Postponed Power

(a) A power of appointment is presently exercisable if it is exercisable by the donee at the time in question, whether or not it is also exercisable by will.

(b) A power of appointment is testamentary if it is exercisable only in the donee's will.

(c) A power of appointment is postponed if it is not exercisable until the occurrence of a specified event, the satisfaction of an ascertainable standard, or the passage of a specified period of time. A postponed power becomes presently exercisable upon the occurrence of the specified event, the satisfaction of the ascertainable standard, or the passage of the specified period of time.

Comment:

a. Presently exercisable power. A power of appointment is presently exercisable if it is exercisable by the donee at the time in question, whether or not it is also exercisable by will. Typically, in fact, a presently exercisable power of appointment is exercisable at the time in question during the donee's lifetime and also exercisable by the donee's will. Thus, a power of appointment that is exercisable "by deed or will" is a presently exercisable power.

A power that is exercisable by the donee's last unrevoked instrument in writing is a presently exercisable power. The donee can make an exercise of such a power irrevocable by explicitly so providing in the writing exercising the power. See § 19.7, Comment *b*.

Illustration:

1. Donor transferred property in trust, directing the trustee to pay the income "to Donee for life, remainder in principal to such person

or persons as Donee shall appoint; in default of appointment, remainder to X." Donee's power is a presently exercisable general power. It is presently exercisable because Donor did not expressly restrict the exercise of the power either to a will or to an inter vivos instrument. The power is general because Donor did not forbid Donee from exercising the power in Donee's own favor.

b. Presently exercisable even though any appointment remains revocable or subject to a condition. A power of appointment is presently exercisable even though, at the time in question, the donee can only appoint an interest that is revocable or is subject to a condition. For example, the interest presently created by the donee in a permissible appointee of a power of appointment in a revocable trust remains subject to the settlor's power of revocation, unless the exercise of the power removes the appointive asset from the trust. The appointive asset may itself be subject to a condition, in which case the interest created by the exercise of the power will be subject to the same condition. For example, suppose that a trust directs the trustee to pay the income to Donee for life, then to distribute the principal by representation to Donee's issue who survive Donee. The trust further provides that, if Donee leaves no issue who survive Donee, the principal is to be distributed "to such persons as Donee shall appoint." Donee is the donee of a presently exercisable power, but the appointive property is a remainder interest that is conditioned on Donee leaving no surviving issue.

c. Testamentary power. A power is testamentary if it is exercisable only in the donee's will.

Illustration:

2. Donor transferred property in trust, directing the trustee to pay the income "to Donee for life, remainder in principal to such of Donee's descendants as Donee shall by will appoint; in default of appointment, remainder to X." Donee's power is a nongeneral testamentary power. It is testamentary because the donor made the power exercisable only "by will." Thus, any purported inter vivos exercise of this power by Donee would be invalid. Donee's power is nongeneral because Donee is authorized to appoint only among her own descendants, a group that does not include Donee. This power would be classified as a *special* power under the older nomenclature because the permissible appointees are reasonable in number.

d. Postponed power. A power is a postponed power (sometimes called a deferred power) if it is not exercisable until the occurrence of a specified event, the satisfaction of an ascertainable standard, or the passage of a specified period of time. A postponed power becomes presently exercisable upon the occurrence of the specified event, the satisfaction of the ascertainable standard, or the passage of the specified period of time.

e. Power exercisable "by deed." When the terms of a power provide that the power can or must be exercised "by deed," it is to be inferred that these words mean a written instrument or an act that would be formally sufficient under the applicable law to transfer an interest to the appointee in the donee's lifetime if the donee owned the appointive assets.

f. "Relation-back" theory. No general theory underlies the whole of power-of-appointment law. The theory traditionally thought to explain the operation of a power of appointment is the "relation-back" theory. The relation-back theory is that the donee acts as the donor's agent, so that the donee's exercise of the power is treated as an act of the donor, relating back to and becoming part of the document creating the power. Under this theory, the exercise of a power is treated as a transfer of the donor, not of the donee.

This Restatement does not rely upon the relation-back theory for resolving the full array of questions that arise under power-of-appointment law. The reason is that the theory is not uniformly applied and does not predict the outcome in any particular case.

The relation-back theory provides that the donor is always the owner-transferor, but there are many instances in which the donee is treated as the owner-transferor. It is, in fact, not possible to render a generalized answer to which party, the donor or the donee, is appropriately treated as the owner-transferor. The answer depends on what type of power the donee has, on what the legal question is, and, in some instances, on whether the donee has exercised the power or not. Accordingly, this Restatement approaches such questions by asking whether (after the power was created) the donor or the donee is appropriately treated as the owner-transferor of the appointive property. See Restatement Third, Trusts § 56, Comment *b*.

f(1). Presently exercisable general power. A presently exercisable general power of appointment is an ownership-equivalent power. See Restatement Third, Trusts § 74. The donee of a presently exercisable general power is almost always treated as the owner-transferor. Relation back is inapplicable. As noted in the Restatement of Property, "The power to become the owner at will is in essence ownership[.]" 3 Restatement of Property, Introductory Note to Chapter 25 (Powers of Appointment) at p. 1812. Although the donee of such a power is not the technical owner of the appointive property, the donee is the owner in substance. See, e.g., § 9.1(c), Comment *j*, and § 23.1, treating property owned in substance as subject to the elective share of the surviving spouse, even under a statute that applies the elective share to the decedent's "estate." See also UPC § 2–205(1). For purposes of the rule against perpetuities as adopted in this Restatement, the donee of a presently exercisable general power of appointment is treated as the transferor, whether the donee exercises the power or not. See § 27.1, Comments *j(1)* and *j(2)*.

f(2). Nongeneral power. In nearly all cases, the donor of a nongeneral power is treated as the owner-transferor of the appointive property, not the donee. See Illustration 3. Accordingly, if the relation-back theory has any predictive value, it is with respect to a nongeneral power.

Illustration:

3. Donor transferred property in trust, directing the trustee to pay the income to Donee for life, then to pay the principal to such of Donee's descendants as Donee shall by will appoint. Donee dies leaving a will that exercises the power in favor of Donee's children, C1 and C2. Under the relation-back theory, Donor's original transfer is treated as if it directed the trustee to pay the income to Donee for life, then to pay the principal to C1 and C2.

For purposes of the rule against perpetuities as adopted in this Restatement, the donor of a nongeneral power of appointment is treated as the transferor. See § 27.1, Comment *j(3)*.

f(3). General testamentary power. The most difficult type of power to characterize is the general testamentary power. For some purposes, including the federal estate tax (see I.R.C. § 2041), the donee of a general testamentary power of appointment is treated as the owner-transferor (rejecting relation back). For other purposes, including the rule against perpetuities as adopted in this Restatement (see § 27.1, Comment *j(3)*), the donor is treated as the owner-transferor (accepting relation back).

A general testamentary power that was created by the donee instead of by another is more often treated as an ownership-equivalent power because the appointive power is property that was once owned by the donee. The reservation of a general testamentary power over property once owned by the donee allows the donee to maintain control of the death-time disposition of that once-owned property.

§ 17.5. Whether Power Is Exclusionary or Nonexclusionary

A power of appointment whose permissible appointees are defined and limited is either exclusionary or nonexclusionary. An exclusionary power is one in which the donor has authorized the donee to appoint to any one or more of the permissible appointees, to the exclusion of the others. A nonexclusionary power is one in which the donor has specified that the donee cannot make an appointment that excludes any permissible appointee or one or more designated permissible appointees from a share of the appointive property. In determining whether a power is exclusionary or nonexclusionary, the power is exclusionary unless the terms of the power expressly provide that an appointment must benefit each permissible appointee or one or more designated permissible appointees.

Comment:

a. Terminology. The traditional term used for what this Restatement calls an *exclusionary power* is "exclusive power," and for what this Restatement calls a *nonexclusionary power* is "nonexclusive power." The terms used in this Restatement are preferred as being more descriptive than the traditional terms.

b. Scope. Only a power of appointment whose permissible appointees are defined and limited (see Comment *c*) can be nonexclusionary. Hence, a nonexclusionary power is almost always a nongeneral power (compare Comments *h* and *i*). It is conceivable, however, that a general power will have permissible appointees who are defined and limited, and if so, the general power might be nonexclusionary (see Comment *g*). A power can be nonexclusionary with respect to part of the appointive property and exclusionary with respect to the other part.

The donee of a nonexclusionary power is not under a duty to exercise the power, but if the donee does exercise the power, the donee's appointment must abide by the nonexclusionary nature of the power.

c. Permissible appointees who are defined and limited. The permissible appointees are defined and limited if they are defined and limited to a reasonable number. Typically, permissible appointees who are defined and limited are described in class-gift terms—a single-generation class such as "children," "grandchildren," "brothers and sisters," or "nieces and nephews" (see §§ 14.1, 14.2), or a multiple-generation class such as "issue" or "descendants" (see §§ 14.3, 14.4) or "heirs" (see § 16.1). Permissible appointees need not be described in class-gift terms to be defined and limited, however. The permissible appointees are also defined and limited if one or more permissible appointees are designated by name or otherwise individually identified.

d. Language unambiguously creating a nonexclusionary power. Language that would unambiguously create a nonexclusionary power would include language granting the donee the power to appoint to "all and every one" or to "each and every one" of a defined and limited class of permissible appointees, or language specifying the share of the appointive property from which one or more individually designated permissible appointees may not be excluded by an appointment.

e. Language clearly creating an exclusionary power. Language that would clearly create an exclusionary power would include language granting the donee the power to appoint to "any one or more" or to "such of" the permissible appointees as the donee selects or to "such person or persons" as the donee selects.

f. Ambiguous language—exclusionary power presumed. Whether or not a power with permissible appointees who are defined and limited is exclusionary or nonexclusionary is a question of construction of the language creating the power. Ambiguous language is construed in favor of an exclusionary power. A power is nonexclusionary only if the terms of the power provide that an appointment must benefit each permissible appointee or one or more designated permissible appointees. Thus, for example, a power to appoint "to," "among," or "between" a defined and limited class of permissible appointees is exclusionary.

The rationale for construing ambiguous language as creating an exclusionary power is that one of the major purposes served by a power of appointment is to give the donee the flexibility to alter the donor's disposition in response to changing conditions. Maximum flexibility results when the donee is not restricted in the selection of the permissible appointees. Thus, it is to be presumed that the donor intended the donee to have as broad a power of selecting among the permissible appointees, including the power to exclude one or more, as the donor would have had at the time of creating the power or as the donee has with reference to owned property.

Illustration:

1. Donor died, leaving a will that devised Blackacre to Donee (Donor's wife) for life, then "to my children as Donee may by will appoint." Donor has four children. Because Donor has not provided that every permissible appointee must be benefited by an appointment, Donee's power is exclusionary. In exercising her power, Donee may appoint to one or more of Donor's children, but need not appoint to all four.

g. General power. A general power to appoint "to such person or persons, including the donee, the donee's estate, or the creditors of either" has no defined and limited class of permissible appointees, and hence is always an exclusionary power. Any attempt by the donor to require the donee to appoint some specified share, such as at least $X, to each permissible appointee of the power, is ineffective because the permissible appointees of the power are unlimited in number, and it would be administratively impossible to carry out the donor's intent. In such case, the donor's restriction is disregarded, and the donee may exclude one or more of the permissible appointees in exercising the power.

A power to appoint only to the donee's creditors or to the creditors of the donee's estate is a general power (see § 17.3). The permissible appointees of this type of general power are defined and limited. Such a general power could be nonexclusionary if, for example, the language creating the power provided that the donee's power is a power to appoint "to such of the donee's estate creditors as the donee shall by will appoint, but if the donee exercises the power, the donee must appoint $X to a designated estate creditor or must appoint in full satisfaction of the donee's debt to a designated estate creditor."

Illustration:

2. Donor died, leaving a will that devised property in trust, directing the trustee to pay the income to Donee (Donor's wife) for life, then to distribute the trust property "to such person or persons, including Donee's estate, as Donee may by will appoint, but in exercising this power Donee must appoint at least half of the trust property among our children." Donee has two separate powers. One is a general exclusionary power over half of the trust property, and the other is a nongeneral exclusionary power over half of the trust property. The two powers are coordinated because a condition of the exercise of the general power is that the nongeneral power also be exercised.

h. Nongeneral power in which permissible appointees are not defined and limited—power is exclusionary. If the permissible appointees of a nongeneral power are "such person or persons other than the donee, the donee's estate, the creditors of the donee, and the creditors of the donee's estate," the donee has an exclusionary nongeneral power. An attempt by the donor to require the donee in connection with any exercise of the power to appoint at least $X to each permissible appointee of the power would be ineffective because the permissible appointees of the power are so numerous that it would be administratively impossible to carry out the donor's expressed intent. In such case, the donor's expressed restriction is disregarded, and the donee may exclude any one or more of the permissible appointees in exercising the power. . . . .

i. Nongeneral power in which permissible appointees are defined and limited—power is nonexclusionary only if the terms of the power provide that an appointment must benefit each permissible appointee or one or more designated permissible appointees. If the permissible appointees of a nongeneral power are a defined and limited class (see Comment *c*), the power is either exclusionary or nonexclusionary. In construing the power, any ambiguity is to be resolved in favor of concluding that the power is exclusionary (see Comment *f*). The power is nonexclusionary only if the terms of the power provide that an appointment must benefit each permissible appointee or one or more designated permissible appointees. . . . .

j. Doctrine of illusory appointments. If a power is determined to be nonexclusionary because its terms provide that an appointment must benefit each permissible appointee, it is to be inferred that the donor intends to require an appointment to confer a reasonable benefit upon each permissible appointee. An appointment under which a permissible appointee receives nothing violates the requirement that each receive something. So also would an appointment that causes a permissible appointee to receive only a nominal sum. What constitutes a reasonable benefit depends upon the number of permissible appointees and the value of the appointive property. In the case of a nonexclusionary power to appoint among four permissible appointees, $1000 is a reasonable benefit from a fund of $10,000 but not from a fund of $1,000,000.

k. Hotchpot clause. To minimize unintended inequalities of distribution among permissible appointees, the language creating a power sometimes provides that no appointee shall receive any share in default of appointment, unless the appointee consents to allow the amount of the appointment to be taken into account in calculating the fund to be distributed in default of appointment. Such a clause does not make the power nonexclusionary, because the terms do not prevent the donee from making an appointment that excludes a permissible appointee.

CHAPTER 18

CREATION OF A POWER OF APPOINTMENT

Introductory Note: Chapter 18 covers two topics. Section 18.1 addresses how a power of appointment is created, and § 18.2 addresses the authority of the donor to revoke or amend a power after the power has been created.

§ 18.1. Power of Appointment: How Created

A power of appointment is created by a transfer that manifests an intent to create a power of appointment.

Comment:

a. Preliminary requirement: effective transfer. A transfer cannot create a power of appointment if the transfer itself is ineffective. In order for a transfer to be effective, it must be properly executed (see §§ 3.1 to 3.3, 6.1 to 6.3, 7.1). In addition, the transferor must have capacity to make the transfer (see §§ 8.1 to 8.2) and be free from undue influence and other wrongdoing (see §§ 8.3 to 8.4).

b. Manifestation of requisite intent. If the transfer is otherwise effective (see Comment *a*), the manifestation of intent necessary to create a power of appointment does not require the use of particular words or phrases. Any words or phrases are sufficient to create a power of appointment if they establish that the transferor so intended. Careful drafting should leave no doubt about the transferor's intent. Many of the Illustrations that follow in this section instance lack of forethought in drafting, which then requires construction to determine the transferor's intent. On construction generally, see Division IV (Chapters 10, 11, and 12).

Illustrations:

1. Donor's will devised property in trust, directing the trustee to pay the net income to Donee (Donor's daughter) for life. The terms of the trust further provided that "Donee shall have the right to dispose of the remainder interest among her children as she pleases." Although Donor's will did not use the words "power of appointment," the quoted language gives Donee a nongeneral power to appoint to her children. Although the quoted language does not expressly say that Donee's power is presently exercisable, the language is not inconsistent with a power in Donee to make an immediate appointment of the remainder interest. Consequently, Donee's nongeneral power is presently exercisable.

2. Same facts as Illustration 1, except that the quoted language is changed to read: "and Donee shall have the right to devise the trust property among her children." The use of the word "devise" limits the exercise of Donee's power to an appointment by will. Consequently, Donee's nongeneral power is testamentary.

c. Legal life estate coupled with unrestricted power of disposition. Sometimes a document of transfer gives the transferee a legal life estate in property and also a presently exercisable general power of appointment over the property in which the life estate exists. The combination of the power and the life estate in the same person does not change the person's ownership interest into a fee simple absolute, even though the presently exercisable general power enables the owner of the life estate to accomplish most of the things that an owner in fee simple could accomplish. The principal difference concerns the devolution of the property on the owner's death. On the death of the owner of a fee simple absolute, the property passes as part of the owner's estate. On the death of the owner of a life estate coupled with a power of appointment, the property passes to the donee's appointees or, if the power has not been exercised, to the takers in default, if any. See Illustration 3. On classification of this type of life estate, see § 24.5, Comment *h*. . . . .

c(1) Ambiguous language. If the terms of a transfer are ambiguous about whether the owned interest that is created is a life estate or a fee simple, the presence of language that would otherwise create a general power presently exercisable tends to indicate that an interest in fee simple is intended rather than a life estate with a power. See Illustration 4.

Illustration:

4. Donor's will devised Blackacre "to Donee (Donor's wife) to enjoy as her property as long as she lives, with absolute power to dispose of the property in fee simple." Donor's will makes no specific provision for the disposition of Blackacre after Donee's death, but the will contains a residuary clause that disposes of any property not otherwise disposed of by Donor. Donee is given a fee-simple interest in Blackacre and not a life estate with a general power of appointment.

d. Fee simple coupled with restricted power of disposition. Sometimes a document of transfer gives the transferee an interest in fee simple absolute but also contains language purporting to give the transferee a power of disposition that is restricted with regard to permissible appointees or to time or manner of disposition. This restricted power of disposition tends to indicate that the transferor did not intend to give to the transferee the unrestricted power of disposition that is an attribute of a fee simple absolute. Therefore, if there is no specific language defining the transferee's interest, although the interest would otherwise be a fee simple absolute, when the interest is coupled with a restricted power of disposition, the interest may be a life interest coupled with a nongeneral power of appointment. No such construction is justified, however, if the power of disposition given to the transferee is a general power presently exercisable, because giving such a power merely reaffirms the intent of the transferor to create an interest in fee simple absolute. In this connection, it should be noted that a disabling, forfeiture, or promissory restraint on the alienation of a fee-simple interest may be invalid (see Restatement Second, Property (Donative Transfers) §§ 4.1–4.3). Regarding the effect of a gift over of a fee-simple interest if the owner dies intestate, see id. § 4.2, Comment *o*. . . . .

e. Precatory words. Words that merely express a suggestion, hope, or desire that a transferee of property will make a certain disposition thereof do not, in the absence of other circumstances, impose an obligation on the transferee to follow the transferor's suggestion, i.e., to create a trust. See Restatement Third, Trusts § 13, Comment *d*. An intent not to impose an obligation is made unequivocally clear if the words are accompanied with a statement that the transferor "does not intend to create any trust in law or in equity with respect to this transfer." . . . . Precatory words may, however, be a sufficient indication of intent to give the transferee a power of appointment over an interest not given to the transferee . . . .

f. Provision in a will directing executor to make decisions regarding distribution of certain property. On the proper construction of a provision in a will *directing* the executor to make decisions regarding the persons who will receive specified estate property or regarding the particular items of estate property that designated persons will receive, see Restatement Third, Trusts §§ 45, 46.

g. Powers created by implication. A power of appointment may be created by implication. The nature of the gift over on the termination of a transferred interest may manifest an intent to give the owner of the terminating interest a power to dispose of the remainder.

Illustration:

10. Donor's will devised Blackacre "to Donee (Donor's wife) for life and if Donee should die intestate, then to my daughter D in fee simple." Since D is to take on Donee's death only if Donee dies intestate, Donee has a general testamentary power of appointment by implication, and D has a gift in default of appointment.

h. All permissible appointees of power die before power is created or before power can be exercised. An intended power of appointment is not created if all the possible permissible appointees of the power are deceased when the transfer that is intended to create the power becomes legally operative. Cf. § 19.12(b) and (c). If all the possible permissible appointees of a power die after the power is created and before the donee exercises the power, the power terminates. . . . .

i. Permissible appointees of power not ascertainable. A power of appointment is invalid if the permissible appointees are so indefinite that it is impossible to identify any person to whom the donee can appoint. If the description of the permissible appointees is such that one or more persons are identifiable, but it is not possible to determine whether other persons are within the description, the power is validly created, but an appointment can only be made to persons who can be identified as within the description of the permissible appointees.

Illustration:

15. Donor's will devised property in trust, directing the trustee "to pay the net income to Donee (Donor's wife) for life, and on Donee's death, to distribute the trust property to such of the friends of Donor and Donee as Donee may by will appoint, and in default of appointment, to the X charity." The description of the permissible appointees of Donee's testamentary power is such that certain persons are identifiable and a valid appointment to such persons may be made.

j. Power of appointment cannot be created in a donee who is deceased. For the proposition that a power of appointment cannot be created in a donee who is deceased, see § 19.11.

§ 18.2. Donor's Authority to Revoke or Amend Power

The donor of a power of appointment lacks the authority to revoke or amend the power, except to the extent that the donor

reserved a power of revocation or amendment when creating the power.

Comment:

a. *Scope.* This section recognizes that the donor of a power of appointment lacks the authority to revoke or amend the power, except to the extent that the donor reserved a power of revocation or amendment when creating the power.

b. *Power created in a revocable inter vivos trust.* The donor's power to revoke or amend a revocable inter vivos trust carries with it the authority to revoke or amend any power of appointment created in the trust. However, to the extent that an irrevocable exercise of the power by the donee removes appointive property from the trust, the donor's authority to revoke or amend the power is eliminated, unless the donor expressly reserved the authority to revoke or amend any transfer from the trust after the transfer is completed. To the extent that the donee's exercise of the power does not remove appointive property from the trust, the donor's authority to revoke or amend the trust, and hence to override any exercise of the power by the donee, continues to apply. . . . .

c. *Power created in an irrevocable inter vivos trust.* If an irrevocable inter vivos trust confers a presently exercisable power on someone who is not the settlor of the trust (the settlor being the donor of the power), the donor of the power of appointment lacks authority to revoke or amend the donee's power, except to the extent that the donor expressly reserved the authority to do so. If the donor did reserve the authority to revoke or amend the donee's power, that authority is only effective until the time that the donee irrevocably exercises the power. . . . .

d. *Same person is both donor and donee.* If the same person is both the donor and the donee of a power of appointment, the donor in his or her capacity as donee can indirectly revoke or amend the power by a partial or total release of the power (see Chapter 20). After the power has been irrevocably exercised, the donor as donor is in no different position in regard to revoking or amending the exercise of the power than the donor would be if the donor and donee are different persons. Regarding whether a donee can revoke or amend an exercise of the power, see § 19.7. . . . .

e. *Power exercisable by the donee only in conjunction with the donor.* If a power of appointment is exercisable by the donee only in conjunction with the donor, the donor's authority to refuse to consent to any exercise by the donee gives the donor an indirect means of achieving a revocation-like result, by refusing to join in its exercise. Similarly, the donor has the leverage to amend the power in effect, by refusing to join in any exercise unless the power is exercised within limits prescribed by the donor. After the power has been exercised irrevocably, however, the donor as donor is in no different position in regard to revoking or amending the exercise of the power than the donor would be if the donor is not a co-donee. Regarding whether the donee can revoke or amend an exercise of the power, see § 19.7.

f. *Power exercisable by co-donees, none of whom is the donor.* If a power of appointment is conferred on co-donees, none of whom is the donor, the donor lacks the authority to revoke or amend the power, except to the extent that the donor reserved a power of revocation or amendment when creating the power.

CHAPTER 19

EXERCISE OF A POWER OF APPOINTMENT

Introductory Note: Chapter 19 covers aspects of the donee's exercise of a power of appointment, including the effectiveness of an attempted exercise and the consequences of an ineffective exercise or of a failure to exercise the power.

§ 19.1. Requisites for Exercise of a Power of Appointment

A power of appointment is exercised to the extent that:

(1) the donee manifests an intent to exercise the power in an otherwise effective document;

(2) the donee's expression of an intent to appoint satisfies the formal requirements of exercise imposed by the donor and by applicable law; and

(3) the donee's appointment constitutes a permissible exercise of the power.

Comment:

a. *Otherwise effective document.* In order for an exercise of a power of appointment to be effective, the writing purporting to exercise the power must be contained in an otherwise effective document. Thus, the document must be properly executed (see §§ 3.1 to 3.3, 6.1 to 6.3, 7.1). See §§ 19.9 to 19.10. The donee must also have the capacity to make an effective transfer of owned property (see §§ 8.1 to 8.2) and be free from undue influence and other wrongdoing (see §§ 8.3 to 8.4). See § 19.8.

b. *Intent to exercise.* On whether the donee has manifested an intent to exercise the power, see § 19.2.

c. *Compliance with requirements of exercise.* On whether the donee's expression of an intent to appoint complies with the requirements of exercise imposed by the donor and by applicable law, see §§ 19.9 and 19.10.

d. *Effective exercise.* On whether the donee's appointment constitutes a permissible exercise of the power, see §§ 19.8 to 19.16.

e. *Choice of law.* The law of the donee's domicile governs whether the donee has effectively exercised a power of appointment, unless the instrument creating the power expresses a different intention. See Restatement Second, Conflict of Laws § 275, Comment *c*.

Part A. Intent to Exercise

§ 19.2. Determining the Donee's Intent to Exercise

Whether or not the donee has manifested an intent to exercise a power of appointment is a question of construction.

Comment:

a. *Determining the donee's intent.* Determining whether the donee has manifested an intent to exercise a power of appointment is a process of construction, conducted in accordance with the principles for determining donative intent as prescribed in Division IV (Chapters 10, 11, and 12).

b. *Capable drafting.* Capable drafting will leave no doubt regarding the donee's intent to appoint or not to appoint. Ideally, the donee or the donee's drafting agent will have the instrument creating the power at hand, and will formulate the language intended to express the donee's intent in light of the creating instrument.

Language expressing an intent to exercise a power is clearest if it makes specific reference to the creating instrument and exercises the power, if that is the intention, in unequivocal terms and with careful attention to the requirements of exercise that the donor has imposed.

c. *Specific-exercise clause.* The recommended method for exercising a power of appointment is by a specific-exercise clause, using language such as the following: "I hereby exercise the power of appointment conferred upon me by [my mother's will] as follows: I appoint [fill in details of appointment]."

d. *Blanket-exercise clause.* A blanket-exercise clause purports to exercise "any power of appointment" the donee may have, using language such as the following: "I hereby exercise any power of appointment I may have as follows: I appoint [fill in details of appointment]."

Although a blanket-exercise clause does manifest the donee's intent to exercise any power of appointment that the donee may have, such a clause raises the often-litigated question of whether it satisfies the requirement of specific reference frequently imposed by the donor in the document creating the power. See § 19.10.

e. *Blending clause.* A blending clause purports to blend the appointive property with the donee's own property in a common disposition. The exercise portion of a blending clause can take the form of a specific exercise or, more commonly, a blanket exercise. For example, a clause providing "All the rest, residue, and remainder of my estate, including the property over which I have a power of appointment under my mother's will, I give, devise, and bequeath as follows" is a blending clause with a specific reference. A clause providing "All the rest, residue, and remainder of my estate, including any property over which I have a power of appointment, I give, devise, and bequeath as follows" is a blending clause with a blanket exercise.

This Restatement seeks to eliminate any significance heretofore attached to the use of a blending clause. A blending clause has traditionally been regarded as significant in the application of the doctrines of "selective allocation" and "capture." This Restatement eliminates the significance of such a clause under those doctrines. See §§ 19.19 and 19.21. The use of a blending clause is more likely to be the product of the forms used by the donee's lawyer than a deliberate decision by the donee to facilitate the application of the doctrines of selective allocation or capture.

f. *Nonexercise clause.* If the donee decides not to exercise a specific power or any power that the donee might have, it is important for the donee to consider whether to depend on mere silence to produce a nonexercise or to take definitive action to assure a nonexercise. Definitive action can take the form of a release during life (see Chapter 20) or a nonexercise clause in the donee's will or other relevant document. A nonexercise clause can take the form of a specific-nonexercise clause (for example, "I hereby do not exercise the power of appointment conferred on me by my uncle's trust") or the form of a blanket-nonexercise clause (for example, "I hereby do not exercise any power of appointment I might have").

In certain circumstances, different consequences depend on the donee's choice. Under § 19.4, a residuary clause in the donee's will is treated as manifesting an intent to exercise a general power in certain limited circumstances if the donee silently failed to exercise the power, but not if the donee released the power or expressly refrained from exercising it. Under § 19.22, unappointed property passes to the donee's estate in certain limited circumstances if the donee silently failed to exercise a general power, but passes to the donor or to the donor's successors in interest if the donee released the power or expressly refrained from exercising it.

§ 19.3. Disposition of Appointive Property

A disposition by the donee of property over which the donee has a power of appointment manifests an intent to exercise the donee's power over that property.

Comment:

a. *Rationale.* The rule of this section is that a disposition by the donee of property over which the donee has a power of appointment manifests an intent to exercise the donee's power over that property, even though the donee's document of transfer does not refer to the power. The rationale of this rule is that the donee's objective is to cause the designated recipient to receive the property, and the means by which that objective is achieved is secondary. Therefore, the donee's words are construed as an expression of intent to appoint. . . . .

b. *Ambiguity arising when donee owns another interest in the same property.* Documents creating a power often give a life interest to the donee with a power of appointment over the remainder interest. Occasionally, the creating instrument gives the donee ownership of an undivided fractional interest and a power of appointment over the other undivided interest.

In these situations, the donee owns an interest in the property and has a power to appoint a different interest. When the purported disposition is effective to pass the owned interest, it is a question of construction whether the disposition also exercises the power of appointment over the appointive interest. If the disposition makes it clear that the donee's intent was to transfer to the beneficiary more than the owned interest, the disposition exhibits an intent by the donee to exercise the power.

Illustration:

6. Donor died, leaving a will that devised Blackacre "to Donee (Donor's son) for life, remainder to such person as Donee shall appoint, and in default of appointment to Donee's children." Donee executes a general warranty deed purporting to convey Blackacre to P in fee simple. The consideration paid by P for the transfer equals the full value of a fee simple in Blackacre. Donee has manifested an intent to exercise his general power, because the intended fee-simple interest will not pass to P if the deed were construed only to pass Donee's owned life estate. . . . .

c. *Ambiguity arising when donee disposes of separate pieces of property, some owned and some appointive.* An ambiguity arises when the donee's instrument of conveyance uses language that identifies separate pieces of property, some owned and some appointive. Suppose, for example, that the donee's will disposes of "all my real estate located in X city." The donee owns one piece of real estate and has a power of appointment over an entirely different piece of real estate, both pieces being located in X city. In the absence of additional facts indicating a different intent, the donee has not manifested an intent to exercise the donee's power of appointment, because the provision in the donee's will is effective without construing it to be an exercise of the donee's power of appointment.

§ 19.4. Donee's Residuary Clause

A residuary clause in the donee's will or revocable trust does not manifest an intent to exercise any of the donee's power(s) of appointment, unless the power in question is a general power and the donor did not provide for takers in default or the gift-in-default clause is ineffective.

Comment:

a. *Scope and rationale.* This section provides that a residuary clause (such as "All the rest, residue, and remainder of my estate, I devise to . . .") in the donee's will or revocable trust does not manifest an intent to exercise any of the donee's power(s) of appointment, unless the power in question is a general power and the donor did not provide for takers in default or the gift-in-default clause is ineffective. A disposition of all of the testator's property (such as "All of my estate, I devise to. . . .") is the equivalent of a residuary clause.

In a well-planned estate, a power of appointment, whether general or nongeneral, is accompanied by a gift in default. The gift-in-default clause is ordinarily expected to take effect; it is not merely an afterthought interjected just in case the power is not exercised. A power should not be exercised in such a case without positive evidence of an intent to appoint.

In a poorly planned estate, on the other hand, there may be no gift-in-default clause. Or, if there is such a clause, the clause may be wholly or partly ineffective. To the extent that the donor did not provide for takers in default or the gift-in-default clause is ineffective, it is more efficient to attribute to the donee the intent to exercise a general power in favor of the donee's residuary devisees. The principal benefit of attributing to the donee the intent to exercise a general power is that it allows the property to pass under the donee's will instead of as part of the donor's estate. Because the donor's death would normally have occurred before the donee died, some of the donor's successors might themselves have predeceased the donee. It is more efficient to avoid tracing the interest through multiple estates to determine who the present successors are. Moreover, to the extent that the donor did not provide for takers in default, it also seems more in accord with the donor's probable intent for the donee's residuary clause to be treated as exercising the power.

Illustration:

1. Donor transferred property in trust, directing the trustee to pay the income to Donee for life, then to pay the principal to such persons as Donee shall by will appoint; in default of appointment, by representation to Donee's issue who survive Donee. Donee subsequently dies, leaving a will containing a residuary clause that provides: "All the rest and residue of my property, real and personal, wheresoever situated, and to which I am in any manner whatsoever entitled, I devise

and bequeath as follows. . . ." Donee left issue who survived Donee. Donee's residuary clause does not exercise Donee's power of appointment. If, however, there had been no gift-in-default clause or if Donee had not left any surviving issue, Donee's residuary clause would be construed to have manifested an intent to exercise the power in favor of Donee's residuary devisees.

b. Absence of takers in default. A gift-in-default clause can be ineffective or partially ineffective for a variety of reasons. The clause might only cover part of the appointive property. The clause might be invalid, because it violates the common-law Rule Against Perpetuities in a state that still follows that rule (see Chapter 27) or because it violates some other rule, or it might be ineffective because it conditioned the interest of the takers in default on an uncertain event that did not happen, the most common of which is an unsatisfied condition of survival.

c. Rule inapplicable if donee released or expressly refrained from exercising power. Because the donee's probable intent supplies the rationale for treating the donee's residuary clause as manifesting an intent to exercise a general power in these limited circumstances, the donee's residuary clause is not so treated if the donee released the general power (see Chapter 20) or expressly refrained from exercising it by, for example, using a nonexercise clause such as described in § 19.2, Comment *f*.

d. Rule inapplicable to nongeneral power. Under no circumstance does a residuary clause manifest an intent to exercise a nongeneral power. A residuary clause disposes of the donee's own property, and a nongeneral power is not an ownership-equivalent power. In addition, there is no similar need in most cases to attribute to the donee the intent to exercise the power in favor of the donee's residuary devisees, because the appointive property passes to the permissible appointees of the power, assuming they are a defined and limited class (see § 19.23), and would not return to the donor's estate in any event. Moreover, the donee's residuary devisees might not be within the class of permissible appointees of a nongeneral power.

e. Rule inapplicable if donor imposed specific-reference requirement. Even if the donee's residuary clause would otherwise be deemed to manifest an intent to exercise a general power, the intended exercise is not effective if the donor has imposed the requirement (which is common) that the power can only be effectively exercised by language that makes specific reference to the power. See § 19.10, Comment *d*.

f. Dispositive provision referring to all property subject to disposition by donee. The rule stated in this section applies to a residuary clause that disposes of the donee's own estate. A residuary clause that disposes of all property that is subject to disposition by the donee is treated as a blanket-exercise clause (see § 19.2, Comment *d*).

Illustration:

2. Same facts as Illustration 1, except that the residuary clause in Donee's will provides: "All the rest and residue of the property, real and personal, wheresoever situated, and which I am entitled to dispose of, I devise and bequeath as follows." Donee has manifested an intent to exercise Donee's power to appoint by will. If there was no gift-in-default clause or if Donee did not leave any surviving issue, Donee's residuary clause manifests an intent to exercise the power in favor of Donee's residuary devisees.

§ 19.5. Other Circumstances Indicating That Donee Intended to Exercise Power

A disposition manifests an intent to exercise a power of appointment if the disposition, read with reference to the property that the donee owned and other relevant evidence of intent, indicates that the donee understood that he or she was disposing of property covered by the power.

Comment:

a. Determining the donee's intent. As noted in § 19.2, Comment *a*, determining whether the donee has manifested an intent to exercise a power of appointment is a process of construction, conducted in accordance with the principles for determining donative intent as prescribed in Division IV (Chapters 10, 11, and 12).

Any relevant evidence of intent may be considered. Factors that may be considered include but are not limited to the donee's knowledge and relationships; the donee's knowledge of the value of the appointive property in comparison with the donee's own property; the donee's knowledge of the existence of the power; advice given to the donee that he or she should make a will in order to dispose of the property covered by the power; the donee's expectation that death was imminent and therefore he or she did not expect to acquire significant additional property; whether the residuary beneficiary was the natural object of the donee's affection and the taker in default was not; and whether the donee had contracted to exercise the power.

Although the process of construction primarily focuses on the donee's intention when the donee executed the dispositive provision, post-execution events can sometimes be relevant in determining the donee's intention. See § 10.2, Comment *g*. Post-execution evidence of intention may properly be considered in resolving an ambiguity, if it sheds light on the donee's intention at the time of execution or on what the donee's intention would probably then have been had the ambiguity been recognized or had the subsequent event been anticipated. As with any other evidence bearing on the donee's intention, the probative force of post-execution evidence of intention is for the trier of fact to evaluate.

If the donee executes a codicil to the will, the will is construed as of the date of the codicil, unless the effect would be inconsistent with the donee's intent. On the doctrine of republication by codicil, see § 3.4.

b. Dispositions exceeding donee's owned property. The rule of this section applies to a disposition that appears to be excessive if its coverage is limited to the donee's owned property, but becomes understandable when appointive assets are considered.

If the relation between the disposition and the amount of property owned at the time of its execution is not such as to indicate that the donee understood that property covered by the power was included in the disposition, subsequent changes in value later in the donee's life do not change the outcome.

Illustration:

1. Donor died, leaving a will that devises $500,000 to Trustee in trust. Trustee is directed to pay the income "to Donee (Donor's wife) for life and on Donee's death to pay the trust property as Donee shall by will appoint, and in default of appointment to pay the trust property to the

X charity." Donee's will provides for pecuniary devises totaling $375,000, and it devises the residue of her estate in trust for the benefit of two sisters. At the time of the execution of her will, Donee's owned assets were worth $80,000. She knew that this was the extent of her owned assets but that she had a power of appointment over the $500,000 in the trust established by Donor's will. Donee has manifested an intent to exercise her general testamentary power.

c. Other applications of rule. Circumstances other than those discussed in Comment *b* may cause a dispositive provision to manifest an intent to exercise a power.

Illustrations:

4. Donor died, leaving a will that devised Blackacre to "Donee (Donor's brother) for life, remainder to such persons as Donee shall by will appoint, and in default of appointment remainder to the X charity." Donee contracts to exercise the power in favor of F, a close friend of Donee, who is providing support for Donee and for whom Donee has frequently expressed great affection and gratitude. (Regarding the validity of the contract, see § 21.2.) Donee has no close relatives. The day after executing the contract to appoint, Donee executes a will providing as follows: "All my estate, real and personal, I give to my friend F." Donee has manifested an intent to exercise his general testamentary power.

5. Donor died, leaving a will that devised property to Trustee in trust. Trustee is directed to purchase or build a residence for Donee, Donor's widow, and allow her to occupy it for her life and at her death to transfer it to such person or persons as Donee shall by will appoint. Trustee buys a lot with a 25-foot frontage, and Donee with her own funds buys an adjoining strip of eight-foot frontage. Trustee builds a residence using both the 25-foot frontage and the eight-foot frontage as though they constituted one lot. Donee then executes a will that provides, "I give, devise and bequeath all my estate, real and personal, which I now have, may die possessed of or may be entitled to, to my sister." Donee has supported her sister for some years and has shown great affection for her. Donee at her death owns no land other than the eight-foot strip. It is to be inferred that Donee considered the eight-foot strip and the 25-foot lot as a single parcel, that she did not want them separated, and that she expected the sister would have the benefit of both. Donee has manifested an intent to exercise her general testamentary power.

d. Specific-reference requirement. Even if the donee's disposition would otherwise be deemed to manifest an intent to exercise a power, the intended exercise is not effective if the donor has imposed the requirement (which is common) that the power can only be effectively exercised by language that makes specific reference to the power. See § 19.10, Comment *d*.

§ 19.6. Exercise of After-Acquired Power

Unless the language or circumstances indicate that the donee had a different intention, a blanket-exercise clause extends to a power of appointment acquired by the donee after the donee executed the document that contains the blanket-exercise clause.

Comment:

a. *Scope.* Nothing in law prevents a donee from exercising a power of appointment in a document that the donee executed before the donee acquired the power. The only question is one of construction—whether the donee intended to exercise the after-acquired power. If the donee's exercising document specifically identifies the power that the donee is exercising, the donee's exercise clause unambiguously expresses an intent to exercise that power, whether the power is an after-acquired power or not (see Comment *e*). A blanket-exercise clause, however, raises a question of construction. The rule of this section is that, unless the language or circumstances indicate that the donee had a different intention, a blanket-exercise clause extends to a power of appointment acquired by the donee after the donee executed the document that contains the blanket-exercise clause. Reference to then-present circumstances, such as "all the powers I have" or like expressions, is not a sufficient indication of an intent to exclude after-acquired powers.

b. *Donee's exercising document.* The donee's exercising document is any document that the donee executes that contains an exercise clause. Thus, the donee's exercising document could be the donee's will, a testamentary trust, a revocable or irrevocable inter vivos trust, or any other document that contains an exercise clause.

c. *After-acquired power.* A power of appointment is an after-acquired power if the instrument creating the power becomes effective after the donee executed the exercising document.

If, for example, the power is created in the donor's will and the donor dies after the execution of the donee's will, the power is an after-acquired power, whether or not the donor's will antedates that of the donee. If the donee executes a codicil, the doctrine of republication by codicil may be applied to treat the date of the codicil as the date that the will is executed for purposes of determining whether a power is an after-acquired power. On the doctrine of republication by codicil, see § 3.4. . . . .

d. *Language or circumstances indicating that the donee did not intend to exercise an after-acquired power.* Although reference to then-present circumstances, such as "all the powers I have" or like expressions, is not a sufficient indication of an intent to exclude after-acquired powers, more precise language, such as "all powers I have at the date of execution of this will," does indicate an intent to exclude after-acquired powers.

If the donee subsequently executes a codicil, the doctrine of republication by codicil (see § 3.4) could be invoked to exercise any power acquired by the donee after execution of the will but before execution of the codicil.

If the donor and donee are the same person, a blanket-exercise clause in the donor-donee's preexisting will is rebuttably presumed not to manifest an intent to exercise a power that the donor later reserved to himself or herself in another donative transfer, unless the donor did not provide for takers in default or the gift-in-default clause is ineffective.

Illustration:

2. Donee's will contains a residuary clause that purports to exercise all powers he has in favor of his daughter M. When Donee executed his will, he was the donee of a power to appoint by will under a trust established by the will of his father. Subsequent to the execution of Donee's will, Donee establishes a revocable inter vivos trust and funds

it with most of his owned assets. Donee reserves the income for life, with remainder to such persons as Donee may by will appoint, and in default of appointment the trust property to pass in equal shares to his daughter M and his son S, both of whom survived Donee. Since a revocable inter vivos trust is in practical effect a substitute for a will, it is not likely that Donee intended that the provisions of his existing will should in effect nullify the provisions of the gift-in-default clause in Donee's subsequently executed revocable trust. Consequently, the manifestation of intent in the blanket-exercise clause in Donee's will is presumed not to have been intended to apply to the after-acquired power. If, on the other hand, there was extrinsic evidence that Donee intended his previously executed will to exercise the power of appointment, or if the inter vivos trust did not contain an effective gift-in-default clause, the blanket-exercise clause in Donee's will would do so.

e. Donor precludes exercise of power if it is an after-acquired power. Although the donee's exercising document manifests an intent to exercise after-acquired powers, the donee's intent is ineffective if the document creating the power precludes exercise in a document that was executed before the power was created.

In the absence of an indication to the contrary, however, it is inferred that the time of the execution of the donee's exercising document is immaterial to the donor. Even if the donor declares that the property shall pass to such person as the donee "shall" or "may" appoint, these terms of futurity do not suffice to indicate an intent to exclude exercise by an exercising document previously executed, because these words of futurity may be construed to refer to the time when the exercising document becomes effective.

f. Specific-reference requirement. A specific-reference requirement does not necessarily preclude exercise of an after-acquired power.

Illustration:

3. Donor and his wife, Donee, execute their wills at the same time. Donor's will creates a trust for Donee under which she is to receive the income for life, with a general power to appoint the trust property by a will in which she makes specific reference to her power under Donor's will. Donee, knowing the terms of Donor's will, makes specific reference to the power under Donor's will and purports to exercise the power. Donor dies, then Donee dies. Donee's will effectively exercised the power.

g. Multiple exercising documents; which one controls. If the donee executes multiple exercising documents containing a blanket-exercise clause, the question is which one controls if the terms of the appointments are different. The presumption is that the exercising document last executed controls. The presumption is rebuttable.

h. Cross-reference. For the proposition that a power of appointment cannot be conferred on a donee who is deceased, see § 19.11. Consequently, the term "after-acquired power" in this section refers to a power acquired on or before the donee's death.

§ 19.7. Donee's Authority to Revoke or Amend Exercise

The donee of a power of appointment lacks the authority to revoke or amend an exercise of the power, except to the extent that

the donee reserved a power of revocation or amendment when exercising the power, and the terms of the power do not prohibit the reservation.

Comment:

a. Scope. This section recognizes that the donee of a power of appointment lacks the authority to revoke or amend an exercise of the power, except to the extent that the donee reserved a power of revocation or amendment when exercising the power, and the terms of the power do not prohibit the reservation.

A donee of a power of appointment who exercises the power is like any other transferor of property in regard to authority to revoke or amend the transfer. Hence, unless the donee in some appropriate manner manifests an intent that an appointment is revocable or amendable, the appointment is irrevocable.

b. Power exercisable by donee's last unrevoked instrument. A power that is exercisable by the donee's last unrevoked instrument in writing is a presently exercisable power. See § 17.4, Comment *a*. The donee can make an exercise of such a power irrevocable by explicitly so providing in the writing exercising the power.

c. Testamentary exercise. Because a will does not become effective as a dispositive instrument until the testator dies (see § 3.1, Comment *a*), a testamentary exercise of a power—whether the power is testamentary or presently exercisable—may be revoked or amended by the donee to the same extent as any other provision of the donee's will. If the power is presently exercisable, an irrevocable inter vivos appointment may defeat a testamentary exercise. . . . .

d. Donor prohibits revocable or amendable exercise—effect. If the donor of a power of appointment manifests an intent that any exercise of the power shall be irrevocable, the effect differs with respect to a general power and a nongeneral power. Such a manifestation will never be found in a testamentary power of appointment, because when the will takes effect the donee will not be alive to revoke or amend the exercise of the power. In the case of a general power presently exercisable, a provision that a revocable or amendable appointment cannot be made could have no effect, because the donee could simply appoint the appointive assets to himself or herself and then make a revocable or amendable transfer of the then-owned property. Any appointment contrary to a prohibition against a revocable or amendable exercise of a general power presently exercisable is construed as an appointment to the donee followed by a transfer by the donee of the then-owned property.

The donee of a presently exercisable nongeneral power cannot appoint the appointive assets to himself or herself. Hence, if the donor prohibits the donee from making a revocable or amendable appointment, the donor's manifested intent is effective. In such a case, the donee can only make an irrevocable and unamendable appointment, and any effort by the donee to retain a power to revoke or amend an exercise is ineffective.

If the same person is both the donor and the donee, a provision that an exercise of the power cannot be revoked or amended is ineffective, because the donor can release the donee from the prohibition. When the same person is both the donor and donee, a revocable or amendable exercise of the power by the donee is treated as including a release by the donor of the prohibition against a revocable or amendable exercise.

e. *Manner of revoking or amending a revocable or amendable exercise of power.* If the donee is not prohibited by the donor from making a revocable or amendable exercise of a power of appointment and the donee makes such an exercise, the donee may specify the manner of revoking or amending the exercise. In the absence of such a specification, the requirements imposed by the donor that must be met to exercise the power are applicable. There may also be formalities imposed by statute in regard to the revocation or amendment of an exercise of a power relating to certain property (e.g., real property).

f. *Exercise of power after revocation of exercise.* An effective revocation of the exercise of a power of appointment restores the donee's options to what they were before the power was exercised. If the power would be exercisable had there never been an exercise followed by a revocation of it, the power is exercisable to the same extent after the revocation.

Part B. Effectiveness of Donee's Attempted Exercise

Introductory Note: Part B considers factors that may prevent an intended appointment from being effective. The donee may lack the capacity to exercise a power or may be the victim of wrongdoing (§ 19.8). The formal requisites for an appointment may not be satisfied (§ 19.9), although donor-imposed formalities may be satisfied by substantial compliance (§ 19.10). An attempt may be made to exercise a power of appointment created after the donee's death (§ 19.11). The consequences of an appointment to a deceased appointee are also examined (§ 19.12).

§ 19.8. Capacity of Donee to Exercise a Power of Appointment; Freedom from Wrongdoing

(a) In order for an attempted exercise of a power of appointment to be effective, the donee must have capacity to exercise the power. The donee has capacity to exercise the power if the donee has capacity to make a similar transfer of owned property.

(b) In order for an attempted exercise of a power of appointment to be effective, the donee must be free from undue influence and other wrongdoing.

Comment:

a. *Cross-references.* On questions of capacity to make a transfer of owned property, see §§ 8.1 (Mental Capacity) and 8.2 (Minority). On questions of undue influence and other wrongdoing, see §§ 8.3 (Undue Influence, Duress, or Fraud) and 8.4 (Homicide—the Slayer Rule).

b. *Incapacitated donee; validity of power.* A power of appointment can be validly conferred on a donee who is incapacitated, whether on account of the donee's mental condition or minority. Cf. § 8.1, Comment *n;* § 8.2, Comment *e.* A power of appointment that was previously conferred on a donee who then had capacity is not invalidated if the donee subsequently becomes incapacitated, nor does subsequent incapacity invalidate an exercise of the power that was executed when the donee had capacity.

c. *Testamentary exercise.* A donee who lacks the mental capacity to execute a valid will (see § 8.1(b) and Comment *c*) also lacks the capacity to make a testamentary exercise of a power of appointment. Because a minor donee lacks the capacity to execute a valid will (see § 8.2(a) and Comment *c*), a minor donee also lacks the capacity to make a testamentary exercise of a power of appointment.

d. Inter vivos exercise of presently exercisable general power by or on behalf of mentally incapacitated donee. Unless the donor has manifested a contrary intent, it is assumed that the donor intends that the legal representative or agent under the authority of a durable power of attorney of the incapacitated donee of a presently exercisable general power is to be permitted to exercise the power for the benefit of the donee to the same extent the legal representative or agent could make an effective transfer of similar owned property for the benefit of the donee.

The Uniform Power of Attorney Act § 211 provides: "Unless the power of attorney otherwise provides, language in a power of attorney granting general authority with respect to estates, trusts, and other beneficial interests authorizes the agent to . . . exercise for the benefit of the principal a presently exercisable general power of appointment held by the principal."

e. Inter vivos exercise of presently exercisable power by minor donee. A purported inter vivos exercise of a presently exercisable power by a minor is subject to ratification or disaffirmance by the minor when the minor becomes of age, as with a purported transfer by a minor of owned property. See § 8.2(b). The legal representative of a minor donee may make an effective exercise of a nonfiduciary general power to appoint by deed for the minor's benefit to the same extent the legal representative could make an effective transfer of similar owned property of the minor for the minor's benefit, unless the donor of the power has manifested a contrary intent.

f. Court authorization for legal representative of incapacitated donee to exercise power. The rule of Comment *d* regarding the exercise of an incapacitated donee's power by the donee's legal representative relates to the legal representative's authority without advance court approval. A court may have jurisdiction apart from the donative document to authorize a legal representative to exercise the incapacitated donee's power.

g. Freedom from wrongdoing. A purported exercise of a power of appointment is invalid to the extent it was procured by undue influence or by other wrongdoing (see §§ 8.3 and 8.4).

§ 19.9. Formal Requirements of an Appointment

In order for an attempted exercise of a power of appointment to be effective, the document purporting to exercise the power must be executed in compliance with (i) the formalities required by law for the transfer by the donee of owned property of a similar type and (ii), except as provided in § 19.10, any additional formalities required by the donor.

Comment:

a. Cross-references. The formal requirements for the execution of various types of donative documents are covered in §§ 3.1 to 3.3 (wills), 6.1 to 6.3 (gifts), and 7.1 (will substitutes). For relief of strict compliance with formal requirements imposed by law, see § 3.3 (harmless-error rule for wills), which by this Comment is made applicable to a will that makes a testamentary exercise of a power of appointment; and see § 6.1, Comment *o* (mistake in perfecting inter vivos gift), § 6.2, Comment *z* (mistake in perfecting inter vivos gift of personal property), and § 6.3, Comment *p* (mistake in perfecting inter vivos gift of land), which by this Comment are made applicable to a document that makes an inter vivos exercise of a power of appointment.

b. Power exercisable "by will." A power of appointment that is exercisable "by will" (as in "to such persons as the donee shall by will appoint") is a testamentary power and is exercisable by an instrument that is formally sufficient to be admitted to probate under applicable law. Although the power is exercised even if the will is not submitted for admission to probate, the power is not exercised if the will is submitted for admission to probate and probate is denied. The applicable law is the law that would apply with respect to the formalities for a will if the appointive assets were the owned assets of the donee. See §§ 3.1 (Attested Wills), 3.2 (Holographic Wills), and 3.3 (Excusing Harmless Errors). Because a revocable trust operates in substance as a will, a power of appointment exercisable "by will" can be exercised in a revocable-trust document, as long as the revocable trust remained revocable at the donee's death.

A power of appointment that is exercisable "by will admitted to probate" is exercisable only by a will that is actually admitted to probate.

c. Power exercisable "by an instrument in the nature of a will." At an earlier time, it was customary to make a power conferred on a married woman exercisable by "an instrument in the nature of a will." The usage arose because a married woman was not then permitted to make a will, a prohibition that has long since been abrogated. In modern circumstances, absent any further manifestation of a contrary intent, a power exercisable "by an instrument in the nature of a will" is construed as a power exercisable "by will," as interpreted in Comment *b*.

d. Power exercisable "by deed." A power that is exercisable "by deed" (as in "to such persons as the donee shall by deed appoint") is exercisable by an instrument that would be formally sufficient under applicable law to be legally operative in the donee's lifetime to transfer an interest to the appointee if the donee owned the appointive assets. At one time, "deed" required the use of seal, but seal is now archaic and is no longer required. The exercise of a power of appointment by a revocable trust would be an exercise "by deed." A power to revoke a revocable trust is effectively exercised by the methods provided in Restatement Third, Trusts § 63. See also Uniform Trust Code § 602(c).

e. Power exercisable "by deed or will." A power that is exercisable "by deed or will" (as in "to such persons as the donee shall by deed or will appoint") is a presently exercisable power and is exercisable by an instrument that is formally sufficient under applicable law to be either (i) legally operative in the donee's lifetime to transfer an interest to the appointee if the donee owned the appointive assets or (ii) formally sufficient to be admitted to probate under applicable law.

f. Power exercisable "by written instrument" or by "last unrevoked written instrument." A power exercisable "by written instrument" or by "last unrevoked written instrument" is exercisable by deed or will (see Comment *e*).

g. Document of exercise not specified. A power in which the document of exercise is not specified (as in "to such persons as the donee shall appoint") is exercisable by deed or will (see Comment *e*).

h. Additional formalities imposed by donor. See § 19.10 for the treatment of additional formalities imposed by the donor.

§ 19.10. Substantial Compliance with Donor-Imposed Formal Requirements

Substantial compliance with formal requirements of an appointment imposed by the donor, including a requirement that the instrument of exercise make reference or specific reference to the power, is sufficient if (i) the donee knew of and intended to exercise the power, and (ii) the donee's manner of attempted exercise did not impair a material purpose of the donor in imposing the requirement.

Comment:

a. *Scope.* This section adopts a substantial-compliance rule for donor-imposed formal requirements. This section only applies to formal requirements imposed by the donor. It does not apply to formal requirements imposed by law. That topic is covered in § 19.9.

b. *Historical note.* The English courts of Chancery developed the rule that "equity will aid the defective execution of a power." Such aid was given only for the benefit of persons favored by courts of equity.

Restatement Second of Property (Donative Transfers) § 18.3 followed the historical rule. Under the Restatement Second, the donee's attempted appointment had to approximate the manner of appointment prescribed by the donor, and the appointee had to be a natural object of the donee's affection, a person with whom the donee had a relationship akin to that with someone who would be a natural object of the donee's bounty, a creditor of the donee, a charity, a person who has paid value for the appointment, or some other person favored by a court applying equitable principles. A court wishing to continue to adhere to the historical rule should give the term "natural objects of the donee's bounty" the meaning attributed to it in § 8.1, Comment *c.*

This Restatement continues the requirement that the donee's attempted appointment approximate the manner of appointment prescribed by the donor, but changes the word "approximate" to the more familiar term "substantial compliance." This Restatement also requires that the evidence establish that the donee knew of and intended to exercise the power, and that the donee's manner of exercise did not impair the donor's purpose in imposing the requirement.

This Restatement does not require that the appointee be someone favored by equitable principles. The substantial-compliance standard supersedes that limitation. The Restatement Second's list of those who are favored covers virtually anyone to whom the donee would normally appoint.

c. *Additional requirements imposed by the donor.* Whenever the donor imposes formal requirements with respect to the instrument of appointment that exceed the requirements imposed by law, the donor's purpose in imposing the additional requirements is relevant to whether the donee's attempted exercise satisfies the rule of this section. To the extent that the failure to comply with the additional requirements will not impair the accomplishment of a material purpose of the donor, the donee's attempted appointment in a manner that substantially complies with a donor-imposed requirement does not fail for lack of compliance with that requirement.

Illustration:

1. Donor transfers Blackacre to Donee (Donor's son) for life, with remainder as Donee shall appoint by a deed under seal. The applicable

law has abolished the necessity of a seal on a deed of real property. In the controlling jurisdiction, a deed is a recordable document though it lacks a seal; and when it has been recorded, no one can be a bona fide purchaser who will cut off the equitable rights acquired by the appointees under the defective appointment. Donee executes a deed not under seal disposing of the fee-simple title to Blackacre in favor of his children. Donee's deed substantially complies with the requirement of a document under seal.

d. Specific-reference requirement. A formal requirement commonly imposed by the donor is that, in order to be effective, the donee's attempted exercise must make specific reference to the power. Specific-reference clauses were a pre-1942 invention to prevent an inadvertent exercise of a general power—an exercise produced, not by the donee's deliberate decision to exercise the power, but by case law or statutory law attributing such an intent to the residuary clause in the donee's will. The federal estate-tax law then provided that the value of property subject to a general power was included in the donee's gross estate only if the general power was exercised. The Massachusetts rule then provided that a general residuary clause in the donee's will presumptively exercised a general power of appointment. The idea of requiring specific reference was designed to thwart the Massachusetts rule from unnecessarily causing estate taxation.

The federal estate-tax law provides that the value of property subject to a general power is included in the donee's gross estate whether the power is exercised or not, if the power was created after October 21, 1942. See I.R.C. § 2041. Consequently, an inadvertent exercise of a general power created after October 21, 1942, no longer has adverse estate-tax consequences. Moreover, the Massachusetts rule is no longer followed in Massachusetts, is not widely followed, and is not followed in this Restatement. See § 19.4.

Nevertheless, donors continue to impose a specific-reference requirement. Because the original purpose of the specific-reference requirement was to prevent an inadvertent exercise of the power, it seems reasonable to presume that that was the donor's purpose in doing so. Consequently, a specific-reference requirement overrides any applicable state law that presumes that a residuary clause was intended to exercise a general power. See § 19.4, Comment *e*.

A more difficult question is whether a blanket-exercise clause (see § 19.2, Comment *d*) satisfies a specific-reference requirement. If it could be shown that the donee had knowledge of and intended to exercise the power, the blanket-exercise clause would be sufficient to exercise the power, unless it could be shown that the donor's intention was not merely to prevent an inadvertent exercise of the power but was to prevent any exercise of the power, intentional or inadvertent. The possibility of applying § 12.1 to reform the donee's attempted appointment to insert the required specific reference should also be explored.

e. Appointment not intended. Under the rule stated in this section, the donee must have intended to exercise the power. If, for whatever reason, the donee did not intend to exercise the power, the rule stated in this section does not apply. See § 19.2. The donee could not have intended to exercise the power if the donee released the power (see Chapter 20), or if the donee's will or other document contained a nonexercise clause (see § 19.2, Comment *f*). Particularly in the case of an instrument not carefully drafted, language of the donee partaking of futurity is not necessarily inconsistent with a present intent to exercise the power.

Illustrations:

5. Donor died, leaving a will that devised property to Trustee in trust. Trustee is directed to pay the income to Donee (Donor's son) for life, with remainder as Donee may appoint by deed or will, and in default of appointment to Donee's issue. Donee dies leaving a memorandum as follows: "Although this is not a legal document, I hope that my issue will comply with my desire to have $10,000 of the trust property of the trust under Donor's will go to my wife." The inference is justified that the precatory language of the memorandum does not indicate an intent on Donee's part to exercise the power. Therefore, the rule of this section is not applicable.

6. Donor died, leaving a will that devised Blackacre to Donee (Donor's daughter) for life, with remainder as Donee shall appoint by a deed with two witnesses. Donee, about to undergo a serious operation, writes an unwitnessed memorandum as follows: "I want my daughter Mary to have Blackacre and will make it over to her if my life is spared." Donee dies during the operation. The inference is justified that Donee intended a present exercise of the power, but had in mind executing a confirmatory instrument because she feared that her memorandum would not suffice. Therefore, the rule of this section is applicable, and Mary will be entitled to Blackacre.

§ 19.11. Death of Donee Before Power Created

If the donee dies before the effective date of a document purporting to confer on the donee a power of appointment, the power is not created, and any attempted exercise of the power is ineffective.

Comment:

a. *Scope.* Just as property cannot be transferred to a person who is deceased (see § 1.2), a power of appointment cannot be conferred on a deceased person. A power of appointment is created when the document purporting to create it becomes effective. Until then, no power is created and no appointment can be made.

b. *Power created in donor's will.* A power of appointment created in the donor's will is created when the donor dies, not when the donor executes the will. If the donee does not survive the donor, any attempt by the donee to exercise the power is ineffective.

If the donee survives the donor, the power is created, and can be exercised by a document executed before or after the donor's death (see § 19.6). If the document exercising the power is the donee's will, the exercise is revocable until the donee dies. If the document exercising the power is an inter vivos document of exercise, the exercise is revocable until the donor's death, unless the exercise is expressly revocable, in which case it is revocable beyond the donor's death as provided in § 19.7.

c. *Power created in donor's inter vivos trust.* A power of appointment created in the donor's inter vivos trust is created when the trust is established, even if the trust is a revocable trust. (For principles controlling when a trust is established, see Restatement Third, Trusts § 10.) If the donee does not survive the establishment of the trust, any attempt by the donee to exercise the power is ineffective.

If the donee survives the establishment of the trust, the power is created, and can be exercised by a document executed before or after the establishment of the trust. If the document exercising the power is the donee's will, the exercise is revocable until the donee dies. If the document exercising the power is an inter vivos document of exercise, the exercise is revocable until the establishment of the trust, unless the exercise is expressly revocable, in which case it is revocable beyond the establishment of the trust as provided in § 19.7.

If the inter vivos trust is revocable, an exercise by the donee after the trust is established that does not remove the appointed property from the trust remains subject to the donor's power to revoke or amend the trust, which includes the authority to revoke or amend the power created in the trust. See § 18.2, Comment *b*.

d. When purported exercise of power ineffective; alternative theories for giving effect to donee's direction—incorporation by reference and independent significance. Although a purported exercise of a power is ineffective under the rule of this section, there are alternative theories for giving effect to the donee's direction in certain cases. The alternative theories are the doctrine of incorporation by reference (see § 3.6) and the doctrine of independent significance (see § 3.7).

d(1). Incorporation by reference. Under the doctrine of incorporation by reference, a provision in the donee's will or other appointive document may be incorporated into the donor's will if the donee's will was in existence when the donor's will was executed and if the donor's will manifests an intent to incorporate a provision in the donee's will directing the devolution of the appointive property.

d(2). Independent significance. Under the doctrine of independent significance, the meaning of a provision in the donor's will creating a power may be supplied by the donee's will or by another appointive document of the donee. The opportunity to rely on the doctrine of independent significance when the donee's attempted exercise of a power is ineffective under the rule of this section would arise principally in a case in which the donor's testamentary gift is to persons named or to be named in the donee's will or in a revocable trust established by the donee, as such trust may be amended from time to time before the donor's death. If the donee predeceases the donor, the rule of this section would make ineffective any exercise of the power in the donee to designate who would take under the power provided for in the donor's will. However, the donee's will or revocable trust has independent significance, because it is primarily directed at the disposition of the donee's property and does not purport to dispose of the donor's property, whether by the exercise of the power to change the trust or otherwise. Consequently, under the doctrine of independent significance, the meaning of a provision in the donor's will creating a power may be supplied by the donee's will or revocable trust even if the donee predeceased the donor.

§ 19.12. Appointment to Deceased Appointee or Permissible Appointee's Descendants; Application of Antilapse Statute

(a) An appointment to a deceased appointee is ineffective, but an applicable antilapse statute may apply to pass the appointed property to the deceased appointee's descendants or other substitute takers.

(b) Even when the applicable antilapse statute does not expressly address an appointment to a deceased appointee, its purpose and policy should apply to an appointment to a deceased appointee (i) as if the appointed property were owned by either the donor or the donee, and (ii) so that the substituted takers are treated as permissible appointees of the power.

(c) The donee of a nongeneral power is authorized to appoint to the descendants of a deceased permissible appointee, whether or not the permissible appointee's descendants are included within the description of the permissible appointees, but not if the deceased permissible appointee died before the execution of the instrument that created the power. This subsection does not apply if the donor specifically prohibited an appointment to the descendants of a deceased permissible appointee.

Comment:

a. Appointment to deceased appointee ineffective. Just as property cannot be transferred to a person who is deceased (see § 1.2), a power of appointment cannot be effectively exercised in favor of a deceased appointee.

b. Antilapse statutes. Several antilapse statutes expressly apply to the exercise of a power of appointment. . . . Under these statutes, a testamentary exercise in favor of an appointee who predeceases the donee triggers the substitution of the deceased appointee's descendants (or other substitute takers), unless the donor or donee expresses a contrary intention (see Comments *c* and *g*). In order for the statute to apply, the deceased appointee must be in the class of protected relatives (see Comment *d*). The applicable antilapse statute is the one that would apply if the donee of the power owned the appointive property and made the disposition described in the appointment.

Even when an antilapse statute does not expressly address the exercise of a power of appointment, it should nevertheless be construed to apply to such an exercise, unless the applicable statute expressly excludes appointments. See § 5.5, Comment *l*. The rationale underlying antilapse statutes—that of presumptively attributing to the testator the intent to substitute the descendants of a predeceased devisee—applies equally to the testamentary exercise of a power of appointment. Consequently, in construing an antilapse statute that does not expressly apply to the exercise of a power of appointment, the donee is treated as the "testator" and the appointee is treated as the "devisee or legatee."

Illustrations:

1. Donor dies, devising Blackacre to Donee (Donor's son) "for life, remainder to such persons as Donee shall appoint and in default of appointment to Donee's children who survive him as tenants in common in fee simple." Donee has a general power; and consequently, any substituted takers provided by an applicable antilapse statute would necessarily be permissible appointees of the power. Donee executes a will in which he appoints Blackacre "to my eldest son, John." John dies before Donee. The applicable antilapse statute applies in this situation to the same extent it would apply if Blackacre had been owned by Donee.

3. Same facts as Illustration 1, except that Donee's power is a nongeneral power to appoint to Donee's issue. John dies before Donee. The applicable antilapse statute applies in this situation to the same extent it would apply if Blackacre had been owned by Donee.

4. Same facts as Illustration 1, except that Donee's power is a nongeneral power to appoint to Donee's children. A substituted taker provided by the applicable antilapse statute would not be an original permissible appointee of the power, but, under the rule of subsection (b) of this section, the application of the antilapse statute makes the substituted taker a permissible appointee of the power. John dies before Donee. Consequently, the applicable antilapse statute applies to the same extent it would apply if Blackacre had been owned by Donee.

c. Contrary intent expressed by donee. Because an antilapse statute is a rule of construction (see § 5.5, Comment *f*; § 11.3, Comments *b*, *d*, and *j*), the statute yields to a contrary intent. For discussion regarding a contrary intent, see § 5.5, Comments *f*, *g*, *h*, and *i*. The clearest way of stating a contrary intent is to do so directly, in language that is understandable to the donee-testator, language that leaves no doubt that the donee-testator considered the possibility of the appointee failing to survive the donee-testator and decided against substituting the appointee's descendants. Language such as "and not to [the appointee's] descendants if [the appointee] fails to survive me" is an unmistakable expression of a contrary intent.

An alternative appointment also indicates a contrary intent, and hence overrides an antilapse statute, if the alternative appointee survives the testator and is otherwise entitled to take (i.e., is not prevented from taking because of an unsatisfied condition). The appointive property goes to that alternative appointee rather than to the primary appointee's descendants under the antilapse statute. If the alternative appointment is in the form of a class gift, at least one class member but not necessarily all class members must survive and be otherwise entitled to take. See § 5.5, Comment *g*.

Illustration:

5. Donor died, leaving a will that devised property to Trustee in trust. Trustee is directed to pay the income to Donee (Donor's son) for life, remainder in principal to such persons as Donee shall by will appoint, and in default of appointment by representation to Donor's descendants who survive Donee. Donee executes a will appointing the remainder interest "to my daughter Mary, but if Mary predeceases me, to my son, Sam." Mary predeceases Donee, leaving descendants who survive Donee. Sam survives Donee. Sam is entitled to the principal of the trust, not Mary's descendants. Donee's alternative appointment expresses a contrary intent and overrides the antilapse statute. If, however, Sam had predeceased Donee, Mary's descendants would be entitled to the principal, because the alternative appointee, Sam, would not have been entitled to take.

d. Protected relatives. In order for the applicable antilapse statute to apply, the deceased appointee must be in the class of relatives who are protected by the statute (see § 5.5, Comment *c*). In the case of an appointment, this requirement is satisfied if the specified relationship exists with respect to either the donor or the donee of the power.

Illustration:

6. Donor transfers property to Trustee in trust. Trustee is directed to pay the income to Donee (Donor's wife) "for life with remainder to such persons as Donee shall appoint and in default of appointment to Donor's issue who survive Donee, such issue to take by representation." The applicable antilapse statute requires that the deceased devisee or legatee be a descendant of the testator. Donee

executes a will in which she appoints one-half of the appointive assets to her son S by a previous marriage and one-half to Donor's daughter M by a previous marriage. Both S and M predecease Donee. The applicable antilapse statute applies to half of the appointive assets as though that half were owned by Donee and she was the testator and to the other half as though that half were owned by Donor and he was the testator.

e. Substitute takers under antilapse statute treated as permissible appointees. Although the deceased appointee must be in a class of protected relatives (see Comment *d*), the substitute takers provided by the antilapse statute (typically the descendants of the deceased appointee) are treated as permissible appointees even if the description of permissible appointees provided by the donor does not expressly cover them. This rule corresponds to the rule applying antilapse statutes to class gifts. Antilapse statutes substitute the descendants of deceased class members, even if the class member's descendants are not members of the class.

f. Descendants of deceased permissible appointee treated as permissible appointees. Under subsection (c), the descendants of a deceased permissible appointee are treated as permissible appointees, but only if the deceased permissible appointee was alive when the power was created or was born thereafter. This rule is a logical extension of the application of antilapse statutes to appointments. If an antilapse statute can substitute the descendants of a deceased appointee, the donee of the power should be allowed to make a direct appointment to one or more descendants of a deceased permissible appointee.

Although the rules of subsections (a) and (b) apply to both general and nongeneral powers, the rule of subsection (c) can only apply to nongeneral powers.

g. Contrary intent expressed by donor. The donor of a power, general or nongeneral, can prohibit the application of an antilapse statute to the donee's appointment and, in the case of a nongeneral power, can prohibit an appointment to the descendants of a deceased permissible appointee, but must do so expressly. A traditional gift-in-default clause does not express a contrary intent in either case, unless the clause expressly provides that it is to take effect instead of the descendants of a deceased permissible appointee.

Part C. Permissible Appointments

Introductory Note: Part C addresses the permissible appointments that the donee of a general power has the authority to make (§ 19.13) and those that the donee of a nongeneral power has the authority to make (§ 19.14).

§ 19.13. General Power—Permissible Appointments

(a) The donee of a general power that permits appointment to the donee or to the donee's estate is authorized to make any appointment, including one in trust and one that creates a power of appointment in another, that the donee could make by appointing to the donee or to the donee's estate and then disposing of the appointive assets as owned property.

(b) The donee of a general power that permits appointment only to the donee's creditors or to the creditors of the donee's estate is restricted to appointing to those creditors.

Comment:

a. Rationale. When the donor creates a general power under which an appointment can be made outright to the donee or outright to the donee's estate, the necessary implication is that the donee can accomplish by an appointment to others whatever the donee could accomplish by first making the appointive assets owned property and then disposing of the owned property.

b. Variations in terms of general power. A general power as defined in § 17.3 is one that permits appointment to the donee, the donee's estate, or the creditors of either. A power that restricts appointment just to the donee or just to the donee's estate or just to the creditors of the donee or just to the creditors of the donee's estate is a general power.

A general power to appoint only to the donee (even though it says "and to no one else") does not prevent the donee from exercising the power directly in favor of others. There is no reason to require the donee to transform the appointive assets into owned property and then, in a second step, to dispose of the owned property. Likewise, a general power to appoint only to the donee's estate (even though it says "and to no one else") does not prevent an exercise of the power by will directly in favor of others. There is no reason to require the donee to transform the appointive assets into estate property and then, in a second step, to dispose of the estate property by will.

A general power to appoint only to the donee's creditors or to appoint only to the creditors of the donee's estate permits only an appointment to the donee's creditors or the creditors of the donee's estate, as the case may be.....

c. Multiple appointments under general power to appoint by deed. A general power to appoint to the donee may purport to allow only one exercise of the power. Such a restriction is ineffective and does not prevent multiple partial exercises of the power under the rule of this section.....

d. Appointment in trust. A general power to appoint to the donee or to the donee's estate may purport to restrict appointment to outright interests not in trust. Such a restriction is ineffective and does not prevent an appointment in trust.....

e. Appointment with conditions, charges, and restraints on alienation. A general power to appoint to the donee or to the donee's estate may purport to forbid the donee from imposing conditions, or charges or restraints on alienation, or other qualifications upon the enjoyment of the property by the appointee. Such restrictions are ineffective and do not prevent an appointment subject to such restrictions under the rule of this section.

f. Creation of power of appointment in another. The donee of a general power of appointment that permits appointment to the donee or to the donee's estate may exercise the power by creating a power of appointment in another.

Illustrations:

5. Donor died, leaving a will that devised Blackacre to Donee (Donor's wife) for life, with power to appoint Blackacre by will "to any person or persons, including Donee's estate." Donee exercises her general power by appointing Blackacre to her daughter Mary for life, "with power to appoint Blackacre to such one or more of Mary's issue as Mary may appoint by her will," and with provision made for the disposition of Blackacre in default of appointment. Donee has made a

permissible appointment in creating in Mary a nongeneral power of appointment.

6. Same facts as Illustration 5, except that Donor provided that any exercise of the general power by Donee not result in the creation of any power in another. Donor's restriction is ineffective. Donee has made a permissible appointment in creating in Mary a nongeneral power of appointment.

g. "Delegation" by donee to another of right to exercise donee's power. An appointment that creates a power of appointment in another in effect delegates to the other the right to complete the exercise of the donee's power. The result is the same under the rule of this section if the donee, without in form making any exercise of the power, delegates to another the right to decide how and to what extent the donee's power is to be exercised.

Illustration:

7. Donor died, leaving a will that devised Blackacre to Donee (Donor's wife) for life, with power in Donee to appoint Blackacre by deed or by will "to any person or persons, including Donee and her estate." Donee contracts to sell Blackacre to P, and gives a power of attorney to her agent to execute for her all the papers that may be required in carrying out her obligations under the contract. Donee's agent may make a permissible appointment of Blackacre to P under Donee's general power to appoint by deed.

§ 19.14. Nongeneral Power—Permissible Appointments

Except to the extent that the donor has manifested a contrary intention, the donee of a nongeneral power is authorized to make an appointment in any form, including one in trust and one that creates a power of appointment in another, that only benefits permissible appointees of the power.

Comment:

a. Rationale. Except to the extent that the donor has manifested a contrary intention, the donee of a nongeneral power has the same breadth of discretion in appointment to permissible appointees that the donee has in the disposition of the donee's owned property to permissible appointees of the power.

Illustration:

1. Donor died, leaving a will that devised Blackacre to Donee (Donor's wife) for life, "remainder to such one or more of Donor's issue as Donee shall appoint by deed or will," and in default of appointment to Donor's issue who survive Donee by representation, and if no issue of Donor survives Donee, to the X charity. Donee, in her lifetime, appoints half of the remainder interest in Blackacre to Donor's daughter Mary. Donee by her will appoints the other half of Blackacre to Mary and Donor's son Sam in equal shares. Donor placed no restriction on multiple appointments at different times by Donee. Donee's appointments are valid, because she has appointed only to permissible appointees.

b. Family definitions. In the absence of a contrary manifestation of intent by the donor, family definitions in the donor's document apply to the permissible appointees. For example, if the donor's document expressly excludes adopted children from the definition of "children" or "descendants," the donee of a nongeneral power whose permissible appointees are the donee's descendants would not be permitted to appoint to the donee's adopted child.

c. Permissible appointee. See § 19.12(c) for the proposition that the descendants of a deceased permissible appointee are permissible appointees in certain circumstances.

d. Donor's manifestation of contrary intent. Language that creates a nongeneral power by the use of customary language referring in general terms to the manner of exercise is not to be construed as a manifestation of intent to curtail what would otherwise be the freedom that the donee would have in making appointments. If the nongeneral power has only one permissible appointee, however, only an outright appointment or one in trust in which the permissible appointee is the sole beneficiary is permissible. . . . .

e. Appointment in trust. Except to the extent that the donor has manifested a contrary intention, the donee of a nongeneral power has the authority to exercise the power by an appointment in trust. In order to express a contrary intent, the creating language must expressly prohibit an appointment in trust. Language merely authorizing the donee to make an outright appointment does not suffice. . . . .

f. Exercising a fiduciary distributive power to create another trust. Subject to fiduciary standards and the terms of the power, a trustee or other fiduciary can exercise a fiduciary distributive power such as a power of invasion to create another trust.

g. Creation of power in another. Except to the extent that the donor has manifested a contrary intent (see Comment *g(5)*), the donee of a nongeneral power has the authority to exercise the power by creating a general power in a permissible appointee (an object) of the original nongeneral power (see Comment *g(1)*) or by creating a nongeneral power in any person to appoint to permissible appointees (objects) of the original nongeneral power (see Comments *g(3)* and *g(4)*).

g(1). Creation of general power in a permissible appointee. Except to the extent that the donor has manifested a contrary intent (see Comment *g(5)*), the donee of a nongeneral power has the authority to exercise the power by creating a general power in a permissible appointee. Because the donee can appoint outright to a permissible appointee, it follows that the donee can create a presently exercisable general power in a permissible appointee, because such an exercise is, in substance, the equivalent of appointing outright to the second donee. If the general power created in the second donee is a testamentary power, the second donee does not have, in substance, the equivalent of ownership, but the second donee is close to having the equivalent of ownership, especially in a case in which the second donee is given a life interest in the appointive assets. In such a case, the second donee can appoint to any person, including himself or herself, whether or not the second donee's appointees are permissible appointees of the original nongeneral power. . . . .

g(2). Creation of general power in an impermissible appointee. The donee of a nongeneral power does not have the authority to exercise the power by creating a general power in an impermissible appointee (a nonobject). See § 19.15.

g(3). Creation of nongeneral power in a permissible appointee. Except to the extent that the donor has manifested a contrary intent (see Comment *g(5)*), the donee of a nongeneral power has the authority to exercise the power by creating a nongeneral power in a permissible appointee (an object) to appoint to permissible appointees (objects) of the original nongeneral power. An appointment that creates a nongeneral power in a second donee to appoint to permissible appointees, no one of whom is an impermissible appointee of the first power, in effect delegates to the second donee the final selection of the persons to take under an exercise of the first donee's power. The inference is that the donor, in creating a nongeneral power, did not intend to do more than to restrict appointments to the permissible appointees of the power. Accordingly, the second donee can only be authorized to appoint to permissible appointees of the first nongeneral power, excluding himself or herself. The second donee cannot be authorized to appoint to himself or herself, because the second donee, even if the second donee is a permissible appointee of the first power, has been given a nongeneral power.

Illustration:

8. Donor died, leaving a will that devised property to Trustee in trust. Trustee is directed to pay the income to Donee-1 (Donor's son) for life, then to such of Donee-1's descendants as Donee-1 shall by will appoint. Donee-1 dies, leaving a will that exercised his nongeneral power, providing that the trust is to continue beyond Donee-1's death, paying the income to Donee-2 (Donee-1's daughter) for life, then to deliver the trust principal to such of Donee-2's descendants as Donee-2 shall by will appoint; in default of appointment, to Donee-2's descendants who survive Donee-2, by representation. Donee-1's appointment creating a nongeneral testamentary power in Donee-2 is a permissible appointment because the permissible appointees of Donee-2's nongeneral power are restricted to permissible appointees of Donee-1's nongeneral power.

g(4). Creation of nongeneral power in an impermissible appointee. Except to the extent that the donor has manifested a contrary intent (see Comment *g(5)*), the donee of a nongeneral power has the authority to exercise the power by creating a nongeneral power in an impermissible appointee (a nonobject) to appoint to permissible appointees (objects) of the original nongeneral power. Because the donor has imposed confidence in the donee to select which permissible appointees to benefit by an appointment, the donee is authorized to grant the selection power to any other person.

Illustration:

10. Donor died, leaving a will that devised property to Trustee in trust. Trustee is directed to pay the income to Donee-1 (Donor's wife) for life, then to such of Donor's descendants as Donee-1 shall by will appoint. Donee-1 dies, leaving a will that exercised her nongeneral power, providing that the trust is to continue beyond Donee-1's death, paying the income to Donor's son John for life, then to deliver the trust principal to such of Donor's descendants as Donee-2 (Donee-1's brother) shall appoint; in default of appointment, to Donor's descendants who survive John, by representation. Donee-1's appointment creating a nongeneral power in Donee-2 is a permissible appointment, because the permissible appointees of Donee-2's nongeneral power are restricted to permissible appointees of Donee-1's nongeneral power.

g(5). Manifestation of contrary intent. In order to express a contrary intent, the creating language must expressly prohibit the creation of new powers by the donee. Language merely conferring the power on the donee does not suffice. . . . .

Part D. Impermissible Appointments

Introductory Note: Part D deals with impermissible appointments—appointments that attempt to frustrate the donor's direction that the appointive property be devoted exclusively to permissible appointees (objects) or pass in default.

Section 19.15 considers the consequences when the donee attempts to benefit an impermissible appointee by a direct appointment to an impermissible appointee, including an appointment partly to an impermissible appointee and partly to a permissible appointee. Such an appointment is frequently referred to as a "fraud on the power."

Section 19.16 covers various situations in which the appointment is made to a permissible appointee, but with the purpose and expectation that some or all of the appointed property or some collateral benefit will pass to an impermissible appointee. An attempt to benefit an impermissible appointee through the appointment to a permissible appointee is also frequently referred to as a "fraud on the power."

The term "fraud on the power" is not necessarily descriptive, for the donee might reasonably believe that the exercise is authorized. Or the permissible appointee to whom the appointment is made or the impermissible appointee sought to be benefited might be unaware of the power, the power's exercise, or the result that the donee seeks to accomplish.

Section 19.17 deals with the case of the fiduciary who distributes appointed property pursuant to the terms of the wrongful exercise of the power.

Section 19.18 deals with the case of the bona fide purchaser of the appointed assets. The common issue these situations present is the extent to which the improper purpose of benefiting an impermissible appointee adversely affects the fiduciary or the bona fide purchaser.

§ 19.15. Appointment to Impermissible Appointee—"Fraud on the Power"

An appointment that benefits an impermissible appointee is ineffective.

Comment:

a. *Rationale.* The donor of a power of appointment sets the range of permissible appointees by designating the permissible appointees of the power. Any attempt by the donee to exceed that authority by an appointment that benefits an impermissible appointee is ineffective.

b. *General powers.* A general power under which the donee is free to appoint to himself or herself or to his or her estate has no impermissible appointee. Even if the instrument creating such a general power expressly excludes certain persons as permissible appointees of the power, the donee can make a direct appointment of a beneficial interest in favor of such excluded persons, because the donee could have achieved the same result by exercising the power in favor of the donee or the donee's estate and then disposing of it by deed or by will to the excluded persons (see § 19.13). A general power under which the donee is only authorized to appoint to the donee's creditors or the creditors of the donee's estate can only be exercised in favor of those creditors; any other appointment is to an impermissible appointee.

c. Nongeneral powers. The donee of a nongeneral power can make a valid appointment only to a permissible appointee (an object of the power). An attempted appointment to an impermissible appointee (a nonobject of the power) is ineffective.

d. Permissible appointees of nongeneral power. The donor may define the permissible appointees of a nongeneral power by exclusion, by inclusion, or by a combination of the two. If they are defined by exclusion, the donor lists the persons to whom a valid appointment cannot be made. If they are defined by inclusion, the donor lists the persons to whom a valid appointment can be made.

If the permissible appointees are defined by exclusion, the list must include the donee, the donee's estate, and the creditors of either; otherwise, the power would be a general power. The common way of identifying the permissible appointees by exclusion is to authorize the donee to appoint to "any person other than the donee, the donee's estate, and the creditors of either." A nongeneral power to appoint to "any person other than the donee, the donee's estate, and the creditors of either" gives the donee an almost unlimited choice of permissible appointees. The list of excluded persons may be expanded beyond just the donee, the donee's estate, and the creditors of either, however, and include other excluded persons. For example, the donee may be authorized to appoint to "any person other than the donee, the donee's estate, the creditors of either, my brother Bob, Bob's wife, Bob's descendants, and the XYZ Charity." An attempted appointment of a beneficial interest to any person that is excluded as a permissible appointee is ineffective.

If the permissible appointees are listed by inclusion, the list of permissible appointees must not include the donee, the donee's estate, and the creditors of either; otherwise the power would be a general power. A well-drafted list usually takes the form of a defined and limited class, such as "children," "grandchildren," "issue," "descendants," "brothers and sisters," "nieces and nephews," or "heirs." If, for example, the permissible appointees are the donee's descendants, an appointment to the donee's brother or sister is impermissible and ineffective. For the meaning of various class-gift terms, see Division V (Chapters 14 through 16). See also § 19.12(c) for the proposition that the descendants of a deceased permissible appointee of a nongeneral power are permissible appointees in certain circumstances.

e. Appointment in trust. The donee of a power to appoint may make an appointment in trust for the benefit of permissible appointees, unless the donor has manifested an intent to exclude an appointment in trust (see § 19.14). An appointment in trust necessarily involves a nominal direct appointment to an impermissible appointee, unless the trustee is a permissible appointee of the power. The appointment to an impermissible appointee-trustee, however, does not give the impermissible appointee a beneficial interest and hence does not violate the rule of this section.

f. Appointment to impermissible appointee at direction of permissible appointee. If the donee of a power makes a decision to exercise the power in favor of a permissible appointee, the permissible appointee may request the donee to transfer the appointive assets directly to an impermissible appointee. The appointment directly to the impermissible appointee in this situation is effective, being treated for all purposes as an appointment first to the permissible appointee, followed by a transfer by the permissible appointee to the impermissible appointee. The rule of this section does not prohibit the appointment.

g. *Ineffective appointment to impermissible appointee.* An attempted appointment of a beneficial interest to an impermissible appointee fails. The impermissible appointee receives no better title than the impermissible appointee would receive in any other case in which a nonowner purports to transfer property to another. If the donee attempts to make simultaneous appointments, some to permissible appointees and some to impermissible appointees, the ineffectiveness of the appointments to the impermissible appointees does not affect the appointments to the permissible appointees, unless the pattern of the appointments reveals that the donee would not have intended any appointment to stand unless all appointments were effective (see § 19.20).

h. *Application of cy pres if appointment is to an impermissible appointee-charity.* If the donee of the power appoints to one or more designated charities, and the donee appoints to a charity not designated as a permissible appointee of the power, the appointment to the impermissible appointee-charity is ineffective. The court, however, may apply cy pres in such situations and will select from among the charities that are the permissible appointees of the power the one or more that have charitable purposes similar to the charity selected by the donee as recipient of the appointive assets. On the cy pres doctrine, see Restatement Third, Trusts § 67.

§ 19.16. Appointment to Permissible Appointee for Benefit of Impermissible Appointee—"Fraud on the Power"

An appointment to a permissible appointee is ineffective to the extent that it was (i) conditioned on the appointee conferring a benefit on an impermissible appointee, (ii) subject to a charge in favor of an impermissible appointee, (iii) upon a trust for the benefit of an impermissible appointee, (iv) in consideration of a benefit conferred upon or promised to an impermissible appointee, (v) primarily for the benefit of the appointee's creditor, if that creditor is an impermissible appointee, or (vi) motivated in any other way to be for the benefit of an impermissible appointee.

Comment:

a. *Rationale.* If, in making an appointment to a permissible appointee, the donee's purpose was to circumvent the donee's scope of authority by benefiting an impermissible appointee (a nonobject), the donee has acted impermissibly. Therefore, to the extent that the appointment to the permissible appointee is induced by such a purpose, the appointment is ineffective.

Comments *b* through *f* cover the situations that most commonly arise and the devices that are most commonly employed to commit fraud on the power. Any appointment whose essential purpose is to benefit an impermissible appointee is to that extent ineffective even though these particular devices are not used; and Comment *g* so provides.

b. *Appointment to permissible appointee conditioned on permissible appointee conferring benefit on impermissible appointee.* If the instrument of appointment provides that the appointment to a permissible appointee is conditioned on the appointee conferring a benefit on an impermissible appointee, there is no doubt about the donee's motive. The only question is whether any part of the appointment is free from the improper motive.

Illustrations:

3. Donor died, leaving a will that devised property to Trustee in trust. Trustee is directed to pay the income to Donee (Donor's wife) for life, then to distribute the trust property "to such of our children as Donee shall appoint by will, and in default of appointment to our children equally." Donor and Donee have two children, John and Mary. Donee remarries and has a child by her second husband. Donee's will appoints the trust property to her daughter Mary upon condition that she will transfer one-third of the trust property forthwith to Donee's child by her second marriage; and if Mary does not perform the condition, the trust property shall pass to Donee's son John. It is to be inferred from these facts that the share of the trust property that Donee intends Mary to keep is offered to her only as an inducement to comply with the condition. The appointment to Mary is ineffective, and the trust property passes in default of appointment to John and Mary in equal shares. The alternative outright appointment to John cannot stand as it is motivated by the purpose to induce Mary to comply with the condition that would benefit an impermissible appointee.

4. Same facts as Illustration 3, except that Donee's will appoints one-third of the trust property to her son John and two-thirds of the trust property to her daughter Mary on condition that Mary give one-half of what she receives to W's child by her second marriage. It is to be inferred that the appointment to Donee was motivated by the desire to benefit Donee's child by her second marriage only to the extent of one-half of the appointment to Mary. Consequently, the appointment to John of one-third of the trust property is effective and the appointment to Mary of one-half of two-thirds (or one-third) of the trust property is effective and ineffective as to one-third of the trust property, which one-third passes in default of appointment to John and Mary in equal shares. In this case, the end result is the same if the entire appointment is ineffective and the entire trust property passes to John and Mary under the gift in default of appointment. A difference in the final result would obtain if the taker in default of appointment included a person in addition to John and Mary, such as a third child of Donor and Donee.

c. *Appointment to permissible appointee subjected to a charge in favor of impermissible appointee.* If the instrument of appointment imposes a charge on the appointive assets in favor of an impermissible appointee, there is no doubt about the donee's purpose. The only question is whether any part of the appointment is not infected by the improper motive and can stand. The charge is unenforceable in any event.

Illustrations:

5. Donor died, leaving a will that devised Blackacre to Donee (Donor's daughter) for life, with remainder "to such of Donee's children as Donee shall appoint by will, and in default of appointment to Donee's children as tenants in common." Donee has three children. Donee by will appoints Blackacre to one of her children, charged with the payment of an annuity of $10,000 to Donee's husband, H. The net annual income from Blackacre is $20,000. There are no facts tending to show that Donee would have preferred one of her children over the other two for any reason other than that of having the annuity paid. The appointment is ineffective, and Blackacre passes in default of appointment to Donee's three children as tenants in common.

6. Same facts as Illustration 5, except that the child to whom Donee appointed Blackacre subject to the charge depended on Donee for support. Thus, it is to be inferred that Donee's improper motivation related to only the property funding the annuity, or one-half of the appointment. A one-half interest in Blackacre passes to the dependent child under the appointment, and the other one-half passes to the three children of Donee, including the dependent child, in default of appointment. Thus, the dependent child owns an undivided two-thirds interest in Blackacre, and each of the other two children owns an undivided one-sixth interest in Blackacre.

d. Appointment to permissible appointee in trust for the benefit of an impermissible appointee. If the instrument of appointment imposes a trust on the appointive assets for the benefit of an impermissible appointee with a permissible appointee as trustee, there is no doubt that the donee's motive is improper. The only question is whether any part of the appointment can be allowed to stand because not being infected by the improper motive. The terms of the trust in favor of the impermissible appointee are unenforceable in any event.

Illustration:

7. Donor died, leaving a will that devised property to Trustee in trust. Trustee is directed to pay income to Donee (Donor's son) for life, then as Donee shall appoint by will "to one or more of Donee's issue, and in default of appointment, the trust property shall be distributed to Donee's issue then living, such issue to take by representation." Donee has three children, and each child of Donee has two children (grandchildren of Donee). Donee by will appoints the trust property to Donee's oldest child, John, in trust with directions to pay one-half of the income to Donee's wife, W, for life and to pay the other one-half of the income to himself and on the death of Donee's wife, W, to distribute the trust property to Donee's issue then living by representation. It is to be inferred from these facts that the only reason Donee's oldest child is preferred over the other issue of Donee during the lifetime of Donee's wife, W, is for the purpose of benefiting W, an impermissible appointee. The beneficial interest under the trust in favor of W is invalid. The appointment in trust is ineffective. The three children of S will take the trust property in default of appointment.

e. Appointment to permissible appointee in consideration of benefit conferred upon or promised to impermissible appointee. An appointment to a permissible appointee in consideration of a benefit conferred upon or promised to an impermissible appointee is ineffective to the extent that it was motivated by the purpose to confer a benefit on the impermissible appointee. The rule applies whether the benefit that is conferred or promised came from the permissible appointee or from a third person, or whether the person upon whom the benefit is conferred or promised is the donee or some other impermissible appointee. The rule applies whether the benefit conferred or promised was the transfer of the property appointed, the transfer of other property, or the doing of an act unrelated to any property.

When the donee seeks to benefit an impermissible appointee through an appointment to a permissible appointee who promises to confer the desired benefit, the promise need not be expressed in the instrument of appointment, but may be oral or evidenced by a separate writing. Because validating the appointment will be to the advantage of the appointee, the parties to the agreement have an incentive to conceal the agreement. Such concealment may render proof of the exact terms of the promise, or the date upon which it was made, difficult or impossible. The agreement may be inferred from the appointment made, the circumstances of the donee at the time of the appointment, and the action of the appointee subsequent to the appointment.

If the appointment is ineffective because it was made in consideration of a benefit conferred upon or promised to an impermissible appointee, restitution of the consideration given for the appointment may be obtained if the person who furnished the consideration was ignorant of the wrongful character of the transaction but not if such person's conduct was knowingly wrongful.

The promise made to benefit an impermissible appointee given in consideration of an appointment cannot be enforced either by the donee or the impermissible appointee sought to be benefited.

Illustrations:

8. Donor died, leaving a will that devised property to Trustee in trust. Trustee is directed to pay the income to Donee (Donor's son) for life, with power in Donee to appoint the principal by deed or by will "to such one or more of Donee's issue as Donee shall determine, and in default of appointment the principal shall pass on Donee's death to Donee's issue then living, such issue to take by representation." Donee and his wife, W, have a son and daughter. Donee wants a divorce, and W agrees to proceed with the divorce if, and only if, Donee appoints the trust property to their daughter. Donee makes the appointment, and W obtains the divorce. The conclusion is justified that the appointment is ineffective, because the donee's purpose is to circumvent the donor's intention in limiting the appointment to specified permissible appointees.

10. Same facts as Illustration 8, except that no promise was made by Donee to W in regard to any appointment if she obtained a divorce, but Donee informed their daughter that Donee would appoint by will $50,000 out of the trust property to the daughter if the daughter would promise to turn over $25,000 of that amount to W. The daughter sent an electronic message to Donee in which she said that, if the appointment of the $50,000 was made, $25,000 of it would be turned over to W. W obtained a divorce from Donee. In his will, Donee appointed $50,000 to the daughter who made the promise, and she turned over $25,000 to W. In a prior will, which was revoked by the will that appointed $50,000 to the daughter, Donee had appointed $25,000 to the daughter and nothing to his son. Under these facts, it may be inferred that Donee would have preferred the daughter over his son to the extent of $25,000 even if the daughter had made no promise. The conclusion is justified that the appointment in Donee's will is effective to the extent of $25,000 and ineffective as to the balance.

f. Appointment primarily for the benefit of impermissible appointee-creditor of a permissible appointee. If the creditors of a permissible appointee are not permissible appointees of the power, an appointment to a permissible appointee to relieve the permissible appointee of outstanding debt benefits both the permissible appointee and the permissible appointee's impermissible appointee creditor. Such an appointment is ordinarily effective, because the appointment is primarily intended to be for the benefit of the permissible appointee. Nevertheless, circumstances can raise an inference that the appointment is primarily for the benefit of the permissible appointee's impermissible appointee-creditor. An inference of improper motive arises if the donee or some person with whose welfare the donee is concerned is the creditor of an appointee.

Illustration:

12. Donor died, leaving a will that devised property to Trustee in trust. Trustee is given discretion "to pay the income and principal, from time to time, to such one or more of Donor's issue living from time to time as Trustee in Trustee's uncontrolled discretion may determine until the death of Donor's last surviving child; on the death of Donor's last surviving child, the then remaining trust property shall be distributed to Donor's issue then living, such issue to take by representation, and if no issue of Donor is then living, the same shall be distributed to the X charity." Donor has four children, and each child has issue. A child of Donor tells the trustee he is heavily in debt; unless these debts are paid, the child will have to go into bankruptcy, and this will have adverse long-range consequences to the child's business opportunities. Neither Trustee nor anyone Trustee is concerned about is a creditor of the child. Trustee distributes trust property to the child in the exact amount of the child's outstanding debts, and the child uses the distribution to pay the debts. The conclusion is justified that Trustee was not motivated, to any extent, in exercising the power in favor of the child by the purpose of benefiting the child's creditors. The appointment is effective so far as the rule of this section is concerned.

g. Other circumstances in which donee's motivation was to benefit impermissible appointee. Situations in which a donee may desire to use property covered by a power to confer benefits upon impermissible appointees and the methods for doing so are numerous. Comments *b* through *f* cover the situations most commonly arising and the devices most commonly employed. Any appointment whose essential purpose is to benefit an impermissible appointee is, to that extent, ineffective even though these common devices are not used.

Fulfillment of the intent of the donor that property be devoted exclusively to the benefit of permissible appointees requires that an appointment is ineffective so far as it is motivated by the purpose of benefiting an impermissible appointee. That policy does not require the entire appointment to be invalidated in all cases. Circumstances may indicate that the desire to benefit impermissible appointees was the predominant motive for the appointment, that such desire affected only the amount of the appointment, or that such desire had no substantial effect. Ineffectiveness ensues only so far as necessary to overcome the impropriety of motive.

Whenever an appointment is made to a permissible appointee, the appointee is free to use the appointed property as he or she wishes. The appointee is under no constraint to limit his or her uses of the appointed property for his or her exclusive benefit or for the benefit of other permissible appointees. The appointee can and may be likely to give, devise, or use the appointed property to or for the benefit of impermissible appointees, including his or her spouse, children, other family members, or favorite charities, even if they are not permissible appointees of the power. It can be expected that the donee understands this, and views such uses as benefiting the appointee. It would be unreasonable to invalidate an appointment merely on that ground, even if the donee knows or expects that the appointee intends, for example, to use the appointed property to buy a new car or remodel a room that will be used and enjoyed by impermissible appointee members of the appointee's family. It is only when the evidence establishes that the donee's essential purpose was to confer direct benefits on impermissible appointees that the appointment fails under the rule of this Comment.

The function of the court in all these cases is the same: to examine the substance of the appointment (regardless of its form), in the light of the circumstances of its formulation, for the purpose of arriving at a conclusion as to what part of the appointment would have been made by the donee if there had been no desire on the donee's part to benefit the impermissible appointees. The fact that, in some cases, evidence sufficient to justify a segregation of part of the appointment may be lacking does not justify a failure to make such a segregation when the language and circumstances indicate that a portion of the appointment was not infected by the improper motive.

In cases covered by this Comment *g*, the ascertainment of the motive of the donee involves a subjective test. Hence, only factors known to the donee can be considered in determining whether the donee was motivated in making the appointment to a permissible appointee to confer a benefit on an impermissible appointee.

In the typical situation in which the rule stated in this Comment is applicable, the donee appoints outright to a permissible appointee in the expectation that an impermissible appointee will indirectly receive the appointed property by descent . . ., gift . . ., or otherwise. The rule applies whether or not the appointee is aware of the donee's purpose to benefit the impermissible appointee.

The factor that vitiates appointments that fall within the rule stated in this section and especially in this Comment is the purpose of the donee, a subjective element. The circumstances of the appointment are relevant only as they are known to the donee and permit drawing inferences regarding the state of his or her mind. . . . .

h. Appointments to permissible appointees that are motivated by considerations other than the welfare of the permissible appointee. The rule of this section stops short of invalidating all appointments that are dictated by considerations other than the welfare of the permissible appointees of the power. If the donee is the parent of the permissible appointees of the power, the mere creation of the power does not manifest an intent of the donor that the donee shall exclude from consideration those sentiments of personal affection, gratitude, or displeasure upon which parents often determine the disposition of their own property. Provided there is no essential purpose to benefit an impermissible appointee, the donee may be guided by considerations not germane to the well-being of the permissible appointees. . . . .

i. Appointment to permissible appointee for purpose of benefiting another permissible appointee. The rule of this section applies only when the donee attempts to confer a benefit on an impermissible appointee. The rule of this section does not invalidate an appointment to a permissible appointee for the purpose of conferring a benefit on another permissible appointee. The donor of the power may, in the instrument creating the power, prohibit such an appointment.

j. Cross-references. The extent to which a fiduciary who carries out an appointment that is ineffective under the rule of this section may be liable is covered in § 19.17. The protection given to a bona fide purchaser of property received by a permissible appointee under an appointment that is ineffective under the rule of this section is considered in § 19.18.

§ 19.17. Liability of Fiduciary Who Transfers Property Pursuant to an Ineffective Appointment

(a) A fiduciary who transfers property pursuant to a direct appointment to an impermissible appointee commits a breach of trust.

(b) A fiduciary who transfers property pursuant to an appointment to a permissible appointee commits no breach of trust, unless the fiduciary knows or has reason to know that the appointment was in violation of the donee's scope of authority under § 19.16.

Comment:

a. Rationale. A fiduciary is required to exercise reasonable diligence in determining that the terms of a power of appointment have been complied with. Consequently, a fiduciary who transfers property pursuant to a direct appointment to an impermissible appointee that is ineffective because the appointment is in violation of § 19.15 commits a breach of trust.

A fiduciary who transfers property pursuant to an appointment to a permissible appointee that is ineffective because the appointment is in violation of § 19.16 commits no breach of trust, unless the fiduciary knows or has reason to know that the appointment was in violation of the donee's scope of authority. If the fiduciary is the donee of the power, the fiduciary knows what motivated the appointment and commits a breach of trust if the appointment is ineffective under § 19.16. If the fiduciary is not the donee, the fiduciary is chargeable with knowledge of the facts revealed by the appointing instrument in determining whether the fiduciary has committed a breach of trust in transferring property pursuant to the terms of the appointing instrument. Restatement Third, Trusts § 76, Comment *f*; Uniform Trust Code §§ 1006, 1007. . . . .

b. Remedies against fiduciary or appointee when fiduciary has transferred property pursuant to an ineffective appointment. If the fiduciary has not committed a breach of trust by transferring the trust property pursuant to the terms of the appointment, the person entitled to the appointive assets may recover those assets from the appointee if the appointment is ineffective under § 19.16. If the trustee committed a breach of trust in transferring the appointive assets pursuant to the terms of the appointment, the person entitled may recover from the trustee. If the fiduciary did not commit a breach of trust in transferring the appointive assets but learns subsequently that the appointment was ineffective under the rule stated in § 19.16, the fiduciary is obligated to notify the persons entitled to the appointive assets of their rights and to initiate action against the mistaken payee to recover the wrongfully dispensed assets. A fiduciary who is in doubt about whether a requested appointment is permissible may petition for instruction under Restatement Third, Trusts § 71.

§ 19.18. Purchaser for Value Without Notice

If an appointee of an ineffective appointment transfers the appointive assets to a purchaser for value, the purchaser is protected from liability, unless the purchaser knows or has reason to know that the appointment was in violation of the donee's scope of authority.

Comment:

a. *Rationale.* If an appointment is made to a permissible appointee that is ineffective under the rule in § 19.16, the title passes to the appointee subject to an equitable right to set aside the transfer. The equitable right to set aside the transfer, like other equitable interests, cannot be asserted against a bona fide purchaser. See Restatement Third, Trusts § 108; Restatement Second, Trusts § 285. . . . .

b. *Remedies when appointee has transferred to a bona fide purchaser.* When the appointee of an ineffective appointment has made a transfer to a bona fide purchaser, the person entitled to the appointive assets is entitled to recover from the appointee the consideration received for the property ineffectively appointed or the value of such property, whichever is greater. See Restatement Third, Trusts §§ 100, 108; Restatement Second, Trusts § 202.

Part E. Selective Allocation of Owned and Appointive Assets to Achieve Maximum Effectiveness of Donee's Intent

Introductory Note: Part E propounds rules of construction that deal with the allocation of appointive assets when a dispositive instrument serves the combined purpose of disposing of owned property and exercising a power of appointment. The rules of construction in Part E are based on the constructional preference for the construction that renders the document more effective than other plausible constructions (see § 11.3(c)(2)) and, in certain cases, on the constructional preference for favorable tax consequences (see § 11.3(c)(4)). Under these rules of construction, appointive property is, to the extent possible, allocated in a way that validates the exercise of the power of appointment and produces favorable tax consequences.

Selective allocation is restricted to cases in which the donee exercises a power of appointment and disposes of owned property in the same document. The document that usually does so is the donee's will, but might be a revocable trust created by the donee. The donee's will might appoint the appointive assets to the revocable trust. It is somewhat unusual, although possible, for a donee of a presently exercisable power to combine in one inter vivos instrument the exercise of the power and the transfer of owned property.

One situation that often calls for the selective allocation of owned and appointive assets is when the donee of a general testamentary power or a nongeneral power creates a trust that would run into perpetuity problems if appointive assets are allocated to the trust but would not do so if owned assets are allocated to the trust. See § 27.1, Comments *j*, *j(1)*, *j(2)*, and *j(3)*.

Another situation that can call for selective allocation is when the donee disposes of property to permissible and impermissible appointees; by allocating owned assets to the dispositions favoring impermissible appointees and allocating appointive assets to permissible appointees, the appointment is rendered effective.

The result of applying selective allocation is always one that the donee could have provided for in specific language, and one that the donee most probably would have provided for had he or she been aware of the difficulties inherent in the dispositive scheme. By these rules of selective allocation, the courts undertake to prevent the dispositive plan from being frustrated by the ineptness of the donee or the donee's counsel. The result desired by the donee is reached by a route which, though never actually contemplated, is nevertheless not excluded by the language used—a judicial approach adopted as early as Roe v. Tranmer, 2 Wils. 75, 95 Eng. Rep. 694 (C.P. 1757).

The process of selective allocation of owned and appointive assets is sometimes referred to as "marshalling." The term "marshalling" is not used in this Part to describe the process of allocation based on the assumed intent of the donee, because that term more commonly applies to situations in which the rights of two or more creditors of a common debtor are at issue. When one creditor is entitled to obtain satisfaction out of two funds and another creditor out of only one fund, a court applying equitable principles normally adjusts the matter so that the claim of the former creditor is satisfied so far as possible out of the fund to which the latter creditor does not have access. This process of "marshalling" as between creditors is an outgrowth of general equitable principles and differs from the rules stated in this Part, which are rules of construction.

§ 19.19. Allocation of Property Appointed in Document That Also Disposes of Owned Property

If the donee of a power of appointment exercises the power in a document that also disposes of owned property, the owned and appointive property are deemed to be allocated in the manner that best carries out the donee's intent.

Comment:

a. *Scope.* The rule of this section is commonly known as the doctrine of *selective allocation.* This section only applies if the donee uses the same document to exercise a power of appointment and to dispose of property that the donee owns. For purposes of this section, the donee's will, any codicils to the donee's will, and any revocable trust created by the donee that did not become irrevocable before the donee's death are treated as the same document.

The rule of this section does not interfere with the freedom of the fiduciary responsible for distributing owned and appointive assets to dispose of the different assets in the manner most appropriate in the light of all the circumstances in administering the estate. *Allocation,* as provided in this section, does not control *distribution.* Allocation simply means that the allocation is treated as if it were made as provided in this section for purposes of furthering the donee's intent.

This section applies to the exercise of both general and nongeneral powers. A principal difference between a general and a nongeneral power, however, is that a nongeneral power has permissible and impermissible appointees. Consequently, in the case of a nongeneral power, selective allocation cannot be used to deem the use of appointive property for the payment of the donee's creditors, the death taxes that arise as a result of the donee's death, or the expenses of administering the donee's estate.

b. *Historical note.* The doctrine of selective allocation has traditionally been limited to cases in which the donee not only used the same document to exercise a power of appointment and to dispose of owned property, but also "blended the owned and appointive assets in a common disposition" (see § 19.2, Comment *e*). The previous Restatements of Property adhered to this limitation. See Restatement Second, Property (Donative Transfers) § 22.1; Restatement of Property § 363. Under the previous view, the doctrine did not apply if the donee exercised the power in a nonblending specific-exercise clause or a nonblending blanket-exercise clause (see § 19.2, Comments *c* and *d*). The donee's use of a nonblending specific-exercise clause or a nonblending blanket-exercise clause was thought to require that the appointive assets be allocated to the disposition contained in the clause.

This section departs from the traditional doctrine and from the previous Restatements by providing for selective allocation even though the donee has not blended owned and appointive assets in a common disposition. The use of a blending clause is more the product of the forms used by the donee's lawyer than of any deliberate decision by the donee to facilitate selective allocation to save the donee's appointment if it turns out to be ineffective. As noted in § 19.2, Comment *e*, and except as provided in Comments *c* and *d*, this Restatement seeks to eliminate any significance heretofore attached to the use of a blending clause.

c. Presumptive allocation if owned and appointive property not blended. If the donee of a general power of appointment exercised the power in a document that also disposed of owned property, and if the power was exercised in a manner that did not blend the owned and appointive property, the owned property is presumptively allocated to the dispositions of owned property and the appointive property is allocated to the appointees. The owned and appointive property are so allocated, because ordinarily such allocation best carries out the donee's intent. If, however, such allocation results in defeating the donee's intent, and if a different allocation would carry out the donee's intent, the presumption is rebutted, and the property is allocated in the manner that best carries out the donee's intent. See Comment *e*.

d. Presumptive allocation if owned and appointive property blended. If the donee of a general power of appointment exercised the power in a document that also disposed of owned property, and if the power was exercised in a manner that blended the owned and appointive property, the owned and appointive property is presumptively allocated ratably to the various interests, including claims of creditors, taxes, and expenses of administration. The owned and appointive property is so allocated, because ordinarily such allocation best carries out the donee's intent. If, for example, the donee, in the same document, transferred owned property worth $60,000 and appointed appointive property worth $40,000 to A, B, and C, the allocation is treated as if each recipient received owned and appointive property in the proportion of six to four. If, however, such allocation results in defeating the donee's intent for some reason, and if a different allocation would carry out the donee's intent, the presumption is rebutted and the property is allocated in the manner that best carries out the donee's intent. See Comment *e*.

Under ratable allocation, a ratable share of each owned and appointive asset need not actually be distributed to the various interests, including claims of creditors, taxes, and administration expenses. Ratable allocation simply means that the allocation is treated as if it were made ratably for purposes of furthering the donee's intent.

e. Selective allocation. The presumptive allocation described in Comments *c* and *d* controls, unless that allocation defeats the donee's intent, and a different allocation would preserve the donee's intent. In that case, the presumptive allocation yields to the allocation that best carries out the donee's intent. See § 11.3(c)(2).

Under selective allocation, a selective share of each owned and appointive asset need not actually be distributed to the various interests, including claims of creditors, taxes, and administration expenses. Selective allocation simply means that the allocation is treated as if it were made selectively for purposes of furthering the donee's intent.

f. Timing of selective allocation. A selective allocation of owned and appointive assets is deemed to be made whenever it becomes apparent that selective rather than ratable allocation will result in increased effectiveness of the donee's dispositions. A decision to apply selective allocation will never make improper something that the personal representative or other fiduciary may have previously done. Selective allocation can only produce a deemed result that will improve the effectiveness of the donee's dispositions.

g. General testamentary powers and nongeneral powers—selective allocation in perpetuity cases. Division VIII of this Restatement adopts a new version of the Rule Against Perpetuities (the Restatement Rule). With certain qualifications and exceptions, the Rule—as promulgated in Division VIII—limits dead-hand control to two generations younger than the transferor. By contrast, the traditional version of the Rule (the traditional Rule) limited dead-hand control to lives in being at the creation of the interest plus 21 years.

Under either the Restatement Rule or the traditional Rule, the benefit of applying selective allocation only arises in the case of the exercise of a general testamentary power or a nongeneral power. Selective allocation operates similarly under both versions. The main difference is the terminology. Under the Restatement Rule, the key question is who is the transferor. Under the traditional Rule, the key question is when was the interest created. In the case of the exercise of a general testamentary power or a nongeneral power, the transferor is the donor of the power, not the donee (see § 27.1, Comments *d(1)* and *j*), and the time of creation is when the power was created, not when the power was exercised. The theory is relation back: The exercise of a general testamentary power or a nongeneral power relates back to the donor's document. See § 17.4, Comments *f(2)* and *f(3)*. In the case of a disposition of the donee's own property, however, the owner is the transferor and the interest is created when the owner created it. Consequently, a perpetuity problem can sometimes be avoided by allocating the donee's own property to a trust rather than allocating appointive property to the trust.

Illustration:

1. Donor died, leaving a will that devised property worth $100,000 to Trustee in trust. Trustee is directed to pay the net income to Donee (Donor's son) for life, and then "to pay the principal to such persons as Donee shall by will appoint; in default of appointment, to pay the principal by representation to Donee's issue then living, and if no issue of Donee is then living, to pay the principal to the X charity." Donee dies. At Donee's death, the property over which he has the general power is worth $200,000, and his owned property is worth $800,000. Donee's will provides as follows: "I hereby devise, bequeath, and appoint all property I own or over which I have any power of appointment to Trustee in trust to pay the net income to my granddaughter Ann for life and then to pay the principal by representation to Ann's issue who survive her, and if no issue of Ann survives her, to pay the principal to the X charity." Ann is more than two generations younger than Donor but is not more than two generations younger than Donee. Ann was not yet born when Donor died. Consequently, a perpetuity problem arises under either the Restatement Rule or the traditional Rule if appointive assets are allocated to the trust. Donee's debts plus the death taxes payable on

Donee's death plus the expenses of administering Donee's estate total $200,000. Under the rule of this section, the $200,000 of appointive assets are deemed to be used to pay debts, taxes, and expenses of administration. Only assets owned by Donee at his death will go into the trust for Ann and her issue, thereby increasing the effectiveness of the dispositions under Donee's will by eliminating any possibility of a perpetuity problem. This allocation is deemed without regard to what assets are in fact used to pay debts, taxes, and administration expenses.

h. Selective allocation in previous estate in perpetuity cases. Suppose that the donee of a general testamentary power dies leaving a will that disposes of owned and appointive assets and creates a general testamentary power or a nongeneral power in a second donee over these assets. Or, suppose that the donee of a nongeneral power dies leaving a will that disposes of owned and appointive assets and creates a general testamentary power or a nongeneral power in a second donee over these assets.

In determining the validity of the interests created by the second donee's exercise of the second power, the owned assets and appointive assets are treated differently for perpetuity purposes.

Regarding the first donee's own assets, the first donee is the transferor for purposes of the Restatement Rule. For purposes of the traditional Rule, the exercise of the second power relates back to the creation of the second power (the first donee's death).

Regarding the appointive assets, the donor is the transferor for purposes of the Restatement Rule. For purposes of the traditional Rule, the exercise of the second power relates back to the creation of the first power.

Under the rule of this section, the selective allocation of the appointive assets in the first donee's estate to reduce or eliminate the amount of those assets to which the second power applies is called for because such an allocation increases the probability that the second power will be effectively exercised. . . . .

i. Nongeneral powers—selective allocation to avoid appointment to impermissible appointees. As noted in Comment *a*, a principal difference between a general and a nongeneral power is that a nongeneral power has permissible and impermissible appointees. In rare cases, a general power also has impermissible appointees—when the power only authorizes the donee to appoint to the donee's creditors. See § 19.13(b).

An appointment to impermissible appointees is ineffective (see Part D of this Chapter). Hence, when owned and appointive assets are disposed of and appointed in the same document, some of the various interests may be in favor of permissible appointees and some in favor of impermissible appointees. The rule of this section requires selective allocation in this situation to the extent greater effectiveness is thereby achieved.

i(1). Allocation of owned assets to impermissible appointees. In the case of a nongeneral power, selective allocation cannot be used to deem the use of appointive property for the payment of the donee's creditors, the death taxes that arise as a result of the donee's death, and the expenses of administering the donee's estate. However, selective allocation of owned assets to such payments may increase the effectiveness of the donee's dispositions over that which would result if the appointive property were allocated ratably to the various interests. . . . .

i(2). Allocation of appointed assets to permissible appointees. Just as owned property can be allocated to impermissible appointees, the rule of this section contemplates that appointed assets can be selectively allocated to permissible appointees. . . . .

j. Selective allocation when appointive property is effectively appointed without allocation. If the combined disposition of owned and appointive assets in a residuary clause is fully effective, but the owned assets of the donee are not sufficient to pay in full a general devise, the allocation of appointive assets to the payment of the general devise will deprive the residuary beneficiaries of an amount that would otherwise pass to them. In such a situation, there may or may not be a basis for assuming an intent of the donee to prefer the general devisee rather than the residuary devisee in the disposition of appointive assets. A significant factor in determining the donee's intent is the past relationship of the donee to the general devisee and the residuary devisee. . . . .

k. Disposing of owned and appointive assets in a nonresiduary clause. Suppose that the donee's will contains a nonresiduary clause that disposes of owned and appointive assets as a single fund to various purposes. In such a case, it is assumed that the donee intends the two types of property to be so allocated as to give maximum effect to all the dispositions of that fund; but it is also assumed, from the fact that the donee did not dispose of the appointive assets with owned assets in the residuary clause or other dispositive clauses of the will, that the donee did not intend the appointive assets to be subject to the claims of general devisees and to the payment of debts, taxes, and expenses of administering the donee's estate. If selective allocation of appointive property within the single fund does not increase the total effectiveness of the dispositions of the single fund, it is assumed that the donee intended owned and appointive assets to be allocated to the various dispositions of the single fund ratably. . . . .

l. Disposing of owned and appointive assets in inter vivos document—presently exercisable general power. If the donee of a presently exercisable general power transfers owned and appointive assets by an inter vivos transfer in a single document, no violation of the common-law Rule Against Perpetuities will occur with respect to the appointive assets that would not likewise occur with respect to the owned assets. Hence, no allocation will increase the validity of the different dispositions under the common-law Rule.

m. Disposing of owned and appointive assets in inter vivos document—presently exercisable nongeneral power. When the donee of a presently exercisable nongeneral power transfers owned and appointive assets by an inter vivos transfer in a single document, a violation of the common-law Rule Against Perpetuities might occur with respect to the appointive assets, and not occur with respect to owned assets, because the validity of interests created by the inter vivos exercise of the nongeneral power is measured by lives in being when the nongeneral power was created. Selective allocation of owned and appointive assets should be applied if doing so increases the effectiveness of the donees' dispositions.

Part F. Consequences of Ineffective or Partially Ineffective Appointments

Introductory Note: Part F addresses the consequences of an ineffective or a partially ineffective exercise of a general or a nongeneral power of appointment. In the case of a partially ineffective appointment, the question addressed in § 19.20 is whether the effective part of the appointment stands or is also rendered ineffective.

Section 19.21 deals with a question that is raised only with respect to an ineffective or a partially ineffective exercise of a general power—whether the ineffective part of the appointment is captured for the donee's estate under the so-called capture doctrine.

§ 19.20. Effect of Partially Ineffective Appointment on Otherwise Effective Portion of Appointment

If part of an appointment is ineffective and another part, if standing alone, would be effective, the effective part is given effect, except to the extent that the donee's scheme of disposition is more closely approximated by concluding that some or all of the otherwise effective part should be treated as ineffective.

Comment:

a. Rationale. The rule of this section is an application of the general principle that partial ineffectiveness of a disposition can distort the transferor's scheme of disposition so significantly that it would better carry out the transferor's intent if otherwise effective parts are rendered ineffective. This principle is sometimes known as the doctrine of infectious invalidity.

Whether the ineffective part of an appointment renders otherwise effective parts ineffective depends upon whether the donee's general dispositive scheme is more nearly approximated by treating as effective some or all of the remaining parts or by allowing some or all of the remaining parts to pass to those persons who would receive it if no appointment had been attempted. On the disposition of unappointed property, see Part G (§§ 19.22, 19.23).

b. Ineffective and effective parts. The ineffective and effective parts of an appointment are easily identifiable in the following cases: the appointment divides the appointive property into present and future interests, and the present interest is ineffective because in favor of an impermissible appointee, but the remainder interest is not ineffective because in favor of permissible appointees; the appointment creates fractional interests in the appointive property, with the appointment being ineffective regarding some of the fractional interests and effective regarding others; the appointment is partly in favor of a deceased appointee.

The only issue in these cases is whether the general scheme that the donee undertook to carry out is more nearly approximated if some or all of the effective appointments also fail under the doctrine of infectious invalidity.

Illustrations:

1. Donor died, leaving a will that devised a fund to Trustee in trust. Trustee is directed "to pay the income to Donee (Donor's daughter) for life and then to dispose of the principal in trust or otherwise for Donee's issue as Donee shall by will appoint, and in default of appointment, Trustee shall pay the principal to Donee's issue who survive Donee, such issue to take by representation, and if no issue of Donee survives Donee, Trustee shall pay the principal to the X charity." Donee dies, leaving a will that directs that the appointive assets remain in trust for the lifetime of her husband H, the trust income to be paid "to H for his life, and on H's death, the trust principal shall be paid to Donee's issue then living, such issue to take by representation." Because H is an impermissible appointee of the power, the appointment to him

is ineffective. The appointment of the principal to Donee's issue living on the death of H is effective. The income of the trust during the lifetime of H will be paid to the takers in default of appointment. On H's death, the principal will be paid to Donee's issue then living. Donee's general scheme is not more closely approximated by defeating the effective part of the appointment.

2. Same facts as Illustration 1, except that Donee's will appoints one-third of the appointive assets to her husband H, one-third to her daughter D1, and one-third to her daughter D2. Donee has one son in addition to her two daughters. The appointment of one-third to H is ineffective, because he is an impermissible appointee of the power. Donee's general scheme appears to be to prefer her daughters over her son so far as the appointive assets are concerned. If the appointments to her daughters stand, the ineffective appointment of one-third will pass under the default clause to Donee's issue, including her daughters and son, but the preference for her daughters will still be carried out. Hence, the ineffectiveness of the appointment of one-third of the appointive assets does not upset the effective appointment of two-thirds.

c. *Perpetuity violations.* In states following the common-law Rule Against Perpetuities, an appointment is partly ineffective if the remainder interest but not the present interest violates the common-law Rule. Perpetuity violations do not arise, however, in states that have reformed the common-law Rule by adopting the wait-and-see-plus-deferred-modification version, because in those states the remainder interest would not be invalid but would be modified to make it valid. The Rule as adopted in this Restatement also adopts wait-and-see-plus-deferred-modification and also switches from time of vesting to time of termination. See § 27.1. For application of the Restatement Rule to the exercise of a power of appointment, see § 27.1, Comments *j*, *j(1)*, *j(2)*, and *j(3)*.

Illustration:

5. Same facts as Illustration 2, except the appointment of one-third is to Donee's only son S for life (rather than to H) with remainder to S's issue who survive him. S was not yet born when Donor died. Donee's general scheme appears to be to have her three children, D1, D2, and S, and their respective families, share equally in the appointive assets. Because the remainder interest in S's issue who survive him may not vest within a life in being plus 21 years, the remainder interest in S's issue is invalid under the common-law Rule. Donee's general scheme will be better carried out by holding the entire appointment ineffective, so that one-third will pass to each child of S under the gift-in-default clause.

d. *Identifying ineffective and effective parts depends on subsequent developments.* In some cases, identifying ineffective and effective parts of an appointment may depend on facts that can occur well into the future. The delay may be so great that the donee's scheme of disposition will be more closely approximated by rendering the whole appointment ineffective.

Illustrations:

6. Donor died, leaving a will that devised a fund to Trustee in trust. Trustee is directed to pay the income to Donee (Donor's son) for life and then "to dispose of the principal in trust or otherwise for Donee's issue as Donee shall by will appoint, and in default of appointment to pay the principal to Donee's issue who survive Donee on a

representational basis," with provision for the disposition of the principal if no issue of Donee survives Donee. Donee by his will directs Trustee to pay the death taxes that arise on Donee's death and the debts and expenses of administration of Donee's estate, and to hold the balance in trust during the life of his son S1, and "to expend the income and principal for the benefit of S1, and S1's issue as Trustee in Trustee's uncontrolled discretion may determine, and on the death of S1, to pay the then remaining trust property to S1's issue then living, such issue to take by representation." S1 was alive when Donor died. S1 and S1's daughter D survived Donee; they are the takers in default. Since the payment of death taxes that arise on Donee's death and the payment of debts and expenses of administration of Donee's estate would be payments to impermissible appointees, that part of the appointment is ineffective. The portion of the appointive assets that is ineffectively appointed will not be known until the death taxes on Donee's estate, Donee's debts, and the expenses of administering Donee's estate are known. If the circumstances are such that these facts will be known within a reasonable time, the effective part of the appointment will stand. If the nature of Donee's estate is such that the facts very likely will not be known for a long period of time, the court may provide S1 with immediately usable property, by allowing all the appointive assets to pass in default of appointment to S1 and D.

7. Same facts as Illustration 6, except the direction given to Trustee regarding the payment of death taxes and debts and administration expenses is deleted, but the discretion given to Trustee regarding the payment of income and principal is "for the benefit of S1, S1's wife Mary, and S1's issue." S1's wife Mary is an impermissible appointee of Donee's nongeneral power and no payment could be made to her by Trustee in the exercise of Trustee's discretion. In this situation, the entire appointment by Donee must fail or the entire appointment must be allowed to stand, with S1's wife deleted as a beneficiary. If S1's wife Mary had predeceased Donee, the appointment would be treated as though she had not been named as a member of the group to whom Trustee in Trustee's discretion could have paid income and principal. The exclusion of S1's wife from the group of beneficiaries to whom discretionary payments may be made as though she predeceased Donee will closely effectuate Donee's scheme. The end result is that there is no ineffective part of the appointment.

e. Ascertaining the general scheme of the donee. In ascertaining the donee's general scheme of disposition, the normal evidentiary rules apply, as set forth in Division IV (Chapters 10, 11, and 12). A gift-in-default clause that provides that the takers in default take "in default of appointment" or take "to the extent the appointive assets are not effectively appointed" is of no evidentiary value in ascertaining whether the general scheme of the donee is more closely approximated by defeating all or some part of an otherwise effective appointment.

f. Excessive appointment. If the donee has a power to appoint a particular property or a particular sum of money, and appoints a larger interest, the appointment is effective with respect to the property covered by the power but ineffective with respect to the excessive portion of the appointment.

§ 19.21. Disposition of Ineffectively Appointed Power Under General Power

(a) To the extent that the donee of a general power makes an ineffective appointment, the gift-in-default clause controls the disposition of the ineffectively appointed property to the extent that the gift-in-default clause is effective.

(b) To the extent that the donor did not provide for takers in default or the gift-in-default clause is ineffective, the ineffectively appointed property passes to the donee or to the donee's estate rather than under a reversionary interest to the donor or to the donor's transferees or successors in interest.

Comment:

a. *Scope.* This section applies when the donee of a general power makes an ineffective appointment.

The black-letter rule of this section does not apply to a donee's ineffective appointment of a power of revocation, amendment, or withdrawal. That topic is covered in Comment *f*.

If the donee of a general power fails to exercise the power, completely releases the power, or expressly refrains from exercising the power, the disposition of the unappointed property is governed by § 19.22.

b. *Historical note—the "capture doctrine."* The rule of this section is a modern variation of the so-called capture doctrine adopted by a small body of earlier case law and followed in Restatement Second of Property (Donative Transfers) § 23.2. Under that doctrine, the ineffectively appointed property passed to the donee or the donee's estate, but only if the donee's ineffective appointment manifested an intent to assume control of the appointive property "for all purposes" and not merely for the limited purpose of giving effect to the attempted appointment. If the donee's ineffective appointment manifested such an intent, the donee's ineffective appointment was treated as an implied alternative appointment to the donee or the donee's estate, and thus took effect even if the donor provided for takers in default and one or more of the takers in default were otherwise entitled to take.

The capture doctrine was developed at a time when the donor's gift-in-default clause was considered an afterthought, inserted just in case the donee failed to exercise the power. Today, the donor's gift-in-default clause is typically well thought out, carefully drafted, and intended to take effect, unless circumstances change that would cause the donee to exercise the power. Consequently, if the donee exercises the power effectively, the donee's exercise divests the interest of the takers in default. But if the donee makes an ineffective appointment, the donee's intent regarding the disposition of the ineffectively appointed property is problematic.

Whether or not the donee's ineffective appointment manifested an intent to assume control of the appointive property "for all purposes" often depended on nothing more than whether the donee's ineffective appointment was contained in a blending clause (see § 19.2, Comment *e*). The use of a blending clause rather than a direct-exercise clause, however, is typically the product of the drafting attorney's forms rather than a deliberate choice of the donee.

The rule of this section alters the traditional capture doctrine in two ways: (1) the gift-in-default clause takes precedence over any implied alternative appointment to the donee or the donee's estate deduced from the use of a blending clause or otherwise; and (2) the ineffectively appointed property passes to the donee or the donee's estate only if there is no gift-in-default clause or the gift-in-default clause is ineffective. Nothing turns on whether the donee used a blending clause or somehow otherwise manifested an intent to assume control of the appointive property "for all purposes."

c. Construction of gift-in-default clause. To the extent that the donee of a general power to appoint a future interest makes an ineffective appointment, the ineffectively appointed property passes under the gift-in-default clause. The gift-in-default clause, such as one that provides "to the extent that the donee does not effectively exercise this power of appointment . . . ," is construed as providing "to the extent that the donee does not expressly exercise this power of appointment effectively, ..." So construed, the clause forecloses any argument that the donee's ineffective appointment has created an implied alternative appointment to the donee or the donee's estate that could divest the interest of the takers in default.

d. Absence of takers in default. To the extent that the donor did not provide for takers in default or the gift-in-default clause is ineffective, the donor's trust or other property arrangement was not well planned. A gift-in-default clause can be ineffective or partially ineffective for a variety of reasons. The clause might only cover part of the appointive property. The clause might be invalid because it violates some rule of law such as the common-law Rule Against Perpetuities in jurisdictions that still follow that rule, or it might be ineffective because it conditioned the interest of the takers in default on an uncertain event that did not happen, the most common of which is an unsatisfied condition of survival.

To the extent that the gift-in-default clause is ineffective, the donee's ineffective appointment is construed as creating an implied alternative appointment to the donee or the donee's estate. This is the construction regardless of whether the donee's appointment was made in a blending clause or somehow otherwise manifested an intent to assume control of the appointive property "for all purposes."

e. Ineffective exercise of general power. An ineffective exercise of a general power may result from a variety of causes. The appointment may violate the common-law Rule Against Perpetuities in jurisdictions that still follow that rule. The donee's attempted exercise may fail to comply with some formality and not be saved by the harmless-error rule. If the appointee predeceases the donee, the appointment may lapse. An appointment is effective, however, if, although an appointee predeceases the donee, the donee's instrument of appointment provides an alternative appointment or if an antilapse statute produces a substitute for the deceased appointee (see § 19.12). If an appointee disclaims the appointment, the result is the same as if the appointee had predeceased the donee.

Illustration:

1. Donor died, leaving a will that created two testamentary trusts—Trust A and Trust B. Trust A provided that the income was to go to Donee (Donor's wife) for life, remainder to such persons as Donee shall by will appoint; in default of appointment, the property of Trust A shall be added to Trust B. Donee died, leaving a will that purported to exercise her general testamentary power to Appointee. Appointee predeceased Donee, without leaving any descendants who survived Donee, making the antilapse statute inapplicable. Consequently, Donee's appointment is ineffective. Regardless of whether Donee's purported exercise of her general testamentary power was contained in

a blending clause, the principal of Trust A is added to Trust B, as provided in Donor's gift-in-default clause.

f. Consequence if donee makes an ineffective exercise of a power of revocation, amendment, or withdrawal. The black-letter rule of this section and Comments *a* through *e* do not apply to an ineffective exercise of a power of revocation, amendment, or withdrawal. To the extent that the donee of this type of general power makes an ineffective appointment, the ineffectively appointed property remains in the trust as originally written.

Part G. Disposition of Unappointed Property

Introductory Note: Part G addresses the disposition of appointive property when the donee allows a power to lapse. A power of appointment is personal to the donee. If the donee dies without exercising the power, the power lapses at the donee's death if it has not lapsed earlier. Upon the donee's death, an unexercised power is not and cannot be passed to the donee's successors in interest. When the donee of a power of appointment fails to exercise the power, completely releases the power, or expressly refrains from exercising the power, in whole or in part, the question is: what disposition is to be made of the unappointed appointive property?

Section 19.22 deals with the disposition of unappointed property when the donee had a general power. Section 19.23 deals with the disposition of unappointed property when the donee had a nongeneral power.

§ 19.22. Disposition of Unappointed Property Under Lapsed General Power

(a) To the extent that the donee of a general power fails to exercise the power, completely releases the power, or expressly refrains from exercising the power, the gift-in-default clause controls the disposition of the unappointed property to the extent that the gift-in-default clause is effective.

(b) To the extent that the donor did not provide for takers in default or the gift-in-default clause is ineffective, the unappointed property passes to the donee or to the donee's estate if the donee merely failed to exercise the power, but if the donee released the power or expressly refrained from exercising the power, the unappointed property passes under a reversionary interest to the donor or to the donor's transferees or successors in interest.

Comment:

a. Scope. Section 19.22 applies to a case in which the donee of a general power does not exercise the power.

The black-letter rule of this section does not apply to a donee's release or failure to exercise a power of revocation, amendment, or withdrawal. That topic is covered in Comment *f*.

b. Rationale. To the extent that the donee of a general power fails to exercise the power, completely releases the power, or expressly refrains from exercising the power, thus causing the power to lapse, the gift-in-default clause controls the disposition of the unappointed property, to the extent that the gift-in-default clause is effective. A gift-in-default clause creates an interest in favor of the takers in default. If the gift-in-default clause is in the form of a class gift, the class gift is construed in accordance with Division V (Chapters 13, 14, 15, and 16).

To the extent that the donor did not provide for takers in default or the gift-in-default clause is ineffective (see Comment *d*), the disposition of the unappointed property depends on whether the donee merely failed to exercise the power or whether the donee released the power or expressly refrained from exercising it by, for example, using a nonexercise clause such as described in § 19.2, Comment *f*. If the donee merely failed to exercise the power, the unappointed property passes to the donee or to the donee's estate. The rationale is the same as when the donee makes an ineffective appointment. See § 19.21, Comment *d*. If, however, the donee released the power (see § 20.1) or expressly refrained from exercising it, the donee has affirmatively chosen to reject the opportunity to gain ownership of the property, and the unappointed property passes under a reversionary interest to the donor or to the donor's transferees or successors in interest.

Illustration:

1. Donor by deed transfers property to Trustee in trust, directing Trustee to pay the income to Donee (Donor's son) for life, with a general testamentary power in Donee to appoint the principal of the trust, and "in default of appointment, to Donee's descendants who survive Donee, such descendants to take by representation, and if no descendant of Donee survives Donee, to X charity." Donee dies, leaving a will that does not exercise the power. Donee was survived by three of his four children; one of Donee's children died without issue two years before Donee's death. The principal of the trust passes under the gift-in-default clause to Donee's three children who survived Donee.

c. *Time when power lapses.* The time when a power lapses is almost invariably at the death of the donee. See Illustration 1. In rare cases, a power lapses during the donee's lifetime. If the donee has a general power to appoint the future interest following an income interest or a life estate that terminates during the donee's lifetime (for example, if the income interest or life estate were held by someone other than the donee), the donee's power lapses upon the termination of the income interest or life estate. The power also lapses during the donee's lifetime if the donee releases the power (§ 20.1). Incapacity of the donee does not cause the power to lapse (see § 19.8, Comment *b*).

d. *Absence of takers in default.* To the extent that the donor did not provide for takers in default or the gift-in-default clause is ineffective, the donor's trust or other property arrangement was not well planned. A gift-in-default clause can be ineffective or partially ineffective for a variety of reasons. The clause might only cover part of the appointive property. The clause might be invalid because it violates some rule of law such as the common-law Rule Against Perpetuities in jurisdictions that still follow that rule, or it might be ineffective because it conditioned the interest of the takers in default on an uncertain event that did not happen, the most common of which is an unsatisfied condition of survival.

Illustrations:

2. Same facts as Illustration 1, except that Donor's gift-in-default clause only covered half of the principal and Donee died intestate. Half of the principal passes under the gift-in-default clause to Donee's three surviving children. The gift-in-default clause is ineffective with respect to the other half. Because Donee died intestate, the other half of the principal of the trust passes to Donee's intestate heirs. If Donee had released the power or if Donee had died with a will that stated "I

intentionally do not exercise the power of appointment I have over the principal of the trust created by Donor," the other half of the principal of the trust would have passed to Donor's transferees or successors in interest.

3. Same facts as Illustration 1, except that Donee died without any surviving descendants. The principal of the trust passes under the gift-in-default clause to X charity.

4. Same facts as Illustration 3, except that Donor's gift-in-default clause did not contain the alternative gift in default to X charity. Donee died intestate. The principal of the trust passes to Donee's intestate heirs. If Donee had released the power or if Donee had died with a will that stated "I intentionally do not exercise the power of appointment I have over the principal of the trust created by Donor," the principal of the trust would have passed to Donor's transferees or successors in interest.

5. Donor died, leaving a will that devised property to Trustee in trust, directing Trustee to pay the income to Donee (Donor's daughter) for life, with a general testamentary power in Donee to appoint the principal of the trust, and "in default of appointment, the trust is to continue and Trustee is directed to pay the income to Donee's children who survive Donee for the life of the survivor, and upon the death of Donee's last surviving child, to pay the principal to Donee's then living descendants, such descendants to take by representation." Donee dies intestate. Applicable perpetuity law follows the common-law Rule Against Perpetuities. The remainder interest in favor of Donee's descendants who survive Donee's last surviving child violates the common-law Rule and is invalid. Consequently, the gift-in-default clause is ineffective to that extent. The invalid remainder interest passes to Donee's intestate heirs.

Because the donee died intestate in Illustrations 2, 4, and 5, the donee merely failed to exercise the power. Cases in which there is either no gift-in-default clause or the gift-in-default clause is ineffective and in which the donee has merely failed to exercise the power will be few, however. Moreover, if the donor did not require a specific reference in order to exercise the power, and if the donee had died with a will that did not expressly refrain from exercising the power and that contained a general residuary clause, the donee's general residuary clause would presumptively have exercised the power to the extent that the donor did not provide for takers in default or the gift-in-default clause is ineffective. See § 19.4.

e. Effect of partial exercise of general power by donee. If the donee of the general power effectively appoints some portion of the appointive property, the rule of this section applies to the unappointed portion of the appointive property.

Illustration:

6. Donor died, leaving a will that devised property to Trustee in trust. Trustee is directed to pay the income to Donee (Donor's wife) for life, and then to pay the principal to such person or persons, including Donee's estate, as Donee may by will appoint. Donee dies, leaving a will that appoints half of the trust property to her child by a previous marriage. The unappointed half of the trust property passes to Donee's estate. If, however, Donee's will had not only appointed half of the trust

property to her child by a previous marriage, but also had stated that she chose not to exercise her power over the other half, that other half would have passed to Donor's transferees or successors in interest.

f. Consequence if donee releases or fails to exercise power of revocation, amendment, or withdrawal. The black-letter rule of this section and Comments *a* through *e* do not apply to a release of or a failure to exercise a power of revocation, amendment, or withdrawal. If the donee releases or dies without exercising a power of revocation or amendment, the power to revoke expires and, unless someone else continues to have a power of revocation or amendment, the trust becomes irrevocable and unamendable at the donee's death. If the donee releases or dies without exercising a power to withdraw principal of a trust, the principal that the donee could have but did not withdraw remains part of the trust.

§ 19.23. Disposition of Unappointed Power Under Lapsed Nongeneral Power

(a) To the extent that the donee of a nongeneral power fails to exercise the power, completely releases the power, or expressly refrains from exercising the power, the gift-in-default clause controls the disposition of unappointed property to the extent that the gift-in-default clause is effective.

(b) To the extent that the donor did not provide for takers in default or the gift-in-default clause is ineffective, the unappointed property passes under an implied gift in default to the permissible appointees of the power (including those who are substituted for permissible appointees under an antilapse statute) living when the power lapses, if:

(1) the permissible appointees are a defined and limited class and

(2) the donor has not manifested an intent that the permissible appointees shall receive the appointive property only so far as the donee elects to appoint it to them.

(c) If subsection (b) is inapplicable, the unappointed property passes under a reversionary interest to the donor or to the donor's transferees or successors in interest.

Comment:

a. Rationale. To the extent that the donee of a nongeneral power fails to exercise the power, completely releases the power, or expressly refrains from exercising the power, thus causing the power to lapse, the gift-in-default clause controls the disposition of the unappointed property, to the extent that the gift-in-default clause is effective. A gift-in-default clause creates an interest in favor of the takers in default. If the gift-in-default clause is in the form of a class gift, the class gift is construed in accordance with Division V (Chapters 13, 14, 15, and 16).

To the extent that the donor did not provide for takers in default or the gift-in-default clause is ineffective (see § 19.22, Comment *d*), the unappointed property passes to the permissible appointees of the power (including those who are substituted for permissible appointees under an antilapse statute) living when the power lapses, if the permissible appointees are a defined and limited class and the donor has not manifested an intent that the permissible appointees shall receive the appointive property only so far as the donee elects to appoint it to them. This rule of construction is based on the assumption that the donor intends the permissible appointees of the power to have the benefit of the property. The donor focused on transmitting the appointive property to the permissible appointees through an appointment, but if the donee fails to carry out this particular method of transfer, the donor's underlying intent to pass the appointive property to the defined and limited class of permissible appointees should be carried out. Subsection (b)(1) effectuates the donor's underlying intent by implying a gift in default of appointment to the defined and limited class of permissible appointees who are living when power lapses. In regard to when the defined and limited class will include those who are substituted takers under an antilapse statute, see § 19.12.

No implied gift in default of appointment to the permissible appointees arises if the permissible appointees are identified in such broad and inclusive terms that they do not form a defined and limited class. In such case, the donor has no underlying intent to pass the appointive property to such permissible appointees.

If the donor manifests an intent that the defined and limited class of permissible appointees are to receive the appointive property only by appointment, the donor's manifestation of intent eliminates any implied gift in default to the permissible appointees.

b. Constructive-trust theory supporting the rule of subsection (b). The rule of subsection (b), under which the unappointed property passes under an implied gift in default to the defined and limited class of permissible appointees, has sometimes been explained on the ground that the donee holds the power "in trust" or that the power is a "mandatory" or "imperative" power. Under these characterizations, the donee's failure to appoint is treated as wrongful (i.e., a breach of trust), justifying the imposition of a constructive trust in favor of the permissible appointees.

c. When the permissible appointees are not a defined and limited class. The permissible appointees of a power are not a defined and limited class unless they are so described that they are members of an identifiable class of persons and are not so numerous as to be unmanageable as takers in default of an appointment.

Illustrations:

1. Donor died, leaving a will that devises property to Trustee in trust. Trustee is directed to pay the income to Donee (Donor's daughter) for life, and then to pay the principal "to such one or more persons, other than Donee, Donee's estate, Donee's creditors, and creditors of Donee's estate, as Donee may appoint by her will." Donor's will contains no gift-in-default clause. Donee dies without exercising her nongeneral power. The unappointed appointive property passes to Donor's successors in interest.

2. Same facts as Illustration 1, except that permissible appointees of Donee's power are defined as "such one or more persons as are friends of Donee." Donee's "friends" do not form an identifiable class. See Restatement Third, Trusts § 46, Comment *a*. Even though Donee could have made an effective appointment to persons she selected as her friends, Donee's failure to appoint results in the unappointed property passing to Donor's successors in interest.

d. Various terms of relationship used to describe permissible appointees of nongeneral power. Various terms of relationship, such as "children," "grandchildren," "issue," "descendants," "brothers," "sisters," "nephews," "nieces," "relatives," and "heirs" of a designated person may be used to describe the permissible appointees of a nongeneral power. These terms of relationship as construed in Division V (Chapters 13, 14, 15, and 16) describe a defined and limited class.

e. Permissible appointees of power living when power lapses; time of expiration of the power. The time when a power lapses is almost invariably at the death of the donee. In rare cases, the power lapses during the donee's lifetime; thus, if there is a power to appoint to the children of A at any time before the youngest reaches the age of 30, the power lapses when the youngest reaches 30 if the donee is then living. Incapacity of the donee does not cause the power to lapse (see § 19.8, Comment *b*).

If the nongeneral power lapses at the death of the donee, the implied gift in default of appointment is in favor of the permissible appointees who survive the donee of the power. The implied gift in default is limited to then living permissible appointees, because the donor's fundamental intention is to benefit those persons to whom the donee could have appointed when the power lapses. The donee could have appointed only to then living permissible appointees (see § 19.12). The permissible appointees of the power may include substituted takers under the applicable antilapse statute (see § 19.12).

If the nongeneral power lapses during the donee's lifetime, the implied gift in default is in favor of permissible appointees who are living when the power lapses.

f. Manifestation of intent that permissible appointees take only as appointees. The donor has the authority to prohibit an implied gift in default, by manifesting an intent that the permissible appointees shall only take by appointment. If the donor has indicated that the donee shall have discretion to determine, not only which members of the defined and limited class of permissible appointees shall receive the appointive property, but also whether any members of the class shall benefit, the donor has manifested an intent that the permissible appointees are to take only under an appointment.

Illustration:

3. Donor died, leaving a will that devised property to Trustee in trust. Trustee is directed to pay the income to Donor's brother Donee and then "if Donee desires that all or any portion of the trust property shall pass to his children, Trustee shall pay over all or such portion as Donee shall direct to such children of Donee as Donee shall by will appoint." Donor, by providing that the appointive property shall pass to Donee's children "if Donee desires that all or any portion of the trust property shall pass to his children," has manifested an intent that the permissible appointees of Donee's power shall receive the appointive property only by appointment. Hence, if Donee allows the power to lapse, the unappointed property passes to Donor's successors in interest.

g. Gift in default subject to conditions. If the donor expressly created a gift in default of appointment that is subject to conditions, and the conditions are unsatisfied when the power lapses, the permissible appointees of the implied gift in default may take possession of the unappointed property pending the performance of the conditions.

Illustration:

4. Donor died, leaving a will that devised property to Trustee in trust. Trustee is directed to pay the income to Donee (Donor's son) for life, and then to pay the principal "to such one or more of Donee's children as Donee by will appoints, and in default of appointment, to pay the principal to Donee's children who attain 21." Donee dies without exercising his nongeneral power. Donee is survived by three children, ages 14, 15, and 17. The beneficiaries of the express gift in default are entitled to take possession of the unappointed property because no child of Donee has attained 21, and it is possible that none ever will. Under the rule of subsection (b), there is an implied gift in default of appointment to Donee's three children, as they are the permissible appointees of the power living when the power lapsed. This implied gift is subject to divestment in favor of Donee's children who attain 21.

Part H. Effect of Appointment to Taker in Default

Introductory Note: Part H addresses the effect of an appointment to takers in default. An appointment to a taker in default raises two potential questions. The situation addressed in § 19.24 is what happens if the donee appoints part of the appointive assets to a taker in default, and leaves the other assets unappointed. Does the appointee share equally with the other takers in default with respect to so much of the appointive assets as pass in default of appointment?

Section 19.25 considers this question: if the appointment made by the donee is to all of the takers in default of appointment, do the takers in default take under the appointment or under the gift in default of appointment?

§ 19.24. Partial Appointment to Taker in Default—Disposition of Unappointed Property

If the donee of a power of appointment makes a valid partial appointment to a taker in default, the taker in default-appointee also takes his or her full share of any unappointed property as taker in default, unless the donor or the donee manifests a contrary intent.

Comment:

a. *Rationale.* If the donee of a power of appointment makes a valid partial appointment to a taker in default, the intent of the donor controls whether the taker can take both as taker in default and as appointee. In the absence of any indication of the donor's intent, it is assumed that the donor intends that the taker can take in both capacities. This rule presupposes that the donor contemplated that the taker in default who is an appointee could receive more of the appointive assets than a taker in default who is not an appointee. The donor can defeat this rule by manifesting a contrary intent, thereby restricting the donee's freedom to benefit an appointee who is also a taker in default in both capacities.

If the donor has not manifested a contrary intent, the donee is free to exercise the power in favor of a taker in default of appointment, assuming that the taker in default is a permissible appointee. Unless the donee manifests a contrary intent in the terms of the appointment, it is assumed that the donee does not intend to affect in any way the disposition of any unappointed property.

b. *Manifestation of contrary intent by the donor.* The donor has the authority to provide that an appointment by the donee to a taker in default eliminates the appointee as a taker in default with respect to all or some part of any unappointed property. The donor also has the authority to provide that the appointee is eliminated as a taker in default unless the appointee takes the value of the appointed property into account in determining the appointee's share as a taker in default. Such a provision is known as a "hotchpot clause" and the action of the appointee in electing to take the appointment into account is known as "bringing the appointee's share into hotchpot."

Illustrations:

1. Donor died, leaving a will that devised $100,000 to Trustee in trust. Trustee is directed to pay the income to Donee (Donor's wife) for life and then to pay the principal "to such person or persons, including Donee's estate, as Donee by will appoints, and in default of appointment, to pay the principal in equal shares to our children." Donor and Donee have three children, C1, C2, and C3. Donee dies, leaving a will that appoints half of the appointive property to C1, and makes no appointment of the other half. The mere fact that the gift-in-default clause provides that the takers in default of appointment are to take "in equal shares" does not justify the conclusion that Donor manifested an intent that an appointment to a taker in default of appointment is to be taken into account in a distribution of the unappointed property to the takers in default of appointment.

2. Same facts as Illustration 1, except that Donee's power of appointment is "to our children as Donee may by will appoint, and in default of appointment to our children in equal shares." The fact that Donee's power is a nongeneral power rather than a general power does not change the result reached in Illustration 1.

3. Same facts as Illustration 1, except that Donor's will contains the following additional clause: "No child of ours to whom an appointment is made by Donee shall share in any property that may pass in default of appointment, unless such child shall bring such child's appointed share into the fund of unappointed property to be distributed in default of appointment." C1 will not receive a share in default of appointment if she does not bring the appointed property into hotchpot. C1 is not likely to do so, because if she did she would receive only one-third of the appointive property. If the appointment by Donee to C1 had been of one-fourth of the appointive property, C1 would receive one-third of the appointive property by electing to bring the appointive property into hotchpot.

c. Manifestation of contrary intent by the donee. The donee has the authority to provide that the appointment to a taker in default is to be treated as an advancement to the appointee to be taken into account in the distribution of any unappointed property to the takers in default of appointment. Such a manifestation of intent by the donee is controlling unless it violates a restriction placed by the donor on the exercise of the power.

Illustration:

4. Donor died, leaving a will that devised $100,000 to Trustee in trust. Trustee is directed to pay the income to Donee (Donor's son) for life and then to pay the principal "to such one or more of Donee's issue as Donee by will appoints, and in default of appointment, to pay the principal to Donee's issue by representation." Donee has two children

and four grandchildren. Donee dies, leaving a will that appoints $25,000 to a grandchild and directs that this appointment be taken into account as an advancement to such grandchild in the distribution of unappointed property. The unappointed property passing in default of appointment would normally be divided equally between Donee's two children. The question is whether Donee's direction that the appointment be treated as an advancement requires that it be taken into account in determining the share of Donee's child who is the parent of the grandchild to whom the appointment is made. The conclusion is justified that it is to be taken into account, because otherwise the language used in the appointment to the grandchild would be meaningless.

d. Extent to which appointee who brings appointed property into hotchpot takes under the appointment. Usually it will make no difference whether the appointee who brings the appointed property into hotchpot takes in part under the appointment and in part under the gift in default of appointment. For situations in which it does make a difference, see § 19.25.

§ 19.25. Appointment to Taker in Default—Appointee Takes as Taker in Default Rather than as Appointee

To the extent that an appointee would have taken the appointed property as a taker in default of appointment had the appointment not been made, the appointee takes under the gift in default of appointment and not under the appointment.

Comment:

a. Rationale. Takers in default of appointment take future interests that may be defeated by an exercise of the power. To whatever extent the donee purports to appoint to a person an interest already held in default of appointment, the donee does not exercise the power to alter the donor's disposition, but merely declares an intention not to alter it. If, however, the total that the appointee would receive as appointee exceeds that which the appointee would receive as taker in default, the excess passes under the appointment.

Illustrations:

1. Donor died, leaving a will that devised property to Trustee in trust. Trustee is directed to pay the income to Donee (Donor's wife) for life, and then to pay the principal "to such person or persons, including Donee's estate, as Donee by will appoints, and in default of appointment, to pay the principal to Donor's son S." Donee dies, leaving a will whose residuary clause provides: "I give all the rest and residue of my estate, including any property over which I may have any power of appointment, to my son S." If Donee had not exercised her power of appointment, S would have received the appointive assets. S takes the appointive assets as the taker in default and not as the appointee.

2. Same facts as Illustration 1, except the gift in default is to Donor's children. Donor has three children, S, C2, and C3. If Donee had not exercised her power of appointment, S would have taken one-third of the appointive assets under the gift in default. S takes one-third of the appointive assets as taker in default and takes two-thirds of the appointive assets as appointee.

3. Same facts as Illustration 2, except that Donee's will appoints half of the appointive assets to S. The total amount passing to S will be

four-sixths of the appointive assets (one-half plus one-third of the one-half of unappointed property). S would have received two-sixths of the appointive assets if no appointment had been made. S takes two-sixths of the appointive assets as taker in default and two-sixths as appointee.

b. Appointment to takers in default that takes effect before the expiration of the power. A donee who has a presently exercisable power may make successive inter vivos appointments. At the time of the initial appointment to a taker in default, it cannot be known whether the total that the appointee will receive under successive appointments will exceed that which the appointee would receive as taker in default. In such case, the appointee will be deemed to take under the gift in default of appointment until the total of the successive appointments exceeds that which the appointee would be entitled as taker in default. The appointee takes any excess as appointee.

Illustration:

4. Donor died, leaving a will that devised property to Trustee in trust. Trustee is directed "to pay the trust property during Donee's lifetime to such one or more persons, including Donee, in such amount or amounts and from time to time, as Donee may appoint by deed; and on Donee's death, the then remaining trust property shall be paid to Donor's children in equal shares." Donee is Donor's widow. Donor and Donee have three children, C1, C2, and C3. Donee makes successive appointments to C1. Until the successive appointments to C1 exceed the one-third of the trust property that C1 would take if no appointments were made, C1 takes as taker in default. Any excess passes to C1 by appointment.

c. Appointment to taker in default of lesser interest than taker would take in default of appointment. The interest of a taker in default of appointment will usually be absolute ownership of all or a fractional share of the appointive assets. If the donee appoints a lesser estate to the taker in default than otherwise would pass to the taker, the appointee receives a different interest than the interest given by the donor in default of appointment. Hence the appointee's only basis of taking is under the appointment.

Illustration:

5. Donor died, leaving a will that devised property to Trustee in trust. Trustee is directed to pay the income to Donee (Donor's widow) for life, and then "to pay the principal to such one or more persons, including Donee's estate, as Donee by will appoints, and in default of appointment to pay the principal to Donor's children." Donor and Donee have three children, C1, C2, and C3. Donee dies, leaving a will that exercises her power of appointment by directing Trustee "to continue to hold the property in trust for C1's lifetime and to pay C1 during the continuance of the trust all of the trust income." The appointment in favor of C1 gives C1 a life-income interest. If Donee had made no appointment, C1 would have taken an absolute possessory interest in one-third of the trust property. As a result of the appointment, C1 has a life-income interest in all of the trust property and, under the rule of § 15.4, an unconditional remainder interest along with C2 and C3 in the trust property in default of appointment. All of C1's life-income interest passes to C1 under the appointment, even though in theory, C1's one-third interest in default of

appointment, if there had been no appointment, would have included within it the right to enjoy the income for life.

d. Legal consequences of appointee taking under appointment or under gift in default of appointment. Usually it makes no difference in legal consequences whether the appointee takes as appointee or as taker in default. The appointee takes the same total amount in either capacity. The principal difference arises in jurisdictions that follow the rule that the estate creditors of the donee of a general testamentary power that was conferred on the donee by another have no claim on the appointive property unless the donee has exercised the power. Although this Restatement does not follow that rule regarding creditor's rights (see § 22.3), some jurisdictions do.

For general powers of appointment created on or before October 21, 1942, the value of the appointive property is included in the donee's gross estate for federal estate-tax purposes only if the donee exercised the power. See I.R.C. § 2041(a)(1).

e. Election by appointee. Appointed property passes in default of appointment to the extent stated in this section without any election by the appointee. Nothing is changed by a formal election by the appointee to take the property in default of appointment. The appointee cannot, by election, cause the property to pass by appointment, rather than in default of appointment.

f. Several appointees, only some of whom are takers in default. The rule stated in this section may apply to one or more of several appointees although it does not apply to others.

Illustration:

6. Donor died, leaving a will that devised property to Trustee in trust. Trustee is directed to pay the income to Donee (Donor's wife) for life, and then Trustee is to pay the principal "to such one or more persons, including Donee's estate, as Donee by will appoints, and in default of appointment, to pay the principal to Donor's children." Donor and Donee have three children, C1, C2, and C3. Donee dies, leaving a will that appoints half of the appointive property to her brother and half to C1. If the appointment to C1 had not been made, C1 would have taken one-third of the one-half of the unappointed property. C1 takes one-third of one-half (one-sixth of the trust property) in default of appointment and takes two-sixths of the trust property under the appointment.

g. Types of interests in default of appointment. The rule stated in this section applies whether the interests of the takers in default are vested or contingent and whether such interests are created by an express gift, implied gift, or by way of reversion. The form of the gift in default of appointment is immaterial.

h. Transfer by taker in default. A person who is a taker in default of appointment has a transferable interest unless it is subject to a valid restraint on alienation (a spendthrift restraint, for example). If a taker in default validly transfers the interest to another, the transferee becomes a taker in default, and the rule of this section applies to an appointment to the transferee. It does not apply to an appointment to the transferor of the interest in default.

i. Indefeasibility of interest appointed to taker in default. When the donee appoints an interest to a taker in default, and, under the rule of this section, that interest passes to the appointee in default of appointment, and is not subject to divestment by an appointment, the appointment operates as a release of the power to defeat the appointed interest.

CHAPTER 20

RELEASE AND DISCLAIMER OF A POWER OF APPOINTMENT

Introductory Note: Chapter 20 addresses the validity of a release and of a disclaimer of a power of appointment. A complete release and a valid disclaimer assure that the power of appointment will never be exercised, but the difference is that a disclaimer operates as a nonacceptance, whereas a complete release causes a power that was not disclaimed to lapse. Because both a complete release and a disclaimer are irrevocable, they produce certainty that the appointive property will be distributed as unappointed property, as provided in Chapter 19, Part G (§§ 19.22, 19.23).

A partial release operates differently. A partial release does not cause the power to lapse, but alters the terms and nature of the power. A partial release can be used to convert a general power into a nongeneral power.

Chapter 20 develops the release and disclaimer of powers of appointment in four sections. Section 20.1 discusses the release of a general power, regardless of whether it is presently exercisable or not.

Section 20.2 considers the release of a nongeneral power, which can be a power whose permissible appointees are almost as inclusive as a general power or whose permissible appointees form a defined and limited class of persons. This section examines the releasability of a nongeneral power, whether it is presently exercisable or not, and whether it is a power that the donor has mandated shall be exercised.

Section 20.3 deals with the question of what constitutes a release of a power of appointment.

Section 20.4 deals with disclaimers. The law applicable to disclaimers is largely statutory.

§ 20.1. Release of General Power

The donee of a general power of appointment can release the power, in whole or in part, except to the extent that the donor effectively manifested an intent that the power not be releasable. A release is irrevocable unless the donee expressly reserves a power to revoke or amend the release.

Comment:

a. Rationale. The donee of a general power, regardless of whether the power is presently exercisable or testamentary, has the authority to release the power in whole or in part, in the absence of a valid restriction on release imposed by the donor.

The donee's authority to release a presently exercisable general power is easily justified, because the donee has the current authority to achieve the same result by exercising the power in favor of the persons who will take upon release.

The donee's authority to release a general testamentary power is more problematic, because the donee does not have the current authority to achieve the same result by exercising the power. Restatement Second of Property (Donative Transfers) justified the releasability of a general testamentary power on the ground that "no significant desires of the donor are defeated by allowing the release" "[i]n light of the wide-open discretion given the donee of the power to appoint by will in regard to the ultimate destination of the appointive assets." Id. § 14.1, Comment *a*.

b. Consequences of release. See § 19.22 for the consequences of the donee completely releasing a general power of appointment over a future interest. See § 19.22, Comment *f*, for the consequences of the donee releasing a power of revocation, amendment, or withdrawal.

c. Restraint on release; general power created by donee. If the donee created the general power, so that the donee is also the donor, the donor-donee cannot effectively impose a restraint on release. A self-imposed restraint on release resembles a self-imposed restraint on alienation, which is ineffective when the settlor of an inter vivos trust attempts to impose a spendthrift restraint on the settlor's beneficial interests in the trust. See Restatement Third, Trusts § 58.

d. Restraint on release; general power not created by donee. If the donee did not create the general power, so that the donee and donor are different persons, the donor can effectively impose a restraint on release, but the donor must affirmatively manifest an intent to impose such a restraint. . . . .

e. Partial release. The donee may release a general power of appointment in whole or in part. A partial release is a release that narrows the freedom of choice otherwise available to the donee but does not eliminate the donee's power of appointment. A partial release may relate either to the manner of exercising the power or to the persons in whose favor the power may be exercised. A partial release converts a general power into a nongeneral power if, after the release, an appointment cannot be made to the donee, the donee's creditors, the donee's estate, or to creditors of the donee's estate. Even if the power is not a general one after a partial release, the rule of this section continues to apply in determining the validity of a further release of the power. . . . .

f. Jointly held powers. If the exercise of a power of appointment requires the joint action of two or more persons, each donee has a power of appointment. Each donee has a general power of appointment if each of them (or their creditors, or their estates, or creditors of their estates) is a permissible appointee of the power. If only one (or the creditors, estate, or estate creditors of only one) is a permissible appointee of the power, that one has a general power and any other joint donee has a nongeneral power. The rule of this section applies to the release by the joint donee who holds the general power, and the rule of § 20.2 applies to the release of the nongeneral power by the other donee.

If one but not the other joint donee releases his or her power, the issue is whether the power survives in the hands of the nonreleasing joint donee. The inference is that the power does so survive, unless the continuation of the power in the hands of a nonreleasing donee is inconsistent with the donor's purpose in creating the joint power. . . . .

g. Lapse of power. If the donor provides that the power is to be exercised within a specified period of time or it will cease to exist, the donee's failure to exercise the power within the specified period of time causes the power to lapse. Allowing the power to lapse is the equivalent of the donee releasing the power.

h. Successive lapses of a series of powers. If the donor imposes a limit on the amount of the appointive property that can be appointed within each of successive periods of time, the donee is possessed of a series of separate powers, each one subject to lapsing to the extent that the specified amount is not appointed in each of the successive periods. If the amount that is not appointed in one period of time can be carried over and added to the amount that can be appointed in a succeeding period, the failure to appoint the full amount in any one period does not cause the lapse of any power. . . . .

i. Power subject to a standard. If an appointment to the donee can be made from time to time if a specified standard is met (such as when needed for the donee's support and maintenance), the donee has a general power that is presently exercisable only when the standard is met. The rule of this section applies in regard to the release of the power.

j. Release of after-acquired power. Section 19.6 provides that, unless the language or circumstances indicate that the donee had a different intention, a blanket-exercise clause extends to a power of appointment acquired by the donee after the donee executed the document that contains the blanket-exercise clause. The same rule applies to a specific-release or a blanket-release clause.

§ 20.2. Release of Nongeneral Power

The donee of a nongeneral power of appointment can release the power, in whole or in part, except to the extent that the donor effectively manifested an intent that the power not be releasable. A release is irrevocable unless the donee expressly reserved a power to revoke or amend the release.

Comment:

a. Rationale. The donee of a nongeneral power, regardless of whether the power is presently exercisable or testamentary, has the authority to release the power in whole or in part, in the absence of a valid restriction on release imposed by the donor.

The authority to release a presently exercisable nongeneral power is easily justified if the persons who would take the appointive property in case of lapse are permissible appointees of the nongeneral power, because the donee has the current authority to achieve the same result by exercising the power. If the persons who would take in case of lapse are impermissible appointees of the nongeneral power, the authority to release the power is more problematic. Restatement Second of Property (Donative Transfers) justified the releasability of a presently exercisable nongeneral power in the latter case on the ground that "the fact that the objects of the power are not takers in default of an exercise indicates they are not of primary concern to the donor." Id. § 14.2, Comment *a*.

The authority to release a nongeneral testamentary power is also problematic, because the donee does not have the current authority to achieve the same result by exercising the power. A nongeneral power cannot be exercised in favor of the estate of a deceased permissible appointee, unless the estate is also a permissible appointee of the power; but if a deceased permissible appointee had a vested interest as a taker in default, subject only to being defeated by the exercise of the power, a complete release of the power would cause the successor to the deceased permissible appointee's owned property to have an indefeasibly vested interest. The successor might be the deceased permissible appointee's estate or some individual who acquired the deceased permissible appointee's interest by sale, gift, judgment, or descent. Restatement Second of Property (Donative Transfers) justified the releasability of a nongeneral testamentary power on the ground that "no significant desires of the donor are defeated by allowing the release." Id. § 14.2, Comment *a*.

b. Restraint on release; nongeneral power created by donee. If the donee created the nongeneral power, so that the donee is also the donor, the donor-donee cannot effectively impose a restraint on release. A self-imposed restraint on release resembles a self-imposed restraint on alienation, which is unenforceable when the settlor of an inter vivos trust attempts to impose a spendthrift restraint on the settlor's beneficial interests in the trust. See Restatement Third, Trusts § 58.

c. Restraint on release; nongeneral power not created by donee. If the donee did not create the nongeneral power, so that the donee and donor are different persons, the donor can effectively impose a restraint on release, but the donor must affirmatively express an intent to impose such a restraint. . . . .

d. Partial release. The donee may release a releasable nongeneral power in whole or in part. A partial release is a release that narrows the area of choice otherwise available to the donee, but does not extinguish the power. The donee may make a partial release that relates to the manner of exercising the power, or relates to the persons in whose favor the power may be exercised, or relates to a portion of the appointive assets. . . . .

e. Change in circumstances that will cause nonreleasable power to be releasable. If a change in circumstances would produce undesirable and unanticipated consequences unless a nonreleasable power is released, the power becomes releasable. An example of a change in circumstances that would justify making a power releasable is a change in the tax laws that would subject the trust property to adverse tax consequences that could be avoided by the release of the power. See § 12.2; Restatement Third, Trusts § 66.

f. Jointly held powers. In regard to the release of a power of appointment that requires the joint action of two persons to exercise the power, see § 20.1, Comment *f*.

g. Release of after-acquired power. Section 19.6 provides that, unless the language or circumstances indicate that the donee had a different intention, a blanket-exercise clause extends to a power of appointment acquired by the donee after the donee executed the document that contains the blanket-exercise clause. The same rule applies to a specific-release or a blanket-release clause.

§ 20.3. Methods of Releasing a Releasable Power

The donee of a releasable power can release the power, in whole or in part, by:

(1) delivering a writing declaring the extent to which the power is released to a person who could be adversely affected by an exercise of the power;

(2) joining with some or all of the takers in default in making an otherwise effective transfer of an interest in the property that is subject to the power, in which case the power is released to the extent that a subsequent exercise of the power would defeat the interest transferred;

(3) contracting with a person who could be adversely affected by an exercise of the power not to exercise the power, in which case the power is released to the extent that a subsequent exercise of the power would violate the terms of the contract;

(4) communicating in any other appropriate manner an intent to release the power, in which case the power is released to the extent that a subsequent exercise of the power would be contrary to manifested intent; or

(5) utilizing any method authorized by the donor or by applicable statute.

Comment:

a. Paragraph (5)—method of release specified by donor of power or by applicable statute. If the donor of a power specifies a method of release of a releasable power that is different from those described in paragraphs (1), (2), (3), and (4), the donor's specification does not preclude using other methods of release described in these paragraphs, unless the donor clearly manifests an intention that the specified method of release is to be exclusive.

If an applicable statute provides a method of release, the statute is not construed to mean that the statutory method is the only permissible method of release, in the absence of express statutory language to this effect.

b. Paragraph (1)—delivery of writing. The donee of a power "delivers" a writing that releases the power, in whole or in part, by the same method of delivery that would make an instrument of transfer effective (see § 6.2, Comment *u*; § 6.3, Comment *d*).

Illustration:

1. Donor died, leaving a will that devised a tract of land to Donee (Donor's daughter) for life, with remainder to such persons as Donee by will appoints, and in default of appointment, remainder "to Donee's natural-born children." The remainder to Donee's natural-born children excludes adopted children. Donee, who is 50 years old, has three adult children. In order to make it possible for Donee and her three children to transfer the land in fee simple subject only to partial divestment by the birth of another child, Donee executes and delivers to her three children a writing that states that Donee releases her general testamentary power. Donee's power is released.

c. Paragraph (2)—"joining" with others in a transfer. The donee of a releasable power "joins" with some or all of the takers in default in a transfer of an interest in the property subject to the power whenever the conduct of the donee, in relation to the transfer, would mislead the transferee were the power to continue to be fully and freely exercisable. . . . .

d. Paragraph (3)—"contracting" not to appoint. If the donee of a releasable power enters into a valid and enforceable contract to appoint some or all of the appointive assets to a taker in default of the exercise of the power, the contract constitutes a release of the power. If the donee subsequently attempts to exercise the power, the purported exercise is ineffective to the extent necessary to enable the donee to fulfill the contractual obligation to the promisee. The extent to which a contract to appoint is valid is developed in Chapter 21.

If the donee of a releasable nongeneral power benefits from a contract not to exercise a power, the contract is not valid and enforceable and hence the power is not released (see §§ 19.15, 19.16 in regard to an appointment that is a fraud on the power). . . . .

e. Paragraph (4)—communicating in any other appropriate manner an intent to release the power. Paragraph (4) is illustrated by the following example:

Illustration:

7. Same facts as Illustration 1, except that Donee executes an instrument in which she states that she releases her power. Donee then files the instrument with land records relating to the area where the land is located. Although the takers in default do not discover the instrument until after Donee's death, Donee released her power upon recording the instrument. Any subsequent attempt by Donee to exercise her power by will would be ineffective.

§ 20.4. Disclaimer of Power by Donee

A person who would otherwise be a donee of a power of appointment can, by a disclaimer, avoid acquiring the power or any part of it.

Comment:

a. Rationale. A prospective donee of a power of appointment cannot be compelled to accept the power, just as the prospective donee of a gift cannot be compelled to accept the gift. See § 6.1, Comment *i*; Restatement Third, Trusts § 35.

b. What constitutes a disclaimer. A disclaimer is to be contrasted with a release of a power of appointment by the donee. A release occurs after the donee accepts the power. See §§ 20.1, 20.2. A disclaimer prevents acquisition of the power, and consequently the donee who has accepted the power can no longer disclaim. Under the Uniform Disclaimer of Property Interests Act (1999) (UDPIA), a disclaimer, in whole or part, of the future exercise of a power not held in a fiduciary capacity is not barred by its previous exercise unless the power is exercisable in favor of the disclaimant. See UDPIA § 13(d).

Disclaimer statutes frequently specify the time within which a disclaimer must be made. The Uniform Disclaimer of Property Interests Act (1999) (UDPIA) does not specify a time limit, but allows a disclaimer until a disclaimer is barred (see UDPIA § 13 . . .).

Disclaimer statutes customarily specify the methods for filing a disclaimer. Section 12 of the UDPIA provides that the statutory methods must be followed. In the absence of such a requirement, statutory formalities for making a disclaimer of a power are not construed as exclusive, and any manifestation of the donee's intention not to accept the power may also suffice.

c. Partial disclaimer. A partial disclaimer of a power of appointment leaves the donee possessed of the part of the power not disclaimed.

d. Disclaimer by donee's representative or agent. If the donee of a power is a minor, a mentally incapacitated person, or a deceased person, and thus does not have the legal capacity to decide whether to disclaim the power, the donee's authorized representative or the donee's agent acting under the authority of a durable power of attorney may disclaim on the donee's behalf. . . . .

e. Using a disclaimer to avoid adverse tax consequences. The donee of a power can in many instances avoid adverse tax consequences by filing a "qualified" disclaimer in accordance with the requirements of the Internal Revenue Code.

f. Disclaimer by permissible appointee, appointee, or taker in default. Just as a person who would otherwise be a donee of a power of appointment can avoid acquiring the power by filing a disclaimer, a person who otherwise would be a permissible appointee, appointee, or taker in default can avoid acquiring that status by filing a disclaimer. If the persons who would otherwise be permissible appointees of a power form a definite class, and if all of them are in existence and disclaim, the effect is to extinguish the power of appointment.

g. Disclaimer of after-acquired power. Section 19.6 provides that, unless the language or circumstances indicate that the donee had a different intention, a blanket-exercise clause extends to a power of appointment acquired by the donee after the donee executed the document that contains the blanket-exercise clause. The same rule applies to a specific-disclaimer or a blanket-disclaimer clause.

CHAPTER 21

CONTRACTS TO APPOINT

Introductory Note: Chapter 21 addresses the enforceability of a contract to appoint. A contract to exercise a power of appointment in a certain way in the future is enforceable if the donee has the authority currently to make the promised appointment. Section 21.1 addresses the enforceability of a contract to appoint a presently exercisable power. Section 21.2 addresses the enforceability of a contract to appoint a power that is not presently exercisable.

§ 21.1. Enforceability of Contract to Appoint a Presently Exercisable Power

(a) If the donee of a presently exercisable general power of appointment contracts to make an appointment, the contract is enforceable.

(b) If the donee of a presently exercisable nongeneral power of appointment contracts to make an appointment, the contract is enforceable, unless the contract or the promised appointment confers a benefit upon an impermissible appointee.

Comment:

a. *Rationale.* A contract to exercise a presently exercisable general power is enforceable, because the donee of such a power has the authority to make the promised appointment—whatever it is—currently.

A contract to exercise a presently exercisable nongeneral power is enforceable if the donee has the authority to make the promised appointment currently. The donee of a presently exercisable nongeneral power has the authority to exercise the power currently, but is limited in the permissible appointees. Consequently, the enforceability of a contract to exercise a presently exercisable nongeneral power depends on whether the contract confers a benefit upon a person who is not a permissible appointee. . . . .

b. *Presently exercisable.* A presently exercisable power is normally also exercisable by the donee's will. If the power is restricted to an exercise that takes effect in the donee's lifetime, a contract to appoint, if enforceable, is an act of the donee that takes effect in the donee's lifetime. Hence, the contract may be in the form of a promise to appoint by the donee's will, even though the power could not be exercised by the donee's will absent such contract.

c. *Remedies of the promisee when the donee is deceased at the time the contract to appoint is broken.* A contract to make a testamentary exercise of a presently exercisable power is breached at the time of the donee's death if the donee's will does not make the promised appointment. Any appointment made by the donee's will that is not in accord with the donee's obligation under the contract is ineffective, either on the ground that the power is not exercisable by will, or if exercisable by will, on the ground that the contract released the power except to the extent that an appointment is made pursuant to the contract.

The promisee may recover damages for the donee's failure to perform the contract to appoint, either from the donee's owned assets or from the appointive assets. The final result should be as near the result that would have been obtained if the donee had performed the contract, which means that the damages to the promisee are payable out of the appointive assets. If the donee's estate is initially forced to pay the damages, the donee's estate is entitled to reimbursement out of the appointive assets.

The promisee may desire to have the specific property that the promisee would have received if the donee had performed the contract. A will cannot be made for the donee that would exercise the power, but the takers in default of appointment who become entitled to the property as a result of the failure of the donee to exercise the power may be subjected to a contract-based decree of specific performance to transfer the property to the promisee.

The donee may be deceased when the contract to appoint is broken, even though the promise is to appoint other than by a will, for example, if the appointment under the contract is to be made by a deed on some specified future date, and the donee dies before that date .... Failure of the donee's executor to perform the contract causes it to be broken. The remedies available are the same as when the contract calls for an appointment by the donee's will; and in addition, a decree of specific performance may direct the donee's executor to exercise the power as required by the contract. ....

d. Remedies of the promisee when the donee is alive at the time the contract to appoint is broken. If the donee is alive when the contract to appoint is broken, the promisee may proceed directly against the donee for damages or specific performance. The damages recoverable, or specific performance when appropriate, eliminates the interest of the takers in default of appointment. The donee's owned assets are not available to satisfy a judgment for damages.

e. Contract to make partial appointment. A contract to appoint a specified part of the appointive assets has no effect on the part of the appointive assets not covered by the contract. Such a contract has the effect of a partial release of the power regarding the part of the appointive assets subject to the contract. If the promise is broken, any recovery by the promisee can be satisfied only out of the part of the appointive assets that are subject to the contract to appoint.

f. Contract or promised appointment that confers benefit on impermissible appointee. A contract to appoint relating to a power presently exercisable is unenforceable if the contract or the promised appointment confers a benefit on an impermissible appointee. If the power is a general power presently exercisable, it is not possible for the contract or the promised appointment to confer a benefit on an impermissible appointee. A general power presently exercisable that permits the donee to appoint to himself or herself, no matter whom the contract or the promised appointment benefits, is treated as though the donee appointed to himself or herself and then contracted to dispose of owned property.

If the presently exercisable power is a nongeneral power of appointment, the permissible appointees of the power may be so inclusive that only the donee of the power and the donee's creditors are impermissible appointees. When the permissible appointees of the power are a defined and limited class that does not include the donee, the impermissible appointees are very numerous. A contract confers a benefit on an impermissible appointee if the consideration given by the promisee for the contract inures to the benefit of an impermissible appointee. The promised appointment inures to the benefit of an impermissible appointee whenever the property appointed pursuant to the terms of the contract would be an appointment in fraud of the power (see §§ 19.15, 19.16). If the contract to appoint is unenforceable because the contract or the promised appointment confers a benefit on an impermissible appointee, the promisee nevertheless may obtain restitution of value given for the promise, if the promisee was ignorant of the defect in the transaction on account of mistake of fact or of law, but not if the promisee's conduct was consciously wrongful (see Restatement Third, Restitution and Unjust Enrichment §§ 9, 32, 34, and 34, Comments *e–f*).

g. *Contract not to appoint.* A contract not to appoint, if enforceable, assures that the appointive property will pass to takers in default. A contract to appoint to the takers in default, if enforceable, has the same effect as a contract not to appoint. In regard to such contracts, see § 20.3, Comment *d*.

§ 21.2. Enforceability of Contract to Appoint a Power Not Presently Exercisable

(a) Except as provided in subsection (b), a contract to exercise a power that is not presently exercisable is unenforceable. Though the promisee cannot obtain damages or the specific property if the promise is not performed, the promisee is entitled to restitution of value that the promisee gave in exchange for the promise.

(b) A contract to exercise a power that is not presently exercisable is enforceable if the donee was also the donor of the power and reserved the power in a revocable inter vivos trust.

Comment:

a. *Rationale.* Except in the case of a postponed power reserved by the donor in a revocable inter vivos trust, a contract to exercise a power of appointment that is not presently exercisable is unenforceable, because the donee of such a power does not have the authority to make a current appointment. If the donee was also the donor of the power and created the power in a revocable inter vivos trust, however, a contract to appoint is enforceable, because the donor-donee could have revoked the trust and recaptured ownership of the trust assets or could have amended the trust to change the power into one that is presently exercisable.

In all other cases, the donor of a power not presently exercisable has manifested an intent that the selection of the appointees and the determination of the interests they are to receive is to be made in the light of the circumstances that exist on the date that the power becomes exercisable. Were a contract to appoint to be enforceable, the donor's intent would be defeated.

If something of value moves from the promisee to the donee of the power in exchange for the donee's promise to appoint, and the donee or the donee's estate is not a permissible appointee of the power (the power is not a general power), the contract would be invalid on the independent ground that it confers a benefit on an impermissible appointee. In such a case, restitution of value is limited to the extent provided in § 21.1, Comment *f*. If, however, the value did not confer a benefit on an impermissible appointee, the restitution to the promisee of the value that the promisee gave for the unenforceable promise is necessary to prevent the unjust enrichment of the one who received such value. If the value is not measurable in dollars, no restitution is available . . . .

A release of a power not presently exercisable can achieve a result somewhat close to a contract to appoint. A release, however, operates negatively by eliminating possible appointees. A contract to appoint, if enforceable, operates affirmatively to select an appointee as well as to eliminate other possible appointees. . . . .

b. Promise not to revoke a will making an appointment. A promise not to revoke an existing will that makes an appointment to the promisee is unenforceable, unless the donee was also the donor of the power and reserved the power in a revocable inter vivos trust.

c. Performance of the promise. Although a contract to exercise a power not presently exercisable is unenforceable, the donee is free to make an appointment in performance of the contract, so long as the appointment does not confer a benefit on an impermissible appointee. The donee-promisor is not liable for damages if the promise is not performed and is not benefited by being relieved of liability if the promise is performed. If the donee received value for the promise, the received value may have to be restored if the promise is not performed. Performance of the contract relieves the donee of the obligation of making restitution if the donee is a permissible appointee of the power. If the donee is not a permissible appointee, performance of the contract does not relieve the donee of the obligation of making restitution, because otherwise performance of the contract would confer a benefit on an impermissible appointee.

d. Contract not to appoint. A contract not to exercise a power that is not presently exercisable, if enforceable, assures that the appointive property will pass to the takers in default of appointment. A contract to appoint to the takers in default, if enforceable, has the same effect as a contract not to appoint. In regard to such contracts, see § 20.3, Comment *d*.

CHAPTER 22

RIGHTS OF THE DONEE'S CREDITORS IN APPOINTIVE ASSETS

Introductory Note: Chapter 22 deals with situations in which the creditors of the donee, seeking to satisfy claims, undertake to reach appointive assets. Section 22.1 addresses creditors' rights regarding a nongeneral power. Sections 22.2 and 22.3 address creditors' rights regarding a general power.

§ 22.1. Creditors of the Donee—Nongeneral Power

Property subject to a nongeneral power of appointment is exempt from claims of the donee's creditors and from liability for expenses of administering the donee's estate.

Comment:

a. *Rationale.* Because a nongeneral power of appointment is not an ownership-equivalent power, the donee's creditors have no claim to the appointive assets, irrespective of whether or not the donee exercises the power. . . . .

b. *Fraudulent transfer.* If the donee formerly owned the appointive assets covered by a nongeneral power and transferred them in fraud of the donee's creditors, reserving the nongeneral power, the creditors can reach the appointive assets under the rules relating to fraudulent transfers. . . . .

c. *Gift in default of appointment to donee's estate.* If the gift in default of appointment is to the donee's estate, the donee's power, though in form a nongeneral power, is in substance a general power to appoint by will, and the rights of the donee's creditors are governed by § 22.2.

d. *Federal bankruptcy.* Section 541(b)(1) of the federal Bankruptcy Code of 1978 (11 U.S.C. § 541(b)(1)) provides that "Property of the estate does not include any power that the debtor may only exercise solely for the benefit of an entity other than the debtor." This provision excludes from the federal bankruptcy estate property subject to a nongeneral power of the donee-bankrupt.

§ 22.2. Creditors of the Donee—General Power Created by Donee

Property subject to a general power of appointment that was created by the donee is subject to the payment of the claims of the donee's creditors to the same extent that it would be subject to those claims if the property were owned by the donee.

Comment:

a. Rationale. If a person makes a transfer but retains a general power of appointment over the transferred property, public policy does not allow this formal change in the control of the transferred property to put the property beyond the reach of the donor-donee's creditors. The Restatement Third of Trusts adheres to the same position with respect to a revocable inter vivos trust. See Restatement Third, Trusts § 25, Comment *e*.

The general power created by the donee may be one presently exercisable or one not presently exercisable. The application of the rule of this section is not affected by the presence of a spendthrift provision, nor by whether the claim of the creditor arose before or after the transfer. . . . .

b. Relation to fraudulent transfer. The rule of this section presupposes that the transfer creating the power does not constitute a fraudulent transfer.

c. Effect of exercise of general power. An irrevocable exercise of the general power by the transferor-donee in the donee's lifetime in favor of someone other than the donee or the donee's estate eliminates the applicability of the rule of this section to the extent of the appointive assets appointed by the exercise of the power. The rules relating to fraudulent transfers, however, are applicable to the exercise of the power.

d. When donee treated as creating the general power. The rule of this section can apply even if the general power was not created in a transfer made by the donee. It is sufficient if the donee paid the purchase price for the transfer, or otherwise contributed the value represented by the transfer. . . . .

e. Effect of availability of owned property of donee. The rule of this section ordinarily applies without regard to any owned assets of the donee, except to the extent the donee establishes the order in which available assets are to be used to satisfy claims against the donee's estate. The donee's act of creating the general power justifies the inference that the donee intended the appointive assets to be used to satisfy claims against the donee's estate only after other available assets have been used, unless the donee manifested a contrary intention.

f. Procedure for subjecting appointive assets to payment of claims and administration expenses. A creditor or personal representative can usually take advantage of the rule stated in this section by filing a bill in equity against the parties interested in the appointive assets, to compel delivery to the creditor of so much of the appointive assets as are necessary to satisfy the claim. If the appointive assets are held under a trust, the trustee may be joined as garnishee in an action against the transferor-donee. Other methods of taking advantage of the rule of this section may be available under governing procedural and remedial law.

g. Federal bankruptcy. Section 541(b)(1) of the federal Bankruptcy Code of 1978 (11 U.S.C. § 541(b)(1)) provides that "Property of the estate does not include any power that the debtor may only exercise solely for the benefit of an entity other than the debtor." The bankruptcy estate includes general powers of the bankrupt that are presently exercisable because they inherently are exercisable for the benefit of the bankrupt. A general power not presently exercisable, such as a general testamentary power, is excluded from the bankruptcy estate under the quoted language because it is exercisable "solely for the benefit of an entity other than the debtor."

The effect of the inclusion in the bankruptcy estate of a power of the debtor gives the trustee in bankruptcy the ability to exercise the power for the benefit of the creditors of the bankrupt. It is immaterial that the instrument creating the general power presently exercisable provides that "no interest of any beneficiary, whether in principal or income shall be assignable or subject to the claims of creditors."

§ 22.3. Creditors of the Donee—General Power Created by Someone Other than the Donee

(a) To the extent that the property owned by the donee is insufficient to satisfy the claims of the donee's creditors, property subject to a presently exercisable general power of appointment that was created by someone other than the donee is subject to those claims to the same extent that it would be subject to those claims if the property were owned by the donee.

(b) Upon the death of the donee, to the extent that the donee's estate is insufficient to satisfy the claims of creditors of the donee's estate, property subject to a general power of appointment that was created by someone other than the donee and that was exercisable by the donee's will is subject to those claims and expenses to the same extent that it would be subject to those claims and expenses if the property had been owned by the donee.

Comment:

a. Rationale. A presently exercisable general power of appointment is an ownership-equivalent power. See § 17.4, Comment *f(1)*; accord Restatement Third, Trusts § 74, Comment *a*. As noted in the Restatement of Property: "The power to become the owner at will is in essence ownership. . . . The general power presently exercisable is the practical equivalent of ownership, since it gives to the donee the power to acquire ownership at any time by appointing to himself." 3 Restatement of Property, Introductory Note to Chapter 25 (Powers of Appointment) at pp. 1812–1813.

Consequently, property subject to a presently exercisable general power of appointment is subject to the claims of the donee's creditors, to the extent that the property owned by the donee is insufficient to satisfy those claims. Furthermore, upon the donee's death, property subject to a general power of appointment that was exercisable by the donee's will is subject to creditors' claims to the extent that the donee's estate is insufficient to satisfy the claims of creditors of the estate and the expenses of administration of the estate.

Whether the donee has or has not purported to exercise the power is immaterial.

b. Postponed general power. A general power of appointment is not subject to the rule of this section if it is a postponed power (see § 17.4(c)).

c. Historical note. The common-law rule was that the donee's creditors could not reach appointive assets covered by an unexercised general power of appointment if the power had been created by a person other than the donee. The thought was that until the donee exercised the power, the donee had not accepted sufficient control over the appointive assets to give the donee the equivalent of ownership of them.

Restatement Second of Property (Donative Transfers) still adhered to the common-law rule, but recognized that statutory law in a number of states had abrogated the common-law rule. The Restatement Second implemented the historical rule in three sections. Section 13.2 provided that "Appointive assets covered by an unexercised general power of appointment, created by a person other than the donee, can be subjected to payment of claims of creditors of the donee, or claims against the donee's estate, but only to the extent provided by statute." Section 13.4 provided that "Appointive assets covered by an exercised general power to appoint by will, created by a person other than the donee, can be subjected to the payment of claims against the donee's estate." Section 13.5 provided that "Appointive assets covered by an exercised general power to appoint by deed, created by a person other than the donee, can be subjected to the payment of the claims of creditors of the donee to whatever extent they could have been thus subjected, under the rules relating to fraudulent conveyances, if the appointive assets had been owned by the donee and transferred to the appointee."

The Restatement Third of Trusts has now diverged from the common-law rule. See Restatement Third, Trusts § 56, Comments *b* and *c*. The Restatement Third of Trusts represents the current position of the Institute, and is the rule adopted in this section, § 22.3.

d. Expressions of contrary intent by donor or donee. The rule stated in this section applies in spite of a contrary intent manifested by the donor or the donee or both. Thus, should the donor provide in the instrument creating the general power that the appointive assets shall in no circumstances be subjected to the claims of the donee's creditors, the creditors will nevertheless prevail. Likewise, should the donee provide in the instrument of appointment that the appointive assets shall not be subjected to the claims of the donee's creditors, the creditors will prevail.

e. Procedure for administration of appointive assets when general power exercised by will. When the donee exercises a general power by will, there is no reason for the appointive assets to be included in the donee's probate estate and administered by the donee's personal representative together with the donee's owned assets, except to the extent that the appointive assets are to be used to pay the donee's debts and other estate obligations. Thus, generally, the appointive assets will pass directly to the appointees, subject to being reached by the donee's personal representative to pay the donee's debts and other estate obligations.

f. Inter vivos appointment to a creditor in satisfaction of creditor's claim. If the donee of a general power makes an inter vivos appointment to a creditor in total or partial satisfaction of the creditor's claim, other creditors have no right to share in the appointive assets covered by the appointment, unless in bankruptcy proceedings the other creditors succeed in having the appointment avoided as a preference. Apart from bankruptcy proceedings, there is no objection to a living debtor preferring one creditor over another with regard to owned property; and the same is true with regard to appointive assets covered by the appointment.

g. Federal bankruptcy. See § 22.2, Comment *g*.

CHAPTER 23

ELECTIVE-SHARE RIGHTS OF THE DONEE'S SURVIVING SPOUSE IN APPOINTIVE ASSETS

Introductory Note: The elective share of the surviving spouse is a statutory provision common to most probate codes in non-community-property states. Elective-share statutes protect a decedent's surviving spouse against disinheritance. The subject is discussed comprehensively in Chapter 9. This chapter, Chapter 23, addresses a narrow question concerning the elective share: In what circumstances does the donee's surviving spouse have a right to take an elective share in appointive assets?

§ 23.1. Elective-Share Rights of the Donee's Surviving Spouse in Appointive Assets

For the purpose of determining the elective-share rights of the donee's surviving spouse, property is treated as owned by the donee at death to the extent that the property is subject to:

(1) a presently exercisable general power of appointment exercisable by the donee immediately before death; or

(2) a general testamentary power of appointment exercisable by the donee if the donee was also the donor of the power.

Comment:

a. *Presently exercisable general power*. Elective-share statutes based on the Uniform Probate Code expressly provide that property subject to a presently exercisable general power of appointment is subject to the elective share of the surviving spouse. See § 9.2, Comment *e*; UPC § 2–205.

Non-UPC elective-share statutes often provide only that the decedent's "estate" is subject to the surviving spouse's elective-share rights. With respect to such statutes, § 9.1(c) of this Restatement provides:

> In a state whose statute subjects the decedent's "estate" to the elective share, the elective share is applied to the value of the decedent's estate which, for purposes of calculating the elective share, includes . . . the value of property . . . owned in substance by the decedent immediately before death that passed outside of probate at the decedent's death to [persons] other than the surviving spouse. . . .

Section 9.1, Comment *j*, explains that property owned in substance includes property subject to a "power to revoke, withdraw, invade, or sever, or to appoint the decedent or the decedent's estate as beneficiary."

The rationale of §§ 9.1 and 23.1 is that a presently exercisable general power of appointment is an ownership-equivalent power. See § 17.4, Comment *f(1)*; Restatement Third, Trusts § 74, Comment *a*. As noted in the Restatement of Property: "The power to become the owner at will is in essence ownership. . . . The general power presently exercisable is the practical equivalent of ownership, since it gives to the donee the power to acquire ownership at any time by appointing to himself." 3 Restatement of Property, Introductory Note to Chapter 25 (Powers of Appointment) at pp. 1812–1813.

Consequently, property subject to a presently exercisable general power of appointment exercisable by the donee immediately before death comes within the rule of § 9.1 as property that is owned in substance by the donee-decedent immediately before death. Unless the donee-decedent exercises the power in favor of his or her surviving spouse, or unless the donee-decedent does not exercise the power and his or her surviving spouse is the taker in default, such property passes outside of probate at the donee-decedent's death to persons other than the surviving spouse and, under the rule of § 9.1, is subject to the surviving spouse's right of election.

b. *General testamentary power*. A general testamentary power is treated as an ownership-equivalent power for some but not all purposes. See § 17.4, Comment *f(3)*. For purposes of the elective share, a general testamentary power that was created by the donee instead of by another is treated as an ownership-equivalent power, because the appointive power is property that was once owned by the donee. The reservation of a general testamentary power over property once owned by the donee allows the donee to maintain control of the death-time disposition of that property.

Consequently, this Restatement continues the position of Restatement Second of Property (Donative Transfers) § 13.7, which treats a general testamentary power as an ownership-equivalent power for purposes of the elective share of the surviving spouse if the donee was also the donor of the power. . . . .

c. *Power created before or after marriage*. The application of the rule of this section does not depend on whether the power was created before or after the donee's marriage to the surviving spouse. This rule is based on an analogy to the elective-share treatment of property that is owned by the decedent at death. Property owned at death is subject to the spouse's elective-share rights, without distinction between property that the decedent acquired before or after marriage.

d. *Power created by donee or another*. Because a presently exercisable general power is an ownership-equivalent power, the application of the rule of this section does not depend on whether the power was created by the donee or by another. This rule is based on an analogy to the elective-share treatment of property that is owned by the decedent at death. Property owned at death is subject to the spouse's elective-share rights, without distinction between property the decedent acquired by gift from another or by other means. . . . .

e. *Nongeneral power*. Under § 9.1(c), the value of an irrevocable gift made by the decedent-spouse in anticipation of imminent death is subject to the elective share of the surviving spouse. Although property subject to a nongeneral power is not ordinarily subject to the elective share of the surviving spouse, a transfer by the decedent-spouse in anticipation of imminent death might create a nongeneral power, in which case property subject to a nongeneral power would be subject to the elective-share rights of the decedent-spouse's surviving spouse.

f. Power exercisable by the donee alone. Although this section is ordinarily limited to powers exercisable by the donee alone, a power that is exercisable by the donee in conjunction with another person or a power conferred on a nonadverse party could come under the rule of this section, if the evidence establishes that the donee created the power in this manner for the purpose of evading the elective-share rights of the surviving spouse.

DIVISION VII

PRESENT AND FUTURE INTERESTS

Scope of Division VII. Division VII addresses present and future interests. Chapters 24 and 25 deal with questions of classification. The system of classification developed over the centuries in English land law to serve a variety of purposes, originating in feudal, military, and fiscal arrangements that have long since become archaic.

Today, present and future interests are predominantly created as equitable interests in trust, not as legal interests in land. For modern purposes, the system of classification based on English land law is unnecessarily complex. As noted in a prominent treatise on the English law of real property: "English real property law has tended to have an unenviable reputation for its complexity." Much of the complexity serves no purpose in modern circumstances. England simplified its land law by legislation in 1925. This Restatement simplifies classification for American law. The principal function of classification today is descriptive—a short-hand way of labeling an interest that has specific characteristics. . . . .

Chapter 26 shifts to mandatory rules and rules of construction that apply to present and future interests. Chapter 26 is related to Division V on class gifts. Chapter 26 provides rules of construction that apply to present and future interests generally, including class gifts, but is not restricted to class gifts.

CHAPTER 24

PRESENT INTERESTS: CLASSIFICATION

Introductory Note: Chapter 24 identifies the different types of present interests (sometimes called possessory interests or estates) in property: the fee simple absolute or its personal-property counterpart, absolute ownership (sometimes called outright ownership); the fee simple defeasible; the life estate; the fee tail; and the term of years. Historically, the fee simple defeasible was divided into three subcategories: the fee simple determinable, the fee simple subject to a condition subsequent, and the fee simple subject to an executory limitation. Section 24.3 takes the position that perpetuating these subdivisions is no longer useful. Section 24.4 takes the position that the fee tail estate, with its convoluted subrules described in Restatement of Property §§ 59 through 106, has become archaic and is no longer recognized.

§ 24.1. Present Interest Defined

A present interest is an ownership interest in property that entitles the owner to possession or enjoyment of the property.

Comment:

a. Historical note; freehold and nonfreehold estates. Historically, the different categories of present interests were developed with respect to land, not personalty, and were called "estates." The estates in land were divided into "freehold estates" and "nonfreehold estates." The "freehold estates" were the fee simple absolute, the fee simple defeasible (the fee simple determinable, the fee simple subject to a condition subsequent, and the fee simple subject to an executory limitation), the fee tail, and the estate for life. The "nonfreehold estates" were the estate for years, the estate from period to period, the estate at will, and the estate at sufferance.

Because the term "freehold estate" was only significant in the feudal land system of England, the distinction between freehold and nonfreehold estates is archaic and not recognized in this Restatement.

b. Scope. This Restatement only deals with property interests that have importance in the law of wills and other donative transfers. These are the fee simple absolute, the fee simple defeasible, the life estate, and the term of years. The term of years is used in both the law of donative transfers and the commercial law of landlord and tenant. For coverage of the commercial use of the term of years and of the other varieties of the so-called nonfreehold estates, see Restatement Second, Property (Landlord and Tenant).

c. *Trusts.* If property is held in trust, the trustee has a nonbeneficial interest of unlimited duration in the trust property and not an interest limited to the duration of the trust, unless a different intention is manifested or the settlor owned only a lesser interest. See Restatement Third, Trusts § 42. The extent of the beneficial ownership interest of a trust beneficiary depends upon the intention manifested by the settlor, except as limited by law or public policy. See id. § 49. See also id. § 2, Comment *d;* § 3, Comments *c* and *d.*

d. *Possession or enjoyment.* The term "possession or enjoyment," which appears in the black letter of this section, is a term of art widely used in the law of estates and trusts and in the law of taxation. The owner of a fee simple absolute, a fee simple defeasible, a life estate, or a terms of years is entitled to possession. Enjoyment includes a right to have the income paid directly to or paid for the benefit of the beneficiary, such as discharging the beneficiary's legal obligations—paying the beneficiary's bills (mortgage, taxes, utilities, credit card, insurance, automobile, or other bills) or satisfying the beneficiary's legal obligations of support.

§ 24.2. Fee Simple Absolute; Absolute Ownership

The estate in "fee simple absolute" is the present interest in land that is unlimited in duration. "Absolute ownership" is the present interest in personal property that is unlimited in duration.

Comment:

a. *Historical note.* The terms "fee," "fee simple," and "fee simple absolute," like the terms "freehold" and "nonfreehold," were developed in the feudal land system of England. (The word "fee" derives from "fief," a feudal landholding.) These terms are not intuitively descriptive. The term "absolute ownership," applicable to personalty, would be more descriptive of the unlimited present interest in land. The civil-law systems use various terms for the unlimited present interest in land, such as "ownership," "absolute ownership," or "perfect ownership." Because the terms "fee," "fee simple," and "fee simple absolute" remain in common use in the legal profession, this Restatement continues these terms for unlimited present interests in land.

b. *No succeeding future interest.* Because the fee simple absolute (land) and absolute ownership (personal property) are present interests that are unlimited in duration, they are never followed by a future interest.

Illustration:

1. Grantor conveyed land by deed "to Grantee and his heirs." Grantee has a fee simple absolute. Grantee's fee simple absolute is not followed by a future interest. The words "and his heirs" are "words of limitation." Words of limitation are words that define the estate granted to Grantee, as opposed to "words of purchase," which would grant a property interest to Grantee's heirs.

c. *General words of inheritance not necessary.* Historically, the conveyance by deed of a fee simple absolute required that general words of inheritance ("and his [or her] heirs") be appended to the name of the grantee, as in Illustration 1. Without that language, the grantee received a life estate. A devise in a will, however, never required the appended language in order for the devisee to receive a fee simple absolute.

Today, in deeds as well as in wills, it is not necessary to add "and his [or her] heirs" to create a fee simple absolute. A conveyance in a deed to the grantee creates a fee simple absolute. To create a life estate, additional words such as "for life" are necessary. . . . .

§ 24.3. Fee Simple Defeasible

The estate in fee simple defeasible is a present interest that terminates upon the happening of a stated event that might or might not occur. The subcategories historically known as the fee simple determinable, the fee simple subject to a condition subsequent, and the fee simple subject to an executory limitation are no longer recognized but are absorbed under the term fee simple defeasible.

Comment:

a. Scope and rationale. Historically, the law recognized three defeasible fee simple estates: (1) the fee simple determinable; (2) the fee simple subject to a condition subsequent; and (3) the fee simple subject to an executory limitation. Continued differentiation among these subcategories is no longer useful, because the future interests formerly recognized as taking effect on the occurrence of the stated event are now the same. See § 25.2. Consequently, this Restatement recognizes only one defeasible fee simple estate. A defeasible fee simple terminates on the happening of a stated event that might or might not occur. The probability that the event will or will not occur is irrelevant. An estate that terminates on the happening of an event that must occur (e.g., the death of an individual or the expiration of a term certain) cannot be a fee estate. To be a fee estate, the estate must be potentially unlimited in duration, except as its duration is limited by the Rule Against Perpetuities. On the application of the Rule Against Perpetuities to a fee simple defeasible, see § 27.2, Comment *d*.

b. Historical note: fee simple determinable. Section 44 of the Restatement of Property defined the "fee simple determinable" as an estate that "is created by any limitation which, in an otherwise effective conveyance of land, (a) creates an estate in fee simple; and (b) provides that the estate shall automatically expire upon the occurrence of a stated event." A fee simple determinable could be followed by either a reversionary or a nonreversionary future interest. If the following future interest was a reversionary future interest, it was called a "possibility of reverter" (see Restatement of Property § 154, Comment *g*). If the following future interest was a nonreversionary future interest, it was called an "executory interest" (see Restatement of Property § 158).

c. Historical note: fee simple subject to a condition subsequent. Section 45 of the Restatement of Property defined the "fee simple subject to a condition subsequent" as an estate that "is created by any limitation which, in an otherwise effective conveyance of land, (a) creates an estate in fee simple; and (b) provides that upon the occurrence of a stated event the conveyor or his successor in interest shall have the power to terminate the estate so created." The future interest in the transferor that followed a fee simple subject to a condition subsequent was called a "power of termination" by the Restatement of Property § 155, but also went by a number of other names such as "right of entry," "right of reentry," or "right of entry for condition broken."

d. Historical note: fee simple subject to an executory limitation. Section 46 of the Restatement of Property defined the "fee simple subject to an executory limitation" as an estate that "exists when any limitation, in an otherwise effective conveyance of land, (a) creates an estate in fee simple in a conveyee, or leaves an estate in fee simple in the conveyor or his successor in interest; and (b) provides that the estate subject thereto, upon the occurrence of a stated event is to be divested, before the normal expiration thereof, in favor of another interest in a person other than the conveyor, or his successor in interest." The future interest in a person other than the conveyor was a nonreversionary future interest called an "executory interest" (see Restatement of Property § 158).

e. Historical note: language of "limitation" versus language of "condition." The language that characterized the fee simple determinable and the fee simple subject to an executory limitation was called "language of limitation"—language such as "during," "until," "while," "so long as," or "for so long as." The idea was that a fee simple determinable or a fee simple subject to an executory limitation terminated naturally, by its own terms, if and when the specified terminating event happened. The difference between the two estates depended on whether the future interest that followed it was retained by the transferor or conferred on a transferee. If the future interest was retained by the transferor, the future interest was a possibility of reverter and the fee was a fee simple determinable. If the future interest was conferred on a transferee, the future interest was an executory interest and the fee was a fee simple subject to an executory limitation.

The language that characterized the fee simple subject to a condition subsequent was called "language of condition" (also called "language of condition subsequent")—language such as "on condition that," "provided that," "but if," or "and if." The idea was that a fee simple subject to a condition subsequent terminated by being cut short or divested if and when the specified terminating event happened. The fee simple subject to a condition subsequent could be followed by either a power of termination (created in the transferor) or an executory interest (created in a transferee). If the fee simple subject to a condition subsequent was followed by a power of termination, the happening of the specified terminating event did not automatically divest the estate; rather, it empowered the grantor or his or her successor in interest to divest the estate by exercising the power of termination.

f. Simplified terminology adopted in this Restatement. Under the simplified terminology adopted in this Restatement, the estate in fee simple defeasible is a present interest that terminates upon the happening of a stated event that might or might not occur. The subcategories historically known as the fee simple determinable, the fee simple subject to a condition subsequent, and the fee simple subject to an executory limitation are no longer recognized but are absorbed under the term fee simple defeasible.

g. Illustrations. The following Illustrations develop the simplified terminology adopted in this Restatement and compare the resulting classification with the classification that would have been reached under the historical system.

Illustrations:

1. Grantor conveyed land "to Grantee School District so long as the land is used for school purposes; upon the land being used for non-school purposes, the land reverts to Grantor if Grantor is then living; if not, to Grantor's then living descendants by representation." Grantee has a fee simple defeasible, because Grantee's fee simple will terminate upon the happening of a stated event that might or might not occur (the land being used for non-school purposes). Grantor's descendants have a remainder. Regarding the application of the Rule Against Perpetuities

to this disposition, see § 27.2, Comment *d*. Historically, Grantee would have had a fee simple determinable.

3. Grantor conveyed land "to Grantee School District on condition that the land be used for school purposes, and if the land is ever used for non-school purposes, Grantor is to have the right to reenter and take possession." Grantee has a fee simple defeasible, because Grantee's fee simple will terminate upon the happening of a stated event that might or might not occur (the decision to retake possession if the land is ever used for non-school purposes). Regarding the application of the Rule Against Perpetuities to this disposition, see § 27.2, Comment *d*. Historically, Grantee would have had a fee simple subject to a condition subsequent.

4. Grantor conveyed land "to Grantee School District, but if the land is ever used for non-school purposes, the land goes to my brother B if B is then living, but if not, to B's then living descendants by representation." Grantee has a fee simple defeasible, because Grantee's fee simple will terminate upon the happening of a stated event that might or might not occur (the land being used for non-school purposes). Regarding the application of the Rule Against Perpetuities to this disposition, see § 27.2, Comment *d*. Historically, Grantee would have had a fee simple subject to an executory limitation.

§ 24.4. Fee Tail Estate Not Recognized

The fee tail estate is not recognized in American law. A disposition "to A and the heirs of A's body" or the like creates a fee simple absolute in A. A disposition "to A for life, then to the heirs of A's body" or the like creates a life estate in A followed by a future interest in fee simple absolute in A's issue who would take from A under the applicable statute of intestacy.

Comment:

a. *Historical note*. Historically, the fee tail estate was created by a disposition "in favor of a natural person as to whom the conveyance contains words of inheritance; and in specific words confines the succession to the issue of the first taker or to a designated class of such issue" or by a disposition that "contains a limitation of an estate for life; and contains a limitation of a remainder of potentially infinite duration in favor of either the issue of the person named as life tenant or a designated class of such issue. . . ." Restatement of Property §§ 59, 60 (internal subsection letters omitted). The fee tail estate terminated upon the death of the last living descendant of the tenant in tail. This event was known as an indefinite failure of issue, as distinguished from a definite failure of issue. An indefinite failure of issue occurs when the tenant's descending line dies out, whenever in the future that might occur. See § 26.8, Comment *a*; Restatement of Property § 61, Comment *e*. At its core, the fee tail estate provided for a continuum of successive life estates in the transferor's issue from time to time living forever.

b. *Scope*. The rule of this section declaring that the fee tail estate is not recognized as part of American law means that the fee tail estate, with all of its characteristics and subrules described in Restatement of Property §§ 59 to 106, is not created by a disposition "to A and the heirs of A's body," "to A for life, then to the heirs of A's body," or any other short-hand formulation such as "to A in fee tail."

A disposition "to A and the heirs of A's body" (or the like, such as "to A in fee tail") creates a fee simple absolute in A.

A disposition "to A for life, then to the heirs of A's body" (or the like, such as "to A for life, then in fee tail") creates a life estate in A, followed by a future interest in A's issue who would take from A under the applicable statute of intestacy. See §§ 14.3, Comment *e*; 14.4; 15.3. The future interest is construed as effecting the definite-failure-of-issue construction (see § 26.6, Comment *b*), as distinguished from the indefinite failure of issue characteristic of the fee tail estate as described in Comment *a*. A definite failure of issue occurs if, at the death of the life tenant, the life tenant then has no living issue, but if the life tenant then has living issue, they take in fee simple absolute, not for life followed by a continuum of successive life estates in their issue. Restatement of Property § 61, Comment *f*.

c. Creation of substantially equivalent estate; the perpetual or centuries-long trust. The rule of this section does not mean that a transfer cannot be made that would create a substantially equivalent estate. A disposition "to A for life, then to A's issue from time to time living forever" creates an estate that is, at its core, substantially equivalent to a fee tail estate. Such a disposition is valid except as curtailed by the Rule Against Perpetuities. Recent years have seen the creation of perpetual or centuries-long trusts in some states that have abolished or modified the Rule Against Perpetuities. See Introductory Note to Chapter 27. A perpetual or centuries-long trust has a strong similarity to the fee tail estate, and might be called an equitable fee tail. Such trusts typically provide that trust income, after the settlor's death, is to be paid, or in the discretion of the trustee is to be paid, to the settlor's issue living from time to time forever or for several hundred years, i.e., the equivalent or substantial equivalent of a continuum of successive life estates in income.

§ 24.5. Life Estate

The life estate is a present interest that terminates on the death of an individual whose life serves as the governing life. A life estate can be qualified by language specifying one or more events that can terminate the estate before or extend the estate beyond the death of the individual whose life serves as the governing life.

Comment:

a. Governing life. The governing life is the individual whose life governs the duration of the life estate. The grantor, the grantee, or a third person can serve as the governing life, or one of the governing lives, of an estate for life. The governing life must be a human life; the governing life cannot be the life of a corporation, an animal, or any other nonhuman entity. Unless the life estate is for the life of another or others (see Comments *c* and *d*), the governing life is that of the tenant in possession.

Historically, the life estate was treated as an estate subject to a "limitation." For a list of words that constitute language of "limitation," see § 24.3, Comment *e*. Thus, the italicized words in the following expressions were classified as language of limitation: "to A *for* life"; "to A *so long as* A lives"; "to A *until* A's death"; "to A *during* A's lifetime"; "to A to have and to hold *during* her natural life"; "to A for her use and benefit *during* her natural life"; "to A *during* his life and the life of his wife"; "to A *during* the lifetime of A"; "to A *until* she dies." See Restatement of Property § 16, Comment *b*; § 107, Comment *e*.

Illustration:

1. Grantor transferred land "to A for life." A has a life estate. A's life estate is sometimes called a legal life estate.

b. *Periodic income or other payments.* The life estate that is commonly created in a donative transfer is an income interest in a trust or a right to other payments for life. See § 15.1, Comment *p* (treating a class gift of income as a series of individual class gifts). The interest of a trust beneficiary who has the right to the income from a trust for his or her lifetime is sometimes called an "equitable life estate."

Illustration:

2. Grantor transferred property in trust, directing the trustee to pay the income "to A for life." A has an income interest for life. A's life estate is sometimes called an equitable life estate.

c. *Estate for life of another or others.* A life estate need not be governed by the life of the tenant in possession, but can be governed by the life of another or others. Historically, this type of estate was called a life estate *pur autre vie* or a life estate *d'autre vie.*

Illustrations:

3. Grantor transferred land "to A for the life of B." A's life estate is a life estate for the life of B. If A predeceases B, the remaining portion of the life estate passes through A's estate to A's successors in interest. After A's death, A's successors in interest have a life estate for the life of B. If B predeceases A, the life estate terminates on the death of B even though A is still alive.

4. Grantor transferred land "to A until the death of the last survivor among B, C, and D." A's life estate is a life estate for the life of B, C, and D.

5. Grantor transferred land "to A for life." A subsequently transferred her life estate to B. B has a life estate for the life of A.

d. *Two or more governing lives.* When two or more individuals are designated as the governing lives, the duration of the estate can be governed either by the life of the survivor or by the continuance of the joint lives. The governing lives may not be so numerous that it would be impractical to track them all.

Illustrations:

6. Grantor transferred land "to A for the lives of B and C and of the survivor of them." A receives an estate for life governed by the life of whoever as between B or C dies later.

8. Grantor transferred land "to A for the lives of all persons listed in the current edition of the city directory of X City." Because of the administrative difficulty and cost of tracing the lives of all listed persons, A receives a life estate governed by A's life only.

e. *Life estate qualified by language that might cause the life estate to terminate before the death of the individual who serves as the governing life.* A life estate can be qualified by language that specifies one or more events that might cause the life estate to terminate before the death of the individual who serves as the governing life. Such a life estate is called a defeasible life estate. Historically, depending on whether the stated event was described by language of limitation or condition (see § 24.3, Comment *e*), the estate was variously called a life estate subject to a "special limitation," "an executory limitation," or "a condition subsequent."

Illustrations:

9. Grantor transferred land "to A for life or until A remarries." Or, Grantor transferred land "to A during widowhood." Assuming the validity of the restriction (see Restatement Third, Trusts § 29, Comment *j*, and Illustration 1), A's life estate is called a defeasible life estate, because it is qualified by language that might cause it to terminate before the death of the governing life. Historically, such a life estate would have been called a "life estate subject to a special limitation" or a "determinable life estate."

10. Grantor transferred land "to A for life, then to B; but if A remarries, to B immediately." Assuming the validity of the restriction (see Illustration 9), A's life estate is called a defeasible life estate, because it is qualified by language that might cause it to terminate before the death of the governing life. Historically, such a life estate would have been called a "life estate subject to an executory limitation."

11. Grantor transferred land "to A for life on condition that A not remarry; and if A remarries, Grantor is to have the right to reenter and take possession." Assuming the validity of the restriction (see Illustration 9), A's life estate is called a defeasible life estate, because it is qualified by language that might cause it to terminate before the death of the governing life. Historically, such a life estate would have been called a "life estate subject to a condition subsequent."

f. *Life estate qualified by language that extends or might extend the life estate beyond the death of the individual who serves as the governing life.* A life estate can be qualified by language that specifies one or more events that causes or might cause the life estate to extend beyond the death of the individual who serves as the governing life. Such a life estate is called an extended life estate if the specified event causes the life estate to extend beyond the death of the individual who serves as the governing life, and is called an extendable life estate if the specified event might cause the life estate to extend beyond the death of the governing life. Historically, depending on whether the stated event was described by language of limitation or condition, such a life estate was variously called a life estate subject to a "special limitation," an "executory limitation," or a "condition subsequent."

Illustration:

13. Grantor transferred land "to A for life or for 10 years, whichever event (the death of A or the expiration of 10 years) occurs later." A's life estate is called an extendable life estate, because it is qualified by language that might cause it to extend beyond the death of the governing life.

g. *Successive life estates.* A disposition such as "to A for life, then to B for life" creates successive life estates, in which the right to possession automatically shifts to B upon A's death.

h. *Life estate coupled with power to dispose of larger estate.* A life estate is sometimes coupled with a power to sell or dispose of a larger estate or to consume the whole. Historically, such an estate would have been called a life estate coupled with a power to sell, consume, or dispose, but in function the estate is a life estate with a power of appointment in the life tenant (see § 18.1, Comment *c*).

Illustration:

15. Grantor transferred land "to A for life with full power to sell, consume, or dispose of the fee thereof at will." A's estate is a life estate coupled with a presently exercisable general power of appointment over the appointive property.

i. Combining life estates and terms. A life estate can be combined with a term of years (see § 24.6), such as in the disposition "to A for life, then to B for 10 years." Any such combination is permissible, such as "to A for life, then to B for 10 years, then to C for life, then to D for 15 years" or "to A for life, then to B for life, then to C for 10 years, then to D for 15 years."

j. Trusts for noncharitable purposes. This section restricts the life-estate label to an estate governed by the life of a human. That restriction is not inconsistent with the validity of a trust for noncharitable purposes in which the term of the trust is governed by the life of a nonhuman such as an animal. See Restatement Third, Trusts § 47.

§ 24.6. Term of Years

The term of years is a present interest that terminates on the expiration of a term that is measured in one or more years, in units of a year, or in multiples or divisions thereof. A term of years can be qualified by language that specifies one or more events that can terminate the estate before or extend the estate beyond the expiration of the term.

Comment:

a. Historical distinction between freehold and nonfreehold estates. Historically, the term of years was classified as a nonfreehold estate. Thus, a grant "to A for 10 years, then to B" was not classified as a term of years in A followed by a future interest in B. Rather, B was characterized as owning the land in fee simple absolute subject to A's term of years.

Today, the distinction between freehold and nonfreehold estates has no continuing importance in the law of donative transfers. Characterizing B as owning the land subject to a term of years in A may still be appropriate regarding a commercial transaction, such as a case in which B, as lessor, leases the land to A, as lessee, for 10 years. As noted in § 24.1, Comment *b*, however, the term of years as used in the commercial law of landlord and tenant is beyond the scope of this Restatement. For coverage of the commercial use of the term of years and of the other varieties of the so-called nonfreehold estates, see Restatement Second, Property (Landlord and Tenant). In the setting of noncommercial transactions, however, the ancient characterization was abolished in the Restatement of Property § 156, Comment *e*, and Illustration 9. Comment *e* states:

> The creation of a remainder in land does not require . . . that the estates preceding the future interest be freehold estates. . . . Historically, an interest created subsequent to a non-freehold estate was not a remainder. If it was not subject to a condition precedent, it was a present interest. If it was subject to a condition precedent, it was a springing executory interest. Modern usage has broadened the inclusiveness of the word remainder. . . .

This Restatement follows the modern usage as described in the Restatement of Property.

b. Mode of expressing duration. The term of years is an estate whose duration is measured in one or more years, in units of a year, or in multiples or divisions thereof.

Illustrations:

1. An estate in A "for one year and three weeks" is an estate for years.

4. An estate in A "until [a date certain]" is an estate for years.

5. An estate in A "until A reaches the age of 21" is an estate for years.

c. Periodic income or other payments. In a donative transfer, it is common to create a term of years in the form of an income interest in a trust or a right to other payments for one or more years, or units, multiples, or divisions of years. See § 15.1, Comment *p* (treating a class gift of income as a series of individual class gifts). The interest of a trust beneficiary who has the right to the income from a trust for a term of years is sometimes called an "equitable term."

d. Term of years qualified by language that might cause the estate to terminate before or extend the estate beyond the expiration of the term. A term of years can be qualified by language that specifies one or more events that might terminate the estate before or extend the estate beyond the expiration of the term. Such a term of years is called a defeasible term or an extendable term, as the case may be. Historically, depending on whether the event was described by language of limitation or condition, such a term was called a term of years subject to a "special limitation," an "executory limitation," or a "condition subsequent."

Illustrations:

6. Grantor transferred land "to A for 10 years or until A remarries." Assuming the validity of the restriction (see Restatement Third, Trusts § 29, Comment *j*, and Illustration 1), A's estate is called a defeasible term, because it is qualified by language that might cause it to terminate before the expiration of the term. Historically, such an estate would have been called a "term of years subject to a special limitation" or a "determinable term of years."

7. Grantor transferred land "to A for 10 years, then to B; but if A remarries, to B immediately." Assuming the validity of the restriction (see Restatement Third, Trusts § 29, Comment *j*, and Illustration 1), A's estate is called a defeasible term, because it is qualified by language that might cause it to terminate before the expiration of the term. Historically, such an estate would have been called a "term of years subject to an executory limitation."

8. Grantor transferred land "to A for 10 years on condition that A not remarry; and if A remarries, Grantor is to have the right to reenter and take possession." Assuming the validity of the restriction (see Restatement Third, Trusts § 29, Comment *j*, and Illustration 1), A's estate is called a defeasible term, because it is qualified by language that might cause it to terminate before the expiration of the term. Historically, such an estate would have been called a "term of years subject to a condition subsequent."

10. Grantor transferred land "to A for 10 years or for life, whichever event (the expiration of 10 years or the death of A) occurs later." A's estate is called an extendable term, because it is qualified by language that might cause it to extend beyond the expiration of the term.

e. Successive terms. A disposition such as "to A for 10 years, then to B for 15 years" creates successive terms, in which the right to possession automatically shifts to B or to B's successors in interest on the expiration of A's 10-year term.

f. Combining terms and life estates. A term of years can be combined with a life estate (see § 24.5), such as in the disposition "to A for 10 years, then to B for life." Any such combination is permissible. Examples include "to A for 10 years, then to B for life, then to C for 15 years, then to D for life" and "to A for 10 years, then to B for 15 years, then to C for life."

CHAPTER 25

FUTURE INTERESTS: CLASSIFICATION

Introductory Note: The system of classification of present and future interests originated in feudal patterns of land holding and governmental finance that have been obsolete for centuries. This Restatement simplifies classification for its present purposes. The principal function of classification today is descriptive—a short-hand way of describing an interest that has specific characteristics.

The previous chapter simplifies the classification of present interests. This chapter simplifies the classification of future interests.

§ 25.1. Future Interest Defined

A future interest is an ownership interest in property that does not currently entitle the owner to possession or enjoyment of the property. The owner's right to possession or enjoyment is postponed until some time in the future and may be contingent or vested.

Comment:

a. *Present ownership interest.* A future interest is a present ownership interest in property, even though the owner's right to possession or enjoyment is postponed until some time in the future and may be contingent or vested (see § 25.3). A future interest arises when it is created, not in the future when or if the right to possession or enjoyment matures.

b. *Historical note; multiple categories.* Historically, future interests were divided into multiple categories. There were five types of future interests: (1) remainders; (2) executory interests; (3) reversions; (4) possibilities of reverter; and (5) rights of entry. This Restatement simplifies the terminology by reducing the categories to reversions or remainders. See § 25.2.

Future interests were also categorized in terms of vesting: (1) indefeasibly vested; (2) vested subject to complete defeasance; (3) vested subject to open (also called vested subject to partial defeasance); and (4) contingent. This Restatement simplifies the terminology by reducing the categories to contingent or vested. See § 25.3. If the future interest is in favor of a class that is open to new entrants, the interest is also subject to open. See § 25.4.

c. *Possession or enjoyment.* The term "possession or enjoyment" is a term of art widely used in the law of estates and future interests (see, e.g., §§ 24.1, 25.1, 25.3) and in the law of taxation. A future interest takes effect in possession when the beneficiary becomes entitled to possession as, for example, in the case of a remainder interest in fee simple or for life or for a term of years. A future interest takes effect in enjoyment when the beneficiary becomes entitled to enjoyment as, for example, in the case of a remainder interest in income.

§ 25.2. Reversion or Remainder

A future interest is either a reversion or a remainder. A future interest is a reversion if it was retained by the transferor. A future interest is a remainder if it was created in a transferee.

Comment:

a. Rationale. Historically, the law divided future interests into five types, each with different characteristics and legal consequences: (1) remainders; (2) executory interests; (3) reversions; (4) possibilities of reverter; and (5) rights of entry. As explained in Comments *b* through *d*, the category into which a future interest was properly placed depended largely on the form of the language used to create it. Today, no legal consequences depend upon placing a future interest in one category or another. For that reason, there is no longer any reason to retain all of the different categories. Consequently, this section abandons the distinctions differentiating executory interests from remainders and differentiating possibilities of reverter and rights of entry from reversions and from each other.

This section reduces the categories to two—reversions and remainders. A future interest that was previously categorized as a possibility of reverter or a right of entry is absorbed under the category of reversion. A future interest that was previously categorized as an executory interest is absorbed under the category of remainder. Even these two categories could be combined, because the distinction between reversions and remainders no longer serves any substantive purpose. The two categories are retained simply because they are in common usage in the legal profession, in other Restatements, in uniform statutes, and in tax law. See Comment *e*.

b. Historical note. Remainders and executory interests were classified as nonreversionary future interests, because they were created in a transferee. Reversions, possibilities of reverter, and rights of entry (called powers of termination in Restatement of Property § 155) were classified as reversionary future interests, because they were retained by the transferor.

A *remainder* was a future interest created in a transferee that could become possessory upon the termination of a life estate or a term of years. To be a remainder, the future interest had to be created simultaneously with the creation of the life estate or term of years. See Restatement of Property § 156.

An *executory interest* was a future interest created in a transferee that could become possessory (i) by divesting a remainder interest or a fee simple subject to an executory limitation or (ii) upon the termination of a fee simple determinable. Executory interests were further divided into springing and shifting executory interests, the former divesting an interest retained by the transferor and the latter divesting an interest conferred on one or more transferees.

A *reversion* was a future interest retained by the transferor that could become possessory upon the termination of a life estate or a term of years.

A *possibility of reverter* was a future interest retained by the transferor that could become possessory upon the termination of a fee simple determinable.

A *right of entry* was a future interest created in the transferor that could become possessory upon the termination of a fee simple subject to a condition subsequent.

c. Distinction between remainders and executory interests discontinued. The principal legal consequences that turned on whether a future interest was a remainder or an executory interest were the application of the Rule of Destructibility of Contingent Remainders and the Rule in Shelley's Case. Remainders in land, if contingent and legal rather than equitable, were subject to destruction under the Destructibility Rule. A remainder in land in the life tenant's heirs or in the heirs of the life tenant's body passed to the life tenant under the Rule in Shelley's Case. An executory interest was not subject to either rule. Both the Destructibility Rule and the Rule in Shelley's Case are now widely abolished, and neither is recognized in this Restatement. See § 16.2 (Rule in Shelley's Case Not Recognized); § 25.5 (Rule of Destructibility of Contingent Remainders Not Recognized).

d. Distinction among reversions, possibilities of reverter, and rights of entry discontinued. The principal distinction between a reversion and either a possibility of reverter or a right of entry was that the reversion was always vested even if subject to a condition, whereas the possibility of reverter and the right of entry were considered to be contingent. The contingent-vested distinction, however, does not justify continuation of the distinction between reversions and possibilities of reverter-rights of entry, because the principal consequence of the contingent-vested distinction was found in the Rule Against Perpetuities, and all three reversionary interests were exempt from perpetuity law regardless of whether they were classified as contingent or vested. The contingent-vested distinction and the reversion-remainder distinction are irrelevant under the Rule Against Perpetuities as formulated in this Restatement. As formulated in this Restatement, the Rule requires a trust or other donative disposition of property to terminate on or before the expiration of the perpetuity period. See Comment *e*.

The principal distinction between a possibility of reverter and a right of entry was that the holder of a right of entry had to exercise the right to take possession of the property if and when the specified terminating event happened, whereas the holder of a possibility of reverter became automatically entitled to take possession if and when the specified terminating event happened. The different means of enforcement, however, turned out to be elusive in practical effect. The early common-law rule was that a right of entry could be exercised only by a physical entry on the land. In most states now, the commencement of an action to regain possession satisfies the requirement of an election to divest the possessory estate, and the holder of a possibility of reverter often must institute a similar action in order to enforce his or her "automatic" interest. In addition, after the stipulated event has occurred, the time allowable under the law of many states for bringing an action to enforce a possibility of reverter is the same as that for making an election under a right of entry. The statute of limitations in several states begins running upon the occurrence of the specified event against both a possibility of reverter and a right of entry; in other states, the statute has been so interpreted; and in still others, the statute is open to such an interpretation. The two interests are thus in alignment on the question of adverse possession. Finally, although the statute of limitations in some states is held not to begin running until an election under a right of entry has been effected, the courts, drawing an analogy to the equitable doctrine of laches, have required that an election be made within a "reasonable time" after the breach of the condition; and there is authority that the period of the statute of limitations constitutes a "reasonable time."

Other differences, once recognized at common law, have now largely disappeared. These include alienability and descendability. At common law, a possibility of reverter was alienable inter vivos but a right of entry was not. Legislation and case law have now moved in the direction of making the right of entry alienable also.

In the end, functional considerations no longer justify continuing to divide reversionary interests into the historic categories.

e. Limited retention of distinction between reversionary and nonreversionary interests: reversions and remainders. By recognizing that a future interest is either a reversion or a remainder, the distinction between reversionary and nonreversionary future interests is retained to that limited extent. The reason for categorizing future interests as either reversions or remainders is that the legal profession, especially in describing future interests created in a trust, is accustomed to referring to a future interest retained by the transferor as a "reversion" and a future interest created in a transferee as a "remainder." In addition, the Restatement Third of Trusts refers to a resulting trust as a "reversionary, equitable interest" (see Restatement Third, Trusts § 7), and the Restatement Third of Trusts and the Restatement Third of Restitution and Unjust Enrichment variously refer to property as "reverting" or "reverting back" to the transferor or the transferor's estate or successors in interest in certain cases. Finally, various uniform statutes, such as the Uniform Trust Code and the Uniform Principal and Income Act, refer to the future interest in trust principal as a "remainder."

No legal consequences in property law attach to the choice of labels, because there is no longer any persuasive reason for continuing to recognize the distinction between reversionary and nonreversionary interests. Until recently, the principal consequence of the distinction was that the reversionary interests were exempt from the Rule Against Perpetuities. See Comment *d*. This Restatement reforms the common-law Rule Against Perpetuities by requiring termination of a trust or other donative disposition of property on or before the expiration of the perpetuity period. Adopting a termination rather than a time-of-vesting Rule makes the distinction between a reversion and a remainder of no consequence. See §§ 27.1, 27.2. Consequently, the only property-law purpose served by separating future interests into two categories, reversions and remainders, is that recognizing the two categories accords with usage within the legal profession, in other Restatements, and in uniform statutes.

Although no legal consequences in property law attach to the choice of labels, tax law relies on the distinction between reversionary and nonreversionary future interests for various tax purposes. . . . .

f. Alienability, devisability, and inheritability. All future interests are alienable and are also devisable and inheritable if the owner's death does not terminate the interest, unless the transferor has imposed a valid restraint on alienation. The validity of restraints on the alienation of future interests held in trust is considered in Restatement Third of Trusts, Chapter 12 (§§ 57 to 60). The validity of restraints on the alienation of legal future interests is considered in Restatement Second of Property (Donative Transfers), Chapter 4 (§§ 4.1 to 4.3).

g. Effect of subsequent transfers. Under the old rule, once a future interest was classified as reversionary or nonreversionary, subsequent transfers of the future interest did not change the classification. The source of that rule, in part, was the historical definition of a remainder as a future interest in a transferee that was created simultaneously with the creation of the preceding estate. See Restatement of Property § 156. For example, if in Illustration 5, below, B had transferred his remainder to Grantor, Grantor would have had a remainder, not a reversion. If, in Illustration 10, below, Grantor had transferred her reversion to B, B would have had a reversion, not a remainder.

Strict application of this section's black letter suggests the continuation of the rule that subsequent transfers do not cause the initial classifications to change. However, because no property-law consequence turns on whether a future interest is labeled as a reversion or a remainder (see Comment *e*), it makes no difference which label is applied when there is a subsequent transfer. Whichever label seems more suitable in the circumstances is acceptable. Insofar as tax law is concerned, the focus is on the retention of a reversionary interest, not on the classification of a retained interest in the hands of a transferee of that interest.

h. Effect of subsequent events. Historically, subsequent events could cause an executory interest to change into a remainder and could cause a remainder to change into an executory interest. For example, in Illustration 8, below, C's executory interest would have changed into a remainder if B predeceased A. In Illustration 6, below, B's interest when created was a remainder, but it would have changed into a springing executory interest if B was under age 21 when A died, unless B's remainder was a legal remainder in land, in which case it would have been destroyed under the Rule of Destructibility of Contingent Remainders. See § 25.5.

The simplified terminology eliminates the need to reclassify future interests based upon subsequent events. In Illustration 8, C's interest continues to be a remainder regardless of whether B predeceases A. . . . .

i. Illustrations. The following Illustrations apply the terminology adopted in this section and compare the resulting terminology with the terminology that would have been applied under the historical doctrine of estates.

Illustrations:

1. Grantor conveyed land "to Grantee School District so long as the land is used for school purposes; upon the land being used for non-school purposes, the land reverts to Grantor if Grantor is then living; if not, to Grantor's then living descendants by representation." Grantee has a fee simple defeasible. See § 24.3, Comment *g*, Illustration 1. Grantor has a reversion. Grantor's descendants have a remainder. Regarding the application of the Rule Against Perpetuities to this disposition, see § 27.2, Comment *d*. Historically, Grantee would have had a fee simple determinable, Grantor would have had a possibility of reverter, and Grantor's descendants would have had an executory interest.

3. Grantor conveyed land "to Grantee School District on condition that the land be used for school purposes, and if the land is ever used for non-school purposes, Grantor is to have the right to reenter and take possession." Grantee has a fee simple defeasible. See § 24.3, Comment *g*, Illustration 3. Grantor has a reversion. Regarding the

application of the Rule Against Perpetuities to this disposition, see § 27.2, Comment *d*. Historically, Grantee would have had a fee simple subject to a condition subsequent, and Grantor would have had a right of entry.

4. Grantor conveyed land "to Grantee School District, but if the land is ever used for non-school purposes, the land goes to my brother B if B is then living, but if not, to B's then living descendants by representation." Grantee has a fee simple defeasible. See § 24.3, Comment *g*, Illustration 4. B and B's descendants have remainders. Regarding the application of the Rule Against Perpetuities to this disposition, see § 27.2, Comment *d*. Historically, Grantee would have had a fee simple subject to an executory limitation, and B and B's descendants would have had executory interests.

5. Grantor transferred property "to A for life, then to B." B's future interest is classified as a remainder. Historically, B's future interest was also classified as a remainder.

8. Grantor transferred property "to A for life, then to B, but if B predeceases A, to C." B's and C's future interests are classified as remainders. Historically, B's future interest was also classified as a remainder, but C's future interest was classified as a shifting executory interest.

10. Grantor transferred property "to A for life." Grantor's future interest is classified as a reversion. Historically, Grantor's future interest was also classified as a reversion.

11. Grantor dies, leaving a will that devised property "to A for life." Because Grantor's will does not contain a residuary clause, Grantor died partially intestate. The future interest following the life estate in A passes to Grantor's heirs by intestacy. Although the future interest in Grantor's heirs is labeled a reversion, the label carries no substantive consequences. Historically, Grantor's heirs also took a reversion.

§ 25.3. Contingent or Vested

A future interest is either contingent or vested. A future interest is contingent if it might not take effect in possession or enjoyment. A future interest is vested if it is certain to take effect in possession or enjoyment. A contingent or a vested future interest may additionally be classified according to the present interest into which the future interest will ripen once and if it takes effect in possession or enjoyment—as a fee simple absolute (or absolute ownership), a fee simple defeasible, a life estate, or a term of years.

Comment:

a. Historical note. Historically, there were four vesting categories: (1) indefeasibly vested; (2) vested subject to complete defeasance; (3) vested subject to open (also called vested subject to partial defeasance); and (4) contingent. This section addresses the categories of indefeasibly vested, vested subject to complete defeasance, and contingent. Section 25.4 addresses the category of vested subject to open.

An *indefeasibly vested* future interest was not subject to a condition or a limitation that might prevent it from taking effect in possession or enjoyment and not subject to a limitation that would prevent it from becoming a fee simple absolute once it became possessory.

A future interest that was *vested subject to complete defeasance* was a future interest that was subject either to a limitation or to a condition that was stated in subsequent rather than precedent form. The Restatement of Property refined this category further, by distinguishing a future interest that was subject to a condition subsequent (called *divestment*) and one that was subject to a limitation. See Restatement of Property § 157, Comment *o*.

A future interest that was *vested subject to open* (also called *vested subject to partial divestment*) was a future interest that was not subject to a condition precedent and was in favor of a class.

A *contingent* future interest was a future interest other than a reversion that was subject to a condition that was stated in precedent rather than subsequent form. A future interest was also contingent if it was subject to an implicit though unstated condition, that is, a future interest in favor of an unborn, unadopted, or unascertained person or class. An executory interest was regarded as contingent, but the term "contingent" was not customarily expressed. A reversion was required to be classified as vested even if it was subject to a condition that was stated in precedent form. The purpose of requiring a reversion to be classified as vested was to facilitate the application of the rule of destructibility of contingent remainders (see § 25.5) and to assure that a reversion was not subject to the common-law Rule Against Perpetuities. That distinction is no longer relevant, however, because the Rule as formulated in this Restatement requires a trust or other donative disposition of property to terminate on or before the expiration of the perpetuity period. See § 27.1.

b. *Historical note: condition precedent and subsequent distinguished.* A central tenet of the classification of future interests was the distinction between a condition precedent and a condition subsequent. A condition precedent provided that the owner was entitled to take in possession or enjoyment "if" a specified event happened, as in "to A for life, then to B if B survives A; if not, to C." B's remainder was classified as contingent. A condition subsequent provided that the owner was entitled to take in possession or enjoyment, "but not if" a specified event happened, as in "to A for life, then to B, but if B fails to survive A, to C." B's remainder was classified as vested subject to divestment.

Although C's future interest was subject to a condition precedent in both cases, it did not bear the same classification. The rule was that if the first future interest was a contingent remainder, the alternative future interest was also a contingent remainder. See Restatement of Property § 278. Both contingent remainders were sometimes called alternative contingent remainders. If the first future interest was a vested remainder subject to divestment, the alternative future interest was an executory interest. See Restatement of Property § 277. Although the executory interest was subject to a condition precedent, the term "contingent" was not customarily expressed; it was simply understood that an executory interest was contingent. . . . .

c. *Historical note: classification irrelevant to whether a future interest was subject to a requirement of survival.* Whether a future interest is subject to a requirement of survival is a question of construction. See §§ 26.3, 26.4. Whether a future interest is vested or contingent is a question of classification. Under the historical system, a vested future interest could be subject to a requirement of survival (as is B's interest in "to A for life, remainder to B, but if B fails to survive A, to C"). A contingent future interest could be subject to conditions unrelated to its holder's survival (as is C's interest in "to A for life, remainder to B, but if B fails to survive A, to C").

d. Historical note: constructional preference for vested interests and for vesting at the earliest possible moment. Historically, there was a constructional preference for vested interests and for vesting at the earliest possible moment. See Restatement of Property § 243, Comments *i* and *j*. Neither constructional preference is endorsed in this Restatement. See §§ 11.3; 15.4, Comment *d*; 26.3, Comment *d*.

e. Historical note: technical reversion. Historically, there was always a reversion when a life estate was followed by contingent remainders. For example, if Grantor disposed of property "to A for life, then to B if B survives A, but if not, to C," Grantor retained a reversion. Grantor's reversion, in this case, was classified as merely "technical," because at A's death the property will either pass to B, C, or C's successors in interest; it cannot pass to Grantor. The technical reversion served only one purpose. It facilitated the application of the rule of destructibility of contingent remainders. The remainders in B and C could be destroyed if Grantor conveyed his reversion to A or if A conveyed her life estate to Grantor. In either case, the reversion and the life estate would merge to become a fee simple absolute, thus destroying the contingent remainders in B and C.

Technical reversions are not recognized in this Restatement, because they now serve no purpose. Their only function was to facilitate the application of the rule of destructibility of contingent remainders, a rule that is not recognized in this Restatement as part of American law. See § 25.5.

f. Simplified terminology adopted in this Restatement. Under the simplified terminology adopted in this Restatement, a future interest is either contingent or vested. The distinction is based on substance rather than on form.

A future interest is contingent if, for any reason, it might not take effect in possession or enjoyment. It is irrelevant whether the interest is subject to a condition that is stated in precedent or subsequent form or is unstated (e.g., to an unborn, unadopted, or unascertained person or class) or is subject to a limitation. The determining factor is the possibility, not the probability, that the interest will not take effect in possession or enjoyment.

A future interest is vested if it is certain to take effect in possession or enjoyment. The question is whether the future interest is certain to take effect in possession or enjoyment, not whether it is certain to take effect in possession or enjoyment in the owner personally. It is sufficient if it is certain to take effect in possession or enjoyment either in the owner personally or in the owner's successors in interest. A vested future interest is sometimes referred to as "vested in interest," as opposed to a present interest, which can be referred to as "vested in possession."

A contingent or a vested future interest can be subject to open. A future interest is subject to open if it is in favor of a class that is open to future entrants. See § 25.4.

A contingent or a vested future interest may additionally be classified according to the present interest into which it will ripen once and if it takes effect in possession or enjoyment—as a fee simple absolute (or absolute ownership), a fee simple defeasible, a life estate, or a term of years.

g. Illustrations. The following Illustrations develop the simplified terminology adopted in this Restatement and compare it with the historical classification. Under the simplified terminology, the classification of an interest can change as post-creation events unfold. Under the historical system, the classification of an interest could also change as post-creation events unfold, except that a subsequent transfer could not change a reversionary interest into a nonreversionary interest.

Illustrations:

1. Grantor conveyed land "to Grantee School District so long as the land is used for school purposes; upon the land being used for non-school purposes, the land reverts to Grantor if Grantor is then living; if not, to Grantor's then living descendants by representation." Grantee has a fee simple defeasible. See § 24.3, Comment *g*, Illustration 1. Grantor has a reversion and Grantor's descendants have a remainder. See § 25.2, Comment *i*, Illustration 1. Grantor's reversion is classified as contingent, because it might not take effect in possession or enjoyment. It can only take effect in possession or enjoyment if the land is used for non-school purposes during Grantor's lifetime. The remainder in Grantor's descendants is classified as contingent, because it might not take effect in possession or enjoyment. It can only take effect in possession or enjoyment in Grantor's descendants who are living if and when the land is used for non-school purposes after Grantor's death. Regarding the application of the Rule Against Perpetuities to this disposition, see § 27.2, Comment *d*. Historically, Grantee would have had a fee simple determinable, and Grantor would have had a possibility of reverter.

3. Grantor conveyed land "to Grantee School District on condition that the land be used for school purposes, and if the land is ever used for non-school purposes, Grantor is to have the right to reenter and take possession." Grantee has a fee simple defeasible. See § 24.3, Comment *g*, Illustration 3. Grantor has a reversion. See § 25.2, Comment *i*, Illustration 3. Grantor's reversion is classified as contingent, because it might not take effect in possession or enjoyment. It can only take effect in possession or enjoyment if the land is used for non-school purposes and if Grantor or Grantor's successors in interest (see § 25.2, Comment *f*) subsequently elect to take possession. Regarding the application of the Rule Against Perpetuities to this disposition, see § 27.2, Comment *d*. Historically, Grantee would have had a fee simple subject to a condition subsequent. Grantor would have had a right of entry.

4. Grantor conveyed land "to Grantee School District, but if the land is ever used for non-school purposes, the land goes to my brother B if B is then living, but if not, to B's then living descendants by representation." Grantee has a fee simple defeasible. See § 24.3, Comment *g*, Illustration 4. B and B's descendants have remainders. See § 25.2, Comment *i*, Illustration 4. B's remainder and the remainder of B's descendants are classified as contingent, because they might not take effect in possession or enjoyment. B's remainder can only take effect in possession or enjoyment if the land is used for non-school purposes during B's lifetime. The remainder in B's descendants is contingent because it might not take effect in possession or enjoyment. It can only take effect in possession or enjoyment in Grantor's descendants who are living if and when the land is used for non-school purposes after B's death. Regarding the application of the Rule Against Perpetuities to this disposition, see § 27.2, Comment *d*. Historically, Grantee would have

had a fee simple subject to an executory limitation, and B and B's descendants would have had executory interests.

5. Grantor transferred property "to A for life." Grantor's reversion is classified as vested, because A is certain to die and therefore Grantor's reversion is certain to take effect in possession or enjoyment on A's death, either in Grantor personally or in Grantor's successors in interest. Grantor's reversion can also be classified by the present interest into which it will ripen once it takes effect in possession or enjoyment, in which case it is classified as a vested reversion in fee simple absolute. If Grantor predeceases A, Grantor's vested reversion would pass to Grantor's successors in interest. Historically, Grantor's reversion would have been classified as indefeasibly vested, because it was not subject to a condition or a limitation that might have prevented it from taking effect in possession or enjoyment and was not subject to a limitation that would have prevented it from becoming a fee simple absolute once it became possessory. If Grantor had predeceased A, Grantor's reversion would have passed to Grantor's successors in interest, but it would have remained a reversion in their hands.

6. Grantor transferred property "to A for life, then to return to me if I am then living; if not, to B." Grantor's reversion is classified as contingent, because it might not take effect in possession or enjoyment. It can only take effect in possession or enjoyment if Grantor survives A. B's remainder is classified as contingent, because Grantor might outlive A and therefore B's remainder might not take effect in possession or enjoyment, either in B personally or in B's successors in interest. These future interests can also be classified by the present interest into which they will ripen once and if they take effect in possession or enjoyment, in which case Grantor's reversion is classified as a contingent reversion in fee simple absolute and B's remainder is classified as a contingent remainder in fee simple absolute. If Grantor predeceases A, B's remainder would become vested and Grantor's reversion would terminate. At Grantor's death before A, the disposition in effect becomes "to A for life, then to B." Historically, Grantor's reversion would have been classified as vested subject to complete defeasance (divestment), although it was subject to a condition that was stated in precedent form (to return to me "if" I am then living); the form of the condition would have been overridden by the rule that a reversion had to be vested. B's executory interest would have been contingent, because it was subject to a condition stated in precedent form (to B "if" Grantor predeceases A). Were it not for the rule that a reversion had to be vested, Grantor's reversion would have been classified as contingent and B's future interest would have been classified as a contingent remainder. If Grantor had predeceased A, B's remainder would have become indefeasibly vested, and Grantor's reversion would have terminated.

7. Grantor transferred property "to A for life, then to return to me, but if I am not then living, to B." Grantor's reversion is classified as contingent, because it might not take effect in possession or enjoyment. It can only take effect in possession or enjoyment if Grantor survives A. B's remainder is classified as contingent, because Grantor might outlive A and therefore B's remainder might not take effect in possession or enjoyment, either in B personally or in B's successors in interest. These future interests can also be classified by the present interest into which they will ripen once and if they take effect in possession or enjoyment, in which case Grantor's reversion is classified as a contingent reversion

in fee simple absolute and B's remainder is classified as a contingent remainder in fee simple absolute. If Grantor predeceases A, B's remainder would become vested and Grantor's reversion would terminate. At Grantor's death before A, the disposition in effect becomes "to A for life, then to B." Historically, Grantor's reversion would have been classified as a vested reversion subject to complete defeasance (divestment), because of the rule that a reversion had to be vested and because Grantor's reversion was subject to a condition that was stated in subsequent form (to return to me, but not if I am not then living). B's executory interest would have been contingent, because it was subject to a condition stated in precedent form (to B "if" Grantor is not then living). If Grantor had predeceased A, B's remainder would have become indefeasibly vested and Grantor's reversion would have terminated.

8. Grantor transferred property "to A for life, then to B." B's remainder is classified as vested, because it is certain to take effect in possession or enjoyment, either in B personally or in B's successors in interest. If B predeceases A, B's remainder passes to B's successors in interest. Historically, B's remainder would have been classified as indefeasibly vested, because it was not subject to a condition or a limitation that might have prevented it from taking effect in possession or enjoyment and not subject to a limitation that would have prevented it from becoming a fee simple absolute once it became possessory. If B had predeceased A, B's remainder would have passed to B's successors in interest.

9. Grantor transferred property "to A for life, then to B for life, then to C." B's remainder is (sometimes referred to as a secondary life estate) classified as contingent, because it might not take effect in possession or enjoyment. It can only take effect in possession or enjoyment if B survives A. C's remainder is classified as vested, because it is certain to take effect in possession or enjoyment, either in C personally or in C's successors in interest. If B predeceases A, B's remainder would terminate, and C's remainder would remain vested. At B's death before A, the disposition would in effect become "to A for life, then to C." Historically, B's remainder would have been classified as vested subject to defeasance, because it was subject to a limitation that might have prevented it from taking effect in possession or enjoyment and subject to a limitation that would have prevented it from becoming a fee simple absolute once it became possessory. C's remainder would have been classified as indefeasibly vested, because it was not subject to a condition or a limitation that might have prevented it from taking effect in possession or enjoyment and not subject to a limitation that would have prevented it from becoming a fee simple absolute once it became possessory. If B had predeceased A, B's remainder would have terminated, and C's remainder would have remained indefeasibly vested.

11. Grantor transferred property "to A for life, then to B, but if B fails to survive A, to return to me." B's remainder is classified as contingent, because it might not take effect in possession or enjoyment. It can only take effect in possession or enjoyment if B survives A. Grantor's reversion is classified as contingent, because B might survive A and therefore Grantor's reversion might not take effect in possession or enjoyment in Grantor personally or in Grantor's successors in interest. These future interests can also be classified according to the present interest into which they will ripen once and if they take effect in

possession or enjoyment, in which case B's remainder is classified as a contingent remainder in fee simple absolute and Grantor's reversion is classified as a contingent reversion in fee simple absolute. If B predeceases A, B's future interest would terminate and Grantor's reversion would become vested. At B's death before A, the disposition would in effect become "to A for life, then to return to me." Historically, B's remainder would have been classified as vested subject to complete defeasance. Grantor's reversion would have been classified as vested subject to complete defeasance. If B had predeceased A, B's remainder would have been divested and Grantor's reversion would have become indefeasibly vested.

12. Grantor transferred property "to A for life, then to B, but if B fails to survive A, to C." B's remainder is classified as contingent, because it might not take effect in possession or enjoyment. It can only take effect in possession or enjoyment if B survives A. C's remainder is classified as contingent, because B might survive A and therefore C's remainder might not take effect in possession or enjoyment. These future interests can also be classified by the present interest into which they will ripen once and if they take effect in possession or enjoyment, in which case B's and C's remainders are classified as contingent remainders in fee simple absolute. If B predeceases A, B's remainder would terminate and C's remainder would become vested. At B's death before A, the disposition would in effect become "to A for life, then to C." Historically, B's remainder would have been classified as vested subject to complete defeasance (divestment). C's executory interest would have been contingent. If B had predeceased A, B's remainder would have been divested and C's executory interest would have become an indefeasibly vested remainder.

13. Grantor transferred property "to A for life, then to B if B survives A." B's remainder is classified as contingent, because it might not take effect in possession or enjoyment. It can only take effect in possession or enjoyment if B survives A. Grantor's reversion is also classified as contingent, because B might survive A and therefore Grantor's reversion might not take effect in possession or enjoyment. These future interests can also be classified according to the present interest into which they will ripen once and if they take effect in possession or enjoyment, in which case B's remainder is classified as a contingent remainder in fee simple absolute, and Grantor's reversion is classified as a contingent reversion in fee simple absolute. If B predeceases A, B's remainder would terminate and Grantor's reversion would become vested. At B's death before A, the disposition would in effect become "to A for life, then to Grantor." Historically, B's remainder would have been classified as contingent. Grantor's reversion would have been classified as vested subject to defeasance, because of the overriding rule that reversions are always vested. If B had predeceased A, B's remainder would have terminated and Grantor's reversion would have become indefeasibly vested.

14. Grantor transferred property "to A for life, then to B if B survives A, but if not, to C." B's remainder is classified as contingent, because it might not take effect in possession or enjoyment. It can only take effect in possession or enjoyment if B survives A. C's remainder is classified as contingent, because B might survive A and therefore C's remainder might not take effect in possession or enjoyment. Grantor has no future interest. If B predeceases A, B's remainder would terminate

and C's remainder would become vested. At B's death before A, the disposition would in effect become "to A for life, then to C." Historically, B's remainder would have been classified as contingent, because the condition of surviving A was stated in the form of a condition precedent—"to B if." Once B's interest had been classified as a contingent remainder, C's interest would also have been a contingent remainder, by virtue of the rule that if the first future interest was a contingent remainder, the alternative future interest would have to be a contingent remainder. C's remainder was subject to the condition that B not survive A. That condition was also stated in the form of a condition precedent—"if [B does not survive A], to C." Grantor would have retained a technical reversion. There would always have been a reversion when a life estate was followed by contingent remainders. Because the contingencies with respect to the interests of B and C exhausted all of the possibilities, the reversion would be said to have been merely "technical." If B had predeceased A, C's interest would have become an indefeasibly vested remainder.

15. Grantor transferred property "to A for life, then to B if B survives A, but if not, to C if C survives A." B's remainder is classified as contingent, because it might not take effect in possession or enjoyment. It can only take effect in possession or enjoyment if B survives A. C's remainder is classified as contingent, because it can only take effect in possession or enjoyment if B predeceases A and C survives A. Grantor has a reversion that is classified as contingent, because it can only take effect in possession or enjoyment if B and C predecease A. If B predeceases A, B's remainder would terminate. If C also predeceases A, C's remainder would terminate, and Grantor's reversion would become vested. At B's death, if B dies before A, the disposition would in effect become "to A for life, then to C if C survives A." At C's death, if C also dies before A, the disposition would in effect become "to A for life." At C's death, if C dies before A, the disposition would in effect become "to A for life, then to B if B survives A." At B's death, if B also dies before A, the disposition would in effect become "to A for life." Historically, B's and C's remainders would have been classified as contingent. C's remainder was subject to two contingencies that were stated in the precedent form ("if" B does not survive A or "if" C predeceases A). Grantor would have had a reversion that would have been classified as vested subject to defeasance (divestment). Grantor's reversion would not have been a technical reversion as it would have been in Illustration 14, because now there was a set of circumstances under which it could have become possessory, i.e., if both B and C had predeceased A.

§ 25.4. Postponed Class Gifts; Subject to Open

In the case of a postponed class gift that is open to new entrants, the future interest of each class member existing from time to time is classified as subject to open. Under the rule of § 25.3, the future interest can be either vested or contingent. The future interest of a potential class member is always classified as contingent.

Comment:

a. Cross-reference. On class gifts in general, see Division V (Chapters 13 through 16).

b. Meaning of the term "postponed class gift." The term "postponed class gift" refers to a future interest in favor of a class.

c. *Historical note.* As noted in § 25.3, Comment *a*, historically there were four vesting categories: (1) indefeasibly vested; (2) vested subject to complete defeasance; (3) vested subject to open (also called vested subject to partial defeasance); and (4) contingent. This section addresses the category of vested subject to open. Section 25.3 addresses the categories of indefeasibly vested, vested subject to complete defeasance, and contingent.

In the case of a postponed class gift that was open to new entrants, and that was not otherwise contingent, the interest of an existing class member was classified as vested subject to open (partial divestment), and the interest of a potential class member was classified as an executory interest. Although the executory interest of a potential class member was subject to the condition precedent of becoming a class member (by birth, adoption, marriage, or any other means), the term "contingent" was not customarily expressed; an executory interest was simply understood to be contingent.

If the postponed class was otherwise contingent because it was subject to a condition precedent, such as a condition of surviving the life tenant, the interests of both living and potential members of the class were classified as contingent. It was customary to say that the class gift was contingent, without separating the interests of living and potential class members. That the interest of an existing class member was also subject to open (partial divestment) was not customarily expressed.

d. *Simplified system adopted in this Restatement.* Under the simplified system adopted in this Restatement, the term "subject to open" is attached to the classification of any postponed class gift that is open to new entrants. The benefit of adding the term "subject to open" is increased clarity, regardless of whether the future interest is vested or contingent.

The future interest of a potential class member is contingent on becoming a class member, by birth, adoption, marriage, or any other means.

e. *Illustrations.* The following Illustrations show the simplified system of classification adopted in this Restatement and compare the resulting classification with the classification that would have been reached under the historical system.

Illustrations:

1. Grantor transferred property "to A for life, then to A's children." Each class member existing from time to time has a remainder that is classified as vested subject to open. As a single-generation class gift, the class gift is not subject to an implied condition of survival of A, except as otherwise provided by statute. See § 15.4. The interest in each of A's unborn or unadopted children is classified as a contingent remainder. Upon birth or adoption before the class closes (on the class-closing rules, see § 15.1), the interests of the existing class members are partially diminished in quantity, because the property must now be divided among a larger number of beneficiaries. The interest of the new class member is classified as a vested remainder subject to open. Historically, if A had one or more living children, the remainder created in A's children was classified as vested subject to open. More specifically, the remainder in each of A's living children was classified as vested subject to open or, under an older terminology, as vested subject to partial defeasance (divestment). The interest in A's unborn or unadopted children was classified as an executory interest. Upon birth or adoption before the class closed, the interests of the

existing class members were partially divested and the interest of the new class member was vested subject to open.

2. Grantor transferred property "to A for life, then to A's children who survive A." Each class member existing from time to time has a remainder that is classified as contingent subject to open. Historically, the remainder created in A's children was classified as contingent. Although it was also subject to open, that term, by custom, was not expressed.

3. Grantor transferred property "to A for life, then by representation to A's issue." Each class member existing from time to time has a remainder that is classified as contingent subject to open. Historically, the remainder created in A's issue was classified as contingent because, as a multiple-generation class gift, the class gift to A's issue was (and still is: see § 15.3) subject to an implied condition precedent of survival of A. Although the class gift was also subject to open, that term, by custom, was not expressed.

4. Grantor transferred property "to A for life, then by representation to A's issue who survive A." Each class member existing from time to time has a remainder that is classified as contingent subject to open. Historically, the remainder created in A's issue was classified as contingent. Although it was also subject to open, that term, by custom, was not expressed.

§ 25.5. Rule of Destructibility of Contingent Remainders Not Recognized

The Rule of Destructibility of Contingent Remainders is not recognized as part of American law. A legal contingent future interest in land is not destroyed by failing to vest on or before the time when the preceding life estate terminates.

Comment:

a. Historical note. The Rule of Destructibility of Contingent Remainders provided that a legal contingent remainder in land was destroyed if it did not vest by the time that the preceding freehold estate terminated. The destructibility rule was a rule of law, not construction.

The destructibility rule rested on two key premises. First, a remainder interest could not follow an estate in fee simple. The only nonreversionary future interest that could do so was an executory interest, which was an interest that could not be destroyed. Pells v. Brown, Cro. Jac. 590, 79 Eng. Rep. 504 (K.B. 1620). Second, a contingent remainder could not change into an executory interest. Purefoy v. Rogers, 2 Wm. Saund. 380, 85 Eng. Rep. 1181 (K.B. 1670). In consequence of these rules, a legal contingent remainder in land was destroyed in three situations—gap in possession, merger, and forfeiture.

b. Historical note: destruction by gap in possession. Destruction by gap in possession was possible when the condition precedent might remain unsatisfied at the life tenant's death. If the condition precedent was not fulfilled when the life tenant died, a gap in possession arose. The gap in possession was filled by the grantor's reversion in fee simple, which then became possessory. The grantor's fee simple could not support a remainder interest, and the remainder interest could not change into an executory interest. As a result, the contingent remainder was destroyed, and the grantor's fee simple became a fee simple absolute. See Illustration 1, below.

The indestructibility of executory interests afforded the conveyancer a means of avoiding the destructibility rule as applied to the gap-in-possession case. The method was to interject an intentional and certain time gap between the natural termination of the life estate and the right to possession of the contingent future interest, thus creating an indestructible executory interest rather than a destructible contingent remainder.

c. *Historical note: destruction by merger.* The premature termination of a life estate caused the destruction of a contingent remainder. One way of causing a premature termination of a life estate was by merger. If a life estate and a successive vested future interest in fee come into the hands of the same person, the doctrine of merger provides that the life estate terminates by being merged into the other interest. The resulting fee simple could not support a remainder interest, and the remainder interest could not change into an executory interest. As a result, the fee simple became a fee simple absolute, and the contingent remainder was destroyed. See Illustration 2, below.

d. *Historical note: destruction by forfeiture.* At common law, a life estate could be terminated before the life tenant's death by forfeiture. Under the Statute of Gloucester, 6 Edw. 1, c. 7 (1278), forfeiture occurred if the life tenant conveyed a greater estate, a fee, than he owned. The conveyance gave the conveyee a "tortious fee," thus destroying any contingent remainder previously supported by the life estate.

Forfeiture of a life estate is not recognized in the United States. If a life tenant purports to convey a fee, the transferee only receives a life estate. The principle is that a grantor can convey no greater estate than the grantor owns. See § 6.1, Comment *c.* Consequently, this method of destroying a contingent remainder was not available in states that adhered to the Destructibility Rule.

e. *Destructibility rule not recognized as part of American law.* The Rule of Destructibility of Contingent Remainders is not recognized as part of American law. A legal contingent future interest in land is not destroyed by failing to vest on or before the time when the preceding life estate terminates.

f. *Illustrations.* The following examples illustrate situations in which the rule of destructibility of contingent remainders would have destroyed a contingent remainder and show the result under this Restatement without the destructibility rule.

Illustrations:

1. Grantor transferred land "to A for life, then to B if B lives to age 21." At A's death, B was under 21. Grantor's reversion in fee simple defeasible becomes possessory, followed by B's contingent remainder. If, after A's death, B reaches 21, B would become entitled to possession. If B dies before her 21st birthday, Grantor's fee would ripen into a fee simple absolute. (If this disposition had been in trust, and if A had died while B was under 21, B, not Grantor or Grantor's successors in interest, would have a right to the income between the time of A's death and B's 21st birthday. See § 26.9, Comment *c.*)

Historically, the gap in possession would have been filled by Grantor's reversion in fee simple, which would then have become possessory. Grantor's fee simple could not have supported a remainder interest, and the remainder interest could not have changed into an executory interest. As a result, B's contingent remainder would have been destroyed, and Grantor's fee simple would have become a fee simple absolute. By a slight manipulation of the disposition, B's future interest could have been treated as an indestructible executory interest. Had the disposition been "to A for life, and one day after A's death, to B if B lives to age 21," B would have had an indestructible executory interest.

2. Grantor devised land "to A for life, then to B if B survives A." Grantor's will contained no residuary clause, and Grantor's sole heir at law is R. R has a reversion. If R conveys his future interest to A, A's life estate and R's reversion would merge, giving A a fee simple defeasible, followed by B's contingent remainder. If B survives A, B would become entitled to possession. If B predeceases A, A's fee simple defeasible would ripen into a fee simple absolute. Historically, Purefoy v. Rogers would have prevented the transformation of B's contingent remainder into an executory interest, and the merger would have destroyed B's contingent remainder. A's fee simple would have become a fee simple absolute. B's contingent remainder could also have been destroyed by the same process if A had conveyed her life estate to R or if both A and R had conveyed their estates to a third person. The person who would have ended up with both the life estate and the reversion would have gotten a fee simple absolute.

CHAPTER 26

PRESENT AND FUTURE INTERESTS: CONSTRUCTION

Introductory Note: Chapter 26 addresses questions of construction that arise in connection with present and future interests. The chapter is divided into four Parts. Part A reiterates the rule of law that a beneficiary who dies before the donative document takes effect takes no interest. Part B moves to express and implied conditions of survival. Part C deals with gifts over on death or on death without issue. Part D covers how incomplete dispositions can be remedied by construction.

The rules of construction in this chapter sometimes apply to class gifts but are not restricted to class gifts. Chapters 14 and 15 also address questions of construction, but those chapters are restricted to questions of construction of class gifts.

Part A. Mandatory Requirement of Survival of the Effective Date of the Transfer

Introductory Note: Part A has one section. Although the rule of § 26.1 is a mandatory rule, not a rule of construction, satisfaction of the rule is a preliminary requirement for the rules of construction in Parts B, C, and D. The rules of construction in Parts B, C, and D only apply to a present or future interest that has satisfied the requirement of survival stated in § 26.1.

§ 26.1. Beneficiary Who Is Deceased When Donative Document Takes Effect

A beneficiary of a present or a future interest who is deceased when the donative document takes effect as a dispositive instrument takes no interest.

Comment:

a. Scope and cross-references. The rule of this section, as applied to class gifts, is duplicated in § 15.2. Section 26.1 applies the rule of § 15.2 to a beneficiary who takes as an individual and to a group of multiple beneficiaries taking as individuals and not as a class. See § 13.2 for the distinction between multiple beneficiaries taking as individuals and not as a class. See also § 1.2 for the rule that an individual who fails to survive the decedent cannot take as an heir or a devisee.

b. Rationale. A donative transfer cannot be made to a person who is deceased, because a decedent lacks juridical personality. This is a mandatory rule, not a rule of construction. Consequently, language in a donative document expressly requiring survival until the time when the donative document takes effect is surplusage. The requirement of survival derives from the law, not from the document. An attempt to confer a property interest on a beneficiary who dies before the donative document takes effect as a dispositive instrument is ineffective. Although the transferor cannot override the rule of this section, he or she can create an express gift over to a substitute taker, even to the "estate" or "executor" of a predeceased beneficiary (for the preferred construction of such a gift over, see § 1.2, Comment *g*). An antilapse statute in many cases also provides a gift over to a substitute taker (see Comment *d*).

The rule of this section applies whether the beneficiary died before or after the donative document was executed. The rule of this section also applies to a beneficiary who is treated as if the beneficiary is deceased when the donative document takes effect as a dispositive instrument. See, e.g., Uniform Probate Code § 2–702.

c. Wills. A will takes effect as a dispositive instrument at the testator's death, not when the will was executed. See § 3.1, Comment *a*. Hence, a devisee in a will must survive the testator. See § 1.2, Comment *a*; § 5.5, Comment *a*. A devisee who fails to survive the testator does not take. Unless an antilapse statute applies (see Comment *d*; § 5.5, Comment *j*) or unless there is an effective express gift over, the failure of the devisee to survive the testator causes the devise to lapse.

Illustration:

1. Grantor died, leaving a will that devised $15,000 "to X." X predeceased Grantor without leaving any descendants who survived Grantor. The devise to X lapses and passes under the residuary clause of Grantor's will.

d. Antilapse statutes. Under a typical antilapse statute, property devised to a devisee who is in the protected class, who predeceases the testator, and who leaves descendants who survive the testator passes to the predeceased devisee's descendants. See § 5.5. An antilapse statute yields to a contrary intention. The following Illustrations assume that there is no contrary intention.

Illustration:

5. Grantor died, leaving a will that devised $15,000 "to X." X predeceased Grantor, leaving descendants who survived Grantor. X is in the class of relatives who are protected by the applicable antilapse statute. The devise to X passes by representation to X's descendants under the antilapse statute.

e. Revocable trusts and other will substitutes. Revocable trusts and other will substitutes are treated as wills for purposes of requiring survival of the settlor and applying the applicable antilapse statute. See § 5.5, Comment *p*; § 7.2, Comment *f*. If the donative document in Illustration[ ] 5 . . . had not been a will, but a revocable trust with the income payable to Grantor for life, the result would have been the same . . . .

f. Deeds. A deed is effective as a dispositive instrument when the transferor manifests the intention that the deed is to be operative as a present transfer, such as by delivery. See § 6.2, Comment *u*; § 6.3, Comment *d*. If the grantee is then deceased, the deed is ineffective.

Part B. Express and Implied Conditions of Survival

Introductory Note: Section 26.2 serves as an introduction to the topic of express and implied conditions of survival. A condition of survival or any other condition can be expressed in either condition precedent or subsequent form. The form in which the condition is expressed has no classificatory consequence, since either form of expression means that the future interest is classified as contingent, not vested. See § 25.3. In terms of construction, however, the form in which the condition is expressed can, in some cases, produce different meanings.

The remaining sections in Part B address express and implied conditions of survival in particular forms of expression.

§ 26.2. Conditions Precedent and Subsequent: Meaning When Attached to a Future Interest

A condition attached to a future interest can be expressed in either precedent or subsequent form. If expressed in precedent form (e.g., "to B if . . ."), the event described in the condition must occur in order for the future interest to take effect in possession or enjoyment. If stated in subsequent form (e.g., "to B, but not if . . ."), the event described in the condition must occur in order for the future interest not to take effect in possession or enjoyment.

Comment:

a. Scope. This section addresses the meaning of conditions precedent and subsequent as applied to future interests. A present interest, by contrast, cannot be subject to a condition precedent but can be subject to a condition subsequent. A condition subsequent attached to a present interest, if satisfied, extinguishes the owner's right to possession or enjoyment.

b. Conditions precedent and subsequent: how differentiated. The distinction between a condition precedent and a condition subsequent is a distinction that is traditionally recognized in the law of future interests.

A *condition precedent* is a condition that is expressed as a condition that must be satisfied in order for the future interest to take effect in possession or enjoyment. A condition precedent provides that a future interest takes effect in possession or enjoyment *if* the condition is satisfied. (A *condition precedent* also exists if the future interest is in favor of an unborn, unadopted, or unascertained person, the condition being birth, adoption, or ascertainment.)

A *condition subsequent* is a condition that is expressed as a condition that, if satisfied on or before the distribution date, extinguishes the possibility that the future interest will take effect in possession or enjoyment. A condition subsequent provides that a future interest is to take effect in possession or enjoyment, *but not if* the condition is satisfied. If a condition subsequent continues to be operative after the future interest takes effect in possession or enjoyment, the future interest becomes a present interest subject to defeasance.

More often than not, a disposition creates a series of future interests expressed in the alternative. As noted in § 25.3, Comment *b*, if the first future interest is subject to a condition precedent or subsequent, that condition typically serves the additional role of operating as a condition precedent to the alternative future interest(s). See Illustrations 3 and 4.

Illustrations:

1. Grantor died, leaving a will that devised property in trust, directing the trustee to pay the income to A for life, then to distribute the trust principal to B if B survives A. B's remainder is subject to a condition precedent ("to B if . . .").

2. Grantor died, leaving a will that devised property in trust, directing the trustee to pay the income to A for life, then to distribute the trust principal to B, but not if B fails to survive A. B's remainder is subject to a condition subsequent ("to B, but not if . . .").

3. Grantor died, leaving a will that devised property in trust, directing the trustee to pay the income to A for life, then to distribute the trust principal to B if B survives A; if not to C. B's remainder is subject to a condition precedent ("to B if . . ."). C's remainder is also subject to a condition precedent ("if [B does not survive A], to C").

4. Grantor died, leaving a will that devised property in trust, directing the trustee to pay the income to A for life, then to distribute the trust principal to B, but if B fails to survive A, to C. B's remainder is subject to a condition subsequent ("to B, but if . . ."). C's remainder is subject to a condition precedent ("if [B does not survive A], to C").

c. *Classification.* Traditionally, the distinction between a condition precedent and a condition subsequent had two consequences: classification and construction. This Restatement declines to perpetuate a difference in classification between a condition precedent and a condition subsequent. Under § 25.3, a future interest is classified as "contingent" if, for any reason, it might not take effect in possession or enjoyment.

d. *Construction when condition precedent and condition subsequent are same in substance.* In matters of construction, there is no difference between a future interest that is subject to a condition precedent and one subject to a condition subsequent, if the substance of the condition, however expressed, is identical. Any condition can be expressed in precedent or subsequent form. The substance of the conditions in Illustrations 1 and 2 is identical: B is entitled to take in possession upon A's death only if B is then living. The substance of the conditions in Illustrations 3 and 4 is identical: B is entitled to take in possession upon A's death only if B is then living; if B is not then living, C or C's successors in interest take.

e. Construction when condition precedent and condition subsequent are not same in substance. Although any condition can be expressed in the precedent or the subsequent form, the meaning of the condition is more apparent when it is stated in the precedent form. Stating a condition in the subsequent form can lead to a construction that might not have been fully understood by the transferor. The conditions in Illustrations 5 and 6, below, are not identical, although a casual examination of the language might suggest that they are.

Illustrations:

5. Grantor died, leaving a will that devised property in trust, directing the trustee to pay the income to A for life, then to distribute the trust principal to A's children who survive A; if none, to C. A had two children, X and Y. X survived A, but Y predeceased A. On A's death, the trust principal passes to X.

6. Grantor died, leaving a will that devised property in trust, directing the trustee to pay the income to A for life, then to distribute the trust principal to A's children, but if none survives A, to C. A had two children, X and Y. X survived A, but Y predeceased A. On A's death, half of the trust principal passes to X and half to Y's successors in interest.

The condition in Illustration 5 is more precise because it is stated in the precedent form. In Illustration 6, a trier of fact cannot be completely confident that Grantor fully understood that the right to half of the trust principal would pass through Y's estate rather than to X. Had the condition in Illustration 6 been stated in the precedent rather than the subsequent form (for example, had the condition been "to A's children who survive A and the estates of those who predecease A if one or more of A's children survives A"), the trier of fact could be confident that that result represents Grantor's intent, because a transferor who was given that language by his or her drafting attorney would have had the opportunity to indicate that that is or is not what he or she wanted.

Additional examples of imprecision produced by the condition-subsequent form occur in Illustrations 7 and 8.

Illustrations:

7. Grantor died, leaving a will that devised property in trust, directing the trustee to pay the income to A for life, then to distribute the trust principal to B, but if B fails to survive A leaving issue who survive A, to such issue. If B survives A, B takes. If B predeceases A leaving issue who survive A, B's issue take. If B predeceases A without leaving issue who survive A, the right to the trust principal passes through B's estate to B's successors in interest. See § 26.5, Comment *c*, Illustration 3.

8. Grantor died, leaving a will that devised property in trust, directing the trustee to pay the income to A for life, then to distribute the trust principal to B, but if B fails to survive A, to C if C survives A. If B survives A, B takes. If B predeceases A and C survives A, C takes. If both B and C predecease A, the right to the trust principal passes through B's estate to B's successors in interest. . . . .

The transferor in Illustration 7 might not have anticipated that the right to trust principal would pass through B's estate if B predeceases A without leaving descendants who survive A. The transferor in Illustration 8 might not have anticipated that the right to trust principal would pass through B's estate if B and C predecease A. The transferor in both Illustrations would have been more likely to have understood the full meaning of the disposition if the condition had been expressed in the precedent form. In Illustration 7: "Income to A for life, then to B if B survives A or to B's estate if B predeceases A without leaving descendants who survive A." In Illustration 8: "Income to A for life, then to B if B survives A or to B's estate if B and C predecease A; to C if B predeceases A and C survives A." The condition-subsequent form in both Illustrations allows the possibility that the property will pass through B's estate to go unstated and possibly unnoticed by the transferor.

The condition-subsequent form produces much litigation, whereas the precedent form tends to avoid ambiguity, and hence avoids the need to litigate the meaning of the disposition. The precedent form pressures the drafter to identify with more care the various events that might transpire in the future, especially those that are improbable but not impossible, in order to bring each eventuality to the transferor's attention, and to implement the transferor's intention regarding each potential event in unambiguous language. See § 26.5, Comment *c*, for additional discussion of the perils of using the condition-subsequent form.

§ 26.3. No Implied Condition of Survival

Except in the case of a postponed multiple-generation class gift (see § 15.3), or unless an applicable statute provides otherwise, a future interest is not subject to an implied condition requiring the beneficiary or beneficiaries to survive the distribution date or survive any other post-creation time or event.

Comment:

a. Scope. This section applies to a future interest in which the beneficiary is not deceased when the donative document takes effect as a dispositive instrument (see § 26.1).

The question examined in this section is whether a future interest is subject to an implied condition requiring the beneficiary or beneficiaries to survive the distribution date or any other post-creation time or event. Sections 15.3 and 15.4 address this question with respect to a future interest that is in the form of a class gift. Section 15.3 adopts the traditional rule of construction by providing that a future interest in favor of a multiple-generation class is subject to an implied condition requiring the class members to survive the distribution date. Section 15.4 adopts the traditional rule of construction by providing that a future interest in favor of a single-generation class is not subject to an implied condition requiring the class members to survive the distribution date or any other post-creation time or event, unless an applicable statute provides otherwise.

This section dovetails with §§ 15.3 and 15.4 by adopting the traditional rule of construction that, except in the case of a postponed multiple-generation class gift, or unless an applicable statute provides otherwise, a future interest is not subject to an implied condition requiring the beneficiary or beneficiaries to survive the distribution date or any other post-creation time or event.

b. Distribution date. As used in this Restatement, the term "distribution date" with respect to a future interest in a trust refers to the time when a future interest is to take effect in possession or enjoyment. The distribution date for a future interest taking effect in possession or enjoyment on the death of a life beneficiary is the time of death of the life beneficiary, not the beginning or end of the calendar day of the income beneficiary's death and not when the trust principal is actually distributed.

c. Rationale of the rule of this section—traditional doctrine. This section adopts the traditional rule of construction that, except in the case of a postponed multiple-generation class gift, or unless an applicable statute provides otherwise, a condition requiring the beneficiary or beneficiaries to survive the distribution date or any other post-creation time or event is not implied. As explained in § 15.4, Comment *e*, this rule of construction is the rule best suited within the confines of the common-law tradition to approximate the likely preference of the transferor, and is supported by the constructional preference for the construction that does not disinherit a line of descent (see § 11.3(c)(3)). A rule better suited to the transferor's purposes would not only recognize an implied condition of survival, but also an implied substitute gift to the descendants of a deceased beneficiary who survive the distribution date. The traditional technique of the common law, however, is to effectuate intent by construction, and not by the creation of substitutionary shares not expressed by the transferor. There are judicial decisions in which the courts have found an implied gift on the basis of the facts and circumstances of a particular case. For example, in the case of a disposition "to A for life, and if A dies without issue, to B," courts have found an implied gift to A's issue if A dies with issue. See § 26.9. But the courts, unlike the legislatures in enacting antilapse statutes, have not presumed to create substitute gifts in all cases.

d. Historical rationale no longer convincing. The traditional rule had its origin in the constructional preference for vested interests and its corollary, the constructional preference for vesting at the earliest possible moment. Although the origin of the constructional preference for early vesting is somewhat obscure, the constructional preference is generally thought to be based on the desire to avoid the now-defunct rule of destructibility of contingent remainders (see § 25.5) and the once overly harsh but now widely liberalized or abolished Rule Against Perpetuities (see Division VIII). Neither the constructional preference for vested interests nor that for vesting at the earliest possible time is endorsed in this Restatement. See § 11.3.

e. Modern rationale—"trickle-down" theory. The strongest justification for the rule of this section is the "trickle-down" theory. Under this theory, the share of a deceased beneficiary will descend through the beneficiary's estate and, when the trust is dissolved at some later time, might end up benefiting the deceased beneficiary's descendants. The traditional rule produces the best chance within the common-law tradition of protecting a descending line that has one or more living members on the distribution date.

It would probably be within the traditional technique of the common law to construe future interests as presumptively subject to an implied condition requiring the beneficiary or beneficiaries to survive the distribution date, as is already done with respect to multiple-generation class gifts (see § 15.3). By itself, however, an implied condition of survival would make it impossible for the trickle-down theory to work. Unless a court is willing to couple a survival requirement with a blanket presumption creating a substitute gift to the descendants of a deceased beneficiary, merely implying a condition of survival in all cases would extinguish the possibility of benefit to the deceased beneficiary's descendants. Another possible approach would be to restrict the rule of construction against implying a condition of survival to instances in which the deceased beneficiary left descendants who survived the distribution date. That approach, while recommended to courts for consideration, is not adopted in this Restatement because of lack of judicial or legislative authority.

The principal weakness of the traditional rule is this: Although the share of a deceased beneficiary might end up in the hands of the deceased beneficiary's descendants, it might not. The deceased beneficiary might die without issue. The deceased beneficiary might die intestate, in which case there might be multiple heirs, one or more of whom also predecease the distribution date. On the distribution date, the deceased beneficiary's share can easily pass to complete strangers. To be sure, a beneficiary who survives the distribution date can also pass his or her share to complete strangers, but at least the beneficiary who survives the distribution date has the right to enjoy his or her share personally.

Another weakness of the traditional rule is the administrative cost of identifying the owner or owners of the interest on the distribution date. Identifying the current owners requires tracing the nonpossessory future interest through the estate of any beneficiary who died before the distribution date and perhaps tracing fractional shares of the interest through the estates of the beneficiary's successors in interest if any of them have also died before the distribution date.

Consequently, the traditional rule is a crude and costly means of protecting the deceased beneficiary's descendants from disinheritance, but probably is the only means of doing so within the traditional constructional technique of the common law.

The traditional rule applies equally to cases in which the future interest is not subject to any other conditions, as in Illustration 1, and to cases in which the future interest is subject to an express condition other than a condition of survival, as in Illustration 2.

Illustrations:

1. Grantor created a revocable inter vivos trust, directing the trustee to pay the income to Grantor for life, then to pay the income to Grantor's daughter A for life, then to distribute the trust principal "to A's children, X, Y, and Z." X survived A. Y predeceased A, leaving descendants who survived A. Z predeceased A. Z had one child, GC, who also predeceased A. GC had no descendants. Under the rule against implied conditions of survival, one-third of the trust principal goes to X, one-third goes to Y's estate, and the remaining one-third goes to Z's estate. Y's share might trickle down to Y's descendants. Z's share cannot trickle down to Z's descendants because there are none. Z's line has no living members on the distribution date.

2. Grantor died, leaving a will that devised property in trust, directing the trustee to pay the income to Grantor's daughter A for life, and at her death to distribute the trust principal "to A's children who survive her, but if A leaves no children surviving her, to my three other children B, C, and D." Grantor was survived by A, B, C, and D. A died without children. B survived A. C and D predeceased A. C left descendants who survived A, but D left no surviving descendants. One-third of the trust principal goes to B, one-third goes to the estate of C (and hence might end up in the hands of C's descendants), and one-third goes to the estate of D (even though D left no surviving descendants). It

is irrelevant that the future interest "to B, C, and D" was conditioned on A dying without children surviving her.

f. Future interest subject to condition other than a condition of survival. As noted in Comment *e*, and as illustrated in Illustration 2, the general rule of this section applies to a future interest that is subject to a condition other than a condition of survival.

Illustrations:

3. Grantor died, leaving a will that devised property in trust, directing the trustee to pay the income to Grantor's son A for life, then to distribute the trust principal "to B if B survives A, but if B does not survive A, to C." C's remainder is subject to the condition that B not survive A. That condition does not cause C's remainder to be subject to an implied condition that C survive either B or A.

4. Grantor created a revocable inter vivos trust, directing the trustee to pay the income to Grantor for life, then to pay the income to Grantor's daughter A for life, then to distribute the trust principal "to A's children who survive A, but if A leaves no children surviving her, to C." C's remainder is subject to the condition that A leave no children surviving her. That condition does not cause C's remainder to be subject to an implied condition that C survive A.

g. Contrary intent—express condition of survival. The rule of this section is a rule of construction that yields if the language or circumstances establish that the transferor had a different intention. If a condition of surviving the distribution date is stated expressly and unambiguously, the language of the disposition expresses an intent contrary to the rule of this section. In Illustrations 1 and 2, for example, if the trusts had provided that the trust principal was to go "to A's children X, Y, and Z who survive A," one-third of the trust principal of both trusts would pass to X. The other two-thirds would pass under the residuary clause. Nothing would pass through the estates of Y or Z. In Illustrations 3 and 4, if the trusts had provided that the trust principal was to go to C if C survived A, nothing would pass through C's estate if C had failed to survive A.

h. Antilapse-type statutes. A few states have enacted legislation that extends antilapse-type coverage to future interests. Most of these statutes are based on § 2–707 of the Uniform Probate Code, which only applies to future interests created in a trust. These statutes provide a more direct and efficient means of protecting equality among different lines of descent than the rule of this section. Under UPC § 2–707, a beneficiary of a future interest who fails to survive the distribution date by 120 hours is excluded, but the beneficiary's descendants who survive the distribution date, if any, take by representation in the beneficiary's place. To prevent the statute from being intent-defeating, the substitution of descendants only applies if the trust document fails to create an alternative future interest that is entitled to take effect in possession or enjoyment. In effect, this provision applies the antilapse statute applicable to wills and will substitutes (see § 5.5) as if the transferor were a testator who died on the distribution date. Section 2–706 of the UPC applies the same approach to beneficiary designations under life-insurance policies and similar arrangements.

UPC § 2–707 self-adjusts to different situations by saving a future interest when the deceased beneficiary left living descendants at the distribution date and extinguishing a future interest when the deceased beneficiary did not leave living descendants at the distribution date.

In Illustrations 1 and 2, UPC § 2–707 would pass one-third of the trust principal to X and one-third to Y's descendants who survived the distribution date. No part of the trust principal in either case would pass down Z's descending line, because that descending line had died out by the distribution date. In Illustrations 3 and 4, if C had predeceased A and had left descendants who survived A, C's descendants would take.

The Restatement Second of Property (Donative Transfers), which only addressed class gifts and did not address future interests not in class-gift form, endorsed the approach of such statutes, by stating that "it would be a better overall result to provide a substitute taker for the deceased class member and avoid involvement of the class member's share in his or her estate." Restatement Second, Property (Donative Transfers) § 27.3, Comment *b*. The Restatement Second also took the position that "[t]he policy of these statutes commends itself to decisional law." Restatement Second, Property (Donative Transfers) § 27.3, Comment *i*. A court that is willing to adopt this antilapse-type approach judicially should prefer it to the rule of this section. . . .

i. Divide-and-pay-over rule rejected. This Restatement follows the Restatement of Property § 260 in rejecting the so-called divide-and-pay-over rule. That rule provided that language attached to a future interest directing the trustee to divide and pay over the principal, or to convert and pay over the principal, to the beneficiaries of the future interest created a condition precedent of survival.

§ 26.4. Express Condition of Survival: Construction When Ambiguous Regarding Time to Which Survival Is Required

Unless the language or circumstances establish that the transferor had a different intention, an express condition of survival that is ambiguous regarding the time to which survival is required is construed to require the beneficiary or beneficiaries to survive the distribution date.

Comment:

a. Scope. The rule of this section as applied to a multiple-generation class gift is set forth in § 15.3, Comment *f*; and as applied to a single-generation class gift is set forth in § 15.4, Comment *g*. Section 26.4 extends the same rule to an ambiguous condition of survival attached to a future interest in favor of a beneficiary who takes as an individual and to a group of multiple beneficiaries taking as individuals and not as a class.

b. Rationale. Unless the language or circumstances establish that the transferor had a different intention, an express condition of survival that is ambiguous regarding the time to which survival is required is construed to require the beneficiary or beneficiaries to survive the distribution date, because that is the more natural meaning of the dispositive language and hence represents the probable intent of the transferor.

Illustrations:

1. Grantor died leaving a will that devised property in trust, directing the trustee to pay the income to A for life, then to distribute the trust principal to B if B survives. The condition of survival is ambiguous because it does not specify whether B must survive Grantor or A. The law requires that B survive Grantor. See § 26.1. The ambiguity

in the language of the disposition is resolved by construing the condition as requiring B also to survive A.

2. Grantor died leaving a will that devised property in trust, directing the trustee to pay the income to A for life, then to distribute the trust principal to those of B, C, and D who survive. The condition of survival is ambiguous because it does not specify whether B, C, and D must survive Grantor or A. The law requires that they survive Grantor. See § 26.1. The ambiguity in the language of the disposition is resolved by construing the condition as requiring them also to survive A.

§ 26.5. Alternative Future Interests Expressed Only in the Disjunctive

Unless the language or circumstances establish that the transferor had a different intention, the meaning of alternative future interests expressed only in the disjunctive (e.g., "to A for life, then to B or B's issue" or "to A for life, then to B or C") is that the interest of the primary beneficiary is subject to a condition of survival of the distribution date.

Comment:

a. Scope. This section only addresses whether the interest of the primary beneficiary is subject to a condition of survival of the distribution date when alternative future interests are expressed only in the disjunctive. Whether the interest of the substitutionary beneficiary is also subject to a condition of survival of the distribution date is a different question. Under the principles of § 26.3, there is no implied condition of survival on the substitutionary beneficiary unless the interest is in favor of a multiple-generation class.

b. Rationale. The rule of construction adopted in this section gives effect to the natural meaning of the language. When alternative future interests are expressed only in the disjunctive, the natural meaning of the language is that the primary beneficiary must survive the distribution date.

When the substitutionary future interest is in favor of the issue of the primary beneficiary (e.g., "to A for life, then to B or B's issue"), the rule of construction adopted in this section has the added benefit of disinheriting a line of descent that has no living members on the distribution date but not disinheriting a line of descent that has living members on the distribution date. As such, the rule of construction is supported by the constructional preference for the construction that does not disinherit a line of descent (see § 11.3(c)(3)).

c. Restricted versus unrestricted conditions of survival; supplanting versus disjunctive form. The rule of construction adopted in this section is sometimes referred to as an unrestricted condition of survival, as distinguished from a restricted condition of survival. Alternative future interests expressed in the disjunctive form produce an unrestricted condition of survival. An unrestricted condition of survival means that the primary future interest is extinguished if the primary beneficiary fails to survive the distribution date.

Alternative future interests expressed in the supplanting (condition-subsequent) form produce a restricted condition of survival. A restricted condition of survival means that the primary future interest is extinguished only if the primary beneficiary fails to survive the distribution date and the substitutionary beneficiary is entitled to take. If the primary beneficiary fails to survive the distribution date and the substitutionary beneficiary does not exist or otherwise is not entitled to take, the future interest passes through the estate of the primary beneficiary. See § 26.2, Comment *e*, for additional discussion concerning the condition-subsequent form.

The future interests in Illustration 1 are expressed in the disjunctive form. The future interests in Illustrations 2 and 3 are expressed in the supplanting (or condition-subsequent) form. The difference between Illustrations 2 and 3 is that Illustration 2 deals with a primary future interest that is not in the form of a class gift and the primary future interest in Illustration 3 is in that form.

Illustrations:

1. Grantor died, leaving a will that devised property in trust, directing the trustee to pay the income to A for life, then to distribute the trust principal to B or B's issue. B failed to survive A. Because B failed to survive A, B's interest is extinguished. If B left issue who survived A, the trust principal would pass to B's issue who survived A. If B did not leave issue who survived A, the trust principal would pass through Grantor's estate to Grantor's successors in interest.

2. Grantor died, leaving a will that devised property in trust, directing the trustee to pay the income to A for life, then to distribute the trust principal to B, but if B predeceases A leaving issue, then to such issue. B died without issue before A's death. B's remainder interest is not extinguished, but instead passes through B's estate to B's successors in interest. See § 26.2, Comment *e*, Illustration 7.

3. Grantor died, leaving a will that devised property in trust, directing the trustee to pay the income to A for life, then to distribute the trust principal to Grantor's brothers and sisters, but if any brother or sister predeceases A leaving issue, to such issue. B (Grantor's brother) died without issue before A's death. C (Grantor's sister) survived A. Because the remainder to Grantor's brothers and sisters is in the form of a class gift, B's interest passes to C. Had B survived A, B would have been entitled to half of the trust principal. Had B predeceased A leaving issue who survived A, half of the trust principal would have passed to B's issue who survived A. If both B and C had predeceased A without leaving issue who survived A, half of the principal would have passed through B's estate to B's successors in interest and half through C's estate to C's successors in interest, demonstrating again that conditions stated in subsequent form can produce unanticipated consequences.

d. Substitution of "children." The rule of this section applies to a future interest that expressly provides for the substitution of the beneficiary's children, but in such a case, the court should examine whether there are grounds for construing "children" to mean "issue." See § 14.1, Comment *g*.

e. Variety of alternative future interests. The rule of this section applies to alternative future interests in various combinations.

Illustrations:

4. Grantor established an inter vivos trust, directing the trustee to pay the income "to A for life, then to distribute the trust principal to B or C or D." B's future interest is subject to a condition of survival of A. C's future interest is subject to a condition of survival of A and a

condition that B not survive A. D's future interest is subject to a condition that B and C fail to survive A.

5. Grantor established an inter vivos trust, directing the trustee to pay the income "to A for life, then to return the trust principal to me or distribute it to C." Grantor's future interest is subject to a condition of survival of A. C's future interest is subject to a condition that Grantor fail to survive A.

6. Grantor established an inter vivos trust, directing the trustee to pay the income "to A for life, then to distribute the trust principal to B or return it to me." B's future interest is subject to a condition of survival of A. Grantor's future interest is subject to a condition that B fail to survive A.

7. Grantor established an inter vivos trust, directing the trustee to pay the income "to A for life, then to distribute the trust principal to B or B's heirs." B's future interest is subject to a condition of survival of A. The future interest in favor of B's heirs is subject to a condition that B fail to survive A. See § 16.1 for the meaning of the class gift to B's heirs.

§ 26.6. Age Specification: Implied Condition of Survival

Unless the language or circumstances establish that the transferor had a different intention, a future interest that is distributable upon reaching a specified age is conditioned on the beneficiary's living to that age.

Comment:

a. *Scope and cross-references.* See § 15.1, Comment *m* (Class gift distributable as each class member reaches a specified age); § 15.1, Comment *o* (Class gift distributable when youngest member of class reaches a specified age).

b. *Rationale.* This section establishes, as a rule of construction, that a future interest that is distributable upon reaching a specified age is conditioned on the beneficiary's survival to that age because that is the more natural meaning of the dispositive language. The case law across the broad spectrum is generally considered to be difficult to reconcile and is sometimes based on small differences in wording that often appear to be inconsequential. See Comment *c*. One recurrent theme has been a tendency to rely on the constructional preference for early vesting to find that survival to the specified age is not required. That constructional preference, however, is no longer convincing and is not followed in this Restatement. See § 15.4, Comment *d*; § 26.3, Comment *d*.

Illustration:

1. Grantor's will bequeathed $90,000 to be paid to Grantor's grandchildren at age 21. Unless other language or circumstances establish that Grantor had a different intention, any grandchild who survives Grantor but dies under 21 is excluded from the class. Under §§ 15.2 and 26.1, any grandchild who fails to survive Grantor is also excluded from the class, regardless of whether the grandchild reached 21 before Grantor's death. On when this class closes, see § 15.1, Comment *m*.

c. Historical note. An old English case, Clobberie's Case, 2 Vent. 342, 86 Eng. Rep. 476 (Ch. 1677), has been the principal source for the rules of construction regarding a future interest distributable to a beneficiary upon reaching a specified age. Although *Clobberie's Case* has continued to influence the law into modern times, the rules laid down by that case turn on small differences in wording. *Clobberie's Case* laid down three rules:

Rule 1: A disposition to X "at" age 21 is not conditioned on X reaching 21 if the disposition gives X the income during the period that X is under 21.

Rule 2: A disposition to X "at" age 21 is conditioned on X reaching 21 if the disposition does not give X the income during the period that X is under 21.

Rule 3: A disposition to X "to be paid at" age 21 is not conditioned on X reaching 21 whether or not the disposition gives X the income during the period that X is under 21.

Although *Clobberie's Case* did not deal with a class gift, but one to an individual, the rules of that case have been extended to class gifts.

d. Express condition of survival. If a condition of surviving to the specified age is stated expressly and unambiguously, that language is controlling. Unambiguous language requiring survival would include such language as "when and if" the beneficiary reaches the specified age or a disposition to class members "who attain [the specified age]" or a disposition to be distributed among those class members "who reach [the specified age]." In § 15.1, Comment *m*, Illustration[ ] 13 . . ., the class members' shares are expressly and unambiguously conditioned on reaching the specified age.

e. Contrary intent—language of present gift with possession postponed. The rule of this section is a rule of construction that yields if the language or circumstances establish that the donor had a different intention. Language providing that the share is "to be paid at" a specified age is treated as a factor but not necessarily a controlling factor suggesting that there is no condition of survival to the specified age.

f. Contrary intent—intermediate income. A provision directing that income from the beneficiary's presumptive share be paid to the beneficiary while the beneficiary is under the specified age is taken as a strong but not necessarily a controlling factor that there is no condition of survival to the specified age.

g. Contrary intent—adverse tax consequences. If requiring survival to the specified age would have adverse tax consequences to the donor, that is a factor weighing against a requirement of survival. For example, one of the requirements for a trust for a minor to qualify for the annual gift-tax exclusion allowed by IRC § 2503(c) is that the property must "pass to the donee on his attaining the age of 21 years, and in the event the donee dies before attaining the age of 21 years, be payable to the estate of the donee or as he may appoint under a general power of appointment. . . ."

h. Contrary intent—absence of gift over. The absence of an express gift over to another beneficiary in case the class member fails to survive to the designated age is taken as a factor but not necessarily a controlling factor suggesting that there is no condition of survival to the specified age.

i. Contrary intent—beneficiary leaves descendants who survive the distribution date. In § 26.3, Comment *e*, it was noted that the trickle-down theory could be judicially effectuated by restricting the rule of construction against implying a condition of survival to instances in which the deceased beneficiary left descendants who survived the distribution date. Although that rule is not adopted in this Restatement as a rule of construction due to lack of supporting judicial or legislative authority, a court is free to do so or to treat it as a factor favoring the conclusion that there is no condition of survival to the specified age. Thus, in Illustration 1, any grandchild who died under 21 would not be excluded from the class if the deceased grandchild had left surviving descendants. And in Illustration 2, that rule would mean that any niece or nephew who died under 21 would not be excluded from the class if the deceased niece or nephew had left surviving descendants.

j. *Antilapse-type statutes.* The UPC provisions described in § 15.4, Comment *i*, and in § 26.3, Comment *h*, apply to future interests distributable at a specified age. As noted in those Comments, a court that is willing to adopt an antilapse-type approach judicially should do so rather than adopt the rule of this section.

Part C. Gifts Over on Death or on Death Without Issue

Introductory Note: The two sections in Part C state rules of construction applicable when a disposition contains a gift over on death or on death without issue.

§ 26.7. Meaning of "Death" When Death Is Referred to as a Conditional Event

Unless the language or circumstances establish that the transferor had a different intention, the word "death" in a disposition that refers to death as a conditional event is construed as referring to death before the distribution date.

Comment:

a. *Rationale.* Because death is an inevitable event, a disposition that refers to death as a conditional event is ambiguous. The construction that has been accepted in the case law and in the Restatement of Property §§ 263 and 264, and that is followed in this Restatement, is that the transferor, by using conditional language, intended to describe an uncertain event. Under that assumption, the only means of introducing an uncertainty into the disposition is to construe the reference to death as referring to death before the distribution date.

b. *Distribution date.* As used in this Division, the term "distribution date" refers to the time when a present or a future interest is to take effect in possession or enjoyment. The distribution date for a present interest taking effect on the death of the testator is the time of death of the testator, not the beginning or end of the calendar day of the testator's death and not when the testator's estate is actually distributed. The distribution date for a future interest taking effect in possession or enjoyment on the death of the income beneficiary is the time of death of the income beneficiary, not the beginning or end of the calendar day of the income beneficiary's death and not when the trust principal is actually distributed.

c. *Present interest "conditioned" on death.* In the case of a present interest that is conditioned on the death of a designated person or class, the distribution date is the effective date of the transfer.

Illustration:

1. Grantor died, leaving a will that devised land "to A, but if A should die, to B." B's interest is conditioned on A's death. The presumed construction is that the phrase "but if A should die" means "but if A should die before Grantor." Under this construction, the land passes to B in fee simple absolute at Grantor's death if A predeceases Grantor and B survives Grantor. If A survives Grantor, A takes the land in fee simple absolute at Grantor's death and B takes nothing.

d. Present interest "conditioned" on death—effect of antilapse statute. Under § 5.5, Comment *g*, an alternative devise overrides an antilapse statute, if the alternative devisee survives the testator and is otherwise entitled to take (i.e., is not prevented from taking because of an unsatisfied condition). The following Illustration applies that principle to a present interest "conditioned" on death.

Illustration:

4. Grantor died, leaving a will that devised land "to my sister A, but if A should die, to my brother B." Both A and B are in the class of relatives protected by the applicable antilapse statute. See § 5.5, Comment *c*. If A predeceases Grantor leaving descendants who survive Grantor, and if B survives Grantor, the land passes to B in fee simple absolute at Grantor's death; the alternative devise to B defeats the antilapse statute. If A predeceases Grantor leaving descendants who survive Grantor, and if B predeceases Grantor without leaving descendants who survive Grantor, the land passes under the antilapse statute to A's descendants in fee simple absolute at Grantor's death; the alternative devise to B does not defeat the antilapse statute because B is not entitled to take. If A predeceases Grantor without leaving descendants who survive Grantor, and if B predeceases Grantor leaving descendants who survive Grantor, the land passes under the antilapse statute to B's descendants in fee simple absolute at Grantor's death. If A predeceases Grantor leaving descendants who survive Grantor, and if B also predeceases Grantor leaving descendants who survive Grantor, the land passes under the antilapse statute to A's descendants in fee simple absolute at Grantor's death.

e. Future interest "conditioned" on death. In the case of a future interest taking effect in possession or enjoyment on the death of the income beneficiary (or life tenant), the distribution date is the time of death of the income beneficiary, not the beginning or end of the calendar day of the income beneficiary's death and not when the trust principal is actually distributed.

Illustration:

5. Grantor died, leaving a will that devised property in trust, "income to A for life, then trust principal to B, but if B should die, to C." A, B, and C survived Grantor. The presumed construction is that the phrase "but if B should die" means "but if B should die before A." Under this construction, the trust principal passes to C if B predeceases A. If B survives A, B's remainder becomes a fee simple absolute.

f. Contrary intent. The rule of this section is a rule of construction, which yields if the language or circumstances establish that the transferor had a different intention. The language in Illustration 1 would establish a contrary intention, and the rule of construction of this section would be rebutted, if the disposition in Illustration 1 had stated "to A, but if before or after Grantor's death A should die, to B." Likewise, if the disposition in Illustration 5 had stated "income to A for life, then trust principal to B, but if before or after A's death B should die, to C," the terms of the instrument would rebut the rule of this section.

§ 26.8. Meaning of "Death Without Issue"

Unless the language or circumstances establish that the transferor had a different intention, a disposition that refers to "death without issue" is construed as referring to death without leaving issue who are living on the distribution date.

Comment:

a. Historical but now rejected meaning of "death without issue": indefinite failure of issue. In early English law (see § 24.4, Comment *a*; Restatement of Property § 266, Comment *a*), the phrase "die without issue" (or terms of like import) meant an indefinite failure of issue. Under that construction, the term "die without issue" meant the ultimate extinction of a descending line whenever in the future such extinction might occur. In a disposition "to A and her heirs, but if A dies without issue, to B," the indefinite-failure-of-issue construction in effect converted A's estate into something akin to the fee tail, because that construction meant that A's death survived by issue would not render A's interest absolute and would not terminate B's interest. A's interest would continue to be defeasible because A's descending line could completely die out later, and if and when that should occur, B's interest would become possessory.

b. Definite failure of issue. Along with the abolition of the fee tail estate (see § 24.4), the indefinite-failure-of-issue construction has now been replaced in both English and American law by the definite-failure-of-issue construction. See Restatement of Property §§ 266 to 270. Under the definite-failure-of-issue construction, the question whether a person or class has died without issue is resolved with finality as of the distribution date.

Illustrations:

1. Grantor died, leaving a will that devised land to A and her heirs, but if A should die without issue, to B. After Grantor's death, A died survived by issue. A's death survived by issue extinguishes B's remainder.

2. Grantor died, leaving a will that devised land to A for life, then to B, but if B should die without issue, to C. After Grantor's death, A died survived by B. B's survival of A extinguishes C's remainder. If B had predeceased A survived by issue who also survived A, C's remainder would also terminate. If B had predeceased A without leaving issue who survived A, C's remainder would become possessory and absolute at A's death.

c. Terms of like import. Terms of like import to "die without issue" include terms such as "die without leaving issue," "die without having issue," "die without issue to inherit," "on failure of issue," "in default of issue," "for want of issue," "have no issue," "die without descendants," "die issueless," "die without heirs of his/her body," "have no issue."

The term "die without children" is also a term of like import in cases in which "children" is construed to mean "issue." See § 15.4, Comment *h*, and references cited therein. Even if "children" is not construed to mean "issue," the form of the disposition is sufficiently similar to those described in this

Section, and, unless a contrary intent of the conveyor is found from additional language or circumstances (see Comment *d*), a rule analogous to that stated in this Section is applicable. The interest that is conditioned on the designated person dying without children becomes a present interest if, but only if, the designated person is not survived by children on the distribution date.

The term "die without heirs" is also a term of like import in cases in which "heirs" is construed to mean "issue." That construction frequently arises in cases in which the gift over "on failure of heirs" is to collateral relatives of the designated person, who themselves would be heirs of the designated person on his or her death without issue. In such a disposition, the term "heirs" is construed to have been used inexpertly to mean issue.

d. Contrary intent. The rule of this section is a rule of construction, which yields if the language or circumstances establish that the transferor had a different intention. For example, the language in Illustration 1 would establish a different intention, and the rule of construction of this section would be rebutted, if the disposition had stated "to A and her heirs, but if before or after A's death A's descending line should die out, to B."

e. Implied remainder to issue. A remainder conditioned on death without issue (see Comment *a*) provides the basis for implying a remainder in favor of the designated person's issue if that person dies with issue. See § 26.9, Comment *b*. If the court finds an implied remainder to issue, the case is put on the same basis as it would have been had there been express alternative present or future interests, one conditioned on the death with issue of a designated person or class and the other conditioned on death without issue of the designated person or class. See Comment *g*. For rules governing the presumptive meaning of "issue" in the implied remainder to issue, see §§ 14.3 through 14.9 and 15.1 through 15.3.

f. Death with issue. The rule of this section also applies to a disposition that refers to death with issue. Such a disposition is construed as referring to death leaving issue who are living on the distribution date.

Illustrations:

4. Grantor died, leaving a will that devised land to A and her heirs, but if A should die with issue, to such issue. After Grantor's death, A died survived by issue. A's death survived by issue causes A's defeasible fee to terminate and the land to pass at A's death to A's then-living issue. If A had died without any then-living issue, A's death without issue would have caused A's defeasible fee to become absolute.

5. Grantor died, leaving a will that devised land to A for life, then to B, but if B should die with issue, to such issue. After Grantor's death, B died survived by A. B left issue who survived A. The land passes at A's death to B's then-living issue. If B had predeceased A without leaving issue who survived A, B's remainder would have vested in possession at A's death in B's successors in interest as a fee simple absolute. If B had survived A, B's remainder would have vested in possession in B at A's death as a fee simple absolute.

g. Death with or without issue. In the case of alternative gifts over, one conditioned on the death of a designated person or class with issue and the other conditioned on death of the designated person or class without issue, the condition is resolved on the distribution date.

Illustration:

7. Grantor died, leaving a will that devised land to A for life, then to B, but if B should die with issue, to such issue, and if B should die without issue, to C. After Grantor's death, B died survived by A. B left issue who survived A. The land passes at A's death to B's then-living issue. If B had predeceased A without leaving issue who survived A, C's remainder would have vested in possession in fee simple absolute at A's death. If B had survived A, B's remainder would have vested in possession at A's death in fee simple absolute.

Part D. Incomplete Dispositions

Introductory Note: The one section in Part D addresses incomplete dispositions that justify the implication of a future interest to fill the gap and make the disposition complete.

§ 26.9. Filling Gaps by Construction—Implication of Future Interests

A gap in a disposition may be filled by construction.

Comment:

a. Rationale. Theoretically, there can be no gap in a disposition, because, under the doctrine of estates, any gap is automatically filled by a future interest in favor of the transferor or the transferor's successors in interest. Thus, in a disposition "to A for life," the transferor retains a reversion even though the language of the disposition does not expressly reserve that reversion. It is sometimes said that the transferor's reversion arises by operation of law. See § 25.2. In such a case, there is no basis for implying a future interest that would take effect in possession at A's death in place of the transferor's reversion.

Nevertheless, when the disposition is more complex, and it appears that the gap was not anticipated by the transferor, there is a basis for implying a future interest by construction if doing so furthers the transferor's overall dispositive plan. An implied future interest takes effect in possession in place of the transferor's reversion that would otherwise become possessory.

b. Implication of a remainder to issue. One of the cases that justifies implying a remainder is the case of the implication of a remainder to issue. Such an implied remainder arises in the case of a disposition in trust, "income to A for life, and if A dies without issue, trust principal to B." If A dies with issue who survive A, an implied remainder to those issue arises by construction. If A dies without issue who survive A, the trust principal passes to B outright. See § 26.8.

The same proposition applies to a disposition in trust, "income to A for life, and if A dies without children, trust principal to B." If A dies with children who survive A, an implied remainder to those children arises by construction. If A dies without children who survive A, the trust principal passes to B outright. See § 26.8. The possibility of construing "children" to mean "issue" should also be considered, if doing so would prevent the disinheritance of a descending line that had one or more living members at A's death. See §§ 15.4, Comment *h*; 26.5, Comment *d*.

Although this section is mainly concerned with the implication of a remainder by construction, the same principle is also applicable to a present interest. For example, suppose that a testator devises property "to A, but if A dies without issue, to B." This devise creates a fee simple defeasible in A (see § 24.3) and a contingent remainder to B (see §§ 25.2, 25.3). But what if, before the testator's death, A dies with issue? In this case, there is a basis for implying a present interest to A's issue. If, on the other hand, A dies with issue after the testator's death, the preferred construction is that A's fee becomes absolute.

c. *Time gap.* A gap in possession arising on the distribution date can supply the basis for implying a remainder. A typical case is a disposition in trust "income to A for life, then to B if B attains 21." If A dies while B is under 21, the logical conclusion is that the income is paid to B during the interim. In some states, this result is supported by legislation such as Cal. Civ. Code § 733, which provides: "When . . . there is a suspension of ownership during the continuation of which the income is undisposed of, and no valid direction for its accumulation is given, such income belongs to the persons presumptively entitled to the next eventual interest." . . . . If, after A's death, B lives to age 21, B's remainder becomes possessory in fee simple absolute. If, after A's death, B dies under 21, B's remainder and entitlement to future income payments are extinguished.

d. *Implication of a cross future interest in trust principal.* A gap in the disposition of a portion of trust principal can give rise to an implied cross remainder in favor of the beneficiary or beneficiaries who are entitled to the other portion of trust principal.

Illustration:

1. Grantor died, leaving a will that devised property in trust, directing the trustee to pay the income to my son, A, and my daughter, B. On the death of the first to die, all of the income is to be paid to the survivor. The trust also provided that on the death of the survivor, half of the trust principal is to be distributed to A's issue and half to B's issue. The trust also provided that should both A and B have no living issue on the death of the survivor of A and B, the trust principal is to be distributed to X charity. A died first, without issue. B later died, survived by issue. Under the clear terms of the trust, half of the trust principal is distributable to B's issue. The gap in the disposition arises regarding the distribution of the other half of the trust principal. X charity is not entitled to that half because the remainder to X charity is conditioned on both A and B dying without issue. On the basis of Grantor's overall plan of disposition, the preferred result is to fill the gap by implying a cross remainder to B's issue. B's issue are therefore entitled to all of the trust principal on the death of B. Similarly, if A had died with issue who survived B, and if B had died without issue, A's issue would be entitled to all of the trust principal on the death of B.

e. *Gap in the disposition of income when there are multiple income beneficiaries.* When the income of a trust is payable to two or more beneficiaries, a gap in the disposition of the income share of a deceased income beneficiary may arise.

e(1). Gap when trust principal distributable on death of last living income beneficiary. A gap potentially arises if the terms of the trust direct that the trust principal is to be distributed on the death of the last living income beneficiary, and if the terms of the trust make no express provision for the distribution of the share of income that a deceased income beneficiary other than the last living income beneficiary had been receiving.

If the income beneficiary's income interest is not limited to the beneficiary's lifetime, no gap arises because the income beneficiary's interest is a life estate for the life of the last living income beneficiary (a life estate pur autre vie). See Illustration 2; § 24.5, Comment *c*.

A gap arises if the income beneficiary's income interest is limited to the beneficiary's lifetime. The traditional rule of construction is that the gap is filled by an implied cross remainder to the living income beneficiary or beneficiaries. See Restatement of Property § 115; Illustration 3. An exception, however, arises if the remainder in trust principal is to pass to the issue of the beneficiaries upon the survivor's death. In such a case, filling the gap by implying an income interest in favor of the deceased beneficiary's issue from time to time living would be more consistent with the transferor's overall plan of disposition. This result pertains whether or not the beneficiaries are described in class terminology. See Illustrations 4 and 5; Restatement Third, Trusts § 49, Comment *c(3)*. For the analysis in the case of a single-generation class gift, see § 14.1, Comment *g(4)*.

Illustrations:

2. Grantor died, leaving a will that devised property in trust, directing the trustee to "pay one-half of the income to my son, A, and one-half to my daughter, B, for the life of the survivor of the two; upon the death of the survivor of my children, the trust principal is to be distributed to my then-living descendants, by representation; if none, to X charity." A died first. A's income interest is a life estate pur autre vie. Half of the trust income is payable to A's successors in interest for the lifetime of B.

3. Grantor died, leaving a will that devised property in trust, directing the trustee to "pay one-half of the income to my son, A, for life and one-half to my daughter, B, for life; upon the death of the survivor of my children, the trust principal is to be distributed to X charity." A died, survived by B. All of the trust income is now payable to B.

4. Grantor died, leaving a will that devised property in trust, directing the trustee to "pay one-half of the income to my son, A, for life and one-half to my daughter, B, for life; upon the death of the survivor of my children, the trust principal is to be distributed to my then-living descendants, by representation; if none, to X charity." A died, survived by descendants. If the trust instrument fails to state who is now entitled to A's share of income, Grantor's overall plan of disposition provides a basis for concluding that A's descendants who are living at the time of each distribution are to receive half of the trust income until the death of B. See Restatement Third, Trusts § 49, Comment *c(3)*, Illustration 3. If A had died without surviving descendants, all of the trust income would be payable to B.

5. Grantor died, leaving a will that devised property in trust, directing the trustee to "pay one-third of the income to my son, A, for life, one-third to my daughter, B, for life, and one-third to my son, C, for life; upon the death of the survivor of my children, the trust principal is to be distributed to my then-living descendants, by representation; if none, to X charity." A died first, survived by descendants. Grantor's overall plan of disposition provides a basis for concluding that A's share of the income passes to A's descendants who are living at the time of each distribution date. Then B died without surviving descendants. Grantor's overall plan of disposition provides a basis for concluding that half of B's share of the income passes to C and half passes to A's

descendants who are living at the time of each distribution until the death of C.

e(2). No gap when proportionate share of trust principal distributable on the death of each income beneficiary. No gap concerning the disposition of a deceased income beneficiary's share of income arises if the terms of the trust direct that a proportionate share of the trust principal is to be distributed on the death of each income beneficiary.

Illustration:

6. Grantor died, leaving a will that devised property in trust, directing the trustee to "pay one-half of the income to my son, A, for life and one-half to my daughter, B, for life; upon the death of each, the proportionate share of trust principal is to be distributed to the then-living descendants of the deceased child, by representation; if none, to X charity." A died, survived by descendants. A's descendants who survive A are entitled to half of the trust principal. If A had died without any surviving descendants, half of the trust principal would have been distributable to X charity. Whether A died with or without surviving descendants, the other half of the trust principal remains in trust for the benefit of B.

f. Accrued share. A gap arises when the language of a dispositive instrument does not expressly provide for the disposition of a share received by the recipient of a gift over (the accrued share) when the recipient's original share is subject to a gift over. The problem is whether the accrued share is also subject to the gift over that expressly applies to the recipient's original share. The position of this Restatement is that, unless the language or circumstances establish that the transferor had a different intention, the transferor's overall dispositive plan is better carried out by implying a gift over of the accrued share.

Illustration:

7. Grantor devised a tract of land "to my three sons, A, B, and C, but if any son dies without leaving issue surviving him, the portion devised to such son shall go to my said sons then living." After Grantor's death, A died without issue; then B died without issue. C is still living. When A died without issue, A's one-third share passed equally to B and C. When B died without issue, B's original one-third share passed to C. There is a gap in the disposition, however, regarding the one-sixth share that B received when A died. That gap is filled by implying a gift over to C of that one-sixth share. C now owns a present interest (a defeasible fee) in all of the property. When C later dies, the disposition of the property depends on whether he dies with or without issue. If C dies with issue, the property passes to his issue. See Comment *b*. If C dies without issue, C's defeasible fee ripens into a fee simple absolute and passes through C's estate to his successors in interest.

g. Power of appointment created by implication. For the proposition that a power of appointment may be created by implication, see § 18.1, Comment *g*.

DIVISION VIII

PUBLIC-POLICY LIMITATION ON DEAD-HAND CONTROL: THE RULE AGAINST PERPETUITIES

Scope of Division VIII. Although freedom of disposition is a core principle in the field of donative transfers (see § 10.1), public policy places limits on that freedom. Public policy has traditionally placed a limit on dead-hand control by means of the Rule Against Perpetuities (the Rule). This Restatement maintains that tradition by adopting a reformulated Rule that—with certain qualifications and exceptions—places a durational limit of two generations on dead-hand control.

This Restatement does not cover all of the rules that fall under the category of rules of public policy that limit freedom of disposition. Other such rules are covered in the Restatement Third of Trusts and the Restatement Second of Property (Donative Transfers).

[See Restatement Third of Trusts § 29(c), Comments *i–m*; Restatement Second of Property (Donative Transfers) §§ 3.1–3.4, 4.1–4.5.]

CHAPTER 27

RULE AGAINST PERPETUITIES

Introductory Note: Chapter 27 addresses the Rule Against Perpetuities in three sections. Section 27.1 states the Rule as adopted in this Restatement. Section 27.2 gives guidance regarding how a disposition is to be modified in cases in which a trust or other donative disposition of property is subject to judicial modification under § 27.1. Section 27.3 lists the transactions that are excluded from the Rule.

The following account of the history and purposes of the Rule Against Perpetuities (the Rule) provides background for the Rule adopted in this chapter.

The limited-dead-hand-control policy of the Rule Against Perpetuities. The Rule began to be developed in the late 17th century. The starting point was Lord Nottingham's decision in the Duke of Norfolk's Case, 3 Ch. Cas. 1, 22 Eng. Rep. 931 (Ch. 1682), which did not announce a rule as such and upheld the trust at issue, but suggested that there was a limit "when any inconvenience appears; nowhere before." The courts developed the Rule case by case over a long period of time. The "world in which the Rule evolved was that of a landed aristocracy and gentry, and [the Rule's] function was to impose limits which seemed reasonable in that world to the degree to which the head of the family, the patriarch for the time being, could make binding dispositions of the family estates which controlled their destination long into the future."

In later times, some writers attributed to the Rule the purpose of facilitating commerce by promoting free alienability of property, especially land. Legal historians have concluded, however, that promoting free alienability of land was not the original purpose of the Rule: "[The] connection [of the common-law Rule] with the value of freedom of disposition was not originally established because of some economic theory about the merits of a free market in land; 17th century lawyers had not read Adam Smith." If the Rule had any effect in promoting the alienability of land, that effect has receded in importance with the rise of the management trust in which the trustee normally has the power to buy and sell trust assets.

Modern thinking about the purpose of the Rule has centered on the Rule's original purpose—preventing a long deceased transferor from keeping property out of the control of the living for an unreasonable period of time. As Professor A.W.B. Simpson has written: "The policy was this: given that one can, to a limited extent only, foresee the future and the problems it will generate, landowners should not be allowed to tie up lands for periods outside the range of reasonable foresight."

Professor Lewis M. Simes argued that the function of the Rule is to "strike[ ] a fair balance between the desires of members of the present generation, and similar desires of succeeding generations, to do what they wish with the property which they enjoy." Sir Arthur Hobhouse suggested that the fair balance be drawn on the basis of a know-and-see standard: "A clear, obvious, natural line is drawn for us between those persons and events which the Transferor knows and sees, and those which he cannot know or see." Professor W. Barton Leach and Owen Tudor expanded on the know-and-see theory: "In establishing the balance between private right and public interest the courts arrived at a solution which permitted the following: . . . In a will a man of property could provide for all of those in his family whom he personally knew and the first generation after them upon attaining majority." The Reporter [for this Restatement Third, Professor Lawrence Waggoner] has suggested a further refinement of the theory: "[T]he [know-and-see] standard [implies] that donors should be allowed to exert control through the youngest generation of descendants they knew and saw, or at least one or more but not necessarily all of whom they knew and saw." An underlying premise of the know-and-see theory is that "it was the function of the courts to favour prudent and sensible dispositions, and, as a corollary, invalidate foolish ones."

The common-law Rule. In developing the common-law Rule following the *Duke of Norfolk's Case*, the "judges accepted the idea that dispositions were to be void if they depended upon contingencies which could happen at too remote a time in the future; indeed the rule came to be called a rule against remoteness of *vesting*." As finally distilled in the late 19th century by Professor John Chipman Gray from two centuries of case law, the accepted statement of the common-law Rule is: "No interest is good unless it must vest, if at all, not later than twenty-one years after some life in being at the creation of the interest."

In hindsight, the mechanism embodied in the common-law Rule was ill chosen. The common-law Rule is difficult to master. Applying the common-law Rule to a specific case requires determining whether there is an individual—a life in being at the creation of the interest—whose life makes an interest valid. Determining whether there is such an individual requires a process considered by many to be mysterious and confusing. Part of the confusion is traced to the counterintuitive position, established in the English case of Jee v. Audley, 1 Cox 324, 29 Eng. Rep. 1186 (Ch. 1787), that every individual, man or woman, is irrebuttably presumed to be physically capable of having a child until death, a proposition known as the conclusive presumption of lifetime fertility. Further confusion arises from the practice of referring to the life in being as the "measuring life," as if the common-law Rule measured out a period of time during which an interest must vest or fail to vest. That part of the mystery has been somewhat demystified by referring to the life in being as the "validating life." The term validating life is more accurate because an interest is valid only if there is a validating life. The absence of a validating life means that an interest is invalid.

Moreover, the common-law Rule serves the limited-dead-hand-control policy poorly, because it defeats dispositions that do not violate that policy. Leach pressed this insight by focusing on the cases that he labeled the fertile octogenarian, the unborn widow, and the administrative contingency.

Illustrations:

1. *"Fertile octogenarian."* Grantor died, leaving a will that devised property in trust, directing the trustee to pay the income "to A my daughter for life, then to A's children for the life of the survivor, and upon the death of A's last surviving child, to pay the trust principal to

A's grandchildren." Grantor died at age 75, survived by his 55-year-old daughter A, who had passed the menopause, and by A's adult children, C1 (age 35) and C2 (age 30). Under the common-law Rule, the future interest to A's grandchildren is invalid because it is deemed possible that A will become pregnant and have a third child or that A will adopt a child and that that third child will outlive by more than 21 years A, C1, C2, and anybody else one can think of who was in being and has any connection to the transaction. Under this chain of events, the interest in the trust principal in favor of A's grandchildren would vest beyond a life in being plus 21 years. Of course, it is improbable that such far-fetched chain of events will occur. It is far more likely that A will have no more children, and the future interest will vest on the death of either C1 or C2, who were in being at the creation of the trust.

2. *"Unborn widow."* Grantor died, leaving a will that devised property in trust, directing the trustee to pay the income "to my son A for life, then to A's surviving spouse for life, and upon the death of A's surviving spouse, to pay the trust principal to A's grandchildren." Under the common-law Rule, the future interest to A's grandchildren is invalid because it is possible that A's surviving spouse will be someone who was not in being at the creation of the interest.

3. *"Administrative contingency."* Grantor died, leaving a will that devised real property "to such of my grandchildren, born before or after my death, as may be living upon final distribution of my estate." Grantor was survived by her children (A and B) and her four grandchildren. Under the common-law Rule, the grandchildren's interest was invalid, by the majority view. Though unlikely, there is a possibility that the final distribution of Grantor's estate will not occur within 21 years after Grantor's death. This possibility eliminates validating the interest on the basis of the 21-year part of the period. In addition, there are no lives in being that can validate it. Not only are afterborn grandchildren presumed, but also presumed is the possibility that final distribution of Grantor's estate will occur after such afterborn grandchildren have outlived by more than 21 years the deaths of A, B, and Grantor's four grandchildren who were living at Grantor's death.

The common-law Rule does not necessarily shorten the duration of a trust whose duration extends beyond lives in being plus 21 years. It merely changes who takes the trust principal on termination.

Illustration:

4. Grantor died, leaving a will that devised property in trust, directing the trustee to pay the income to Grantor's children for life, then to Grantor's grandchildren for life, and at the death of the last living grandchild, to distribute the trust principal to Grantor's then living descendants. Under the common-law Rule, only the future interest to Grantor's then living descendants is invalid. Because the future interest in income to Grantor's grandchildren is valid, even though the last living grandchild might be born after Grantor's death and outlive by more than 21 years all of the children and grandchildren who were in being at Grantor's death, the trust itself is not cut short. The only effect is that when the trust terminates, the trust principal cannot be distributed to Grantor's then living descendants, but has to return to Grantor's estate. Since Grantor would typically have died decades earlier, the current owners of the right to trust principal can only be determined by tracing the reversion through the estates of those successors who also died

before the termination of the trust. It would not be unusual to find that the current owners were far removed from Grantor's bloodline.

The movement from the common law to wait-and-see. As Illustrations 1 through 3 demonstrate, the common-law Rule's what-might-happen approach invalidates contingent future interests on the basis of highly improbable chains of post-creation events. Leach proposed modifying the common-law Rule so that contingent future interests would not be invalidated on the basis of what might happen but on the basis of what does happen. Under the what-does-happen approach, which has come to be known as wait-and-see, the affected future interests would almost certainly be valid. Under both approaches, the assumption is that the law should not allow a contingent future interest to continue to exist, neither vesting nor failing to vest, beyond a life in being plus 21 years.

Although both the common law and wait-and-see use the life-in-being-plus-21-years period, the two approaches use that period differently. Validity under the common law depends on identifying an individual who was in being and whose life validates the interest, hence the term validating life. If no validating life can be identified, the contingent future interest is invalid. Validity under wait-and-see depends on whether the contingent future interest vests or fails to vest within the period. Wait-and-see requires a true measuring life—an individual whose life measures the permissible vesting period.

In 1978, Reporter A. James Casner brought a proposal to adopt wait-and-see before the floor of The American Law Institute. Following a momentous debate involving spirited exchanges between Professor Casner and Professor Richard R. Powell, who was the Reporter for the Restatement of Property, the Institute in 1979 adopted wait-and-see combined with judicial modification for cases in which a contingent future interest failed to vest on or before the expiration of the wait-and-see perpetuity period. See Restatement Second, Property (Donative Transfers) §§ 1.1 through 1.6. The Restatement Second used a list of measuring lives for measuring the wait-and-see perpetuity period. . . . .

In order to avoid disagreements about whom to use as measuring lives for purposes of wait-and-see, the Uniform Law Commission promulgated a wait-and-see statute known as the Uniform Statutory Rule Against Perpetuities (USRAP) in 1986. USRAP adopted wait-and-see combined with judicial modification, but abandoned the use of actual measuring lives and instead adopted 90 years as a rough approximation of the life-in-being-plus-21-years period. USRAP was enacted in over half of the states, and still is the most widely enacted perpetuity reform measure.

Today, no state follows the common-law Rule in its pure form.

Before enactment of the federal generation-skipping transfer tax (GST tax) in 1986, transferors lacked desire to establish perpetual trusts. Before 1986, three states—Wisconsin, South Dakota, and Idaho—had abolished the Rule by statute or had never adopted the Rule in the first place, but it appears that transferors had little desire to take advantage of the absence of a Rule in those states in order to establish perpetual trusts for their descendants from time to time living forever.

A transferor by nature prefers to benefit known descendants, not remote unknown descendants. Instinctively, though perhaps not consciously, a transferor understands that his or her genetic relationship with his or her descendants will be diluted at each step down the generational ladder. On average, and disregarding nongenetic descendants such as adoptees, a transferor's genetic relationship with his or her genetic descendants is cut in half at each succeeding generation. Specifically, a transferor's genetic relationship with his or her children is 50 percent, with grandchildren is 25 percent, and with great-grandchildren is 12.5 percent. Seldom does a transferor think beyond great-grandchildren and contemplate benefiting more remote generations. For example, the great-grandchildren of the transferor's great-grandchildren—the transferor's great-great-great-great-grandchildren—are six generations removed from the transferor: They will be born about 100 years after the transferor's death and the transferor's genetic relationship with them will be a mere 1.5625 percent. At the 14th generation below the transferor, the genetic relationship will be about 0.0061035 percent, which—due to our common origins—is about the same relationship that one has with any randomly selected member of the population.

As the transferor's genetic relationship with his or her descendants becomes diluted with each step down the generational ladder, the number of beneficiary-descendants increases geometrically. Government statistics indicate that the average birth rate per woman in the United States is slightly more than two children. If, for simplicity, we assume that two children and four grandchildren are living at the transferor's death, that the average interval between generations is 25 years, that at least three generations of descendants are living in any particular time frame, and that the transferor and each member of the senior descendant generation dies at age 75, the following projections can be made: On average, a transferor will have about 450 living descendants (who are beneficiaries of the trust) 150 years after the trust is created, over 7000 living beneficiaries 250 years after the trust is created, and about 114,500 living beneficiaries 350 years after the trust is created. To visualize a trust with 114,500 beneficiaries, bear in mind that this group would be larger than the crowd that can now fit into the largest American football stadiums, such as Michigan Stadium or the Rose Bowl. Three hundred and fifty years after creation, the transferor's descending line will have divided into thousands of branches. Assuming that a branch is composed of a parent, two children, four grandchildren, and up to sixteen great-grandchildren, each branch will have between seven and fifteen living members. A trust with 114,500 living beneficiaries will have between 7633 and 16,357 branches. Four hundred and fifty years after the trust is created, the number of living beneficiaries could rise to 1.8 million and have between 120,000 and 257,143 branches. . . . .

These demographics of descent put the perpetual or near-perpetual trust on a collision course with core principles of trust administration. A trustee operates under a strict duty to distribute trust funds only to those persons who qualify as beneficiaries under the terms of the trust. Restatement Second, Trusts § 226 [Restatement Third, Trusts § 76]. The trustee who makes a mistaken distribution to a person who is not a beneficiary "is liable although [the trustee] reasonably believes that the person to whom [the trustee] pays or conveys is the beneficiary. . . ." Id. at Comment *b*. Because a trustee acts at peril for mistaken distributions, the trustee must investigate whether a person who claims to be a beneficiary does in fact qualify. If, however, a trust were to have thousands or tens of thousands of potential beneficiaries, centuries removed from the transferor by descent, the task of ascertaining which persons qualify as beneficiaries would become enormously complex and expensive.

In addition to the duty to avoid distributing trust assets to persons who do not qualify as beneficiaries, a trustee also operates under the duty of impartiality, which provides that "in investing, protecting, and distributing the trust estate, and in other administrative functions, the trustee must act impartially and with due regard for the diverse beneficial interests created by the terms of the trust. . . ." Restatement Third, Trusts § 79(1)(a); accord Uniform Trust Code § 803 (duty to give "due regard to the beneficiaries' respective interests"). The Restatement of Trusts observes that the duty of impartiality "is important not only, for example, in balancing the naturally conflicting concerns of life and remainder beneficiaries but also whenever multiple income beneficiaries have significantly differing needs and tax positions, or when multiple remainder beneficiaries have significantly different objectives and risk tolerance." Restatement Third, Trusts § 79(1)(b), Comment *a*. Moreover, in discharging the duty of impartiality, "a trustee will often find it desirable, and sometimes important or even necessary, to consult with beneficiaries and obtain information from them concerning their financial needs and circumstances and perhaps their preferences concerning matters of trust administration." Id., Comment *d*. Just how the trustee of a perpetual trust with thousands of beneficiaries with conflicting interests could appropriately consult them, investigate their "needs and circumstances," and give "due regard" to the interests of each, is difficult to comprehend. The trustee will have to employ and assign more and more trust officers, each with primary operational responsibility—aided by ever-advancing technologies—for a manageable number of branches. The costs of trust administration could become significant. The trustee is entitled to be reimbursed out of the trust property for properly incurred administrative costs. See Restatement Third, Trusts § 38; Uniform Trust Code § 709.

As a perpetual trust drifts deeper and deeper into its second century and beyond, and long after the settlor and the attorney responsible for proposing and drafting the trust have died, administrative and other costs in keeping up with births, adoptions, deaths, marriages, and so on will act as a drag on investment performance. How much of a drag remains to be seen, because no trustee has experience in administering a centuries-old private trust with thousands upon thousands of beneficiaries who continue to multiply as more than twice as many beneficiaries are born or adopted than die. The perpetual or near-perpetual trusts now in existence are only in their first or second decade and have, on average, only six to fourteen beneficiaries. As the number of beneficiaries increases, so will the costs of administration and the trustee's fees.

Statutory movement to allow perpetual or near-perpetual trusts. Before 1986, transferors had little desire to establish perpetual or near-perpetual trusts for their descendants from time to time living forever, even though permitted to do so under the law of Wisconsin, South Dakota, or Idaho. The federal generation-skipping transfer tax (GST tax) created an artificial incentive for the wealthy to establish such trusts. (Enacted in 1986, the GST tax was in abeyance in 2010 but reemerged in 2011.)

The GST tax led to a movement in the states to abolish the Rule Against Perpetuities in order to allow transferors to create perpetual or near-perpetual trusts. What sparked the movement was the large GST exemption—in 2006, $2 million per donor ($4 million for a married couple). In 2009, the GST exemption, which is equal to the applicable estate-tax exclusion amount, increased to $3.5 million per donor ($7 million for a married couple), and in 2010 increased to $5 million per donor ($10 million for a married couple), plus an inflation adjustment. . . . .

Although a GST-exempt trust of a few million dollars, even $5 million or $10 million, represents a small portion of the net worth of the truly wealthy, various estate-planning techniques can be used to leverage the amount exempted beyond the exemption's ceiling. For example, the trustee can be authorized to purchase or retain assets such as second-to-die life-insurance policies, start-up businesses, and minority or non-voting interests in existing family businesses at discounted values through note-sales or other devices. Under current trust law, the interests of the beneficiaries can be insulated from creditors through the use of spendthrift clauses. Potentially, the perpetual or near-perpetual trust movement could, over time, lead to large concentrations of wealth within a relatively small number of family dynasties and financial institutions, contrary to longstanding federal tax policy.

In fashioning the GST exemption, Congress relied on state perpetuity law to control the length of GST-exempt trusts, placing the duration of GST-exempt trusts in the hands of the states, some of which have exhibited greater interest in generating trust business for in-state institutional trustees than in protecting the federal fisc. Hence was born a movement to abolish the Rule Against Perpetuities, or at least to modify the Rule to permit trusts of hundreds of years. The movement began slowly, but accelerated as local lawyers and banking institutions in state after state learned of the potential for attracting or retaining trust business that the GST-exempt perpetual or near-perpetual trust provides.

Despite the growing state-level movement to permit GST-exempt perpetual or near-perpetual trusts, Congress has not acted to curb the duration of GST-exempt trusts. Under current tax law, once a trust qualifies for the GST exemption, the exemption continues as long as the property remains in the trust. A GST-exempt trust remains GST-exempt, no matter how long the trust lasts and no matter how much its value increases beyond the GST-exempt amount. Because of the commercial interests of banks and local attorneys, states are in full-scale competition with one another for trusts that potentially last for hundreds of years and in some cases forever. . . . .

Allowance of perpetual or near-perpetual trusts has brought considerable trust business into states allowing them. Wealthy transferors have responded to the tax incentive to create GST-exempt perpetual or near-perpetual trusts. An empirical study based on data through 2003 from the annual reports that institutional trustees filed with federal banking authorities found that roughly $100 billion in trust assets had flowed into states allowing perpetual or near-perpetual trusts. Considerably more wealth has undoubtedly moved into these states in the years following 2003. Moreover, the $100 billion figure undercounts the actual value of trust assets flowing into these states, because the sources on which the study was based were reports from federal regulatory agencies. These reports contain no data on trusts in which the trustee is a family trust company, organized for the limited purpose of administering trusts of one family. Family trust companies, which are becoming popular vehicles for administering perpetual trusts of the very wealthy, are regulated if at all by state law, not federal law, and consequently do not report to federal agencies.

The states that attracted the most perpetual or near-perpetual trust business were those states that do not tax trust income produced by funds originating from out of state. States that levied an income tax on trust funds attracted from out of state experienced no observable increase in trust business.

Position of The American Law Institute. It is the considered judgment of The American Law Institute that the recent statutory movement allowing the creation of perpetual or near-perpetual trusts is ill advised. The movement to abrogate the Rule Against Perpetuities has not been based on the merits of removing the Rule's curb on excessive dead-hand control. The policy issues associated with allowing perpetual or near-perpetual trusts have not been seriously discussed in the state legislatures. The driving force has been the effort to compete for trust industry (financial services) business from other states.

A rule that curbs excessive dead-hand control is deeply rooted in this nation's history and tradition, and for good reason. A 360-year trust created in the year 2010 could endure until the year 2370 and have over 100,000 beneficiaries. A 1000-year trust created in 2010 could terminate in the year 3010 and have millions of beneficiaries. No transferor has enough wisdom to make sound dispositions of property across such vast intervals and for beneficiaries so remote and so numerous. A 1000-year or 360-year trust created in 2010 might incorporate what are currently considered to be flexible provisions for a trust that could last that far into the future. To put that claim into perspective, consider the devices for controlling family wealth through subsequent generations that were available 360 or more years ago, in the year 1650 or earlier. Such devices, drafted before the invention of the typewriter, first took the form of the unbarrable entail and, after the entail became barrable, the strict settlement. These devices became archaic long ago. If that which was considered sophisticated 360 or more years ago is considered primitive today, there is reason to suspect that that which is considered sophisticated today will be considered primitive 360 or more years from now. . . . .

An important reason for maintaining a reasonable limit on dead-hand control is that the limit forces control of encumbered property to be shifted periodically to the living, free of restrictions imposed by the original transferor. The living can then use the property as they wish, including retransferring it into new trusts with up-to-date provisions. By way of example, consider one set of provisions that are likely to become increasingly obsolete as time goes by—family class-gift definitions. A perpetual or near-perpetual trust drafted today might appear to be flexible if it grants the trustee discretionary powers to distribute income or principal among the settlor's descendants from time to time living. Such a trust, however, will often define the class of descendants according to time-of-creation standards, standards that run the serious risk of becoming out of date as concepts of family change over time. No trust drafted in 1650 or earlier could have contained provisions anticipating the possibility of adopted children, children of assisted reproduction, or children born to a surrogate mother, much less second-parent adoptions or posthumously conceived children. Likewise, no perpetual or near-perpetual trust drafted today will be able to anticipate concepts of family and descent as they change and adjust over vast intervals in the future. This Restatement contains up-to-date class-gift rules of construction that address these and other questions of status, and subsequent law may eventually catch up with concepts of family as they continue to change over time. Because trust-document definitions prevail over contrary rules of construction, however, and control the permissible appointees of a nongeneral power of appointment, definitions that become out of date over time will constrain the ability of a trust to adjust to evolving concepts of family. Without a limit on dead-hand control, the living would not be able to retransfer the property into new trusts with up-to-date family definitions.

The political pressure on the states to remove the limit entirely or to extend the limit to several centuries would not have arisen were it not for the artificial incentive created by the GST exemption. In fashioning the GST exemption, Congress did not intend to encourage states to modify or repeal state perpetuity law to facilitate perpetual or near-perpetual trusts. On the contrary: Congress displayed a lack of foresight in relying on state perpetuity law to limit the length of GST-exempt trusts. An unintended consequence of tax law should not determine policy on so fundamental a matter as state perpetuity law, especially since history suggests that tax loopholes do not last indefinitely.

The shift from lives in being to a generations-based limit on dead-hand control. This Restatement continues to recognize the desirability of a rule of public policy that curbs excessive dead-hand control, but implements that rule in a more tailored manner than the limit based on lives in being plus 21 years. An unexamined assumption of the common-law Rule and the wait-and-see movement is that the perpetuity period—the maximum limit—must be measured by lives in being at the creation of the interest. Requiring the lives to be in being at the creation of the interest prevents the perpetuity period from adjusting to the trust and family circumstances, because that requirement often divides members of the same generation into measuring and non-measuring lives. Although trusts commonly confer lifetime benefits on members of one generation before passing benefits to the next generation, the life-in-being requirement means that only those members of a generation who are in being at the creation of the interest can be used to measure the perpetuity period. Members of the same generation who come into being later cannot be used. This Restatement replaces the "in being" requirement with a rule that measures the perpetuity period by generations. With certain qualifications and exceptions, the Rule—as promulgated in this Restatement—limits dead-hand control to granting benefits through but not beyond two generations younger than the transferor. The result is that the perpetuity period becomes more consistent with the know-and-see theory than the lives-in-being approach and is tailored to the individual trust and family circumstances.

The objective of switching to a generations-based perpetuity period is not to produce a materially longer or shorter maximum period. Under the traditional lives-in-being approach, the longest-living individual who serves as a measuring life will eventually die, but that individual can be someone who is more than two generations younger than the transferor and can outlive the transferor by many decades, maybe even a century, but not much more and often less. Under the two-younger-generations approach, the longest-living individual who serves as a measuring life will eventually die, but that individual can be someone who is conceived and born after the transferor's death and can outlive the transferor by many decades, maybe even a century, but not much more and often less. Although the length of the two periods will be different in individual cases, the average length will probably work out to be about the same.

Time of vesting versus time of termination. Historically, the Rule has focused on contingent future interests and the time of vesting. The Rule has been formulated to prevent a contingent future interest from continuing to exist beyond the allowable perpetuity period. That mechanism has some merit but is not well aligned with the purpose of the Rule, which is to limit dead-hand control. The rule of this Restatement focuses on the time at which the trust or other disposition of property terminates. The time of termination as opposed to the time of vesting coordinates more purposively with the Rule's objective of limiting dead-hand control, because the time of termination is when the property comes under the control of the ultimate beneficiaries. Another benefit of shifting from the time of vesting to the time of termination is that the distinction between a contingent and a vested future interest becomes irrelevant.

Judicial modification. Judicial modification of an otherwise noncomplying trust or other donative disposition of property is an integral part of the Rule Against Perpetuities adopted in this Restatement. A trust or other donative disposition of property that does not terminate on or before the expiration of the perpetuity period is not invalid. The property does not return to and then through the estate of the long-deceased transferor. Instead, the trust or other donative disposition is subject to judicial modification. In most cases, the form of modification will accelerate the right to possession of the beneficiaries of the trust or other disposition. Instead of benefiting remote beneficiaries, the benefit accrues to beneficiaries who satisfy the know-and-see theory.

§ 27.1. Statement of the Rule Against Perpetuities

(a) A trust or other donative disposition of property is subject to judicial modification under § 27.2 to the extent that the trust or other disposition does not terminate on or before the expiration of the perpetuity period, except that if, upon the expiration of the perpetuity period, the share of a beneficiary is distributable upon reaching a specified age and the beneficiary is then younger than the earlier of the specified age or the age of 30, the beneficiary's share may, without judicial modification, be retained in trust until the beneficiary reaches or dies before reaching the earlier of the specified age or the age of 30.

(b) The perpetuity period expires at the death of the last living measuring life. The measuring lives are as follows:

(1) Except as otherwise provided in paragraph (2), the measuring lives constitute a group composed of the following individuals: the transferor, the beneficiaries of the disposition who are related to the transferor and no more than two generations younger than the transferor, and the beneficiaries of the disposition who are unrelated to the transferor and no more than the equivalent of two generations younger than the transferor.

(2) In the case of a trust or other property arrangement for the sole current benefit of a named individual who is more than two generations younger than the transferor or more than the equivalent of two generations younger than the transferor, the measuring life is the named individual.

Comment:

a. *Scope.* The principal rule of public policy for curtailing excessive dead-hand control is the Rule Against Perpetuities (the Rule). Over the centuries, the Rule has taken various forms. As formulated in this Restatement, the Rule continues the wait-and-see approach of the Restatement Second of Property (Donative Transfers), but measures the perpetuity period by generations rather than by lives in being at the creation of the interest. This Restatement also shifts to a termination rule. The Rule is no longer a rule against remoteness of vesting that only applies to a contingent future interest: The distinction between a contingent and a vested future interest is irrelevant.

Under this section, a trust or other donative disposition of property is, with one exception described in the next paragraph, subject to judicial modification under § 27.2 to the extent that the trust or other disposition does not terminate on or before the expiration of the perpetuity period. A corollary of this proposition is that if the terms of the trust or other disposition require the trust or other disposition to terminate on or before the expiration of the perpetuity period, the trust or other disposition is valid from its inception and will never be subject to judicial modification. The perpetuity period is defined in subsection (b) (see Comment *b*).

There is no 21-year period automatically tacked on at the end of the perpetuity period as there was at common law and under the Restatement Second. Although the tack-on 21-year period was a period in gross and not tied to the actual minority of any beneficiary, it is generally understood that the 21-year period was designed to allow the transferor to continue the trust or other disposition throughout the minority of a remainder beneficiary. Under this section, the tack-on 21-year period is replaced by a provision specifically targeted to an age contingency that has not yet been satisfied. If, upon the expiration of the perpetuity period, the share of a beneficiary is distributable upon reaching a specified age and the beneficiary is younger than the earlier of the specified age or the age of 30, the beneficiary's share may, without judicial modification, be retained in trust until the beneficiary reaches or dies before reaching the earlier of the specified age or the age of 30.

b. *Generations-based perpetuity period: rationale.* Under subsection (b), the perpetuity period expires at the death of the last living measuring life. Under subsection (b)(1), and except as otherwise provided in subsection (b)(2), the measuring lives constitute a group composed of the following individuals: the transferor (see Comment *d(1)*), the beneficiaries of the disposition who are related to the transferor and no more than two generations younger than the transferor (see Comments *d(2)* and *e*), and the beneficiaries of the disposition who are unrelated to the transferor and no more than the equivalent of two generations younger than the transferor (see Comments *d(2)* and *f*). In a narrow but important exception, the measuring life can be a beneficiary who is more than two generations younger than the transferor or more than the equivalent of two generations younger than the transferor. That exception relates to a trust or other property arrangement for the sole current benefit of a named individual. Under subsection (b)(2), the measuring life is the named individual. See Comment *c*.

Subsection (b) switches perpetuity law from the traditional *lives-in-being-plus-21-years* perpetuity period to a generations-based period. Historically, the Rule has measured the perpetuity period by lives in being at the creation of the interest plus 21 years. The requirement that the measuring lives be "in being" at the creation of the interest serves as a means of limiting the length of the perpetuity period, but the requirement produces a perpetuity period that is not tailored to the individual trust and family circumstances (see Illustration[ ] 1 . . .). The Restatement Second continued the lives "in being" requirement, but this Restatement measures the perpetuity period by generations, without regard to whether each or any member of the measuring generation was "in being" when the interest was created. The subsection (b)(1) measuring life is the last living individual among (1) the transferor and (2) the beneficiaries of the trust who are not more than two generations or the equivalent of two generations younger than the transferor.

A generations-based perpetuity period is more responsive to the purposes of the Rule than one based on lives in being, because the generational approach produces a period that self-adjusts to the individual trust and family circumstances and hence imposes a more tailored outer limit on dead-hand control. Trusts commonly confer lifetime benefits on members of one generation before passing benefits to the next generation. Subsection (b)(1) produces a perpetuity period that is tailored to the family, by counting beneficiaries of the same generation as measuring lives whether they were in being at the creation of the interest or not. The traditional lives-in-being period does not self-adjust because it excludes after-born members of the same generation and, as a result, can require judicial modification if an after-born member outlives the in-being members. Subsection (b) allows dead-hand control to go no farther than benefiting children and grandchildren, with the possible continuation of a trust or other property disposition if, upon the expiration of the perpetuity period, the share of a beneficiary is distributable upon reaching a specified age and the beneficiary is then younger than the earlier of the specified age or the age of 30. In such a case, the beneficiary's share may, without judicial modification, be retained in trust until the beneficiary reaches or dies before reaching the earlier of the specified age or the age of 30. See Comment *i*.

Illustration:

1. Grantor died, leaving a will that devised property in trust, directing the trustee to pay the income "to my son C for life, then to C's children for the life of the survivor, and on the death of C's last surviving child, to distribute the trust principal to C's then-living descendants." Grantor was survived by C and by C's two children, GC1 and GC2. After Grantor's death, C and his wife (W-1) were divorced. Subsequently, C remarried and he and his second wife (W-2) had another child (GC3). C, GC1, and GC2 were in being at the creation of the interest but they have now died survived by GC3. GC3 outlived C, GC1, and GC2. The trust is valid at its outset because its terms require the trust to terminate no later than the death of Grantor's last living grandchild. The trust will never be subject to judicial modification under § 27.2. The measuring lives are C, GC1, GC2, and GC3. If the measuring lives were limited to those in being at the creation of the interest, only C, GC1, and GC2 could qualify as measuring lives. Although GC3 came into being after the creation of the trust, GC3 is a measuring life under subsection (b)(1) because GC3 is a beneficiary who is related to Grantor in the second generation below Grantor's generation. Treating GC3 as a measuring life means that the trust is valid and not subject to judicial modification under § 27.2.

To put the generations-based perpetuity period into perspective, it should be noted that the common-law Rule itself would not cut a two-generations trust short. In Illustration[ ] 1 . . ., the only effect of violating the common-law Rule would be to invalidate the remainder interest to C's then-living descendants that was to take effect on the death of C's last living child (Grantor's grandchild), thus forcing the right to the trust principal to revert to Grantor's estate on the death of GC3 (Grantor's last living grandchild). Because Grantor would typically have died many decades earlier, the final owners of the right to trust principal could only be determined by tracing the reversion through the estates of those successors who also died before the termination of the trust. It would not be unusual to find that some and perhaps most or all of the final owners were far removed from Grantor's family. The two-generations approach does nothing more than save the validity of the remainder interest, thus preserving Grantor's intention regarding the ultimate distributees of the trust and removing the inefficiency of forcing the right to the trust principal to revert to and through Grantor's estate and then through the estates of Grantor's successors.

c. Subsection (b)(2)—Measuring life in the case of a trust or other property arrangement for the sole current benefit of a named individual who is more than two generations younger than the transferor or the equivalent of more than two generations younger than the transferor. Subsection (b)(2) provides that the measuring life in the case of a trust or other property arrangement for the sole current benefit of a named individual who is more than two generations younger than the transferor or more than the equivalent of two generations younger than the transferor is the named individual. See Comment *h*.

d. The subsection (b)(1) measuring lives. Under subsection (b)(1), the measuring lives constitute a group composed of the following individuals: the transferor, the beneficiaries of the disposition who are related to the transferor and no more than two generations younger than the transferor, and the beneficiaries of the disposition who are unrelated to the transferor and no more than the equivalent of two generations younger than the transferor. Only an individual (i.e., a human) can be a measuring life. A non-human (e.g., an animal or an entity such as a government, corporation, or trust) cannot be a measuring life.

d(1). Transferor. The transferor is a measuring life whether or not the transferor is a beneficiary of the trust or other donative disposition of property. Consequently, the perpetuity period can never expire before the transferor's death.

Identifying the transferor is important, not only because the transferor is a measuring life, but also because the other measuring lives are identified by their relationship to the transferor. As discussed in more detail in Comment *j*, the transferor in the case of a trust or other donative disposition created by the exercise of a power of appointment is the donor of the power, unless the exercised power was a presently exercisable general power. If the exercised power was a presently exercisable general power, the transferor is the donee of the power, whether or not the donee is also the donor. Because a presently exercisable general power is an ownership-equivalent power, the transferor is the donee of the power even if the donee does not exercise the power and the appointive property passes under a gift-in-default clause.

Any attempt to disguise the identity of the true transferor by the use of reciprocal transfers or any other deceptive means is ineffective. For example, if by prearrangement a parent gives money outright to his or her child or exchanges money or property with his or her child for the purpose in either case of creating a trust that the parent would otherwise have created, the transferor of the trust is the parent, not the child.

d(2). Beneficiaries of the trust or other donative disposition of property. Other than the transferor, the subsection (b)(1) measuring lives must be beneficiaries of the trust or other donative disposition of property. For purposes of this category, the term "beneficiaries of the trust or other donative disposition of property" refers to those individuals who take beneficial interests in the trust or other disposition and those individuals who have a power of appointment or have a reversionary interest arising by operation of law or otherwise. The term also includes individuals who have succeeded to an interest of a beneficiary by assignment, inheritance, or otherwise. See Restatement Third, Trusts § 48 and Comment *a* thereto.

An appointee of a general or a nongeneral power of appointment is a beneficiary. A permissible appointee of a nongeneral power is a beneficiary if the individual is identified by name or is a member of a defined and limited class. See § 19.15, Comment *d*. Similarly, in the case of a discretionary trust, a permissible recipient of income or principal or both is a beneficiary.

e. Beneficiaries related to the transferor who can be subsection (b)(1) measuring lives. The beneficiaries of the trust or other donative disposition of property who are related to the transferor can be measuring lives under subsection (b)(1) only if they are not more than two generations younger than the transferor. It is immaterial whether they were or were not in being at the creation of the interest.

e(2). Adopted child. With one exception (see below), an adoptee is assigned to the generation immediately below the adoptive parent's generation. Consequently, an adoptee is a measuring life if the adoptee is assigned to a generation that is not younger than two generations below the transferor's generation and is a named beneficiary of the trust or other donative disposition of property or a class member under § 14.5 or § 14.6. If GC1, GC2, or GC3 in Illustration 1 . . . were adopted by C and C's second spouse, the result . . . would be the same.

The one exception to the rule assigning an adoptee to the generation immediately below the adoptive parent's generation arises in the case in which, before the adoption, the adoptee was a descendant of the transferor or a descendant of an ancestor of the transferor. In that case, the adoption does not cause the adoptee to be reassigned to a higher generation than his or her previous assignment. For example, if a parent of the transferor adopts a child of the transferor, the child remains assigned to the generation immediately below the transferor.

e(3). Child of assisted reproduction. A child of assisted reproduction is assigned to the generation immediately below the child's parent. Consequently, a child of assisted reproduction is a measuring life if the child is assigned to a generation no younger than two generations below the transferor's generation and is a named beneficiary of the trust or other disposition of property or a class member under § 14.8. If GC1, GC2, or GC3 in Illustration 1 . . . were conceived by assisted reproduction, the result . . . would be the same.

e(4). Spouse or domestic partner. A spouse or domestic partner or a surviving spouse or surviving domestic partner of the transferor or of a relative of the transferor is treated as related to the transferor and is assigned to the same generation as his or her spouse or domestic partner. Consequently, a spouse or domestic partner or a surviving spouse or surviving domestic partner is a measuring life if he or she is a beneficiary of the trust or other disposition of property and is married to or partnered with a relative of the transferor who is no younger than two generations below the transferor's generation. Divorce, dissolution of the partnership, or death does not cause the former spouse or domestic partner to be removed from the list of measuring lives, unless the divorce, dissolution, or death causes the former spouse or domestic partner to cease being a beneficiary. For purposes of this Restatement, the term "domestic partner" includes a person who qualifies as a domestic partner under § 6.03 of the [American Law Institute's] Principles of the Law of Family Dissolution: Analysis and Recommendations. The term also includes an unmarried partner under any other relationship entitling the partners to intestacy or other spousal-equivalent rights under applicable law, such as a civil union or domestic-partner relationship.

The generation assignment of a current or former spouse or domestic partner is similar to the generation assignment of a current or former spouse under the federal generation-skipping transfer tax (GST tax). Currently, the GST tax assigns a current or former spouse of the transferor or of a lineal descendant of a grandparent of the transferor to the same generation as the transferor or the transferor's relative. IRC § 2651(c) provides: "An individual who has been married at any time to the transferor shall be assigned to the transferor's generation [and an] individual who has been married at any time to an individual [who is a lineal descendant of a grandparent of the transferor] shall be assigned to the generation of the individual so described."

Marriage or domestic partnership between two beneficiaries who are related to the transferor but in different generations does not change the generation assignment of either beneficiary.

Illustration:

3. Grantor died, leaving a will that devised property in trust, directing the trustee to pay the income "to my nephew N for life, then to N's surviving spouse for life, and upon the death of N's surviving spouse, to pay the trust principal to N's then living descendants by representation." Grantor was survived by N and N's wife, W-1. After Grantor's death, W-1 died. Subsequently, N married W-2, who was not in being at Grantor's death. W-2 outlived N and W-1. If the measuring lives were limited to those in being at the creation of the interest, only N and W-1 could qualify as measuring lives. Although W-2 came into being after the creation of the trust, W-2 is a measuring life under subsection (b)(1) because she is a beneficiary who is related to the transferor in the first generation below the transferor's generation. Treating W-2 as a measuring life means that the trust is valid and not subject to judicial modification under § 27.2.

e(5). Relatives of spouse or domestic partner. Because, under Comment *e(4)*, a spouse or domestic partner or a surviving spouse or surviving domestic partner of the transferor or of a relative of the transferor is treated as related to the transferor and is assigned to the same generation as his or her spouse or domestic partner, a relative of a spouse or domestic partner or of a surviving spouse or surviving domestic partner is treated as related to the transferor and assigned to the generation to which he or she would be assigned if the spouse or domestic partner or surviving spouse or surviving domestic partner had been the transferor.

f. Beneficiaries who are unrelated to the transferor who can be subsection (b)(1) measuring lives. The beneficiaries of the trust or other donative disposition of property who are unrelated to the transferor can be measuring lives under subsection (b)(1) only if they are not more than the equivalent of two generations younger than the transferor. It is immaterial whether they were in being at the creation of the interest. The generation assignment of individuals who are unrelated to the transferor is determined by the number of years that they are younger than the transferor. This Restatement follows the federal generation-skipping transfer tax (GST tax) to determine whether an unrelated beneficiary is no more than the equivalent of two generations younger than the transferor. Currently, the GST tax assigns an unrelated beneficiary on the basis of the age difference between the beneficiary and the transferor. IRC § 2651(d) provides that such an individual is "assigned to a generation on the basis of the date of such individual's birth with-(1) an individual born not more than 12½ years after the date of the birth of the transferor assigned to the transferor's generation, (2) an individual born more than 12½ years but not more than 37½ years after the date of the birth of the transferor assigned to the first generation younger than the transferor, and (3) similar rules for a new generation every 25 years."

g. No subsection (b)(1) measuring life other than the transferor. If there is no measuring life under subsection (b)(1) other than the transferor, and there is no subsection (b)(2) measuring life, the transferor is the only measuring life and the perpetuity period expires at the transferor's death. See Comment *d(1).*

h. Beneficiary who can be a subsection (b)(2) measuring life. In the case of a trust or other property arrangement for the sole current benefit of a named individual who is more than two generations younger than the transferor or more than the equivalent of two generations younger than the transferor, the measuring life is the named individual. Requiring the beneficiary to be a named individual is intended to assure that the beneficiary is in being when the trust or other property arrangement is established. Subsection (b)(2) thus facilitates the establishment of a trust or other property arrangement for the sole current benefit of a beneficiary such as a living great-grandchild. If the trust or other property arrangement is created by a transfer from an existing trust or fund, the named individual is the measuring life so long as the named individual was named in the original trust or fund and the transfer occurs on or before the expiration of the perpetuity period under subsection (b)(1).

To qualify as the sole current beneficiary, the individual must be the only one who can then receive or benefit from mandatory or discretionary payments or distributions of income or property. The fact that a trustee, a custodian, or another has discretion to withhold income or property for future distribution to someone else does not disqualify the individual from being the sole current beneficiary and hence the measuring life. The beneficiary is the measuring life only so long as the beneficiary continues to be the sole current beneficiary. If, during the beneficiary's life, the beneficiary ceases being the sole current beneficiary, the beneficiary can no longer be a measuring life and, unless there are subsection (b)(1) measuring lives who are still living, the perpetuity period then expires.

Among the types of trusts or other property arrangements that would satisfy the requirement that the beneficiary be the sole current beneficiary are a special-needs trust, a "529 educational savings plan," a "Coverdale Education Savings Account," a "section 2503(c) trust" for a minor, and a custodianship under the Uniform Transfers to Minors Act, the Uniform Gifts to Minors Act, or the Uniform Custodial Trust Act.

A trust or other donative disposition of property is not subject to judicial modification merely because on or before the expiration of the perpetuity period described in subsection (b)(1) the trust or other disposition divides into one or more trusts or other property arrangements that are described in subsection (b)(2).

i. Share distributable at a specified age beyond expiration of the perpetuity period. Subsection (a) provides an exception to the rule that a trust or other donative disposition is subject to judicial modification to the extent that the trust or other disposition does not terminate on or before the expiration of the perpetuity period. If, upon the expiration of the perpetuity period, the share of a beneficiary is distributable upon reaching a specified age and the beneficiary is then younger than the earlier of the specified age or the age of 30, the beneficiary's share may, without judicial modification, be retained in trust until the beneficiary reaches or dies before reaching the earlier of the specified age or the age of 30. Illustration 4 demonstrates the application of this exception.

Illustration:

4. Grantor died, leaving a will that devised property in trust, directing the trustee to pay the income "to my son C for life, then to C's children for the life of the survivor, and on the death of C's last surviving child, to distribute the trust principal to C's grandchildren who reach the age of 30." At Grantor's death, Grantor had one child, C, and one grandchild, GC1. After Grantor's death, C had another child, GC2. C had no more children. The measuring lives are C, GC1, and GC2. C died, survived by GC1 and GC2. GC1 then died, survived by GC2. GC2 has now died. The perpetuity period expired at GC2's death. At GC2's death, GC1 and GC2 had three children, GGC1, GGC2, and GGC3. GGC1 was then 28, GGC2 was then 26, and GGC3 was then 22. The shares of GGC1, GGC2, and GGC3 may, without judicial modification, be retained in trust until each great-grandchild reaches 30 or dies before reaching 30. The same result would be reached if the specified age in Grantor's trust had been age 35. If the specified age in Grantor's trust had been age 25, the shares of GGC1 and GGC2 would be distributable immediately upon GC2's death and the share of GGC3 could be retained in trust until GGC3 either reached the age of 25 or died before reaching 25.

j. Trust or other donative disposition created by the exercise of a power of appointment. In determining whether a trust or other donative disposition created by the exercise of a power of appointment is subject to judicial modification under this section, the question is whether the donor or the donee of the power is the transferor. As noted in Comment *d(1)*, the transferor in the case of a trust or other donative disposition of property created by the exercise of a power of appointment is the donor of the power, unless the exercised power was a presently exercisable general power. If the exercised power was a presently exercisable general power, the transferor is the donee of the power, whether or not the donee is also the donor. On the possibility of determining who is the transferor under the doctrine of selective allocation, see Chapter 19, Part E (§ 19.19).

j(1). Trust or other donative disposition created by the exercise of a presently exercisable general power. In the case of a trust or other donative disposition created by the exercise of a presently exercisable general power, the transferor is the donee of the power, whether or not the donee is also the donor. In the case of a presently exercisable general power, the relation-back doctrine is not followed. See § 17.4, Comment *f(1)*.

Illustration:

5. Donor's will created a trust that provided for the income to go to Donee (Donor's son) for life, then to deliver the trust principal to such person or persons, including Donee, his estate, his creditors, or the creditors of his estate, as Donee shall appoint; in default of appointment, to Donee's descendants who survive Donee, by representation. Donee's general power is exercisable because it was presently exercisable upon its creation at Donor's death. Donee died leaving a will that exercised his presently exercisable general power by providing that the trust is to

continue beyond Donee's death, paying the income to Donee's daughter, C, for her lifetime, then to deliver the trust principal to C's descendants who survive C, by representation. C was born after Donor's death. The trust is not subject to judicial modification because Donee is the transferor and the trust terminates on the death of C, who is a beneficiary who is only one generation younger than Donee.

j(2). Unexercised presently exercisable general power. Because a presently exercisable general power is an ownership-equivalent power, the transferor is the donee of the power even if the donee does not exercise the power and the appointive property passes under a gift-in-default clause. Consequently, in Illustration 5, Donee would be the transferor if Donee had died without exercising his power and the gift-in-default clause had provided that the trust is to continue beyond Donee's death, paying the income to Donee's daughter, C, for her lifetime, then to deliver the trust principal to C's descendants who survive C, by representation.

j(3). Trust or other donative disposition created by the exercise of a general testamentary power or a nongeneral power. In the case of a trust or other donative disposition created by the exercise of a general testamentary power or a nongeneral power, general principles of property law adopt the relation-back doctrine. See § 17.4, Comments *f(2)* and *f(3)*; § 19.19, Comment *g*. Under that doctrine, the donor of the power is the transferor of the trust or other donative disposition created by the exercise of the power.

If the trust or other donative disposition was created by the exercise of a nongeneral or testamentary power that was created by the exercise of a nongeneral or a testamentary power, the relation-back doctrine is applied twice and the donor of the first power is the transferor of the trust or other donative disposition created by the second donee's exercise of his or her power.

Illustrations:

6. Donor's will created a trust that provided for the income to go to Donee-1 (Donor's son) for life, then to such of Donee-1's descendants as Donee-1 shall by will appoint. Donee-1 died leaving a will that exercised his nongeneral power by providing that the trust is to continue beyond Donee-1's death, paying the income to Donee-2 (Donee-1's daughter) for life, then to deliver the trust principal to such person or persons, including Donee-2, her estate, her creditors, or the creditors of her estate, as Donee-2 shall appoint; in default of appointment, to Donee-2's descendants who survive Donee-2, by representation. The transferor of the trust created by Donee-1's exercise of his power of appointment is Donor. Because the trust created by Donee-1's exercise of his power will terminate on the death of Donee-2 or will continue as a result of Donee-2's exercise of her presently exercisable general power, and because Donee-2 is two generations younger than Donor, the trust created by Donee-1's exercise of his nongeneral power is not subject to judicial modification under this section. If Donee-2 exercises her presently exercisable general power of appointment, Donee-2 is the transferor of any trust that she would create by the exercise of her power of appointment.

7. Donor's will created a trust that provided for the income to go to Donee-1 (Donor's son) for life, then to such of Donee-1's descendants as Donee-1 shall by will appoint. Donee-1 died leaving a will that exercised his nongeneral power, providing that the trust is to continue beyond Donee-1's death, paying the income to Donee-2 (Donee-1's

daughter) for life, then to deliver the trust principal to such of Donee-2's descendants as Donee-2 shall by will appoint; in default of appointment, to Donee-2's descendants who survive Donee-2, by representation. Under the doctrine of relation back, Donor is the transferor of the trust created by Donee-1's exercise. Donee-2 died leaving a will that exercised her nongeneral power by appointing outright to her descendants. Or, Donee-2 died leaving a will that did not exercise her nongeneral power and the property passed outright under the gift-in-default clause. Because in either case the trust terminated on the death of Donee-2, who is two generations younger than Donor, the trust created by Donee-1's exercise of his nongeneral power is not subject to judicial modification under § 27.2. If Donee-2's will exercised her nongeneral power in further trust, however, the trust created by Donee-1's exercise of his nongeneral power would not terminate on or before the expiration of the perpetuity period and the trust would be subject to judicial modification under § 27.2.

j(4). Trust or other donative disposition created by the exercise of a fiduciary distributive power. As noted in § 17.1, Comment *g*, a fiduciary distributive power is a nongeneral power of appointment for purposes of the Rule Against Perpetuities. Consequently, the transferor in the case of a trust or other donative disposition of property created by the exercise of a fiduciary distributive power is the donor of the power.

k. Directed accumulations of trust income. On the possibility of a court preventing directed accumulations of trust income that are capricious even if the trust is not subject to judicial modification under this section, see Restatement Third, Trusts § 29, Comment *h(2)*.

l. Contracts. The Rule Against Perpetuities only applies to dispositions of property. The Rule does not apply to a contract even if the contract creates contractual obligations extending beyond the perpetuity period.

m. Effective date. This Restatement does not adopt an effective-date rule for the generations-based perpetuity rule adopted in this Chapter. A court or legislature adopting the rule of this Chapter will need to address the effective-date question and fashion its own effective-date rule.

At a minimum, a court or legislature will likely want to protect the validity of trusts or other donative dispositions that are in effect when the new Rule is adopted and that are valid under the then-current Rule, including trusts or other dispositions that contain a traditional perpetuity saving clause.

A traditional perpetuity saving clause is comprised of two components: the perpetuity-period component and the gift-over/termination component. In one form, the perpetuity-period component establishes a period of time that runs parallel with the continuation of the trust or other property arrangement as provided in its dispositive terms. In another form, the perpetuity-period component directly governs the length of the trust or other property arrangement. In either form, a clause that validates the trust or other donative disposition under the common-law Rule keys the period of time to the death of or no more than 21 years after the death of the last living member of a group of individuals expressly designated in the clause. Such a clause makes all interests to which the clause applies valid under the common-law Rule. Because the clause designates its own validating lives, there is no need for an independent search for a validating life.

Such a clause is valid unless the designated validating lives are unreasonable in number or include individuals who were not in being at the creation of the interest. The validating lives are unreasonable in number if it would be impractical to keep track of them all to determine when the last living member dies.

The gift-over/termination component creates a gift over that is guaranteed to vest in possession at the termination of the period established in the perpetuity-period component.

Once a jurisdiction adopts the generations-based perpetuity rule, practice should shift to the use of a new type of valid perpetuity saving clause, one that fixes the perpetuity period to the period adopted in this section.

§ 27.2. Judicial Modification

Upon the petition of an interested person, the court shall modify a disposition that is subject to judicial modification under § 27.1(a). The form of the modification must be in a manner that most closely approximates the transferor's manifested plan of distribution and is within the perpetuity period provided in § 27.1(b).

Comment:

a. Scope. This section establishes standards for modifying a disposition that is subject to judicial modification under § 27.1(a). The primary goal is to modify the disposition so that the trust or other donative disposition of property terminates on or before the expiration of the perpetuity period.

Because the modification will take the form of ordering the trust or other disposition to terminate, the modification will primarily relate to determining who is then entitled to the property outright and should be fashioned in a manner that most closely approximates the transferor's manifested plan of distribution. See, e.g., Illustrations 1 and 2. Ordering a defeasible fee to become absolute is appropriate in cases such as Illustrations 3 and 4.

b. Petition of an interested person. Only an interested person has standing to bring a suit for judicial modification. The trustee of a trust has standing to bring such a suit. Any person having a claim to trust or nontrust property eligible for modification under § 27.1 would also have standing to bring such a suit. For example, in Illustrations 1 and 2, the trustee or any one of Grantor's descendants living at the expiration of the perpetuity period would have standing to bring a suit for judicial modification. In Illustrations 3 and 4, Grantee School District would have standing to bring a suit for judicial modification.

c. Modifying a potentially perpetual or near-perpetual trust. Illustrations 1 and 2 demonstrate the manner of modification in the case of a potentially perpetual or near-perpetual trust.

Illustrations:

1. Grantor died, leaving a will that devised property in trust, directing the trustee to distribute the income at the trustee's discretion among Grantor's descendants from time to time living. The terms of the trust require the trust to terminate when Grantor no longer has any living descendants. On termination, the trustee is directed to distribute the trust principal to a specified charity. At Grantor's death, Grantor had two adult children, C1 and C2, four grandchildren, GC1, GC2, GC3,

and GC4, and two minor great-grandchildren, GGC1 and GGC2. No more grandchildren were born or adopted after Grantor's death. The measuring lives are Grantor's children and grandchildren, C1, C2, GC1, GC2, GC3, and GC4. GC4, the last living measuring life, died at age 88. GC4's death marked the expiration of the perpetuity period. At GC4's death, Grantor had fifty living descendants—eight great-grandchildren, sixteen great-great-grandchildren, and twenty-six great-great-great-grandchildren. The trust is subject to judicial modification, because the trust did not terminate on or before the expiration of the perpetuity period. The court should modify the trust by requiring it to terminate on the death of GC4 and order the trust principal to be distributed by representation to Grantor's descendants living when the perpetuity period expired. If Grantor's descending line had died out when or before the perpetuity period expired, no modification would be required because the trust would have required distribution to the specified charity when Grantor's last living descendant died.

2. Grantor created an irrevocable inter vivos trust, directing the trustee to distribute the income at the trustee's discretion among Grantor's descendants from time to time living. The terms of the trust require the trust to terminate at the earlier of 360 years after creation or when Grantor no longer has any living descendants. On termination, the trustee is directed to distribute the trust principal to Grantor's then-living descendants by representation; if none, to a specified charity. At the creation of the trust, Grantor had two adult children, C1 and C2, and two grandchildren, GC1 and GC2. After the trust was created, two more grandchildren, GC3 and GC4, were born. GC4 was born after Grantor's death. The measuring lives are Grantor and Grantor's children and grandchildren, C1, C2, GC1, GC2, GC3, and GC4. GC4, the last living measuring life, died at age 88. GC4's death marked the expiration of the perpetuity period. At GC4's death, Grantor had fifty living descendants—eight great-grandchildren, sixteen great-great-grandchildren, and twenty-six great-great-great-grandchildren. The outcome is the same as in Illustration 1.

d. Modifying a fee simple defeasible. This Restatement continues the position of the Restatement Second of Property (Donative Transfers) § 1.5, Comments *b* and *c*, by providing that if the future interest following a fee simple defeasible has not vested in possession on or before the expiration of the perpetuity period, the manner of modification is to terminate the future interest and render the fee simple a fee simple absolute.

Illustrations:

3. In a donative transfer, Grantor conveyed land "to Grantee School District so long as the land is used for school purposes; upon the land being used for non-school purposes, the land reverts to Grantor if Grantor is then living; if not, by representation to Grantor's descendants who are then living." When Grantor executed the conveyance, Grantor had two adult children, C1 and C2, and two grandchildren, GC1 and GC2. After making the conveyance, two more grandchildren, GC3 and GC4, were born. GC4 was born after Grantor's death. The measuring lives are Grantor and Grantor's children and grandchildren, C1, C2, GC1, GC2, GC3, and GC4. GC4, the last living measuring life, died at age 88. GC4's death marked the expiration of the perpetuity period. At GC4's death, the land was still being used for school purposes. The conveyance is subject to judicial modification. The court should order the conveyance to be modified so that the future interests to Grantor and

Grantor's descendants are terminated and Grantee's fee simple defeasible becomes a fee simple absolute. The same result would be reached if the conveyance had been "to Grantee School District on condition that the land is used for school purposes, and if the land is used for non-school purposes, Grantor is to have the right to reenter and take possession if Grantor is then living; if not, by representation to Grantor's descendants who are then living."

4. In a donative transfer, Grantor conveyed land "to Grantee School District so long as the land is used for school purposes; and upon the land being used for non-school purposes, the land goes to Grantor's daughter C if C is then living; if not, by representation to C's descendants who are then living." When Grantor executed the conveyance, C had one child, GC1. After Grantor's death, C had another child, GC2. C had no more children. The measuring lives are Grantor and Grantor's children and grandchildren, C, GC1, and GC2. C died, survived by GC1 and GC2. GC1 then died, survived by GC2. GC2 has now died. The perpetuity period expired at GC2's death. At GC2's death, the land was still being used for school purposes. The conveyance is subject to judicial modification. The court should order the conveyance to be modified so that the future interests to C and C's descendants are terminated and Grantee's fee simple defeasible becomes a fee simple absolute. The same result would be reached if the conveyance had been "to Grantee School District, but if the land is used for non-school purposes, the land goes to Grantor's daughter C if C is then living; if not, by representation to C's descendants who are then living."

e. Judicial modification before expiration of the perpetuity period. With one exception pertaining to an unsatisfied age contingency, § 27.1 provides that a trust or other donative disposition of property is subject to judicial modification if the trust or other disposition has not actually terminated on or before the expiration of the perpetuity period. Nevertheless, in cases in which it is possible that the trust or other disposition will not actually terminate on or before the expiration of the perpetuity period, judicial modification is permissible before the expiration of the perpetuity period. For example, if a petition for modification were filed before the expiration of the perpetuity period in Illustration 1 or 2, a court should exercise its inherent equitable powers by granting the petition. The modification order should provide that, if the trust does not terminate on or before the expiration of the perpetuity period, the trust must terminate on the expiration of the perpetuity period and the trust property must be distributed by representation to Grantor's descendants who are then living and, if none, to the specified charity. Because neither Illustration involved an age contingency, the perpetuity period will expire in both Illustrations at the death of the last living measuring life. In Illustration 1, the measuring lives are Grantor's children and grandchildren. In Illustration 2, the measuring lives are Grantor and Grantor's children and grandchildren.

f. Other modifications. The previous Comments and Illustrations do not exhaust the many situations that can arise that call for judicial modification. The authority to modify includes authority to alter existing interests or powers and to create new interests or powers by implication or construction based on the transferor's manifested plan of distribution as a whole. If necessary to carry out the transferor's manifested plan of distribution, one or more related dispositions may also be modified.

§ 27.3. Exclusions from the Rule Against Perpetuities

The Rule Against Perpetuities does not apply to:

(1) commercial transactions, except that the Rule does apply to a trust or other disposition of property arising out of (a) a premarital or postmarital agreement, (b) a separation or divorce settlement, (c) a spouse's election, (d) any other arrangement arising out of a prospective, existing, or previous marital relationship between the parties, (e) a contract to make or not to revoke a will or trust, (f) a contract to exercise or not to exercise a power of appointment, (g) a transfer in satisfaction of a duty of support, or (h) a reciprocal transfer;

(2) a trust or other donative disposition of property solely for charitable purposes as defined in Restatement Third, Trusts § 28;

(3) an honorary trust and a trust for the care of an animal to the extent authorized by applicable law;

(4) a trust or other property arrangement forming part of a pension, profit-sharing, stock bonus, health, disability, death benefit, income deferral, or other current or deferred benefit plan for one or more employees, independent contractors, or their beneficiaries or spouses or domestic partners, to which contributions are made for the purpose of distributing to or for the benefit of the participants or their beneficiaries or spouses or domestic partners the property, income, or principal in the trust or other property arrangement, except a trust or other donative disposition of property that is created by an election of a participant or a beneficiary or spouse or domestic partner; and

(5) a trust or other disposition of property, a property interest, a power of appointment, or an arrangement that was not subject to the common-law Rule Against Perpetuities or is excluded by an applicable statute.

Comment:

a. Scope. This section lists four exclusions from the Rule Against Perpetuities. Paragraph (5) preserves all exclusions recognized by the common law or an applicable statute.

b. Paragraph (1)—commercial transactions excluded; rationale. Paragraph (1) excludes (with certain enumerated exceptions) commercial transactions, even commercial transactions that create a contingent property interest. The reason is that the perpetuity period—whether that period is measured by a life in being plus 21 years or by two younger generations—is only appropriate for measuring the allowable duration of family-oriented trusts and other donative dispositions of property.

Commercial transactions that do not create a contingent property interest are not subject to the Rule Against Perpetuities. Certain commercial transactions—such as options in gross, rights of first refusal, leases scheduled to commence in the future, at a time certain or on the happening of a future event such as the completion of a building, contingent easements, and top leases and top deeds with respect to interests in minerals—create contingent property interests. Such transactions are often entered into with or between corporate or other business entities, and directly or indirectly restrain the alienability of property or provide a disincentive to improve property. There is therefore a case for limiting the duration of such commercial transactions. But the perpetuity period is inappropriate for measuring the allowable duration of such commercial transactions. A more appropriate measurement for limiting the duration of such transactions is a fixed number of years. . . . . [L]egislation in some states imposes a durational limit of either 30 years or 40 years on one or more of these types of commercial transactions.

c. Consideration does not necessarily make the transfer a commercial transaction. A transfer can be supported by consideration and still be donative in character and hence not excluded from the Rule. A transaction that is essentially gratuitous in nature, accompanied by donative intent on the part of at least one party to the transaction, is not to be regarded as a commercial transaction simply because consideration is also present. Thus, for example, the exclusion would not apply if a parent purchases a parcel of land for full and adequate consideration, and directs the seller to make out the deed in favor of the purchaser's daughter for life, remainder to such of the daughter's children as reach 25. For purposes of § 27.1, the transferor would be the parent. The deed would not be subject to judicial modification under § 27.2, because the deed requires the disposition to terminate on or before the expiration of the perpetuity period (see § 27.1(a) and (b)).

d. Transactions not excluded even if considered a commercial transaction. Some types of transactions—although bilateral and therefore in some sense supported by consideration and hence arguably commercial in nature—arise out of a domestic situation, and should not be excluded from the Rule. To avoid uncertainty with respect to such transactions, paragraph (1) specifies that a trust or other donative disposition of property arising out of any of the following transactions is not excluded by paragraph (1)'s commercial-transactions exclusion: a premarital or postmarital agreement; a separation or divorce settlement; a spouse's election, such as the "widow's election" in community-property states; any other arrangement arising out of a prospective, existing, or previous marital relationship between the parties; a contract to make or not to revoke a will or trust; a contract to exercise or not to exercise a power of appointment; a transfer in full or partial satisfaction of a duty of support; or a reciprocal transfer.

e. Paragraph (2)—trust or other donative disposition of property solely for charitable purposes. Paragraph (2) excludes from the Rule Against Perpetuities a trust or other donative disposition of property solely for charitable purposes as defined in Restatement Third, Trusts § 28. The exclusion under this paragraph extends to a trust or other donative disposition of property in which the charitable beneficiary shifts from one or more charitable organizations to one or more other charitable organizations on the passage of time or the occurrence of a certain or uncertain event.

f. Paragraph (3)—honorary trust and trust for care of an animal to the extent authorized by applicable law. Paragraph (3) exempts from the Rule Against Perpetuities an honorary trust (a trust for noncharitable purposes) and a trust for the care of an animal to the extent authorized by applicable law. The Restatement Third of Trusts, which provides for trusts for noncharitable purposes including a trust for the care of a pet animal, limits the duration of an honorary trust to a specified or reasonable period of time normally not to exceed 21 years or of a trust for a pet to the life of the pet. See Restatement Third, Trusts § 47 and Comment *d(2)* thereto. See also Uniform Probate Code § 2–907 (duration of honorary trust limited to 21 years; duration of trust for pet limited to life of pet); Uniform Trust Code

§§ 408, 409 (duration of honorary trust limited to 21 years; trust for animal limited to life of animal).

g. Paragraph (4)—trusts for employees and others; trusts for self-employed individuals. Paragraph (4) excludes from the Rule Against Perpetuities a trust or other property arrangement forming part of a pension, profit-sharing, stock bonus, health, disability, death benefit, income deferral, or other current or deferred benefit plan for one or more employees, independent contractors, or their beneficiaries or spouses, to which contributions are made for the purpose of distributing to or for the benefit of the participants or their beneficiaries or spouses the property, income, or principal in the trust or other property arrangement, except a trust or other donative disposition of property that is created by an election of a participant or a beneficiary or spouse. The exclusion under this paragraph extends to a trust or other property arrangement, whether part of a "qualified" or "unqualified" plan under the federal income-tax law, forming part of a bona fide benefit plan for employees (including owner-employees), independent contractors, or their beneficiaries or spouses. The exclusion under this paragraph does not, however, extend to a trust or other donative disposition of property created by an election of a participant or beneficiary or spouse.

CONCISE RESTATEMENT OF TRUSTS

PART 1

NATURE, CHARACTERISTICS, AND TYPES OF TRUSTS

CHAPTER 1

DEFINITIONS AND DISTINCTIONS

Introductory Note: A trust is one of several legal devices by which one person is enabled to deal with property for the benefit of another person. Among other such devices are agency and guardianship, devices that in some form are to be found in all mature systems of law. The trust, however, is peculiarly a product of the Anglo-American legal system.

The principles, rules, and standards of the law of trusts owe their origin and development in large part to the circumstance that in England there were for centuries separate courts of common law and chancery. The distinction between legal interests and equitable interests, now fundamental to the American law of trusts, is traceable to this separateness of judicial functions. In spite of the merger of courts of law and equity in England and generally in the United States, the distinction between legal interests and equitable interests persists with rare exception, and the associated essentials of the law of trusts remain.

Also crucial to the development of the trust as a device for flexible, long-term settlement of family property has been the partially parallel evolution of an Anglo-American law of future interests. Peculiar to that body of law is a tolerance for time-divided ownership that permits a variety of legal (as well as equitable) present and future interests, even in potential, unborn beneficiaries and including conditions and powers of appointment, that would surprise most lawyers familiar only with other legal systems.

Although in many respects the courts in this country have dealt with equitable interests as they have dealt with legal interests, there has generally been less rigidity in the judicial treatment of equitable interests. Among the most important characteristics of the trust device is its flexibility, both in the law and in practice. It may be used for purposes the accomplishment of which would be impermissible or impractical if reliance had to be placed on the more limited legal interests. The trust is used not only for family settlements during life and for the flexible disposition of decedents' estates, but it also is used in many kinds of commercial transactions and business relationships.

Coverage of this Restatement. The special characteristics and uses of trusts make it desirable to treat them in a separate Restatement subject, though closely allied to the subject of Property and especially to its topics of donative transfers and future interests.

The trust, as the term is used in this Restatement (see § 1, Comments *a–c*, and §§ 2 and 5), is most frequently a method of disposing of property and of enabling the transferor to provide flexibly for varied purposes and for a number of beneficiaries, often in sequence over time and often including persons yet to be born. Inherent in the Anglo—American trust is a separation of interests in its subject matter, the beneficiaries having equitable property interests and the trustee having a property interest that is normally a legal interest. The creation of a trust includes also the creation of a personal relationship involving rights and duties between the beneficiaries and the trustee. In the origin of trusts and the early "uses" out of which the modern trust has developed, the emphasis was laid on the personal relation; but in the course of time the emphasis has shifted and is now generally placed on the trust as a property disposition and as a means of allocating beneficial rights in the property.

This Restatement deals only in limited ways with a number of matters that are fully dealt with in Restatement Third, Property (Wills and Other Donative Transfers). These include the rule against perpetuities, rules regulating accumulations, rules concerning class gifts, general rules of interpretation and construction, rules concerning powers of appointment, and rules about successive legal estates and legal future interests.

The Restatement of Trusts does not deal with such devices as business trusts, trusts used for purposes of security, and many pooled investment arrangements that use a trust concept. See § 1, Comment *b*, and § 5, Comment *l*. Nor does it, except incidentally, deal with matters of trust taxation and the roles trusts play in the tax aspects of estate planning. This Restatement also does not deal with questions of conflict of laws, which are dealt with in the Restatement Second of Conflict of Laws.

Finally, this Restatement does not deal with constructive trusts, except insofar as they may arise as a result of the creation or attempted creation of express trusts. Constructive trusts, as remedial devices, are dealt with primarily in the Restatement of Restitution. See § 1, Comment *e*. This Restatement does, however, cover the subject of resulting trusts.

Analogous, nontrust relationships. There are a number of widely varying relationships that more or less closely resemble trusts but are not trusts, although the terms "trust" and "trustee" are often used loosely in relation to some of these relationships. It is important to differentiate trusts from these other relationships because many of the rules applicable to trusts are not applicable to them. Some of these relationships were recognized by the courts before the courts of chancery enforced trusts; some of them were developed later. Some of them were developed by courts of law, some by courts of chancery, and some by the ecclesiastical courts.

The term "trust" is sometimes used to encompass all fiduciary relationships. This Restatement does not use the term in this broad sense, given that so many of the rules applicable to trustees are not applicable to other fiduciaries. Thus, an executor, guardian, agent, or corporate officer or director is a fiduciary, but the fiduciary duties and relationships involved differ in many ways from those of a trustee.

In some of the relationships distinguished in this chapter from trusts there is no fiduciary element. A debtor, for example, is not a trustee. Yet it is sometimes difficult to determine whether a debt or trust has been created, although the distinction may be of considerable importance because the rules applicable to trusts differ significantly from those applicable to debts. So also, it is important to distinguish trusts from, for example, mortgages, equitable charges, and contracts to convey property.

In this Restatement there is no attempt to state the rules governing any of these various nontrust relationships, whether fiduciary or not, but the characteristic differences between trusts and these relationships are considered later in § 5 of this chapter.

§ 1. Scope of This Restatement

Trusts dealt with in this Restatement include:

(a) trusts as defined in § 2;

(b) charitable trusts (see § 28); and

(c) resulting trusts (see §§ 7, 8, and 9).

Comment:

a. Matters included. The law relating to charitable trusts and resulting trusts is included in this Restatement, as well as the law relating to trusts as defined in the next section.

The law in this Restatement relates not only to trusts that are created by will or other written instrument but also to trusts the terms of which do not appear in any writings but are ascertained from the spoken words or other conduct of the parties.

In addition, the law in this Restatement applies: (i) to trusts that are established by statute or court order to be administered as express trusts; and (ii) to trusts (including "virtual trust" relationships) created by express reference to a statute that supplies the terms of the trust, as typified by the so-called "custodial trusts" and "custodianships" under uniform acts ... dealing, respectively, with transfers or declarations by mature property owners and with gifts or transfers to "minors" (including, under some statutes, beneficiaries a few years beyond minority).

The custodianships under the various states' versions of the Uniform Gifts to Minors Act and (more recently) the Uniform Transfers to Minors Act are technically not "trusts" but are substantively so similar to express private trusts in their characteristics, applicable legal principles, and role in the donative transfer of family property that, as "virtual trusts," they are treated as trusts within the meaning of this Restatement. It is therefore intended that the rules of trust law as stated in this Restatement apply to these types of custodianships except as otherwise provided, expressly or by necessary implication, by the applicable statute. This exception to the applicability of trust-law rules is itself consistent with trust-law principles, because the provisions of the statute constitute terms of the custodianship much as the provisions of a governing instrument supply the "terms of the trust" (see definition in § 4) in regular express trust relationships—terms that may change most of the generally applicable rules of trust law.... See also discussion in § 5, Comment *a*, following Illustration 1.

To be contrasted with minor's custodianships are the many and varied other forms of custodial arrangements that are not trusts. See generally § 5, especially Comment *e*.

a(1). Qualified inclusion of certain trusts. Several bodies of state and federal legislation dealing with various types of charitable, public, or pension (governmental and private) funds expressly or impliedly incorporate rules of the general trust law that is the subject of this Restatement.....

The principles of this Restatement are generally appropriate to those statutory bodies of rules, both by analogy and insofar as those rules expressly or impliedly incorporate general principles of trust law. Specific provisions and special circumstances or relationships involved in the application of those statutory rules, however, often present fundamentally different considerations, thus expressly or impliedly calling for application of different rules that are not within the scope of this Restatement except as similar circumstances are taken into account in the elaboration of general trust-law principles.

b. Matters excluded. The law relating to the use of trusts as devices for conducting business and investment activities outside the express private- and charitable-trust context is not within the scope of this Restatement. Although many rules of trust law may also apply to business and investment trusts, many of these rules do not; instead other rules are drawn from other bodies of law that are specially applicable to those activities even when conducted in trust form. Thus, the business trust is a business arrangement that is best dealt with in connection with business associations; and most pooled investment vehicles are properly governed by laws applicable to investment companies and to the issuance and sale of securities.

The law relating to the use of a trust as a security device or as an arrangement for the benefit of creditors also is not within the scope of this Restatement. Again, although many of the rules set forth in this Restatement apply to deeds of trust in the nature of mortgages, to assignments for the benefit of creditors, and to other trust arrangements for similar purposes, different rules are often applicable. For similar reasons, rules relating to trustees in bankruptcy are not within the scope of this Restatement. See generally § 5.

c. Charitable trusts. Whenever it is desirable to emphasize the contrast between a trust defined in § 2 and a charitable trust, the term "private trust" is used in this Restatement to indicate a trust that is not a charitable trust.

The fundamental distinction between private trusts and charitable trusts is that, in the case of a private trust, property is devoted to the use of specified or described persons who are designated as beneficiaries of the trust; in the case of a charitable trust, property is devoted to purposes the law deems appropriately beneficial to the public.

Much of the law stated throughout this Restatement applies to charitable trusts. A few of the rules applicable to private trusts, however, do not apply to charitable trusts, and there are rules applicable to charitable trusts that are not applied to private trusts.

Specific rules defining charitable purposes are set out in § 28. A special rule (*cy pres*) for modification of charitable trust purposes is stated in § 67. Also, the definite beneficiaries requirements of § 44, applicable to private trusts, does not apply to charitable trusts; and see § 47(2) on noncharitable "purpose trusts."

d. Resulting trusts. Resulting trusts are described and the rules applicable to them are stated in §§ 7–9. The term "express trust" is used in this Restatement to indicate a trust as defined in § 2 whenever it is desirable to emphasize the contrast between a trust as there defined on the one hand and either a constructive trust (see Comment *e*, below) or a resulting trust on the other hand.

In brief, a resulting trust differs from an express trust in that the beneficial interest or interests involved in the former are implied by law. In addition, resulting and express trusts generally differ in the nature and extent of the duties of the trustee, although occasionally a resulting-trust interest is simply a reversionary part of the beneficial-interest structure of a continuing express trust. See § 7, Comment *e*.

Although many of the rules applicable to express trusts are also applied to resulting trusts, others of these rules are not; and there are also rules applicable to resulting trusts that are not applied to express trusts.

e. *Constructive trusts*. A constructive trust is a relationship with respect to property usually subjecting the person by whom its title is held to an equitable duty to convey the property to another on the ground that the title holder's acquisition or retention of the property is wrongful and that unjust enrichment would occur if the title holder were permitted to retain the property. See Restatement of Restitution § 160 [Restatement Third, Restitution and Unjust Enrichment § 55]. On the meaning of unjust (or "unjustified") enrichment, see Restatement Third, Restitution and Unjust Enrichment § 1 . . . .

Both express trusts and resulting trusts are based upon an intention of the person who creates them. An express trust is created by a settlor's manifestation of an intention to create it (see § 13), while a resulting trust (Comment *d*) arises because of circumstances that raise an inference that the transferor of the property did not intend that the person taking or holding title is to have the beneficial interest (see § 7). On the other hand, a constructive trust is imposed, not necessarily to effectuate an expressed or implied intention, but to redress a wrong or to prevent unjust enrichment. A constructive trust is thus the result of judicial intervention and is remedial in character.

Except as a constructive trust establishes an express trust or arises out of an express trust or an attempt to create an express trust, the rules applicable to constructive trusts are not dealt with in this Restatement. These rules are more broadly dealt with in the Restatement of Restitution.

§ 2. Definition of Trust

A trust, as the term is used in this Restatement when not qualified by the word "resulting" or "constructive," is a fiduciary relationship with respect to property, arising from a manifestation of intention to create that relationship and subjecting the person who holds title to the property to duties to deal with it for the benefit of charity or for one or more persons, at least one of whom is not the sole trustee.

Comment:

a. *Terminology*. When the term "trust" is used in this Restatement without any qualifying adjective or description, it denotes a trust (private or charitable) as defined in this section, and an express trust rather than a resulting or constructive trust. See also § 1, Comment *a*. The term "trust" also includes public funds and public and private pension-fund arrangements in trust form; but see the observations in § 1, Comment *b*, about the frequent influence of state or federal legislation and special circumstances in limiting the applicability of rules governing private and charitable trusts as stated in this Restatement.

Increasingly, modern common-law and statutory concepts and terminology tacitly recognize the trust as a legal "entity," consisting of the trust estate and the associated fiduciary relation between the trustee and the beneficiaries. This is increasingly and appropriately reflected both in language (referring, for example, to the duties or liability of a trustee to "the trust") and in doctrine, especially in distinguishing between the trustee personally or as an individual and the trustee in a fiduciary or representative capacity. See, for example, Chapter 21 of this Restatement. . . . .

The term "express trust" is used in this Restatement to indicate a trust as here defined whenever it is desirable to emphasize the contrast between such a trust on the one hand and a resulting trust or a constructive trust on the other.

The term "private trust" is used in this Restatement to indicate a trust as here defined whenever it is desirable to emphasize the contrast between a private trust and a charitable trust.

For examples of fairly typical kinds of express private trusts, see the Illustrations in Comment *i*, below.

On the doctrine of merger, where a sole trustee is the sole beneficiary, see § 69.

b. *Fiduciary relationship*. The trust relationship is one of many forms of fiduciary relationship, each of which reflects the legal principles of the substantive area of law in which it has developed. In § 5, trusts are compared and contrasted with some of these other fiduciary relationships, as well as with some confidential and other business, personal, and property relationships.

Despite the differences in the legal circumstances and responsibilities of various fiduciaries, one characteristic is common to all: a person in a fiduciary relationship to another is under a duty to act for the benefit of the other as to matters within the scope of the relationship. (Fiduciary duties may, in the circumstances of certain trust relationships, technically exist but not be effectively enforceable; the situation arises to the extent the trustee holds a power of revocation or a presently exercisable general power of appointment or withdrawal. See §§ 74 and 97, and compare Restatement Second, Trusts § 216, Comments *h* and *i*.)

In matters *within the scope* of a fiduciary relationship, the fiduciary is under a duty not to profit at the expense of the other and not to enter into competition with the other without the latter's consent, unless properly authorized to do so by a court or by the terms of the arrangement under which the relationship arose. In such matters, if the fiduciary enters into a transaction with the other and fails to make full disclosure of all relevant circumstances known to the fiduciary, or if the transaction is unfair to the other, the transaction can be set aside by the other. On the especially strict duty of loyalty in trust relationships in particular, see § 78, and compare Restatement Second, Trusts § 170.

A fiduciary is normally under a duty not to delegate to a third person the performance of the fiduciary duties. In the interest of the beneficiaries of a trust, however, a trustee may delegate if and as a prudent person would. See § 80; compare Restatement Second, Trusts § 171. In addition, trust terms or statutes often expressly authorize delegation, at least in some matters or circumstances.

Fiduciary relationships include not only the relation of trustee and beneficiary but also, among others, guardian-ward, agent-principal, attorney-client, and partnership relationships. The scope of the transactions affected by the relationship and the extent of the duties imposed are not identical in all fiduciary relationships. The duties of a trustee are more rigorous than those of most other fiduciaries. As to the duties of a trustee, see §§ 70–84, and Restatement Second, Trusts §§ 169–185.

b(1). Confidential relationship. Although the relationship between two persons is not a fiduciary relationship, it may nevertheless be a confidential relationship. Conversely, a fiduciary relationship may exist even though the parties do not enjoy a confidential relationship.

A confidential relation exists between two persons in many circumstances in which one has gained the confidence of the other and purports to act or advise with the other's interests in mind. Thus, a confidential relation may exist although there is no fiduciary relation and is particularly likely to arise between family members or close friends or on the basis of the confidence that arises between physician and patient or priest and penitent.

If one stands in a confidential but not fiduciary relation to another, a transaction between them will not be set aside at the instance of one of them unless in fact he or she placed confidence in the other and the other abused that confidence by fraud, undue influence, or otherwise. The importance of confidential relationships in attempts to create trusts and the potential in those situations for relief against unjust enrichment are discussed in § 24(2) and § 24, Comment *f*. Cf. § 24(3) and (4).

Although a fiduciary relationship exists, an otherwise valid transaction between the parties that is *not within the scope* of the fiduciary relation will be set aside if and only if there is an abuse of a confidential relation between the parties.

Illustration:

1. T is trustee of certain property for B and B's issue. T purchases B's beneficial interest in Blackacre, which is an asset of the trust, and also purchases Whiteacre from B, who is full legal and beneficial owner of Whiteacre. B can set aside the sale of his equitable interest in Blackacre if T failed to disclose to B facts known to her affecting the value of Blackacre. B cannot, however, set aside the sale of Whiteacre unless T stood in a confidential relation to him and abused this relation, such as by affirmative actions inducing B to refrain from seeking independent advice.

In neither of the transactions in Illustration 1 has T engaged in self-dealing, within the prohibition of § 78 (and see Restatement Second, Trusts § 170, Comments *b*, *h*, and *j*). Self-dealing would have been involved if T individually purchased Blackacre from herself as trustee, rather than dealing with B in the purchase of B's equitable interest in Blackacre (see § 78 and Restatement Second, Trusts § 170(2), and § 170, Comment *w*).

c. Property. The term "property" usually denotes interests in things and not necessarily the things themselves. See original Restatement of Property, Introductory Note to Chapter 1.

The expression "trust property" denotes the property interests that are held in trust. The phrase "subject matter of the trust" denotes the things themselves, some or all interests in which are held in trust. Either of the foregoing terms, or a reference to "trust assets" or "the trust estate," may be used in this Restatement when the foregoing distinctions are unimportant and there is no perceived danger of confusion.

Where the owner of land transfers an estate for life or for a term of years to another as trustee, the life or term estate is the trust property and the land itself is the subject matter of the trust. Rules concerning the trust property are discussed in §§ 40–42.

d. Title, ownership, and interests. A person who holds an interest has "title" to the interest whether that interest is held for the person's own benefit or for the benefit of another. The term "owner" is used in this Restatement to indicate a person by whom one or more interests are held for the person's own benefit.

Thus, unlike "ownership," the term "title" without more does not indicate whether the title holder holds the property beneficially or as trustee.

Although trust beneficiaries have equitable title, a trustee's title to trust property may be either legal or equitable. Although it is usually true (and is, unfortunately, often stated without qualification in cases and texts) that the trustee has legal title, in some instances the trustee will hold only an equitable title.

Illustration:

2. S is the life beneficiary of a trust established by his mother, M. He transfers his beneficial interest in M's trust to T, who is directed to hold that interest in trust for certain others. T holds an equitable interest as trust property for the benefit of those designated by S as the beneficiaries of this second trust.

The distinction between legal and equitable interests is due to the historical circumstance that these two types of interests were originally enforced in different tribunals and by different forms of procedure. The rules governing equitable interests as developed by the courts of chancery were more flexible than the rules governing legal interests, due in large part to conceptions concerning the role of the chancellor. Statutes have been passed in most states today abolishing the separation between courts of law and courts of equity and purporting to abolish most of the distinctions between actions at law and suits in equity. Equity powers have also been extended in many states to courts of probate, along with the legislative trend toward expanding the traditionally limited jurisdiction of those courts.

The various changes in procedures have not necessarily affected the substantive rules concerning legal and equitable interests, which still retain some characteristic differences. These differences generally involve methods by which the interests may be created, the types and characteristics of permissible interests, and some rules concerning relations to third parties. Also, an equitable interest in a thing is traditionally extinguished by the transfer of the legal interest in it to a bona fide purchaser when a legal interest in the thing would not be so extinguished. Recording statutes in the various states, however, have exposed many unrecorded legal interests to similar risks of subsequent transactions and have also afforded protection for recorded equitable interests, thus illustrating the reduced distinction between legal and equitable interests in these important matters.

e. Manifestation of intention. The phrase "manifestation of intention" in this Restatement means the external expression of an intention as distinguished from an undisclosed intention. See § 4.

Sometimes it is important to distinguish between an external expression (i.e., manifestation) of intent that may and one that may not be considered in court to establish that intent for purpose of giving it effect by way of express trust. This is particularly so when a statute of frauds or a wills act requires a writing or other formalities. In such cases, reference may be made in this Restatement to intentions that are "properly" or "improperly" manifested, or the like. See § 4, Comments *a* and *b* . . . . See also § 12.

f. *The elements of a trust.* In the strict, traditional sense, a trust involves three elements: (1) a trustee, who holds the trust property and is subject to duties to deal with it for the benefit of one or more others; (2) one or more beneficiaries, to whom and for whose benefit the trustee owes the duties with respect to the trust property; and (3) trust property, which is held by the trustee for the beneficiaries. In a more comprehensive sense, the trust purpose is often included in discussions of the elements of trusts, as in Part 3 (specifically Chapter 6) of this Restatement.

Although all of these elements are present in a complete trust, either or both of elements (1) and (2) above may be temporarily absent without destroying the trust or preventing its creation.

g. *Necessity of a trustee.* An express trust can be created, or having been created can continue, although for a period of time there is no trustee. Thus, if the owner of property devises or bequeaths it in trust, a trust may arise although no trustee is named in the will or the person named as trustee refuses to accept the trusteeship or is dead or otherwise incapable of taking title to the property. See § 14, Comment *b*. Once a trust has been created, it does not fail merely because the trustee subsequently dies, resigns, is removed, or otherwise ceases to serve as trustee. See § 31. On the special though analogous problem presented in attempts to create trusts by inter vivos conveyance, see § 14, Comment *d*, and § 16, Comments *b* and *c*.

In short, a trust will not fail *merely* (cf. § 31, Comment *b*) for lack of a trustee; if necessary, a trustee will be appointed by court or by other method appropriate to the terms of the trust. See § 34.

h. *Necessity of a beneficiary.* An express trust can be created, or having been created can continue, although for a period of time there is no designated beneficiary in being. None of the intended beneficiaries need be identified or in existence at the time of the creation of the trust, provided one or more beneficiaries may become ascertainable pursuant to the terms of the trust within the requirements of the applicable rule against perpetuities. See §§ 43–45; cf. § 46. (In a more comprehensive sense, even at the outset such a trust has existing beneficiaries by implication of law: the reversionary beneficiaries whose interests may or may not eventually materialize by way of resulting trust. See §§ 7–8.)

Thus, for example, a trust can be created for the benefit of a child not born or conceived at the time of the creation of the trust (see § 44, Comment *c*), or for the benefit of a definite class of persons although the identity of the individuals comprising its membership is not ascertained or ascertainable at the time of the trust's creation. See § 45. In these cases, protection will be provided against improper acts of the trustee; and the trust cannot be revoked by a settlor who has not retained a power of revocation. See § 65.

On the other hand, if property is transferred upon an intended private trust and no definite or validly ascertainable beneficiaries are provided, no express trust is created. See § 46(1); but cf. § 46(2). A charitable trust, however, can be created although no definite beneficiary is provided. See § 28, Comment *c*.

On who is a "beneficiary," see . . . also § 48, Comment *a*.

That no trust exists when the intended sole trustee is the sole beneficiary, see § 69 on the doctrine of merger and the narrow circumstances in which it operates.

i. *Necessity of trust property*. A trust cannot be created unless there is trust property in existence and ascertainable at the time of the creation of the trust. That property, however, may consist of such diverse rights as an undivided interest, a term of years, a future interest (legal or equitable, vested or contingent), or a *chose in action*, even with respect to things that are neither in existence nor ascertainable when the trust is created. See §§ 40–41.

In the absence of trust property there is at most an instrument of trust, or a plan or promise to create a trust. Whether a promise to create a trust is enforceable depends upon whether the requirements for the creation of a contract are satisfied. In fact, the rights under an enforceable promise constitute "property" (a *chose in action*) so that, if so intended, they may be held immediately in trust rather than giving rise only to a contract to create a trust in the future. See § 10, Clause (e) and Comment *g*, and § 15, Comment *b*.

Although merely entering into or executing an agreement or instrument of trust does not initially create a trust because of the absence of trust property, a trust may nevertheless be created later if and when a transfer of property to the trustee is made with reference to that agreement or instrument. See generally § 23, Comment *e*, § 20, and §§ 17(2)(b) and 19.

If a trust is created and subsequently the whole of the trust property ceases to exist, the trust is terminated because the trustee no longer holds anything in trust. If, however, there remains so much as a claim against the trustee or another on behalf of the beneficiaries, the claim constitutes trust property that continues to be held in trust for the beneficiaries. See . . .also § 41, Comment *c*.

The Illustrations that follow offer examples of a fairly representative but far from exhaustive array of express private trusts.

Illustrations:

3. S's will leaves his residuary estate to T in trust to distribute the net income to L for life, and upon L's death to distribute the trust estate to R, if then living, and if not then to R's issue who are then living. S, who is now dead, is the settlor and T the trustee of an express private trust. L, R, and R's issue are beneficiaries of this trust, a type often referred to as a "testamentary" trust, and S's residuary estate is, initially at least, the trust property. (See § 17.)

4. The will of W, who is now dead, leaves Greenacre, all of her stock in X and Y corporations, and $250,000 to T, as trustee, to pay or apply periodically "such amounts from the trust income and principal as T deems appropriate to support my husband H in his accustomed life-style," and upon H's death to distribute the trust estate to the then living descendants of H and W. W has created an express private trust of the properties devised to T.

5. H transfers certain properties to T in trust, setting forth certain provisions for H's own benefit during his lifetime and other provisions thereafter for the benefit of his wife W during her lifetime, with the remainder on the death of the survivor of H and W to be distributed to various named and described relatives of H. H reserves the right during life to revoke and amend the trust, in whole or in part, from time to time. This is an express private trust of a type often referred to as a revocable inter vivos or "living" trust. (See § 25.)

6. S transfers certain cash and securities to his daughter D in trust for the benefit of his grandson B. D is instructed to pay or apply trust income and principal in her discretion to or for the benefit of B until he reaches age 21, at which time D is to distribute the entire trust estate to him; if B dies before reaching age 21, D is to distribute the trust property to B's estate. S, who retained no power of revocation or amendment, has created an express private trust; it is an irrevocable inter vivos trust of a type often used to qualify the transfer for the federal gift-tax annual exclusion.

§ 3. Settlor, Trust Property, Trustee, and Beneficiary

(1) The person who creates a trust is the settlor.

(2) The property held in trust is the trust property.

(3) The person who holds property in trust is the trustee.

(4) A person for whose benefit property is held in trust is a beneficiary.

Comment:

a. *The settlor.* The term "settlor" includes a person who creates a trust by will as well as a person who creates a trust inter vivos. A trust may have more than one settlor.

The settlor is sometimes called the "trustor," or particularly in tax contexts the "grantor," but these terms are not used elsewhere in this Restatement. The terms "transferor" and "testator" are used occasionally in this Restatement in referring to a settlor, as well as to another who makes a transfer of property.

In some contexts significant questions may arise concerning the person who is properly to be treated as the settlor of a trust. See, e.g., § 58, Comments *e* and *f*. See also § 10, Comment *g* . . . .

b. *The trust property.* The term "trust property" denotes things or the interests in things that are held in trust. By contrast, when the distinction is important, the expression "subject matter of the trust" is used to denote the things themselves, one or more interests in which are held in trust. See § 2, Comment *c*. When it is desired to refer to the trust property as a whole, the term "trust estate" is often used. Although property held in trust usually consists of legal interests in tangible or intangible things, equitable interests also can be held in trust. See § 2, Illustration 2. See more generally §§ 40–42 on what may be trust property and on the trustee's title.

The trust property is sometimes called the "trust res," but that term is not used elsewhere in this Restatement.

c. *The trustee.* The "trustee" is the person who holds trust property. The settlor may serve as trustee, as may a beneficiary. A trust may have two or more trustees, who are commonly referred to as "co-trustees." See further §§ 31–39.

d. The beneficiary. A trustee holds the trust property for the benefit of a person or persons who are referred to as the "beneficiary" or "beneficiaries." A trust beneficiary is sometimes called "cestui que trust," but that expression is not used elsewhere in this Restatement.

The settlor or the trustee, or both, may be beneficiaries; but a sole trustee may not be the sole beneficiary (see § 69 on the doctrine of merger). Thus, the trustee must hold property for the benefit of one or more persons, at least one of whom is not the sole trustee (§ 2), and whose interests will suffice to prevent merger when the trustee is also a beneficiary, regardless of whether those interests are present or future, vested or contingent.

Most express trusts are created for the benefit of multiple beneficiaries. These beneficiaries may be named or described, often through the use of class-gift terminology, and the beneficial interests in a private trust usually involve an array of present and future interests.

On trust beneficiaries more generally, see §§ 43–48.

e. Meaning of "person." The term "person" includes corporations and unincorporated associations.

f. Cross-references. On the question of who may serve as a trustee, see §§ 32–33. On the question of who may be a beneficiary, see § 43. On what may be trust property, see §§ 40–41. On the question of who has capacity to be a settlor, see § 11.

§ 4. Terms of the Trust

The phrase "terms of the trust" means the manifestation of intention of the settlor with respect to the trust provisions expressed in a manner that admits of its proof in judicial proceedings.

Comment:

a. What is included in "terms of the trust"? The phrase "the terms of the trust" is used in a broad sense in this Restatement, as in many statutes and cases. It includes any manifestations of the settlor's intention at the time of the creation of the trust, whether expressed by written or spoken words or by conduct, to the extent the intention is expressed in a manner that permits proof of the manifestation of intent in judicial proceedings. The terms of the trust may appear clearly from written or spoken words, or they may be provided by statute, supplied by rules of construction, or determined by interpretation of the words or conduct of the settlor in the light of all of the circumstances surrounding the creation of the trust.

Among the circumstances that may be of importance in determining the terms of the trust, either in the absence of a written instrument declaring those terms or in matters about which a written instrument is silent or ambiguous, are the following: (1) the situations of the settlor, the beneficiaries, and the trustee, including such factors as age, legal and practical competence, personal and financial circumstances, and the relationships of these persons and these factors to each other; (2) the value and character of the trust property; (3) the purposes for which the trust is created; (4) relevant business and financial practices at the time; (5) the circumstances under which the trust is to be administered; (6) the formality or informality, the skill or lack of skill, and the care or lack of care with which any instrument containing the manifestation in question was drawn.

The intention of the settlor that determines the terms of the trust is the intention at the time of the creation of the trust and not a subsequent intention. The settlor's intention at the time of the trust's creation may be shown, however, not only by facts that occurred before or at that time but also by facts occurring thereafter to the extent evidence of those facts may be considered under the applicable rules of evidence to show the intention in question.

See generally Restatement Third, Property (Wills and Other Donative Transfers) § 10.2; and cf. id. §§ 11.1–11.3, 12.1, and 12.2. . . . .

a(1). Default law and law of the instrument. As shall be seen throughout this Restatement, many (but not all) of trust law consists of "default rules," as opposed to mandatory or restrictive rules, and is therefore subordinate to the terms (or "law") of the trust. (This is particularly apparent in the subsequent volumes of this Restatement.) On statutes as provisions of wills or inter vivos instruments by incorporation, see Comments *c, d,* and *g*.

b. What is not included in "terms of the trust"? A manifestation of the settlor's intention does not constitute a term of the trust if evidence of such manifestation may not be considered in the judicial proceedings in which the terms of the trust are in question. Thus, if the manifestation may not be considered because of a statute of wills, a statute of frauds, the parol-evidence rule, or some rule of the law of evidence, it is not a term of the trust. See Comments *c, d,* and *e* below. See generally Restatement Third, Property (Wills and Other Donative Transfers) § 10.2 and §§ 11.1–11.3. On occasional references in this Restatement to "proper" or "improper" manifestations of intention, see § 2, Comment *e*.

The mere fact, however, that an admissible manifestation of intention is not legally effective does not prevent it from being one of the terms of the trust. Thus, a provision in a trust instrument that is impossible to comply with or that violates the rule against perpetuities (§ 29(b)) or is otherwise invalid (§ 29(a), (c)) is nevertheless one of the terms of the trust.

c. Trusts created by will. If a trust is created by will, the terms of the trust are determined by the provisions of the will as interpreted in light of all the relevant circumstances and direct evidence of intention in accordance with the general rules of law governing interpretation of wills. These rules of interpretation are not peculiar to the law of trusts and are not generally within the scope of this Restatement. On Wills Acts, see §§ 17–19. See generally Restatement Third, Property (Wills and Other Donative Transfers) § 10.2 and §§ 11.1–11.3.

The "provisions of the will" (and thus the terms of the testamentary trust) include the terms of any statute incorporated or made applicable by other will provisions.

d. Trusts created inter vivos by written instrument. If a trust is created by a transaction inter vivos and is evidenced by a written instrument, the terms of the trust are determined by the provisions of the governing instrument as interpreted in light of all the relevant circumstances and such direct evidence of the intention of the settlor with respect to the trust as is not denied consideration because of a statute of frauds, the parol-evidence rule, or some other rule of law. On the statutes of frauds, see §§ 22–24 (and cf. § 20), and on the parol-evidence rule, see § 21. See generally Restatement

Third, Property (Wills and Other Donative Transfers) § 10.2 and §§ 11.1–11.3.

The "provisions of the governing instrument" include the terms of any statute incorporated or made applicable by other provisions of that instrument.

e. *Trusts orally created inter vivos.* If a trust is created by a transaction inter vivos and is not evidenced by a written instrument, the terms of the trust are determined by such evidence of the intention of the settlor with respect to the trust as is not barred from consideration because of a statute of frauds or some other rule of law. See §§ 20–24.

f. *Trusts created by court order.* If a trust is established by an order of court and is to be administered as an express trust, the terms of the trust are determined by the provisions of the court order as interpreted in accordance with general rules governing interpretation of judgments.

g. *Trusts created by statute.* Some forms of trusts that are created by statute, especially public retirement systems or pension funds, and sometimes public land trusts, school land trusts, or trusts for benefit of native populations, are administered as express trusts, the terms of which are either set forth in the statute or are supplied by the default rules of general trust law. See § 10, Comment *b*.

h. *Cross-reference.* As to the effect of the terms of the trust in determining the nature and extent of the duties and powers of the trustee, see § 70. On the duty of the trustee to administer the trust in accordance with the terms of the trust (and applicable law), see § 76.

§ 5. Trusts and Other Relationships

The following are not trusts:

(a) successive legal estates;

(b) decedents' estates;

(c) guardianships and conservatorships;

(d) receiverships and bankruptcy trusteeships;

(e) durable powers of attorney and other agencies;

(f) bailments and leases;

(g) corporations, partnerships, and other business associations;

(h) conditions and equitable charges;

(i) contracts to convey or certain contracts for the benefit of third parties;

(j) assignments or partial assignments of choses in action;

(k) relationships of debtors to creditors;

(l) mortgages, deeds of trust, pledges, liens, and other security arrangements.

Comment:

a. *Trusts in general.* A property arrangement may constitute a trust, as that term is used in this Restatement, even though such terms as "trust" or "trustee" are not used (§ 13, Comment *b*), or the parties to the arrangement are unfamiliar with the trust concept as such. Conversely, use of the word "trust" or "trustee" does not necessarily mean that a trust relationship is involved (id.). A property arrangement is a trust as long as it has the characteristics, and gives rise to the rights and duties, the law recognizes as a trust.

Illustration:

1. A wishes to make a gift to B but wishes to provide fiduciary management of the funds until B is likely, in A's view, to attain practical as well as legal capacity to manage her own financial affairs. A therefore executes and delivers, and C cashes, a check made payable to C. The check is accompanied by a writing instructing C to "invest, manage, and expend the funds as may appear appropriate for B's benefit until she reaches age 21, and then to turn the property over to her." There is no written or spoken reference to a trust or to the role of trustee. Nevertheless, this transfer is properly construed as creating a trust, of which A is the settlor, C is the trustee, B is the beneficiary, and the funds received by C upon cashing the check are the initial trust property. The terms of the trust (see § 4) are those expressed in the writing, supplemented by those supplied through interpretation and by state law.

a(1). Custodianships for minors. A disposition quite similar in result to that in the above Illustration may be made, simply and with a complete set of terms, by A's check made payable to (and cashed by) "C as custodian for B under the Uniform Transfers to Minors Act of State X." This so-called "custodianship" is sometimes referred to in this Restatement as a "virtual trust" and is a relationship to which the rules of this Restatement apply. See § 1, Comment *a*. Thus, A, B, and C are included in references in this Restatement to the settlors, beneficiaries, and trustees of express private trusts, even though the above reference to a "virtual trust" acknowledges that custodianship statutes generally state or are interpreted as meaning that the beneficiary has full title of the custodial assets. For Restatement purposes, however, trust treatment for this particular form of custodianship is appropriate because other elements of the trust relationship are present. Furthermore, the language and substance of these statutes are generally consistent with the custodian having title-based authority over the property and with the beneficiary having all of the beneficial rights and interests.

Thus, although custodianships under the various versions of the Uniform Transfers to Minors Act (and of the predecessor Uniform Gifts to Minors Act) technically are not trust entities, this Restatement treats these particular custodianships and custodians respectively as trusts and trustees. . . . . Accordingly, these relationships are subject to the rules of trust law stated in this Restatement, except as the provisions of the applicable statute expressly or by necessary implication require otherwise. (Even in this respect these custodianships parallel trust relationships, the terms of which displace the rules of trust law insofar as those rules are nonmandatory, or "default," rules.) The terms of the illustrative custodial relationship in the preceding paragraph are the provisions of the State X custodianship statute, together with the above-quoted gift language referring to that statute and designating B as the beneficiary. See § 4, Comments *a*, *c*, and *d*.

To be contrasted are the many and varied other "custodial" relationships that serve quite different and ordinarily more limited roles. See especially Comment *e*.

a(2). Determining whether trust intended. Whether or not a trust is intended is usually evident from the general nature of a relationship or is readily apparent from its terms, that is, from the parties' written or spoken words in context. In any event, and often crucial in determining the character of a relationship, there can be no trust without identifiable trust property.

Occasionally, however, situations arise in which it is difficult to determine the intended legal relationship. Furthermore, it is possible for an arrangement to involve more than one legal relationship.

The difficult cases of arguable trust relationships arise only when there is a possibility of identifying trust property, so that general intentions and the expectations of parties then become determinative—even though the specific question of trust or no trust may never have entered the consciousness of the parties. In such a situation, the legal characterization of the arrangement may become important in order to determine rights and duties among the parties to the relationship, and sometimes liabilities or priorities with respect to third parties. Yet, in these situations, it is not uncommon or inappropriate for courts to rely on reasoning that, based on common sense or experience, inquires into the likelihood that the parties would have contemplated that certain obligations or expectations normally associated with a particular relationship should apply. . . . .

b. Trusts and successive legal estates. In their objectives and in the nature of the beneficial rights involved, many trusts bear a close resemblance to relationships between legal life tenants and remainder beneficiaries and to other relationships involving successive legal estates. This is particularly so in situations in which the beneficiary for life serves, or arguably serves, as trustee.

Despite the separation of legal and equitable interests that typifies the trust, parallels exist not only between the successive rights of enjoyment in these different types of time-divided property ownerships arrangements but often also between: a trustee's power to invade principal and a life tenant's power of consumption; the powers of appointment that may be granted to legal life tenants or others and those that are often given to trust beneficiaries (and, to a lesser degree, fiduciary powers granted trustees to determine some of the beneficial rights of some beneficiaries); and the normal management authority of trustees and the powers of sale and management authority often expressly conferred on legal life tenants, or on others either alone or in conjunction with the life tenant.

The similarities, and thus the potential for confusion, are further illustrated by the fact that the life (or other) beneficiaries of trusts may serve as trustee, while life tenants in successive legal-estates arrangements may hold one or more of their powers with respect to the subject matter in a fiduciary capacity that is somewhat similar to that of trusteeship. Beyond this, it is not unusual for instruments creating successive legal estates to provide expressly that, on sale of one or more of the assets originally subject to the arrangement, the person who was the life tenant is to become trustee of the proceeds.

Thus, although the language used in transferring property for the benefit of two or more persons in succession is usually clear enough to avoid uncertainty concerning the intended legal relationship, the extensive flexibility allowed by the law in the creation of trust and nontrust arrangements sometimes leads to difficulties in categorization. In such cases, it is a question of the transferor's intention whether the property is to be held in trust for the persons who are to be benefited or whether those persons take successive legal estates. In close cases involving cash and securities, as distinguished from land and chattels, there is a slight preference for construing the terms of a transfer as creating a trust, with the life beneficiary standing also in the role of trustee holding full legal title, rather than as creating successive legal interests. Even when successive legal interests are created, there is some modern tendency, particularly by statute, to make some of the rules of trust law applicable to those interests.

Absent a grant of additional authority by statute or the terms of the disposition, the life tenant and other holders of successive legal estates may deal only with their own respective interests in the subject matter. Individually, they have no power to sell or otherwise deal with the underlying property, or with the interests or potential interests of others in that property. Unlike a trustee, the life tenant as such does not stand in a fiduciary relationship to the other beneficiaries of successive legal interests, although the life tenant's rights in the assets involved are subject to an array of limitations and obligations for the protection of the holders of the future interests. The rights, powers, and duties of successive holders of legal interests are dealt with at length in the original Restatement of Property at §§ 187–210.

c. Trusts compared to decedents' estates and guardianships. Personal representatives of decedents' estates and guardians, conservators, and their counterparts, by whatever name, are fiduciaries but they are not trustees. Although many of the rules applicable to trustees are applicable to executors and administrators and also to guardians and conservators, many other rules of trust law are not.

A trustee has title to the trust property. Guardians and, traditionally, conservators do not; this is increasingly true also of executors and administrators, but technicalities of the passage of title vary from state to state. It is particularly likely that traditional concepts of probate law may still place title to personal property in a decedent's personal representative. Many modern statutes also grant a conservator title to a conservatee's property. With frequent exception for personal representatives serving under a will, the powers and duties of these nontrust fiduciaries are generally fixed by statute and are often narrower in scope than those of trustees.

An executor or administrator owes duties to estate creditors in addition to the general duties the fiduciary owes to the beneficiaries of the estate. In the absence of a statute otherwise providing, the fundamental duties of personal representatives are: (1) to determine and, if appropriate, take possession of the estate assets; (2) to determine and pay the decedent's debts, taxes, and expenses of administration; and (3) to determine and make distribution to the beneficiaries. In the course of discharging these responsibilities, the executor or administrator is also under a duty to preserve, and liquidate as appropriate, estate assets and their product. The personal representative's investment authority and responsibilities, however, tend to be more limited than those of trustees but vary from state to state and may well be affected by the terms of a will or statute. The details and problems of these matters are beyond the scope of this Restatement.

If a testator names the same person to serve as both executor and trustee, or imposes duties normally associated with trusteeship on one referred to in the will only as an "executor," that person acts as executor in performing the duties mentioned above but as trustee in performing additional duties. The fiduciary may also act as trustee with respect to a part of the estate while still acting as executor with respect to the rest.

d. Trusts and estates in receivership or bankruptcy. When a corporation or an individual is insolvent, and in some other situations, the court may appoint a receiver to administer the corporation's or individual's property under court supervision. The receiver is a fiduciary but does not hold title to the property under administration and is not a trustee.

Statutes in some states provide that, on dissolution of a corporation, its assets pass to a designated person for the purpose of winding up the corporation. Although such a statutory successor may hold title to the corporate property and is considered to be a trustee for some purposes, the successor is not a trustee within the rules stated and terminology used in this Restatement.

Even a trustee in bankruptcy does not hold the bankruptcy estate in a trust as that term is used, or within the rules stated, in this Restatement.

e. Trusts and durable powers of attorney and other agencies. Traditional agency relationships terminate automatically on the legal disability or death of the principal. The durable power of attorney is a modern form of agency that, by its terms, survives the legal incapacity of the principal or springs into effect upon the principal's loss of legal capacity. An agent as such does not acquire title to the property of the principal, although the agent may have powers with respect to some or all of that property. An agent may be entrusted with possession of property of the principal, but this does not make the agent a trustee. See Comment *f* (on bailments). An agent may even be entrusted with title in some contexts (see Comment *f*), resulting in a technical trust relationship, but one that is generally subject to rules of agency law insofar as they differ from the rules of this Restatement.

An agency is created by the consent of principal and agent (see Restatement Second, Agency § 1 [Restatement Third, Agency §§ 1.01, 3.01]), but a trust may be created without the consent or even the knowledge of either the beneficiaries or the trustee (see § 14 and § 2, Comment *g*). An agency may be terminated at the will of either the principal or the agent, but a trust is ordinarily not terminable at the will of either the trustee or the beneficiaries, or by the death or incapacity of either. Furthermore, the fact that, by the terms of the trust, powers of revocation and amendment are reserved to the settlor does not make the trustee an agent (see § 25(1)).

An agent undertakes to act on behalf of the principal and subject to the latter's control. Although a trustee is under a duty to deal with the trust property in accordance with the terms of the trust and can be compelled to do so by the beneficiaries, a trustee is not subject to the control of either the settlor or the beneficiaries except to the extent the terms of the trust reserve or confer some such power over the trustee—power that is not readily inferred (although compare problems of interpretation sometimes arising with regard to inter vivos trusts, § 63, Comments *b* and *c*).

Agents may subject their principals to personal liability to third persons, but trustees as such cannot subject beneficiaries to such liabilities (see generally Chapter 21).

An action against a third person with respect to property of the principal can ordinarily be maintained by the principal and not by the agent, although an agent in possession of the principal's property can maintain such actions as may be maintained by other persons in possession of the property of another. A trustee can maintain an action with respect to trust property, but ordinarily a beneficiary cannot. (See generally Chapter 21.)

Although an agent is not a trustee and is subject to rules of the law of agency, many of the same legal principles that are applied to trustees may be applied to agents, particularly an agent serving under a durable power of attorney during the principal's legal incapacity.

f. *Trusts and bailments or leases.* The owner of a chattel may give another person possession of the chattel without granting that person title to it. In such a case, a bailment and not a trust is created. Whether the bailment is for the benefit of the bailor, the bailee, or a third person, or some combination of these, the bailee is not a trustee. Similarly, an owner of land who leases the property or simply gives a term of years to another does not create a trust or thereby become trustee of the land for the other's benefit. (This does not mean that, with further agreement or understanding, a trust could not be created of a term interest, for such an interest is *property* for purpose of § 40 and § 40, Comment *b*.) The interests of both lessor and lessee are legal interests, as are the interests of both bailor and bailee.

Delivery of a chattel to another, with no writing, may suffice either to pass title or merely to give possession. When the act is done for the benefit of the owner or a third person, or for the benefit of the bailee as well as for another, the potentially difficult question of whether a trust or a bailment is created depends on the intention manifested by the parties.

An agent who has possession of a chattel of the principal is a bailee as well as an agent. If the principal also gives the agent title to the chattel, the relationship is technically one of trust as well as agency but remains subject to the rules applicable to agents rather than to those applicable to trustees.

g. *Trusts compared to corporations, partnerships, and other business associations.* There are many similarities and also differences in the roles and duties of trustees and those of corporate officers or directors, partners of various types of partnerships, and member-managers of limited-liability companies.

For example, trustees and corporate officers and directors, as fiduciaries, manage the affairs, respectively, of the trust or the corporation for the benefit of the beneficiaries or the shareholders. Corporate officers and directors, however, do not hold title to the property of the corporation and therefore are not trustees; accordingly their fiduciary duties are not within the scope of this Restatement.

Even the members of the managing board of a charitable corporation, whether called directors or trustees, are not "trustees" in the strict sense because they do not hold title to the property of the corporation. On charitable *trusts*, however, see §§ 28 (charitable trust purposes) and 67 (*cy pres*).

Similarly, partners as mutual agents (cf. Comment *e*), and particularly general partners of limited partnerships and member-managers of limited-liability companies, perform roles and have fiduciary responsibilities to other partners or members in many respects similar to those of trustees. Yet they differ in many respects from trustees and are subject to responsibilities and rules that differ significantly from those of trustees based on separate bodies of legislation and case law. . . . . Thus, although an occasional statute and numerous cases refer to these others generically as "trustees," their fiduciary duties and other governing rules are not the subject of this Restatement.

h. *Trusts compared to conditions and equitable charges.* An owner of property may transfer it, inter vivos or by will, to another person and provide that, if the latter should commit or fail to perform a specified act, the transferred interest shall be forfeited. The condition may be for the benefit of one or more third persons or, if the transfer is inter vivos, for the benefit of the transferor. On breach of the condition, the transferor, the successors in interest of the transferor, or some designated person will be entitled to recover the property from the transferee.

In situations of these types, the interests of the transferees are subject to a condition subsequent and are not held in trust. The condition does not create a fiduciary relationship. Unlike a trust beneficiary's right to compel performance of a trustee's duties, neither the transferor nor a person to be benefited may compel or prevent performance of the act upon which a condition depends, nor can they have the transferee removed and replaced by another. (Cf. § 37 on removal and replacement of trustees.)

Whether a property transfer accompanied by a requirement for the performance of a particular act gives rise to a trust or a condition depends on the manifested intention of the transferor. The mere fact that the word "condition" is used is not necessarily determinative.

When the transfer is "on condition" that the transferred property be dealt with in a manner beneficial to the transferor or a third person, a trust is created if the transferor manifested an intention (a) that the transferee should be subject to a duty to use the specific property for the transferor's or a third person's benefit, rather than (b) that the transferee's interest should be divested upon failure to perform the act specified. In the absence of other evidence, a transfer "on condition" that the property be dealt with in a manner beneficial to a *third person*, without language directing forfeiture, indicates an intention to create a trust rather than an intention to make a transfer upon condition. The opposite inference is generally drawn, however, when an inter vivos transfer is made "on condition" that the property be dealt with in a manner beneficial to the *transferor*. In such a case, there is no reluctance to infer that a condition was intended.

Even if a transfer is made "on condition," if the settlor manifests no intention to create either a condition or a trust, it is also possible that the settlor's intention is to create an equitable charge.

Thus, an owner may transfer property inter vivos or by will to another person for the latter's own benefit but subject to the payment of a sum of money (or subject to some other action beneficial) to one or more third persons. In such a case, the third person has an equitable charge or lien upon the property. The relationship between the parties here is different from that created by a transferor's direction that the particular property being transferred is to be used in part for the benefit of one or more third persons, in which case a trust is created. For example, the holder of property subject to an equitable charge may properly transfer the property to a donee or purchaser, provided the purchaser is notified of or otherwise takes subject to the charge. On the other hand, it is a breach of trust for a trustee to transfer trust property to another unless the transfer is authorized by the terms of the trust, by court order, or under some circumstances by the beneficiaries.

Both trusts and equitable charges involve transferees who hold title to property subject to equitable interests in others. In addition, equitable interests as well as legal interests may be subject to equitable charges, just as equitable interests as well as legal interests may be held in trust.

The equitable charge, however, creates a security interest, rather than a beneficial interest, in the transferred property; and there is no fiduciary relationship. Enforcement of the benefit intended for the third person is thus predicated on a lien against the property rather than on a duty imposed on the transferee.

A transfer subject to an equitable charge is beneficial to the transferee as well as to the person to be benefited by the charge. Although this may also be true in the case of a trust, the intention to confer a beneficial interest as well as title upon a trustee is not readily inferred, the usual inference being that a resulting trust arises with respect to the remaining beneficial interest. See § 8, Comment *f*.

In short, the question in these cases is whether by accepting the property the transferee assumes an obligation to the third person, who holds a security interest in the property, or whether the latter simply has a beneficial interest in the property.

Ordinarily a transfer of property to another "subject to" the making of a payment or payments to a third person creates an equitable charge and not a trust, because the transferor does not thereby manifest an intention to impose a duty on the transferee to deal with the property itself for the benefit of the third person. If, however, property is transferred to another "with" or "subject to" a direction that the payment or payments are to be made to a third person out of the transferred property or its product or proceeds, a trust and not an equitable charge is created. This is because the transferor manifests an intention to impose a duty on the transferee to deal with the property, in part at least, for the benefit of the third person.

Thus, if A devises Blackacre to B "subject to the payment of" A's debts and legacies, an equitable charge is created in the absence of evidence of a different intention; whereas, A's devise of Blackacre to B with a direction to sell the property and to pay debts and legacies from its proceeds, in the absence of evidence of a different intention, creates a trust. In the latter case, the transferor has manifested an intention to impose duties on the transferee with respect to the property. In the former, there is no manifestation of such an intention but merely an intention to create a security interest in the property, giving rise to an equitable charge.

When one person transfers property to another as consideration for the other's promise to make certain payments to the transferor or to a third person, and the transferor manifests neither an intention to impose a duty on the transferee to deal with the property for another nor an intention to create a condition or a security interest, but merely manifests an intention to impose a personal liability upon the transferee, no trust or condition or equitable charge is created. Thus, if a person transfers securities to another in consideration of an agreement by the other to make certain payments to a third person, the third person does not acquire any interest in the securities but, as beneficiary of a contract, has rights against the transferee. See Comment *i*.

Both the equitable encumbrancer and the transferee who takes subject to an equitable charge have property rights. Thus, the interest of either may be held in trust. Similarly, an interest subject to a condition precedent or subsequent, like other property interests, may be held by the transferee in trust. (See § 40.) Or a transfer may create a trust that is to arise or terminate upon some condition. In addition, by the terms of a trust, the equitable interest of a trust beneficiary may be subjected to a condition. (On unlawful or other impermissible trust conditions, see § 29.)

i. Trusts and contracts to convey or certain contracts for the benefit of third parties. If a contract to convey property is not specifically enforceable, the purchaser acquires no interest in the property before the conveyance is made but has merely a personal claim against the vendor. Even if the contract is specifically enforceable and the purchaser therefore acquires an interest in the property, the relation between the vendor and the purchaser is not a trust; nor is it a fiduciary relationship.

Thus, even though a purchaser has paid the purchase price, the vendor who has not yet conveyed is not a trustee of the property for the purchaser. And prior to payment of the purchase price, the purchaser is not trustee of the purchase money for the vendor. The latter is the case not only because there is no fiduciary relationship but also because there is no specific money in which the vendor has an interest.

A promisee under a contract to convey property may, however, hold the rights as promisee in trust for a third person if an intention to that effect is manifested. See § 40, Comment *b*; cf. § 10, Clause (e) and Comment *g*, and § 15, Comment *b*.

If property is transferred by one person to another and the transferee agrees to sell that property and to pay its proceeds or a certain amount of the proceeds to a third person, ordinarily a trust of the property is created. If, however, property is transferred by one person to another who agrees in consideration thereof to assume a personal liability to a third person, a contract for the benefit of the third person and not a trust is created. Again, the beneficiary of the contract has only a personal claim against the promisor, unless the contract is specifically enforceable. Even in the latter case, the equitable interest is not that of a trust beneficiary. Also, by contrast with the trust situation, there is no fiduciary relation between a promisor or promisee and the beneficiary of the contract. Although the promisee as well as the beneficiary may, in many instances, sue upon a contract for the benefit of a third party (see Restatement Second, Contracts §§ 302 and 304), a trust ordinarily cannot be enforced by a settlor who is not also a beneficiary (see § 94).

To be distinguished from a contract for the benefit of a third party is (i) the situation in which a contract right is held by the promisee in trust for one or more third parties and (ii) the situation in which the beneficiary of a contract for the benefit of a third party may hold the rights under the contract in trust for one or more others. See § 40.

When a person pays money to another with instructions that the latter is to pay a debt or the debts of the former to one or more third persons, it depends on the manifestation of intention of the parties whether a trust or an agency or a different type of contract is created. If the person receiving the money is entitled to use it as his or her own, the transaction merely creates a contract for the benefit of the payor's creditor, a contract that may or may not be subject to revocation or modification by the payor. See generally Restatement Second, Contracts § 311. If the person receiving the money is not entitled to use it for his or her own purposes, a trust or agency is created. Depending on the circumstances and manifestations of intention, the person receiving the money may be an agent of the payor or of the creditor; or the person receiving the money may be a trustee for the payor or the creditor or both. If the latter, the trust may or may not be revocable by the payor (§ 63, Comments *b* and *c*).

j. Trusts and assignments or partial assignments of choses in action. The obligee of a *chose* in action may effectively declare himself or herself trustee of the rights as obligee, and thereby hold those rights for the benefit of one or more third persons. Or the obligee may assign the chose in action to another to hold in trust for the benefit of one or more third persons, with the assignee thereby becoming a trustee for those beneficiaries. (See § 40.) On the other hand, if the obligee of a chose in action assigns his or her rights as obligee to and for the benefit of a third person, no trust is created, and there is no fiduciary relationship between the assignor and the assignee.

One who is the trustee of a chose in action owes duties to the trust beneficiaries to enforce the *chose* and then pay the proceeds to, or hold and manage the proceeds for, the beneficiaries.

By contrast, the assignor of a chose in action has no active duties to the assignee, the assignor's only duties being negative, namely, not to enforce the claim, not to make an assignment of it to a third person, and not otherwise to interfere with the assignee's right to enforce the chose in action. An assignor who does nevertheless enforce the assigned claim holds the proceeds upon constructive trust for the assignee (whether beneficially or as trustee for others).

The assignee of a chose in action can maintain an action at law against the obligor directly without joining the obligee, although the procedural details will depend on the laws of the state involved. When a trustee improperly refuses or neglects to enforce a chose in action held in trust, a beneficiary can sue in equity to compel the trustee to bring an action against the obligor or, in order to prevent multiplicity of suits, may join the obligor as a codefendant in the suit against the trustee; if it is impossible or impracticable to make the trustee a party to the suit, the beneficiary can maintain the suit on behalf of the trust against the obligor alone. See Chapter 22.

The obligor of a chose in action held in trust by the obligee discharges the liability by paying the trustee and in doing so is not liable to the beneficiary. An exception exists if the obligor has notice that the trustee is committing or intends to commit a breach of trust and nevertheless pays the trustee, thereby participating in the breach. (See Chapter 22.) On the other hand, the obligor of a chose in action that has been assigned by the obligee discharges the liability by paying the assignee. Payment to the assignor, however, will not discharge that liability to the assignee unless the payment is made without notice of the assignment.

Similar principles apply when a partial assignment is made of the chose in action. There is no fiduciary relationship between the assignor and the assignee, with the former's only duties to the latter being negative. The duty of the obligor is to pay an appropriate share of the obligation to the partial assignee and to pay the balance to the assignor; the obligor remains liable to the partial assignee after paying the whole amount to the assignor if payment is made with notice of the partial assignment.

Again, of course, it is possible for the obligee: (i) to assign a chose in action to another in trust, partially for the benefit of the assignor (or assignee) and partially for the benefit of one or more third parties; (ii) to make a partial assignment to another as trustee for one or more third parties; or (iii) to make a total or partial declaration of trust by which the obligee holds all or an undivided interest in the chose in action as trustee for the benefit of one or more others.

k. *Trusts and debt relationships, secured and unsecured.* When a trust is created there is a fiduciary relationship between the trustee and the beneficiaries, and the beneficiaries of a trust have equitable interests in the trust property. A debtor does not as such stand in a fiduciary relationship to his or her creditors. A creditor as such has against the debtor merely a personal claim, which can be enforced by judicial proceedings to reach the debtor's property.

The debtor is not a trustee, although in some circumstances (such as when insolvent) a debtor may not be entitled to dispose of his or her own property as he or she likes, such as by making gifts or preferential payments.

If the subject matter of a trust is lost or destroyed without fault of the trustee, the trustee is not liable to the beneficiaries. If loan funds are lost by the borrower, the debt is not discharged and the liability to the lender continues.

If a trustee becomes insolvent or bankrupt, the trustee's personal creditors (ordinarily at least) may not reach the trust property (§ 42); the beneficiaries retain their equitable interests in that property if it can be identified, or in its product if the property can be traced into a product. (The trust beneficiaries are therefore entitled to that trust property as against the general creditors of the trustee.) When a loan has been made and the borrower becomes insolvent or bankrupt, the lender is not entitled to priority over other creditors of the borrower with respect to the borrowed funds (or their traceable product) in the hands of the borrower.

When one person transfers funds to another, it depends on the manifested intention of the parties whether the relationship created is that of trust or debt. If the intention is that the money shall be kept or used as a separate fund for the benefit of the payor or one or more third persons, a trust is created. If it is intended, however, that the person receiving the money shall have the unrestricted use of it, being liable to pay a similar amount to the payor or a third person, whether with or without interest, a debt is created.

The intention of the parties is ascertained by considering their words and conduct in light of all the terms and circumstances of the transaction. Among the factors that may be of importance in determining the intention of the parties are: (1) the amount of money involved and the relative financial situations of the parties; (2) the presence or absence of an agreement to pay interest on the money; (3) the time that is to elapse before the payee is to perform the agreement and its various components; (4) relationships between the parties, the nature and handling of prior transactions between them, and their respective business roles and activities; and (5) business customs and usage in such transactions or similar ones.

If there is an understanding between the parties that the person to whom funds are transferred is to pay "interest" thereon (at a fixed or current rate, and not merely such interest or other earnings as the funds, being invested, may earn), it becomes close to certain that the relationship is a debt rather than a trust. Interest is normally paid for the "use of funds." Accordingly, recipients of funds who pay interest are, in the absence of a definite understanding to the contrary, borrowers who are entitled to use the funds for their own purposes.

A person who, as agent, receives funds for a principal is an agent-trustee (subject to the rules of agency law but not to all rules of trust law) if title to the money is received (see Comment *e*); but the person is an agent-bailee if mere possession but no title is received (see Comment *f*). In either case, unless the principal manifested an intention that the agent should be entitled to use the money as its owner, the agent is not a debtor to the principal. This is true, for example, of so-called collection agents, real-estate brokers, and auctioneers. It is also true of attorneys who receive funds for or from their clients to be applied for the clients' purposes. . . . .

Although the same inference of agent-trustee status is appropriate to stockbrokers who receive money from their customers or from the sale of their customers' securities, there is a greater likelihood in these than in other situations of finding implied agreements that the brokers may use these funds as their own. This is because of behavior patterns and understandings that have become fairly common in broker-customer relations. An agreement that would make the broker simply a "debtor" normally is implicit when the customer has a running account with the broker. A like understanding may appear in other ways from the course of the dealings between the parties, particularly where the broker is to pay the customer interest on the funds. On the other hand, when a broker purchases securities for a customer, the customer has the beneficial interest in the securities in the broker's hands. This is so regardless of whether the broker has mere possession (holding the securities as bailee) or also has legal title (thus holding title also as trustee), and even though the customer is indebted to the broker for some or all of the purchase price. In the latter case, the broker also holds the stocks or bonds as security.

Often agreements are made between an employer and its employees under which the employer is to deduct certain amounts from the wages of the employees and is either to hold those amounts as trustee or to transfer the amounts to another as trustee of a fund (such as a retirement fund) for the benefit of the employees. In such a case, a trust arises as to the amounts deducted as soon as they are either set aside by the employer for the employees' purposes or paid over to another person for those purposes. Until then, the employer's obligation is merely a debt, with the "obligee" (the employer or other person) holding a chose in action (the claim against the employer) in trust. The claim that is held in the trust estate is like the claims of the other general creditors of the employer except to the extent of any preference that may be conferred by statute or other rules of law or equity, preferences that are not peculiar to the trust law.

Sometimes the beneficiary of a life-insurance policy is entitled, under the selected settlement option, to receive deferred payments from the insurance company. The insurance company is not a trustee in such a case unless by the terms of the policy it has a duty to segregate, hold, and administer the policy proceeds as a separate fund, and in fact does so. Where, as is almost always the case, the payments are to be made out of the general assets of the insurance company, it is a debtor and holds nothing in trust. . . . . Even though the insurance company is not a trustee, however, courts in some jurisdictions may choose to apply to this type of contract some of the rules normally applicable to trusts rather than those normally applicable to ordinary debts.

On insurance trusts—that is, trusts in which the payee of life-insurance proceeds is to hold those proceeds in trust for others—see § 25, Comment *c*.

A general deposit of money in a commercial bank creates not a trust but a relation of debtor and creditor, with the depositor having certain contract rights against the bank in addition to ordinary rights as a creditor. This is true although the depositor is already a trustee of the funds for the benefit of others. Thus, if a trustee properly makes a general deposit of trust money in a commercial bank, the bank is a debtor to the trustee, whose claim against the bank is a part of the trust estate held for the beneficiaries.

Even if money is deposited in a bank for a special purpose, the bank is not a trustee of the money unless it is the clear understanding of the parties that the bank is not free to use funds so deposited for its own purposes. When money is deposited in a bank to be paid to a third person, it depends on the manifestation of intention of the depositor whether the bank's obligation to pay the money can be enforced by the third person or only by the depositor. A deposit may be made in escrow. That is, the money on deposit is to be paid to a third person on the happening of a designated event, and in the meantime the depositor has no right to withdraw the money. In such a situation, it depends on the manifestation of the intention of the parties whether the bank may use the deposited money as its own or whether the money is to be held in trust. Ordinarily, the strong inference accompanying escrow deposits is that the bank may use the money, with the bank undertaking (as a debtor) to pay the amount of the deposit on the happening of the designated event.

Where a person deposits money with another as security for the faithful performance of obligations owed to the other, it depends on the manifestation of intention of the parties whether the person holding the money is a debtor or is a trustee with a security interest in the money. If it is understood that the money is to be kept for the depositor and returned when the depositor has performed the obligations, the money is held in trust. If the understanding is that the money may be used as the holder's own, with the amount of it to be paid to the depositor when the latter's obligations have been performed, the relationship is one of debt. This question most commonly arises when tenants deposit funds with their landlords as security for the performance of their obligations as lessees. The landlord's duties are beyond the scope of this Restatement and may be affected by statute or municipal ordinance; the nature of those duties may in turn affect the classification of the relationship.

A mortgage is not a trust even though both the debtor (the mortgagor) and the creditor (the mortgagee) have interests in the same property. Even a mortgagee who takes possession of the mortgaged premises and is accountable to the mortgagor for receipts during this possession is not a trustee, although under a fiduciary duty to pay due regard to the rights of the mortgagor. A mortgage is created for the purpose of giving the creditor a security interest in the mortgaged property.

Similarly, other security interests such as pledges and liens, legal or equitable, are not trusts as that term is used in this Restatement. Nor is the trust law in this Restatement generally applicable to the trustee under a deed of trust that is in the nature of a mortgage. Although it holds title under this security arrangement and stands in a fiduciary relation to both debtor and creditor, this type of trustee is not subject to all of the fiduciary duties and rules stated in this Restatement.

In some states, if title to land is transferred to a purchaser before the purchase price has been fully paid, the transferor has an equitable lien upon the land as security for the claim against the purchaser for the unpaid purchase price. In this situation also, a trust is not created and the purchaser is not a trustee for the vendor.

In short, even when trust concepts are used and some rules applicable to trust relationships are applied, security relationships are not "trusts" as that term is used in this Restatement, regardless of the title theories applied and the varied terminology used in different jurisdictions. See generally Restatement Third, Property (Mortgages) § 1.1 and § 4.3, Comment *a*.

As with the rights of property holders under other relationships discussed in the Comments to this section, creditors may hold their rights as creditors in trust for others, or they may transfer those rights to another as trustee for the benefit of others. (On a *chose* in action as trust property, see § 40, Comment *b*.) It is a breach of trust, however, for a trustee to transfer the trust property to a third person unless authorized to do so by the terms of the trust, by court order, or, under some circumstances, by the beneficiaries.

Furthermore, by agreement between a debtor and creditor, a novation may be effected by which the debt is discharged and a trust is created. Conversely, by the terms of a trust, or by agreement between a trustee and beneficiaries who have the right to terminate a trust, a novation may be effected whereby the trust is extinguished and the trustee becomes a debtor to the beneficiary or beneficiaries.

l. Trusts and other devices using a "trust" label. Some other relationships or arrangements are often referred to in terminology that includes the word "trust," and to some extent employ the trust concept, but are not trusts in the sense in which that term is used in this Restatement.

Examples are so-called voting trusts, business trusts, land trusts, and investment trusts. These relationships are generally and more properly governed or regulated by other bodies of law, such as state or federal laws concerning business associations or investment companies, or concerning the issuance and sale of securities. The rules of these relationships, however, may borrow from the law of trusts and thus resort to some of the rules set out in this Restatement. On the other hand, some rules of this Restatement apply to the use by trustees of some of these devices insofar as they offer pooled investment opportunities for the funds of express private and charitable trusts. See § 90 (Restatement Third, Trusts (Prudent Investor Rule) § 227), Comment *m*.

Usually there is no practical difficulty in distinguishing trusts as that term is used in this Restatement and these various other arrangements that bear the "trust" label.

CHAPTER 2

RESULTING TRUSTS

§ 7. Nature and Definition of Resulting Trusts

A resulting trust is a reversionary, equitable interest implied by law in property that is held by a transferee, in whole or in part, as trustee for the transferor or the transferor's successors in interest.

Comment:

a. *In general.* Unless qualified by the term "resulting," references to "trusts" in this Restatement do not refer to resulting trusts; and rules applicable to trusts generally do not apply to resulting trusts except as a consequence of applying these rules to express trusts in which resulting trust (i.e., reversionary) interests are impliedly retained by settlors or their successors in interest.

A resulting trust arises when a person (the "transferor") makes or causes to be made a disposition of property under circumstances (i) in which some or all of the transferor's beneficial interest is not effectively transferred to others (and yet not *expressly* retained by the transferor) and (ii) which raise an unrebutted presumption that the transferor does not intend the one who receives the property (the "transferee") to have the remaining beneficial interest.

Because the transferee under such a disposition is not entitled to the beneficial interest in question and because that beneficial interest is not otherwise disposed of, it remains in and thus is said "to result" (that is, it reverts) to the transferor or to the transferor's estate or other successor(s) in interest. The transferee is said to hold the property, in whole or in part, upon a resulting trust for the transferor (the "beneficiary" of the resulting trust) or for the transferor's successors in interest (the "beneficiaries"). Therefore, the beneficial interest that is held on resulting trust is simply an equitable reversionary interest implied by law, with the "resulting trust" terminology ordinarily being applied if and when the reversionary interest materializes as a present interest.

Thus, unlike the express trust, which arises from a transferor's manifestation of intention to create it, a resulting trust arises from an intention that is legally attributed to a transferor based on the nature of the transaction, rather than from manifested intent.

Resulting trusts arise in two fundamentally different types of situations (see Comments *b* and *c*), one of which is and one of which is not associated with express trusts. Compare § 8 with § 9. In each of these situations, however, (i) it appears that the person receiving legal title to the property was not, in the circumstances that have occurred, intended to have the beneficial interest, and (ii) no effective disposition was otherwise made of the beneficial interest in question.

Because resulting trusts and resulting-trust interests are reversionary in nature, they are property rights of a default, or last-resort, character. Thus, in express-trust situations, they arise only when anti-lapse statutes, interpretation, construction, reformation, and other comparable statutes or processes fail to fill voids on the equitable side of the trust disposition. See § 8, Comments *b* and *g*. (See also Comment *e* of this section on the duty not to interfere with purposes of the express trust.) Similarly, in the purchase-money situations that are mentioned in Comment *c* and examined more fully in § 9, the resulting trust for the payor of the purchase price is recognized only after any relevant circumstances, written and oral statements, associated agreements or understandings, and other admissible parol evidence have been considered in an effort to ascertain and give effect to any discernible, actual *intentions* of the payor or *objectives* of the parties.

The transferor, successor in interest, or other person seeking to establish the existence of a resulting trust does not do so by showing that the transferor manifested an intention to create it. The case is made by showing circumstances which raise a presumption that the person making the transfer or causing it to be made did not intend to give the transferee the beneficial interest in question, and thus that the interest remained in the transferor or payor or his or her estate. Accordingly, the resulting trust is imposed for the purpose of carrying out a legally implied intention. Thus, in the usual express-trust context, the resulting trust gives effect to what appears from the circumstances probably would have been intended if the person making the disposition had foreseen the situation that has occurred but with no opportunity to "rewrite," or add to, the equitable interests.

The presumption of resulting trust makes it unnecessary to prove by affirmative evidence an intention to create a trust, or to reserve a trust interest, in favor of the transferor. In fact, if it is shown that the transferor manifested in proper form an intention that the property or the interest in question is to be held in trust wholly or partially for the transferor's own benefit, the provision creates an express trust or an express-trust interest. Accordingly, in this latter situation, there is no resulting trust.

b. *Resulting trusts in express-trust context.* In property law generally, a reversion arises whenever a property owner makes an effective transfer of less than the owner's entire interest in the property.

For example, assume that O, the fee-simple owner of Blackacre, transfers it to L for life, remainder to R if living at L's death and otherwise to R's issue who are then living. By normal interpretation, this disposition creates a life interest in L and alternative contingent remainders in R and R's issue, but it also leaves a reversionary interest in O. O's interest may or may not materialize in the sense of becoming a present interest. That is, it may be very likely that either R or R's issue will receive full ownership of Blackacre when L's life estate terminates at her death. But if R should predecease L and leave no issue who survive L, Blackacre reverts to O, if then living, and otherwise to O's successors in interest. O's reversionary interest has now materialized as a present interest, here one in fee simple.

Usually, resulting-trust situations are simply equitable counterparts of the above situation. Resulting trusts usually, though not always (see, e.g., Comment *c*), arise in express-trust situations in which an owner of property transfers its full *legal* title to a trustee but fails to make full, effective disposition of the beneficial—that is, *equitable*—interests in the property.

Illustration:

1. S deeds Blackacre to T in trust to hold and administer, or in T's discretion to sell and invest the proceeds, for the benefit of L for life and upon L's death to distribute the trust estate to R, if living at L's death, and if not then to R's issue who are then living. If events develop as apparently anticipated by S, the trust will terminate on L's death with full disposition of the trust estate either to R or to issue of R. If, however, none of the designated remainder beneficiaries survives L, S's equitable reversion will have materialized so that T will then hold upon a resulting trust for S. Or, if S has assigned the reversion or died, T will hold for S's assignees or for the testamentary or intestate successors to S's interest.

If the trust in Illustration 1 had been established by the residuary clause of S's will, S would have died partially intestate. This is because the will failed to provide for all possible eventualities. Thus, S's heirs at law immediately took an equitable reversionary interest, one that under the terms of this disposition might or might not eventually materialize in present enjoyment. If and when the reversionary interest does materialize, it will cause the trust estate to be held by T on resulting trust for these heirs or their successors in interest, who together then comprise the successors in interest of S.

Just as reversions in grantors may arise in many different contexts involving successive legal interests in real or personal property, so too may resulting trusts arise from many varied situations involving the creation or attempted creation of express trusts. These usually are (i) situations in which (as in Illustration 1) the terms of a private or charitable trust fail to provide beneficial interests for certain situations apparently overlooked by the settlor. Others are (ii) situations in which some of the interests provided by the terms of the trust fail because of invalidity or disclaimer, leaving gaps that are not filled by interpretation or rules of construction, and (iii) situations in which a private or charitable trust is fully performed without exhausting the trust estate. (Whether a trust is fully performed occasionally depends on difficult questions of interpretation concerning a trust's terms or purposes.) Still others are (iv) situations involving an invalid purpose or a failure to designate the beneficiary in language that satisfies applicable requirements with regard to both formality and definiteness. On these various situations, see § 8, Comments *b–e*.

c. *Purchase-money resulting trusts.* Sometimes a transfer of property is made to one person and the purchase price is paid by another, and no express trust is declared and no other agreement is made to allocate the beneficial rights in the property. Often the presumption in these cases is that the transferee is intended to take no beneficial interest and therefore holds the property on resulting trust for the person who paid the purchase price. See § 9. If, however, the transferee in a case of this type is the spouse, child, or other natural object of the bounty of the payor, the presumption is not of resulting trust but of gift, with the transferee presumptively taking the beneficial interest. See § 9, Subsection (2) and Comment *b*. In either of these situations, the presumption, whether of resulting trust or gift, may be rebutted in whole or in part by evidence of a different intention. See § 9, Comment *e*.

Like other resulting-trust situations, the so-called purchase-money resulting trust is a form of equitable reversionary interest. When a person purchases property and instructs the seller to transfer that property to another, and the payor does not manifest nor the law imply the beneficial interest on the transferee, the law then presumes that the beneficial interest remains in the payor as, in effect, the "transferor." Again, this is not based on a manifestation of the transferor's intention but on a legally attributed intention that is not overcome by evidence of a different intention.

A fundamentally different situation is presented, however, when an owner of property transfers it directly to another without declaring a trust and without other manifestation of intention concerning beneficial enjoyment. In these facts, there is no presumption that the transferee holds the property on resulting trust even though the transfer is gratuitous. Instead, the presumption is that the transferor in such a case intends to make a gift to the transferee. See § 9, Comment *a*. The early common law had inferred that the feoffee in such a situation took title subject to a use in reversion in favor of the feoffor, but that rule has not been applied in modern trust or property law.

d. Resulting trust distinguished from constructive trust. A constructive trust is imposed not because of the legally inferred intention of the parties but because the court concludes that the person holding the title to the property, if permitted to keep it, would profit by a wrong or would be unjustly enriched. Thus, unlike either a resulting trust or an express trust, a constructive trust is remedial in character. See generally Restatement of Restitution § 160 [Restatement Third, Restitution and Unjust Enrichment § 55].

e. Duties of trustee of resulting trust. Ordinarily the trustee of a resulting trust, like the trustee of a passive express trust (see § 6, Comment *e*), is under a duty merely to transfer the trust property or the reversionary portion thereof to the reversionary beneficiary or in accordance with that beneficiary's directions. Until the property is so transferred, the title holder remains trustee with a duty to preserve the affected property and its product and to perform any other duties appropriate to the resulting-trust relationship.

Thus, if (within the basic rule of Subsection (1) of § 9) a transfer of property is made to one person and the purchase price is paid by another, it is the duty of the transferee to convey the property upon demand to the payor or the payor's successors in interest, in the absence of other direction by the payor or successor. Similarly, where an express trust fails in whole or in part or is fully performed without exhausting the trust estate, it is ordinarily the duty of the trustee to convey the trust estate or affected part thereof to the person who created or attempted to create the trust or to that person's successors in interest.

Sometimes, however, the express trust in which a resulting-trust interest arises does not terminate, because one or more of the beneficiaries of the express trust have continuing interests thereunder. In this type of case, the trustee does not have an immediate duty to make distribution of the property that is subject to the resulting trust. Assume, for example, that a trust is created for one beneficiary for life and for others in remainder, and that the life beneficiary disclaims but the interests of the remainder beneficiaries do not accelerate for some reason . . . . In this situation, there is a resulting trust of the benefits that flow from the disclaimed interest during the life of the disclaimant. Here the trustee's duty is to pay the income, but not the principal, to the settlor or to the settlor's successors in interest.

In any event, in situations of this latter type the resulting trust is not to interfere with the performance of the express trust or with any remaining active duties of the trustee with respect to that trust. The resulting-trust interest in such a case is simply a reversionary interest, implied by law, in the ongoing express trust; it is merely a part of the overall beneficial-interest structure of that trust. Therefore, the trustee's duties with respect to the resulting trust may be to administer the trust property in a manner consistent with any remaining beneficial interests and purposes of the express trust and, to the extent consistent with those interests and purposes, to make distributions from income or principal to the settlor or other reversionary beneficiaries.

f. *Transfers by beneficiary or trustee.* The beneficiary of a resulting trust or potential resulting trust has power to transfer the reversionary interest either during life (§ 51) or by will (§ 55), either outright or in further trust. This applies to the equitable reversion in an express trust at any time after that trust has been created. The reversionary interest is transferable even if the terms of the trust restrain alienation of the expressed beneficiaries' interests. This is because these "spendthrift" restraints, even if otherwise valid, are not effective with respect to the interests of settlors or their successors in interest (see § 58(2)).

Similarly, on the death intestate of the beneficiary of a resulting trust, the devolution of the reversionary equitable interest is governed by the same rules of descent and distribution as govern the devolution of corresponding legal interests. See § 55, Comment *c*.

In addition, the creditors of the beneficiary of a resulting trust can, by appropriate proceedings, reach the beneficiary's reversionary interest and thereby subject it to the satisfaction of their claims. See § 56 and (on spendthrift trusts) § 58(2).

If the trustee of a resulting trust transfers the trust property in breach of trust, the rights and liabilities of the transferee are subject to the same rules that apply to transferees of property subject to an express trust. See Chapter 22.

g. *Resulting trusts and statutes of frauds.* Although a statute provides that all declarations or creations of trusts of land shall be manifested and proved by some writing signed by the party who is by law enabled to create such a trust, no writing is required for the creation of a resulting trust. These statutory provisions (and their occasional counterparts applicable to personal property) apply to express trusts but not to either resulting or constructive trusts. These exceptions were expressly stated in § 8 of the original English Statute of Frauds, 29 Car. II, ch. 3 (1677).

Statutes of this type, however, together with rules about their operation and exceptions, generally apply to attempts by a settlor or successors in interest, without a writing, to convey the resulting-trust interest to another or to surrender it to the trustee.

In the case of a purchase-money resulting trust, however, the resulting trust that arises in favor of the person by whom the purchase price was paid can be extinguished by the payor's or successor's oral surrender of the equitable interest to the trustee of the resulting trust (usually the original transferee). Just as the inference of resulting trust in such a case can be rebutted without a writing, so can it be extinguished without a writing; in either case the required writing, the deed to the transferee, exists and is consistent with the desired result.

Such a transaction is different from the attempt by a beneficiary of a purchase-money resulting trust to transfer the equitable ownership to a third person by oral conveyance. In this case, the statute requiring a writing, and the rules concerning its operation and effect, apply if the subject matter is property of a type encompassed by the statute's provisions.

h. Other matters. The rights of beneficiaries of resulting trusts to enforce their rights against the trustee or third persons are subject to the same rules regarding the doctrine of laches and statutes of limitations as apply in the case of express trusts. See § 98, and also compare §§ 96 and 97.

The so-called doctrine of merger, which applies to express trusts (see § 69), also applies to resulting trusts. . . . .

§ 8. When Express Trust Fails in Whole or in Part

Where the owner of property makes a donative transfer and manifests an intention that the transferee is to hold the property in trust but the intended trust fails in whole or in part, or the trust is or will be fully performed without exhausting or fully utilizing the trust estate, the transferee holds the trust estate or the appropriate portion or interest therein on resulting trust for the transferor or the transferor's successors in interest, unless

(a) the transferor manifested an intention that a resulting trust should not arise, or

(b) the trust fails for illegality and the policy against permitting unjust enrichment of a transferee is outweighed by the policy against giving relief to one who has entered into an illegal transaction.

Comment:

a. In general. Except as otherwise provided in this section, where the owner of property makes a donative transfer of it inter vivos upon an express trust that fails at the outset, the trustee holds the property on resulting trust for the transferor. See Comment *c*.

Except as otherwise provided in this section, if property is devised upon a trust that fails at the outset, in whole or in part, the property or an appropriate share or interest therein is held by the devisee on resulting trust for the testator's successors in interest, except as, in circumstances defined by applicable law, a doctrine concerning passive trusts (§ 6) or a court order causes the property to pass directly to the successors in interest without vesting title in the devisee. See Comment *c*. (Consistent with modern usage, the terms "devised," "devise," and "devisee" are generally used in this Restatement to include "bequeathed," "bequest," and "legatee.")

Except as otherwise provided in this section, if the intended trust fails in whole or in part at a later time, or has been or is being fully performed without exhausting or fully utilizing the trust estate, the transferee then holds the trust property, or an appropriate part thereof or interest therein, upon a resulting trust for the transferor or for the successors in interest of the transferor. See Comment *d*.

If, however, a deed or will is ineffective to transfer title to the property to the intended trustee or a substitute trustee, no resulting trust arises by reason of the failure of the intended inter vivos or testamentary trust. The title to the property remains (with no need of the resulting-trust device) either in the would-be transferor or in the personal representative or beneficiaries of the testator's estate.

a(1). Successors in interest defined. If a testamentary disposition is not a residuary disposition, the decedent's successors in interest are normally determined by the residuary provisions of the will. Otherwise—that is, if the will contains no applicable residuary clause or if the trust disposition is itself residuary and there is no alternative disposition—the successors in interest are the testator's intestate successors, specifically the decedent's heirs at law.

If a testamentary trust comes into operation but thereafter is fully performed, or subsequently fails in whole or in part, the trustee then holds the appropriate property or interests on resulting trust for the testator's successors in interest. The initial step in determining these successors is as stated in the preceding paragraph. This is because the testator died leaving this reversionary interest to (that is, the possibility of a resulting trust later arising for) those original residuary or intestate successors from the very outset. Then, when the resulting trust eventually occurs, the interests of those various successors will have to be traced, if and as necessary, through possible subsequent assignments, insolvency proceedings, and decedents' estates, and ultimately then into the hands of the initial successors' respective successors in interest, who at the time of the resulting trust will also be successors in interest to the testator. In any of the foregoing situations, the successor in interest (or one of the successors) may be the State, for want of other successors.

Similarly, if an inter vivos express trust comes into existence but later is fully performed or wholly or partially fails, the reversionary interest based on this possibility remained in the settlor from the outset. If the settlor is dead when the resulting trust arises, and if the reversion has by then been voluntarily or involuntarily alienated, the successors in interest are determined by tracing the retained interest through the settlor's estate, or assignments or insolvency proceedings, and onward into the hands of the current interest holders, essentially as described in the preceding paragraph. The beneficiaries of the resulting trust are those so determined.

On situations in which statutory or other rules of construction provide implied *express-trust* interests in persons not named or described in the trust instrument (e.g., a typical anti-lapse statute), even interests in persons who at a later time "would be the heirs" of the settlor if he or she were to have died at a date later than his or her actual death (see UPC § 2–707(d)(2), with § 2–711), so that no reversionary interest results, see Comment *b* and Illustration[ ] 11 . . . of Comment *d*.

On circumstances manifesting an intention that no resulting trust should arise on the failure of an express trust, see Comment *f*.

On situations in which transferees or third persons have given consideration for the original transfer in trust, see Comment *f*.

On the handling of situations in which an express trust fails for illegality, see Comment *i*.

b. Situations to which the rule of this section applies: in general. The rule stated in this section is applicable to a broad variety of situations in which, at the outset or as events develop, the settlor of an express trust has not made full and complete disposition of all of the present and future beneficial rights in the property transferred to the trustee. Under the rule of this section, a resulting trust may arise when, at the outset or at a later time, an intended express trust has been or will be fully performed without exhausting or fully utilizing the trust property, or when for any of a variety of reasons an intended express trust fails in whole or in part.

Although a transfer has been properly made to establish an express trust, the intended trust or some interest therein may fail because no beneficiary has been named for the trust or interest; or the trust or interest may fail because (i) the designated beneficiary or beneficiaries are nonexistent, (ii) one or more of the beneficiaries disclaim some or all of their interests, (iii) the trust or interest is not legally effective by reason of the rule against perpetuities or an improper designation of the beneficiary, or (iv) a designated beneficiary is disqualified from or incapable of taking the beneficial interest. In addition, the purpose or purposes of a properly established trust may be fully accomplished without exhausting the trust property or, especially in the case of a charitable trust, may become certain of accomplishment without continued commitment of the full trust estate to the trust purpose or purposes.

On the other hand, an express trust has not failed or been fully performed, and therefore resort to a resulting trust is not called for, as long as the beneficiary, interest, or need for funds that appears to be lacking can be supplied through interpretation, by application of rules of construction or an anti-lapse statute, or through some form of reformation based, for example, on curable mistake (see § 62), the doctrine of *cy pres* (see § 67), or equitable approximation under modern perpetuities legislation or decisions (see § 29, Comment *g*, and Restatement Second, Property § 1.5 [Restatement Third, Property (Wills and Other Donative Transfers) § 27.2]). See generally § 7, Comment *a*, that resulting trusts occur by default or as a last resort when other rules and processes fail to preserve an express trust or to fill gaps in the equitable interests.

On the comprehensive meaning of the "terms of the trust," see § 4.

c. *Situations that arise at inception.* Various situations can arise at the time a trust is created that may cause the failure of the intended express trust, in whole or in part, so as to require the trustee to hold all or some of the trust estate upon a resulting trust. The Illustrations below exemplify and examine a number of these situations. All of the Illustrations that follow here involve private trusts; situations involving charitable trusts are discussed below in Comment *g*.

Illustrations:

2. B transfers Blackacre inter vivos to T in trust for C. Unknown to B, C is dead at the time of the transfer. T holds Blackacre on resulting trust for B.

4. F devises Blackacre to T in trust for such persons as F may name in a letter to be found in F's safe-deposit box after his death. The letter is never written, and there is no allegation of wrongdoing. T holds Blackacre on resulting trust for the estate of F.

In facts that are otherwise like those in Illustration 4, above, if a letter is found in the safe but was written after execution of the will (and thus cannot be incorporated by reference), and if the intended trust fails in the jurisdiction and circumstances involved (see § 17, Comment *g*), T would hold the property on resulting trust for F's estate. . . . . .

c(1). Contributions to a fund. If two or more persons make contributions to a fund to be held in trust for a noncharitable purpose, but the express trust fails for some reason, the funds are held on resulting trust for the contributors, each being entitled to the amount he or she contributed. If the contributions are of property that is not fungible, the property is to be returned in specie to the person who contributed it. If part of the fund has been expended or expenses have been incurred prior to the failure of the trust, ordinarily the contributors are entitled to share in the balance in proportion to the amounts of their respective contributions. The order in which contributions are made normally is immaterial. If funds are received from some contributors after the trustee knows that the trust has failed, these contributors are entitled to return of their contributions in full. Their contributions do not increase the amount to which the prior contributors are entitled.

If some of the contributors in the above situations cannot be ascertained, or disclaim their reversionary entitlements, the shares to which they would be entitled by way of resulting trust ordinarily are held for the State. Absent a contrary statute or trust provision, the trustee will not be permitted to hold these otherwise unclaimed shares free of trust or to apply them to other purposes.

On situations in which a charitable trust fails, see Comment *g*.

On trusts that fail for illegality, see Comment *i*.

On situations in which either the intention to create a trust or the designation of beneficiaries is not properly manifested, see Comment *h*. See more generally §§ 43–46.

d. *Situations that arise at a later time.* The most frequent applications of the rule stated in this section involve situations in which a trust has been in operation for a period of time and subsequently fails in whole or in part. Thus, if the owner of property transfers it in trust to pay the income to one beneficiary for life and thereafter to convey the principal to others on a contingency that does not in fact occur, on the life beneficiary's death the trustee holds the property on resulting trust for the settlor or his or her successors in interest. Occasionally, the rule stated in this section applies because, without exhausting the property held in an express trust, the trust purposes have been fully accomplished. Potential cases of these types are considered in the Illustrations that follow.

A different situation is presented when the owner of property transfers it in trust for a sole beneficiary and the terms of the trust provide for income, or some fixed or discretionary amounts, to be paid to that beneficiary for a fixed or ascertainable period, with principal thereafter to go to the beneficiary or, if dead, to the beneficiary's estate. If the beneficiary in this case dies testate or intestate before the expiration of the trust period, the beneficial interest passes to the testate or intestate successors of the beneficiary, all in fulfillment of the express trust. All beneficial interests having been disposed of, there is no need for a resulting trust in favor of the settlor or the settlor's successors in interest. This is true even if the beneficiary dies intestate leaving no heir or next of kin, with the beneficial interest therefore passing to the State as the beneficiary's escheated intestate property. In short, in this type of case the beneficiary effectively has the entire equitable interest in the trust property. On the beneficiary's death, that interest simply passes to those who are the successors to the beneficiary's estate, whoever they may be. Hence, there is no failure of the express trust for purposes of the rule stated in this section.

Similarly, if the owner of property transfers it in trust for one beneficiary for life and for another in remainder, and if the latter has (pursuant to the usual, traditional rule of construction) the entire beneficial interest in the trust property subject only to the life interest of the former, on the death of the remainder beneficiary before the death of the life beneficiary the equitable remainder interest passes by express trust to the remainder beneficiary's successors in interest. . . . Accordingly, no resulting trust will arise.

Illustrations:

10. A's will leaves property to T in trust to pay the income to B for life, remainder thereafter to the issue of B living at B's death. B dies leaving no issue. There is a resulting trust for the estate of A. (The successors in interest are determined as described above in Comment *a*.)

11. C devises to T in trust for D for life, remainder to E. E dies after C's death but before D's. As traditionally construed, the remainder to E does not fail by reason of her death in these circumstances. Thus, there is no failure of the express trust. Because E is dead, her interest now belongs to *her* successors in interest, to whom T will make distribution in fulfillment of the terms of the express trust. There is no resulting trust.

All of the foregoing Illustrations involve private trusts. On situations involving charitable trusts, see Comment *g*.

The rule stated in this section applies where a settlor transfers property to a trustee upon an express trust either (i) as to only a part of the property (for example, "to sell Blackacre and to pay half of the proceeds to X") or (ii) for a period less than that of the estate transferred to the trustee ("to pay the income to L for life"), provided the settlor manifests no intention as to the beneficial interests in the rest of the property or for the rest of the period. On the other hand, if the legal interest transferred to the trustee in the situation in (ii) is limited in duration to the period of the trust (L's lifetime), with the trustee having no active duties requiring a greater title, the settlor or the successors in interest of the settlor have a legal reversionary interest. Accordingly, no resulting trust arises. Such a limitation of the trustee's legal interest may be expressly stated in the trust terms (see § 42), or it may be based on interpretation or on the Statute of Uses or some statutory or court-developed counterpart thereof applicable to so-called passive trusts. On the Statute of Uses and its counterparts, see § 6.

If a trust is created for the benefit of a noncharitable association, as such, and the association ceases to exist, any of the trust property remaining after dissolution of the association is held on resulting trust for the contributors to the trust in proportion to their contributions (cf. Comment *c(1)*). As to the validity of such a trust, see § 43, Comment *d*. If, however, a trust is created for the benefit of the members of a noncharitable association, and not for the benefit of the association as such, the members of the association at the time it is dissolved are entitled to the trust property as beneficiaries of the terminating express trust. Accordingly, no resulting trust need arise in favor of the contributors.

On the failure of a charitable trust, see Comment *g*.

On trusts that fail for illegality, see Comment *i*.

On situations in which either the intention to create a trust or the designation of beneficiaries is not properly manifested, see Comment *h*. See more generally §§ 17–24.

e. *Application to powers of appointment*. By the terms of many trusts, one or more powers of appointment are conferred upon one or more beneficiaries or others. Fairly typical is a trust established primarily for the benefit of a designated person (possibly the settlor's spouse or child) for life, with the remainder to be distributed by the trustee as that beneficiary (the "donee" of the power) may appoint, in compliance with the limitations and other terms of the power. These terms can vary considerably from trust to trust. Sound drafting would supply a clear, expressed remainder to take effect in the absence of an effective and complete appointment.

Assume that the donee does not exercise or attempt to exercise the power and that the terms of the trust provide neither an expressed nor implied gift in default of appointment to or for the benefit of other beneficiaries. On the death of the donee-life beneficiary in such a case, the trustee holds the appointive property on a resulting trust for the settlor (the "donor" of the power) or the settlor's successors in interest. In cases in which there is a gift in default of appointment, whether expressed or implied, there is no failure of the express trust and therefore no need for a resulting trust.

A gift in default of appointment is normally implied when, absent an express default gift, the power of appointment is a special power that is exercisable (whether by deed or by will) in favor of a sufficiently definite and limited class that distribution can reasonably be made among the class members on some objective basis, such as: equally to all of them (as, for example, in the case of "children," "grandchildren," or "brothers and sisters"); to persons and shares determined (as in the case of "issue" or "descendants") by right of representation or by using the appropriate jurisdiction's preferred pattern of distribution among descendants; or even by applying rules of intestate succession (as, by the preferred view, in the case of "family," "relatives," or "kindred"). See Restatement Second, Property (Donative Transfers) § 24.2(1), and id., Comment *d* [Restatement Third, Property (Wills and Other Donative Transfers) § 19.23, and id., Comment *d*].

There will be no gift implied in default of appointment, however, when the unexercised power of appointment is general or is one exercisable in favor of an indefinite class such as "friends" or (in language fairly typical of many tax-motivated trusts) in favor of "any person, persons or entities other than the donee, the donee's estate, or the creditors of the donee or of the donee's estate." Restatement Second, Property (Donative Transfers) § 24.1 and 24.2, Comment *c* [Restatement Third, Property (Wills and Other Donative Transfers) § 19.22, and § 19.23, Comment *c*]. In these types of cases, except as mentioned below, under traditional doctrine at least, the trustee holds the unappointed property on resulting trust for the donor, or the donor's successors in interest, whenever the terms of the trust fail to express a gift in default of appointment. (In the case of a *general* power of appointment, however, this result has its critics, and some statutes or decisions may provide that the trustee holds for the donee or the donee's successors in interest. In that event, the implied disposition is by express trust and no resulting trust is needed.)

When the donee attempts to exercise a general power of appointment, and the attempted exercise is defective in whole or in part, in many circumstances the property the donee has attempted to appoint will be treated as if it were property owned and transferred by the donee. This is the so-called "capture" doctrine, described in Restatement Second, Property (Donative Transfers) § 23.2 [Restatement Third, Property (Wills and Other Donative Transfers) § 19.21]. In this type of case, even under traditional doctrine, the donee is substituted for the donor and is treated as the settlor with respect to the property subject to the attempted exercise. Accordingly, the appropriate trustee, either of the original trust or of a partially defective trust appointed by the donee, holds the appointive property on resulting trust for the donee (as a substitute settlor) or for the donee's successors in interest to whatever extent the attempted appointment fails.

f. Rebutting the presumption of resulting trust. If the settlor properly manifested an intention that, in the event of the failure or complete performance of the purposes for which the trust was primarily established, a different disposition or use should be made of the property, and assuming that the substitute disposition or use will be implemented, the express trust does not fail. Therefore no resulting trust arises. Or, if the terms of the trust provide that in such an event the trustee is to reconvey the property to the settlor or the settlor's estate, this provision would then be a feature of the express trust and again would avoid the need for a resulting trust.

Furthermore, as noted and illustrated above in Comments *c*, *d*, and *e*, what may initially appear to be gaps in an incomplete or failed trust disposition may be filled with express-trust interests by application of an anti-lapse statute or other legislation, by acceleration of future interests, by implication, or otherwise by either interpretation or application of rules of construction. These various results often serve to prevent the occurrence of situations in which express trusts would have failed or been fully performed. Thus, they serve to avoid a need to recognize the equitable reversionary interests called for by the rule of this section.

Even in cases in which a resulting-trust presumption does arise, that inference may be overcome by a finding that the settlor intended that, in the circumstances presented, the trustee should hold the property beneficially and free of trust. Although that intention is not ordinarily to be found by implication, it is ultimately a matter of interpretation whether the circumstances and admissible evidence reveal the existence or likelihood of an intention that the trustee is to retain the trust property as beneficial owner.

Among the circumstances that may be of importance in determining the existence or nonexistence of an intention that the trustee may retain the property free of trust are: (1) the language used in the trust instrument; (2) the likelihood that the situation appearing to involve a failure or full performance of the trust would have been apparent to the settlor when the trust was created; (3) the relationship between the settlor and the trustee and any other dispositions made by the settlor, especially in the same instrument; and (4) whether the trustee is an individual or a corporation, and, if the latter, whether it is a charitable corporation. On what constitute the terms of a trust and on the admissibility of evidence of a settlor's manifestations of intention, see § 4 . . . . See also §§ 22–24 (on statutes of frauds), §§ 17 and 18 (on Wills Acts), and § 21 (on the parol-evidence rule).

Where the owner of property transfers it upon a trust that fails or is fully performed, the usual presumption of resulting trust is not applicable if the transferor received from the transferee consideration for the transfer as an agreed exchange. The inference then is that the transferee holds the property free of trust. (Compare the purchase-money resulting-trust situations in § 9, especially in Comment *e* of that section.) Here, usual reasons for inferring that on the failure of a trust the property should be returned to the settlor are not present. The situation is analogous to a transfer of property free of trust to a purchaser who thereupon voluntarily declares himself or herself trustee of the property. In this latter case (assuming no obstacle to merger of legal and equitable titles), the purchaser would simply hold the property beneficially, as owner and with no need of a resulting trust, on the failure or full performance of the trust.

If, however, the consideration is not intended by the parties as the full purchase price of the property, or of the transferee's claimed beneficial interest, the parties have created the trust jointly. When reversionary rights materialize in such a case, absent agreement by the parties, the court will order such disposition of the property as is equitable in light of the circumstances, including the amounts contributed by each of the parties and the other rights, relationships, and general objectives of the parties.

Similar principles apply when, rather than a transfer in trust, there is a *declaration of trust* by a property owner (see § 10, Clause (c) and Comment *e*) who receives from another consideration that is intended as either a full or partial purchase price. In this type of situation, if the express trust fails or is fully performed, the presumption is that the person who paid the consideration is entitled either to the property or to an appropriate share thereof. Cf. § 9. In these circumstances, the payor's beneficial right is by resulting trust.

g. Application to charitable trusts. Often property is given in trust to be applied to a specific charitable purpose, or to a limited set or type of charitable purposes. Sometimes in such cases the particular purpose or purposes are or become illegal, impossible, or impracticable to carry out, or are fully performed without exhausting the trust estate. In other cases, the purpose ceases to be charitable, or it becomes clear that continued application of all of the trust funds solely to the particular purpose or purposes would be unreasonable and wasteful.

In these various circumstances, unless the settlor manifested an intention to substitute one or more other charitable purposes or a valid noncharitable purpose, or unless the doctrine of *cy pres* (see below and, more fully, § 67) is applicable, a resulting trust normally arises. Thus, if the settlor has provided no other purpose and has directed that *cy pres* not be applied, the trustee holds the trust estate, or an appropriate portion thereof or interests therein, upon resulting trust for the settlor or the settlor's successors in interest. (This assumes, of course, that the settlor has manifested no intention that the trustee should hold the property beneficially and free of trust. See Comment *f*.)

When the particular charitable purpose or purposes fail or leave a surplus as described above, the doctrine of *cy pres* will ordinarily apply. This doctrine allows an appropriate court to direct application of the trust property or surplus to some charitable purpose that closely approximates the charitable intention of the settlor, unless the terms of the trust provide otherwise. See generally § 67, especially Comments *b* through *d*. If *cy pres* is applied, there will be no need for a resulting trust.

Illustration:

17. S transfers certain funds inter vivos to T in trust to apply all of the trust income in perpetuity for a designated charitable purpose. It is no longer possible to use trust income for that purpose, and the terms of the trust direct that the doctrine of *cy pres* not be applied but provide no substitute purpose or disposition. T holds the trust estate on resulting trust for S or, if he is then dead, for his successors in interest.

If two or more persons contribute to a fund that is to be held in trust for one or more charitable purposes that fail, are fully performed, or leave a surplus as described above, and if the doctrine of *cy pres* is inapplicable, the inference in the absence of contrary intention or applicable legislation is that the trustee holds the trust estate or surplus on resulting trust for the contributors (or their successors in interest) in proportion to their contributions (see further § 67, Comment *f*). The order in which their contributions were made is ordinarily immaterial. If, however, contributions are received after the trustee knows that the purposes have failed, or that sufficient funds have already been received to accomplish the trust purposes, the later contributors are normally entitled to return of the amounts of their contributions. These later contributions, therefore, do not increase the amounts to which prior contributors are entitled.

h. Trust intention or intended beneficiaries not properly manifested. The rule stated in this section is not applicable where the transferor's intention to create a trust is not properly manifested—that is, where the intended trust cannot be enforced as an express trust because of either a statute of frauds or a statute of wills.

In some of these cases, the transferee will be allowed to retain the property free of trust, despite an allegation that the transferor had intended to create a trust or that the transferee had promised to hold in trust, because evidence in support of the allegation either is not admissible as the result of the failure to comply with the statute's formal requirements or because, if admissible, the evidence is not sufficiently persuasive. In some other circumstances, an express trust can be established despite the settlor's failure to comply with mandated statutory formalities. In still other cases, a constructive trust remedy may be imposed on the transferee, whether in favor of intended beneficiaries or for the transferor or the successors in interest of the transferor, based on wrongdoing by or the prospect of an unjust enrichment of the transferee. The matters in this paragraph are discussed in §§ 17 and 18 (testamentary transfers) and in §§ 22–24 (inter vivos transfers).

None of these outcomes, however, involves a resulting trust. This is because the transferee takes the beneficial interests, as well the title, or because either the intended purpose or restitution will be accomplished by constructive trust or under an exception that removes the case from the statute's prohibition.

Quite different are cases in which property is transferred, either inter vivos or by will, accompanied by a proper manifestation of the intention that the property be held by the transferee in trust but without proper manifestation of the intended beneficiaries or purposes. In these cases, in the absence of another remedy (again, either by constructive trust or statutory exception), a resulting trust arises.

Assume, for example, that an owner of land transfers it to another person or a testator devises property to another, and that the deed or the will states that the transferee is to hold the property "as trustee" or "in trust." Assume further, however, that the intended trust beneficiary or beneficiaries are not designated in the instrument (see § 22 or § 17(2)(a)) or through either a properly incorporated writing or facts of independent significance. (See § 17(2)(b) or (c).) In these situations, if the failure to properly designate the intended beneficiaries prevents the intended express trust from being carried out, and if a constructive trust is not imposed on the transferee either to carry out the intended trust or to return the property to the transferor or successors in interest (§ 24 or § 18), a resulting trust arises.

In the circumstances described in the two preceding paragraphs, unlike those in the earlier paragraphs of this Comment, it is clear on the face of the deed or will that the property is to be held in trust and that the transferee does not take the property beneficially. Thus, when neither an express trust nor a constructive trust establishes the entitlement to the equitable interests in the property, there is no disposition of those interests. The equitable interests therefore revert, and the transferee holds the property on resulting trust for the transferor or for the testator's estate or other successors.

On the related situations of intended trusts for indefinite beneficiaries or for specific noncharitable purposes, see §§ 43–47.

i. Where trust fails for illegality. Sometimes an owner of property transfers it inter vivos upon an intended trust that is unenforceable because the purpose or the performance of the trust is unlawful. (See § 29(a).) A resulting trust does not arise in such a case if the policy against permitting unjust enrichment of the transferee (i.e., the intended trustee) is outweighed by the policy against giving relief to a person who has entered into an illegal transaction.

This rule is based on a principle of public policy that is directed not only against the enforcement of an intended trust that is unlawful, but also against aiding a participant in an illegal transaction to obtain restitution. For this reason, not only do the courts refuse to enforce the unlawful purpose or provision, but they also may refuse to assist the party to an illegal transaction to recover the transferred property, even though the transferee would thereby be unjustly enriched.

Whether to aid or to refuse to aid the transferor requires a weighing of the interests of the public and the parties. As between the parties, a resulting trust would normally be imposed in order to prevent the transferee's unjust enrichment at the expense of the transferor; but the public interest may require allowing the transferee to be enriched unjustly at the transferor's expense. When the latter result is found to be justified, it is on the grounds that the result tends to deter illegal transactions and that the public should not be burdened with the expense of adjusting claims based on illegal transactions.

It is not possible to state a definite rule that will determine in all cases whether a resulting trust will be imposed. The court must take account of the circumstances involved in the particular case. Among the factors to be considered and weighed are the following: (1) whether the transferor was aware of or had suspicions about the law or the facts that make the trust unlawful; (2) whether, if so, the settlor's conduct involves moral turpitude; (3) whether the transferee was more at fault than the transferor; (4) the nature and force of the legal policy making the transaction unlawful; and (5) whether enforcement of a resulting trust would tend to prevent the accomplishment of the unlawful purpose. The last of these depends on whether the purpose has already been fully accomplished or become impossible of accomplishment. If the transferor was not in equal fault with the transferee, this tends to support the enforcement of a resulting trust unless the transaction nevertheless involves sufficiently serious moral turpitude on the part of the transferor to overcome this tendency.

Thus, a transferor is not necessarily precluded from recovering the property by resulting trust merely because enforcement of the intended trust would be against public policy. If, for example, property is transferred upon a trust that is partially invalid because some of the intended interests are excessively remote (see § 29(b)), in that as written they might vest at a time beyond the period of the rule against perpetuities, a resulting trust arises unless a modern rule of reformation applies (see, e.g., Uniform Statutory Rule Against Perpetuities § 2–903 and Restatement Second, Property (Donative Transfers) § 1.5 [Restatement Third, Property (Wills and Other Donative Transfers) § 27.2]).

So also, where part of a trust fails because of conditions in restraint of marriage (§ 29(c)), the court will attempt to give effect to what the settlor probably would have wished instead (see § 29, Comment *i(1)*), even in the unlikely event that this should involve enforcement of a resulting trust. In these cases, when the transferee is not permitted to carry out the intended purpose and no adapted purpose is substituted, the transferor's conduct ordinarily is not blameworthy in a way that precludes recovery of the property.

Similarly, if a trust is lawful at the time of its creation but owing to a change of law or circumstances later becomes unlawful, the transferor is not precluded from enforcing a resulting trust, because the conduct involved is not blameworthy.

If the will of a deceased property owner devises property upon a trust that fails for unlawfulness of purpose, the devisee ordinarily holds the property on resulting trust for the testator's estate. This is because the reversionary interest will prevent the accomplishment of the illegal purpose without aiding the testator personally. Assuming the beneficiaries of the estate are innocent of the wrongdoing, they are merely protected from being deprived, by an unlawful act, of what they would otherwise receive.

If, however, after transferring property inter vivos upon a trust that fails for illegality, the settlor conveys the potential reversionary interest inter vivos to another, the transferee ordinarily stands in no better position than the settlor even though the transferee was not a participant in the unlawful transaction or was unaware of its illegality. So also, the later death of the settlor who cannot enforce a resulting trust ordinarily will not enable the settlor's testate or intestate successors in interest to do so.

§ 9. Purchase-Money Resulting Trusts

(1) Except as stated in Subsection (2), where a transfer of property is made to one person and the purchase price is paid by another, a resulting trust arises in favor of the person by whom the purchase price is paid unless

(a) the latter manifests an intention that no resulting trust should arise, or

(b) the transfer is made to accomplish an unlawful purpose, in which case a resulting trust does not arise if the policy against unjust enrichment of the transferee is outweighed by the policy against giving relief to a person who has entered into an illegal transaction.

(2) Where a transfer of property is made to one person and the purchase price is paid by another and the transferee is a spouse, descendant, or other natural object of the bounty of the person by whom the purchase price is paid, a resulting trust does not arise unless the latter manifests an intention that the transferee should not have the beneficial interest in the property.

Comment:

a. In general. Under early common law in England, a resulting use was held to arise in favor of a person who made a transfer of land by feoffment in fee simple to another, if no consideration was given for the feoffment and no express use was declared by the feoffor. This rule was understandable as a reflection of the widespread practice of English landowners during the 15th and 16th centuries of having legal title held for their use by others. The rule is not recognized in the modern property and trust law, the inference in a situation of this type being that the transferor intended to make a gift to the transferee.

On the other hand, a counterpart rule that presumed a resulting use to arise when a vendor transferred land to another at the direction of the person who paid the purchase price generally remains a part of the law of property and of resulting trusts today in states that have not abolished the presumption by statute. . . . . Although rebuttable by evidence of other intention, the presumption in this situation generally is that the payor of the purchase price does not intend the transferee to have the beneficial interest in the property but that the beneficial interest is to remain in the payor. See Comment *d*.

In the latter situation, if the transaction is accompanied by an actual intention that the transferee is to hold the property in trust for the payor and if that intention is properly manifested to be provable in court, the transferee holds the property upon an express trust for the payor. There is then no need in such a case for the payor or successors in interest to resort to the rules of this section concerning so-called "purchase-money resulting trusts."

A purchase-money resulting trust arises in the absence of circumstances supporting the contrary presumption of gift in Subsection (2) and also absent evidence or circumstances showing the payor's actual intention, or an agreement of the parties involved, that some other purpose is to be served by the transaction (see Comment *e*). Circumstances that support a presumption of gift in purchase-money situations are stated in Subsection (2). In these circumstances, the rule stated in Subsection (1) is not justified because a fundamental element of its rationale is missing.

When the transferee is not a natural object of the bounty of the person who paid the purchase price, the rationale of the presumption of a purchase-money resulting trust is: first, that it is no more reasonable to believe that such a transferee is intended to take beneficial ownership than that the purchaser wished to acquire the property but to have its title appear in the name of another; and second that, when this uncertainty of intention is present, it is preferable to run the less serious risk that an intended gift may later be disavowed by a donor than the more serious risk that intended ownership would be lost by one who paid the purchase price. . . . .

When the payor arranges for the property to be transferred to a natural object of the payor's generosity, the first element of this rationale is missing because a presumption of gift reflects a distinctly more likely intention. See Comment *b*.

The rules stated in this section are of primary importance whenever no persuasive, admissible evidence is available of the payor's intention or of an agreement of the parties. See Comments *c* and *e*. In these cases, the rule of the applicable subsection determines whether a resulting trust arises or the transferee has the beneficial interest.

The rules stated in this section are applicable to transfers of either personal property or real property. These rules apply regardless of whether the purchase price is paid with money or other property; and they apply not only where the purchase price is paid directly to the vendor by a person other than the transferee but also where the purchase price is paid by the transferee with funds belonging to another with the latter's consent.

Parol evidence to show the source of payment is not barred by the parol-evidence rule, even when the instrument recites that consideration was paid by the transferee; nor is it precluded by a statute of frauds. Section 7 of the English Statute of Frauds, 29 Charles II, c. 3, provided that all declarations or creations of trust shall be manifested and proved by some writing signed by the party who is by law enabled to declare such a trust. Section 8 of the statute, however, provided that no such writing is necessary in the case of a trust that may "arise or result by the implication or construction of law." With or without similar provisos, statutes of frauds in the United States do not require a memorandum evidencing the intention to create a resulting trust. . . . .

b. Relatives or "natural objects" to whom Subsection (2) applies. The rule presuming a gift rather than a resulting trust, despite payment of the purchase price by a person other than the transferee, applies when the transferee and payor have a relationship that makes it probable that the payor intends to make a gift to the transferee. That is, the exception in Subsection (2) of this section applies when the transferee is a natural object of the bounty of the payor.

Even when Subsection (2) does not apply, the existence of a relationship that is insufficient to raise an inference of gift is nevertheless a circumstance that can be shown along with other circumstances as tending to rebut the presumption of resulting trust under the rule of Subsection (1) of this section.

The rule stated in Subsection (2) applies where the payor and transferee are spouses and where the transferee is a child or other descendant of the payor, or is the spouse of a descendant of the payor; and it applies regardless of whether the descendant's relationship to the payor is based on adoption or on birth in or out of marriage. The rule also applies: where the payor, whether or not a relative of the transferee, stands in loco parentis by having assumed to act in the place of a parent to the transferee; where the payor and transferee are engaged to be married or have cohabited for a significant period of time; and where the transferee is a parent of the payor. In addition, the rule of Subsection (2) applies where the transferee is a descendant of a parent of the payor, particularly if the payor is without issue at the time of the transfer. The circumstances or relationship upon which a presumption under Subsection (2) is based may affect the weight of the presumption—that is, the difficulty of rebutting the presumption.

Illustration:

1. W pays the purchase price to the vendor, V, who at W's direction transfers the land to her husband, H. Absent evidence of other intention to rebut the presumption in Subsection (2), W has made a gift to H. No presumption of resulting trust arises, as Subsection (1) is inapplicable.

The presumption of gift under the rule of Subsection (2) arises regardless of whether the transferee is an adult or a minor. . . . .

c. Rebutting the presumption of gift in Subsection (2). Where one person pays the purchase price for property that is transferred at the payor's direction to another who is a spouse, descendant, or other natural object of the bounty of the payor (see Comment *b*), parol evidence is admissible to show that the payor intended that the transferee should not have the beneficial interest in the property. This proposition holds even though a statute of frauds (see Comment *a*) would apply to the declaration or creation of an express trust of that same property.

The intention not to make a gift to the transferee may be shown not only by the payor's oral or written declarations but also by the circumstances under which the transfer is made. Thus, statements or conduct by either the payor or the transferee, in context, may indicate that the transferee was to hold the property for the payor's benefit. So also, the fact that it would be improvident for the payor to make a gift to the transferee is some indication that the payor did not intend to make a gift, as are circumstances in which the payor would have reason for taking title in the name of another while intending to retain the beneficial interest.

It is the payor's intention at the time of the transfer and not at some subsequent time that determines whether a resulting trust arises. The conduct of the payor and the transferee before or after the transfer, however, may be such as to show that at the time of the transfer the payor did not intend to make a gift to the transferee. Thus, the fact that the payor manages the property or directs its management, collects rents, pays taxes and insurance premiums, pays for repairs and improvements, or otherwise acts as an owner would act, especially with the transferee's acquiescence, is evidence that tends to rebut a presumption that the payor intended to make a gift to the transferee.

Where a person pays the purchase price and directs that property be transferred to another who is a natural object of the payor's bounty, and it is shown that the payor intended merely to have a partial interest in the property, a resulting trust arises in favor of the payor only as to that interest. The presumption of gift under Subsection (2) is thus rebutted in part. Similarly, if in a transaction of the general type described in Subsection (2) it is shown that the payor intended to have the beneficial interest only upon the happening of a designated event, a resulting trust arises in favor of the payor upon the happening of the event; or, if it is shown that the payor intended to retain a beneficial interest that is to terminate on the happening of a designated event, a present interest by resulting trust arises, but the transferee holds the property free of trust on the happening of that event.

Where one person pays the purchase price and directs that the property be transferred to a natural object of the payor's bounty, the rule of this subsection does not apply if the payor properly manifests an intention to create an express trust for one or more third parties. A resulting trust does not arise in favor of the payor, nor can the transferee keep the property free of trust, for there is instead an express trust for the third person. If the intention of the payor to create the express trust is not properly manifested, however, and the transferee refuses to perform the trust or to make a binding commitment to perform it, there is neither evidence nor a presumption (the presumption being one of gift) to support a resulting trust. Nevertheless, a constructive-trust remedy may be available in such a case. See generally § 24.

d. Applications of the rule stated in Subsection (1). Where the purchase price of property is paid by a person at whose direction the property is transferred to another who is not a natural object of the payor's bounty, a resulting trust arises unless the payor manifests a contrary intention. An intention contrary to the resulting-trust presumption is manifested by a showing of intention that the transferee is to hold the property beneficially. A contrary intention is also indicated by any showing that the transfer was intended to serve a different donative, business, or other purpose.

More generally on circumstances manifesting an intention that no resulting trust should arise because of a contrary intention, see Comment *e*.

Where the purchase is in the name of a spouse, descendant, or other natural object of the bounty of the payor, see Comments *b* and *c*.

Where the contrary intention is one to accomplish an unlawful purpose, see Comment *g*.

Illustration:

4. A purchases land from B, who at A's direction transfers the land to C, who is not a natural object of A's bounty. In the absence of evidence of a different intention on the part of A, under the rule of Subsection (1) C holds the land on resulting trust for A.

The rule stated in Subsection (1) applies as well when one person deposits money in a bank in the name of another, who is not a natural object of the depositor's bounty.

In addition, the rule of Subsection (1) applies when a portion of the purchase price is paid by one or more persons, the rest being paid by the transferee. In a case of this type, the presumption is that the transferee holds the property proportionately for the transferee's own benefit and for the benefit of each of the contributors. This inference may be rebutted by a showing of a gift intention on the part of a contributor or of a different agreement among the parties (see Comment *e*).

Legislation in a number of states enacts the rule stated in Subsection (1).

In a few other states, statutes reject or abolish the presumption of resulting trust when land is conveyed to one person for consideration paid by another and provide that a trust for the payor arises only where it appears by agreement that the transferee was to hold the land or some interest therein for the payor's benefit. Several statutes provide, in effect, that a trust results in favor of the payor only in certain cases involving misconduct, situations for which a constructive trust would ordinarily be appropriate in any event, and also that transfers to one person paid for by another are presumed fraudulent as against the payor's creditors. In these states, the rule of Subsection (1) does not apply.

e. Rebutting the resulting-trust presumption in Subsection (1). Where a transfer of property is made to one person and the purchase price is paid by another, a resulting trust does not arise if the person by whom the purchase price is paid manifests a contrary intention.

The normal inference of a purchase-money resulting trust may be overcome by written or spoken words or by the conduct of the parties, or by other evidence, showing in the circumstances an intention that a resulting trust should not arise but rather that the transfer was to serve another purpose. That intention may be found in evidence of either an intention of the payor or an agreement of the payor and transferee that the transaction is to serve some donative, business, or other purpose.

Thus, like other resulting trusts (see §§ 7–8), the purchase-money resulting trust is a reversionary equitable interest left in a transferor (here, the person who paid the purchase price) when no other disposition has been made of all of the beneficial rights in the property. The resulting trust is, in effect, a last resort based on a legally presumed intention when no other explanation for the transfer is established.

When one person pays the purchase price for a transfer to another, the presumption that a resulting trust was intended is rebutted if it appears that the payor intended the transferee to have the beneficial interest in the transferred property. This is the case where it appears that the payor: (i) intended to make a gift of the property to the transferee; (ii) had the property transferred to discharge a debt or other obligation owed to the transferee; or (iii) was making a loan of the purchase price to the transferee, who thereby becomes indebted to but does not hold the property for the payor.

The presumption of resulting trust in favor of the payor of the purchase price also may be rebutted by manifestations of intention with respect to some purpose other than either that the beneficial interest is to pass to the transferee or that it is to remain in the payor. For example, parol evidence may establish a business purpose with the underlying agreement providing for the involvement or participation of the payor and others, including possibly the transferee, in any of a variety of roles. The various parties may make contributions to a common enterprise to which only one or several contribute money or property while others contribute special skills or status, with rewards being allocated among the parties to such arrangements in any of an unlimited variety of ways. If those rewards provide for allocation of all of the beneficial interests in the transferred property, no interest remains for the transferee to hold upon a resulting trust. Also, a transaction may involve a security arrangement in which the transferee advances the purchase price to another, who, effectively as "payor," uses the borrowed funds to pay the purchase price for the property, with the transferee receiving title not beneficially but as security for repayment of the loan.

Among the factors that may be of relevance in determining the donor's intention, or in determining the existence of an agreement between the donor and the transferee, are: (1) declarations of the payor's intention or of the wishes or objectives of the payor and transferee, or the conduct of the payor and transferee, occurring before, at, or after the time of the transfer; (2) the relationship between and the relative financial positions of the payor and the transferee; (3) whether the transferee is an individual or a corporation, and if a corporation whether it is a charitable corporation; (4) whether a gift by the payor to the transferee would be improvident or surprising; and (5) the presence or absence of any probable reason for taking title in the name of, without giving the beneficial interest to, the transferee.

The fact that one who pays the purchase price takes title to the property in the name of another jointly with the payor, whether as tenants in common or as joint tenants, indicates the payor's intention to make a beneficial gift of an undivided interest in the property to the other person. Accordingly, in the absence of evidence of a different intention in such a case, the other person does not hold the interest on resulting trust for the payor.

Where the payor has property transferred solely to another and it is shown, by written or oral declarations, by agreement of the parties, or by conduct or other circumstances, that the payor intended the transferee to have a partial beneficial interest in the property (such as an undivided interest, a life estate, or a future interest), with no manifestation of intention as to the rest, a resulting trust arises in favor of the payor as to the balance of the beneficial interest.

Where a person pays the purchase price and has the property transferred to another, accompanied by a properly manifested intention to create an express trust for the payor or others, or for some combination of the transferee, the payor, and others, there is an express trust for the intended beneficiaries. Accordingly, there is no occasion for a resulting trust to arise.

Sometimes, however, the intention to create an express trust is not properly manifested, because the property is land and statute-of-frauds requirements are not satisfied. See generally §§ 22–23. In a case of this type, if there is neither performance nor a binding commitment to perform by the transferee, nor some other basis for enforcing the express trust as such, a resulting trust may nevertheless arise (by unrebutted inference of law) or a constructive-trust remedy may be available, depending on the circumstances. If the intended trust was solely to benefit the payor, evidence of that trust intention is admissible, because this is evidence that serves merely to reinforce the resulting-trust presumption that remains in these facts. If any other trust intention is found in this type of situation, however (that is, an unenforceable trust intended wholly or partially in favor of third parties), the presumption of Subsection (1) is rebutted, and therefore a resulting trust is prevented from arising in favor of the payor. In such a case, however, a constructive-trust remedy may be available. See generally § 24.

f. Other matters. The rule of Subsection (1) does not apply, and no presumption of resulting trust arises, where the transferee obtains transfer of the property by undertaking an obligation to pay the transferor the purchase price and another subsequently pays or assumes an obligation to pay some or all of that price.

Where a resulting trust arises from a transfer of property to one person with the purchase price being paid by another, and a third person relying on the apparent ownership of the property extends credit to the transferee who holds upon a resulting trust, the third person can obtain satisfaction of the claim out of the property that is subject to the resulting trust on the same basis and under the same circumstances as when the property is held on an express trust. See generally Chapter 22.

Where a transfer of an interest in land is made to one person and the purchase price is paid by another, a resulting trust in favor of the payor can be extinguished by an oral surrender of the beneficial interest to the trustee by the beneficiary of the resulting trust. The equitable reversionary interest can be extinguished without a writing, just as the presumption that a resulting trust arises from payment of the purchase price can be rebutted without a writing. Compare § 8, Comment *g*, on extinguishment by surrender of resulting-trust interests in situations in which an express trust of land fails or is fully performed.

f(1). Burden of proof. Under either Subsection (1) or Subsection (2), the party alleging the purchase-money resulting trust has the burden of proving by clear and convincing evidence that the claimant (or a predecessor in interest) paid or furnished the purchase price or claimed a portion thereof.

If that initial showing is made in a case under Subsection (1), and the transferee introduces evidence tending to show that the funds were paid or furnished by the payor as a loan or with an intention to make a gift, or for other intended or agreed purpose that might rebut the resulting-trust inference, the ultimate burden then is on the payor (or a successor in interest) to establish the existence and extent of the resulting-trust interest by a preponderance of the evidence.

In a case under Subsection (2), one who has proved a claim of having provided the purchase price has the further burden of rebutting the inference of gift by a preponderance of the evidence, weighed in light of the circumstances of the parties and the nature of the particular natural-object relationship.

g. Unlawful purpose. Sometimes, in an attempt to accomplish an unlawful purpose, a transfer of property is made to one person and another pays the purchase price. In such a case, a resulting trust does not arise if the policy against unjust enrichment of the transferee is outweighed by the policy against giving relief to a person who has entered into an illegal transaction. This aspect of the rule stated in Subsection (1) is based upon the same policy and is subject to the same principles as are stated with respect to other resulting-trust situations discussed in § 8, Comment *i*.

The most frequent applications of the principle stated in Clause (b) of Subsection (1) of this section involve situations in which the purchaser of property takes title in the name of another for the purpose of defrauding creditors of the former. In a case of this type, the property is subject to a constructive trust for the creditors of the purchaser. To the extent the property is not needed for the satisfaction of the creditors' claims, this aspect of the rule of Subsection (1) will ordinarily preclude the payor from enforcing a resulting trust in the property held by the transferee.

Sometimes a person deposits money in a savings account in a bank in the name of another person when the depositor already had on deposit the maximum amount permitted to a single depositor by a statute or the bylaws of the bank. Even though the deposit was made in the other's name for the purpose of evading the statute or bylaw, the person in whose name the deposit was made ordinarily holds the claim against the bank on resulting trust for the depositor. Generally, in this type of case, the purpose of the depositor is not so seriously against public policy as to justify the particular sanction of preventing enforcement of the resulting trust.

Sometimes a person who is not eligible to acquire government land provides the funds for the purchase of the land in the name of another. In such a case, the payor, being ineligible to acquire the land, ordinarily cannot do so by enforcing a resulting trust of that land, even though the government takes no steps to set aside the transaction for fraud.

In some places, land or certain interests in land may not be acquired by certain categories of persons, and the prohibition and associated forfeiture applies by statute or decision to equitable interests as well as legal interests. In a case of this type, if an ineligible person pays the purchase price and has the title to the land placed in the name of an eligible person under circumstances that would give rise to a resulting trust if the payor were an eligible person, a resulting trust ordinarily arises in favor of the ineligible person but subject to the prescribed forfeiture.

PART 2
CREATION OF TRUSTS

CHAPTER 3

BASIC PRINCIPLES AND REQUIREMENTS

Introductory Note: There are numerous methods of disposing of property during life and at death. Outright transfers may be made at death by devise or by intestate succession. During life, a transferor may dispose of all or part of his or her interest in real or personal property by sale or by gift to a person outright or to multiple transferees as concurrent owners. Tolerant Anglo—American common law also permits property owners not only to transfer limited present interests or future interests to their transferees, retaining the other interests, but also to create powers of appointment and combinations of successive legal interests, present and future, in named and described transferees, some of whom may be unborn or unascertained at the time the disposition is made.

The creation of a trust is another method—a particularly flexible and useful method—of making property dispositions, either inter vivos or by will. As appears from the rules and commentary in this chapter, the requirements for the creation of a trust are quite simple, even if they sometimes give rise to difficult issues.

In order to create a trust, there must be a proper manifestation of the intention to do so (§ 13), either by the settlor or in communications between the settlor and the intended trustee; and the settlor ordinarily must make an effective inter vivos or testamentary transfer of the trust property to the trustee (§ 10), just as other means of disposition ordinarily require that the property owner make an effective transfer to create property interests in others. An important exception to the transfer requirement is that trust dispositions also may be accomplished by the property owner's declaration that certain of the declarant's own property is now held by the declarant in trust for one or more others or for both the declarant and others. In addition, trusts are occasionally created by contract even before the promised transfer occurs, or by transfers eventually made pursuant to promises or pursuant to insurance or retirement-plan beneficiary designations, even after the settlor's death.

No consideration is required for the creation of a trust. See § 15. In fact, most trusts are created by gratuitous transfer. Ordinarily, however, if the property owner does not manifest an intention immediately to create a trust, but only the intention to create a trust in the future, no trust is created. Nor is the property owner bound later to create the trust in such a case, unless the requirements for the formation of a contract are complied with. See § 15, Comment *b*, and also § 10, Comment *b*. The result is the same (that is, no trust and no obligation later to create one) where, in the absence of consideration (although language of present transfer is used), the would-be settlor does not at the time own the property purportedly transferred in trust.

Thus, a trust is normally created by an effective disposition of property, either during life or at death, and not by a mere attempt or undertaking to make a disposition in the future. Although a settlor can gratuitously and effectively make a present disposition of property in trust by declaration, an attempt to make a present, outright gift inter vivos that is ineffective (for lack of delivery, for example) will not be treated as a declaration of trust. Similarly, an undertaking to make a disposition at some future date that is not binding as a contract will not be salvaged by treating it as a declaration of trust. See § 16, Comment *d*.

If the trust property is an interest in land, statutes of frauds in nearly all states require that the creation of an enforceable trust be manifested and proved by written instrument. See generally §§ 20–24. If the trust is to be a testamentary trust, it is ordinarily necessary to satisfy the requirements of the state's wills act. See generally §§ 17–19.

§ 10. Methods of Creating a Trust

Except as prevented by the doctrine of merger (§ 69), a trust may be created by:

(a) a transfer by the will of a property owner to another person as trustee for one or more persons; or

(b) a transfer inter vivos by a property owner to another person as trustee for one or more persons; or

(c) a declaration by an owner of property that he or she holds that property as trustee for one or more persons; or

(d) an exercise of a power of appointment by appointing property to a person as trustee for one or more persons who are objects of the power; or

(e) a promise or beneficiary designation that creates enforceable rights in a person who immediately or later holds those rights as trustee, or who pursuant to those rights later receives property as trustee, for one or more persons.

Comment:

a. *In general.* In each of the methods of trust creation stated in this section, the trustee, including a settlor-trustee in Clause (c), may also be a beneficiary of a trust that has multiple beneficiaries.

On the doctrine of merger, where a sole trustee is the sole beneficiary, see § 69. (But contrast § 17, Comment *a*, and § 25, Comment *b*, pointing out that a trust may exist even though the only interests of other beneficiaries are contingent, subject to revocation, or otherwise highly uncertain. See § 69, Comment *c*.)

b. *Other trust situations.* After a trust is created by one of the methods stated in this section, additional property ordinarily may be added to the trust by the original settlor or settlors or by one or more others.

A trust may also be created by statute. In some states, for example, amounts recovered under a wrongful-death action conferred upon an executor or administrator are received by that personal representative not as assets of the decedent's estate but in trust for persons specially designated in the statute. Also, statutes in some states provide for the forced share elected on behalf of an incapacitated surviving spouse to be held upon a special trust for the spouse and certain successors in interest of the predeceased spouse.

In addition, on public retirement systems and pension funds, see . . . also § 4, Comment *g*.

On trusts created by court decree, see § 4, Comment *f*.

Comment on Clause (a):

c. *Transfers by will.* A trust may be created by a property owner's devise to someone in trust for the benefit of one or more others or for the benefit of the trustee and one or more others. See § 15, Comment *b*, and § 17. (The term "devise" is generally used today, and in this Restatement, to include the traditional term "bequest.") . . . .

On the situation in which no trustee is named in the will, or in which the person named as trustee is dead or otherwise unable or unwilling to take title to the property, see § 14, Comment *b*.

On the effect of an agreement by a devisee or intestate successor to hold in trust property received from a decedent, see § 18.

On the creation of a trust by a testamentary disposition (a so-called "pour-over") to a trustee named in a trust instrument, with or without prior funding of the intended trust, see § 19.

Comment on Clause (b):

d. *Transfer inter vivos.* A trust may be created by an owner's inter vivos transfer of property to another person as trustee for the benefit of the transferor, for one or more third persons, or both, whether or not the trustee is also a beneficiary. See § 25 (on revocable living trusts) and § 69 (on merger).

Illustration:

2. S transfers certain of his land and securities to T as trustee upon an active trust for B for life, remainder to B's issue. T is trustee of that property for the benefit of the beneficiaries designated by S.

On the situation in which the owner of property attempts to make a transfer in trust but the actions taken are not effective to transfer the property, see § 16.

Comment on Clause (c):

e. *Declaration of trust.* If the owner of property declares himself or herself trustee of the property for the benefit of one or more others, or for the declarant and one or more others, a trust is created, even though there is no transfer of the title to the trust property to another and even though no consideration is received for the declaration.

Illustration:

3. S declares herself trustee of certain of her own property for the benefit of herself for life and thereafter for the benefit of her husband H for life, remainder at the death of the survivor of S and H to S's then living descendants. S is trustee of the property for the benefit of herself and the other designated beneficiaries.

A statute of frauds may require a signed writing in order for a declaration of trust to be enforceable. See § 22.

Assuming neither the terms of the declaration nor the terms of an applicable statute provide otherwise, the trust in Illustration 3 is presumptively revocable because of S's retained beneficial interest. See § 63, Comment *c*; and cf. § 14, Comment *c* (possible effect on terms of trust if S's declaration not communicated to beneficiaries).

Upon the death of S in Illustration 3 or upon her incompetency or resignation, the remaining provisions of the trust will be carried out by the successor trustee (if any) named in the declaration, or a successor trustee may be appointed either by a process provided in the terms of the trust or by the court. See § 34.

In this Restatement, the declaration of trust is generally considered to be an additional means of creating a trust inter vivos, and is thus an exception to or substitute for the usual requirement that there be a transfer of the trust property to the trustee. Conceptually, however, it is not inappropriate for the declaration of trust to be viewed as a form of "transfer" from the property owner individually to the property owner in a representative capacity. Cf. § 2, Comment *a*. Accordingly, regardless of which of these views may be preferred in a particular jurisdiction, an owner of property may create a trust by executing an instrument worded either simply as a declaration of trust or as a transfer of the property to himself or herself as trustee.

Illustration:

4. S, the owner of Blackacre, executes, acknowledges, and records a deed conveying Blackacre to S "as trustee" or "in trust" for certain designated beneficiaries. S holds Blackacre in trust for those beneficiaries.

The above instrument of transfer is as effective to create a trust as if the owner had simply executed an instrument using language of declaration of trust. In either case, the transaction may be viewed (i) as one in which there is and need be no transfer of title to the property, because the settlor-trustee already has title to it, or (ii) as a transaction involving a transfer of title from the property owner individually to himself or herself as trustee, that is, in a separate, representative capacity.

In neither Illustration 3 nor Illustration 4 does the law ordinarily require acknowledgment or recordation, or other formal change in ownership records or documents of title, for the effective creation of the trust. Even additional statutory formalities, such as those applicable to transfers of land requiring that a document be sealed, attested, acknowledged, or recorded, ordinarily are not essential to effect a valid transfer as between transferor and transferee. See Restatement Second, Property (Donative Transfers) § 32.3, Comment *a* [Restatement Third, Property (Wills and Other Donative Transfers) § 6.3]. See also § 14 infra (on transfers to *others* in trust). For practical reasons, steps to conform ownership documents or records and to perfect the rights and interests of the parties with respect to third persons should ordinarily be taken at the time a trust is created. As long as the trust is effectively established, however (and assuming no inconsistent third-party rights have by then intervened, see Chapter 22), these steps may be taken later by the settlor or may be accomplished, following the settlor's death or incompetency, by court order or other procedures appropriate to the circumstances and applicable law or practice. Compare § 16, Comment *b*.

In addition, except as precluded by statute, a trust may be established by the settlor's signing of an instrument that begins, essentially, "I hereby declare myself trustee of the property listed in Schedule A attached hereto" or "O, as settlor, hereby transfers to O, as trustee, the property listed in the attached Schedule A," even though in either case the document is not supported at the time of execution, or by the time of the settlor's death or incompetency, by other acts or other documents of transfer or title. In short, the trust instrument may serve as an instrument of transfer (i.e., as a "deed" of gift or conveyance).

Comment on Clause (d):

f. Transfer by exercise of a power of appointment. If a person (the "donee") has been given a power of appointment and makes an appointment to another person as trustee, a trust is created, provided the power is properly exercised.

On the capacity of the donee to exercise a power of appointment, see § 11, Comment *d.* See also Restatement Second, Property (Donative Transfers) § 18.1 [Restatement Third, Property (Wills and Other Donative Transfers) § 19.8].

On matters of form and timing in the exercise of powers, see Restatement Second, Property (Donative Transfers) §§ 18.2–18.4 [Restatement Third, Property (Wills and Other Donative Transfers) §§ 19.6, 19.9, 19.10].

On the scope of the donee's authority, see Restatement Second, Property (Donative Transfers) § 12.2 [Restatement Third, Property (Wills and Other Donative Transfers) Ch. 17, Part B, Intro. Note, and § 17.3, Comment *a*], and more specifically id. §§ 19.1–19.4 [§§ 19.13–19.14] on permissible beneficiaries and permissible forms of disposition.

If the donee has an inter vivos general power of appointment (including a power of withdrawal over trust property) that can presently be exercised by appointing the property outright to himself or herself, the donee has the same power to appoint in trust as an outright owner of the same property would have.

On the other hand, the donee may have either (i) a special or other nongeneral power of appointment or (ii) a general power of appointment that is exercisable only by will (or by the last unrevoked writing delivered during life) or that is otherwise applicable only to the remainder of the property after the donee's death. In these situations, the donee can effectively appoint the property subject to the power, or any portions of or interests in that property, in trust for the benefit of permissible appointees (the "objects") of the power unless the terms of the trust or other disposition that created the power of appointment clearly manifest the creator's (the "donor's") contrary intention. Even when an appointment in situation (ii) can properly be made to the donee's estate, a prohibition against appointment in trust will be given effect. Similarly, with respect to the extent and nature of the interests that can be appointed to or for the benefit of any one or more of the permissible appointees, it is to be inferred that the donor of such a power intended the donee to have the same breadth of authority in making appointments that the donee would have in making a disposition of the donee's own property in favor of those permissible appointees.

Thus, the donee of a power of appointment ordinarily may appoint, outright or in trust, in present and future interests for the benefit of any one or more of the objects of the power, and may create new powers of appointment, including general powers of appointment, even presently exercisable general powers, in objects of the original power. The donee also ordinarily may impose otherwise valid conditions, restraints on alienation, charges, and other qualifications on the enjoyment of the property by the appointee. On the nature and extent of the ability of the donee of a nongeneral power to create powers of appointment in others, see Restatement Second, Property (Donative Transfers) § 19.4 [Restatement Third, Property (Wills and Other Donative Transfers) § 19.14].

When the donee of a power of appointment appoints in trust, the trustee need not be an object of the power unless the terms of the power so require. This is true even if the trustee is granted discretionary authority with respect to the benefits to be enjoyed by objects of the power who are made beneficiaries of the appointed trust.

Illustration:

6. S devised Blackacre to T in trust for the benefit of B for life, with a testamentary power in B "to appoint the remainder among any one or more of her issue as she may choose and in such manner and in such shares and interests as she may determine, remainder in default of appointment by right of representation to the issue of B who are living at her death." B exercises her power by her will, appointing to her husband, H, in trust for certain of her issue. A trust is created, to be administered in accordance with the terms of B's appointment.

Comment on Clause (e):

g. Trust created by enforceable promise or beneficiary designation. Where a property owner makes a nonbinding promise to create a trust in the future, no trust is thereby created. If the property owner later establishes the trust by inter vivos or testamentary transfer or by declaration, the trust is created by the transfer or declaration (see Comments *d* and *e*) and not by the promise.

Similarly, when a property owner makes a contractually binding promise to establish a trust by inter vivos or testamentary transfer or by declaration and later performs by making the promised transfer or declaration, ordinarily the trust is created at the time of performance, whether the transfer or declaration is made voluntarily or involuntarily. In this situation, the trust and the trustee's fiduciary duties ordinarily come into existence at the time of the settlor's performance and not at the time the binding promise is made. See § 15, Comment *b*.

If, however, a person makes or causes to be made an enforceable promise to pay money or transfer property to another as trustee, and if the person (with the expressed or implied acceptance of the intended trustee) also manifests an intention immediately to create a trust of the promisee's rights, a trust is created at the time of the contract, with a *chose in action* (the rights under that contract) then being held for the beneficiaries by the trustee.

On when a trust arises when a beneficiary designation calls for payments (such as of the proceeds of a life-insurance policy or the death benefits under a retirement arrangement) to be made to a person as trustee, see § 25, Comment *c* (also explaining that the trust is not "testamentary" merely because it is created by a transfer that occurs after the death of the insured, plan participant, or other settlor).

If a promise to create a trust is made for a consideration and the promised trust is thereby or thereafter created, the person who supplies the consideration is the "settlor," as that term is used in this Restatement. If the enforceable promise is partially donative, in that its value is intendedly greater than the consideration paid for it, both the promisor and the payor of the consideration are the settlors. . . . .

On the possibility of relief being granted for reasonable, detrimental reliance on an otherwise unenforceable promise to create or declare a trust, see Restatement Second, Contracts § 90 . . . . See also Restatement of Restitution § 164.

Promises to create trusts in the future are different from situations in which the promisee of another's enforceable promise either declares that he or she holds the rights as promisee in trust or transfers those rights to another as trustee. In these latter types of cases, a trust is presently created at the time of the promisee's declaration (Clause (c) and Comment *e*) or at the time of the transfer (Clause (b) and Comment *d*); the trust property in these situations is a *chose in action*, that is, the promisee's rights under the promissory note or other contract.

Irrevocable life-insurance trusts, or even revocable insurance trusts, that are created by transfer (assignment) of the life-insurance policy to the trustee fall within Clause (b) and Comment *d* (trust created by inter vivos transfer) of this section and not within Clause (e) or this Comment *g* (trust created by contract or beneficiary designation).

Illustrations:

9. O, the owner of certain securities, tells B that before the end of the year she will declare herself trustee of those securities for B. No trust is created unless and until O declares herself trustee.

10. In consideration of valuable services that have subsequently been performed by B, A promised B that on the first of the next month he (A) will transfer certain securities to T in trust for B. Although no trust arises until A transfers the securities to T in trust, A is liable for breach of contract if he fails to create the trust.

12. S has designated T as payee of the proceeds of an insurance policy on S's life, pursuant to an independent agreement between S and T that T will hold the proceeds in trust for S's spouse for life, with remainder thereafter to be distributed to S's issue. S dies. T holds the insurance proceeds upon the agreed trust.

§ 11. Capacity of a Settlor to Create a Trust

(1) A person has capacity to create a trust by will to the same extent that the person has capacity to devise or bequeath the property free of trust.

(2) A person has capacity to create a revocable inter vivos trust by transfer to another or by declaration to the same extent that the person has capacity to create a trust by will.

(3) A person has capacity to create an irrevocable inter vivos trust by transfer to another or by declaration to the same extent that the person has capacity to transfer the property inter vivos free of trust in similar circumstances.

(4) A person has capacity to create a trust by exercising a power of appointment to the same extent that the person has capacity to create a trust of his or her own property under Subsection (1), (2), or (3) above, as appropriate to the type of transfer and trust being created.

(5) Under some circumstances, an agent under a durable power of attorney or the legal representative of a property owner who is under disability may create a trust on behalf of the property owner.

Comment on Subsection (1):

a. Testamentary trusts. An owner of property who has capacity to devise the property outright to another person has the capacity to transfer the property by will to be held by the transferee in trust. (The term "devise," generally today and in this Restatement, includes "bequeath.") A property owner who lacks this testamentary capacity does not have capacity to create a trust by will.

Different courts may define this degree of capacity in slightly different terms. As ordinarily stated, however, the essence of what is required is that the testator be able to understand the natural objects of his or her bounty and the nature and extent of his or her property, and be able to understand and make decisions about how he or she wishes to dispose of that property. (Also, a will may be invalidated because of minority or a derangement that affects the will.) The rules of testamentary capacity are not peculiar to the law of trusts, and further discussion or a precise statement of these rules is not within the scope of this Restatement.... See also Restatement Third, Property (Wills and Other Donative Transfers) § 8.1 and id., Comments *c* (general standard), *m* (lucid interval), and *s* (insane delusion, or derangement). See also id., Comment *f*, on burden of proof.

Comment on Subsection (2):

b. Revocable inter vivos trusts. An owner of property who has capacity to create a trust by will (see Comment *a*) also has capacity to create a revocable trust during life. Conversely, one who lacks testamentary capacity also lacks capacity to create a revocable inter vivos trust.

Ordinarily, the revocable trust serves as a will substitute with respect to all or part of the settlor's estate and has as its primary significance the determination of the persons who will receive the trust property, and in what interests, at the settlor's death. Therefore, the standards applicable to wills are also applicable in determining whether a revocable trust is valid or fails when later challenged by persons who would otherwise be the settlor's successors in interest.

Insofar as the establishment of a revocable trust may also present issues of the settlor's ability to understand matters beyond those involved in making a testamentary disposition, the consequences of inadequate understanding of those matters may be dealt with by reformation or other appropriate remedies that will not jeopardize the plan of disposition by making it dependent on a standard different or higher than that for making a will. Thus, for example, a trustee may be removed and replaced (§ 37), terms of administration may be modified (cf. § 62), and past transactions may be reviewed in a manner that is flexible and fair to all concerned, particularly when issues are raised after a settlor has ceased to function as trustee or has lost the capacity to monitor the actions of another as trustee. Cf. § 74.

Comment on Subsection (3):

c. Irrevocable inter vivos trusts. A property owner who has capacity to transfer property by outright gift inter vivos ordinarily has capacity to create an irrevocable trust during life. A property owner who does not have the capacity to make a gift lacks capacity to establish an irrevocable trust.

Rules concerning gift-making capacity are not peculiar to the law of trusts and are not within the scope of this Restatement. See generally Restatement Third, Property (Wills and Other Donative Transfers) § 8.1, Comment *d*. In general, however, this is a standard slightly higher than that for a will because, in addition to factors that testators must be capable of understanding, irrevocable donative transfers during life require an ability to understand the effects the disposition may have on the future financial security of the settlor/donor and of those who may be dependent on him or her.

Some irrevocable inter vivos trusts, however, are not donative, or at least not entirely. Trusts are sometimes created as a result of negotiations, as in the case of a trust that is established as part of a commercial transaction or in settlement of an adversary legal proceeding, such as an action for divorce. For these situations, higher standards are normally appropriate. Again, however, these rules are not peculiar to the law of trusts and are not within the scope of this Restatement. See generally Restatement Second, Contracts § 12, on capacity to contract.

Comment on Subsection (4):

d. Capacity of donee of power to appoint in trust. The donee of a power of appointment has the capacity to make an effective appointment in trust if the donee has capacity to make an effective transfer of owned property of like type to the trustee of a trust that is similar in testamentary, revocable, or irrevocable character. See Comments *a*, *b*, and *c*. Also, see generally Restatement Second, Property (Donative Transfers) § 18.1(1) and Comments *a* and *b* thereto [Restatement Third, Property (Wills and Other Donative Transfers) § 19.8].

Thus, a person holding a testamentary power of appointment may appoint in trust if, but only if, the power holder has testamentary capacity. The donee of a presently exercisable general power of appointment may exercise that power by appointing in revocable trust if, and only if, the donee has testamentary capacity. And a person who holds a presently exercisable power of appointment may appoint to a person as a trustee of an irrevocable trust if, and only if, the person has capacity to make an inter vivos transfer of property in which the power holder has a similar interest, by way of gift—or, if appropriate to the circumstances, by way of a commercial or negotiated disposition. See Comments *a*, *b*, and *c*.

General Comment:

e. Acts by owner under incapacity. A transfer in trust or a declaration of trust by a minor or incompetent adult is voidable, rather than void. It may therefore be ratified in the same manner as a purported transfer free of trust, either by the purported settlor after attaining or recovering legal capacity or, following the purported settlor's death, by those who would succeed to the property if the purported transfer were repudiated. Ratification may occur in these circumstances by failure of the purported settlor or successors in interest to repudiate the purported trust within a reasonable time. See Restatement Third, Property (Wills and Other Donative Transfers) § 8.1, Comment *g*; and Restatement Third, Restitution and Unjust Enrichment § 16.

Comment on Subsection (5):

f. Acts on behalf of owner under disability. Transfers of property belonging to minors and legally incompetent adults may be made in the course of managing their financial affairs by their guardians, conservators, or other legal representatives, or by the agent (attorney in fact) of an incompetent adult appointed and acting under a durable power of attorney executed before the principal's incapacity. The legal representative or holder of a durable power of attorney may also make charitable and other inter vivos gifts of the property of a minor or incompetent person, including gift-transfers in trust, but only to the extent authorized by the appropriate court or, expressly or impliedly, by the terms of the durable power.

Ordinarily, under principles of "substituted judgment" . . ., a court may authorize a legal representative to make such transfers of the minor's or mentally incompetent person's property as would be reasonable as a matter of the property owner's personal, family, tax, and estate-planning objectives. Under many statutes, however, by express provision or judicial interpretation, courts do not have power to authorize legal representatives to make wills for minors or legally incompetent persons. Similarly, under many durable-power-of-attorney statutes, it is not legally permissible for the terms of a durable power to authorize an agent to make a will for an incapacitated principal.

Nevertheless, even under statutes that preclude the making of wills for persons under legal disability, a court or the terms of a durable power may for some purposes authorize a legal representative or agent to create, amend, or revoke, or to transfer additional property to, a revocable trust or other will-substitute arrangement. See Uniform Trust Code § 602(e) and (f); and compare generally Restatement Third, Property (Wills and Other Donative Transfers) § 8.1, Comments *k* and *l*, and Restatement Second, Property (Donative Transfers) §§ 34.4(2) and 34.5. For example, despite a restriction against making a will for an incompetent person, it is proper for a court or principal to authorize a legal representative or agent to establish, modify, or enlarge a revocable inter vivos trust to serve purposes that are financially advantageous to the estate, such as probate avoidance and managerial efficiency.

The trust's distributive provisions, however, present more sensitive issues, which turn on the policy underlying the typical statute's will-making prohibition. Distributions directed or authorized by the provisions of a revocable trust established by a legal representative or agent must be consistent either: (i) with inter vivos gifts the legal representative or agent could be empowered to make directly (supra); or (ii) with post-death dispositions that, under the statute, the court may, or the terms of the durable power may and do, authorize the legal representative or agent to make of the affected property of the incompetent person.

In the second situation (alternative (ii), above), the effect of a statutory prohibition against will making by legal representatives or agents depends on the reasons underlying that prohibition. The underlying policy may reflect a narrow purpose (based on efficiency and tradition) of precluding the use of a particular device (a will) that relies on the safeguards of probate and of specific, well-established statutory formalities; or the will-making prohibition may instead manifest a more general, substantive policy against post-death dispositions by these fiduciaries that would alter the plan of disposition established by intestate succession or by an existing will executed by a person who has subsequently become incompetent.

The breadth and generality of the latter policy would ordinarily apply by analogy (cf. § 25(2) and Comments *d* and *e* thereto) to limit the post-death distributive provisions of a revocable inter vivos trust created by a legal representative or agent to dispositions that conform to the disposition of the affected property that would result, as the case may be, by operation of law or under the incompetent person's existing estate plan. Any departure from that pre-incompetency scheme of disposition would then be permissible only to the extent the adversely affected, expectant beneficiaries consent to relinquish some or all of their expected interests.

On the other hand, if the underlying policy is a narrow one that applies only to the making of wills by legal representatives or agents, and not to their use of will substitutes, the foregoing limitations on post-death distributive provisions (preceding paragraph) do not apply to the creation of revocable trusts by these fiduciaries.

Ultimately, the nature and breadth of the policy indicated by a will-making prohibition are matters of statutory interpretation. Durable-power-of-attorney legislation and principles of substituted judgment under conservatorship, guardianship, and other such statutes are designed to preserve for persons under disability much of the flexibility in financial management and planning that other property owners enjoy. Estate planning is fundamental to the objectives ordinarily implicit in such statutes; and sound, flexible planning requires actions that reflect not only the property owner's evolving circumstances and likely objectives but also changes in the law and in the personal and financial circumstances of potential beneficiaries. Furthermore, these statutes allow donative dispositions only with court authorization or as a result of authorization granted by a competent principal, with judicial scrutiny available for cases in which it is alleged that an agent's fiduciary authority has been exceeded or abused.

Accordingly, prohibitions against will making are generally to be strictly construed to prevent only the use of a particular device, the will, and not as reflecting a more general, substantive policy that extends to and prohibits the use of other methods of planning and accomplishing properly justified post-death disposition of estates of persons under disability.

In many states, the general preference for narrow construction is reinforced by statutes that, while prohibiting the making of wills, expressly enable a court or principal to authorize the use or amendment of certain other post-death dispositions or will substitutes. Some such statutes, for example, refer specifically to creating, amending, or enlarging revocable trusts, whereas other statutes or sections may authorize the closely related actions of selecting or changing post-death beneficial rights—such as beneficiary designations and payment options—under life-insurance policies, retirement plans, and the like.

A conservator, guardian, or other legal representative or an agent under a durable power of attorney may be authorized by court or the terms of a durable power to exercise a settlor's expressed or implied rights to withdraw funds or amend terms of a revocable trust in accordance with the foregoing principles applicable to the creation of revocable trusts by these fiduciaries. That is, legal representatives and agents may be authorized to exercise the incompetent settlor's reserved powers not only in circumstances and ways that are appropriate to the current needs of the settlor and the settlor's family but also as appropriate to the settlor's estate-planning objectives, based on (i) the principles of substituted judgment or the terms of the durable power and on (ii) what is proper in light of the policies underlying any applicable statutory prohibition against the making of wills by such fiduciaries. . . . .

§ 12. Trust Creation Induced by Undue Influence, Duress, Fraud, or Mistake

A transfer in trust or declaration of trust can be set aside, or the terms of a trust can be reformed, upon the same grounds as those upon which a transfer of property not in trust can be set aside or reformed.

Comment:

a. In general. Where no consideration is paid for the creation of a trust, it can be set aside or reformed upon the same grounds, such as fraud, duress, undue influence, or mistake, as those upon which a gratuitous transfer of property not in trust can be set aside or reformed. . . . . See also § 62 ("Rescission and Reformation"). If the settlor is deceased, the trust may be set aside by the person to whom the property would belong if the transfer or declaration had not been made, and reformation of the trust may be sought by persons whose authority or rights have been affected by the circumstances justifying the reformation.

Rules governing avoidance, reformation, and the effects of wrongful conduct and mistake with respect to gratuitous inter vivos transfers and testamentary dispositions are not peculiar to inter vivos and testamentary trusts. Thus, details of the law governing these matters are not within the scope of this Restatement. See more generally Restatement Second, Property (Donative Transfers) § 34.7. Also see Restatement Third, Property (Wills and Other Donative Transfers) §§ 12.1, 12.2 . . . .

Where the owner of property receives consideration for making a declaration of trust or a transfer in trust, or for causing a transfer to be made in trust, the rules governing rescission, reformation, and the effects of wrongful conduct, mistake, and failure of consideration are the rules applicable to contracts or transfers for value, including rules concerning bona fide purchase. Details of the law governing these matters is not within the scope of this Restatement. Compare Restatement Second, Contracts §§ 159–177 (Ch. 7 dealing with "misrepresentation, duress and undue influence"), and cf. id. §§ 71–109 (Ch. 4 on "formation of contracts—[failure of] consideration"); also compare Restatement Second, Property (Donative Transfers) § 34.9.

The settlor cannot set aside or reform a trust to the extent or in a manner that would be inequitable to a beneficiary who has changed position without notice of the grounds for rescission or reformation. . . . . Compare § 10, Comment *g* . . . .

b. Trust creation wrongfully procured. Where no consideration is paid for the creation of a trust, the settlor can set the trust aside if its creation was induced by fraud, duress, or undue influence. This is true not only when the wrongful conduct was that of a beneficiary or trustee but also when it was that of a third person and the beneficiaries and trustee did not personally know or have reason to know of the improper conduct.

On the question of whether a settlor has been induced to create a trust by undue influence, the following factors may be of importance: (1) whether and to what extent a fiduciary or confidential relationship existed between the person charged with undue influence and the settlor at the time the settlor was persuaded to create the trust; (2) whether it was the trustee, a beneficiary, or a third person who persuaded the settlor to create the trust; (3) whether and to what extent it was improvident for the settlor to create the trust; (4) the settlor's age, health, intelligence, and business experience and whether the settlor had independent legal advice at the time of the decision to create the trust; and (5) whether the character and provisions of the trust are such that it would have been unnatural for a person in the settlor's position to create it. Most of these factors are also likely to be of importance in cases involving allegations of fraud.

On the nature, proof, and effects of fraud, undue influence, and other initial wrongdoing, compare § 24, Comments *e* and *f* (and cf. § 18), dealing with failure to comply with formal requirements for the creation of trusts.

On the possible effects of change of position by innocent beneficiaries, see Comment *a*.

c. *Mistake.* The settlor may be able to rescind or reform a trust created as a result of a material mistake. See § 62.

Where no consideration is paid for the creation of the trust, it is sufficient to show that the settlor was induced by mistake to create the trust, although neither the trustee nor the beneficiary shared in the mistake or knew or had reason to know of it. . . . Also see generally Restatement Third, Property (Wills and Other Donative Transfers) § 8.3.

On the other hand, where the owner of property receives consideration for making a transfer of the property in trust, a mistake on the part of the transferor alone ordinarily is not sufficient ground for setting aside the transfer. See generally Restatement Second, Contracts §§ 151–158 (Ch. 6 on "mistake").

On the possible effects of change of position by innocent beneficiaries, see Comment *a*.

More generally on termination, modification, and splitting of trusts by settlors, trustees, courts, and beneficiaries, see §§ 63–68.

d. *Cross-reference: incapacity of settlor.* General rules for setting aside transfers of property on the ground that the transferor was under incapacity, such as infancy or legal incompetency, are also applicable to an owner's purported creation of a trust by declaration or transfer. See generally § 11, Comment *e*.

§ 13. Intention to Create Trust

A trust is created only if the settlor properly manifests an intention to create a trust relationship.

Comment:

a. *In general.* In order to create a trust the settlor, alone or together with the trustee, must properly manifest an intention to create a relationship that constitutes a trust as defined in § 2. (On what is a "proper" manifestation of trust intent, see Comment *b* and §§ 4, 17, and 22.)

It is immaterial whether or not the settlor knows that the intended relationship is called a trust, and whether or not the settlor knows the precise characteristics of a trust relationship.

The manifestation of intention requires an external expression of intention as distinguished from undisclosed intention. See § 4. There may, however, be a sufficient manifestation of the intention to create a trust without communication of that intention to the beneficiary or to the trustee or any third person. See Comment *b*. See more generally § 14.

On the other hand, no trust is created unless the settlor manifests an intention to impose enforceable duties. See Comment *c*. Also, a property owner's manifestation of an intention to transfer property to another as an outright gift is not a manifestation of an intention to declare a trust. See § 16(2).

In addition, the manifestation of intent to create a trust inter vivos ordinarily requires that the intention be to create the trust at that time. Thus, an intention to create a trust at some time in the future ordinarily does not create an express trust. See § 10, Comment *g*, and § 16, Comments *b* and *c*. (On contractual situations, compare § 10, Clause (e) and Comment *g*.) Nor will the mere manifestation of intention to transfer property inter vivos to another as trustee for one or more third persons, when not accompanied by an effective transfer (§ 16(1)), ordinarily be treated as a manifestation of an intention by the property owner to make a declaration of trust. See § 16(2) and Comment *d* thereto.

On the possibility that subsequent actions, considered together with an initial manifestation of intention to create a trust in the future, may suffice to create a trust by declaration or transfer, see § 16, Comment *b* . . . .

b. *Mode of manifesting trust intention*. Except as otherwise provided by statute, such as a statute of frauds (see § 22) or a wills act (see § 17), the required manifestation of intention to create a trust may be by written or spoken words or by conduct.

No particular manner of expression is necessary to manifest the trust intention. Thus, a trust may be created without the settlor's use of words such as "trust" or "trustee," and the fact that a transferor uses the word "trust" or "trustee" does not necessarily indicate the intention to create a relationship that constitutes a trust as defined in § 2.

In interpreting the words and conduct of property owners, circumstances that shed light upon their intentions are relevant. Evidence of such circumstances is admissible except when excluded by the parol-evidence rule (see § 21), by a statute of frauds or of wills, or some other rule of law. (If a statute requires a particular method of manifesting the trust intention, as in the case of trusts of interests in land or trusts to be created by will, the manifestation of intention normally must comply with the statute. See § 22 and § 17.) Acts or communications prior to and subsequent to, as well as those contemporaneous with, the transfer or other act that is claimed to create a trust may be relevant in determining whether a property owner had the requisite intention to create a trust. See § 4. . . . .

On the question of whether a trust is created when A deposits $10,000 in a savings account in the name of "A, trustee for B," or the like, see § 26.

c. *Communication of intention*. Although there is no manifestation of trust intention unless there is an external expression of that intention (see Comment *a*), there is no requirement in the absence of a statute that the intention to create a trust inter vivos must be manifested in any particular language (Comment *b*), form, or manner. What is essential is that some oral statement, writing, or action (including, for example, an act of delivery in the context of prior communications with or from the intended trustee) manifest the settlor's intention that a trust should arise at that time.

The intention to create a trust may be sufficiently manifested by a settlor without handing an instrument evidencing that intention or otherwise communicating the intention to the trustee, the beneficiary, or any other person. See § 14. The failure of a property owner (other than a testator) to communicate such an intention to anyone, however (such as the failure to hand anyone the instrument an owner had drawn up declaring an intention to hold certain property in trust), is some, but not conclusive, evidence that the property owner had not arrived at a definite, present intention to create a trust. See, e.g., § 14, Comment *c* (where it is also suggested that, in the context of a possible declaration of trust, noncommunication may be some evidence of an intention to create a revocable trust). See also, on possible revocability, § 63, Comments *b* and *c*.

d. *Precatory language.* Unless a testator or other transferor manifests an intention to impose enforceable duties on the transferee, the intention to create a trust is lacking and no trust is created. Whether a transferor intended to impose the obligations essential to a trust, or merely intended to explain the motivation for a bequest or to express a nonbinding wish or recommendation, is sometimes unclear and is therefore a matter for interpretation.

The inference normally to be drawn from precatory language accompanying a transfer, suggesting that the transferee use or dispose of the property in a certain manner, is that the transferor intends to leave it to the transferee to decide whether or not to follow the suggestion. It is no longer the case, as it once appeared to be in England, that the wish of a testator, like that of a sovereign, is to be taken as a command. And no trust is created if the transferor manifests an intention merely to impose a moral obligation on the transferee.

In determining the intention of the transferor, the following circumstances among others may be important: (1) the specific terms and overall tenor of the words used; (2) the definiteness or indefiniteness of the property involved; (3) the ease or difficulty of ascertaining possible trust purposes and terms, and the specificity or vagueness of the possible beneficiaries and their interests; (4) the interests or motives and the nature and degree of concerns that may reasonably be supposed to have influenced the transferor; (5) the financial situation, dependencies, and expectations of the parties; (6) the transferor's prior conduct, statements, and relationships with respect to possible trust beneficiaries; (7) the personal and any fiduciary relationships between the transferor and the transferee; (8) other dispositions the transferor is making or has made of his or her wealth; and (9) whether the result of construing the disposition as involving a trust or not would be such as a person in the situation of the transferor would be likely to desire.

Vagueness or uncertainty with respect to possible purposes or beneficial interests tends to suggest that the transferor did not intend to create a trust. Nevertheless, if the language of the disposition and other evidence establish the transferor's intention to create a trust, its specific terms may be supplied by interpretation and construction, with application of resulting-trust doctrine (§§ 7–8) as necessary. If these processes fail to supply the elements and provisions essential to a valid trust (see § 3 and also Part 3, Chapters 6–9 (§§ 27–48)), however, the intention to create an express trust that cannot be carried out requires the transferee to hold upon a resulting trust for the transferor or for the transferor's estate or other successors in interest.

Illustrations:

5. A devises Blackacre to B "hoping he will continue it in the family." In the absence of other evidence of A's intention, B is entitled to the property beneficially and does not take it in trust.

8. H devises all of his property to his wife, W, adding his "request that she use whatever of it she thinks necessary for the support and care of my brother, B." B is elderly, in bad health, and unable to provide for his own needs, and for some time had been supported by H. W's independent wealth is very large relative to what may reasonably be needed for her future security and comfort. These circumstances of B and W existed at the time H executed his will, as well as at his death. In the absence of other evidence of H's intention, W takes H's estate in trust for her own benefit as well as B's, with a duty imposed upon W as trustee to make reasonable provision for B's support and care. The circumstances here overcome the inference normally drawn from precatory words; and they also overcome the inference that a trustee holds excess funds (or interests not expressly granted to others) upon resulting trust rather than beneficially. See § 8, Comment *f*. On the possibility that a disposition such as that in this Illustration might create an equitable charge, and on the distinctions involved, see § 5, Comment *h*.

If property is transferred to a person to dispose of in any manner or to any persons the transferee may choose, this is not a manifestation of trust intention and the transferee takes the property beneficially. If, on the other hand, a disposition is made for the benefit of the transferee and the transferee's family, it is a question of interpretation whether the manifested intention of the transferor is to create a trust or to make a beneficial gift to the transferee with an expression of the motive for making the gift. On the meaning of "family" if a trust is intended, see § 45, Comment *e*; cf. Restatement Second, Property (Donative Transfers) § 24.2 [Restatement Third, Property (Wills and Other Donative Transfers) § 19.23].

Illustration:

10. A bequeaths $50,000 to B "to be used for the support of his wife and himself." In the absence of evidence of a contrary intention, a trust is created. (If property remains after the deaths of B and his wife, the ordinary inference would be that the property reverts to A's successors in interest. See § 8.)

§ 14. Notice and Acceptance Not Required to Create Trust

A trust can be created without notice to or acceptance by any beneficiary or trustee.

Comment:

a. In general. Frequently, prior to the testator's death, the terms of a will that creates a testamentary trust are communicated neither to any of its beneficiaries nor to the trustee it names. In fact, in the case of a holographic will, the existence and contents of the document are often communicated to no one. The necessary transfer to create a testamentary trust is effectuated simply by the combination of the testator's death and the prior execution of a valid, unrevoked will containing the essential terms of the intended trust. See § 17. The beneficiaries remain free thereafter to disclaim the interests provided for them (cf. § 51, Comment *f*), and a person who is named as trustee may decline to act in that capacity (§ 35).

Much the same can be said of trusts created by declaration or by inter vivos transfer. Such a trust may come into existence with no communication to anyone when a written declaration (§ 10(c)) is neither lawyer-assisted nor initially disclosed. Even though an effective present transfer of the property is required (§ 10(b)) to create a trust by the settlor's inter vivos transfer to another as trustee, the desired result does not require disclosure of the trust intention or other contents of a writing at the time of its delivery.

b. Trusts created by will. Where a will manifests the testator's intention to create a trust and the terms of the trust are set forth in the will, the trust will come into existence upon the death of the testator. This is true despite the testator's loss of testamentary capacity before death but after the execution of the will.

The trust is also effectively created even though the will names no trustee or the designated trustee predeceases the testator or otherwise fails or declines to serve as trustee. If the will makes no provision for filling the vacancy in the trusteeship in a case of this type, an appropriate court ordinarily will do so. An exception exists for the extraordinary situation in which the settlor manifests an intention that the trust shall not arise or the purposes of the trust cannot be carried out unless the designated person acts as trustee. On the general principle that, once created, a trust will not fail for want of a trustee, see § 31.

If property is devised or bequeathed to a sole trustee who declines to act or predeceases the testator, or to several co-trustees who all decline appointment or predecease the testator, title to the property passes instead to the substitute or successor trustee designated in the will. If no such trustee is designated, title passes to the testator's executor subject to a constructive trust requiring the executor to transfer the trust property upon the intended trust to a new trustee appointed pursuant to procedures prescribed in the will or applicable statute or to a trustee appointed by the court. In many states by statute, however, title to the trust property is in a court or is simply suspended until a new trustee is appointed. On appointment of trustees generally, see § 34. . . . .

On situations in which one of several testamentary trustees predeceases the testator or declines to serve, see Comment *e*. See also § 34, Comments *d* and *e*.

c. Trusts created by declaration. An inter vivos trust, revocable or irrevocable, may be created by declaration without acceptance by any of the beneficiaries. Once the trust comes into being as the result of a property owner's declaration that he or she presently holds certain of his or her own property upon a particular trust, it is immaterial that the settlor dies or becomes legally incompetent or bankrupt before any of the beneficiaries or anyone else is informed of the existence of the trust.

Although notice to the beneficiaries is not essential to the creation of a trust by declaration, the failure of the property owner to notify anyone of the declaration may be some but not conclusive evidence that the property owner did not intend immediately to create a trust; or it may be some evidence that although a trust is created the declarant reserves a power to revoke it. See § 12, Comment *c*. Compare § 26, Comment *a*; § 63, Comments *a* and *b*. . . . .

c(1). Beneficiary's disclaimer. If, upon learning that a trust has been created and without expressly or impliedly accepting its benefits, an intended beneficiary disclaims a beneficial interest, that interest is eliminated retroactively. The trust nevertheless continues for the other beneficiaries. A disclaimed interest may be absorbed by the interests of other beneficiaries, such as by acceleration of future interests, or otherwise through construction or interpretation. If these processes fail to fill the void left by a disclaimer, a reversion will be left in the settlor or the settlor's successors in interest. On resulting trusts of this type, see §§ 7–8.

In the event of disclaimer by a sole beneficiary or by all beneficiaries, the person who declared the trust or that person's successors in interest will hold the property free of trust.

d. Trusts created by inter vivos transfer. If the owner of property intends to create a trust by transferring the property to another but title does not pass to the intended trustee for want of delivery of the property or deed, no trust is created. Ordinarily title to the property remains in the owner free of trust. See § 16, Comment *b*.

Delivery to a third person, however, may be effective to pass the title to the intended trustee, even though the trustee has no knowledge of the transfer. For example, if delivery is made in this fashion, ordinarily at least (but see § 16, Comment *c*), the intended express trust is established. If, however, in receiving the property or the deed of conveyance, the third person is to act solely as the property owner's agent for purpose of making delivery but has not done so, there is no transfer. In that event, the intended trust is not created, since the property still belongs to the principal. Whether in such a situation an intended trust may be given effect by constructive trust under some circumstances, see § 16, Comment *c*.

Once created a trust is not affected by the death, legal incompetency, or bankruptcy of the settlor (assuming no fraudulent conveyance, see § 29, Comment *b*), even before the trustee learns of the trust or accepts it. Nor is the trust affected by the settlor's death, loss of competency, or bankruptcy before any of the beneficiaries learn of or accept the trust.

When a trust is to be created by a property owner's inter vivos transfer to another as trustee (whether by delivery to the trustee or to a third person), the trustee may decline to act as trustee if he or she has not by words or conduct previously manifested consent to serve. See § 35. The effect of the intended trustee's disclaimer of the trusteeship after delivery is to vest the title in a successor trustee if any is named in the terms of the trust, and if not then to restore to the transferor the title that had passed to the intended trustee, but not the beneficial interests. The transferor thereupon becomes constructive trustee of the property for the intended beneficiaries and purposes. As constructive trustee, unless the intended express trust was revocable, the transferor is under a duty either to make (expressly or impliedly) a declaration of trust or to transfer the property to a new trustee (to be selected by the transferor or, if necessary, by the court) upon the intended express trust. Compare Comment *b*. This is an application of the principle that, normally, a trust having once been created will not fail for want of a trustee. See § 31. . . . .

Although delivery of the trust property or a deed of gift to a third person can effectively pass title to the intended trustee even without the latter's knowledge, where there is an attempted delivery to the intended trustee personally and the intended trustee refuses to accept delivery, title to the trust property does not pass. Accordingly, no trust is created, and title to the property remains in the owner free of the intended express trust. If the transferor wishes, of course, the desired trust may be created by declaration or by a new transfer to a new trustee of the transferor's choice; but the transferor is under no obligation to do so. On the other hand, if the settlor agrees, the intended trustee may accept the delivery and permit the title to the property to pass to him or her but reserve the power to decline to act as trustee (see § 35), thereby avoiding the failure of the intended trust (see § 16, Comment *b*).

On the possibility that the owner's acts of attempted transfer may provide a basis for the imposition of a constructive trust if the intended trustee refuses to accept delivery and the owner dies or becomes incompetent without having a reasonable opportunity to establish the desired trust, see § 16, Comment *c*.

If an intended trust beneficiary has not expressly or impliedly manifested acceptance of a beneficial interest, the beneficiary may disclaim that interest. The disclaimed interest is retroactively eliminated but the trust will continue for the other beneficiaries, with adaptation through construction or interpretation or, if necessary, by partial reversionary interest. Compare Comment *c(1)*.

In the event of disclaimer by a sole beneficiary or by all beneficiaries, the trustee holds the property upon resulting trust for the settlor or the settlor's successors in interest. See generally §§ 7, 8.

e. *Disclaimer by (or death of) one of several trustees.* If property is transferred inter vivos to two or more persons as co-trustees, title passes to them as joint tenants in trust. If one of them declines the trusteeship, the title passes to and is held in trust by the other or others alone.

If property is transferred by will to multiple persons as trustees and one of them declines to act or predeceases the testator, title passes under the will in trust to the other or others alone.

On the question whether a new co-trustee will be appointed to take the place of the disclaiming or deceased trustee, see § 34, especially Comments *d* and *e*.

§ 15. Consideration Not Required to Create Trust

The owner of property can create a trust of the property by will or by declaration or transfer inter vivos, whether or not consideration is received for doing so.

Comment:

a. *In general.* Most trusts are created gratuitously. The absence of consideration to the settlor is immaterial to the validity of such a trust, whether created by a properly executed will or declaration or by an effective transfer inter vivos. It is also immaterial that the trustee receives no consideration apart from the transfer of the trust property. . . . .

b. *Promise to create a trust.* A promise to create a trust in the future is enforceable if, but only if, the requirements for an enforceable contract are satisfied. This is true whether the promise is one to create the trust by declaration or by inter vivos or testamentary transfer.

Where a possible declaration of trust is involved, it often becomes a question of interpretation whether the property owner intends to create a trust of the property at that time of the statement or is merely promising to become trustee of the property by a declaration to be made at some time in the future.

Where the promise to create a trust is legally enforceable, the usual inference is that the trust does not come into being until the promise to hold or transfer in trust is voluntarily or involuntarily performed. On the possibility, however, that the trust may arise at the time the enforceable promise is made, see § 10, Comment *g*; and also see § 25, Comment *c* (on insurance trusts and the like).

A promise to create a trust in the future is fundamentally different from the situation in which the promisee of *another's* enforceable promise either declares that he or she holds the rights as promisee in trust or transfers those rights to some person as trustee. In these latter types of cases, a trust is created at the time of the promisee's declaration or transfer. The trust property in such a case is a *chose* in action; that is, the trust property is the promisee's rights under the promissory note or other contract. See § 10, Comment *g*.

§ 16. Ineffective Inter Vivos Transfers

(1) If a property owner undertakes to make a donative inter vivos disposition in trust by transferring property to another as trustee, an express trust is not created if the property owner fails during life to complete the contemplated transfer of the property. In some circumstances, however, the trust intention of such a property owner who dies or becomes incompetent may be given effect by constructive trust in order to prevent unjust enrichment of the property owner's successors in interest.

(2) If a property owner intends to make an outright gift inter vivos but fails to make the transfer that is required in order to do so, the gift intention will not be given effect by treating it as a declaration of trust.

Comment:

a. In general; scope of section. Except for trusts that are created by declaration (see § 10(c) and related Comment *e*) or by contract (see § 10(e), and related Comment *g*, and § 15, Comment *b*), a transfer of the intended trust property is required for the creation of an express trust, whether during life or at death.

The effectiveness of a transfer for these purposes, that is, to establish an inter vivos or testamentary trust, respectively, is determined either by rules that govern the making of gifts or by those governing devises. These bodies of rules are not peculiar to trust dispositions and therefore are not comprehensively discussed in this Restatement. See generally Restatement Second, Property (Donative Transfers) §§ 31.1–32.4 (on "accomplishing a donative transfer in the donor's lifetime") [Restatement Third, Property (Wills and Other Donative Transfers) §§ 6.1–6.3] and §§ 33.1, 33.2 (on "accomplishing a donative transfer by a will") [Restatement Third, Property (Wills and Other Donative Transfers) §§ 3.1–3.3].

Special issues of trust law, however, often arise in connection with the effectiveness or ineffectiveness of apparent attempts to make donative transfers inter vivos. These are the subject of this section.

Testamentary trusts do not present the special transfer problems discussed in this section. The transfers that are necessary to create the equitable interests of testamentary trust beneficiaries, like those that create outright devises, simply require the execution of a valid will that remains unrevoked at the time of the testator's death, and that also manifests the trust intention when a trust objective is involved. See § 10, Comment *c*; § 14, Comment *b*; and § 17.

Apart from the issues in this section involving the effectiveness of intended transfers during life, there are several related problems specially associated with the creation of inter vivos trusts. These are considered in § 13 and in § 14, Comment *d.* See also § 15, Comment *b.* On special problems associated with declarations of trust, see § 10, Comment *e.*

b. Intended inter vivos transfer to another as trustee: effective or ineffective? When an owner of property intends to create an inter vivos trust other than by declaration, the owner must transfer the property to the intended trustee. If the property owner attempts to make a transfer in trust but the intended transfer is not effective, no express trust is created.

An intended or contemplated transfer in trust may be ineffective for a number of reasons. The transfer may not be completed for want of delivery of the subject matter or instrument of transfer; or it may be ineffective because a would-be settlor does not own the intended trust property at the time of the purported transfer. In cases of these types, no trust is created. In the latter of these situations, however, actions of the would-be settlor after acquiring the intended trust property, considered together with the initial manifestation of trust intent, may serve to perfect the transfer and thereby create the trust at the later time. . . . .

In the first of the above-mentioned situations, where there has been no delivery, the title to the property ordinarily (but see Comment *c*) remains in the owner free of trust. Even when an owner of property surrenders possession of it or of a document of transfer in a manner that otherwise would be sufficient to transfer the property to a trustee, if the property owner does not intend to make a presently effective transfer there is no transfer of the title. Accordingly, no trust is created and the owner retains title to the property, ordinarily free of trust. Again, however, subsequent actions of the property owner, considered together with the initial manifestation of trust intention, may constitute delivery, thereby completing the transfer and bringing the trust into being.

On the other hand, delivery sufficient to pass title to a trustee, like transfers to others as donees of outright gifts, may occur without handing over the property or an instrument of transfer to the intended trustee. Thus, a delivery may be made in escrow or may be accomplished by acts of constructive or symbolic delivery performed with the requisite intention to make a present transfer. On donative transfers without using a document of transfer, see Restatement Second, Property (Donative Transfers) § 31.1, Comments *b* and *c* (and compare id. Comment *g* on gifts relating to registered personal property); on delivery of a document of transfer, see id. § 32.2 . . . (property other than land) and § 32.3 (land) [Restatement Third, Property (Wills and Other Donative Transfers) § 6.2].

Furthermore, if the owner of property transfers it to another with the intention that it be held immediately in trust, a trust may then arise even though by the terms of the trust the settlor reserves the power to revoke and modify the trust in whole or in part. See § 17, Comment *a,* and particularly § 25, Subsection (1) and Comments *a* through *c.* Similarly, a declaration of trust is not incomplete, nor is it a mere expression of an intention to create a trust in the future, simply because of the declarant's reservation of power to revoke and amend (§ 25(1)). In either of these situations the revocable inter vivos trust may be created even though the terms of the revocable trust also include the reservation to the settlor of a life interest in the property, and even though the transfer or declaration of trust thereby serves primarily as a substitute for a will (id.). See generally Restatement Second, Property

(Donative Transfers) § 32.4 [Restatement Third, Property (Wills and Other Donative Transfers) § 7.1].

If the owner of property attempts ineffectively to transfer it inter vivos to another as trustee but has received consideration for the purported transfer, the property owner is under a duty to complete the transfer similar to the duty that would exist if the property owner had made a contract to convey the property free of trust (see § 10, Clause (e) and Comment *g*, and § 15, Comment *b*). In a proper case, specific performance may be had. See Restatement Second, Contracts §§ 359, 360.

Similarly, if the owner of property makes a defective transfer of it to another in trust and the intended beneficiary so changes position in reliance on the purported transfer that it is inequitable to permit the owner to retain the property, the property owner may be compelled in equity to transfer the property upon the intended trust, or other appropriate relief may be granted. See Restatement of Restitution § 164 and Restatement Second, Contracts § 90 . . . .

Illustrations:

2. O, the owner of Blackacre, executes a deed by which he might convey Blackacre to T in trust for B for life, remainder to B's issue, but makes no delivery of the deed. The title to Blackacre remains in O free of trust.

3. At a time when her father is alive but terminally ill, O executes an instrument whereby she purports gratuitously to transfer "all my rights and interests in the estate of my father" to T as trustee for B for life, remainder to B's issue, and she delivers the instrument to T. No trust is created because O's bare expectancy with respect to her father's assets is not property that O can gratuitously transfer or that T can hold in trust.

4. The same facts as in Illustration 3, except that O's father had died shortly before she executed and delivered the instrument to T. Even though her father's estate remains subject to administration and is not ready for distribution, a trust is created by O's assignment of her then existing property rights to T as trustee for the intended beneficiaries and purposes. (On the "trust property" aspect of this Illustration and Illustration 3, see §§ 40–41.)

Unless the contrary is expressly provided in an applicable statute, or is necessarily implied from its provisions, formalities prescribed for the creation of a recordable document, or otherwise for protection of or from third parties, need not be satisfied in order to make a valid donative transfer, that is, one that is effective as between the transferor and the transferee(s). See Restatement Second, Property (Donative Transfers) § 32.3, Comment *a* [Restatement Third, Property (Wills and Other Donative Transfers § 6.3, Comment *c*].

Good practice certainly calls for the use of additional formalities and the taking of appropriate further steps, such as changes of registration, or the execution and recordation of deeds to land. Nevertheless, a writing signed by the settlor, or a trust agreement signed by the settlor and trustee, manifesting the settlor's present intention thereby to transfer specified property (such as all property listed on an attached schedule) is sufficient to create a trust. . . .

The rights and interests of transferees may be later perfected with respect to third parties, and for the protection of third parties, by steps taken by the settlor or, even following the settlor's death or incompetency, by court order or other procedures appropriate to the circumstances and applicable law or practice. Compare also the discussion of declarations of trust in the last two paragraphs of § 10, Comment *e*.

c. *Incomplete transfer sometimes given effect by constructive trust.* Sometimes an attempted inter vivos transfer is ineffective to create an express trust even though the property owner has taken all the steps that would be required of the owner personally in order to implement the transfer in the intended manner. In such a case, the acts and circumstances may nevertheless satisfy the underlying legal policy of determining, by objective and reliable evidence, that the property owner had arrived at a definite, considered intention to create a trust either immediately or soon thereafter.

Cases of this type may arise because the title to intended trust property remains in a would-be settlor as a result of some technical defect or incompleteness in the intended transfer. For example, a person named as trustee may be dead or otherwise incapable of taking title to the intended trust property, or the trustee may have been insufficiently designated. Thus, an attempted transfer of intended trust property to the intended trustee may fail despite the property owner's delivery of the property or the document of transfer in escrow. Similarly, an intended transfer may remain incomplete because an essentially ministerial act has not been performed. For example, a property owner may have placed property in the hands of his or her own agent with instruction to complete delivery promptly or as soon as conveniently possible (or at some time or upon the occurrence of some event that would have been expected to occur soon within the property owner's lifetime) but without need of further direction or action by the property owner.

In these various situations, if the property owner becomes legally incompetent or dies, it may be appropriate for a court of equity to compel the legal representative of the incompetent property owner or the deceased property owner's successors in interest to transfer property upon the intended trust. Provided the property owner had not expressly or impliedly by inaction manifested an intention to retain or reacquire the property free of trust, a constructive trust may be enforced to prevent the unjust enrichment that would occur if the property owner's successors in interest were allowed to retain or acquire property that is satisfactorily shown to have been intended to benefit others. This is so even though, at the time of death or incompetency, the property owner personally had the right to terminate or modify the agent's authority or to refuse to correct a defect in the intended transfer. . . . . Also see generally and compare Restatement of Restitution § 164.

In some of these cases, of course, it may be difficult to determine whether the property owner had formed a sufficiently definite intention presently to proceed with the creation of the trust, or whether the owner had simply manifested an intention gratuitously to create a trust at some future time. Such questions are inevitably ones for interpretation. The critical issue in these cases is likely to be whether or not, under the chosen manner of making the transfer, it had been contemplated that the property owner personally would take some further action or make some further manifestation of intention before the transfer to the intended trustee was to be completed. Events and circumstances, however, may provide a negative answer to this question and satisfy the underlying policies by supplying both the evidentiary certainty and the likelihood of deliberation that support carrying out a trust intention. Thus, in a given situation the steps actually taken may supply the objective, reliable manifestations of intention needed to show that the now deceased or legally incompetent property owner had made a serious, definite decision to proceed with a transfer in trust (whether revocable or irrevocable), with no showing that this objective had been abandoned.

On disclaimer by the intended trustee and the possibility of using a constructive trust to implement the intended disposition, see § 14, Comment *d*.

Illustration:

7. O, the owner of Blackacre, executes a deed by which she might convey Blackacre to T as trustee for B for life, remainder to B's issue. Because of her imminent departure on a business trip to Europe, O hands the deed to her financial adviser, A, asking him to act as her agent to make delivery to T as soon as A has an opportunity to do so. O dies in an automobile accident in Europe shortly after arriving there and before A has an opportunity to make delivery to T. Although O could have telephoned A immediately before her death to terminate his authority as her agent, and although title to Blackacre remained in A, her personal representative or other successors in interest can be compelled to transfer Blackacre to T in trust for the intended purposes and beneficiaries.

The result in Illustration 7 is not based on dilatory conduct on the part of A or otherwise confined to cases that invite application of the maxim that equity treats as done what ought to have been done.

Illustration:

8. Same facts as in Illustration 7, above, except that the instrument executed by O and handed to A is not a document of transfer but one authorizing A, as O's agent, to receive on her behalf distribution of certain valuable chattels from the executor of her deceased father's will, with instructions to A thereafter to deliver those chattels to T, as trustee, to sell them and to hold and invest the proceeds upon a trust for B for life, remainder to B's issue. Prior to A's receipt and transfer of the property to T, no trust is created. Accordingly, if A dies under these circumstances, the express trust she had intended to establish does not exist because the transfer which she contemplated would create the trust has not been completed. T or the intended beneficiaries, however, can by constructive trust compel O's successors in interest to transfer the property upon the intended trust.

d. Incomplete gift or declaration of trust. If the owner of property attempts to transfer it inter vivos to another person for that person's benefit but the conduct is not sufficient to constitute a gift, the property owner's conduct will not be treated as a declaration of trust. The reason is, in part at least, that the property owner had no intention to act as a trustee. (On declarations of trust generally, see § 10(c) and Comment *e* thereto. The possibility that an incomplete transfer, intended as an *outright* gift, may be given effect by constructive trust under some circumstance is not within the scope of this Restatement. Compare, however, Comment *c*.)

The foregoing rule is simply stated but not always easy to apply, for it is often difficult to determine whether the property owner's actual intention was to make an outright gift or to make a declaration of trust. An effective declaration of trust does not require an express reference to "trust" or "trustee," or the use of an expression such as "I hereby hold" the property for another's benefit. The settlor need not even know that the relationship that is being created is called a trust, as long as the intended relationship and rights and duties are those the law treats as a trust. See § 5, Comment *a*, and § 13, Comment *b*.

Thus, for example, it may be difficult to determine (i) whether a property owner's actions and statements merely express what amounts to a tentative plan or expectation of making an outright gift to a certain family member when the donee is of sufficient age to assume responsibility for managing and expending the funds, or (ii) whether they express something equivalent to "I hereby hold this property in trust for X, to be distributed to her when she reaches age 22." If the former is what the property owner has in mind, the intention is too indefinite and tentative to be given effect should the owner die or become legally incompetent before the contemplated gift is implemented. On the other hand, if the property owner's intention is immediately to assume a role the law considers to be that of trusteeship, there is a declaration of trust. Thus, with no further action being needed to establish the trust, the intended beneficiary would be entitled to the intended property rights even in the event of the declarant's death or incompetency.

The process of interpreting a property owner's actions and oral or even written statements in such a case is complicated not only by the endless variations of language and conduct but also by the variety of dispositions a transferor is permitted to make. For example, the law allows the immediate creation of presently existing future interests, and even presently existing interests (legal or equitable, present or future, vested or contingent) that are subject to revocation and amendment. See Introductory Note to Chapter 3, Comment *a* to § 17, and § 25(1).

If the manifestations of intention provide reliable, objective evidence of a deceased property owner's intended purpose and there is no indication that this purpose has been abandoned, the conduct and words ordinarily are interpreted as intending a type of transaction that would be effective to accomplish this purpose under the circumstances. That is, the preferred interpretation in marginal cases of this type is not that the property owner was merely expressing an intention to make a gift in the future but rather that the owner intended a declaration of trust. (If tenable under the circumstances, it is also possible that marginal acts that might or might not constitute delivery would be treated as a delivery based on a finding that they were in fact undertaken with the intention of making a present, outright gift. See Restatement Second, Property (Donative Transfers) § 31.1 and § 32.1, Comment *g* [Restatement Third, Property (Wills and Other Donative Transfers) § 6.2].)

Illustration:

9. O, the owner of certain bonds, signs a brief writing that states: "These bonds are for X when he becomes 22." Shortly following O's death, the writing and the bonds are found together in her safe-deposit box. Absent additional evidence of O's intention, she has (by declaration, § 10(c)) created a trust of the bonds for X. In the circumstances, her written words, securely stored and segregated with the bonds, are interpreted as meaning that "I hereby hold these bonds [as trustee] for X, to be turned over to him when he reaches age 22," rather than that "these are bonds of which I plan to make a gift to X when he reaches age 22."

Inasmuch as O in the above Illustration has not sought to revoke the trust, it does not matter that O may have failed to communicate her trust intention to X or anyone else, even though this circumstance may be some evidence that the trust, with the vague terms in which it was declared, was intended to be revocable. See § 14, Comment *c*; cf. § 63, Comments *a* and *b*.

CHAPTER 4

FORMALITIES: TRUSTS CREATED BY WILL

Introductory Note: Section 16 of Chapter 3 reviews the frequently troublesome problems of the transfer requirement associated with the creation of inter vivos trusts other than by declaration or contract. By contrast, the transfer requirements for a testamentary trust may be satisfied simply by the execution of a will followed by the testator's death without having revoked the will or its trust provisions. A trust is then created if the will reasonably manifests the trust intention (§ 13) and supplies the essential trust terms (described in § 17). Even the testator's failure to name a trustee will not cause a testamentary trust to fail, because this necessary element of the trust relationship can be supplied by court appointment. See generally § 14, Comment *b*, § 16, Comment *a*, and §§ 31 and 34.

Despite this relative simplicity, as this brief Chapter 4 reveals, a variety of problems may arise from casual or uninformed attempts to create testamentary trusts without following the foregoing prescription, or from special circumstances or objectives that occasionally invite a would-be settlor to depart from that simple prescription. For problems of this type, the rules stated in this chapter are designed to avoid failure of a decedent's trust objectives whenever this can be accomplished without undue disregard for the purposes and policies underlying the formal requirements prescribed by Wills Acts. This is consistent not only with the objectives and rules of other chapters of Part 2 of this Restatement but also . . . with objectives and rules of the Restatements, Second and Third, of Property ([Wills and Other] Donative Transfers).

More generally, the rules stated in this chapter and elsewhere in Part 2 of this Restatement seek to accommodate, within reason, the diverse circumstances, objectives, and preferences of persons wishing to use trusts. Thus, for example, individuals may choose to accomplish their post-death property dispositions, in trust or otherwise, either by will or by revocable inter vivos trust, even when the latter is used openly as a substitute for a will and serves to avoid the formal safeguards and normal procedures applicable to wills. See § 25(1), and also Restatement Second, Property (Donative Transfers) § 32.4 [Restatement Third, Property (Wills and Other Donative Transfers) § 7.1].

References to "testamentary trusts" or "testamentary dispositions" are not used in this Restatement (as they unfortunately often have been in cases and texts in the past) to refer to will substitutes, or more ominously to dispositions that are intended as inter vivos transfers but are threatened with failure because they are "too similar" to dispositions by will. Under modern principles recognized in this Restatement, it is clear that a trust established by declaration or transfer inter vivos is not objectionable—or "testamentary"—merely because the settlor reserves beneficial interests for life or powers to revoke, amend, or appoint during life or at death, or even the right to serve as trustee. Nor is a trust testamentary merely because all beneficial rights of others are future interests, even "contingent" or revocable, throughout the settlor's lifetime.

A "testamentary trust" is simply one that is created by will—even if the settlor may not realize that the instrument being used is a will.

A will must be executed in a manner that complies with the formalities prescribed by the applicable Wills Act, or at least that qualifies under legislative rules or judicially developed doctrine allowing admission to probate based on "substantial compliance," "harmless error," "power of dispensation," or some such terminology. Then, in order for an intended express testamentary trust to be upheld, the trust intention (§ 13) and the essential terms of the trust (§ 17) must be supplied either by the provisions of the will itself or in other ways described in §§ 17 and 19 of this chapter.

§ 17. Creation of Testamentary Trusts

(1) A testamentary trust is one created by a valid will.

(2) Except as provided in § 19, a trust is created by a will if the intention to create the trust and other elements essential to the creation of a testamentary trust (ordinarily, identification of the trust property, the beneficiaries, and the purposes of the trust) can be ascertained from

(a) the will itself; or

(b) an existing instrument properly incorporated by reference into the will; or

(c) facts referred to in the will that have significance apart from their effect upon the disposition of the property bequeathed or devised by the will.

Comment:

a. Dispositions that are testamentary. Aside from transfers based on an enforceable promise or beneficiary designation (§ 10(e)), an intended transfer is testamentary when the property owner had no intention of making a transfer inter vivos. Similarly (again excepting contract and beneficiary-designation cases), when a person intends to create a trust but does not intend to transfer the trust property during life to another as trustee or to declare the trust and hold the property as trustee during life, the intention is to create a testamentary trust. Such a trust can be created only by will.

A will is a validly executed document intended to transfer property upon the transferor's (or "testator's") death. The term also includes a codicil and any other testamentary instrument, such as one that merely appoints an executor or guardian, exercises a testamentary power of appointment, revokes another will, or expressly excludes or limits the right of an individual or class to succeed to intestate property. Restatement Second, Property (Donative Transfers) § 33.1; Restatement Third, Property (Wills and Other Donative Transfers) § 3.1, Comment *a*.

Statutes in the various states, referred to in this Restatement as "Statutes of Wills" or "Wills Acts," provide that a will is validly executed if it complies with specified statutory formalities. See further Comment *b*.

A "testamentary trust" is one that is created by will, even if the settlor does not understand that the instrument being executed is a will. Thus, a trust that a property owner intends to create is testamentary, and must therefore satisfy the requirements of this section, if the property owner does not intend the instrument to transfer the intended trust property during life to another as trustee, and the owner also does not intend to serve as trustee or to be bound in contract to create the trust. Accordingly (except for post-death transfers based on contracts and beneficiary designations), if an instrument provides for a transfer to a trustee who cannot be identified until the transferor's death, or to make a disposition of property that cannot be identified until the transferor's death, the instrument is one that attempts to create a testamentary trust and that can therefore be effective only if it satisfies the requirements of the applicable Wills Act.

On the other hand, a trust is not "testamentary" and not subject to the rules of this section merely because the settlor, in establishing the trust by declaration or inter vivos transfer (see § 10(b) and (c)), reserves any or all of the following: rights to possession or enjoyment of the trust property; rights to receive mandatory or discretionary distributions of trust income or principal; powers of revocation, withdrawal, or amendment; powers of appointment, whether exercisable during life or at death; powers to advise, direct, or replace the trustee; and even the right to serve as a co-trustee or as the sole trustee. See § 25(1). In such a trust, it does not matter that all the beneficial interests of others are future interests, even "contingent" interests throughout or beyond the settlor's lifetime, and even though those interests are subject to control by amendment or revocation by the settlor. Nor does it matter that the settlor has deliberately used a revocable living trust as a substitute for a will and as a means of avoiding the estate administration procedures and formal safeguards normally associated with wills, or that the law for many important substantive purposes (§ 25(2)) treats the beneficiaries' interests in the same manner it would treat bare expectancies, while treating the settlor's rights as the equivalent of ownership. See generally § 25.

Illustrations:

1. O executes and delivers to T an instrument purporting to transfer to T, as trustee for B, such property as O may own at the time of his death. The instrument does not satisfy the requirements of a will. O dies intestate. No trust is created, either at the time of the execution and delivery of the instrument or at the time of O's death, and all of the property he owns at death is to be administered as an intestate estate.

2. O executes an instrument purporting to transfer certain of her securities, in trust for B, to such person as O may name as trustee in her will. The instrument is executed without consideration and does not comply with the requirements for a valid will; O never executes a will. The contemplated trust does not arise either at the time the instrument was executed or on O's death, because there was no transfer inter vivos for want of a trustee to whom delivery and transfer could be made; and the instrument, of a testamentary nature that neither creates enforceable rights (cf. § 10(e)) nor attempts to create a trust until O's death, was not valid as a will and therefore could not create a testamentary trust for which a court could appoint a trustee.

3. Same facts as in Illustration 2, except that the instrument complies with the requirements for a valid will under applicable law, and O dies without revoking the instrument or executing a later inconsistent will. Because the instrument itself is valid as a will and therefore supplies the transfer in trust, a valid *testamentary* trust is

created; it is immaterial that no trustee was named, for a court will appoint a trustee (see Comment *e*, below, § 14, Comment *b*, and §§ 31 and 34).

4. O transfers securities to T in trust to manage and apply funds for O's benefit during his life and thereafter to distribute to or hold for such person as O may later designate in a letter of instructions delivered to T. (If O were to die in these circumstances without writing the contemplated letter, regardless of its testamentary or nontestamentary character the express trust would fail at O's death for want of a beneficiary and T would hold on resulting trust for O's estate. That, however, does not occur.) Before his death, O delivers a letter to T instructing her to distribute the property to B upon O's death. The letter makes a valid inter vivos disposition of what had been a legally implied equitable reversion, and B is entitled to the trust property. The trust provision is not rendered testamentary merely because B's possession and enjoyment are postponed until O's death.

5. Same facts as in Illustration 4, except that the contemplated letter of instruction (marked "Do not open until my death") is found at O's death in his safe-deposit box, signed by him and designating intended trust beneficiaries and, expressly or impliedly (see Comment *e*), a trust purpose. The apparently intended disposition by O is testamentary. If the letter of instruction is neither holographic nor attested and does not otherwise satisfy the requirements for a will under applicable law, the trust beneficiaries have not been properly designated and the trust fails at O's death. T holds the property on resulting trust (see §§ 7, 8) for O's estate.

If the letter of instruction found at O's death in Illustration 5 had been executed in compliance with the formalities prescribed by the applicable Wills Act, or if admissible to probate under applicable law on the basis of a rule of harmless error, substantial compliance, or judicial dispensation, the situation—and the result—would be different. The written instructions, although not delivered during life and therefore testamentary, would constitute a will. The terms of the trust would therefore be validly completed. If the will does not satisfy the requirements for an effective exercise of O's reserved power to appoint or to amend the remainder provision (cf. § 63, Comment *i*), the beneficiaries would be entitled to the rights set out in the letter, as a disposition of O's equitable reversion. T would hold not on resulting trust, however, but on an express trust for the beneficiaries and purposes prescribed by O. If it matters procedurally, because of its origin in O's inter vivos transfer to T, the trust should be administered as a nontestamentary trust unless O has manifested a contrary intention. In effect, O's will merely disposed of his equitable future interest, retained by implication of law, to a trust created during his lifetime. (See also the inference of nontestamentary trust in § 19, Comment *i*, for "pour-over" situations, including the situation in which the disposition by a valid will provides the initial funding and thereby creates the trust at death.)

b. *Wills Act execution requirements*. Although differing in specific detail, statutes in the various states provide that a will is validly executed if it is in writing, signed by the testator and by a specified number of attesting witnesses, and complies with any other formalities that may be prescribed by the particular statute. . . . . Statutes in many states also authorize, again in varying detail, holographic wills; such a will, though unwitnessed, is validly executed if it is handwritten and signed by the testator, and satisfies any dating or other requirements the statute may prescribe. In addition, some states allow oral (or "nuncupative") wills to dispose of property other than land in certain strictly limited circumstances.

Statutes in a growing number of states, usually based on Uniform Probate Code § 2–503, provide that wills not executed in compliance with the applicable statutory formalities are nevertheless treated as validly executed and admissible to probate if the proponent of the will establishes by clear and convincing evidence that the decedent intended the document to be a will. Even in the absence of one of these so-called dispensing-power statutes, courts in some states admit wills to probate despite their failure to comply with statutory formalities based on doctrines of "harmless error" or "substantial compliance." Restatement Third, Property (Wills and Other Donative Transfers) § 3.3, provides that a will is validly executed if the will was executed in substantial compliance with the statutory formalities and the proponent establishes by clear and convincing evidence that the decedent intended the document to constitute a will.

Detailed discussion of Wills Act execution requirements is beyond the scope of this Restatement . . . .

c. Incorporation by reference. In most states, an instrument in existence at the time of the execution of a will and referred to in the will can be incorporated by reference into the will and can be admitted to probate or otherwise given effect as a part of that will. Some states impose additional requirements, and the various states differ in the strictness with which they insist on conformity to the stated requirements for incorporation by reference.

A few states have not recognized the doctrine of incorporation by reference.

Because the law of incorporation by reference applies not only to trusts but also to other testamentary property dispositions, a thorough discussion of it is not within the scope of this Restatement. . . . . See also § 19, on the doctrine's role in pour-over wills, and more generally Restatement Third, Property (Wills and Other Donative Transfers) § 3.6.

d. Facts of independent significance. Wills frequently refer to beneficiaries or to property devised (a term used, generally now and in this Restatement, to include "bequeathed") in terms of descriptions that require resort to extrinsic facts. Under many circumstances, a testator's references to matters and events outside the will are not only quite safe but are essential to the ambulatory character of modern wills, applying as they do to property owned at death and to persons alive at or after the testator's death. An illustration of such facts involving both property and beneficiaries is a disposition of the "residue" of a testator's estate "by right of representation to those of my issue who are living at my death." Yet, other references may be to facts of a type that are peculiarly within the knowledge or control of the testator and thus may involve attempts to complete or alter wills on the basis of excessively casual, unclear, or unreliable indications of intention, or may even be excessively vulnerable to misconduct on the part of others.

Under the so-called doctrine of facts of independent significance, beneficiaries or property may be ascertained from facts that have significance (or a "substantial significance") apart from their effect on the dispositions in a will. An act has significance of this type if it is one that is naturally done for some reason other than the effect it would have on the testamentary disposition. It may be and often is an act that, in itself, has nothing to do with the disposition of property, such as taking persons into one's employ; or it may have to do with the disposition of nonprobate property. It may be an act done either by the testator or by some third person, and the act may occur after the execution of the will.

Because the doctrine of facts of independent significance is not peculiar to the law of trusts, a full discussion of it is not within the scope of this Restatement. . . . . See also § 19, on the doctrine's role in "pour-over" wills, and Restatement Third, Property (Wills and Other Donative Transfers) § 3.7.

e. *Essential trust elements.* Ordinarily a trust (see "elements" in § 3) cannot be created by will unless the intention to create the trust (see § 13), the identity of the beneficiaries (see §§ 44–46) and trust property (see § 40), and the purposes of the trust (§ 27) can be ascertained from the will itself or from some combination of the will and the doctrines of incorporation by reference and facts of independent significance. It is sufficient, and often necessary, that "purposes" can reasonably be inferred from the instrument's identification of beneficiaries and their interests. (The "pour-over" disposition discussed in § 19 is, in some limited circumstances, an exception to this set of requirements.)

The other essential element of a trust relationship—the trustee (§ 3)—will, ordinarily at least, be supplied by court if no trustee is named in the will or if the named trustee predeceases the testator or is unable or unwilling to serve (§§ 31, 34, and § 14, Comment *b*).

The requirement that a trust that is to be established other than by contract or declaration be created by a "transfer" of property to the trustee applies to testamentary trusts, but the transfer occurs automatically upon the death of a settlor who leaves a valid, unrevoked will. (Contrast §§ 10(b) and 16 on transfers inter vivos.)

f. *Testamentary trust properly expressed.* A valid testamentary trust may be created, satisfying the requirements stated in Comment *e*, even though ascertainment of one or more of the essential trust elements requires resort to rules of construction or to the process of interpretation. (On the "terms of the trust," see § 4 . . . .) And a trust may be valid even though some of the equitable interests are reversionary interests supplied by operation of law. (On resulting trusts, see §§ 7–9, especially § 8.)

Also, some of the terms of most modern trusts will almost inevitably involve some application of the "independent significance" concept (Comment *d*), especially for future-interest dispositions relying on class gifts to identify remainder beneficiaries, and often as well in residuary trusts in order to identify the trust property. Occasionally, however, a settlor devises property in trust relying on facts that have a substantial significance apart from their effect on the will as the means of identifying the primary beneficiaries of the trust.

In addition, in states that recognize the doctrine of incorporation by reference (Comment *c*), a trust that is not sufficiently expressed in the will itself is valid when its essential terms are sufficiently provided or completed by the contents of an instrument that is properly incorporated into the will by reference.

Illustrations:

6. A bequeaths $250,000 to T in trust to pay from income or principal the sum of $1000 per month for one year to each person who is a full-time employee of A at the time of her death, remainder to the church of which she "is a member" at the time of her death. When A dies,

Butler and Cook are her only full-time employees, and she regularly attended services and assisted with social functions at Divinity Church during the last years of her life. The trust is valid because the employees and church are identifiable as beneficiaries by facts that have significance apart from their effect on the trust disposition in her will.

7. X devises all of "the furniture in my house and the funds on deposit in my checking and saving accounts at B Bank" to Y in trust for Z's support and education until age 20, with principal thereafter to go outright to Z. The trust property is identifiable by facts of independent significance, and the trust is valid.

On precatory language (such as "wish" or "hope") as a possible expression of trust intention, see discussion and Illustrations in § 13, Comment *d*.

g. Intended testamentary trust not properly expressed. Except as provided in § 19, if the purposes of an intended testamentary trust and the identity of the beneficiaries and trust property cannot be ascertained from the will itself or from the will together with an instrument properly incorporated by reference, or together with facts extrinsic to the will but having significance apart from their effect on the dispositions in the will, the intended testamentary trust is invalid.

On the question of whether in a case of this type the devisee can be compelled to hold the property upon a constructive trust, see § 18.

If the intention of the testator to create a trust appears in the will in a case of this type, and if no constructive trust is imposed to carry out that intention, the devisee holds the property upon a resulting trust for the estate of the testator. See §§ 7 and 8. Even if willing to perform the intended trust in this situation, the devisee cannot properly do so. (In this respect, the Wills Act cases differ from the Statute of Frauds cases in § 24(1)(a) and Comment *b* thereto.)

Illustration:

10. A bequeaths $10,000 to B in trust for such person or persons as A shall name in a memorandum that he will prepare and place in his safe-deposit box along with his will. On A's death, a memorandum is found as described and names C as trust beneficiary. The memorandum bears a date later than that of the will and is not executed with the formalities prescribed by the applicable Wills Act. The memorandum neither has independent significance (Comment *d*) nor, as a subsequent writing, can it be incorporated by reference (Comment *c*). Therefore, unless the memorandum and its circumstances satisfy the requirements of an applicable rule of judicial dispensation, substantial compliance, or harmless error (see Comment *b*), the intended testamentary trust for C is not valid. But compare § 18.

A will may include more than one instrument, a supplemental instrument usually being referred to as a codicil. Thus, for example, if the essential terms of a trust appear in multiple instruments all executed with the formalities required by the applicable Wills Act, the trust is valid. If the memorandum in Illustration 10 had satisfied the applicable requirements for an attested or holographic will, directing (or being interpreted to mean) that B is to hold the money devised to her in trust to pay it to C on reaching the age of majority, the intended trust would be valid.

h. Disposition in accordance with directions of a third person. When a will directs that property devised or bequeathed by a testator shall be disposed of in accordance with the directions of a third person, the will confers a power of appointment upon the third person. The power may thereafter be exercised in the manner provided by the testator, and may be exercised by appointing in trust (see Clause (d) of § 10) or by prescribing beneficiaries and purposes for a trust created by the testator's will.

Where the power of appointment is to be exercised by will, a variety of situations and potential issues may arise. If the donee of the power survives the testator and thereafter executes a will exercising the power of appointment and dies, it is clear that the power is properly exercised. If, however, the donee had executed the will prior to the testator's death but survived the testator, is the power properly exercised? Ordinarily, the answer would be that the power is properly exercised by such a will, but the testator may have manifested an intention that the power should not be exercised by a previously executed will, or the donee may have manifested an intention not to exercise a power subsequently acquired, and such an intent would be honored. See § 10, Comment *f*; see also Restatement Second, Property (Donative Transfers) § 17.6; cf. id. § 17.1 [Restatement Third, Property (Wills and Other Donative Transfers) §§ 19.6, 19.2].

On the other hand, if the donee of the testamentary power of appointment predeceases the testator, he or she cannot exercise the power that the testator's will attempts to confer because the power cannot be exercised before it is created. See Restatement Second, Property (Donative Transfers) § 18.4 [Restatement Third, Property (Wills and Other Donative Transfers) § 19.11]. This does not necessarily mean, however, that the property devised or bequeathed by the testator will not pass in accordance with the provisions of the will of the intended donee of such an intended testamentary power of appointment. The disposition may be effective on one of the grounds stated in the three paragraphs that follow.

The disposition may be effective under the doctrine of incorporation by reference (see Comment *c*), as would be the case where the testator devises property to persons to be identified by the provisions of the will of a person who is already dead or, if so intended, by the provisions of a *particular existing* will of a person who is still living even though that person happens thereafter to predecease the testator. See Restatement Second, Property (Donative Transfers) § 18.4, Comment *d* [Restatement Third, Property (Wills and Other Donative Transfers) § 19.11, Comment *d(1)*].

So also, the disposition may be effective under the doctrine of facts of independent significance (see Comment *d*), such as where a testator devises property to such persons as may take the property of another under the other's will. Such a disposition is valid, whether the other predeceases or survives the testator, since the disposition of the other's own property has significance apart from its effect on the disposition of the testator's property. See Restatement Second, Property (Donative Transfers) § 18.4, Comment *e* [Restatement Third, Property (Wills and Other Donative Transfers) § 19.11, Comment *d(2)*].

Even apart from the doctrines of incorporation by reference and facts of independent significance, the disposition may be upheld provided the safeguards imposed by the Wills Act are preserved. Assume, for example, that a testator makes a devise to such person or persons as a third person shall appoint by will, whether or not the third person survives the testator, and that the third person predeceases the testator leaving a will purporting to dispose of the property in question. This disposition in accordance with the third person's will is effective even though the testator did not or could not incorporate that will by reference and even though the third person's will does not have independent significance (because it does not give any of the third person's own property to the person or persons to whom the property of the testator would be given). See Restatement Second, Property (Donative Transfers) § 18.4, Comment *f*.

i. *Other matters.* On the effect of an agreement by a devisee with the testator to hold the devised property upon a trust not stated or insufficiently stated in the will, see § 18.

As to the effect of a disposition to the trustee of an inter vivos trust, or to the trustee named in an inter vivos trust instrument, and purporting by "pour-over" to enlarge or to fund that trust, see § 19.

On various forms of revocable inter vivos trust, including life-insurance trusts, see § 25; and see § 26 on "tentative" (or "Totten") trusts.

§ 18. Secret Trusts

(1) Where a testator devises or bequeaths property to a person in reliance on the devisee's or legatee's expressed or implied agreement to hold the property upon a particular trust, no express trust is created, but the devisee or legatee holds the property upon a constructive trust for the agreed purposes and persons.

(2) Where a property owner dies intestate relying upon the expressed or implied agreement of an intestate successor to hold upon a particular trust the property acquired by intestate succession, no express trust is created, but the intestate successor holds the property upon a constructive trust for the agreed purposes and persons.

General Comment:

a. *In general.* Sometimes decedents by will or intestate succession leave property to a devisee or intestate successor who has agreed to hold the property upon a particular trust pursuant to an expressed or implied agreement with the decedent, but the terms of the trust (and often the intention to create a trust) do not appear in a will. (The term "devisee," here and generally today, includes "legatee.")

Where the person dies intestate, or the testator's will manifests no intention to create a trust, the expression "secret trust" is commonly used, as it is in this Restatement. Where the will reveals the intention to create the trust but not its terms, the expression "semi-secret trust" is used, generally and in this Restatement.

When a constructive trust is imposed under the rules stated in this section in a situation of this type, it arises out of an intended express trust that is unenforceable because of the failure to satisfy the requirements of the Wills Act. In such a case, the testate or intestate successor would be unjustly enriched if permitted to retain the property, and is therefore chargeable as a constructive trustee.

It is arguable that, if a secret-trust agreement is shown, the testate or intestate successor should be chargeable as a constructive trustee (or, in the case of a semi-secret trust, as trustee of a resulting trust) for the estate of the decedent rather than for the intended beneficiaries. This would suffice to prevent the recipient from being unjustly enriched. The same evidence that shows the intended trust, however, also shows that the other (albeit innocent) beneficiaries of the decedent's estate would be unjustly enriched by such a result. In addition, the rule of this section is supported by the great weight of authority in secret-trust cases (in Comments *b* and *g*) and by the lesser risk of unwarranted litigation in the semi-secret-trust cases (in Comment *c*).

Comment on Subsection (1):

b. *Secret agreement by devisee to hold in trust.* A testator may devise property to a person, with no reference being made in that or another will (that is, in the will or its codicils) to an intended trust, and before or after the execution of the will, but prior to the death of the testator, the devisee may agree to hold the property upon a certain trust. In such a case, no express testamentary trust is created. See § 17(2). The devisee, however, can be compelled to hold the property on constructive trust for the agreed beneficiaries.

If the intended trust involves continuing duties on the part of an intended trustee who does not volunteer to perform as agreed, the court ordinarily will order the devisee to transfer the property to another to carry out the intended purposes in the manner of an express trust.

Although the intention to create a trust is not evidenced by the will in cases of this type, the devisee would be unjustly enriched if permitted to keep the property free of trust. Similarly, an unjust enrichment would occur if a constructive trust were imposed for the benefit of the estate of the testator, whose devisee had agreed to hold certain property in whole or in part for other beneficiaries or purposes.

It is immaterial whether the agreement of the devisee was made prior to or at the time of the execution of the will, or after the execution of the will but before the death of the testator. A devisee's promise that induces a testator to refrain from revoking a will is as effective as an agreement that induces a testator to make a will.

Furthermore, it is immaterial whether the agreement by the devisee was in specific words, whether written or oral, or was shown by the devisee's conduct. Thus, if the intention of the testator to create a trust and the terms of the intended trust are communicated to a devisee who does not decline to hold the property upon the intended trust, the mere silence of the latter is ordinarily sufficient indication of the agreement to hold the property upon the intended trust.

If a testator's will would leave a certain sum or certain property to a person who agrees to hold that sum or property in trust for a designated person, and the testator thereafter increases the amount of the disposition by a new will or a codicil with the intention of increasing the amount of the intended trust but without further communication to the devisee, the latter holds the full, enlarged disposition upon the intended trust. (Without an undertaking to the contrary, however, this additional responsibility may provide sufficient grounds for an otherwise willing and committed devisee to decline (cf. § 35) or resign (§ 36) from the trusteeship.) On the other hand, if it is shown that the testator intended only the original sum or property to be held upon the trust and that the excess should be held by the devisee beneficially, this intention will be given effect. . . . .

c. *Where trust intent appears in the will.* Sometimes a testator devises property to a person and the will states that the property is to be held upon such trust as has been or may be directed by the testator, and the devisee agrees to hold the property upon that trust. In such a case, the trust cannot be carried out as a testamentary trust because the Wills Act requirements (§ 17(2)) are not met.

It is also clear, however, that the devisee is not permitted to keep the property, because it appears in the will itself that he or she was not to take it beneficially. The devisee would therefore be unjustly enriched if permitted to retain the property. Instead, the devisee can be compelled to hold the property upon a constructive trust for the purposes for which he or she had agreed to serve as trustee.

Although in such a case it would be possible to impose a resulting trust for the benefit of the estate of the testator, this would unjustly enrich the other beneficiaries of the estate (unless they and their interests happen to be entirely identical to those provided in the intended trust). The policy reasons for compelling the devisee to hold the property upon a constructive trust for the intended purposes are as strong as where the devise appears absolute on its face; and this case does not involve the inevitable risk of spurious claims against devisees who might have been intended to take beneficially in the wholly secret-trust situations in Comment *b*.

As in the case where the devise discloses no trust intention, the agreement in the semi-secret-trust case may be expressed or it may be implied from words or conduct. Again, it is immaterial whether the devisee's consent was given prior to or at the time of the execution of the will or after the will's execution but before the death of the testator. . . . .

d. No intention to impose legal obligation. A testator may devise or bequeath property to a person with no reference in the will to any intended trust, but may tell the devisee of the testator's hope that the property will be used for certain purposes. Unless it is found that the testator intended to impose a legal obligation that the property be devoted to those purposes, the devisee is entitled to hold the property free of trust. See § 13.

Similarly, if a testator leaves property to another, mentioning in the will the testator's wish that the property be used for purposes the testator has discussed with the devisee, unless the testator's intention was to impose a legal obligation, the devisee is permitted to hold the property beneficially and free of trust.

On precatory language generally, see § 13, Comment *d*.

e. No designation of beneficiary. A devisee may agree with or be instructed by the testator to hold property received under the testator's will for such person or persons and purposes as the testator shall thereafter designate. Whether or not the will discloses the intention to create a trust, if the testator dies without designating a trust purpose or beneficiaries, no express trust is created. (See § 17, Comments *e* and *g*.) Furthermore, there is no purpose for which a constructive trust can be imposed. In such a case, however, the presumption is that the devisee is not entitled to retain the property free of trust.

If the intention that the devisee is to take the property in trust appears on the face of the will, but the beneficiaries and purposes are never provided, the devisee holds upon a resulting trust (§§ 7, 8) for the testator's estate. There is no need for a constructive trust and no purpose for which one could be fashioned.

If a trust intention does not appear in the will but the devisee's agreement to hold in trust is proved, and if the terms of the trust are not, the devisee cannot retain the property beneficially but holds it upon a constructive trust for the testator's estate.

The above situations are different from one in which a devisee agrees to hold property in trust for a person or persons to be designated in an instrument to be delivered to the devisee during the testator's lifetime and the instrument is so delivered in an envelope the devisee does not open until after the death of the testator. In such a case, based on the promise of the devisee, the intended beneficiaries can enforce a constructive trust in their favor.

Similarly, if the devisee agrees to hold property in trust for such person or persons as the testator shall designate in a letter to be found with his or her will, and if a beneficiary is so designated, a constructive trust may be enforced for the intended beneficiary even though during the lifetime of the testator the devisee does not learn of the specific trust purposes to which the agreement relates. . . . .

f. No agreement by devisee: intention to create trust not communicated. Assume that a testator devises property to another in a will that makes no reference to an intended trust, and the testator has not communicated the trust intent to the devisee, so that the latter has neither expressly nor impliedly . . . agreed to hold the property in trust. Ordinarily, the devisee in this situation can hold the property free of trust although the testator allegedly intended it to be held upon a certain trust. This result is based on a fundamental Wills Act policy of protecting beneficiaries of a properly executed will from spurious charges and the risks of litigation without sufficient reason that, based on some alleged conduct on the part of the legatee or devisee, justifies exposing that beneficiary to those risks.

The foregoing result is not changed by the fact that, after the death of the testator, a letter allegedly written by the testator is found directing the devisee to hold the property upon a certain trust, unless that letter not only is intended as a "will," that is, as an instrument making or completing the terms of a testamentary disposition of the decedent's property, but also either complies with the formalities prescribed by the Wills Act (for example, as a holographic will) or satisfies the requirements for its admission to probate under a judicially recognized or statutory rule of substantial compliance, harmless error, or dispensation by court.

On the other hand, intended beneficiaries may be able to obtain relief in some cases of this general type on the basis of initial wrongdoing, not only if committed by the devisee but also if done by a third person (possibly involving undue influence, duress, or fraud, on which see § 12, Comment *b*, and compare § 24), or on the basis of mistake (§ 12, Comment *c*, and compare Restatement Third, Property (Wills and Other Donative Transfers) § 12.1).

Comment on Subsection (2):

g. Agreement by heir or next of kin to hold in trust. A property owner may die intestate relying upon the expressed or implied agreement of an intestate successor to hold upon a particular trust some or all of the property that he or she acquires as a result of the property owner's intestacy. In such a case, no express trust is created (§ 17(2)). Nevertheless, the intestate successor will be compelled, in accordance with the terms of that agreement, to hold the property upon a constructive trust for the designated beneficiaries and purposes.

Although the intention of the decedent to create a trust is not evidenced by a will, the intestate successor is not permitted to keep the property acquired through the decedent's intestacy because the successor would be unjustly enriched if permitted to do so.

As in situations under Subsection (1) of this section, it is immaterial in cases under Subsection (2) whether the agreement by the intestate successor is in specific words, written or oral, or is shown by conduct (compare Comment *b*); but, again, the decedent must have intended to impose a legal obligation (compare Comment *d*). . . . .

General Comments—Other Matters:

h. *Burden of proof.* The burden of proving facts necessary to support a constructive trust under the rules of this section (and the risk of nonpersuasion) is upon those claiming to be beneficiaries of the expressed or implied agreement between the devisee or intestate successor and the testator or intestate decedent.

In the secret-trust cases, the existence of the agreement to hold the property in trust must be shown by clear and convincing evidence. This is because the proof must overcome either what appears on the face of the will to be an outright bequest or devise or an intestate right conferred by law, and because the proof must therefore, in either case, substitute for the normal statutory requirements of the Wills Act. No such special burden is placed on the intended beneficiaries in a semi-secret-trust case because the testator's trust intention appears in the will itself and calls for clarification. In fact, to contradict the manifestation of trust intention on the face of the will in the latter case, the devisee seeking to keep the property beneficially must prove initial wrongdoing or mistake. (On these matters, see generally § 12.)

In both secret-trust and semi-secret-trust situations, those claiming as intended beneficiaries and seeking to impose a constructive trust have the burden of proving the essential terms of the intended trust by a preponderance of the evidence.

If the expressed or implied agreement of a legatee or devisee to hold in trust is established but the essential terms of the intended trust are not, the legatee or devisee in a semi-secret-trust situation holds upon resulting trust or, in a secret-trust situation, upon constructive trust for the estate of the testator.

On burden of proof generally, compare Restatement Third, Property (Wills and Other Donative Transfers) § 10.2, Comment *i*, distinguishing between ambiguous (cf. the semi-secret trust) and unambiguous (cf. the secret trust) documents, and requiring clear and convincing evidence only for cases of the latter type.

i. *Restrictions on testamentary disposition.* Statutes in some states provide that property cannot be devised to a particular class of individuals or entities, or limit the amount that can be left to such individuals or entities. If a testator or intestate decedent in such a state leaves property to a person who is not within the restricted class but who agrees to hold the property in trust for an individual or entity included within that class, the devisee or intestate successor holds the property (or excess over the limit) neither beneficially nor upon a constructive trust for the intended beneficiary. In the semi-secret-trust situation, the devisee holds upon resulting trust for the estate of the testator. In the secret-trust situation, the devisee or intestate successor holds upon constructive trust for the estate of the decedent.

Thus, in some states there have been statutes limiting the portion of a testator's estate that could be devised for charitable purposes. Limitations of this type often applied only where the testator died within a certain time after executing the will, leaving certain near relatives surviving. See § 28, Comment *b*, ... Similarly, a few states have statutes that bar or limit testamentary gifts to persons involved in a nonmarital relationship with the testator.

These various statutes are ordinarily applicable not only to outright devises and to testamentary dispositions upon express trust but also to cases in which a decedent leaves property pursuant to a so-called secret-trust or semi-secret-trust arrangement. In cases of these latter types, the devisee or intestate successor cannot be compelled to hold the property or the excess amount of property upon a constructive trust for the prohibited private or charitable purpose, and also will not be permitted to hold the property free of trust. Instead, the testate or intestate property or excess will be held by the recipient upon either resulting or constructive trust for the estate of the decedent. Cf. spousal elective shares, § 25(2), Comment *d*.

j. *Taxes and constructive trusts.* Questions may arise concerning the determination of and liability for estate or inheritance taxes in secret-trust or semi-secret-trust situations, or concerning the income-tax accountability for earnings on the intended trust property. These matters are not within the scope of this Restatement; nor are the possible gift-tax consequences of constructive trusts or voluntary performance of intended trusts in secret-trust or semi-secret-trust situations.....

§ 19. "Pour-Over" Dispositions by Will

Where a will contains a testamentary disposition for the purpose of adding property to an irrevocable or revocable inter vivos trust, or for the purpose of funding a trust pursuant to the terms of an instrument of trust executed but not funded during the testator's lifetime, the intended disposition is effective if and as:

(a) provided by statute;

(b) validated by the doctrine of incorporation by reference or by the doctrine of facts of independent significance; or

(c) the trust instrument, together with the will, either

(i) satisfies an applicable rule of substantial compliance, harmless error, or judicial dispensation, or

(ii) otherwise satisfies the policies underlying the formal safeguards of the applicable Wills Act.

Comment:

a. *In general.* Often a settlor who has created a trust inter vivos wishes, by will at death, to add property to that trust to be held, administered, and distributed in accordance with the terms of the trust—or, as it is usually expressed, to "pour over" some or all of the settlor's probate assets into the trust. The receptacle is usually a funded revocable trust, but is sometimes an irrevocable trust or an unfunded trust, maybe of the "insurance trust" variety (see § 25, Comment *c*).

a(1). *Devise to another's trust.* Sometimes a testator wishes to make a testamentary addition to a trust established by another person during life or at death. This arrangement is readily validated, according to the rule of § 17, by the doctrine of facts of independent significance, if not also by incorporation by reference, and is not further considered in this section.

a(2). Nonprobate transfer to testamentary trust. In addition, persons sometimes wish to provide in the terms of an irrevocable or revocable inter vivos trust, or by the terms of a contract or beneficiary designation, for trust property, pension benefits, insurance proceeds, or other funds to be "poured up" into a testamentary trust to be created by that person's or another's will. Compare § 17, Comment *h*. Arrangements of these various types also are valid and not further discussed here, being based on a receptacle trust the provisions of which are set out in an instrument that satisfies the Wills Act and are accompanied by one or more pour-over dispositions that are made under the terms of a valid inter vivos transfer, or pursuant to another will or an enforceable contract or directive.

a(3). Unfunded trust. In addition to the usual case of a pour-over to an existing inter vivos trust, this section is also concerned with situations in which the testamentary "pour-over" disposition is to provide the initial funding for, and thereby to create upon the testator's death, a trust the terms of which are set out in an independent writing. Such an inter vivos instrument of trust would ordinarily be one executed on a standby basis at a time when it is contemplated that the trust might be funded later in the testator's life (possibly even by the holder of the testator's durable power of attorney, as discussed in § 11, Comment *f*), an inter vivos funding that may or may not in fact occur. When the "trust"—really, then, only a trust document—remains unfunded at the time of the testator's death, and does not control the disposition of property from any source other than the property of the testator's probate estate, the arrangement is not supportable under the doctrine of facts of independent significance. Other rationale must therefore be considered (see Clause (c) and Comment *h*) unless the arrangement is validated by statute.

a(4). Special pour-over statutes. Legislation has been enacted in most United States jurisdictions authorizing pour-overs to trusts in existence at the testator's death or to trustees named in independent instruments of trust. Most of these statutes are based on the Uniform Testamentary Additions to Trusts Act (UTATA) or the 1991 revised version of that Act.

The principal provision of the revised Act (only slightly different from the original Act) provides that a will

> may validly devise property to the trustee of a trust established or to be established during the testator's lifetime by the testator, by some other person, or by the testator and some other person, including a funded or unfunded life insurance trust, although the settlor has reserved any or all rights of ownership of the insurance contracts, or
>
> at the testator's death by the testator's devise to the trustee, if the trust is identified in the testator's will and its terms are set forth in a written instrument, other than a will, executed before, concurrently with, or after the execution of the testator's will or in another individual's will if that other individual has predeceased the testator, regardless of the existence, size, or character of the corpus of the trust.

The above provision adds that "[t]he devise is not invalid because the trust is amendable or revocable, or because the trust was amended after the execution of the will or the testator's death"; and a subsequent provision makes clear that the property is to "be administered and disposed of in accordance with the provisions of the governing instrument setting forth the terms of the trust, including any amendments thereto made before or after the testator's death." (The original Act had provided that, absent contrary provision in the will, the pour-over assets were subject only to amendments made before the testator's death.)

The analysis in the ensuing Comments to this section recognizes that a given jurisdiction may not have pour-over legislation, and also that questions may arise that are not covered by the statute in the particular jurisdiction. The analysis therefore examines the ways in which the doctrines of incorporation by reference and facts of independent significance, and other concepts, might apply in various sets of circumstances.

b. Governing principles absent pour-over statute. A testamentary disposition in trust is valid not only where the terms of the intended trust are set forth in the will, but also where the will refers to an instrument of trust that was executed inter vivos in a manner that satisfies the requirements of an applicable Wills Act, and also where the disposition satisfies the requirements of rules permitting resort to facts of independent significance or, where recognized, rules permitting incorporation by reference.

Under the doctrine of incorporation by reference, a writing in existence when a will is executed may be incorporated by reference if the will manifests this intention and describes the writing sufficiently to permit its identification, with further technical requirements sometimes imposed by the law of a given jurisdiction. See § 17, Comment *c*.

Under the doctrine of facts of independent significance, there is no requirement that a fact (or entity) be one existing at the time of the execution of the will. See § 17, Comment *d*.

Under both of these rules, it is immaterial whether the inter vivos trust to which testamentary assets are to be poured was created by the settlor's declaration of trust or by a transfer of property to another as trustee.

If no property was placed in the purported inter vivos trust prior to the testator's death, and no assets from other sources (such as proceeds of a life-insurance policy or retirement arrangement) are governed by the terms of that trust, the disposition by will cannot be upheld on the ground of resorting to facts of independent significance, because the instrument of trust is not a separate entity and it does not otherwise have a significance apart from its effect on the testamentary disposition. Furthermore, if a merely nominal amount of property is included in the inter vivos trust, it is questionable whether it can be considered to have the independent significance necessary for the doctrine's application. See generally § 17, Comment *d* . . . .

Such a trust disposition by will can be upheld on the ground of incorporation by reference, however, if but only if the requirements of that doctrine are satisfied. Under all versions of the doctrine, this would require that the writing be in existence at the time of the will's execution. See generally § 17, Comment *c* . . . .

With these principles in mind, the following types of situations will be considered below on the assumption that there is no applicable statute validating pour-overs: (1) where the inter vivos trust is not subject to revocation or modification; (2) where it is subject to revocation or modification but is not in fact revoked or modified; (3) where it is subject to modification and is in fact subsequently modified; (4) where it is subject to revocation and is subsequently revoked; and (5) where the purported trust is unfunded and therefore is merely an instrument in writing.

Before proceeding with these analyses, however, it should be noted (with respect to situation (5) above) that the revised version of the Uniform Act (UTATA) mentioned in Comment *a(4)* not only validates "testamentary additions to trusts" that exist outside the will in question, but also validates testamentary dispositions that provide the entire initial trust funding (and therefore actually *create* the trust) at the testator's death by testamentary reference to the inter vivos instrument of trust in each of the foregoing situations. See provision (ii) of the lengthy Revised UTATA excerpt set out in Comment *a(4)*. The original Act (in UTATA and in the UPC) is properly interpreted to achieve the same result.

c. Inter vivos trust not subject to revocation or modification. Where the inter vivos trust is created by an instrument in which the settlor has reserved no power to modify or revoke the trust, and the settlor in his or her will identifies that trust and leaves property to its trustee or "to be held upon the trust stated in that instrument," the disposition made by the will is valid on two grounds.

First, the instrument, being in existence at the time of the execution of the will that manifests the intention to incorporate, is validly identified and incorporated by reference (at least in the absence of some highly technical defect in the will's wording under some rule of applicable law). Even in states that do not ordinarily permit incorporation by reference, or that might find a technical flaw, incorporation of a relatively formal instrument that is typical of these arrangements should be permitted.

Second, the inter vivos trust is a fact of independent significance. The settlor is simply adding testamentary property to a trust entity already in existence. (On trusts as entities, see § 2, Comment *a(1)* . . . .) . . . .

d. Inter vivos trust subject to revocation or modification but not revoked or modified. Where an inter vivos trust is created by an instrument in which the settlor has reserved the power by subsequent instruments to revoke or modify the trust, and the settlor leaves property by his will to be added to the trust, which is not thereafter revoked or modified, the disposition made by the will is valid on two grounds.

First, the trust instrument is incorporated by reference because it was in existence at the time of the execution of the will, which manifested the intention to incorporate it. For the reasons indicated in Comment *c*, if the trust instrument is carefully prepared and executed, the disposition should not be held invalid even in a jurisdiction that normally does not permit incorporation by reference. And in a jurisdiction that does recognize incorporation by reference but in terms that recite highly technical requirements for the doctrine's application, the disposition should not fail merely because the will is construed as referring also to possible future instruments of revocation or modification (an objection sometimes expressed in terms of "words of futurity").

Second, the inter vivos trust is a fact of independent significance. The settlor is simply adding property to an entity, the trust, that has an independent existence both at the time of the execution of the will and at the time of death, and thus has a significance apart from its effect on the disposition in the settlor's will. . . . .

e. Inter vivos trust subject to modification or revocation and subsequently modified. Where an inter vivos trust is created by an instrument in which the settlor has reserved power to revoke or amend the trust, and the settlor's will leaves property to be added to the trust and thereafter executes an instrument modifying the trust, the disposition made by the will is valid under the doctrine of facts of independent significance.

If, contrary to usual practice and also to the normal inference to be drawn in a situation like this, the testator manifested an intention that the property should be held upon the terms of the trust as they existed at the time of the execution of the will, the disposition may be upheld on the ground that the settlor has incorporated the existing trust instrument by reference into the will. If so intended, this type of disposition may also be upheld on the ground that the terms of the trust, as they existed at the time of the execution of the will, were facts of independent significance.

If the settlor's will states (as it usually would) or is given the ordinary interpretation that the property devised to a trust that is revocable and amendable is to be held upon the terms of the trust as they exist at the time of the settlor's death, the disposition is valid on the ground of resort to facts of independent significance. The inter vivos trust and any amendment or amendments at the time of the settlor's death are facts of independent significance. It is immaterial that the trust is in fact modified after the execution of the will, because the amendments as well as the remaining terms of the original trust have independent significance because they determine the disposition of the property in the inter vivos trust as well as the property disposed by the settlor's will.

On the other hand, the disposition in this latter situation could not be supported on the ground of incorporation by reference (unless the will is republished by codicil after the last amendment), because one or more of the instruments that were to govern the testamentary disposition, namely the actual instrument(s) of modification, did not exist at the time of the execution of the will. . . . .

f. Inter vivos trust subject to revocation and subsequently revoked. Where an inter vivos trust is created by an instrument in which the settlor has reserved power to revoke it and the settlor's will provides for probate property to be added to that trust, as stated in the above Comments the testamentary addition will be valid if the settlor does not revoke the trust. When a settlor *does* revoke the trust, however, it would be appropriate and normal for the settlor to take further steps by will (or another trust instrument) to reestablish a testamentary (or pour-over) trust plan or to establish some other testamentary disposition.

If the testator-settlor does not take further relevant action after *expressly* revoking the inter vivos trust, whether by a writing, by declaration(s) accompanying an act of destruction or cancellation, or otherwise (on methods of revocation, see § 63, Comments *h* and *i*), it is presumed that the pour-over provision fails. This presumption, based on the normally inferred intention of the settlor in executing a pour-over will and in later expressly revoking the trust (cf. UTATA below), may be rebutted by clear and convincing evidence of an intent that the pour-over is to be given effect in accordance with the terms of the revoked trust.

On the other hand, if the settlor merely withdraws all of the assets of the inter vivos trust and leaves it unfunded at the time of death, it is a question of interpretation whether the settlor intended thereby to revoke the pour-over trust plan. In such a case, however, there would ordinarily be no reason to believe that the settlor was dissatisfied with the trust plan, and the presumption (rebuttable by clear and convincing evidence) is that the settlor intended the pour-over trust plan to be given effect. The reasons for withdrawal of the trust assets are sufficiently diverse and so likely to be unrelated to any dissatisfaction with the existing estate plan that this presumption arises even in the absence of evidence to explain the reasons for withdrawing all of the property.

Sometimes a pour-over trust plan uses as the intended receptacle a trust established by (or to be established by a particular will of) another person, or by the settlor and another with either having the power unilaterally to "revoke" and terminate the trust and thereby have the trust property restored to the settlors. In cases of these types, the other person's complete revocation of the trust of which the settlor-testator has no knowledge or opportunity to respond does not revoke the pour-over trust plan. If the settlor-testator knows of the other's revocation and takes no action before death, the effect is a matter for interpretation and depends on the intention or probable intention of the settlor-testator. (On the special problems of revocation and amendment associated with trusts of community property, or other trusts with multiple settlors, see § 63, Comment *k*.)

Sometimes a settlor expresses an intention in the will that, should the trust thereafter be revoked, the probate property subject to the pour-over provision is nevertheless to be held upon the terms of the trust. This would be the normal interpretation if a settlor's will simply expresses the intention that his or her probate property is to be held upon the trust terms as they existed at the time the will was executed. In such a case, the intended disposition can readily be upheld on the ground of incorporation by reference, if recognized in the jurisdiction. If necessary, however, it can be upheld by looking to the trust, as it existed at the will's execution, as a fact of independent significance.

If the intention manifested by the settlor was that the testamentary disposition is to be held upon the terms of the trust as they might be modified by any subsequent amendment, even if the inter vivos trust should thereafter be revoked prior to the settlor's death, the disposition to the trust as subsequently amended prior to the revocation can be upheld, not as an incorporation by reference, but under the doctrine of facts of independent significance. Thus, there is an effective reference to the remaining terms of the original trust instrument and selectively to any amendments but not to any act of revocation.

When, however, the settlor has manifested an intention that the property subject to a pour-over provision should be held in or upon the terms of the inter vivos trust only if it should not be revoked, the property does not pass to the trustee designated in the revoked trust and will not be held in trust pursuant to the terms of that trust instrument. The property goes instead to the residuary beneficiaries of the will; or, if (as is often the case) the terms of the pour-over disposition are included in the residuary clause of the settlor's will without manifestation of a contingent, substitute disposition, the property will pass to the settlor's intestate successors. It is immaterial that the testator is thus enabled, by revoking the trust, to nullify or alter the testamentary disposition without complying with formalities prescribed by the Wills Act.

f(1). Statutes. Legislation in many states, based on the original or revised version of the Uniform Act (UTATA or via the UPC) noted in Comment *a*, specifies simply and without qualification that "[u]nless the testator's will provides otherwise, a revocation or termination of the trust before the testator's death causes the devise to lapse." See Uniform Probate Code § 2–511(c). . . . .

g. Pour-over to insurance trust. The rules stated in Comments *c* through *f* are applicable to devises to life-insurance trusts, whether established by assignment of one or more insurance policies to the trustee or by mere designation of the trustee as payee of the proceeds, and regardless of whether the trust is funded inter vivos with other assets to be used for the payment of insurance premiums or other purposes. The insurance trust itself is valid, whether or not the trustee has active duties to perform until the death of the insured and even though the insured or other settlor-policy owner reserves the powers to change the beneficiary of the policy and to revoke or modify the trust. See § 25, Comment *c*.

Under each of the variations of terms and circumstances in the preceding Comments of this section and for the reasons there indicated, the provision in a will adding property to an insurance trust is valid on the ground that the terms of the trust and any amendments thereto have, apart from their effect on the testamentary disposition, an independent significance in that they govern the administration and disposition of the insurance proceeds. In addition, in some of the circumstances and for reasons previously discussed, the pour-over disposition pursuant to the terms of the insurance-trust instrument may be upheld on the ground of incorporation by reference.

h. Inter vivos trust instrument not funded during life. Sometimes a testator executes an inter vivos instrument of trust but dies without having transferred property to the trustee, and thus without having actually created an inter vivos trust. A provision of that testator's will providing for disposition of property to that "trust," or to the trustee named (or pursuant to the terms set out) in that instrument of trust, may present greater difficulty than is presented by the situations in Comments *c* through *g*.

In many situations of this general type, however, the trustee named in the instrument of trust will also be named as beneficiary of one or more other dispositions or contracts. (This may or may not create a trust before payment is received; if so, the trustee's right under the contract—a *chose in action*—constitutes trust property. See § 10, Comment *g*; § 15, Comment *b*; and § 25, Comment *c*. See also § 40, Comment *b*.) Most frequently the trustee will be designated as primary or contingent beneficiary of life-insurance policies or of annuity contracts, employee-benefit or pension plans, or other retirement arrangements. The independent-significance principles discussed above in Comments *c* through *g* are applicable because these other funding sources or potential funding sources provide an independent, nontestamentary significance to the terms of the original trust instrument and any amendments that might be made to it. Often, also, an originally unfunded trust will be funded later in the testator's lifetime either by the testator personally or by the testator's conservator or agent under a durable power of attorney (see § 11, Comment *f*). . . . .

Thus, the special problems addressed below in this Comment, of a purported pour-over disposition pursuant to the terms of an inter vivos instrument of trust, arise only when the testamentary disposition serves as the only means of actual funding and thus as the only means of creating a trust. Even in this situation, modern legislation enacted in most of the states will validate this intended trust arrangement. See Comments *a* and *b*.

Absent such legislation, however, even the flexible doctrine of facts of independent significance will not apply to this situation, and offers dubious support even if the inter vivos trust has nominal funding, because the trust or trust instrument lacks substantial significance apart from its effect on the disposition in the will.

If the jurisdiction, though lacking modern pour-over legislation, recognizes the doctrine of incorporation by reference, that doctrine will sometimes sustain the intended trust arrangement. This will certainly be so if the trust terms are set out in a writing that exists at the time the will was executed and if either the trust terms are not subject to modification or the will purports only to incorporate the terms as they exist at the time of its execution. The doctrine should also sustain the intended arrangement in the common situation in which the terms of the trust instrument are subject to modification but are not in fact changed by the settlor after execution of his or her will. See Comment *c*. In addition, the doctrine of incorporation by reference, together with that of republication by codicil . . ., will validate the will disposition to an amended trust provided the testator executes a codicil at the time of or after executing the last trust amendment.

Depending on the form and circumstances of the execution of the inter vivos instrument of trust, and on the applicable jurisdiction's law of wills with respect to possible rules of substantial compliance, harmless error, or judicial dispensation (see § 17, Comment *b*), the intended trust arrangement may be sustained by finding that the trust plan satisfies the applicable Wills Act requirements. See generally Restatement Third, Property (Wills and Other Donative Transfers) § 3.3.

Beyond that, in light of growing legislative and judicial acceptance of these more lenient concepts (supra), plus the widespread, successful experience with modern pour-over legislation (Comment *a*), it will ordinarily be appropriate in other jurisdictions for courts to uphold the intended arrangement. The testamentary disposition and the testator's intent are expressed in a properly executed will, and the devise is made to a trustee to be held, administered, and distributed pursuant to a writing in circumstances that usually provide circumstantial assurance that upholding the disposition will fulfill a considered intention of a testator who died believing, even if mistakenly, that the normal requirements for a valid estate plan had been met. Compare § 12, Comment *d* . . . and § 16, Comment *c*. Also compare § 62, and Restatement Third, Property (Wills and Other Donative Transfers) §§ 12.1 and 12.2, as well as id. § 3.3 (supra). . . . .

i. *Single trust created by pour-over.* Where a testator who has created a trust inter vivos leaves a will adding property to the trust, a single trust is thereby created. This trust is to be administered as an inter vivos trust and not as a testamentary trust, where that distinction may be significant, because the trust is an entity that is not created by will even though property is being added to it by a testamentary disposition. (On trusts as entities, see § 2, Comments *a(1)* and *i* . . . .) The trust is an inter vivos trust even though there is no express provision in the terms of the trust authorizing testamentary additions, and even though the trust that serves as a receptacle for the pour-over is otherwise funded only at the time of a testator's death from such sources as life-insurance proceeds or distributions from employee-benefit or retirement arrangements.

The single, inter vivos trust result applies even if, in sustaining the disposition, a court relies on an incorporation-by-reference rationale, and even if the pour-over will itself appears to rely on that rationale, unless the testator otherwise manifests the intention to create a testamentary trust separate from the inter vivos trust.

If, however, the testamentary disposition is to a trustee pursuant to the terms of an inter vivos instrument of trust that is not funded from any other source during life or at the death of the testator, the matter is at least theoretically somewhat different. In such a case, the single trust that is thereby created may be either an inter vivos trust or a testamentary trust, where the distinction may matter, depending on the intention of the testator. Still, however, unless the testator expresses an intent on this matter, the question is one of interpretation, with the inference being that the trust is intended to be nontestamentary.

CHAPTER 5

FORMALITIES: CREATION OF INTER VIVOS TRUSTS

Introductory Note: Chapter 4 explores various formal aspects of the creation of testamentary trusts, and § 16 of Chapter 3 reviews the frequently troublesome "transfer" problems arising from efforts to create inter vivos trusts by means other than declaration or contract (see § 10). This Chapter 5 deals, primarily at least, with formalities issues related to the requirements, or to failure to comply with the requirements, for establishing express inter vivos trusts.

Most of the problems dealt with in this chapter arise from the typical statute-of-frauds requirement that trusts of land be created or proved by a writing (generally referred to in cases and literature, including the prior Restatements of Trusts, as a "memorandum"). Under typical statute-of-frauds provisions, trusts of personal property need not be in writing. In most jurisdictions, therefore, associated issues arise about what properties constitute "interests in land."

The terms and interpretations of statutes in the various American jurisdictions differ somewhat. In any particular state, for example, one may find that inter vivos trusts of personal property must be in writing, or that trusts of land need not be. One may even find that a writing is required for a declaration of trust but not for a transfer in trust, some extra measure of security for the latter being provided by the relatively objective nature of the required act of transfer. Some recent statutes may be more "forgiving" than their predecessors, and a few others now impose requirements more rigorous than the traditional.

In any event, it is common for statutes or decisions to require clear and convincing evidence of an intended oral trust, even when and where these trusts are valid. Furthermore, parol-evidence-rule problems may arise when a writing is used, whether or not the writing was required.

As mentioned in the Introductory Note to Chapter 4, one objective of the rules throughout this Restatement is to allow property owners meaningful opportunity to choose among various forms for the disposition of their property. This particularly includes choice between the use of wills and the use of will substitutes.

So, too, a goal of this Part 2 (Chapters 3 through 5) is to give effect to property owners' objectives either by validating intended express trusts or, as necessary, by resort to constructive trusts, to the extent this goal can be achieved without unduly undermining the safeguards, channeling and deliberative functions, and other policy objectives underlying the formal mandates of wills acts and statutes of frauds.

Because this Chapter 5 deals with "inter vivos" trusts, and because rules often differentiate these from "testamentary" trusts, it should be noted here that the former may include not only trusts created during life but also those that actually come into being after the settlor's death as a result of enforceable directives or contracts made during life. A contract, for example, may create a trust immediately, with the trustee holding a *chose in action* as the trust property; or the later performance of the contract may bring about the creation of a trust at the time the promised transfer occurs. See § 10, Comment *g*, and § 15, Comment *b*. In either event, the trust is an inter vivos trust, and not a testamentary trust—that is, not one created by will—even if the promised payment or other transfer occurs after the settlor's death.

Fortunately, it is rarely significant to determine *when* a trust that is initially "funded" by a payment of life-insurance proceeds after the settlor-insured's death, or by death benefits distributed under a retirement plan, comes into existence—although, for example, the distinction may determine whether fiduciary duties existed or not at a given point in time.

What is important, and regularly so even if no longer a matter requiring frequent litigation, is whether these types of trusts must satisfy, as "testamentary trusts" must, the requirements of Wills Acts. The answer given to that question in this Restatement (and also, now, quite consistently given in the case law, despite often awkward rationale) is "no." See § 25(1); also see § 17, Comment *a*. Similarly, revocable living trusts are not "testamentary" and need not be executed with Wills Act formalities (id.). This is so even though throughout this Restatement (and in an increasing number of jurisdictions and circumstances) the settlor's rights are treated the same way they would be treated if the settlor were still the owner of the trust property for purposes of rules of substantive policy, as distinguished from matters of form and the avoidance of probate procedures. Section 25(2). Similarly, during the settlor's lifetime the rights of post-death beneficiaries of revocable trusts are generally treated the same way as they would be treated if they were bare expectancies, including for purpose of applying certain statutes designed for dispositions by will (id.).

§ 20. Validity of Oral Inter Vivos Trusts

Except as required by a statute of frauds, a writing is not necessary to create an enforceable inter vivos trust, whether by declaration, by transfer to another as trustee, or by contract.

Comment:

a. Common-law and statutory rules. Most states have enacted statutory provisions like Section 7 of the English Statute of Frauds, specifically requiring a writing for the inter vivos creation of enforceable trusts of interests in land. In some of the remaining states, statutory provisions requiring a writing for certain contracts or conveyances affecting land have been held applicable to the creation of trusts of interests in land; and some state-court decisions have treated Section 7 of the Statute of Frauds as part of the common law.

In a few states, statutes require a writing for the creation of enforceable inter vivos trusts of personal property.

All of the foregoing requirements, however worded, whether expressly stated in a statute or judicially recognized by construction or as common law, are referred to in this Restatement as "statutes of frauds."

Unless a statute of frauds requires a writing for the creation of an enforceable inter vivos trust, a property owner may declare a trust or transfer property during life to another in trust without a writing. Thus, in all but a few jurisdictions, during the settlor's lifetime, enforceable trusts of personal property may be created orally. Similarly, absent a statute-of-frauds requirement, enforceable trusts of personalty may be created by contract, or (as often occurs) by receipt of payments under contracts, without a writing even if the promisor's performance is expected to occur after the settlor's death.

In addition, judicial decisions in several jurisdictions that have no express counterpart of Section 7 of the English Statute of Frauds allow enforceable inter vivos trusts of land to be declared or created by transfer without need of a writing. . . . .

b. *Cross-references.* On the requirements imposed by a statute of frauds, see §§ 22 and 23.

On the situation when a statute-of-frauds requirement of a writing has not been satisfied, see § 24.

On the validity and effects of revocable trusts as inter vivos trusts, see § 25. See also § 26 (on so-called "tentative trusts").

On the parol-evidence rule where a writing is used, whether or not required, see § 21.

§ 21. The Parol-Evidence Rule

(1) In the absence of fraud, duress, undue influence, mistake, or other ground for reformation or rescission, if the owner of property:

(a) transfers it inter vivos to another person by a writing that states that the transferee is to take the property for the transferee's own benefit, extrinsic evidence may not be used to show that the transferee was intended to hold the property in trust; or

(b) transfers it inter vivos to another person by a writing that states that the transferee is to hold the property upon a particular trust, extrinsic evidence may not be used to show that the transferee was intended to hold the property upon a different trust or to take it beneficially; or

(c) by a writing declares that the property owner holds the property upon a particular trust, extrinsic evidence may not be used to show that the owner intended to hold the property upon a different trust or to hold it free of trust.

(2) If the owner of property transfers it inter vivos to another person by a writing that does not state either that the transferee is to take the property for the transferor's own benefit or that the transferee is to hold it upon a particular trust, except as excluded by a statute of frauds or other statute, extrinsic evidence may be used to show that the transferee was to hold the property in trust for either the transferor or one or more third parties, or for some

combination of the transferor, the transferee, and one or more third parties.

Comment:

a. *The parol-evidence rule in general.* Even in circumstances in which a statute of frauds does not apply, whenever a written instrument evidences the transfer of legal title to property, questions may arise concerning whether and to what extent extrinsic evidence is admissible to show the transferor's intention to create or not to create a trust.

Under the parol-evidence rule, where the manifestation of the settlor's intention is integrated in a writing, that is, if a written instrument is adopted by the settlor as the complete expression of the settlor's intention, extrinsic evidence is not admissible to contradict or vary the terms of that instrument in the absence of fraud, duress, undue influence, mistake, or other ground for reformation or rescission (§ 62). On reformation based on mistake, however, see § 62, Comment *b*, and Restatement Third, Property (Wills and Other Donative Transfers) § 12.1, under which the rule of Subsection (1) should have a less inhibiting effect than might initially appear.

If the writing is an incomplete expression of the settlor's intention or if the meaning of the writing is ambiguous or otherwise uncertain, evidence of the circumstances and other indications of the transferor's intent are admissible to complete the terms of the writing or to clarify or ascertain its meaning, unless the evidence is excluded by the Statute of Frauds or some other rule. On the Statute of Frauds, see §§ 22–24. On the limited applicability of other restrictive rules, see generally Restatement Third, Property (Wills and Other Donative Transfers) § 10.2, Comment *h*.

On the application of the parol-evidence rule to contracts, see Restatement Second, Contracts §§ 213–216; and id. §§ 209, 210 on "integrated" and "partially integrated" writings.

b. *Recital of consideration.* Although the instrument of transfer recites that consideration was paid by the transferee, the parol-evidence rule does not preclude admission of evidence intended to show that the transferee did not pay consideration and thus that the transfer was not made to the transferee beneficially, but upon trust wholly or partially for the benefit of the transferor or others, or both.

Similarly, the parol-evidence rule does not prevent showing that consideration was in fact paid by a third person and that a resulting trust was created in the payor's favor. See § 9. Compare Restatement Second, Contracts § 218.

c. *Transfer "to the use of" a transferee, or to transferee "as trustee."* Where a transfer of land is made "to the use of" the transferee, these words do not necessarily show that the disposition is for the transferee's own benefit. As a result of the Statute of Uses (see § 6), these words have long been used in some conveyancing practices, and sometimes continue to be used even if unnecessarily, in order that the transferee might retain *legal* title. Thus, because of uncertainty of usage and purpose, these words do not prevent admission of extrinsic evidence that the transferee was intended to hold the property in trust.

Similarly, if property is transferred to a person "as trustee" or "in trust," without stating the terms of any trust, the parol-evidence rule does not prevent the admission of extrinsic evidence intended to complete the terms of the apparent trust or even to show that no express trust was intended to be created.

In either of the foregoing situations, however, otherwise admissible extrinsic evidence may be excluded because of a statute of frauds. See § 22.

§ 22. Writing Required by Statute of Frauds

(1) In order to create an enforceable express inter vivos trust of property for which a statute of frauds requires a writing, the writing must be signed as provided in § 23 and must

(a) manifest the trust intention, and

(b) reasonably identify the trust property, the beneficiaries, and the purposes of the trust.

(2) The writing required by a statute of frauds

(a) may consist of several writings,

(b) need not be intended as the expression of a trust, and

(c) continues to satisfy the statute-of-frauds requirement even though later lost or destroyed.

Comment:

a. The Statute of Frauds. In an English statute entitled "An Act for the Prevention of Frauds and Perjuries," 29 Charles II, c. 3, enacted in 1677 and commonly known as the Statute of Frauds, it was provided in § 7 that "all declarations or creations of trusts or confidences of any lands shall be manifested and proved by some writing, signed by the party who is by law enabled to declare such trust, or by his last will in writing, or else they shall be utterly void and of none effect."

In most American jurisdictions statutes have been enacted based on this provision. In some others, counterparts of § 1 or § 4, or both, of the English Statute of Frauds, dealing respectively with conveyances of and certain contracts concerning interests in land, are interpreted as requiring that inter vivos trusts of interests in land be proved in writing. In still others, the requirement of a writing for inter vivos trusts of interests in land has been held to be a part of the common law.

In a few jurisdictions, the statute-of-frauds writing requirement has been extended to trusts of personal property (although occasionally applicable to declarations of trust but not to transfers to others in trust). And in a small number of states, there is or appears to be no statute-of-frauds requirement that inter vivos trusts, even trusts of land, be created or proved in writing.

The term "statute of frauds" is used in this Restatement to refer to all of these rules requiring that inter vivos trusts be created or proved in writing, including those rules that are based on judicial decisions finding the requirement in the common law, and those rules that apply to some or all inter vivos trusts of personal property.

Despite differences in the wording of the various statutes of frauds, and even in the sources from which they are derived, there is much similarity in the interpretations given them in this country and in the manner in which their requirements may be satisfied. See generally Restatement Second, Contracts § 110, Comment *c*. There is also general agreement that an inter vivos trust that is created without compliance with the Statute is not void but merely unenforceable. See id. § 146, Comment *b*.

As expressly provided in the English statute, it is accepted with or without a like provision in this country that a writing is not necessary for the enforcement of resulting or constructive trusts. See § 7, Comment *g* . . . .

b. *Meaning of "interest in land."* The typical statute of frauds applies, expressly or by interpretation, only to "interests in land." On what constitutes an interest in land, see generally Restatement Second, Property (Donative Transfers) § 31.4 [Restatement Third, Property (Wills and Other Donative Transfers) § 6.3]; and Restatement Second, Contracts § 127.

The typical statute of frauds therefore does not apply to trusts of personal property, and this is so even though the trustee subsequently uses that property to acquire land. Nor does the typical statute of frauds apply if the owner of a note secured by a mortgage of land declares himself or herself trustee of the note or transfers the note inter vivos to another person in trust; an enforceable trust of personal property is created, even though ordinarily the security interest in land follows the debt by operation of law.

On the other hand, leasehold interests are interests in land for purposes of the typical statute-of-frauds trust provisions, as are condominiums, although the stock of a housing cooperative is not. Compare Restatement Second, Property (Donative Transfers) § 31.4, Comments *a–f* [Restatement Third, Property (Wills and Other Donative Transfers) § 6.3].

If the owner of land orally declares himself or herself trustee of the land and subsequently sells it, the beneficiary cannot enforce a trust of the proceeds; if, however, after receiving the proceeds the owner orally declares or reaffirms the trust, it will be enforceable. Similarly, if the owner of land makes an oral declaration of trust to sell the land and to hold the proceeds in trust, the intended beneficiary cannot compel the sale of the land or, if it is sold, cannot enforce a trust of the proceeds, unless the owner also reaffirms the trust or declares a trust of the proceeds after the sale.

Slightly different is the situation of a transfer of land to another upon an oral trust. Again, however, if the owner of the land transfers it to another person who is orally instructed or who orally promises to hold the land in trust and who subsequently sells the land, the beneficiary cannot enforce an express trust of the proceeds. And if the transferee, after receiving the proceeds, orally declares himself or herself trustee thereof, there is then an enforceable express trust of the proceeds. (On whether the transferee in the former situation may be held as a constructive trustee of the land or the proceeds, see § 24.) On the other hand, the difference between the declaration and transfer situations exists where the owner of land transfers it to another upon an oral trust to sell the land and to hold the proceeds in trust. In this case, although the beneficiary still cannot compel the transferee to sell the land, if in fact the transferee does sell the land there is a valid contract to hold the proceeds in trust; the proceeds are personal property so that, under a typical statute of frauds, this promise is enforceable without a writing, even though the consideration for the contract is the transfer of the land. . . . .

Comment on Subsection (2):

c. *Several writings.* The writing requirement of a statute of frauds may be satisfied by several separate writings (i) if each is signed by the party to be charged and the writings indicate that they relate to the same transaction, or (ii) though only one writing is signed, if that writing is physically annexed to the other(s) by the party to be charged, or refers to the unsigned writings in a manner that allows their identification, or was signed, as shown by an examination of all the writings and the circumstances, with reference to the unsigned writings. Compare Restatement Second, Contracts § 132.

d. Writing not intended as memorandum. The writing need not be intended as the expression of a trust in order to satisfy the requirements of the statute of frauds.

Thus, the writing may take the form of a letter signed by the trustee, regardless of whether or to whom it is mailed; or it may even be a signed writing in which the trustee states that he or she is not bound by the trust and does not intend to perform it (except in the case of a pleading setting up the statute of frauds as a defense to a suit brought to enforce the trust). Compare Restatement Second, Contracts § 133.

e. Lost or destroyed writing. The loss or destruction of a writing does not deprive it of its effect as a satisfaction of the requirements of a statute of frauds. Compare Restatement Second, Contracts § 137.

Oral evidence of the contents of the lost or destroyed memorandum is ordinarily admissible. The possibility that some evidence of the contents of a writing may be excluded under the "best evidence rule" (such as where the memorandum is fraudulently destroyed by the beneficiary) is not within the scope of this Restatement.

Comment on Subsection (1):

f. What the writing must contain. A properly signed memorandum (§ 23) is sufficient to satisfy the requirements of a statute of frauds if, but only if, it indicates that a trust is intended and, together with the circumstances, provides a reasonable basis for identifying the trust property and the beneficiaries and purposes of the trust. See generally § 4; and cf. § 17, Comment *e*. A declaration of trust naturally identifies the other essential trust element, the trustee; in the case of a trust created by transfer inter vivos, the instrument of transfer identifies the transferee as also does, ordinarily at least, the accompanying act of delivery. Compare § 14, Comment *b*, and § 17, Comment *e*.

A writing may sufficiently identify these elements of the trust even though it requires resort to interpretation or leaves some reversionary beneficial interest(s) to be supplied by operation of law. See generally § 8. Furthermore, trust purposes may be and often are inferred from the identification of the beneficiaries and their interests, together with the circumstances at the time of the trust's creation.

For example, the owner of property may declare that it is held or may transfer it to another "in trust" for a named person without specifying the purposes of the trust. The circumstances in a case of this type may indicate that the settlor's intention was to create an active trust for the remaining period of minority of the beneficiary. Or it may be inferred in the circumstances that the intention was to create a passive trust for the beneficiary. See § 6, especially Comment *d*.

A memorandum that sets forth with reasonable definiteness the trust property, the beneficiaries, and the purposes of the trust may be a sufficient writing even though it also reveals that the subsequent execution of a more formal instrument was contemplated. Compare Comment *d*; and also compare Restatement Second, Contracts § 131.

§ 23. Signing Requirement: When and By Whom?

(1) Where the owner of property declares that he or she holds it upon a trust for which a statute of frauds requires a writing, a writing evidencing the trust as provided in § 22 is sufficient to satisfy the statute if it is signed by the declarant

(a) before or at the time of the declaration, or

(b) after the time of the declaration but before the declarant has transferred the property.

(2) Where the owner of property transfers it inter vivos to another person upon an inter vivos trust for which a statute of frauds requires a writing, a writing evidencing the trust as provided in § 22 is sufficient to satisfy the statute if it is signed:

(a) by the transferor before or at the time of the transfer; or

(b) by the transferee

(i) before or at the time of the transfer, or

(ii) after the transfer was made to the transferee but before the transferee has transferred the property to a third person.

General Comment:

a. By whom writing should be signed: in general. The typical statute of frauds provides or is construed as providing, essentially, that the writing it requires shall be signed by a party "who is by law enabled to declare the trust."

In the case of a trust created by inter vivos transfer, the transferor is a party who is "enabled" to create the trust at any time until the transfer is made. Because the transferee is the person to be bound by the trust, the transferee is also a party who is "enabled to declare the trust" prior to or at the time of the transfer; in addition, the transferee can create the trust at a time subsequent to the transfer.

When a person declares himself or herself trustee of his or her own interest in property to which a statute of frauds applies, the declarant is the only proper person to sign the writing. This is true regardless of whether the signing occurs before the declaration of trust, at the time of the declaration, or after the trust is declared.

Comment on Subsection (1), Clause (a):

b. Writing signed before or as a declaration of trust. The requirements of a statute of frauds are satisfied when the owner of an interest in land (or other property interest subject to the statute) signs a writing declaring that the declarant holds that interest in trust on terms as specified in § 22, intending thereby to create the trust.

If a writing setting forth the terms of the trust as prescribed in § 22 is signed by the declarant prior to making an oral declaration of trust, that writing is sufficient to satisfy the requirements of a statute of frauds if it was made with reference to that declaration or if the declaration is made with reference to the writing, or if the declarant adopts the writing at a time subsequent to the declaration but before the declarant has transferred the interest to another.

Comment on Subsection (1), Clause (b):

c. Writing signed after property transferred by declarant to another. Where under a typical statute of frauds the owner of an interest in land orally declares himself or herself trustee of that interest, a writing signed by the property owner after transferring the interest to a third person does not satisfy the requirements of a statute of frauds and therefore does not make the intended express trust enforceable.

Once the property owner transfers the land to a third person, whether by sale or mortgage or gift, a signed writing thereafter declaring the trust is ineffective because the declarant no longer owns the property. The transferee may keep the property free of trust, and this is so even though the transferee had knowledge of the oral declaration of trust prior to the transfer. . . . .

d. Writing signed after declaration but before transfer of settlor's interest to another. Where under a typical statute of frauds the owner of an interest in land orally declares that he or she holds that interest in trust, the trust is not void but merely unenforceable. See Restatement Second, Contracts § 146, Comment *b*. A subsequent writing will make the express trust enforceable if signed by the declarant before having transferred the interest to another.

The writing is effective for this purpose even though a creditor has attached the interest or, after judgment, has levied execution upon it, unless it has been sold on execution before the signing of the memorandum or unless by a recording act or estoppel the creditor is in the position of a bona fide purchaser. See Chapter 22 (also see Restatement Second, Trusts §§ 308, 313).

Ordinarily, the writing is similarly effective even if, between the oral declaration of trust and the signing of the memorandum, the property owner has married subject to the laws of a jurisdiction that recognizes common-law dower or an inchoate spousal interest in the nature of dower. . . . .

Prior to 1938, it was held that a memorandum signed by a debtor after becoming bankrupt was sufficient to make the trust enforceable. Since that time, however, the Bankruptcy Act has provided that the trustee in bankruptcy has the benefit of all defenses available to the bankrupt as against third persons, expressly including statutes of frauds, and that a waiver of such defenses by the bankrupt after bankruptcy shall not bind the bankruptcy trustee. . . . .

Comment on Subsection (2), Clause (a):

e. Writing signed by transferor at or before time of transfer in trust. Where, under a typical statute of frauds, the owner of an interest in land transfers it inter vivos to another person in trust, a writing properly evidencing the trust (§ 22) signed by the transferor at the time of the transfer satisfies the requirements of a statute of frauds, whether the writing is contained in the instrument of conveyance or in a separate instrument.

Where the owner of property transfers it inter vivos to another person with an oral direction or agreement that the transferee is to hold the property upon a trust to which a statute of frauds applies, the transferor's previously signed writing properly evidencing the trust (§ 22) is sufficient to satisfy the requirements of a statute of frauds if the writing was made with reference to the transfer or is adopted by the transferor when the transfer occurs. . . . .

f. Writings signed by transferor subsequent to transfer. The requirements of a typical statute of frauds are not satisfied by a memorandum signed by the transferor subsequent to the time an interest in land is transferred to an intended trustee by a deed that makes no mention of the trust intention.

When trust provisions are not contained in the instrument of conveyance but are set out in a separate document, it is not sufficient merely to prove that the separate writing was in fact signed by the transferor, because if it was signed subsequent to a transfer that makes no mention of an intended trust it does not satisfy the requirements of the statute.

If the deed by which the transferor conveys land to the intended trustee shows the trust intention but not the intended beneficiaries or purposes, a subsequent writing signed by the transferor and setting forth the essential terms of the trust is ordinarily sufficient to make the trust enforceable. This is because, at the time the transferor executes the instrument, the transferee holds the property on resulting trust for the transferor, who thereby still holds the equitable interest affected by the subsequent memorandum. See § 24, Comment *g*.

Comment on Subsection (2), Clause (b):

g. Memorandum signed by transferee at or before time of transfer. A writing properly evidencing the trust (see § 22) signed by the transferee at the time of the transfer is sufficient to satisfy the requirements of a statute of frauds.

Where the owner of an interest in property for which a statute of frauds requires a writing transfers it inter vivos to another person by an instrument that does not mention the intended trust, a written statement of the trust signed by the transferee before the transfer is made satisfies the requirement of the statute of frauds if the writing was made with reference to the transfer or is adopted by the transferee either at the time of the transfer or at a subsequent time while the transferee still has title to the property.

h. Writing signed by transferee after transfer. If the owner of an interest in property for which a statute of frauds requires a writing transfers it inter vivos to another person with an oral direction or pursuant to an oral agreement that the transferee is to hold the property in trust, a memorandum thereafter signed by the transferee is sufficient to satisfy the statute of frauds if it is signed while the transferee still has title to the property. The subsequent memorandum, however, is not sufficient to satisfy the statute if it is signed after the transferee has transferred the property to a third person.

Thus, if a transferee upon an unenforceable oral trust transfers the property by sale, mortgage, or gift to another person and thereafter signs the memorandum evidencing the trust, neither the original transferee nor the other person holds the property subject to the intended express trust. It does not matter that the other person had knowledge of the oral trust before receiving the transfer.

In a situation of this type, however, see § 24 on the possibility that the original transferor or the intended beneficiaries may obtain a remedy of constructive trust. On the further possibility that the subsequent transferee, if a bona fide purchaser, may take the property free of the remedy of constructive trust as well, compare Chapter 22 (and see Restatement Second, Trusts §§ 308, 313).

A writing subsequently executed by a transferee upon an unenforceable oral trust is sufficient although a creditor of the transferee has attached the property or has levied execution upon it after judgment, unless the interest has been sold on execution before the signing of the memorandum or unless by a recording act or estoppel the creditor is in the position of a bona fide purchaser. Also, ordinarily, the beneficiaries can enforce the express trust even though the subsequent memorandum is signed by the transferee after marriage in a jurisdiction that recognizes common-law dower or an inchoate spousal interest in the nature of dower. On both of these matters, compare Comment *d*. . . . .

Prior to an amendment of the Bankruptcy Act in 1938, it was held that a memorandum signed by the transferee after becoming bankrupt was sufficient to make the trust enforceable. As amended, however, the statute currently provides that the trustee in bankruptcy has the benefit of all defenses available to the bankrupt as against third persons, expressly including a statute-of-frauds defense, and that the bankrupt's waiver of the defense after bankruptcy does not bind the bankruptcy trustee. . . . . Nevertheless, if the transferee upon an unenforceable express trust can be compelled to hold the property upon a constructive trust for the transferor or the intended beneficiaries (see § 24), the trustee in bankruptcy is not entitled to the property, whether or not the bankrupt transferee signs a memorandum, except as one or more of the creditors, by a recording act or estoppel, is in the position of a bona fide purchaser. Compare Chapter 22 (and see Restatement Second, Trusts §§ 308, 309).

i. Writing signed by transferee stating a different trust. If the owner of an interest in property for which a statute of frauds requires a writing transfers it inter vivos to another person upon an oral trust for the transferor or a third person, and a memorandum is thereafter signed by the transferee declaring that the transferee holds the property upon a trust different from the oral trust upon which it was transferred, the oral express trust remains unenforceable.

If, however, in a case of this type, the transferee can be compelled to hold the property upon a constructive trust for the transferor or the intended beneficiary (see § 24), the signing of the memorandum stating a different purpose will not preclude the beneficiaries or transferor from enforcing the constructive trust.

On the other hand, if, in the absence of the memorandum, the beneficiaries or transferor are unable to prove circumstances necessary to compel a constructive trust and the transferee would therefore be permitted to hold the property free of trust, the signing of the memorandum would ordinarily be effective as a declaration of trust by the transferee. This assumes that the transferee properly manifests an intention to declare the trust and is not precluded by intervening rights of third persons from creating a trust at the time the writing is signed.

j. Other matters. Whether the signature of an agent of one who can properly sign a writing evidencing a trust is sufficient to satisfy a statute of frauds, and if so whether the agent's authority must be in writing, depends on the language and interpretation of the applicable statute of frauds.

On the question of whether, if the requirements of a statute of frauds are not satisfied, the transferee is entitled to keep the property transferred or whether the transferee holds upon a resulting or constructive trust either for the transferor or for the intended beneficiaries, see § 24.

On the parol-evidence rule when a signed writing exists, see § 21.

On the possible effects of unlawful objectives in connection with undisclosed trust intentions, compare § 8(b) (and Comment *i*) and § 9(1)(b) (and Comment *g*).

§ 24. Result of Noncompliance with Statute of Frauds

(1) Where a property owner creates an oral inter vivos trust for which a statute of frauds requires a writing, the trustee

(a) can properly perform the intended express trust, or

(b) can be compelled to perform the intended express trust if it later becomes enforceable on the basis of part performance.

(2) Where an owner of property transfers it to another upon an inter vivos trust for which a statute of frauds requires a writing, but no writing is properly signed (§ 23) evidencing the intended trust (§ 22), and the transferee refuses and cannot be compelled to perform it as an express trust under Clause (b) of Subsection (1), the transferee holds upon a constructive trust for the intended beneficiaries and purposes if

(a) the transfer was procured by fraud, undue influence, or duress, or

(b) the transferee at the time of the transfer was in a confidential relation to the transferor.

(3) Where an owner of property transfers it to another upon an inter vivos trust for which a statute of frauds requires a writing, but no writing is properly signed (§ 23) evidencing the intended trust (§ 22) and the rule of Subsection (2) does not apply, and the transferee refuses and cannot be compelled under Clause (b) of Subsection (1) to perform the intended express trust, the transferee can be compelled to hold the property either upon resulting trust or upon constructive trust for the transferor, except when the transferor is incompetent or dead and a constructive trust for the intended beneficiaries and purposes is necessary as a means of preventing unjust enrichment of successors in interest of the transferor.

(4) Where an owner of property orally declares a trust that is unenforceable because of a statute of frauds and cannot be compelled to perform the trust under Clause (b) of Subsection (1), the declarant holds the property free of enforceable trust, except when the declarant is incompetent or dead and a constructive trust for the intended beneficiaries and purposes is necessary as a means of preventing unjust enrichment of successors in interest of the declarant.

General Comment:

a. Background and scope of section. In most American jurisdictions, an oral trust of personal property is enforceable as an express trust because the statute of frauds does not apply; and, in a few jurisdictions, the statute of frauds does not require a writing even for the creation of an enforceable express trust of land. See § 20. The present section is primarily concerned with those situations in which a property owner has transferred property upon an oral inter vivos trust to a person who may assert a defense under a typical statute of frauds because land is involved, or under the rare statute of frauds that requires a writing even when personal property is involved.

Subsection (1) applies not only to these situations arising from transfers to others as trustee but also to situations in which a property owner makes a declaration of trust. Subsections (2) and (3) are not applicable to declarations of trust; but Subsection (4) deals with the possible settlor-trustee counterpart of Subsection (3).

Even though a statute of frauds requires a writing for the property involved, an oral inter vivos trust created by declaration or transfer is not void but simply unenforceable in most circumstances as an express trust because of the failure to comply with the statutory mandate. Compare Restatement Second, Contracts § 146, Comment *b*. And restitution is ordinarily available as a "standard remedy" in such a case. Id. § 110, Comment *d*, and § 375; see also Restatement of Restitution § 108.

a(1). Who may assert statute-of-frauds defense? Although an oral trust is created of property subject to a statute of frauds, no one except the trustee or a person succeeding to the trustee's interest may take advantage of the unenforceability of the trust.

Thus, the personal representative of a deceased trustee may assert a statute-of-frauds defense against persons claiming to be beneficiaries of the oral trust, as may a transferee from the trustee—even a transferee without consideration or with knowledge of the trust. So also may a creditor levying on the trustee's interest (but see Comment *b* on *voluntary performance* by the trustee and § 23, Comments *d* and *h*, on the effect of a *subsequent writing* signed by the trustee).

A statute-of-frauds defense is not available to others, however, such as the insurer under a fire-insurance policy taken out by the beneficiary on the beneficiary's interest in a building on property held by the trustee of the oral trust. Compare generally Restatement Second, Contracts § 146.

On possible effects of possible unlawful objectives in connection with undisclosed trust intentions, compare § 8(b) (and Comment *i*) and § 9(1)(b) (and Comment *g*).

Comment on Subsection (1):

b. Voluntary performance of oral trust. The trustee of an unenforceable, oral inter vivos trust can properly perform the trust if the trustee has not transferred the property. Thus, under a typical statute of frauds, where an oral trust of an interest in land is created inter vivos, whether by declaration or by transfer, the trustee who still has title to the property can voluntarily carry out the trust. The trust can properly be performed under the same circumstances under which it can be made enforceable by the trustee's signing of a memorandum evidencing the trust. See § 23, Comments *d* and *h*.

Illustration:

1. O orally declares himself trustee of Blackacre for B. O is free to perform the intended trust despite the lack of a required writing. If O does not do so, however, and instead, several days after his declaration, conveys Blackacre to X, X may keep Blackacre. O may no longer perform the trust.

On the power of the transferee under a will to perform an intended trust that is invalid for failure to comply with the Wills Act, compare § 18, Comment *g*.

c. Part performance. Although a trust of property for which a statute of frauds requires a writing is orally expressed and no memorandum is signed, the express trust becomes enforceable if conduct occurs that satisfies the doctrine of part performance. See Restatement Second, Contracts §§ 129 and 139 (discussing more generally "Action in Reliance").

In order to seek enforcement of the oral express trust, as distinct from restitution (for which evidence of the intended trust is admissible despite a statute of frauds), circumstances must be shown that estop the trustee to assert the defense of the statute. Enforcement of the intended express trust that does not satisfy the writing requirement of a statute of frauds is based on the existence of a compelling substantive basis for relief necessary to avoid injustice, as well as circumstances that help satisfy the evidentiary purposes of the statute. In the trust context, except when the oral trust is created by declaration, the focus is on the latter of these elements, that is, on circumstances involving "action or forbearance" that corroborates other "evidence of the making and terms of the promise," in the language of § 139(2)(c) of the Restatement Second of Contracts, supra; also see id. § 129, Comment *b*. . . . .

Thus, the payment of consideration or a transfer of property for the creation of a trust is not alone sufficient to make the trust enforceable under a part-performance theory. Also important to the doctrine of part performance is some evidence, such as conduct on the part of the trustee, that is consistent with the existence of a contractual or trust obligation and that would ordinarily not be expected to occur in the absence of some such obligation, or some evidence of actions taken by a beneficiary with the awareness and acquiescence of the trustee that tend to corroborate other evidence of the alleged trust relationship.

The latter is illustrated by a situation in which, in addition to a settlor's transfer or payment of consideration, a beneficiary enters into possession of the land or makes valuable improvements thereon, or the beneficiary irrevocably changes position in reliance on the trust. In cases involving a declaration of trust, the improvements or change of position are also of importance in order to provide an element (supra) of "relief necessary to avoid injustice."

Illustration:

3. O, the owner of Blackacre, orally declares herself trustee of Blackacre for B until he attains age 30 and then to transfer the property to B. B, with O's knowledge, enters into possession of Blackacre and makes valuable improvements. The trust is enforceable on the basis of part performance.

The rule stated in this Comment *c* is similar to the rule under which oral gifts of land and contracts for the sale of land or other purposes subject to a statute of frauds become enforceable on the ground of "part performance," or "action in reliance," in Restatement Second, Contracts §§ 129 and 139. Compare promises to create trusts in § 10, Comment *g*, and § 15, Comment *b*.

Comment on Subsection (2):

d. Transferee orally agrees but later refuses to hold in trust: general principles. If a person transfers property to another upon an express trust that is unenforceable for failure to comply with the requirements of a statute of frauds (§§ 22, 23), and the transferee refuses to perform the trust (Comment *b*) and cannot be compelled to do so on a ground of part performance (Comment *c*), the question arises whether the transferee holds the property free of trust or whether the transferee can be compelled to hold the property upon a constructive trust; and if the latter, whether the constructive trust is for the transferor or for the intended beneficiaries and purposes.

As appears in the Comments that follow, a constructive trust for the beneficiaries will be enforced where the transfer was wrongfully obtained (Comment *e*) or where the transferee stood in a confidential relation to the transferor (Comment *f*). These situations within the rule of Subsection (2) involve transfers in which a written instrument of conveyance does not disclose the existence of a trust intention, but the circumstances present special considerations that favor giving effect to the trust objectives despite the transferor's failure to comply with a statute of frauds. In these cases, it does not matter whether the intended express trust was for the benefit of the transferor or for the benefit of other beneficiaries.

In some cases of initial wrongdoing or confidential relationship, the instrument of conveyance discloses that the transfer is in trust but does not disclose the beneficiaries and purposes of the trust. In such a case, it could be argued that a resulting-trust situation exists on the face of the document and that a constructive trust is therefore not needed to prevent unjust enrichment. This potential distinction, however, is rejected (Comment *g*). Applicable here, as well as in the cases described in the preceding paragraph, is the rationale underlying all of Subsection (2): a statute of frauds yields and the trust intention will be effectuated by constructive trust when necessary to avoid harm that would otherwise result to the intended beneficiaries from the transferee's initial wrongdoing or violation of a confidential relationship.

On the other hand, where there was merely an unenforceable oral promise to hold in trust that the transferee later refuses to perform, with no initial wrongdoing or confidential relationship, the considerations are different relative to the matter of respecting the terms and policy of a statute of frauds. These situations fall within the rule of Subsection (3) and the Comments thereto (Comments *h* and *i*).

d(1). Preventing unjust enrichment in general. There are many analogous, nontrust situations in which it is well established that evidence of an oral agreement that is unenforceable because of a statute of frauds can be shown for the purpose of preventing unjust enrichment of the promisor.

Thus, the owner of land, which is about to be sold to satisfy a claim against the owner, might be induced not to prevent the sale (or otherwise protect his or her interest) by another's oral promise to purchase the land at the sale and reconvey it to the debtor. If the promisor in fact buys the land but refuses to perform as agreed, the promise will be unenforceable in most states because of the statute of frauds. Nevertheless, the promisor in such a case can be compelled to hold the property upon a constructive trust for the debtor. See Restatement of Restitution § 181.

So also if the owner of an interest in land transfers it to another upon an oral agreement for other land in exchange, and if the transferee relies on a statute of frauds in refusing to perform the agreement, the transferee holds the interest thereby acquired on constructive trust for the transferor. See Restatement of Restitution § 180. Similarly, if money is paid or services are rendered to another under an oral agreement for the transfer of land and the owner of the land refuses to transfer it, relying on a statute of frauds, the purchaser is entitled to restitution of the money paid or to the value of the services in quasi-contract. See generally Restatement Second, Contracts § 375 and §§ 141–144; and Restatement of Restitution § 108.

e. Transfer induced by initial wrongdoing. Where the owner of property transfers it inter vivos to another in trust for the transferor, but without a signed writing as required by an applicable statute of frauds, the transferee will be compelled to hold the property on constructive trust for the transferor if the transfer was procured by fraud, undue influence, or duress. Although the intended express trust is not enforceable because of the failure to comply with the requirements of the statute of frauds, the transferee would be unjustly enriched if permitted to keep the property.

Thus, under a typical statute of frauds, if at the time of a transfer of land the transferee orally agreed with the transferor to hold the land in trust for the latter, but at the time the agreement was made the transferee did not intend to perform it, the transferee is guilty of fraud and not merely of a breach of promise. The making of a promise by a transferee who did not at the time intend to perform is a conscious misrepresentation of fact relating to present intention and thus a fraud for which specific restitution by constructive trust is an appropriate remedy. A transferee's subsequent refusal to perform the promise is some but not conclusive evidence of the transferee's intent at the time of the transfer not to perform.

Furthermore, a constructive-trust remedy is available also where the transfer is intended to benefit persons other than the transferor. Assume, for example, that an owner of property transfers it inter vivos to another in trust wholly or partially for the benefit of one or more third persons, and that the transfer was procured by fraud, undue influence, or duress but no memorandum properly evidencing the intention to create a trust is signed as required by an applicable statute of frauds. The transferee who refuses to perform the intended express trust will be compelled to perform its objections by holding the land on constructive trust for the intended beneficiaries and purposes. In such a situation, a wrong is committed not merely against the transferor but also against the third persons, for whom the wrongful conduct effectively prevented the transferor from creating enforceable interests. Accordingly, a court of equity will specifically redress the wrong by putting the parties in the position they would have been in had the wrong not been committed.

Thus, in a jurisdiction that has a typical statute of frauds, if an owner of land transfers it to another pursuant to an oral agreement that the transferee will hold the land in trust for certain beneficiaries and purposes, and the transferee never intended to perform as promised, the transferee is guilty of fraud and not merely of a breach of promise. Accordingly, having committed a wrong against the beneficiary for whom it is to be inferred the transferor otherwise would have created an effective trust, the transferee will be compelled to hold the land upon a constructive trust for the intended purposes.

A somewhat analogous situation arises when an owner of property is induced by wrongful means to transfer it to another in trust for one or more third persons for whom the transferor would not have created the trust but for the wrongful conduct. In a case of this type, the transferee will not be permitted either to keep the property or to perform the trust, but will be compelled to hold the property on constructive trust for the grantor. Thus, if a transferee obtains property to be applied to the benefit of a third person as the result of a fraudulent representation that the third person was in needy circumstances, the transferor is entitled to specific restitution by means of constructive trust. Similarly, if it had been the transferor's intention to create a trust for a needy individual but the terms of the trust are broadened to include provision for another individual as a result of fraud or other misconduct, a constructive trust will be imposed or reformation may be obtained to carry out only the original, properly intended purpose. Because of the wrongdoing, neither the statute of frauds nor the parol-evidence rule prevents the remedy.

More generally on constructive trusts that arise from wrongful conduct, and also those arising from mistake, see Restatement of Restitution §§ 163–171 [Restatement Third, Restitution and Unjust Enrichment § 55] (on constructive trusts).

Illustration:

6. A transfers Blackacre to B, who orally agrees to hold it in trust for A. At the time of the transfer, B does not intend to perform her promise. Although the applicable statute of frauds prevents enforcement of the intended express trust, B holds Blackacre upon a constructive trust for A, who can compel B to reconvey Blackacre to him.

f. Transferee in confidential relation to transferor. Where the owner of property transfers it inter vivos to another upon an oral trust for which a statute of frauds requires a writing, and the transferee refuses to perform or to sign a writing evidencing the trust, the transferee will be compelled to hold the property on constructive trust for the intended beneficiaries and purposes if the transferee at the time of the transfer stood in a confidential relationship with respect to the transferor.

This is true whether the trust was solely for the benefit of the transferor or for the benefit of one or more others, or for some combination of the transferor, transferee, and third persons. It is also true even though, at the time of the transfer, the transferee intended to perform the oral trust and was not guilty of undue influence or other abuse of the confidential relationship in procuring the transfer.

A remedy is not barred by the statute of frauds in these situations, nor is it limited to restitution, because of the weight of the policy in favor of protecting reliance on confidential relationships and of carrying out the objectives of transactions undertaken on the basis of that reliance. Accordingly, the remedy for the breach of an oral trust agreement by a party to a confidential relationship is not limited to restoring the parties to their original position but includes going forward with the intended trust.

A confidential relationship exists not only when there is a fiduciary relationship, such as that between attorney and client, trustee and beneficiary, agent and principal, or conservator and conservatee, but also where there is a confidential relationship as a matter of applicable law or on the basis of the particular facts involved. Illustrative of the latter are situations in which, because of family relationship or otherwise, the transferor is in fact accustomed to relying on the guidance or judgment of the transferee or is otherwise specially justified in assuming that the transferee will act in the interest of the transferor. Compare § 2, Comment *b*. More is required for this purpose, however, than the trust and confidence implicit in the transferor's reliance on the transferee's oral promise in making the particular transfer to him or her as an intended trustee.

Illustration:

8. S deeds Blackacre to B, her brother, in reliance on B's oral agreement to hold and manage it in trust for her. S is accustomed to relying on B's advice and has often trusted B to act on her behalf in financial matters. At the time of the transfer, B intends to perform his

promise but subsequently changes his mind and refuses to do so. B holds Blackacre upon constructive trust for S.

g. Where conveyance is "in trust." Sometimes an owner of property transfers it to another by an instrument that states that the transfer is made "in trust," or is made to the transferee "as trustee," but the beneficiaries and purposes to which the transferee has orally agreed are not set forth as required by a statute of frauds. In such a case, it is clear from the express terms of the instrument of conveyance that the transferee takes only the legal title and is not entitled to hold the property free of trust.

Under the circumstances stated in Clause (a) or Clause (b) of Subsection (2), the transferee, if unwilling to perform or to sign a writing evidencing the trust, will be compelled to hold the property on constructive trust for the intended beneficiaries and purposes.

Even in the absence of circumstances stated in Subsection (2), the instrument still reveals that the transferee does not hold beneficially; on whether the apparent resulting trust (see §§ 7 and 8) is necessarily appropriate if the transferee refuses to perform the oral trust and the transferor is not its sole beneficiary, see Subsection (3), and especially Comment *i* thereto.

Comment on Subsection (3):

h. Other cases: mistake or simple breach of promise. Many instances of unenforceable oral trusts involve neither confidential relationship (Comment *f*) nor provable initial wrongdoing (Comment *e*) but merely a transferee's subsequent refusal to perform the intended express trust. Although a statute of frauds prevents enforcement of the express trust, the transferee does not hold the property free of trust because the statute does not bar proof of the oral agreement to prevent the transferee's unjust enrichment. See Comment *d*. The normal remedy of restitution (Comments *a* and *d*), requiring the transferee to hold on constructive trust for the transferor, provides appropriate and adequate relief in situations in which the transferee has orally promised to hold solely for the benefit of the transferor.

On the other hand, if the unenforceable express trust was intended in whole or in part to benefit other beneficiaries, restoring the property to the transferor fulfills neither the original objectives of the transferor nor the expectations of the beneficiaries. Nevertheless, that remedy ordinarily applies and provides an appropriate balance between competing policies. It prevents unjust enrichment and yet gives force to the statute of frauds by not enforcing a trust that fails to satisfy the statutory requirement, the special circumstances of Subsection (2) (see above) being absent. Although the transferor has failed properly to create the intended trust, availability of the remedy of specific restitution (i) removes the incentive for the transferee to refuse to execute a proper memorandum or (ii) provides an opportunity, ordinarily at least, for the transferor to take the further steps necessary to create an enforceable express trust. Even a change of mind by the transferor would not be inappropriate because the transferor has not yet taken the steps legally required to create an effective express trust.

Special circumstances may exist, however, when the unenforceable oral trust was to benefit third parties and, by the time the issue is presented, the transferor has died or become legally incapacitated without having either expressly or impliedly repudiated the trust objectives. Developments by that time may or may not support enforcement of the intended express trust on the ground of part performance (Comment *c*). If not, unless the testate or intestate successors of the transferor and their interests happen to be the same as the intended beneficiaries and interests of the oral trust, the transferee can be compelled to hold the intended trust property upon constructive trust for the beneficiaries and purposes of the intended express trust.

The remedy of going forward with the intended trust is here justified in order to avoid unjust enrichment not only of the transferee but also of persons other than those the transferor attempted but is no longer able to benefit. This unjust enrichment of the transferor's successors in interest would occur, of course, in a case of this type if the transferor has died intending and expecting the trust intentions to be carried out. Where, however, the transferor is alive but has become incompetent without repudiating the trust, greater refinement in the remedy may be required. The court will exercise equitable discretion in determining whether the constructive trust should be one to give effect directly to the purposes of the oral trust or should restore the property to the transferor upon a similar constructive trust but also subject to the financial needs and possible mental recovery of the transferor.

That the constructive trust is a proper remedy to avoid innocent as well as culpable unjust enrichment, see § 1, Comment *e* . . . . More generally see Restatement of Restitution § 160 [Restatement Third, Restitution and Unjust Enrichment § 55]; Restatement Third, Restitution and Unjust Enrichment, Chapter 1 (General Principles) . . . .

Illustration:

> 11. In a jurisdiction having a typical statute of frauds, O conveys Blackacre to T orally in trust for O. At the time of the transfer, T intends to perform her promise and is not in a confidential relation to O, but subsequently changes her mind and refuses to perform her promise. T holds Blackacre upon a constructive trust for O, who can compel T to convey Blackacre to him.

Similar rules apply where a property owner's inter vivos transfer to another upon an unenforceable trust is the result of such a mistake as to entitle the transferor to rescind. The transferee can be compelled to hold the property on constructive trust for the transferor, whether the intended express trust was to benefit the transferor or third persons, or both, unless at the time the constructive trust is to be imposed the transferor is dead or incompetent and the trust purposes would not be fulfilled if the property is allowed to pass to the successors in interest of the transferor. Again, if necessary to avoid unjust enrichment of the transferor's successors, a constructive trust will be imposed for the intended beneficiaries and purposes.

h(1). Burden of proof. In a proceeding to impose a constructive trust under this Comment *h*, where the transfer to the alleged trustee was accomplished by an instrument of transfer that does not disclose the existence of an intention to create a trust, the proof of that intent must be by clear and convincing evidence. A preponderance of the evidence is then sufficient to establish the intended interests of the beneficiaries.

i. Other cases: transfer "in trust." Where the owner of property transfers it inter vivos to another by a deed that states that the transfer is made "in trust" or to the transferee "as trustee," but the trust is unenforceable under a statute of frauds because the instrument does not provide the necessary terms of a trust, the transferee who refuses to perform the trust will not be permitted to retain the property free of trust.

On the face of the instrument of transfer it appears that the transferee takes only the legal title, and therefore holds upon resulting trust for the transferor unless the intended express trust is voluntarily performed (Comment *b*) or can be enforced on the basis of part performance (Comment *c*), or unless the rule of Subsection (2) applies. Ordinarily, the apparent resulting trust will be recognized and the transferee will be required to hold for the transferor by implication of law. See §§ 7 and 8. There is no need of a constructive trust to prevent a transferee's unjust enrichment.

A constructive trust may nevertheless be required in some situations, upon the same circumstances and rationale that support constructive trusts for intended beneficiaries of oral trusts in Comment *h*. That is, the transferee will hold upon such a constructive trust for the intended beneficiaries and purposes when necessary to avoid unjust enrichment of some or all of the transferor's successors in interest.

Illustrations:

16. In a jurisdiction that has a typical statute of frauds, O conveys Blackacre to T by a deed that recites that the transfer is "in trust" or is to T "as trustee" but that does not state the beneficiaries or purposes of the trust. T subsequently refuses to perform the intended trust but was neither in a confidential relation to O nor guilty of procuring the transfer by fraud or other wrongful conduct. No grounds exist for enforcing the intended express trust on the basis of part performance, and O is alive and legally competent. Regardless of the intended beneficiaries and purposes, T holds Blackacre on constructive trust for O.

17. The facts are as stated in Illustration 16, except that O is dead when T refuses to perform the intended express trust. Unless the oral trust was solely for the benefit of O or O's successors in interest, T holds upon constructive trust for the intended beneficiaries and purposes.

Comment on Subsection (4):

j. Oral declaration of trust not performed. If an owner of property declares himself or herself trustee of an express trust that is unenforceable because of a statute of frauds and that cannot be enforced on grounds of part performance, the declarant ordinarily holds the property free of trust—free, therefore, to perform the trust or to sign a writing evidencing it, if he or she wishes, or to abandon the original trust objectives.

An exception applies, allowing the intended beneficiaries to obtain a constructive trust for the intended purposes, based on the same circumstances and rationale that support the constructive trust for intended beneficiaries and purposes under the rule of Subsection (3).

Beneficiaries seeking a constructive trust under this Subsection (4) must prove the declaration of trust by clear and convincing evidence, while the intended interests of intended beneficiaries may be established by a preponderance of the evidence. Cf. Comment *h(1)*.

Illustration:

18. O orally declares that she holds Blackacre in trust for B until age 30, at which time the trust is to end and the property is to be distributed to B. The intended express trust is unenforceable under a typical statute of frauds; at this point, O can properly repudiate the trust

and keep Blackacre free of trust. Thereafter, however, and before either an expressed or implied repudiation by O or any acts of part performance (or reliance), O dies intestate leaving X, Y, and Z as her sole heirs. B can now obtain a constructive trust to carry out the terms of O's oral declaration of trust.

§ 25. Validity and Effect of Revocable Inter Vivos Trust

(1) A trust that is created by the settlor's declaration of trust, or by inter vivos transfer to another, or by beneficiary designation or other payment under a life-insurance policy, employee-benefit or retirement arrangement, or other contract is not rendered testamentary merely because the settlor retains extensive rights such as a beneficial interest for life, powers to revoke and modify the trust, and the right to serve as or control the trustee, or because the trust is funded in whole or in part or comes into existence at or after the death of the settlor, or because the trust is intended to serve as a substitute for a will.

(2) A trust that is not testamentary is not subject to the formal requirements of § 17 or to procedures for the administration of a decedent's estate; nevertheless, a trust is ordinarily subject to substantive restrictions on testation and to rules of construction and other rules applicable to testamentary dispositions, and in other respects the property of such a trust is ordinarily treated as though it were owned by the settlor.

General Comment:

a. Scope, background, and rationale of this section. Revocable inter vivos (or living) trusts are useful and widely used as a legitimate means of avoiding the costs and delays typically associated with the processes of administering decedents' estates in this country. This is because probate administration is not required for assets transferred to the trustee inter vivos, or for funds payable to the trustee by nonprobate arrangements, such as pension or life-insurance beneficiary designations. Assets added to the trust by will, however, are subject to estate administration before they are distributed to the trustee. (On such "pour-over" arrangements, see § 19.)

Living trusts are also used as means of providing property management for settlors late in life, often on a contingent or standby basis by settlors who initially at least serve as their own trustees but designate successors to assume responsibility in the event the settlor resigns or becomes incompetent. Thus, for management of the trust estate, the relatively developed principles and processes associated with trust administration (see §§ 74 and 97, as well as §§ 76–89) are in general substituted for the heavily court-dependent concepts and procedures of conservatorship.

Occasionally, settlors find additional motivation for the use of revocable trusts rather than wills—reasons such as privacy or, in some states, the avoidance of probate courts' retained jurisdiction over testamentary trusts, with what may be perceived as more intrusive supervision than the relationship of equity courts to inter vivos (or "non-court") trusts. Under some state inheritance-tax systems, tax considerations may also encourage the use of living trusts as receptacles for life-insurance proceeds or death benefits under retirement plans.

In short, despite modern efforts to simplify the probate process and the modern and ongoing development of the durable powers of attorney for property management, revocable trusts created by declaration or by transfer to another are often preferred by property owners as means of holding and disposing of their property. Accordingly, the revocable trust is widely used as a legally accepted substitute for the will as the central document of an estate plan, usually in conjunction with pour-over wills (§ 19) and often with durable powers of attorney (§ 5, Comment *e*), the latter more for trust funding than for asset management.

The law offers a variety of different means of transferring property to others or of creating property rights and interests in beneficiaries, each with its own set of procedures and formalities. These same means are available for creating trusts and conferring equitable property interests on trust beneficiaries, with the declaration of trust offering an additional means of trust creation. See generally § 10. Thus, for example, just as it is not necessary to comply with the formalities of Statutes of Wills for a beneficiary to receive insurance proceeds or periodic payments after the death of an insured-policy owner, or to receive death benefits under under various settlement options under a decedent's pension plan, so, too, may insurance proceeds or plan benefits be paid to a trustee on the death of the insured or plan participant based on the usual policy or plan formalities and without need to comply with those of a Wills Act.

With widespread legislative and judicial endorsement over the years, supported by experience as well as popular interest, the revocable trust has become well established in American law as a socially useful and successful device for property management, especially late in life, and for the disposition of property (outright or in further trust) following the settlor's death. The revocable trust satisfies all of the essential elements of a trust (§ 3), provided a competent *settlor* (§ 11, and cf. § 12) makes a proper (§§ 17–24) *declaration* or inter vivos or nonprobate *transfer* (§ 10, Comments *b–e*) with the *intention* (§ 13) of creating a relationship the law defines as a trust (§ 2), and funds it with trust *property* (§§ 40, 41), title to which is held by a *trustee* (§§ 31–37), to be administered for a lawful trust *purpose* (§§ 27–29) for the benefit of appropriately ascertainable *beneficiaries* (§§ 43–46), primarily and properly (§ 43, Comment *a*) for the settlor while alive.

Issues of formality and procedure aside, however, the availability of nontestamentary methods of making disposition should not mean that substantive policies applicable to testamentary dispositions have no application. Thus, increasingly, statutes and case law in the various states are coming to recognize, as this Restatement provides, that the rights of the spouses and creditors of testators and of settlors of revocable trusts are fundamentally alike, because both the testator and the settlor have retained their complete control over the property that is subject to the will or trust instrument. Similarly, whatever the technicalities of concept and terminology, the interests the revocable-trust beneficiaries will receive on the death of the settlor should, generally at least, receive the same treatment and should be subject to the same rules of construction as the "expectancies" of devisees.

Thus, this Restatement recognizes and gives effect to a property owner's right to choose among different forms and procedures for disposition of property. Yet it seeks to treat functional equivalents similarly, and not to allow choice of form either to provide an escape from serious, substantive policies or to cause the loss of properly relevant aids in essentially constructional matters. Such a policy of treating revocable trusts and their settlors and beneficiaries in like manner to the treatment accorded testators and will beneficiaries, both during life and after the death of the settlor or testator, has long been explicit in the federal income and transfer tax systems. See, e.g., Internal Revenue Code §§ 671–677 (income tax), §§ 2036 and 3038 (estate tax), § 2511 with Treasury Regulation § 25.2511–2(c) (gift tax), and § 2652(a) (generation-skipping transfer tax). Early, traditional, and still-developing doctrine in trust and probate law has been neither so clear nor so consistent.

In brief, the fundamental and pervasive policy underlying this section and related rules of this Restatement is that diverse forms of revocable trusts (i) are valid without compliance with Wills Act formalities but (ii) absent persuasive reason for departure, are subject to the same restrictions (such as spousal rights) and other rules and constructional aids that are applicable to wills. In other substantive respects (such as creditors' rights), the property held in a revocable trust is ordinarily to be treated as if it were property of the settlor and not of the beneficiaries.

Unless a contrary intent is manifested or the rights of the spouses are significantly altered by the trust terms, community property transferred by husband and wife to a jointly created revocable inter vivos trust remains community property. Compare § 63, Comment *k*; and Restatement Second, Property (Donative Transfers) § 1.2, Comment *b*. On issues concerning powers to revoke and amend jointly created living trusts in community-property states, see § 63, Comment *k* (last paragraph).

On who is the "settlor" of a trust, see § 10, Comment *g* . . .; and § 58, Comment *f*.

Beyond the observation above concerning the treatment of revocable trusts, the tax treatment and tax considerations applicable to trusts are not within the scope of this Restatement. . . . .

Comment on Subsection (1):

b. *Settlor's reservation of powers and interests.* If a property owner intends and takes steps to create a trust by declaration or transfer during life, the trust is not "testamentary" as that term is defined in § 17, Comment *a*, and is not subject to the Wills Act and the formal requirements of § 17. Its validity as an inter vivos trust is not affected by the fact that the interests of all beneficiaries other than the settlor do not take effect in possession or enjoyment before the settlor's death, or that they are contingent or subject to conditions subsequent, including the exercise of a power of revocation, withdrawal, amendment, or appointment reserved to the settlor, whether exercisable during life or by will.

Nor is a trust testamentary because possession or enjoyment is reserved to the settlor during life or because the settlor serves as sole trustee or co-trustee, or reserves the right to veto, direct, or otherwise control the acts of another trustee in the administration or distribution of the trust estate. (As a practical matter, a settlor's control over the trustee is essentially implicit in a reserved power of revocation and amendment. Compare § 63 with §§ 74 and 97.)

The validity of an inter vivos trust as a means of disposition is not affected by the fact that property is added to it after the settlor's death by either testamentary (§ 19) or nontestamentary (Comment *c*) disposition, or both. Nor is a trust testamentary because its only funding during the settlor's lifetime is a *chose in action* under a contract that is not to be performed during the settlor's life, or even because the trust and the trustee's fiduciary duties do not come into being during the settlor's lifetime after which the trust is funded wholly (or partially, see also pour-over provisions, § 19) by nontestamentary dispositions. See Comment *c*. Furthermore, the settlor may grant powers to administer or appoint or withdraw trust property, during or after the settlor's lifetime, to others who may be trustees or beneficiaries, or persons otherwise unconnected with the trust, and who may hold powers alone or jointly in fiduciary or nonfiduciary capacities (Cf. § 64).

The foregoing is not an exhaustive list of the rights a settlor may reserve during life or confer upon others. In short, there is no specific limit on the nature or extent of the beneficial interests or powers the settlor may reserve or confer on others. . . . .

On the trustee's responsibilities when a power of control or direction is reserved to the settlor or given to another, see § 70; cf. § 74 (see also Restatement Second, Trusts § 185); and on rules concerning powers to revoke and amend trusts, see §§ 63 and 64.

On the distinction between trust and agency, see § 5, Comment *e*.

c. Insurance and related trusts. If a person takes out (or otherwise owns) a policy of insurance and designates, as primary or contingent payee of the proceeds, a third person as trustee, the trust is not testamentary or subject to the Wills Act even though the settlor reserves the power to change the beneficiary of the policy and the power to revoke or modify the trust.

The validity of the life-insurance trust is not affected by the fact that neither the policy nor other assets are transferred inter vivos to the trustee, by the fact that the trustee of such a trust sometimes has no duties to perform during an insured-settlor's lifetime, or by whether the trustee is designated as such in the policy or is designated as beneficiary without mention of any trust but pursuant to an agreement with the insured (or other policy owner) to hold the proceeds upon the agreed trust.

c(1). When trust arises. An insurance arrangement of this type may result in the creation of a present trust, with the trustee immediately holding, in trust, the rights acquired as designated beneficiary under the policy; or it may instead result in a nontestamentary trust that comes into existence upon the death of the insured, if and when the trustee's right to the proceeds materializes.

The revocable life-insurance trust is usually created with the express agreement, or at least with the knowledge and acquiescence, of the trustee. These circumstances result in the creation of a present trust with a *chose in action* as the trust property, unless the settlor manifests a contrary intention. A trust does not come into existence until the death of the insured, however, if before that time the trustee is unaware of the intended trust, such as where the policy shows that the proceeds are to be paid to the designated beneficiary "in trust" or "as trustee" and the trust terms are set forth by the settlor in a separate writing (see § 22, Comment *c*).

On when a trust that is created by an enforceable promise comes into existence in other contexts, see generally § 10, Comment *g*, and § 15, Comment *b*.

c(2). Other trust and insurance arrangements. Revocable inter vivos life-insurance trusts may be but rarely are created in the same manner as the widely used irrevocable life-insurance trust—that is, by a transfer of the life-insurance policy to the trustee. In cases of these types, the trust property is the policy itself, and additional property may and often is transferred to the trustee as well. In any event, the revocable or irrevocable trust comes into existence in these situations by reason of and at the time of the insured's (or other owner's) assignment of the policy to the trustee.

In addition, the trustee of a revocable or irrevocable trust funded with other assets (thus, not an "insurance trust") may also be the designated beneficiary of one or more insurance policies.

Furthermore, the proceeds of life-insurance policies may be paid to testamentary trusts, when the trustee named or to be named in a will is designated as the primary or alternate beneficiary by the insured or other owner of the policy.

c(3). Trusts and retirement benefits. Similar in concept, validity, and nontestamentary character are (i) inter vivos trusts that are created (or enlarged) by beneficiary designation under such arrangements as employee-benefit plans, individual retirement accounts, and other pension arrangements, and (ii) trusts that are later created at the time they are funded by the receipt of death benefits from such sources by trustees named in beneficiary designations and instruments of trust executed during the plan participant's lifetime. (As in the case of insurance trusts, the inference is that the trust is intended to arise at the time the designated trustee is informed of the arrangement.) Again, it is also possible and valid for additions to be made to testamentary trusts by these types of beneficiary designations in favor of trustees named or to be named in wills. . . . .

On revocation and amendment of trusts that are to receive proceeds of community property life-insurance policies and pension arrangements, cf. § 63, Comment *k*.

Comment on Subsection (2):

d. Applicability of restrictions on testamentary disposition. Although revocable inter vivos trusts are nontestamentary and therefore need not meet the *formal* requirements imposed on testation, a different situation is presented by what might be called *substantive* policies restricting testation. The history of the trust reveals the role it has played, for good or for bad, in avoiding some of the undesired consequences of legal ownership.

One of the contributions of the trust device has been its use in avoiding outmoded rules or technical disabilities in advance of legal reform or, as can be seen in the preceding Comments to this section, as a means of providing choice and alternatives in matters of form and procedure, alternatives that are not inconsistent with serious policies relating to the disposition of property following death. (See more generally Comment *a*.)

Although serious policies *restricting* disposition of property after the owner's death would seem to make most sense if expressly made applicable as well to will substitutes, they are often expressed in narrow statutory language referring only to wills or to decedents' estates. Despite the narrow wording of a relevant statute, however, and although the trust is otherwise valid, a trust may be subject to a restrictive policy and, as appropriate to the circumstances, may be set aside in whole or in part because the trust or part of it involves a disposition that could not effectively have been made by will. Thus, a revocable inter vivos trust generally will not be given effect to the extent the settlor is prohibited from disposing of similar property for a similar purpose by will. This result is not dependent on a finding that the trust is "illusory" or that it was "intended to evade" the restriction on testamentary disposition.

For example, in most American jurisdictions the surviving spouse of a married decedent is entitled to a share of the estate of which the spouse cannot be deprived by the decedent's will in the absence of an election by the spouse to accept something less or different, or nothing, as may be provided by the decedent's will. Although modern versions of these so-called "forced" or "elective" share statutes vary considerably in language and in details of implementation, a married property owner cannot properly circumvent the policy of such statutes through the use of an inter vivos trust that is revocable, directly or indirectly (such as through an unrestricted power of amendment or appointment), by the settlor. This is true even though an *outright gift* by a married property owner would operate to diminish the eventual elective share of the donor's spouse. See more generally Restatement Second, Property (Donative Transfers) §§ 13.7 and 32.1(3) [Restatement Third, Property (Wills and Other Donative Transfers) §§ 9.1–9.2, 23.1].

Similarly, in some American jurisdictions there have been and may again be statutes limiting the portion of a testator's estate that can be devised or bequeathed for charitable purposes, particularly if the testator leaves certain near relatives surviving and dies within a certain period after executing the will. (See § 28, Comment *b*.) Under the rule stated in this subsection, this type of restriction is applicable as well to provisions for charitable purposes taking effect after the death of the settlor of a revocable inter vivos trust. . . . .

e. Rights of creditors and other matters. Although a revocable trust is nontestamentary and is therefore not subject to the Wills Act or to the usual procedures of estate administration, property held in the trust is subject to the claims of creditors of the settlor or of the deceased settlor's estate if the same property belonging to the settlor or the estate would be subject to the claims of the creditors, taking account of homestead rights and other exemptions.

This result is not dependent on the trust being "illusory" or "testamentary," or on the transfer being a fraudulent conveyance, but is based on the sound public policy of basing the rights of creditors on the substance rather than the form of the debtor's property rights. Nor is the result affected by the presence of a spendthrift provision in the terms of the trust (see § 58(2)) or by whether a creditor's claim arose before or after the transfer.

Whether other assets of the settlor must first be exhausted and other questions involving priority among creditors or among various categories of intended beneficiaries of a deceased debtor are not within the scope of this Restatement. . . . .

e(1). Statutory protections against oversight and aids in construction. In addition to the limitations on testamentary disposition represented by statutes discussed in Comment *d* and less directly by claims of creditors (above), an array of statutes are found throughout the various American jurisdictions that are designed as protections or aids against oversight or inadequacies in the planning and drafting of wills. These statutes often fail specifically to address revocable inter vivos trusts or other will-substitute dispositions. (*Common law* rules or principles of construction normally apply to revocable and irrevocable inter vivos trusts as well as to testamentary trusts. . . . .)

Illustrative are pretermitted-heir statutes that, despite differences in their breadth and other details, usually provide intestate shares of a decedent's estate at least for children born after the making of a will that does not by class gift or otherwise make provision, as defined by the statute, for them. Analogous statutes in some states, especially where intestate shares of surviving spouses are significantly greater than their elective shares, make provision in certain circumstances for survivors of marriages entered after the execution of wills.

Other examples include anti-lapse statutes, usually providing substitute gifts for the issue of certain legatees and devisees who predecease testators, and statutes primarily providing for revocation of will provisions for spouses in cases in which divorce occurs after the making of a will.

Statutes of these various types are generally based on legislative judgments concerning probabilities of intention and yield to contrary intent that is shown by types of evidence allowed by the legislation. Sound policy suggests that a property owner's choice of form in using a revocable trust rather than a will as the central instrument of an estate plan should not deprive that property owner and the objects of his or her bounty of appropriate aids and safeguards intended to achieve likely intentions. Thus, although a particular statute of this general type fails to address trusts that are revocable but nontestamentary, the legislation should ordinarily be applied as if trust dispositive provisions that are to be carried out after the settlor's death had been made by will.

e(2). Limits on public benefits and resources. Somewhat analogous problems may arise from quite different types of federal and state legislation or administrative regulations, involving such matters as public benefit programs and governmentally allocated opportunities. Examples range from matters of eligibility and reimbursement for welfare benefits and services to issues about the allocation of entitlements or licenses with respect to water resources, communications media, and the like. . . . .

f. Cross-references. On the subject matter of this Comment, see generally Restatement Third, Property (Wills and Other Donative Transfers) § 7.2, Comments *a–c* and *e–h*; and Restatement Second, Property (Donative Transfers) Chapter 34, and also compare id. Chapter 13.

§ 26. Tentative ("Totten" or Bank-Account) Trusts

Where a person makes a deposit in an account with a bank or similar financial institution in the depositor's own name "as trustee" or "in trust" for another, the presumption is that the depositor intends to establish a "tentative trust." The depositor may modify or revoke a tentative trust and may, from time to time, withdraw any or all of the funds on deposit. On the death of the depositor, the trust is enforceable by the beneficiary as to any funds then remaining on deposit, unless the depositor has revoked the trust.

Comment:

a. The depositor's intention. A person may make a savings deposit in a bank, savings and loan association, credit union, or other similar financial institution in the depositor's own name "in trust" or "as trustee" for another named person. The depositor's intention may be to create a trust or not to create a trust. If the former, the deposit constitutes a declaration of trust, in which the depositor is the trustee and the claim against the financial institution is the trust property. Even in such a case of intended trust, however, the intention may be to create a form of revocable trust or to make a gift by means of an immediate, irrevocable trust. And even this last interpretation leaves uncertain the duration and terms of the trust and the extent of the interest given to the person named as beneficiary.

Evidence may be admitted to show which of the various above results was intended by the depositor. In the absence of sufficient evidence of a depositor's different intention, the mere fact that the deposit was made in the name of the depositor "as trustee" or "in trust" for another person, or for other persons, manifests an intention to create the special type of revocable trust to which the rules stated in this section apply. Such a trust is called a "tentative trust" in this Restatement, and in cases and literature is often called a "savings account" or "bank account" trust, or a "Totten trust," for the leading case establishing its validity, Matter of Totten, 179 N.Y. 112, 71 N.E. 748 (1904).

Unlike the usual rule concerning trusts, however, including trusts created by taking title to corporate stocks or bonds as "trustee" or "in trust" for another (on the circumstances of presumed revocability or irrevocability more generally, see § 63, Comment *e*), mention of a trust or trustee in a savings-account form carries no inference of irrevocability, but rather the opposite. See Comment *c*. Furthermore, the casual, uncertain nature of the tentative trust also justifies the occasional differences in treatment prescribed for it in cases and in this section (see Comment *c*), as compared to the treatment of revocable living trusts generally, as stated in § 25 . . . .

Although notice to the beneficiary is not essential to the creation of a trust (see § 14), the fact that the depositor notified the beneficiary of the deposit is some evidence of an intention that the trust is to be irrevocable. This is so whether the notification is given at or before the time of the deposit or subsequently. Delivery of the account book to the beneficiary is also some evidence that the trust is intended to be irrevocable, as are statements by the depositor to third persons of an intention to create an irrevocable trust. Strong evidence of intended irrevocability is the depositor's filing of a gift-tax return reporting the transfer establishing the account as a gift. On the other hand, failure to file a gift-tax return is no evidence of the depositor's intent when the amount deposited is less than the amount of the gift-tax annual exclusion, and is only slight evidence supporting the inference of revocability when the deposit exceeds the annual exclusion amount.

Evidence may also be admitted to show that the depositor did not intend to create a trust at all, either revocable or irrevocable, despite the use of the word "trust" or "trustee." See § 13, Comment *b*. Thus, evidence may be admitted to show a reason why the depositor wished not to have the account reveal his or her individual ownership.

Evidence that the funds in the account were treated as the depositor's own property after making the deposit serves to counter evidence or allegation of irrevocability, but is not evidence at all that would tend to rebut the presumption of a tentative-trust intention.

Illustrations:

1. D deposits her own funds in a savings account in her name "as trustee" for her niece, N. Absent other evidence of her intent, D has created a tentative (i.e., revocable) trust for herself and N in accordance with the rules of Comments *b* through *d* of this section.

2. Same facts as in Illustration 1, except that D turns the passbook over to N's father and tells friends that she has set up a "college fund" for N (referring to the savings account). This establishes an

irrevocable trust for N, not a tentative trust as defined and described in this section.

5. X uses her funds to purchase shares in a stock mutual fund, "as trustee" for her child, C, checking the form option calling for the dividends to be reinvested—that is, to be used to purchase additional shares in that fund. Absent other evidence of X's intent, this type of "trust" arrangement is not of a type that is subject to the tentative-trust presumption and rules of this section.

Unlike the stock fund in Illustration 5, deposits in money-market mutual funds and similar accounts with investment companies, banks, and other financial institutions are potentially subject to the rule and principles of this section, although typical forms used and information supplied in establishing such accounts are likely to overcome (or prevent) the tentative-trust presumption.

b. Validity of tentative trust. Even though a settlor who creates a tentative trust reserves complete control over the deposit during life, the disposition is not invalid as an "illusory" or "testamentary" disposition. To the contrary, it is upheld as a convenient and permissible method of disposing of money at death. The tentative trust is an accepted form of will substitute that need not comply with the requirements of the Statute of Wills and, ordinarily at least (compare Comment *d*), will be implemented without involvement in estate administration.

c. Revocation and termination of tentative trust. A tentative trust can properly be revoked by the depositor at any time during life by a manifestation of intention to do so. No particular formalities are necessary to manifest that intention.

Thus, the trust is terminated by withdrawal of all the funds or by transferring them to a different account. If any part of the deposit is withdrawn during the depositor's lifetime, this operates as a revocation of the trust to the extent of the withdrawal; and the beneficiary will be entitled only to the amount remaining on deposit at the death of the depositor. The nature or terms of the account may be changed by the depositor's direction to the savings institution. In addition, the right to funds remaining in the account at the depositor's death may be changed by agreement between the beneficiary and the depositor. . . . .

Where there are multiple depositors, or if there are multiple persons designated as trustees, one of whom is the depositor, it is presumed that there is a right of survivorship between or among the "trustees" of the trust, which remains a tentative trust as long as a trustee and a beneficiary survive. The death of the beneficiary (or of the last survivor of multiple beneficiaries) of a tentative trust prior to the death of the depositor (or last trustee) terminates the trust, even though the depositor (or last trustee) later dies without having manifested an intention to revoke the trust and without having withdrawn the amount on deposit. In such a case, the personal representative of the depositor (or last trustee), not the personal representative of the beneficiary, will be entitled to the amount on deposit; and even an anti-lapse statute that ordinarily applies to other revocable trusts (§ 25, Comment *e(1)*) does not apply to tentative trusts. . . . .

In the absence of a statute to the contrary, a tentative trust may be revoked in whole or in part by the depositor's will, either by express provision or by necessary implication. The conservator of a depositor who becomes incompetent may, with such court permission as may be required by law, withdraw some or all of the tentative-trust funds as necessary for the welfare of the depositor and appropriate members of his or her family. A successor "trustee" will not be appointed (contrast §§ 31, 34).

Illustrations:

6. D sets up a tentative-trust account, the filled-in bank form showing B as beneficiary. Later, a few months before his death, D executes a will expressly bequeathing one half of the funds on deposit in that account to X. At D's death (assuming no statute to the contrary), B and X are entitled to share equally in the account, by reason of D's partial revocation.

7. Same facts (and assumption) as in Illustration 6, except that D's will simply leaves his entire estate to X. This does not revoke the tentative trust; B is entitled to the funds in the account at D's death.

8. The same facts (and assumption) as in Illustration 6, except that D has little property other than his home and the funds on deposit in the tentative-trust account, and his will leaves the home to X, $50,000 to Y, $50,000 to Z, and the rest of his estate, "if any," to C Church. D was aware when he made his will that his "other" property was worth about $20,000, which was also its value when he died. The trust account had about $75,000 in it when he executed his will and about the same at his death. Absent any evidence showing a contrary intention of D, the tentative trust is revoked by implication by D's will.

d. Creditors' rights, family protection, and rules of will construction. The creditors of a person who establishes a tentative trust can reach the funds on deposit, as may the personal representative of a deceased depositor if assets otherwise available in the estate administration are insufficient to pay debts and funeral, last-illness, and administration expenses.

The tentative trust, like other revocable inter vivos trusts, is subject to restrictions on testamentary disposition and also to pretermitted-heir and omitted-spouse protections. On these latter, see § 25, Comment *e(1)*; and on the elective share of a depositor's surviving spouse and restrictions on dispositions for charitable purposes, see § 25, Comment *d*. Statutes revoking will provisions for former spouses following divorce (§ 25, Comment *e(1)*) also apply to tentative-trust beneficiaries, but anti-lapse statutes (§ 25, Comment *e(1)*) do not. See Comment *c*.

e. Statutory provisions. Statutes in most states provide protections for financial institutions that make payments in reliance on the forms in which deposits are made, such as deposits "as trustee" or "in trust." Also increasingly common are statutes (many based on the original or amended version of Uniform Probate Code, Article 6) that make detailed provisions concerning the interpretation of savings deposits "in trust" or "as trustee" (as a form of "POD account" under the UPC) or supply details concerning the nature and treatment of tentative trusts and the rights of depositors and beneficiaries. . . . .

PART 3
ELEMENTS OF TRUSTS

CHAPTER 6

TRUST PURPOSES

Introductory Note: It is often stated, including in some statutes, essentially, that trusts may be created "for any purpose that is not illegal" or "for any purpose for which a person may contract." In a comprehensive sense these statements are true, for, with its flexibility and its highly developed, prototypical, default body of ready-made fiduciary principles, the trust device is widely used in a broad variety of arrangements serving diverse purposes. Illustrative are trusts to pay or secure creditors, to operate employee-benefit and pension programs, to manage property, and to conduct business or collective-investment activities. Although usually subject in significant part to other bodies of federal or state law and not specifically within the subject matter of this Restatement (see § 1, Comments *a* and *b*, and § 5, Comment *l*), these various trust forms also draw heavily upon the concepts, principles, and rules of the law of trusts as set forth throughout this Restatement. . . . . In addition, revocable trusts (see § 25) can be used for virtually any purpose their living settlors personally could pursue.

Nevertheless, the trusts that are the primary subject of this Restatement are those associated with the planned, usually donative, testamentary or nontestamentary disposition of family property. The use of these trusts, once they become irrevocable, is subject to rules and policies that limit trust purposes and provisions in various ways. A price is exacted by modern common-law legal systems for their unique tolerance of the deadhand control that typifies these trusts. Beyond its regulation of perpetuities (see § 29(b)), for example, the common law does not allow trusts for capricious or frivolous purposes, even purposes with which the law would not interfere if pursuit of those purposes merely involved the use of property by living, current owners (§ 29(c)).

Specifically, with exceptions that are limited in both purpose and duration, trusts must be for objectives that qualify as either charitable or private. (See §§ 27 and 28, and compare the recognition of what have often been called "purpose" or "honorary" trusts in § 47. On the importance of whether a trust is "charitable" rather than private, or honorary, see § 28, Comments *a–d* . . . .) Furthermore, even in otherwise valid trusts, certain provisions may not be given effect because the trust law views them as serving purposes that are contrary to public policy although the acts or decisions of a person who owned the property would not be similarly constrained.

Throughout not only this chapter but this entire Restatement, reference is regularly made to "the purpose(s) of the trust" and to the importance of trust "purposes" in the handling of specific issues. Unfortunately, the purposes of a given trust are often not stated in the trust provisions, especially with precision or in comprehensive terms. As a result, the ascertainment or clarification of settlor purposes is frequently difficult and left to some speculation. Whatever identification and understanding of trust purposes is possible is often the result of inferences drawn from the nature and terms of the various beneficial interests created by the settlor.

More thoughtful guidance by drafters would often be helpful to trustees, beneficiaries, and courts in seeking to understand trust purposes and to carry out settlor intentions. Yet, it is important to note as well that hasty, casual, or rote expressions of trust objectives are often incomplete and can even be seriously misleading, and are thus likely to do more harm than good.

§ 27. Purposes for Which a Trust Can Be Created

(1) Subject to the rules of § 29, a trust may be created for charitable purposes (see § 28) or for private purposes, or for a combination of charitable and private purposes.

(2) Subject to the special rules of §§ 46(2) and 47, a private trust, its terms, and its administration must be for the benefit of its beneficiaries, who must be identified or ascertainable as provided in § 44. (On charitable trusts, see § 28.)

Comment on Subsection (1):

a. *Charitable and private purposes.* Except as provided in §§ 46(2) and 47 (on certain trust provisions for "indefinite beneficiaries" and "noncharitable purposes," respectively), permissible purposes of trusts that are the subject of this Restatement are confined to those that are charitable ("charitable trusts") and those that are for the benefit of persons who are definite or will be ascertainable in compliance with rules regulating perpetuities ("private trusts"). Furthermore, trust purposes and provisions must not be unlawful or contrary to public policy (§ 29).

Trusts may have mixed charitable and private purposes. Thus, for example, a trust may be created to provide concurrent benefits for both charitable and private purposes, either by fixed portions or discretionary distributions. More frequently, so-called "split-interest" trusts are created to benefit the settlor or family members for term or life periods and thereafter to benefit charity, or vice versa. See further § 28, Comment *e*. The use and details of these mixed arrangements are likely to be dominated by tax objectives and requirements, which are not within the scope of this Restatement.

The subject of charitable trusts and purposes is specifically addressed in the next section (§ 28), and the principles for determining whether a purpose qualifies as a charitable purpose are discussed in that section. (Trust-law definitions of charity may differ from those used in federal, state, and local tax law.) Some purposes that a reasonable individual might believe worthwhile may fall short of the standard of charity for which a charitable trust may be established. On such cases, see § 47.

Often the purposes of private trusts are not specified but must be inferred from the interests conferred on the various beneficiaries, whose identities and interests are subject to the requirements of definiteness discussed in Chapter 9 (especially §§ 44 through 47).

On the possibility of treating intended trusts that are not capricious (see § 29, Comment *h*, and § 47, Comment *e*), but are neither charitable nor entirely private, as powers under adapted trusts (sometimes called "honorary trusts"), see § 47, Comments *c* and *d*.

Comment on Subsection (2):

b. Private trusts. The general purpose of a private trust is to benefit identified or identifiable beneficiaries (see §§ 44–46) in accordance with their respective interests in the trust. Within this general private purpose, a given trust may and most likely will serve multiple objectives or purposes (see *b(1)* below).

The settlor of a particular trust has considerable latitude in specifying the manner in which a trust purpose is to be pursued. In order to be valid, however, administrative and other provisions must reasonably relate to a trust purpose and must not have the effect of diverting the trust's funds or administration from that purpose in support of a purpose that does not meet the private- or charitable-purpose requirement of Subsection (1), as qualified by § 47 (on general and specific noncharitable "purpose" trusts).

Also, on the trustee's duty of loyalty, and to administer in a manner consistent with the trust purposes, see § 78 and also § 87.

b(1). Uses of private trusts. It is not possible to enumerate all of the diverse reasons that motivate settlors to create private trusts for themselves or for others. . . . . Common motivations, however, range from the avoidance of probate, to providing property management for those who cannot, ought not, or wish not to manage for themselves, to providing for limited and successive enjoyment of property over several generations, and including as well such objectives as the saving of taxes and the insulation of trust property from the claims of beneficiaries' creditors.

§ 28. Charitable Purposes

Charitable trust purposes include:

(a) the relief of poverty;

(b) the advancement of knowledge or education;

(c) the advancement of religion;

(d) the promotion of health;

(e) governmental or municipal purposes; and

(f) other purposes that are beneficial to the community.

General Comment:

a. The general nature of charitable trusts and purposes. The general scope of charitable purposes in England was indicated over four centuries ago in the preamble to the Statute of Charitable Uses, 43 Eliz. I, c. 4 (1601). The listing there was similar in substance to that set forth above in this section, although differing in style, language, and detail.

The validity of charitable trusts in the United States is not dependent upon the adoption of a statute to that effect or upon the reception of the English Statute of Charitable Uses as part of the law of the particular state.

The discussion in this section of dispositions that are charitable does not necessarily provide a complete enumeration of charitable purposes. Other purposes of the same general character are likewise charitable. The common element of charitable purposes is that they are designed to accomplish objects that are beneficial to the community—i.e., to the public or indefinite members thereof—without also serving what amount to private trust purposes (see *a(1)* of this Comment). As long as the purposes to which the property of the trust is to be devoted are charitable, however, the motives of the settlor in creating the trust are immaterial.

A trust purpose is charitable if its accomplishment is of such social interest or benefit to the community as to justify permitting the property to be devoted to the purpose in perpetuity and to justify the various other special privileges that are typically allowed to charitable trusts.

There is no fixed standard to determine what purposes are of such interest to the community, for the interests of the community vary with time and place. Trust-law definitions of charity are not limited by those used in federal, state, and local tax law; nor are tax-law definitions necessarily limited to charitable purposes recognized by the trust law. Of the generally agreed purposes stated in this section, it is Clause (f) (Comment *l*) that provides the greatest flexibility and also presents the most definitional issues at the margin.

A charitable trust can be created for one or more charitable purposes and thus may fit within more than one of the purposes as stated in this section. For example, a trust to establish a scholarship for poor children is a trust for the relief of poverty as well as for the advancement of education.

Charitable trusts are favored not only in regard to the rules to which they are subject (see, e.g., Comments *c* and *d* . . .) but also in matters of interpretation. Thus, courts prefer to find that a purpose is limited to charity and qualifies as a charitable purpose when uncertain language is susceptible of a broader, not strictly charitable interpretation. Accordingly, a trust for "charitable and benevolent purposes," or even for "charitable *or* benevolent purposes," would likely be interpreted as intended to include only charitable purposes; if the term "benevolent" is given its broader meaning, however, the trust is not charitable. In the latter case, however, see § 47.

A trust need not designate a specific charitable purpose or a method of accomplishing such a purpose in order to be charitable. Thus, a trust "for such charitable purpose or purposes as my trustee shall select," or "as T or her successor trustee may from time to time select," is charitable. So also is a trust simply "for charitable purposes" or even a devise simply to "Charity," for which the intention to create a charitable trust will be implied, with the trustee to have power and a duty to select one or more charitable purposes. In either of the latter cases, when a trustee is not named one will be appointed by the court, for a trust created in such terms will not fail for want of a trustee (see § 31).

An outright devisee or donation to a nonproprietary hospital or university or other charitable institution, expressly or impliedly to be used for its general purposes, is charitable but does not create a trust as that term is used in this Restatement. A disposition to such an institution for a specific purpose, however, such as to support medical research, perhaps on a particular disease, or to establish a scholarship fund in a certain field of study, creates a charitable trust of which the institution is the trustee for purposes of the terminology and rules of this Restatement.

a(1). Public not private benefit. It does not matter in the latter case that, for example, only one student or two may receive a scholarship from the fund as long as the potential class of recipients will be drawn from an indefinite group . . . rather than from a group so narrowly defined (e.g., the settlor's descendants or relatives) as to make the trust a private trust (see further Comment *f*, last paragraph).

The fact that a medical facility, school, home for the poor, or similar institution, whether public or private, charges a fee for its services or for the use of its facilities does not prevent the institution from being charitable, or a trust to support its programs from being a charitable trust, as long as the institution is not proprietary—i.e., does not seek to make a profit to benefit its shareholders or otherwise to serve a noncharitable purpose. . . . .

a(2). Controversial ideas and unpopular causes. If the general purposes for which a trust is created are such that they may be reasonably thought to promote the social interest of the community, the mere fact that a majority of the people or of the members of a court believe that the particular purpose of the settlor is unwise or not well adapted to its social objective does not prevent the trust from being charitable. Thus, a trust to promote a particular religious doctrine or a particular system of taxation is charitable even though the view to be promoted has but a modest number of adherents. The role of the court in deciding whether a purpose is charitable is not to attempt to decide which of conflicting views of the social or community interest is more beneficial or appropriate but to decide whether the trust purpose or the view to be promoted is sufficiently useful or reasonable to be of such benefit or interest to the community, including through a marketplace of ideas, as to justify the perpetual existence and other privileges of a charitable trust. Thus, a trust to establish a museum to exhibit what a testator regarded as objects of art but which testimony establishes to be of no artistic value, or a trust to publish and distribute a testator's views that are irrational or other writings that are of no literary or educational value, is not charitable. The line between what is charitable and what is not is sometimes a difficult one to draw, for the difference may be one of degree and the line may be drawn differently at different times and in different places. For trusts that do not qualify as either private or charitable trusts, see the limited duration and acceptance of "trusts for noncharitable purposes" in § 47.

On trust purposes that were initially charitable but cease to be of interest to the public or otherwise to have the social utility necessary to be charitable, see § 67 on the doctrine of cy pres, especially id., Comment *c*.

b. Restrictions on creation of charitable trusts. Except as otherwise provided by statute, there are no restrictions on the right of property owners to create charitable trusts that are not equally applicable to the creation of private trusts. . . . .

Statutes restricting, by amount or timing, the creation of charitable trusts apply to secret or semi-secret trusts (§ 18) for charitable purposes and to attempted testamentary additions (see § 19) to existing charitable trusts. If reasonably possible, a statute of this type should be construed as applicable, or its policy applied by analogy, to revocable living trusts (see § 25(2)).

c. Indefinite beneficiaries. A charitable trust can be created although it has no definite or definitely ascertainable beneficiary. (Contrast §§ 44–46 on the beneficiary requirement of private trusts.)

Charitable trusts are ordinarily enforceable upon suit by the Attorney General, as representative of the community, although there may also be beneficiaries with a special interest in the trust who can maintain a suit to enforce it. See Chapter 17.

d. Duration of charitable trusts. A charitable trust is not invalid although by its terms it is to continue for an indefinite or unlimited period of time. This is unlike the rules for private trusts, in which the interests of the beneficiaries must vest within the period of the applicable rule against perpetuities, and under which a provision that a private trust shall be indestructible (i. e., is not to be terminated even upon the consent of all beneficiaries) beyond the period of the rule is invalid. See § 29(b) and § 29, Comments *g* and *h*.

Charitable trusts may be of unlimited duration, although dispositions over to charitable purposes following private trusts are subject to the rule against perpetuities, as are dispositions over to private purposes upon termination of charitable trusts. On the other hand, even after the perpetuities period would have expired, a shift over from one charitable purpose or trust to another is permissible because, it is often said, the property is "vested in charity." See § 29, Comment *g*. Also see id., Comment *h* and (on accumulations) Comment *h(2)*.

e. *Trusts with mixed charitable and other purposes.* A trust is not invalid, although it might not be a *charitable* trust, merely because it includes private trust interests (§ 27(2)) or a "noncharitable purpose" (§ 47) as well as the designated charitable purpose.

If the charitable and other purposes are distinctly divided either by time or into separate and independent shares, the period or share devoted to charity will be treated as a charitable trust just as if separate trusts had been created for the different purposes. Where there is no such separation by time or by independent shares, the trust is valid, but such a mixed charitable and *private* trust is subject to the rule against perpetuities as a private trust; and if the trust similarly combines charitable purposes with a *noncharitable purpose*, the trust is subject to the rules and limitations of noncharitable-purpose trusts under § 47. . . . .

f. *Consistency with law and public policy.* Like other trusts, charitable trusts are subject to the rule of § 29 that trust purposes and provisions must not be unlawful or contrary to public policy.

It is particularly common, however, for provisions to be included in various types of charitable trusts, especially those created for educational or health purposes or for the relief of poverty, limiting the direct benefits or eligibility to persons of a particular national origin, religion, gender, sexual orientation, age group, political affiliation, or other characteristics or background. Of course, federal and state constitutions, legislation, and other binding expressions of applicable law and policy are to be respected in the administration of trusts and in determining the enforceability of the terms of trusts. These matters, and such implicit issues as what may constitute state action, are beyond the scope of this Restatement. The issue for present purposes, however, remains what provisions of this general type may, as a matter of trust law and policy, be inconsistent with the nature of charitable purposes.

Provisions of these types in charitable trusts are not valid if they involve *invidious* discrimination (see below). Where a restriction or preference is invalid, or the particular charitable disposition cannot be carried out because the intended recipient refuses to accept it due to a restrictive provision or preference the intended recipient deems objectionable, an issue arises concerning the application of the doctrine of cy pres. See § 67. Unless the terms of the trust manifest a valid contrary intention, the doctrine will be applied to remove a provision that is unlawful or contrary to public policy. Where an intended recipient objects to a provision that is not invalid, the doctrine would ordinarily be applied *either* by removing that provision *or* by substituting a different recipient, in accordance with principles described in § 67, Comment *d*, for closely approximating probable settlor intention.

It is not always possible to state with certainty what constitutes an "invidious" form of discrimination for these purposes. What the law of charitable trusts does or does not allow inevitably varies from time to time and place to place, as well as from context to context. For example, trust-law policies regarding restrictions on gender, sexual orientation, or age are especially sensitive to *context*, as the scope of more general statutory and constitutional protections evolve in these matters. . . . . Some generalizations are nevertheless possible.

When a scholarship or other form of assistance or opportunity is to be awarded on a basis that, for example, explicitly excludes potential beneficiaries on the basis of membership in a particular racial, ethnic, or religious group, the restriction is ordinarily invidious and therefore unenforceable. Thus, a trust to provide land and maintenance for a playground from which Black children are excluded, or a trust to support a scholarship program for which no Roman Catholic may apply, is not enforceable under those terms as a charitable trust. Similarly, although the exclusions are not *explicit*, a trust to provide research grants for which only "white, Anglo-Saxon Protestants" may apply is invidious and noncharitable.

This does not mean that a criterion such as gender, religion, or national origin may not be used in a charitable trust when it is a reasonable element of a settlor's charitable purpose and charitable motivation. Thus, the requirement that the purpose be of charitable character does not prevent alumnae or friends of a women's college from endowing a professorial chair or library fund for that college, or a Jewish man from leaving money to a university to establish a scholarship program, in the betterment of his religion as he sees it, to enable a rabbi or two each year to study in that university's philosophy department. Nor does it mean that a Norwegian immigrant who became wealthy in this country cannot establish a program of an otherwise charitable nature to aid, solely or by preference, other Norwegian immigrants or the children of Norwegian immigrants. Similarly, the law of charitable trusts as such does not object to what is sometimes called "affirmative action," attempting to respond to a social problem in its own terms, at least as reasonably perceived by a substantial (even if not majority) segment of society or of the affected community.

A trust may be charitable if its purpose is, for example, to relieve poverty or health problems among: persons over or under a certain age; members of a particular labor union, fraternal organization, or church parish to which the settlor belonged; or persons who are or have been engaged in, or the surviving spouses and orphaned children of persons who had engaged in, a particular profession or trade, such as writers, actors, teachers, or employees of a particular business.

Thus, a trust with one or more of the purposes stated in Clauses (a) through (f) of this section may be a charitable trust despite limitations of types described in the two preceding paragraphs. The class of potential beneficiaries, however, may not be so narrowly defined as to benefit only named individuals or a class of friends, descendants, or other relatives of the settlor. The private character of a trust with potential beneficiaries so narrowly defined prevents it from being a charitable trust, even though it is concerned, for example, with education or health care. See more generally Comment *a*. Such a trust may nevertheless be upheld as a private trust (see

§§ 43–46) and may be enforced within the rules and limitations (e.g., § 29(b)) applicable to private trusts.

Comment on Clause (a):

g. Relief of poverty. A trust for the relief of poverty is charitable. To assist the poor is a charitable purpose whether the method of assistance provided by the terms of the trust is by the distribution of money or goods among the needy, by leasing the land or making loans to them at a low rent or at low or no interest, by assisting them to secure employment, by providing soup kitchens, or by establishing a home or other facility to meet their needs, or if the settlor provides that the means of assistance is within the discretion of the trustee.

A trust for the relief of poverty generally, with no specification of the means to be employed, is valid as a charitable trust. Thus, a trust "for the benefit of the poor" or simply "for the poor" is charitable.

A trust may be valid as a trust for the relief of poverty even though the terms of the trust do not state specifically that the beneficiaries must be poor. Thus, a trust for the benefit of "widows, widowers, and orphans" is ordinarily to be interpreted as meaning "needy widows, widowers, and orphans." Similarly, a trust for the benefit of the "elderly inhabitants" of a particular community may be construed as including only such of them as are poor or otherwise in need of special assistance (compare, e.g., promotion of health, Comment *j*).

A trust to help persons who are in some need of financial aid is a charitable trust under Clause (a) although the persons to be assisted are not destitute. For example, a trust is charitable if its purpose is to provide financial assistance to persons who have an income that does not afford the reasonable comforts of life that most others enjoy. Thus, a trust to provide rent or rental subsidies for secure, sanitary housing for such persons is charitable.

A trust to establish or maintain a home for the poor which is not conducted for private profit is charitable, although it is provided that the residents shall pay an admission fee or otherwise contribute to the expense of maintaining the home. The relief of poverty is charitable even though an incidental effect of assisting those in need is to help those better off, or even the wealthy, by diminishing the amount of taxes they might otherwise be compelled to pay. And a trust is no less charitable because one of its effects may be to relieve relatives of the assisted persons from a legal duty or sense of moral obligation to provide for their support.

A trust for the relief of poverty is charitable although the beneficiaries are limited to inhabitants of a specific place, whether a particular country, state, city, town, or parish. The relief need not extend to all persons in need but may be limited to those of a particular cause or type of need, provided the class is not so limited or defined as to be invidiously discriminatory or more consistent with the nature of a private trust (see Comment *a*).

Comment on Clause (b):

h. Advancement of knowledge or education. A trust for the advancement of knowledge or education is charitable. Trusts for the promotion of education include trusts: to establish, maintain, or help to maintain schools, colleges, or other educational institutions or associated facilities; to establish professorships, lectureships, or fellowships; to pay or increase salaries or pensions of teachers or staff; to establish scholarships, academic prizes, or otherwise to assist students in acquiring an education, regardless of whether financial need is a criterion; or to establish or maintain public libraries, museums, or other facilities. Also supportive of education or enhancement of knowledge are trusts to promote or support research, or to promote the dissemination of knowledge or beliefs by the publication of books and pamphlets or through conferences or the delivery of lectures or media presentations.

A trust to promote knowledge or education generally, without specifying the method to be employed, is valid as a charitable trust. Thus, a trust simply "for educational purposes" or "for the promotion of research" is charitable.

A trust for the purpose of providing training in citizenship, character, and leadership is charitable. Thus, a trust to support an organization such as the Girl Scouts is charitable, as is a trust for the instruction of immigrants or others in duties and responsibilities of citizenship.

A trust for the dissemination of beliefs or doctrines may be charitable although the views are out of harmony with those of a majority of the public. Thus, a trust to publish and distribute books and pamphlets or to deliver lectures or hold conferences on the nature and advantages of a phonetic alphabet is charitable. A trust, however, for the dissemination of beliefs or doctrines that are irrational or apparently so foolish as to be of no significant interest to members of the community is not a charitable trust, even though the dissemination is not illegal. A trust to provide instruction in the performance of a criminal act or to induce the commission of such acts is not charitable, although a trust to support the dissemination of literature advocating or explaining the nature and societal benefits of conduct or procedures that are illegal in the state (e.g., assisted suicide) would ordinarily be an educational and thus charitable purpose.

A trust that gives funds to or expends funds for the benefit of an educational or research institution is charitable, whether that institution is public or private, provided the institution is not proprietary. An institution is charitable even if it seeks to make a profit, so long as those profits are to be used for a charitable purpose. Nor is a trust to establish or maintain an educational institution noncharitable because it is provided that the pupils shall pay fees or otherwise contribute to the expense of maintaining the institution, unless it is a proprietary institution—that is, one the profits of which go to shareholders or noncharitable purposes. Similarly, a trust to establish a loan fund to assist students in acquiring an education is charitable, although the borrowers are required to pay interest on the loans provided the interest is to be used for the same or other charitable purposes.

Comment on Clause (c):

i. Advancement of religion. A trust for the advancement of religion is charitable. Included are trusts: to build or maintain a church building; to erect or maintain a monument, memorial window, or other part of the church building; to maintain a burial ground in connection with the church; to supply music for the church; to pay the salary of a clergyman; to disseminate religious beliefs or doctrines; to establish or maintain domestic or foreign missions; or to distribute Bibles and other religious literature.

A trust for the saying of masses for the soul of the settlor or of others is charitable, because the funds support religious activity and the intended benefits are not confined to the particular souls but extend to others. Similarly, a trust to promote the doctrines of a particular religious sect is charitable, although the doctrine is adhered to by only a small portion of the community. So also is a trust charitable if it seeks to promote independent religious beliefs unless those beliefs are not of community interest. On the other hand, a trust to promote actual participation in activities or practices that are unlawful, such as polygamy, is noncharitable even though the belief is one of the tenets of a religion.

A trust for the promotion of religion generally, without reference to any particular sect or method, is charitable. Thus, a trust for such religious purposes as the trustee might select, or a trust "for the worship of God" or "for the spread of the gospel" is charitable. A trust may be charitable as one for the advancement of religion although the terms of the trust do not state in specific terms that its purpose is religious. Thus, the fact that a devisee is a religious organization or a person holding a religious office may indicate that it is to be applied solely for religious purposes, although the terms of the trust do not specifically so limit its purposes. The question is one of interpretation of the language involved in light of all the circumstances, for a devise to a particular person currently holding a religious office is not charitable if it is for his or her personal use and benefit.

Comment on Clause (d):

j. Promotion of health. A trust for the promotion of health is charitable. A trust for the prevention or cure or treatment of diseases (or of a particular disease) is charitable. Thus, a trust to establish or maintain a hospital, or to maintain a ward or a bed in a hospital, is charitable, as is a trust for the study of the causes or treatment of diseases. Similarly, a trust to maintain conditions conducive to health, as by draining swamps, disposing of sewage, establishing pest houses, or otherwise preventing the spread of disease, is charitable, and so is a trust simply for the promotion of health with no provision as to the means of doing so.

A trust for the promotion of mental health is charitable. Thus, a trust to provide a home of comfort and care for persons who suffer from a particular mental disorder, or a home of rest for persons who suffer from the stress of overwork or who are otherwise in need of mental relaxation is charitable. So, too, is a trust for the prevention of mental as well as physical cruelty to children.

A trust for the promotion for health need not extend to all persons but may be limited to those residing in a particular district, or to persons who are members of a particular class or fit a particular description that is not invidious (Comment *f*), provided the eligible group is not in the nature of a private trust or so small that relief to the class is not of benefit to the community. Thus, a trust to establish or maintain a hospital for members of a particular trade or for the employees of a particular company would ordinarily be charitable.

A trust is charitable if it provides funds for the support of a hospital or health facility, whether public or private, provided it is not a proprietary institution . . . . Similarly, a trust to establish or maintain a health facility is charitable although patients are required to pay fees, if profits from its operation are to be used to maintain or improve the institution or are to be applied to some other charitable purpose.

Comment on Clause (e):

k. Governmental or municipal purposes. A trust for the construction or maintenance of public buildings, bridges, streets, highways or other public facilities, or for other governmental or municipal purposes, is charitable under Clause (e) of this section.

A trust for the purpose of supplying a community with facilities ordinarily supplied at the expense of taxpayers is charitable. Charitable trusts therefore include: trusts to erect or maintain a town hall; trusts to provide land for public parks or for developing or maintaining such parks; trusts for the planting of trees along public roadways; trusts to supply or improve the quality of water for the inhabitants of a town or area; trusts to protect the inhabitants from loss by fire or flood, or to provide relief or financial assistance to those who have suffered damage; and trusts to erect monuments to commemorate the contributions of noteworthy individuals.

Clearly, different types of charitable purposes overlap, as can be seen particularly in the case of governmental purposes. For example, a trust to establish or maintain or to assist in the establishment or maintenance of a public school or library or a municipal hospital is charitable not merely on the ground that such a trust is for the advancement of education or the promotion of health but also on the ground that it is to provide the community with facilities or services ordinarily provided at public expense.

A trust may have governmental or municipal purposes, and thus be charitable, although it is not created to provide the community with any specified facilities or services. Thus, a devise to or in trust for the benefit of a certain village or city, without specifying the purposes of the devise or the method of applying the funds of the trust, is charitable. So also, is a trust to defray the general expenses of a town, county, state, or country, or one to contribute toward the reduction of public debt.

Comment on Clause (f):

l. *Promotion of other purposes beneficial to the community.* A trust is charitable if it is established for the promotion of purposes that are of a character sufficiently of interest or beneficial to the community to justify permitting the property to be devoted forever to their accomplishment and to justify whatever other special privileges may be accorded to charitable trusts.

Thus, for example, a trust is charitable if its purpose is to promote the arts and culture (as may be implicit in Comments *h* and *k*) or environmental quality (also see Comments *j* and *k*).

The trusts encompassed by this Comment may involve any of a large, indefinite array of purposes in addition to (or overlapping) those that are dealt with in the preceding Comments but that are nevertheless held to promote the social interests of the community, and are therefore upheld as falling within the scope of charity. It is not possible adequately and accurately to enumerate all purposes of this type, for in deciding whether a particular purpose falls within the present clause, much depends on the time and the place at which the question arises. In each such case, as under some other clauses of this section, particularly some cases involving purposes that are arguably educational, the question for potential judicial determination is whether at the time when the question arises and in the state in which it arises the purpose is one that might reasonably be held to be of community or social interest. The mere fact that a trust is created for the benefit of members of a community outside the state, however, does not prevent the trust from being charitable. Thus, a trust for the benefit of impoverished residents of another state, or to establish a school or hospital in a foreign country, is charitable.

A trust to prevent or alleviate the suffering of animals is charitable. Thus, a trust for the prevention of cruelty to animals, or for the prevention, cure, or treatment of injuries or diseases of animals, is charitable. So also is a trust to establish or support a home or to provide care for stray animals, although a trust to provide for the settlor's own pets is not charitable (see, however, § 47).

A trust for the promotion of national security is charitable. This is so even if it is not clear that a particular trust of this type serves a governmental purpose as described in Comment *k*. Such a trust is charitable whether the means to be employed are the promotion of peace through disarmament or the promotion of preparedness for national defense. So also is a trust that tends to promote efficiency, health, quality of life, or morale among members of the military services. Similarly, a trust to promote patriotism or patriotic purposes is charitable, such as a trust to aid in the celebration or commemoration of important historical dates or events by appropriate ceremonies.

A trust to promote expanded social or economic opportunities for members of the community is charitable although those to be aided are not poverty stricken but merely have less than ordinary opportunities for recreation, enjoyment, or economic advancement. Thus, a trust to assist in providing low-cost housing is charitable, as is a trust to lend money at low rates of interest to persons desirous of entering a trade, profession, or business venture. Similarly charitable is a trust to establish or maintain an institution to improve the moral, intellectual, and physical standards of a community's youth, such as the local Young Men's or Young Women's Christian Association, or other facilities for social meetings, health activities, reading, or the offering of board or lodging to community members or visitors at reasonable rates.

A trust to promote the contentment or well being of members of the community is charitable. Thus, a trust to beautify a city or to preserve the beauties of nature, or otherwise to add to the aesthetic enjoyment of the community, is charitable. Similarly of benefit to the community, and charitable, is a trust to support public concerts or to provide sports or other recreational facilities for the inhabitants of a town. Although some of these examples may be trusts that also promote health or involve a form of education or municipal services, it is sufficient for charitable status under Clause (f) that a trust contribute to the general happiness or the quality of life within the community. . . . .

A trust for the promotion of temperance in the use of intoxicating liquors or other addictive substances is charitable, whether or not the manufacture, sale, or use of such substances is forbidden by law. Such a charitable trust may promote temperance through education or through legislation, and may seek to induce total abstinence or moderation.

A transfer of property with a direction to apply it to the erection or maintenance of a grave, tomb, or monument may not in some circumstances create a charitable trust (but compare "noncharitable purpose" trusts under § 47). If, however, the grave or monument is to be included in, and the funds are to help maintain, even a limited part of, a churchyard or a cemetery that is open to the public, or a not-too-narrow segment thereof, the trust is charitable and thus may provide for maintenance over an unlimited period of time. (By statute in many states dispositions of property for the perpetual care of graves, tombs, and monuments are permitted, and some such expenditures are proper as costs of administering a decedent's estate.)

A trust may be charitable although the accomplishment of the purpose for which the trust is created involves a change in the existing law. If the purpose of the trust is to bring about a change in the law by illegal means, however, such as by revolution, bribery, or illegal lobbying, or bringing improper pressure to bear upon members of the legislature, the purpose is not charitable. Cf. § 29. Certainly a trust to promote general improvement in the law, whether by financial support of the work of a law-revision commission or through the support of research projects so directed, is charitable. The mere fact, however, that the purpose of a trust is to advocate and bring about a *particular* change of law does not prevent the purpose from being charitable. This is so whether the change is pursued indirectly through the education and persuasion of the electorate, so as to bring about a public sentiment favorable to the change, or through more direct but lawful influences, such as by proper lobbying and other persuasion brought to bear upon legislators. And a trust to improve the structure and methods of government is charitable, whether by promoting the development of initiative or referendum processes on the one hand or by the promotion of representative government on the other.

Although a trust to promote the success of a particular political party is not charitable, the development and dissemination of information advocating or seeking to improve understanding of a particular set of social, economic, or political views is charitable, whether because it is educational (Comment *h*) or because it contributes to a marketplace of ideas that is beneficial to the community. Thus, on the one hand, a trust the income of which is to be used in the discretion of the chairperson of a political party to assist in the election of members of that party or otherwise to promote its interests is not charitable. On the other hand, if the promotion of a particular cause or socio-economic perspective is charitable, the mere fact that one or another of the political parties advocates that cause or viewpoint does not make the promotion of that cause or set of views noncharitable. Accordingly, a trust to promote a policy either of free trade or of protective tariffs is charitable although different political parties may take different stands on these policies or their current applications.

§ 29. Purposes and Provisions That Are Unlawful or Against Public Policy

An intended trust or trust provision is invalid if:

(a) its purpose is unlawful or its performance calls for the commission of a criminal or tortious act;

(b) it violates rules relating to perpetuities; or

(c) it is contrary to public policy.

General Comment:

a. Scope; types of impermissible purposes or effects. An intended trust or trust provision is invalid if its purpose or performance is unlawful or against public policy. More specifically, an intended trust or a particular provision in the terms of a trust is unenforceable: if it calls for the performance of criminal or tortious acts by the trustee or its purpose is fraudulent or otherwise unlawful (Comments *c–e*); if its implementation would violate the applicable rules regulating perpetuities (which are treated briefly in Comments *g* and *h*, but are otherwise beyond the scope of this Restatement (see cross-references in Comment *e*)); or if its performance would be contrary to public policy (Comments *i–m*).

This list is not necessarily exclusive. Compare, e.g., § 27(2) and . . . § 58, Comments *b* and *e* (on impermissible restraints on alienation).

With the subject matter of this section, compare generally Restatement Second, Contracts §§ 178 et seq.

Comment on Clause (a):

b. *Voidable transfers contrasted.* The types of situations addressed in Clause (a) involve impermissible purposes or provisions of the trust itself. Analogous but different are trusts that may fail in whole or in part because a third party is entitled to set aside the settlor's transfer to the trustee or to reach the property in the trustee's hands. Illustrative are cases in which the settlor's property had been illegally acquired by the settlor and cases in which the settlor's transfer to the trust constitutes a fraudulent transfer under applicable creditors' rights law. (The law of fraudulent conveyances is not within the scope of the Restatement of this subject.)

Trusts in situations of these types are not invalid, and the beneficiaries may ordinarily enforce their rights under the terms of the trust if or to the extent the third party's right of avoidance is not exercised. In brief, trust beneficiaries generally may enforce their beneficial interests in a trust to the same extent they would be allowed to retain the property if it had been transferred to them directly and free of trust.

Compare: § 56, § 58, Comment *e*, and § 60, Comment *f* (all on the rights of the creditors of a settlor to reach the latter's retained interests in an irrevocable trust); § 25(2), Comments *d* and *e* (on the rights of a settlor's surviving spouse, pretermitted heir, or creditors to reach property held in a revocable trust); and §§ 56 through 60 (on the rights of creditors of a beneficiary to reach the latter's beneficial interest in a trust).

c. *Performance criminal or tortious.* If an intended trust or trust provision calls for the commission of a criminal or tortious act by the trustee, the trust provision is invalid. Thus, where several persons establish a fund to be held in trust for the purpose of securing, through bribery, legislation or administrative action favorable to their business activities, the intended trust is unenforceable. Similarly, an intended trust or provision to participate in an unlawful business, such as the marketing of legally prohibited substances or the unlicensed practice of medicine or law, is unenforceable; and a direction to operate a factory on certain land is unenforceable if the factory operation would be a tortious nuisance to the owners of adjoining lots or would be in violation of environmental law.

If a settlor transfers property upon a trust the terms of which provide for the trustee to engage in conduct that at the time of creation of the trust is lawful but that, owing to a change of law or circumstances, subsequently becomes unlawful, the terms in question become unenforceable. (On modification of the terms of such a trust, see § 66; also, in the case of a charitable trust, compare § 67.)

Whether an intended trust in any of the foregoing situations fails altogether depends on whether the unlawful provision can be appropriately modified (supra) or can be separated from the other provisions without defeating the purpose of the settlor in creating the trust. See Comment *e*, below.

d. *Fraudulent or otherwise unlawful purposes.* Although not invalid because of the inherent nature of the trust provisions or the fiduciary conduct they require, a trust may be invalid and thus unenforceable under this section because of the purposes those provisions are to serve.

For example, the owner of property might transfer it to another who agrees to hold it in trust for the transferor or another with the purpose being to conceal the interest of the transferor or other person, not merely for reasons of privacy but in order to mislead the government or others with respect to the true beneficial interests in the property. Such a case may arise where a person pays money to another pursuant to an oral agreement that the funds will be held in trust for the payor and returned upon demand, intentionally creating a deceptive appearance of ownership in the payee and thereby inducing a third person to make a loan to the payee. Or a person may purchase land or securities and, for the purpose of defrauding creditors or of evading a prohibition or limitation in a statute, have title placed in the name of another, who agrees to hold the property upon a trust for the purchaser.

Similarly, a trust or provision is invalid if the trust is created or the provision is included for a consideration that is unlawful. Thus, if, in consideration of another's agreement to commit certain felonious acts, a person transfers property in trust for the purpose of compensating the other from time to time for the performance of the various agreed criminal acts, the trust is unenforceable.

e. *Consequences of illegality; cross-references.* In general, the fact that a trust purpose is not enforceable or that the settlor directs or suggests an unlawful means of performing a trust does not invalidate the trust if it has a substantial purpose that is valid and can be achieved by methods that are not unlawful. This is not the case, however, if the purpose or method directed is so essential to the settlor's objective(s) that the permissible and impermissible purposes cannot be separated.

A trustee is ordinarily under a duty to the beneficiaries not to carry out a trust purpose or provision that the trustee knows or has reason to know is unlawful. If the trust does not fail, however, the trustee is under a duty to administer the trust property in a lawful manner to accomplish the valid trust purpose(s).

On the question of whether and under what circumstances a resulting trust arises in favor of the settlor or the settlor's successors in interest when an intended trust fails in whole or in part for unlawful purpose, see § 8, Comment *i*, and § 9, Comment *g*.

On the consequences of analogous situations in which a transfer constitutes a fraudulent conveyance or involves property unlawfully acquired, see Comment *b*. Also, more generally, see Restatement Second, Property (Donative Transfers) §§ 34.1–34.3 (rights of spouse, issue, and creditors of transferor) [Restatement Third, Property (Wills and Other Donative Transfers) § 9.1–9.6].

The consequences of trust interests or conditions that violate rules regulating perpetuities or other public policies are treated in the discussion of those types of violations in the Comments below. See more generally: Restatement Second, Property (Donative Transfers) § 1.5 (remote vesting), § 2.1 (trust duration), and § 2.2 (accumulations); id. Chapter 4 (restraints on alienation); and id. Chapters 5 through 9 (restraints on beneficiary conduct) [Restatement Third, Property (Wills and Other Donative Transfers) §§ 8.5, 27.1, 27.2, and Scope Note to Division VIII].

General Comment on Clauses (b) and (c):

f. *In general.* A beneficial interest, a condition attached to a beneficial interest, or other provision in the terms of a trust is invalid if carrying out or enforcing the provision would be against public policy, even though the provision does not have a fraudulent purpose and does not involve the trustee in the performance of a criminal or tortious act (as in Comments *c* and *d*).

For example, under Clause (b) of this section, a provision in a trust is invalid insofar as it purports to create an interest that by its terms is to vest at too remote a time or purports to direct accumulation of income or to restrain alienation or trust termination for too long a period. See Comments *g* and *h*.

Similarly, under Clause (c), some conditions or provisions are invalid because their enforcement would tend to induce the commission of unlawful or immoral acts by beneficiaries or would create an improper motive tending to induce conduct that is not in itself unlawful or immoral. These latter supply a socially undesirable inducement for beneficiaries to exercise or not to exercise fundamental rights that seriously affect their personal interests and lives, and usually also those of others. See Comment *i*, especially last paragraph of *Scope note* at end of that Comment. See also Comments *j* through *l*. Public policy also forbids or limits trust provisions that tend to undermine proper administration of trusts. See Comment *m*. . . .

It is typical of situations under Clause (c), as it is not of situations falling under Clause (a), that a provision in the terms of a trust may be held invalid although the settlor personally might have been legally allowed to make payments under similar circumstances, free of trust, to the same persons. See Comment *i*; see also Introductory Note to this chapter.

Comments on Clause (b):

g. Remoteness of vesting. An attempt to create a private trust fails unless the trust has one or more definite beneficiaries or provides for one or more beneficiaries to be ascertained within the requirements of the applicable rule against perpetuities. See § 2, Comment *h*, and §§ 44 and 46. Although a trust may satisfy the definiteness-of-beneficiaries requirement and be a valid trust, the terms of the trust may nevertheless purport to create one or more beneficial interests or powers of appointment that are invalid for violating Clause (b) of this section.

The rule against perpetuities regulates remoteness of vesting and applies not only to legal estates but also to the equitable interests of trust beneficiaries. Although a comprehensive treatment of the rule is beyond the scope of the Restatement of this subject, its relationship to trusts is briefly summarized in this Comment.

Under the traditional common-law rule against perpetuities, no trust interest is good unless, by the terms and time of its creation, it is certain to vest or fail no later than 21 years after some life in being at the creation of the interest. See generally original Restatement of Property, Division IV. Modern statutes and statements of the rule tend to ease its most treacherous and harsh features, either: (i) by allowing some form of wait-and-see approach, rather than judging the validity of future interests or powers at the moment of their creation and on the basis of what might possibly happen thereafter; or (ii) by providing for reformation (rather than reversion) of offending dispositions to approximate a settlor's intention within the mandates of the rule; or (iii) by some form of both, as in the Uniform Statutory Rule Against Perpetuities and in Restatement Second, Property (Donative Transfers), Chapter 1 (§§ 1.1–1.6).

g(1). When interest "created." In general, a beneficial interest or power in a trust is created for purposes of the rule against perpetuities at the time the trust is created—that is, when the transfer is made to create an inter vivos trust or at the time of a testator's death in the case of a testamentary trust. In the case of a revocable living trust, however, the interests are deemed to be created, and thus the perpetuities period begins to run, when the settlor dies or the trust otherwise becomes irrevocable.

An equivalence of ownership similar to that of revocability is recognized, preventing the running of the perpetuities period, while a person holds a general power of appointment that is presently exercisable.

Also, interests in property later added to a trust are not "created" until the addition occurs, or until a beneficiary designation becomes irrevocable when insurance or pension proceeds are made payable to a trustee.

g(2). Charitable interests. Although the rule against perpetuities is somewhat relaxed where charitable purposes are involved, this is only so to the extent the property is "vested in charity" within the period allowed by the rule. Thus, where there is a trust for one charity, with a gift over upon a remote contingency to or in trust for another charity, the disposition is valid.

On the other hand, where a trust is established initially for private purposes but provides for a gift over to or in further trust for a charity upon an excessively remote contingency, the charitable disposition violates the rule against perpetuities. Similarly, private interests that follow charitable interests are subject to the timely vesting requirements of the rule against perpetuities. On charitable trusts more generally, see § 28.

h. Duration of trusts; accumulations. A trust is not invalid, either in whole or in part, merely because its duration may exceed the period of the rule against perpetuities, provided the vesting requirement of the applicable rule is satisfied. In such a trust, the trustee may continue to have and exercise administrative powers (to sell, lease, invest, and the like), but the trustee no longer may have discretion with respect to distributions to beneficiaries; discretionary interests must not be subject to a condition precedent of the trustee's exercise of discretion beyond the perpetuities period.

Although spendthrift trusts are generally valid (see § 58), restraints on voluntary or involuntary alienation of beneficiaries' interests are not effective beyond the perpetuities period, not by reason of the rule itself against perpetuities but by an analogous rule that uses the same time limit.

h(1). Indestructibility. Furthermore, also by analogous rule, a private trust may not be indestructible beyond the perpetuities period. Thus, a "material purpose" of the settlor that would otherwise preclude termination of a trust even though its sole beneficiary or all beneficiaries wish to terminate it (see § 65(2) on the so-called *Claflin* doctrine) is no longer respected in this manner after the period of the rule against perpetuities has expired. The public policy against permitting an indestructible trust of excessively long duration, however, does not invalidate the trust itself. Nor does it enable less than all of the beneficiaries to terminate the trust, unless the terms of the trust so provide. The rule allowing premature termination by beneficiaries (see § 65(1)) continues normally to require consent of all of them, although independent and separable shares of a single trust are treated as separate trusts for these purposes.

On matters of trust duration, see more generally Restatement Second, Property (Donative Transfers) § 2.1, especially Comment *d* and Comments *g* through *i* [Restatement Third, Property (Wills and Other Donative Transfers) §§ 27.1–27.3].

h(2). Accumulations. An expressed or implied provision in the terms of a private trust directing or authorizing the income of the trust estate to be accumulated by the trustee is invalid beyond the period of the rule against perpetuities. Accumulations in charitable trusts are not limited to the perpetuities period.

In both charitable and private trusts, however, a court may prevent, by appropriate reformation, *directed* accumulations that are capricious, even within the perpetuities period. . . . . See more generally, and contrast, Restatement Second, Property (Donative Transfers) § 2.2 [Restatement Third, Property (Wills and Other Donative Transfers) § 27.1, Comment *k*]. Judicious management of a trust (see id. § 2.2, Comments *j–l*) does not result in an "accumulation" for these purposes; nor does a growth-oriented investment policy that is not inconsistent with the trustee's duty of impartiality. On trust investment principles, see Chapter 17; and on the duty of impartiality, see § 79. See also Restatement Third, Trusts (Prudent Investor Rule) § 227, Comment *i*, and id. §§ 232, 240.

Comments on Clause (c):

i. Nature and rationale of public-policy limits on trust provisions. The rules allowing and limiting the use of trusts, and the time-divided property ownership usually associated with deadhand control, reflect a compromise between free disposition of private property and other values (see § 27 and Introductory Note to this chapter). So also does the rule of Clause (c) of this section, and ensuing Comments *j–l* involving trust benefits conditioned upon the beneficiary's future conduct.

The private trust is tolerated, even treasured, in the common-law world for the flexibility it offers to property owners in planning and designing diverse beneficial interests and financial protections over time, individually tailored as the particular property owner deems best to the varied needs, abilities, and circumstances of particular family members and others whom the owner chooses to benefit. Yet these societal and individual advantages are properly to be balanced against other social values and the effects of deadhand control on the subsequent conduct or personal freedoms of others, and also against the burdens a former owner's unrestrained dispositions might place on courts to interpret and enforce individualized interests and conditions.

The simplest examples of trusts or provisions that offend public policy are those that tend to encourage criminal or tortious conduct on the part of beneficiaries. (Compare Comment *c*, on provisions that involve the trustee in such conduct.) Thus, if certain persons are likely to engage in the commission of certain types of crimes, a trust to pay the fines of any of them who may be convicted of committing such acts is invalid; the payment of fines is not illegal, but the direct tendency of the trust is to undermine the deterrent effect of the fines imposed by the law. Similarly invalid would be a trust to pay someone's liabilities for operating a nuisance. Less objective is the possibility that a trust provision may be invalid because of a tendency to encourage immorality, or because of the array of more common inducements described hereafter and considered more specifically in Comments *j* through *l*.

Policies concerned with deadhand control limit the use of trusts in ways that do not apply to living individuals in the direct disposition of their property. Thus, a policy of fostering free family interaction or privacy between individuals, or simply society's tolerance of human frailty, traditionally exempts acts of property owners (and even their outright dispositions by will) from restrictions that would apply to personally intrusive or socially dubious conditions in the distributive provisions of irrevocable trusts. Furthermore, the "rigor mortis" of deadhand control is not present while a property owner is able to respond to persuasion and evolving circumstances.

Thus, although one is free to give property to another or to withhold it, it does not follow that one may give in trust with whatever terms or conditions one may wish to attach. This is particularly so of provisions that the law views as exerting a socially undesirable influence on the exercise or nonexercise of fundamental rights that significantly affect the personal lives of beneficiaries and often of others as well. See *Scope note,* Comment *i(2),* below. Also compare § 28, Comment *f,* on "invidious" restrictions in charitable trusts.

In cases of the types considered in the Comments that follow, simple and precise rules of validity or invalidity frequently cannot be stated. This is particularly so because of the need to weigh the often worthy concerns and objectives of settlors against the objectionable effects or tendencies of conditions attached to beneficial interests, each of which involves specific terms and personal and overall estate-planning contexts that may vary subtly but significantly from situation to situation. Furthermore, in these various situations, remedial flexibility is required to reconcile (i) the policy objection to a provision with (ii) a motive or goal of the settlor that is legally acceptable in whole or in part as an effort to protect the beneficiary's interest or the trust property.

i(1). Consequences of invalidity; reformation. Ordinarily, if a beneficial interest in a trust is to be conferred or is to terminate upon an invalid condition (whether, in form, precedent or subsequent), the interest becomes effective or continues as if the condition had not been imposed, or as if the settlor's requirements or restrictions were satisfied. A different result may be reached, however, to avoid distorting the settlor's underlying general plan for allocating his or her estate among family members. Furthermore, if the settlor provides for a certain disposition in case of a condition's invalidity, that direction will be respected unless it would have the effect of deterring a beneficiary from asserting the rule of this Clause (c) of this section.

In addition, a provision that is not to be upheld as written but is susceptible of adaptation to accommodate both public-policy concerns and legitimate settlor objectives may be so adapted by the court. The rule allowing reformation under the Comments that follow is rather like the use of equitable approximation (i.e., reformation) in cases of violations of the rule against perpetuities (Comment *g*).

i(2). Scope note. The policies restraining deadhand control in Clause (c) of this section do not apply to outright dispositions conditioned on conduct prior to the death of the testator, or prior to the time a revocable trust becomes irrevocable. See Restatement Second, Property (Donative Transfers) § 6.1, Comment *c;* although the Property Restatement's rules on behavior restraints apply to nontrust as well as trust dispositions in various forms, those rules (as here) only address restraints on "future conduct."

Some of the personal relationships or freedoms considered in Comments *j* through *l* may be protected in some fashion by federal or state statutes or constitutions (such as religious freedom). These Comments, however, involve rules and policies of the trust law and limit the purposes and terms of trusts in ways that are not based on statutory or constitutional safeguards, although trust law may be influenced by policies underlying such protections.

j. *Family relationships.* A trust or a condition or other provision in the terms of a trust is ordinarily (see below) invalid if it tends to encourage disruption of a family relationship or to discourage formation or resumption of such a relationship. See also Restatement Second, Contracts §§ 189–191.

Thus, a trust provision normally may not terminate a beneficial interest if a beneficiary and spouse who are living apart should resume living together, or confer a beneficial interest upon a beneficiary if he or she obtains a divorce or legal separation. Similarly, a trust provision is ordinarily invalid if it would tend to induce termination of a long-established relationship of cohabitation without marriage.

In addition, a trust provision is ordinarily invalid if it tends seriously to interfere with or inhibit the exercise of a beneficiary's freedom to obtain a divorce (creating a risk, e.g., of encouraging financial dependency upon an abusive relationship) or the exercise of freedom to marry, either by limiting the beneficiary's selection of a spouse or by unduly postponing the time of marriage. A fundamental exception, however, permits termination of a beneficial interest of the settlor's spouse in the event of the spouse's remarriage or, if the restraint is reasonable under all the circumstances . . ., termination of a beneficial interest of the surviving spouse of one who is or would have been a natural object of the settlor's bounty (cf. definition in § 9, Comment *b*).

The policy against undermining family relationships applies as well to trust provisions that discourage a person from living with or caring for a parent or child or from social interaction with siblings.

Clause (c) of this section is generally concerned with the objective effects of a provision rather than with the settlor's underlying motive(s). Nevertheless, a subjective inquiry into the settlor's reasons for including a provision in a trust may be relevant. Thus, it may be shown that the settlor's motive was to provide for special needs that might arise in the event of the beneficiary's divorce, or to provide support for a beneficiary until marriage or for a child who feels unable to return to a parent's home. A provision of this type may be upheld despite the incidental influence it may have on the beneficiary's decision(s) affecting a marriage or family relationship. Such a condition may even relieve financial pressure on a beneficiary to remain in or enter a marriage. Similarly, in making or increasing provision for a beneficiary upon divorce from a particular spouse, a settlor may be motivated by reasonable concern over that spouse's financial irresponsibility or an apparent gambling or substance addiction.

The credibility of any such explanation is diminished, however, and its socially undesirable influence aggravated, when the provision does not take the form of discretionary distributions appropriately tailored to the alleged risk or to the beneficiary's needs and the availability of other means of meeting those needs. Moreover, a provision may reflect a mixture of motives or may provide some other basis for finding it invalid as written despite an acceptable purpose. In cases of these various types, a provision may fail in its original form but nevertheless be judicially reformed to accomplish the permissible objectives (possibly with fiduciary discretion over distributions) while removing or minimizing socially undesirable effects. Speculation about a settlor's motives and other difficulties inherent in these cases may be eased by this remedial flexibility under which an all-or-nothing decision is not required. . . .

k. *Religious freedom.* Individuals are normally free during life to promote their theological views among others, and to create charitable trusts during life or at death to support or advance a chosen religion (see § 28, Clause (b)). But the use of private trusts that create financial pressure regarding the future religious choices of beneficiaries is a different matter. A trust provision is ordinarily invalid if its enforcement would tend to restrain the religious freedom of the beneficiary by offering a financial inducement to embrace or reject a particular faith or set of beliefs concerning religion. Illustrative is a provision granting or terminating a beneficial interest only if the beneficiary should adopt or abandon a particular religious faith. . . . .

On the other hand, trust provisions would ordinarily be upheld if reasonably designed (or reformed) to protect beneficial interests or trust property from adverse financial implications associated with a beneficiary's present or future religious commitments. . . . .

l. *Careers and conduct.* It is not contrary to public policy for a trust provision to encourage a beneficiary to be a productive member of society or to pursue a particular career or form of training, as long as the effect of the provision is not punitive or so rewarding as to be coercive. Thus, a settlor may validly create a trust or include a provision solely to finance a beneficiary's higher education, or a particular type of education, or to facilitate pursuit of a particular type of career (such as religious or social service) by compensating for the financial sacrifices that tend to be associated with the career choice.

Different policy considerations are presented, however, by a provision to distribute the corpus of a trust to its income beneficiary only if the beneficiary becomes a surgeon, or to terminate a beneficiary's interests for abandoning a particular career or for failing to take it up by a stated age. In cases of this type, society's interest in a property owner's freedom of disposition must be weighed against the risk of excessive influence on a personal decision significantly affecting the life of the beneficiary and perhaps others. The social concerns here involve not only the increased risk of an unsuitable decision being made or adhered to by the beneficiary but also the burdens and difficulties of judicial interpretation and enforcement of such interpretations.

Trust provisions intended or likely to induce a change or continuation of a beneficiary's personal habits or conduct ordinarily are not against public policy. But compare Comments *j* and *k*, above, that where a provision is unnecessarily punitive or unreasonably intrusive into significant personal decisions or interests, or involves an unreasonable restraint on personal associations, the provision may be invalid.

Some restraints may be unenforceable for indefiniteness; or the settlor's selection of an arbiter to determine whether a beneficiary is in violation of a condition may give rise to conflicting interests or a variety of problems of fairness or enforcement. See generally Restatement Second, Property (Donative Transfers) § 8.2, Comment *b*. A requirement, however, that a beneficiary abstain from "gambling" or "smoking," or from "indulging in intoxicating liquor" or "using illegal substances," at least with the aid of interpretation, is ordinarily sufficiently clear to be enforced.

m. *Capricious purposes; sound administration of trust.* It is against public policy to enforce a trust provision that would divert distributions or administration from the interests of the beneficiaries to other purposes that are capricious or frivolous (§ 47, Comment *e*), detrimental to the community, or otherwise (with limited exceptions, see § 47, Comments *b*, *c*, and *d*) neither private nor charitable in character. See § 27.

Similarly, a trust provision may not be enforced if to do so would undermine proper administration of the trust. Thus, a provision that purports to prevent a court from removing a trustee will be disregarded if removal appears appropriate to proper administration of the trust; and an arbitrary restriction on the appointment of trustees or successor trustees may be invalid if not reasonably related to the trust purposes. A provision is also invalid to the extent it purports to relieve the trustee altogether from accountability and the duty to provide information to beneficiaries (see §§ 82, 83), or to relieve the trustee from liability even for dishonest or reckless acts (see § 87, § 96, and §§ 76–79). See generally Chapters 14 through 18, and cf. Restatement Second, Property (Donative Transfers) § 9.2 and Restatement Third, Property (Wills and Other Donative Transfers) § 8.5.

This principle does not, however, prevent a settlor from prescribing administrative provisions designed to serve a reasonable view of the beneficiaries' best interests or to express a widely even if not generally held view of business ethics or morality. See § 27, Comment *b* . . .; and cf. Principles of Corporate Governance: Analysis and Recommendations § 2.01(b) and its Comments *h* and *i*.

On the validity and effect of provisions restraining contests of wills, trusts, or other donative transfers, see § 96. Also, see generally Restatement Third, Property (Wills and Other Donative Transfers) § 8.5 and Restatement Second, Property (Donative Transfers) § 9.1; and compare "*Consequences of invalidity; reformation*" in Comment *i(1)*, supra this section.

§ 30. Impossibility and Indefiniteness

A private trust, or a provision in the terms of a trust, may be unenforceable because of impossibility or indefiniteness.

Comment:

a. Impossibility. If all of the purposes for which a private trust is created are or become impossible of accomplishment, the trust will be terminated. Whether the property will then be turned over to one or more of the beneficiaries (when the impossibility is not due to failure of intended beneficiaries) or will revert to the settlor, or to the settlor's successors in interest, is a matter for interpretation when the matter is not covered by the terms of the trust. On trust termination generally, see § 61; also, on the possibility of a resulting trust in general, see §§ 7 and 8.

On charitable trusts and the *cy pres* doctrine see § 67.

If a particular administrative provision in the terms of the trust fails for impossibility, ordinarily the trust does not terminate but will be administered as if that provision had not been included in the trust. If necessary, the court may authorize deviation from the terms of the trust based on unanticipated circumstances. See § 66.

Where a condition precedent or subsequent is or becomes impossible of performance, the impossibility excuses the performance unless this result would be contrary to the purposes of the settlor. Thus, if a trust provides that a beneficial interest shall only arise (or shall terminate) if the beneficiary performs (or fails to perform) a specified act, such as serving in the U.S. armed forces, and it is impossible for the beneficiary to perform the act, such as for reason of disqualifying physical disability, the beneficiary will acquire the interest in question (or the interest will not terminate), unless it is shown that this result would be inconsistent with a more general purpose of the settlor. Cf. Restatement Second, Property (Donative Transfers) § 5.2.

On the application of the doctrine of *cy pres* when performance of a charitable trust is or becomes impossible, see § 67.

b. *Indefiniteness.* If all of the purposes for which a trust is created are so indefinite that the trust cannot be enforced, the intended trust fails. Thus, a trust may fail because of the indefiniteness of the beneficiaries, or of their interests or the purposes for which the trust is created. On possibilities for enforcement and alternatives to complete failure of the settlor's intended purposes, when beneficiaries or purposes are initially indefinite, see §§ 46 and 47. Cf. Restatement Third, Property (Wills and Other Donative Transfers) § 11.2.

A condition precedent or subsequent may be of such a character that it is or becomes impossible to determine whether it has been performed. It is a matter for interpretation whether the beneficial interest in question takes effect as if the condition had been satisfied (the result usually to be inferred), whether the trust is to be carried out without regard to that interest, or whether a resulting trust (§§ 7 and 8) arises. Compare Restatement Second, Property (Donative Transfers) § 8.1, Comment *e*, and § 8.2, Comment *b*.

On the effect upon a charitable trust of the settlor's failure to state a definite charitable purpose, see § 28, Comment *a*, and § 67 (on *cy pres*). . . . .

CHAPTER 7

THE TRUSTEE

Introductory Note: This chapter deals with questions about what persons have capacity to serve as trustees, how they are appointed and compensated, how they accept or resign trusteeships, how and for what they may be removed from office, and how and when substitute and successor trustees are appointed.

Section 39 provides that multiple trustees of private trusts ordinarily act by majority vote. Although contrary to traditional common-law doctrine, this rule is consistent with the modern statutory trend, drafting tendencies, and long-standing rules applicable to the trustees of charitable trusts.

Later chapters deal with such related matters as the fiduciary duties, powers, rights, and potential liabilities of trustees (Chapters 14–19), as well as rules applicable to their dealings with beneficiaries and third parties (see especially Chapter 21).

§ 31. Trust Does Not Fail for Lack of Trustee

A trust does not fail because no trustee is designated or because the designated trustee declines, is unable, or ceases to act, unless the trust's creation or continuation depends on a specific person serving as trustee; a proper court will appoint a trustee as necessary and appropriate (see § 34).

Comment:

a. *General rule.* Even though a trustee is essential to a trust, a trust does not fail simply because no trustee is provided by the terms of the trust or because, before or when or after the trust is created, the designated trustee dies, is unable or unwilling to act, or is removed. Absent provision for the situation in the terms of the trust, and except as provided in Comment *b*, the court will appoint a trustee. See § 34. . . . .

b. *Trust creation or duration dependent on specific trustee.* A settlor may manifest an intention that the creation of a trust is contingent on acceptance of the trusteeship by a particular trustee, or that the trust continue only for as long as a particular person serves as trustee. In these cases, the rule that a court will appoint a substitute or successor trustee does not apply. The settlor's intention is being respected in such a case, for the settlor's contemplated trust was conditioned upon and limited to service by the designated trustee. Cases of this type are most unusual. See also § 14, Comment *b*.

On the analogous possibility that a particular power conferred upon a designated trustee may be personal and therefore not pass to a successor trustee, see § 70. Also cf. § 46, Comment *d*, and § 47, Comments *c*, *d*, and *f*.

A trust may fail if no competent trustee can be found to serve at a cost that can be justified. Compare generally § 66 (on unanticipated circumstances and equitable deviation) and id., Comment *b* (that appropriate judicial action may occasionally involve termination).

§ 32. Capacity of Individual to Be Trustee

A natural person, including a settlor or beneficiary, has capacity

(a) to take and hold property in trust to the extent the person has capacity to take and hold the property as beneficial owner; and

(b) to administer trust property and act as trustee to the same extent the person would have capacity to deal with the property as beneficial owner.

Comment:

a. *Scope; general principles.* This section is concerned with questions of whether an individual as a trustee can legally acquire and hold property in trust, or can legally act as a trustee of the property. It is not concerned with the individual's practical fitness or suitability to serve as trustee; those matters are considered hereafter in §§ 34 and 37.

This section also does not deal with questions concerning the validity or failure of an intended trust. That an intended trust ordinarily will be given effect despite the transferee-trustee's inability to take title to the property, see § 31, § 14, Comment *d*, and § 16, Comments *b* and *c*; and that once created, a trust ordinarily will not fail for want of a trustee, see §§ 31 and 34 (court will ordinarily appoint a substitute or successor trustee).

Whether and to what extent a witness to a will may benefit from the will is not strictly a matter of capacity to take title and is beyond the scope of this Restatement. See Restatement Third, Property (Wills and Other Donative Transfers) § 3.1, Comment *o*. The role of witness, however, ordinarily does not disqualify a person from taking and acting as trustee, because service in that fiduciary role (even with compensation) does not constitute a "beneficial interest" under the will. . . . .

One who lacks capacity to administer a trust need not be formally removed by court order. Thus, if the terms of the trust designate or provide a procedure for a substitute or successor trustee to assume the vacant trusteeship, no judicial action is required. As necessary or appropriate, however, a court will replace a trustee or will confirm a successor's appointment or title to trust property. See § 37; see also § 34.

b. *Settlor or beneficiary as trustee.* An owner of property who gratuitously declares a trust (see § 10(c) on declarations of trust) is both settlor and trustee, and is sometimes also a beneficiary. The settlor may also be one of several trustees by transferring property to several persons (including the settlor) as co-trustees; and the settlor may become a successor trustee or co-trustee.

A person who receives both the sole legal title to property and the entire beneficial interest in that property, whether by will or by inter vivos transfer, takes the property free of trust because of the doctrine of merger (§ 69). This rarely happens because most trusts have multiple beneficiaries, and merger does not occur even if all beneficiaries are co-trustees (id., Comment *c*). On termination when all legal and beneficial interests in a trust become united in a single person after the trust's creation, see § 69, Comments *a* and *b*.

It is virtually inherent in the nature of trusts and trustees' responsibilities that, in many matters of trust administration, personal interests of a beneficiary-trustee will come into conflict with the interests of other beneficiaries, to whom the trustee owes fiduciary duties. Illustrative are matters ranging from the exercise of discretion regarding distributions (see especially § 50, Comment *b*) to the trustee's selection of investments. (In general, on the duties of loyalty and impartiality, see §§ 78 and 79.) Because of considerations of this type, a court will generally not appoint a beneficiary as trustee (see § 34, Comment *f(1)*). Nevertheless, settlors often select beneficiaries as trustees or co-trustees, and the existence of conflicting interests is not ordinarily a basis for a court to remove (or deny appointment to) a trustee of the settlor's choice. See generally § 37 on grounds for removal. In any event, these are not issues of capacity to act as a trustee but issues of suitability, or of fitness to serve as trustee of a particular trust.

Possible tax consequences of settlors or beneficiaries serving as trustees are beyond the scope of this Restatement. . . . .

c. *Minors and others under legal disability.* A minor or incompetent adult can acquire and hold property either beneficially or as trustee. Because transfers and contracts by persons under legal disability are voidable, however, such an individual cannot act as trustee, at least until the disability is removed.

d. *Nonresidents and aliens as trustees.* A natural person who is not a citizen of the United States, or who does not reside in the state in which a trust is created or to be administered or in which trust property is situated, can receive and administer property as trustee. Those characteristics, however, may be relevant to questions of suitability or the fitness of a particular individual to serve or to continue as trustee or co-trustee of a particular trust. See §§ 34 and 37 on judicial appointment and removal of trustees.

In a few jurisdictions, statutes or constitutional provisions may limit the capacity of certain categories of natural persons to take or hold title to property. The significance of these restrictions on capacity to administer property in trust depends on the terms and underlying policies of the statutory or constitutional provision. These terms and policies may also affect the place and manner in which the trust will be administered.

Statutes in some jurisdictions purport to limit the ability of nonresidents or noncitizens to serve as trustees. Such statutory provisions may raise constitutional issues . . . . In any event, these statutes should be construed not to impose stricter limits than are appropriate to fiduciary suitability and convenience in the administration of trusts. Compare § 33, Comment *c*, and more generally §§ 34 and 37.

§ 33. Corporations and Other Entities as Trustees

(1) A corporation has capacity to take and hold property in trust except as limited by law, and to administer trust property and act as trustee to the extent of the powers conferred upon it by law.

(2) If a partnership, unincorporated association, or other entity has capacity to take and hold property for its own purposes, it has capacity to take, hold, and administer property in trust.

Comment on Subsection (1):

a. Statutory restrictions on corporations holding property. Statutes in some jurisdictions may restrict the amount or purposes of corporate property holdings. These statutes do not invalidate an intended trust; a proper court will normally appoint a substitute trustee (see § 31) if the terms of the trust do not provide for a replacement or for a co-trustee who can carry out the trust.

b. Capacity to administer a trust. A corporation's capacity to administer a trust is determined by constitutional or statutory provisions and by the corporation's charter or certificate of incorporation. If property is transferred to a corporation in trust for a purpose germane to the purposes for which the corporation is created, it has capacity to administer the trust. . . . .

b(1). National banks. The Federal Reserve Act of 1913 authorized the Federal Reserve Board to grant (or revoke) authority to national banks to act as trustees, when not in contravention of state law. The authority over trust powers of national banks was shifted in 1962 to the Comptroller of the Currency, whose Regulation 9 supersedes Regulation F issued pursuant to the 1913 Act. The Comptroller can revoke a national bank's authority to provide trust services for continued improper conduct without removal proceedings under state law.

c. Foreign corporations. A corporation organized and authorized to act as trustee under the laws of one state has capacity to act as trustee in another state except as limited by a statute of the latter state.

Many states have legislation limiting or conditioning the ability of foreign corporations to act as trustees within the legislating state. Statutes of this type should be construed not to apply when the trust will be administered in a state in which the corporation is authorized to act as trustee, even if that state is not the settlor's domicile or the situs of some or all of the trust property. On the other hand, if the distance between the trustee and beneficiaries interferes with the proper administration of the trust, this may be a ground for removal or other remedy. See § 37.

Use of a corporation outside the United States as trustee may raise tax problems, which are not within the scope of this Restatement.

d. Municipal corporations. The powers of a municipal corporation may be limited by the express provisions of statutes. Otherwise, a municipal corporation may act as trustee for purposes that fall within the scope of permitted activities of municipalities. Ordinarily, these include such charitable purposes as promotion of health and education, relief of poverty, construction and maintenance of public parks, buildings and works, and the like; but religious purposes, although charitable, would generally be inappropriate because of principles of separation of church and state.

Municipal functions would not ordinarily include administration of wholly private trusts.

e. *Effect of inability to act as trustee.* Even if a corporation designated as trustee lacks capacity to administer the trust property, the trust does not fail. Compare Comment *a*, and see § 31.

Illustration:

2. S's will leaves property to Helpful Savings & Loan in trust for the benefit of the testator's widow and children. Although Helpful is not authorized by applicable law to act as a trustee, a proper trustee can be appointed to carry out the trust.

In the above Illustration, if Helpful nevertheless undertakes to administer the trust and mismanages the property, it may be held liable as a trustee.

Comment on Subsection (2):

f. *Capacity of partnership, unincorporated associations, and other entities to administer a trust.* To the extent, by statute or otherwise, a partnership, unincorporated association, limited-liability company, or other entity can, as such, take and hold property beneficially, it can take, hold, and administer property in trust.

Legislation has been widely enacted to provide or confirm that various forms of partnerships and unincorporated associations are legal entities and are capable of holding title to property. . . . .

g. *Lack of capacity to take and hold property.* To the extent a partnership or unincorporated association cannot take or hold title to property, it cannot take or hold property in trust. The trust, however, does not fail. See § 31. (On the effect of an attempted transfer outright to such an unincorporated association see § 43, Comment *d.*)

Under the law of some jurisdictions, a transfer of property to a partnership or an unincorporated association for its own benefit places the title to the property in the partners or the members of the association. In these jurisdictions, a purported transfer to the partnership or association in trust similarly will have the effect of passing the property to the partners or members of the association in trust. The members of the association may be insufficiently definite or it may appear that the settlor would not have intended the individual partners or association members to serve as trustees; or having them serve as trustees may be an unsuitable or inefficient arrangement. In such cases, a proper court will appoint one or more suitable trustees, possibly including one or more of the partners or association members.

§ 34. Appointment of Trustees

(1) Except as required by statute, a trustee designated by or selected in accordance with the terms of a trust may act without being appointed or confirmed by an order of court.

(2) If the appointment of a trustee is not provided for or made pursuant to the terms of the trust, the trustee will be appointed by a proper court.

(3) A trustee need not provide a performance bond except as required by statute, trust provision, or court order.

General Comment:

a. When court appointment necessary; bonding. Some statutes require that testamentary trustees be appointed by a court in the manner of personal representatives. (The grounds upon which a court may refuse to appoint a designated trustee are discussed in § 37, Comment *a.*) These statutes, however, do not invalidate the acts of a trustee who fails to obtain the court appointment. Acts undertaken without formal appointment constitute an acceptance of fiduciary responsibility, subjecting the person designated as trustee to the duties of trusteeship. See § 35 and compare § 33, Comment *e.* . . . .

a(1). Bond of trustee. A trustee is not required to give bond to secure performance of the duties of the fiduciary office unless required by the terms of the trust or a statute, or unless ordered by court upon a finding that bonding is necessary to protect the interests of the beneficiaries. Such an order is reviewable for abuse but is not precluded by a provision in the trust stating that no bond is required.

The cost of a bond is normally paid from the trust.

Comment on Subsection (1):

b. Judicial role: trustee provided for in terms of trust. If the terms of a testamentary or inter vivos trust designate or provide a procedure for designating a trustee, including a substitute, successor, or additional trustee, no court appointment or confirmation is needed in the absence of a statutory requirement. . . . .

c. Terms of trust or statute. By statute in some states, certain defined trustees or beneficiaries are authorized to appoint new trustees to fill vacancies without court action.

It is also common for the terms of trusts to provide for the appointment of new trustees, thereby avoiding need for court involvement. For example, the terms of a trust may reserve to the settlor a power to appoint trustees or may grant such a power to one or more named or described beneficiaries, trustees, or other persons. Trust terms imposing limitations on those powers (or on judicial appointments), such as requiring the selection of a corporate trustee, ordinarily must be respected. On the possibility of court-ordered deviation in appropriate circumstances, see § 29, Comment *h,* and § 66.

Although appointments made in compliance with these statutes or trust provisions are effective, a proper court may remove an unsuitable trustee so appointed. See § 37.

The tax consequences of settlor or beneficiary powers to designate or replace trustees are beyond the scope of this Restatement. . . . .

c(1). Appointment by beneficiaries. To the extent the beneficiaries have power to terminate or modify the trust under § 65 (but note id., Comment *f*), they also have the power even without specific trust provision to fill a vacancy in the trusteeship or to remove and replace the trustee. Otherwise, except as authorized by statute or the terms of the trust (supra), the beneficiaries are not entitled to select a trustee, although the court will ordinarily consider the wishes of beneficiaries in making an appointment (see Comment *f*).

Comment on Subsection (2):

d. Judicial power: remaining co-trustee. If several persons are named as trustees and one of them dies, declines to serve or resigns, is removed, or is or becomes incapable of acting as trustee, a replacement trustee is required only if the settlor manifested an intention, or it is conducive to proper administration or purposes of the trust, that the number of trustees should be maintained. Otherwise, the remaining trustee or trustees are entitled to administer the trust.

e. *Appointment of additional trustees.* Even when there is no vacancy, a proper court may appoint one or more additional trustees when this would promote better administration of the trust.

f. *Judicial power to fill vacancies.* Application to fill a vacancy in the trusteeship may be made by any beneficiary, the settlor, a continuing or retiring trustee, or a trustee who is named by the settlor but unwilling to serve as trustee; or by a person having an interest in the subject matter of the trust (see § 3, Comment *b*) or in the administration of the trust (see § 25, Comment *e*); or, in the case of a charitable trust, by the Attorney General.

f(1). Factors considered in court's selection of trustee. In exercising its discretion in appointing a trustee, a court will consider: (1) the objectives and probable intentions of the settlor, as well as any guidance provided by the terms of the trust; (2) the interests and wishes of beneficiaries; and (3) the promotion of the proper administration of the trust. The last of these naturally looks to the basic fiduciary duties of prudence (care, skill, and caution, § 77), loyalty (§ 78), and impartiality (§ 79), as well as respect for the terms and purposes of the trust (§ 76). (Compare generally § 37 on removal of trustees.)

A court may refuse to appoint a person who applies or is nominated for court appointment as trustee even though the court would not have removed that person if appointed by the settlor or by person(s) upon whom a trustee-appointment power was conferred by the terms of the trust. Thus, the court will not normally appoint as trustee a person who would have a conflict of interests, such as one of the beneficiaries or even a relative of some but not others of the beneficiaries, unless the appointment of such a person is supported by an apparent intention or objective of the settlor.

§ 35. Acceptance or Renunciation of Trusteeship

(1) A designated trustee may accept the trusteeship either by words or by conduct.

(2) A designated trustee who has not accepted the trusteeship may decline it.

Comment:

a. *Scope of section.* A person who has not accepted the office cannot be compelled to act as trustee. To be distinguished from the rejection of a trusteeship is a trustee's resignation after acceptance of the office (see § 36); also to be distinguished is a disclaimer in the trustee's fiduciary capacity either of property that would otherwise be transferred to the trust or of specific powers that would otherwise accompany the trusteeship (see § 85 and also § 70).

A trust may be created despite the designated trustee's refusal to accept the trust (see § 31; § 14, Comment *d;* and § 16, Comments *b* and *c*), and a court can appoint a new trustee (§§ 31 and 36).

The requirements, effectiveness, and consequences of a designated trustee's renunciation of the trusteeship for trust-law purposes are not the same as for a disclaimer for tax purposes under Internal Revenue Code

§ 2518. The state and federal income- and transfer-tax considerations in accepting or rejecting a trusteeship, however, are not within the scope of this Restatement.

b. Manifestation of intention to accept or decline. No particular formalities are necessary for a designated trustee to manifest a refusal to accept the trusteeship. Similarly, unless otherwise provided by the terms of the trust, no particular formality is necessary to constitute an acceptance by the trustee of the fiduciary office. Thus, although trustees usually indicate acceptance by signing a trust agreement or other writing to that effect, an acceptance can be expressed orally or inferred from conduct.

It is a question of fact in each case whether the trustee has manifested an intention to accept or to reject the trusteeship. Dealing with trust property in a manner that would be proper only by a trustee normally constitutes an acceptance, but merely protecting the property temporarily until a trustee is appointed does not.

Failure to accept a trusteeship for a long period of time normally indicates an intention to reject it. Contrast Restatement Second, Property (Donative Transfers) § 32.2(2) (failure to disclaim *beneficial* interest as acceptance) [Restatement Third, Property (Wills and Other Donative Transfers) § 6.1, Comment *i*]. If the trustee, before the creation of the trust, made a promise to accept the trust, such a promise does not preclude the trustee from declining; but under these circumstances a failure promptly to decline may constitute an acceptance. Compare Restatement Second, Contracts § 69(1)(c) (silence may be acceptance of an offer "where because of previous dealings or otherwise, it is reasonable that the offeree should notify the offeror if he does not intend to accept").

Even if one designated as trustee has not accepted the office, in some circumstances it may be appropriate for a court to impose liability for unreasonable delay in acting or in declining the trusteeship if this conduct causes harm to beneficiaries who reasonably relied on the designated trustee to protect their interests.

On the duties and liabilities of a trustee who has accepted the office, see generally Chapters 14–19 and 21.

c. Withdrawal of renunciation. In the case of an inter vivos trust, a designated trustee who declines the office cannot thereafter accept it without the settlor's consent. As to the effect on creation of the trust and on title to the trust property, see § 14, Comment *d*, and § 31.

In the case of a testamentary trust, a proper court may allow a trustee to withdraw a renunciation made while the probate estate is still in administration if doing so would not prejudice the interests of the beneficiaries.

d. Partial renunciation. A person designated both as executor and trustee under a will may accept the executorship and renounce the trusteeship, or vice versa, unless the testator manifests a different intention. If two separate trusts are created, by the settlor or by the court (see § 68), a person named as trustee may accept one and decline the other, unless this would be contrary to the purposes of the settlor or the sound administration of the trusts.

This is to be distinguished from a disclaimer of part of the trust property or of particular trustee powers, as noted above in Comment *a*.

§ 36. Resignation of Trustee

A trustee who has accepted the trust can properly resign:

(a) in accordance with the terms of the trust;

(b) with the consent of all beneficiaries; or

(c) upon terms approved by a proper court.

Comment:

a. Terms of the trust. The terms of a trust may allow a trustee to resign without court proceedings. For example, where there are several trustees or a provision naming a successor trustee, unless the terms of the trust provide otherwise a trustee may resign by written notice to the co-trustee(s) or to the person named as successor trustee. Or a trustee may be authorized to resign by notice to or with consent of certain designated beneficiaries.

Under any such provision, the trustee's resignation becomes effective only upon the acceptance of the trusteeship by a new trustee.

Also, a trustee may not exercise a power of resignation or otherwise resign for the purpose of facilitating a breach of trust by the remaining co-trustee(s) or of escaping adverse circumstances without disclosing the breach or circumstances to the beneficiaries, settlor, or court, as the case may be. That all trustee powers are subject to a duty of good-faith exercise, see § 187; see also §§ 70 and 76–78.

b. Consent of beneficiaries. Even in the absence of a provision in the terms of the trust, statutes in some states facilitate trustee resignation without court proceedings by allowing certain defined beneficiaries to act for all of them in accepting a trustee's resignation.

If the consent of all the beneficiaries of a trust can be obtained, they may authorize and accept the resignation of the trustee even in the absence of a trust or statutory provision to that effect. On obtaining consent on behalf of all beneficiaries, see § 65, Comment *b*. (On the requirements for effective consent by a beneficiary, see § 97 (and also § 65, last sentence of Comment *a*).) On trust modification by beneficiaries generally see § 65, but the material purpose ("*Claflin*") doctrine (§ 65(2) and id., Comment *d*) need not be satisfied in a resignation under Clause (b) of this section (but contrast *removal* by beneficiaries, discussed in § 65, Comment *f*).

The consent of a settlor holding a power to revoke a trust (and thus able to act for all beneficiaries, see §§ 74 and 97) is sufficient to enable a trustee to resign. Even without the settlor's consent, however, a trustee of a revocable trust may resign if the addition of property or a change in the trust terms significantly changes the trustee's responsibilities. See § 63, Comment *g*.

c. Authorization of court. It is within the discretion of the court to determine the conditions upon which a trustee's resignation becomes effective. The purpose of this discretion is not to force involuntary service by a trustee but to protect the interests of the beneficiaries and to assure continuity and efficiency in the administration of the trust. . . . . Of particular importance in this respect is the ability to find a suitable successor to the resigning trustee.

d. Liability and duties of resigning trustee. Resignation does not relieve the trustee from liability for breaches of trust committed prior to the time the resignation becomes effective. Normally the trustee has a duty to account to the beneficiaries, and this accounting may have the effect of determining any liability of the resigning trustee and of relieving the trustee of other liability. See §§ 83, 97, 98. The trustee also has a duty to administer and preserve the trust property until a successor is properly appointed and assumes the duties of the trusteeship. . . . .

e. *Transfer of trust estate.* Upon resignation, the trustee is under a duty to transfer the trust property to a successor trustee unless by statute, the terms of the trust, or court order the trust property vests in the new trustee without such an act of transfer.

It is a breach of trust for a trustee to transfer the trust estate to another as trustee except under the circumstances of resignation stated in this section. Cf. § 80.

§ 37. Removal of Trustee

A trustee may be removed

(a) in accordance with the terms of the trust; or

(b) for cause by a proper court.

Comment:

a. *Refusal to appoint* If a statute requires testamentary trustees to be appointed by a court (§ 34, Comment *a*), the court will refuse to appoint a person as trustee under circumstances that would warrant the person's removal as trustee. In similar circumstances, even if no statute requires court appointment, while a settlor's estate is in administration a court may replace a person designated by the settlor to serve as a testamentary trustee.

Courts are less hesitant to reject a designated trustee's appointment at the outset than to remove an acting trustee, because of the severity of the action and the disruption in administration that the latter entails.

Trustees may be disqualified for reasons that predate the creation of the trust. For example, a spouse named as a fiduciary in a will may be ineligible to serve as testamentary trustee if the settlor and the spouse are later divorced. Also, undue influence or inappropriate taking advantage of a confidential relationship in procuring the designation as trustee may be a ground for rejecting the appointment, or for the trustee's removal if later discovered. . . . .

b. *Removal by beneficiaries.* The beneficiaries cannot compel removal of a trustee except for cause (see Comments *d* and *e* on removal by court), unless the terms of the trust authorize them to remove the trustee (see Comment *c*) or they have the power by unanimous consent to terminate or modify the trust (see § 65, especially Comment *f*).

c. *Terms of the trust.* The settlor may remove the trustee if the power to do so is reserved in the terms of the trust, or if the settlor has retained the power to revoke (or unrestricted power to amend) the trust. See also § 74.

Also, power to remove a trustee may be conferred by the terms of the trust upon one or more beneficiaries or others. Such a power allows removal without court proceedings, although its exercise must conform to any valid (see § 29, Comment *h*) requirements or limitations imposed by the trust terms. . . . .

The tax consequences of the retention or grant of removal powers are beyond the scope of this Restatement. . . . .

d. Removal by court; judicial discretion. A court may remove a trustee whose continuation in that role would be detrimental to the interests of the beneficiaries. See Comment *e*. The matter is largely left to the discretion of the trial court, but is subject to review for abuse of discretion.

The court may act on the petition of any beneficiary, co-trustee, or other interested party, or on its own motion (see generally § 94). The trustee is entitled to due process, with notice and an opportunity to be heard, although the court may suspend a trustee's powers (including, if necessary, by appointing a temporary trustee) pending a removal hearing.

e. Grounds for removal. The following are illustrative, but not exhaustive, of possible grounds for a court to remove a trustee: lack of capacity to administer the trust (see § 32); unfitness, whether due to insolvency, diminution of physical vigor or mental acuity, substance abuse, want of skill, or the inability to understand fiduciary standards and duties; acquisition of a conflicting interest (cf. Comment *f(1)*); refusal or inability to give bond, if bond is required (see § 34, Comment *a*); repeated or flagrant failure or delay in providing proper information or accountings to beneficiaries (see §§ 82 and 83); the commission of a crime, particularly one involving dishonesty; gross or continued inadequacies in matters of investment (see §§ 90–92); changes in the place of trust administration, location of beneficiaries, or other developments causing serious geographic inconvenience to the beneficiaries or to the administration of the trust; unwarranted preference to the interests of one or more beneficiaries; a pattern of indifference toward some or all of the beneficiaries; or unreasonable or corrupt failure to cooperate with a co-trustee.

Not every breach of trust warrants removal of the trustee (cf. Comment *g*), but serious or repeated misconduct, even unconnected with the trust itself, may justify removal. . . . .

e(1). Friction between trustee and beneficiaries. Friction between the trustee and some of the beneficiaries is not a sufficient ground for removing the trustee unless it interferes with the proper administration of the trust. Beneficiaries may be resentful when property they expected to inherit is placed in trust, or of reasonable exercise of a trustee's discretion with regard to matters of administration or the alleged underperformance of the trustee's investment program. Such resentment ordinarily does not warrant removal of the trustee; but a serious breakdown in communications between beneficiaries and a trustee may justify removal, particularly if the trustee is responsible for the breakdown or it appears to be incurable.

Serious friction between co-trustees may also warrant removal of one or both of them. . . . .

f. Trustee named by settlor. The court will less readily remove a trustee named by the settlor than one appointed by a court. Courts may also show some but a lesser degree of deference with regard to a trustee appointed by beneficiaries or others pursuant to the terms of a trust. Such deference, however, may no longer be justified if, after being designated, a corporate trustee undergoes a significant structural change, such as by merger, or any trustee significantly reduces the level or quality of service to the trust or its beneficiaries.

If the trustee named by the settlor is unfit to act as trustee—for example, is under an incapacity, or is shown to be dishonest or entirely lacking the qualifications necessary for proper administration of the trust—a court will remove or refuse to confirm the trustee. Compare § 29, Comment *m*.

Ordinarily, a court will not remove a trustee named by the settlor upon a ground that was known to the settlor at the time the trustee was designated, even though a court would not itself have appointed that person as trustee. In cases of unfitness to serve (supra), however, a court may remove a trustee even upon a ground known to the settlor at the time of designation.

f(1). Conflicting interests. Thus, the fact that the trustee named by the settlor is one of the beneficiaries of the trust, or would otherwise have conflicting interests, is not a sufficient ground for removing the trustee or refusing to confirm the appointment. This is so even though the trustee has broad discretion in matters of distribution and investment.

A trustee's removal may be warranted, however, by a conflict of interests that existed but was unknown to the settlor at the time of the designation, or that came into being at a later time.

Furthermore, when a beneficiary serves as trustee or when other conflict-of-interest situations exist, the conduct of the trustee in the administration of the trust will be subject to especially careful scrutiny. See § 78. See also § 87, and compare § 50, Comment *c*.

Illustrations:

8. W's will left her residuary estate to T, in trust, to pay "all of the net income, and such amounts of principal as the Trustee in his sole discretion may deem appropriate, to my husband H," and on H's death to distribute the principal "by right of representation to my then living descendants," all of whom were issue of W by a prior marriage. T predeceased W, and W's daughter D has petitioned to be appointed as trustee to fill the vacancy, for which W's will makes no provision. Even though D is an adult with suitable skills to act as a trustee, the court will ordinarily deny D's petition because of the conflict of interest. See § 79 on the duty of impartiality.

9. The same facts as in Illustration 8 except that, after learning of T's death, W executed a codicil naming her daughter D as trustee in the place of T. The court will not remove D (or refuse to appoint her) as trustee.

Although D in Illustration 9 may properly proceed to act as trustee, the court will remove her from the trusteeship upon a showing that she has not fairly exercised the discretion conferred upon her with respect to distributions to H or has, through her investment authority or otherwise, unduly favored her own interests. On the duty of impartiality, see § 79.

Illustration:

10. The same facts as in Illustration 8, except that T survived W and thereafter married W's daughter. This may justify a court in removing (or refusing to appoint) T as trustee.

g. Alternatives to removal of trustee. Courts may grant more limited relief to deal with cases in which removal is not necessary or appropriate.

For example, conflict-of-interest problems might be ameliorated by the appointment of an additional trustee, or by the appointment of a trustee *ad litem* to handle a specific, conflict-sensitive transaction. Insolvency concerns might be dealt with by requiring a bond (see § 34, Comment *a*) or other security for the proper administration of the trust. When a national bank fails, its responsibilities may be transferred to a successor, thereby obviating the need for removal proceedings under state law. . . . .

§ 38. Trustee's Compensation and Indemnification

(1) A trustee is entitled to reasonable compensation out of the trust estate for services as trustee, unless the terms of the trust provide otherwise or the trustee agrees to forgo compensation.

(2) A trustee is entitled to indemnity out of the trust estate for expenses properly incurred in the administration of the trust.

General Comment:

a. Individual and corporate trustees. The rules stated in this section apply to both private and charitable trusts, and to family members or friends who act as trustee as well as to corporate or professional trustees.

The trustee's experience, skill, and facilities, however, are factors in determining the reasonableness of compensation. See Comment *c(1)*. Also, a family relationship or friendship may be relevant to the parties' expectations (and therefore intentions) concerning compensation. Compare Comment *g*, infra.

b. Lien for compensation and indemnification. The right of indemnification in Subsection (2) entitles a trustee to pay directly from funds of the trust, or to obtain reimbursement from the trust estate if the trustee has personally paid, expenses of the trust properly incurred in the course of administration.

Before distributing income or principal of the trust, the trustee may withhold funds for such reimbursement or for appropriate compensation.

On what constitutes proper administration expense generally, see § 88. Also compare Comment *c*.

On the possibility and basis of indemnification for expenses *improperly* incurred, see § 88.

Comment on Subsection (1):

c. Amount of compensation. Some state statutes still prescribe formulas for determining the amount of a trustee's compensation. They usually provide that trustees' fees are to be based on specified percentages of the principal or of the income and principal of the trust. Normally, the statute in effect at the time the compensation is claimed controls, regardless of when the trust was created. If the trustee has negligible active duties, statutes fixing compensation for trustees are usually held not to apply. Furthermore, statutes are normally to be interpreted as allowing the court to authorize additional or reduced compensation if the court determines that the statutory formula would result in a trustee's fee that is unreasonably high or low.

Many statutes merely provide that trustees are entitled to reasonable compensation. The reasonable compensation rule applies where there is no statute dealing with trustee compensation.

Trustees ordinarily receive some compensation periodically and, when the trust terminates, additional compensation for their special responsibilities at that time.

c(1). Determining reasonable compensation. Trial courts have discretion in determining reasonable compensation, but their determinations are subject to review for abuse of discretion.

Local custom is a factor to be considered in determining compensation. Other relevant factors are: the trustee's skill, experience and facilities, and the time devoted to trust duties; the amount and character of the trust property; the degree of difficulty, responsibility, and risk assumed in administering the trust, including in making discretionary distributions; the nature and costs of services rendered by others; and the quality of the trustee's performance.

The amount of compensation received by a trustee is relevant in determining whether certain costs of others' services are reimbursable under Subsection (2). This is particularly so of costs of hiring advisors, agents, and others to render services expected or normally to be performed by the trustee. Conversely, even proper expenses of this type may affect what is reasonable compensation for the trustee. . . . . On the requirement that expenses be properly incurred, see generally § 88.

Absent a statute so requiring, the trustee's compensation need not be approved by a court, but a trustee who has taken excessive compensation may be ordered to refund it. To make the possibility of judicial review meaningful, beneficiaries should be informed of compensation being taken by the trustee. On the extent to which a trustee is protected by a court decree, or by approval or acquiescence of beneficiaries, see § 83 (on accounting) and §§ 97 (beneficiary consent) and 98 (laches). . . . .

d. Special services. A trustee who renders special services in the administration of the trust, for example as attorney or real-estate agent, may be awarded compensation for such services when it is advantageous to the trust that the trustee rather than another perform those services. This is particularly relevant under a statutory fee schedule. Compare § 78 on the duty of loyalty. . . . .

e. The terms of the trust. When the terms of a trust provide that the trustee is to receive a certain compensation or no compensation, the trustee's right to compensation is ordinarily governed by that provision. It is a question of interpretation whether such a provision applies also to successor trustees.

If the amount of compensation provided by the terms of the trust is or becomes unreasonably high or unreasonably low, the court may allow a smaller or larger compensation, or may allow the trustee to resign. See § 36.

A trustee who has expressly agreed with the settlor to act for a certain compensation, however, is entitled only to the agreed compensation, unless there are unanticipated circumstances that are substantial and relevant to compensation (cf. § 66).

If a trust provides a benefit for the person designated as trustee or is created by a will that also makes a devise to the trustee, it is a question of interpretation whether the benefit or devise is in addition to or in lieu of the trustee's regular compensation, and whether it is conditional upon the beneficiary or devisee performing the duties of trustee. In the absence of evidence of a different intention, the presumption is that a devise or benefit is in addition to compensation as trustee and is not conditional on performing the duties of trustee. . . . .

f. Agreement with beneficiaries. The amount of compensation or indemnification to which the trustee would otherwise be entitled may be enlarged or diminished by agreement between the trustee and the beneficiaries. Such an agreement will bind only the beneficiaries who are parties to it, directly or by virtual representation. Cf. § 65, especially Comment *b*, and § 97. An agreement enlarging the trustee's compensation or indemnification will not bind a beneficiary who personally consented but was under incapacity and was not otherwise bound by representation; nor will it bind a consenting beneficiary if the trustee failed to disclose all the relevant circumstances that the trustee knew or should have known, or if the agreement is unfair to the beneficiary. See §§ 78, 97, and 65, Comment *b*.

g. *Waiver.* A trustee may voluntarily forgo any claim to compensation or indemnification. A waiver may be inferred from conduct in some circumstances, for example, when upon termination (with no showing of mistake) the trustee distributes the trust property without withholding any compensation.

That the absence of compensation does not diminish the trustee's normal duties, see § 70.

h. *Double commissions for double roles.* A person who acts both as executor and as trustee is entitled to such compensation as is reasonable in view of all the duties performed. See generally discussion in Comment *c*. Compare Comment *d* and also § 78, dealing with the duty of loyalty where self-hiring is involved.

i. *Several trustees.* When there are two or more co-trustees, compensation that is fixed by statute or trust provision ordinarily is to be divided among them in accordance with the relative value of their services. Where the rule of reasonable compensation applies, see generally Comment *c*, and especially Comment *c(1)*.

In the aggregate, the reasonable fees for multiple trustees may be higher than for a single trustee, because the normal duty of each trustee to participate in all aspects of administration (see § 81, and cf. § 80) can be expected not only to result in some duplication of effort but also to contribute to the quality of administration. And see Comment *c(1)* on factors (time, skill, etc.) relevant to establishing the compensation of each of the co-trustees.

j. *Successive trustees.* If a trustee fails to complete the administration of the trust because of death, resignation, or removal, each trustee (or a deceased trustee's estate) is entitled to reasonable compensation for such services as the trustee has performed.

k. *Cross-references.* On the effect of a breach of trust on the trustee's compensation, see Chapter 19.

On the trustee's power to incur expenses, and also on indemnification for expenses not properly incurred, see § 88.

On the allocation of costs of trustees' compensation between income and principal, see Chapter 23; and also Revised Uniform Principal and Income Act (1997) §§ 501(2), 502(a)(2); Revised Uniform Principal and Income Act (1962) § 13; and Uniform Principal and Income Act (1931) § 12.

§ 39. Exercise of Powers by Multiple Trustees

Unless otherwise provided by the terms of the trust, if there are two trustees their powers may be exercised only by concurrence of both of them, absent an emergency or a proper delegation; but if there are three or more trustees their powers may be exercised by a majority.

Comment:

a. *Basic rule and rationale.* If a trust has two trustees, they must concur in order to exercise powers of the trusteeship. If there are three or more trustees and they disagree, the decision of the majority controls, although when feasible all trustees must be consulted before decisions are made. . . . .

For purposes of this rule, the number of trustees in office at the time of the action is controlling, rather than the original number of trustees. As to delegation see Comment *d*.

Traditionally, the majority-rule principle has applied only to charitable trusts; in private trusts all the trustees had to agree in order to take action. Considerations of sound and efficient administration, however, tend to be better served by the rule stated in this section. This is evidenced not only by widespread drafting practice but also by the fact that most states today provide for majority rule by statute. . . . . See also Uniform Trustees Powers Act § 6; Uniform Trusts Act (1937) § 11; and Uniform Trust Code § 703(a).

These statutory provisions and the rule of this section ordinarily protect a dissenting trustee from liability for an act authorized by the majority, while preserving the co-trustee's duty normally to participate in deliberations and decisionmaking and to act reasonably to prevent a breach of trust. See . . . also § 81.

Illustrations:

1. A trust has five trustees. Three of them join in a conveyance of land belonging to the trust. Absent a contrary provision in the trust, such as one stating that the trustees "shall act by unanimous vote," the conveyance is valid. If the conveyance is a breach of trust, the two trustees who did not join in it will not be liable, unless they failed to act reasonably to prevent the breach of trust, such as by failing to bring suit to prevent or set aside the conveyance.

2. A deed purporting to convey trust property is signed by only one of two trustees. The deed is subject to rescission and the rights of the beneficiaries are ordinarily unaffected. (On the protection of bona-fide purchasers, and on the question of who is a bona-fide purchaser, see generally Chapter 22.)

b. *Ratification or acquiescence by co-trustee.* An action taken by one trustee with the consent of the other trustee(s) is valid. When a trustee has acted without the others' consent, they can ratify the action.

Thus, a contract to sell trust property signed by one of two trustees with the knowledge and acquiescence of the other is valid. If the other trustee did not know of the contract when it was signed but later learned of it and failed to object within a reasonable time, this would be an effective ratification. Compare § 97 on affirmance of a breach of trust by a beneficiary.

c. *Emergencies.* If an action important to the purposes of the trust is required by an emergency to be carried out before consent can be obtained from the other trustee(s) or from the court, one or more of multiple trustees (including a majority of the available trustees) can properly exercise powers conferred upon the trustees.

d. *Delegation.* To the extent that a trustee can properly delegate authority to a co-trustee (see . . . § 81), acts can properly be performed pursuant to the delegation.

e. *Breaking deadlocks.* If multiple trustees are deadlocked with regard to the exercise of a power, on application of a co-trustee or beneficiary a proper court may direct exercise of the power or take other action to break the deadlock.

Illustration:

5. A provision of a trust having two trustees grants them discretion from time to time to select charities to which trust property is to be distributed. The trustees cannot agree on charities to receive distributions. Unless it is appropriate for no action to be taken in the circumstances, the court may make selections, ordinarily among charities proposed by the trustees; or it may appoint a temporary or permanent third trustee to participate in a specific decision or transaction, or may appoint a trustee *ad litem* . . . to handle the matter.

f. Terms of the trust. The terms of a trust may provide that the powers of multiple trustees are to be exercised in a manner that differs from that prescribed by the rule of this section. Thus, for example, a trust provision may require that all of the trust's three trustees concur in exercising powers or a particular power, or may provide that the decision of a particular trustee prevails in the event two trustees are deadlocked with regard to certain matters.

Illustration:

6. The terms of a trust with three trustees provide that one of them, X, has sole responsibility for the operation of a business held by the trust. A lease renewal for real estate used in the operation of the business is executed only by X. The lease renewal is valid. A lease executed by a majority consisting only of the other two trustees would not be valid. On the duties of the other two trustees in such a situation, see § 81.

It is a matter of interpretation whether a provision in a trust instrument stating that "the trustees shall act jointly" sufficiently manifests an intention contrary to the rule stated in this section with respect to decisionmaking by three or more trustees. The inference is that it does. In the context of a trust that is initially established with multiple trustees, one of whom dies, however, the quoted language alone is not sufficient to require the appointment of a successor trustee; thus, the normal result . . . applies, allowing the surviving trustee(s) to act alone in exercising the powers of the trusteeship.

CHAPTER 8

TRUST PROPERTY

Introductory Note: A trust is a fiduciary relationship with respect to property (§ 2), and the creation of a trust is a method of making a disposition of property, with the beneficiaries acquiring equitable interests in the subject matter of the trust. As earlier mentioned (§ 2, Comment *c*, and § 3, Comment *b*), the expression "trust property" (or "trust assets" or "trust estate") denotes things or interests in things that are held in the trust, whereas the phrase "subject matter of the trust" refers to the things themselves, some or all interests in which are held in the trust. Thus, if S transfers an undivided interest in a fund or fungibles, or a remainder interest in Blackacre, to T as trustee, the trust property held by T is the undivided interest, or the remainder, but the fund or fungible property, or Blackacre, is the subject matter.

Except as provided in § 29(a) (trust purpose or performance unlawful), no policy of trust law limits the property interests that may be held in trust; any forms or types of property are appropriate for a trustee to hold. Not all legally protected rights or interests are property interests, nor are mere hopes or expectations of acquiring property in the future.

Other bodies of law or the contractual or other governing terms of a property interest may prevent the transfer or limit the transferability of certain interests or types of property. This affects an owner's ability to transfer the property to a trustee, and usually even to declare a trust of it, but is not necessarily the same as saying that such property cannot be held in trust (§ 40, Comment *d*).

§ 40. Any Property May Be Trust Property

Subject to the rule of § 29, a trustee may hold in trust any interest in any type of property.

Comment:

a. Scope note. This section is primarily concerned with the fundamental question of whether trust law in any way limits the forms of property that can be held in trust. This section also addresses problems posed by other bodies of law or private arrangements that might prevent or limit a property owner's ability to place property in trust (Comment *d*) and problems that might arise because of a property owner's failure to adequately identify the property of an allegedly intended trust (Comment *e*).

This section does not address again the general requirements that there be trust property (see § 2, Comments *f* and *i*) and a legally effective declaration or transfer (§§ 10, 14, and 16) in order to create a trust. Nor does it address issues of illegality (§ 29(a)) or the trustee's possible duty to dispose of particular trust property in order to make investments in accordance with the terms of a trust or statute or the general principles of the Prudent

Investor Rule. On trust investing see §§ 90 through 92 [§§ 227–229 of Restatement Third, Trusts (Prudent Investor Rule)].

Section 41 considers closely related questions about hopes or expectations that relate to property but that are not themselves "property" interests.

b. The basic rule: any property may be trust property. Subject to requirements of lawful purpose and administration (§ 29(a)), no policy of the trust law restricts the types of property interests a trustee may hold in that fiduciary capacity. See also qualifications discussed in Comment *d* and those implicit in Comment *c*.

Property denotes interests in things, not necessarily the things themselves, but necessarily things that are legally capable of being owned (and, ordinarily, transferred) and to which property interests can attach. See generally original Restatement of Property, volume I, Introductory Note, page 3. . . . . Nevertheless, what the law includes within the definition of "property" has evolved over common-law history and can be expected to continue doing so in the future. Trust law continues to reflect such developments in property law, especially the law of gifts.

Trust property may be real or personal, tangible or intangible. It may consist of such diverse rights as undivided interests, terms of years, contingent future interests, and *choses in action,* even *choses* with respect to things that are not specifically ascertainable (cf. Comment *e*) at the time the trust is created, or with respect to things that are not owned by the settlor or in existence (cf. § 41) at that time.

Thus, a trademark, patent, or copyright, even an unpatented invention or uncopyrighted literary production, can be held in trust, as can the interest of a person designated as beneficiary of a life-insurance policy. Also, legal or equitable present interests in real or personal property for life or for a term of years, and presently existing future interests, whether legal or equitable, whether reversionary interests, executory interests, or remainders (contingent, vested, or vested subject to being divested), may be held in trust.

Trust property may also take the form of a fractional or undivided interest, whether it is clearly and specifically designated as such or it results from an assignment, bequest, or declaration with respect to a dollar (e.g., $25,000) portion of a designated bank account or of "my X Corporation stock." Segregation is not required as long as the portion of a fund or of fungible items can be ascertained from the expressed or implied terms of the disposition.

Despite some early expressions of a contrary view, a *chose in action* consisting of a legally enforceable claim against the trustee may be held in trust. See § 2, Comment *i* . . . . Trust property may also take the form of claims against the settlor or a beneficiary, as well as against some other person.

Although trust beneficiaries have equitable title to the trust property and it is generally stated and usually true that the trustee has legal title, in some instances the trustee will hold only an equitable interest because that is the character of the interest owned and placed in trust by the settlor. See Illustration 2 of § 2.

c. Transferable property. Any property interest of which an owner may make disposition by will can be the subject of a testamentary transfer in trust. Any property interest of which an owner may make a present transfer by way of outright gift can be the subject of a declaration of trust or of an inter vivos transfer to another to be held in trust.

d. Nontransferable property. Because trusts serve as a means of disposing of equitable interests in property, and of the legal title as well unless the trust is created by declaration, difficulties are presented when property that a settlor seeks to hold or transfer in trust is nontransferable or may be transferred only upon certain conditions or circumstances.

The problems arise not from any prohibition or policy of trust law but from other bodies of statutory or common law, from articles or bylaws of business entities, or from the terms of private agreements, deeds, or other governing instruments. If the owner of property cannot transfer it to another to be held for the other's own benefit, usually (but see below) the owner will not be able either to transfer it to another to be held in trust or to make an effective declaration of trust. Thus, the problem is not one of acceptability as trust property but of whether or how an owner is able to place certain property in a trust.

Limitations on the transfer of property rights include restrictions on alienation of participants' rights under public and private pension programs, the inalienability of certain future interests under antiquated common-law property doctrines, and privately imposed restrictions on alienation of the interests of trust beneficiaries (see §§ 58 and 59 on spendthrift trusts). Other types of restrictions may apply to some government bonds, tort and contract claims, seats on financial or commercial exchanges or boards, governmental life-insurance programs, and shares of corporations or other business entities or of cooperative housing projects or condominiums.

These or other impediments to transfer may frustrate a particular owner's wishes or efforts to hold a particular form of property in trust by declaration or to transfer it to another in trust. Nevertheless, absent some policy against separation of legal title from the equitable or beneficial rights, there is no objection to nontransferable property interests being held in trust if those interests somehow either arise in trust or come to be held by a trustee.

The latter can occur if a restriction on transfer can be waived or is only partial. Partial restrictions, for example, may allow transfers to or for certain relatives of the owner, dispositions at death, or inter vivos donative transfers; or they may apply only to the legal title (that is, to the identity of the obligee), so that the asset may be held by the title holder in trust by declaration. Except for the subject of spendthrift trusts (see §§ 58 and 59), comprehensive review of the nature, validity, effect, and interpretation of rules or arrangements that may inhibit the transfer of property are beyond the scope of this Restatement. . . . . [O]n various types of privately imposed restraints on alienation, see Restatement Second, Property (Donative Transfers), Chapters 3 (§§ 3.1–3.4) and 4 (§§ 4.2–4.5).

A nontransferable property interest may be held in trust when, as occasionally occurs, it is created in trust by act of the trustee or it accrues to a trustee of a trust that is already in existence. Ordinarily, these or other nontransferable interests that are held in trust will pass to successor trustees. . . . .

e. Indefinite subject matter. The subject matter of a trust must be definite or ascertainable. There is no trust property if the identity of the intended subject matter remains wholly in the control of the settlor or if its description is so indefinite that it cannot be ascertained. Thus, although S may declare himself trustee of all of the stocks and bonds he owns at the time of the declaration, if he declares himself trustee of "the bulk of my securities" or purports to transfer "some substantial portion of my X Co. stock" to T in trust, no trust is created.

It is not necessary that the trustee or beneficiary have the entire legal or beneficial interest in the subject matter. Nor is it necessary that the extent of the interests of the various beneficiaries be definite at the time the trust is created, or when the property is transferred to an existing trust, as long as the extent of the interests will be ascertained within the requirements of the applicable rule regarding perpetuities (see § 29(b)). Furthermore, it is not necessary that the parties actually know what the subject matter is as long as its identity can be ascertained from existing facts.

Illustration:

4. S directs her stockbroker to buy a thousand shares of X Corporation stock or any part thereof that can be purchased at no more than $100 per share. After the broker has bought 650 shares for S but before S knows whether any shares have been bought for her, she declares herself trustee of such shares of X Corporation as the broker may have bought for her. A trust of the 650 shares is created.

Although no trust can be created where the subject matter is not definite or ascertainable, a trust may subsequently arise when the intended trust property becomes definite or ascertainable if the settlor at that subsequent time expressly or impliedly manifests an intention to hold the property in, or add it to, the intended trust. See § 16, Comment *b*; compare § 41.

§ 41. Expectancies; Nonexistent Property Interest

An expectation or hope of receiving property in the future, or an interest that has not come into existence or has ceased to exist, cannot be held in trust.

Comment:

a. Expectation of receiving property by testate or intestate succession. A person who expects to receive property in the future by the will of a living person or by intestate succession has no presently existing interest of which to make a declaration of trust or a transfer to another in trust. Such an expectancy is not a contingent future interest (cf. § 40, Comment *b*) but a mere hope or expectation, however well founded or likely to materialize. By all traditional and current concepts of property, expectancies are not property interests.

Although the holder of a contingent future interest in a clear and growing majority of states (cf. § 40, Comment *d*) has property of which present disposition can be made, by gift or otherwise, a person cannot transfer an expectancy. The hope of an expectant heir, for example, is not property; it cannot be reached by creditors of the expectant heir; nor does it ordinarily (but cf. conservatorship proceedings) entitle the expectant heir to notice of proceedings involving the assets in question while the owner is still alive.

Once a testator has died leaving a will under which a particular person will be entitled to receive distribution of property on completion of estate administration, or on the happening of some future event(s), that person has an interest that can be held or transferred in trust. This is true even if the chance is remote that the person will ever receive the property.

On the other hand, if the testator has not yet died, a beneficiary named in the will has only a bare expectancy in the testator's property even though the testator is unlikely (or even hopelessly without capacity) to change the will. Similarly, one who is expected to inherit the property of a person who has made no will has no existing interest in that person's property of which to make a gift or other present transfer, or to create a trust.

Illustration:

1. S's father, F, died some years ago leaving most of his estate in a testamentary trust for S's mother, M, for life, remainder to S if then living and if not to S's then living issue. M also has a substantial estate of her own, which she plans to leave to S. For tax and other reasons, S executes and delivers a deed purporting immediately to transfer to T, as trustee, both his remainder interest in the trust created by F and any property he may receive from the estate of M. A trust is created of S's equitable contingent remainder interest in the trust previously created by his father, but not of his expectancy in the estate of his mother.

Note: Illustration 1 assumes a typical modern body of property law, freely allowing voluntary transfer of all future interests (see § 51), and that S's interest is not subject to a spendthrift restraint (§ 58). In this Illustration, T takes S's remainder interest subject to the same uncertainties it had in S's hands (here, at least his survival of M). S's adult children also have existing future interests of which any of them can make a present assignment, outright or in trust, or a declaration of trust.

A person has a property interest even though his or her interest is subject to being divested at the will of another, even if the interest is also subject to some condition precedent. See § 40, Comment *b*. (For example, if M in Illustration 1, above, had been given an inter vivos or testamentary power of appointment, the result of the Illustration and the observations noted after it would not change.)

So also, under traditional and currently accepted principles of property law, the beneficiaries of revocable inter vivos trusts have existing property interests (see § 25(1)) that can be transferred outright or in trust, even though in other important respects (see § 25(2)) the trust property is treated as if it belongs to the settlor holding the power of revocation rather than to the beneficiaries designated in the trust instrument. . . . . See also § 69, Comment *c* (that no merger occurs even if the settlor of a revocable trust is its sole trustee).

b. Nonexistent interests. An interest may not be in existence because the thing that would be the subject matter of the interest is not itself in existence or, although the thing exists, no one has an interest in it. In these cases, no one has an interest in anything of which there could be a declaration of trust or a transfer to another in trust. A person can make a promise to create a trust of an interest in such a thing should it thereafter be acquired, but such an agreement is not binding unless the requirements of the law of contracts are satisfied. See Comment *c*.

Thus, if A gratuitously declares herself trustee of the next picture she paints or of such shares as she may thereafter acquire in a corporation not yet organized, without more a trust is not created. The result is the same if A purports to transfer the contemplated painting or shares to another as trustee. Similarly, one cannot create a trust of property of which another has sole and complete ownership. In these situations, there is at most a gratuitous undertaking to create a trust in the future.

The rule of this section applies even though the would-be settlor once owned or has reason to expect, but no legally enforceable right, to acquire the thing or an interest in it in the future (Comment *a*). Difficulties may be encountered in drawing lines between property to be acquired in the future and the future yield of an existing property right. See . . . observations concerning "property" in § 40, Comment *b*.

c. Contractual liability. If consideration is received for a purported declaration of trust or assignment in trust of a bare expectancy or nonexistent property, the purported declaration or transfer is treated as a contract to create a trust even though it is worded as a present declaration or transfer.

On legally enforceable promises to create a trust in the future, and the possibility that a contract to create a trust in the future may create an immediate trust of a *chose in action* (i.e., of the rights under the contract), see § 10, Comment *g*, and § 15, Comment *b*.

d. Intended trust property subsequently acquired. A person gratuitously purports to declare a trust, or to make a transfer to another in trust, of a bare expectancy or nonexistent property. No trust arises when the person later acquires the intended trust property in the absence of some express or implied manifestation at the later time of an intent to give effect to the trust. See § 16, Comment *b*; compare § 40, Comment *e*.

e. Other matters. The rule of this section is applicable to property the person hopes to acquire by gift inter vivos.

To the extent a right to expected compensation in the future under an existing contract of employment is assignable (see Restatement Second, Contracts § 321), a trust of such rights can be created, either by declaration or transfer.

On tortious interference with expectancies, see Restatement of Restitution § 133(1) and § 169, Comment *c*; and compare id. § 184 [Restatement Third, Restitution and Unjust Enrichment § 46 (wrongful interference with donative transfer)]. See also Restatement Second, Torts § 774B.

§ 42. Extent and Nature of Trustee's Title

Unless a different intention is manifested, or the settlor owned only a lesser interest, the trustee takes a nonbeneficial interest of unlimited duration in the trust property and not an interest limited to the duration of the trust.

Comment:

a. Scope and rationale. The rule stated in this section is applicable although the trust is passive in whole or in part, and applies even if a statute of uses or counterpart doctrine (see § 6) immediately passes some or all of the trustee's title through to some or all of the beneficiaries.

The statement in this rule that the interest taken by the trustee is nonbeneficial (and see Comment *c*) is standard common-law doctrine. It reflects the basic concept that the beneficiaries hold the beneficial interests (or "equitable title") in the trust property, while the trustee (ordinarily) holds "bare" legal title to the property. See § 2, Comment *d*.

The rule of this section concerning the extent of the trustee's interest is long established for trusts of personal property. A more limited view . . . is sometimes expressed with regard to the extent of the trustee's title to real property held in trust, but that view is counterproductive and no longer justified. Furthermore, the rule stated here accords with modern doctrine eliminating distinctions between real and personal property. In any event, the narrower concept of the extent of the trustee's estate in land is, in modern circumstances, virtually consumed by its own qualifications or exceptions; and whatever utility the concept may have had is adequately and more properly served by statutes of uses (§ 6).

The rule that a trustee ordinarily takes an interest of unlimited duration reflects the extent of administrative powers normally granted trustees in modern trust instruments, and also by implication of law (§§ 70 and 85), in addition to typical provisions and rules relating to the manner of winding up a trust's affairs and making distributions upon termination (§§ 70 and 89). In addition, it provides certainty and a generally sound, simple set of concepts for the management of trust property, for fiduciary dealings with third parties, and for procedural aspects of litigation involving trust property. Furthermore, the rule serves simply and appropriately to establish the extent to which a fiduciary relationship exists between trustees and beneficiaries (especially remainder beneficiaries, cf. § 2), the extent to which restraints on alienation may be made applicable to future interests (§ 58), and the extent of a court's equitable authority to deal with unanticipated circumstances (§ 66). . . . .

b. Extent of the trustee's interest: effect of the rule. When a settlor transfers property to another as trustee or declares a trust of that property, unless the transferor manifests a different intention, the trustee takes the settlor's full title or interest in that property. The trustee's interest, therefore, ordinarily will not be limited in duration to the duration of the trust. Thus, if the owner of land, chattels, or securities transfers them to another in trust for a designated beneficiary for life, with remainder to others, the trustee takes a legal title of unlimited duration and not one limited to the lifetime of the life beneficiary.

The settlor may limit the duration of the trustee's interest by manifesting the intention to do so. Thus, O, who owns the full fee-simple title to Blackacre, conveys "to T a life estate in Blackacre for the life of B, with T to manage the property and distribute its rents and profits to B for as long as B lives, and I convey the remainder interest in Blackacre to R." Although this deed clearly grants T only a legal life estate *pur autre vie* (for B's life), it would be possible for O to supplement that interest by a grant of what are usually referred to as powers in trust. These powers might be designed to enable T to mortgage Blackacre or to rent it for a period that might run beyond B's lifetime, or might even include a power to sell Blackacre, thereby allowing T to encumber or even divest B's legal remainder interest in the original trust property.

It would be possible also for O to confer an interest of limited duration upon T by language less explicit than the foregoing. Thus, that intention might be found by implication from the fiduciary powers specified and particularly those expressly withheld, from the disposition's overall context within the document by which the trust is created, and from the circumstances surrounding the transaction and other admissible evidence tending to show that intention (see § 4).

In cases of trustees who take typical titles of unlimited duration, however, the terms of a governing instrument may withhold specific powers. On the other hand, it is usual (though unnecessary) for trust instruments to recite fiduciary powers that would otherwise be implied by law.

As a result of similarities of appearance in the various situations in the preceding paragraphs, difficult questions of interpretation may arise when the settlor has not expressly stated the extent of the trustee's title. In such cases, an interpretation is preferred that does not displace the general rule of this section, because of likely intention and the practical advantages (Comment *a*) inherent in that result.

c. Nature of trustee's interest: bare, nonbeneficial title. The observation in the rule of this section that a trustee takes only a nonbeneficial interest in the trust property refers to the quality of the title taken in the trustee's fiduciary role. The trustee may, of course, also be a beneficiary of the trust (§ 32, Comment *b*; § 43, Comment *a*), but the resulting *beneficial* interest is not held in the trustee's fiduciary capacity.

Thus, a trustee, *as* trustee, ordinarily takes only what is generally described as the "bare" legal title to the trust property. (Occasionally, however, the trustee takes a non-beneficial, "bare" equitable title because that is the nature of the interest the settlor owned and transferred to the trust. See § 2, Illustration 2.)

Although a beneficial interest in a trust may generally be reached by creditors of the beneficiary (§ 56, but cf. §§ 58–60 on spendthrift and discretionary trusts), the trustee's personal creditors or trustee in bankruptcy may not reach either the trust property or the trustee's nonbeneficial interest therein. Also, unlike the general rule that beneficiaries may transfer their beneficial interests during life or by will (§ 51, Comment *b*, and § 55, Comment *b*, but cf. §§ 58–60), the trustee may not transfer the trust property or the nonbeneficial interest therein, except as incidental to procedures for replacement of trustees (§§ 34–37) or, acting in a fiduciary capacity as trustee, in the course of administration by exercising a power of sale or other power of the trusteeship (§ 85 and §§ 70, 76). (But, on claims against the trust estate—i.e., against the trustee in its representative capacity—and on the rights of bona fide purchasers, cf. Chapters 21 and 22.)

CHAPTER 9

BENEFICIARIES

Introductory Note: This chapter deals with the question of who may be a trust beneficiary and with the requirement that a private trust have definite beneficiaries, together with related problems that arise when qualified or definite beneficiaries are lacking in various recurring, intended trust contexts. The definite-beneficiary requirement (§ 44) does not apply to trusts for charitable purposes.

A valid trust can be created even though for a period of time there is no designated beneficiary in being, as long as one or more beneficiaries may be validly ascertained within applicable rules relating to perpetuities. As noted in § 2, Comment *h* (and hereafter in § 44), however, an intended private trust fails if it has no definite or validly ascertainable beneficiary. Some intentions that have failed entirely under traditional applications of this rule may nevertheless be salvaged by the rules of §§ 46(2) and 47.

Trust beneficiaries, in the terminology of this Restatement, include not only persons intended to have enforceable rights in the trust property (contrast "Incidental Benefits" in § 48), including in the form of powers of appointment, but also those who take legally implied reversionary interests (that is, "by resulting trust") and the successors in interest of those who earlier had held beneficial interests either under the terms of an express trust or by resulting trust (§ 48, Comment *a*).

§ 43. Persons Who May Be Beneficiaries

A person who would have capacity to take and hold legal title to the intended trust property has capacity to be a beneficiary of a trust of that property; ordinarily, a person who lacks capacity to hold legal title to property may not be a trust beneficiary.

Comment:

a. In general. If a person has capacity to take and hold legal title to property, that person may take and hold equitable title as a trust beneficiary to the same extent and of like property. (The term "person" includes corporations, unincorporated associations, and, for this purpose at least, other trusts, as well as individuals. See § 3, Comment *e*.)

An individual, although a minor or otherwise lacking capacity to transfer property or to enter into contracts, may be a trust beneficiary. A corporation, municipal or private, including a nonprofit corporation (whether or not for charitable purposes), may be a beneficiary of trust property to the extent it has capacity to take and hold legal title to like property (Comment *c*). Also, the United States or a state may be a beneficiary of a trust, which to the extent of the governmental interest would normally be a charitable trust.

Ordinarily, but not necessarily (see Comment *d*), a person who lacks capacity to take legal title to property lacks capacity to become the beneficiary of a trust of that property; and a person who becomes a trust beneficiary ordinarily has capacity to continue as beneficiary of the trust property only to the extent the person has capacity to hold legal title to that property.

A settlor of a trust may be the sole beneficiary or one of the beneficiaries of the trust. A trustee may also be a trust beneficiary, provided the trust has at least one other beneficiary or another trustee. See § 69 on the doctrine of merger.

An animal or a "purpose" is not a person and may not hold title to property or be a beneficiary of a private trust (but compare § 47 on what have often been called "purpose" or "honorary" trusts). A charitable purpose (see § 28), however, will support a charitable trust, to which the definite-beneficiary requirement of § 44 does not apply (see § 44, Comment *a*).

b. *Noncitizens.* Noncitizens generally have capacity to take legal title to property and therefore have capacity to become trust beneficiaries. If by statute, however, land held by a noncitizen is subject to forfeiture to the government . . ., the equitable interest of a noncitizen beneficiary of a trust of land in such a jurisdiction is likewise subject to forfeiture.

c. *Corporations.* If, by statute or the terms of its charter or articles, a corporation cannot take title to land, or to land of more than a certain value or for other than certain purposes, it cannot become the beneficiary of a trust of land, or of land of more than the designated value or for other than the designated purposes. If the corporation can take but cannot hold title to certain land against the objection of the state or a shareholder, it cannot continue to hold a beneficial interest in a trust against the objection of the state or shareholder.

d. *Unincorporated associations.* In nearly all jurisdictions today, unincorporated associations of various types may take and hold legal title to property, but that matter is not within the scope of this Restatement. . . . Whether or not it has capacity to take or hold legal title to property, however, an unincorporated association has capacity to be the beneficiary of a trust, the disability being a technical and historical one rather than one based on current substantive policy. Accordingly, if property is left by will directly to an unincorporated association that is incapable of taking or holding title to property, the disposition does not fail; a trust arises for the intended purpose, and the court will appoint one or more trustees (§ 34) to hold the property in trust for the association.

This rule applies where the trust is for the benefit of the association, as such, rather than for the benefit of its members (see and contrast Comment *e*, below, and § 45, Comment *a*). It does not matter that all potential members of the continuing entity may not be ascertainable at any point in time. Ordinarily, the association's rights in the trust are enforceable in a suit in the name of the association by an appropriate officer or, if necessary, in a representative suit by members of the association.

e. *Associated perpetuities issues.* The intended duration of trusts for corporations or unincorporated associations may conflict with policies related to the rule against perpetuities. If the corporation or association has capacity to hold title to property, however, and its interest in the trust is not subject to a condition precedent, the problem is not one of "vesting" (§ 29, Comment *g*). In such a situation, an apparent problem of trust duration is avoided by the related rule (§ 29, Comment *h(1)*) that a trust is valid but not indestructible, regardless of a "material purpose" of the settlor (see § 65(2)), after the period of the rule against perpetuities has expired. The corporation or association may then, as sole beneficiary (see § 65), terminate the trust and acquire the property outright by action taken in accordance with its governing procedures.

This solution is not available, however, if distribution to an unincorporated association is precluded (as may still be the case in a few states) by its incapacity to take title at the time the perpetuities period expires. Nevertheless, in this situation, the trust is valid for a perpetuities period . . ., with a severable disposition of the property thereafter to depend on the terms of the trust and the rules applicable to the association. If the trust provisions can be interpreted as so providing, either (i) the trust property is to be distributed to the association members ascertained when the trust can no longer continue or (ii), if the governing law of the association empowers it to determine the disposition of property, a disposition may be made accordingly. Otherwise, the property is held upon resulting trust for the settlor, or his or her successors in interest (§ 8).

e(1). Perpetuities and association members, rather than association itself, as beneficiaries. Rather than creating a trust for the association as such, a settlor may create a trust for the individual members of the association as then constituted. In such a case, the beneficiaries are definite and ascertained (for purposes of § 44) at the outset, and the trust is enforceable.

On the other hand, a trust might be intended to benefit the individual members of the association as constituted from time to time. Although those beneficiaries might be susceptible of ascertainment from time to time (in the terms of § 44), their interests would not comply with the vesting requirements of the traditional rule against perpetuities. A consideration of the results that follow from this noncompliance, under the various types of rules regulating perpetuities in this country, is not within the scope of this Restatement. (Illustratively, however, compare reformation in § 29, Comment *g*.) . . . .

§ 44. Definite-Beneficiary Requirement

A trust is not created, of if created will not continue, unless the terms of the trust provide a beneficiary who is ascertainable at the time or who may later become ascertainable within the period and terms of the rule against perpetuities.

Comment:

a. Scope of section; general principles. The rule stated in this section is not applicable to charitable trusts. See § 28, Comment *c*. On the effect of a transfer upon an intended trust for a specific or general noncharitable purpose, without designating a definite or ascertainable person as beneficiary, see § 47.

The creation or continuation of a trust, or the validity of a trust provision purporting to create a beneficial interest, requires that there be a person to receive and hold the beneficial interest in the trust property—an identifiable person by whom or on whose behalf the trust or the provision in question can be enforced.

It is not necessary that the intended beneficiary or beneficiaries be known at the time of the creation of the trust. A beneficiary must be either: (1) specifically named or capable of ascertainment from facts existing at the time the trust or interest is to be created (cf. the doctrine of facts of independent significance in § 17, Comment *d*), or at the time when a question of the trust's continuance is to be resolved; or (2) capable of becoming existent and ascertainable in the future from facts that will be determinable within the period and terms of the rule against perpetuities, including by exercise of a power of appointment. (The operation and effects of common-law and statutory rules against perpetuities are not within the scope of this Restatement, but see § 29(b) and especially § 29, Comment *g*, for a summary discussion.)

A trust may have a single beneficiary or multiple beneficiaries whose interests may be enjoyable concurrently or successively. And just as legal interests may be held in tenancy in common or joint tenancy, so may the equitable interests of trust beneficiaries.

The interests of some trust beneficiaries may be valid although the intended interests of others are not, including invalidity for indefiniteness, unless the failure of some interests defeats the entire plan of the settlor in creating the trust.

b. *Beneficiaries ascertainable by description.* Beneficiaries need not be named in the terms of the trust, but may be designated by class terminology or by description. Thus, wills often establish trusts for the primary or eventual benefit of classes consisting of the testator's children and other descendants. Other forms of description also may be used.

Illustration:

1. S's will leaves her residuary estate to T in trust to pay $10,000 to each person who is a full-time employee of S at the time of her death, and to pay $25,000 to each of S's brothers and sisters who are living at her death, with the rest of the trust estate to be held in trust (in accordance with terms described in the will) for S's issue. A trust is created, and all of the beneficiaries mentioned here are ascertainable by description.

c. *Trusts for unborn or subsequently ascertainable beneficiaries.* A trust or trust provision may be created, and once created may continue, for the benefit of a person or persons not in existence or not ascertainable at the time of the creation or continuation of the trust if they and their interests will be ascertainable, or the beneficial interests will fail, within the period and the terms of the applicable rule against perpetuities. Thus, a child who has not been born or conceived at the time of the creation of a trust can be a beneficiary of the trust.

Illustrations:

2. O declares himself trustee of certain securities to pay the income of the trust to B during her lifetime and following her death to accumulate the income and to pay the principal and accumulated income to B's children who attain age 21. The trust, including the remainder interest, is valid whether or not B had any children at the time of the declaration of trust. If at B's death she leaves children then living, the trust will continue (or be distributed) pursuant to its terms. If she dies leaving no children, or if no children who survive her live to age 21, the trust, although valid throughout its existence, will terminate (assuming no other disposition is provided in the terms of O's declaration), and the

trust property will revert to O, if living, or to his successors in interest, in either case by resulting trust (see §§ 7 and 8).

3. X, a childless bachelor, transfers Blackacre to T in trust to manage the property and to accumulate or expend the rents and profits for the benefit of X's first-born child and to convey Blackacre, together with any accumulated rents and profits, to that child on attaining majority. A trust is created. If X later dies without ever having a child, the trust will not continue, and T will hold the trust property for X's estate (or other successor(s) in interest, possibly even by assignment by X during life).

4. S's will leaves $50,000 to T in trust to invest and manage and to pay such amounts from the income or principal of the trust as S's husband H may direct, during his life or by will, to or for the benefit of such relatives, friends, charities, or others as H may select (but excluding H, his estate, or the creditors of H or his estate); and to the extent H does not so direct the disposition of the trust property, the trustee is to distribute the remainder of the trust estate in equal shares to those of S's nieces and nephews who have graduated from high school by the time of H's death. A trust is created with H being granted a valid power of appointment by which beneficiaries may be ascertained in the future, and also with beneficiaries, ascertainable by description, to take in default of appointment.

As in Illustrations 2 and 3, the validity of the trust in Illustration 4 is not affected by the fact that the beneficial interests provided by the terms of the trust may eventually fail to materialize and that the trustee may then hold upon resulting trust for the settlor's successors in interest.

Although the reversionary beneficiaries in these Illustrations take by operation of law rather than by the terms of the trusts, they are nevertheless beneficiaries of the trusts and their interests are legally protected and enforceable. See § 48, Comment *a*.

c(1). Corporation not yet organized. Subject to limits imposed by the rule against perpetuities, a trust may be created in favor of a corporation (see § 43) that is not organized at the time of the creation of the trust. Thus, a corporation to be formed by the settlor may be a trust beneficiary because the described corporation will necessarily be organized, if at all, within the settlor's lifetime. If no corporation is so organized, the trust reverts (by resulting trust, § 8) to the settlor's successors in interest.

d. Predeceased beneficiary. A person who has died prior to the creation of a trust cannot be a beneficiary of the trust. Thus, if property is devised in trust for a person who predeceases the testator, the devise of the beneficial interest lapses. If other beneficiaries are not provided by the terms of the trust (or by anti-lapse statute), the designated trustee ordinarily holds the property upon resulting trust for the estate of the testator (see § 8).

So also, if property is transferred inter vivos in trust, or a property owner makes a declaration of trust, for a designated person who is dead at the time of the transfer or declaration, in the absence of other beneficiaries no express trust is created. Ordinarily (§ 8, Comment *f*), in such a case the transferee holds upon a resulting trust for the transferor, or the declarant holds the property free of trust.

In the case of a revocable trust, however, the interest of a designated beneficiary who is alive at the time the trust is created but dies before the trust becomes irrevocable, under traditional doctrine, does not fail unless that interest is subject to an expressed or implied condition of survival. Statutes or modernized doctrine may bring such dispositions under lapse rules and anti-lapse statutes. See § 25(2), and particularly § 25, Comment *e* . . . .

§ 45. Members of a Definite Class as Beneficiaries

The members of a definite class of persons can be the beneficiaries of a trust.

Comment:

a. Application of the rule. A class of persons is definite within the meaning of the rule stated in this section and the rule of § 44 if the identity of all the individuals comprising its membership is ascertainable at the time the trust is created or will become ascertainable within the period and terms of the rule against perpetuities. A class is not indefinite for this purpose merely because it consists of a changing or shifting group, the number of whose members may increase or decrease.

Typical of provisions for definite classes are trust provisions for the "children" or "grandchildren," the "issue" or "descendants," or the "heirs" or "next of kin" of a designated person, or for a person's "brothers and sisters" or "nieces and nephews." Also, under ordinary circumstances, a provision for the members of an unincorporated association on the date of the disposition, or on a date five or 10 years later, is or will timely become sufficiently definite to permit the intended beneficiaries to be ascertained (§ 43, Comment *e*).

b. Shares of class members. If the shares in which class members are to take are specified, or the manner in which they are to benefit is stated, those directions in the terms of the trust will be followed. A settlor's unclear directions can be clarified by interpretation or construction. (On the meaning of "per capita," "per stirpes," and similar expressions, with relevance also to construction of class gifts, compare Restatement Third, Property (Wills and Other Donative Transfers) §§ 2.3, Comments *b* through *g*.)

If the settlor fails to specify the shares of class members or to provide for the manner in which they are to benefit, class members described as "children," "grandchildren," "brothers and sisters," or "nieces and nephews" are presumed to take equally. Those described as "issue," "descendants," "heirs," or "next of kin" of a person are presumed to take in the manner in which those class members would take the person's property as intestate successors under applicable law. (The various distribution systems are discussed in Restatement Third, Property (Wills and Other Donative Transfers) § 2.3.)

c. Power of selection. A trust may be created for the benefit of selected members of a definite class when the terms of the trust authorize the trustee or another person to determine the recipients and the portions in which they are to take. (On power to select beneficiaries from the members of an indefinite class, see § 46, Comment *d*.)

If the trustee or other person having the power of selection fails to exercise it, the trust property will be divided among the members of the definite class, as determined at the time of the expiration of the power, in equal shares or in other shares appropriate to the class term (see Comment *b*), unless the transferor has manifested a different intention.

d. "Relatives." Whether the term "relatives" is a definite class depends on the settlor's intended meaning in using the term.

If it is shown that, in using the word "relatives," the settlor intended to create a trust for all individuals who are related to the designated person, the intended class is not sufficiently ascertainable to sustain a trust, because a person has an indefinite number of close and remote relatives. Thus, an intended trust to divide the trust property equally among all relatives of a designated person fails under the rule stated in the section.

On the other hand, under the preferred construction, an intended trust for "relatives" is to be interpreted not to mean all relatives (supra) but to mean some definite group of near relatives or some other ascertainable group of relatives. Absent evidence of the settlor's actual intention (or a power of selection, see below and Comment *c*), the term will be construed to refer to the heirs of the designated person. Under any such construction, the class is definite within the rule stated in this section.

d(1). Selected "relatives." A trust for the benefit of "relatives" of the settlor or other designated person does not fail if the trustee has power to select who among the relatives shall take and in what portions. See Comment *b*. In such a case, the trustee may select any person or persons who reasonably fit within the meaning of the term, whether or not they would be heirs of the designated person.

If the trustee fails to make a selection, however, the property will be divided among those relatives who would be the heirs of the designated person as determined at the time the power expires and in shares determined by the applicable intestacy statute, unless the transferor has manifested a different intention.

e. "Family." In the case of a trust for members of the "family" of a designated person, a difficult question of interpretation arises. The term may be construed to include the designated person and his or her spouse and children, or such of these persons or other relatives or others as are living with the designated person, or it may include certain other relatives. In any event, once the meaning is determined, by interpretation, the term supplies a definite class for purposes of the rules stated in this section and in § 44, unless the term is found to include relatives generally, in which case it falls within the principles of Comment *d*.

Where a trust is created for members of the family of a designated person, the extent of the interests of the various family members involves a further question of interpretation. The settlor may have intended that each member of the "family" be entitled to an equal share, especially in the case of a prompt distribution of the trust property. On the other hand, the settlor may have intended successive life and remainder interests, or that one member of the family be entitled to the whole beneficial interest except to the extent funds are needed for the support of other members of the family. Or the settlor may have intended the trustee to have discretion concerning the benefits to be received by the various members of the family.

An analogous question is whether a transfer to A for the benefit of "himself and his family" manifests an intention to create a trust or merely an intention to make a beneficial gift to A, with an expression of motive for making the gift. That question is discussed in § 13, Comment *d* (and compare § 13, Illustration 10). On the treatment of a class gift directly to a person and his or her family, see original Restatement of Property § 303(2).

f. Persons who can enforce the trust. When a trust is created for members of a class, suit to redress or enjoin a breach of trust can be maintained by any member of the class. See generally § 94. This is true even though the trustee has power to select which members of the class shall take and has not yet exercised the power; each member of the class is a beneficiary of the trust until excluded by the trustee's exercise of the power in favor of other class members (cf. § 48, Comment *a*). The fact that a member of the class may ultimately take nothing does not prevent that beneficiary from maintaining suit; each of the beneficiaries of such a trust is in this position, for if none could sue the trustee might commit a breach of trust with impunity.

Illustrations:

1. S's will leaves $100,000 to T in trust to pay the income to B for life and upon B's death to pay the principal to such of the issue of B and in such proportions as T may select. During B's lifetime and with B's consent, T commits a breach of trust by borrowing some of the trust fund. Any of B's issue can maintain a suit to compel T to redress the breach of trust.

2. Same facts as in Illustration 1, except that upon B's death T decides not to exercise his power of selection. T is to distribute the property to such of B's then living issue and in such shares as called for by that form of representation prescribed by the applicable statute of intestate succession. At that time, only one or more of the issue so determined may enforce the trust. (The choice-of-law rule for determining the applicable statute is not within the scope of this Restatement.)

g. Declaration of trust. The rules stated in this section apply where the owner of property makes a declaration of trust, as well as where the owner conveys or devises property to another in trust. Thus, if S effectively declares herself trustee of property for such of her issue as she may thereafter appoint, until the power is exercised, assuming the trust is irrevocable, it may be enforced by any of S's issue, because the issue constitute a definite class that would take by implied remainder in default of appointment.

§ 46. Members of an Indefinite Class as Beneficiaries

(1) Except as stated in Subsection (2), where the owner of property transfers it upon intended trust for the members of an indefinite class of persons, no trust is created.

(2) If the transferee is directed to distribute the property to such members of the indefinite class as the transferee shall select, the transferee holds the property in trust with power but no duty to distribute the property to such class members as the transferee may select; to whatever extent the power (presumptively personal) is not exercised, the transferee will then hold for reversionary beneficiaries implied by law.

General Comment:

a. When class is "indefinite." A class of persons is indefinite under the rule of this section if the identity of all individuals comprising its membership cannot be ascertained. Although it is possible to determine that certain persons fall within a class and that others do not, it may be impossible to determine *all* of the persons who fall within it. In such a situation, the class or group is indefinite. This is the case, for example, of a class consisting of all of the "friends" of the settlor or of another person. So also, a class is indefinite if it includes all persons other than the transferee or the transferee's estate.

A different situation is presented where a class reference is merely precatory and the transferor is found to have intended a beneficial gift to the transferee, rather than to create a trust. See § 13, Comment *d.*

Comment on Subsection (1):

b. Where an equal division is directed among, or a specified amount is to be paid to, all members of the class. If the only beneficial provision of an intended trust directs the trust property to be divided in equal shares among all of the members of an indefinite class, no member of the class can maintain a proceeding to enforce the intended trust, nor can anyone else. Because the intended trustee is under no enforceable duty to carry out the testator's direction, no trust is created. Moreover, since the total membership of the class cannot be ascertained, it is impossible to make an equal distribution among all of the members of the class, even if the intended trustee wishes to do so.

Similarly, where a testator directs the trustee to pay a specified sum to every member of an indefinite class, the intended trust provision for those class members fails. Accordingly, in these circumstances, the intended trustee holds the property upon resulting trust for the testator's estate.

Although a disposition is expressed simply as a trust for the members of an indefinite class, a literal interpretation would seem doubtful as a matter of transferor intention and (unless the transferor is alive to take by resulting trust) would wholly defeat whatever specific objective the transferor had in mind. An interpretation is therefore preferred that would give the disposition some effect reasonably consistent with the transferor's general objective. Thus, the disposition may be interpreted as intended to create a trust for members of the described class as determined or selected by the designated trustee, in which case the situation falls within Subsection (2). See Comment *d.* Or, if the disposition is interpreted as one intended to benefit those members of an otherwise indefinite class that are or may become identifiable in a manner described in § 44, Comments *a* and *b*, a valid trust is created. See § 45.

Illustration:

1. S leaves all of his property to T in trust to distribute it in equal shares among S's friends and relatives. Under a literal interpretation, the intended trust fails, and S's estate will be distributed by resulting trust to S's next of kin. By interpretation, however, it may be found either (i) that some ascertainable group of friends and relatives was intended (in which case see § 45) or (ii) that an implied term of the trust authorizes T to determine who the friends and relatives are or to select distributees from among S's friends and relatives, with the direction then being to distribute the property in equal shares to all of those so determined or selected (in which case see Comments *c–g*).

Comment on Subsection (2):

c. Background and comparison: powers of appointment. Subsection (2) addresses situations in which a property owner conveys or devises property to a person who is directed, not merely authorized, by the terms of the intended trust to distribute the property to persons to be selected by the trustee from an indefinite class of intended beneficiaries. This situation is discussed hereafter in Comment *d.*

Different from those situations and much more frequent are instances of valid transfers in trust for the benefit of definite beneficiaries under which one or more of the beneficiaries, or occasionally a trustee or other person, is granted a power of appointment by which the trust property or remainder may be (i.e., is authorized but not required to be) appointed to or for one or more "objects" (permissible appointees) of the power.

Under well-established doctrine, the objects of powers of appointment may properly consist of classes that are either definite or indefinite; powers of appointment may even be general, with no limit whatever with respect to permissible appointees. Thus, a fairly typical trust might direct T to pay the income to A for life and thereafter to distribute the remainder as A may appoint by her will to or for any one more of her issue (a special testamentary power), with T directed to distribute the remainder in default of appointment to A's issue by some form of representation prescribed by the trust terms. The validity of the trust would not be affected if A's power of appointment had allowed her to appoint by will among "her or my friends and relatives" or to "any one or more persons or entities she may choose, including her estate," or, as is sometimes provided for tax purposes, "to any one or more persons or entities, excluding her estate or the creditors of herself or her estate." Nor would the validity of the power or trust be affected if she had been allowed to exercise her power inter vivos.

The donee (holder) of one of the above powers of appointment is under no duty to exercise the power—unlike the intended mandate to a trustee to make selections in the situations considered in Comment *d* and falling within the rule of Subsection (2). (Unfortunately, judicial opinions or texts sometimes use confused terminology, such as "power held in trust," to express the typical result that, in the absence of an express gift in default of appointment, cures the drafting defect simply by implying a gift in default of an appointment when the class of objects is definite. Illustrative would be the first of the powers in the preceding paragraph if the settlor had omitted the default provision providing for A's issue to take by right of representation. See § 45, and particularly compare § 45, Comments *b* and *d*. Also cf. Restatement Second, Property (Donative Transfers) § 24.2 [Restatement Third, Property (Wills and Other Donative Transfers) § 19.23.)

A trust can be created for beneficiaries whom the settlor, or another, is authorized later to designate or "appoint." See § 44, Comment *a*, and especially § 44, Comment *c*, and Illustrations 3 and 4. Also see § 45, Comment *g*.

d. *Beneficiaries to be selected by trustee.* Occasionally, a testator leaves property to another upon an intended trust for members of an indefinite class to be selected by the devisee, intending thereby to impose upon the devisee, as trustee, a *duty* to make selections and to hold and administer the property in the meantime solely for the members of the class. This presents a problem that differs significantly from that in Comment *b* but that similarly arises from the requirement that a trust have definite beneficiaries.

d(1). Example. Instead of attempting to create a trust simply for all of the members of an indefinite class (as in Subsection (1) and Comment *b*), the testator leaves property to a person who, as trustee, is directed to liquidate the property and to distribute all of its proceeds in equal shares to those of the testator's "friends" whom the trustee shall select.

This trust, as written, fails for lack of definite beneficiaries capable of enforcing the intended fiduciary duty of selection. . . . The settlor's intended trust purpose, however, need not fail altogether: That the trustee cannot be *required* to select the beneficiaries, and that a court will not direct a recalcitrant trustee to make equal distribution to class members too indefinite to be ascertained, nor even remove and replace the trustee, does not mean that the trustee cannot be *allowed* to make the selections if willing to do so.

The result of this example is that the devisee holds the property upon a trust, adapted by operation of law, for reversionary beneficiaries (the same persons who would take by resulting trust under § 8 if the trust had immediately and completely failed), subject to the interests of potential beneficiaries later to be identified by the devisee's exercise of a nonmandatory power of selection. (On the validity of such a trust, cf. § 44, Comments *a* and *c*; Comment *c*, above, on powers of appointment; and § 45, Comment *g*.) Thus, the law simply treats the defective disposition as having a trust effect approximating that stated by the testator. Instead of complete failure, with an immediate resulting trust, there is a legally implied reversion to take effect only in default of selection.

d(2). Rationale. A testator can create a trust expressly for the people who would be his or her own heirs (or residuary beneficiaries), subject to an *express power of appointment* by which the trustee is allowed to appoint among an indefinite class of objects. (See Comment *c*.) Or the testator could have created a trust for beneficiaries *authorized* to be appointed later by the trustee, with either an express gift or one implied by law (a reversionary or "resulting trust" interest) in favor of the testator's estate (see § 44, Comments *a* and *c*).

Therefore, if an intended trust that purports to *require* the trustee to select distributees from an indefinite class (such as "friends") fails as written, then, rather than to have the purpose fail altogether, the testator's purpose would be better served—and no policy of the law is violated (see Comment *c*)—by *treating* the will as having created an adapted version of the intended trust. This results in an enforceable trust for a definite though unexpressed (legally implied) class of reversionary beneficiaries, whose interests are subject, by legal adaptation, to a nonmandatory power in the trustee to select other distributees.

In brief, if a devisee can properly make distributions where merely authorized to do so, there is no reason why a devisee should be precluded from doing so where directed to do so. In neither case can the devisee be compelled to make the distributions, but in both cases a willing devisee should be permitted to carry out the testator's intention. This rule also serves to remove (or at least to reduce to technical questions) any issue of whether a particular power was or was not intended by the settlor to be mandatory.

Under the rule of Subsection (2), the primary purpose of the adapted trust will fail only to the extent the trustee (i) refuses to make selections, (ii) selects beneficiaries to receive some of the property but declines to make additional selections, (iii) fails to make selections within the specified time or the otherwise implied "reasonable period" for doing so, or (iv) dies without having exercised the power.

d(3). Selection power presumed personal. The preceding paragraph assumes, as is normally presumed, that the power of selection in any such case (like the typical power of appointment) was intended by the settlor to be personal to the designated trustee. (It is not presumed that the general administrative duties of the trusteeship are also personal to the named trustee; the person so designated may decline or cease to serve as trustee while retaining the power of selection. See Illustration 4, below, and more generally § 47, Comment *f*. Also, see § 34(2) on court appointment of substitute and successor trustees generally; and cf. § 70(2), that powers conferred upon a designated trustee, unless personal to that trustee, may properly be exercised by a successor or substitute trustee.)

On the other hand, if the testator in the *Example* above (Comment *d(1)*) had designated or provided a means for designating a substitute or successor trustee, the power of selection in the adapted trust would pass to the substitute or successor upon the initially designated trustee's disclaimer, resignation, incapacity, or death before the power is exercised or expires.

Similarly, if no substitute or successor was designated but the testator's intention is shown not to depend on the designated person serving as trustee (cf. observation following Illustration [2] of § 47, Comment *c*), then the selection power as well as the trusteeship in the adapted trust would pass to a court-appointed substitute or successor trustee.

Illustrations:

3. S's will leaves her residuary estate to T, in trust, "to administer and liquidate the property and to distribute its proceeds, within five years after my death, equally to such of my friends and relatives as T shall select." The intended trust will not be enforced as written, but T holds S's residuary estate upon an adapted trust with the power but no duty to distribute the trust property equally among any persons T may select, but excluding anyone he selects who does not reasonably qualify as a friend or relative of S. Thus, by adaptation, T holds S's residuary estate in trust for S's heirs at law (a definite class of beneficiaries), who have power to enforce the trust but whose interests are subject to divestment by an exercise of T's nonmandatory power to select one or more qualified distributees.

4. The same facts as in Illustration 3, except that T wishes to make the selections entrusted to him but does not feel able to handle all of the fiduciary responsibilities of the trusteeship. T may retain and perform the presumptively personal, nonmandatory power of selection while declining to serve as trustee. A court will appoint a substitute trustee to manage and liquidate the trust property and to distribute it as instructed by T.

e. Rule against perpetuities. An intended disposition of the type considered in this subsection may fail altogether on the ground that the power in the adapted trust violates the severe, traditional common-law rule against perpetuities. See § 29(b). Powers of this type, however, as we have seen (Comment *d(3)*), are usually personal to named individuals and thus are not likely to involve risks of invalidity under the rule; nor would other powers that are expressly or impliedly limited by their terms to being exercised within the period of the rule. Examples of the latter are powers even in corporate trustees that may be exercised only "within 21 years of my death" or only in favor of a class of persons necessarily alive at the testator's death (e.g., "my friends"). Furthermore, modernized rules regulating perpetuities would preserve nearly all adapted trusts recognized under this subsection. See § 29, Comment *g*.

f. Transfers inter vivos; declarations of trust. The rule of Subsection (2) applies to a transfer inter vivos directing the transferee to liquidate the property and to distribute all of its proceeds among such members of an indefinite class as the transferee shall select. The adapted trust, however, is revocable (cf. § 63, Comment *c*) until the earlier of the settlor's death or the exercise of the power of selection and distribution. This is the case even if the settlor had manifested the intention to create an irrevocable trust, which as written cannot be enforced.

On the other hand, if the property owner executes a declaration of trust stating that the property is held for such members of an indefinite class of persons as the declarant may select, no trust is created. The declarant holds the property free of trust, but free to perfect the contemplated dispositions by later selecting those who are to benefit.

g. Enforcement of adapted trust. In no event is the devisee in the situation in Subsection (2) permitted to keep or misappropriate the property. Either the power of selection must be exercised or the trust property must be returned to the settlor's estate. See Comment *d.*

The heirs or other successors in interest of the settlor can maintain a proceeding to prevent or redress a breach of trust, or to compel the trustee to convey the trust property to them if the power is not exercised within the period specified in the will or, if none is specified, within a reasonable period fixed by the court. Thus, the devisee holds the property upon an enforceable trust for the legally implied reversionary beneficiaries, subject to a power in the devisee (trustee) voluntarily to select and make distribution among members of the class.

A situation may arise in which the named trustee disclaims the office or resigns, dies, or becomes incapacitated before the power in the adapted trust is exercised and, although the power is not personal to that trustee (see Comment *d(3)*), no substitute or successor is designated in the will. In such a case, either the testator's successors in interest or a person who fits within the class description may petition the court for appointment of another trustee. So may the testator's personal representative if the named trustee in such a case predeceases the testator, as may the personal representative, conservator, or guardian of a trustee who survives the testator but dies or becomes incapacitated before the exercise or expiration of a nonpersonal power. On nonjudicial means of obtaining a substitute or successor trustee, see § 34, Comments *c* and *c(1)*.

§ 47. Trusts for Noncharitable Purposes

(1) If the owner of property transfers it in trust for indefinite or general purposes, not limited to charitable purposes, the transferee holds the property as trustee with the power but not the duty to distribute or apply the property for such purposes; if and to whatever extent the power (presumptively personal) is not exercised, the trustee holds the property for distribution to reversionary beneficiaries implied by law.

(2) If the owner of property transfers it in trust for a specific noncharitable purpose and no definite or ascertainable beneficiary is designated, unless the purpose is capricious, the transferee holds the property as trustee with power, exercisable for a specified or reasonable period of time normally not to exceed 21 years, to apply the property to the designated purpose; to whatever extent the power is not exercised (although this power is *not* presumptively personal), or the property exceeds what reasonably may be needed for the purpose, the trustee holds the property, or the excess, for distribution to reversionary beneficiaries implied by law.

General Comment:

a. *Scope and basic principles.* This section is concerned with what are often called "purpose" or "honorary" trusts. These are a special form of noncharitable trust in which the purpose as expressed by the settlor is normally unenforceable. Thus, a testator may seek to establish a trust (1) for a noncharitable purpose that is general or indefinite (compare § 46(2) dealing with indefinite *beneficiaries*) or (2) for a specific noncharitable purpose. In either case, for lack of a definite beneficiary, the trust is not enforceable in accordance with its intended terms.

Although reversionary interests arise in these cases by operation of law (compare §§ 7, 8 on "resulting trusts"), the primary question is whether the intended purpose should fail entirely or whether the devisee who wishes to do so may carry out the intended purpose. That is, does the devisee hold the property in trust for the testator's successors in interest, with a "power" (rather than a duty) to divest those successors in whole or in part by making distributions for the noncharitable purpose? Cf. § 46(2) on "adapted trusts" in the private-trust context.

The rule of this section also applies to trust provisions for either general or definite noncharitable purposes. In either case, there is no definite beneficiary to enforce the particular provision, even if the trust has identifiable express beneficiaries (§§ 44 and 45) to enforce it in other respects. The provision for the noncharitable purpose is unenforceable as written, leaving again the question of whether that purpose may be carried out through a power, even at the expense of express interests of ascertainable beneficiaries.

These questions are addressed, with affirmative answers, in Subsections (1) and (2) of this section and are further considered in Comments *c* and *d*. The underlying principles are similar to those applicable to the indefinite-beneficiaries situations in § 46(2). See particularly § 46, Comments *c* through *g*.

The *adapted trust* rule of this section does not apply to intended trusts for purposes that are capricious (see Comment *e*) or otherwise contrary to public policy. See generally § 29(c).

Perpetuities issues are considered hereafter in Comment *b*.

On the application of the rules of this section to trusts, or trust provisions, intended to be created by inter vivos transfer, see Comment *g*.

The rules of this section do not apply if the transferor intended a beneficial gift to the transferee. See § 13, Comment *d*, and cf. § 46, Comment *a*. Nor do they apply to trusts or provisions that have an indefinite *charitable* purpose. See Comment *c*, and also § 28, Comment *c*. Charitable trusts are enforceable by the attorney general or similar official of the state. See generally §§ 28, 67, and 94.

b. *Perpetuities issues and limits.* Both powers of appointment (except presently exercisable general powers) and trustees' discretionary powers over income or principal distributions are subject to the rule against perpetuities. They are therefore void at their inception under traditional concepts if the rule is violated. See § 29(b) and § 29, Comments *g* and *h*.

In all but the exceptional situations involving care of graves or pets (Comment *d(2)*), however, perpetuities issues are eliminated by the associated rule in Comments *c* and *d* limiting the duration of powers under adapted trusts. As in other "associated rules" on perpetuities matters (see

§ 29, Comment *h*, and Restatement Second, Property (Donative Transfers), Chapter 2 [Restatement Third, Property (Wills and Other Donative Transfers), Chapter 27]), the maximum allowable period for these powers is derived, by analogy, from the "lives in being and 21 years" vesting period of the rule against perpetuities itself.

Because a suitable measuring life is usually absent in cases under this section, the time allowed for the exercise of devisees' powers is normally confined to 21 years. More precisely, the allowable period in these situations is that specified in the will or, if none, a "reasonable time" for accomplishing the settlor's intended purpose, but no more than 21 years, except for the special cases under Comment *d(2)*.

Comment on Subsection (1):

c. *Trusts for indefinite noncharitable purposes.* This subsection and Comment address questions that arise when a testator leaves property upon an intended trust for such "benevolent" or "worthy" or "charitable or benevolent" objects as the devisee may select, or uses other language of purpose that is not limited to charity. In such cases, if a power of selection is not expressed it is implied.

A preliminary question of interpretation in these situations is whether the testator's words were intended to be limited to charitable objects. A constructional preference favors that meaning, resulting in an enforceable charitable trust. See § 28. This subsection and Comment deal with the effect of dispositions in which the objects are *not* so limited.

When the intended trust is for general or indefinite purposes that are not limited to charitable purposes, although they may include charitable purposes, no one can maintain a proceeding to enforce that aspect of the intended trust. Therefore, under the rule of Subsection (1), the devisee holds the property as trustee (of an adapted trust) for the testator's successors in interest (i.e., those who would take by resulting trust under § 8 if the trust had immediately and completely failed), subject to a nonmandatory power in the trustee to apply the property to the designated purposes. To the extent the trustee is unwilling to exercise the power, fails within a reasonable time to do so, or dies without having done so, ordinarily (but see Comment *f*) the property is held in trust for distribution to the testator's successors in interest.

Illustration:

1. S devises funds to T in trust to dispose of it to such objects of benevolence and liberality, charitable or otherwise, as T may select. T dies without having made any selection. Unless the power of selection is shown not to be personal to T (Comment *f*), the trust property is to be distributed to the residuary beneficiaries of S's estate.

If willing and able to do so, however, the devisee (T in the above Illustration) will be permitted to distribute or apply the trust property to purposes falling within the scope of the testator's directions. Thus, the devisee holds the devised property in trust, upon terms adapted by operation of law.

The adapted trust in a case of this type is a trust for the testator's residuary beneficiaries (or heirs if the devise is residuary), but subject to the devisee's power, with no duty, to select and make distributions for one or more of the testator's intended purposes. To the extent the devisee has not fully exercised the power by the time of its expiration (Comment *b*), or declines to exercise the power or dies without having fully done so (unless the power is exercisable by a successor trustee, see Comment *f*), the property then held in trust is to be distributed to the reversionary (residuary or intestate) beneficiaries.

That borderline situations might arise in which it would be difficult to say whether a decision by the devisee falls within the testator's directions does not prevent recognition of the adapted trust or preclude the devisee from selecting purposes that can be determined to fall within the intended purposes.

c(1). Rationale: The rationale underlying the rule of this subsection is essentially the same as that stated in § 46, Comment *d*. See also § 46, Comment *c*.

Illustration:

2. The same facts as in Illustration 1, except that T is willing and able to carry out S's intended purposes. T holds upon adapted trust with a nonmandatory power to dispose of the property in favor of one or more objects of benevolence and liberality of her choosing. If within a reasonable time she fails to do so, she then holds in trust for distribution to the residuary beneficiaries of S's estate.

Where the devisee or designated trustee is a corporation or simply anyone who may serve as "executor," the usual presumption that the power is personal to the designated trustee may be inapplicable. The question is one of interpretation. See generally Comment *f*.

Comment on Subsection (2):

d. Intended trust for a specific noncharitable purpose. If property is devised to a person on an intended trust for a specific noncharitable purpose without a definite or ascertainable beneficiary, the devisee cannot be compelled to apply the property to the designated purpose, there being no beneficiary to enforce the intended trust (§ 44) and no charitable purpose to be enforced by the attorney general or other appropriate officer of the state (see §§ 28 and 94). If willing to do so, however, the devisee can properly apply the property to the designated purpose, provided that purpose is not capricious (see Comment *e*).

Such a willing devisee holds the property in trust, adapted by operation of law, for the successors in interest of the testator, subject to the devisee's nonmandatory power to carry out the testator's intended purpose. To the extent the trustee fails within the allowable time (see Comment *b*, above, but also see Comment *f*, below) to apply the property to the designated purpose or the trustee or a court determines at the outset or later that the amount of the property exceeds what is reasonably necessary to carry out the purpose, the trustee is under a duty to distribute the unexpended or unneeded property to the successors in interest of the testator. The trustee may not misappropriate or keep the property. (On who may bring enforcement proceedings, see Comment *f*.)

While the adapted trust continues, the trustee has the usual duties with respect to protecting and managing the trust property (see §§ 70, 76–84, and 90–92). These include a fiduciary duty to the beneficiaries (testator's successors in interest) to proceed efficiently and within a reasonable time either to implement the noncharitable purpose or to distribute to these reversionary beneficiaries any property that is not to be so applied.

The usual remedies for breach of trust are available to the beneficiaries to enforce this duty. In addition to surcharge, denial or reduction of compensation, and the like, these remedies include removal of the trustee. See generally §§ 37, 95. Removal may result in termination of the trust, or it may result in the appointment of a successor trustee provided the adapted power is not personal to the original trustee and it is reasonable to expect that the appointment of a successor trustee is a reasonable means of accomplishing the noncharitable purpose. See generally Comment *f*.

d(1). Application and rationale. The rule stated in this subsection and its Comments applies (i) to such purposes (where not charitable) as the care of graves and the erection or maintenance of tombstones or cemetery monuments, the support and care of animals, and the saying of masses and (ii) to the continuation or support of activities that are worthwhile or meritorious but fall short of constituting charitable activity. As under Subsection (1), the rationale here is essentially that stated in § 46, Comment *d* (also cf. § 46, Comment *c*).

The purposes stated in the Illustrations that follow can be upheld as written, or with modest modification, in many states: (i) because of legislation (particularly common for the situations in Illustrations 4 . . . and 8); or (ii) as trusts for religious, educational, humane, or other charitable purposes (as particularly may be the case with the situations in Illustrations 6 . . . and 8); or (iii) simply as part of or by inference from some other statutory or nonstatutory policy or process, such as an expenditure incident to estate administration (see Illustration[ ] 4 . . .). Otherwise, the matters in the Illustrations fall within the rule of Subsection (2).

Illustrations:

4. S's will leaves (a) $10,000 to his friend F "in trust" for the erection of a monument on S's grave and (b) $10,000 to brother-in-law B for the erection of a monument on the grave of S's predeceased wife. Unless the dispositions are otherwise enforceable (e.g., as a funeral expense), F and B cannot be compelled to expend the funds but have power to do so; if either refuses or fails within a reasonable time to do so, the funds in question are held for S's residuary estate, except as a successor may be appointed (Comment *f*) to exercise the power, there being no presumption under Subsection (2) that the powers are personal to F and B.

6. S's will leaves $10,000 to T "in trust" to expend it for the offering of masses for the repose of the souls of S and his predeceased wife, W, the principal and any interest to be expended for that purpose within a five-year period from S's death. In a state in which this disposition is not enforced as a charitable trust (as it would be under § 28, Comment *i*) or otherwise, T cannot be compelled to expend the money for the designated purpose but, as trustee for the specified five-year period, has power to do so. To the extent T fails to spend the funds for masses, presumptively she can be replaced within the five-year period (Comment *f*); otherwise she holds the funds for S's residuary estate.

8. S's will leaves $100,000 to T "in trust" to use the income and principal as necessary for the support and care of S's dog. Unless the intended trust is otherwise enforceable in the state in question . . ., T cannot be compelled to use the funds for the dog, but she (or probably, if necessary, a substitute or successor trustee, see Comment *f*) has power under an adapted trust to do so for as long as the dog lives, unless an

earlier termination of the trust is required by a rule against perpetuities (see Comment *b* and particularly Comment *d(2)*). Subject to this power, T (or a successor) holds upon an adapted trust for the settlor's successors in interest as described in this Comment; if, however, the fund exceeds what is reasonably likely to be required for the dog's needs, the excess funds are to be distributed to the residuary beneficiaries of S's estate.

d(2). Special duration rule: care of pets and graves. An adapted trust is allowed a period reasonably appropriate to accomplish the settlor's legally permissible purpose, although a period specified by the settlor is normally accepted if reasonably related to the purpose. Generally, however, regardless of how the reasonable period is determined, the period may not exceed 21 years, by analogy to the period of the rule against perpetuities. See Comment *b*.

The 21-year period is neither sacred nor necessarily suitable to all cases of adapted trust powers. If an adapted trust for the care of a pet is worth allowing at all (see Illustration 8), it makes sense to allow it to continue for the life of the pet, although not a human "life in being" for perpetuities purposes (but see below). Also, a trust power to maintain a grave should be allowed for the lifetime of the decedent's spouse and children, or of other concerned individuals designated in the will . . ., all lives in being at the testator's death.

These exceptions to the 21-year limit are based on the special nature of the permissible noncharitable objective and the modest commitment of resources involved.

The power to support the dog in Illustration 8 is likely to be validated by modern versions of the rule against perpetuities either by use of an alternative statutory period (90 years under the Uniform Statutory Rule Against Perpetuities § 1(c)(2)) or by the wait-and-see or reformation features adopted by many statutes and some judicial decisions. See § 29, Comment *g*; and Restatement Second, Property (Donative Transfers) § 1.4, Comment *a*, and § 1.5 [Restatement Third, Property (Wills and Other Donative Transfers), Chapter 27]. Furthermore, the rule against perpetuities, as such, may be held to have no application to powers of this type under adapted trusts. . . . .

Further General Comments:

e. Capricious purposes. The rule of this section does not apply when the specific noncharitable purpose is capricious. Nor does it allow the devisee in making distributions from an adapted trust under Subsection (1) to select purposes that are capricious. Furthermore, in a trust that has definite or ascertainable beneficiaries, a provision intended to allow property to be used for a capricious purpose is to that extent invalid.

A clear line cannot be drawn for purposes of this rule between objectives that are capricious—or "frivolous" or "whimsical"—and those that are not. A purpose is not capricious merely because no living person benefits directly from its performance, if it satisfies a desire that many (even if not most) people have with respect to the disposition of their property (see Illustrations following Comment *d(1)*) and the amount of the property to be devoted to the purpose is not unreasonably large. On the other hand, it is capricious to provide that money shall be thrown into the sea, that a field shall be sowed with salt, that a house shall be boarded up and remain unoccupied, or that a wasteful undertaking or activity shall be continued. Also, an intended trust for the progeny of particular pets, or for the maintenance of a menagerie under circumstances that are inhumane or not of reasonably widespread interest to others (i.e., not charitable, see § 28(f) and Comment *l*), may be invalidated as capricious even within the "reasonable time" limit allowed in this section.

Although one may deal capriciously with one's own property, self-interest ordinarily restrains such conduct. In any event, society may be properly reluctant to interfere with such a use of property by its current owner. Where, however, a former owner has attempted to confer such a power upon another who is not the beneficial owner of the property, it is contrary to sound public policy to allow the exercise of the power. Thus, a trust or trust provision, even as a power, is not allowed for capricious purposes, although the line is sometimes difficult to draw and policies inevitably vary from time to time and place to place. See generally § 29(c) and Comment *m*.

f. *Successor trustee; enforcement.* In the case of an adapted trust under either Subsection (1) or Subsection (2), the devisee may retain the power to direct the distribution or application of trust funds while declining or resigning from the trusteeship. A substitute or successor may be appointed by court, or by other means described in § 34, Comments *c* and *c(1)*, to hold and administer the trust property. See § 46, Illustration 4.

Where the terms of the disposition neither designate nor make provision for the appointment of a substitute or successor trustee, it is generally presumed that the power of selection and distribution under an adapted trust under Subsection (1) is personal to the named devisee. Cf. § 46(2). There is no such presumption, however, where the intended trust is for a definite noncharitable purpose under Subsection (2) (and see Comment *d*). The power in the adapted trust is more a power of implementation than one of personal selection. In such a case, if the designated trustee effectively refuses the power or resigns, becomes incapacitated, or dies before its expiration, absent a contrary trust provision a successor trustee may be appointed by the court or by other means described in § 34, Comments *c* and *c(1)*.

A proceeding to prevent or redress a breach of trust, or to replace a trustee-power holder, may be brought (i) by the personal representative of the settlor or of a trustee who dies while in office, (ii) by any of the settlor's successors in interest, or (iii) by a person identifiably interested in the purpose of the power, such as the person caring for a pet or a member of the immediate family of a decedent for whom masses, grave care, or a monument is to be provided. (The trustee's fiduciary duties and the available remedies are briefly noted in the last two paragraphs of Comment *d*, above.)

g. *Transfer inter vivos; declaration of trust.* If a settlor transfers property inter vivos to another upon an adapted trust, the transferee has power to distribute or apply the property for the intended purpose(s) as described in Comments *c* and *d*, but the trust is revocable (cf. § 63, Comment *c*) as to undistributed property during the settlor's lifetime. This is the case even if the settlor had manifested the intention to create an irrevocable trust, which as written cannot be enforced.

If the owner of property declares that he or she holds the property as trustee for a noncharitable purpose, no trust is created and the declarant holds the property free of trust. If, however, in a situation falling within Subsection (2), the declarant dies believing that a trust has been created that will be continued by a successor trustee, an adapted trust will then be given effect by constructive trust. Compare § 24(3) and (4).

§ 48. Beneficiaries Defined; Incidental Benefits

A person is a beneficiary of a trust if the settlor manifests an intention to give the person a beneficial interest; a person who merely benefits incidentally from the performance of the trust is not a beneficiary.

Comment:

a. Persons who are beneficiaries: in general. The "beneficiaries" of a trust are the persons or classes of persons, or the successors in interest of persons or class members, upon whom the settlor manifested an intention to confer beneficial interests (vested or contingent) under the trust, plus persons who hold powers of appointment (special or general) or have reversionary interests by operation of law. Also included are persons who have succeeded to interests of beneficiaries by assignment, inheritance, or otherwise.

Persons who may incidentally benefit in some manner from the performance of the trust are not beneficiaries of the trust and cannot enforce it. Cf. Restatement Second, Contracts § 302 (on incidental beneficiaries of contracts). Those persons, however, may have other rights, for example, as creditors.

Illustrations:

1. S leaves her residuary estate to T, in trust, to pay the income to S's brother B during his lifetime and thereafter to distribute the principal to C Charity; S further directs that T retain her shares in a specified stock mutual fund of M Investment Co. and continue to invest at least half of the trust principal in that mutual fund. M Investment Co. is not a beneficiary of the trust and cannot compel T to retain or purchase shares of the designated fund. On the rights of B and C Charity as beneficiaries and T's duty to them under this investment direction, see § 94 (on standing to enforce trusts) and § 76 (on duty to administer in accordance with the terms of the trust).

2. S leaves the S Proprietorship and other assets to T in trust for L for life, remainder to R or R's issue, authorizing T to continue the business and to pay from the trust property any debts T may properly incur in the operation of the business. T incurs several such debts. The creditors are not beneficiaries of the trust.

3. S transfers $100,000 to T upon irrevocable trust to apply as much of the income and principal as needed to cover the tuition, living expenses, and other costs of education for his recently deceased sister's child, N, in a specified private boarding school. The school is not a beneficiary of the trust.

b. Directions to employ a designated person. Where the terms of a trust call for the trustee to employ one or more designated persons in the administration of the trust, those persons are not beneficiaries of the trust unless the settlor intended to give them a right to compel the trustee to employ them. Such a provision may be merely precatory (see § 13, Comment *d*). Even if mandatory, it is presumed not to be for the benefit of the designated person but to promote the administration of the trust. In such a case, the trustee has no duty to the designated person.

Thus, a direction to employ a named lawyer as attorney for the trustee is ordinarily intended merely to promote the efficient administration of the trust rather than to confer a benefit on the lawyer. Similarly, where a settlor's business is placed in trust, with a direction to employ a particular person as manager of the business, that person cannot enforce the direction unless the settlor manifested an intention to confer such a beneficial right upon the person.

Even if a settlor intended to confer a right to the employment, the trustee is not necessarily obliged to employ the person. Thus, there is no such obligation to that person where the employment is of such a character that it might seriously interfere with the trustee's proper administration of the trust. A direction to employ a specified attorney, for example, is not enforceable because the relationship is highly fiduciary and personal in character.

Although the services involved may be such that the trustee cannot be compelled to employ a designated person, a trust provision may be found to manifest the settlor's intention that the person be entitled to damages if denied the employment, or be paid an appropriate amount as a beneficiary, at least as long as the person is willing to perform the specified services. A settlor might, for example, provide for the payment of a specified sum periodically to a named person with a further provision that, upon refusal to perform certain services, the person should lose the right. On the other hand, a provision for a person's employment may have been intended as a gift or legacy, as in the case of an elderly person who has been in the settlor's employ for many years. Absent clear answers in the terms of the trust, these issues are all matters for interpretation.

c. Trustee or administrative power holder as beneficiary. A person who is a trustee may also be a beneficiary of the trust (§ 43, Comment *a*). The fact that a trustee is entitled to compensation for serving in that capacity (see § 38(1)), however, does not make the trustee a beneficiary of the trust. Compare § 65, Comment *a*, that a trustee, as such, need not consent to the termination of a trust by action of all of its beneficiaries.

It is possible, however, that a person's designation as trustee, or as holder of a power to direct or veto actions of a trustee, was intended by the settlor as a means of conferring a special benefit on that particular person through control over some or all of the trust property or decisions. For example, a testator may leave one-third of the probate estate outright to one child while leaving the rest of the estate to that child as trustee for the testator's other two children and their families, with the purpose being to assure the trustee-child control over a farm or business that passes in part to that child and in part to the trust for the others.

Because of the diversity of trust situations and objectives, and of family or other relationships, subtle questions of interpretation may be presented concerning the existence, degree, and significance of any such "beneficiary" status. The degree and character of the person's fiduciary responsibility in such a case also are matters of interpretation that inevitably inquire into the purposes of the person's role, and can particularly determine the nature and extent of the duty of impartiality (§ 79) in the exercise of fiduciary powers.

PART 4

NATURE OF BENEFICIARIES' RIGHTS AND INTERESTS

Introductory Note: This Part includes three chapters on the nature of the interests of trust beneficiaries. The first (Chapter 10) deals with the extent, interpretation, and enforcement of those interests, especially discretionary interests; the second (Chapter 11) deals with general principles of voluntary and involuntary alienation; and the third (Chapter 12) deals with restrictions on alienation, particularly spendthrift trusts.

The definitions in § 2 of this Restatement state that the beneficiary's interest is not a mere *chose in action* but is an equitable interest in the trust property. See § 2, Comment *d* . . . .

"Real" or "personal property." In traditional concept, as stated in earlier Restatements of the Law of Trusts (e.g., Restatement Second, Trusts § 130(a) and (b)): "If the trust property is personal property, the interest of the beneficiary is personal property" and "if the trust property is real property, the interest of the beneficiary is real property unless the interest of the beneficiary is so limited in duration that if it were a legal [i.e., a nonfreehold] interest it would be personal property." Furthermore, it is generally recognized (see id. § 131(1)) that, if "real property is held in trust and by the terms of the trust a duty is imposed upon the trustee to sell it and hold the proceeds in trust or distribute the proceeds, the interest of the beneficiary is personal property," under the doctrine of equitable conversion; and the converse (stated in id. § 131(2)) is generally recognized in the case of personalty that is to be converted to real property. Although accepted as well for purposes of this Restatement, these definitional rules are not further considered in this Part except in the context of other trust-law matters for which the issue may still be significant. See, e.g., § 522 on inheritance of beneficial interests. Even where such characterization issues are relevant, their proper resolution depends on the purpose and policies underlying the particular inquiry and thus frequently on other bodies of law. Also, the question of "real" or "personal" property may not be quite the right question. E.g., see Restatement Second, Conflict of Laws § 265 ("movable" or "immovable") and more generally id. §§ 239–282. Even in statute-of-frauds cases involving the creation of trusts (§ 22, Comment *b*) or the assignment of beneficiaries' interests (§ 53), the question is usually presented in terms of whether the beneficiary has an "interest in land." . . . .

CHAPTER 10

EXTENT AND ENFORCEABILITY OF BENEFICIAL INTERESTS

Introductory Note: Section 49 deals primarily with the rights of a trust beneficiary who is entitled to the income of a trust, although it does not address matters of principal and income accounting (see Chapter 23). It considers the implied authority of trustees when distributees lack competency or when their legal or practical capacity is in doubt. The section also examines a few problems of construction, the nature of annuity and unitrust interests, and, on an introductory basis, rights in principal.

Section 50 addresses fiduciary issues and beneficiary rights in discretionary trusts. These matters have become highly significant in both drafting and administration as a result of current tax and nontax planning practices. Involved are not only invasion of principal for income beneficiaries and others but also discretionary authority to distribute income to a life beneficiary or among various beneficiaries. The section describes the nature and limits of discretionary authority, discusses the bases upon which courts might interfere with fiduciary judgment, and examines a series of recurring issues of construction and interpretation. These issues mainly concern the meaning of various standards, the relevance of discretionary beneficiaries' other resources, and the effect of liberalizing language (such as "absolute" or "sole and controlled") in a grant of discretion. The discussion in § 50 is also relevant to the rights of discretionary beneficiaries' creditors, considered in § 60 (Chapter 12).

§ 49. Extent of Beneficiaries' Interests

Except as limited by law or public policy (see § 29), the extent of the interest of a trust beneficiary depends upon the intention manifested by the settlor.

Comment:

a. In general. The interests of beneficiaries are usually prescribed with reasonable clarity by the express provisions of a trust. When this is not the case, uncertainties may be resolved through the process of interpretation or by application of rules of construction. See generally § 4 on "terms of the trust." On interpretation and construction more generally, see Restatement Third, Property (Wills and Other Donative Transfers), Chapters 10 and 11. The terms of the trust in these matters will be respected and given effect unless contrary to public policy. See §§ 27 and 29, particularly § 29(c) on conditions that may be unenforceable as against public policy. See also Chapter 12 (§§ 57–60) of this Part 4.

Words of inheritance (such as "to A and his heirs") are unnecessary to the creation of an equitable interest in fee simple, whether the trust is created by declaration, by transfer inter vivos, by will, by the exercise of a power of appointment, or by order of court.

a(1). Future interest in heirs of settlor or another. At early common law there were rules of law, known as the doctrine of worthier title and the rule in Shelley's Case, that essentially prohibited the creation of a remainder interest in land in the heirs of a grantor (treating that interest as a reversionary interest) and the creation of a remainder in the heirs of another following a freehold interest in that other person (treating the remainder as belonging instead to that person and often resulting in a beneficial interest in fee simple). Over time, these rules were narrowed in application or softened into rules of construction. They have now been abolished by legislation or rejected as a part of the common law in nearly all jurisdictions.

No such rules of law or construction are recognized by this Restatement [or by the Restatement Third, Property (Wills and Other Donative Transfers)]. Compare Restatement Second, Property (Donative Transfers), Chapter 30. There remains only a question of construction, with the presumption being that language expressing an apparent intention to create a remainder in someone's heirs is so intended and is to be given that effect. Thus, the potentially destructive effects of antiquated doctrine have been removed while the potential advantages often perceived in some retention of those doctrines have been provided by other adaptations of doctrine. See, e.g., § 65 and cf. § 66 on modification and termination of trusts.

On the creation of trusts for members of a definite or indefinite class of persons, see §§ 45 and 46; and on the many questions of construction that arise from the varied language used in expressing class gifts, see Restatement Second, Property (Donative Transfers) §§ 29.1–29.8 (on "heirs" and related terms) and §§ 25.1–28.5 (on other class-gift terms) [Restatement Third, Property (Wills and Other Donative Transfers), Division V].

b. Definiteness of extent of beneficiary's interest. The extent of the interests of the beneficiaries of a trust need not be definite at the time of the creation of the trust. It is sufficient if the extent of an interest will become ascertainable within the period and terms of the rule against perpetuities.

The interest of a beneficiary may be a present or future interest; and an interest may or may not be subject to conditions with respect to the recipients or the extent of the interest. Furthermore, an interest may be subject to the discretionary decisions of a trustee or another (see § 50), or subject to a power of appointment or a power of revocation or amendment. In fact, there is practically no limit to the variety of interests a settlor may create. But see § 29(b) (perpetuities matters) and § 29(c) (other policy limitations).

c. Dispositions of income. If a disposition of income is limited to the lifetime of the designated beneficiary, and no other disposition is made of the income thereafter or of the principal, on the designated beneficiary's death the trustee holds the trust property upon resulting trust for the settlor or for the settlor's successors in interest (see § 8 and also §§ 51 and 55). If by the terms of a trust a person is entitled to the income from the trust property perpetually and there is no other disposition of the beneficial interest, that person is the sole beneficiary of the trust and has the full and absolute equitable interest in the trust property. (On the rights of such a beneficiary or his or her successors in interest to terminate the trust, see § 65; and on succession to the beneficiary's rights at death, see § 55.) If the trust terms are unclear on the matter, it is a question of interpretation whether a direction simply to pay income to a designated beneficiary is intended to include a right to the income perpetually or is limited to income during the life of the person.

c(1). Right to and timing of distributions. Where a trustee is directed to pay the trust's income to a beneficiary for life or a designated period, in the absence of other direction the trustee is under a duty to pay the beneficiary the net income of the trust property at reasonable intervals, normally monthly or quarter-annually, but at least annually, whether or not the beneficiary needs the income. On what is included in "income," see Chapter 23. . . . .

Despite a duty to distribute all income periodically, the trustee can properly withhold a reasonable amount of income receipts to meet present or anticipated expenses that are properly chargeable against income, or temporarily for the trustee's and beneficiaries' protection where there is reasonable doubt as to the amount of income properly payable to the income beneficiary. Also, the trustee may rely on reasonable projections and adjustments in the scheduling and making of income distributions, particularly in order to facilitate frequent, relatively stable distributions (monthly, for example, even though dividends tend to be received by the trust on a quarterly basis).

Furthermore, a court may permit or direct the trustee to distribute or apply trust principal or otherwise undistributable income to or for the support, care, or other needs of a beneficiary before the time when, by the terms of the trust, the beneficiary would be entitled to the enjoyment of that principal or accumulated income, if the interest of no other beneficiary of the trust is thereby impaired. On these and further possibilities for deviation from or modification of administrative and distributive provisions under other circumstances, see § 66 (judicial authority) and § 65 (consent of beneficiaries).

c(2). Beneficiary under incapacity. Where a beneficiary who is entitled to receive trust income is legally incapacitated, such as by minority or judicial declaration of incompetency, what disposition should the trustee make of the income that is required to be distributed? If the terms of the trust authorize the income to be applied by the trustee directly for the benefit of a beneficiary, the trustee can properly do so. Absent either express authorization or a contrary provision, it is implied from a direction to distribute income (or other amounts) that the trustee has authority to apply the funds for the beneficiary's benefit so long as no objection is raised by or on behalf of the beneficiary.

It is further implied that, if the trustee has good-faith doubt concerning a beneficiary's practical or legal capacity to handle the funds, distributions to which the beneficiary is entitled may be retained and managed by the trustee as a separate fund belonging to the beneficiary, subject to a continuing right of withdrawal upon demand by or on behalf of the beneficiary. (Compare § 66 on unanticipated circumstances and principles of equitable deviation.) This tentative power of retention will often make it unnecessary for a personal fiduciary (guardian, conservator, or the like) to be appointed for the beneficiary, or, if one has been appointed, for the trustee to make distribution to the personal fiduciary (including an agent holding the beneficiary's durable power of attorney) until the personal fiduciary asserts the right of withdrawal. Also, in these various circumstances, in the absence of a duly appointed personal fiduciary, the trustee has discretionary authority to select and distribute the funds to a suitable statutory custodian for the beneficiary, or to act as that custodian, unless this is contrary or inappropriate to the terms of the applicable Uniform Transfers to Minors Act, Uniform Custodial Trust Act, or other custodianship statute. On the effect of such retention or distribution on a spendthrift restraint, see § 58, Comment *d*. (In all of the

foregoing situations, the trustee's implied authority to retain funds to which a beneficiary is entitled, or to distribute them to a custodian, is inapplicable if that authority is contrary or inappropriate to the purposes of the trust, such as an objective of qualifying for the federal estate tax marital deduction. . . . .)
. . . .

A trustee who is under a duty to apply the income for the benefit of the beneficiary in the event of incompetency can properly pay the income to a personal fiduciary for this purpose, provided the manner and cost of so delegating the trustee's duty are appropriate and reasonable. (On authority and duties with respect to delegation generally, see § 80.)

A trustee who improperly applies or distributes income in good faith for the support, care, or other needs of the beneficiary (whether or not under a legal disability) is entitled to credit in the trust accounts to the extent the beneficiary would otherwise be unjustly enriched. See generally § 76; also see Chapter 19.

If the terms of a trust validly (see § 29, Comment *h(2)*) authorize or direct the trustee to accumulate some or all of the income of the trust, the trustee is not under a current duty to pay that income to the beneficiary. Similarly, if the terms of the trust direct or authorize the trustee merely to apply or distribute income as needed for the support of a beneficiary, the trustee is neither required nor permitted to pay the beneficiary income that is not needed for that purpose. . . . .

On the disposition of income accrued or received in the trust but undistributed on the death of the life-income beneficiary, see Chapter 23. Compare the duty of the trustee, upon termination of the trust, to pay principal to the beneficiaries entitled thereto (§ 76).

c(3). Multiple life beneficiaries: income share(s) not expressly disposed of. Where trust property is distributable to a class, or otherwise to multiple beneficiaries, the rules for determining the eligibility of potential recipients and the shares in which they take (of income or principal currently or later) are the same as those for legal interests. On these matters generally, see Restatement Second, Property (Donative Transfers) §§ 25.1 et seq. [Restatement Third, Property (Wills and Other Donative Transfers), Division V].

Where the income of a trust is payable to two or more life beneficiaries with a gift over on the death of the survivor, and an income beneficiary dies, the disposition of the income share the deceased beneficiary had been receiving depends upon the terms of the trust. Where the terms of the trust make no express provision for the situation, the normal inference is that the settlor intended the income share to be paid to the issue (if any) of the deceased income beneficiary in the typical case of this type in which the remainder is to pass to the descendants of the income beneficiaries upon the survivor's death. This presumed result applies whether or not the beneficiaries are described in class terminology. It may appear from language of the trust or the circumstances, however, that the settlor would have preferred: (i) that the income be paid to or divided among the surviving income beneficiary or beneficiaries (as "cross remainders"), even if the beneficiaries are not described as a class; or (ii) that the income share be paid to the estate, or successors in interest, of the deceased income beneficiary (whose interest is thus one "pur autre vie"); or (iii) that it be paid to or accumulated for all of the remainder beneficiaries; or (iv) that it be paid (by reversion) to the *settlor's* successors in interest as property not disposed of by the terms of the trust (see § 7, Comment *b*, and § 8, Comment *d*, . . . on resulting trusts). . . . .

d. *Invasion of principal.* Questions of whether, under what circumstances, and to what extent a beneficiary who is entitled to receive trust income may also be entitled to receive principal depend upon the terms of the trust. The terms of the trust may, expressly or impliedly, authorize the trustee to pay or apply principal to or for the income beneficiary as appropriate for support or for other specific or general purposes. In the absence of such authority the trustee has no power to invade principal for an income beneficiary. But cf. the judicial power to authorize deviation from the terms of the trust in § 66.

So also, a beneficiary may be empowered to require the trustee to pay the beneficiary or another some or all of the trust principal. The extent of any such power, as well as the fiduciary or nonfiduciary character of the power, depends upon the terms of the trust. Thus, a beneficiary may be authorized by the terms of the power to require the payment only of such sums as the beneficiary reasonably believes to be necessary for support or other current expenditure; or the beneficiary may be authorized to demand the payment of any part or all of the principal with no limitation.

d(1). Related issues; cross-reference. In these various trust situations, whether the trustee can properly distribute or apply the principal for the intended purposes when the beneficiary has personal resources available for those purposes depends on the language used by the settlor, as interpreted in light of the circumstances and other admissible evidence (§ 50, Comment *e*). So does the question (§ 50, Comment *d*) of whether and for what purposes the trustee may make discretionary payments of income or principal to the estate of a deceased beneficiary. Similar issues arise also in the increasingly common situations in which a trustee's discretion applies to distribution of income as well as principal. In either event, a court will not interfere with the exercise of discretion conferred upon the trustee except to prevent its abuse. These and other questions of construction involving discretionary powers over distributions are considered hereafter in § 50.

e. *Annuities and unitrust interests.* The terms of the trust may provide that a beneficiary is to receive periodically a stated sum (an annuity) or a sum to be determined by some mathematical formula, such as a stated percentage of the trust estate's value determined annually (a unitrust). The required sum is payable from the funds of the trust without regard to distinction between income and principal unless the settlor has manifested an intention that the annuity or unitrust amount is payable only from income.

In the latter situation, in which the trustee may not use principal when the income is insufficient to pay the stated or formula amount, further questions of interpretation may arise. Is the deficiency in one year to be made up from excess income of subsequent years? And is the trustee to use excess trust-accounting income of earlier years to prevent possible deficiencies in subsequent years? When the settlor's language is unclear on these points, there is no generally applicable rule of construction and the questions are necessarily ones of interpretation. . . . . On accumulations generally, see § 29, Comment *h(2)*.

f. *Conditions.* Sometimes the terms of a trust provide that a beneficiary is to take an interest in income or principal only on the happening of a designated event, or that the beneficiary's interest in income is to terminate on the happening of a designated event. Unless contrary to public policy (see § 29(c) and § 57), such a condition is valid.

As to the effect of indefiniteness or impossibility of performance of such conditions, see § 30.

On whether a gift to a person on reaching a certain age is conditional on his or her reaching that age, or is an absolute gift with mere postponement of enjoyment, see Restatement Second, Property (Donative Transfers) § 27.3, Comment *f* . . . [Restatement Third, Property (Wills and Other Donative Transfers) § 15.1, Comment *o*]. On the general question of whether the interest of a remainder beneficiary is subject to an implied requirement of survival, see id. §§ 27.1–27.3, 28.2(1), and 29.5. Cf. Restatement Third, Property (Wills and Other Donative Transfers) § [§§ 15.3–15.4], on future interests to classes. . . . .

§ 50. Enforcement and Construction of Discretionary Interests

(1) A discretionary power conferred upon the trustee to determine the benefits of a trust beneficiary is subject to judicial control only to prevent misinterpretation or abuse of the discretion by the trustee.

(2) The benefits to which a beneficiary of a discretionary interest is entitled, and what may constitute an abuse of discretion by the trustee, depend on the terms of the discretion, including the proper construction of any accompanying standards, and on the settlor's purposes in granting the discretionary power and in creating the trust.

General Comment:

a. Scope of section. The powers of trustees and the discharge of trusteeship responsibilities regularly involve the exercise of discretion, or fiduciary judgment, with which courts do not interfere except to prevent abuse. On discretionary powers in trust administration generally, see § 87. On investment matters, see § 90 [§ 227 of Restatement Third, Trusts (Prudent Investor Rule)], and Comment *j* thereto; § 91 [id. § 228], Comment *g*; and § 92 [id. § 229], Comment *d*. On grants of discretion in principal-and-income accounting matters, see Chapter 23.

This section deals with situations in which trustees are granted discretion with respect to beneficiaries' rights to trust benefits. For these situations, the terminology "discretionary trust" or "discretionary interest" is used in this Restatement whether or not the terms of the trust provide standards (see Comments *d, e,* and *f*) to limit or guide the trustee's exercise of the discretionary power.

Situations of this type range from the typical power to invade principal for an income beneficiary to the discretionary trust that calls for distributions or applications of income, or of income and principal, for the support of a designated beneficiary (often a surviving spouse, elderly parent, or underage child) or for the benefit of "any one or more" of a group of beneficiaries, such as the settlor's spouse and issue. The trustee may have discretion whether or not to make payments to a particular beneficiary; or the trustee may have discretion only to determine the time, manner, and amount of distributions, pursuant to a particular standard or otherwise. A power's "discretionary" character may be implied from its being attached to a standard, such as a simple direction to pay "amounts appropriate to B's support."

The commentary that follows is concerned not only with the trustee's duties but also with the ability of beneficiaries of these discretionary interests to enforce their rights, and thus with the extent of the beneficiaries' interests. Comments *b* and *c* address the limited but important judicial authority to control a trustee's exercise of discretion, while Comments *d*, *e*, and *f* examine the meaning and effects of various standards and omissions frequently encountered in trust terms accompanying a grant of discretion.

A trustee's discretionary power with respect to trust benefits is to be distinguished from a power of appointment. The latter is not subject to fiduciary obligations and may be exercised arbitrarily within the scope of the power. That an appointment may not be made to persons who are not objects (i.e., not permissible appointees) of a power of appointment, see Restatement Second, Property (Donative Transfers) § 20.1; "fraud on powers" is discussed in id. §§ 20.2–20.4; and cf. §§ 16.1, 16.2 (on contracts to appoint) [Restatement Third, Property (Wills and Other Donative Transfers) § 19.15 (on "fraud on the power"), §§ 21.1–21.2 (on contracts to appoint)]. (Tax law generally does not categorize powers in this manner, and even traditional property-law distinctions between fiduciary powers and powers of appointment may be difficult to draw; this is especially so because a true power of appointment can be conferred upon one who is also a trustee, although a power that runs with the office of trustee is strongly presumed to be a fiduciary power.) Also to be distinguished are nonfiduciary powers to demand or direct trust distributions based on "ascertainable" (Internal Revenue Code § 2041) or "objective" (case law under id. § 2038) standards; nevertheless, the discussion in Comments *d*, *e*, and *f* may have relevance to these powers. Compare the inclusion of these powers in the discussion of "discretionary interests" in § 60 (rights of creditors). Also, on powers granted others to terminate or amend, or to direct the trustee, see §§ 64, 75, and 87.

Comment on Subsection (1):

b. Judicial review and control of trustee's discretion. A court will not interfere with a trustee's exercise of a discretionary power when that exercise is reasonable and not based on an improper interpretation of the terms of the trust. Thus, judicial intervention is not warranted merely because the court would have differently exercised the discretion.

On the other hand, a court will not permit abuse of discretion by the trustee. What constitutes an abuse depends on the terms of the trust, as well as on basic fiduciary duties and principles (§§ 76–83). Of particular importance are the purposes of the power and the standards, if any, applicable to its exercise (see Comments *d–f*) and the extent of the discretion conferred upon the trustee (Comment *c*). Relevant fiduciary principles include (i) the general duty to act, reasonably informed, with impartiality among the various beneficiaries and interests (§ 79) and (ii) the duty to provide the beneficiaries with information concerning the trust and its administration (§ 82). This combination of duties entitles the beneficiaries (and also the court) not only to accounting information but also to relevant, general information concerning the bases upon which the trustee's discretionary judgments have been or will be made. See Comment *e(1)*.

Court intervention may be obtained to rectify abuses resulting from bad faith or improper motive, and to correct errors resulting from mistakes of interpretation. Absent language of extended (e.g., "absolute" or "uncontrolled") discretion (Comment *c*), a court will also intervene if it finds the payments made, or not made, to be unreasonable as a means of carrying out the trust provisions. For example, a beneficiary may be entitled to amounts sufficient to provide support, or to meet some other standard, and the amounts being paid by the trustee may be clearly excessive or inadequate for the purpose. It is not necessary, however, that the terms of the trust provide specific standards in order for a trustee's good-faith decision to be found unreasonable and thus to constitute an abuse of discretion.

Furthermore, a court will intervene where the exercise of a power is left to the judgment of a trustee who improperly fails to exercise that judgment. Thus, even where a trustee has discretion whether or not to make any payments to a particular beneficiary, the court will interpose if the trustee, arbitrarily or without knowledge of or inquiry into relevant circumstances, fails to exercise the discretion.

Illustrations:

1. S's will left her residuary estate in trust to pay the income to her husband, H, and also to distribute to him "as much of the principal as the trustee deems appropriate for H's comfortable support," remainder to S's descendants, all of whom are issue by her prior marriage. She appointed H to serve as trustee "if and for as long as he is willing and able to serve," with S's and H's friend and financial advisor, T, designated as substitute or successor trustee. A few years after S's death, with H serving as trustee, two of S's children challenge the extent of H's principal invasion for his own benefit. H has a permissible, settlor-created conflict of interest, but his acts are to be carefully scrutinized for abuse (see § 37, Comment *f*, and also § 78 on the duty of loyalty). Nevertheless, the court will not substitute its judgment for H's merely because it would have exercised the discretion differently. It will, however, intervene if it finds that H has acted unreasonably, after considering in this situation not only such matters as the standards set out in the terms of the trust (see Comments *d* and *e*) but also the fact that S has trusted H to serve as trustee with the fiduciary authority to determine the amounts of principal appropriate to his own comfortable support.

2. Same facts as in Illustration 1, except that T has succeeded H as trustee. The court will interfere with T's exercise of discretion only in the event of abuse. Despite T's personal relationship with H, which was known to S, or T's possible irritation with the complaints of S's children, T's fiduciary duties include a duty of impartiality (see § 79).

When judicial intervention is required, a court may: direct the trustee to make or refrain from making certain payments; issue instructions (§ 71) to clarify the standards or guidelines applicable to the exercise of the power; or rescind the trustee's payment decisions, usually directing the trustee to recover amounts improperly distributed and holding the trustee liable for failure or inability to do so. (On the elements of a trustee's liability for breach of trust, see Chapter 19.) The court may also deny or diminish the trustee's compensation, establish safeguards against abuse in the future, or even remove the trustee for repeated or serious abuse of the discretionary power. See § 37, Comments *e* and *g*.

c. *Effect of extended discretion.* Although the discretionary character of a power of distribution does not ordinarily authorize the trustee to act beyond the bounds of reasonable judgment (Comment *b*), a settlor may manifest an intention to grant the trustee greater than ordinary latitude in exercising discretionary judgment. How does such an intention affect the duty of the trustee and the role of the court?

It is contrary to sound policy, and a contradiction in terms, to permit the settlor to relieve a "trustee" of all accountability. (Cf. § 87, and also § 76.) Once it is determined that the authority over trust distributions is held in the role of trustee (contrast nonfiduciary powers mentioned in Comment *a*), words such as "absolute" or "unlimited" or "sole and uncontrolled" are not interpreted literally. Even under the broadest grant of fiduciary discretion, a trustee must act honestly and in a state of mind contemplated by the settlor. Thus, the court will not permit the trustee to act in bad faith or for some purpose or motive other than to accomplish the purposes of the discretionary power. Except as the power is for the trustee's personal benefit, the court will also prevent the trustee from *failing* to act, either arbitrarily or from a misunderstanding of the trustee's duty or authority.

Within these limits, it is a matter of interpretation to ascertain the *degree* to which the settlor's use of language of extended (e.g., "absolute") discretion manifests an intention to relieve the trustee of normal judicial supervision and control in the exercise of a discretionary power over trust distributions.

Illustrations:

3. Following S's death his previously revocable trust has been administered for nearly a decade by T Bank, which is directed to pay income to S's widow, W, and also empowered to pay her "such additional amounts from the principal of the trust as the Trustee, in its sole and uncontrolled discretion, believes appropriate for W's comfortable support and care," with the remainder upon W's death to pass to S's then living issue. In response to requests by W, T Bank has begun to pay substantially increased amounts to her to enable her to accumulate funds from which she may aid C (her child by a prior marriage) in his plans to obtain control and expand the activities of X Co., of which C has been an officer and shareholder for a number of years. S's children petition the court to instruct T Bank that principal distributions for that purpose are improper and that it must recover amounts previously paid to W for that purpose. Nothing in relevant circumstances or in other terms of the trust indicates a broader purpose for the invasion power than the support-related (see Comment *d*) language quoted above. The court will issue the order requested by the remainder beneficiaries. Despite S's grant of extensive discretion, and without a finding of bad faith, T's judgment was not exercised in an appropriate state of mind, that is, for a purpose falling within the quoted standard.

4. S's testamentary trust grants T, as trustee, the "absolute and uncontrolled discretion to pay or apply such amounts of income or principal or both to or for the support and benefit of my wife W and any one or more of my descendants, as T may consider desirable and in their best interests." On W's death, the trust estate will be distributed to S's then living issue, if any, and otherwise to others. After a meeting with W (who does not expect to need funds from the trust), her tax accountant, and D (S's only child), T made a large distribution to D to enable her to acquire a home and to advance her career and investment objectives, and has begun to implement a plan of modest distributions to D's two children (ages 14 and 15) to develop funding for their career and personal objectives. Assuming no showing of bad faith or of settlor intention contrary to the quoted trust provisions, T has not abused the

extended discretion it has in pursuing the broad standard (see generally Comment *d*) set out in S's will. (On a trustee's duties to provide information to beneficiaries and to act with impartiality, see Comment *b*.)

Extended discretion serves to discourage challenges by remainder beneficiaries to the generosity of trustees, as in Illustration 4. On the other hand, it may also make it difficult for a discretionary beneficiary to obtain judicial intervention when a trustee's judgments are highly conservative with regard to matters that fall within the settlor's authorized purposes. The overall tenor of the terms of a power may, however, in the context of the trust's more general purposes, lead to an interpretation granting the trustee ordinary discretion with respect to the benefits to which the discretionary beneficiary is minimally entitled (e.g., reasonable support), with the extended discretion applicable to the trustee's allowance of more. This "one-sided" liberalization of the discretionary authority, where a court finds the settlor's language was intended to assure generosity in favor of a life beneficiary, would thus tend to encumber the efforts of remainder beneficiaries who seek to challenge what might otherwise be excessively generous decisions by a trustee.

Comment on Subsection (2):

d. Meaning of frequently used standards. The terms of trusts usually provide some standards or guidelines concerning the purposes the settlor has in mind in creating a discretionary interest. Reasonably definite or objective standards serve to assure a beneficiary some minimum level of benefits, even when other standards are included to grant broad latitude with respect to additional benefits. On the trustee's duty to inform beneficiaries of the bases upon which discretionary distributions have been or will be made, see Comment *b*.

Sometimes trust terms express no standards or other clear guidance concerning the purposes of a discretionary power, or about the relative priority intended among the various beneficiaries. Even then a general standard of reasonableness, or at least of good-faith judgment, will apply to the trustee (Comment *b*), based on the extent of the trustee's discretion, the various beneficial interests created, the beneficiaries' circumstances and relationships to the settlor, and the general purposes of the trust.

d(1). General observations. This Comment is concerned with the construction of expressions frequently used in the terms of discretionary powers, and particularly with the types of benefits likely to be encompassed by typical standards. (The manner in which other resources available to a beneficiary relate to various standards is considered hereafter in Comment *e*; and Comment *f* discusses multiple beneficiaries or groups as concurrent discretionary distributees.) Presumed meanings yield to findings of actual contrary intention and also may be affected by context and the more general purpose(s) of the trust and the estate plan of which it is a part. See Comment *g*. Thus, distributions to which a discretionary beneficiary would ordinarily be entitled by a standard might properly be withheld if distribution would divert funds from other beneficiaries or purposes without achieving the purpose of the discretionary power.

d(2). Support or maintenance. The terms "support" and "maintenance" are normally construed as synonyms, even when this treats the terms as redundant. Probably the most common guides used in grants of discretion, these terms are sometimes accompanied by a reference to the beneficiary's accustomed standard of living or station in life. That level of intended support is normally implied from "support" or "maintenance" even without an express reference to the beneficiary's customary lifestyle. Whether this accustomed style is expressed or implied, a lower level of distributions may be justifiable if the trust estate is modest relative to the probable future needs of the beneficiary.

The accustomed manner of living for these purposes is ordinarily that enjoyed by the beneficiary at the time of the settlor's death or at the time an irrevocable trust is created. The distributions appropriate to that lifestyle not only increase to compensate for inflation but also may increase to meet subsequent increases in the beneficiary's needs resulting, for example, from deteriorating health or from added burdens appropriately assumed for the needs of another. See Illustration 5. Also, if a beneficiary becomes accustomed over time to a higher standard of living, that standard may become the appropriate standard of support if consistent with the trust's level of productivity and not inconsistent with an apparent priority among beneficiaries or other purpose of the settlor. Furthermore, distributions allowing the beneficiary an increased standard of living may be appropriate if, in light of the productivity of the trust estate, the eventual result would otherwise favor the remainder beneficiaries over the present beneficiary to a degree unlikely to have been intended by the settlor. "Productivity" for these purposes refers not only to trust income but also to a pattern of appreciation beyond maintenance of purchasing power, such as might result from a growth-oriented investment program.

Illustrations:

5. S's residuary estate was left to T, in trust, to pay "to my wife W all of the income and also such amounts of the principal as the trustee may deem necessary to maintain her in her customary manner of life," remainder to S's issue. W is dependent on the distributions from this trust to continue the comfortable lifestyle she enjoyed during H's lifetime. A number of years after H's death, C, an adult child of W's prior marriage, became unable to care or provide for himself and has returned to his mother's home to live with her. T can properly increase the payments to W to preserve her accustomed standard of living, taking account of the additional expenses of having D reside with her, assuming that these additional distributions will not jeopardize W's future security or other purposes of the trust.

6. S's will left her residuary estate to T, in trust, to pay or apply "as much of the income and principal as T deems appropriate for the support of my [adult] daughter B," remainder to B's issue. Except during a brief period while her children were in college, B has received no distributions from S's trust and has relied on her own earnings and those of her husband, H, to enjoy an increasingly comfortable standard of living until the time of H's death and her retirement shortly thereafter. The trust estate is now quite sufficient to permit a level of distributions that will enable B to maintain the standard of living to which she has become accustomed. This standard, although considerably beyond what she enjoyed at the time of S's death, is appropriate to the reasonable exercise of T's discretion.

Under the usual construction of a support standard (supra) it would not be reasonable (Comment *b*), or even a result contemplated by the settlor (Comment *c*), for the trustee to provide only bare essentials for a beneficiary who had enjoyed a relatively comfortable lifestyle. (This is so even though the discretionary power is couched in terms of amounts the trustee considers "necessary" for the beneficiary's support.) The standard ordinarily entitles a beneficiary to distributions sufficient for accustomed living expenses, extending to such items as regular mortgage payments, property taxes, suitable health insurance or care, existing programs of life and property insurance, and continuation of accustomed patterns of vacation and of charitable and family giving. Reasonable additional comforts or "luxuries" that are within the means of many individuals of like station in life, such as a special vacation of a type the beneficiary had never before taken, may be borderline as entitlements but would normally be within the *permissible* range of the trustee's judgment, even without benefit of a grant of extended discretion (Comment *c*).

Without additional language suggesting a broader standard (infra), however, even with extended discretion, the terms "support" and "maintenance" do not normally encompass payments that are unrelated to support but merely contribute in other ways to a beneficiary's contentment or happiness. Thus, these terms do not authorize distributions to enlarge the beneficiary's personal estate or to enable the making of extraordinary gifts. See Illustration 3; but also compare Comment *g*.

A support standard normally covers not only the beneficiary's own support but also that of persons for whom provision is customarily made as a part of the beneficiary's accustomed manner of living. This generally includes the support of members of the beneficiary's household and the costs of suitable education (infra) for the beneficiary's children. The beneficiary is entitled also to receive reasonable amounts for the support of a current spouse, and of minor children who reside elsewhere but for whom the beneficiary either chooses or is required to provide support. Additional amounts to cover the beneficiary's support obligation to a former spouse would normally be within the trustee's reasonable discretion. (These matters of construction differ from but may be relevant to the question, discussed in § 60, whether a beneficiary's discretionary interest may be reached in satisfaction of claims for spousal or child support.)

d(3). Other standards and supplementary language. Other terms or language may be used with or instead of a support standard to define or guide a trustee's discretionary authority with respect to trust distributions. These provisions may permit or even entitle beneficiaries to receive greater or lesser, or different, benefits than would have been authorized under a support provision standing alone. Sometimes, however, additional language adds little or nothing to what "support" might imply.

Supplementary terminology may affect the degree of generosity appropriate to a beneficiary's support, or it may suggest a special emphasis. For example, the term "education," without elaboration, is ordinarily construed as extending to payment of living expenses as well as fees and other costs of attending an institution of higher education, or the beneficiary's pursuit of a program of trade or technical training, and the like, as may be reasonably suitable to the individual and to the trust funds available for the purpose.

Similarly, without more, references to "health," "medical care," and the like in the terms of a discretionary power may be useful to inform beneficiary expectations or guide an inexperienced trustee, but presumptively they provide merely for health and medical benefits like those normally implied by a support standard. Thus, if the intention is to assure the beneficiary some special form of education, or expensive home care when not cost efficient, further elaboration would be helpful. Even a grant of extended discretion is likely to make it more difficult, if the trustee does not act generously, for a beneficiary to compel a trustee to follow a particular course of action (see Comment *c*).

Language of "comfort" often accompanies a support standard. Whether modifying support (e.g., "comfortable support" or "support in reasonable comfort") or as an additional standard ("support and comfort"), the normal construction is the same: the language adds nothing to the usual meaning of accustomed support (supra) for a beneficiary whose lifestyle is already at least reasonably comfortable. Such terms, however, would tend to elevate the appropriate standard for a beneficiary whose accustomed lifestyle has been more modest. "Comfort," in isolation, normally has like effect, impliedly referring to a comfortable level of support. On the other hand, stronger language, such as "generous" support, may permit and encourage the trustee to allow, and may even require, some reasonable enhancement of the beneficiary's lifestyle; but it falls short of a "happiness" standard (infra) in that the benefits still must normally be support-related. . . . .

Although one effect of authorizing distributions for the "benefit," "best interests," or "welfare" of a beneficiary is to suggest a support standard, these terms tend also to authorize discretionary expenditures that fall beyond the usual scope of a purely support-related standard. For example, a "benefit" standard might make it reasonable for a trustee to make substantial distributions to provide a beneficiary with capital needed to start a business. (See also loans to beneficiaries, infra this Comment.) Terms of this type, however, lack the objective quality of a term such as "support." Thus, they may not facilitate a beneficiary's efforts to obtain judicial intervention to compel distributions by the trustee. On the other hand, the presence of less objective terminology in a discretionary standard may diminish the relevance of the beneficiary's other resources, except a parent's obligation to support a minor beneficiary. See Comment *e*.

The terms of a discretionary standard occasionally include stronger language, such as the word "happiness." Such language suggests an intention that the trustee's judgment be exercised generously and without relatively objective limitation. Although "happiness" alone expresses no objective minimum of entitlements (which to some extent may nevertheless be readily implied), the primary effect of such a term is to immunize from challenge by remainder beneficiaries almost any reasonably affordable distributions. This, however, does not mean that the trustee cannot properly resist any reasonable request by the beneficiary, because the decision remains one within the fiduciary discretion of the trustee.

Illustration:

7. T is trustee of the residuary trust under S's will and holds a discretionary power to distribute principal to the life beneficiary, B (S's widow), "for her comfortable support and happiness." B has requested T to make a special distribution for an extended overseas vacation—something she and S had never done during his lifetime—and to provide the funds for B's sister (a person of modest means) to accompany her. This request, readily affordable by the trust, falls within the permissible range of T's discretion.

d(4). Restrictive terminology. Illustrative of terms that tend to be highly restrictive are those that authorize invasion of principal or other discretionary payments in the event of an "emergency," "severe hardship," "disability," or the like. These are construed as authorizing distributions only when the described conditions or circumstances arise, and then only to the extent appropriate to alleviate the emergency, hardship, or special need.

d(5). Post-death obligations. A question may arise, following the death of the beneficiary of a discretionary interest, whether a support or other standard authorizes or requires the trustee to pay the beneficiary's funeral and last-illness expenses and debts incurred by the beneficiary for support. Ultimately, the question is one of interpretation when the terms of the trust are unclear, with the presumption being that the trustee has discretion to pay these debts and expenses.

A duty to do so is presumed only to the extent that (i) probate estate, revocable trust, and other assets available for these purposes are insufficient or (ii) the trustee, during the beneficiary's lifetime, either agreed to make payment or unreasonably delayed in responding to a claim by the beneficiary for which the terms of the trust would have required payment while the beneficiary was alive. (A deceased beneficiary's estate may also recover distributions the trustee had a duty to make but did not make during the beneficiary's lifetime.)

d(6). Loans to beneficiaries. Sometimes a beneficiary requests funds for a purpose that falls within the reasonable discretion of the trustee but which the applicable standard would not require the trustee to furnish. If the trustee is reluctant for some reason to make the requested distribution, and particularly if the trustee's concern is one of impartiality, the trustee has discretion to make a loan or advance to the beneficiary. The loan need not qualify as a prudent investment under § 90 [Restatement Third, Trusts (Prudent Investor Rule) § 227]. It is a form of discretionary benefit, and may be made at a market rate of interest or at low or no interest; and funds may be advanced with recourse only against the beneficiary's interest, without personal liability. See also Comment *f*, final paragraph.

e. Significance of beneficiary's other resources. It is important to ascertain whether a trustee, in determining the distributions to be made to a beneficiary under an objective standard (such as a support standard), (i) is *required* to take account of the beneficiary's other resources, (ii) is *prohibited* from doing so, or (iii) is to consider the other resources but *has some discretion* in the matter. If the trust provisions do not address the question, the general rule of construction presumes the last of these.

Specifically, with several qualifications (below), the presumption is that the trustee is to take the beneficiary's other resources into account in determining whether and in what amounts distributions are to be made, except insofar as, in the trustee's discretionary judgment, the settlor's intended treatment of the beneficiary or the purposes of the trust will in some respect be better accomplished by not doing so.

One qualification is that, if the discretionary power is one to invade principal for (or to distribute additional income to) a beneficiary who is entitled to all or a specific part of the trust income, or to an annuity or unitrust amount, the trustee must take the mandatory distributions into account before making additional payments under the discretionary power. Where a beneficiary is entitled to payments from another trust created by the same settlor (e.g., nonmarital and marital deduction trusts for a surviving spouse), or as a part of coordinated estate planning with another (such as the settlor's spouse), required distributions from the other trust—and the purposes of both trusts—are to be taken into account by the trustee in deciding whether, in what amounts, and from which trust(s) discretionary payments are to be made.

Another qualification is that, to the extent and for as long as the discretionary interest is intended to provide for the support, education, or health care of a beneficiary (or group of beneficiaries, Comment *f*) for periods during which a beneficiary probably was not expected to be self-supporting, the usual inference is that the trustee is *not* to deny or reduce payments for these purposes because of a beneficiary's personal resources. (But contrast the effect of *another's* duty to support the beneficiary, Comment *e(3)*).

Furthermore, in cases of nonobjective standards (e.g., "benefit" or "happiness"), other resources have less direct relevance than with regard to additional amounts necessary to maintain an accustomed lifestyle, for example. Those resources, however, may have some bearing on the overall reasonableness of an exercise of the discretionary authority.

As a rule of construction, the above presumption, with its qualifications, does not apply when the settlor expresses a different intent or if the presumption is contrary to purposes or terms of the trust as interpreted in light of circumstances and other evidence of the settlor's intention (§ 4). Thus, the settlor may manifest an intention that other resources *are not* to be taken into account (as in an absolute gift of support) or that they *must* be (as in a provision for payments "only if and as needed" to maintain an accustomed standard of living), with the trustee to have no discretion in the matter. (Contrast, however, the common phrase "necessary for support," which without more normally does not limit the trustee's discretion in this way.) On factors relevant to this question of interpretation, see Comment *g*.

A grant of extended discretion (Comment *c*) does not relieve the trustee of a duty to take into account, or of a duty to disregard, a beneficiary's other resources, although the extended discretion is a factor to be considered in the process of interpretation. If, under the general rule of construction, the trustee has discretion in the matter the trustee has greater latitude in exercising that discretion when the settlor has used language of extended discretion in granting the power of distribution.

e(1). Underlying fiduciary duties: ascertaining needs and resources; informing beneficiaries. The trustee has a duty to act in a reasonable manner in attempting to ascertain the beneficiary's needs and, under the usual rule of construction, other resources that may be appropriately and reasonably available for purposes relevant to the discretionary power. The trustee generally may rely on the beneficiary's representations and on readily available, minimally intrusive information requested of the beneficiary. This reliance is inappropriate, however, when the trustee has reason to suspect that the information thus supplied is inaccurate or incomplete.

Conversely, the trustee's duty to keep beneficiaries reasonably informed (§ 82), together with the trustee's duty of impartiality (§ 79), entitles the beneficiaries to disclosure of the bases upon which the trustee's discretionary decisions concerning distributions have been or will be made. See Comment *b*. Appropriate disclosure can usually be provided in general terms that allow reasonable protection for confidential, private, or sensitive information.

e(2). What other resources are to be considered? Where a trustee is to take a beneficiary's other resources into account in deciding whether and in what amounts to make discretionary payments to satisfy a standard, those resources normally include the beneficiary's income and other periodic receipts, such as pension or other annuity payments and court-ordered support payments.

A trustee may have discretion, and perhaps a duty, to take account of the principal of the beneficiary's personal estate, depending on the terms and purposes of the discretionary power and other purposes of the trust. The settlor's relationships and objectives with respect to both the beneficiary in question and the trust's other current and remainder beneficiaries are of particular relevance. Also important are any income, estate, and other tax purposes the trust may serve (see Comment *g*), as well as the liquidity (including marketability and income-tax basis) of the discretionary beneficiary's assets.

e(3). Others' duties of support. It is a question of interpretation whether and to what extent the duty of another to support a beneficiary is to be taken into account by the trustee in determining distributions to be made to or for the beneficiary under a discretionary power.

The question may arise with regard to the normally mutual support obligations between married individuals, one of whom is the designated beneficiary of a discretionary interest and the other of whom has resources from which to provide their support. Whatever duty or discretion the trustee has generally in the matter of other resources presumptively extends also to the right of spousal support.

Regardless of the trustee's general duty and authority with regard to a beneficiary's personal resources, however, the presumption is that the trustee *is* to take account of a parental duty to support a youthful beneficiary under applicable state law. (The presumption may be reinforced when the governing standard for the discretionary power is to "benefit" the child, for only the parents would be likely to *benefit* economically if the trustee provides what the child is entitled to in any event.) Thus, the trustee's discretionary authority normally should be exercised only to provide types of support or other benefits that fall beyond the parental obligation. This is particularly so when a parent is trustee or co-trustee; the presumption then is that the usual further element of discretion, allowing the trustee sometimes to disregard other means of the beneficiary, does not apply to disregarding a child's support entitlements. (This avoids attributing to a settlor the unlikely intention to create a conflict of interest or to expose the parent to adverse tax consequences, which may result even if the power is not in fact exercised in a way that benefits the parent. . . . .)

These usual presumptions concerning a parental duty of support and the trustee's discretion are inapplicable when the child's only parent is a widow or widower at the time the trust is created (e.g., by the other parent's will or by a grandparent). Ultimately, in such a case, as in others, a trustee's duty and authority with respect to other resources are matters of settlor intention, and it may be determined through interpretation that a particular settlor intended to provide for, or allow, the beneficiary's full support to come from the trust, and thus to assist and benefit the parent indirectly.

A rare but potentially important exception to the foregoing principles applies to parental support obligations that result from the adoption of a discretionary beneficiary *after* the creation of the trust. It is presumed in such a case that this parental duty of support is to be disregarded by the trustee, except that the trustee has the reasonable discretion that a trustee generally has in these matters to depart from the applicable rule of construction concerning a beneficiary's other resources. (Thus, the construction is the inverse of the usual presumption and discretion described in the first two paragraphs of Comment *e* above.) Even while recognizing that adopted children have the same family entitlements as children by birth, the presumption is based on the likelihood that the settlor(s) contemplated that trust distributions would provide for the beneficiary's support and other needs through the period of the trust. It is further based on a likely settlor preference for a construction that will be neutral with respect to possible future adoption decisions—more specifically, for terms that will not tend to discourage adoption by imposing what might be prohibitive, added financial burdens on a potential adoptive family. (Also, compare Illustration 14 and especially the last three sentences of the paragraph thereafter.)

Illustration:

8. B and C were orphaned, at ages seven and 10 respectively, by the accidental deaths of their parents. The parents' wills poured their modest probate estates into their (previously revocable) life-insurance trust, funded mainly with the proceeds of substantial policies on their lives. The terms of the trust provide for termination, essentially, when B attains age 23; until then the trustee is to pay or apply such amounts as it deems appropriate for the children's support, health care, education, and general welfare. The parents' wills designated their good friend F as guardian of the persons (and property, if necessary) of B and C; F and her husband, H, have three children of their own, ranging in age from seven to 11 at the inception of the guardianship. About four years later, B and C are adopted by F and H. Unless the terms of the trust (§ 4) reveal a different intention of the settlors, the trustee should, presumptively at least, continue distributions to provide support (as well as other benefits) for B and C, even though this has the effect of relieving F and H of support obligations newly resulting from the adoption. The trustee, however, has reasonable discretion (cf. Comment *e*, supra) not only to consider the adequacy of the trust funds to meet expected future needs of B and C and the educational and other purposes of the trust, but also to consider the overall financial burdens and resources of F and H and their likely ability to provide all five of their children with an accustomed level of support and suitable educational opportunities.

The presumption in Illustration 8 is, of course, rebuttable. And this exceptional presumption will have no application in many of the diverse situations in which adoptions occur, even situations in which an adopted child *subsequently* inherits property or becomes a trust beneficiary. In these latter cases, there would be no inference that the decedent's or settlor's purpose, or the perceived need, was to meet the child's basic support requirements or to assist the adoptive family.

e(4). Public benefits. If a discretionary beneficiary is or may be eligible to receive public benefits, this factor, like the availability of other resources generally, is to be taken into account by the trustee under the usual rule of construction. Thus, to the extent consistent with the terms and purposes of the trust, and allowable by applicable benefits statutes . . ., the presumption is that the trustee's discretion should be exercised in a manner that will avoid either disqualifying the beneficiary for other benefits or expending trust funds for purposes for which public funds would otherwise be available.

e(5). Other and related matters. Many specific issues cannot properly be addressed by rules of construction or constructional preferences. Absent some guidance from the settlor, such questions inevitably become matters for interpretation, on a case-by-case basis. An example is whether a trustee is to take account of an unemployed or underemployed beneficiary's earning capacity after completion of his or her education.

Another example involves the negative side of the resources issue: the liabilities of the beneficiary. Payments to an insolvent beneficiary, even if literally conforming to the language of the discretionary standard, might fail to achieve the settlor's purposes or run counter to the trustee's duty of impartiality. The trustee's duty may turn on the identity of an attaching creditor, such as whether the creditor is a person (e.g., a minor child) whose needs the settlor would normally expect to be met, albeit indirectly, by distributions to the beneficiary. See § 60, Comment *e*.

It is normally appropriate, and often necessary, for a trustee to take tax considerations into account in determining what discretionary distributions to make, and often to whom (see Comment *f*), considerations usually affected by the nature and amount of the beneficiary's independent resources. An often more troublesome question is whether distributions can properly be made purely for tax reasons to selected beneficiaries under a flexible power (as in Comment *f* and its Illustration[ ] 9 . . .). . . . . An appropriate answer may require careful consideration of the other resources of the various beneficiaries, as well as their income-tax and estate-tax positions, the tax circumstances of the trust, and the underlying purposes of the settlor (Comment *g*).

f. Multiple beneficiaries or groups as concurrent discretionary distributees. Questions about the presumed meaning of standards and the significance of beneficiaries' other resources are complicated when a trust has multiple discretionary beneficiaries, whether of the same or different generations. Difficulty of generalization through rules or preferences is aggravated by the number and interrelatedness of issues and alternative meanings to be considered, and by diversity in the terms of these discretionary powers, in the purposes and size of trusts, and in the beneficiaries' circumstances and their relationships to the settlor and to one another.

Illustrative is a trust in which the income is required to be distributed to B (usually the settlor's spouse or adult child), with discretion in the trustee to invade principal for the benefit of B and others, often a class consisting of B's or the settlor's children or descendants. A wholly discretionary variation of such a trust simply provides for discretionary distributions of income as well as principal to "any one or more of a group consisting of B and my [or B's] issue." Another example is a discretionary trust for "my children and their issue" (or, more simply, for "my descendants"), or for "X, Y, and Z and their issue." (In all of the above, the provisions for different individuals and classes may be separately stated, sometimes by generation, with the same or different standards for each.) A somewhat different prototype involves discretionary distributions among beneficiaries of one generation (e.g., "my children"), probably with contingent provision for distributions to the issue of any deceased members of that generation. A familiar version of this is the family trust providing collectively for the young children of a deceased couple (or of a deceased parent under a grandparent's will) until some age or other condition is satisfied.

In all of these cases, the structure and terms of the interests may suggest a priority to be accorded various individuals or classes. Complex issues of management and distribution (as well as taxation) can be eliminated or simplified if the trust directs or allows either administration as separate shares or division into separate trusts, one for each member of the first beneficiary generation. This, however, is likely to be both impractical and undesirable in a trust for the support and education of orphaned children.

Most questions arising in these various situations must be resolved through case-by-case interpretation. Nevertheless, a few appropriate inferences and constructional preferences can be identified, and can be quite useful as starting points. Structure and context often suggest that someone is the trust's primary beneficiary or has "favored status" (see Illustration 9, infra), or that a particular person (e.g., an elderly in-law or collateral relative) stands lower in the settlor's priorities, perhaps to benefit only in the event of need or hardship. In any event:

> Relationship to the settlor is relevant, leading in the most common situations to an inference that the beneficiary at the top of a line of descendants is favored over his or her own issue, with the settlor's spouse also so favored whether or not an ancestor of the others (e.g., settlor's issue by prior marriage).
>
> Among multiple lines of descent (e.g., all of the settlor's issue) there is an inference of priorities *per stirpes*, that is, that (i) the various lines are entitled to similar, impartial (see § 79, but not necessarily equal) treatment, with disparities to be justified on a principled basis consistent with the trust purposes, and that (ii) the inference of favored status within a descending line begins with the person(s) at the top (e.g., the settlor's child or the children of a deceased child).
>
> The preceding inference applies to the typical family trust for the support and education of minor or youthful beneficiaries following the death of one or both of their parents, with a preference for a common standard of living and similarity of opportunity to be balanced against usually modest funding and almost inevitably different beneficiary needs, capacities, and interests.
>
> Because these various situations do not involve "substantially separate and independent shares" for different lines of beneficiaries . . ., it is presumed that differences in benefits received by remainder beneficiaries or their ancestors during the trust period are not later to be taken into account in determining shares upon subsequent distribution, or in dividing the original trust for continuation thereafter in separate shares or trusts for separate lines of issue.

Illustrations:

> 9. As trustee of a trust created by H, T is directed to pay all of the income to W (H's widow) for life, with further grant of discretionary power to make principal distributions "to W and to any one or more of my issue, as T may deem appropriate for her or their comfortable support, health, education, and general best interests"; the remainder is to be distributed on W's death to S's then living issue. "Context" suggests that W is the primary beneficiary of this trust, with a favored position for T's exercise of discretion. This is reinforced by an inference based on her "relationship to the settlor."

Note: "Favored status" (or status as a "primary" beneficiary) does not necessarily mean that W should receive principal payments greater than—or even equal to—the distributions made to others; nor does it mean either that the trustee *may not* withhold principal payments to her because of her other resources or that in considering and making distributions to H's descendants T *must* take account of their independent resources (see Comment *g*). What W's favored status does mean is that, in the absence of compelling considerations, T is to give priority to providing what she needs, if anything, to continue her lifestyle and to have appropriate care and other suitable benefits. (On the significance of standards and independent resources, see Comments *d* and *e*; on the relevance of a settlor's tax and other objectives, see generally Comment *g*.)

9 (continued). A similar significance attaches to the favored status S's children hold in relation to their own issue by reason of both their relationship to S and their position at the top of their respective stirps, with a further inference of impartiality among the various lines of descent. It is both common and proper for trustees in these circumstances, for tax reasons and other considerations of common family interest, to make rare or no principal payments to the surviving spouse, while, for example, making principal distributions to each child whose best interests and wishes are thereby served and making similar distributions to the issue of each of the other children (i.e, of those children needing or wishing no personal benefits). The latter distributions, especially to grandchildren, generally serve purposes that fall outside the support obligations of the children.

14. M and F died in a plane crash while returning from a business trip together. Their wills (or revocable trusts) create a single trust for the support, health, care, and education of their three children, and also for the family of any child who might thereafter die before the trust terminates; termination is to occur as soon as no living child is under the age of 24. The concept of impartiality described in the paragraph preceding these Illustrations applies. (See also Comment *e* on the possible relevance of a child's independent means.)

Difficult problems of judgment may be presented to the trustee in Illustration 14. These are exemplified by differences in the duration and costs of education sought by various beneficiaries; or a child may make a reasonable request for assistance in acquiring a home, or in beginning a business or profession, while the youngest child is still under age. Although the trustee may lack authority to charge these differences in educational or other benefits against different distributive shares on termination, the trustee does have discretion—instead of possibly denying an appealing but troubling request—to make loans or advances from the trust estate for all or part of the requested amount (see final paragraph of Comment *d*), with a lien or right of offset against the ultimate distributive share of the beneficiary or his or her issue. The trustee may also contribute suitably to the common expenses of the family of the guardian or other person by whom the children are being raised, without itemizing or directly applying funds for the beneficiaries. To the extent safely consistent with the size of the trust fund and the probable future needs of the beneficiaries, the trustee may assist those other family members financially when to do so would be in the overall best interest of the beneficiaries. In short, in the family trust in Illustration 14, the trustee has quite flexible discretion to carry out the probable purposes of the trust within a general duty of impartiality of the type described above.

Comment on Subsections (1) and (2):

g. General observations on relevant factors in the interpretation of discretionary powers. Many factors may be influential in a process of interpretation that seeks to determine whether, based on evidence of the intention of a particular settlor, a relevant rule of construction or some aspect of it is inapplicable or modified with respect to the discretionary trust in question, or to decide how some inference may apply in a particular situation.

This is evident in judicial opinions involving matters considered in the preceding commentary. Many reported cases have proceeded without *acknowledging* any applicable presumption or constructional preference as a starting point.

Factors often cited in opinions as influential range from the particular language used in the grant of discretion (e.g., details of wording such as whether "may" or "shall" was used, whether discretion was about amounts "necessary" rather than "appropriate" to a beneficiary's support, and whether remainder beneficiaries were to take "the principal" or "whatever principal remains") to the relationships between the settlor and one or more of the beneficiaries. Relevant relationships include not only family relationships but also the settlor's personal feelings about a beneficiary, and occasionally about the beneficiary's spouse, and whether it had been customary or would be "natural" for the settlor to provide for the beneficiary's needs. Among many other factors cited as influential are whether the trustee is also a beneficiary of the power, whether the discretion is applicable to income as well as principal, whether the settlor made other provision for the discretionary beneficiary (or other beneficiaries) under the same document or otherwise, whether the settlor was aware of the beneficiary's other resources or of other circumstances, whether a spendthrift restraint was imposed on the beneficiary's interest, and whether a given interpretation might incidentally benefit someone other than the designated beneficiary.

Specific language, facts, and circumstances in a situation are properly to be considered in the process of interpretation, and may overcome, alter, or reinforce a particular presumption. Realistically, however, these factors often reveal little of a settlor's actual intent. The settlor may have formed no intention on the matter at issue, or whatever intention may have existed might not have been ascertained by counsel or preserved in the drafting. In any event, the significance of particular facts and circumstances is often highly speculative, or they may cut both or several ways even if judicial opinions sometimes mention but one side. Furthermore, to be influenced by and draw meaning from subtle details of wording may well ignore the realities of how drafting is done, not to mention that the words were those of one whose work product suggests inattention to the particular issue or circumstances for which it has become necessary to discover, or attribute, an intention.

Frequently, therefore, the most revealing and reliable guides for resolving these types of questions are the underlying or general purposes of the trust or provision in question. From these it may be deduced what objectives the settlor had in mind, and thus what intention might appropriately be attributed to the settlor on the matter at issue. Accordingly, rather than relying on speculation about the import of specific details of fact or wording, it is often more instructive to analyze the variety of beneficial interests and other provisions of the trust as a whole, with any other available evidence, in a broader effort to ascertain why the trust was created and what role the particular discretionary power was to play in the trust plan.

g(1). An illustrative situation. A common and revealing example is that of a trust that can be readily recognized as tax motivated and planned, with further indication that the discretionary beneficiary was of first concern to the settlor, even if others were also important beneficiaries of the plan. A discretionary beneficiary's favored status may be discerned, collectively, from the trust terms and other provisions of the governing instrument, from other actions and prior estate plans of the settlor, from records of the lawyer who interviewed the settlor and drafted the trust, and the like. It may be discovered, for example, that the settlor had intended to leave everything outright to that beneficiary, often the settlor's spouse, until counsel pointed out tax-planning opportunities and the importance to other family members of avoiding unnecessary taxation. The lawyer may have further explained that these tax objectives can be achieved without significantly sacrificing the security and comfort—and wishes—of the spouse, while avoiding management burdens, risks associated with aging, and probate when the spouse dies. Similar considerations and comparable examples are frequently found in trusts for a settlor's mature, well-to-do children.

Without the tax-planning element prominently in mind, the discretionary beneficiary's favored position might have suggested various conclusions, such as that the independent resources of the beneficiary, especially the principal of his or her estate, should not be taken into account by the trustee in determining distributions to be made pursuant to a standard of generous support. With a fuller understanding of the settlor's purposes, however, and perhaps the beneficiary's own wishes and expectations in developing a common estate plan, the appropriate and almost natural conclusions would be: (i) that the trust purposes and thus the settlor's intentions would be best served by a liberal and generous construction of any discretionary standards in question, and of the lifestyle and luxuries the beneficiary should enjoy; but that those same purposes and intentions would be served by recognizing (ii) that the trustee should have flexible discretion with respect to the question of considering other resources, and (iii) that in this trust the discretion should be exercised, when advantageous and not a cause of feelings of insecurity, to encourage consumption of substantial principal of the beneficiary's potentially taxable wealth.

g(2). Tax-sensitive trusteeships. An understanding of a trust's underlying purposes and estate-planning context is also important in appropriately resolving issues of interpretation in frequent situations involving tax-sensitive trusteeships. It is proper, and also realistic in ascertaining settlor intention, that the interpretation of discretionary powers should reflect circumstances, and tax (and other) rules, that are relevant to the settlor's tax (and other) objectives. These circumstances include the fact that, when the trust instrument was drafted, a discretionary beneficiary or other economically interested individual was being designated as trustee or co-trustee.

h. Cross-references. On ascertaining the meaning and effect of donative transfers generally, see § 4 . . .; §§ 62 and 66; and Restatement Third, Property (Wills and Other Donative Transfers) § 10.1 (donor's intention controls to extent allowed by law), § 10.2 (on evidence admissible in determining intent), §§ 11.1–11.3 (on resolving ambiguities), and §§ 12.1 (reformation to correct mistakes) and 12.2 (modification to achieve tax objectives).

CHAPTER 11

VOLUNTARY AND INVOLUNTARY TRANSFERS OF BENEFICIAL INTERESTS: GENERAL PRINCIPLES

Introductory Note: This chapter discusses the general principle that trust beneficiaries can transfer their interests in the trust, during life or at death, and that their creditors can reach those interests. Limitations imposed by law on transfers or on the rights of creditors that apply to legal interests apply as well to equitable interests in a trust.

Special rules of trust law allowing the settlor to impose restraints on voluntary and involuntary transfer of beneficial interests (spendthrift and forfeiture provisions), and limitations on the effectiveness of the assignment or attachment of discretionary interests, are discussed in Chapter 12.

The voluntary or involuntary transfer of a beneficiary's interest does not refer to transfer of the trust property itself, for the beneficiary cannot assign, nor generally can the creditors reach, more than the beneficiary has.

§ 51. Voluntary Transfers Inter Vivos

Except as provided in Chapter 12, a beneficiary of a trust can transfer his or her beneficial interest during life to the same extent as a similar legal interest.

Comment:

a. Scope of section. The general principle stated in this section does not apply if there is a valid restriction on transfer, such as a spendthrift restraint. Such restrictions are discussed in §§ 57–59, and also see § 60 (on discretionary interests). Statutes in some states limit the power of trust beneficiaries to transfer their interests.

The rule of this section applies to transfers as security as well as outright assignments.

The transfer of the interests of trust beneficiaries at death are dealt with in § 55. The claims of creditors of beneficiaries are discussed in § 56. On the problems presented by successive transfers of the same interest, see § 54. The necessity and form of manifesting the intention to make a transfer are considered in §§ 52 and 53. On a transferee's status as a "beneficiary" of the trust, with right to enforce it, see § 48, Comment *a*.

b. Power to transfer beneficial interests. Except as stated in Chapter 12, a trust beneficiary can voluntarily transfer inter vivos the whole or part of his or her interest in the trust. A transfer may be to another beneficiary, to the trustee, or to a third person to the extent that person has capacity to be a trust beneficiary (see § 43).

A purported transfer of an interest that the beneficiary does not have is ineffective. The fact that an interest is a contingent future interest, however, does not preclude its transfer. . . . . (Contingent or other uncertain interests are to be contrasted with expectancies. See § 41.)

Illustration:

2. A trust gave an interest to B for life, remainder to his issue who survive him. During B's life, his daughter D assigned her interest in the remainder to X. The assignment is effective. If D survives B, X is entitled upon distribution to the principal share to which D would have been entitled. If D predeceases B, the assignment gives X nothing (even though X is then alive and the transfer was valid), because D's interest was contingent on her surviving B, and X acquired only what D had.

On whether the assignment of a beneficiary's interest to another beneficiary allows the latter to terminate the trust, see § 65. On the assignee's status as a trust beneficiary, see § 48, Comment *a*. On the right of a beneficiary to set aside a transfer of his or her interest to the trustee if the trustee abuses the fiduciary relation between them, see § 78. On the ability of a beneficiary to transfer a beneficial interest to another upon a different trust or to declare a trust of the interest, see § 10(b) and (c) and § 40, Comments *c* and *d*.

c. Capacity. A trust beneficiary has capacity to transfer a beneficial interest to the same extent the person would have capacity to transfer a legal interest. Compare § 11 (dealing with capacity to create a trust). See generally Restatement Second, Property (Donative Transfers) § 18.1 (capacity to exercise powers of appointment), § 34.4 (donative transfers by minors), and § 34.5 (mentally incompetent donor) [Restatement Third, Property (Wills and Other Donative Transfers) § 8.1 (mental capacity), § 8.2 (incapacity due to minority), § 19.8 (capacity to exercise powers of appointment)].

d. Notice to and consent of trustee. Notice to or consent of the trustee is not necessary for an effective transfer of a beneficiary's interest, unless it is otherwise provided by the terms of the trust.

On the liability of a trustee who continues to deal with a beneficiary after receiving notice of a transfer of that beneficiary's interest, see § 76.

e. Notice to and acceptance by transferee. A transfer by a beneficiary is not ineffectual or revocable merely because of lack of notice to or an affirmative act of acceptance by the transferee, but lack of such notice is some evidence that the beneficiary did not intend to make a present transfer. Compare § 14 (dealing with notice, acceptance, and disclaimer by beneficiaries in the creation of trusts).

f. When disclaimer of interest or power is a transfer. A proper disclaimer of a beneficial interest by a trust beneficiary is not an assignment or "transfer" of the interest for purposes of this section. (On what constitutes a proper disclaimer, see Restatement Second, Property (Donative Transfers) §§ 32.2(2), 32.3(2), and 31.1, Comment *e* [Restatement Third, Property (Wills and Other Donative Transfers) § 6.1, Comment *i*]. On the different and quite strict requirements for a "qualified disclaimer" for tax purposes, see Internal Revenue Code § 2518. . . . .)

If, however, a person purporting to disclaim redirects the disposition and recipient(s) of the renounced interest, this exercise of dominion constitutes an acceptance of the interest and results in a *transfer* of the beneficial interest to the intended recipient(s).

If, without directing the disposition of the interest, the person purporting to disclaim has otherwise expressly or impliedly accepted the interest, or has failed to meet statutory requirements for an effective disclaimer, the purported disclaimer will constitute a *release.* A release is treated for many purposes, but not all (see, e.g., § 58, Comment *c*), as a transfer of the renounced interest to those who benefit from the release, generally to be determined as if the beneficiary had died at the time of the release. . . . . Also see generally Restatement Second, Property (Donative Transfers) § 31.1, Comment *l;* § 32.2(2), Comment *e;* § 32.3(2), Comment *e;* and § 32.2, Comment *d;* and also id. § 26.1, Comment *j,* and § 26.2, Comment *i.*

f(1). Powers of appointment. Similarly, a proper disclaimer by the donee of a power of appointment is not a *transfer* within the meaning of this section. Again, however, a purported disclaimer after expressed or implied acceptance of the power, or after failing to meet statutory requirements for an effective disclaimer, constitutes a *release* of the power. In the case of a general power of appointment, a release, which also includes a "lapse" by allowing a power to expire unexercised, is for most purposes (see § 58(2), Comment *f*) treated as if it were a transfer by the donee of the property or interest that is subject to the power. See generally Restatement Second, Property (Donative Transfers) § 14.1, Comments *a* and *e,* and compare id. § 14.5, Comments *b* and *e* [Restatement Third, Property (Wills and Other Donative Transfers) §§ 19.22–19.23 (on lapse of power of appointment), §§ 20.1–20.4 (on release or disclaimer of power of appointment)].

Although the holder of a power of appointment cannot transfer the power . . . , if the donee of a presently exercisable general power of appointment or a power of revocation purports to transfer the trust property, that act manifests an intention to make a transfer (§ 52), with the effect of withdrawing the subject property from the trust and then transferring that property.

On the importance of finding a "transfer" in these various cases, see § 58(2) and § 60, Comment *f* (whether and to what extent a person is settlor of a trust). . . . .

§ 52. Intention to Transfer

(1) To transfer a beneficial interest in a trust, the beneficiary must manifest an intention to make a present transfer; consideration is not essential to such a transfer.

(2) A promise to transfer an interest in the future is enforceable only if the requirements for an enforceable contract are satisfied.

(3) A transfer by a beneficiary can be rescinded upon the same grounds as the transfer of a legal interest.

Comment:

a. Manifestation of intention. Although some external manifestation of intention is required to transfer a beneficial interest, the beneficiary may manifest the intent to transfer without communicating it to anyone as long as the intention can be established by competent evidence. A failure to communicate, however, is some evidence of lack of the essential intent to make an immediate transfer.

Acts and communications prior or subsequent to an alleged transfer may be relevant in determining whether the beneficiary had the requisite intention. Compare § 13 (dealing with the intention to create a trust) and § 53 (on the need of a writing).

b. Authorization to receive or transfer trust benefits. If a beneficiary authorizes a third person to receive and retain distributions that the beneficiary would be entitled to receive from the trustee, this does not show an intent to transfer the beneficiary's interest. Nor does the beneficiary's authorization or direction to the trustee to make payments to a third person show an intention to transfer the beneficiary's interest.

Such authorizations are presumed merely to give the third person or trustee a revocable right to receive or authority to make distributions. Compare Restatement Second, Contracts § 325, Comment *a* ("a written instrument addressed to the debtor, directing the debtor to pay all or part of the debt to [a third person] . . . is not an assignment unless there is some additional manifestation of intention to assign").

Illustration:

1. T holds property in trust to convey it to B, who writes a letter to T in which she says, "I authorize you to convey to C the property which you hold in trust for me." Before T does so, B changes her mind and directs T to convey the property to her instead. Because, without more, B's earlier letter merely manifested an intention to authorize T to transfer the property to C, T's duty now is to transfer it to B.

c. Assignment as security. A beneficiary may manifest an intent to assign an interest only as security for a loan.

Illustration:

2. B has a remainder interest in a trust, contingent upon surviving her mother, who is receiving the income for life. B executes an instrument assigning her remainder interest to C. In conjunction with this assignment, C writes B a $50,000 check, which B promptly cashes. If the assignment is intended only as security for a loan of the $50,000, a fact that can be shown by evidence extrinsic to the instrument of transfer, C will have no interest in the trust after the loan obligation is satisfied.

d. Intention to transfer in the future. A manifestation of intention to transfer an interest in the future is not effective as a transfer. Treated as a promise, it is enforceable only if the requirements of an enforceable contract are satisfied. Compare § 15, Comment *b*. See also Restatement Second, Contracts § 330.

e. Rescission. A transfer by the beneficiary of a trust can be rescinded upon the same grounds as the transfer of a legal interest. Compare § 12.

§ 53. Need for a Writing

(1) A writing is not necessary to transfer a trust beneficiary's interest.

(2) If a statute requires the assignment of an interest in a trust to be in writing and signed by the assignor, the applicable principles are as stated in §§ 22–24.

Comment:

a. Statutory provisions. In some states a writing is required for a transfer of the beneficiary's interest in a trust of land only; in some a writing is required for the transfer of a beneficial interest in any trust. In others no writing is required, even in a trust of land. Compare § 22, Comment *a*, dealing with the creation of trusts, and Restatement Second, Property (Donative Transfers) § 31.4 [Restatement Third, Property (Wills and Other Donative Transfers) § 6.3], on donative transfers of interests in land.

b. What is necessary to comply with the Statute of Frauds. Statutory provisions dealing with assignments of interests in a trust may differ somewhat from those governing the creation of trusts. It is nevertheless appropriate to resolve comparable issues arising under comparable provisions the same way. Thus, for example, a sufficient writing that is later lost or destroyed continues to satisfy the statute. Compare § 22(2)(c).

§ 54. Effect of Successive Transfers

Where the beneficiary of a trust makes successive transfers of an interest, the first transferee is entitled to the interest unless the subsequent transferee prevails under principles of estoppel.

Comment:

a. Scope of the rule. The rule of this section may be affected by statute in many states, particularly in the case of interests in land.

If the first transfer involves only a part of the beneficiary's interest or is given as security, the subsequent transferee is entitled to any balance of the interest after the prior transferee's rights have been satisfied.

With the rule of this section compare Restatement Second, Contracts § 342, which also makes the right of an earlier assignee superior to that of later ones, with certain exceptions.

b. Estoppel of prior transferee. If the prior transferee of a beneficiary's interest induced the subsequent transferee to believe that no transfer had occurred, and the subsequent transferee in reliance thereon paid value without notice of the earlier transfer, the prior transferee is by estoppel postponed to the subsequent transferee. Compare Chapter 22.

c. Where prior transfer revocable or voidable. If a prior transfer is revocable or voidable, a subsequent transfer constitutes an implied revocation or avoidance, and the subsequent transferee prevails. Compare Restatement Second, Contracts § 342(a).

d. Where subsequent transferee obtains title from trustee. A subsequent transferee who, without notice of a prior transfer, gives value for an assignment of a beneficiary's right to trust property, and who pursuant thereto receives legal title to that property from the trustee, is entitled to retain the property free of the first assignee's equitable interest. . . . . Compare Restatement Second, Contracts § 342(b).

§ 55. Transfers at Death

(1) If the interest of a deceased beneficiary of a trust does not terminate or fail by reason of the beneficiary's death, the interest devolves by will or intestate succession in the same manner as a corresponding legal interest.

(2) Where a statute gives a surviving spouse an elective share of the deceased beneficiary's estate, equitable interests of the deceased beneficiary's estate are included in determining that share.

Comment:

a. Scope of section. The interests of trust beneficiaries are usually designed not to survive the beneficiary's death. This is the case, for example, where the beneficiary has only an interest for life or has a future interest that is subject to an expressed or implied survival requirement that is not satisfied. The rule of this section has no application to interests of this type.

On the disposition of trust income that has been received or accrued in the trust but has not been distributed prior to a life beneficiary's death, see Chapter 23. See also § 49, Comment *c*, on the rights to income shares not expressly disposed of during the lifetime of the survivor of multiple life beneficiaries. On the effect of the death of a class member before the time for distribution of a class gift, see Restatement Second, Property (Donative Transfers) § 27.3 ("children" and other one-generation classes) and § 28.2 ("issue" and other multi-generation classes) [Restatement Third, Property (Wills and Other Donative Transfers) §§ 14.1–14.2 (single-generation classes), §§ 14.3–14.4 (multiple-generation classes]. . . . .

Statutes in several states provide that, if the owner of property disappears and is not heard from for a designated period, the property devolves as if the owner were dead. These statutes apply to equitable as well as legal interests.

b. Disposition by will or will substitute. The principles governing wills and will substitutes apply also to devises and voluntary transfers by trust beneficiaries of their interests that do not terminate at death. See § 17, Comment *b*, and § 25. See also Restatement Third, Property (Wills and Other Donative Transfers) §§ 3.1–3.9 (statutory requirements for wills) and § 7.1 (validity of will substitutes). On formal requirements for exercising powers of appointment, see Restatement Second, Property (Donative Transfers) §§ 18.2 and 18.3 [Restatement Third, Property (Wills and Other Donative Transfers) §§ 19.9–19.10].

c. Intestate succession. Beneficial interests that do not terminate at a trust beneficiary's death, and are not disposed of by the beneficiary's will or by will substitute, pass by intestate succession. Modern law has eliminated or reduced the historical differences in the devolution of real and personal property, but where they still apply they extend to equitable interests as well as to legal interests.

If the beneficiary of a trust dies intestate without heirs, a beneficial interest that does not terminate devolves upon the state.

d. Spouse's rights. The historical question whether spouses were entitled to dower or curtesy in equitable interests is of little importance today since most states have abolished dower and curtesy. . . . .

The right of a surviving spouse to a statutory elective share in the estate of a deceased spouse applies to equitable interests that do not terminate at death. The community-property rights of spouses include equitable interests that are assets of the community by origin, tracing, or conversion.

On the rights of settlors' surviving spouses in revocable trusts, see § 25, Comment *d*.

§ 56. Rights of Beneficiary's Creditors

Except as stated in Chapter 12, creditors of a trust beneficiary, or of a deceased beneficiary's estate, can subject the interest of the beneficiary to the satisfaction of their claims, except insofar as a corresponding legal interest is exempt from creditors' claims.

Comment:

a. *Scope of section.* The rule of this section and the rights of beneficiaries' creditors are subject to the rules of §§ 57–60 dealing with spendthrift or other restrictions or limitations on transfer imposed by the terms of the trust or resulting from the nature of the beneficiary's interest. In a few states, comparable restraints on alienation are imposed by statute.

The rule of this section applies to all beneficial interests in a trust. Thus, subject to the rules of Chapter 12 and applicable exemptions (Comment *d*), creditors may reach a beneficiary's right to receive the trust income or an annuity or unitrust payments. They may also attach a beneficiary's right to discretionary distributions, subject to the practical limitations described in § 60. The rule of this section applies as well to all forms of future interests in trust, except to the extent that a policy of applicable law precludes or limits creditors' access to contingent or other uncertain legal interests. . . . .

Creditors may also reach a beneficiary's right to withdraw trust property or to demand distribution of a stated or formula amount (see Comment *b*), including a power periodically to compel payments of stated or percentage amounts. This power to require periodic distributions (although arguably a series of general powers) is treated for this purpose as an annuity or unitrust interest. On powers held by beneficiaries to demand distributions for purposes of "support" or pursuant to some other standard, see § 60, Comment *g*. Compare § 50(2) and especially Comment *d* thereto.

Matters of procedure, including limited protections for debtor-beneficiaries, and matters of priority between legal and equitable assets of a beneficiary-debtor, are dealt with hereafter in Comment *e*. The order of abatement among those beneficially interested in the estate of a deceased trust beneficiary, and among beneficiaries of his or her nonprobate transfers that are subject to estate obligations, is a matter of state law related to probate and is not within the scope of this Restatement.

On trusts that are created by transfers in fraud of creditors, see § 29, Comment *b* ("*Voidable transfers contrasted*").

That the personal creditors (or trustee in bankruptcy) of the trustee cannot reach the trust property, see § 42, Comment *c*.

b. *Powers of revocation or appointment.* The rights of creditors of the settlor of a revocable trust are discussed in § 25(2), which for these and other purposes of substance (as distinguished from form or procedure) treats the trust property essentially as if it were owned by the settlor. . . . . The other beneficiaries of a revocable trust are *treated*, for many of these purposes, *as if* they had no existing property interests (that is, their rights may be treated like the bare expectancies of will beneficiaries) so long as the power to revoke exists. Accordingly, these revocable interests are not reachable by the creditors of those beneficiaries. . . .

The rights of creditors with respect to trust property over which the debtor has a power of appointment depend on the nature of the power. For example, the creditors of the donee of a nongeneral power of appointment (one that cannot be exercised for the economic benefit of the power holder), whether or not presently exercisable, cannot reach the property subject to the power for the satisfaction of their claims; nor is the property subject to the expenses of administering the donee's estate.

Trust property subject to a presently exercisable general power of appointment (a power by which the property may be appointed to the donee, including one in the form of a power of withdrawal), because of the power's equivalence to ownership, is treated as property of the donee of the power. It can therefore be subjected to the satisfaction of the claims of the donee's creditors. (This is and long has been the law under the federal Bankruptcy Act.) Conversely, the interests of the other trust beneficiaries in that property cannot be reached by their creditors. Thus, the treatment of the assets subject to a presently exercisable general power is like the treatment of revocable trust assets under § 25(2). (That it is immaterial that the terms of a trust creating such a power include a spendthrift restraint, see § 58, Comment *b*.)

Furthermore, assets that were subject to a presently exercisable general power of appointment immediately preceding the donee's death thereafter remain subject to the satisfaction of claims against the donee's estate, including expenses of estate administration.

A general power to appoint only by will (or by other instrument that is revocable during life) does not give the donee the equivalent of ownership of the appointive assets. Hence, it does not enable creditors of the donee to reach the trust remainder during the donee's lifetime. The advantages of such a power, however, are sufficiently close to beneficial ownership when the power becomes exercisable upon the donee's death that the appointive assets can then be reached to satisfy creditors' claims and other obligations of the deceased donee's estate.

On other interests of deceased trust beneficiaries, see Comment *c*. On a beneficiary's power to require periodic payments of stated or percentage amounts, see Comment *a*. On a beneficiary's power to demand distributions subject to a standard, see § 60, Comment *g*.

c. Creditors of deceased beneficiaries. Creditors of a deceased trust beneficiary can subject the beneficiary's interest to the satisfaction of their claims to the extent that interest survives the beneficiary's death. See also Comment *b* on powers of appointment held by the beneficiary.

The priorities allowed by statute to certain classes of creditors of decedents apply to equitable as well as legal interests.

d. Exemptions. In all states, and under the federal Bankruptcy Act, certain kinds or amounts of property are exempt from creditors' claims within specified limits. These exemptions apply to equitable as well as legal interests.

e. Procedure for reaching beneficiary's interest. Except as modified by statute, a creditor can subject the beneficiary's interest to the satisfaction of a claim under the rule of this section after having attempted to satisfy the claim out of legal interests of the beneficiary, or when it appears that an attempt to do so would be unsuccessful or insufficiently productive.

In the appropriate proceedings, the court will give creditors relief that is fair and reasonable under the circumstances. If the beneficiary has only a right to the trust income or a right periodically to receive ascertainable or discretionary (but see § 60) payments, the court will normally direct the trustee to make the payments to the creditor until the claim, with interest, is satisfied. The court, however, may order less than all of the payments to be made to the creditor, leaving some distributions for the actual needs of the beneficiary and his or her family. ("Actual needs" are not based on a "station-in-life" standard of support and require that account also be taken of the beneficiary's other available resources.) . . . .

In some circumstances, the court may order a sale of the beneficiary's interest and payment of the creditor's claim from the proceeds. Sale may be appropriate when it appears unlikely that the debt can be satisfied from distribution(s) within a reasonable time, particularly when the beneficiary's interest is a future interest. Even then the uncertainty or remoteness of the interest may be such that its forced sale would produce little relative to its value to the beneficiary, and perhaps also too little to satisfy the creditor's claim. In that case, unless a loan or other arrangement can be obtained, it would be appropriate for the court to grant the creditor a lien on the beneficiary's interest, to be realized if and when it falls into possession.

Statutes in some states allow creditors to reach a beneficiary's interest by some form of legal execution, such as by levying directly upon the beneficial interest. Unless inconsistent with such a statutory provision, a court has discretion to prevent execution sale of a beneficiary's interest and to direct that creditors' claims be satisfied out of future distributions, provided that claims (with interest) will thereby be satisfied within a reasonable period of time. Some statutes allowing attachment of the beneficiary's interest limit the portion of periodic distributions that may be diverted from the beneficiary to the satisfaction of the creditor's judgment.

Illustrations:

1. A trust provides that the trustee is to pay B all of the trust income and such amounts of principal as the trustee deems appropriate for B's support, with the remaining principal to be paid upon B's death to R if she is then living and if not to her issue. (The trust contains no spendthrift clause. See § 58.) C, a judgment creditor of B, seeks to reach B's interest in the trust through the locally appropriate proceeding. C's claim, with interest, can be satisfied within a reasonable period of time from the income payments to which B is entitled; in fact, the claim can be satisfied sooner if principal payments are also made, with a portion of those payments directed to be paid to C, an inducement that the court finds reasonable and within the terms of the trustee's discretionary authority (see § 60). The court may properly direct that the trust income, plus a specified portion of any principal distributions the trustee decides to make, be paid to C instead of B.

2. The same facts as in Illustration 1, except that C is a creditor of R, rather than B, and seeks during B's lifetime to reach R's remainder interest in satisfaction of its judgment against her. (Applicable property law does not preclude forced sale of uncertain future interests. . . . .) The uncertainties of B's life expectancy and of the trustee's decisions concerning principal invasion for B, together with the risk that R may not survive B, lead the court to conclude that requiring sale of R's interest would have unduly harsh results to R even though the proceeds might be sufficient to pay C's claim. The court may properly impose a

lien on R's interest, to be enforced upon the death of B if some other alternative is not arranged for earlier payment of the claim.

A beneficiary's interest may also be reached through federal bankruptcy proceedings when available. . . . . Under the present Bankruptcy Act, the trustee in bankruptcy acquires for the benefit of the creditors "all legal or equitable interests of the debtor . . . as of the commencement of the case," except that (i) the bankruptcy estate does not include "any power that the debtor may exercise solely for the benefit of an entity other than the debtor" (compare Comment *b*) and (ii) the Code will honor a "restriction on the transfer of a beneficial interest of the debtor in a trust that is enforceable under applicable nonbankruptcy law" (see § 58).

CHAPTER 12

SPENDTHRIFT AND RELATED TRUSTS

Introductory Note: Despite its relatively restrictive rules concerning restraints on alienation of legal interests in property, American law departed from its English antecedents and has long been lenient with respect to disabling as well as forfeiture restraints on the alienation of the equitable interest of trust beneficiaries. See Restatement Second, Property (Donative Transfers) §§ 4.1–4.5 (the Introductory Note to Chapter 4 expressly acknowledging that its rules on the validity of restraints on alienation generally "do not apply to equitable interests under a trust"). Trust law also allows a settlor to require the retention of particular property in a trust, thus restraining alienation of legal interests by the trustee. See § 85; but cf. § 66.

The rules stated in this chapter deal with the validity and effect of trust provisions imposing forfeiture for voluntary or involuntary alienation of beneficiaries' interests (§ 57) and spendthrift provisions that disable beneficiaries from transferring their interests and their creditors from reaching those interests (§§ 58 and 59). This chapter also deals with the indirect restraint that results from the nature of discretionary trusts, limiting the effectiveness of assignment or attachment of beneficiaries' interests (§ 60). . . . . In all of these rules, the law's acceptance of restraints or limits on alienation does not extend to those that settlors may attempt to attach to their own retained interests in trusts that they, directly or indirectly, have created. . . . .

The rules in this chapter reflect a general acceptance of a fundamental common-law principle that a property owner, being free either to bestow property rights and benefits upon others or to withhold them, can bestow those rights and benefits through the trust device with the settlor's chosen conditions and restraints so long as those conditions and restraints are not, in the conventional terminology of trust law, unlawful or contrary to public policy. The rules stated in this chapter also reflect the difficulties inherent in balancing freedom of disposition against other relevant policies, as a special subset of issues and answers involving broader, ongoing controversies over the permissible extent of "deadhand" control by former owners of property. See § 29(c) (primarily on restraints on the behavior of beneficiaries) and compare § 29(b) (on perpetuities) . . . .

§ 57. Forfeiture for Voluntary or Involuntary Alienation

Except with respect to an interest retained by the settlor, the terms of a trust may validly provide that an interest shall terminate or become discretionary upon an attempt by the beneficiary to transfer it or by the beneficiary's creditors to reach it, or upon the bankruptcy of the beneficiary.

Comment:

a. Scope of rule. The rule stated in this section applies even where disabling restraints (spendthrift trusts, allowed by the rule of § 58) are not permitted. . . .

The discussion in this commentary assumes that the provision concerning alienation does not violate the rule against perpetuities, considered in § 29(b). Conditions relating to alienation or solvency are to be distinguished from conditions that relate to the personal conduct of trust beneficiaries, considered in § 29(c).

b. Termination of interests in income or principal. Where an interest entitles the beneficiary to receive income or principal during life or for a term of years, or to receive principal on termination of the trust, the terms of the trust can validly provide that the interest shall terminate upon an attempt by the beneficiary to transfer it, upon an attempt by the beneficiary's creditors to reach it, or in the event of the beneficiary's bankruptcy or insolvency.

The foregoing, however, does not apply to beneficial interests retained by the settlor; otherwise, a settlor could use the trust device to make what amounts to a delayed disposition of a retained interest in disregard of future transfers or in anticipation of insolvency. This comes objectionably close to a pre-planned fraudulent conveyance that is to become effective on insolvency.

Illustrations:

1. S transfers property to T in trust to pay the net income to B for life, and to pay the principal on B's death to R or to R's issue if she is then dead. The terms of the trust provide that if "any beneficiary should transfer his or her interest or his or her creditors should attempt to reach it, or if the beneficiary should become bankrupt, his or her interest under the trust shall cease; the trust shall then be administered as if that beneficiary had died at the time of the termination of his or her interest." If B becomes bankrupt, his interest terminates. Under the above trust provisions, so does the trust, with principal being distributed to R if living. If it is R (instead of B) who becomes bankrupt, on later termination of the trust at B's death the principal will be distributed to R's issue.

2. The facts are as stated in Illustration 1, except that the trust was created by B. On B's bankruptcy, neither the trust nor B's interest terminates, but his trustee in bankruptcy is entitled to his life interest under the trust.

A forfeiture restraint for attempted voluntary transfer applies to any attempt to assign the interest, including as security, unless the terms of the trust limit the scope of the restraint.

A forfeiture provision restraining alienation of a beneficiary's interest is valid even in states that prohibit spendthrift restraints or limit their effect. . . . .

c. Interest becoming discretionary on alienation. The terms of a trust can validly provide that the interest of a beneficiary other than the settlor shall cease upon voluntary or involuntary alienation of the interest and that, instead, the trustee shall thereafter have discretionary authority with respect to any further payments to the beneficiary. These are often called "protective" provisions, and often authorize discretionary distributions also to the original income beneficiary's family or other relatives. These arrangements are particularly common in England and in states that reject or severely restrict spendthrift trusts, but they are also used elsewhere to prevent creditors from seizing spendthrift trust funds following distribution (§ 58, Comment *d*).

On the nature of the beneficiary's interest in a discretionary trust, see § 50; and on the rights of transferees and creditors of beneficiaries of discretionary trusts, see § 60.

Illustration:

3. S creates a trust to pay all of its income to B for life, remainder to R or R's issue, but if B shall ever become insolvent then "the trustee, in its sole discretion, may accumulate income or pay such amounts of income as it shall determine to or for the benefit of any one or more of B, her husband, and her issue." B becomes insolvent. Her right to the trust income ceases and cannot be reached by her creditors. The trust becomes discretionary. (On the rights of B's creditors, see § 60, Comments *c–e(1)*.)

d. Solvency as a condition precedent. The terms of a trust can validly provide that a beneficiary who is not the settlor shall be entitled to the principal of the trust or other benefits only after the beneficiary becomes financially solvent or receives a discharge in bankruptcy.

Because a contingent future interest would otherwise be subject to creditors' claims in most states (see § 56), there is a presumption that a condition precedent of solvency carries with it an implied spendthrift restraint (see § 58, Comment *b*) until the condition is met. Such an interest cannot be reached by the beneficiary's creditors until after the condition has been satisfied. . . . .

§ 58. Spendthrift Trusts: Validity and General Effect

(1) Except as stated in Subsection (2), and subject to the rules in Comment *b* (ownership equivalence) and § 59, if the terms of a trust provide that a beneficial interest shall not be transferable by the beneficiary or subject to claims of the beneficiary's creditors, the restraint on voluntary and involuntary alienation of the interest is valid.

(2) A restraint on the voluntary and involuntary alienation of a beneficial interest retained by the settlor of a trust is invalid.

General Comment:

a. Terminology, background, and scope of section. The term "spendthrift trust" refers to a trust that restrains voluntary and involuntary alienation of all or any of the beneficiaries' interests. The extent of the protection such a trust offers is considered hereafter in Comment *d*. Spendthrift protection is not limited to beneficiaries who are legally incompetent or who, as a practical matter, lack the ability to manage their finances in a responsible manner.

A spendthrift trust is to be distinguished from a discretionary trust but may or may not also contain discretionary interests, which are considered in § 60 (and § 50). A spendthrift restraint may or may not also contain a forfeiture provision of the type discussed in § 57.

The rules stated in this section and its commentary address the validity and application of spendthrift restraints, with special exceptions for certain categories of claimants being treated in § 59. These rules apply to interests in principal as well as in income, and also to possessory interests under trusts.

Spendthrift restraints are not permitted under English law and have been rejected by a few American cases. The vast majority of decisions in this country, however, have accepted the spendthrift trust doctrine essentially as stated above in Subsections (1) and (2) but differ in some matters discussed hereafter in this commentary, and also in matters discussed in § 59.

A number of states have enacted legislation codifying the law of spendthrift trusts. A few statutes contain significant departures from the rules stated here, such as by allowing restraints on income but not principal interests or otherwise limiting the extent of the protection allowed (e.g., to the beneficiary's support). Some statutes make all trusts spendthrift trusts unless the settlor provides otherwise, or restrain involuntary but not voluntary alienation with respect to all trusts.

The rules of this section have long been recognized under federal bankruptcy law. Current Bankruptcy Code § 541(c)(2) states that a "restriction on the transfer of a beneficial interest of a debtor in a trust that is enforceable under applicable nonbankruptcy law" is to be honored in bankruptcy. The rule of Subsection (1) of this section, often without the exception in Subsection (2), has been codified in various state and federal statutes that provide spendthrift restraints or require or authorize their inclusion in pension trusts, most notably the provisions in the Employee Retirement Income Security Act. Federal estate and gift tax regulations permit marital-deduction trusts under Internal Revenue Code §§ 2056 and 2523 to include spendthrift clauses, provided any accompanying forfeiture restraint (§ 57) is inapplicable to the spouse's interest. Further discussion of these various bodies of legislation is beyond the scope of this Restatement . . . .

Comment on Subsection (1):

b. Requirements for a valid spendthrift trust. Subsection (2) invalidates a spendthrift clause to the extent it is intended to apply to any interest of a beneficiary who is also the settlor of the trust. Furthermore, if the settlor is the sole beneficiary during life and reserves a general power of appointment, even a testamentary general power (one allowing appointment to the settlor's estate), creditors of the settlor can reach not only the beneficial interest(s) retained for life but the trust property itself. See further Comments *e* and *f*.

b(1). Absence of ownership equivalence. An intended spendthrift restraint is also invalid with respect to a nonsettlor's interests in trust property over which the beneficiary has the equivalent of ownership, entitling the beneficiary to demand immediate distribution of the property. Thus, if an income beneficiary also holds a presently exercisable general power of appointment (that is, a power currently to compel distribution of trust property to the power holder), a spendthrift restraint will not prevent the beneficiary's creditors or transferees from reaching the property that is subject to the power. (A general power exercisable only at death does not give a nonsettlor sole life beneficiary the equivalent of ownership for this purpose. Compare, however, § 56, Comment *b*.)

Similarly, a spendthrift clause is ineffective to the extent the trust is or becomes either passive (whether or not subject to a statute of uses, see § 6) or subject to the doctrine of merger because the debtor or assignor is both sole beneficiary and sole trustee (see § 69). Except in this latter situation, a spendthrift provision is not invalid with respect to a beneficiary's interest(s) merely because the beneficiary is also the trustee or a co-trustee.

Illustrations:

1. S transfers property to T in trust to pay the income to B for life and to distribute the principal on B's death to R or R's issue. The terms of the trust provide that the interests of the beneficiaries cannot be transferred by them or reached by their creditors. The trust is a spendthrift trust, and B cannot assign his right to the trust income, nor can the creditors of B reach the trust income before it is distributed to him. R also has no power to transfer her remainder interest, and her creditors cannot reach it.

2. The facts are the same as in Illustration 1, except that B is also granted the power at any time after reaching age 30 to withdraw all or any part of the principal and thereby terminate the trust in whole or in part. Although the restraint on alienation of B's interest is initially valid, once B reaches age 30 the spendthrift provision is no longer effective because he has the equivalent of complete ownership of the entire trust estate (compare § 29, Comment *g*, on the rule against perpetuities). This does not invalidate spendthrift restraints with respect to the interests of other beneficiaries; but under the rule of § 25(2) and its Comment *e* (and also see § 56, Comment *b*), once B reaches age 30 the remainder interests in this Illustration have little substance and, for creditor purposes, are treated in the same manner as if they were bare expectancies of devisees under a will.

b(2). Restraint on both voluntary and involuntary alienation. A spendthrift trust is one that restrains both voluntary and involuntary alienation.

For reasons of policy, a spendthrift restraint that seeks only to prevent creditors from reaching the beneficiary's interests, while allowing the beneficiary to transfer the interest, is invalid under the rule of Subsection (1) (but compare Comment *c*). A restraint only on voluntary transfer does not protect the interests from creditors and is thus insufficiently effective as a practical matter to justify a departure from the law's general policy against restraints on alienation. (On a purchaser's status as a creditor, compare paragraph following Illustration 7 in Comment *d(1)*.)

Illustration:

3. S transfers property to T in trust to pay the income to L for life, remainder to R or R's issue. The terms of the trust provide that the interests of the beneficiaries can be voluntarily transferred by them but that their interests cannot be reached by their creditors. The trust is not a spendthrift trust, and the intended protection from creditors is invalid. Thus, not only can L and R assign their interests but their interests can be reached by their respective creditors as well.

b(3). Required manifestation of spendthrift intention. The settlor must manifest the intention to create a spendthrift trust. No particular form of wording is necessary for this purpose, as long as the requisite intention can be discerned from the terms of the trust (as defined in § 4). It is sufficient if a settlor simply provides that the trust "is to be a spendthrift trust." A spendthrift restraint is implied from language stating that a beneficial interest is subject to a condition precedent of the beneficiary's becoming solvent or receiving a discharge in bankruptcy (see § 57, Comment *d*).

Furthermore, language in a trust instrument that only expresses the settlor's intention to restrain *voluntary* alienation is sufficient to create (by implication) a spendthrift trust with involuntary alienation restrained as well; and when an instrument (unlike that in Illustration 3) merely states an intention to restrain involuntary alienation, an intention to restrain voluntary alienation is presumed.

Illustrations:

4. S's will leaves property to T in trust to pay the income "to B for life, the payments not to be anticipated by her or subject to interference by others." On B's death the terms of the trust direct T to distribute the principal to R or R's issue. The quoted language manifests S's intention to impose a spendthrift restraint on B's interest. Without more, however, it does not manifest an intent to restrain voluntary or involuntary alienation of the remainder interest. (If, however, the trust had simply stated in general terms that "this is a spendthrift trust," this would manifest an intention to restrain alienation of both income and principal interests.)

5. The facts are the same as in Illustration 4, except that the language following the direction to T to pay the trust income to B states simply that "her right to these payments is not to be transferable." The trust is a spendthrift trust as to her interest. The quoted language has the effect of restraining involuntary as well as voluntary alienation.

That a beneficiary's interest is discretionary is not itself sufficient evidence of the settlor's intention to impose a spendthrift restraint upon that interest. However, a discretionary provision accompanied by additional language or other evidence of a settlor's intention to restrain alienation may provide a sufficient basis for inferring the intention to create a spendthrift trust.

Illustration:

6. S left property to T in trust to pay such amounts of income and principal to B as T deems appropriate for B's support and comfort, remainder on B's death to R or R's issue. The nature of this discretionary trust is not alone a sufficient basis for finding the required manifestation of intent to create a spendthrift trust. (On other effects of the interest's discretionary character, see § 60.)

c. What acts are precluded "transfers"? A spendthrift restraint prevents the transfer of a trust beneficiary's interest to another, whether the attempted assignment is by gift, sale, or exchange, or as security for a new or existing debt. On other effects of an attempted transfer, however, see Comment *d*.

A designated beneficiary of a spendthrift trust is not required to accept or retain an interest prescribed by the terms of the trust. Thus, an intended beneficiary may reject a beneficial interest or power of appointment by a proper disclaimer. Even the release of an interest in a spendthrift trust, including by purported disclaimer following expressed or implied acceptance, is permissible and serves to terminate the beneficiary's interest even though the release is treated for some other purposes as a transfer. On the other hand, a purported disclaimer by which the beneficiary attempts to direct who is to receive the interest is a precluded transfer and will not be given effect because of the spendthrift restraint. But cf. limited exception in § 65, Comment *e* (on termination of trusts by beneficiaries). See generally § 51, Comment *f*, on disclaimers and releases as possible "transfers" of beneficiaries' interests or of property subject to powers of appointment. See also Comment *f* below.

If an income beneficiary also holds a presently exercisable power to appoint principal of the trust only to others, the power does not invalidate spendthrift protection of the income interest. Exercise of such a power (although a corpus distribution would carry with it the income interest in the property) is not a transfer prevented by the spendthrift restraint, as long as the beneficiary does not attempt to so exercise the power as to appoint only the income interest.

d. Effect of spendthrift restraint. Spendthrift trusts provide only limited protection against the creditors or improvidence of beneficiaries. Spendthrift protection prevents anticipation of the beneficiary's rights but does not extend beyond the point of distribution. See also exceptions for certain claimants in § 59.

d(1). Rights of beneficiary's purported transferees. Persons who have received a purported assignment of a beneficiary's interest in a spendthrift trust do not thereby acquire that beneficial interest. This does not mean, however, that the purported transfer has no effect. The beneficiary's act has the effect of an authorization to the trustee to distribute to the purported transferee whatever distributions the beneficiary is entitled to receive and has purported to assign, but the authorization is revocable at any time. Thus, a spendthrift restraint merely prevents the beneficiary from making an *irrevocable* transfer of his or her beneficial interest.

A trustee who pays funds to a purported assignee in accordance with a beneficiary's unrevoked assignment is protected, but must cease doing so upon instruction from the beneficiary. A trustee, however, is under no duty either to the beneficiary or to the purported assignee to accept this authorization to act on behalf of the beneficiary. (On a trustee's duty not to misdeliver trust funds, and duty to transferees of nonspendthrift interests, see § 76.)

Illustration:

7. S devises to T upon a spendthrift trust to pay the income to B for life, remainder on his death to R or R's issue. The terms of the trust instruct T to pay the income "to B personally and not to any attaching creditor or other person." B subsequently assigns his interest under the trust to A and directs T to pay the income thereafter to A. T pays the trust income to A for several years until receiving instructions from B to cease doing so. T is not liable to B for the payments made to A before receiving this instruction, but will be liable if any further payments are made to A rather than B. A can properly keep the payments that have been made but cannot compel T to make further payments. (Whether A can keep a payment improperly made to him by T after B has revoked T's authority, leaving B with a remedy only against T, depends on whether A is a bona fide purchaser. See Chapter 22.)

If the beneficiary of a spendthrift interest purports to transfer it to another for value but later revokes the assignment and the trustee's authority pursuant to it, the beneficiary is liable to that other person. Although that person cannot reach the beneficiary's interest under the trust, satisfaction of the claim can be obtained from other property of the beneficiary or from trust funds after they have been distributed to the beneficiary.

d(2). Rights of beneficiary's creditors. A spendthrift trust protects the income and principal interests of its beneficiaries from the claims of their creditors as long as the income or principal in question is properly held in the trust. Thus, a beneficial interest that is subject to a valid spendthrift restraint cannot be attached by judgment creditors of the beneficiary, nor does it become an asset of the beneficiary's bankruptcy estate under § 541 of the Bankruptcy Code.

After the income or principal of a spendthrift trust has been distributed to a beneficiary, however, it can be reached by creditors through the same procedures and in accordance with the same rules that apply generally to property of the beneficiary.

In addition, property that has become distributable to the beneficiary but is retained by the trustee beyond a time reasonably necessary to make distribution to the beneficiary, and thus to which the beneficiary has a right to demand immediate distribution, is then subject to attachment by creditors of the beneficiary. Compare Comment *b*, on trust property of which a beneficiary has the equivalent of ownership.

Comment on Subsection (2):

e. Where the settlor is a beneficiary. A spendthrift trust cannot be created for the benefit of the settlor. That is, a spendthrift restraint is not valid with respect to any interest retained by the settlor. Accordingly, a retained right to trust income for life or a term of years, or a certain or uncertain future right retained in the principal of the trust, is subject to attachment by creditors of the settlor. Such rights will also pass to the settlor's trustee in bankruptcy as "a beneficial interest . . . in a trust that" is not subject to a restriction on transfer "that is enforceable under applicable nonbankruptcy law" under the terms of Bankruptcy Code § 541(c)(2).

The rule of this subsection does not depend on the settlor having made a transfer in fraud of creditors or upon the retention of a power of revocation. (Compare § 57 on forfeiture restraints and § 60, Comment *f*, on discretionary interests of settlors.) The rule does not invalidate a spendthrift restraint with respect to the interests of others.

If the settlor reserves not only a right to receive the income of a trust for life but also a general power to appoint the remainder by will, neither the life interest nor the remainder subject to the right to appoint can be protected from the creditors of the settlor by a spendthrift restraint. The settlor's creditors can reach the principal of the trust, provided there are no interests in others who can receive benefits during the settlor's lifetime. See Restatement Second, Property (Donative Transfers) § 13.3 [Restatement Third, Property (Wills and Other Donative Transfers) § 22.2]. (And compare § 25(2) on the rights of the settlor's creditors to reach property held in a revocable trust.)

This situation is to be distinguished from one in which a testamentary (or equivalent) general power of appointment is held by another. See Comment *b* and compare § 56, Comment *b*. Also, where a settlor has a life interest and a general power exercisable only at death, the *creditor* rule is different from the general rule that applies to *voluntary transfer* during life, which allows the settlor to transfer only the life interest but not the trust property.

Illustration:

8. S transfers property to T in trust to pay the income to S for life and to pay the principal on S's death to R or R's issue. The terms of the trust provide that S's interest under the trust cannot be transferred or reached by her creditors. She can nevertheless transfer her interest, and her creditors can reach it. If the spendthrift provision encompasses the interests of R and the issue as well, their interests cannot be transferred by them or attached by their creditors.

If the terms of the trust in the above Illustration had authorized T to invade principal for the benefit of S, or if the trust had been a wholly discretionary one for S's lifetime, the discretionary interest could also be subjected to the claims of S's creditors. On what a creditor can reach by attaching a discretionary interest retained by a settlor, see § 60, Comment *f*.

f. Circumstances in which beneficiary is settlor. The rule of Subsection (2) is not limited to cases in which the beneficiary actually conveyed the property to the trust or executed the trust instrument, or was designated as settlor. It is sufficient, for example, that the beneficiary pay the consideration in return for which another transferred the property to fund the trust.

If a beneficiary transfers part of the property or supplies part of the consideration to fund a trust, the beneficiary is ordinarily settlor to the extent of a fractional portion appropriate to reflect his or her proportionate share of the funding. (A beneficiary might be treated as settlor of the whole of his or her interest, rather than as settlor of a proportionate part of the entire trust, in a situation in which the beneficiary purchased the interest, or if the beneficiary paid, either to the settlor or by contributing to the trust, a consideration reasonably consistent with the value of the beneficiary's own interest in a trust that otherwise would have been created solely for the benefit of others. . . . .)

Illustrations:

9. S transfers $500,000 to T in trust to pay the income to S's brother B for life, remainder to B's issue. At about the same time, pursuant to their prearrangement, B creates a similar trust, also of $500,000, for S and her family. Each trust contains a spendthrift clause. Nevertheless, as settlor of the trust ostensibly created for her by B, she can transfer her interest, and her creditors can reach that interest. . . . . The restraint on alienation is valid, however, with respect to the remainder interests.

10. B's father F transferred $500,000 to T to be held by it in trust pursuant to the terms of an instrument executed by F and signed by him as settlor, and to pay the income to B for life, remainder at her death to her issue. The terms of the trust included a spendthrift clause. Upon learning of her father's plan to establish this trust, B contributed $250,000 of her own funds to the trust. B is settlor of a one-third portion of this trust. Her creditors or assignees can reach a one-third share of her income interest, while her right to income from the other two-thirds of the trust is protected by the spendthrift restraint. (If, instead, B had made her $250,000 contribution to the trust at a later time, when the trust estate had appreciated by 50 percent to $750,000, she would become settlor of a one-quarter share of the then $1 million trust fund.)

A life beneficiary of a spendthrift trust created by another who pays off encumbrances on the trust property becomes to that extent settlor of the trust. The beneficiary's creditors or transferees can reach a portion of the life interest appropriate to this contribution.

If an heir contests a will that would leave the testator's property to others, and in order to settle the litigation a spendthrift trust is created in the heir's favor, by agreeing to the settlement of a genuine dispute the heir has given consideration and is settlor of the trust within the rule of this subsection. The same is true when the contestant is an outright devisee under a prior will. If, however, others contest a will that would leave the testator's estate in spendthrift trust, the beneficiaries of that trust do not become settlors by reason of a settlement that gives a portion of the estate to the contestants and preserves the rest of it in the trust as prescribed by the testator. Similarly, if the beneficiaries of a spendthrift trust under a prior will contest a later will that leaves the testator's estate to others free of trust, and under a bona fide settlement a portion of the estate is placed in trust in accordance with the prior will, the trust beneficiaries are not settlors of the trust.

Where a spendthrift trust is created by the will of one spouse in favor of the other, the surviving spouse does not become the settlor of the trust for purposes of the rule of this section merely because she or he waives a right to insist on a statutory forced share of the deceased spouse's estate. . . . .

f(1). Renunciations. Where the income beneficiary of a residuary trust under the will of another is also designated to receive a specific devise under that will but properly disclaims the devise, the disclaimer is not a transfer to the residuary trust even though it would normally have the effect of enlarging that trust (see § 51, Comment *f*). Thus, the beneficiary is not the settlor of the enlarged portion of the trust, and a spendthrift provision in the trust terms is valid with respect to the beneficiary's life interest in all of the enlarged trust.

If, however, the beneficiary's renunciation is not a proper disclaimer, it would be treated as a transfer (id.); if the devised property then passes to the residuary trust the beneficiary would be treated as settlor to the extent of the property so added.

Similarly, if an income beneficiary of a trust properly disclaims a power of withdrawal or other presently exercisable general power of appointment over all or a portion of the trust estate, the beneficiary has not acquired an equivalent of ownership that invalidates a spendthrift restraint applicable to the income interest in the appointive property under the rule of Comment *b*; and the disclaimer is not treated as a transfer of the appointive property to the trust (see § 51, Comment *f*) to cause the beneficiary to be treated as settlor of the trust or portion thereof.

On the other hand, if the beneficiary had made a belated renunciation or other release (including a lapse, by allowing expiration) of the power, the beneficiary would have the equivalent of ownership until the time of the release, which—as a transfer (id.)—would have made the beneficiary settlor of the trust thereafter to the extent of the property previously subject to the power. Thus, any spendthrift restraint that would otherwise be applicable to the beneficiary's interest would be invalid, initially under Comment *b* and subsequently under this Subsection (2).

Illustration:

11. W and H (a married couple) transfer $20,000 to T in trust to pay the income to their grandchild, G, for life and to pay the principal at G's death to his then living issue. The trust instrument gives G the right

to withdraw the $20,000, and also the right thereafter to withdraw any additional contributions anyone might make to the trust; any power of withdrawal is to expire at the end of the calendar year in which the transfer to the trust occurs. The terms of the trust also include a spendthrift clause applicable to all beneficiaries. The spendthrift restraint is valid with respect to the interests of G's issue but not with respect to G's income interest, because (i) he has the equivalent of ownership until his withdrawal power lapses and because (ii) he becomes settlor of the trust thereafter. The same result will apply to each of the contributions H and W make, as they contemplate doing in subsequent years.

General Comment:

g. Death or legal disability of beneficiary. If the beneficiary of a spendthrift trust is under legal disability, a guardian or conservator of his or her property has the right to demand the income or other distributions to which the beneficiary is entitled to the same extent as if the trust were not a spendthrift trust (see § 49, Comment *c*). The beneficiary's agent under a durable power has the same right, on behalf of the beneficiary, to demand distributions from the trustee.

The executor or administrator of a deceased beneficiary of a spendthrift trust is entitled to income or other distributions that have accrued but have not been paid at the time of the beneficiary's death to the same extent as if the trust were not a spendthrift trust (see Chapter 23).

Because income or principal received by the personal representative is distributed and no longer subject to the trust, these funds are subject to creditors' claims and other obligations of the deceased beneficiary's estate, and to disposition by the beneficiary's will or by intestate succession. See Comment *d*. Also, if an interest survives (that is, is not terminated by) the beneficiary's death (see § 55 and also § 49, Comment *c*), the interest is an asset of the beneficiary's probate estate. As such it passes, subject to administration and creditors' claims, to the deceased beneficiary's testate or intestate successors, or in satisfaction of spousal rights, in the same manner as an interest in a nonspendthrift trust. . . . .

h. Cross-references. On the effect of the consent of a spendthrift-trust beneficiary to a breach of trust, or of a spendthrift-trust beneficiary's participation in a breach of trust, see § 97. On impounding the share of a spendthrift-trust beneficiary who is also a trustee and has committed a breach of trust, see § 59, Comment *a*, and, more generally, Chapter 20. On the effect of a trustee's advance or loan of trust funds to the beneficiary of a spendthrift trust (set-off), see id.

On the effect of a transfer of the trust property by the trustee to the beneficiary of a spendthrift trust before the purposes of the trust have been fully accomplished, see § 65, Comments *a* and *e*.

On the termination of a trust created for the settlor's own benefit, see § 65. And on the modification and termination of spendthrift trusts generally, see § 65, Comment *e*, and § 66.

On the validity of restraints on alienation of legal estates and equitable estates other than those arising under a trust, see Restatement Second, Property (Donative Transfers), Part II, Chapter 3 (§§ 3.1–3.4 on definitions) and Chapter 4 (§§ 4.1–4.5, the first three sections dealing with the validity of, respectively, disabling, forfeiture, and promissory restraints).

§ 59. Spendthrift Trusts: Exceptions for Particular Types of Claims

The interest of a beneficiary in a valid spendthrift trust can be reached in satisfaction of an enforceable claim against the beneficiary for

(a) support of a child, spouse, or former spouse; or

(b) services or supplies provided for necessities or for the protection of the beneficiary's interest in the trust.

General Comment:

a. Scope of the rule. The rule stated in this section allows certain categories of creditors to reach beneficial interests in spendthrift trusts that are valid under the rule of § 58, including discretionary interests in those trusts. The creditor's special advantage in being able to attach a discretionary interest is limited by the nature of the interest, as described in § 60.

a(1). Governmental claims. It is implicit in the rule of this section, as a statement of the common law, that governmental claimants, and other claimants as well, may reach the interest of a beneficiary of a spendthrift trust to the extent provided by federal law or an applicable state statute. Governmental claims and claims under governmentally assisted programs are often granted this special status. . . . .

a(2). Other exceptions. The exceptions to spendthrift immunity stated in this section are not exclusive. Special circumstances or evolving policy may justify recognition of other exceptions, allowing the beneficiary's interest to be reached by certain creditors in appropriate proceedings (on which see § 56, Comment *e*).

In some circumstances, to permit attachment despite the spendthrift restraint may not undermine, and may even support, the protective purposes of the trust or some policy of the law. On the other hand, the advantage thus conferred on select creditors over others who cannot attach the interest but must pursue funds in the hands of the beneficiary, after distribution (see § 58, Comment *d*), is not always appropriate as a matter of fairness and sound policy. Unlike the exceptions in Comments *b* through *d*, possible exceptions in situations of this type require case-by-case weighing of relevant considerations or evolving policies.

The nature or a pattern of tortious conduct by a beneficiary, for example, may on policy grounds justify a court's refusal to allow spendthrift immunity to protect the trust interest and the lifestyle of that beneficiary, especially one whose willful or fraudulent conduct or persistently reckless behavior causes serious harm to others.

Also, the interest of a beneficiary who receives a loan or advance of trust funds from the trustee, or who—by breach of duty as trustee or otherwise—causes harm to the trust estate and the beneficial interests of others, may ordinarily be reached by set-off or impounding to satisfy the resulting obligation, even in the case of a spendthrift trust. See more generally Chapter 20.

Comment on Clause (a):

b. Support claims. A beneficial interest in a spendthrift trust can be reached to satisfy an enforceable claim by the beneficiary's spouse or children for support. It can also be reached in satisfaction of a claim by a former spouse for support or alimony (or "compensatory spousal payments" . . .).

Although a spendthrift clause can often be construed as not intended to exclude the beneficiary's dependents, that is neither the rationale nor the limit of this exception to the general effect (§ 58, Comment *d*) of spendthrift protection. On public-policy grounds, the beneficiary should not be permitted to enjoy a beneficial interest in a trust while neglecting the support of dependents. The resulting advantage over other creditors (compare § 58, Comment *d*) is also based on policy considerations. . . . .

The right to benefits under the spendthrift interest, however, cannot be anticipated by execution sale, even in the case of a future interest. Nor can the support claimant assign to others the rights he or she acquires by attachment.

The beneficiary's interest may be attached through an appropriate proceeding in which the court has equitable discretion to determine whether all or only a portion of the trust distributions should be allocated to the support claimant, taking account of the beneficiary's actual need for some part of the distributions. Compare § 56, Comment *e*. The exception to the spendthrift protection is not measured by the amount of payments called for by a support order; the result is as if the trust had been created for the benefit of the dependents as well as the beneficiary. . . . .

Comment on Clause (b):

c. Debts incurred for beneficiary's necessities. The interest of a beneficiary of a spendthrift trust can be reached to satisfy an enforceable claim by one, such as a physician or grocer, who renders necessary services or furnishes necessary supplies to the beneficiary. To the extent the person's claim is excessive in amount, however, or if the person has acted officiously, the claim cannot be enforced against the spendthrift interest.

Failure to give enforcement to appropriate claims of this type would tend to undermine the beneficiary's ability to obtain necessary goods and assistance; and a refusal to enforce such claims is not essential to a settlor's purpose of protecting the beneficiary.

d. Debts incurred to protect beneficiary's interest. The interest of a beneficiary in a spendthrift trust can be reached to satisfy an enforceable claim for services rendered or materials furnished to the beneficiary for the purpose of preserving his or her beneficial interest. Also, one who has an enforceable claim against the beneficiary for goods and services that have increased the value of the beneficiary's interest can reach that interest to the extent of the increased value of the interest.

The beneficiary in these cases would be unjustly enriched if the claimant were prevented from reaching the beneficial interest; and a beneficiary of modest means would find the spendthrift restraint an obstacle to obtaining services essential to the protection or enforcement of his or her intended rights under the trust. (These cases are to be distinguished from obligations properly incurred by the *trustee*, or for which the trust estate would otherwise be unjustly enriched if it were permitted to retain benefits without paying for them. See § 88.) . . . .

§ 60. Transfer or Attachment of Discretionary Interests

Subject to the rules stated in §§ 58 and 59 (on spendthrift trusts), if the terms of a trust provide for a beneficiary to receive

distributions in the trustee's discretion, a transferee or creditor of the beneficiary is entitled to receive or attach any distributions the trustee makes or is required to make in the exercise of that discretion after the trustee has knowledge of the transfer or attachment. The amounts a creditor can reach may be limited to provide for the beneficiary's needs (Comment *c*), or the amounts may be increased where the beneficiary either is the settlor (Comment *f*) or holds the discretionary power to determine his or her own distributions (Comment *g*).

Comment:

a. Scope of the rule. The rule of this section allows a beneficiary's assignee to receive discretionary distributions to which the beneficiary would otherwise be entitled, and allows creditors of the beneficiary to attach his or her discretionary interest. The rule does not apply if the beneficiary's interest is subject to a valid spendthrift restraint under the rules of § 58 unless the situation falls within an exception under § 59.

This section recognizes special rules for discretionary interests retained by a settlor (compare § 58(2)) and for trusts in which the beneficiary, as trustee or otherwise, holds the discretionary authority to determine his or her own distributions (compare § 58, Comment *c*). These rules (in Comments *f* and *g*, respectively) expand the amount such a beneficiary's creditors may reach.

The rules stated in this section and its commentary apply to whatever extent a beneficiary's interest is discretionary. Thus, if the beneficiary is entitled to all of the trust's net income but only to principal in the trustee's discretion, the section applies to the provision for invasion of principal but not to the income interest. Also, the section prevents the trustee not only from making payments to the beneficiary but also from making "distributions" by applying funds directly for the beneficiary's benefit contrary to the rights of the transferee or creditor. (On the latter, see especially Comment *c*.)

"Discretionary interests" for purposes of this section include those encompassed by § 50 (see especially § 50, Comment *a*). Thus, this section applies where trustees are granted discretionary authority over benefits, regardless of whether the trust terms provide simply for the beneficiary's support, provide other or additional standards, or express no standards to limit or guide the trustee's exercise of discretion. For purposes of this section, however, unlike § 50 (see § 50, Comment *a*), discretionary interests also include powers by which beneficiaries who are not trustees may determine their own benefits pursuant to any form of standards, but which are not equivalent to ownership under § 58, Comment *c*. Thus, Comment *g* deals with nonfiduciary as well as fiduciary powers under which beneficiaries may distribute trust funds to themselves subject to some expressed or implied standard, often the "ascertainable" or "objective" standards dictated by Internal Revenue Code § 2041 or cases under id. § 2038.

b. Application to transferees. In the absence of a valid restraint on voluntary alienation, the beneficiary of a discretionary interest can properly assign that interest to another. The assignee, however, acquires only what the beneficiary had. Thus, if the interest is for the designated beneficiary's lifetime, the assignee takes a life interest *pur autre vie*—that is, for the life of the assigning beneficiary. (See Chapter 11, Introductory Note.) Standards governing the trustee's exercise of discretion still refer to the assigning beneficiary and his or her circumstances. Thus, to the extent the trustee may refuse or limit payments to or for the beneficiary, the trustee may refuse or limit payments to the assignee.

Whether or not the transferee could compel the trustee to make distributions (see Comments *e*–*e(2)*), if the trustee with knowledge of the assignment does make discretionary distributions they must be made to the transferee and not to the beneficiary-assignor. A trustee who knows of an assignment and nevertheless distributes trust funds to the original beneficiary is personally liable to the transferee in the absence of a valid spendthrift (§ 58) or complete forfeiture (§ 57) provision. (On the duty of trustees not to misdeliver trust funds, and to honor the rights of transferees of beneficial interests, see generally § 76 and § 48, Comment *a*.)

Illustrations:

1. S devises property to T in trust to pay to B such amounts of income or principal as T deems appropriate, and on B's death to distribute the remaining trust estate to R or R's issue. The trust does not restrain alienation by its beneficiaries. B transfers his interest in the trust to his daughter, D, and informs T of his assignment. T decides to make distributions pursuant to its discretionary authority. The distributions are to be made to D and cannot be properly be made to B.

2. The facts are the same as in Illustration 1, except that the assignment is made to A. T, although aware of the assignment, applies trust funds for the benefit of B. T is personally liable to A for this improper application of trust funds.

c. *Rights of creditors.* In the absence of a valid restraint on involuntary alienation (under § 58 or a statute), the creditors of the beneficiary of a discretionary interest may attach that interest and may subject it to the satisfaction of enforceable claims by appropriate process as described in § 56, Comment *e*. The interest, however, is not subject to execution sale. Furthermore, if an expressed or implied purpose of the discretionary interest is to provide for the beneficiary's support, health care, or education, in establishing the portion of each distribution allocated to the payment of claims the court is to take account of the beneficiary's actual needs in maintaining a reasonable level of support, care, and education. (Compare the court's equitable discretion in the spendthrift-trust exception in § 59, Comment *b*, and more generally in § 56, Comment *e*. Also contrast the generous station-in-life standard typical of discretionary "support" provisions, § 50, Comment *d*, and the flexibility a trustee usually has in considering a beneficiary's other resources, § 50, Comment *e*, neither of which is appropriate here.)

If the trustee has been served with process in a proceeding by a creditor to reach the beneficiary's interest, the trustee is personally liable to the creditor for any amount paid to or applied for the benefit of the beneficiary in disregard of the rights of the creditor, in the absence of a valid spendthrift provision (§ 58) applicable to the creditor (see § 59). (Compare the protective provision in Illustration 3, below; but contrast an improper payment to the beneficiary following *complete* forfeiture (§ 57), which renders the trustee liable not to the creditor but to other, adversely affected trust beneficiaries.)

Illustration:

3. S's will leaves property to T in trust to pay all of the income and as much principal as T deems appropriate to or for the benefit of B, with remainder upon her death to R or R's issue. The trust contains a "protective" forfeiture provision, as described in § 57, Comment *c*, thus

providing that upon forfeiture of the original provisions for B the trustee has "absolute" discretion (see § 50, Comment *c*) to make payments to B or to others. C, holding a judgment claim that cannot be satisfied from B's other property, obtains a court order attaching her discretionary interest under the protective provision of the trust. By reason of the attachment, T is liable for any distributions it makes under this provision to B in disregard of C's rights (described supra).

d. Discretionary trust for a class or group of beneficiaries. Sometimes a trust is created for the members of a class or group of persons, with the trustee having discretion whether and in what amounts to make payments to them. (See also the protective provision above in Illustration 3.) In such a case, a trustee who knows of the assignment of a particular beneficiary's interest, or who has been served with process in a proceeding by a creditor to reach that interest, is personally liable for any amounts paid to or applied for the benefit of that beneficiary in disregard of the rights of a transferee or creditor.

Illustration:

4. S's will left property to T in trust to pay or apply such amounts of the income or principal to or for the benefit of any one or more of the group consisting of B, his wife, and his issue as the trustee deems appropriate, and on the death of the survivor of B and his wife to distribute the trust estate to B's then living issue. C, a judgment creditor who is unable to satisfy the claim from other property of B, attaches his interest in the trust. T will be personally liable for any amounts distributed to B or applied for his benefit in disregard of C's rights (Comment *c*) under the attachment.

Sometimes a trustee is directed or authorized to make payments to a designated beneficiary for the benefit of the beneficiary and his or her family. Such a beneficiary's right to receive distributions can be reached by creditors, whose allocations in satisfaction of their claims are to be determined by the court in its equitable discretion (Comment *c*), having due regard for the actual needs of the beneficiary and relevant family members. (Compare § 50, Comment *d*, on the inclusion of family members within a support standard applicable to a designated beneficiary. . . . .

e. Can discretionary distributions be compelled by beneficiary's transferee or creditors? A transferee or creditor of a trust beneficiary cannot compel the trustee to make discretionary distributions if the beneficiary personally could not do so. It is rare, however, that the beneficiary's circumstances, the terms of the discretionary power, and the purposes of the trust leave the beneficiary so powerless. The exercise or nonexercise of fiduciary discretion is always subject to judicial review to prevent abuse. What might constitute an abuse, however, is not only affected by the extent of the trustee's discretion, standards applicable to its exercise, and purposes of the trust, but also by the beneficiary's circumstances and the effect discretionary decisions will have on the discretionary beneficiary and on others in relation to the fulfillment of trust purposes. See generally § 50 and its commentary, especially Comment *d(1)*.

The rights of a discretionary beneficiary's assignee or creditor are also entitled to judicial protection from abuse of discretion by the trustee. On the other hand, a trustee's refusal to make distributions might not constitute an abuse as against an assignee or creditor even when, under the standards applicable to the power, a decision to refuse distributions to the beneficiary might have constituted an abuse in the absence of the assignment or attachment. This is because the extent to which the designated beneficiary might actually benefit from a distribution is relevant to the justification and reasonableness of the trustee's decision in relation to the settlor's purposes and the effects on other beneficiaries. See § 50, Comments *d–d(4)*, *e–e(3)*, and *g*. Thus, the balancing process typical of discretionary issues becomes, in this context, significantly weighted against creditors, and sometimes against a beneficiary's voluntary assignees.

Illustration:

5. F devised property to T in (nonspendthrift) trust to pay "such amounts of income or principal as T may deem appropriate to or for the support and welfare of my son, B," and to distribute the trust estate upon B's death to his issue. B's interest has been attached by several of his creditors, one of whom has a very large property and personal-injury judgment against B resulting from an automobile accident. T has decided that, despite the support standard in the terms of the discretion, the limited benefit B would receive from trust distributions over the years (in excess of any amounts reserved for him under the attachment order, Comment *c*) would not justify the significant impairment of the intended remainder interest of S's grandchildren. Absent other factors that would make this an unreasonable exercise of T's judgment, this decision is not an abuse of discretion. Thus, the creditors cannot compel distributions by T.

In some attachment situations an indebted beneficiary's circumstances will be neither hopeless nor dire, so that it may be reasonable for the trustee to assist the beneficiary by making discretionary distributions. Faced with the prospect of providing much less than the settlor's intended level of benefits, even if creditors could not compel distributions, the trustee might be justified in making distributions that would benefit creditors, as a permissible exercise of discretion. In some circumstances, however, a court might conclude that an abuse of discretion would result from withholding or severely limiting distributions that would normally be called for under the standards prescribed by the settlor, thereby allowing creditors to compel distributions. Furthermore, in many cases a trustee might properly make distributions pursuant to an arrangement with the attaching creditor(s) that would serve the beneficiary's interests in a manner consistent with the trustee's duty of impartiality, the terms of the discretionary power, and the more general purposes of the settlor. (See, e.g., § 56, Illustration 1, involving in part a power to invade principal.)

e(1). Special claimants. A creditor who has provided services or materials either for the protection of the beneficiary's interest in the trust or necessary for the beneficiary's support or care (cf. § 59(b)) should be able to compel a trustee to make a distribution for those goods or services when it would be an abuse of discretion for the trustee not to do so.

Similarly, a creditor seeking to enforce a support right or judgment against the trust beneficiary (cf. § 59(a)) may be able to compel the trustee to make a distribution on the ground that a refusal to do so would constitute an abuse of discretion. A beneficiary's right to distributions for "support" usually includes amounts appropriate to the support of certain dependents (see § 50, Comment *d*).

The general policy favoring creditors of these types is properly to be taken into account in this context.

Illustration:

6. The facts are the same as those in Illustration 5, except that the attaching creditors are B's minor children of his prior marriage. B is under court order to support the children but has failed to do so, and the children have exhausted other resources of B that are not exempt. If T refuses to make distributions that would be reasonably appropriate to the support standard, the court will order it to do so.

e(2). Transferees. The identity of a beneficiary's assignee and the purpose of a voluntary assignment may be such as to make it reasonable, within the settlor's objectives, for the trustee to make distributions, all of which would go to the assignee (Comment *b*). See Illustration 7, and compare Illustration 1 above.

Illustration:

7. The facts are the same as those in Illustration 5 except that, instead of attachment by creditors, B gratuitously assigns two-thirds of his interest to his children, all of whom are adults. It would be within T's reasonable discretion to make distributions, which would go one-third to B and the rest to the children, who are remainder beneficiaries of the trust and would share equally under the terms of the assignment.

If the terms of the trust in Illustration 7 prohibit T from considering B's other resources (see § 50, Comment *e*) in determining the amounts to be distributed for B's support (§ 50, Comment *d*), so that B could compel T to make some minimum amount of payments for his support, the children also should be able to compel those distributions if the payments to them pursuant to the objective standard for their father would not undermine a purpose of the trust. A conflict with a trust purpose would be unlikely where B chooses mainly to use his own resources for his support and to allow some trust payments to go instead to his children—a situation that might well produce greater income-tax advantages to the beneficiary-family than a gift of comparable value from B's own property.

f. Where discretionary beneficiary is settlor. Where the trustee of an irrevocable trust has discretionary authority to pay to the settlor or apply for the settlor's benefit as much of the income or principal as the trustee may determine appropriate, creditors of the settlor can reach the maximum amount the trustee, in the proper exercise of fiduciary discretion, could pay to or apply for the benefit of the settlor. Where the beneficiary is the settlor of only a portion of the trust, the amount the creditor can reach under this rule is limited to that portion of the trust estate.

The special rule of this Comment normally does not apply to the settlor-beneficiary's transferees. A purchaser who is entitled to restitution based on fraud or mistake, or the like, however, is a creditor of the beneficiary and may thus attach the settlor-beneficiary's interest for the satisfaction of that claim.

On whether and to what extent a beneficiary is the settlor of a trust, see § 58, Comment *f*.

Illustration:

8. S irrevocably transfers property to T in trust to pay the income, and principal as T deems necessary, to B for life, remainder to R for R's issue; but the trust terms further state: "provided, however, that at any time, in its absolute discretion, T may pay or apply any amounts of income or principal it deems appropriate to or for S to provide

for her comfortable support and care." Although S's transfer was not in fraud of creditors, and regardless of whether the terms of the trust include a spendthrift clause, S's creditors may attach her interest and thereby obtain the right to receive from time to time the maximum amount T can properly distribute to S in accordance with the rules and principles of § 50 and its commentary. (The court's equitable discretion to reserve amounts for a beneficiary's needs under Comment *c* does not apply to the settlor.)

g. Where beneficiary holds discretionary power. Sometimes a beneficiary is trustee of the discretionary trust, with authority to determine his or her own benefits. In such a case, a rule similar to that of Comment *f* applies, with creditors able to reach from time to time the maximum amount the trustee-beneficiary can properly take. As in other nonsettlor-beneficiary situations, the court may reserve a portion of that amount for the beneficiary's actual needs for reasonable support, health care, and education (Comment *c*). The beneficiary's rights and authority represent a limited form of ownership equivalence analogous to certain general powers under the rule of § 56, Comment *b*; thus the rule of this Comment is similarly unaffected by a purported spendthrift restraint (see § 58, Comment *b*).

The special rule of this Comment also applies to the discretionary right of a beneficiary who is not a trustee but is given power to demand trust distributions pursuant to an expressed or implied standard, whether or not the standard is an objective one (e.g., "support"). See Comment *a*.

The rule does not apply, however, if the discretionary power is held jointly with another person who, in exercising the discretionary authority, has fiduciary duties to other beneficiaries of the trust. Nor does this rule apply on behalf of *transferees* of the beneficiary's interest, although a purchaser who is entitled to restitution based on fraud or mistake, or the like, is a creditor of the beneficiary and may attach the beneficiary's interest for satisfaction of that claim.

Illustrations:

9. S's will leaves his residuary estate to his daughter D, as trustee, "to pay income or principal to or for the benefit of any one or more of D, her children, and their issue in such amounts, if any, as the trustee deems appropriate and desirable for the particular beneficiary's support, education, and care, taking account of the beneficiary's other resources if and to whatever extent the trustee deems appropriate." D's creditors may reach the maximum amount of trust funds that she may, without abuse of her discretion, distribute to herself for the authorized purposes (see generally § 50), without reduction for other resources available to her for those purposes, but subject to a possible reservation the court may make for D's actual support needs.

10. The facts are the same as in Illustration 9, except that T serves as co-trustee with D, and they together hold the discretionary power to determine trust distributions. The special rule of this Comment does not apply. The creditors may still attach D's interest, absent a spendthrift restraint, but under the general rule of this section.

11. S transfers property to T, in trust, to pay the income to B and also "to pay B from the principal of the trust any additional amounts B may request from time to time for his health, education, support, and maintenance in his accustomed standard of living," remainder at B's death to R or R's issue. The rule of this Comment applies. Thus, in

addition to their right to reach B's income interest (or, in the case of a spendthrift trust, the income in his hands following distribution), B's creditors can attach his discretionary interest in the principal, measured by the maximum amount he could properly call for (cf. § 50) under the above-quoted standard. (This latter interest would not be protected by a spendthrift restraint. See last sentence of first paragraph of this Comment.)

The beneficiary may resign as trustee or otherwise release the discretionary power; but a creditor who has already attached the discretionary interest may nevertheless reach the same amount as if the beneficiary had continued to hold the power. The same result follows from a release of the power, or the discretionary interest, under circumstances that would constitute a transfer in fraud of creditors in the case of other transfers. Unlike the release of a power that is the full equivalent of ownership, however, the release of a beneficiary's discretionary power, or the prior failure to exercise the power for his or her own benefit, does not cause the beneficiary to become a partial settlor of the trust for purposes of Comment *f* or the rules of § 58, Comments *e* and *f*.

PART 5

MODIFICATION AND TERMINATION OF TRUSTS

CHAPTER 13

MODIFICATION AND TERMINATION OF TRUSTS

Introductory Note: This chapter deals with rules applicable to the termination and modification of trusts. It begins with termination pursuant to the original terms and plan of the trust, as described in § 61; that section covers generally routine situations and probably most trust terminations. (It is worth noting, however, that this section applies in the common-law context and that different issues—and different planning and drafting considerations—may arise with respect to trusts of indefinite duration in jurisdictions that have adopted legislation to abolish the rule against perpetuities.)

The next section, § 62, mainly recognizes and briefly illustrates the applicability to trusts of general doctrine dealing with remedies, most particularly reformation, for mistake or for the wrongdoing of others.

More challenging and important issues of trust law are examined in the rest of this chapter. These are issues that arise from efforts by parties to a trust to make or obtain changes in its terms or duration. Sections 63 and 64 deal with powers of revocation and amendment expressly or impliedly reserved to settlors and with powers of termination or modification conferred upon others—trustees, beneficiaries, and, increasingly, third parties. Section 63 reflects the expanded use (both in frequency and function) of inter vivos trusts, particularly the increase in those that are or may be revocable and may be planned with inadequate advice.

The qualified right of beneficiaries collectively to terminate a trust or alter its provisions is dealt with at length in § 65.

The next two sections deal with the authority of courts to intervene in cases involving unanticipated circumstances, modifying or allowing deviation from specific provisions of a trust in order to carry out its more fundamental purposes and to give effect to the probable or presumed wishes of the settlor. The "equitable deviation" doctrine of § 66 enables the court to protect the settlor's private or charitable objectives by adjusting, to unforeseen conditions, the means by which the objectives were originally to be accomplished. Under § 67, however, applicable only to charitable trusts and then only if the settlor has not provided otherwise, the cy pres doctrine allows the court to change the trust purpose itself when the settlor's designated purpose cannot reasonably be accomplished or can no longer reasonably be pursued as the sole purpose of the trust.

Section 68 allows a trustee to divide or combine trusts without court approval when this can be done without impairing the rights of any beneficiary.

Section 69 deals with termination (or the nonexistence) of a trust under the doctrine of merger.

This chapter does not specifically address powers of appointment in their traditional sense (a matter left to the Restatement of Property), although the exercise of such powers may extend or cut short the duration of a trust and normally changes its terms by adding beneficiaries or at least altering their rights.

Liberalized rules and their rationale. At various points throughout this chapter, traditional rules concerning revocation, termination, and modification are relaxed somewhat, or in some instances clarified, to facilitate the making of changes in the terms of trusts. This reflects both (i) modern trends in legislative policy and judicial decisions and (ii) practical considerations arising from other developments in or affecting estate planning. . . . . See also § 63, Comment *c(1)* ("Rationale") . . . . A number of practical considerations (below) suggest the desirability of the greater flexibility in this area of the trust law, and thus the desirability of the selective "liberalization" of rules stated in this chapter.

As life in the estate-planning world becomes increasingly complex, mainly with changing tax rules and concerns, which tend also to invite the use of longer-term trusts, the parties to trusts and the courts increasingly, and understandably, encounter instances of apparent oversight and human error. The desire, for tax and possibly other reasons, to use trusts of long or indefinite duration is reflected in the recent movement to abolish the rule against perpetuities . . .; and the problems resulting from changed circumstances and the risks of inadequacies in trust design and detail can be expected to be exacerbated by this trend.

Furthermore, problems of error and oversight appear to have increased as broader segments of the population have come to recognize the utility of trusts for an expanding variety of purposes, with many settlors relying on advice and implementation not only by less expert or independent members of the legal profession but also by nonlawyers. (Recently illustrative is the living trust that was found "valid," despite the preparer's "unauthorized practice of law," in Miller v. Miller, 139 Ohio App. 3d 512, 744 N.E.2d 778 (2000). . . . .

Still another set of reasons underlying the selective liberalization of the rules considered in this chapter is possibly more fundamental: the growing recognition that trusts should serve the beneficiaries' best interests (§ 27(2)); and also the growing recognition that, realistically, this greater flexibility is more likely to aid than to undermine settlor objectives (e.g., § 66, Comment *a* . . .).

§ 61. Completion of Period or Purpose for Which Trust Created

A trust will terminate in whole or in part upon the expiration of a period or the happening of an event as provided by the terms of the trust; in the absence of such a provision in the terms of the trust,

termination will occur in whole or in part when the purpose(s) of the trust or severable portion thereof are accomplished.

Comment:

a. Scope of section; cross-references. On the meaning of "terms of the trust," see § 4. (This expression and the rule of this section refer to valid trust provisions, so that a termination provision that violates a perpetuities rule would not, as written, control. See § 29, Comment *g*, and cf. § 29, Comment *h*.)

On the possibility of trusts of indefinite duration, with no time of termination as described in this section, see Introductory Note to this chapter . . . noting the abolition of the rule against perpetuities in a growing minority of states. . . . .

The apparent terms of a trust may be invalid (see, e.g., § 29(b) and (c)) or subject to reformation (§ 62); and the application of the rule of this section may be affected (resulting in early or delayed termination) by other rules set forth in this chapter.

On termination when the purposes of a private trust become unlawful or impossible to accomplish, see § 66, Comment *c*. On charitable trusts and the *cy pres* doctrine, see § 67.

b. Period may be stated or implied by terms of trust. In various words, trusts may be created to last for a definite period of years, or for the duration of one or more lives or periods of minority, or until the happening of a designated event. Otherwise a trust will terminate upon the fulfillment of its purpose(s).

Thus, a fairly typical trust may provide for the support of a designated beneficiary for life, with the trust instrument specifically stating that upon the life beneficiary's death the trust is to terminate and that the trust property is then to be distributed to one or more designated remainder beneficiaries. . . . .

On the other hand, the terms of a trust for such a purpose might fail to specify when the trust is to terminate, or when the property is to be distributed, but instead leave the settlor's intention to be inferred from the words and purposes of the trust. For example, if the settlor transfers property in trust for the support of a designated beneficiary for life and then for the benefit of another or others absolutely, the inference from the terms of the trust is that the settlor intended the trust to terminate on the life beneficiary's death even though that time of termination or distribution is not stated in specific language. Sometimes in a case of this type the inference to be drawn is not so readily recognizable and becomes a matter for interpretation.

Illustration:

2. H devised a portion of his estate to T "in trust to provide for the support and care of W during her lifetime, remainder in trust for our grandchild, G." At the time of W's death, G is an adult. The stated purpose of the trust having been completed, with no further purpose indicated or shown, the trust terminates at W's death and the property is to be distributed to G.

In this Illustration, if G had been a minor at the time of W's death, in the absence of other evidence it would be appropriate, from the "in trust for" language, to infer that the trust should continue for the remaining period of G's minority, with termination thereafter. . . . .

c. *Partial termination.* The terms of a trust may provide that, at the expiration of a certain period or on the happening of a certain event, the trust shall terminate as to part of the trust property but shall continue as to the rest of the property. Thus, it may be provided that, when the first of two designated beneficiaries reaches a specified age, a certain sum or portion of the trust estate shall be distributed to that beneficiary, with the remaining property to continue in trust for the other beneficiary. Similarly, a trust in which no time of termination or distribution is provided will terminate, in whole or in part, upon the fulfillment of the purpose(s) of the trust or of a separate and independent portion thereof.

§ 62. Rescission and Reformation

A trust may be rescinded or reformed upon the same grounds as those upon which a transfer of property not in trust may be rescinded or reformed.

Comment:

a. *Grounds for rescission or reformation; scope of section.* Where no consideration is involved in the creation of a trust, it can be rescinded or reformed upon the same grounds, such as fraud, duress, undue influence, or mistake, as those upon which a gratuitous transfer of property not in trust can be rescinded or reformed. Where consideration is involved in the creation of a trust, the rules governing transfers for value and contracts are applicable. The law governing the rescission or reformation of a transfer inter vivos applies to declarations of trust as well as to inter vivos transfers in trust. The law governing the validity and reformation of testamentary dispositions applies to testamentary trusts. On the foregoing matters generally, and equitable limitations thereon, see § 12. The law more broadly governing these various matters is not within the scope of this Restatement. . . . .

On standards of capacity for the creation of various types of trusts and the effects of incapacity, see § 11.

b. *Clarification and correction of terms of trust.* On resolving uncertainties of meaning where the terms of a donative document are ambiguous, see Restatement Third, Property (Wills and Other Donative Transfers) §§ 11.1–11.3.

Even if the will or other instrument creating a donative testamentary or inter vivos trust is unambiguous, the terms of the trust may be reformed by the court to conform the text to the intention of the settlor if the following are established by clear and convincing evidence: (1) that a mistake of fact or law, whether in expression or inducement, affected the specific terms of the document; and (2) what the settlor's intention was. Restatement Third, Property (Wills and Other Donative Transfers) § 12.1 (noting that direct evidence of intention contradicting the plain meaning of the text, as well as other evidence of intention, may be considered).

Illustration:

1. S established a testamentary trust for the benefit of his brother and sister and their families. The language of S's will expressly states that the trust is to terminate and be distributed on the death of S's sister. Clear and convincing evidence establishes that S had intended

to provide for the trust to terminate on the death of the survivor of his brother and sister and that the erroneous time of termination stated in the will was the result of a "scrivener's error" by S's lawyer. The termination provision of the trust will be reformed to reflect S's intention.

c. *Cross-reference: modification for tax objectives.* On the power of a court to modify a donative document, in a manner that does not violate the probable intention of the settlor or other donor, in order to achieve the donor's tax objectives, see Restatement Third, Property (Wills and Other Donative Transfers) § 12.2.

§ 63. Power of Settlor to Revoke or Modify

(1) The settlor of an inter vivos trust has power to revoke or modify the trust to the extent the terms of the trust (§ 4) so provide.

(2) If the settlor has failed expressly to provide whether the trust is subject to a retained power of revocation or amendment, the question is one of interpretation. (See presumptions in Comment *c*.)

(3) Absent contrary provision in the terms of the trust, the settlor's power to revoke or modify the trust can be exercised in any way that provides clear and convincing evidence of the settlor's intention to do so.

General Comment:

a. *Scope of section; cross-references.* The rule of this section applies whether the inter vivos trust was created by the settlor's transfer of property to another as trustee or by a declaration of trust under which the settlor holds the property as trustee.

That revocable trusts are not "testamentary" for purposes of formalities and procedure see § 25. Nevertheless, for purposes of serious substantive policy (e.g., spousal elective share, rights of creditors), the trust property is generally to be treated in the same manner as if it were still owned by the settlor. See § 25(2) and Comments *d* and *e* to § 25. Also compare § 26 (Totten trusts).

The harmless-error rule of Restatement Third, Property (Wills and Other Donative Transfers) § 3.3, applies to revocation and amendment of trusts (and notably to matters discussed hereafter in Comments *h* and *i*). Doctrines set forth in Restatement Third, Property (Wills and Other Donative Transfers), Chapters 10, 11, and 12, apply to the interpretation, construction, reformation, and modification of trusts.

Comment on Subsections (1) and (2):

b. *The "terms of the trust."* The phrase "terms of the trust" means the settlor's intention concerning the trust provisions, manifested in a manner that admits of its proof in judicial proceedings. See § 4.

If the terms of the trust are otherwise expressed in writing but fail to provide whether or to what extent the settlor reserves the power to revoke or modify the trust, the writing is incomplete and its meaning uncertain. Accordingly, the writing does not prevent the admission of extrinsic evidence to prove the settlor's intention to either retain or relinquish power to revoke or amend the trust, or the admission of evidence to prove an intent to limit any such power. Cf. § 21(2) (on the parol-evidence rule and the intention to create a trust). On resolving ambiguities generally, see Restatement Third, Property (Wills and Other Donative Transfers) §§ 11.1–11.3.

c. Presumptions regarding revocability. Where the settlor has failed expressly to provide whether a trust is subject to revocation or amendment, if the settlor has retained no interest in the trust (other than by resulting trust, § 8), it is rebuttably presumed that the settlor has no power to revoke or amend the trust. If, however, the settlor has failed expressly to provide whether the trust is revocable or amendable but has retained an interest in the trust (other than by resulting trust), the presumption is that the trust is revocable and amendable by the settlor. For these purposes, a power of appointment retained by the settlor (including a power of withdrawal, even if subject to a standard) is a retained interest, although the fact that a power of appointment is limited (e.g., a testamentary or special power) weakens, but does not eliminate, the rebuttable presumption that the settlor also retains broader authority.

c(1). Rationale. The differing presumptions concerning settlors' unstated intentions, and thus concerning the rebuttably implied terms of trusts, on the question of revocability reflect different principles or considerations applicable to the different situations just mentioned.

On the one hand, when a trust is comparable to an outright gift, with the settlor reserving no beneficial interests or nonfiduciary powers, the presumption of irrevocability reflects the traditional general rule of the law of inter vivos gifts. (Cf. Restatement Third, Property (Wills and Other Donative Transfers) § 6.2, Comment *b*; on exceptions and possible exceptions for gifts causa mortis and for wedding presents and gifts in anticipation of marriage, see Restatement Third, Property (Wills and Other Donative Transfers) § 6.2, Comments *l* and *m*.) This presumption that such a trust is irrevocable and unamendable may fairly reflect the understanding and expectation of a settlor whose trust provides for the immediate or exclusive benefit of others, and this presumption also supports the intended tax objectives of many trusts of this general type.

On the other hand, in cases of more complicated trusts involving retained interests in settlors, a presumption of revocability is justified by the risk of confusion and doubts about a settlor's understanding, uncertainties that are aggravated by the patently deficient performance of counsel in failing expressly to deal with the obviously important matter of revocability. (On the increasingly diverse uses and sources of living trusts, compare the next to last paragraph of the Introductory Note to this chapter. . . . .) In this context, an implied power to revoke also tends to protect the settlor from unanticipated, adverse tax consequences, without jeopardizing tax objectives that are likely in other types of inter vivos trusts (above). In addition, the presumption of revocability reflects a principle that, when this type of uncertainty in a donative disposition becomes important, reasonable doubt generally should be resolved in favor of the settlor. . . . .

Illustrations:

1. S transfers property to T in trust for B's support and education until B attains age 23, at which time the trust property is to be distributed outright to B or, if B dies before reaching age 23, to B's then living issue. The language of the trust makes no mention of powers of amendment or revocation, and there is no evidence of S's intention on the matter. S has no power to amend or revoke the trust. (It does not matter that S here has a reversionary interest by operation of law—i.e.,

that there would be a resulting trust—in the event of B's death without issue before age 23.)

2. S transfers property to T, in trust, to pay the income to S for life, plus such amounts of principal as T deems necessary for S's support, remainder on S's death to R or R's issue. The language of the trust makes no mention of powers of amendment or revocation, and there is no evidence of S's intention on the matter. S has, by implication, the power to revoke (and amend) the trust.

3. The facts are the same as in Illustration 2, except that evidence shows that S's attorney believed, and told S, that the trust was irrevocable. This showing is sufficient to rebut the presumption of revocability and to resolve the uncertainty concerning the intended terms of the trust.

Similarly, the result of Illustration 2 would be changed, and the presumption of revocability rebutted, if the only evidence of intent on the issue of revocability showed that S had filed a gift-tax return (such a return not being required in the case of a revocable trust). On the other hand, the *failure* of S to file a gift-tax return in Illustration 1 would not suffice to overcome the presumption of irrevocability, because failure to file even a required gift-tax return is too common to be revealing of S's intention or understanding of the trust. In that Illustration, however, proof that counsel had advised S that the trust was revocable would serve to rebut the presumption of irrevocability.

In general, any circumstances or competent testimony that sheds light on the settlor's intention may properly tend to rebut or reinforce the presumption applicable to a particular type of case. Thus, for example, in a case involving a trust of which the settlor is a beneficiary, the nature of other interests reserved by a settlor, or particularly the fact that a trust was otherwise designed to qualify for a charitable deduction, or to remove property from the settlor's estate for tax purposes, may be influential. Compare Restatement Third, Property (Wills and Other Donative Transfers) § 6.2, Comment *zz,* on language and circumstances that may negate a gift causa mortis.

d. Reformation for omission or mistake. If an intended provision is omitted or an unintended provision is included in the terms of the trust dealing with the settlor's power to amend or revoke, and if that omission or inclusion resulted from a mistake, the terms of the trust may be reformed to properly reflect the settlor's intention. See § 62.

If, for example, the settlor intended the terms of the trust to provide that the trust is irrevocable and unamendable, or to limit the settlor's power with respect to revocation or amendment in some manner, but by mistake that provision was omitted from the terms of the trust, the trust instrument may be reformed to conform to the settlor's intention. See § 62, Comment *b*. Similarly, if a provision is included in the terms of the trust expressly declaring it to be irrevocable and unamendable, and that provision was the result of a mistake, the settlor can have the instrument reformed. Section 62, Comment *b* (requiring, in this latter situation, there being no ambiguity in the instrument, clear and convincing proof of both the mistake and the settlor's intent).

e. Partial revocation. The settlor may reserve a power "to revoke the trust as to all or any part" of the property, or a power to revoke only as to a stated portion of the trust property. A power simply to revoke the trust, however, is interpreted as including also the power to revoke the trust in part, thus allowing withdrawal of some rather than all of the property from the trust, if that is all the settlor wishes to do.

f. *Repeated exercise of power.* If the settlor holding a power of revocation exercises the power by withdrawing a part of the trust property, the power is not thereby exhausted but may be exercised from time to time with respect to property then remaining in the trust, unless the terms of the trust or of the exercise of the power provide otherwise.

Similarly, a settlor's exercise of a power of amendment does not prevent its repeated exercise to make further amendments, unless the terms of the power or its exercise provide otherwise.

g. *Power either to "revoke" or to "amend" as including the other.* If the settlor reserves a power to *modify* (or "amend") the trust, it is a question of interpretation to be determined in view of the language used and all of the circumstances whether or to what extent the power is subject to restrictions. If the power to modify is subject to no restrictions, it includes a power to revoke the trust.

A power to *revoke* the trust includes the power to modify the terms of the trust, and a power to revoke only a portion of the trust includes the power to modify that portion. It is not necessary for the settlor first to revoke the trust (or part thereof) and then to create a new one. If, however, the effect of the modification is to significantly increase the burdens or risks of the trusteeship in a manner not reasonably anticipated by the trustee, this provides a ground for the trustee's resignation and is a circumstance to be taken into account in determining any conditions upon which the resignation is to become effective (see § 36, Comment *c*).

Comment on Subsection (3):

h. *Form of exercise when no method is specified.* If the settlor reserves the power to revoke or modify the trust but does not specify the manner or form in which the power is to be exercised, the power can be exercised in any way that provides clear and convincing evidence of the settlor's intention to do so. Thus, the power can be exercised by a will or codicil that is executed after the creation of the trust and remains unrevoked at the settlor's death, and that refers expressly to the trust or the power or that otherwise clearly manifests the settlor-testator's intent to exercise the power.

Similarly, a definitive manifestation by the settlor during life of his or her intention that the trust is thereby revoked is sufficient. If, for example, the settlor writes a letter to the trustee stating that the trust is revoked and mails the letter but dies before it is received by the trustee, the revocation is effective and the interests of the beneficiaries in the trust property are extinguished. (Although the settlor has revoked the trust, the trustee incurs no liability for acts done in accordance with the terms of the trust before receiving information of the revocation.)

Furthermore, a power of revocation or amendment may be exercised by the settlor's execution and delivery to the trustee of a new trust instrument expressing the present intention to establish a trust different from that prescribed by the original terms of the trust.

i. *Where method of revocation or amendment specified.* If the terms of the trust reserve to the settlor a power to revoke or amend the trust *exclusively* by a particular procedure, the settlor can exercise the power only by substantial compliance with the method prescribed. Thus, if a settlor reserves the power to revoke the trust "only by a notice in writing delivered to the trustee," revocation requires the delivery of such a notice to the trustee. It is sufficient delivery, however, if the notice is mailed to the trustee by the settlor even though it is not received by the trustee until after the settlor's death.

Although the terms of the trust provide a method for the exercise of a power of revocation or amendment, if the terms do not make that method exclusive, this is not a "contrary provision" for purpose of Subsection (3). Thus, the settlor's power can be exercised *either* in the specified manner or by a method described in Comment *h*, above.

Compare § 62 on mistake; also compare, on mistake, Restatatement Third, Property (Wills and Other Donative Transfers) § 12.1. And that the harmless-error rule of id. § 3.3 applies to the revocation and amendment (as well as the creation) of a "will substitute," such as a revocable trust, see id. § 7.2, Comment *d*.

j. Power to revoke or modify with another's consent. If the settlor reserves a power to revoke or modify the trust with the consent of one or more others, such as the trustee, one or more of the beneficiaries, or a third party, the power normally cannot be exercised without that consent. Under some circumstances, however, depending on the terms of the provision requiring the consent, a court may intervene if a person whose concurrence is required improperly withholds (or grants) the consent. For example, the person might have acted in bad faith or from an improper motive.

Furthermore, as in other matters, the discretionary decision of a trustee to consent or not is subject to judicial control if and as necessary to prevent an abuse of the discretion. What may constitute an abuse in a case of this type depends on whether a standard is provided or a purpose can be discerned against which the reasonableness of the trustee's judgment can be measured, and if not whether the trustee has acted in bad faith or from an improper motive. Cf. § 64, and more generally see §§ 87 and 50.

Other General Comment:

k. Trust with multiple settlors. If a revocable trust has more than one settlor, unless the terms of the trust provide otherwise, each settlor ordinarily (but see exceptions below) may revoke or amend the trust with regard to that portion of the trust property attributable to the settlor's contribution.

Illustration:

4. Both H and W transfer property to T, in trust, for the benefit of themselves and the survivor of them, remainder thereafter to their issue. The trust instrument states merely that the trust "may be revoked or amended by a signed writing delivered to the trustee." While H and W are both alive, they may together revoke or amend the trust in whole or in part as they may agree; but either acting alone may revoke or amend only with respect to the part of the trust traceable to his or her contributions. Following the death of one of them, the trust becomes irrevocable and unamendable as to the portion of the trust traceable to the decedent's contributions, with the survivor having power to revoke or amend with respect to the rest of the trust—i.e., only with respect to the part traceable to the survivor's contributions. (If a different result is intended, the settlors should expressly so provide; but even if they have failed to do so, the vague language quoted above concerning revocation and amendment may be clarified by extrinsic evidence showing the intended terms of the trust on this matter.)

One exception to this general principle applies when the references in the trust provisions to the "settlor," in light of the circumstances of the instrument's execution and of the trust's funding, are interpreted as referring to a particular person rather than to the other person(s) who contributed to the funding of the trust.

Illustration:

5. Several years after his marriage, X established a revocable trust for the benefit of himself and his family, funding it with a modest amount of assets and referring to himself in the instrument as the "Settlor." A few months later, his parents donated a substantial amount of securities to the trust and periodically thereafter made cash contributions to it. Although, technically, the parents are also settlors of the trust, absent evidence to the contrary they have no power of revocation, but X instead has the power not only to revoke the portion of the trust traceable to his contributions but also the power to withdraw (even if not quite accurately referred to as a power to revoke), and the power to amend, the portions of the trust traceable to the contributions made by his parents.

The other exception to the earlier generalization applies to a trust established by spouses and consisting of their community property. In the absence of a contrary provision in the terms of the trust, the trust may be *amended* only by the joint action of both spouses during their joint lifetime; but it may be *revoked* by either spouse acting alone, thereby terminating the trust and causing the property to be restored to the spouses, free of trust, as their community property. This construction of the spouses' revocable living trust is consistent with the community-property character of the assets and is appropriate to preserve that character while the assets are held in the trust. The trust terms, of course, may make contrary provision; sometimes, for example, joint action is required for revocation as well as amendment, with the community-property right of testation preserved by allowing each spouse a power of amendment (or appointment) over his or her community share of the trust with respect to the interests taking effect following his or her death.

l. *Settlor under legal incapacity.* Where a settlor who has retained the power to revoke or amend a trust becomes legally incompetent, the power may be exercised by an agent under a durable power of attorney if and to the extent expressly authorized by the terms of the durable power or by the terms of the trust. The agent in such a case acts in a fiduciary capacity and, except as the settlor-principal specifies otherwise, for purposes similar to the substituted-judgment concept in conservatorship law.

Similarly, unless the trust terms provide otherwise, the settlor's power to revoke or amend a revocable trust may be exercised by a conservator, guardian, or other legal representative if and to the extent authorized by the appropriate court. (Even though a trust provision forbids such exercise by the settlor's legal representative, the court may direct withdrawal of trust funds as needed for the benefit of the settlor and his or her family.)

On substituted judgment and related matters, see generally § 11, Comment *f*. . . .

§ 64. Termination or Modification by Trustee, Beneficiary, or Third Party

(1) Except as provided in §§ 65 and 68, the trustee or beneficiaries of a trust have only such power to terminate the trust or to change its terms as is granted by the terms of the trust.

(2) The terms of a trust may grant a third party a power with respect to termination or modification of the trust; such a third-party power is presumed to be held in a fiduciary capacity.

General Comment:

a. *Duties; fiduciary responsibility.* If the terms of a trust confer a power of termination or modification upon a trustee, beneficiary, or third party, the power must be exercised within any limitations, conditions, and other terms imposed by the terms of the trust.

It is a question of interpretation whether and to what extent the person to whom the power is granted is subject to fiduciary duties in exercising it. Also compare § 75.

Comment on Subsection (1):

b. *Trustee's power.* Unless otherwise provided by the terms of the trust, a power of termination or modification that runs with the office of trustee is held by the trustee in a fiduciary capacity, even in the absence of express standards by which the reasonableness of the trustee's judgment can be measured. On judicial review of a trustee's exercise of discretion generally, see §§ 87 and 50, and cf. § 63, Comment *j*.

c. *Power of beneficiary.* A power of termination or modification conferred upon a beneficiary may be fiduciary in character (cf. Comment *d*), or may be beneficial to the power holder (donee), or in the nature of a power of appointment (see § 46, Comment *c*; cf. § 48, Comments *a* and *c*); or it may be subject to fiduciary obligations in some respects and not in others.

Except so far as the terms of the trust are clear on the character of the power and any obligations of the beneficiary, these are (as noted in Comment *a*) matters of interpretation. As such, a determination of fiduciary or nonfiduciary character will depend on the scope, terms, and general nature and purpose of the power, the nature and extent of the donee's and others' beneficial interests, the donee's relationship to other beneficiaries, the general plan of the trust, and other relevant circumstances, ordinarily including other aspects of the settlor's overall estate plan.

Even if the power is nonfiduciary, the donee must respect any limitations or other terms of the power, and in some situations may also have a duty not to exercise it in a manner that is unnecessarily harmful or unfair to other beneficiaries.

Comment on Subsection (2):

d. *Third-party power.* In the absence of some contrary indication, and despite the broad terms and purposes of powers of termination or amendment sometimes granted to third parties . . ., such powers are normally fiduciary in character. This is true even if the extent of the third party's discretion (e.g., if the grant of authority is accompanied by such terms as "absolute" or "sole and uncontrolled") is such as to limit judicial intervention to situations in which the grantee acts in bad faith, from improper motives, or without regard to the purposes of the trust or power. Cf. § 87, § 50, Comment *c*, and § 75.

§ 65. Termination or Modification by Consent of Beneficiaries

(1) Except as stated in Subsection (2), if all of the beneficiaries of an irrevocable trust consent, they can compel the termination or modification of the trust.

(2) If termination or modification of the trust under Subsection (1) would be inconsistent with a material purpose of the trust, the beneficiaries cannot compel its termination or modification except with the consent of the settlor or, after the settlor's death, with authorization of the court if it determines that the reason(s) for termination or modification outweigh the material purpose.

General Comment:

a. *Scope, background, and general principles.* With the rule of this section *contrast* the rule of § 66, which depends upon a finding of unanticipated circumstances but does not require beneficiary consent.

The rule of this section applies to both testamentary trusts and irrevocable inter vivos trusts. It defines the conditions upon which beneficiaries may join together to modify a trust or to compel its termination, in whole or in part, although the period fixed by the terms of the trust for its duration (§ 61) has not expired.

For purposes of the rule of this section, separable and independent shares of a single trust are to be treated as separate trusts.

Although Subsection (2) is not a part of the English law, that subsection recognizes the prevalent American view under the so-called *Claflin* doctrine (Claflin v. Claflin, 149 Mass. 19, 20 N.E. 454 (1889)).

While the rule against perpetuities requires only the timely vesting of interests and does not directly limit the duration of trusts, the rule of Subsection (2) ceases to apply after the perpetuities period has expired, and the *Claflin* doctrine no longer restricts the beneficiaries' power to terminate or modify the trust under Subsection (1). See § 29, Comment *h*. . . . .

The consent of the settlor of an irrevocable trust cannot cure a lack of full beneficiary consent under Subsection (1). Nor does the objection of a settlor who is not also a beneficiary prevent termination or modification of the trust if the requirement of Subsection (1) is satisfied and there is no "material purpose" obstacle under Subsection (2). (Of course, a settlor's testimony would be relevant in a material-purpose inquiry.) Similarly, unless the trustee is also a beneficiary, termination or modification under the rule of this section does not require the consent of the trustee.

If the beneficiaries can compel termination or modification of a trust under this section, it is not necessary that they obtain a court decree directing or authorizing termination or establishing the modification. As a practical matter, however, the trustee is under a duty to assure that all requirements of the rule are satisfied before acting on a beneficiary plan for termination or modification. (On a trustee's right to petition the court for instructions, see § 71.)

If the trustee takes action, reasonably and in good faith, on the basis of the consent of the beneficiaries, but it turns out that the action was contrary to a material purpose of the trust or that consent was not properly obtained from or on behalf of all beneficiaries, the *consenting* beneficiaries may not hold the trustee liable for damages resulting from action taken by the trustee before becoming aware of the impropriety. When the trustee's action was not taken reasonably and in good faith, the court, in determining whether estoppel applies or the amount of damages recoverable, may consider the relative fault of the various parties and the nature of the trust purposes or other obstacle to the requested termination or modification. (In this commentary, as elsewhere in this Restatement, a reference simply to "consent" refers to a consent that was not improperly obtained, including by inadequacy of disclosure where disclosure is required.)

Comment on Subsection (1):

b. Requirement that all beneficiaries consent. The rule of Subsection (1) requires that consent be obtained from or on behalf of all potential beneficiaries, including those who lack capacity. This requirement of unanimous consent also includes, for example, beneficiaries who are relatively unlikely ever to receive distributions, those whose interests arise by operation of law (i.e., reversionary, or "resulting trust," interests), and persons who hold powers of appointment under the trust, as well as those who would take in default of the exercise of any but a presently exercisable general power (on which see § 74). See generally § 48, Comment *a*, defining trust beneficiary. Also included among those whose consent is required are successors in interest of prior beneficiaries, and the potential unborn (including after-adopted) or unascertainable beneficiaries so often provided for by class description, as in a seemingly simple trust designed to pay income to A for life and then to distribute the principal to A's descendants who are living at her death.

Illustrations:

1. S created an irrevocable inter vivos trust for his mother M for life, remainder to his daughter D if she survives M, and if she does not, remainder to S's friend F. Under traditional rules of construction (which would not impliedly require F to survive M), Subsection (1) is satisfied if M, D, and F all agree to a proposed termination or modification. Subsection (1) does not require S's consent (although his consent may be important if there would otherwise be a material-purpose obstacle under Subsection (2)).

2. The same trust as in Illustration 1, except that its terms also require that F be alive at M's death in order to take. Under common-law rules of construction applicable in this state (i.e., with no substituted gift to the issue of a deceased remainder beneficiary), there is now a reversionary interest in the trust, to take effect if both D and F predecease M. Therefore, Subsection (1) also requires the consent of S (as a reversionary *beneficiary* not as *settlor*), unless he has died before the time of the agreement, in which case the reversioner(s) whose consent would be required would be S's successor(s) in interest.

In cases more complicated than those in the foregoing Illustrations (and more typical of properly drawn, modern dispositions), the requirements of Subsection (1) are likely to be difficult to satisfy. The consent of potential beneficiaries who cannot consent for themselves, however, may be provided by guardians ad litem, by court appointed or other legally authorized representatives, or through representation by other beneficiaries under the doctrine of virtual representation. . . . .

As a practical matter, however, the necessary consents may not be obtainable in many situations. This is not only because some beneficiaries may dissent from a termination or modification plan but also because of fiduciary inhibitions on the part of those called upon to represent the interests of others. The technical and practical problems of representing others are particularly challenging whenever more is involved than mutually beneficial modification of administrative provisions.

Illustrations:

3. The terms of the trust provide for income to be distributed to L for life, remainder at his death to be distributed to his then living descendants. L's only descendants are his daughter, D, and his son, S (both young adults). L would like to receive increased distributions from the trust, and D and S have indicated that they would be happy to support a modification that would authorize the trustee to invade principal for L's benefit, which the present terms of the trust do not allow. The need to obtain consent on behalf of potential unborn remainder beneficiaries (possible issue of D or S who might take should D or S predecease L) presents the question whether a guardian ad litem, or S and D as virtual representatives (acting in an essentially "donative" frame of mind), could properly provide that consent because invasions of principal would impair the value of the remainder interests of absent beneficiaries, who receive nothing in return. (This is not to suggest that the cause is necessarily hopeless. . . . .)

4. The same facts as in Illustration 3, except that the desired trust amendment (again, suggested by L and supported by D and S) is one that would free the trust-investment program of a restriction imposed by the terms of the trust and that could be expected to be beneficial to all and particularly to the remainder beneficiaries. Obtaining consent on behalf of potential unborn remainder beneficiaries, either by guardian ad litem or virtual representation, does not appear difficult.

c. Required consent not obtained. Where consent of all beneficiaries cannot be obtained, the other beneficiaries cannot compel termination or modification under this section. Even in such a case, however, if the court is satisfied that the best interests of the beneficiaries as a whole would be served by a proposed termination or modification and if continuation of the trust is not required by Subsection (2), a court may order a partial termination of the trust (or other arrangement that might involve bonding, insurance, or impounding of some trust property) in a manner that will not prejudice the interests of nonconsenting beneficiaries.

Comment on Subsection (2):

d. The material-purpose restriction. Under the rule of Subsection (2), even all of the beneficiaries acting together ordinarily cannot compel termination of a trust if its continuance is necessary to carry out a material purpose of the trust. Similarly, the beneficiaries ordinarily cannot compel modification of the trust if the modification is inconsistent with a material purpose of the trust.

Because the rights of the beneficiaries are thus limited out of respect for serious objectives that appear to have motivated the settlor in creating the trust, however, the material-purpose restriction does not apply if the settlor is alive, legally competent, and content to waive it. Also, the restriction becomes unimportant and does not apply if the material purpose is no longer relevant or cannot be accomplished in any event. Furthermore, following the death or incapacity of the settlor, an appropriate court may authorize the termination of a trust under this section if it determines that the reason(s) offered in support of the beneficiaries' petition for termination outweigh, at the time, the concerns or objectives reflected in the material purpose.

The line is not always easy to draw between a "material purpose" on the one hand and, on the other, specific intentions that are deemed less important so that the *Claflin* doctrine does not protect them. Occasionally, a settlor expressly states in the will, trust agreement, or declaration of trust that a specific purpose is the primary purpose or a material purpose of the trust. Otherwise, the identification and weighing of purposes under this section frequently involve a relatively subjective process of interpretation and application of judgment to a particular situation, much as purposes or underlying objectives of settlors in other respects are often left to be inferred from specific terms of a trust, the nature of the various interests created, and the circumstances surrounding the creation of the trust. The question is narrower and more focused, although not necessarily easier, when applied to a specific modification rather than to the termination of the trust (see Comment *f*).

Material purposes are not readily to be inferred. A finding of such a purpose generally requires some showing of a particular concern or objective on the part of the settlor, such as concern with regard to a beneficiary's management skills, judgment, or level of maturity. Thus, a court may look for some circumstantial or other evidence indicating that the trust arrangement represented to the settlor more than a method of allocating the benefits of property among multiple intended beneficiaries, or a means of offering to the beneficiaries (but not imposing on them) a particular advantage. Sometimes, of course, the very nature or design of a trust suggests its protective nature or some other material purpose.

Illustrations:

5. S devised a portion of her estate to T in trust to pay to her grandson B (then age 14) such amounts as T may deem appropriate for B's support and education, and after B attains age 21 to pay him all of the trust income, plus additional amounts of principal in T's discretion, and then to distribute one-third of the trust estate to B at age 25 and to terminate the trust and distribute the remaining property to B when he reaches age 30. B has now reached age 22, has completed his college education, and wishes to use the funds held in the trust to purchase a home and establish his own business. (Under the terms of the trust, B is the sole beneficiary, with no other provision for the disposition of the property even in the event of his death before age 30.) The nature and evident protective purpose of the trust are such that B cannot compel its termination earlier than provided by its terms.

6. S devised a portion of his estate to T as trustee, "to apply such amounts of the trust income and principal as T deems appropriate for the education of my grandchildren, X, Y, and Z," and when "the youngest of them reaches age 26, or at such earlier time as T, in her sole discretion, believes they have all completed their education," the trust is to terminate, with the trust estate then to be distributed to those grandchildren in equal shares. (Under traditional rules of construction applicable to this trust, the remainder interests of the three grandchildren, except as they may be diminished by distributions for education, are indefeasibly vested.) When the grandchildren are ages 19, 21, and 23, they all agree to have the trust terminated and request T to distribute the trust property to them. T declines to do so. The trust terms

reveal, presumptively at least, a material purpose that prevents the beneficiaries from compelling termination.

The mere fact that the settlor has created a trust for successive beneficiaries does not prevent the beneficiaries from terminating or modifying the trust to reallocate the beneficial interests among themselves if they wish to do so. A trust plan to provide successive enjoyment is not itself sufficient to indicate, for example, that the settlor had a material purpose of depriving the beneficiaries of the property management or otherwise of protecting them from the risks of their own judgment. In the absence of additional circumstances indicating a further purpose, the inference is that the trust was intended merely to allow one or more persons to enjoy the benefits of the property during the period of the trust and to allow the other beneficiary or beneficiaries to receive the property thereafter.

Thus, if the beneficiaries of such a trust are under no incapacity and they all consent to the termination of the trust, they can compel distribution of the trust property as they agree. Similarly, if a beneficiary who is entitled to the income acquires the interest of the sole remainder beneficiary, or vice versa, there is no protective or other purpose implicit in a plan of successive enjoyment that would indicate that the person who thus becomes the sole beneficiary should not be allowed to compel termination of the trust.

Illustrations:

8. H leaves property to T in trust to pay the income to W for life and on W's death to pay the principal to such of the children of H's deceased brother D as are then living, and if none is then living then to X. Under traditional construction, W, X, and D's children are the only beneficiaries of the trust. If they all consent, in the absence of other evidence of trust purpose, they can terminate the trust and have the property distributed as they agree.

9. S left her residuary estate in trust to T to pay the income to L for life, and on L's death to distribute the remainder to R if then living and otherwise to R's issue. R subsequently dies leaving no issue, and the trust interest, which thereby fails, passes by resulting trust to L as S's sole intestate successor. L has thus become the trust's sole beneficiary and can compel T to convey the trust property to her in the absence of a showing that S had a purpose in creating the trust other than to provide for R or his issue following the provision for L.

10. The same facts as in Illustration 9, except that it is shown that a primary purpose for S's creation of the trust was her concern over what she perceived as L's unsound financial judgment and inability to manage the property. L, though she has become sole beneficiary, cannot compel termination of the trust.

e. *Discretionary and spendthrift trusts.* If the interests of one or more of the beneficiaries of a trust are subject to restraints on alienation (see §§ 58, 59), or if the terms of the trust provide support or other discretionary benefits for some or all of the beneficiaries (see § 50), this may supply some indication that the settlor had a material purpose—a protective purpose—that would be inconsistent with allowing the beneficiaries to terminate the trust. Nevertheless, spendthrift restrictions are not sufficient in and of themselves to establish, or to create a presumption of, a material purpose that would prevent termination by consent of all of the beneficiaries. This is also true, in many contexts, of discretionary provisions.

A spendthrift clause may be included as a routine or incidental provision of a trust (unimportant or even unknown to the settlor) as a part of a trust established for tax purposes, merely to provide successive enjoyment, or for other reasons not inconsistent with allowing premature termination upon application of all of the beneficiaries. Thus, for example, the fact that a lawyer had explained the effect and advised the inclusion of a spendthrift provision is not alone sufficient to establish that it represents more than an advantage that the beneficiaries are free to relinquish by consenting to termination of the trust.

Similarly, discretionary provisions, like other provisions involving successive enjoyment, may represent nothing more than a settlor's plan for allocating the benefits of his or her property flexibly among various beneficiaries rather than revealing some significant concerns or protective purposes that would prevent the beneficiaries from joining together to terminate a trust and divide or distribute the property as they wish under the rule of this section. This is particularly so when the trust is created to provide, as needed, for the life beneficiary's support and care, with remainder to others. Many trusts, however, have broader discretionary purposes and beneficiary classes. The nature of the interests and terms of trusts of this latter type may, without more, justify a finding that it was a significant or "material" purpose of the settlor to secure the ongoing, flexible (and possibly expert) judgment of the trustee regarding the amount, timing, and recipients of distributions over the duration of the trust, as circumstances and opportunities might develop (cf. Comment *f*).

Illustration:

11. Upon W's death, her revocable trust was divided by T (W's successor trustee) by prescribed formula into two trusts. Trust A provided for all of its income, "plus additional amounts of principal in T's discretion," to be paid to W's husband, H. Trust B authorized T to pay "such amounts of income or principal or both to any one or more of H, my issue, and the spouses of my issue as T may deem appropriate, taking into account any personal, financial, tax, and other considerations T deems appropriate." On H's death, both trusts are to terminate and be distributed to W's then living issue. The terms of Trust B indicate a material discretionary purpose sufficient to prevent its termination by the beneficiaries. The above-described terms of Trust A, however, reveal no material purpose that would bar termination under the rule of this section.

f. Material purpose and modification. Although a trust may have a material purpose that would preclude complete or even partial termination of the trust, a particular modification agreed to by the beneficiaries might not be inconsistent with any material purpose of the trust. In such a case, all of the beneficiaries could join together to modify the terms of the trust to that extent. Thus, where modification is involved, under Subsection (2) of this section the material-purpose inquiry focuses on the particular amendment sought by the beneficiaries.

For example, a proposed modification might change the trustee or create a simple, inexpensive procedure for appointing successor trustees, or it might create or change procedures for removing and replacing trustees. Modifications of these types may well improve the administration of a trust and be more efficient and more satisfactory to the beneficiaries without interfering with a material purpose of the trust. On the other hand, repeated modifications to change trustees or even a particular change of trustee, or an amendment of provisions relating to the trusteeship, might have the effect of materially undermining the contemplated qualities or independence of trustees. A given change might even have the effect of shifting effective control of the trust in such a way as to be inconsistent with a protective management purpose or other material purpose of the trust. Thus, changes of trustees or in trustee provisions are to be particularly but sympathetically scrutinized for possible conflict with a material trust purpose.

g. Material purpose and charitable trusts. Where a specific charitable purpose is designated in the terms of a trust, that designation reflects a material purpose of the settlor under the rule of this section, so that the specific charitable purpose cannot be changed or exchanged for a trust or other benefits serving a different charitable purpose. (Compare, however, § 67 on the cy pres doctrine.)

h. Compromise of contest. The fact that the beneficiaries could not terminate a trust because to do so would be inconsistent with a material purpose of the settlor does not preclude the court from approving a compromise under which a part of the trust would be terminated in order to settle a bonafide contest of the will that would create the trust or to settle bonafide litigation challenging the validity of an inter vivos trust.

§ 66. Power of Court to Modify: Unanticipated Circumstances

(1) The court may modify an administrative or distributive provision of a trust, or direct or permit the trustee to deviate from an administrative or distributive provision, if because of circumstances not anticipated by the settlor the modification or deviation will further the purposes of the trust.

(2) If a trustee knows or should know of circumstances that justify judicial action under Subsection (1) with respect to an administrative provision, and of the potential of those circumstances to cause substantial harm to the trust or its beneficiaries, the trustee has a duty to petition the court for appropriate modification of or deviation from the terms of the trust.

Comment on Subsection (1):

a. Scope and purpose of section. With the rule of this section, *contrast* the rule of § 65, which requires the consent of all beneficiaries but does not depend on a finding of unanticipated circumstances.

This section—the so-called "equitable deviation" doctrine—applies to both charitable and private trusts. Although the unanticipated circumstances in cases falling under this section are likely to be circumstances that have changed since the creation of the trust, the rule of the section does not require changed circumstances. It is sufficient that the settlor was unaware of the circumstances in establishing the terms of the trust.

It is not necessary under this section that the situation be so serious as to constitute an "emergency" or to jeopardize the accomplishment of the trust purposes.

The objective of the rule allowing judicial modification (or deviation) and the intended consequences of its application are not to disregard the intention of a settlor. The objective is to give effect to what the settlor's intent probably would have been had the circumstances in question been anticipated.

b. Operation of section. The terms of the trust that the court may modify, or from which the court may authorize deviation by the trustee, may be provisions governing the management or administration of the trust estate or they may be provisions defining the beneficial interests or entitlements of the various trust beneficiaries. Thus, for example, the provision subject to modification or deviation may be one expressly directing or expressly forbidding the sale of certain properties or the acquisition of certain types of investments. Or the modification or deviation may, for example, involve trust terms that do not allow invasion of principal or accumulation of income.

If appropriate to the circumstances prompting the court action, and to the purposes and other circumstances of the trust, the court may so modify the terms of the trust as to require prompt termination. If this result appears premature to the court, it may authorize the trustee subsequently to terminate the trust if the trustee concludes from further experience (or despite lesser modification) that the purposes of the trust would be better served by termination. In the event of termination under the rule of this section, the trust property is to be distributed in accordance with the trust purposes and the settlor's probable intention.

Upon a showing of changed circumstances, or a petitioner's credible presentation that relevant circumstances were unknown to the settlor, the burden of persuasion shifts to the person(s) seeking to show that the circumstances were anticipated by the settlor during the formulation and execution of the trust. Failure to provide in the terms of trust for subsequent developments involved in a case reinforces an inference that the circumstances were not anticipated by the settlor.

Then, upon a finding of unanticipated circumstances, the court must further determine whether a proposed or contemplated modification or deviation would tend to advance (or, instead, possibly detract from) the trust purposes. This latter inquiry is likely to involve a somewhat subjective process of attempting to infer the relevant purpose or purposes of a trust from the general tenor of its provisions and from the nature of the beneficial interests, together with the family or personal relationships involved in the trust. In this process, it is appropriate that courts act with particular caution in considering a modification or deviation that can be expected to diminish the interest(s) of one or more of the beneficiaries in favor of one or more others.

Illustration:

1. The terms of the trust being administered by T require the retention of a modest-sized apartment complex that the settlor had owned and operated during her lifetime. It has subsequently become clear that this apartment complex cannot be administered efficiently and can be expected to continue to detract from the overall performance of the trust estate, to the disadvantage of all of the beneficiaries. The court may authorize deviation from the terms of the trust, enabling the trustee to sell the apartment complex and reinvest the proceeds.

c. Illegality or impossibility. If it is or becomes unlawful or impossible to accomplish the purposes of a private trust, and the terms of the trust make no provision for the situation, this constitutes an unanticipated circumstance for purposes of this section. Thus, the court may terminate the trust and direct distribution of the property in accordance with the settlor's probable intention. (On charitable trusts, however, see § 67.) If it becomes unlawful or impossible to comply with certain terms of the trust, the court may modify those terms or authorize deviation from them in order to further the intended purposes of the trust.

d. *Inefficiency of small trust.* If the trust estate is or becomes so small that the interest of the beneficiaries, or the trust purposes, would be better served by terminating the trust, the court may so order and shall then direct distribution in a manner consistent with the probable intention of the settlor.

Comment on Subsection (2):

e. *Duty and authority of trustee.* If circumstances exist that would justify judicial action with respect to an *administrative* provision under Subsection (1) of this section, and if the trustee knows or should know of those circumstances and that substantial harm may result to the trust or its beneficiaries from adhering to the existing terms of the trust, the trustee is under a duty to initiate proceedings to seek appropriate modification of or deviation from that administrative provision.

This duty under Subsection (2) ordinarily does not apply to the initiation of proceedings for modification of or deviation from *distributive* provisions of a trust. The trustee may, however, upon or without request by a beneficiary, seek modification or deviation where judicial action may be justified under Subsection (1) with respect to distribution provisions. Furthermore, if the trustee is *actually* aware that a purpose of the settlor would be jeopardized by adhering to existing provisions governing distribution when judicial action under Subsection (1) would be justified, the trustee has a duty to petition the court for instructions or for appropriate deviation or modification. . . . .

Illustration:

7. The trust and circumstances are as stated in Illustration 1. The trustee has a duty to petition the court for authority to disregard the settlor's direction to retain the apartment complex.

In a situation involving an emergency, that is, a situation of unanticipated circumstances in which the trustee believes substantial harm will result to the trust or its beneficiaries if action is not taken promptly, the trustee may deviate from the terms of the trust without prior authorization of court. If the court should subsequently determine that deviation was not justified under the principles of this section, the trustee will not be liable in the absence of bad faith or unreasonable disregard of the terms of the trust.

§ 67. Failure of Designated Charitable Purpose: The Doctrine of Cy Pres

Unless the terms of the trust provide otherwise, where property is placed in trust to be applied to a designated charitable purpose and it is or becomes unlawful, impossible, or impracticable to carry out that purpose, or to the extent it is or becomes wasteful to apply all of the property to the designated purpose, the charitable trust will not fail but the court will direct application of the property or appropriate portion thereof to a charitable purpose that reasonably approximates the designated purpose.

Comment:

a. *The cy pres doctrine: background and scope of the rule.* The rule stated in this section is called the doctrine of cy pres. The expression indicates the principle that, when the exact intention of the settlor is not to be carried out, the intention will be given effect "as nearly" as may be.

At common law in England, a prerogative power of cy pres, exercisable by the Crown in certain circumstances and without regard to the settlor's intent, developed in addition to the judicial power in the Chancellor. The prerogative power (or legislative counterpart) has not been recognized in the United States, although legislation may reasonably regulate the extent and exercise of the cy pres power of courts. The judicial power of cy pres has evolved in this country along lines generally similar to the equity power under English common law. . . . .

The cy pres doctrine's modern rationale rests primarily in the perpetual duration allowed charitable trusts and in the resulting risk that designated charitable purposes may become obsolete as the needs and circumstances of society evolve over time, not to mention the sometimes unanticipated extent of decrease or increase in the funds available from a given trust. Nevertheless, the doctrine may also apply to a charitable trust if, at the time of its creation, the particular purpose of the trust has been fully accomplished or cannot possibly or practicably be accomplished. On the other hand, if at the time of the trust's creation its intended purpose is of no value at all to the community, or is otherwise not charitable by its nature, the trust is not enforceable as a charitable trust and is not subject to the rule of this section.

The cy pres doctrine is not applicable to private trusts. There are, however, narrower but analogous principles that apply to both private and charitable trusts, as particularly illustrated by the rule of equitable deviation in § 66 allowing courts, in certain circumstances, to modify the means of accomplishing a trust purpose. Also compare § 29, Comment *g*, and also Comment *i* (on consequences of invalidity), and §§ 45–47 (adaptation of certain intended trusts). (Occasionally, the term "cy pres" is casually used to refer to reformations or judicial modifications in other contexts in which some modified effect is given to dispositions that would otherwise exceed what the law allows, such as under the rule against perpetuities.) . . . .

b. *Contrary intention of settlor.* Just as it is against the policy of the trust law to permit wasteful or seriously inefficient use of resources dedicated to charity, trust law also favors an interpretation that would sustain a charitable trust and avoid the return of the trust property to the settlor or successors in interest. See § 28, Comment *a*. Accordingly, when the particular purpose of a charitable trust fails, in whole or in part, the rule of this section makes the cy pres power applicable (thus presuming the existence of what is often called a general charitable purpose) unless the terms of the trust (defined in § 4) express a contrary intention. . . . .

A trust provision expressing the settlor's own choice of an alternative charitable purpose will be carried out, without need to apply the cy pres doctrine, assuming not only that the initially specified purpose cannot be given effect or continued but also that the alternative purpose is one that properly can be given effect.

Effect will also be given to terms of a trust providing that, under circumstances described in this section, the charitable trust is to terminate and that the property or surplus portion thereof is to be held upon resulting trust (see § 8, Comment *g*, and Illustration 17), or that the trust property or surplus is to pass pursuant to a noncharitable disposition that can be given effect under applicable rules regulating perpetuities (see § 29(b)). If the substitute disposition is of this latter, nonreversionary type and cannot be given effect, the further presumption then is that the cy pres power is to be exercised because of the failure of its alternative.

The mere fact that the terms of the trust provide that property shall be devoted "forever" to a particular charitable purpose, or that it shall be devoted "only" to that purpose, or that the property is given "upon condition" that it be applied to that purpose, does not necessarily indicate the absence of a more general charitable commitment on part of the settlor. Such language may merely emphasize the intention of the settlor that the property should not be applied to other charitable purposes as long as it is practicable to apply it to the specific purpose. Thus, such language alone does not sufficiently express an intention that cy pres should not apply and that the trust is to terminate if it should become illegal, impossible, or impracticable to carry out the particular purpose.

Even though the terms of a trust contain an express provision precluding the application of cy pres to alter the trust purpose, this does not prevent application of the so-called equitable-deviation doctrine of § 66 to modify the *means* by which the purpose is to be accomplished.

c. Causes for failure of designated purpose. Under what circumstances will the particular purpose intended by the settlor not be carried out or continued, so that the court will either modify the trust cy pres or give effect to a trust provision calling for termination? It is not sufficient merely that it can be demonstrated that the trust funds could be better spent on some other purpose. Certainly, however, the particular purpose will fail if it is or becomes illegal or impossible to carry it out, or if the purpose is no longer charitable (as defined in § 28, see especially Comment *a*). The doctrine of cy pres may also be applied, even though it is *possible* to carry out the particular purpose of the settlor, if to do so would not accomplish the settlor's charitable objective, or would not do so in a reasonable way. In such a case, it is "impracticable" to carry out the particular purpose in the sense in which that word is used in this section.

Thus, if a testator devises property in trust to establish and maintain an institution of a particular type but a similar institution already exists and is sufficiently effective that the testator's plan would serve no useful purpose, the intended purpose will not be enforced. Similarly, if a settlor provides for a trust to establish or support a school or other institution but prescribes a curriculum for the school or directs the conduct of the institution in a manner that prevents the offering of a proper education or seriously undermines the usefulness of the institution, the court may modify the terms of the trust to allow a similar but more general charitable purpose to be accomplished.

If property is given in trust for a particular charitable purpose and the amount given is insufficient to accomplish the intended purpose in a socially useful manner, the specified purpose fails and may be modified cy pres in the absence of a trust provision preventing the court from doing so. Thus, for example, if the trustee is directed to erect a hospital but the trust assets are insufficient, the court may direct the trustee to apply the funds to enlarge an existing hospital.

If property is given in trust to be applied to a particular charitable purpose that cannot be carried out without the consent or cooperation of a third party, who refuses that consent or cooperation, the particular charitable purpose fails and, unless precluded by the terms of the trust, cy pres will be applied. Thus, if a testator devises property in trust to erect a public library in a town provided the town agrees to accept and to maintain it, and the town refuses to do so, the property will be applied cy pres for a reasonably similar purpose. Or, if a testator leaves funds to a college in trust to provide scholarships solely for defined categories of students and the college refuses (or is legally unable) to accept the devise under those terms, the court will modify the terms of the devise to relieve it of the objectionable restrictions if to do so would suitably approximate the testator's intended purpose. See further Comment *d* and also § 28, Comment *f*, especially the third paragraph of each Comment.

c(1). Surplus funds. Another type of case appropriate to the application of cy pres, when not precluded by the terms of the trust, is a situation in which the amount of property held in the trust exceeds what is needed for the particular charitable purpose to such an extent that the continued expenditure of all of the funds for that purpose, although possible to do, would be wasteful. (The term "wasteful" is used here neither in the sense of common-law waste nor to suggest that a lesser standard of merely "better use" will suffice.)

Faced with circumstances of the type required for cy pres intervention in a surplus-funds case, a court might broaden the purposes of the trust, direct application of the surplus funds to a like purpose in a different community, or otherwise direct the use of funds not reasonably needed for the original purpose to a different but reasonably similar charitable purpose. (On the result if cy pres modification is prohibited by the settlor, see § 8, Comment *g* . . . .)

d. New purpose; manner of cy pres application. In applying the cy pres doctrine, it is sometimes stated that the property must be applied to a purpose as near as possible to that designated by the terms of the intended trust. Increasingly, however, courts have recognized (as does the rule of this section) that the substitute or supplementary purpose need not be the *nearest possible* but one reasonably similar or close to the settlor's designated purpose, or "falling within the general charitable purpose" of the settlor. This is especially so when the particular purpose becomes impossible or impracticable of accomplishment long after the creation of the trust or when, among purposes reasonably close to the original, one has a distinctly greater usefulness than the others that have been identified. This more liberal application of cy pres is appropriate both because settlors' probable preferences are almost inevitably a matter of speculation in any event and because it is reasonable to suppose that *among relatively similar purposes* charitably inclined settlors would tend to prefer those most beneficial to their communities.

In framing a scheme for the application of property cy pres, the court will consider evidence suggesting what the wishes of the settlor probably would have been if the circumstances had been anticipated. Such an assessment may look to whatever evidence is available concerning the attitudes and interests that appear to have motivated the settlor's selection of the particular purpose. Thus, it would be especially appropriate to consult the donor if available. In other situations, the circumstances of the trust's creation may be revealing, as may the settlor's relationships, social or religious affiliations, personal background, charitable-giving history, and the like. For example, a settlor's adviser may be able to reveal that a devise to a particular institution for a specific project or purpose began with a desire to benefit that institution and was then shaped to address some institutional interest, need, or opportunity; or the opposite might be revealed, with the settlor having a strong desire to encourage a particular field of study or research, or a particular charitable activity, and then settling upon an institution that appeared suitable. In the former case, if the precise plan does not work out or the funds prove to be excessive for the purpose, a court would probably decide to look for a different but related subject or activity at the chosen institution. In the latter case, the court would probably decide that the special interest of the settlor should be pursued at a nearby or comparable institution.

The cy pres power is vested in the court, not in the trustee or the Attorney General, who is, however, a necessary party entitled to notice of the proceeding. Cy pres proceedings are normally initiated by trustees or Attorneys General, but they are occasionally brought by institutions or individuals having a special interest in the charitable purpose. (See generally § 94 on standing to enforce trusts. Cf. Restatement Second, Trusts § 391.) In its effort to select a substitute purpose, the court may refer the matter to a master, who, after receiving evidence as well as suggestions from interested parties, will frame an alternative plan or two and submit a recommendation or recommendations to the court.

If under circumstances described in this section a trustee (e.g., a recipient institution or community foundation), without prior court authorization, applies property to a purpose other than that designated in the terms of the trust, the trustee is subject to liability for breach of trust. If, however, the application made by the trustee is such as the court would have directed, the court may approve the application, and such approval will be as effective as though the court had authorized the application before it was made.

e. Gift to corporation or association. If a testator devises property to a charitable corporation or association that refuses to accept it, or that is incapable of taking or holding it or is not in existence, the disposition will not fail if the testator manifested an intention to devote the property to charitable purposes and not merely to make a gift to the particular corporation or association. Thus, if the testator leaves money to a particular university to teach courses in dianetics, and the university refuses to accept the funds on that basis, the court may permit the legacy to be applied to the establishment of such a course in another university, assuming the settlor has not provided otherwise.

Similarly, if gifts are made to a charitable corporation that is subsequently dissolved, the doctrine of cy pres applies and the court may direct that the property be given to another corporation or association having similar purposes, in the absence of a contrary statute or provision in the terms of the gift. So too, if property is given in trust to be applied for the support of a particular institution, and the institution subsequently merges with another established for similar purposes, the court will ordinarily permit the property to be used for the support of the new institution.

f. Multiple settlors. If several persons contribute to a fund to be applied to a particular charitable purpose, and it is or becomes illegal, impossible, or impracticable to carry out the particular purpose, or the funds are or become excessive for the purpose, and if the doctrine of cy pres is not applicable, a resulting trust will arise in favor of the contributors or their successors in interest (see further § 8, Comment *g*). If some of the fund has been expended, the contributors are entitled to share in the balance in proportion to their contributions. If some of the contributors cannot be ascertained, usually there will be a resulting trust of their shares for the State in the absence of applicable legislation on the matter.

§ 68. Dividing and Combining Trusts

The trustee may divide a trust into two or more trusts or combine two or more trusts into a single trust, if doing so does not adversely affect the rights of any beneficiary or the accomplishment of the trust purposes.

Comment:

a. Purpose and scope of section. Although a broader power may be conferred upon the trustee by the terms of the trust (§ 64), the rule of this section allows trusts to be divided (e.g., for tax reasons) or combined (e.g., for administrative efficiency) by a trustee without the cost or delay of court proceedings.

When combining or dividing trusts involves more than is authorized by this section, such as where the interests of beneficiaries will be materially altered, the court may be able to modify the trust terms or authorize the trustee to divide or combine trusts under § 66 in situations of unanticipated circumstances. See also § 65 on the possibility of dividing or combining trusts upon consent of the beneficiaries.

b. Application of section. The trustee's general duty to provide information to beneficiaries on a reasonable basis (see § 82) would ordinarily mean that the trustee, before taking action under this section, should advise appropriate beneficiaries of the contemplated action. It is not necessary that all beneficiaries be notified but, so far as practical, the information should be provided to legally competent beneficiaries who are entitled or eligible to receive distributions currently from the trust and those to whom distributions would be made if the present interest(s) of the trust were to terminate at the time of the notification. (The purpose of notification is not to obtain consent, or to suggest that beneficiaries have veto power, but to allow beneficiaries' views to be heard, for the trustee's information and consideration.)

If two or more trusts that are to be combined have different trustees and one is willing to resign, the other trustee may combine the trusts and act as trustee without court appointment provided the change of trustees can be accomplished in a manner authorized by the terms of the trust or by statute. Illustrative would be a trust provision allowing a resigning trustee to appoint a successor or allowing certain beneficiaries to appoint a trustee. See § 34, Comments *b* and *c*.

Illustration:

1. W's will has left her estate to T to divide into two trusts, one for son S and his family and one for daughter D and her family. Her husband, H, had died a number of years earlier leaving his estate to T in trust for W for life and on her death to establish two trusts, one for S and his family and the other for D and her family. The terms of H's and W's trusts for the S family are identical, as are their trusts for the D family, the estate planning for H and W having been done at the same time by the same lawyer. T may combine the two trusts for the S family without court approval, having advised S and his adult children of his plans to do so; T also may combine the two trusts for the D family on a similar basis. If the trusts created by H have a shorter period remaining for purposes of the rule against perpetuities than those created by W (for example, because of grandchildren or great grandchildren born between

the two deaths), and if this conceivably may matter, the problem can be dealt with by proper accounting (i.e., as separate shares).

§ 69. Merger

If the legal title to the trust property and the entire beneficial interest become united in one person, the trust terminates.

Comment:

a. Acquisition of beneficial interest by trustee. If by inter vivos transfer, will, or operation of law the entire beneficial interest in trust property passes to the trustee, the trust terminates and the trustee holds the property free of trust.

Thus, if the sole beneficiary of a trust dies intestate and his interest passes to the trustee as his heir, merger occurs and the trust terminates. Similarly, if the trustee is also the life beneficiary of the trust, and if the sole remainder beneficiary, holding an indefeasibly vested remainder interest in the trust, assigns her interest to the trustee or dies and leaves her interest to the trustee, the trust terminates.

b. Acquisition of legal title by beneficiary. If, by operation of law, the legal title to the trust property passes to the beneficiary who has the entire beneficial interest, merger occurs, the trust terminates, and the beneficiary holds the property free of trust.

Thus, if the sole beneficiary is one of two trustees and the other trustee dies or resigns, and if under the law (see § 34, Comment *d*) or the terms of the trust the beneficiary-trustee becomes the sole trustee, the trust terminates.

c. Where one person is not both sole beneficiary and sole trustee. A trust does not terminate merely because one of several beneficiaries becomes one of several trustees or the sole trustee, or because the sole beneficiary becomes one of several trustees, or because the several beneficiaries become the co-trustees. Thus, if the sole trustee becomes one of several beneficiaries, merger does not occur and the trust is not terminated. Nor is the trust terminated if the trust has two beneficiaries who become the co-trustees of the trust, or if the two trustees of a trust become its only beneficiaries. . . . .

d. Application. The doctrine of merger applies to terminate a trust even though all of its purposes have not been accomplished, and even though some or all of the equitable interest(s) of the trustee-beneficiary are subject to a spendthrift restraint.

A sole beneficiary, however, may avoid becoming sole trustee by refusing to accept appointment as trustee or by promptly declining to serve as sole trustee following the death or resignation of a co-trustee. Similarly, a trustee-beneficiary may avoid becoming sole beneficiary by a timely disclaimer of an assignment, devise, or inheritance of the remaining beneficial interest.

e. Cross-references. This section deals with a trust that is *extinguished* by the doctrine of merger. Compare § 10 to the effect that a trust is not *created* when, at the outset, a single person acquires all legal and all equitable interests in the trust property—i.e., would be both sole trustee and sole beneficiary, as might result from a partial intestacy of the would-be settlor of an intended testamentary trust.

With this section, compare § 17, Comment *a*, and § 25, Comment *b*, making clear that a trust is created even though the only interests of other beneficiaries are contingent, subject to revocation, or otherwise uncertain. . . . .

PART 6
TRUST ADMINISTRATION

Introductory Note: This Part 6 deals with the administration of trusts, including associated relationships among trustees, beneficiaries, and third parties.

After Chapter 14, setting out certain general principles applicable to trust administration, Chapter 15 addresses the duties trustees owe to the beneficiaries, and Chapter 16 deals with trustees' powers and how the exercise of those powers is affected by the trustees' fiduciary duties. Chapter 17 discusses trust-investment law (the Prudent Investor Rule), applying the foregoing principles concerning the authority and responsibilities of trustees to the primary management function of most trusts—the investment function.

Chapters 18 through 22 deal with trustees' liabilities and beneficiaries' remedies for breach of trust, and also with the rights and liabilities of third parties, as well as other liability issues arising from trust relationships.

Chapter 23 addresses trust principal-and-income accounting and related issues involving the rights of successive beneficiaries.

Most of the rules stated in black letter and commentary throughout this Part 6 represent default law, that is, rules that apply in the absence of a contrary provision in the terms of the trust. (The traditional definition of "terms of the trust" is set out in § 4, and would include terms as established by reformation (§ 62) as well as by interpretation; but for purposes of this Part 6, the expression also includes terms added or as revised by settlors or designated others (§§ 63, 64), by the beneficiaries (§ 65), or by court order (§§ 66, 67).) As revealed in the statement or discussion of the various rules, however, some rules or bodies of rules, especially some principles of fiduciary behavior or remedy, are mandatory or at least subject only to limited modification. Also worth noting here is that, although legislation in the various states may be contrary to some of the common law of trusts as stated in this Part 6, the trend of modern legislation, and especially the statutory law based on relevant uniform acts, is to narrow these differences. . . . .

Related Matters. Numerous matters that are closely related to trust administration are dealt with in other portions of this Restatement. Of particular relevance is Chapter 7 on "The Trustee," dealing with the appointment and removal of trustees, the manner in which multiple trustees exercise their powers, and various other matters concerned with the office of trustee, including trustees' rights to compensation and indemnification. Illustrative of the interrelationships among matters considered here and elsewhere in this Restatement is the right of indemnification, which is closely tied to § 88 of Chapter 16 of this Part 6; that section recognizes the trustee's power and duty to incur only reasonable and appropriate expenses, thus limiting the amounts of expense for which a trustee will be entitled to indemnification.

CHAPTER 14

TRUSTEE POWERS AND DUTIES: GENERAL PRINCIPLES

Introductory Note: This Chapter 14 sets forth some basic principles applicable to trust administration generally, and more specifically to ensuing Chapters 15, 16, and 17.

These general principles begin in § 70 with summary statements concerning the powers and duties of trustees. This section (by reference to the more detailed provisions of § 85) reflects persistent, long-term trends in drafting practices, case law, and legislation (as illustrated by the Uniform Prudent Investor Act and the Uniform Trust Code) by (a) recognizing the desirability of comprehensive empowerment of trustees, absent restrictions in the terms of the trust or of a statute, and (b) leaving the protection of settlor objectives and beneficiary interests primarily to the fiduciary duties imposed upon trustees in exercising their powers. For situations in which reasonable doubt exists concerning a trustee's powers or duties under the law or the terms of a trust, the right of the trustee or a beneficiary to seek clarification through judicial instructions is described in § 71.

The next two sections deal with the responsibilities of trustees to the trust beneficiaries in situations in which trust provisions are unlawful or contrary to public policy (§ 72) or in which the performance of a direction in the terms of a trust is or appears to be impossible, or at least impracticable (§ 73). See also § 30 (on impossibility) and § 29 (for detailed consideration of the nature and effect of provisions that are unlawful or contrary to public policy); cf. also § 66 (on equitable deviation).

The rules of trust administration, and the principles applicable to the authority and responsibility of trustees, are fundamentally affected by trust provisions that grant others the power to control trustees in the exercise of some or all of their powers, and particularly by situations involving revocable trusts or in which a beneficiary has similar, ownership-equivalent power over the trust or portion thereof by reason of a presently exercisable general power of appointment or power of withdrawal. The greatly increased use of revocable living trusts, particularly as a means of avoiding probate at death and conservatorship late in life, requires that more attention be given to these trusts than appeared necessary at the time of the prior Restatement of Trusts. Accordingly, § 74 addresses, in some detail, the ways in which a trustee's powers and duties are affected by a settlor's power of revocation or by a donee's unrestricted power to appoint or withdraw trust property. (Also, compare § 25.) Section 75 then addresses the obligations of holders of powers to control a trustee's actions (as well as the associated duties of the trustee) in circumstances other than those covered by § 74.

§ 70. Powers and Duties of Trustees

In administering a trust, a trustee:

(a) has, except as limited by statute or the terms of the trust, the comprehensive powers described in § 85 to manage the trust property and to carry out the terms and purposes of the trust, but

(b) in the exercise or nonexercise of those powers, is subject to the fiduciary duties stated and explained hereafter in Chapter 15 and elsewhere in this Restatement.

General Comment:

a. Broad powers with fiduciary safeguards. Clause (a) of this section refers to § 85, which states the authority of trustees in the broadest of terms, with no powers per se or presumptively excluded by that default rule, while Clause (b) provides the appropriate safeguards for trust beneficiaries and purposes by requiring that trustees' powers be exercised only in accordance with the rigorous standards of fiduciary conduct.

This section thereby provides a summary statement of a basic principle of trust administration: that a trustee presumptively has comprehensive powers to manage the trust estate and otherwise to carry out the terms and purpose of the trust, but that all powers held in the capacity of trustee must be exercised, or not exercised, in accordance with the trustee's fiduciary obligations.

Thus, even a power expressly conferred by the trust instrument, or by statute, is subject to the fundamental duties of prudence, loyalty, and impartiality, to a duty to adhere to the terms of the trust, and to the other fiduciary duties of trusteeship, all as stated, qualified, and applied in Chapters 15 through 17 and elsewhere in this Restatement.

a(1). Implications of the rules of this section. Fiduciary litigation involving an alleged breach of trust has traditionally charged the trustee with one (or both) of two forms of misconduct: (i) that the trustee undertook to perform an act that the trustee was not empowered, either by law or by terms of the trust, to perform; or (ii) that, even if the act in question was one the trustee had power to perform, the trustee exercised that power in a manner inconsistent with the applicable standards of fiduciary conduct. Because of the rule of Clause (a) and § 85, except as the trustee's powers are limited by statute or by terms of the trust, issues of misconduct will focus on point (ii), that is, on the trustee's compliance or noncompliance with the fiduciary duties of the trusteeship (Clause (b)).

Similarly, under the rule of Clause (a), instructions (§ 71) concerning a trustee's *powers* will essentially be confined to the interpretation of statutes or trust provisions that might have the effect of limiting those powers.

b. Cross-references. On the meaning of the phrase "terms of the trust," see § 4, and also Part 6, Introductory Note, and § 76, Comment *b(1)*. On court instructions where a trustee's duties or powers are unclear, or where the proper interpretation of the trust terms is otherwise uncertain, see § 71.

On the manner in which powers are exercised by co-trustees, see § 39 (default rule of majority control when there are more than two trustees). On the normal duties of co-trustees (even dissenting or minority trustees) to participate in trust decisions and deliberations and to protect the trust estate, see § 81.

On the nature and effect of terms that are unlawful or contrary to public policy, see § 72 and, more fully, § 29. On the effects of impossibility, impracticability, and unanticipated circumstances, see § 73 and also §§ 30, 66, and 67.

On the responsibilities and authority of trustees upon trust termination, see § 89.

On the effects of a settlor's power to revoke the trust, see §§ 74 and 97 (and cf. § 63); on the effects of another's power to direct the trustee in matters of trust administration, see § 75 (and cf. § 64).

Comment on Clause (a):

c. *In general.* The comprehensive statement of the powers of trustees in the default rule of § 85, briefly incorporated here in Clause (a), not only is simple but also has the advantage of facilitating efficient use of family resources, foreclosing no courses of action. In addition, the rule offers both the flexibility suitable to the varied purposes and circumstances of trusts today and the adaptability needed to accommodate changing economic conditions and asset-management practices over time. The breadth and simplicity of the rule also should diminish the need of trustees for instructions under § 71.

The breadth of Clause (a) is consistent with pervasive trends in modern American trust law, as illustrated by Uniform Trust Code § 815(a)(2) (2000). Also compare the "prudent investor rule" (prohibiting no investment or investment course of action), adopted in the preliminary volume (1992, now incorporated in Chapter 17) of this Restatement and in most states, usually by enactment of the Uniform Prudent Investor Act (1994).

On the early background, evolution, and rationale of the law of trustee powers, see § 85, Comment *a*.

Comment on Clause (b):

d. *Fiduciary duties of trustees.* A trustee, in deciding whether and how to exercise the powers of the trusteeship, even those expressly authorized by trust provision or statute, has a duty to the beneficiaries to act in good faith, with prudence, and in accordance with the trustee's other fiduciary duties. (See particularly Chapter 15 and § 86 of Chapter 16.)

Although a trustee's duties, like trustee powers, may be affected by the terms of the trust, the fiduciary duties of trusteeship are subject to minimum standards that require the trustee to act in good faith and in a manner consistent with the purposes of the trust and the interests of the beneficiaries. These fundamental standards of trusteeship are implicit in and normally (but see § 74, Comment *a(1)*) essential to the trust relationship. See, e.g., § 50, Comments *b* and *c*, § 86, § 87, especially Comment *d*, and § 96, as well as discussion generally throughout Chapters 15 through 17.

d(1). Duties not dependent on whether trustee is compensated. Whether or not a person receives compensation for serving as trustee, the person is subject to a duty to administer the trust in accordance with its terms (§ 76), with prudence (§ 77), and in good faith and conformity with other fiduciary duties referred to in Clause (b) (see especially §§ 78–84). On the matter of trustee compensation (unless waived by the trustee or precluded by the trust terms) and the manner in which the amount of compensation is to be determined, see § 38(1) and id., Comments *a* and *c–f*.

§ 71. Application to Court for Instructions

A trustee or beneficiary may apply to an appropriate court for instructions regarding the administration or distribution of the trust if there is reasonable doubt about the powers or duties of the trusteeship or about the proper interpretation of the trust provisions.

Comment:

a. *Rationale.* A trustee commits a breach of trust not only by violating a duty as a result of negligence or misconduct but also, ordinarily (but see . . . § 77, Comment *b(2)*), by violating a duty because of a mistake concerning the nature or extent of the trustee's powers and duties under the terms of the trust or applicable law. On breach of trust generally, see § 93. To avoid undue risk of liability when reasonable doubt exists in these matters, a trustee may seek protection by applying for instructions from an appropriate court. This power to grant instructions to trustees has long been viewed, in prior Restatements and in most states, as inherent in the equitable powers of courts having jurisdiction over trusts, although this authority is generally now based on declaratory-judgment legislation, such as the Uniform Declaratory Judgments Act. . . . .

Similarly, as a protection against harm that might be caused by a breach of trust resulting from a mistake concerning the trustee's powers and duties, a beneficiary may petition the court to instruct the trustee with regard to the powers and duties of the trusteeship. The settlor, as such, ordinarily (see § 94) does not have standing to apply to the court for instructions.

b. *Effect of instructions.* Subject to the right of appeal, and absent misrepresentation (or concealment by a trustee), instructions provided by an appropriate court will bind the trustee and beneficiaries who, either personally or by representation, are properly made parties to the proceeding. Rules more generally concerning the preclusive effect of court instructions are part of the law relating to judgments and procedure and are not within the scope of this Restatement. . . . .

c. *Matters about which instructions are appropriate.* In circumstances of reasonable uncertainty, whether of law or of terms of the trust, the trustee or a beneficiary is entitled to instructions of the court to clarify the trustee's powers or duties or other matters involving the meaning and effect of the trust provisions. Illustrative are such matters as uncertainties concerning the identity of the trust beneficiaries, the nature and extent of their interests, the proper allocation or apportionment of receipts or expenditures between income and principal (Chapter 23), and the propriety of a trustee's plan of distribution on trust termination (§ 89).

d. *Matters about which instructions are not appropriate.* Because of concern regarding burdens on the judicial system and unwarranted costs and delays in trust administration, a trustee or beneficiary normally is not entitled to instructions with respect to the administration of a trust unless there is some reasonable doubt about the extent of the trustee's powers or duties or about proper interpretation of the trust provisions. Nor will the court instruct the trustee as to a question that may never arise, or that may arise only in the future, unless some need is shown for current resolution of the matter. Thus, a court ordinarily will not instruct a trustee on the distribution of trust property before the time arrives for making, or at least planning, that distribution.

If a matter rests within the sound discretion of the trustee, or is a matter of business judgment, the court ordinarily will not instruct the trustee how to exercise that discretion or judgment. Thus, for example, after having determined and instructed that the purposes of a charitable trust include certain purposes about which reasonable doubt had existed, and that the trustee's discretion includes the making of distributions for those purposes, it would not be proper for the court, either upon its own motion or at the request of the trustee or a beneficiary, to go further and instruct the trustee in advance on matters of judgment concerning the amounts of income or the portions of the trust estate the trustee should expend for the particular purposes in question.

As a qualification upon the rule of this Comment, a court may be justified in accepting as "reasonable" doubt or uncertainty a trustee's legitimate concern that a particular beneficiary's insistence upon an unreasonable position might, without instruction on the matter, lead to significantly more costly and disruptive litigation; on resulting costs, see Comment *e*, below.

e. *Costs of instructions*. Expenses incurred by a trustee in applying to the court for instructions are payable from the trust estate unless the application for instructions was plainly unwarranted, there being no reasonable uncertainty about the powers or duties of the trustee or about the relevant law or proper interpretation of the trust. In such a case it is normally improper for a trustee to incur the expenses of making the application. See generally § 88 (on proper costs of administration); but see also exception at end of Comment *d*, above.

Expenses incurred by the trustee as a result of a beneficiary's application for instructions are payable or reimbursable from the trust estate, provided the expenses and the trustee's conduct were reasonable and appropriate to the trustee's fiduciary duties (see particularly §§ 76–79 and § 88). On the costs incurred by the beneficiary in making or responding to an application for instructions, see § 88, Comment *d*; and compare generally Chapter 19 on trustees' liabilities to beneficiaries.

f. *Cross-references*. On the trustee's usual duty of impartiality in instruction proceedings, see § 79, Comment *a*.

On the power of the court to permit or direct deviation from, or modification of, the terms of the trust, see § 66; also see §§ 72 and 73, and cf. § 67.

Occasionally, under state law or the circumstances, instructions may be unavailable even in a situation of doubt concerning a trustee's duties or powers; on the possible effects of a trustee's reasonable reliance on advice of counsel in such a case, see § 77, Comment *b(2)*.

Although a settlor expressly grants a trustee the power to interpret the trust instrument (or to make a "binding" determination of its meaning and effect) in cases of doubt or controversy, the trustee's discretion is nevertheless subject to judicial review for abuse. . . . . Generally, on grants of discretion or "absolute" discretion, see § 87; also see § 50, Comments *b* and *c*.

§ 72. Terms That Are Unlawful or Against Public Policy

A trustee has a duty not to comply with a provision of the trust that the trustee knows or should know is invalid because the provision is unlawful or contrary to public policy.

Comment:

a. Background, general observations, and cross-references. This section and its Comments reflect the rules of § 29, dealing with trust purposes and provisions that are unlawful or against public policy. Under that section, as further explained in its extensive commentary, a trust provision is invalid if: it is unlawful or its performance calls for the commission of a criminal or tortious act (§ 29(a)); it violates rules regulating perpetuities or accumulations (§ 29(b)); or it is contrary to public policy (§ 29(c)). A trustee's normal duty to comply with the terms of the trust (§ 76) does not apply to a trust provision that is invalid on these grounds (id., Comment *b(1)*).

Situations involving the variety of public-policy issues considered in § 29, Comments *i–m*, are particularly likely to justify trustees in seeking court instructions (§ 71) due to uncertainty or the age of case authority in a given jurisdiction. Also, a provision that is invalid under § 29 may be subject to modification (either by court under § 66 or by beneficiary consent under § 65) or to reformation (§ 62), which is especially likely to be available for cases under § 29(b) or § 29(c) (see Comments *g* and *i(1)* to § 29).

It is immaterial to the rule of this section that compliance with the provision in question was not unlawful or contrary to public policy at the time of the creation of the trust if it becomes so before the time of performance. On the other hand, if performance of the provision was illegal or contrary to public policy at the time the trust was created but subsequently becomes lawful or ceases to be contrary to public policy, the trustee is subject thereafter to the normal duty to comply with the trust provision unless the trust has already failed altogether on the ground of invalidity (see § 29, Comment *e*) or unless, or to the extent that, a modification or reformation of the trust renders compliance with the provision impractical.

b. Duty not to comply. Not only is the trustee under no duty to comply with a term of the trust that is invalid (Comment *a*), but, as stated by the rule of this section, the trustee ordinarily has a duty to the beneficiaries not to comply. Thus, the trustee is not justified in complying with a direction if the trustee knows or should know that to do so would be a criminal offense and thus potentially harmful to the trust or its beneficiaries. Similarly, a trustee has a duty not to comply with a trust provision that the trustee knows or should know violates rules regarding perpetuities or is contrary to public policy. The trustee's compliance with a provision of this type might, for example, result in a distribution that would violate the rights of one trust beneficiary while exposing another to an obligation of restitution.

Furthermore, a trustee has a duty not to comply with a trust provision that directs the trustee to refrain from doing an act, if it is unlawful or against public policy for the trustee not to perform that act. For example, a trustee is not to comply with a term of the trust that would prevent the trustee from making a particular distribution or payment that is required to be made under a rule against accumulations (§ 29, Comment *h(2)*) or under a rule against restraints on certain beneficiary behavior (id., Comments *i–l*).

c. What trustee should know. A trustee "should know" what the trustee would have learned through the exercise of reasonable care (e.g., that a course of action in question was prohibited by an applicable zoning ordinance). See duty of prudence, § 77, Comment *b*. A trustee who is uncertain about the validity of a provision, or who has reason to believe (e.g., because of a beneficiary's assertion) that its performance may be unlawful or contrary to public policy, has a duty not to comply with the provision without consulting legal counsel or otherwise investigating the matter. If reasonable doubt remains, the trustee is justified in applying to an appropriate court for instructions (§ 71) and ordinarily should do so. (Cf. § 77, Comment *b(2)*, on possible effects of advice of counsel.)

In determining whether a trustee should have known that a provision was unlawful or contrary to public policy, or should have investigated the provision's validity, among the relevant factors for a court to consider are the particular trustee's experience, familiarity with trust law and practice, and representations concerning competence to serve as a trustee. Cf. § 77(3) (recognizing that, although all trustees are held to at least the standard of an "individual" of ordinary intelligence (§ 77, Comment *b*), a trustee who possesses or purports to possess greater-than-ordinary skill may be held to a higher standard).

§ 73. Impossibility or Impracticability

A trustee has a duty not to attempt to comply with a trust provision directing the trustee to do an act if the trustee knows or should know

(a) that compliance is impossible, or

(b) that the expense of attempting to comply is unreasonable.

Comment:

a. *Background: no duty to comply.* A trustee is not under a duty to attempt to comply with a trust provision directing the trustee to do an act the performance of which is impossible or reasonably appears to be impossible. Section 76, Comment *b(1)*. It is not sufficient to relieve a trustee of the normal duty of compliance that the trustee believes the act to be impossible, unless the trustee makes such an investigation as is reasonable under the circumstances, and it then reasonably appears that performance is impossible.

b. *Duty not to comply.* If compliance with a term of the trust is in fact impossible, and the trustee knows or should know that compliance is impossible, the trustee is not justified in incurring expense in attempting to comply with the trust provision.

Similarly, a trustee is not justified in incurring expense in complying or attempting to comply with a trust provision if it would be unreasonable to incur the expense of doing so in view of all the circumstances, including the amount of the expense, the chance of failure, and the advantages likely to result to the trust if the attempt is successful.

On what a trustee "should know," see § 72, Comment *c*.

c. *Uncertainty regarding impossibility or impracticability.* If the trustee is in doubt whether it is possible or reasonable to comply with a provision of the trust, application may be made to the proper court for instructions concerning the trustee's duty. See § 71. If it appears to the court that compliance with a trust provision is not possible, or that it would be wasteful to attempt to comply, and if the impossibility or impracticability is a result of unanticipated circumstances, not only may the court direct or authorize the trustee to deviate from the provision, but it may modify the terms of the trust. See § 66 (under which unanticipated circumstances justify judicial intervention to "further the purposes of the trust" upon a less rigorous standard than required for the trustee to disregard a trust provision under the present section).

d. *Temporary impossibility.* If the terms of the trust direct a trustee to do an act the performance of which is temporarily impossible or impracticable, the trustee has a duty to the beneficiaries not to attempt to do the act as long as the impossibility or impracticability continues. The trustee, however, would come under a duty to perform the act in question after a temporary impossibility or impracticability is removed, unless performance is then prevented by judicially directed or authorized modification of or deviation from the terms of the trust under the rule of unanticipated circumstances stated in § 66.

e. *Cross-references.* On when an intended trust fails altogether for impossibility or indefiniteness of its purposes, and on the effect of the impossibility of (e.g., a beneficiary's) performance of a condition, see § 30.

On modification of or deviation from the terms of a trust in furtherance of its purposes in the event of unanticipated circumstances, see § 66. On charitable trusts and the doctrine of cy pres, see § 67.

If a trustee through a breach of trust has made it impossible to comply with the terms of the trust, the trustee may be liable to the beneficiaries for resulting damages. See generally Chapter 19.

§ 74. Effect of Power of Revocation

(1) While a trust is revocable by the settlor and the settlor has capacity to act:

(a) The trustee

(i) has a duty to comply with a direction of the settlor even though the direction is contrary to the terms of the trust or the trustee's normal fiduciary duties, if the direction is communicated to the trustee in writing in a manner by which the settlor could properly amend or revoke the trust; and

(ii) may comply with a direction or act in reliance on an authorization of the settlor although the direction or authorization is contrary to the terms of the trust or the trustee's normal fiduciary duties, even if the direction or authorization is not manifested in a manner by which the settlor could properly amend or revoke the trust.

(b) The rights of the beneficiaries are exercisable by and subject to the control of the settlor.

(2) To the extent that a trust is subject to a presently exercisable general power of appointment or power of withdrawal and the donee of the power has capacity to act, the donee has authority similar to the authority that the settlor of a revocable trust has under Subsection (1).

General Comment:

a. *Scope of section; rationale.* This section deals with situations in which a person currently has, by reason of a power of revocation, appointment, or withdrawal, the equivalent of ownership of the trust property, even though the legal title to the property is held by the trustee. A power of this type allows the trust property to be taken by and vested personally in the settlor or other holder (the "donee") of the power, thereby eliminating all interests of other beneficiaries. Such a power also allows the settlor or donee to amend the terms of the trust. See § 63, Comment *g*. Ownership-equivalent powers are held by the settlor or donee individually and not in a fiduciary capacity, even if the power holder also serves as trustee.

Subsection (1) most obviously applies to a power of revocation expressly reserved to the settlor of a revocable trust. Although a power of revocation is not expressly reserved, however, the power to revoke may be found by implication in appropriate circumstances (§ 63(2), and see Comments *b–c(1)* of § 63) or may be supplied by reformation upon a proper showing (§ 62 and § 63, Comment *d*); and an unrestricted power to amend (or "modify") a trust includes a power to revoke the trust (§ 63, Comment *g*). Furthermore, as a practical matter and for purposes of Subsection (1), if the terms of a trust merely provide that the settlor reserves a power of withdrawal, and the power is unrestricted and subject to no unfulfilled condition precedent, that power constitutes a power of revocation, as does a retained presently exercisable general power of appointment—that is, one by which the property can properly and immediately be appointed to the settlor. (That a trust is not invalid merely because the settlor has power to revoke or amend it or to control the actions of the trustee, or even because the settlor serves as trustee, see § 25; but that such a trust and its property may be subject to some of the same statutory restrictions and other substantive rules or policies that apply to wills and to property owned by the settlor, see § 25(2).)

Subsection (2) applies to situations in which a person (the "donee") who is not the settlor has the equitable equivalent of ownership. This situation exists when the donee holds a presently exercisable general power of appointment (i.e., a power by which the donee currently may appoint directly to himself or herself) or a power of withdrawal that is subject to no unfulfilled condition precedent and is unrestricted, except as to amount (see Comment *h*). A power of withdrawal is not the equivalent of ownership and does not fall within Subsection (2) if its exercise is subject to a standard. A standard has this effect whether it is "objective," such as the common, tax-motivated "ascertainable standard" power to withdraw or compel distribution to the donee based on his or her "health, education, support, or maintenance" (I.R.C. §§ 2041 and 2514), or "nonobjective," such as an implied "general standard of reasonableness" (§ 50, Comment *d*).

On powers exercisable only with the consent of another, see Comment *g(1)*. On ownership-equivalent powers that apply only to a portion of trust, see Comment *h*. On revocable trusts with multiple settlors, see Comment *f*.

Because the ownership-equivalent powers described above allow the settlor or donee to modify the trust (see, e.g., § 65 and § 63, Comment *g*) or to acquire or reacquire ownership of some or all of the property free of trust (and then to establish a new trust on different terms), it would seem pointless—and unnecessarily cumbersome and costly—not to recognize the essentially lesser included authority described in this section. Also, because the settlor or donee can properly, by exercise of the power and with no need to justify or explain, eliminate the interest of any or all beneficiaries or give binding consent on their behalf to trustee conduct that may be contrary to normal standards of trust law or the terms of the trust (§ 97), the authority and rights of settlors and donees under this section are not subject to fiduciary obligations, as long as exercised personally by a legally competent settlor or donee. (Contrast Comment *a(2)* on the more limited possibility of exercise, in a fiduciary capacity, by an agent under a durable power of attorney or by a conservator or similar legal representative.)

a(1). Where settlor or donee is also trustee. The principles and rationale underlying this section, and therefore the rules of this section, apply to the settlor or donee who also serves as trustee, even though in such a situation there ordinarily would be no articulation of a "direction" or "authorization" or release from liability by the power holder. The settlor's or donee's plenary authority under this section is properly exercised in such cases by implication when, in administering the trust, action is taken or not taken in the settlor's or donee's concurrent role as trustee. Accordingly, the trustee-settlor under a declaration of revocable trust (Comment *b*), or the trustee-beneficiary (id.) who is donee of a presently exercisable general power to appoint or power to withdraw the trust property, cannot be compelled to provide information (under § 82) or an accounting or report (under § 83) and is not subject to surcharge by other beneficiaries or a successor trustee for breach of trust. On breach of trust generally, see § 93; on normally applicable rules of trustee liability, see Chapter 19. . . . .

a(2). Required capacity of settlor or donee. The rules stated in this section apply to settlors or donees who have the mental capacity to exercise the power to revoke, withdraw, or appoint and to make and understand the business, financial, personal, and other judgments appropriate to the matters involved in an exercise of authority or control under this section. Compare generally § 11; also, on the requirement of *informed* consent, compare § 97. In the absence of reason for the trustee to believe that the settlor or donee lacks the requisite capacity, the trustee is entitled to proceed on the assumption that the settlor or donee possesses that capacity. . . . .

When the settlor or donee lacks the requisite mental capacity, the authority described and rules stated in this section generally do not apply. A conservator's or agent's withdrawal of revocable trust property for the needs and obligations of a settlor (see § 63, Comment *l*), for example, is quite different from an exercise of the types of authority emphasized in this section. Therefore, except as the settlor or donee *personally* intervenes, the matters contemplated here tend to be matters for which a trust was the settlor's chosen property-management device, and the trustee (rather than a conservator or agent) was the fiduciary selected by the settlor for the exercise of administrative judgment and discretion. Thus, it is the trustee who is normally to carry out the settlor's trust plan and to assume responsibility for the fiduciary duties that are owed to the settlor or donee and also, even if secondarily, to the settlor's other chosen beneficiaries.

Sometimes, however, the authority of a settlor or donee under this section may be exercisable (i) by the power holder's conservator (or guardian or other legal representative) if and to the extent authorized by the appropriate court, or (ii) by an agent under a durable power of attorney if and to the extent the terms of the durable power or the trust expressly authorize the agent to exercise the power of revocation, appointment, or withdrawal. (See and compare § 63, Comment *l*, on incapacitated settlors' powers to revoke and amend.) Whether an aspect of the authority described in this section may be so exercisable depends on the nature and purposes of the particular action contemplated under this section, and particularly on whether the action will serve or protect the conservatee's or principal's own needs or financial interests. Also relevant is whether some action on behalf of the settlor has become necessary to advance the apparent or probable objectives of the settlor in creating the trust, or whether there are trust-administration needs that have arisen from unanticipated circumstances for which the existing trust provisions are inadequate.

If allowed to act on behalf of the power holder in a matter described in this section, the agent or conservator (or other legal representative)—unlike a settlor or donee personally—acts in a fiduciary capacity. Furthermore, a conservator, for example, acting pursuant to prior order of the court, generally acts in accordance with principles of substituted judgment . . ., while the acts of an agent are subject to subsequent review (but with no need of prior judicial authorization) under similar principles of substituted judgment, absent other guidance in the terms of the durable power. (See § 11, Comment *f*, and § 63, Comment *l* . . . .)

In short, conservatorship action (or action by an agent who is expressly authorized to exercise the settlor's power to revoke or amend) may be appropriate to substitute for the judgment an incapacitated *settlor* can no longer exercise when need appears—for example, to compensate for shortcomings in the planning of the trust or to make necessary or desirable gifts from the trust; but conservatorship or agency action exercising a settlor's power would normally not be appropriate to substitute for (i.e., to interfere with) the judgments the *trustee* was expected and adequately empowered to make.

On the right of a trustee to petition for instructions in situations of reasonable uncertainty concerning the trustee's duties in these matters, see § 71. . . . .

See further, on other aspects of situations in which a settlor or donee holding an ownership-equivalent power lacks the required capacity, Comments *e* and *g*.

Comment on Subsection (1), Clause (a):

b. Duty to comply with direction of settlor. Whether or not the terms of the trust expressly authorize the settlor in some respects or in general to control the conduct of the trustee in the administration of the trust, the settlor of a revocable trust can properly direct the trustee in the performance (or nonperformance) of acts involving the management or distribution of the trust estate. Even if the settlor directs the trustee to perform acts that are contrary to the terms of the trust or inconsistent with the trustee's normal fiduciary responsibilities, the trustee has a duty to comply with the direction if it is communicated to the trustee in writing and in a manner that would be effective to amend or revoke the trust. (On methods of exercising a power to amend or revoke a trust, see § 63, Comments *h* and *i*, and also see id., Comments *j* and *k*.)

Sometimes a trust provision or applicable law allows a trust to be amended without a writing communicated to the trustee. See § 63(3). As a matter of fairness and to afford reasonable evidentiary protection for the trustee, not only regarding the existence of the direction but also regarding its terms, the duty of compliance under this section applies only when the trustee receives a written communication or confirmation from the settlor. A trustee who receives only an oral direction from the settlor, and who intends not to comply with the direction (also, cf. Subsection (1)(a)(ii) and Comment *c*), has a duty to inform the settlor of the need for an appropriate writing.

Illustration:

2. S is settlor, and T trustee, of a revocable trust, the corpus of which includes several antique cars, which the trust terms instruct T "not to sell or in any way encumber" during S's lifetime. S recently telephoned T to direct her promptly to sell a specified one of these cars to F, a collector friend of S, for a price upon which S and F had tentatively agreed. (There being no inconsistent provision in the trust instrument, S could revoke or amend the trust "in any way that provides clear and convincing evidence of [his] intention to do so." See § 63, Comments *h* and *i*.) T made careful notes of her conversation with S, but then became concerned that, should a sale at the directed price later be questioned by S or by another beneficiary after S's death, her testimony and notes might appear self-serving and be unpersuasive as evidence of S's direction. She therefore transcribed her notes and sent them by e-mail to S several hours after their conversation. The next day S mailed T a brief, handwritten note confirming the conversation and the contents of T's e-mail. T has a duty promptly after receiving S's note to attempt to conclude the contemplated sale to F.

If S in the above Illustration does not provide a confirmation (or new direction) in writing, T may comply (Comment *c*) but is under no duty to do so. If T does not comply with the oral direction, should S die or become incapacitated without confirming in writing or withdrawing the direction, an appropriate court may find that S has amended the trust if consistent with S's intention in giving the oral direction (cf. Comment *i*) and if the unwritten direction satisfied the requirements for an amendment of the trust in question. In the difficult circumstances of this case, the writing requirement in this section has protected T from the element of unfair risk, and yet the opportunity of the court to prevent failure of a sufficiently evidenced intention fulfills the purpose of the flexible rule of § 63(3).

A trustee is not liable to the beneficiaries for a loss that results from compliance with a settlor's direction in accordance with the terms of that direction. The trustee remains subject to fiduciary duties, however, and thus has potential liability, with respect to those aspects of the directed conduct that are not prescribed by the terms of the settlor's direction. Thus, if the settlor of a revocable trust simply directs the trustee to sell certain real property held in the trust, the trustee must, for example, act with prudence in arranging the price and other terms of the sale.

Illustration:

3. The same facts as in Illustration 2, except that S merely directed T to sell the specified antique car but with no instructions concerning the buyer, price, or other terms. Upon receiving written confirmation of that direction, T has a duty to sell the car but in doing so must act with prudence and otherwise conform to her normal fiduciary duties.

c. Trustee's reliance on less formal direction or authorization by settlor. Although under no duty to do so, under Subsection (1)(a)(ii) a trustee may properly act in reliance on a direction or authorization of the settlor, even if the direction or authorization, whether oral or in writing, is not manifested in a manner by which the settlor could properly amend or revoke the trust. If, however, the trustee intends not to comply with such a direction or authorization, the trustee has a duty to inform the settlor of the trustee's need for a proper writing (as called for by Subsection (1)(a)(i) and Comment *b*).

Except as noted in the last paragraph of Comment *b*, above, the trustee is not liable to the beneficiaries for action taken, or for inaction, in compliance with an informal *direction* of the settlor, even though the direction is inconsistent with the terms of the trust or the trustee's normal fiduciary duties.

On the other hand, although a mere *authorization* by the settlor may permit action or inaction that would otherwise be inconsistent with the prohibitions or requirements of trust law or the terms of the trust, in deciding whether as well as how to exercise this type of empowerment, the trustee is not excused from the normal fiduciary duties that require the trustee to act in good faith, with prudence, and in accordance with other duties of trusteeship (see § 86 and § 70, Comment *a*), except as provided or clearly implied by the terms or nature of the authorization.

Subsection (1)(a)(ii) is essentially an extension of the rule of beneficiary consent in § 97. (Cf. Comment *d*, below.) The justification here for allowing (without requiring) compliance with an informal direction by the settlor of a revocable trust, or for allowing action in reliance on the settlor's informal authorization, is that such conduct by a trustee, particularly by a family member, friend, or other inexperienced trustee, is not unreasonable. Therefore, if action has been taken under such circumstances, the trustee should not be denied the above-described degree of consent-based protection from liability merely because of the lack of formality. (See § 97.) As a practical matter, however, in the event of a surcharge action, the trustee does run a risk in relying on unwritten evidence to support a defense based on settlor direction or authorization.

Comment on Subsection (1), Clause (b):

d. *Powers and rights of settlor*. Because the settlor who holds a power of revocation has full authority to revoke or amend the trust, the settlor can properly extinguish or modify the rights and interests of any and all of the beneficiaries. This comprehensive power to modify the terms of the trust also enables the settlor, without actually amending the trust, to bind all beneficiaries in order, for example, to clarify that a particular action may be taken by the trustee when the matter might otherwise be uncertain under the existing terms of the trust. The settlor may even consent to, and thereby authorize on behalf of all beneficiaries (§ 97), certain acts or inaction for which the trustee would otherwise clearly be liable for breach of trust. In addition, settlors who hold powers of revocation may and often do consent to accountings by trustees or, via accountings or otherwise, approve prior acts that might or do constitute a breach of trust, thereby binding all beneficiaries and relieving the trustee of liability to them. The consent of a settlor in such matters, however, like that of any other beneficiary, must be an *informed* consent. (See § 97, and also, on accountings, see § 83.)

e. *Trustee's duties owed primarily to settlor*. For as long as, and to the extent that, the trust is revocable by the settlor and the settlor is legally competent (as described in Comment *a(2)*, above), the settlor may enforce the trust on behalf of all beneficiaries, and the trustee's duties are owed primarily to the settlor, or solely to the settlor insofar as the rights of other beneficiaries are preempted by conduct of the settlor. Thus, competent settlors of revocable trusts can properly bring or prevent suits to surcharge trustees, may remove, replace, or add trustees, and are entitled to receive from trustees all of the information and accountings to which trust beneficiaries are entitled under §§ 82 and 83.

Furthermore, as long as the settlor has capacity to understand and evaluate information provided by the trustee regarding the administration of the trust, the trustee of a revocable trust is not to provide reports or accountings or other information concerning the terms or administration of the trust to other beneficiaries without authorization either by the settlor or in the terms of the trust or a statute.

If, however, the settlor lacks this required capacity, the other beneficiaries are ordinarily entitled to exercise, on their own behalf, the usual rights of trust beneficiaries, and the trustee is ordinarily under a duty to provide them with accountings and other information concerning the trust and its administration in accordance with §§ 82 and 83. The terms of the trust, however, may direct that the trustee in these circumstances not provide the beneficiaries (or that the trustee provide only selected beneficiaries) a copy of the trust instrument or other information disclosing trust provisions; such a direction is effective to the extent this information is not currently needed by the beneficiaries in order to protect against mismanagement of the trust estate, or to remedy breaches of trust for which the settlor has not previously granted informed consent, approval, or release. . . . .

For more general discussion of the trustee's duty to provide information to the beneficiaries, see §§ 82 and 83.

General Comment on Subsection (1):

f. Where revocable trust has multiple settlors. Because a settlor's exercise of authority under this section is similar to a temporary amendment of the trust (see Comment *i*), application of the rules of Subsection (1) to multiple-settlor situations parallels the rights of the settlors, jointly or independently, to amend the trust either under its terms or under the default rules stated in § 63, Comment *k*. The manner of exercise and the extent of authority under this section become particularly significant when one of the settlors has died or has become legally incapacitated or is unwilling to join with the other(s) in an exercise of authority.

Thus, for example, if siblings B and S established a revocable trust and contributed equally to its funding, absent a contrary trust provision each would be able to amend (or revoke) as to a one-half share of the trust (§ 63, Comment *k*); similarly, authority of each acting alone under this section would extend only to that one-half share. If, however, spouses H and W established a revocable trust and funded it entirely with their community property, absent other provision in the terms of the trust or applicable statute, while H and W are both alive they would have to act jointly in order to amend the trust (id., last paragraph); accordingly, neither would be able alone to exercise the authority of a settlor under this section (except by what would amount to a revocation or partial revocation, id.). Joint exercise would also be required for a direction under this section if B and S (or H and W) had contributed individual (or separate) property to fund the trust if its terms expressly require joint action in order to accomplish an amendment.

On the possibility that, in the event of one settlor's incapacity, the other might act jointly with the conservator or agent of the legally disabled settlor, compare Comment *a(2)*, above, and also § 63, Comment *l*.

On situations in which the authority of a settlor (or a donee of an ownership-equivalent power) under this section extends only to a portion of a trust, see Comment *h*.

Comment on Subsection (2):

g. Authority of donee of certain powers of appointment or withdrawal. The donee of a presently exercisable general power to appoint or power to withdraw trust property has the equivalent of the ownership of that property. Like the settlor of a revocable trust, the donee has the power to extinguish the rights of the other beneficiaries by acquiring the trust property and retaining it or transferring it to (or declaring) a new trust on different terms. Rather than having to act by indirection, the donee also has the power to amend the trust. For these reasons (and see Comment *a*), the donee has the same substantive rights and powers under this section as the settlor of a revocable trust, although the manner of exercising this authority may be somewhat different. (See below.)

Accordingly, the trustee has a duty to comply with a direction of the donee of an ownership-equivalent power, or action may be taken or not taken by the trustee in reliance on an authorization of the donee, even though the direction or authorization may be contrary to the terms of the trust and the normal fiduciary duties of trusteeship. Insofar as the direction or authorization does not supersede the trust terms or the trustee's normal duties, however, the trustee remains subject to those terms and duties. (Cf. last paragraph and Illustration 3 of Comment *b*.) To be effective, a direction must be communicated by the donee to the trustee in writing and also conform to any additional formalities or acts that may be required to exercise the power of appointment or withdrawal.

The donee of an ownership-equivalent power may also act for and bind the other beneficiaries of the trust in such matters as the clarification of trust provisions, the removal, replacement, and addition of trustees, the bringing or prevention of suits to surcharge a trustee, and approval of reports or accountings or otherwise relieving a trustee from liability for prior acts of administration. Nevertheless, a trustee in this situation (unlike the revocable-trust situation) is ordinarily under a duty to provide reports or accountings and other information about the trust and its administration to the other trust beneficiaries, as well as to the donee, in accordance with §§ 82 and 83. This is because the donee, unlike the settlor of a revocable trust, is not the source of the beneficiaries' rights, and the beneficiaries are entitled to know of the donee's actions and to know of and verify the donee's authority over the trust. After initial information has been provided to others in accordance with § 82(1)(a) and Comment *b*, however, the donee has the right to direct that further information be provided solely to the donee, if and for as long as the donee is legally competent to understand and evaluate reports and other information concerning the trustee's conduct in administering the trust.

g(1). Donee power held jointly or requiring consent of another. The rule of Subsection (2) generally does not apply where a donee's power to appoint or withdraw trust property can be exercised only with the consent of another beneficiary or a trustee, or of a third party not otherwise interested in the trust. A power of this type is not the equivalent of ownership of the trust property.

Presumptively, however, a different case is presented by a power of withdrawal or appointment that is held jointly by two or more donees who can properly, by acting together, exercise the power by requiring the trust property to be distributed to themselves, immediately and free of trust. If it is reasonable to infer from the terms or form of the power that the settlor would have anticipated that the donees might agree to divide the property, such an exercise by the donees is not a fraud on the power. In such a case, the donees together have the equivalent of ownership and may exercise the rights and authority described in Subsection (2) by the joint action of both (or all) donees. Their situation is like that of multiple settlors who have power to amend a revocable trust only by joint action, as discussed in Comment *f*. Also, compare Comment *h*.

Additional General Comment:

h. Power over portion of trust. Although an ownership-equivalent power is not held in a fiduciary capacity and can properly override other provisions of the trust, when the settlor's or donee's power applies only to a portion of the trust, the authority recognized in this section does not extend beyond that portion to the rest of the trust. In such a case, the authority of the settlor or donee may not be exercised to affect the administration of the other portion or portions of the trust in a way that alters the rights or interests of, or the trustee's duties to, the beneficiaries (or *other* beneficiaries) of the other portion(s). The settlor or donee may exercise the power of revocation, appointment, or withdrawal to create a separate trust of some or all of the property subject to the power and may then or later exercise the authority described in this section with respect to that separate trust. Similarly, if the power applies only to a separate share of the trust, or if the power over a portion of the trust is exercised to establish a separate share, the authority under this section may be exercised with respect to that share insofar as the exercise does not intrude upon the administration of, or the rights of others in, the other share or shares of the trust. (See also Comment *f* on trusts with multiple settlors.) . . . .

i. Direction or authorization: trust amendment compared. As an exercise of ownership-equivalent rights, the exercise of a power holder's authority under this section, without more, does not have the effect of a lasting amendment to the terms of the trust. The period during which a settlor's or donee's direction or authorization is effective—somewhat like a temporary trust amendment—depends on the terms and nature of the direction or authorization. For an action of this general type to have the effect of a trust amendment applicable beyond the period of ownership equivalence, however, the settlor or donee would have to manifest the intention to amend the trust and would have to do so in a manner authorized for such an amendment by the terms of the trust or by applicable default law.

Thus, for example, a settlor's direction to a trustee to invest the entire trust estate only in tax-exempt municipal bonds, or only in some specified mix of such bonds and certain described common stocks, terminates upon the settlor's death or any earlier termination of the settlor's power to revoke. Whether the direction would also terminate on the settlor's loss of the capacity required to cancel or modify an investment directive (see Comment *a(2)*) is a matter of interpretation, depending primarily on the terms, nature, and purpose of the direction.

Unlike an exercise of ownership-equivalent authority (see last paragraph of Comment *a* and, e.g., § 29, Comment *i(2)*), an enduring amendment is (after the ownership-equivalent period expires) subject to the various policy limitations on enforcement and validity generally applicable to the terms of a trust, as described in Chapter 15 and elsewhere in this Restatement (e.g., §§ 29(c) and 96).

§ 75. Effect of Power to Control Acts of Trustee

Except in cases covered by § 74 (involving powers of revocation and other ownership-equivalent powers), if the terms of a trust reserve to the settlor or confer upon another a power to direct or otherwise control certain conduct of the trustee, the trustee has a duty to act in accordance with the requirements of the trust provision reserving or conferring the power and to comply with any exercise of that power, unless the attempted exercise is contrary to the terms of the trust or power or the trustee knows or has reason to believe that the attempted exercise violates a fiduciary duty that the power holder owes to the beneficiaries.

Comment:

a. *Scope of section; general observations.* The terms of a trust may reserve to a settlor or grant a designated person the authority to control the trustee in certain matters, by direction or by withholding a required consent. The person who holds a directory or veto power may be designated by name, by class or other description, or by inclusion in the trust provision of a list of persons to serve in the role concurrently or in sequence.

This section is concerned with situations in which the designated power holder is a settlor or beneficiary but is not covered by § 74, and with situations in which a designated person is a third party otherwise unconnected with the trust. The power holder's relationship to the trust is unimportant, except as it may be a factor in determining the nature or extent of the power. See Comment *c*. Situations in which a *trustee* is granted power to control the actions of co-trustees are considered in § 81, Comment *b*.

a(1). Cross-references. Situations involving the use of advisors or consultants are considered in § 77 (prudence), § 79 (impartiality), and § 88 (reasonableness of expenses). Situations in which a trustee delegates authority to an agent are considered in § 80.

Analogous though usually broader powers conferred upon a trustee, beneficiary, or third party to modify or terminate a trust are considered in § 64. . . . .

b. *Ordinary duty of trustee to comply.* Where the terms of the trust provide that, in administering the trust, the trustee shall take certain actions if so directed by another person, it is ordinarily (but see Comments *d* and *e*) the trustee's duty to comply with that person's direction; the trustee would ordinarily be liable for a loss resulting from failure to do so. (See generally Chapter 19.) Similarly, where a trust provision states that the trustee shall not do certain acts without the consent or direction of another, the trustee is ordinarily under a duty not to do such an act unless that consent or direction has been received, and the trustee would ordinarily be liable for a loss resulting from taking action without the required authorization. On the other hand, the trustee is ordinarily protected from liability for actions taken or not taken in accordance with a direction or veto (i.e., refusal of required consent) by the designated person.

Thus, for example, if the terms of a trust provide that the trustee shall acquire or sell such investments as the designated person shall direct, or that the trustee shall not acquire or sell any trust assets without that person's consent, the trustee must ordinarily comply with a direction, or refrain from acting without the required consent, of the designated person. The trustee ordinarily will be liable for a loss resulting from failure to comply with the trust provision, and ordinarily will not be liable for action or inaction resulting from compliance. But see Comments *d* and *e*.

A provision expressly purporting to relieve the trustee from liability for complying with the designated person's direction or veto does not necessarily insulate the trustee from liability in situations of improper compliance (Comments *d* and *e*), although the provision may narrow the conditions of liability in the manner of other exculpatory provisions. (See § 96.)

Illustration:

1. The terms of a trust instruct T, the trustee, to sell (and reinvest the proceeds of) any property held in the trust if D so directs, even though the property is a prudent trust investment. D directs T to sell certain trust property. T has a duty to sell that property within a reasonable time and is not liable merely for doing so; but, absent further direction that D may be authorized to give regarding the terms of the sale, the direction to sell does not exempt T from a trustee's normal fiduciary duties and liability with respect to the price and other terms of the sale. (Cf. § 74, Illustration 3, and immediately preceding text in Comment *b* of § 74.)

b(1). Trustee's duty to provide power holder with information and opportunity to respond. The duties of a trustee under a trust provision of this type include a duty to provide the designated person with such information and opportunity to respond as may be expressly or impliedly called for by the terms of the provision. This matter itself may present a problem of interpreting the trust instrument.

Where certain actions the trustee may wish to take are not to be taken without the consent, direction, or authorization of a designated person, the provision is not likely to be unclear in this respect; even without further instruction in the instrument or from the power holder, it is implicit in the nature of the provision that the trustee must inform that person of any desired actions and allow a reasonable opportunity to respond. Nor is a provision likely to be unclear when it simply mandates that certain types of action be taken "only" upon the direction of the power holder; absent greater specificity, the wording of the provision implies that the trustee must advise the power holder of any particular needs for direction, as well as supplying general information on matters relevant to the power holder's possible exercise of the directory power.

Conversely, a provision may be carefully drafted to make clear that the trustee is to proceed with the administration of the trust as if the power to direct or prevent action did not exist, until the power holder takes the initiative by directing either that the trustee take certain action or that the trustee not act without receiving further direction or consent, possibly for some period of time specified by the power holder. Even in such a case of power-holder initiative, the trustee has a duty to keep the designated person reasonably informed of trust information and circumstances of relevance to the power holder's authority. Cf. § 82 on a trustee's general duty to provide information to beneficiaries.

Less clear is a trust provision simply requiring the trustee to make or retain "such investments as my wife, W, shall direct," or a provision simply stating that "my husband, H, shall have" the power or right "to direct the trustee with regard to the purchase, sale, or retention of trust investments," or with regard to certain specified assets or matters. Is the trustee under a duty to proceed with administration in the absence of some direction from the designated person? That is, is this trustee in the position of the trustee in the immediately preceding paragraph?

Where the trust terms are unclear, leaving doubt as to the duties of the trustee in this respect, the trustee is justified in applying to the appropriate court for instructions (§ 71). See further, on the importance of these questions, Comment *g*.

c. Whether power is held in fiduciary capacity or for benefit of power holder. A power to direct the actions or to prevent proposed actions of a trustee is often conferred upon a designated person for the benefit of the trust beneficiaries generally. Sometimes, however, such a power may be granted for the sole benefit of the designated power holder, or just for one or more of the beneficiaries or even for some person whom the trustee could not otherwise benefit. Or a power may be intended to serve some combination of these purposes.

Ultimately, the purposes of a power and the nature and extent of the rights, duties, and liabilities of the power holder, and thus also of the trustee, depend upon trust language and all relevant circumstances. Although no precise rules on the matter can be stated, some generalizations are possible.

c(1). Power holder other than settlor. If the designated person has expertise in matters of investment, for example, a power to control the trustee in the acquisition or disposition of trust investments would presumptively be a power for the benefit of the beneficiaries of the trust generally, and thus (see Comment *e*) a power held in a fiduciary capacity. A power given to the settlor's widow or widower, however, to prevent the sale of residential property held in the trust by refusing to consent to its sale would presumptively be a power for the benefit of the occupant-power holder. Thus, it would not be held in a fiduciary capacity. (See, however, Comment *d*.)

A power conferred on a parent of the income beneficiary of a trust to direct the trustee to pay that beneficiary additional amounts from trust principal ordinarily would be a power for the benefit of the income beneficiary. The parent would nevertheless hold the power in a fiduciary capacity, although presumptively with broad discretion in its exercise so that there would be no violation of the parent's fiduciary duties in the absence of bad faith or indifference to the competing interests of other beneficiaries or to the purposes of the trust or power. (Compare § 50, Comments *b* and *c*, and, more generally, § 87.) It is even possible, however, that the wording of the power and other admissible evidence of settlor intention (see § 4) might justify an interpretation that a power such as this is a power of appointment, with the only duty of the trustee then being to ascertain whether an attempted exercise is within the terms of the power. Cf. Restatement Third, Property (Wills and Other Donative Transfers) §§ 19.15–19.17.

Illustrations:

2. F, a financial planner and friend of the settlor (S), is empowered to direct T, the trustee of S's testamentary trust, in all matters of investment involving the trust estate, which is held for L for life, remainder to L's issue. F holds the directory power in a fiduciary capacity.

3. S's will established a trust for his daughter, D, for life, with remainder thereafter to go to D's issue. Included in the trust estate is the residential property that S and D had shared as their home at the time of S's death. The terms of the trust forbid the trustee from selling or encumbering that property without D's consent. Absent evidence to

the contrary, D holds her veto power solely for her own benefit and not in a fiduciary capacity.

c(2). Power reserved by settlor. A question of interpretation arises when the settlor of an irrevocable trust (contrast § 74 on revocable trusts) reserves a power to control the trustee in making or retaining trust investments—or just certain trust investments. The power may be one that is exercisable for the settlor's own benefit, for the benefit of the trust beneficiaries generally, or, especially when the settlor is a beneficiary, for some combination of these.

Illustrative of circumstances tending to show that a reserved power of control regarding certain investments is for the sole benefit of the settlor would be that the settlor had placed one-half of the shares of a corporation in trust while retaining the other half, or that the settlor had placed an undivided interest in real property in the trust while retaining the remaining interest. In such a case, the circumstances suggest a purpose of protecting the settlor's position with respect to the retained property. Yet, the advantage to the trust generally of a settlor's special knowledge of the particular investment might suggest a broader or mixed purpose. Extrinsic evidence is admissible in such cases of conflicting inferences. (For an analogous situation involving an apparently beneficial veto power conferred by a settlor upon another, see § 49, Comment *c*.)

If a settlor's power is for the benefit of the beneficiaries generally or for both the settlor and other beneficiaries, the power is held by the settlor in a fiduciary capacity (Comment *e*). Nevertheless, it would ordinarily be permissible for the settlor to exercise somewhat broader investment discretion than might be appropriate for the trustee alone. Illustrative are judgments involving such matters as portfolio risk-and-return objectives (see § 77 and § 90(a)) or tilting the ingredients and benefits of overall return in favor of certain beneficiaries (see § 79(2) and § 90(c)(1)), although a settlor who lacks power to revoke or directly amend the trust must exercise a directory power in a manner reasonably consistent with the original purposes of the trust. Cf. § 87, Comment *d*.

d. Duties of trustee where power is for sole benefit of power holder. A power that is for the sole benefit of the person holding the power is not a fiduciary power. Nevertheless, the power holder must respect any limitations or other terms of the power. So also, the power holder must not abuse the power by exercising it in a manner that is harmful or indifferent to the interests of other beneficiaries when such exercise is not reasonably related to the benefit intended for the power holder. Cf. § 64, Comment *c* (on nonfiduciary power of a beneficiary to modify or terminate the trust).

The primary duty of the trustee in regard to such a power is to ascertain whether an attempted exercise is within the terms of the power and to refuse to comply if it is not. If the trustee knows or has reason to believe that an attempted exercise exceeds the scope or would otherwise constitute an abuse of the power (supra), the trustee would have a duty not to comply with the direction given by the holder of the power. If inquiry does not satisfy the trustee's concerns on one of these grounds, and the power holder insists upon compliance notwithstanding the trustee's objection, the trustee may apply to the court for instructions (§ 71).

e. Duties of trustee where power holder is subject to fiduciary obligations. If a power to control the actions of a trustee is for the benefit of the beneficiaries generally, or in whole or in part for the benefit of someone other than the holder of the power, the power holder is subject to fiduciary duties in the exercise of the power. On the potential liability of the holder of a power of control, see Comment *f*. The trustee in such a case is under duties generally comparable to those of a trustee with respect to the actions of a co-trustee. Cf. § 81.

If the trustee has reason to believe that the holder of a power may be attempting to exercise it in violation of a fiduciary duty to which the holder is subject, the trustee has a duty not to comply and may be liable for compliance in disregard of that duty. If inquiry does not satisfy the trustee's concerns, and the power holder insists upon compliance notwithstanding the trustee's objection, the trustee may apply to the court for instructions (§ 71).

Even though the person holding the power of control holds it as a fiduciary and in fact violates a fiduciary duty in exercising the power, the trustee is not liable for acting in accordance with the exercise of the power unless the trustee knows or should have known (cf. § 72, Comment *c*) that the power holder acted in violation of the fiduciary duty. Thus, where the terms of the trust provide that the trustee shall make such investments as a designated person may direct, and the person directs a trustee to purchase certain securities, the trustee is not liable for doing so merely because it is later shown that the designated person had a personal interest in having the trust purchase the securities, provided the trustee neither knew nor had reason to believe that (and thus a duty to investigate whether) this conflict of interests existed. Similarly, if the designated person directs the trustee to purchase certain real estate for the trust at a particular price that is excessive, the trustee is not liable merely because the power holder had failed to exercise due diligence in assessing the quality and value of the property if the trustee had no knowledge or reason to believe that this failure had occurred.

f. *Duties of power holder*. A person designated by a settlor to hold a power of control has no duties under the provision unless the person has expressly or impliedly accepted the power. (Cf. § 35, Comment *b*.) Even after acceptance, a power holder may terminate his or her duties and rights under the directory or veto provision by release of the power. (Cf. § 36, especially Comments *c* and *d*. Also see § 82 on the trustee's duty to inform beneficiaries of significant developments or changes in administration.)

Where a designated person has power to control the action of a trustee and holds that power as a fiduciary, and if the terms of the trust do not permit the trustee to act without the direction or consent of that person, the power holder is liable for any loss resulting to the trust estate from a breach of a fiduciary duty as power holder, whether as a result of improper exercise of the power or improper failure to exercise it. (Relevant to this failure of the power holder to act, however, is the trustee's duty to inform under Comment *b(1)*.) The designated person's fiduciary duties and liabilities with respect to the power are generally comparable to those of a trustee.

If the terms of the power merely authorize the designated person to direct a trustee who is otherwise under a duty to proceed with the administration of the trust so long as the power is not exercised, ordinarily the only duty of the power holder is not to exercise the power in a manner inconsistent with the fiduciary duties owed to one or more of the beneficiaries. Circumstances, however, may justify one or more of the beneficiaries in relying on the holder of such a power to monitor the administration of the trust, so that there may be an affirmative duty to act when the power holder knows or should know that the purposes of the power call for some action to be taken.

That the power holder is entitled to be kept reasonably informed by the trustee, see Comment *b(1)*. On limitations and duties of the power holder even when the power is one for the power holder's sole benefit, see Comment *d*.

g. Duties of trustee in absence of required direction or consent. Where the terms of the trust provide that the trustee shall not act except at the direction of another, the trustee is ordinarily justified in doing nothing until such direction is given. If, however, the trustee knows, or reasonable attention to trust matters would reveal, that the failure of the other to exercise the directory power is likely to damage the trust or violates its terms or a fiduciary duty of the power holder, the trustee has a duty to make the power holder aware of the need for the power to be exercised. If the holder of the power refuses to exercise the power notwithstanding the trustee's recommendation, the trustee may apply to the court for instructions (§ 71). If appropriate (see § 66(1)) and necessary (e.g., urgency and unavailability or recalcitrance of the power holder), the trustee should apply for court authorization to deviate from the terms of the trust (§ 66(2)).

Where the terms of the trust do not allow the trustee to act without the consent of another, the trustee is not necessarily justified in doing nothing merely because the consent has not been received. The trustee should undertake to obtain that consent if the circumstances are such that the trustee believes that action ought to be taken. If the other person refuses to give consent, the trustee may be justified in doing nothing further, but if the trustee knows, or a reasonable inquiry would reveal, that the failure of the other to consent is likely to damage the trust or violates its terms or a fiduciary duty of the power holder, the trustee may have a duty to apply to the court for instructions (§ 71), or for authorization to deviate from the trust provision if necessary and appropriate. (See § 66.)

See also Comment *b(1)* on the trustee's general duty to provide information relevant to the role of the power holder and to allow reasonable opportunity to respond.

g(1). Designated person's death, disability, or release. On the death of the holder of a power to direct or prevent certain actions by the trustee, or after the holder's release of the power, unless a replacement power holder is designated or otherwise provided for in terms of the trust, the trustee's duties under the directory or veto provision terminate. The trustee is thereafter to proceed with the administration of the trust as if the provision had not been included in the terms of the trust. Cf. § 76, Comment *b(1)*, and § 73, Comment *a* (no duty to comply with trust provision when impossible to do so); but cf. § 82 on duty to keep beneficiaries informed.

Similarly, in the event of the power holder's lack of capacity to understand the type of financial, business, personal, or other judgments that would be involved in an exercise of the power (cf. § 74, Comment *a(2)*), with no replacement power holder provided for, the trustee's duties under the directory or veto provision generally terminate, or are at least suspended, with administration of the trust generally to proceed as if the provision had not been included in its terms. If, however, a provision conferring the power is one for the benefit of the power holder, the trustee's duties are likely to be uncertain. In such a case the trustee is justified in applying for court instructions to determine whether, to what extent, and for what purposes a conservator (or other legal representative) or an agent under a durable power of attorney may exercise the power on behalf of the power holder. (Compare the possible exercise of an incapacitated settlor's (i) power to revoke or amend in § 63, Comment *l*, and (ii) power to direct the trustee in § 74, Comment *a(2)*.) The questions presented for instruction may require the court to interpret not only the terms of the trust but perhaps also the terms of an instrument creating a durable power of attorney.

CHAPTER 15

SPECIFIC DUTIES OF TRUSTEESHIP

Introductory Note: This chapter (§§ 76–84) deals with the duties owed by a trustee to the beneficiaries during the period of trust administration, including on trust termination (on which see further § 89 on Powers and Duties on Termination). A violation of one or more of a trustee's duties is a breach of trust. The liabilities of trustees and remedies of the beneficiaries arising from a breach of trust are considered in Chapters 18 and 19.

Section 76 begins by instructing the trustee to proceed diligently with the administration of the trust and to comply with its terms and applicable law. It also lists and briefly examines basic functions or responsibilities typically encompassed by the duty to administer a trust.

The core of trust fiduciary law is found in §§ 77 through 79—the fundamental standards of fiduciary conduct in trust administration. These three sections deal, respectively, with the trustee's duties of *prudence* (so fundamental to the investment function and further developed in §§ 90–92), *loyalty* (often called the "cardinal" principle of fiduciary relationships, but particularly strict in the law of trusts), and *impartiality* (balancing the diverse interests and competing claims—concurrently and over time—of the various beneficiaries or objectives of typical modern trusts).

The other sections of this chapter deal with fiduciary duties that are ancillary to and supportive of these core duties. Sections 80 and 81 describe the standards of conduct that apply when a trustee relies on or works with others (agents or co-trustees) in performing the duties of trusteeship. Sections 82–84 essentially prescribe a fiduciary standard of openness and transparency in trust administration, examining the duties of trustees regarding disclosure of information to beneficiaries, maintenance and availability of records of administration, and identification of trust assets, all in order to facilitate the enforcement of the trustee's duties, the rights of the beneficiaries, and the purposes of the trust.

Except as accompanying language or context indicates otherwise, references in this chapter (as generally in this Restatement) to a trustee's "duties" are to duties the trustee owes to the trust beneficiaries—i.e., the trustee's fiduciary duties—rather than to duties or obligations that may for some reason run to others. On trustees' liabilities to third parties, see Chapter 21.

§ 76. Duty to Administer the Trust in Accordance with Its Terms and Applicable Law

(1) The trustee has a duty to administer the trust, diligently and in good faith, in accordance with the terms of the trust and applicable law.

(2) In administering the trust, the trustee's responsibilities include performance of the following functions:

(a) ascertaining the duties and powers of the trusteeship, and the beneficiaries and purposes of the trust;

(b) collecting and protecting trust property;

(c) managing the trust estate to provide returns or other benefits from trust property; and

(d) applying or distributing trust income and principal during the administration of the trust and upon its termination.

General Comment:

a. *Duty depends on acceptance of trusteeship.* A trust can be created without notice to or acceptance by the person designated as trustee (§ 14), but that person has no duty to administer the trust unless he or she accepts the trusteeship. Absent expressed or implied acceptance, a designated person is free to disclaim the office of trustee and normally incurs no risk of liability. (See § 35.) Once having accepted the office, however, a trustee has a duty to administer the trust as long as he or she continues to serve as trustee.

That the duty to administer the trust applies even though the trustee serves without compensation, see § 70, Comment *d(1)*. On the effect of another's power to control a trustee's actions upon the trustee's responsibilities in administering the trust, see §§ 74 and 75.

On resignation by a trustee, see § 36, and cf. §§ 37 (on removal) and 34 (on appointment and replacement of trustees). On the duties and powers of successor or substitute trustees, see § 85(2), and cf. §§ 81 and 39 on co-trusteeship.

Comment on Subsection (1):

b. *Duty to administer: in general.* The trustee's duty to administer the trust as stated in this section is an affirmative duty. Thus, a trustee may commit a breach of trust by improperly failing to act, as well by improperly exercising the powers of the trusteeship.

A trustee has a duty in administering a trust not only to act in furtherance of its purposes but also to act in accordance with its terms and applicable law. On the interplay of law and trust provisions, see Comment *b(1)*.

The duties of a trustee in administering a trust also encompass the performance of the basic functions described hereafter in Comments *c–f* under Subsection (2).

b(1). Administration in accordance with terms of the trust and applicable law. References in this section, and elsewhere in Part 6, to the terms of the trust (defined generally in § 4) also refer to trust terms as reformed (§ 62) or modified (§§ 66, 67) by court decree, and as modified by the settlor (§ 63 and cf. § 74(1)) or others (§ 64, and cf. § 74(2)) or by consent of all beneficiaries (§ 65). See Introductory Note to Part 6.

A trustee has both (i) a duty generally to comply with the terms of the trust and (ii) a duty to comply with the mandates of trust law except as permissibly modified by the terms of the trust. Because of this combination of duties, the fiduciary duties of trusteeship sometimes override or limit the effect of a trustee's duty to comply with trust provisions; conversely, the normal standards of trustee conduct prescribed by trust fiduciary law may, at least to some extent, be modified by the terms of the trust. Briefly stated, much of trust law, especially trust fiduciary law, is default law—but some is not. The interaction of fiduciary law and trust provisions is considered in more detail as various fiduciary duties are stated and explained, in general in §§ 77–84, in regard to investments in §§ 90–92, and in other respects elsewhere in this Restatement. For example, "absolute discretion" purportedly granted in the terms of a trust instrument is *not absolute* under principles of trust law described in general in § 87 and specifically with regard to discretionary distributions in § 50, Comments *b* and *c*.

The normal duty of a trustee to obey the terms of the trust also does not apply to provisions that are invalid because they are unlawful or against public policy. See § 29 and § 72, Comment *a*. Also, on the effects of impossibility and impracticability, see §§ 30 and 73, and cf. §§ 66 and 67; on permissible trust purposes, see §§ 26, 29, and 47. In situations of uncertainty, see § 71 and cf. § 77, Comment *b(2)*.

b(2). *Appropriate place of administration*. A trustee's duty to administer a trust includes an initial and continuing duty to administer it at a location that is reasonably suitable to the purposes of the trust, its sound and efficient administration, and the interests of its beneficiaries. Terms of the trust, however, may establish expressly or by implication a place of administration, initially at least, and may affect the trustee's duty in the matter. . . . .

This continuing duty will sometimes limit a trustee's inherent general authority to change the place of a trust's administration, or it may require the appointment of an agent to handle some matters. Under some circumstances the trustee may have a duty to change or to permit (e.g., by resignation) a change in the place of administration. Changes in the place of administration by a trustee, or even the relocation of beneficiaries or other developments, may result in costs or geographic inconvenience serious enough to justify removal of the trustee. (See § 37, Comment *e*.)

If a trustee is considering making a significant change in the place of administration, the trustee has a duty to so inform beneficiaries (see § 82) and to invite their comments. This does not mean that objecting beneficiaries have a right to veto a contemplated change, but in the event of objection, either a beneficiary or the trustee may seek court instructions (§ 71).

Comment on Subsection (2):

c. *Clause (a): Ascertaining the duties and powers of the trusteeship; ascertaining the beneficiaries and purposes of the trust*. Promptly upon undertaking administration of the trust, a trustee or successor trustee should review the terms of the trust for the purpose of understanding the powers and duties of the trusteeship and also to determine the beneficiaries and purposes of the trust, with the aid and guidance of counsel as necessary.

On the availability of court instructions on matters of reasonable doubt, see § 71. That the trustee should promptly advise interested parties of the existence of the trust or of a change in the trusteeship, as well as providing certain basic information, see § 82.

d. Clause (b): Collection and protection of trust property. The trustee's duty to administer the trust includes a duty, at the outset of administration, to take reasonable steps to ascertain the assets of the trust estate and to take and keep control of those assets.

In the case of a testamentary trust, these initial steps should include obtaining and examining an accounting from (or the records of) the settlor's executor. Similarly, a successor trustee ordinarily (but cf. § 74, Comments *a(2)*, *d*, and *e*) should obtain an accounting from or review the records of the predecessor trustee. Furthermore, in cases of these types, the trustee ordinarily has the associated responsibility of taking reasonable steps to uncover and redress any breach of duty committed by a predecessor fiduciary.

The manner of acquiring and maintaining control of the trust property depends on the nature of the property, the terms of the trust, and what is appropriate to the prudent administration of the trust. Accordingly, except as it may be reasonable for the trustee to entrust possession to an attorney, broker, banker, or other agent (§ 80), the trustee is responsible for taking and keeping possession of securities. Also, the trustee is ordinarily to take and keep possession or control of chattels, except as a beneficiary may be entitled to possession or control under or consistent with the terms of the trust. If land is held in the trust, it depends on the trust terms and on considerations of prudent management whether the trustee has a duty to retain possession, to lease the property to others, or to give possession of it to a beneficiary; if the land was subject to a lease at the time of the trust's creation, the lessee should be notified of the trust and directed to pay the rent to the trustee. If the trust property includes a chose in action, the trustee should take necessary steps to inform the obligor of the trust, to receive payments of income and principal, and to enforce the chose on maturity.

The duty of protecting the trust estate includes taking reasonable steps to enforce or realize on other claims held by the trust and to defend actions that may result in a loss to the trust estate. Reasonable steps may include taking an appeal to a higher court, compromise or arbitration of claims by or against the trust, or even abandoning a valid claim or not resisting an unenforceable claim if the costs and risk of litigation make such a decision reasonable under all the circumstances. . . . .

The trustee also owes to the beneficiaries a duty to act with prudence—that is, to use reasonable care and skill (see § 77)—to preserve trust property. This duty includes the use of reasonable care to protect trust property from loss or damage, and to make such repairs (cf. § 88, Comment *b*, on improvements), obtain such insurance (fire, theft, liability, etc.), pay such obligations, and bring such actions as a prudent person would for the protection and preservation of trust property. If there is not sufficient money in the trust estate to provide what is needed for the preservation of trust property, and funds cannot reasonably be raised from the trust estate by sale or borrowing or otherwise, it is the duty of the trustee to notify the beneficiaries in order to give them the opportunity to advance the necessary funds; the trustee individually is under no duty to advance money to the trust (and cf. § 78, on self-dealing), although advances by a trustee are permissible under some circumstances (id., Comment *c(6)*).

The terms of the trust may modify the duties of the trustee with respect to securing and preserving the trust property, but the trustee may not act in bad faith or in disregard of the other terms or purposes of the trust. See generally §§ 87 and 96.

d(1). Duty with respect to bank deposits. Although a trustee can properly deposit trust money in a bank (or other financial institution), reasonable care must be used in selecting the bank and in arranging the terms of the deposit (see § 90), and also to earmark the account in the trustee's name as trustee (see § 84). A bank account is an appropriate method for the safekeeping of funds and making them available from time to time for expenses, distribution, or investment; but prudence requires a balancing of convenience and expense against the duty to make trust assets productive (Comment *e*). Thus, the facilities of or available to the trustee for expeditious movement of funds from account to account must be considered, as must restrictions on withdrawal, for the trustee is liable for interest lost by lack of reasonable diligence. (Again, see § 78 (duty of loyalty), Comment *c(6)*).

e. Clause (c): Management to provide returns or other benefits from trust property. The trustee's duty to administer the trust includes a duty to make reasonable efforts to obtain suitable investment returns from trust assets and to provide other benefits consistent with the nature of the property and the terms and purposes of the trust. See generally § 77 on the duty of prudence, § 79 on impartiality and the associated duty with regard to income productivity, § 89, Comment *d*, on management during the process of termination, and §§ 90–92 on the investment function.

f. Clause (d): Application or distribution of trust income and principal. In administering the trust, the trustee has a duty to comply with the terms of the trust and applicable law providing for the distribution or application of trust income and principal to or for the beneficiaries or for the charitable or other purposes of the trust throughout the period of its ongoing administration, and also at the time of its termination. See particularly: §§ 49 and 50 on distribution entitlements of beneficiaries of private trusts; §§ 28 and 47, respectively, on charitable and noncharitable purposes; and § 89 on trust termination.

The trustee has a duty not to misdeliver trust funds or other trust property, and is ordinarily liable for failure to deliver the property to its proper distributee—that is, to the designated beneficiary or his or her assignee. Therefore, a trustee normally (absent, e.g., proper consent or agreement among potential beneficiaries) has a duty to petition the appropriate court for instructions (§ 71) when the remainder or current distributive provisions of a trust are ambiguous or otherwise unclear. A trustee is not liable, however, when a misdelivery results from information the trustee was unable to obtain despite diligent, good-faith efforts or results from reasonable reliance on the express provisions of a trust instrument. (To understand possible causes of misdelivery in this context, note, for example: § 4 that "terms of the trust" may have a meaning broader than just what is expressed in a writing; § 62, Comment *b*, allowing correction of a scrivener's error in seemingly clear trust provisions; § 51, Comment *d*, that a beneficiary's interest may be assigned without notice to the trustee; and the possibility of skillful deception.)

Similarly, if trust property is distributed to one or more persons who would be entitled to it under the provisions of a trust that is later held to be invalid in whole or in part, or that is later found to have been amended or revoked in whole or in part, the trustee may be liable to the person(s) properly entitled to the property. Specifically, the trustee is liable in such a case if, but only if, at the time of the distribution, either the trustee knew that the trust or a trust provision was invalid, amended, or revoked, or the trustee had reason for concern that the trust or provision may be invalid or that it may have been revoked or amended (e.g., was aware of an unbarred claim to that effect). Again, on the availability of court instructions, see § 71.

Although trustees may be relieved of liability for some acts of misdelivery under principles or rules designed to avoid unnecessary costs and delays or unwarranted surcharge (above, and more generally compare § 95), the rules of this Comment do not preclude the imposition of an obligation of restitution on the recipient of an improper distribution. See generally Chapter 20. . . . .

§ 77. Duty of Prudence

(1) The trustee has a duty to administer the trust as a prudent person would, in light of the purposes, terms, and other circumstances of the trust.

(2) The duty of prudence requires the exercise of reasonable care, skill, and caution.

(3) If the trustee possesses, or procured appointment by purporting to possess, special facilities or greater skill than that of a person of ordinary prudence, the trustee has a duty to use such facilities or skill.

General Comment:

a. *Test of prudence.* In matters relating to the administration of the trust, the trustee has a duty to exercise prudence—that is, to act with care, skill, and caution (Comment *b*)—as well as a duty to adhere to the other fiduciary standards described in other sections of this chapter.

The test of prudence is one of conduct not of performance. The trustee's conduct, and compliance with other fiduciary standards, is to be judged as of the time of the decision or action in question.

Thus, the prudence of a trustee's conduct is to be judged on the basis of circumstances at the time of that conduct, not with the benefit of hindsight or by taking account of developments that occur after the time of the action or decision. Also, whether a breach of trust has occurred depends on the prudence or imprudence of the trustee's conduct, not on the eventual results of managerial or other decisions. Investment performance or other results of trustee conduct become relevant, however, when a breach of trust is found and the measure of liability is in issue.

On prudence in the investment function, see §§ 90–92 (the "Prudent Investor Rule"). On prudence in delegation, see § 80 and also § 90, Comment *j*. On prudence and its application to a trustee's exercise of certain powers, see § 86.

Comment on Subsections (1) and (2):

b. *Elements of prudence: care, skill, and caution.* The duty of prudence encompasses the duty to exercise reasonable care and skill in trust administration and the duty to act with a degree of caution suitable to the particular trust and its objectives, circumstances, and overall plan of administration.

The duty of *care* requires the trustee to exercise reasonable effort and diligence in planning the administration of the trust, in making and implementing administrative decisions, and in monitoring the trust situation, with due attention to the trust's objectives and the interests of the beneficiaries. This will ordinarily involve investigation appropriate to the particular action under consideration, and also obtaining relevant information about such matters as the contents and resources of the trust estate and the circumstances and requirements of the trust and its beneficiaries. (More generally, cf. Comment *b(1)*.)

As necessary or appropriate to informed decisionmaking, care may also call for obtaining and considering the advice of others on a reasonable basis (cf. § 88 on proper expenses). It is ordinarily satisfactory that information or advice be obtained from sources on which prudent property owners or managers in the community customarily rely. (On the possible effects of trustees' reliance on the work of agents or on the advice of financial or legal counsel, see Comment *b(2)* and § 80, Comment *g* . . . .)

More is required than the exercise of reasonable care alone, for a trustee may be liable for losses that result from failure to use the *skill* of an individual of ordinary intelligence, despite use of all the skill the particular trustee possesses. A person who serves as trustee should be reasonably able to understand the basic duties of prudent trusteeship. The practical need in trust law for some objective standard in these matters means that some persons are not properly capable of serving as trustees.

The fact that some aspects of a trust's administration may require knowledge and experience greater than that of a particular individual of ordinary intelligence, however, does not normally prevent that person from serving as trustee. This just emphasizes the importance of obtaining competent guidance and assistance (supra) sufficient to meet the standards required by the combination of care and skill in a given situation. Simple, written guidelines prepared by legal counsel may be helpful for a trustee's general reference, or for presentation by an inexperienced trustee in conferring with a financial or other adviser or agent. Cf. § 80 on delegation (and id., Comment *b*, on advice and consultation). Essentially, a trustee may either possess or hire the degree and types of skill needed for a specific transaction or required more generally by the needs and strategies of the particular trust's administration. See Comment *b(1)*.

Thus, these two basic standards of trusteeship are neither excessively demanding nor monolithic, neither precluding conscientious service by friends or family members nor permitting casual, inattentive behavior by trustees who are able to meet a standard of competence and conduct higher than the ordinary. (See Comment *e*.)

In addition to the duty to use care and skill, the trustee must exercise the *caution* of a prudent person managing similar assets for similar purposes. The duty to act with caution does not, of course, mean the avoidance of all risk, but refers to a degree of caution that is reasonably appropriate or suitable to the particular trust, its purposes and circumstances, the beneficiaries' interests, and the trustee's plan for administering the trust and achieving its objectives.

On the standards of care, skill, and caution imposed on a trustee in making and monitoring investments, for which the duty of prudence has its most significant application in most trusts, see §§ 90–92. Also, see generally § 86 for illustrative applications of the requirement of prudence (and other duties) in the exercise of various powers of trustees.

b(1). Prudent administration: relevant circumstances and considerations. It is not possible to state all of the factors that are necessary or appropriate for a trustee to take into account in making decisions or taking action in the many diverse aspects of the investment, management, protection, and distribution of trust property. Some generalizations are nevertheless possible and useful regarding considerations that are likely to be relevant to all or many trusts and their beneficiaries and to require analysis or verification by the trustee.

Among the most obvious of the factors to be considered are the terms and purposes of the trust, the value and nature of the trust estate, the likely duration of the trust, and the amount and timing of its distribution requirements, along with potentially associated needs for liquidity, stability of income flow, and preservation of (or growth in) the purchasing power of capital. Inevitably related to some of the foregoing, insofar as relevant to the trust purposes, are the needs, independent resources, and other personal and financial circumstances and concerns or goals of the various beneficiaries. These various factors together offer illumination regarding such important considerations as the risk tolerance and tax positions of the trust and its beneficiaries, as well as other concerns that are fundamental to prudent decisions and strategies in matters ranging from investment management to discretionary distributions.

Other considerations and circumstances (at some risk of redundancy) that are likely to be important to prudent administration of a trust include: the expected returns (including both income and capital elements) or other benefits of various courses of action that might be pursued, plus their anticipated tax and cost consequences; any special value or relationship an asset or course of action may have to the purposes of the trust or to one or more of the beneficiaries; the skills and facilities of, or reasonably available to, the trustee; and general economic conditions and potential effects of inflation or deflation.

What constitutes due diligence, satisfying the duty of prudence, is inevitably affected by the nature of the transaction or activity and the market(s) involved. . . . . Also see § 86, and the discussion of various types of investments and investment courses of action in § 90, e.g., in Comments *o* (real estate) and *p* (venture capital), and compare id., Comment *h(1)* (passive strategies) with id., Comment *h(2)* (active strategies) . . . .

b(2). Effect of advice of counsel. The work of trusteeship, from interpreting the terms of the trust to decisionmaking in various aspects of administration, can raise questions of legal complexity. Taking the advice of legal counsel on such matters evidences prudence on the part of the trustee. Reliance on advice of counsel, however, is not a complete defense to an alleged breach of trust, because that would reward a trustee who shopped for legal advice that would support the trustee's desired course of conduct or who otherwise acted unreasonably in procuring or following legal advice. In seeking and considering advice of counsel, the trustee has a duty to act with prudence. Thus, if a trustee has selected trust counsel prudently and in good faith, and has relied on plausible advice on a matter within counsel's expertise, the trustee's conduct is significantly probative of prudence.

On the duty of a trustee (or successor trustee) regarding redress of attorney malpractice, see generally § 76, Comment *d*, and compare § 80, Comments *d(2)* and *g*.

c. Ignorance of trust provisions. Lack of awareness or understanding of the terms of the trust normally will not excuse a trustee from liability.

Reasonable care (Comment *b*) requires that the trustee, with advice of counsel or court instructions (§ 71) as necessary, become acquainted with and acquire a reasonable understanding of the terms of the trust, the rights and interests of the beneficiaries, and the nature and circumstances of the trust property. See § 76(2)(a), and especially id., Comment *c*.

d. *Standard fixed by terms of the trust.* Because the normal duty of prudence in matters of administration is default law, the terms of the trust may modify or relax its requirements (§ 76, Comment *b(2)*), especially—but not solely—as regards the element of caution. Trust provisions fixing a standard of prudence lower than that otherwise required of trustees are strictly construed. In any event, trust terms may not altogether dispense with the fundamental requirement that trustees not behave recklessly but act in good faith, with some suitable degree of care, and in a manner consistent with the terms and purposes of the trust and the interests of the beneficiaries (cf. § 86 and § 87, and also § 50, Comments *b* and *c*).

On the effects (and limits) of exculpatory provisions in the terms of trusts, see § 96.

Comment on Subsection (3):

e. *Special skill or facilities and the standard of prudence.* It follows from the requirement of care, as well as from sound policy, that if the trustee actually possesses a degree of skill greater than that of an individual of ordinary intelligence (Comment *b*), the trustee has a duty to make use of that skill, and is ordinarily liable for a loss that results from failure to do so. Similarly, if a trustee, such as a corporate or professional fiduciary, procured the appointment as trustee by expressly or impliedly representing that it possessed greater skill than that of an individual of ordinary intelligence, the trustee may be liable for failure to make reasonably diligent use of that degree of skill. So also, if the trustee has or represents that it has special facilities for administering the trust, the trustee has a duty to make reasonably diligent use of those facilities, and may be held liable for failure to do so.

Even a trustee with special skills and facilities may, as a matter of reasonable care in some circumstances, have a duty to obtain guidance or assistance in carrying out responsibilities appropriate to the plan for administration of the particular trust. See, e.g., § 90 (on investment matters), especially id., Comment *j*; and more generally see § 80 (duty with regard to delegation).

On the power to incur expenses that are reasonable in amount and appropriate to the trusteeship, see § 88.

§ 78. Duty of Loyalty

(1) Except as otherwise provided in the terms of the trust, a trustee has a duty to administer the trust solely in the interest of the beneficiaries, or solely in furtherance of its charitable purpose.

(2) Except in discrete circumstances, the trustee is strictly prohibited from engaging in transactions that involve self-dealing or that otherwise involve or create a conflict between the trustee's fiduciary duties and personal interests.

(3) Whether acting in a fiduciary or personal capacity, a trustee has a duty in dealing with a beneficiary to deal fairly and to

communicate to the beneficiary all material facts the trustee knows or should know in connection with the matter.

General Comment:

a. The trustee and the trust relationship. It follows from the nature of the trust relationship (§ 2) that the trustee stands in a fiduciary relationship with respect to the beneficiaries as to all matters within the scope of the trust relationship, that is, all matters involving the administration of the trust and its property. The duty of loyalty is, for trustees, particularly strict even by comparison to the standards of other fiduciary relationships.

Although the commentary hereafter often refers only to trust "beneficiaries," this section and commentary apply to *charitable* as well as private trusts, with the power to avoid transactions or to seek other relief residing in the appropriate attorney general or others having standing to enforce the trust (§ 94).

Subsection (1) states the trust law's fundamental principle of undivided loyalty. The breadth of this principle is exemplified in Comment *f* (acts serving interest of third parties or nontrust objectives); and cf. Comments *e(1)* and *e(2)*.

With limited exceptions (see Comments *c* and *c(4)-c(8)*, below), the rule of Subsection (2) strictly prohibits the trustee from entering into transactions involving the trust property, or affecting its investment or management, if the transaction is for the trustee's personal account (self-dealing) or otherwise involves or creates a conflict between the fiduciary duties and personal interests of the trustee (see Comment *d*), unless authorized: by a proper court (Comment *c(1)*); expressly or impliedly by the terms of the trust (Comment *c(2)*); or by all of the beneficiaries (Comments *c(3)* and *g*, and cf. § 97 on the effect of consent by less than all beneficiaries). This rule also prohibits the trustee personally from engaging in transactions that, though not involving trust property, place the trustee in a position in which it is reasonably foreseeable that a conflict of fiduciary and personal interests may arise in the future. See Comment *e*.

The rule of Subsection (3) is not so strict, although it is similar to basic loyalty concepts in some other fiduciary relationships. In addition to dealings in the trustee's fiduciary capacity with trust beneficiaries (including obtaining consent from them), this rule also applies to a trustee's personal transactions that fall outside Subsections (1) and (2) but that nevertheless may be affected by the broader confidential relationship the trustee ordinarily has with respect to the trust beneficiaries during the existence of the trust, and thereafter (Comment *h*) for as long as the trustee retains significant influence over the beneficiary or beneficiaries involved in the transaction in question. Thus, in any transaction between a trustee and beneficiary, even one that does not involve the trust property and is not within the scope of the trust relationship, the duty in Subsection (3) requires that the trustee establish that the consent or other transaction was based on full disclosure and was otherwise fair to the beneficiary.

Transactions in violation of the duties stated in Subsection (1), (2), or (3) are not void but may be affirmed or set aside by the beneficiaries, except as the rights of bona fide purchasers intervene (Chapter 22). Remedies for breach of trust are more fully discussed in Chapter 19.

Comment on Subsections (1) and (2):

b. Undivided loyalty: prohibitions and rationale. The rule of Subsection (2) flatly prohibits certain transactions by trustees (see Comment *a*), unless authorized as stated in Comments *c(1)-c(3)*. See also exceptional situations in Comments *c(4)-c(8)*. This prohibition most obviously forbids most self-dealing by trustees. Perhaps more subtle, but broader in application, is the general requirement that trustees act solely in the interest of the beneficiary in matters of trust administration. Furthermore, a trustee must refrain, whether in fiduciary or personal dealings with third parties, from transactions in which it is reasonably foreseeable that the trustee's future fiduciary conduct might be influenced by considerations other than the best interests of the beneficiaries.

In transactions that violate the trustee's duty of undivided loyalty, under the so-called "no further inquiry" principle it is immaterial that the trustee may be able to show that the action in question was taken in good faith, that the terms of the transaction were fair, and that no profit resulted to the trustee. A trustee, therefore, commits a breach of trust by purchasing trust property, even as the highest bidder at a public auction; otherwise the possibility of purchase by the trustee would create a temptation for the exercise of less than the trustee's best efforts and business judgment on behalf of the trust to determine whether sale is appropriate and to obtain the most favorable price and terms from others for the trust property. Further on cases of self-dealing, see Comments *d* and *d(1)*. The principle applies as well to conflict-of-interest situations that do not involve self-dealing. See Comments *e–e(2)*. For example, normal assurances concerning proper fiduciary behavior would be undermined (especially regarding the trustee's future conduct) if a bank were allowed to purchase its own shares for a trust it is administering, even though the shares were purchased from third persons at a market price and would be a prudent investment for the trust.

The fiduciary duty of undivided loyalty in the trust context, as stated in Subsection (1) and amplified in Subsection (2), is particularly intense so that, in most circumstances, its prohibitions are absolute for prophylactic reasons. The rationale begins with a recognition that it may be difficult for a trustee to resist temptation when personal interests conflict with fiduciary duty. In such situations, for reasons peculiar to typical trust relationships, the policy of the trust law is to prefer (as a matter of default law) to remove altogether the occasions of temptation rather than to monitor fiduciary behavior and attempt to uncover and punish abuses when a trustee has actually succumbed to temptation. This policy of strict prohibition also provides a reasonable circumstantial assurance (except as waived by the settlor or an affected beneficiary) that beneficiaries will not be deprived of a trustee's disinterested and objective judgment.

The inherent subjectivity and impracticability of second-guessing a trustee's application of business judgment or exercise of fiduciary discretion are aggravated by the opportunities and relative ease of concealing misconduct—or at least by the absence of timely information and the likely disappearance of relevant evidence—that result from the trustee's day-to-day, usually long-term, management of the trust property and control over the trust records. Viewed from the beneficiaries' perspective, especially that of remainder beneficiaries, efforts to prevent or detect actual improprieties can be expected to be inefficient if not ineffective. Such efforts are likely to be wastefully expensive and to suffer from time lag and inadequacies of information, from a lack of relevant experience and understanding, and perhaps from want of resources to monitor trustee behavior and ultimately to litigate and expose actual instances of fiduciary misconduct.

Also, unlike many other fiduciary situations, trust beneficiaries are neither readily able to dispose of their interests nor able to fire or vote out their fiduciaries.

For reasons of this type, it has often been said that the requirement of undivided loyalty and its mandates are so fundamental to trust fiduciary law that they are unyielding and not to be eroded by exceptions. These statements, however, fail to capture either the experience or the true policy of American trust law in this area. Therefore, before examining particular applications (Comments *d–f*) of the general prohibitions described above, the commentary immediately below (under Comment *c*) reviews, initially, three qualifications that condition these prohibitions and then several types of transactions for which exceptions have evolved over the years, either through judicially accepted practices or through widespread legislation.

c. Qualifications and specific exceptions. Strict prohibitions against transactions that involve conflicting fiduciary and personal interests, or that are likely to give rise to such conflicts in the future, do not apply to the extent transactions of this type are authorized by court order (Comment *c(1)*) or, expressly or impliedly, by the terms of the trust (Comment *c(2)*). The latter include the terms of a trust as modified by the consent of all beneficiaries pursuant to § 65. The strict prohibition also does not apply if all beneficiaries consent to a particular transaction in a manner that is not intended as a continuing modification of the trust under § 65; but if one or more but less than all of the beneficiaries consent to a prohibited transaction, the transaction constitutes a breach of trust, although one for which the trustee is not liable to any beneficiary from whom (or on whose behalf) consent has been properly obtained (Comment *c(3)*).

Even without authorization in the terms of the trust, or by the court or beneficiaries, certain types of transactions do not fall within the strict conflict-of-interest prohibitions generally applicable to trustees. For these exceptional situations, although conflicting-interest temptations *do* exist for the trustee, generalized considerations of efficiency and beneficiary interest, as well as the minimal or manageable degrees of risk involved, justify departure from the trust law's strict, prophylactic approach to issues of fiduciary loyalty. The exceptions described in Comments *c(4)-c(7)* are recognized here as matters of common law (although often codified as well), while Comment *c(8)* describes an exception that has been adopted by (and is dependent upon) legislation enacted in most American jurisdictions.

While relieving a trustee of the otherwise strict prohibition against conduct involving divided loyalty, these qualifications or exceptions do not eliminate the trustee's duty to act fairly, in good faith, and in the interest of the beneficiaries, as well as with prudence.

c(1). Approval of court. A transaction that would otherwise be prohibited under the rules of Subsections (1) and (2) may be undertaken by a trustee with court authorization. Thus, a trustee can properly purchase trust property with the approval of the court.

The court will permit a transaction of this type only if it determines that it is in the interest of the beneficiaries to do so. Ordinarily, for example, the court will not permit a trustee to purchase trust property if there are other available purchasers willing to pay the same price the trustee is willing to pay. In a proceeding of this type, the trustee has an affirmative duty to disclose material information. Cf. §§ 82 and 83.

In many situations involving a conflict of a trustee's fiduciary duties and personal interests, especially in significant matters involving complexity and business judgment, the interests of sound administration may be better served if the court were to appoint a trustee ad litem . . . to reach a decision on the matter in question and then, if appropriate, to arrange the terms of the transaction and its implementation. . . . .

c(2). Authorization in terms of trust. A trustee may be authorized by the terms of the trust, expressly or by implication, to engage in transactions that would otherwise be prohibited by the rules of undivided loyalty stated in Subsections (1) and (2). For example, the terms of a trust may permit the trustee personally to purchase trust property or borrow trust funds, or to sell or lend the trustee's own property or funds to the trust.

Even an express authorization of this type, however, would not completely dispense with the trustee's underlying fiduciary obligations to act in the interest of the beneficiaries and to exercise prudence in administering the trust. Accordingly, no matter how broad the provisions of a trust may be in conferring power to engage in self-dealing or other transactions involving a conflict of fiduciary and personal interests, a trustee violates the duty of loyalty to the beneficiaries by acting in bad faith or unfairly.

Whether and to what extent a trustee may be impliedly authorized to engage in self-dealing, or in other transactions that present loyalty issues, is inevitably a matter of interpretation. See, e.g., discussion in Comment *e(2)*, below, and § 92, Comment *d*; also compare § 37, Comment *f(1)*, and § 34, Comment *f(1)*, on settlor designation or court appointment of trustees with potential conflicts between their fiduciary and personal interests.

As this Comment illustrates, even the vital fiduciary duty of loyalty is a *default rule* that may be modified by the terms of the trust. This is so at least to the degree of allowing the settlor to eliminate strict prohibitions, such as that against self-dealing (discussed in Comment *d*). The second paragraph above, however, recognizes that to some extent the duty of loyalty involves (as do other duties) more than default law—that is, that there are limits to the settlor's freedom, thereby protecting the fundamental fiduciary character of trust relationships recognized by the law. On the other hand, even the statement (concluding that paragraph and reflecting typical judicial and treatise language) about not allowing a trustee to act "unfairly" requires a recognition that, in this context, fairness itself depends on trust provisions and purposes and on benefits the settlor may have intended to confer on the trustee personally, either as a designated beneficiary or as inferred from the terms of the self-dealing authorization. For example, the authorization may allow the trustee to purchase certain trust property at a stated or formula price that amounts to a beneficial (i.e., potentially favorable) option price. Such a purchase would not be "unfair" even though for less than a fair-market consideration.

For further discussion of the limits of the power of settlors to modify default fiduciary law in analogous contexts, see § 76, Comment *b(1)*, and § 87, Comment *d*; and cf. § 50, Comment *c*, on the limits of trustee discretion (e.g., "absolute" discretion) regarding discretionary distributions to beneficiaries.

The common situation in which one or more of a trust's beneficiaries are selected or authorized by the settlor to serve as trustee or co-trustee inevitably presents an array of conflicts between the trustee's interests as a beneficiary and the interests of other beneficiaries; the problems presented by these (usually) implicitly authorized conflicts are most appropriately dealt with as questions of impartiality under § 79 (even if the settlor's designation of the beneficiary-trustee may, as a matter of interpretation, suggest a "tilt" in favor of the beneficiary-trustee in the balancing of divergent interests; see id. Comment *b(1)* and more generally id., Comments *b* and *c*).

c(3). Consent of beneficiaries. A particular transaction that would otherwise violate a trustee's duty of loyalty may be authorized by consent properly obtained from or on behalf of all of the trust beneficiaries (as defined and prescribed in § 65, Comment *b*), even though the consent is not intended to modify the terms of the trust within the meaning of § 65 and of Comment *c(2)*, above. If, however, consent to a prohibited transaction is obtained from or on behalf of one or more of the trust beneficiaries, a trustee who engages in the prohibited transaction nevertheless commits a breach of trust but is not liable to any beneficiary whose consent has been properly obtained. On the duty of the trustee in obtaining the consent of a beneficiary, see Subsection (3) and Comment *g*; more generally on the effect and requirements of proper consent, see § 97.

c(4). Exception for trustee's compensation. The strict prohibitions against transactions by trustees involving conflicts between their fiduciary duties and personal interests do not apply to the trustee's taking of reasonable compensation for services rendered as trustee. On reasonable compensation generally, see § 38. On the trustee's duty of disclosure regarding compensation, see §§ 82 and 83. On dealings between a trustee and one or more of the beneficiaries relating to the trustee's compensation, see Subsection (3) and Comment *g*.

c(5). Exception for certain self-employment. Although under Subsection (2) self-hiring by a trustee is generally prohibited as a form of self-dealing (see Comment *d*), in some circumstances a trustee may provide to the trust, and receive additional compensation for, special services that—while not required of trustees generally—are necessary or appropriate to prudent administration of the trust. It is reasonable to expect that a trustee who possesses special skills and facilities that are useful in trust administration will use those skills and facilities in administering the trust, and also to expect that the trustee's familiarity with the purposes and affairs of the trust will result in efficiency and cost advantages to the trust. Cf. Comment *c(2)*. Also cf. § 77(3) and § 77, Comment *e*, on the duty of trustees to make use of their special skills and facilities, and § 88 on the duty of trustees to be cost-conscious in trust administration. See further § 38, Comment *c(1)*, on factors to be considered in determining trustees' "reasonable compensation," and id., Comment *d*, indicating that a trustee may receive additional compensation for "special services . . ., for example as attorney or real-estate agent, . . . when it is advantageous to the trust that the trustee rather than another perform those services" (noting that this may be "particularly relevant under a statutory fee schedule").

Although the duty of loyalty does not strictly prohibit the trustee from providing this type of compensated services for which the trustee has a special competence, the trustee is not relieved of the normal duty to act with prudence and in the interest of the beneficiaries in determining whether the services are reasonably necessary and by whom they may best be provided. Thus, the risks inherent in sacrificing independence and objectivity of judgment in deciding these matters must be justifiable in terms of the expected benefits to the trust through greater efficiency and reduced time and expense in allowing the trustee to render the services. Furthermore, the trustee has a duty to disclose to the beneficiaries the special services performed and the additional time and compensation involved (see § 82, Comment *d*, and § 83, Comment *c*). Although the special compensation need not be approved by a court, trustee compensation may be challenged in court, and a trustee who is found to have taken excessive compensation will be ordered to refund it.

With this Comment, contrast Comment *d(1)* on outside compensation (but also compare the more lenient observations in that Comment on the matter of trustees voting to elect themselves to corporate officer or director positions).

The exception in this Comment does not apply to conflict-of-interest transactions prohibited under Comment *e*, such as employing family members of the trustee to handle trust transactions (Comment *e(1)*).

c(6). Exceptions for certain loans to the trust and for deposits of trust money. The strict prohibition against transactions that involve a conflict between the fiduciary and personal interests of a trustee does not apply to advances of a trustee's personal funds for proper expenses of administration or for the protection of the trust estate. These are advances for which the trustee is entitled to reimbursement without interest. (See, on a trustee's right of indemnification, § 38, Comment *b*.) Nor does the prohibition apply to loans by a trustee personally, with reasonable interest, when borrowing is necessary for proper needs of administration because (and for as long as) funds for this purpose are not reasonably available from other sources on equally favorable or better terms.

The strict prohibition against self-dealing ordinarily prevents a trustee from borrowing money held in the trust estate, but the prohibition does not preclude the deposit of trust funds in a regulated financial-services institution operated or controlled by, or affiliated with, the trustee. The trustee, however, must be able to show that the amount, duration, and other terms of the deposit (including any provision for interest) fully conform to the trustee's duty of prudence (§ 77) as applied generally to the deposits of trust money awaiting investment, distribution, or payment of expenses (§ 76, Comment *d*), as well as the requirements of any statute or regulation applicable to the deposit. (See, e.g., Comptroller of the Currency Regulation 9, "Fiduciary Funds Awaiting Investment or Distribution," especially 12 C.F.R. §§ 9.10(b) and 9.5(e), as revised in 1997.)

c(7). Exception for transactions with other trusts or fiduciary estates. The duty of loyalty does not preclude trustees in their fiduciary capacity from dealing with other trusts or with decedents' or conservatorship estates, including trusts and estates of which the trustee is a fiduciary. Any such sale, exchange, loan, or other transaction, however, must be consistent with the purposes of each fiduciary relationship and for a consideration that is fair to the beneficiaries of the relationships. Even the fair-consideration requirement does not necessarily apply if the arrangement is appropriate to the terms or beneficial interests of those relationships and to the applicable requirements of impartiality (§ 79).

On this last point, and more generally on a trustee's dealings directly with one or more of the beneficiaries of a trust, compare Subsection (3) and Comment *g*.

c(8). Statutory exception for proprietary mutual funds. Under statutes enacted in most of the states, a trustee is not precluded from investing trust funds in the securities of an investment company or investment trust to which the trustee or an affiliate provides services in a capacity other than as trustee, even though the trustee (or an affiliate) is compensated for those services by the investment trust or company out of fees charged to the trust or investment, provided the investment is prudent (§ 77 and § 90, particularly id., Comment *m*). These statutes require the trustee to satisfy certain requirements set out in the statute concerning information the trustee must report to beneficiaries about the rate of compensation and the method by which the compensation was determined. . . . .

It is essential to note that this statutory exception for corporate trustees' participation in what are generally called "proprietary mutual funds" does not relieve the trustee of its normal duty to exercise prudence (§ 77, including compliance with the prudent investor rule of §§ 90–92). Nor does it dispense with the trustee's fundamental duty to act in the interest of the beneficiaries, its duty of impartiality, or the other fiduciary duties of trusteeship. For example, the trustee cannot properly confine its investments to the proprietary-mutual-fund offerings if this would impair the trustee's ability to manage both uncompensated and compensated risk through proper diversification and through asset allocation appropriate to the particular trust (§ 90); and the trustee must be sufficiently aware of overall costs associated with other mutual-fund alternatives to enable the trustee to fulfill its important responsibility to be cost conscious in managing the trust's investment program (see § 90(c)(3) and more generally § 88). Furthermore, the use of proprietary mutual funds for a trust's investment program must not result in the trustee receiving more than the reasonable overall compensation (§ 38) appropriate to its services to the trust, taking account of the trustee's mutual-fund duties and compensation. . . . .

Comment on Subsection (2):

d. Self-dealing: sales, loans, and other transactions between trust and trustee personally. Except as stated in Comments *c–c(3)* or in Comments *c(4)-c(6)* or *c(8)*, the duty of loyalty prohibits a trustee from engaging on behalf of the trust in transactions with the trustee personally. Thus, it is a breach of trust for the trustee personally to buy property held in the trust, or to sell the trustee's own property to the trust; nor may the trustee personally borrow money from, lend funds to, or exchange property with the trust. Also, except as described in *c(5)*, a trustee, acting in a fiduciary capacity, cannot properly hire the trustee personally to perform services for the trust.

In prohibited self-dealing transactions, under the no-further-inquiry rule, it is immaterial to the question of breach of trust (as distinguished perhaps from the appropriate remedy) that the trustee has acted in good faith and for a fair consideration. It is immaterial whether the property has a market price, whether the trustee makes a profit from the transaction, and whether a sale of trust property is made privately or at auction, or even that the trustee does not actually make the sale. For example, except as provided in Comments *c(1)-c(3)*, if a trustee were personally to purchase trust property at a foreclosure or tax sale, or at a sale on execution of judgment, this would be a breach of trust, with no further inquiry to allow the trustee an opportunity to argue and attempt to show that all reasonable steps had been taken to prevent the sale and to maximize the number and enthusiasm of the bidders.

Self-dealing occurs also when the trustee personally has a financial interest in the transaction of such a nature that it might affect the trustee's judgment. Illustrative would be a sale to or purchase from a firm of which the trustee is a member or a corporation in which the trustee has a controlling or substantial interest. Also, a sale to a third person violates the trustee's duty of loyalty if made with an understanding that the third person is to hold the property for or transfer it to the trustee personally.

Similarly, a corporate trustee violates its duty of loyalty if it enters into a transaction with one of its departments, such as when the trustee purchases property from or sells property to its securities or banking department. Self-dealing is involved because the various departments are not separate persons. Nor may a corporate trustee engage in transactions on behalf of the trust with a subsidiary corporation or affiliate . . . in which it has the entire or a controlling interest or an interest of such a substantial nature that there would be a temptation to consider its own financial advantage in the transaction rather than acting solely in the interest of the trust beneficiaries. The rule is the same when the shares of the purchasing or selling corporation are owned by the shareholders of the corporate trustee.

d(1). Outside compensation for acts performed as trustee. A trustee engages in self-dealing and therefore normally violates the duty of loyalty by personally accepting from a third person any fee, commission, or other compensation for an act done by the trustee in connection with the administration of the trust. But see Comment *c(8)* on proprietary funds, and cf. Comment *c(5)* on self-employment.

Accordingly, if the trustee sells trust property and accepts (and retains) a bonus from the purchaser for making the sale, the trustee commits a breach of trust. So also, if the trustee is employed by an insurance company with which the trustee insures trust property and from which the trustee receives a commission for placing the insurance, the trustee is at least accountable to the trust for the commission (cf. Comment *c(5)*). The same rule applies if a trustee's fiduciary dealings with a third party are subsequently "rewarded" (even by more-than-trivial expression of appreciation) by the third party, and therefore the reward must be accounted for to the trust; even an informal prearrangement, practice, or expectation that the trustee would be so rewarded could render the dealings a breach of trust.

If a trustee were allowed to keep any form of compensation from a third person for acts performed in the administration of the trust, a temptation would exist that would deprive the beneficiaries of the circumstantial assurance of independent and objective fiduciary judgment that the trust law seeks to provide (see Comment *b*).

A special situation arises when a trust holds stock or other interests in an enterprise and the voting power or influence of those shares or interests is used to procure a trustee's election to a position such as director, officer, or manager of the enterprise. Although technically a form of self-dealing results, there is no breach of trust if the trustee's position is procured to serve the interests of the trust and its beneficiaries, provided that the salary is not greater than warranted by the services the trustee performs in the position with the enterprise, or that it is contemplated that the trustee will be accountable to the trust for any excess. (An appropriate arrangement for the situation would be for the trustee to account to the trust for all of the compensation, with the reasonable compensation (or special compensation) as trustee to include the value of the special services rendered in the trustee's role with the corporation or other enterprise.) Compare generally Comment *c(5)*. As in other exceptional situations, the trustee's duty of loyalty continues to apply so that subsequently, for example, in exercising the trust's voting or other rights in the enterprise or in deciding whether to sell (or acquire additional) shares or interests in the enterprise, the trustee has a duty to act in the interest of the trust beneficiaries. A decision on behalf of the trust to have a trustee assume a role in the corporation or other enterprise, however, necessarily carries with it an acceptance on behalf of the trust that the trustee's duties to it will be subordinated to any legal duties to which the trustee is subject when acting in the role of director, officer, manager, or the like. A trustee's election to a role of this type is a matter of which beneficiaries should ordinarily be informed under § 82(1)(c). That duties of prudence, loyalty, impartiality (including re: income productivity), and other fiduciary duties apply to the trustee's decisions and conduct in, e.g., incorporating business or investment activities of the trust, see § 86, Comment *e*.

For purposes of this Comment (and Comment *d* more generally), a trustee's action or decision that is motivated by and taken in the best interest of the beneficiaries does not violate the rule of Subsection (1) or (2) merely because there may be an incidental benefit to the trustee.

Comment on Subsection (1):

e. Other conflicting interests or loyalties: dealings with third persons. Except as provided in Comments *c–c(3)*, the duty of loyalty prohibits the trustee from engaging in transactions, as trustee, with persons with whom the trustee is closely related or associated.

The prohibition also applies to transactions by a trustee, acting in either a fiduciary or personal capacity, with third persons if the transaction would create a reasonably foreseeable risk of future conflict between the trustee's fiduciary duties and personal interests. Although not involving self-dealing (Comment *d*), transactions of this type could expose trustees to the temptation of considering interests other than those of trust beneficiaries.

The duty of loyalty therefore prohibits transactions (including employment transactions, see Comment *e(1)*, below) between the trustee, as trustee, and family members, because these are people for whom the trustee could be expected to have a natural, personal concern. For this purpose, the reference to "family members" includes the trustee's spouse and parents, the trustee's descendants and their spouses, and other individuals who are natural objects of the trustee's bounty (see definition in § 9, Comment *b*). This prohibition, however, does not apply to a trustee's fiduciary dealings with family members who are trust beneficiaries as long as those dealings are consistent with benefits authorized for the beneficiaries by the provisions of the trust (e.g., see § 50, Comment *d(6)*) and with the trustee's duty of impartiality (§ 79). On a trustee's dealings with beneficiaries more generally, see Comment *g*.

Any fiduciary transaction with a personal agent or personal attorney of the trustee is *presumed* to be affected by a conflict between the fiduciary and personal interests of the trustee.

Neither strict prohibition nor a presumption of divided loyalty applies to transactions with more remote relatives or with personal or business acquaintances of the trustee. A breach of trust may nevertheless be established by a beneficiary or successor trustee by showing that the trustee was improperly influenced by relationship to, friendship for, or expectations of reciprocity from the other party to a transaction that was disadvantageous to the trust. Compare Comment *f*.

Similarly, a corporate trustee cannot properly engage in a purchase, sale, or other transaction with one of its officers or directors. Although not involving self-dealing (as would occur in the case of affiliates, as mentioned in Comment *d*), these transactions involve individuals closely associated with a corporate trustee in a manner comparable to family members of an individual trustee.

The prohibition in this Comment also applies to a trustee's *personal* dealings with unrelated third parties when there would be a conflict between the trustee's fiduciary duties and personal interests. Thus, for example, even though no direct dealings with the trust are involved, a trustee must not personally acquire (or establish) a business that competes with the business activities of the trust; nor may a trustee take personal advantage of an opportunity that properly belongs to the trust. . . . .

Furthermore, the prohibition extends to (i) a trustee's *personal* transactions with third parties that would place the trustee in a position in which conflict-of-interest temptations foreseeably may arise in the future, as well as to (ii) a trustee's *fiduciary* transactions with third parties that create such a risk of future conflicts between the trustee's fiduciary and personal interests. Thus, for example, a trustee must not acquire, for the trustee's personal account, a lease or encumbrance held by another on trust property.

Similarly, a trustee cannot properly purchase interests in a business association both for the trust estate and for the trustee personally at the same time, or purchase in either the trustee's fiduciary or its personal capacity an interest of a third party in a business association in which the trustee already holds an interest in the other capacity, if in any of these cases the interest is of such a substantial nature that, at the time of purchase or in the future, there would be a temptation to consider the trustee's own advantage rather than solely the interest of the trust beneficiaries. Temptation might arise, for example, in the exercise of voting rights, in later decisions to sell or retain the interest held either in the trust or by the trustee personally, and in situations in which the trustee might consider making further equity or debt investment in the enterprise.

Illustrations:

3. T purchases for the trust she is administering 100 shares of the common stock of General Motors Corporation, in which T already owns 200 common shares personally. Because neither holding represents a significant portion of the corporation's stock, T's purchase of these shares for the trust does not violate the principle stated in the preceding paragraph.

4. T purchases (for the trust) from the estate of a deceased individual 20 percent of the common stock of Genial Motors Corporation, an automobile dealership of which T already holds 20 percent personally. Unless authorized pursuant to Comments *c(1)-c(3)*, T's purchase of the shares constitutes a breach of trust under the principles of this Comment, even if the shares were a prudent investment under the terms and circumstances of the trust. (Cf. § 90, Comment *p*.)

e(1). Undivided loyalty: employing trustee's family members. A trustee cannot properly hire his or her own family members (see definition in Comment *e*) in the administration of the trust, except as the family member may be a beneficiary of the trust and the employment is consistent with the trust's purposes and beneficial interests, and also with the trustee's duty of impartiality (§ 79). Thus, for example, it would ordinarily be a breach of trust for the trustee to hire his or her spouse or son or daughter to provide legal services for the trust, to manage trust property, or to handle transactions involving the sale or purchase of securities or other property for the trust.

An arrangement of this type would create a temptation for the trustee to consider the interests of others rather than to act solely in the interests of the beneficiaries. It would also deprive the beneficiaries of the circumstantial assurance that the trustee will exercise an independent and objective judgment (Comment *b*) not only in the selection of persons to provide trust services but also in establishing the duties, compensation, and other terms of the employment, in supervising or monitoring the employee, and in exercising business judgment about whether or with what frequency to engage in sales, purchases, or other transactions involving the trust estate.

Illustration:

5. T, as trustee of a trust for the benefit of B and B's issue, has engaged and regularly uses D (a securities broker who is T's daughter-in-law) to handle sales and purchases of stocks and bonds for the trust estate. T's conduct in doing so constitutes a breach of trust—even with no showing that T acted in bad faith or that lower brokerage commissions (or greater discounts) would otherwise be available; and note the impracticability and undesirability of having to evaluate business judgments in an effort to protect against the risk of excessive transactions (or "churning") in the management of a trust portfolio.

e(2). Corporate trustee's own shares as trust investment. Ordinarily, a bank or trust company cannot properly purchase its own stock for the trust estate, even if the shares are purchased from third persons and thus involve no self-dealing. This is so even though a purchase of similar shares of another bank would be a suitable investment for the particular trust. Similarly, it is ordinarily improper for a corporate trustee to retain shares of its own stock received as an original investment on the death of the settlor of a testamentary trust or received as successor to the settlor or another as trustee of an inter vivos trust. (On the duty to sell, see § 92, Comment *c*.)

In either of the foregoing cases, however, the purchase or retention is proper if expressly or impliedly authorized by the terms of the trust (Comment *c(2)*) or if authorized by the consent of all beneficiaries (Comment *c(3)*). Also, the retention of a trustee's own stock is sometimes authorized by statute. In addition, it would normally be permissible for a relatively modest portion of the trustee's stock to be held indirectly through an appropriate holding of shares in a mutual fund or other pooled-investment vehicle.

In any event, in such matters as voting the shares or deciding whether to sell or keep them, an authorization to acquire or retain shares of the trustee does not relieve the trustee of its duties to act with prudence and solely in the interest of the trust beneficiaries.

Whether a trustee is impliedly authorized to retain its own stock as an inception asset is a matter of interpretation. Often trust provisions or statutes do not expressly state that a corporate trustee may retain its own shares in trust, but merely provide general authorization to retain investments received from the settlor. In situations of this type, the question of implied authorization is one of interpreting the terms of the trust or statute. On this matter generally, see § 92, Comments *c* and *d*, and particularly the third paragraph of the latter Comment.

f. Actions serving the interests of third persons or non-trust objectives. In administering a trust the trustee has a duty to the beneficiaries not to be influenced by the interest of any third person or by motives other than the accomplishment of the purposes of the trust. Thus, it is improper for the trustee to sell property of the trust or purchase property for the trust, or to engage an agent or advisor for the trust, either for the purpose of benefiting a third person (whether or not a party to the transaction) rather than the trust estate or for the purpose of advancing an objective other than the purposes of the trust. See further § 90, Comment *c*; also compare § 87, Comments *c* and *d*.

Comment on Subsection (3):

g. Dealings with beneficiaries. Under the rule of Subsection (3) there is no strict prohibition that precludes a trustee, either in a personal capacity or in administering the trust, from dealing with one or more of the beneficiaries. The trustee, however (except for *personal* dealings in limited circumstances, below), must be able to show that the dealings were fair and that all relevant and material information that was known, or that should have been known (cf. § 72, Comment *c*), by the trustee was communicated to the beneficiary or beneficiaries involved. Also, such transactions undertaken as trustee must not violate other fiduciary duties, such as the duty of prudence (§ 77) or impartiality (§ 79), and must not conflict with a trust purpose or violate a spendthrift restraint (§§ 58 and 59) or other provision of the trust (see § 76 on the trustee's duty to comply with the terms of the trust).

Illustrative of a trustee's *fiduciary* dealings with beneficiaries are: seeking and obtaining beneficiary consent to what would or might otherwise be a breach of trust (see Comment *c(3)* and more generally § 97); sales of trust property to a beneficiary or purchase of a beneficiary's property for the trust; lending money to or borrowing money from the beneficiary; leases involving property of the trust or of a beneficiary; and transactions involving the trust's acquisition of a part or all of the equitable interest (or a lien on the interest) of a beneficiary. In all such transactions, in addition to complying with the requirement of full disclosure and with other fiduciary duties of trusteeship (possibly most pointedly, the duty of impartiality among beneficiaries), the transaction must be *fair* to the beneficiary and the trust—normally meaning, in this context, either that the transaction is for a fair and adequate consideration or that it is consistent with the beneficial interests of the beneficiary or beneficiaries in question, such as by making a no—or low—interest loan to a beneficiary as a discretionary benefit under § 50, Comment *d(6)*.

Even though not within the fiduciary relation inherent in trust administration, the trustee's *personal* dealings with beneficiaries of the trust may involve a confidential relationship that is sufficiently natural to the parties' roles in the trust relationship to be recognized by the trust law as an incident or extension of the intense duty of loyalty applicable to trustees. (On fiduciary and confidential relationships, compare § 2, Comments *b* and *b(1)*.) A confidential relationship is not presumed to exist, however, with regard to beneficiaries whose interests in the trust are remote and whose interactions with the trustee as fiduciary are insignificant. In other circumstances, a beneficiary involved in a transaction of this type may set aside the transaction except as the trustee is able to establish that it was based on appropriate disclosure (supra) and was otherwise fair to the beneficiary. (But the latter requirement does not preclude a "natural" disposition that is wholly or partially donative, e.g., by a mother-beneficiary to a son or daughter, even though the son or daughter serves as trustee under the father's will.)

That the rule of Subsection (3) may apply to a former trustee while that person retains significant influence over a beneficiary, see Comment *h*.

Additional General Comment:

h. Pre- and post-trusteeship transactions. The rules of this section do not render voidable those transactions or agreements that were entered into or claims that were acquired by a person before being appointed trustee or contemplating appointment (cf. Comment *e*, on creating potential for future conflicts) as trustee. After becoming trustee, however, with a responsibility for protecting the trust estate (§ 76, Comment *d*), the handling of even a preexisting claim of this type will involve conflicting interests, requiring at least disclosure to beneficiaries and that the trustee act in good faith and in the interest of the beneficiaries. If the transaction or conflict is significant, a trustee ad litem may have to be appointed .... Furthermore, unless the conflict was disclosed or known at the time of the appointment, and thus at least impliedly approved, it may provide a ground for the trustee's removal (§ 37, Comment *f(1)*). In any event, the conflict calls for close scrutiny of potentially affected conduct.

Similarly, the prohibitions against self-dealing and other forms of divided loyalty do not apply to transactions by a former trustee after termination of the trust, or after the person has otherwise ceased to serve as trustee, provided the person obtains no improper advantage as a result of information, influence, or confidence acquired as trustee.

i. Associated duty of confidentiality. Incident to the duty of loyalty, but necessarily more flexible in its application, is the trustee's duty to preserve the confidentiality and privacy of trust information from disclosure to third persons, except as required by law (e.g., rules of regulatory, supervisory, or taxing authorities) or as necessary or appropriate to proper administration of the trust. Thus, the trustee's duty of loyalty carries with it a related duty to avoid unwarranted disclosure of information acquired as trustee whenever the trustee should know that the effect of disclosure would be detrimental to possible transactions involving the trust estate or otherwise to the interests of the beneficiaries.

This duty of confidentiality ordinarily does not apply to the disclosure of trust information to beneficiaries or their authorized representatives (see duties to inform and report, §§ 82 and 83) or, in the interest of one or more trust beneficiaries, to the trustees of other trusts or the fiduciaries of fiduciary estates in which a beneficiary has an interest. Even in providing information to or on behalf of beneficiaries, however, the trustee has a duty to act with sensitivity and, insofar as practical, with due regard for considerations of relevancy and sound administration, and for the personal concerns and privacy of the trust beneficiaries. See § 82, Comment *f*.

§ 79. Duty of Impartiality; Income Productivity

(1) A trustee has a duty to administer the trust in a manner that is impartial with respect to the various beneficiaries of the trust, requiring that:

(a) in investing, protecting, and distributing the trust estate, and in other administrative functions, the trustee must act impartially and with due regard for the diverse beneficial interests created by the terms of the trust; and

(b) in consulting and otherwise communicating with beneficiaries, the trustee must proceed in a manner that fairly reflects the diversity of their concerns and beneficial interests.

(2) If a trust is created for two or more beneficiaries or purposes in succession and if the rights of any beneficiary or the expenditures for a charitable purpose are defined with reference to trust income, the trustee's duty of impartiality includes a duty to so invest and administer the trust, or to so account for principal and income, that the trust estate will produce income that is reasonably appropriate to the purposes of the trust and to the diverse present and future interests of its beneficiaries.

General Comment:

a. *Scope of section and duty.* The rules stated in this section apply whenever a trust has two or more beneficiaries or purposes, whether the purposes of the trust are private, charitable, or mixed. The duty of impartiality applies whether the beneficiaries' interests or the purposes are successive or concurrent. Accordingly, the duty is important not only, for example, in balancing the naturally conflicting concerns of life and remainder beneficiaries but also whenever multiple income beneficiaries have significantly differing needs and tax positions, or when multiple remainder beneficiaries have significantly different objectives and risk tolerance.

For purposes of this section, and particularly for purposes of the rule stated in Subsection (2), a trust is treated as having more than one purpose (e.g., a trust for a specific charitable purpose) when the purpose involves objectives that are competitive over time—that is, when it is necessary for the trustee to balance the concerns of the present against the concerns of the future, as in the case of a charitable trust that is directed to expend all income, or is authorized to expend only income, for its designated charitable purpose. See Comment *h*.

The duty of impartiality is applicable to all duties of the trustee. Thus, the requirements of this section are important: (1) in the making or retention of investments (see § 90); (2) in the management of real property or tangible personal property held in the trust; (3) in the allocation of receipts and expenditures between principal and income accounts (see Chapter 23), especially as fiduciary discretion, or the making of adjustments (Comment *i*), may be involved; (4) in decisions concerning discretionary distributions to one or more beneficiaries (see § 50); and (5) in controversies among beneficiaries concerning their rights and beneficial interests.

b. *Meaning of impartiality.* The duty of impartiality is an extension of the duty of loyalty to beneficiaries but involves, in typical trust situations, unavoidably and thus permissibly conflicting duties to various beneficiaries with their competing economic interests.

It would be overly simplistic, and therefore misleading, to equate impartiality with some concept of "equality" of treatment or concern—that is, to assume that the interests of all beneficiaries have the same priority and are entitled to the same weight in the trustee's balancing of those interests. Impartiality does mean that a trustee's treatment of beneficiaries or conduct in administering a trust is not to be influenced by the trustee's personal favoritism or animosity toward individual beneficiaries, even if the latter results from antagonism that sometimes arises in the course of administration. Nor is it permissible for a trustee to ignore the interests of some beneficiaries merely as a result of oversight or neglect, or because a particular beneficiary has more access to the trustee or is more aggressive, or simply because the trustee is unaware of the duty stated in this section.

It is not only appropriate but required by the duty of impartiality that a trustee's treatment of beneficiaries, and the balancing of their competing interests, reasonably reflect any preferences and priorities that are discernible from the terms (§ 4), purposes, and circumstances of the trust and from the nature and terms of the beneficial interests. Thus, unfortunately, it is often the case that the implications of the duty of impartiality are complicated by the difficulties of determining, and the vagueness of, some relevant aspects of the settlor's intentions and objectives—much of which is left to interpretation and inference.

Therefore, in short, it is the trustee's duty, reasonably and without personal bias, to seek to ascertain and to give effect to the rights and priorities of the various beneficiaries or purposes as expressed or implied by the terms of the trust. On the range of (and factors affecting) reasonable fiduciary judgment in such matters, cf. § 87 (on judicial review of discretion). Also cf. § 50, Comment *f* (and Illustration[ ] 9 . . .), on inferences that might be drawn from the relationships of beneficiaries to the settlor, and relationships among the beneficiaries, in making distributions among multiple discretionary beneficiaries.

b(1). Beneficiary as trustee. In many modern trust situations, the trustee (or one or more co-trustees) will be a life beneficiary or perhaps a remainder beneficiary. In a case of this type, there will inevitably be some conflicts of interest that are approved (see § 78, Comment *c(2)*), implicitly at least, either by the settlor (§ 37, Comment *f(1)*) or through an appointment process that is authorized by the terms of the trust or a statute (§ 34, Comments *c* and *c(1)*) or that is influenced (in the case of judicial appointment) by the trust provisions (§ 34, Comment *f(1)*).

In these circumstances there is, on the one hand, some inference of a preference for or confidence in the trustee-beneficiary but, on the other hand, a general recognition that a trustee-beneficiary's conduct is to be closely scrutinized for abuse, including abuse by less than appropriate regard for the duty of impartiality. Cf. § 50, Comment *b*, especially Illustrations 1 and 2.

Comment on Subsection (1), Clause (a):

c. Balancing of competing interests in the administration of the trust estate. As discussed in Comment *b*, the duty of impartiality does not require an equal balancing of diverse interests but a balancing of those interests in a manner that shows due regard for—i.e., is consistent with—the beneficial interests and the terms and purposes of the trust. This includes respecting any ascertainable preferences of the settlor for some beneficiaries over others, such as the priority frequently discernible from language or circumstances for a life beneficiary (e.g., a surviving spouse or a son or daughter) over that beneficiary's descendants or other recipients of future interests.

The balancing of diverse interests usually involves not only the obviously competitive interests of successive-interest beneficiaries (see Subsection (2) and Comments *e–g*) but also, for example, the competing needs and objectives of multiple life beneficiaries or of multiple remainder beneficiaries. For example, different present-interest beneficiaries may have different needs, objectives, and tax positions, leading to differing preferences (e.g., to emphasize high yield, or capital appreciation, or tax-exempt income) in the trust's investment program. Similarly, different future-interest beneficiaries may have significantly different objectives and concerns (or attitudes) about, for example, the tradeoff between growth and security of capital, or about the types and tax characteristics of assets eventually to be distributed.

That it may be possible to divide one trust into several as a means of lessening impartiality issues and inefficient compromises in asset management, especially in cases involving multiple life beneficiaries or objectives, see § 68 and also § 65.

In what might be called the "substantive" aspects of impartiality (as distinguished from the communication matters considered in Comment *d*), the rule of Subsection (1) directs trustees (i) to avoid injecting their personal favoritism into their decisionmaking and conduct in trust administration and (ii) to make diligent and good-faith efforts to identify, respect, and balance the various beneficial interests when carrying out the trustees' fiduciary responsibilities in managing, protecting, and distributing the trust estate, and in other administrative functions.

The trustee's duty of impartiality is fundamental, along with the duty of prudence, in the investment function, which is discussed comprehensively in § 90 (see particularly id., Comments *e* and *i*), and in the requirement of income productivity when applicable (see Comments *e–i*, below). The duty is also fundamental, along with the duty to comply with the terms of the trust (see § 76), in the exercise of discretion regarding distributions to be made to beneficiaries of discretionary interests or wholly discretionary trusts, discussed comprehensively in § 50. (See especially id., Comments *d–g(2)*.)

Principles of impartiality and the balancing of conflicting beneficiary interests are also fundamental in accounting for principal and income. The duty of impartiality is particularly important in determining principal-and-income rights when a trustee is granted discretionary authority by the terms of the trust (see generally § 87) and whenever fiduciary judgment is otherwise to be exercised. (E.g., on possible duties of trustees regarding equitable adjustments at common law or in making *statutory* adjustments or elections, see Comment *i* . . . .) Further on these matters, see Chapter 23.

In managing real estate and tangible personalty held in the trust estate, impartiality is important in matters ranging from decisions concerning leasing to third parties or allowing one or more beneficiaries the use of trust property, including the duration and other terms of such arrangements, to decisions about insuring, repairing, and possibly improving or replacing trust property. In various respects, it is ordinarily to be expected that, for example, the interest of a life beneficiary in the net income or other enjoyment of the property will conflict with the interests of remainder beneficiaries in eventually receiving distributions of trust property of high value, in good condition, and without unnecessary encumbrances. See generally §§ 86 and 89.

Thus, the duty of impartiality potentially applies to the full range of a trustee's duties in administering the trust estate, and it also applies to situations in which controversies arise among the beneficiaries concerning their rights and beneficial interests in the trust. For example, in petitions for instruction or other litigation involving the interpretation of the beneficial-interest provisions of a trust, or involving principal-income accounting or other disputes strictly among the beneficiaries over matters of trust administration, it is the duty of the trustee not to become an advocate but to remain neutral. Even in the role of a neutral "stakeholder," however, the trustee may have a duty to provide relevant information of which the trustee has knowledge and to make reasonable efforts to assure that all interested beneficiaries are (or have an opportunity to be) adequately represented. (Cf. § 76, Comment *d*, on trustees' duties with regard to claims by or against third parties.)

Comment on Subsection (1), Clause (b):

d. Communication with beneficiaries. A trustee has a general duty to provide information to beneficiaries of the trust (§ 82; see also § 83). Beyond this, a trustee will often find it desirable, and sometimes important or even necessary, to consult with beneficiaries and obtain information from them concerning their financial needs and circumstances and perhaps their preferences concerning matters of trust administration. See, e.g., § 50, Comments *d–f*, on discretionary distributions, and § 90, Comments *c* and *i*, on the investment function. The "procedural" aspect (Clause (b)) of the duty of impartiality applies to the trustee's conduct—when not required and governed by the rule of § 82—in furnishing, obtaining, and discussing useful or necessary information or in consulting the beneficiaries about administration of the trust.

Most communications of these types need not include all available beneficiaries, provided the trustee's selection—or exclusion—of those to be informed or consulted is fair, reasonable, and impartial in light of the context and reasons for the communication. Although trustees are required for some purposes under § 82(1) to provide certain information or reports to "fairly representative beneficiaries" (as described in id., Comment *a(1)*), in other circumstances communication with a narrower group of beneficiaries will satisfy a trustee's duty of impartiality.

Thus, before taking contemplated action, a trustee may wish to consult or to inform and invite comment from one or more of the beneficiaries. In doing so, except as otherwise authorized or directed by the terms of the trust, the trustee should select beneficiaries who appear reasonably to reflect the diverse beneficial interests that are likely to be affected and should avoid arbitrary discrimination among persons similarly situated with respect to the matter involved.

In matters that can be expected to affect the trust beneficiaries generally, such as decisions establishing or altering investment policy, impartiality may call for trustees to communicate—if they do so at all—with both the trust's current beneficiary (or beneficiaries) and its primary future-interest beneficiaries. Thus, it would be ill-advised, and perhaps a breach of trust, if a trustee were to follow a regular practice of informing and consulting with the life beneficiary to the exclusion of readily available persons whose concerns and views could be fairly expected to reflect the general concerns of remainder beneficiaries. On communications regarding discretionary distributions, cf. § 50, Comment *e(1)*.

Illustration (on Comments *c* and *d*):

1. T is trustee of a large, broadly discretionary trust for the benefit of S's widow (W) and descendants. Although the trust provisions make clear that W is the "primary" beneficiary, the terms of the trust authorize distributions to be made from income or principal in T's discretion, from time to time, "to any one or more of W and my children and their issue." The children (B, C, and D) were all adults with children of their own when S died; D had for some time been estranged from her parents and siblings, as T (long a friend of the settlor) was aware. T kept B, C, and W (but not D) well informed of trust affairs and invited them periodically to meet with him to discuss their (independently comfortable) financial circumstances and wishes concerning administration of the trust. As a result, T saw no need to make distributions except as necessary to avoid the heavy income taxation of

the trust that would result if it were to accumulate even the relatively moderate amount of taxable income generated by its "growth-oriented" investment program. Because W wanted to receive no distributions from the trust, the income was distributed at the end of each year equally to the children or, at their request, to their children. D's share arrived with a holiday greeting from T, noting that the money was sent to her at her "mother's request" (followed shortly by the required form reporting income-tax information). D, whose needs considerably exceeded those of her siblings, knew almost nothing about the trust except that it had been established by her father a few years before his death, initially as a revocable trust, and that her mother was the primary beneficiary. In these circumstances, T has violated his duty of impartiality under both Clause (a) (see Comment *c*) and Clause (b) (see Comment *d*) of Subsection (1). (. . . . On remedies and possible damages, see § 95 and Chapter 19.) The rule of Subsection (2), however, does not apply for reasons explained below in Comments *e* and *f*.

Comment on Subsection (2):

e. *Relationship to Subsection (1); scope of productivity requirement.* The rule stated in this Subsection (2) is an application of the broader rule stated in Subsection (1), especially Clause (a), requiring a trustee to administer the trust impartially with regard to multiple beneficiaries or purposes. The rule of Subsection (1) applies whether beneficiaries or purposes are entitled to the benefits of the trust property concurrently or in succession.

The rule stated in Subsection (2) involves the application of the duty of impartiality to frequently encountered situations in which (i) the terms of the trust provide for different beneficiaries or purposes in succession and in which (ii) the entitlements of one or more of the beneficiaries or purposes are measured by reference to the *income* of the trust—that is, the entitlements are based on trust-accounting income. The rule may also apply to a charitable trust even though it has a single charitable purpose, but a purpose that involves conflicting concerns between current expenditures and future needs (see Comment *h*, below).

The trustee's duty to balance the competing interests of present and future beneficiaries or purposes is generally expressed as a duty to make the trust property reasonably productive of trust-accounting income. This duty of "productivity" applies to the trust portfolio as a whole, not asset by asset. The performance of this duty inevitably involves an interplay of principal-income accounting (Chapter 23) and the investment function (Chapter 17).

f. *Trusts to which the rule applies: when do distribution rights depend on "income"?* The trustee's duty with respect to income productivity applies only when a right to distributions or expenditures is based in some respect on the amount of trust income. Therefore, there will be many trusts to which the rule of Subsection (2) will not apply.

The most common example of the latter is the wholly discretionary trust, which involves discretionary beneficial interests (§ 50) that, with or without standards (e.g., "support") to guide the trustee, do not distinguish between income and principal sources and therefore allow the trustee to disregard income productivity in managing trust investments. Also, trusts or interests in which beneficiaries' distributive rights, or expenditures for a purpose, are based *strictly* on annuity or unitrust amounts (§ 49, Comment *e*) do not depend on the amount of trust-accounting income. (These types of trusts may, however, present other impartiality issues in investing, such as issues about possible emphasis on tax-exempt earnings or about tradeoffs between the high total-return objectives of some beneficiaries and the low risk tolerance of others.)

On the other hand, a trust in which a life beneficiary is entitled to the trust income, or a fraction of the income, is the most obvious example of a trust in which distribution rights depend on the amount of trust-accounting income, and thus one to which the reasonable-productivity requirement of this subsection applies. In such a situation, an inherent economic competition exists between the interests of the income beneficiary and the interests of those who may later be entitled to principal.

The fact that an income beneficiary may also receive principal in the trustee's discretion reduces but does not eliminate the productivity issue, much as it eases but does not remove the related principal-income accounting issues. Similarly, if a beneficiary is entitled to discretionary, annuity, or unitrust distributions but these amounts are payable only from income, or must not be less than the trust income, the reasonable-productivity requirement of Subsection (2) may be of modest significance but is not eliminated.

The rule stated in this subsection applies whether the designated period for which the income is to [be] paid to a beneficiary is a period of uncertain duration, such as the beneficiary's lifetime, or one of fixed duration, such as a term of years, or some combination of these, such as until a beneficiary attains a specified age or sooner dies.

Illustration:

2. S devised his residuary estate to T in trust, to pay the income to L for life, principal at L's death to such of her issue as she may appoint by will, and in default of appointment to distribute the principal by right of representation to L's issue who are living at her death. This is a trust created for beneficiaries in succession, and it is subject to the duty of reasonable income productivity.

The trust in Illustration 2 is fairly typical of trusts for beneficiaries in succession and to which Subsection (2) applies. The productivity rule applies to that trust even if T also has power to invade principal for the benefit of L. On the effect of such a power on investment-productivity issues, see § 90, Comment *i*. The trust would also be one to which this subsection applies if L had been granted an inter vivos special power of appointment or a testamentary general power (or even if the remainder had been to L's estate)—that is, as long as the power does not make the interests of a life beneficiary equivalent to full ownership. Contrast § 74(2). Also note that, if a general power or estate remainder (above) follows L's life interest, a distinct preference in her favor can readily be inferred (Comment *b*), and *prudence* would also call for recognition that her support or other needs would likely vary over time (cf. Comment *h*).

Illustration:

3. S's will left $250,000 to each grandchild of hers who is alive at her death, but directs that the devise to a grandchild who is under the age of 25 at S's death shall be held in trust for that grandchild's benefit. G is 16 years old at S's death. Under the terms of the will, the trustee is to pay G such amounts of income or principal or both as necessary to provide for her "comfortable support and education" until she reaches age 25, and then to distribute principal to her. The will further provides that if G dies before that time, the trust is to terminate, with the trust estate to go outright to her issue, if any, and if not, to others. Although

this is a trust for beneficiaries in succession, it is not one to which the requirement of income productivity applies.

Even though in the above Illustration it is highly likely that G will reach age 25 and therefore that distribution will in fact be made to no one other than G, the broader rule of impartiality in this section applies to the trust because of its other potential beneficiaries. But the terms of the trust draw no distinction between income and principal, so the rule of Subsection (2) does not apply to these facts, and there is no requirement of reasonable income productivity to affect the administration of the trust. Nevertheless, the broader duty of impartiality applies to the exercise of the trustee's discretion with regard to distributions to G during the period of the trust, although it may readily be inferred from the nature of the trust that G is the primary beneficiary (see Comment *b*).

If, upon G's death before age 25 in Illustration 3, the trustee had been directed simply to distribute the trust property to G's estate, the trust would not be one that provides for beneficiaries in succession. G is not strictly the sole beneficiary (contrast, e.g., § 74(2)), but is so close as to justify exception (unlike the *life*-beneficiary situation mentioned in the text following Illustration 2). Accordingly, the trust would be subject to neither the duty regarding productivity in Subsection (2) nor the broader duty of impartiality stated in this section.

This would be true even if the trustee had been directed to pay *all* of the trust income to G, commencing, for example, at age 19 or 21. Furthermore, even with this change, Subsection (2) would not apply if, in the event of G's death before age 25, G had a testamentary general power of appointment, with an express gift in default of appointment to others. With respect to this relatively short-term trust, unlike some of the other trusts and variations in this Comment, S's objectives so focus on a single beneficiary, and G's interests so closely approximate a grant of complete ownership, that the interests of takers in default of appointment are treated as incidental and are properly disregarded for purposes of the impartiality rules of this section (unlike rules such as that in § 65 on termination by all beneficiaries).

Whether or not a trust gives rise to a duty of income productivity or of impartiality more generally, the trustee has a duty to comply with the terms of the trust. Accordingly, in Illustration 3 and the variations in the ensuing text, it would be a breach of trust, for example, for the trustee to abuse the discretionary power by making excessive distributions to G or by making distributions for purposes other than G's "comfortable support" or "education."

g. Duty to each of successive beneficiaries. If by the terms of a trust the trustee is directed to pay the income to a beneficiary during a designated period and, on the expiration of the period, to pay the principal to others, the trustee has a duty to exercise care to ensure that a reasonable amount of income will be payable to the income beneficiary. But the trustee is also under a duty to the remainder beneficiaries to exercise reasonable care in an effort to preserve the trust property, a duty that ordinarily includes a goal of protecting the property's purchasing power. In some trust situations the trustee may even invest with a goal of increasing the real value of the principal—a possibility that, like what is "reasonable" productivity, necessarily depends on the terms and purposes of the particular trust (Comment *b*).

It is important to note that the protection or growth of the purchasing power of principal tends as well to preserve or enhance the purchasing power of the income flow over the duration of the income interest. This same effect would be of importance in implementing comparable duties of impartiality and prudence that would exist if there were successive *income* beneficiaries, or even successive periods with expectedly different circumstances during the lifetime of an individual beneficiary. (See and compare Comment *h* on charitable endowments.)

Even with best efforts and prudent conduct by a trustee, however, the combination of objectives with respect to income and principal might not be accomplished, particularly over any given time frame. Tradeoffs inevitably exist in these matters, and a need to generate and distribute significant amounts of income can be expected to impair the trustee's ability to preserve the real value of corpus, especially during periods of serious inflation or declining markets.

The precise meaning of the trustee's duty of impartiality, and the balancing of competing interests and objectives, inevitably are matters of interpretation and fiduciary judgment (see Comment *b*). Thus, the duty and balancing are affected by the purposes, terms, distribution requirements, and other circumstances of the trust, not only at the outset but as they may change from time to time. For example, the trust's risk tolerance and expected duration are factors to be considered, as are distribution requirements and other factors that may affect the trust's investment strategy. On investment standards generally, see § 90.

Similarly, the terms of a trust (including any discernible settlor priorities, whether expressed or by interpretation) may significantly influence the trustee's balancing of competing present and future interests and affect a particular trustee's duty with respect to productivity. (See Comment *b*, above, and also cf. Comment *g(2)*, below.) Thus, although a trustee is ordinarily not to endanger the safety of principal in an effort to produce a large income, the purposes, circumstances, and needs of a particular trust may call for a high yield for the income beneficiary at an increased risk to principal, especially at the risk of failing to maintain its purchasing power. Accordingly, it may be appropriate for the trustee to invest heavily in bonds and other fixed-income securities in order to favor an income beneficiary. (But compare Comment *i*, below, for trusts, even of this type, that have a high risk tolerance and that therefore might more prudently pursue a high level of total return.) Conversely, in the circumstances of a given trust it might be appropriate for the trustee to seek a modest yield for the income beneficiary and a high level of capital appreciation. Trust terms granting the trustee authority to invade principal or to accumulate income tend to alleviate investment inhibitions or pressures based on the duty of impartiality. See § 90, Comment *i*.

In short, trustees have a duty of impartiality with respect to the diverse beneficial interests they serve, and this involves an associated duty of reasonable productivity, from the trust portfolio as a whole, whenever the rights of beneficiaries depend on the amount of trust income. A trustee then has a duty to attempt to balance the income and principal elements of total investment return. (Again, however, note Comment *i*, below.) The balance is to be achieved in a manner that is fair to all beneficiaries as a reflection of their particular beneficial interests—that is, reflecting the trust's purposes, terms, and obligations, in light of the circumstances of the trust and usually the circumstances of its beneficiaries, including the needs of an income beneficiary so far as these needs are relevant to the purposes of the trust. (Hence the importance of the trustee's communication with beneficiaries, as discussed in Comment *d*, and cf. § 82.)

g(1). Duty with respect to underproductive or overproductive property. One result of this aspect of impartiality is that a trustee has a duty generally (but cf. Comment *i*) to the income beneficiary not to retain or purchase unproductive or underproductive (low-income) property to an extent that jeopardizes the proper entitlements of that beneficiary through an inadequate income yield *from the trust estate as a whole*. (Note, however, the possibility of a low yield from some investments being offset by a high yield from others.) Traditionally, this duty has been thought to apply (but see Comment *i*) even though it could be expected that the trust corpus would significantly appreciate in value (and thereby enhance the income flow) over the long term as a result of the underproductive investments.

Beneficiaries of various forms of future interests have counterpart concerns over a trustee's purchase or retention of "wasting" or other overproductive assets (see Chapter 23), insofar as those assets may produce unduly high income at the expense of principal interests. These beneficiaries are also entitled to have reasonable consideration given to their concerns about protection of the purchasing power of trust principal. Thus, under the duty of impartiality, *subsequent* income beneficiaries as well as ultimate remainder beneficiaries have a right that their interests not be disregarded either by inadvertence or as a result of efforts to provide a higher-than-appropriate yield for the current income beneficiary.

Ultimately these matters may be affected not only by applicable provisions of the trust (see Comment *g(2)*, below), and by the possibility of subtle beneficiary priorities, but also indirectly yet importantly by principles governing principal-and-income accounting. See Comment *i* and also Chapter 23; and, on associated matters of investment policy, see § 90, particularly Comments *e* and *i*.

g(2). Terms of the trust. The terms of a trust established for beneficiaries in succession may authorize an underproductive (or overproductive) investment program, much as the terms and purposes of a trust determine the nature and meaning of the trustee's duty of impartiality in other respects. Accordingly, the terms of trusts (§ 4) may and often do permit trustees to purchase or retain unproductive or underproductive property (such as family farms or closely held business interests), or sometimes overproductive property, even though those investments may cause the trust estate as a whole to be underproductive or overproductive. Similarly, the trust terms sometimes authorize trustees to determine principal and income without regard to applicable principal-income law (see Chapter 23 and cf. § 87).

The presence of a power to invade principal for an income beneficiary's support or other purposes may affect the trustee's duty with respect to income productivity. Ordinarily, however, this power would not eliminate the income beneficiary's right to receive income distributions that are reasonable in light of the trust's objectives and circumstances, even if that degree of productivity can be expected regularly to exceed what would be needed (for example) for support. See § 90, Comment *i*.

h. Application to certain charitable trusts. Although the discussion in the preceding commentary has tended to emphasize the rights of successive beneficiaries of private trusts, Subsection (2) applies to some charitable trusts. That is, the rule applies to trusts with successive charitable purposes (e.g., a trust to pay its income to Charity A for 20 years and then to distribute its principal to Charity B) and to what are generally called "split-interest" trusts for charitable and private purposes in succession, in either order—for example, either to an individual for life with remainder to charity, or to charity for 10 years, remainder to family members. (Because of current federal tax requirements, the lead interest in a split-interest trust is ordinarily a form of annuity or unitrust interest that would give rise to productivity issues *only if* (Comment *f*) subject to an "income" ceiling, with or without a "makeup" requirement, . . ., and further see § 49, Comment *e* . . . .)

Special counterparts of these productivity issues (although, arguably, they may be viewed as prudence issues) arise even in purely charitable trusts for a single charitable purpose—usually, ostensibly, in perpetuity. Productivity under Subsection (2) is a concern whenever (as in typical endowment funds) "income" is to be expended for the designated purpose or, in any event, whenever the amount of expenditures is defined by reference to income so that the interests of the "present" may need to be balanced against the interests of the "future" within that charitable purpose. The manner and extent to which income productivity is of concern depends: (i) on the degree to which the continuing charitable purpose (or activity, such as supporting a specialized type of medical service within a community hospital) is expected to be dependent on expenditures from the particular trust, rather than on ongoing fundraising; and (ii) on the degree to which it is properly contemplated that over time the expenditures will meet an expanding need, rather than a stable need that could be provided for simply by maintaining the real value (or purchasing power) of the corpus. . . . .

i. Underproductive or overproductive portfolio; power of equitable adjustment. The aspect of the duty of impartiality that is stated in Subsection (2), requiring a suitable level of income productivity in certain types of trusts (Comments *e* and *f*), imposes a necessarily flexible duty on trustees.

Because of this flexibility, there is no breach of trust if the substance of the trustee's duty, and of the beneficiaries' income-based entitlements, can properly be satisfied within the terms of the trust and applicable law—provided the investment strategy that produces the underproductivity or overproductivity of the trust estate is justified by prudent attention to the risk tolerance of the trust and the collective best interests of its beneficiaries. If it were otherwise, a rigid application of the duty with respect to income productivity would undesirably inhibit the performance of the trustee's vital duties with respect to investment, thereby denying the beneficiaries the advantages of prudent fiduciary efforts to pursue an optimal investment strategy. For example, an insistence upon an appropriate degree of productivity based entirely on net income, as determined solely by normal rules of trust principal-income accounting, might impair the total return (essentially, income plus appreciation) the particular trust could appropriately and reasonably expect over the long term, thereby reducing the assets available to benefit both present and future beneficiaries. . . . .

Absent applicable legislation (below) addressing this matter, when the investment strategy pursued by a trustee is otherwise appropriate but fails to (or is not expected to) achieve the level of productivity to which an income distributee is entitled, the trustee normally has the power and a duty to make appropriate accounting adjustments to comply with the duty of impartiality. Or the trustee or a beneficiary may petition the appropriate court, in a proceeding for instructions (§ 71), accounting (§ 83), or perhaps even equitable deviation (§ 66), for a determination of the beneficiary's rights and the trustee's duties, and for an order directing (or preventing) an equitable adjustment . . . or providing for equitable deviation or other suitable remedy, including a direction or authorization to the trustee with regard to future actions in similar circumstances. Similarly, the trustee or an appropriate court order may resolve the inverse issues that may arise from an overproductive trust portfolio. Also, informal arrangements with proper beneficiary consent may supply appropriate results and facilitate administration, assuming proper representation of all potential or adversely affected beneficiaries. (Cf. § 65, Comment *b*, . . . on representation in trust modification; and § 78, Comments *c* and *c(3)*, . . . on beneficiary consent in the context of *loyalty* issues.)

Increasingly, state legislation, with Internal Revenue Service acceptance, provides for problems of this type, seeking to allow for greater efficiency and suitability in trust-investment programs while providing protections that are consistent with the purposes of the trust and preserving the beneficial interests as originally intended by the settlor. For example, § 104 of the 1997 revision of the Uniform Principal and Income Act grants trustees a special "adjustment power" to be used when proper and beneficial investment programs yield lower or higher trust-accounting income than called for by the trustee's duty of impartiality. As a result of controversies over the details and operation of this adjustment power but in recognition of its sound objectives, legislation has been enacted in a number of states and is under consideration in others to authorize trustees, in some circumstances and upon some conditions, to elect to give effect to some "income" rights by suitable unitrust distributions. (Most jurisdictions have now enacted either the adjustment power or the unitrust option, or both. . . . .) Beginning a couple of decades earlier, the Uniform Management of Institutional Funds Act, enacted in most states and applicable to some charitable trusts, has attempted, with reasonable success, to address comparable investment and productivity concerns (see Comment *h*).

§ 80. Duty with Respect to Delegation

(1) A trustee has a duty to perform the responsibilities of the trusteeship personally, except as a prudent person of comparable skill might delegate those responsibilities to others.

(2) In deciding whether, to whom, and in what manner to delegate fiduciary authority in the administration of a trust, and thereafter in supervising or monitoring agents, the trustee has a duty to exercise fiduciary discretion and to act as a prudent person of comparable skill would act in similar circumstances.

General Comment:

a. Scope of section; cross-references. Except as otherwise provided by statute or trust provision, the delegation rules of this section and its commentary apply to a trustee's delegation of authority to an agent. Because of the different considerations involved, they do not apply to co-trustees' delegation or allocation of functions between or among themselves, on which see § 81. For purposes of this section, an agent is a person (other than a co-trustee) to whom a trustee delegates the performance of specified fiduciary duties or functions and grants authority to exercise corresponding powers of the trusteeship. . . . .

Delegation is to be distinguished from the hiring of consultants and advisors, on which see Comment *b*. See also §§ 77 and 88.

Assuming that compensation is involved, delegation to an agent raises questions not only about reasonableness of the agent's compensation (§ 88) but also questions about the effects on trustee compensation. See § 38, Comment *c(1)* . . .; § 88, Comment *c*; and § 90, Comment *m* . . . (also discussing effects on trustee fees of compensated advice or consultation and analogous costs associated with mutual-fund investing, on which also cf. § 78, Comment *c(8)*).

b. Advice or consultation distinguished. A trustee, in acting personally and without the effect of delegation, may consult with and receive advice from others, such as accountants, legal counsel, and financial advisers. On the duty sometimes to do so, see § 77, Comment *b*. On the duty to incur only expenses that are reasonable and appropriate, see § 88, especially Comment *c*; on the effects of compensated advice or consultation upon the trustee's rights to indemnification and compensation, see id. . . . and § 38, Comment *c(1)*.

It is also permissible, and may sometimes be necessary, for a trustee to consult with beneficiaries on an impartial basis (§ 79, especially Comment *d*). It is therefore normally proper for a trustee to obtain and consider information concerning not only the beneficiaries' circumstances but also their concerns, preferences, and general views with respect to matters of trust administration.

After obtaining advice or consultation, the trustee can properly take the information or suggestions into account but then (unlike delegation) must exercise independent, prudent, and impartial fiduciary judgment on the matters involved.

Comment on Subsection (1):

c. Resignation; delegation of entire administration. A person designated as trustee need not accept the trusteeship, but may simply renounce it. See generally § 35, Comment *b*. Having accepted appointment, however, a trustee cannot properly transfer the trust property to another as trustee and thereby abdicate responsibility; nor may a trustee resign from the trusteeship except in accordance with the terms of the trust or conditions imposed by order of an appropriate court, or as authorized by proper consent of the beneficiaries. See § 36, Comments *a–c*; and also see id., Comments *d* and *e*, on the duties of a resigning trustee. . . . .

A trustee cannot properly commit the entire administration of the trust to an agent or other person, except as permitted to do so by the terms of the trust.

This prohibition does not preclude even extensive temporary delegation on a prudent basis by the trustee for a reasonable period of absence or during the trustee's inability to perform the duties of the trusteeship. Delegation of this type may be justified when it would not be practical or in the interest of sound administration to require appointment of a substitute or temporary trustee or a trustee ad litem. Extensive temporary delegation may be appropriate, for example, to enable the trustee to take reasonable vacations, including overseas travel, or to cover the trustee's absence due to illness or the necessities of other employment that is not inappropriate to the responsibilities and circumstances of the trusteeship. Further on permissible delegation, see Comments *e–f(3)*.

Illustration:

> 2. S devised his residuary estate to T in trust. T then commits the management of the trust indefinitely to A, giving her a general power of attorney with respect to the trust property. T has violated the general duty to administer the trust personally.

d. General fiduciary duty and discretion. A trustee stands in a fiduciary relationship to the beneficiaries of the trust and therefore is under a general duty personally to perform the responsibilities of the trusteeship. (On the nature of the trust relationship, see § 2, Comment *b*.) A flexible exception to this duty allows trustees to delegate to agents the making of those decisions and the performance of those acts of administration that a person of comparable skills could prudently delegate under like circumstances.

Although a corporate trustee has the same responsibilities as an individual trustee with respect to performing or delegating administrative functions of a trust, a corporation acts—and thus may administer trusts without "delegation"—through its directors, officers, and appropriate corporate employees. This does not preclude prudent delegation to others as agents (or the hiring of others as employees) of the trustee in its fiduciary (i.e., its "representative") capacity, on behalf of a particular trust. (Guidelines applicable to the conduct of trust business by national banks are found in Regulations 9.4–9.9 of the Comptroller of the Currency. . . . .) The observations in this paragraph generally apply as well to other organizations serving as trustees.

Decisions of trustees concerning delegation are matters of fiduciary judgment and discretion. Therefore, these decisions are not to be controlled by a court except to prevent abuse of that discretionary authority. On control of discretionary powers generally, see § 87.

d(1). Imprudent failure to delegate. A trustee's discretionary authority in matters of delegation may be abused by imprudent failure to delegate as well as by making an imprudent decision to delegate. See § 77, Comment *b*.

d(2). Prudence in delegation. Abuse of discretion may also be found in failure to exercise prudence in the degree or manner of delegation. Prudence thus requires the trustee to exercise reasonable care, skill, and caution in the selection and retention of agents and in negotiating and establishing the terms of the delegation.

Significant terms of a delegation range from matters of agent compensation, and matters relating to the duration, termination, and other conditions of the delegation, to providing the agent with substantive direction and guidance consistent with the terms and purposes of the trust. Significant terms also include those providing the arrangements for supervision or for reporting and reviewing the agent's activities, and perhaps a provision securing the agent's consent to the jurisdiction of a particular court.

The trustee then has a further duty to act with prudence in supervising or monitoring the agent's performance and compliance with the terms of the delegation. Upon discovering a breach of duty by the agent (Comment *g*), the trustee has a duty to take reasonable steps to remedy it. See generally § 76, Comment *d*. . . . .

Because much of delegation relates to the trustee's investment responsibilities, delegation is considered further in that context in § 90, particularly Comment *j*. On whether and how a trustee might delegate in the context of a challenging investment program, see id., Illustration 23 and accompanying observations.

On the trustee's duty to avoid excessive costs, see § 88, Comments *b* and *c*; and, on effects of delegation upon the trustee's compensation, see § 38, Comment *c(1)* . . . , § 88, Comment *c* . . . , and § 90, Comment *m* . . . .

Comment on Subsection (2):

e. Permissible delegation: in general. Although the administration of a trust may not be delegated in full (Comment *c*), a trustee may for many purposes delegate fiduciary authority to properly selected, instructed, and supervised or monitored agents.

Prudent delegation is not limited to the performance of ministerial acts. In appropriate circumstances delegation may extend, for example, to the selection of trust investments or the management of specialized investment programs, and to other activities of administration involving significant judgment.

It is not possible precisely to define acts that a trustee can properly delegate or the circumstances and conditions of proper delegation. A delegation of fiduciary authority is proper when it is prudently arranged and is reasonably intended to further sound administration of the trust. Certainly it is proper to delegate the performance of acts that it would be unreasonable to expect the trustee personally to perform. More than that is permitted, however, for the trustee has fiduciary discretion to delegate such functions, and in such manner, as a prudent investor or manager with comparable skills and facilities might reasonably delegate in the particular circumstances. See also Uniform Prudent Investor Act § 9.

A trustee's exercise of this discretionary authority is judicially reviewable only for abuse, based ordinarily on unreasonableness of judgment or on failure to exercise the required degree of care, skill, or caution (§ 77), violation of duties of loyalty or impartiality (§ 78, 79), or failure to comply with the relevant terms of the trust (§ 76). See generally § 87. In considering whether and under what circumstances and conditions a particular delegation of fiduciary authority is proper—as well as in considering the terms that are appropriate and the supervision or monitoring that is required—the following circumstances, among others, may be of importance to the trustee or to a reviewing court: (1) the nature and degree of discretion or judgment involved in the delegation; (2) the burdens and complexity of the decisions or activities involved; (3) the relationship of the acts or functions involved to the competence and facilities possessed (or represented to be possessed) by the trustee; (4) the amount of funds or the value and character of the property involved; (5) considerations of efficiency, convenience, and cost in light of the situs of the property or activities involved; and (6) the fairness and appropriateness of the responsibilities in question to the trustee's compensation and the overall burdens of the trusteeship.

In short, consideration should be given to all factors that are relevant to analyzing whether the fact and manner of delegation can reasonably be expected to contribute to the sound, efficient administration of the trust.

f. Permissible delegation: selected applications. The commentary immediately below discusses several illustrative, but not exclusive, applications of the delegation rule of this section, with Comments *f(1)* and *f(3)* addressing some limits on permissible delegation.

f(1). Powers with respect to the investment function. The trustee is not required personally to perform all aspects of the trust's investment activities, even if the trustee is a professional or institutional fiduciary with competence and experience in financial matters.

The qualities and qualifications for which trustees are properly selected for fiduciary roles, and the scope and complexity of the investment programs of some trusts, are so diverse that prescriptions for prudent behavior in the delegation of investment functions cannot be expressed in simple or precise legal rules.

With professional advice as needed, the trustee personally must at least define the trust's investment objectives. In addition, the trustee must personally either formulate or approve the trust's investment strategies and programs. Admittedly, even these limited generalizations are necessarily and desirably couched in terms that are less than self-defining.

In other matters, the trustee must exercise reasonable care, skill, and caution in determining what investment responsibilities to delegate. Then, fiduciary prudence must be exercised as well in selecting an agent and establishing the terms of the delegation, and also in supervising or reviewing the agent's performance and compliance with the terms of the delegation, all in a manner appropriate to the circumstances and conditions of the delegation and the competence of both agent and trustee. See Comments *d* and *e*. Matters of delegation in the investment function are discussed and illustrated in greater detail intermittently throughout § 90, and particularly in id., Comment *j*.

f(2). Powers to buy, sell, lease, and otherwise manage trust property. A trustee can properly appoint an agent to assist in acquiring, selling, leasing, or improving trust property, or otherwise to assist in the management of trust assets.

For example, it is proper for a trustee to employ an agent to secure offers for these purposes, or to perform ministerial acts for the purpose of finalizing contracts or consummating transactions on terms established by the trustee. In appropriate circumstances, however, prudence may well justify delegation of authority to an agent to establish the terms of transactions to be carried out under an agency or employment arrangement that requires no further participation by the trustee. This type of delegation is particularly likely to be appropriate in the case of a trust that conducts a business or other activities the administration of which involves numerous transactions. In situations of these types the trustee may not only be permitted but virtually compelled by considerations of time, efficiency, or even competence, and thus effectiveness of administration, to delegate to properly selected agents the power to hire employees of a trust business, to fix prices or the terms of contracts, and to carry out sales, purchases, and other transactions.

f(3). Powers over discretionary distributions to beneficiaries. If by the terms of a trust the trustee has discretionary power to determine the recipients or amounts of distributions to be made to one or more of the trust's beneficiaries (see § 50), the trustee cannot properly delegate this discretionary authority. Similarly, if terms of a trust provide that a beneficiary is entitled to receive distributions of specified or formula amounts from the trust but also provide that the trustee has discretionary authority to reduce or withhold those amounts, and perhaps to either accumulate or divert them to others, the trustee cannot properly delegate this discretionary authority.

On the other hand, to the extent the trustee properly can determine specific (or objective formula) amounts to be distributed and the timing of those amounts over a forthcoming period of time, the trustee may delegate to an agent the performance of the essentially ministerial duty of making those distributions, as well as the making of any nondiscretionary distributions, to one or more specified trust beneficiaries.

g. Responsibilities of agent; liability of trustee. In accepting the delegation of a trust function from a trustee, an agent assumes a fiduciary role with fiduciary responsibilities. Thus, the agent has a duty to the trust and its beneficiaries to act with reasonable care (cf. § 77, Comment *b*) in performing a delegated function and in complying with the instructions and other provisions in the terms of the delegation, with potential liability for breach of duty.

A trustee who acts with prudence—that is, with reasonable care, skill, and caution—to comply with the requirements of Subsection (2) (described in Comments *d* and *e*, and particularly in Comment *d(2)*, including in redressing an agent's breach of duty) is not personally liable to the trust or its beneficiaries for the decisions or actions of the agent to whom the function was delegated. (On a trustee's liability to third parties in the trustee's fiduciary capacity, including possible liability as principal for the conduct of an agent, see Chapter 21 . . . .)

In monitoring the performance of an agent, the degree to which a trustee may rely on the agent to make decisions and take action without personal investigation by the trustee (or by a consultant) inevitably depends on what is reasonable and appropriate under the circumstances, including the expertise (or reputation) of the agent and the trustee's competence in the matter(s) involved. See discussion in Comment *e*, and also see Comment *d*. . . . .

The combined responsibilities of trustee and agent in a delegation situation supply the reasonable assurance trust law requires that the trust relationship and the interests of the beneficiaries will be protected.

Additional General Comment:

h. Terms of the trust. The terms of the trust may permit a trustee to delegate to agents or other persons (e.g., a co-trustee) the administration of the trust or the performance of acts that could not otherwise properly be delegated. Or trust terms may narrow the scope of permissible delegation. Similarly, the trust terms may broaden the degree of the trustee's discretion in matters of delegation. On judicial control of ordinary and extended (e.g., "absolute") discretionary powers, see generally § 87, especially Comments *b–d* (and cf. § 50).

Trust provisions may thus authorize a trustee to permit an agent to manage trust property or trust activities that the trustee could not otherwise properly delegate, or could not otherwise properly delegate in the particular circumstances, or to delegate without adverse effect on the trustee's compensation.

So also, the trust terms may provide that some elements of authority that a trustee would normally have shall be held instead by some other person. See, e.g., § 75. Thus, it may be provided that the trustee shall make only such investments as may be directed by the settlor, one or more of the beneficiaries, or some third person, or by a co-trustee. As to the duty of the trustee in such a case, see § 75, Comments *b(1)* and *d–g(1)*. On co-trusteeship, see § 81, especially Comment *c(1)*.

i. Power of trustee to cooperate with others. It is not a breach of the trustee's duty to the beneficiaries to cooperate with other persons holding similar interests, provided that it is prudent to do so and that the trustee's duties of loyalty and impartiality are not violated. This is so even though decisions and actions may thereafter be taken by majority vote of those cooperating. Cf. § 86, Comment *e*.

Thus, it is not a breach of duty for a trustee to deposit securities of a corporation in financial distress with a protective committee in circumstances in which it would be reasonable for an individual owner to make such a deposit. Similarly, a trustee may in a proper case join in a representative suit affecting the trust property, although the trustee thereby surrenders control over the suit.

§ 81. Duty with Respect to Co-Trustees

(1) If a trust has more than one trustee, except as otherwise provided by the terms of the trust, each trustee has a duty and the right to participate in the administration of the trust.

(2) Each trustee also has a duty to use reasonable care to prevent a co-trustee from committing a breach of trust and, if a breach of trust occurs, to obtain redress.

General Comment:

a. *Scope of section; cross-references.* This section does not address a trustee's duty in taking over from a predecessor trustee, on which see § 76, Comment *c*. Nor does this section address matters regarding the office of trustee that are treated in Chapter 7, concerning: the capacity to serve as trustee (§§ 32, 33, and cf. § 77, Comment *b*); the appointment (§ 34), resignation (§ 36, and cf. § 35 on renunciation), and removal (§ 37) of trustees; and "reasonable compensation" of trustees in multiple-trustee situations (§ 38, Comment *i*). On the possibility of removal for failure to cooperate with a co-trustee, see § 37, Comment *e*.

That, absent contrary provision in the terms of the trust, fiduciary authority is exercised by majority vote in trusts that have three or more trustees, see § 39, applicable to private as well as charitable trusts.

That, when several persons are designated as trustees and one of them dies, declines to serve or resigns, is removed, or is or becomes incapable of acting as trustee, the remaining trustee or trustees ordinarily are entitled to administer the trust, with a replacement trustee being required only if the settlor manifested an intention (or it is conducive to the proper administration or purposes of the trust) that the number of trustees should be maintained, see § 34, Comment *d*, and § 85, Comment *e*. Also see § 34, Comment *e*, on the authority of courts to appoint additional trustees to promote better administration of a trust even when there is no vacancy.

When a trust has multiple trustees, the fiduciary duties of trustees stated in this chapter, except as modified by the terms of the trust, apply to each of the trustees. Thus, for example, each of the co-trustees is ordinarily to participate and cooperate with the other(s) in the prudent administration of the trust (Comment *c*, and also see §§ 76, 77) and in so doing to conform to the duties of loyalty (§ 78) and impartiality (§ 79). Permissible delegation between or among co-trustees is considered in Comment *c(1)*, below; in respects there described . . ., the rules of such delegation differ from the rules in § 80 for delegation to agents.

b. *Effect of the terms of the trust.* The duties of multiple trustees, as discussed in this section, may be reduced, modified, or specially allocated by the terms of the trust.

Thus, trust provisions may and often should allocate roles and responsibilities among the trustees, or relieve one or more of the trustees of duties to participate in particular aspects of the trust's administration. A settlor may even designate, or provide for the appointment of, a "special trustee" to handle only one or more specified functions or types of decisions (e.g., the exercise of tax-sensitive powers of distribution, when the general trustee or trustees are beneficiaries of those powers), with the special trustee having no authority in or responsibility for other aspects of the trust's administration. The settlor's limiting of a trustee's functions or allocation of functions among the trustees usually, either explicitly or as a matter of interpretation, has the effect of relieving the trustee(s) to whom a function is not allocated of any affirmative duty to remain informed or to participate in deliberations about matters within that function. Similarly, exculpatory provisions (§ 96) may be designed to apply selectively.

Even in matters for which a trustee is relieved of responsibility, however, if the trustee knows that a co-trustee is committing or attempting to commit a breach of trust, the trustee has a duty to take reasonable steps to prevent the fiduciary misconduct. See Comments *d* and *e*. Furthermore, absent clear provision in the trust to the contrary, even in the absence of any duty to intervene or grounds for suspicion, a trustee is entitled to request and receive reasonable information regarding an aspect of trust administration in which the trustee is not required to participate.

The terms of a trust may provide that the decision of a particular trustee to take action in certain matters shall prevail for purposes of breaking a deadlock, or even by overriding a position of the other trustees although they may constitute a majority. Essentially, a provision of this type merely authorizes action upon the decision of one (or possibly more) of the trustees in the event of disagreement but does not relieve the others of their normal duties and rights of informed participation in the trustees' deliberations and decisionmaking. More generally, on the duties and liabilities of minority or dissenting trustees, see Comments *d* and *e*.

Comment on Subsection (1):

c. *Active personal participation: general rule.* The duty of a trustee to administer the trust (§ 76) applies to the trustees of trusts that have two or more trustees. Thus, except as otherwise provided by the terms of the trust, each co-trustee has a duty, and also the right, of active, prudent participation in the performance of all aspects of the trust's administration. Implicit in this requirement of prudent participation is a duty of reasonable cooperation among the trustees.

In hiring counsel for the trustees in their fiduciary capacity, the selection is ordinarily made by majority vote of the co-trustees (§ 39), with all of the trustees entitled to participate in meetings and other aspects of the counseling process and to have access to communications from the trustees' counsel. If separate counsel is reasonably needed to aid a trustee in the performance of a fiduciary duty, as may be necessary under Subsection (2), appropriate attorney fees are payable or reimbursable from the trust estate.

The duty to participate in the trust's administration does not prevent, as a means of participation, prudent delegation by the co-trustees to one or more agents in accordance with § 80. Nor does it preclude proper delegation by a co-trustee to the other co-trustee(s) in accordance with Comment *c(1)*.

The trustee's duty to participate in administering the trust does not require an equal level of effort or activity by each co-trustee, as recognized in the variability of their "reasonable" compensation (§ 38, Comment *i*). Accordingly, the duty of participation by each of the co-trustees does not prevent them from deciding (short of constituting delegation) to allow one or more of the co-trustees to carry more of the burden in regard to various matters, for example, by initiating, analyzing, reporting, and making recommendations for reasonably informed action by all of the trustees. It does, however, normally prevent the trustees from "dividing" the trusteeship or its functions in a manner that is not authorized by the terms of the trust. Cf. Comment *c(1)*.

If and to the extent a co-trustee is unavailable to participate prudently in the performance of a trusteeship function because of absence, illness, or other temporary incapacity, or because of disqualification under other law, the co-trustee is excused from participation. If prudence calls for action to be taken in these circumstances, the remaining co-trustee(s) can properly act for the trust.

In the case of a trust with two co-trustees, joint action or the concurrence of both trustees is required to exercise powers of the trusteeship. See § 39. Also, in trusts having three or more trustees, the terms of the trust or applicable law (rejecting the majority-control rule of § 39) may require action or concurrence by all of the trustees to exercise certain or all of the trustees' powers. If a situation arises in which prudence requires that the trustees reach a decision and they are unwilling or unable to do so, the trustees have a duty to apply to an appropriate court for instructions. See § 71.

c(1). Delegation to other co-trustee(s). The general duty of each co-trustee to participate in performing the functions of the trusteeship does not prevent delegation on a prudent basis between or among themselves with respect to essentially ministerial matters, such as the custody of trust property and the implementation of decisions that have been made by proper vote of the co-trustees. (A trustee may also expressly delegate responsibilities and authority to the remaining co-trustee(s) in anticipation of the trustee's unavailability due to circumstances of the type described above in Comment *c*, involving relief from responsibility during illness or absence.)

Delegation is also permissible in circumstances in which it would be unreasonable to expect the co-trustee personally to perform the function(s) in question. (Compare the earlier standard for delegation *generally*, as stated in Restatement Second, Trusts § 171.)

Furthermore, delegation to a co-trustee may be desirable and appropriate in circumstances in which adherence to the general rule of Comment *c* would not be practical and prudent because of cost or inefficiency, or even because delegation would be consistent with the settlor's expectations in designating, or providing for appointment of, that co-trustee. For example, delegation of investment authority is generally authorized by implication when a settlor designates his or her surviving spouse to serve as co-trustee with a skilled professional trustee (or provides that the co-trustee position should always be filled by one of the settlor's children, to serve with the professional trustee) when the settlor was aware that the spouse (or children) had neither skill nor interest in investment or relevant financial matters.

A trustee's delegation to the other trustee(s) is revocable and does not relieve the other trustee(s) of the duty to provide information to the delegating trustee, on request or in the event of significant, unanticipated circumstances or changes of investment policy.

That co-trustees cannot properly divide up the trusteeship functions except as may be expressly or impliedly authorized by the terms of the trust (cf. Comment *b*), see Comment *c*. Uncertainties concerning permissible delegation among co-trustees are appropriate matters for judicial instruction under § 71, or perhaps even equitable deviation under § 66. . . . .

c(2). Special situations. In appropriate situations, a panel of co-trustees (despite the generalizations in Comment *c*) may, in administering the trust, function in the manner of a corporate board of directors. Of relevance for the purpose of this possibility are not only (though critical) the number of trustees but also their circumstances (skills and experience, compensation, other commitments, etc.) and the nature and scale of the trust's asset holdings, investment programs, and other activities. . . . .

On the powers of trustees to incorporate (or to establish other entities for) some or all of a trust's holdings or operations, see § 86, Comment *e*; and on joining and cooperating with others, see § 80, Comment *i*. . . . .

Comment on Subsection (2):

d. Duty regarding breach of trust by co-trustee. When a trust has multiple trustees, each trustee ordinarily (cf. Comment *b*) has a duty to exercise reasonable care to prevent a co-trustee from committing a breach of trust. Thus, for example, it is a breach of trust for a trustee knowingly to allow a co-trustee to commit a breach of trust. And, if a breach occurs, the trustee must take reasonable steps seeking to compel the co-trustee to redress the breach of trust.

If a trustee needs independent counsel to fulfill these duties, reasonable attorney fees may be paid or reimbursed from the trust. See § 88, Comment *d*.

A trustee is not precluded from maintaining a suit for redress by the fact that the trustee participated in the breach of trust, because the suit is on behalf of the trust and its beneficiaries.

On the duty of a trustee where a power of control is conferred upon another, see § 75.

e. Whether trustee liable for breach of trust by co-trustee(s). A trustee is not liable for a breach of trust committed by a co-trustee, unless the trustee: (i) participated or acquiesced in the breach of trust or was involved in concealing it; (ii) improperly delegated administration of the trust to the co-trustee; or (iii) enabled the co-trustee to commit the breach of trust by failing to exercise reasonable care, including by failing to make reasonable effort to enjoin or otherwise prevent the breach of trust. Furthermore, a trustee may be liable for neglecting to take reasonable steps seeking to obtain redress for the breach of trust. That it might be "reasonable" for a trustee to decide not to bring suit to redress a breach of trust, see § 76, Comment *d*.

A trustee who opposed an action taken upon decision by a majority of the trustees, and who made that opposition known to a co-trustee but thereafter reasonably joined in the action in order to avoid obstructing its execution, is not liable for the action unless the dissenting trustee was aware that the action was a breach of trust.

When several trustees are liable for a breach of trust, either as a breach committed by them jointly or on another of the above grounds, they are jointly and severally liable. On the right of a trustee to contribution or indemnity from co-trustee(s), see Chapter 19.

§ 82. Duty to Furnish Information to Beneficiaries

(1) Except as provided in § 74 (revocable trusts) or as permissibly modified by the terms of the trust, a trustee has a duty:

(a) promptly to inform fairly representative beneficiaries of the existence of the trust, of their status as beneficiaries and their right to obtain further information, and of basic information concerning the trusteeship;

(b) to inform beneficiaries of significant changes in their beneficiary status; and

(c) to keep fairly representative beneficiaries reasonably informed of changes involving the trusteeship and about other significant developments concerning the trust and its administration, particularly material information needed by beneficiaries for the protection of their interests.

(2) Except as provided in § 74 or as permissibly modified by the terms of the trust, a trustee also ordinarily has a duty promptly to respond to the request of any beneficiary for information concerning the trust and its administration, and to permit beneficiaries on a reasonable basis to inspect trust documents, records, and property holdings.

General Comment:

a. *Duty in general; cross-references.* The rule of this section imposes on trustees, absent permissible modification by the terms of the trust (Comment *a(2)*), a duty in some circumstances to provide some types of information to beneficiaries. (Although this section and its commentary usually refer only to "beneficiaries," the references also apply to charities and charitable purposes, with the information entitlements in the appropriate attorney general, and sometimes (cf. § 94) in identifiable charities.) The rule of this section is related to and reinforced by the rule of § 83 on the duty of trustees to maintain books and records and, on request, to provide beneficiaries with reasonably comprehensive reports or accountings concerning the trust's property and administration. Also related is the § 84 requirement regarding segregation and identification of trust property. Together these sections foster a reasonable degree of openness and transparency, as well as accountability, suitable to the underlying principles that, under modern default law, (i) trustees have comprehensive authority (§§ 70, 85), subject to their fiduciary responsibilities (§§ 70, 86), and (ii) a trust is to be administered for and enforceable by its beneficiaries (§ 27(2)).

The information requirements in this section (§ 82) do not apply to revocable trusts while the settlor is alive and competent. See § 74, Comment *a(1)* (settlor as trustee), and more generally id., Comments *d* and *c*; and compare § 74, Comment *g*, on other holders of ownership-equivalent powers. Also relevant for present purposes is § 76, Comment *c*, instructing the trustee promptly after accepting the trusteeship to review the terms of the trust and other information in order (inter alia) to identify parties interested in the trust and their beneficial interests.

Subsection (1) of this section calls for the trustee within a reasonable time to alert a cross section of the beneficiaries (Comment *a(1)*) to the existence of the trust and to give them certain initially useful information about it (Subsection (1)(a) and Comment *b*), and thereafter, if and as circumstances warrant (see Subsections (1)(b) and (1)(c) and Comments *c* and *d*), to apprise various beneficiaries of significant information or developments to enable them to protect their interests. Specifically, because differences in trust and beneficiary circumstances preclude imposing precise, universal rules in all of these matters, the trustee's duty is to exercise reasonable judgment in deciding when, about what, and to whom information is to be provided under this subsection.

In addition, under Subsection (2), all beneficiaries (or their duly appointed representatives) are ordinarily entitled (but see Comment *e* and § 74), at reasonable hours and intervals, to inquire about the terms and asset holdings of the trust and about trust management and distributions (Comment *e*). This entitlement includes an associated right to examine trust accounts, other records, and tangible properties.

a(1). Fairly representative beneficiaries. Language in Subsection (1) refers flexibly to "fairly representative" beneficiaries, balancing considerations of practicality for trustees and the importance in most trusts of reflecting the diversity of the beneficial interests and beneficiary concerns. Thus, the trustee's duty under this requirement is to make a good-faith effort to select and inform a limited number of beneficiaries whose interests and concerns appear fairly representative of—i.e., likely to coincide with—those of the trust's beneficiaries generally, thereby affording a reasonable opportunity for monitoring the trustee's duty of impartial (§ 79) as well as faithful, prudent (§§ 76–78) administration of the trust.

A trustee's duty under Subsection (1) to provide information to fairly representative beneficiaries usually can be satisfied simply by providing the required information (i) to those beneficiaries who are then either entitled or eligible to receive distributions of income or principal and (ii) to those who would be entitled or eligible to receive distributions of income or principal if either the trust or current interests referred to in (i) above were then to terminate. (On corresponding charitable interests, see Comment *a* . . .)

Occasionally, however, the trustee's duty to provide information about a trust will extend also to a donee of a power of appointment who is not covered by (i) or (ii), above (particularly the duty under Comment *b*), or to a person not so covered who is granted power to veto or direct acts of the trustee (§ 75), power to modify the trust (§ 64), or the like. On the other hand, in some circumstances, and for some purposes (particularly under Comment *d*), a dissemination of information on a more limited basis than described in the preceding paragraph may be reasonable, impartial, and sufficient. (For example, cf. § 50, Comment *f*, on trusts with broad classes of discretionary current beneficiaries.)

Illustrations:

1. S created a testamentary trust to pay income to B for life, "remainder per stirpes to B's issue who survive her, and if none do then to her then-surviving brothers and sister or their issue." B's only descendants are all living; they consist of her two adult children and several adult and minor grandchildren. B also has living siblings. The trustee's duty to inform fairly representative beneficiaries of this rather typical trust can readily be satisfied by providing information to B (under (i), above) and to her two children (under (ii), above). Information under Subsection (1) need not be provided to the grandchildren or siblings.

2. The same trust as in Illustration 1, except that the trust terms provide that, if B's husband X survives her, the trust is to continue and

X is eligible for life to receive income distributions in the trustee's discretion, with an appropriate adaptation of the above-quoted remainder to follow. In this situation, information normally should be provided to X (under (ii) above) as well as to B and her two children.

For the limited purpose of fulfilling the duty prescribed by Subsection (1), it is both practical and sufficient for the trustee in the above Illustrations to provide information to remainder beneficiaries by providing it to B's children rather than to some broader cross section or all of the potential remainder beneficiaries. Also, there is no need for the trustee to struggle with difficult, often archaic distinctions between technically "vested" and "contingent" future interests.

Although not required by this section to do so, the trustee may, for some matters and some trustee concerns, provide information to additional beneficiaries (e.g., B's adult grandchildren or one or more siblings in the above Illustrations) if the trustee wishes (see, e.g., Comment *d*, next-to-last paragraph) or deems appropriate to the circumstances (cf. Illustration 3, below).

A duty to provide information to a beneficiary who is under disability may be satisfied for purposes of Subsection (1), by providing the information to the beneficiary's conservator, agent under a durable power of attorney, legal or natural guardian, or other suitable person(s), such as one or more trust beneficiaries whose concerns can be expected reasonably to coincide with those of the disabled beneficiary. For example, if a child of B and X in Illustration 2 were still a minor, information provided to the other child, an adult, would satisfy the trustee's duty to the minor under this subsection during the period of his or her minority.

Illustration:

3. The same trust as in Illustration 1, except that B has no issue, but her sister and two brothers are all alive to constitute a fairly representative set of beneficiaries under (ii) above. The trustee, however, is aware that brother Z is in failing health, inattentive to his financial affairs, and of uncertain mental capacity. The duty imposed by Subsection (1) may be satisfied in these circumstances, without having to resolve uncertainties about Z's capacity, by information provided to Z's siblings as well as to Z; but the trustee may prefer also to provide the required information to Z's adult child or children, if any, as persons who would take in Z's place if he should predecease B.

a(2). Effect of terms of the trust. The terms of a trust may alter the amount of information a trustee must give to the beneficiaries under this section and also the circumstances and frequency with which, and persons to whom, it must be given. (The extent to which trust provisions may modify a trustee's normal duty to provide reports or accounts under § 83 is considered in id., Comment *d*.)

Except as precluded by § 74, Comment *e*, however, a beneficiary is always entitled under Subsection (2) to request such information as is reasonably necessary to enable the beneficiary to prevent or redress a breach of trust and otherwise to enforce his or her rights under the trust. Furthermore, although subject to modification by trust provision, the duty to provide information to certain beneficiaries under Subsection (1), Clauses (a) through (c), may not be dispensed with entirely or to a degree or for a time that would unduly interfere with the underlying purposes or effectiveness of the information requirements. See opening paragraph of Comment *a*, and cf. Comment *d*.

Comment on Subsection (1):

b. Subsection (1), Clause (a): initial information. Except as permissibly modified by the terms of the trust, upon creation of the trust or when a revocable trust becomes irrevocable (and see § 74, Comment *e*, if the settlor becomes incapacitated), the trustee is to inform fairly representative beneficiaries of: the existence, source, and name (or descriptive reference) of the trust; the extent and nature (present or future, discretionary or conditional, etc.) of their interests; the name(s) of the trustee(s), contact and compensation information, and perhaps the roles of co-trustees; and the beneficiaries' right to further information, ordinarily including the usual right to request information concerning the terms of the trust or a copy of the trust instrument (but see Comments *a(2)* and *d* (last paragraph), and cf. § 83, Comment *d*).

It is appropriate, and will ordinarily be simplest, for the trustee to provide a copy of the trust instrument to fairly representative beneficiaries as a part of the initial information at the outset of administration.

c. Subsection (1), Clause (b): significant beneficiary changes. If it later appears that a person should be treated as a fairly representative beneficiary (e.g., because of the death of a "higher" remainder beneficiary), the trustee should ordinarily provide the type of information called for under Subsection (1)(a).

If a beneficiary becomes currently entitled to distributions (such as by obtaining a specified age or because of another's death), or becomes eligible to receive or request discretionary distributions, or if a beneficiary ceases to be entitled or eligible to receive distributions, the trustee should appropriately inform the beneficiary.

d. Subsection (1), Clause (c): disclosure of significant information. The rule of Subsection (1)(c) does not impose a regular or routine requirement of reporting or accounting. It does, however, impose an affirmative requirement that, if and as circumstances warrant over the course of administration, the trustee inform fairly representative beneficiaries of important developments and information that appear reasonably necessary for the beneficiaries to be aware of in order to protect their interests. Because of inevitable differences in trusts and in their terms, objectives, asset holdings, investment or management activities, and other circumstances, it is not realistic to attempt to state precisely or universally what information will be "significant" for these purposes. Accordingly, the trustee's duty under Subsection (1)(c) is to exercise reasonable judgment in determining what matters have such significance. Nevertheless, some generalizations may offer guidance.

For various reasons of prudence, loyalty, or impartiality, or simply as a general matter of proper disclosure, but subject to considerations of practicality as well as sensitivity of negotiations, a trustee's duty to provide information to beneficiaries may apply when there are (inter alia): significant changes in trustee circumstances, including changes in the identities, number, or roles of trustees or in methods of determining trustee compensation; decisions regarding delegation of important fiduciary responsibilities or significant changes in arrangements for delegation; important adjustments being considered in investment or other management strategies; significant actions under consideration involving hard-to-value assets or special sensitivity to beneficiaries (such as liquidating or selling shares of a closely held business or a sale or long-term lease of a major real-estate holding); plans being made for distribution on termination or partial termination (or perhaps subdivision) of the trust; and other transactions or developments of which beneficiaries should be made aware and thereby allowed an opportunity to offer suggestions, comments, or information, or to request reports or accountings under § 83. In addition, a trustee should advise discretionary distributees of information the trustee may need (or desire) regarding the beneficiaries' circumstances, needs, resources, concerns, or wishes, as may be relevant to fiduciary judgments with respect to discretionary distributions, along with disclosure by the trustee of the bases upon which discretion will be exercised. (Cf. § 87 and § 50, Comment *e(1)*; also see § 79.)

These types of disclosures do not afford beneficiaries a right to veto trustee action, although disclosure may eventually afford the trustee a defense based on laches or a statute of limitations (§ 98).

Disclosure is fundamental to sound administration of the trust, and to both the trustee's performance and the beneficiaries' monitoring of associated fiduciary obligations. Therefore, the trustee's duty to provide the type of information described in this Comment is subject to modification only by clear language in the terms of the trust and within limits described in Comment *a(2)*. That trusts and their administration are to be for the benefit of the beneficiaries, see § 27, Comment *b* .... See also §§ 77–79 (on duties of prudence, loyalty, and impartiality), § 87 (on abuse of discretion), § 89 (duties on termination), and more generally § 86.

Comment on Subsection (2):

e. Requested information and access. Under the general rule of Subsection (2), a trustee ordinarily has a duty, with reasonable promptness, to provide information that is requested regarding the trust property or its administration by any beneficiary, a right not limited to fairly representative beneficiaries. The trustee is also to grant access to books and records of the trust, and to permit inspection of the trust's property holdings, on a reasonable basis, at reasonable hours and intervals, to any beneficiary, including with the participation of the beneficiary's accountant, attorney, or other advisor. On petition by the trustee or a beneficiary, however, a court may limit the frequency or extent of such inquiries by one or more of the beneficiaries, weighing the remoteness or substantiality of their interests in the trust against the burdens, intrusiveness, and privacy considerations that may be involved.

Because one's enforcement of his or her rights as a trust beneficiary normally requires an awareness not only of the trust's existence but also of the terms of the trust, a beneficiary is ordinarily entitled to obtain a copy of the trust. Sometimes, a request for the needed terms of the trust can be satisfied by copies of relevant provisions or a suitably redacted copy of the trust instrument. Particularly in situations involving or likely to involve litigation, however, selected or edited terms of the trust will be unsatisfactory. Accordingly, the easiest and most helpful response to a beneficiary's request (and ordinarily *required* if demanded) is for the trustee simply to send a copy of the instrument when the request is made.

By the terms of the trust, however, the settlor can limit the trustee's duty to disclose trust provisions or information on a reasonable basis, in order, for example, to lessen the risk of unnecessary or unwarranted loss of privacy, or the risk of adverse effects upon youthful ... or troubled beneficiaries about whose motivation or responsibility the settlor has concerns. Even limitations of these types, however, cannot properly prevent beneficiaries, even underage beneficiaries (or their duly appointed representatives), from requesting and receiving information to the extent currently necessary for the protection of their interests in accordance with principles stated in Comment *a(2)*. . . . .

Other General Comment:

f. What need not be disclosed? A trustee is privileged to refrain from disclosing to beneficiaries or co-trustees opinions obtained from, and other communications with, counsel retained for the trustee's personal protection in the course, or in anticipation, of litigation (e.g., for surcharge or removal). This situation is to be distinguished from legal consultations and advice obtained in the trustee's fiduciary capacity concerning decisions or actions to be taken in the course of administering the trust. Communications of this latter type are subject to the general principle entitling a beneficiary to information that is reasonably necessary to the prevention or redress of a breach of trust or otherwise to the enforcement of the beneficiary's rights under the trust.

When the roles and objectives of legal consultation are unclear, the question of who has paid for the legal services, or who ultimately will be required to pay those expenses, although potentially relevant, involves other and complicated considerations (see § 88) so that this matter is not determinative in resolving issues of privilege.

When a beneficiary's request for information may encompass sensitive, private information acquired by the trustee about other beneficiaries, the extent of the trustee's duties may require a balancing of competing interests. While recognizing the requesting beneficiary's "need to know" (see Comment *a*, first paragraph, and Comments *d* and *e*, last paragraph of each), a trustee—and ultimately a court—may need to provide some response that offers a compromise between the confidentiality or privacy concerns of some and the interest-protection needs of others. Cf. § 78, Comment *i*. . . . .

§ 83. Duty to Keep Records and Provide Reports

A trustee has a duty to maintain clear, complete, and accurate books and records regarding the trust property and the administration of the trust, and, at reasonable intervals on request, to provide beneficiaries with reports or accountings.

Comment:

a. Duty to keep records. Implicit in the duty to provide information to beneficiaries (§ 82) is the duty stated in this section requiring a trustee to maintain an adequate set of books and records. The performance of these record-keeping responsibilities is also essential to a trustee's duty to collect and safeguard the trust property (§ 76, Comment *d*) and to the beneficiaries' right to enforce the trustee's duty to act with prudence, loyalty, and impartiality (§§ 77–79), as well as the trustee's duty regarding reasonable and appropriate costs of administration (§ 88). Accordingly, the trustee has a duty to maintain books (or accounts) and records that show in detail the nature and amount of the trust property and the trustee's administration thereof.

With regard to the latter, the records of a trust must provide information that will enable the trustee to account for receipts, expenses, and distributions made to beneficiaries, and for the sale, purchase, or exchange of trust properties. In addition, the records must show allocations between the principal and income accounts (Chapter 23) and any other information that may be needed in providing a report to the beneficiaries or in presenting a more formal accounting to the beneficiaries or in court (Comment *b*).

Given the diversity of trusts and trustees, the law recognizes that the duty under this Comment may be satisfactorily discharged by simple, orderly forms of bookkeeping and record maintenance, disclosing information in an understandable manner that will enable beneficiaries to determine whether the trust is being properly administered.

a(1). Consequences of failure to maintain records. A trustee who fails to keep proper records is liable for any loss or expense resulting from that failure. A trustee's failure to maintain necessary books and records may also cause a court in reviewing a judicial accounting to resolve doubts against the trustee. These failures by trustees may furnish grounds for reducing or denying compensation, or even for removal, or for charging the trustee with the costs of corrective procedures or of having to conduct otherwise unnecessary accounting proceedings in court.

b. Duty to provide reports. The right of any beneficiary to request information under § 82(2) includes a right to request and receive accountings or comparable reports (see below) from the trustee at reasonable intervals. Also, in a proper judicial proceeding, a beneficiary may compel the trustee to render an account of trust administration to the appropriate court. (Although a routine requirement of periodic reporting is not imposed on trustees by this section or § 82, matters of court and noncourt accountings are regulated—as to both form and frequency—by statute in many states, particularly with respect to testamentary or court-appointed trustees but increasingly, though often with less burden, with respect to all trustees.)

When a trustee prepares and provides a report in response to a request by a beneficiary, the trustee might wish to follow a simple, routine practice of also sending a copy to other beneficiaries, particularly to fairly representative beneficiaries (described in § 82, Comment *a(1)*) and perhaps to other beneficiaries as well. As noted below, a copy must be sent to other beneficiaries who request it. A beneficiary who receives an accounting or other report of the trustee's administration is not precluded from making requests for additional information under § 82(2).

If a beneficiary is not sent a report (or accounting) at about the time of another's request and later asks for a report, it may be a reasonable and sufficient response for the trustee to provide that beneficiary with a copy of the recent report.

The trustee may be required to report on request not only to beneficiaries who are presently entitled or eligible to receive payments of income or principal (or other "fairly representative beneficiaries" under § 82, Comment *a(1)*), but also to other beneficiaries who will or may be entitled to income or principal in the future, including beneficiaries whose interests are contingent. See, however, Comment *d*, and also § 82, Comment *e*. This breadth of beneficiary rights under this section, and under § 82, is essential to the enforceability of a meaningful duty of impartiality.

A trustee's duty to provide "reports" or "accountings" to a beneficiary may be satisfied by relatively informal reports that reveal trust assets and liabilities, receipts and disbursements, and other transactions involving trust property, and that disclose the amounts and bases of compensation paid to the trustee(s) and any agent(s) during the accounting period covered by the report. Trust assets should be listed with their respective market values (using good-faith estimates as necessary) as of the date of the accounting.

b(1). Cross-references re: accountings. On the general duty of trustees to provide reports or accountings on request, contrast § 74, Comment *a(1)*, that no accounting is required of a trustee-settlor of a revocable trust or a trustee-beneficiary (donee) who holds an ownership-equivalent power; also cf. id., Comments *d*, *c*, and *g*, limiting the rights of beneficiaries in other situations in which a competent settlor or donee holds a power of revocation or withdrawal.

That a successor trustee has a responsibility to ascertain and collect trust assets and to discover and enforce trust claims, thus entitling the successor (as well as the beneficiaries) to obtain an accounting, or to review trust records or other information, upon termination of a prior trusteeship, see § 76, Comment *d*. That distributees are entitled to an accounting on termination of a trust, see § 89, Comment *c*.

c. Effect of report or accounting; adequate disclosure. With respect to beneficiaries who are properly made parties to a judicial proceeding, a court order approving all or part of a trustee's accounts discharges the trustee from liability (or further liability) for matters appropriately disclosed. Because a trustee has an affirmative duty to disclose relevant information, a matter involving sensitive issues must be revealed in the accounting with sufficient clarity to invite attention to the issue if the court order is to protect the trustee as a matter of issue preclusion. Illustrative would be a matter involving self-dealing by a trustee, even a purportedly permissible form of self-dealing (see, e.g., § 78, Comment *c(5)*, and cf. id., Comment *d(1)*).

In the context of a nonjudicial accounting or report, a trustee may be protected from challenge by a beneficiary with respect to matters appropriately disclosed in the accounts or report submitted to the beneficiary, including one who is represented by a guardian ad litem or by virtual representation .... The trustee's protection may result from approval (i.e, informed consent) by or on behalf of the beneficiary (see § 97 and § 78(3), Comment *g*) or from passage of time under an applicable statute of limitations or the doctrine of laches (see § 98).

d. Terms of the trust. Occasionally the terms of a trust provide that the trustee shall have no accountability for his or her conduct in the administration of the trust. Assuming that the settlor intended to create a trust relationship, however, this does not preclude the beneficiaries from holding the trustee liable for a breach of trust or otherwise accountable for the trust property and its administration. A trust provision of this type may be interpreted as having the same effect as an exculpatory clause, and thus as being subject to the same limitations. See § 96, and cf. § 87.

Except as prohibited or limited by statute, the terms of a trust (or waiver by a beneficiary) can properly dispense with or limit the normal requirements for submission of reports or accountings under this section or as imposed by statute. A trust provision of this type, however, does not eliminate the trustee's duty to furnish information in accordance with the rules (and qualifications) stated in § 82; nor does it dispense with the duty to maintain records in some reasonable form (Comment *a*) at the risk of suffering consequences as mentioned in Comment *a(1)*.

The terms of trusts sometimes provide that the trustee need only account or submit reports to a designated person, for example, to one of the beneficiaries of the trust (or to the settlor of an irrevocable inter vivos trust), and that the approval of the trustee's account or report by that person shall discharge the trustee from liability. A provision of this type is effective, provided (i) the other person in giving approval acts neither in bad faith nor in casual disregard of the interests or rights of the nonassenting beneficiaries and (ii) the accounting appropriately discloses material issues about the trustee's conduct. (The provision does not eliminate a beneficiary's right to information under § 82.) The designated person's approval, however, is subject to court review for abuse, with particular attention (see (i) above) to neglect or to the possible effects of a conflict of interests between that person and a beneficiary (or even to a settlor's disregard of beneficiary rights that the settlor has no power to modify). This review is available to a beneficiary regardless of a trust provision to the contrary, such as one purporting to make the trustee's discharge final or conclusive upon the designated person's approval (cf. § 87). The beneficiary's right of review, however, is subject to the doctrine of laches or an applicable period of limitation (see § 98).

§ 84. Duty to Segregate and Identify Trust Property

The trustee has a duty to see that trust property is designated or identifiable as property of the trust, and also a duty to keep the trust property separate from the trustee's own property and, so far as practical, separate from other property not subject to the trust.

Comment:

a. *Duty in general.* It is ordinarily the duty of the trustee: to earmark the trust property as property of the trust (see Comments *d* and *e*); to keep the trust property separate from the trustee's own property (see Comment *b*); and to keep the trust property separate from property held by the trustee upon other trusts (see Comment *c*).

b. *Duty not to commingle trust property with trustee's own.* A trustee has a duty not to commingle property of the trust with the trustee's own property. Thus, it is improper for a trustee to deposit money of the trust in the trustee's personal account in a bank, even if the trustee maintains records continuously and carefully showing the trust's interest in the account. (On questions of remedies, and particularly of damages and causation, see § 95 and Chapter 19.)

The general prohibition against commingling trust property with the trustee's own is strictly applied, based on the duty of loyalty's prohibition against a trustee's creation of potentially conflicting interests. (See § 78.) Particular concern exists when commingling (or lack of identification) might make misconduct or abuses difficult to detect.

An exception is recognized, however, when a commingling results from (and thus, cf. § 78, Comment *c(2)*, is impliedly authorized by) the settlor's creation of a trust to hold an undivided interest in property in which an undivided interest also is given or already belongs to the trustee personally, or is given or already held by the trustee as property of another trust in which the trustee is beneficially interested. More generally, and on identification, see Comment *e*.

c. *Duty not to mingle property of separate trusts.* It is ordinarily the duty of a trustee not to mingle property held upon one trust with property held upon another trust, whether the two or more trusts are created by the same or different settlors. . . . .

Particularly if a trustee administers numerous trusts, it may in some respects be impractical or undesirable, and not important to the protection of the interests of the various trusts, strictly to prohibit the trustee from mingling the properties of the different trusts. Thus, in the absence of a personal financial interest in one of the trusts, ordinarily the trustee can properly deposit the funds of various trusts in a single bank account (one that is not the trustee's personal account), provided the trustee maintains accurate records of the respective deposits and the continuing interests of the various trusts. (As to deposits of trust funds by a trust company in its own banking department, see § 78, particularly Comments *d* and *c(6)*.)

Similarly, a trustee may make joint investments using the property of two or more trusts, as long as the requirements of earmarking (below) are satisfied or, when earmarking is not feasible, the trustee maintains records clearly revealing the respective interests of the different trusts. In the latter case, the trustee still must act carefully and in good faith, even though the risk of error or misappropriation is less serious in the case of pooled investment arrangements on behalf of multiple trusts than it would be if a trustee were allowed to jointly invest trust property with the trustee's personal assets.

On investing funds of multiple trusts in mortgage participations, and on traditional bank practices of maintaining common trust funds, see § 90, Comment *m*; and see § 78, Comment *c(8)*, on corporate trustees' use in more recent times of proprietary mutual funds.

d. *Duty to earmark trust property.* It is ordinarily the duty of a trustee to have trust property designated or made externally identifiable as trust property. Thus, deposits of trust money in a bank should be made in a separate account in the name of the trustee as trustee (more precisely, see below), although it may sometimes be appropriate (Comment *c*) for the funds of more than one trust to be deposited together in one account held by the trustee as trustee. Similarly, title to land acquired by a trustee as such should be taken and recorded in the name of the trustee as trustee. And it would be proper for a trustee to have stock certificates issued and mutual-fund or brokerage accounts opened in the name of the trustee as trustee, and for bonds held in trust to be so registered. (On "bearer" bonds, see Comment *d(2)* below.)

Actually, in situations such as those above it is not sufficient merely to indicate that property is trust property but it should also be shown that the trustee holds it as trustee of a particular trust. For example, the property should be held by T as trustee "under the will of S" or "under a declaration of trust executed by S on [date]" or "of the BFY Family Trust."

Although proper, the foregoing forms for holding trust property are not exclusive or even necessarily the most efficient or satisfactory. What is important in the matter of earmarking is that, to the extent feasible, the property is shown to be property of the trust in records maintained by and within the control of a party other than the trustee or a beneficiary. Accordingly, the interest of the trust often, and properly, appears in records of such third parties as banks, investment companies, brokerage firms, and transfer agents.

d(1). Taking title in the name of a third person. The holding of securities in the name of a third person or a group of persons nominated by the trustee (i.e., "in nominee form") is widely authorized by statute and can be properly authorized by trust provision. Even without such special authorization, with prudence exercised by the trustee, title may be taken in the name of a nominee although registration will not then show the trustee's name as trustee, provided the trust holdings will be sufficiently identifiable as such in account records of a brokerage firm or in other records maintained by an independent party.

d(2). When earmarking is not feasible. Sometimes earmarking is not feasible, as in the case of tangible personal property, bonds payable to bearer, and other assets the ownership of which is not susceptible of being registered or reflected in the records of a custodian or other independent party. In these situations, the trustee must maintain records clearly reflecting that the property belongs to the trust and must keep that trust property separate from property belonging to the trustee personally.

e. Terms of the trust. The terms of a trust may permit trust property to be mingled or jointly held with the trustee's own property. The terms of the trust may expressly so provide or the character of the trust and trust property may be such (see Comment *b*) as to make commingling proper by implication. This, however, does not relieve the trustee of the duty to earmark if and as feasible; thus, the duty recognizes that, for example, in the matter of earmarking property that a trustee holds both personally and in trust, a herd of cattle on the family farm presents a more difficult problem than does the farm itself.

Similarly, the terms of a trust may authorize trust property to be held in the name of the trustee without designating the particular trust, or even without indicating that the property is held in trust at all.

Custom or the character of a trust may also make it proper to mingle the property of one trust with property of another trust. In situations in which the trustee holds the funds of numerous persons it may be proper to mingle the funds of all of them (cf. Comment *c*). Thus, in the case of an attorney, collection agent, or auctioneer, or a stockbroker who receives customers' money for the purchase or from the sale of certain securities, it is ordinarily proper to deposit the funds of various clients or customers in a single fiduciary account, provided accurate records are maintained of the separate contributions. In some situations of this type it may be unclear whether there is a trust or some other relationship (see § 5), but in any event the amount on deposit is not to be diminished by withdrawals, disbursements, or otherwise below the aggregate amount to which the clients or customers are entitled.

CHAPTER 16

EXTENT AND EXERCISE OF TRUSTEES' POWERS

Introductory Note: This chapter begins by defining in § 85 the extent of the powers a trustee holds for the purpose of administering a trust—a comprehensive body of powers, limited only as provided by statute or expressly or impliedly by the terms of the trust. That a trustee possesses a power does not itself justify the exercise or a particular exercise of the power.

As emphasized and illustrated in § 86, a trustee's decision to exercise (or not to exercise) a power, and the manner of its exercise, must comport with the trustee's fiduciary duties (see particularly §§ 76–79 of the prior chapter). As a trustee's judgment in these matters involves fiduciary discretion, it is subject to judicial control for abuse, but not merely because the court would have exercised a power differently, as explained in § 87.

The other sections of this chapter address the trustee's proper exercise of powers to incur expenses to be paid or reimbursed from the trust estate (§ 88) and to manage and distribute trust property in the course of winding up the trust following its termination date (§ 89).

§ 85. Extent of Trustees' Powers

(1) In administering a trust, the trustee has, except as limited by statute or the terms of the trust,

> **(a) all of the powers over trust property that a legally competent, unmarried individual has with respect to individually owned property, as well as**
>
> **(b) powers granted by statute or the terms of the trust and**
>
> **(c) powers specifically applicable to trust administration that are recognized in other sections of this Restatement.**

(2) Except as otherwise provided by the terms of the trust, the powers of a trustee under Subsection (1) pass to and are exercisable by substitute or successor trustees.

Comment on Subsection (1):

a. Background and rationale. Early trust doctrine, especially as developed in England, severely limited the authority of trustees. This reflected concerns at the time over risks of abuse or mismanagement, as well as the limited purposes for which most trusts (usually of land) were then used. Over time, as equitable remedies and fiduciary standards have evolved and as the role of trusts has diversified, the powers allowed to trustees have gradually, rather steadily, expanded through judicial decisions and legislation and also through the drafting practices of experienced lawyers. . . . .

Even today trust instruments frequently contain extensive provisions conferring virtually unlimited powers upon trustees in an effort to assure that no authority that might be needed is either omitted or susceptible of overly conservative interpretation. Leading modern treatises . . ., while listing and discussing the powers of trustees at some length, ultimately rely on rather vague, open-ended language (such as "necessary or appropriate" to the purposes and circumstances of the trust) in describing the powers of trustees, thereby indicating considerable flexibility in the default law—but at a price of uncertain guidance for trustees, beneficiaries, and courts, and also still accompanied by unfortunate statements about powers that are not ordinarily authorized by implication.

The default rule of this section is consistent with the most recent and pervasive trends in American trust law, especially with the terms of § 815(a)(2) of the Uniform Trust Code, promulgated in 2000. It is also consistent with the principles earlier adopted in Restatement Third, Trusts (Prudent Investor Rule) §§ 227–229 (preliminary volume, 1992), hereafter incorporated into Chapter 17 (as §§ 90–92), and under which no investment or investment course of action is per se or presumptively prohibited. The "prudent investor" principles have already been codified in nearly all of the states, usually by enactment of the Uniform Prudent Investor Act, promulgated in 1994. . . . .

The comprehensive statement of the powers of trustees in the default rule of Subsection (1) not only offers ease of practical application but also has the advantages (i) of facilitating fundamental efficiency in the use of family financial resources, with no course of action arbitrarily foreclosed, and (ii) of supplying both the *immediate* flexibility suitable to today's variety of trust purposes and circumstances and the adaptability *over time* to accommodate changing economic conditions and asset-management practices. In addition, the breadth and simplicity of this subsection should minimize the trustee's need for instructions under § 71.

b. General observations and cross-references. Various definitions, principles, and other rules are important to understanding the role and application of Subsection (1).

b(1). Meaning of "terms of the trust." As elsewhere in this Restatement, the phrase "terms of the trust" in this Part 6 means the settlor's intention "with respect to the trust provisions" manifested "in a manner that admits of its proof in judicial proceedings" (§ 4), plus provisions resulting from subsequent modifications (§§ 62–67). See generally Introductory Note to Part 6.

b(2). All powers are subject to fiduciary duties. As noted in § 70, Comment *a*, all powers held as trustee, whether they are expressed or implied, are held in a fiduciary capacity and their exercise or nonexercise is subject to the fiduciary duties of trusteeship. See § 86.

b(3). Powers (and duties) of co-trustees. On the manner of exercising the powers of a trusteeship for which there are multiple trustees, see § 39, which provides for majority control as the default rule for decisionmaking in situations of three or more trustees. That majority control often excuses a dissenting trustee from certain liabilities but not from the normal duties to remain informed, to participate in fiduciary deliberations, and to take action as necessary seeking to prevent or remedy a breach of trust by the majority, see § 81.

c. Terms of the rule. The reference in Subsection (1) to all of the powers that a "legally competent, unmarried individual" has with respect to his or her own property (Clause (a)) is intended to avoid various questions of the default rule's meaning that might otherwise arise. For example, this wording removes limitations or uncertainties that might have resulted: from possible restrictions in corporate law, articles, or bylaws; from conservatorship or guardianship law; or from dower, tenancy-by-the-entirety ownership, or even limited marital disability that might somewhere be resurrected with application to both spouses. No such limitations are contemplated by the rule of Subsection (1) with regard to trustees.

The ensuing references in this Subsection to powers recognized elsewhere in this Restatement (Clause (c)) and those granted by the provisions of trusts or statutes (Clause (b)), seek to assure that powers that would or might have no relevance to an individual property owner, or to his or her individual property, are not left in doubt. Merely illustrative of powers of these types are: the trustee's power to split or combine trusts (§ 68) or, under some circumstances, to withhold income directed to be paid to a beneficiary (§ 49, Comment *c(2)*); a settlor's grant of power to a trustee to modify the trust (considered in § 64) or to terminate it if uneconomically small (compare § 66, Comment *d*); and the power to disclaim fiduciary powers granted by the trust terms, or property initially bequeathed (or later to be added) to the trust, as might be appropriate for a trust because of tax considerations, concerns about environmental liability, or other reasons (see § 86, especially Comment *f*, and, on the duty of prudence generally, see § 77). Powers like any or all of the foregoing Restatement provisions, and others, may be found, expanded, or varied in the terms of trusts or in applicable legislation.

c(1). Limitations on powers: terms of trust or statute. Subsection (1) makes clear that the comprehensive powers of a trustee under the default rule may be narrowed or qualified by statute or by the terms of the trust. Such limitations on the authority of the trustee and related concerns are too varied or individualistic to justify or even permit incorporation more specifically into the rule of the section. Furthermore, respect for the possible concerns of a settlor, even if not set out in trust provisions expressly limiting trustee powers, is implicit in the fiduciary duties mentioned in Comment *b(2)* and in § 86 (as well as in Clause (b) of § 70), especially in requiring that the trustee's powers be exercised in a manner that is consistent with the objectives of the settlor as indicated by the terms of the trust (cf. § 76).

The terms of a trust, or of a statute, may limit a trustee's powers either expressly or impliedly (see, e.g., § 86, Comment *c*), with court instructions available in circumstances of uncertainty (§ 71). In cases of trust provisions specifically conferring certain listed powers upon a trustee, however, the preferred construction is that the provision is not intended to be exhaustive. A similar construction is preferred with regard to statutory provisions, provided the context and language of the statute permit. This preference is reflected in language that is commonly used in the drafting of documents and legislation expressly stating that the powers listed are not intended to be exclusive or exhaustive (see, e.g., Uniform Trust Code § 816). In short, without more (such as language authorizing specified types of transactions or investment in specified types of property, conditioned by specified limitations or characteristics), a general list of trustee powers should not be a sufficient basis for denying a trustee other powers described in Subsection (1).

Further on the powers of trustees, and on recurring issues concerning the exercise of some particular powers, see §§ 86–88. On rights and liabilities of third parties in dealing with trustees, see Chapter 22.

Comment on Subsection (2):

d. General rule on authority and responsibilities of successor trustees. By the terms of some trusts, the powers, duties, and even liabilities of original trustees are expressly expanded or diminished in various respects with regard to successor trustees. In the absence of an express provision of this type in the terms of the trust, however, the powers (and duties, see § 86) of a successor trustee are the same as those of the original (or designated) trustee, unless and until contrary instruction is granted by judicial interpretation of the terms of the trust (§ 71). (References in this Comment to successor trustees include substitute trustees.) On the matter of fiduciary liability, see discussion of exculpatory clauses in § 96.

It should be noted that the occasional suggestion of a general distinction in this matter between powers that are ministerial and those that involve significant fiduciary judgment or discretion, or that affect the beneficiaries' rights to distributions, has not been accepted or reflected in the actual decisions of courts, and is rejected here. Such an approach to determining the authority and duties of successor trustees would undermine not only the effective management of trusts but also discretionary interests that are fundamental to the beneficial provisions of many trusts.

When interpretation is required, however, a court's determination of whether a particular power can be exercised by a successor trustee may be affected, on the one hand, by an appearance from the terms of the trust that the settlor placed some particular confidence in the original trustee, as well as, on the other hand, by whether the power is essential to the sound management of the trust and the intended beneficial interests. Cf. § 31 (that a trust normally does not fail because the designated trustee declines or ceases to act, or is dead or otherwise unable to serve, and that a proper court will appoint a trustee unless the trust's creation or continuation depends on a specific person serving as trustee).

The situation is different in the case of a *power of appointment* conferred upon a beneficiary (or other person), even though that person also is designated (or otherwise serving) as trustee. A power of appointment is personal to the designated donee or donees (i.e., power holder(s)), and is to be distinguished from a fiduciary power that runs with the office of trustee or is conferred upon a person *as* trustee.

e. Surviving co-trustee. If several persons are named as co-trustees and one of them dies, becomes incapacitated, or otherwise ceases to serve as trustee, a replacement trustee is required only if the settlor manifested that intention or it is found conducive to the proper administration of the trust. See § 34, Comment *d.*

In such cases, when no replacement trustee is appointed, the remaining trustee or trustees are entitled to administer the trust and are "successor trustees" as that expression is used here and for purposes of applying the rule of Subsection (2).

§ 86. Fiduciary Duties and the Exercise of Trustee Powers

A trustee, in deciding whether and how to exercise the powers of the trusteeship, is subject to and must act in accordance with the fiduciary duties stated in Chapter 15 and elsewhere in this Restatement.

Comment:

a. Scope of section; cross-references. The purpose of this section is to emphasize the difference between having a power and exercising that power, and the vital relationship between the trustee's fiduciary duties and the trustee's exercise of the generally comprehensive powers of the trusteeship. Commentary here does not attempt to define or generally to explain the trustee's fiduciary duties, a function that is served mainly (though not only) by Chapter 15.

For discussion of a few illustrative applications of the rule of this section, see Comments *c–f*. These Comments address several selected powers for which prudence or other fiduciary concerns may be particularly significant or for which, due to similar concerns, it was unclear under earlier, more restrictive doctrine whether (or for what purposes) the power in question might have been implied as "necessary" or "appropriate" to carrying out the purposes of the trust.

Although it is not possible to address the virtually limitless and evolving powers of trusteeship, a number of other sections address various significant powers and associated fiduciary responsibilities. See § 90 on investment powers; § 50 on discretionary powers over distributions; § 80 on power to delegate; § 89, Comments *d* and *e(2)*, on powers of management and distribution on termination; § 88 on power to incur expenses; and Chapter 23 on discretionary power in principal-income accounting. For more general discussion of trustee powers and abuse of discretion in their exercise, see § 87.

b. All powers are subject to the trustee's fiduciary duties. All powers of trusteeship are held in the trustee's fiduciary capacity and must be exercised in good faith and to serve the interests of the beneficiaries. See § 70, Comment *a*, and § 85, Comment *b(2)*. The exercise or nonexercise of a trustee's powers, even those expressly conferred by the terms of the trust or by statute, are subject: to the fundamental duties of prudence, loyalty, and impartiality (§§ 77–79); to a duty to respect the terms and purposes of the trust (§ 76); and to other fiduciary duties of trusteeship—all as defined, qualified, and explained in Chapter 15 (above), in this chapter and Chapter 17, and elsewhere in this Restatement.

A trustee's duties, like trustee powers, may be modified by the terms of the trust, but the duties of trusteeship are subject to certain minimum standards that are fundamental to the trust relationship and normally essential to it (see, however, § 74, Comment *a(1)*). See generally § 76, Comment *b(1)*. See also § 87, Comment *d* (on extended—e.g., "absolute" or "sole and uncontrolled"—discretion); § 50, Comments *b* and *c* (on extended discretion with respect to distributions to beneficiaries); § 91, Comment *g–g(2)* (on grants of "discretion" regarding investment); and discussion generally throughout Chapters 15 through 17.

c. Lease and sale of trust property. Under the rule of § 85, a trustee ordinarily has broad authority to lease trust property to others and to sell trust property, at public or private sale or in exchange for other property. A trustee's powers in these matters include power to grant, for example, easements, rights to explore and remove natural resources, and options to lease or purchase.

A trustee's powers, however, may be expressly limited by the terms of the trust, and powers or their exercise may be impliedly limited in matters of lease or sale by trust provisions that, for example, direct that specific property be distributed to one or more beneficiaries on termination (cf. § 89, Comment *e(3)*) or entitle a beneficiary to occupy or use specific property during some or all of the trust period. (On the trustee's duty to comply with trust terms, see § 76.) It is a matter of interpretation in such cases whether the implied prohibition against sale of certain property (or even an express prohibition for a purpose of this type) is dependent on the actual or continued interest of certain beneficiaries in using or preserving the property, a matter for which instructions are available under § 71. See also § 97 on beneficiary consent. A similar question of interpretation arises when there is an expressed or implied prohibition against the sale of shares in a corporation controlled by, or in which there is personal involvement of, the settlor or members of the settlor's family.

Although a mere authorization to retain certain property does not prohibit its sale, if a trustee is authorized to sell the property only for a particular purpose or only under certain circumstances, the trustee has a duty not to sell the property except for that purpose or under those circumstances.

That, in the event of unanticipated circumstances, a court may permit or direct a trustee to deviate from a prohibition against sale, see § 66. . . . .

c(1). Fiduciary duties in leasing trust realty. In exercising the power to lease trust property, the trustee has a duty to act with prudence (§ 77) and in a manner that is reasonable in light of the terms and purposes of the trust and its probable duration and other circumstances.

Thus, the trustee must exercise reasonable care, skill, and caution (§ 77, Comment *b*) in selecting a tenant and in establishing the amount of the rent, the duration of the lease, the rights and obligations of the parties, and other terms of the agreement, taking account of the nature and condition of the property and customary practices and circumstances in the relevant real-estate market. (The trustee also has a duty to fulfill or enforce the obligations of lessor and lessee under lease provisions and applicable law.) It may be appropriate for a trustee to agree to reduced rental payments or a longer lease period, or both, in consideration of the lessee's agreement to make improvements that will belong to the trust when the lease expires, with no payment (or a prescribed payment) to be made by the trust. The propriety of such an arrangement, however, depends on: (i) whether it presents a productivity issue (see § 79(2) on impartiality), and, if so, how that issue might be resolved (cf. id., Comment *i*); and (ii) whether the additional "investment" in the property raises diversification issues or other issues of prudence under the principles of § 90.

The duration of a lease may present special fiduciary concerns for the trustee to consider. First, the pervasive concern for balancing risk and return (cf. § 90, Comment *e(1)*) becomes increasingly aggravated as the lease period under consideration increases. Second, a trustee must take seriously into account the remainder beneficiaries' interest in receiving unencumbered title on termination of the trust. Although the trustee has the power to lease beyond the period of the trust, and even where this authority is expressly conferred by statute or trust provision, it is the duty of the trustee to respect this interest of the beneficiaries except as justified by reasonable considerations of productivity and prudent management. The degree of justification required is naturally affected by the extent to which the lease period exceeds or risks exceeding the duration of the trust, and by whether the time for the trust's termination is uncertain (e.g., when the life beneficiary dies) or certain (e.g., a trust that is to end on a specific date or when a designated beneficiary attains a certain age). See § 82(1)(c) on the trustee's possible duty to inform beneficiaries when considering significant actions involving these special concerns.

c(2). Fiduciary duties in selling trust realty. Although a trustee ordinarily has broad authority with regard to the sale of real property held in the trust, and even if confirmed by powers expressly granted in a statute or trust provision, the exercise of the trustee's power of sale requires the exercise of prudence (§ 77), as well as compliance with other relevant fiduciary duties (see, e.g., §§ 76, 78–80, and also see § 82).

In this context, the demands of fiduciary care and skill (Comment *b* of § 77) are likely to be particularly rigorous—requiring the exercise of due diligence and competence, via advisors or agents if and as needed by the trustee—because of the pricing, information, and other challenges presented by the particular market. Compare § 90, Comment *o*, on investing in real estate. If the transaction involves exchanging the trust property for other property whether of similar (perhaps with tax objectives) or dissimilar character, the demands of prudence may well be aggravated.

The terms of many trusts and statutes authorize trustees to sell "for cash or on credit," and this is also the effect of the general rule of § 85. Nevertheless, entering into such a sale transaction is a proper exercise of a trustee's power only insofar as the transaction and its terms are consistent with the trustee's fiduciary duties. Thus, for example, it would be proper for a trustee to sell trust property partly for cash and partly for a secured promissory note that would be suitable to the investment portfolio and strategy of the particular trust. See generally § 90. In some circumstances, however, it may be proper for a trustee to accept from a buyer a note or other asset of a type or in an amount that the trustee would not otherwise acquire for the trust portfolio when it is prudent under the circumstances to do so, considering any special advantages of the sale opportunity along with the tax as well as investment aspects of the transaction.

On matters of loyalty and impartiality in sales of trust property to a trust beneficiary or to another trust or a fiduciary estate, see § 78, Comments *g* and *c(7)*.

d. Power to borrow and encumber trust property. Unless prohibited by statute or the terms of the trust, a trustee has power to borrow money for trust purposes and to pledge, mortgage, grant a deed of trust, or otherwise encumber trust property. The trustee has a duty to exercise caution as well as the duty to exercise care and skill in deciding whether and under what terms to borrow money for trust purposes or to grant a security interest in trust property.

Despite the risks inherent in borrowing, cash may be required in order to meet trust needs ranging from distribution requirements to maintenance of real estate, or even implementation of investment programs. Cf. § 90, Comment *h*, on the role of borrowing and lending in trust investment strategies; also see id., Comment *l*.

As increasingly recognized in legislation and drafting practices, and enabled by the comprehensive empowerment of trustees in § 85, prudent borrowing may have advantages over liquidation of assets to raise funds for trust needs. This may be especially true in the case of relatively short-term requirements in situations involving marital-deduction trusts and revocable (or other estate-tax "grantor") trusts—postponing sale, for example, of a residence or appreciated assets. The power of trustees to borrow, however, with the exercise of fiduciary care and skill, may be of value in trust administration generally as a means of responding to shifting concerns or opportunities as a particular trust's circumstances change and as more general economic conditions, financial concepts or practices, and rules of taxation evolve over time.

Because of a trustee's duty to respect the terms of the trust (§ 76), it is normally improper for a trustee to exercise the power to encumber trust property by granting security interests in assets that are to be specifically distributed to one or more beneficiaries on termination. (Compare implied limitation on power to sell or lease in Comment *c*.) If other sources are not readily available to meet distribution requirements or other needs of trust administration, conflicting fiduciary duties may present an issue of interpretation (see § 71) or even of equitable deviation (§ 66); and eventually perhaps (because the trustee's power to encumber is not confined to the duration of the trust) a question may arise of priority of rights among remainder beneficiaries. (On the latter, compare the familiar doctrines of exoneration, abatement, and ademption in the law of wills, but with material differences likely in irrevocable-trust situations. Compare Uniform Probate Code § 2–606(b) (nonademption) with id. § 2–607 (nonexoneration), and reconciliation in the comment to the latter. See generally Restatement Third, Property (Wills and Other Donative Transfers) § 1.1, Comment *f* (on abatement) and § 5.2, Comment *g* (on ademption), and cf. § 7.2, Comment *f* (on application of wills rules to revocable trusts).)

That a trustee contemplating significant borrowing may have a duty to inform the beneficiaries, see § 82(1)(c).

On advances to the trust by the trustee personally, see § 78, Comment *c(6)*. On lending to (or borrowing from) trust beneficiaries or other trusts or fiduciary estates, see generally §§ 78(2) and 79, and particularly § 78, Comments *c(7)* and *g*; cf. § 50, Comment *d(6)*.

e. Power to form a corporation or other entity to carry on a trust activity. Except as otherwise provided by trust provision, trustees have power under the rule of § 85 to incorporate, or to form limited-liability companies or other entities, for the purpose of carrying on business or investment activities of the trust. In deciding whether and how to exercise this authority, the trustee must act with care, caution, and skill (obtaining competent advice and assistance as needed) in exploring alternative organizational forms and the various legal, business, financial, operational, tax, and other considerations that may be appropriate to the particular activities and trust involved.

Beyond the fundamental requirements of prudence (above, and see § 77), the fiduciary responsibilities of trusteeship will require the trustee to be alert and responsive to considerations of loyalty (§ 78) and impartiality (§ 79), as well as to the trustee's duty sometimes to inform beneficiaries of plans involving significant matters (§ 82(1)(c)). The trustee's various fiduciary duties apply both, initially, to decisions involved in creating an entity and, thereafter, to operation of the entity. A trustee who, for example, establishes a corporation (transferring certain trust assets to it in return for its stock) has a duty as sole shareholder to assure that the enterprise will be conducted in a manner consistent with the purposes of the trust, the interest of its beneficiaries, and other duties of trusteeship. Thus, the trustee must not operate the corporation in a manner that results in self-employment that is improper (but note § 78, Comment *c(5)* and last two paragraphs of id., Comment *d(1)*) or in a way that subverts, through dividend policy or otherwise, any applicable requirement of productivity (§ 79(2), but see flexibility in id., Comments *h* (charitable endowments) and *i* (income beneficiaries)).

A trustee may join with one or more other entities or individuals in restructuring an existing enterprise or in forming a new entity. These joint arrangements may add complexities not specifically addressed in this Comment's brief review of fiduciary concerns likely to arise in a trustee's creation and use of a corporation or other entity; but on the duty of loyalty in these situations, see § 78, Comments *d(1)* and *c(7)*; on cooperating with others, see § 80, Comment *i*; and on impartiality and productivity, see § 79, especially Comment *i*.

f. Power to disclaim or abandon property. Under the rule of § 85, a trustee has power to abandon or disclaim property that is or otherwise would be held in the trust, and also to disclaim (or release) fiduciary powers. No such action may be taken, however, unless it is to serve the interest of the beneficiaries and is consistent with the purposes of the trust (§ 76), as well as with the trustee's other fiduciary duties.

A trustee who relinquishes trust property or a fiduciary power to further a trust purpose, or in the interest of the beneficiaries, may nevertheless serve or continue to serve as trustee. But such action may not be taken merely for the convenience, or to avoid or lessen the responsibilities, of the trustee; a trustee so motivated may decline appointment (§ 35) or resign from the trusteeship (§ 36; on unanticipated burdens resulting from trust additions or modifications as special justification for resigning, see id., Comments *b* and *c*, and § 63, Comment *g*).

The permissible exercise of a power of this type, or the power itself, may be impliedly limited by the objectives of the settlor in establishing the trust. (Compare discussion of implied limitations on power to sell or lease in Comment *c*.) For example, a power to disclaim (even one expressly conferred by general terms of a trust or statute) may not be exercised in a manner that would disqualify the trust for an intended tax deduction or status, because to so exercise the power, and perhaps even to *have* a power that could properly be exercised in such a manner, would be inconsistent with the purposes of the trust.

In addition, in exercising the power to relinquish trust property or powers, the trustee must act in a manner that is consistent with other fiduciary duties of trusteeship. Thus, the trustee must exercise reasonable care and skill, with competent financial, tax, and legal (e.g., environmental, tort, or trust law) advice as needed, to determine: whether and for what purposes action may be needed (and whether the concerns can be cured by reformation or actions of beneficiaries individually); the manner and extent of relinquishment appropriate to the concern or objective in question; the effects the contemplated action would have on various interests and beneficiaries of the trust or another trust, or of the settlor's estate; and other facts and considerations of relevance.

The trustee must also pay due regard to potential issues of impartiality (§ 79), and perhaps loyalty (§ 78). Furthermore, the very nature and diverse implications of actions of this type, not to mention the possibilities of oversight or lack of foresight, may require the trustee to inform beneficiaries (at least potentially affected beneficiaries) in advance of a contemplated action, in accordance with § 82(1)(c). See particularly § 82, Comment *d*.

Often more satisfactory than disclaiming a fiduciary power as a means of curing a drafting defect may be petitioning a court for reformation or possibly, for limited purposes, seeking modification. See § 62, Comments *b* and *c*, and more fully Restatement Third, Property (Wills and Other Donative Transfers) §§ 12.1 and 12.2.

§ 87. Judicial Control of Discretionary Powers

When a trustee has discretion with respect to the exercise of a power, its exercise is subject to supervision by a court only to prevent abuse of discretion.

Comment:

a. Scope of section; cross-references. A trustee generally has discretion (i.e., is to use fiduciary judgment) with respect to the exercise of the powers of the trusteeship. That is, a power is discretionary except to the extent its exercise is directed by the terms of the trust or compelled by the trustee's fiduciary duties. Even in cases of what are often called "mandatory" powers or provisions, for which trustee compliance is required except as provided in § 66 (equitable deviation in unanticipated circumstances), the trustee often has some discretionary authority and responsibility in important matters of detail and implementation. For example, the terms of a trust may require the sale of certain real property but then, by failing to provide more, leave the trustee to exercise fiduciary judgment with respect to the timing (on which see § 92, Comment *b*), price, and other terms of the sale. Similarly, room for fiduciary judgment and responsibility may well remain in situations in which a trustee is directed to take action by the holder of a directory power (see § 75, Comment *b*, Illustration 1) or by the settlor of a revocable trust (§ 74, Comment *b*, Illustration 3).

The most important of the discretionary powers in most trusts are those having to do with various aspects of the investment function, together with, in many trusts, those having to do with discretionary distributions, such as a power to invade principal for an income beneficiary or the power to distribute income to a beneficiary or among a class of beneficiaries. These matters are dealt with in considerable detail in Chapter 17 (§§ 90–92, on "Investment of Trust Funds") and in § 50 ("Enforcement and Construction of Discretionary Interests"). See also Chapter 23 on discretionary powers in principal-income accounting. The rule of this section and the principles described in its commentary apply not only to these matters but also to discretionary powers regarding other aspects of trust administration.

This section applies to discretionary authority that is ordinarily implicit in the powers of trustees (supra) as well as to discretionary authority that is expressly stated in the terms of a trust. Express grants of discretion and accompanying language, however, often present issues of interpretation or effect, sometimes beginning with a question of whether a settlor's "grant" of discretion with regard to a power is merely redundant or confers a broader degree of authority than would normally be implicit in the particular power. See Comment *d*.

b. Judicial intervention only for abuse; remedies. A court will not interfere with a trustee's exercise of a discretionary power (or decision not to exercise the power) when that conduct is reasonable, not based on an improper interpretation of the terms of the trust, and not otherwise inconsistent with the trustee's fiduciary duties (see particularly §§ 76–79). Thus, judicial intervention is not warranted merely because the court would have differently exercised the discretion.

On the other hand, a court may be called upon to intervene for the purpose of preventing a trustee's abuse (including by misinterpretation) of discretionary authority. What constitutes an abuse of discretion depends on the terms and purposes of the trust, and particularly on the terms and purposes of the power and any standards or guidance provided for its exercise, as well as on applicable principles of fiduciary duty. See Comment *c*. Also relevant is the extent of the discretion conferred upon the trustee. See Comment *d*.

When judicial intervention is required, the court may (ordinarily upon petition by a beneficiary) assert control over the exercise of the discretionary power by directing the trustee to act or refrain from acting or by setting aside a transaction in which the trustee has already acted. Or the court may hold the trustee liable for the adverse consequences of improper conduct, as in other breaches of fiduciary duty. The court may also, or instead: issue instructions clarifying the trustee's duties in exercising the discretionary power (cf. § 71) or otherwise establish safeguards against future abuse; deny or diminish the trustee's compensation; or even remove the trustee if there has been repeated or serious abuse of the discretionary power (see generally § 37, Comments *e* and *g*). Further discussion of remedies is beyond the scope of this section, but see Chapters 18 (especially § 95) and 19; also see § 50, Comment *b*.

c. *Abuse of discretion: in general.* An abuse of discretion may result from the exercise of discretionary authority in bad faith or from improper motive. Thus, a discretionary power is abused if a trustee acts dishonestly, such as when the trustee receives an improper inducement for exercising the power in question. Similarly, an abuse of discretion occurs when a trustee acts from an improper even though not dishonest motive, such as when the act is undertaken in good faith but for a purpose other than to further the purposes of the trust or, more specifically, the purposes for which the power was granted. See, e.g., § 50, Comment *d(2)*, that a discretionary power to make distributions for a beneficiary's "support" does not permit the trustee to make well-intentioned, even otherwise reasonable, distributions that are not support-related. More generally, see § 76 (duty to comply with the terms of the trust).

When the exercise of a discretionary power is left to the judgment of a trustee, an abuse of discretion may result from the trustee's improper failure to exercise that judgment. An abuse of this type results if the trustee, arbitrarily or without knowledge of or inquiry into relevant circumstances, fails to exercise the discretion. So also, the court will interpose where a trustee fails to exercise or otherwise abuses discretionary authority because of mistaken interpretation of the terms of the trust or power, or a misunderstanding of applicable fiduciary law. Similarly, an abuse of discretion occurs when a trustee, even in good faith, exercises a power in a manner that is inconsistent with the duty of loyalty (§ 78) or the duty of impartiality (§ 79). . . . .

Perhaps most of the litigation in which it is concluded that a trustee has committed an abuse of discretion involves a finding that the trustee, in exercising a power, has acted unreasonably—that is, beyond the bounds of a reasonable judgment. In some cases there is an objective standard by which the reasonableness of the trustee's conduct can be measured, but expressed standards are not necessary in order for a good-faith decision of a trustee to be found unreasonable; a court may apply what has sometimes been called "a general standard of reasonableness," taking account of other terms and purposes of the trust. In either event, judicial intervention on the ground of abuse is called for, not because the court would have exercised the discretion differently, but because the trustee's decision is one that would not be accepted as reasonable by persons of prudence. Thus, a court may properly interpose if it finds that the trustee's conduct, in exercising a discretionary power, fails to satisfy the applicable standard of care, skill, and caution (§ 77). For example, if discretionary power is conferred upon a designated trustee to appoint a successor or additional trustee, and the designated trustee appoints an unfit person, the court will remove the person so appointed.

Other common examples, and many reported cases, of allegedly unreasonable or otherwise abusive exercise of discretion involve either investment management (see commentary and Illustrations in §§ 90–92 . . .) or discretionary distributions to beneficiaries (see commentary and Illustrations in § 50 . . . .).

Illustrations:

1. The corpus of S's revocable trust passed on her death to T, as her successor trustee, to pay the trust income to S's daughter D during her lifetime, remainder thereafter to go by right of representation to the issue of D who survive her. The terms directed T to sell the real property that had served as S's home and to reinvest the proceeds, "unless T, in his discretion, decides to retain that property for D's use as her residence, which T is hereby authorized to do if and for as long as he believes this to be an appropriate and reasonable use of that property." Shortly after S's death, T received and accepted an offer from P to purchase that residential property (upon terms that no one challenges as unsatisfactory or imprudent if a sale is to be made); but T had made no effort to ascertain D's interest or personal or financial circumstances, or otherwise to investigate or consider whether her use of the property as a residence would be "appropriate and reasonable." By failing to exercise his judgment, T has abused his discretionary power regarding retention of the residential property for D's benefit.

2. The same facts as in Illustration 1, except that in the years between S's creation of the revocable trust and her death, D's husband died and her children became adults, left home, and married. T exercised his judgment, deciding that the residential property was not appropriate to D's needs and circumstances and also finding that D had no desire for the property to be retained for her use. Upon inquiry and investigation, T reached the further conclusion that the residential property would be just right for one of D's sons and his growing family. T therefore decided that the property should be retained and entered into a rental agreement with the son, setting a reasonable rent that could be paid to D as trust income. Absent other facts (e.g., showing grounds for equitable deviation under § 66), T has abused his discretion, even if in good faith, by exercising it for an improper motive—that is, for a purpose other than that for which he was granted discretionary power to retain the property, rather than sell it as otherwise directed.

d. Extended discretion: limitations, interpretation, and effects. Ordinarily, a mere grant of discretion in the terms of the trust, or an express reference to the discretionary character of a power or of powers generally, does not authorize the trustee to act beyond the bounds of reasonable judgment. See, e.g., discussion in § 91, Comments *g–g(2)*. A settlor may, however, manifest an intention to grant greater than ordinary latitude in the trustee's exercise of discretionary judgment.

Once it is determined that the power in question is held in the role of trustee, however, words such as "absolute" or "sole and uncontrolled" or "unlimited" are not interpreted literally. It is contrary to sound policy, and a contradiction in terms, to permit the settlor to relieve a *trustee* of all accountability. See § 50, Comment *a*, and cf. § 75, Comment *c*. Even under the broadest grant of fiduciary discretion, a trustee must act honestly and (as cases have sometimes quoted from prior Restatements) "in a state of mind contemplated by the settlor." What this means is that courts will intervene to prevent trustees from acting in bad faith, or without regard to the terms and purposes of the trust or the interests of its beneficiaries, or for some purpose or motive other than the accomplishment of the purposes of the discretionary power. Except to the extent the power is for the personal benefit of a beneficiary-trustee, the court may also be called upon to prevent the trustee from failing to act, whether capriciously, arbitrarily, or from a misunderstanding of the trustee's powers or duties.

Within these limits, it is a matter of interpretation to determine the degree to which a settlor's use of language of extended discretion (e.g., "absolute discretion") manifests an intention to modify the normal duties of the trustee and the normal grounds of judicial intervention in the exercise of a discretionary power. A primary question is whether and to what extent the settlor's language authorizes the trustee to act beyond the bounds of what would otherwise be a reasonable judgment.

Examination of the overall tenor of language granting powers and other terms of trusts may lead to diverse, refined interpretations on a case-by-case basis. For example, a court may conclude that the language of extended discretion and other evidence before it manifests a settlor intention to authorize the particular trustee to act with a lesser degree of *caution* (e.g., to accept a greater degree of compensated risk), but not a lesser degree of *care*, than would otherwise be appropriate to the particular trust and its circumstances under the duty of prudence (§ 77). Cf., in the investment context, § 91, Comment *g(1)*, and § 90, Comment *g*. Similarly, on the possibility of a "one-sided" liberalization of discretionary authority with regard to distributions (and on likely reasons for granting extended discretion in this context), see § 50, Comment *c* (text following that section's Illustrations 3 and 4).

Illustrations:

3. The same facts as in Illustration 2 (in Comment *c*, above), except that the quoted terms of the trust began "unless T, in his absolute discretion, decides to retain. . . ." The addition of the word "absolute" would not affect the result stated in Illustration 2, because T is still not authorized to retain the property for a purpose other than that for which the extended discretion was granted.

4. The same facts as in Illustration 3, above, except that the language there quoted continues by allowing T to retain "that property for a beneficiary's use as a residence, which T is authorized to do if, and for so long and upon such terms as, T believes appropriate and reasonable." T's actions in retaining the property and in leasing it to D's son are within the range of the authorized discretion (and would appear to be so even without the *extended* discretion).

5. The same trust as in the foregoing Illustrations (essentially, a trust for D for life, remainder to her issue who survive her), except that the terms of the trust grant T "absolute and binding discretion, in the event of any controversy or uncertainty, to construe and finally determine the meaning of the trust provisions." Upon the death of D, T distributes the corpus in three equal shares to D's two then surviving children and the surviving spouse of D's other child, who died shortly before D. This is an abuse even of T's extended discretion, there being no "uncertainty" in (or reasonable grounds for "controversy" over) a disposition "to the issue of D who survive her" (Illustration 1 wording) that would justify a construction including the spouse of a deceased child. (Such a broad grant of discretion, however, should ordinarily be interpreted as allowing T to so construe the remainder to D's "issue" as to include her deceased child's adopted or nonmarital child, even if such a traditionally troublesome question of construction would, at the time, have been subject to a different presumption under applicable case law or statutory rule of construction.)

With grants of extended discretion, contrast § 96 on exculpation clauses. An exculpatory provision is not intended to broaden the authority of the trustee, or to encourage or authorize breach of trust, or even to narrow the *grounds* of judicial intervention, but to relieve the trustee of liability (to the extent provided in the clause and allowed by law) should a breach of trust occur.

§ 88. Power to Incur and Pay Expenses

A trustee can properly incur and pay expenses that are reasonable in amount and appropriate to the purposes and circumstances of the trust and to the experience, skills, responsibilities, and other circumstances of the trustee.

Comment:

a. In general. The comprehensive powers of a trustee (§ 85) include the power to incur and pay expenses in the course of trust administration, but the exercise of this power is subject to the trustee's fiduciary duties (§ 70). Implicit in a trustee's fiduciary duties is a duty to be cost-conscious. See generally § 77 on the duty to act with prudence.

Also implicit in the trustees' fiduciary duties is a duty to respect legal and settlor-imposed limits on the trustee's authority, including the power to incur expenses. See § 76 on the duty to act in accordance with the terms of the trust and applicable law. That certain litigation expenses are payable from the trust estate only upon order of court, see Comment *d*.

The trustee's right of indemnification (§ 38(2)) entitles the trustee either to pay proper expenses directly from the trust estate (exoneration) or to obtain reimbursement from the trust when the trustee has personally paid those expenses.

Conversely, if expenses that are improper have been paid from the trust estate, the trustee ordinarily has a duty to restore the amount of the improper payment(s) to the trust; if improper expenses have been paid from the trustee's personal funds, the trustee ordinarily is not entitled to reimbursement for those expenditures. In either case, however, in order to avoid unjust enrichment of the trust and its beneficiaries, the trustee will be allowed indemnification, as equitable . . ., to the extent the improper expenditure has conferred a benefit upon the trust estate.

b. What expenses are proper and reasonable? A trustee is not limited to incurring expenses that are "necessary" or essential, but may incur expenses that, in the exercise of fiduciary judgment (see § 87), are reasonable and appropriate in carrying out the purposes of the trust, serving the interests of the beneficiaries, and generally performing the functions and responsibilities of the trusteeship. For example, the trustee can properly incur expenses appropriate to the collection and protection of the trust property (§ 76, Comment *d*) and to making the property productive (id., Comment *e*; and see, in the investment context, § 90, particularly Comment *h(2)*). Although a trustee is expressly or impliedly authorized or required to incur a particular type of expense, the trustee has a duty to exercise such care and skill as a person of ordinary prudence would exercise in incurring the expense. See § 77. Thus, if a trustee borrows funds from a third party for use in the administration of the trust, the interest on the loan is payable (or reimbursable) from the trust estate, provided the rate of interest is reasonable and the borrowing serves an appropriate trust purpose and is otherwise consistent with the trustee's fiduciary duties.

Similarly, for example, in managing real property held in a trust, the trustee can properly incur such appropriate expenses as the cost of leasing or other property management and the cost of insuring the trust estate against loss, damage, or liability. Also, the trustee can properly incur expenses, as appropriate to the trust purposes, to keep trust real property or tangible personal property in repair, whether the property is held for the use of the beneficiaries or for the return it may produce as a trust investment. In doing so, the trustee must act with prudence in determining the character, likely benefits, and costs of the repair work. . . . .

Analogous questions may arise when a trustee is considering the possibility of improving trust property. Improvements may serve to make the property more productive, or to make the premises safe or tenantable; therefore a trustee can properly incur improvement costs if and as the property's retention and improvement are prudent and suitable to the purposes of the trust. Issues of retention and improvement, however, are essentially matters of prudent investment (see §§ 90 and 92), often involving diversification issues (§ 90, Comment *g*) and management challenges (see id., Comment *o*, and § 92, Comments *e* and *c*).

Where the terms of a trust direct retention of certain property or forbid the making of improvements or certain types of repairs, deviation may be permitted or directed by the court under the rule stated in § 66.

c. Employing agents and advisors. The trustee can properly incur reasonable expenses in employing lawyers, brokers, or other agents or advisors so far as such employment is appropriate to the sound administration of the trust. The trustee cannot properly incur expenses, however, in employing agents or others to do acts if the employment would involve a violation of the trustee's duties as defined either by law or by the terms of the trust. On the propriety and potential importance of delegation or obtaining advice in administering a trust, see § 80 and § 77, Comment *b* . . . .

Similarly, a trustee cannot properly incur expenses for another to perform functions the trustee is compensated—and thus expected—to perform personally. Thus, the method of fixing a trustee's compensation, and the amount of that compensation, are relevant in determining whether certain costs of other's services are payable or reimbursable from the trust estate. Even proper expenses of this type, that is, expenses that are neither unreasonable nor impermissible, may affect what is appropriate compensation for a trustee under a typical (§ 38(1)) "reasonable compensation" standard. See . . . § 38, Comment *c(1)* . . . . Cf. § 90, Comment *m* . . . .

d. Costs of judicial proceedings. The trustee can properly incur expenses for reasonable counsel fees and other costs in bringing, defending, or settling litigation as appropriate to proper administration or performance of the trustee's duties. For example, see § 71 on petitions for instruction and § 76, Comment *d*, on actions to collect or protect trust property. The right of indemnification applies even though the trustee is unsuccessful in the action, as long as the trustee's conduct was not imprudent or otherwise in violation of a fiduciary duty.

More complicated issues are presented by costs incurred by trustees in controversies, or in anticipation of possible litigation, involving allegations of breach of trust and thus exposing the trustee personally to risks such as surcharge or removal. To the extent the trustee is successful in defending against charges of misconduct, the trustee is normally entitled to indemnification for reasonable attorneys' fees and other costs; to the extent the trustee is found to have committed a breach of trust, indemnification is ordinarily unavailable. Ultimately, however, the matter of the trustee's indemnification is within the discretion of the trial court, subject to appeal for abuse of that discretion.

Illustration:

1. B brought suit against T to surcharge it for losses allegedly caused by T's imprudent retention of certain trust investments, resulting in significant losses to B and other beneficiaries. After finding that T's conduct was prudent and that all costs incurred by T were reasonable, the court acted properly (absent special circumstances) in allowing T reimbursement for attorney fees and other expenses of its successful defense.

A trustee cannot properly pay costs incurred by a beneficiary in a judicial or other proceeding involving the administration of the trust or the beneficiary's interests in the trust, except pursuant to a court order. A court may, in the interest of justice, make an award of costs from the trust estate to a beneficiary for some or all of his or her attorney fees and other expenses. Ordinarily, however, awards of this type are limited to situations in which the beneficiary's participation in the proceeding is beneficial to the trust, usually either because of a recovery that benefits the trust's beneficiaries generally (rather than merely the beneficiary in question) or by clarifying a significant uncertainty in the terms of the trust.

Illustrations:

4. In Illustration 1, above, it would ordinarily be appropriate for the court to deny a request by B for an award of costs.

5. The same facts as in Illustration 1, except that B (one of the trust's numerous beneficiaries and potential beneficiaries) was successful in obtaining a substantial recovery when the court found that T had acted imprudently in retaining the investments in question. It would ordinarily be proper for the court to make an award from the trust of reasonable attorney fees and other expenses to B, based on the resulting benefit to the trust and its beneficiaries generally.

6. T petitions the court for instructions to clarify uncertainties in the meaning of certain distributive provisions of the trust. The court found that there was need to clarify the provisions, which it concluded were ambiguous, and admitted extrinsic evidence that led to interpretations clarifying the uncertainties. The court may award appropriate costs to a group of beneficiaries who, in good faith, urged a reasonable but unsuccessful interpretation, as well as to the side that prevailed.

e. Cross-references. More generally, on remedies and liabilities among beneficiaries and trustees, see § 95 and Chapters 19 and 20.

On the rights of third parties to whom the trustee has incurred liabilities in the course of trust administration, see Chapter 21.

On the allocation of trust expenses between principal and income accounts, see Chapter 23.

§ 89. Powers and Duties on Termination

The powers of a trustee do not end on the trust's termination date but may be exercised as appropriate to the performance of the trustee's duties in winding up administration, including making distribution, in a manner consistent with the purposes of the trust and the interests of the beneficiaries.

Comment:

a. Termination date: meaning. Reference in this section to the "termination date" of a trust means the time at which it becomes the duty of the trustee to wind up administration of the trust. This time ordinarily arrives at the expiration of the period for which the trust was created (see § 61), not at the time when distribution is actually accomplished. Thus, for example, the termination date of a trust for L for life, remainder to R, arrives upon L's death; and the termination date of a trust to pay income to B until age 25, with principal then to go outright to B, ordinarily arrives when B attains age 25. The period for which a trust was originally created, however, and thus the termination date, may be shortened or extended by a power reserved in the settlor (§ 63) or granted to another (§ 64), or under a rule regarding trust modification or termination (see §§ 65–69).

The meaning of this expression parallels the normal meaning of "distribution date" in the law of future interests, essentially looking to the termination of the preceding beneficial interests rather than to the time or times when the corpus of a trust estate is actually distributed. . . . .

b. Termination date: effect in general. Although the termination date for a trust has arrived, the trustee does not thereby necessarily cease to be trustee but normally continues to serve until the trust is finally wound up. The period for winding up the trust refers to the period after the termination date and before trust administration ends by complete distribution of the trust estate.

The duration of this period of continuation properly depends on the circumstances involved. If, for example, the estate is large, especially with tax complications, or if the trust terms or circumstances require the sale of property that is not readily saleable, or if the beneficiaries entitled to distribution or the amounts to which they are entitled are difficult of ascertainment, the period for winding up the trust may properly be longer than it would be in the absence of these or other complicating circumstances.

Also, delay may result because of difficulties in establishing and implementing a plan for distributing the trust estate that both serves the interest of the beneficiaries and is consistent with the trustee's duty of impartiality. See, e.g., Comment *e(2)*. If difficulties of this type are anticipated, however, and if the trust is to terminate at a fixed time or at a time that is reasonably foreseeable, the trustee should begin planning for distribution in advance of the termination date.

The powers and duties of the trustee in winding up the trust are an extension of the powers and duties of the trustee generally in administering the trust, except that the trustee's fiduciary duties in exercising powers of the trusteeship are significantly affected by the fact that the trust is in (or approaching) the process of termination. Accordingly, when the termination date has arrived, the trustee can properly exercise powers of the trusteeship as appropriate to the winding up of the trust (including distribution of the trust estate) in accordance with its purposes and the interests of its beneficiaries. Furthermore, the court retains jurisdiction, when called upon, to settle accounts and to resolve issues regarding trust management and distribution.

If necessary, as when the trust is to terminate on the death of a life beneficiary who also has served as sole trustee, a successor trustee will be appointed, pursuant to the terms of the trust or by court order, to wind up the trust. Cf. § 34.

c. Trustee's responsibilities during windup period: in general. While winding up administration of the trust, the trustee is to continue holding and administering the trust estate, except as one or more preliminary distributions can be made without interfering with the windup process.

During the windup period the trustee has a duty: to determine and satisfy trust obligations, including those to taxing authorities . . .; to ascertain the proper distributees and their shares, and plan and make distribution accordingly (see Comment *e(2)*); and, unless waived by the beneficiaries, to prepare and submit an accounting or report to the court or the beneficiaries (cf. § 83, Comment *b*). In the meantime, the trustee has a duty to preserve and manage the trust property (see Comment *d*). These responsibilities are to be carried out with prudence and special attention to the fact that the trust is in the process of termination, and in accordance with the purposes of the trust and the interests of the beneficiaries.

On a trustee's lien for compensation and indemnification, see § 38, Comment *b*; and cf. § 88.

d. Asset management during the windup period. Although the trust termination date has arrived, the trustee can properly exercise such powers as are reasonable and appropriate for the preservation of the trust property until the process of winding up is completed. Thus, the trustee can properly keep real property and tangible personalty of the trust insured and in repair. There may be also need to convert property to cash or other form appropriate for distribution (see Comment *e*).

So also, the trustee can properly keep trust property productive, as reasonable in the circumstances. Accordingly, suitable new investments or commitments (e.g., renewal of leases on trust-owned apartments) may be appropriate to avoid wasting the potential of trust assets to produce income or other return for the remainder beneficiaries. Sound exercise of fiduciary discretion in this respect requires not only that the trustee take account of the likely period until preliminary or final distribution can be made of the assets in question, but also that this consideration be balanced against the interest of distributees in receiving property that is unencumbered or readily marketable (cf. § 86, Comment *c(1)*, on the duty of a trustee regarding leases that might extend beyond the duration of the trust).

Because distributees are normally ascertainable once the time for termination has arrived (see Comment *a*, last paragraph), it is usually practical as well as proper for a trustee to obtain beneficiary consent (§ 78(2)) in matters of asset management during the winding up of administration. If necessary, uncertainties concerning the trustee's duties and authority may be clarified by judicial instruction (§ 71).

e. *Distribution of trust estate.* Following a trust's termination date, the trustee has a duty within a reasonable time (see Comments *b* and *c*) to distribute the trust property to the persons who are entitled to it, and to make preliminary distributions as appropriate within the period for winding up administration. Ordinarily (cf. Comment *g*) the trustee performs this duty by transferring the trust property to the distributee(s).

On making distribution to minors or other distributees under disability, compare § 49, Comment *c(2)*. . . . .

On the trustee's duty not to misdeliver trust property, see § 76, Comment *f*; if in doubt about the distributees or their shares, the trustee may apply to the court for instructions under § 71.

References to remainder beneficiaries (or distributees) in Comments *e(1)-e(3)* include persons who receive distribution in trust—i.e., as trustee.

e(1). Mode of distribution: sole remainder beneficiary. If a trust has only one beneficiary who is entitled to the trust estate on termination, it is ordinarily appropriate for the trustee to transfer the trust property to that beneficiary in kind, subject to other needs in winding up administration. This normally would not be appropriate, however, if the terms of the trust direct a different form of distribution; and the trustee may depart from the directed method of distribution, either with consent of the beneficiary (cf. § 65, and Comment *e(3)* below) or with court approval (cf. § 66).

The principles described in this Comment apply even though the terms of the trust direct that specific property of the trust be distributed to one or more others, with a single beneficiary to receive the remaining (or residuary) trust estate.

e(2). Mode of distribution: multiple beneficiaries. If on termination of a trust there are several beneficiaries among whom the trust estate is to be distributed, whether and to what extent it would be appropriate for the trustee to convey trust property to the beneficiaries as tenants in common, or to divide and distribute property in kind, or to sell property and distribute the proceeds, depends on the terms of the trust. Absent such terms, or to the extent they do not apply, the mode or modes of distribution to be employed depend upon what the trustee, in the exercise of discretion, determines is in the interest of the beneficiaries and fair and reasonable under the circumstances. The trustee's exercise of discretion in these matters, whether or not conferred by trust provision, is subject to judicial review and intervention for abuse (§ 87). The trustee's duties of prudence and impartiality have particular importance in these situations.

Among the numerous factors that may be of significance to a trustee in developing an appropriate plan for the form and timing of distributions are: the nature of the trust subject matter (the extent to which it consists of securities, chattels, business interests, etc.) and the tax and other characteristics of specific properties; the number of remainder beneficiaries and the size of their various shares; and the preferences, concerns, and circumstances (tax and financial positions, legal capacity or skill level, etc.) of the various distributees. In planning distribution, the trustee should take into account, so far as practical, the likely transaction costs and tax effects (immediate and long-term) to the beneficiaries as well as to the trust. With these and other relevant considerations in mind, the trustee has a duty to act fairly, with reasonable care, and in the interests of the various beneficiaries.

In short, except as otherwise provided by the terms of the trust, a trustee may make, as prudent and appropriate to the circumstances of the trust and its beneficiaries, distributions in cash or in kind or in undivided interests, or in some combination of these, and in making distributions in kind may do so either on a pro rata basis or on a non-pro rata basis (with assets in the latter event to be valued at their date or dates of distribution).

Unless otherwise required by trust provision (Comment *e(3)*), or by fiduciary duties in other aspects of the windup process (Comment *c*), considerations of prudence and impartiality may cause trustees to prefer—so far as practical—to distribute trust property in kind on a pro rata basis, that is, by transferring real property (and possibly other nonfungibles) to the remainder beneficiaries as tenants in common and by dividing and distributing fungibles (e.g., 600 shares of the same class of XYZ Co. stock) among the beneficiaries so that each receives his or her proportionate share of each of the fungible asset holdings. To the extent this form of distribution would be undesirable, however, particularly because of impracticality (e.g., numerous tenants in common) or other disadvantages it may have for some or all of the distributees, distribution can properly be facilitated by some combination of liquidation and non-pro rata division of some or all of the trust estate. Furthermore, if required to meet trust obligations or to make distribution, the trustee may borrow funds on a prudent basis from a third party; or, if authorized by the terms of the trust or approved by the affected beneficiaries (cf. § 78(2)), the trustee may even facilitate distribution through borrowing/lending on fair terms between or among distributable shares, and by including promissory note(s) in the distributive share(s) as appropriate.

Normally, a trustee should inform the distributees of the plan for distribution of the trust estate (see § 82, Comment *d*). Especially if the plan is complicated, the trustee should consider obtaining the informed consent of the beneficiaries when it is practical to do so, although the trustee must also consider the possibility that adverse tax consequences may follow from relying on beneficiary consent—rather than on independent fiduciary judgment in the matter, informed by careful consultation. A trustee may prefer to submit the distribution plan to the court for approval, as is often done, especially with complex plans, at the time (or in advance) of a final accounting if the trustee decides or is required to account in court rather than directly to the beneficiaries. . . . .

e(3). Effect of provisions in the terms of the trust. If the terms of the trust specify the method or methods by which distribution is to be made by the trustee, the provision is normally controlling. Similarly, a remainder disposition of specific property to one or more designated persons is normally binding as a provision implicitly directing distribution of that property in kind. Departure from a normally controlling provision in the trust terms, however, may be authorized or directed by court order pursuant to § 66 or by consent of the affected beneficiary or beneficiaries pursuant to the principles of § 65 (the affected beneficiaries ordinarily being readily ascertainable at the trust's termination date). Also, specific provisions of these types may be subject to the trustee's duty to satisfy obligations of the trust (Comment *c*).

For these purposes, a direction in the terms of the trust to distribute a stated or formula amount (i.e., a monetary value) to a person on the termination of the trust is ordinarily not a trust provision that must be satisfied in cash or that otherwise restricts the methods a trustee may use in making distribution. Generally, the prescribed amount simply establishes a nonresiduary share to which the person is entitled. Thus, absent contrary provision in the terms of the trust, the amount (i) does not function as a fractional share of the trust estate and (ii) may be satisfied in cash or in kind, with any property distributed in kind to be valued at its fair market value at the time or times of actual distribution for purpose of satisfying that amount.

f. Division or partial termination of trust. If the terms of a trust provide that a beneficiary is to receive a fractional (or percentile) share of the trust estate at a designated time and that the rest of the trust property is to be retained in trust (a partial termination), the trustee has, with appropriate adaptation, the powers and duties described in this section and in the above commentary. Similarly, the principles of this section and its commentary apply to situations in which a trustee is to divide the trust estate into fractional shares and is thereafter to retain and administer those shares in two or more separate trusts. . . . .

On substantial distributions (or division into separate trusts) under provisions calling for distribution or allocation to be made either of specific property or of a stated or formula amount, see Comment *e(3)*.

g. Legal title in remainder beneficiary on termination date. Occasionally, when time for termination arrives, the trustee's title to the trust property terminates, with title then vesting in the remainder beneficiary or beneficiaries. See, e.g., § 6 on passive trusts and the Statute of Uses (or counterparts) and § 42, Comment *b*, on the possibility that the trustee may have been granted only an interest of limited duration in the subject matter of the trust. In cases of this type (usually but not necessarily involving doctrines about real property), the beneficiary's title is subject to the trustee's powers and duties so far as necessary to satisfy obligations and wind up trust administration (see particularly Comment *c*, and also see § 38, Comment *b*, on the trustee's lien for compensation and indemnification); and the trustee's duty of distribution is performed by surrendering possession of the subject matter of the trust within a reasonable time and taking steps that may be necessary to enable the beneficiary readily to establish ownership.

CHAPTER 17

INVESTMENT OF TRUST FUNDS (THE "PRUDENT INVESTOR RULE")

Introductory Note: The foundation of trust investment law in the First and Second Restatements has been the so-called "prudent man rule" of Harvard College v. Amory, 9 Pick. (26 Mass.) 446, 461 (1830). The opinion admonished trustees "to observe how men of prudence, discretion and intelligence manage their own affairs, not in regard to speculation, but in regard to the permanent disposition of their funds, considering the probable income, as well as the probable safety of the capital to be invested." Thus, in 1959, the rule of Restatement Second, Trusts § 227 directed trustees "to make such investments and only such investments as a prudent man would make of his own property having in view the preservation of the estate and the amount and regularity of the income to be derived." In generally similar language, influenced by the original Restatement, the prudent-man rule had been adopted at one time by decision or legislation in most American jurisdictions, often displacing the more restrictive, so-called "legal list" statutes.

Unfortunately, much of the apparent and initially intended generality and adaptability of the prudent-man rule was lost as it was further elaborated in the courts and applied case by case. Decisions dealing with essentially factual issues were accompanied by generalizations understandably intended to offer guidance to other courts and trustees in like situations. These cases were subsequently treated as precedents establishing general rules governing trust investments. Specific case results and flexible principles often thereby became crystallized into specific subrules prescribing the types and characteristics of permissible investments for trustees.

Based on some degree of risk that was abstractly perceived as excessive, broad categories of investments and techniques often came to be classified as "speculative" and thus as imprudent per se. Accordingly, the exercise of care, skill, and caution would be no defense if the property acquired or retained by a trustee, or the strategy pursued for a trust, was characterized as impermissible.

Knowledge, practices, and experience in the modern investment world have demonstrated that arbitrary restrictions on trust investments are unwarranted and often counterproductive. For example, understandable concern has existed that widely accepted theories and practices of investment management cannot properly be pursued by trustees under long-standing judicial and treatise statements of the law. Prohibitions that developed under the traditional prudent-man rule have been potential sources of unjustified liability for trustees generally and, more particularly, of inhibitions limiting the exercise of sound judgment by skilled trustees. This is particularly so for trustees whose fiduciary circumstances call for, or at least permit, investment programs that would include some high risk-and-return strategies (such as a venture-capital program) or for the use of abstractly high-risk investments or techniques (such as futures or option trading) for the purpose of reducing the risk level of the portfolio as a whole.

These criticisms of the prudent-man rule are supported by a large and growing body of literature that is in turn supported by empirical research, well documented and essentially compelling. Much but not all of this criticism is found in writings that have collectively and loosely come to be called modern portfolio theory. The need for modernization or at least clarification of the prudent-man rule was also evidenced [prior to the 1992 publication of the "Prudent Investor Rule" Volume] by some legislative trends at both federal and state levels.

In addition, for some time the need for revision had been evident from conflicts between the prudent-man rule and modern asset-management practices. Investment products and techniques have developed and changed over the years. So have information and theories concerning financial markets and prudent investing, backed not only by the extensive research mentioned above but also by the authoritative judgments and investment behavior patterns of expert fund managers.

Trust investment law should reflect and accommodate current knowledge and concepts. It should also avoid repeating the mistake of freezing its rules against future learning and developments.

The rules in this Chapter 17 are intended to reflect the lessons derived from modern experience and research, without either endorsing or excluding any particular theories of economics or investment.

This goal calls for a limited body of legal rules that draw upon the consistent themes of legitimate theories and express only those principles upon which there is general agreement. This much is needed in order to protect trust beneficiaries and settlor objectives while also providing standards by which to judge and guide trustees' conduct. Yet the rules must be general and flexible enough to adapt to changes in the financial world and to permit sophisticated, prudent use of any investments and courses of action that are suitable to the purposes and circumstances of the diverse trusts to which the rules will inevitably apply. Thus, the objectives of the "prudent investor rule" of this Restatement Third range from that of liberating expert trustees to pursue challenging, rewarding, nontraditional strategies when appropriate to the particular trust, to that of providing other trustees with reasonably clear guidance to safe harbors that are practical, adaptable, readily identifiable, and expectedly rewarding.

With modest reformulation of the Harvard College dictum and the basic rule of prior Restatements, the prudent investor rule of this Restatement seeks to modernize trust investment law and to restore the generality and flexibility of the original doctrine. The language of the prudent investor rule and the accompanying Comments in § 90 [§ 227 in 1992 volume] are thus intended to preserve the law's adaptability by confining its mandates to those that seem essential to prudence (based on traditional duties of care, skill, and caution), to the protection of fiduciary goals, and to supplying helpful guidance to courts and trustees. The rule's mandates are limited to principles that are supported by general consensus among various theories and that are adaptable to the differences among various trusts, trustees, and their needs and objectives.

Principles of prudence. In addition to the fundamental proposition that no investments or techniques are imprudent per se, there are a few principles of prudence set out in the sections that follow. These principles instruct trustees and courts that: (1) sound diversification is fundamental to risk management and is therefore ordinarily required of trustees; (2) risk and return are so directly related that trustees have a duty to analyze and make conscious decisions concerning the levels of risk appropriate to the purposes, distribution requirements, and other circumstances of the trusts they administer; (3) trustees have a duty to avoid fees, transaction costs, and other expenses that are not justified by needs and realistic objectives of the trust's investment program; (4) the fiduciary duty of impartiality in most trusts requires, at least under traditional principal-and-income rules, a balancing of the elements of return between production of current income and the protection of purchasing power; and (5) trustees may have a duty as well as having the authority to delegate as prudent investors would.

(1) The first two of these principles are fundamental to risk management. A duty to diversify was included in § 228 of prior Restatements but is so central to modern concepts of prudence that it has been incorporated into the prudent investor rule of § 90 [1992 § 227]. This pervasive duty and its vital role in minimizing "uncompensated" risk are emphasized in the commentary, not only as a matter of caution but also as a basic aspect of due care and skill.

(2) Although carrying uncompensated risk is ordinarily undesirable, the same cannot so simply be said of risks that are compensated by expectations of increased return. This so-called *market* risk is unavoidable in investing, and fiduciary decisions are therefore concerned with the appropriate degree of that risk. These decisions are an integral part of investment strategy because of the direct relationship between market risk and portfolio-return expectations. Thus, the second of the above principles calls for the trustee to make a deliberate assessment and judgment about a suitable level of risk and reward to be pursued in light of the particular trust's return requirements, risk tolerance, general purposes, specific terms, and other pertinent circumstances.

Case law and prior Restatements have condemned "speculation" and excessive risk without definition, as if such risk could be recognized in the abstract without regard to portfolio context and objectives. The prudent investor rule recognizes that investments and courses of action are properly judged not in isolation but on the basis of the roles they are to play in specific trust portfolios and strategies.

(3) Although trustees are entitled to indemnification for reasonable expenses, the duty to avoid unwarranted costs is given increased emphasis in the prudent investor rule. This is done to reflect the importance of market-efficiency concepts and differences in the degrees of efficiency and inefficiency in various markets. In addition, this emphasis reflects the availability and continuing emergence of modern investment products, not only with significantly varied characteristics but also with similar products being offered with significantly differing costs. The duty to be cost conscious requires attention to such matters as the cumulation of fiduciary commissions with agent fees or the purchase and management charges associated with mutual funds and other pooled-investment vehicles. In addition, active management strategies involve investigation expenses and other transaction costs (including capital-gains taxation) that must be considered, realistically, in relation to the likelihood of increased return from such strategies.

(4) Modern experience with inflation—so different from experience with the value of money in the formative periods of trust investment law—dictates a greater sensitivity in investment management to the competition between the income and principal interests in a trust, or, more broadly, to reflect the needs of both today and tomorrow. In addition, tax consequences within the trust and the tax positions of the various beneficiaries have come to have considerable importance in the management of trust funds, and the trustee's investment decisions often affect different beneficiaries quite differently in this respect. For these reasons, trustees must recognize that the traditional insistence on preservation of principal includes a consideration of the real value of corpus and a need to balance this concern against a life beneficiary's typical interest in the production of trust income, with attention to the after-tax worth of each. The prudent investor rule also recognizes that the life beneficiary's concern over trust-accounting income is not the same (or even present) in all trusts, and makes clear in any event that this concern focuses on the portfolio as a whole rather than on each investment. Trust purposes, beneficiary circumstances, and family financial objectives will sometimes allow more than an effort to protect purchasing power and thus may justify a deliberate effort to achieve real growth in some trust estates.

(5) The last of the above-stated principles of prudence recognizes that, with proper attention to cost concerns, prudent investing may require or at least benefit from expert assistance in investment matters. Thus, the prudent investor rule views delegation from a positive perspective. Nonetheless, the terms and manner of delegation, the competence of agents, and the supervision or monitoring of agents' activities all remain critical aspects of prudence. The need for delegation may be most readily apparent when complicated or challenging investment strategies are pursued by trustees managing large, diverse portfolios. In quite different ways, however, delegation is also likely to be important to nonexpert investors who nevertheless may be well situated and qualified to serve as trustees, as will often be the case with family members or friends. Accordingly, the rule stated in § 90 [1992 § 227] recognizes broad authority to delegate in the prudently exercised discretion of the trustee.

Significant cross-references. On powers of trustees in general, see § 85. On prudence generally, see § 77; also cf. § 86. On the trustee's duties of loyalty and impartiality, see respectively § 78 and § 79. On the trustee's general rights and duties with respect to costs, see § 88. On delegation, see § 80, and cf. § 81 (on co-trusteeship).

On the trustee's duty to comply with trust terms and applicable law, see § 76, and cf. § 87 on the effects of instrument language granting "discretion" in the exercise of a trustee's powers.

§ 90. General Standard of Prudent Investment

The trustee has a duty to the beneficiaries to invest and manage the funds of the trust as a prudent investor would, in light of the purposes, terms, distribution requirements, and other circumstances of the trust.

(a) This standard requires the exercise of reasonable care, skill, and caution, and is to be applied to investments not in isolation but in the context of the trust portfolio and as a part of an overall investment strategy, which should incorporate risk and return objectives reasonably suitable to the trust.

(b) In making and implementing investment decisions, the trustee has a duty to diversify the investments of the trust unless, under the circumstances, it is prudent not to do so.

(c) In addition, the trustee must:

(1) conform to fundamental fiduciary duties of loyalty (§ 78) and impartiality (§ 79);

(2) act with prudence in deciding whether and how to delegate authority and in the selection and supervision of agents (§ 80); and

(3) incur only costs that are reasonable in amount and appropriate to the investment responsibilities of the trusteeship (§ 88).

(d) The trustee's duties under this section are subject to the rule of § 91, dealing primarily with contrary investment provisions of a trust or statute.

General Comment:

a. *Scope of the rule.* Except as otherwise provided by the terms of the trust (see §§ 4 and 91), the trustee has a duty to preserve the trust property (see § 76, Comment *d*) and to make it productive (see § 76, Comment *e*). In doing so the trustee must exercise reasonable care, skill, and caution (§ 77) and must act with undivided loyalty to the beneficiaries (§ 78) and with impartiality among them (§ 79). This chapter deals with the trustee's performance of these duties in making and reviewing investments.

The prudent investor rule stated in this section is an extension and clarification of the traditional, so-called "prudent man rule" originally articulated by the Massachusetts Supreme Judicial Court and followed by most states in the recent past. The prudent investor rule or an earlier but comparable rule has been adopted by statute in nearly all jurisdictions. (See Forenote to this chapter.) In several states, the investment authority of trustees remains or may remain somewhat more restricted, at least for some trustees. See § 91.

Several bodies of state and federal legislation dealing with various types of charitable, pension, or public funds have for several decades incorporated rules more or less similar to the prudent investor rule. See § 91. The principles of this section are generally appropriate to those statutory rules, both by analogy and when those rules incorporate general principles of trust law. Specific provisions and special circumstances or relationships involved in the application of those statutory rules, however, may present different considerations. . . .

In the absence of a contrary statutory provision, a trustee may generally invest in such properties and in such manner as expressly or impliedly authorized by the terms of the trust. Assuming no contrary trust provision, however, the rule of this section describes the nature of the investment authority and duties normally to be implied.

Illustrations:

1. The will of S left her residuary estate to T and T's successors, in trust, "to hold, manage, sell, invest and reinvest and to pay all of the net income, plus such amounts of principal as the trustee shall deem appropriate, to L for life, with the remainder at L's death to be distributed to those of my issue who are then living, such issue to take

by right of representation." No investment provisions or powers are included in the will. Under this will, T's duties and authority with respect to trust investments are those prescribed by the prudent investor rule of this section.

2. The same facts as in Illustration 1, except that the trust provision of S's residuary clause contains the following additional language: ". . . by right of representation; provided, however, that the trustee shall not invest any portion of the trust estate in real property." Subject to this expressed restriction on T's investment authority, which T must obey in the absence of extraordinary circumstances (see § 66), T's remaining duties and authority in investing the funds of this trust are those of the prudent investor rule set out in this section.

The Comments that follow in this section describe how the trustee's general fiduciary duties apply to the investment function (Comments *b* through *e*), then explain the trustee's specific responsibilities in regard to risk, diversification, impartiality, and delegation (Comments *f* through *j*), and finally discuss principles and legally relevant considerations applicable to specific types of investments and courses of action (Comments *k* through *p*). The significance and effects of particular investment provisions that may appear in legislation or in the terms of a trust are considered in § 91. The influence an existing portfolio of investments may have on the trustee's duties, especially at the start of administration, is discussed in § 92. . . . .

Comment on Basic Duties of the Prudent Investor:

b. *Duty to conform to fiduciary standards.* Trustees have a general fiduciary duty to comply with the terms of their trusts. See § 91, and more generally § 76. The nature and extent of a trustee's duties and powers are primarily determined by the terms of the trust. See §§ 70 and 85. The phrase "terms of the trust" is broadly defined to include intentions of the settlor manifested in any way that admits of proof in a judicial proceeding. See generally § 4. Thus, the trust terms, expressed and implied, may be derived from written or spoken words, circumstances surrounding the establishment of the trust, and sometimes statutory language that is automatically imported into trusts or by which some trusts are established. Id., Comments *a* and *g*. The terms may also be affected by subsequent modifications and by limitations imposed by applicable law. See § 76, Comment *b(1)*.

In managing investments, as in other matters relating to the administration of the trust, the trustee must adhere to fundamental fiduciary standards. See generally the basic standards referred to in §§ 70 and 86 and set out in Chapter 15 (§§ 76 through 84); and that cost-conscious management is fundamental to prudence in the investment function, see Introductory Note to this chapter ("*Principles of Prudence*," item (3)) . . . and, more generally § 88. The trustee's duties apply not only in making investments but also in monitoring and reviewing investments, which is to be done in a manner that is reasonable and appropriate to the particular investments, courses of action, and strategies involved.

The trustee's compliance with these fiduciary standards is to be judged as of the time the investment decision in question was made, not with the benefit of hindsight or by taking account of developments that occurred after the time of a decision to make, retain, or sell an investment. The question of whether a breach of trust has occurred turns on the prudence and propriety of the trustee's conduct, not on the eventual results of investment decisions. The trustee is not a guarantor of the trust's investment performance. See § 77 and more generally Chapter 19.

Illustrations:

3. Under the same facts as in Illustration 1, above, T invests the funds of the trust with the required degree of care, skill, and caution in short-term and intermediate-term Treasury securities and in several mutual funds holding corporate stocks. The combination is suitable to the circumstances and purposes of the trust. As a result of general market and economic conditions, the value of all of the mutual-fund shares declines suddenly during the second year of the trust. T is not liable for the losses sustained by the trust, even though some trustees and many other investors suffered lesser or no net losses as a result of the same market events during the same period.

4. Under the same set of facts as in Illustration 3, the sudden initial decline in the value of the shares is followed by an eight-month period of a generally declining market that continues to have adverse overall effects on the value of the trust estate. Early in this period and at various times during the period, many investors (including many other trustees) sell their holdings in investments similar to the mutual-fund holdings retained by T, investing instead in short-term debt instruments. These investors thereby avoid much of the loss sustained by S's testamentary trust. T, however, reasonably concludes that it is wise to retain the mutual-fund shares in which substantial losses of value are eventually sustained. T is not liable for the losses that followed from these reasonable judgments that, in retrospect, prove disadvantageous.

5. The same facts as in Illustration 2, above (a simple residuary trust with a special prohibition against investing in real estate). T invests some of the funds of the trust in carefully selected real-estate investments. T was advised that these investments had a good, established record of earnings, represented an excellent investment opportunity, and would contribute to meeting the trust's needs for diversification and a long-term hedge against inflation (see Comment *o*, below). This advice came from experienced, competent sources of investment advice. T conscientiously considered and understood and carefully examined this advice and the available investment alternatives before deciding that the investments would serve the best interests of the trust and its beneficiaries. There are no circumstances present that would have justified a court order authorizing deviation from the terms of the trust under § 66. (See Comment *e* of § 91.) T is liable for any resulting loss from the investment, because T committed a breach of trust in not respecting the trust provision expressly limiting her investment authority. This is so even though the causes of the loss were not foreseeable and even though T acted in a manner that would have been reasonable but for the express prohibition in the trust terms. See § 91(b).

On the effects of legal and other advice concerning a trustee's investment powers and duties and advice concerning the exercise of those powers and the performance of those duties, see § 77, Comment *b(2)*, and compare § 93.

On the meaning of "loss" resulting to the trust estate when a trustee has committed a breach of trust, see Chapter 19.

c. General requirements of loyalty and impartiality. Under the prudent investor rule, the trustee must act with undivided loyalty and solely in the interests of the beneficiaries. See § 78. It is therefore a breach of duty, for example, to make a trust investment by purchasing property owned by the trustee individually. As to the associated general duty to earmark investments made as trustee, see § 84.

The strict duty of loyalty in the trust law ordinarily prohibits the trustee from investing or managing trust investments in a manner that will give rise to a personal conflict of interest. See, e.g., § 78, Comments *d–e(2)*. The prohibition also applies to investing in a manner that is intended to serve interests other than those of the beneficiaries or the purposes of the settlor. Id., Comment *f*.

Thus, for example, in managing the investments of a trust, the trustee's decisions ordinarily must not be motivated by a purpose of advancing or expressing the trustee's personal views concerning social or political issues or causes. Such considerations, however, may properly influence the investment decisions of a trustee to the extent permitted by the terms of the trust or by consent of the beneficiaries. (On the latter, see §§ 65 and 97; also compare (on the duty of impartiality) Comment *i*, below, and § 79.) In addition, social considerations may be taken into account in investing the funds of charitable trusts to the extent the charitable purposes would justify an expenditure of trust funds for the social issue or cause in question or to the extent the investment decision can be justified on grounds of advancing, financially or operationally, a charitable activity conducted by the trust. . . . .

Unlike the financial and other personal interests of the trustee, the divergent economic interests of trust beneficiaries give rise to conflicts of types that cannot simply be prohibited or avoided in the investment decisions of typical trusts. These problems regularly present the trustee with problems of conflicting obligations to diverse beneficiaries. (See generally § 79 on the duty of impartiality.) The interests of a life-income beneficiary, for example, are almost inherently in competition with those of the remainder beneficiaries, especially in light of the risks of inflation; and the different tax circumstances of the various beneficiaries frequently create competing investment preferences, among concurrent as well as successive beneficiaries (id., Comment *a*).

These conflicting fiduciary obligations result in a necessarily flexible and somewhat indefinite duty of impartiality. The duty therefore requires the trustee to balance the competing interests of differently situated beneficiaries in a fair and reasonable manner. See § 79, Comment *b*. With respect to the trust investment function, see id., Comments *c–i*, and particularly the discussion and Illustrations (infra) in Comment *i* of this section.

Illustrations:

6. T is trustee of a trust that is to pay its net income to L for life and to distribute the remainder on L's death to R or R's then living issue by right of representation. Some trust funds are available for short-term investment pending a forthcoming distribution to L. T, in good faith, concludes that the most efficient and rewarding temporary investment of these funds is a loan to herself personally, for which T (who is an excellent risk) is prepared to pay a higher rate of interest than normally available on a short-term basis. This is an improper investment for the trust, because it violates T's duty of undivided loyalty. T is therefore liable to the trust for any personal profits derived from the use of these funds, and for any losses suffered by the trust estate as a result of this loan investment.

7. T is trustee of a trust to pay income to A for life, remainder to B if then living and if not then by right of representation to B's issue who are then living. T invests the trust funds in investments of a type that, despite the broad range of yields that might be appropriate to particular trusts (see Comment *i*, below), appear unduly to favor A's interest in receiving a high income at the expense of the B family's interest in having corpus protected against loss of purchasing power. This constitutes a breach of T's duty of impartiality (see Comment *i*, below) in the absence of satisfactory explanation.

Such an explanation might be based, for example, on the terms and purposes of the trust, including A's needs as they may properly relate to those purposes. See generally § 79, Comments *b* and *g–g(2)*. Even with such a justification, the trustee should recognize that in inflationary times a high-yield and low-growth (or no-growth) investment strategy, adhered to over a long period, would pose a risk not only to principal interests but also with respect to a life beneficiary's future security; the effects of such a strategy would be comparable to a regular practice of invading principal. See also the possibility of a different investment strategy accompanied by an equitable (or statutory) adjustment as described in Comment *i* of § 79.

Illustration:

8. Under a trust similar to that in Illustration 7, above, T invests the trust funds in a manner that appears unduly to favor growth of principal at the expense of the life beneficiary's interest in income. This is a breach of T's duty of impartiality (see Comment *i*, below) in the absence of satisfactory explanation (see generally § 79, Comments *b* and *g–g(1)*), possibly accompanied by equitable (or statutory) adjustment (see id., Comment *i*).

d. General requirements of care and skill. The duty of care requires the trustee to exercise reasonable effort and diligence in making and monitoring investments for the trust, with attention to the trust's objectives. The trustee has a related duty of care in keeping informed of rights and opportunities associated with those investments.

The trustee must give reasonably careful consideration to both the formulation and the implementation of an appropriate investment strategy, with investments to be selected and reviewed in a manner reasonably appropriate to that strategy. Ordinarily this involves obtaining relevant information about such matters as the circumstances and requirements of the trust and its beneficiaries, the contents and resources of the trust estate, and the nature and characteristics of available investment alternatives. To the extent necessary or appropriate to the making of informed investment judgments by the particular trustee, care also involves securing and considering the advice of others on a reasonable basis. It is ordinarily satisfactory that this information and advice be obtained from sources on which prudent investors in the community customarily rely. See generally § 77.

The exercise of care alone is not sufficient, however, because a trustee is liable for losses resulting from failure to use the skill of an individual of ordinary intelligence (§ 77). This is so despite the careful use of all the skill of which the particular trustee is capable. On the duty therefore (as an aspect of prudence) to seek necessary assistance, through delegation or by obtaining advice, see infra this Comment and also § 77, Comment *b*.

On the other hand, it follows from the requirement of care as well as from sound policy that, if the trustee possesses a degree of skill greater than that of an individual of ordinary intelligence, the trustee is liable for a loss that results from failure to make reasonably diligent use of that skill. So also, if a trustee, such as a corporate or professional fiduciary, procured appointment as trustee by expressly or impliedly representing that it possessed greater skill than that of an individual of ordinary intelligence, or if the trustee has or represents that it has special facilities for investment management, the trustee is liable for a loss that results from failure to make reasonably diligent use of that skill or of those special facilities. See § 77(3) and id., Comment *e*.

The duty to exercise both care and skill in investment management may require knowledge and experience greater than that of an individual of ordinary intelligence, depending on the investment strategy to be employed. This does not prevent an ordinarily intelligent person from serving as a trustee. In that role, however, such a person may have to take reasonable steps to obtain sufficient competent advice, guidance, and assistance in order to meet the standards of this section and to formulate and implement a prudent investment strategy for the particular trust. (Also, see Comments *h* and *m*, below, on the use of mutual funds and other investment pools.) In addition, a person who serves as trustee should be capable of reasonably understanding the basic duties of prudent trusteeship. Simple, written guidelines prepared by legal counsel may be helpful for reference or presentation by an inexperienced trustee when conferring with an investment adviser.

The standards of trusteeship are neither excessively demanding nor monolithic. They should neither effectively preclude service by conscientious family members and friends nor permit casual, inattentive behavior by trustees who can, because of their expertise, meet a higher than ordinary standard of conduct and competence. Thus, the applicable requirements of care and skill allow responsible individuals of ordinary intelligence to serve as trustees and to adopt reasonable investment strategies of types that are appropriate to their skills. Yet the standards require fiduciaries possessing special facilities and skills to make those advantages available to the trust and its beneficiaries.

Beyond this, the prudent investor rule, with its adaptable requirements of care and skill and its flexible standard of caution (Comment *e*, below), does not prevent trustees from prudently pursuing an expectedly rewarding investment strategy merely because that strategy is highly demanding, provided it is appropriate both to the purposes and circumstances of the trust and to the skills possessed by or available to the trustee. In the implementation of a permissible investment strategy, the trustee has the power and may have a duty to delegate authority to others, as a prudent investor would in the circumstances. See particularly Comment *j*, below. In so delegating, the trustee must exercise appropriate care and skill in selecting, instructing, and supervising or monitoring agents and in determining the degree and terms of the delegation. See generally § 80.

Illustration:

9. A portion of A's residuary estate was left in trust to help provide for the widow and children of A's deceased son, S, until the youngest child of S reaches age 24. At that time, the trust estate is to be distributed by right of representation to S's then living descendants. The will names A's other son, T, as trustee. T is a successful young chemist

with a pharmaceutical company and is well acquainted with and trusted by the beneficiaries, but he has no experience with investment matters. It appears that T is qualified to serve as trustee; the facts do not suggest that he lacks the skill to which he will be held in that capacity.

In the above Illustration, T may need instruction and guidance from responsible legal and financial advisers on the nature of his investment duties (as well as other fiduciary duties) and on the performance of these duties. He should become reasonably aware of such matters as the importance of diversification, the meaning of caution in risk taking and investment strategy, the need for attention and relevant information in making investment decisions, and the possibilities of assistance through delegation (see Comment *j*, below, and § 80). The cost of advice in these matters, as reasonably necessary to T's needs as trustee, may be paid or reimbursed from the trust estate. See § 88, Comment *c*. On the effects of relying on agents, see § 80(2) and especially id., Comment *g*.

Illustration:

10. The same facts as in Illustration 9, except that, instead of son T, a trust company was named as trustee. This trustee has a duty to make use of facilities and to exercise a degree of skill consistent with the facilities and skills possessed, or those actually or impliedly represented to be possessed, by the trust company. This would include both professional sensitivity to the duty of caution and professional sophistication in establishing and implementing an appropriate investment strategy for the trust for the benefit of S's family.

If both son T and a trust company or professional fiduciary had been appointed as co-trustees of the trust in Illustrations 9 and 10, differing standards of skill would be imposed so that the applicable standard would be that appropriate to each co-trustee. On the exercise of fiduciary powers by multiple trustees, see § 39; on the duty of each to participate in the administration of the trust and to prevent (or to compel redress of) a breach of trust by a co-trustee, see § 81; and on delegation between or among co-trustees, see Comment *c(1)* of § 81. The authority and responsibilities of co-trustees may be divided or otherwise modified by the terms of the trust. See § 81, Comment *b*. Questions of fault, liability, contribution, and indemnity among co-trustees are discussed in Chapter 19.

e. *General requirement of caution.* In addition to the duty to use care and skill, the trustee must exercise the caution of a prudent investor managing similar funds, in similar circumstances, for similar purposes. See § 77, Comment *b*. . . . . In the absence of contrary provisions in the terms of the trust, this requirement of caution requires the trustee to invest with a view both to safety of the capital and to securing a reasonable return. See generally § 79 on the duty of impartiality.

"Safety" of capital includes not only the objective of protecting the trust property from the risk of loss of nominal value but, ordinarily, also a goal of preserving its real value—that is, seeking to avoid or reduce loss of the trust estate's purchasing power as a result of inflation. This objective will also normally tend to protect the purchasing power of the income flow in the future.

Reasonable "return" refers to total return, including capital appreciation and gain as well as trust-accounting income. Thus, return objectives and safety of capital are at least partially interrelated. The capital-growth element of these return objectives, however, is not necessarily confined to the preservation of purchasing power, but may extend to growth in the real value of principal in appropriate cases.

In balancing the return objectives between flow of income and growth of principal, the investment emphasis depends not only on the purposes and distribution requirements of the trust but also on its other circumstances and specific terms, such as the beneficiaries' tax positions and whether the trustee has power to invade principal. On income productivity generally and on the duty of impartiality, see Comment *i*, below, and § 79(2) and id., Comments *e–i*.

It is virtually inevitable that in some periods the trustee will be unable to succeed in the effort to preserve purchasing power. It is also to be expected that the pursuit of this objective carries with it some increase in risk.

e(1). Risk management. All investments, even the nominally excepted short-term U.S. Treasury securities, and all investment strategies involve some risk in the comprehensive sense of possible loss of real, inflation-adjusted value. Therefore, the duty of caution does not call for avoidance of risk by trustees but for their prudent management of risk. For these purposes, risk management is concerned with more than failure of collection and loss of dollar value. It takes account of all hazards that may follow from inflation, volatility of price and yield, lack of liquidity, and the like.

Insofar as the term "risk" is used (as it commonly is in economic literature) to refer to volatility of return, risk management by a trustee requires that careful attention be given to the particular trust's risk tolerance, that is, to its tolerance for volatility. Risk tolerance largely depends on a combination of the regular distribution requirements of the trust and any irregular distributions that may in fact become necessary or appropriate. These obligations in turn are likely, depending on the terms of the trust, to be affected by the needs of one or more of the beneficiaries. Thus, these various distribution requirements facing the trustee effectively serve to define the consequences of the volatility risk with respect to a particular trust.

In understanding a trustee's duties with respect to the management of risk, it is useful to distinguish between diversifiable (or "uncompensated") risk and market (or nondiversifiable) risk that is, in effect, compensated through pricing in the marketplace. The distinction is useful in considering fiduciary responsibilities both in setting risk-level objectives and in diversification of the trust portfolio.

In the absence of contrary statute or trust provision, the requirement of caution ordinarily imposes a duty to use reasonable care and skill in an effort to minimize or at least reduce diversifiable risks. Often called nonmarket risk, or somewhat less precisely "specific" or "unique" risk, these are risks that can be reduced through proper diversification of a portfolio. Because market pricing cannot be expected to recognize and reward a particular investor's failure to diversify, a trustee's acceptance of this type of risk cannot, without more, be justified on grounds of enhancing expected return. What has come to be called "modern portfolio theory" offers an instructive conceptual framework for understanding and attempting to cope with nonmarket risk. The trustee's normal duty to diversify in a reasonable manner, however, is not derived from or legally defined by the principles of any particular theory. . . . .

Another aspect of risk management deals with market risk, often called "systemic" or "systematic" risk, or more descriptively for present purposes, simply nondiversifiable or compensated risk. The trustee's duties and objectives with respect to this second category of risk are not as distinct as those with respect to diversifiable risk. They involve quite subjective judgments that are essentially unavoidable in the process of asset management, addressing the appropriate degree of risk to be undertaken in pursuit of a higher or lower level of expected return from the trust portfolio. In this respect the trustee must take account of the element of conservatism that is ordinarily implicit in the prudent investor rule's duty of caution. Opportunities for gain, however, normally bear a direct relationship to the degree of compensated risk. Thus, although an inferred, general duty to invest conservatively is a traditional and accepted feature of trust law, that duty is necessarily imprecise in its requirements and is applied with considerable flexibility. (Despite the flexibility of the trustee's duty in this respect, it is often possible to obtain useful and, in a sense, objective information about degrees of risk associated with a stock or bond or with a portfolio of securities. . . . .)

For purposes of understanding and applying the fiduciary duty of prudent investing, it is essential to recognize that compensated risk is not inherently bad. Therefore, no objective, general legal standard can be set for a degree of risk that is or is not prudent under the rule of this section. Beneficiaries can be disserved by undue conservatism as well as by excessive risk-taking. Decisions concerning a prudent or suitable level of market risk for a particular trust can be reached only after thoughtful consideration of its purposes and all of the relevant trust and beneficiary circumstances. This process includes, for example, balancing the trust's return requirements with its tolerance for volatility. . . . .

If a trust cannot tolerate adverse outcomes in the short run, the trustee should not adopt a high risk-reward strategy. The principal reason for flexible application of the duty of caution is that trusts differ considerably in their risk-bearing capacities, as well as in their purposes. Risk tolerances also vary from time to time during the life of most trusts, especially private trusts, shifting with the likelihood and proximity of having to liquidate holdings in order to meet major (certain or uncertain) trust obligations.

Normally, in investing the funds of a trust, the trustee's strategy must make preservation of the trust estate (including its purchasing power) a significant consideration. In most trust situations (see Comment *i*, below, and also § 79), the amount and stability of income (again, normally including its purchasing power) must also be given serious consideration.

As a result of the duty of caution and a duty to be cost-conscious (§ 88), the typical trustee's asset-management program generally emphasizes long-term investment. Changes in a company's circumstances, adaptation to trust- and capital-market developments, fine-tuning, and the like may, of course, justify the selling and buying of properties as an aspect of a prudent plan of asset allocation and diversification (see Comment *g*, below). This is consistent with the trustee's ongoing duty to monitor investments and to make portfolio adjustments if and as appropriate, with attention to all relevant considerations, including tax consequences and other costs associated with such transactions.

The usual emphasis on long-term investing, however, does not prevent the use of active management strategies. Nor does it necessarily preclude a trust investment strategy that makes competent use of investments or techniques that are often characterized as risky or "speculative." Such investments (for example, real estate and venture capital) or techniques (for example, borrowing and options or futures transactions) are not prohibited as long as they are employed in a manner that is prudently designed to reduce the overall risk of the trust portfolio or to allow the trust, in appropriate circumstances, to achieve a higher return expectation without a disproportionate increase in the overall level of portfolio risk. Furthermore, although it is ordinarily helpful in justifying the reasonableness of a trustee's conduct to show that an investment or strategy is widely used by trustees in comparable trust situations, the absence of such use does not render imprudent the informed, careful use of unconventional assets or techniques.

In short, the prudent investor rule, despite its requirement of caution, does not classify specific investments or courses of action as prudent or imprudent in the abstract. The rule recognizes that what may be underproductive of trust accounting income or risky—or even characterized as speculative—in isolation, or in a different context, may play a role in an investment strategy that contributes to the trustee's compliance with the requirement of caution. . . . .

Although a general requirement of conservatism in investing is normally inferred from the duty to use caution, the degree of conservatism required and thus the degree of risk permitted for a particular trust is ultimately a matter for interpretation and judgment. This requires that a trustee make reasonable efforts to ascertain the purposes of the trust and to understand the types of investments suitable to those purposes in light of all the relevant circumstances. These investment judgments may also be affected by the fact that a special type of trust is involved, such as certain pension funds and charitable trusts.

Unfortunately, it is much easier to acknowledge the importance of trust purposes than it is to identify them with a specificity that would provide clear guidance in setting trust investment objectives. As a result, especially but not solely with regard to private trusts, the degree-of-risk question sometimes has to be dealt with rather abstractly. It is, however, generally approached with a conservative bias.

Despite variations and flexibility in all of these matters, one pervasive generalization prevails concerning the prudent investor's duty of caution: reasonably sound diversification is fundamental to the management of risk, regardless of the level of conservatism or risk appropriate to the trust in question. Therefore, trustees ordinarily have a duty to diversify investments. See Comment *g*, below. The purpose of diversification (apart from the role it may play in discharging the trustee's duty of impartiality) is not only to moderate risks that are inherent in investing but also to reduce risks that are not justified by some prospect of gain.

Illustration:

11. T is trustee of a trust that pays its income to L for life, with remainder thereafter to pass to R or R's issue. T has adopted a continuous, long-term strategy of investing the trust estate in short-term bank and federal obligations. Although in a sense cautious, this investment program would ordinarily be viewed as failing to take adequate account of the fiduciary duty of caution as it applies to safeguarding the real value of capital, and even of protecting L's longer-range interests with respect to income. Thus, unless specially justified by T, the investment program is improper for a trust with the above beneficial provisions.

The amount and stability of income are important considerations in investing trust funds, but so is preservation of the trust estate. The latter objective ordinarily includes protecting the purchasing power of principal and usually that of its income stream in the future, here over L's lifetime.

Possible justifications for the pattern of investment in Illustration 11 are discussed in connection with Illustration 7, above, involving the often related duty of impartiality. In addition, secure, short-term debt investments like those in Illustration 11 may well be acceptable and prudent in the case of a trust of relatively short duration administered, for example, primarily for the benefit of one beneficiary until he or she attains a specified age. Or, even assuming fundamentally different successive beneficial interests, such a pattern of investment may be suitable to a trust in which either the investment program may properly favor the income beneficiary (for example, if this is a permissible alternative to invading principal) or the amount of income does not determine the rights of the various beneficiaries (such as when income may be accumulated or when distributions are based on support needs). Compare generally Comment *i* (on impartiality) and Comment *g* (on diversification), below. See also § 79, Comments *e* and *f*. See further id., Comment *i*, and Chapter 23, on other means of assuring (through accounting adjustments) a suitable level of distributions to the income beneficiary while using an investment strategy that emphasizes greater total return.

Illustration:

12. W bequeaths her estate to T in trust for H (W's surviving spouse) for life, with any remaining principal at H's death to go to a defined class of W's relatives. T, personally a successful investor, invests the bulk of the trust funds in the common stock of three carefully analyzed and selected corporations of the "emerging growth variety" in which T had made his own fortune. This failure to exercise reasonable caution constitutes a breach of trust. Therefore, if the investments do badly, T will be personally liable for the losses that result from this breach. If the investments are successful, of course, H and the other beneficiaries of the trust will receive and retain the benefits.

The possible surcharge of T in the above Illustration is not simply based on the results obtained. The test of prudence is one of conduct, not one of performance. If liability results in this case it is because T, in violation of his duty of caution, has failed reasonably to diversify the trust's investments and also appears to have undertaken excessive risks in quest of high returns.

Failure to diversify on a reasonable basis in order to reduce uncompensated risk is ordinarily a violation of both the duty of caution and the duties of care and skill. . . . . [A]lso see Comment *m*, below, on the use of mutual funds and other pooled-investment arrangements for this purpose. On the other hand, the prudent investor rule is considerably more flexible in addressing questions concerning the degree of compensated risk, essentially questions of conservatism. This flexibility is appropriate because of the tradeoff between risk and expected return, and because a consideration of the purposes, obligations, and circumstances of the trust is proper in evaluating the suitability of a trustee's investment strategy. Nevertheless, the facts of Illustration 12 suggest no justification for the described degree of commitment to a high-risk-and-reward strategy. The reason, however, is not that the investment of trust funds in relatively unestablished enterprises is impermissible if done in a prudent manner in appropriate trust situations. See Comment *p*, below . . . .

On the measure of loss from a violation of the duty to diversify, or from other breaches of trust, see Chapter 19; and also see id. on the question whether, if one of the corporations in the foregoing Illustration had performed very poorly and the others had done well, the gains and the losses from multiple breaches of trust may be offset.

Comment on Prudent Investing:

f. Background principles for prudent investing. There are no universally accepted and enduring theories of financial markets or prescriptions for investment that can provide clear and specific guidance to trustees and courts. Varied approaches to the prudent investment of trust funds are therefore permitted by the law. This does not mean, however, that the legal standard of prudence is without substantive content or that there are no principles by which the fiduciary's conduct may be guided and judged. A trustee's approach to investing must be reasonably supported in concept and must be implemented with proper care, skill, and caution. Furthermore, although competing theories of investment provide some conflicting signals, they also offer some consistent themes with respect to matters on which there is general agreement.

Generalizations based on the latter are central to understanding and applying the prudence standard of this section. See particularly paragraphs (1) through (5) at the end of the Introductory Note, above, to this Chapter 17 for a summary of the principles developed throughout this section. . . . .

Beyond the general principles discussed in Comments *d* (on care and skill) and *e* (caution), above, several generalizations are appropriate to note concerning prudent investing by trustees:

(1) Trustees, like other prudent investors, prefer (and, as fiduciaries, ordinarily have a duty to seek) the lowest level of risk and cost for a particular level of expected return—or, inversely, the highest return for a given level of risk and cost.

(2) Specific investments or techniques are not per se prudent or imprudent. The riskiness of a specific property, and thus the propriety of its inclusion in the trust estate, is not judged in the abstract but in terms of its anticipated effect on the particular trust's portfolio. (See Comment *g*, below.) The same is true of specific courses of action, such as the "defensive" use of options seeking to reduce the risk of an investment strategy and to do so at a lower "price" in terms of program goals than might be exacted by converting to a more conservative portfolio of assets.

(3) Diversification is fundamental to the management of risk and is therefore a pervasive consideration in prudent investment management. So far as practical, the duty to diversify ordinarily applies even within a portion of a trust portfolio that is limited to assets of a particular type or having special characteristics.

(4) Relatively "passive" investors raise the expected return of efficient, diversified portfolios by increasing their degree of market risk. This increase in risk requires a fiduciary judgment that a trust, in light of the amounts and timing of its cash needs and obligations, is in a position to accept the resulting risk of greater volatility in asset values, and therefore in portfolio performance for any given year or period. (Thus, a particular danger to be considered is that of having to raise significant amounts of cash for distribution in a down market.) The volatility associated with a strategy involving increased risk will ordinarily have considerably more impact on the trust's principal account than on its income account.

(5) Departure from an ordinarily suitable, diversified portfolio may be justified by special circumstances or opportunities of a particular trust or by peculiar risks facing its beneficiary families. Departures might also be justified by: specialized investment capabilities of or available to the trustee; special interests or managerial abilities of beneficiaries; or special settlor objectives, including particular asset holdings that are preferred or encouraged by the terms of the trust (see § 91, Comments *d* through *g*). The greater the departure, the heavier the trustee's burden to justify the strategy in question.

g. Risk and the requirement of diversification. The objective of prudent risk management imposes on the trustee a duty to diversify trust investments unless, under the circumstances, the objectives of both prudent risk management and impartiality can be satisfied without doing so, or unless special considerations make it prudent not to diversify in the particular trust situation. On the relationship of the diversification requirement to the trustee's duty of impartiality, see Comment *i*, below, and also Illustration 7 in Comment *c*, above. See also, especially when Treasury and other essentially "safe" debt securities are involved, Illustration 11 and the accompanying discussion in Comment *e(1)*, above.

Asset allocation decisions are a fundamental aspect of an investment strategy, and are a starting point in formulating a plan of diversification (as well as an expression of judgments concerning suitable risk-return objectives). These decisions deal with the categories of investments to be included in a trust portfolio and the portions of the trust estate to be allocated to each. These decisions are subject to adjustment from time to time as changes occur in the portfolio, in economic conditions or expectations, or in the needs or investment objectives of the trust. Basic asset classifications might begin with cash equivalents, bonds, asset-backed securities, real estate, and corporate stocks, with both debt and equity categories further divided by their general risk-reward or income/growth characteristics, by the domestic, foreign, tax-exempt, or other characteristics of the issuers, and the like.

There is no defined set of asset categories to be considered by fiduciary investors. Nor does a trustee's general duty to diversify investments assume that all basic categories are to be represented in a trust's portfolio. In fact, given the variety of defensible investment strategies and the wide variations in trust purposes, terms, obligations, and other circumstances, diversification concerns do not necessarily preclude an asset-allocation plan that emphasizes a single category of investments as long as the requirements of both caution and impartiality are accommodated in a manner suitable to the objectives of the particular trust.

Investment values are based on projections of future return, which take account of changes in market price as well as cash receipts. Value depends, however, not only on expectations concerning average return from an asset but also on volatility and the risk of departures ("variance") from that average. For example, common stocks can be expected to outperform bonds in the long run but yet to have poorer returns—even negative returns—during some periods. Because investors are risk averse, they require extra compensation for increased risk. The investor's reward for accepting a greater likelihood of volatile returns follows from the lower market price at which the investor is able to purchase the investment.

Events affecting the economy do not affect the value of all investments in the same way. Thus, effective diversification depends not only on the number of assets in a trust portfolio but also on the ways and degrees in which their responses to economic events tend to cancel or neutralize one another. Consequently, an otherwise dubious, volatile investment can make a major contribution to risk management if the shifts in its returns tend not to correlate with the movements of other investments in the portfolio. This is a major reason why diversification is valued and why the prudence of a trustee's investment is to be judged by its role in the trust portfolio rather than in isolation. See Comments *e* and *f*, above.

As a result of the tendency of the value fluctuations of different assets to offset one another, a portfolio's *risk* is less than the weighted average of the risk of its individual holdings. A portfolio's *expected return*, on the other hand, is simply a weighted average of the expected returns of the individual assets. Thus, the expected return is not affected by the portfolio's reduced level of what is often called "specific" or "unique" risk—insofar as those terms are used to refer to risks that can be reduced by diversification. Other types of risk, however, are generally compensated through market pricing, so that the expected return from an investment or portfolio is directly affected by the level of these risks that cannot be diversified away—the so-called "market" or "systematic" risks. Accordingly, a trustee's duty of prudent investing normally calls for reasonable efforts to reduce diversifiable risks, while no such generalization can be made with respect to market risk. See discussion of risk management in Comment *e(1)*, above, dealing with the duty of caution.

Significant diversification advantages can be achieved with a modest number of well-selected securities representing different industries and having other differences in their qualities. Broader diversification, however, is usually to be preferred in trust investing. Broadened diversification may lead to additional transaction costs, at least initially, but the constraining effect of these costs can generally be dealt with quite effectively through pooled investing. See Comment *m*, below. Hence, thorough diversification is practical for nearly all trustees. The ultimate goal of diversification would be to achieve a portfolio with only the rewarded or "market" element of risk.

The rationale of the trust law's requirement of diversification is more than conservatism or a duty of caution, which admonishes trustees not to take excessive risks—that is, not to take risks higher than suitable to a trust's purposes, return requirements, and other circumstances. The general duty to diversify further expresses a warning to trustees, predicated on the duty to exercise care and skill, against taking bad risks—ones in which there is unwarranted danger of loss, or volatility that is not compensated by commensurate opportunities for gain. Thus, while risk-taking cannot realistically be forbidden, or subjected to an arbitrary ceiling, it is required to be done prudently. A central feature of such prudence ordinarily is the reduction of uncompensated risk through diversification.

This generalization does not apply to nondiversifiable, compensated risk. In constructing a portfolio, the degree of such risk in a trust's investment program is properly a matter of conscious decision to be made by the trustee, influencing, for example, the ratings of bonds a trustee will decide to hold in a portfolio of debt securities and the risk level of a stock portfolio. The trustee has an obligation to make this strategic decision after careful consideration of the risk-reward tradeoffs involved and after considering the potential cash-need consequences of the risk element in that choice. This decisionmaking is to be done with the general and flexible fiduciary duty of caution in mind. See Comment *e*, above.

h. Prudent investment: theories and strategies. Diversification is a common theme of modern investment concepts (see Comment *g*, above), and it ordinarily applies at all different levels of risk-return preference. Beyond that, however, there are endless variations in reasonable strategies for investing and for the prudent management of risk, with a variety of legitimate theories of investment to support and incorporate into these strategies.

For example, a relatively small trust pursuing a fairly conservative investment strategy can quite reasonably achieve a desired low-risk portfolio either by relying on suitable mutual funds (or other pooled-investment vehicles) or by holding a number of securities with a proper mix of volatility characteristics. Similarly, when appropriate to the particular trust, a relatively high level of expected return can be achieved by the trustee through the same types of essentially passive techniques but employing a higher-risk portfolio.

The alternative of buying securities of a number of companies, even assuming the trustee has (or obtains through advisers) the understanding and information necessary to select those securities in an appropriate combination, tends to involve relatively high transaction costs for a trust of modest size. Therefore, given the fiduciary duty to avoid excessive administrative expense (see § 88), the alternative of purchasing suitable mutual-fund shares may be more inviting to the trustee because it offers a means of obtaining much greater diversification for what will usually be a lower cost. This approach, however, also requires an understanding of the characteristics of particular funds, and attention as well to their management fees and other charges.

h(1). Passive strategies. Investing in index funds that track major stock exchanges or widely published listings of publicly traded stocks is illustrative of an essentially passive but practical investment alternative to be considered by trustees seeking to include corporate equity in their portfolios. It is one that offers the pricing security and economies of buying in essentially efficient markets. . . . .

Additional benefits may be derived from broadening the market coverage and thus the portfolio's diversification. This can be accomplished by direct purchase of appropriate stocks or through the use of pooled-investment products. The latter includes the possibility of investing in a fund that operates under an index formula encompassing a significant element of over-the-counter securities. Funds, indexed and other, are also available for investing in foreign securities.

Debt instruments are often well suited to simple, diversified trust investment programs and offer a convenient, readily available alternative for reducing the level of risk and expected return. A trustee may find it preferable, for example, to reduce risk by mixing a moderately risky portfolio with essentially "riskless" assets (such as short-term federal obligations), rather than by developing a low-risk portfolio for the entire trust estate. Lending by trusts need not be confined to investments with negligible risk but properly extends to corporate bonds and asset-backed securities, usually diversified through a mix of maturities suitable to the trust's cash-flow needs and the portfolio's risk objectives. The inclusion of debt investments also tends to enhance income productivity, which is usually an important element of the trust's return objectives. See Comment *i*, below.

Borrowing may play an inverse role to that of lending and is permissible for trustees, provided the tactic is employed selectively and cautiously. See

§ 86, Comment *d*. Prudent fund managers sometimes borrow as part of a strategy for appropriate situations (such as for a trust with a relatively high return requirement) in which borrowing serves as a reasonable means of raising anticipated total return. The objective of such strategies is to achieve the desired result with a more modest or efficient risk increase than might result from raising the risk level of the investment portfolio itself.

Other strategies of essentially passive, diversified investment may also be prudently employed by trustees to raise or lower expected return. These programs typically call for adjustments based on various characteristics in the selection or weighting, or both, of securities acquired for the trust estate in a systematic manner that produces a desired higher or lower overall level of portfolio risk.

h(2). Active strategies. Prudent investment principles also allow the use of more active management strategies by trustees. These efforts may involve searching for advantageous segments of a market, or for individual bargains in the form of underpriced securities. . . . .

Prudent risk management continues to call for a trustee's attention to the benefits of informed diversification within these activities. In fact, if appropriate to the particular trust, the use of vigorous research and investigation to introduce assets from the less efficient markets into the trust portfolio can be expected to contribute to its overall diversification and return objectives. For example, real estate tends to have a negative or limited covariance with stocks and bonds. Traditionally, it has also tended to offer a long-term hedge against inflation. See Comment *o*, below; also compare Comment *p* on venture capital.

Active strategies, however, entail investigation and analysis expenses and tend to increase general transaction costs, including capital-gains taxation in private trusts. Additional risks also may result from the difficult judgments that may be involved and from the possible acceptance of a relatively high degree of diversifiable risk. These considerations are relevant to the trustee initially in deciding whether, to what extent, and in what manner to undertake an active investment strategy and then in the process of implementing any such decisions.

If the extra costs and risks of an investment program are substantial, these added costs and risks must be justified by realistically evaluated return expectations. Accordingly, a decision to proceed with such a program involves judgments by the trustee that:

a) gains from the course of action in question can reasonably be expected to compensate for its additional costs and risks;

b) the course of action to be undertaken is reasonable in terms of its economic rationale and its role within the trust portfolio; and

c) there is a credible basis for concluding that the trustee—or the manager of a particular activity—possesses or has access to the competence necessary to carry out the program and, when delegation is involved, that its terms and supervision are appropriate.

In addition, the course of action and the overall strategy of which it is a part must be suitable to the particular trust in light of its objectives, risk tolerance, liquidity requirements, and other circumstances.

Illustration:

13. T is trustee of a moderate-sized, previously revocable trust established by her now deceased brother, B, who had served as trustee during his lifetime. The trust is now to pay its net income, plus principal as needed for support, to B's widow W for as long as she lives, with remainder thereafter to be distributed by right of representation to B's issue of a prior marriage. As encouraged by the trust terms, T liquidated the trust's real-estate holdings that B had managed effectively over the recent past. As this occurred T implemented an investment program that resulted in a portfolio of no-load mutual funds (a high-grade bond fund of mixed maturities, plus a stock index fund that tracked the Standard and Poor's 500 list and another indexed to the New York Stock Exchange), in addition to a small interest-bearing account and some Treasury notes and bills. Assuming these investments are reasonably balanced to suit the needs and purposes of the trust, this is a legally proper way for T to begin discharging her investment responsibilities.

The investment program above illustrates a plan of asset allocation and of diversification within asset categories that would ordinarily be both reasonable and simple for a trustee to follow. This is not to suggest, however, that fewer asset categories (for example, omitting the bond fund) or more (such as including shares in a suitable fund of foreign investments) would be inappropriate. See generally Comment *g*, above, on diversification and also Comment *e(1)*, above, on degree of risk. Nor does the nature of T's mutual-fund holdings in Illustration 13 suggest that pooled investing by trustees must be confined either to index funds or to no-load funds. See Comment *m*, below, on benefits, fund characteristics, and cost considerations in a trustee's use of pooled-investment vehicles; and see generally § 88, Comment *b*, on reasonableness of expenses.

Illustrations:

14. The same facts as in Illustration 13, except that, instead of the two index funds, T purchased common shares of 20 corporations for the equities portion of the trust estate. T made a reasonable effort to achieve informed diversification, which is not simply a matter of numbers (see Comment *g*, above); she gave due consideration to the portfolio risk level and to the size, distribution requirements, and purposes of the trust; and she received professional investment guidance as needed. T's investment program is reasonable and appears appropriate to the discharge of her investment duties, even though many advisers might prefer, if practical, having a greater (and others might reasonably accept having a slightly lower) number of corporations represented in the stock portfolio.

15. X bequeathed $2 million worth of property to a trustee with instructions that the funds be divided between two trusts, one for each of X's adult children and their respective families. These trusts were designed and created almost entirely for tax reasons and have the potential for long duration through special testamentary powers of appointment conferred upon the children. The trust's provisions are broadly discretionary with respect to the distribution or retention of both income and principal. X's children have been successful financially and are now independently well-to-do. They have also received outright the rest of X's substantial estate. As compared with the trust situation described in Illustrations 12 and 13, the trustee of these two trusts properly could pursue considerably more aggressive investment

strategies in which, for example, it might be appropriate to include programs involving real estate and venture capital. See Comments *o* and *p*, below.

The particulars of the investment programs in Illustration 15 should reflect the trustee's analysis of a broad array of considerations with respect to each of the trusts. The relevant considerations would include the beneficiaries' personal objectives, tax positions, independent financial risks and special needs, at least as far as these considerations are consistent with the trustee's duty of impartiality, the trusts' terms, and X's ascertainable purposes. On the absence of concern over income productivity in such a wholly discretionary trust, see Comment *i*, below. See also § 79, Comment *f*. The trustee would probably have considerable discretion to pursue the rewards of a relatively high level of risk. Thoughtful attention to broad diversification would ordinarily remain central even to these more venturesome strategies.

Comment on Some Special Duties of Trustees:

i. *Requirement of impartiality: income productivity.* The typical private trust provides for successive enjoyment by different beneficiaries. The trustee of such a trust has a duty of fairness to all of the beneficiaries and of impartiality among them. See § 79.

The obligation to act impartially applies not only between life and remainder beneficiaries but also among concurrent beneficiaries. Concurrent life beneficiaries may appear to be similarly affected by investment decisions but are likely to differ, for example, in their tax positions and in their needs or desires for income as against growth of principal. These problems may be eased by trust arrangements that provide separate trusts or shares for sibling life beneficiaries, but even then multiple potential remainder beneficiaries of each trust are unlikely to have objectives that are identical either among themselves or to those of a life beneficiary.

Similarly, the terms of charitable trusts may call for expenditure of income and preservation of corpus, thereby imposing on the trustee some duty of fidelity both to the present purposes and to the future protection of those or other objectives. See § 79, Comment *h*. Also, pension-fund management is likely to involve conflicts not only between the interests of employers and employees but between those of current and retired employees as well.

The requirement of impartiality in these varied contexts, usually complicated by vagueness of settlor intentions, has important investment implications. These appear primarily in the form of issues involving the "productivity" of trust investments, here meaning productivity of trust-accounting income. Most pointed and common is the competition between the interests of beneficiaries entitled to income and of those who may later be entitled to the principal.

The fact that an income beneficiary may also receive principal in the trustee's discretion reduces but does not eliminate the productivity problem, much as it diminishes but does not remove the related income-and-principal accounting questions. Similarly, if the life beneficiary's rights are discretionary but payable only from income, the significance of the possible underproductivity or overproductivity of investment properties is lessened but not eliminated. See § 79, Comments *e* and *f*. Wholly discretionary interests, however, with or without standards (such as "support") for the trustee's guidance, involve distributive interests that do not distinguish between income and principal sources, and therefore allow the trustee to disregard income productivity in managing investments. See id. Also, on varied forms of unitrust and annuity trust arrangements, see id.

The nature and significance of these productivity concerns vary with the trust's circumstances and terms. Usually, however, much is left to interpretation and inference. If a beneficiary is entitled to all of the net income of the trust, it is clear that the trustee has a duty to make the trust estate reasonably productive. But this does not make the character and extent of that duty clear. Thus, for example, the extent to which the needs, or any particular needs, of a life-income beneficiary are relevant to the productivity objectives of a trustee's investment program is a question of interpretation. See generally § 79(1), Comment *b*, and § 79(2), Comments *g–g(2)*. Note, however, that this duty with respect to productivity need not necessarily be accomplished through the trustee's investment program as long as it can be accomplished through accounting-related techniques, equitable or statutory. . . . . Also see § 79, Comment *i*.

Facts and circumstances in any given case may offer some illumination concerning the nature and extent of the productivity requirement. The terms of many trusts, however, simply direct that the beneficiary be paid "the net income," rather than, for example, "such amounts as needed for support." If the beneficiary relies substantially on the trust income for maintenance, and if invasion of principal is not authorized, ordinarily the inference is that the beneficiary's customary support needs are particularly relevant, although not controlling, in the trustee's determination of a productivity target. On the other hand, the fact that trust income will clearly exceed the life beneficiary's needs is merely one of various considerations to be taken into account. In any event, this lack of need does not permit the trustee, in setting investment objectives, to disregard altogether other concerns the income beneficiary may have about the degree of productivity, except upon the informed consent or request of that beneficiary. On consent, see generally § 97; and compare Illustration 18, below.

To whatever extent a requirement of income productivity places a trustee under a duty not to pursue an investment strategy unduly favorable to one beneficiary or group of beneficiaries at the expense of others, the requirement applies not investment by investment but to the portfolio as a whole.

It is therefore the trust estate, not any particular asset, that normally must not be underproductive of income. Nor does it matter that particular assets are overproductive, as long as the remainder interests are reasonably protected by a balanced trust portfolio that is not overly productive overall. For example, wasting assets are overproductive in isolation, and even corporate or municipal bonds may be so viewed because of inflation, but the presence of such investments in a portfolio may be offset by the inclusion of growth-oriented (low-yield) stocks in the trust estate. The purposes or provisions of a particular trust, however, may justify a portfolio that otherwise might be considered, as a whole, to be overproductive or underproductive (see § 79, Comment *g(2)*); or administrative adjustments, judicial modifications, or statutory elections may permit the trustee to depart from impartiality norms that would otherwise apply to the investment process (see id., Comment *i*).

In short, only when beneficial rights do not turn on a distinction between income and principal is the trustee allowed to focus on total return (defined in Comment *e*, above) without regard to the income component of that return.

In other trust situations, absent other means of meeting impartiality requirements, there exists a fiduciary duty to make the trust estate productive of trust-accounting income. The trustee then has a duty to consider two aspects of the productivity question. First, what is an appropriate level or range of income productivity for the particular trust? As noted above, this is a matter for interpretation and fiduciary judgment. See also discussion in § 79, Comments *b*, *g*, and *h*. Second, how should that productivity objective be incorporated into an overall portfolio strategy? In resolving the latter question the trustee is not governed by the productivity standard in the selection and retention of each individual investment. The standard applies to the portfolio as a whole.

"Overproductivity" problems involving depreciation, depletion, or other forms of arguable waste are initially problems to be dealt with through the applicable principal-and-income accounting rules. The problems of fairness that remain become matters to be addressed, if practical and prudent, through a balancing of the trust portfolio, or possibly (§ 79, Comment *i*) through equitable adjustment (or statutory adaptation if available). Thus, in such matters, as in the problem of underproductive properties, the trustee has a duty to dispose of or not to acquire an overproductive or underproductive investment only when an appropriate overall balance is not otherwise reasonably and prudently achieved. . . . .

Illustration:

16. T is successor trustee of a revocable trust established and previously administered by S, who recently died. The trust is now designed to pay its net income to S's spouse, L, for life, with remainder thereafter to pass by right of representation to the then-living issue of L and S. S's investment program during life was concentrated almost entirely on growth of capital, with a very low income yield. Now, however, as the trust portfolio is reviewed (as called for by § 92), the duty of impartiality will require that T give attention to L's entitlements as income beneficiary.

S, like the typical individual investor dealing with his or her personal funds, was in a position during life to concentrate on total return, without having to consider the principal or income ingredients of that return. Following his death, two new factors come into the picture. First, implicit in the terms of the trust now is a significant distinction between income and principal—a distinction not previously significant because of S's power of revocation, even if the trust terms had called for distribution of "all net income" to S during life. (Cf. § 74.) Second, there is also now a fiduciary duty of impartiality between the successive beneficial interests of L and the issue. These factors combine to impose a general duty on T to make the trust estate productive of trust-accounting. See § 79(2).

The duty with respect to productivity does not preclude T's retention or acquisition of specific underproductive properties, provided they are otherwise prudent and suitable investments for this trust. The underproductivity of particular assets may be offset by the relatively high income productivity of others. Thus, suitable asset allocation and diversification in such a case can be expected to provide a suitable degree of productivity for the portfolio as a whole.

Furthermore, portfolio reconstruction is not the sole means available to T for fulfilling the productivity obligation to L. . . . . On the principle of equitable adjustment, and on principal-and-income legislation granting trustees adjustment powers and elective unitrust options, see § 79, Comment *i* . . . .

The terms or circumstances of a trust, of course, may eliminate or modify the duty to make trust investments productive. This, however, is not readily to be implied and would not be implied solely from the facts stated in Illustration 16, that is, from the pattern of S's investments during life. On the trustee's duty with respect to original investments generally, see § 92.

Illustration:

17. The same facts as in Illustration 16, except that the trust terms also grant T the power to invade principal as needed in order to maintain L's accustomed standard of living. The significance of this additional fact is a matter of interpretation. The ordinary inference, however, is that this power justifies greater deference being paid to T's judgment concerning the inevitably somewhat vague standard of reasonable productivity.

The power to invade corpus is but one of a number of factors T is to consider in weighing competing obligations and opportunities relevant to an investment strategy for the trust created by S. That power does not abrogate the duty of impartiality. Under the terms of this trust, L is entitled to all of the net income of the trust, without regard to need (§ 49, Comment *c*(*1*)). The investment authority of a trustee may not be exercised in a manner that simply disregards such a life beneficiary's potential interest in receiving income, even if merely to enhance the personal estate of L in this Illustration.

Illustration:

18. The same facts as in Illustration 16 or 17, except that L consents to or encourages an underproductive investment strategy by T. T may now pursue an investment program that produces what would otherwise be an unreasonably low yield overall with an excessive emphasis on growth, provided the standards of the prudent investor rule of this section are otherwise satisfied.

The duty of impartiality is not breached if T proceeds as suggested in this Illustration because L, the only one to be adversely affected, has effectively consented to the underproductive portfolio. This result does not require satisfaction of all of the requirements for the modification or termination of a trust under § 65. It does, however, require a fully informed consent on the part of L. See, generally, § 97 and § 78(3), Comment *g*, for the requirements of effective consent by a beneficiary. Unlike the situations considered in § 65, the material-purpose doctrine (§ 65(2)) does not apply; nor does it matter that L's interest is subject to a valid spendthrift restraint (§ 58).

Illustrations:

19. A bequeathed and devised her residuary estate to B Bank as trustee for A's spouse and descendants. Under the terms of the trust, H (A's widower) is entitled to receive "such amounts of income or principal or both as B Bank shall deem appropriate for H's comfortable support and care," with the remainder to go by right of representation to A's issue upon H's death. (On the meaning and effect of this discretionary authority over distributions, see generally § 50.) Because the terms of this trust make no distinction between income and principal, B Bank's duty of impartiality entails no duty to make the trust property productive. Accordingly, although the normal duties of prudent

investing remain, B Bank may adopt an investment strategy that looks to total return without regard to the amount of the trust accounting income included in that return.

20. Other provisions of A's will in the preceding Illustration bequeathed specified sums to B Bank to be held in two trusts, each to be administered for certain charitable purposes. The initial corpus of one of these trusts is $250,000. B Bank is directed to invest these funds and to pay the net income quarterly to C Church for purposes to be determined from time to time by certain church authorities. The principal is to be held intact in perpetuity. In prudently investing the funds of this trust, B Bank has a duty to make the trust investments productive, as well as a duty to treat preservation of principal, including its purchasing power, as a consideration in setting investment policy. (See § 79, Comment *h*; compare, however, the effects of the Uniform Management of Institutional Funds Act §§ 2 and 6 (1972) or the Uniform Prudent Management of Institutional Funds Act § 4 (2006), if either is applicable.)

21. The terms of the second charitable trust mentioned in Illustration 20, to which A also bequeathed $250,000, direct B Bank to distribute $40,000 annually to C College to fund four $5000 scholarships each semester. This is to continue until the trust estate is exhausted. In investing the funds of this trust, B has no duty to make the investments productive of trust-accounting income and may focus entirely on total return. Prudent management of the assets, however, requires appropriate regard for the cash-flow needs and other objectives of the trust.

j. Duty with respect to delegation. In administering the trust's investment activities, the trustee has power, and may sometimes have a duty, to delegate such functions and in such manner as a prudent investor would delegate under the circumstances. See generally § 80. On the trustee's duty to select agents with care and to exercise prudence in monitoring or supervising their activities, see § 80(2), Comments *d(2)* and *g*. On the trustee's duty to avoid unwarranted or excessive costs generally, see § 88; with respect specifically to the trustee's right to be reimbursed for agents' compensation, see § 88, Comment *c*; and compare the discussion of layered management costs in Comment *m*, below.

The trustee is not required personally to perform all aspects of the investment function. The trustee must not, however, abdicate the responsibilities of the office and must not delegate unreasonably. Prudent behavior in this matter, as in other aspects of prudent investment management, cannot be reduced to a simple, objective formula.

With professional advice as needed, the trustee personally must define the trust's investment objectives. The trustee must also make the decisions that establish the trust's investment strategies and programs, at least to the extent of approving plans developed by agents or advisers. Beyond these generalizations, expressed in terms that are necessarily imprecise, there is no invariant formula concerning functions that are to be performed by the trustee personally.

Many factors affect the nature and extent of prudent and therefore permissible delegation. These factors include the almost infinite variety that exists in trustees and trusteeships, as well as in investment objectives and techniques and in the types, circumstances, and goals of trusts. For example, it would be impractical for delegation decisions not to take account of the scale of a trust's operations and the nature of the trustee's operating structure. Corporate trustees necessarily act through their employees; between that situation and the individual who acts as a trustee or co-trustee, however, there are many variations of trusteeship, encompassing, for example, institutional governing bodies, law firms, and panels of individuals operating with the support of full-time staff.

The trustee's authority to delegate is not confined to acts that might reasonably be described as "ministerial." Nor is delegation precluded because the act in question calls for the exercise of considerable judgment or discretion. The trustee's decisions with regard to delegation are themselves matters of fiduciary judgment and responsibility falling within the sound discretion of the trustee.

As in other matters of fiduciary discretion (see § 87), the trustee must not abuse the discretion to delegate. Accordingly, a court may substitute its judgment for that of the trustee in a matter of delegation if and only if the trustee has acted unreasonably, or has unreasonably failed to act. Similarly, a trustee's liability in a matter of delegation depends on a failure to exercise the required degree of care, skill, or caution.

In deciding what as well as whether to delegate and in selecting, instructing, and supervising or monitoring agents, the trustee has a duty to the beneficiaries to act as a prudent investor would act under the circumstances. The trustee must exercise care, skill, and caution in establishing the scope and specific terms of any delegation, and must keep reasonably informed in order to monitor the execution of investment decisions or plans.

In all of these matters the trustee has a duty to the beneficiaries to take account of all relevant circumstances. These include the knowledge, skill, facilities, and compensation of both the trustee and the prospective agents. Also of importance are such considerations as the size of the trust estate and the burdens and complexity of both the assets to be managed and the strategies to be implemented. Active investment strategies, for example, especially in low-efficiency markets such as real estate and venture capital, are likely to require the hiring of agents with special skills not possessed by many trustees, often not even by professional or corporate fiduciaries.

Illustrations:

22. T is trustee of a modest-sized testamentary trust for the family of the testator. Under the trust terms, T is granted broad discretion over distribution and accumulation of income, as well as power to invade principal. T is a close and trusted friend of the testator's family but is not experienced in investment matters. After an initial briefing by a lawyer and consultation with A, an investment adviser, T decides to invest the bulk of the trust estate in several mutual funds. After a discussion of various types of funds and their characteristics, including the charges associated with each, T approves a plan that calls for holding certain types of funds in approximately equal portions. T then authorizes A to identify suitable mutual funds and to purchase their shares for the trust pursuant to this plan. A is then to report the purchases to T, who is to review those reports as they are received. All of this is done, as planned, promptly at the outset of trust administration. T also authorizes A to continue making and reporting additional investments for the trust pursuant to the plan, as unexpended receipts periodically become available and as adjustments become necessary to maintain the portions of the trust estate to be

allocated to the various types of funds. Assuming adequate care in selecting the agent and adequate subsequent monitoring or supervision by T, this delegation does not constitute a breach of trust. See generally § 80.

23. The trustees of a large trust, after consultations and study, have reasonably concluded that it would be desirable as a part of an overall portfolio strategy to have a portion of the trust estate committed to a venture-capital investment program. They also have reasonable grounds for preferring to do this directly by holding the company shares in the trust estate, rather than by purchasing shares of some suitable stock mutual funds or other venture-capital pools. (See generally Comment *p*, and compare Comment *m*, below.) The trustees therefore wish to hire agents with specialized skills to manage the program. In this situation, substantial but prudent delegation is justifiable.

If a venture-capital program of the type contemplated in Illustration 23 is to be pursued, the trustees would have not only authority but a duty to delegate management activities in some reasonable fashion unless the trustees personally possess both the necessary expertise and the necessary time (even with the use of advisers) to manage the program themselves with the requisite degree of care, skill, and caution. Prudent delegation in turn requires informed, careful planning and arrangements. Thus, even in undertaking to delegate, the trustees must have, or obtain through the advice and assistance of others, the skill and time necessary to make a competent, careful evaluation of potential managers for the venture-capital program and to monitor their performance of their duties. It also requires that the trustees have or obtain the capacity to develop appropriate instructions and working arrangements and to negotiate an appropriate contract with an individual or firm selected for the managerial role.

Without the competence to select managers and to work out proper terms of a prudent delegation—or in the event convincingly qualified managers cannot be found for the program—the trustees may not proceed with their desired direct-investment alternative for accomplishing their objective through program managers. To do so would violate the proper conditions of such a delegation and thus the requirement of caution imposed by the prudent investor rule of this section.

Comment on Specific Investments and Techniques:

k. Background and general considerations. Early development of the law governing trust investments in England and in this country was in the hands of the judiciary. Some courts attempted to define permissible types of investments. Others sought to judge a trustee's investments case by case, asset by asset, sometimes without articulated standards and sometimes with reference to a generally conservative standard of prudence.

Thereafter, and continuing into the 20th century, statutes were widely adopted setting out so-called "legal lists" of permissible investments with varying degrees of specificity. In some other states an evolving "prudent man rule" prevailed in the courts, and through legislation this approach gradually spread to or was reaffirmed in most of the states. In judicial hands, general principles of care, skill, and caution were developed and applied case by case. As generalizations were articulated and guidance was offered to trustees in dicta, opinions tended to transform what had been decided as a predominantly factual issue in one case into a legal precedent for application in others.

Through these processes and experiences, general standards were often crystallized into subrules specifying the permissible types and acceptable characteristics of trust investments. This was done in varying degrees of definiteness and, although usually accompanied by recognition of some general requirement of diversification, tended strongly to judge and classify investments in isolation. Broad categories of properties and techniques came to be branded as "speculative," or not of "investment quality," and to be viewed as per se or presumptively imprudent. This was usually based on some perceived but undefined degree of risk that exceeded what the duty of caution would bear. The exercise of care, skill, and caution in establishing and implementing a suitable investment strategy usually was no defense in a surcharge action attacking a trustee's acquisition or retention of individual assets that were classified as "impermissible."

The terms of a trust or statute may still make a particular type of investment or course of action impermissible. See § 91; cf. §§ 70 and 85. Otherwise, under the prudent investor rule, assets and techniques are no longer so classified in isolation. See Comments *f* through *h*, above. See also discussion of caution in Comment *e*, above.

Thus, there is no arbitrary barrier to the competent use, in proper roles and circumstances, of options and futures transactions and other derivatives or of programs for investing in foreign markets, real estate, or unestablished enterprises. Even when the propriety of an investment turns on an issue of "income" productivity, as an aspect of impartiality rather than strictly as an element of prudence, the trustee or court is to make the decision not in the abstract but within the context of the trust's portfolio and purpose. See Comment *i*, above. Furthermore, beneficial objectives and the investment function may become so intertwined as to justify the purchase of financial products that might not ordinarily be thought of as investments. For example, an annuity may offer a reasonable means of seeking to assure that a trust's periodic distribution requirements can be met; or the acquisition and maintenance of a life-insurance policy may fit within the trust purposes as an appropriate type of benefit or protection for one or more beneficiaries.

Even though assets are not subject to some universal standard of risk, specific types of investments and courses of action certainly differ significantly in the nature and degree of the risks associated with them. Thus, specific types of investments and courses of action are likely to differ in the degree of justification required to support their use by a trustee. Justification will be largely in terms of the portfolio roles and trust purposes these investments or techniques are intended to serve, or perhaps in terms of some special competence of (or available to) the trustee. Accordingly, in selecting an investment with due prudence, the trustee must examine and weigh numerous factors about the asset and the trust circumstances with care and skill, and with an eye toward an overall level of caution appropriate to the trust at the time the investment is made.

Among the characteristics a trustee should consider in examining a contemplated investment are the following:

(1) Expectations concerning the investment's total return, and also the amount and regularity of the income element of that return whenever the beneficial interests or purposes supported by the trust are affected by distinctions between trust-accounting income and principal;

(2) The degree and nature of risks associated with the investment, and the relationship of its volatility characteristics to the diversification needs of the portfolio as a whole;

(3) The marketability of the investment, and the relation between its liquidity and volatility characteristics and the amount, timing, and certainty of the trust's cash flow or distribution requirements;

(4) Transaction costs (including tax costs) and special skills associated with the acquisition, holding, management, and later disposition of the particular investment; and

(5) Any special characteristics of the investment that affect its risk-reward tradeoffs and effective return, such as exposure to unlimited tort liability, the presence and utility of tax advantages, and the maturity dates and possible redemption provisions of debt instruments.

Thus, an analysis of the characteristics of the particular investment is related to the size and composition of the trust estate. Asset selection also requires sensitivity to the trust's investment time horizons and to the goals and needs of the trust.

In addition, as far as consistent with trust purposes, consideration should be given to the needs and financial objectives of the beneficiaries. The federal and state tax positions and other circumstances of the beneficiaries are also relevant, as are the conflicts that may result from the diversity of those tax and other circumstances. For example, a trustee must recognize that pricing and pre-tax returns are affected by the tax-exempt status of certain investments and that different beneficiaries are benefited differently or not at all from tax advantages. A particular trust situation may even involve a need to hedge against the accentuated risks that are likely to follow when there is a direct correlation between the way events tend to affect the investment under consideration and the way those events tend to affect the employment and resources of some or all of the beneficiaries.

On prudence considerations generally, see § 77, Comment *b(1)*.

l. *Stocks and bonds (and other debt instruments).* The investment programs of many modern trusts concentrate on the stocks of established corporations and on a broad array of fixed-income investments. These latter investments include: bonds of federal, state, and local governments; the U.S. government's short- and intermediate-term bills and notes; bonds of established private corporations; and certificates of deposit from banks and savings and loan associations, plus various types of commercial paper. Also widely included in trust portfolios are pooling vehicles for these assets, such as money-market funds and mutual funds holding bonds or stocks or both. See Comment *m*, below.

Under the prudent investor rule of this section, however, the permissible stock and bond investments of trustees are not confined to the "reliable" securities of governments and "established" corporations. See Comments *e* through *h*, above.

The variety of characteristics available in equity and debt securities offers a broad range of risk and expected return levels, plus important variations in other characteristics, all of which are to be considered by trustees. Because the categorization of financial instruments can be greatly misleading, these varied characteristics are to be examined, weighed, and balanced in the selection of individual securities as well as in the underlying (so-called asset-allocation) decisions that trustees have to make with respect to the general types of properties to be held in a particular trust and with respect to the portions of the trust estate to be allocated to each asset category (see Comment *g*, above). In selecting the individual securities to implement a portfolio strategy, trustees must take account of more than just the general or usual differences between debt and equity securities. For example, they should also take account of the differences in terms and circumstances among the bonds and stocks of different issuers, and also of the significant differences in the volatility of various debt instruments resulting from their differing maturity dates.

Historically, corporate stocks have provided greater total return over the long term than bonds but ordinarily entail higher risks to the trust estate, including the possibility of serious losses in principal value. Although dividend yields differ widely from one corporation to another, from a trust-accounting perspective the "income" productivity of common stocks is now considerably lower than that of debt instruments. Nevertheless, dividends tend to be stable relative to the volatility of share prices, and gradual growth of dividends over long time periods has historically served as a protection against declines in the purchasing power of trust income streams. Ordinarily a trustee may also justify the relatively high principal risks associated with stock investments on the basis of a compensating prospect of long-term appreciation in share values. Thus, a primary and proper attraction of common stocks is that they offer trustees a hedge against loss of purchasing power and may even, in appropriate trust situations, contribute to a deliberate effort to increase the real value of the trust estate.

With the flexibility offered by their differences in orientation as between high dividends and growth, the shares of major domestic corporations with solid earnings records have understandably held favor among most trustees. For their diversification benefits and other advantages, the shares of similarly well established foreign corporations have, particularly in recent years, found increasing acceptance as well. . . . . Nevertheless, with risks moderated by diversification (see Comment *g*, above) and with greater value fluctuations expected to be offset by increased gains in the long run, higher-risk domestic and foreign stocks are also permissible investments for trustees under the prudent investor rule. This is true even of the shares of the newer, smaller, expanding corporations referred to hereafter in the discussion of venture capital. The inclusion of high-risk securities in a trust portfolio, of course, requires a selection process and investment strategy suitable to the circumstances and objectives of the trust in question. See Comment *p*, below. . . . .

Similarly, both domestic and foreign fixed-income investments may properly be acquired by trustees, including the bonds of all types of private corporations and the obligations of federal, state, and local governments. Because of their varied characteristics, these securities are sought for a variety of suitable roles in trust portfolios. Overall, these investments tend to reduce both the risk level and the expected total return of the trust estate. They also tend to favor productivity of trust-accounting income, while exposing the principal (and, in the long run, income as well) to the risk of purchasing power impairment as a result of inflation.

At one extreme, the liquidity and virtually risk-free quality of short-term federal issues (currently, "T-bills") enable these investments to play certain useful roles in the management of trust funds. Treasury obligations issued for intermediate terms ("T-notes") offer higher rates of interest while being subject, as a result of their longer maturities, to substantial fluctuations in value as market rates of interest change. The maturity periods of long-term Treasury bonds, whether interest paying or issued at a discount, expose them to sometimes dramatic changes in market value as interest rates fluctuate in the market place. Thus, depending on the period remaining until maturity, these relatively "safe" Treasury securities involve various types and varying degrees of risk and opportunity for the trustee to take into account in constructing an investment portfolio. . . . .

Similar generalizations, with appropriate adaptations, primarily for different risks of nonpayment and potential differences in federal and state tax treatment, may be made with regard to municipal bonds and the bonds and other obligations of private corporations. . . . . A trustee's duties of prudence and impartiality, for example, require that account be taken of the tradeoffs—both the advantages and the disadvantages—involved in investing in municipal bonds, for the potential tax benefits of which a buyer "pays" via interest rates and pricing. The fiduciary should therefore carefully consider whether and to what extent the advantages may be relevant to different types of trust purposes and beneficiaries, noting even the varied tax positions of different individual beneficiaries.

Like stocks, corporate bonds vary widely in the practical characteristics they offer to trust investment programs. They have higher interest yields than comparable Treasury securities but normally have lower total-return expectations than stocks. Some corporate bonds involve little more risk of default than Treasury securities, while others are noticeably more uncertain. Like Treasury bonds, the prices of both corporate and municipal bonds, and thus their overall returns, will be affected by changes in prevailing interest rates. The impact on trust principal will depend on the bonds' maturity dates and also on any redemption rights the issuer may have.

Given the duty of caution, trustees tend to prefer bonds with top ratings and relatively short maturities. The utility and prudence of particular types of bond investments, however, like other assets, are not judged in the abstract. Professional projections of portfolio mixes suitable to specific return objectives may well show that reasonable goals for a particular trustee can be met, at lowest levels of risk, by including bonds of varying yields and maturities in the trust portfolio. With proper diversification, given the risk premiums involved, a trustee might reasonably conclude even that the inclusion in a particular portfolio of high-yield bonds with low ratings (or unrated bonds) would play a useful role in the trust's overall investment program.

In any event, as compared to common stocks, corporate bonds generally play a role of relatively low risk and reward in a trust portfolio, but to a lesser degree than do Treasury securities. And in balancing the income and principal interests of trust beneficiaries, bonds tend to add to current income productivity rather than to purchasing-power protection or growth. The degree to which the latter is so depends on various factors, such as whether the bonds in question are purchased at a significant discount and how applicable law treats bond discount for principal-and-income accounting purposes.

Interest-bearing accounts, certificates of deposit, and money-market funds or accounts serve purposes in the management of trust funds generally similar to the roles played by short- and intermediate-term Treasury instruments. Returns from these investments have traditionally been relatively low, but their convenience, liquidity, and safety (enhanced when federally insured) are especially useful in making modest amounts of trust funds productive for limited periods of time. In addition, money-market funds and other short-term obligations can serve more general roles in trust portfolios, and have been especially attractive to investors in periods of special concern over the prospect of inflation.

Illustrations:

For examples of trust investment programs and problems involving stocks, bonds, and other debt instruments, see Illustrations 7, 11, 12, and 14, above. The first two of these cited Illustrations, and the discussion in Comment *e(1)* accompanying the latter, address the nature and limits of the role diversification plays with respect to both prudence and impartiality when Treasury and other essentially low-risk debt securities are involved.

m. Common trust funds, mutual funds, and other vehicles for pooled investment. Many banks and trust companies have traditionally operated one or a variety of common trust funds in order to pool the investment resources of many trusts under their administration, allocating to each an appropriate number of shares in the fund. This has generally been done without separate compensation, with the trustee receiving only its regular fees for administering each of the participating trusts. (On the more recent practice of many corporate trustees of using proprietary mutual funds, now with near-universal statutory blessing, see § 78, Comment *c(8)*, which briefly reviews the compensation rules and concerns involved, reflecting inherent self-dealing issues; in most other respects the investment considerations are like those of other mutual funds discussed in this Comment.)

Use of common trust funds is supported under state laws either by special systems of statutory and administrative regulation or by enabling legislation (usually the Uniform Common Trust Fund Act) that relies essentially on Regulation 9 of the U.S. Comptroller of the Currency to govern the operation of these bank funds. Some statutes (enacted before the proprietary mutual-fund movement, supra) also authorize the creation of mutual investment companies, in the shares of which participating banks and trust companies may invest the funds of individual trusts under their administration. These various practices are intended to facilitate economical fund management and diversification of investments for small trusts and, in some states, for small corporate trustees.

The Federal Revenue Act of 1936 exempted common trust funds from being treated as "associations" for corporate income-tax purposes, provided the fund is maintained by the bank "(1) exclusively for the collective investment and reinvestment of monies contributed thereto by the bank in its capacity as a trustee, executor, administrator, or guardian; and (2) in conformity with the rules and regulations, prevailing from time to time, of the Board of Governors of the Federal Reserve System pertaining to the collective investment of trust funds by National Banks." In 1962 this regulatory authority was transferred to the Comptroller of the Currency.

Similarly, a vast array of pooled-investment vehicles are now available to investors generally. These investments include the shares of mutual funds and other so-called investment trusts or regulated investment companies. They offer trustees diversified holdings of stocks or bonds, or a mixture of both. Also available are money-market funds (see Comment *l*, above) and a broad variety of pooling vehicles for investing in mortgages and other asset-backed securities, real estate, and venture capital. See, respectively, Comments *n*, *o*, and *p*, below.

The use of pooled-investment vehicles by individual or other trustees is expressly sanctioned by statute in many states and by the terms of many trusts. In the absence of statute or trust provisions authorizing or restricting their use, mutual funds and other pooling arrangements are permissible investments for individual and corporate trustees under the principles of the prudent investor rule of this section. These investment vehicles particularly tend to facilitate diversification and to make specific management skills and facilities available to the trustee.

Like any other investments or techniques, pooling devices can be misused. Therefore, they must be employed or selected with care and with attention to how a particular fund's characteristics fit the trustee's investment strategy and the trust's productivity and other needs or objectives.

In considering or making investments of this type, there are many features of various mutual funds, closed-end funds, and other pooling arrangements for the trustee to take into account. Some funds are primarily oriented toward income and others primarily toward growth, while still others have balanced objectives. There are, for example, long-term, short-term, and mixed bond funds variously described by such more-or-less self-explanatory labels as "high-grade" and "high-yield" funds, each holding a collection of either corporate or tax-exempt municipal bonds; and then there are U.S. government bond funds. Also available are mortgage funds and money-market funds, plus varied types of stock funds. These last may be described in such terms as "growth and income," "long-term growth," and "aggressive growth," as well as "sector" or "specialized" funds and the increasingly important "international" or "global" funds. There are even difficult-to-categorize "hedge funds," as well as "funds of funds." So-called "all weather portfolios" are assembled to offer broad asset allocation as well as diversification within the various markets that are encompassed, all in a single fund. Pooled-investment vehicles may be actively managed or essentially passive, with the latter including (among others) a diverse array of "index" funds that track differently defined markets.

There are no-load funds and funds that have moderate to very high front-end sales charges. Some of the former, however, may have back-end (or "exit") loads or redemption fees when a shareholder later sells. Funds bought through brokers ordinarily involve sales commissions. Cost concerns with respect to funds that have front-end or back-end loads are accentuated when the investments are made for short terms or if early liquidations are likely to be required. Also important are annual deductions for management fees and possibly other charges that effectively reduce the periodic distributions to the trust, and sometimes significantly. Some mutual funds offer charge-free exchange privileges within a family of funds.

Concerns over sales charges, compensation, and other costs are not an obstacle to a reasonable course of action using mutual funds and other pooling arrangements, but they do require special attention by a trustee. Because the differences in the totality of the costs described above can be significant, it is important for trustees to make careful overall cost comparisons, particularly among similar products of a specific type being considered for a trust portfolio. See § 88 on the general duty to incur only appropriate and reasonable expenses.

Even assuming fiduciary care in comparing costs and avoiding excessive charges, fund managers inevitably must be compensated in one way or another. If the trustee also receives commissions from the trust, they must be appropriate to the duties performed; and overall management costs to the trust estate must not be unreasonable in light of alternatives realistically available to the particular trustee. Because multiple layers of investment management costs can be a serious concern, the amount of the trustee's compensation may depend on the nature of the investment program, the role played by the trustee, and the qualifications and services contemplated in the selection and remuneration of the trustee. Compare § 88, Comment *c*, on the expenses of employing agents.

The use of pooling arrangements does not violate prohibitions against commingling. The trust's interest in the fund in question is separate from the interests of other investors for purposes of the duty to segregate and earmark trust assets (see generally § 84) and for the purpose of allowing independence of action by the trustee. In addition, given this independence and a general ease of marketability (and distribution), the varied objectives of different investors are adequately accommodated by the diversity of the funds available.

Nor does pooled investing violate rules concerning delegation. Acquisition, retention, and disposition of the trust's interest in the mutual fund or other pooling arrangement are all within the trustee's control. Thus, for this purpose, the relevant securities are the fund shares held by the trustee, not the corporate, government, or other securities held in the pooled fund, much as any stock investment held in trust involves the shares rather than the internal assets of the issuing corporation. Even viewed as a delegation, however, the action would be justifiable and proper (see Comment *j*, above, and also § 80) as long as the investment is otherwise prudent for the trustee.

Pooled investing potentially offers special advantages to many trustees. These advantages are especially, but not exclusively, important for small trust funds (see diversification requirement, Comment *g*, above) or for trustees who possess the required minimal level of skill but lack specific expertise and facilities for the investment function (see Comment *d*, above). Properly selected funds may also play useful roles in the portfolio of a trustee who is a skilled investor but whose overall asset-management strategy calls for the inclusion of one or more rewarding but challenging investment programs. See, for example, Comments *o* and *p*, below, on real-estate and venture-capital programs.

Illustrations:

For an example involving the use of mutual funds (including index funds) in a trust investment program, see Illustration 13, above. See also Illustrations 3, 4, and 23, above.

n. Mortgages and other asset-backed securities. Secured lending has a long but occasionally unfortunate history in trust investment law. Various types of mortgages, deeds of trust, and other asset-backed securities have often been arbitrarily characterized as "prudent" or "imprudent" for fiduciaries.

These earlier practices of classifying secured-lending devices by some categoric test of prudence are neither justified nor practical. This is especially so in light of modern investment products available to fiduciaries generally and the variety and potential utility of specialized lending arrangements in the hands of trustees possessing the required competence. Thus, the trustee's use and selection of asset-backed securities, and the methods of investing in them, are judged not in isolation or solely on the basis of their particular characteristics but in light of their role and context within the trust portfolio.

The prudent-investor standard recognizes no simple rule of thumb concerning the percentage of an asset's value that may be advanced under a first mortgage, for example, and no arbitrary prohibition against investing in junior mortgages. Ordinarily, although first mortgages have advantages over second mortgages in the reduction of risk, the latter offer the compensating prospect of higher return. These and other generalizations about typical advantages of one class over another, however, may not hold when all of the specific terms and circumstances of particular secured obligations are compared.

The degree of efficiency of the various markets in which mortgages and similar investments are acquired, or the opportunities, challenges, and transaction costs when direct lending and negotiations are involved, are factors for a trustee to consider in this type of investing. So are the value and seniority of the security, the rate and possibly the variability of interest, and the risk of loss not only from default but also from exposure to inflation and fluctuations in market rates of interest. Like the volatility associated with long-term corporate or government bonds, the risks that rate shifts and inflation pose to the trust estate are directly related to the duration or remaining duration of a secured loan. Trustees must also recognize and consider a broad array of other matters, if and as applicable to a particular investment, including: the borrower's financial history and resources aside from the mortgage property; the reliability of appraisals; socio-political factors specific to the security, such as demographic and land-use risks; whether a particular real-estate "enterprise" is established, untested, or developmental; and the possibility that special terms may alleviate some of a junior encumbrancer's difficulties in controlling or influencing events associated with default. Because of the sometimes highly individualistic provisions of asset-backed securities, trustees have a duty to exercise the care and skill necessary to understand the risks and other characteristics of any such investment.

In addition, the trustee must take account of the usual considerations involved in trust investing, such as the confined return potential and the "income" emphasis inherent in this type of investment. Compare discussion of corporate bonds in Comment *l*, above. Also to be considered is the trustee's ability to diversify the debt portion of the trust portfolio.

A trustee's problems of transactional inefficiency and diversification with respect to these investments may often be dealt with through pooling arrangements. For example, an individual or corporate trustee may purchase shares of a mutual fund that sells pooled mortgage investments to the general public. See Comment *m*, above. Similarly, corporate or professional fiduciaries may directly operate mortgage pools, mortgage participation arrangements, and the like. Special problems that may arise concerning the duty to segregate and earmark (see generally § 84) can be handled by proper procedures. The fact that the trustee combines the funds of one trust with funds of other trusts does not make the investment improper. Thus, investing the funds of a trust in a participating interest in mortgages held by the fiduciary for trust investment is proper if the mortgages are properly selected and the particular trust's participation is appropriate to its portfolio and purpose.

The combination of size and marketability problems in mortgages and similar investments can produce special issues that may require sensitivity in handling potential conflicts among participating trusts. Questions of self-dealing by the trustee may also arise. The mere fact, however, that a corporate trustee advances its own money initially in acquiring mortgages for the purpose of investment by trust estates under its administration is not a prohibited form of self-dealing, provided the program can be implemented promptly and without concern over full utilization of the pool.

o. Real estate. Ownership of real estate by a trust differs markedly from a trustee's holding of loans secured by real estate. Earlier court decisions tended to disapprove equity positions in real property as trust investments. Although real-estate ownership involves special risks, investment in land is not prohibited under the flexible principles of the prudent investor rule.

There may be good reasons for a particular trust to hold equity positions in real estate, provided the particular investment or investment program fits the circumstances and purposes of the trust and can otherwise be handled in a prudent manner. In addition, the preferences and experiences of settlors often result in trust terms that encourage trustees to invest in real property and often to manage active real-estate operations.

Because of its importance as a part of the country's capital markets, real estate is a potentially valuable ingredient of a diversification strategy, especially in light of its limited covariance with publicly traded equity and debt securities. Historically, land has also tended to provide long-term protection against inflation. In addition, diversified real-estate holdings have tended to offer, with less apparent volatility, returns comparable to those of a diversified portfolio of marketable securities. Furthermore, with thoughtful selection of properties or structuring of ownership positions, a trustee can organize the elements of the return toward the enhancement of either income productivity or principal appreciation, as might be desired for a particular trust portfolio.

Despite the potential advantages of investing in real estate, it would not be prudent for a trustee to disregard the complexities, burdens, and special risks associated with a decision to commit a portion of the trust estate to such investments. High transaction costs are to be expected. In addition, the absence of regulated and efficient central markets that deal in largely uniform assets creates specialized problems and significant extra risks. Inefficiencies in pricing inevitably cut both ways. This is especially so given the hazards of appraisal. Also, risk as well as opportunity for gain results from the array of uncertainties that relate to location, such as demography and land-use patterns, trends, and regulation.

Furthermore, important differences in the potential for gain enhancement and risk exposure turn on the specifics of the structure, terms, and circumstances of each real-estate investment. Variations may involve matters ranging from financing arrangements to operating form to tax consequences of the diverse interests potentially involved. Some trust investments in real estate are likely to present challenging, ongoing management requirements. In addition, efforts to achieve diversification within the affected portion of the trust estate will be complicated by the combination of high unit costs typically associated with land and the general desirability of diversifying real-estate investments by both geography and property type when practical.

Thus, problems are likely to be presented by the concern many trustees will have, especially trustees of smaller trusts, over diversification objectives; problems are also likely to be presented by a need for the technical competence that is so vital to success in a specialized field. These problems invite cautious, informed consideration of the opportunities of acquiring real-estate limited-partnership interests or publicly traded shares of real-estate investment trusts and other real-estate pooling devices. Investing through real-estate pools may also alleviate liquidity problems, transaction costs, and inefficient pricing that are normally associated with investments in land.

Possibly more than other pooled-investment securities (see Comments *m* and *n*), real-estate investment pools and their management tend to require special care and scrutiny by a fiduciary. The trustee making major investments of this type should generally seek diversity in managers as well as in operational emphasis. Furthermore, reliance on these real-estate securities may detract from some of the above-mentioned advantages of direct ownership of land, particularly in regard to volatility but also in regard to covariance with stocks and bonds.

Despite these concerns, real-estate investment trusts, limited partnerships, and other pooling arrangements offer a means by which trustees can prudently invest in real estate, once a determination is made that such properties are appropriate to the needs and goals of the particular trust.

In brief, a trustee contemplating the investment of trust funds in real estate has the usual fiduciary duty to make, with care, skill, and caution, an analysis of the role the property is to play in the trust's overall portfolio and strategy, and also an analysis of the risk-reward tradeoffs involved. In addition, the trustee must recognize that special sensitivity and attention will be required either in selecting shares of suitable real-estate investment pools or in dealing with the competence and delegation issues that are virtually inherent in holding real estate directly as a part of the trust corpus. Accordingly, special care is required in making the choice between these two divergent approaches to a program of real-estate investment. See Comment *j*, above; also compare Illustration 23, above.

p. Venture capital. The roles venture-capital investments may play in the stock portfolios of trusts, plus some of the difficulties in using these investments, are touched upon in Comments *f* through *h*, above, . . . and also in the discussion of delegation in Comment *j*, above.

Under the traditional "prudent-man rule" as it was evolving, barriers initially existed with respect to trust investment in corporate stocks of any type. And later there remained distinct resistance to allowing trustees to purchase the shares of what are often described as "new and untried enterprises." . . . .

Today the proper use of the stocks of small and growing companies has become well accepted in the strategies of many prudent investors. Modern investment products, the practices of skilled investment managers, some bodies of federal legislation and regulations, and statutes in many states have all helped to modernize this aspect of trust investment standards. . . . . In effect, these developments have helped to bring about a recognition of the potential that venture capital has for a variety of appropriate roles in the current portfolio strategies of many trustees.

Under the prudent investor rule, the stocks of small, expanding companies ("venture capital") are not abstractly characterized as impermissible trust investments. By the time a company has become well established, with a long and stable record of earnings, the price of its shares and their performance in the market tend to offer a trust portfolio quite different rewards and characteristics than those that favorably appraised, newer companies offer to offset the risks inherent in holding their shares. Therefore, as with other investments and investment techniques, the propriety of venture-capital investments is judged not in isolation but in the context of their functions and the other assets in the trust estate. They are also to be evaluated more generally in light of the purposes, return requirements, investment time horizons, general risk tolerance, and other circumstances of the trust.

Even in what are otherwise appropriate circumstances, the trustee has a duty to the beneficiaries to use care, skill, and caution in deciding to proceed with a program of venture-capital investing, because the duty of prudence extends to the implementation of that course of action.

Despite the trustee's exercise of care and skill in selecting the investments in a venture-capital program, some of the enterprises in which the trustee invests are likely to fail, just as some of those selected can be expected to succeed. Accordingly, diversification ordinarily is an important consideration in such programs.

Critical, because of the challenges presented, are the process, criteria, and skill by which the trustee initially determines that the program contemplated can reasonably be expected to reward the risks and costs involved.

Similarly critical, in thereafter executing the plan, are the trustee's determination of the types of pooled-investment vehicles to be used, if that route is chosen. This will involve the selection of specific fund shares to be acquired, along with the monitoring process and related decisionmaking that will thereafter be required.

If, rather than relying on pooling arrangements, the trustee decides to undertake the venture-capital program directly through purchasing and holding the shares of a suitable mix of promising companies as trust assets, then it is essential that the quality of that process measure up. And so, in particular, must the very decision to proceed down this latter course. See discussion accompanying Illustration 23, above.

Whichever of these procedures is followed in implementing the decision to include venture capital in the trust portfolio, even assuming the requisite care is exercised, competence to perform the necessary functions will be needed. Reliance on pooled-investment vehicles may require skilled advice or assistance to a sufficiently informed and capable trustee who has the personal ability or the necessary guidance to understand investment advice and to assure that reasonable judgments are made. For a direct investment program, most trustees, even many corporate and professional trustees, will need to follow a prudent course of delegation. This in turn means that due care, skill, and caution must be exercised not only in the selection and supervision or monitoring of the manager but also in designing the extent, operating conditions, and other terms of the delegation. See generally Comment *j*, above.

In each aspect and stage of these procedures, the trustee has the duty, measured by the standard of a prudent investor, reasonably to ascertain that the necessary competence is brought to bear on the decisions and activities involved. Although supported by the prospect of an increased return for the trust estate, the trustee who departs from more conservative strategies to pursue a venture-capital program must cope with the special risks and burdens encountered in relatively inefficient markets.

Illustrations:

For examples involving questions of venture-capital investments by trustees, see Illustrations 12 and 15, above, in addition to Illustration 23 (mentioned above in this Comment).

p(1). Special situations. Factors comparable to those discussed above are involved when, in appropriate circumstances, a trustee decides to become involved in such "special investment situations" as leveraged buy-outs and purchases of turnaround enterprises. In these undertakings the risk and reward levels are high, liquidity problems are severe, and results turn on skilled, careful selection of the enterprise and its management. Thus, the challenges of advice and delegation are similar to those presented by typical venture-capital investment programs. The trustee must possess or have available the requisite competence to devise and implement a prudent plan of delegation; otherwise it would be imprudent to proceed even if the goals, resources, and other circumstances of the trust would justify an undertaking of this type.

§ 91. Investment Provisions of Statute or Trust

In investing the funds of the trust, the trustee

(a) has a duty to conform to any applicable statutory provisions governing investment by trustees; and

(b) has the powers expressly or impliedly granted by the terms of the trust and, except as provided in §§ 66 and 76, has a duty to conform to the terms of the trust directing or restricting investments by the trustee.

General Comment:

a. Introduction. The prudent investor rule of § 90 is subject to the trustee's duty to respect applicable statutes and the terms of the trust, as that duty is described in this section. See also § 76; and see id., Comment *b(1)*, recognizing that most—but not all—trust fiduciary law is default law and therefore not applicable to the extent permissibly modified by trust terms.

Nearly all states (as of 2006) have enacted a version of the prudent investor rule or comparable principles by statute. (See Forenote to this chapter.) Also, analogous principles have been enacted by statute in most states to govern investment practices of charitable institutions and have been adopted by federal statutes and regulations to govern investment practices of private foundations and major types of pension funds. (On the relationship between these special rules and the prudent investor rule, see § 90, Comment *a*.) In several states the investment authority of trustees remains somewhat more limited by statute, for at least some trustees, in the absence of contrary trust provision.

The terms of trusts often restrict, otherwise alter, or guide the trustee's common-law or statutory authority and responsibilities in investment matters, in either general or specific ways. These provisions sometimes leave important questions of interpretation to be dealt with by courts, trustees, and beneficiaries.

Comment on Clause (a):

b. Statutory investment rules. As noted in Comment *a*, most states have legislation adopting prudent-investor principles to govern investments by trustees; a few of these states have also preserved some traditional language of the so-called "prudent-man rule." The rule of § 90 applies to these various statutory rules, except as clearly inconsistent with specific provisions of the statute. The designedly flexible and general terms and objectives of the modern statutes should not be encumbered by adherence to or rigid interpretation of decisions emanating from different economic circumstances, lesser knowledge of financial markets, and now outmoded investment concepts and offerings.

Although now in general disfavor, more restrictive statutory rules governing investments, by at least some fiduciaries, still exist in several states. So-called "legal list" statutes may limit some trustees (absent contrary trust provision) or other fiduciaries to such specified investments as government securities, first mortgages on land, and, more recently, prescribed types of corporate bonds and perhaps stocks.

c. *Effects of restrictive statutory rules.* The effects of various restrictive provisions may differ from state to state, but restrictions normally are not construed as preventing a settlor from empowering a trustee to make investments other than those authorized by the particular rule. See Comments *d* through *h*, below. Even a trustee who confines investments to those authorized by a legal list may be liable for failure to meet one or more of the underlying duties of loyalty and impartiality or of care, skill, and caution, including a general requirement of reasonable diversification for most situations.

The propriety of a trustee's investment decision is ordinarily determined by the legislation in force when the investment is made, rather than by statutory or other rules in force at the time the trust was created. The terms of a trust, however, may provide otherwise. . . . .

Illustrations:

3. Some years ago, S established the trust of which B Bank is now trustee. At that time the applicable statute prohibited trustees from investing in the stock of private corporations of any type. Subsequent legislation in the state adopts the prudent-investor standard described in § 90. B Bank may now invest funds of the trust in corporate stock.

4. The same statutes and trust in Illustration 3, except that the terms of the trust expressly provide that the trustee may invest only in the manner provided by the statute in existence at the time the trust was established. Despite the subsequent enactment of prudent-investor legislation, corporation stocks are still impermissible investments for this trust.

Comment on Clause (b):

d. *Terms of the trust.* As a general rule a trustee can properly make investments in such properties and in such manner as expressly or impliedly authorized by the terms of the trust. See also § 90, Comment *b*, and more generally § 76. But cf. § 29, Comment *m*, and § 27(2), Comment *b*; see more generally § 76, Comment *b(1)*; and also see § 66 (on unanticipated circumstances).

In the absence of contrary provision in the terms of a trust (or in an applicable statute), the investment authority described in § 90 is normally "impliedly granted" (Clause (b), supra) to the trustee. Cf. § 85.

The widely adopted Uniform Prudent Investor Act (codifying the principles of this chapter) states: "The following terms or comparable language in the provision of a trust, unless otherwise limited or modified, authorizes any investment or strategy permitted under this [Act]: 'investments permissible by law for investment of trust funds,' 'legal investments,' 'using the judgment and care under the circumstances then prevailing that persons of prudence, discretion, and intelligence exercise in the management of their own affairs, not in regard to speculation but in regard to the permanent disposition of their funds, considering the probable income as well as the probable safety of their capital,' 'prudent man rule,' 'prudent trustee rule,' 'prudent person rule,' and 'prudent investor rule.' " Id. § 10.

e. Mandatory provisions. The terms of the trust may limit the trustee's investment authority in various ways. Authority is sometimes narrowed in a general manner, through restrictions or directions that govern investment objectives, policies, and techniques. Other restrictions are more specific in character. These usually either forbid the retention or acquisition of certain investments or types of investments, or they require that certain property or types of property be retained or acquired for the trust estate.

Unless violative of some public policy (see, e.g., § 76, Comment *b(1)*, § 27, Comment *b*, and § 29, Comment *m* . . .), such directions and restrictions are legally permissible and are ordinarily binding on the trustee in managing the trust assets, thus often displacing the normal duty of prudence. The trustee, however, is not under a duty to comply with an investment provision when compliance would be impossible (see § 73) or unlawful (see § 72). Nor is the trustee under a duty to comply with a term of the trust if a court order directs or authorizes noncompliance because, as a result of circumstances not anticipated by the settlor, deviation from or modification of the provision will further the purposes of the trust. See § 66. Indeed, under these circumstances, the trustee may have a duty to apply to the court for permission to deviate from the terms of the trust. See § 66(2) and id., Comment *e*. . . . .

f. Permissive provisions. The terms of a trust may broaden the normal investment authority of the trustee, either in general terms or in terms that are quite specific. For example, a general provision may lessen the degree of conservatism (see § 90, Comment *e*) or productivity (see § 90, Comment *i*) that would otherwise be appropriate to the portfolio of the particular trust. An explicit investment provision, on the other hand, might permit the trustee to invest in a specific security or type of property that would be impermissible, for example, under an otherwise applicable statute or because of the trustee's normal duty of loyalty. Similarly, a provision might specifically permit retention or expansion of the trust's holdings of particular property, such as assets that may be of special interest to some or all of the beneficiaries, even though this might otherwise be inconsistent with a normal standard of prudent diversification (on which see § 90, Comment *g*).

When a term of the trust merely authorizes a particular investment, or a particular type or pattern of investment, the provision is permissive rather than mandatory. (Contrast directions or restrictions in Comment *e*, above.)

The distinction between permissive and mandatory provisions may be significant in several ways. A trustee is not under a duty to make or retain investments that are made merely permissive by trust provision. Less clear is the degree to which the trustee may have to give special consideration to specifically authorized investments, as against simply omitting them from serious consideration. This is a question of interpretation of the particular provision.

In any event, the fact that an investment is permitted does not relieve the trustee of the fundamental duty to act with prudence. The fiduciary must still exercise care, skill, and caution in making decisions to acquire or retain the investment. Compare § 92, Comment *d*, and, more generally, § 86. Nor does mere authorization with regard to an investment or type of investment constitute an exculpatory clause (on which see § 96).

Whether and to what extent a specific investment authorization may affect the normal duty to diversify the trust portfolio (see § 90, Comment *g*) can be a difficult question of interpretation. Because permissive provisions do not abrogate the trustee's duty to act prudently and because diversification is fundamental to prudent risk management, trust provisions are strictly construed against dispensing with that requirement altogether. Nevertheless, a relaxation in the degree of diversification may be justified under such an authorization by special opportunities for the trust or by special objectives of the settlor. The trustee should recognize, however, that more is at stake in this matter than a construction that would attribute to the settlor a preference concerning desired degrees of caution and risk. A settlor may well wish less investment conservatism so that market risk may be increased in pursuit of higher returns, but impaired diversification also invites unrewarded risk for which the duties of care and skill normally require some justification. See also discussion of diversification issues in § 92, Comment *d(2)* . . . .

g. Trust terms conferring "discretion." The terms of many trusts grant the trustee "discretion" with respect to investments, often in relatively standardized language of will and trust forms. It is a question of interpretation whether and to what extent the settlor intended thereby to enlarge the trustee's investment authority or to broaden the scope of permissible investments. See generally § 87.

g(1). Under a prudent investor rule. A trust provision that authorizes investments to be made "in the trustee's discretion," or that confers on the trustee "all of the powers of an owner," is not ordinarily to be construed as granting the trustee wider latitude than conferred by the prudent investor rule. The terms of that rule authorize sound, discretionary asset management and are sufficiently flexible that trust provisions of these types are generally strictly construed. Accordingly, they do not ordinarily result in a broadening of the standard set out in § 90.

Trust investment provisions sometimes purport to grant the trustee "absolute" or "sole and uncontrolled" discretion. Such language broadens the trustee's latitude in investment matters but is not unlimited, and the trustee is subject to liability for abusing it. Extended discretion of this type does not, for example, allow the trustee personally to borrow from the trust estate in violation of the normal duty of undivided loyalty, or to purchase for the trust estate property owned by the trustee individually. See § 78. Nor can the trustee invest recklessly or in a state of mind not contemplated by the settlor. See generally § 87, Comment *d*. Such extended investment discretion, however, is ordinarily interpreted as lessening the degree of caution or conservatism ordinarily required of the trustee (see § 90, Comment *e*), and as permitting in general a greater than normal latitude in the development of an investment strategy. This might involve a more active strategy or a portfolio with a higher or lower level of risk and expected return than might otherwise be thought suitable to the particular trust, or it may allow the trustee greater latitude in judgments concerning the "income" productivity of investments. See § 90, Comment *i*.

Ultimately, the effect of a grant of discretion or of extended discretion is a question of interpretation. Even language of extended discretion, however, is strictly construed so as ordinarily not to relieve the trustee of duties of loyalty and care, or of general responsibility for risk management.

Furthermore, discretion or even extended discretion ordinarily is not given the effect of an exculpatory clause. On the nature and permissible effect of exculpatory provisions, see § 96.

g(2). Under a restrictive statutory rule. In the context of a statutory rule that restricts the investment authority of trustees (see Clause (a) of this section), it remains a question of interpretation whether and to what extent the settlor intends by a grant of discretion to broaden the scope of permissible investments. Here, however, narrow construction of general language concerning investment authority ordinarily is not appropriate.

Thus, the inference is that a grant of power to invest "in the trustee's discretion" or "with all of the powers of an owner" is intended to free the trustee from a "legal list" and to relieve the trustee of other statutory restrictions. The result is to bring the trustee's authority and duties within the prudent-investor principles of § 90. Again, there is a degree of strict construction that resists interpreting language of discretion as evidencing an intention to liberalize the applicable standards beyond those of the prudent investor rule.

Extended discretion, however, couched in terms such as "absolute" or "sole and uncontrolled," generally has a somewhat broader impact. It ordinarily has an effect with respect to statutory rules similar to the effect it has with respect to the prudent investor rule. See discussion above in Comment *g(1)*.

Illustrations:

9. The trust in question grants the trustee, T, "discretion" in making investments for the trust estate. The prudent investor rule prevails under the applicable state law. Absent indication of a different settlor intention, the provision does not affect the ordinary investment standards to which T would be subject, as those standards are discussed in § 90.

10. The same facts as in Illustration 9, except that the jurisdiction involved has a legal list that normally governs trust investments by T. Absent indication of other intention, the settlor's grant of "discretion" liberalizes the principles applicable to T's investment activities and brings the trust under the prudent investor rule of § 90.

11. The same facts as in Illustrations 9 and 10, except that the terms of the trust in each instance grant T "sole and absolute discretion in investing the funds of this trust." In the absence of other evidence, in either a prudent-investor or legal-list context, the provision reduces the degree of conservatism implied by the duty of caution. T is allowed more than ordinary latitude in taking or reducing risks that offer a prospect of higher or lower return, as T deems advisable. Also, absent indication of other intention, the provision allows T greater than ordinary latitude in matters in which income productivity and impartiality might otherwise inhibit a desired investment program, although compare § 79, Comment *i*.

T in Illustration 11 will still be required in all of these matters to act in good faith and in a state of mind contemplated by the settlor (§ 87). In the matter of impartiality, for example, T's program must not create unwarranted hardship to the life beneficiary or other results not likely to have been contemplated by the settlor. In addition, the clause ordinarily does not have an exculpatory effect. Nor, absent other evidence, does it abrogate

T's duties of loyalty and care or dispense with the need for reasonable management of risk.

Illustrations:

12. The same facts as in Illustrations 9 and 10, except that the grant of "discretion" to T is accompanied by form language stating that T has "authority to invest in all types of properties, including properties not normally permissible as trust investments." In a legal-list context this provision converts T's investment authority to that described in § 90. Under a prudent investor rule, the language has no readily apparent purpose and ordinarily is construed as reaffirming but not broadening T's normal authority, under which no investments are per se impermissible in any event. T remains, in both cases, subject to the general duty of exercising the investment authority prudently.

13. The same facts and language as in Illustration 12, except that the quoted provision goes on to add, in language somewhat similar to that found in many will and trust forms, "and without regard to the normal duty of diversification." This language is interpreted and applied with a sympathetic effort to ascertain and give effect to a transferor's purpose, even though the trustee's fundamental duty to act with prudence still applies, including reasonable consideration of the role diversification may play in risk management. (See generally Comment *f*, above, and Comments *e* and *g* of § 90.)

The language quoted in Illustration 13 is too general to reveal a definite purpose and yet too clear not to be respected. Thus, some reasonable effect is to be given to the quoted language, even though it may well be simply a carryover from traditional drafting practices that reflect concern over earlier, more rigid concepts of fiduciary authority and caution than those of § 90.

The effect of this added language is necessarily a matter of interpretation, justifying a court in looking more freely than it otherwise might to other circumstances, background, and settlor objectives that may give meaning and purpose to the words of the instrument. Nevertheless, drastic departures from a reasonable degree of diversification, and therefore of prudence, by taking on avoidable elements of risk without a compensating increase in expected return should be justifiable by T on some reasonable basis. Justification may be found in the settlor's purposes or in some investment objectives, such as that of permitting, for some discernible reason, a major commitment of the trust estate to some particular enterprise or asset holdings. Compare factors affecting interpretation of analogous language in the analogous situations that are considered in § 92, Comment *d* . . . .

When doubt exists regarding the interpretation or proper application of provisions like those above and when questions arise about the nature and extent of the trustee's authority, as distinguished from business judgments concerning the wisdom of a particular exercise of that authority, court instructions are available under the principles of § 71.

Comment on Informal Trusts:

h. *Informal trusts.* All of the states now offer forms of statutory trusts commonly called "custodianships." These may be created simply by complying with the modest mandates of legislation such as a Uniform Transfers to Minors Act. The terms of these trusts, including their investment provisions, usually are set out in some detail in the statutes. On the construction of the investment terms of these acts, see Comment *b*, above.

In some situations express trusts may be created without a writing, with the terms of the trust expressed orally. The trust intention, investment provisions, and other terms of the relationship may be proved by evidence of these oral communications. See § 13. If there is no proof of the intended investment provisions, in the absence of a contrary statute the investment provisions to be implied are those of the prudent investor rule of § 90. See Comment *d*, above.

Other express trusts may be even less formal. These "informal trusts" are created with little or no express statement of important trust terms, and often without express statement that the arrangement is intended to be a trust. See, e.g., § 5, Comments *c* and *e*, and § 13. For example, a person may hand over a check or specific asset to another, with some understanding, often vague, that the latter is to hold and manage the property as a trustee for the benefit of the transferor or one or more others. The beneficiaries are often the minor children or grandchildren of the transferor or transferee. It is not uncommon, for example, for grandparents to establish trusts for their grandchildren by casual payments (such as by mailing checks) to children, or to sons- or daughters-in-law.

The trust terms of a valid informal trust, including the trustee's investment authority and responsibilities, are governed by the intention of the parties, evidenced by their words and other conduct interpreted in light of relevant circumstances. Insofar as a trust's investment terms are thus established, they are controlling in accordance with the principles described in Comments *e* through *g*, above. Otherwise, in the absence of applicable statute to the contrary, the investment powers and duties of the trustee of an informal trust are governed by the prudent investor rule of § 90, with its inherent adaptability to the size and other circumstances of the trust.

Illustration:

14. At the birth of each of her grandchildren, X either delivered or sent a $10,000 check to their mother, X's daughter, D. On holidays and birthdays, X would also send D a check for the intended grandchild in an amount of $1000 or more. These transfers were occasionally accompanied by X's statements to the effect that the money was to "start a fund" or "open an account" for the grandchild's "future" or for his or her "education and other needs." The precise purposes and even the intended duration of the trusts, assuming trusts were intended, are less than clear. In the absence of evidence of contrary intention, however, the investment powers and duties of the trustee-parent are those of the prudent investor rule of § 90.

On investing the funds of informal trusts, often trusts of short duration, with small corpus amounts and administered by a family member for the primary benefit of one beneficiary, see the discussion accompanying Illustration 11 in § 90, Comment *e(1)*.

§ 92. Duty with Respect to Original Investments

The trustee has a duty, within a reasonable time after the creation of the trust, to review the contents of the trust estate and to make and implement decisions concerning the retention and disposition of original investments in order to conform to the requirements of §§ 90 and 91.

Comment:

a. Duty to restructure trust portfolio. The rules of §§ 90 and 91 require the trustee to manage trust investments as a prudent investor would in light of any applicable statutory restrictions and the terms, purposes, distribution requirements, and other circumstances of the trust. Because a trustee rarely receives a trust estate consisting wholly of cash, the relevant circumstances of the trust include its existing investments—so-called "inception assets." Thus, with the trust's investment objectives in mind, the trustee must review the original investments and, if and as necessary, formulate a plan for restructuring the portfolio to achieve a suitable level of risk and expected return with appropriate degrees of diversification and income productivity. See generally § 90, Comments *e*, *f*, and *g*. On the duty of impartiality, see § 90, Comment *i*, and, more generally, § 79.

The trustee must decide which original investments and how much of each to retain and, if adjustments are to be made, when and in what order assets should be sold or exchanged. These decisions must include a determination whether, under any applicable statutes and the terms of the trust, any property received from the settlor is an impermissible investment. The trustee must also determine whether the trust terms direct retention or disposition of any of the inception assets.

With respect to other property, the trustee's decisions about retention and conversion must take account of the suitability of an existing investment to the needs and the contemplated portfolio and strategy of the particular trust. Also relevant to these decisions are transaction costs and the tax consequences of sales or retentions. In some circumstances, for example, tax considerations (looking to the tax positions of both the trust and the beneficiaries) may tend to suggest retention of inception assets, and in others these considerations may tend to suggest that conversion be made promptly. . . . . In addition, the trustee's decision to retain or dispose of certain assets may properly be influenced, even without trust terms expressly bearing on the decision, by the property's special relationship to some objective of the settlor that may be inferred from the circumstances, or by some special interest or value the property may have as a part of the trust estate or that it may have, consistent with trust's purposes and the trustee's duty of impartiality, to some or all of the beneficiaries. Examples of such property might be land used in a family farming operation, the assets or shares of a family business, or stockholdings that represent or influence control of a closely or publicly held corporation. Compare Comment *e*, and also Comments *c* and *d*, below.

The trustee has a duty to make and implement decisions with respect to inception assets within a reasonable time. See Comment *b*, below.

A similar process of review and possibly of restructuring should ordinarily take place when additional assets are contributed to the trust or when there is a change of trustees. On the latter, in addition to noting the possibility of different skills or expertise, see § 76, Comment *c*, and § 85, Comment *d*, on the responsibilities of successor trustees. On the trustee's general, ongoing duty to monitor investments, see § 90, Comment *b*.

b. Reasonableness of delay. When a trustee has a duty to dispose of trust property, whether for the purpose of restructuring the portfolio or because the property is an impermissible investment, the disposition must be made without unreasonable delay following the creation of the trust. No positive rule can be stated with respect to what constitutes a reasonable time for the sale or exchange of such property.

The question in each case is whether, under all the circumstances, the trustee acted with prudence in making or delaying the sale. The question may be affected by the terms of the trust. It may also be affected by the trustee's investment strategy, and by long-term and short-term plans and opportunities for reinvestment. In addition, the reasonableness of the delay in making a disposition depends on such factors as: the nature of the property involved; the reason the trustee is required to sell it; whether appraisals are necessary; whether there is a ready market for the property; and the relative degree of price efficiency in that market. Even though the trustee has opportunities to sell the property, it may be proper for the trustee to delay sale in order to avoid selling at a sacrifice.

A trustee who has a duty to dispose of trust property may apply to the court for permission to delay the sale (see § 71), but is not required to do so.

A trustee may be held liable for losses resulting from imprudently retaining trust property or from unreasonably delaying its sale. An issue of alleged unreasonable delay is inevitably one of due care and judgment, with the reasonableness of the trustee's decision to be judged as of the time it is made rather than on the basis of hindsight. Compare § 90, Comment *b*.

Conversely, the trustee may be liable for a loss that results from accepting an inadequate price in selling at a time when it is imprudent to do so. For example, if inception stock has a special value because it represents or influences voting control in a corporation, it would be a violation of the trustee's duties of care and caution to fail to take that element of value into account in selling the stock. The mere fact, however, that the property appreciates in value or a higher offer is received after the property has been sold is not sufficient to render the trustee liable. In cases of these types the question is whether, under all the circumstances at the time of the sale, the trustee acted with prudence in selling the property.

c. *Retention of normally prohibited investments*. Statutes in a few states may still limit the types of investments a trustee is permitted to make (see § 90, Comment *b*), and even in prudent-investor jurisdictions a particular trustee may be prohibited from acquiring a particular investment because, for example, to do so would violate the duty of loyalty (see § 90, Comment *c*). The terms of a trust, however, may require or authorize the trustee to make investments that would otherwise be impermissible. See § 91, Comments *d* through *g*. A permissive provision of this type also has the effect of authorizing the trustee to retain similar investments if received as a part of the original trust estate. Id.

If the terms of an applicable statute make it improper for trustees to purchase certain types of investments, the trustee cannot properly retain inception assets of these types unless retention of such original assets is authorized by another statutory provision or by the terms of the trust. Statutes in many states and the terms of many trusts expressly provide that a trustee may retain assets received from the settlor at the inception of a trust, and these provisions should be interpreted to apply as well to assets later added by the original settlor or others, whether by inter vivos or testamentary transfer.

If the trust instrument is silent or the terms of the trust are otherwise unclear with respect to the retention of particular inception assets, it is a question of interpretation whether the terms of the trust include an implied authorization to the trustee to retain those investments. Specific mention of certain property in the will or other instrument by which the trust is established is ordinarily some indication of an intention of the settlor to authorize the trustee to retain that property.

If the trustee is in doubt whether the terms of the trust authorize the retention of ordinarily impermissible investments, the trustee may apply to the court for instructions. See § 71.

On the effect of expressed or implied authorization to retain inception assets generally, see Comment *d*, below.

d. Effect of direction or authorization to retain. If the terms of a trust direct the trustee to retain investments that were a part of the trust property at the time of the creation of the trust, the trustee is not liable for retaining them except as stated in § 66(2) or § 72. Except as provided in those sections, however, the trustee is subject to liability for failure to retain such investments. See Chapter 19; and see generally § 91, Comment *e*.

If a statutory provision or the terms of a trust authorize the trustee to retain inception assets, the effect of that authorization is similar to the effect of a settlor's grant of permissive or discretionary authority with respect to the making of investments. See § 91, Comments *f* and *g*. If such a situation arises in a state that has legislation generally restricting trust investments, the trustee's authority and duties with respect to the retention of inception assets are generally those of the prudent investor rule of § 90; in a prudent-investor jurisdiction the authority and duties of the trustee are generally unchanged. See § 91, Comment *g(1)*. Thus, if by the terms of the trust or an applicable statute the trustee is permitted but not directed "to retain investments originally transferred to the trust," the trustee is not liable for retaining them when there is no abuse of discretion in doing so. The authorization to retain, however, ordinarily does not justify the trustee in retaining such assets if, under the circumstances, retention would be imprudent. Compare §§ 86, 87. On the other hand, whether the jurisdiction has the prudent investor rule or a restrictive statute, subtle differences may result from permissive provisions expressly set out in the terms of a trust, particularly if the provision authorizes the retention of specific investments rather than applying to original investments generally. See § 91, Comment *f*.

Authorization to retain inception assets ordinarily does not authorize the trustee to purchase other investments of the same character when a statute makes investments of that character improper for trustees generally. Nor does such an authorization ordinarily modify the investment effects of the duties of loyalty and impartiality, although the question is ultimately one of interpretation. Relevant factors in determining whether an express provision authorizing retention applies to investments that involve a conflict of interest include: whether the authorization was general or specific; whether the conflict of interest was foreseeable by the settlor; and the purposes underlying the authorization. In general, compare the discussion and Illustrations in § 91, Comments *g–g(2)*. On the duty of impartiality, see § 90, Comment *i*, particularly Illustration 16 and ensuing discussion; compare, however, § 91, Comments *g–g(2)*, particularly Illustration 11 and ensuing discussion.

d(1). Extended discretion or exculpatory language. Sometimes a statutory or trust provision expressly grants the trustee "absolute," "sole and uncontrolled," or similar discretion to retain assets received as a part of the trust estate, or expressly states that the trustee shall not be liable for retaining such assets. Language of this type does not wholly insulate the trustee from judicial intervention or liability for abuse of discretion. See § 87. Such language, however, confers upon the trustee greater than ordinary latitude in the exercise of judgment with respect to the retention of inception investments, although it does not allow the trustee to act in bad faith or in a state of mind not contemplated by the settlor. See § 87, Comment *d*. Nor does it allow the trustee to act recklessly or in disregard of the fiduciary duty of loyalty. See generally § 91, Comment *g(1)*, and also § 86.

d(2). Diversification. Except as otherwise provided by the terms of the trust, the trustee is ordinarily under a duty to the beneficiaries to diversify the trust portfolio. Compare § 90, Comment *g*. This may require the trustee to convert investments received as a part of the trust estate even though those assets are not otherwise either improper investments for the trustee or of a type unsuitable to the trust's investment objectives. Thus, if a trustee receives a testator's residuary estate in trust and half of the trust estate consists of the shares of a particular corporation, the trustee is ordinarily under a duty to sell some or all of the shares and to invest the proceeds in other assets so that the trust portfolio will not, without some special justification, include an excessive amount of the securities of a single corporation or carry an unwarranted degree of uncompensated risk.

The duty to diversify, however, is not absolute. See § 90(b) and id., Comment *g*. With or without a general authorization to retain inception assets, other considerations may properly affect the trustee's decisions in these matters. Thus, the advantages of diversification may be offset by other aspects of the fiduciary duty to preserve the trust estate and the general duty, so far as consistent with the purposes of the trust, to serve the best interests of the beneficiaries. For example, the trustee should consider whether (or to what extent) disposition will allow the trust to realize and retain the full value of the property in question, taking account of factors ranging from tax consequences to special value a particular holding may have to the trust or to some or all of its beneficiaries. Settlor objectives, of course, are relevant to any such decision, insofar as they can be ascertained from the trust instrument, circumstances, and other admissible evidence of intention. The trustee's duty of impartiality is not to be overlooked in these matters. (See § 90, Comment *i*.) It usually presents income-productivity considerations that were not of concern during the settlor's lifetime. (See, however, § 79, Comment *i*.) And in some of these situations, the duty will require a difficult balancing or accommodation of significant differences that may exist in the needs or objectives of different beneficiaries.

Illustrations:

1. S bequeathed the residue of his estate to T in trust for C, his adult child, for life, with remainder thereafter to the issue of C. Forty percent of the trust estate distributed to T by S's executor consists of the publicly traded stock of X Co. S's will contains no reference to these shares, which are readily marketable at a fair price. There are no circumstances or other evidence indicating that S intended to encourage retention of the X Co. shares, or that they represent voting influence or other opportunity of special value to C or the trust. Absent special circumstances that might make it prudent to retain the shares, T has a duty to diversify the investments of the trust by selling a major portion of the X Co. stock.

2. A owned a large farm that she had operated with her husband, H, prior to their recent death in an automobile accident. A's will, executed five years before her death, would have specifically devised and bequeathed the real estate and equipment used in the farming operation (representing the bulk of her estate) outright to H had he outlived her,

and otherwise provided for an alternative disposition that would have left these farm assets equally to her two children if they had both attained age 24 by the time of her death. Because at A's death the children, D and S, were age 20 and 17, respectively, the farm assets instead pass with A's other property under the residuary clause of her will. The applicable provision of that clause establishes a trust for the children (with contingent provision for their issue), essentially until the younger attains age 24, when the trust will end, with D and S, if alive, then receiving the corpus. The will contains no language referring to the retention or disposition of the farm assets. Absent evidence of contrary intention, however, or circumstances making it imprudent or otherwise inappropriate to retain and manage the farm assets as part of the trust estate, the trustee's duty with respect to diversification here imposes no requirement that the farm assets be sold. These facts are sufficient to support a reasonable decision the trustee might make to preserve the farm assets and the opportunity they represent for D and S, provided the decision is implemented with care, skill, and caution and with continuing consideration and reasonable balancing of the needs and potentially differing objectives of the individual beneficiaries.

A general authorization in an applicable statute or in the terms of the trust to retain investments received as a part of a trust estate does not ordinarily abrogate the trustee's duty with respect to diversification or the trustee's general duty to act with prudence in investment matters. The terms of the trust, however, may permit the trustee to retain all the investments made by the settlor, or a larger proportion of them than would otherwise be permitted. Thus, a trust may be created by a will that directs or authorizes the trustee to retain all of the securities bequeathed to the trustee; or the will may provide that any or all such securities or some specific securities may be retained, as the trustee deems proper, without regard to the ordinary requirement of diversification.

It is a question of interpretation whether and to what extent an authorization in the trust instrument to retain property received as a part of the trust estate dispenses with or modifies the trustee's normal duty with respect to diversification. Among the factors that may be of importance in this matter are: whether, in effect, the settlor has intended to encourage or merely to authorize retention of the investments; whether an authorization to retain applies to specific investments, to particular types of investments, or to all property received as a part of the trust estate; the character of the original trust property in question; and the purpose of the trust generally, and especially any identifiable purposes underlying the particular grant of authority. See also discussion of extended discretion and exculpatory language in instruments and statutes in Comment *d(1)*, above; and compare § 91, Comments *f* and *g*, and more generally, § 87, Comment *d*.

In most instances, a trustee should not take a settlor's authorization to retain specific investments as special justification indefinitely if retention would otherwise be imprudent, especially if an apparent purpose of the authorization becomes outdated by changed circumstances or passage of time.

e. Duty to wind up settlor's business. Sometimes a settlor's estate is left in trust and the estate includes an interest in a closely held business or property employed in a business carried on by the settlor, alone or with others. In such a case, if the executor has not disposed of the property during estate administration, the trustee cannot properly retain the interest or continue to carry on the business unless authority to do so is expressly or impliedly granted by terms of the trust or unless, considering all the circumstances of the particular trust, it is prudent to do so. (Among the relevant circumstances are the skills of or available to the trustee. Cf. § 77, Comment *b*.) See generally § 90, Comments *e*, *j*, and *p*. See also discussion of diversification in Comment *d(2)*, above. On the reasonableness of a delay in disposing of such property, see Comment *b*, above.

A trustee who improperly continues the settlor's business is liable for losses to the trust estate caused thereby. (On what constitutes a loss, see Chapter 19.) If the business is profitable, however, the trustee is accountable for the profits.

The terms of the trust may authorize the trustee to continue a business in which the settlor was engaged, either for a limited period or for the duration of the trust. In such a case the trustee is not liable to the beneficiaries for losses incurred in carrying on the business in accordance with the terms of the trust, provided the losses are incurred without fault on the part of the trustee. Whether the will or other instrument creating the trust provides special authorization to continue the business is a question of interpretation. Language in the instrument merely granting the trustee discretion with respect to investments, or generally authorizing the trustee to continue "investments" made by the settlor, ordinarily is not sufficient to constitute a special authorization to continue to carry on a business in which a settlor was engaged. On other circumstances that may be important in these cases, see Comments *d–d(2)*, especially the discussion of diversification.

If the trustee is in doubt whether the terms of the trust authorize continuation of the settlor's business, the trustee may apply to the court for instructions. See § 71.

Even when it is not permissible under the circumstances and the terms of the instrument for the trustee to carry on a business in which the settlor was engaged, a beneficiary who, in accordance with the rule stated in § 97, consents to the continuation of the business cannot hold the trustee liable for losses incurred by doing so. Also, a court may empower the trustee to continue a business in which the settlor was engaged so that, for example, the business can be sold as a going concern.

As to the trustee's right to indemnity for expenses incurred in carrying on the business, see § 88.

As to the rights of creditors to whom the trustee has incurred liabilities in carrying on the business, see Chapters 21 and 22.

CHAPTER 18

REMEDYING BREACH OF TRUST: GENERAL PRINCIPLES

Introductory Note: This chapter deals with certain basic principles relevant to the remedies that may be available to beneficiaries (or others on their behalf) or to attorneys general (or eligible others) for the purpose of preventing or redressing a breach of trust by the trustee of a private or charitable trust. (Chapter 19 subsequently addresses matters of trustee liability, especially the measure of recovery for a breach of trust.)

Section 93 of the present chapter briefly defines what constitutes a breach of trust, and § 94 discusses the matter of standing to enforce a trust—that is, the question of who may maintain a suit against a trustee to prevent or redress a breach of trust. The next section, § 95, reviews the types of remedies that might be available to enforce or improve performance of a trust.

The remaining sections of this chapter (as well as the final Comment of § 95 on the possibility of equitable relief) involve matters that might in one way or another eliminate or limit the ability of beneficiaries to hold a trustee liable for breach of trust. Section 96 examines the extent to which an exculpatory clause in the terms of a trust may limit the liability of a trustee who has committed a breach of trust, and whether a no-contest clause may be used to inhibit trust-enforcement suits against trustees. The effect and meaning of informed beneficiary consent to or acceptance of trustee misconduct are the subject of § 97; and the operation and effects of the doctrine of laches and modern statutes of limitations are examined in § 98.

§ 93. What Is a Breach of Trust?

A breach of trust is a failure by the trustee to comply with any duty that the trustee owes, as trustee, to the beneficiaries, or to further the charitable purpose, of the trust.

Comment:

a. *Scope of section; cross-references.* Recognition of what constitutes a breach of trust (Comment *b*) is essential because a trustee is personally liable, ordinarily (cf. §§ 95–98), for losses attributable to a breach of trust, but is not liable for losses that are not attributable to a breach. Even if a breach of trust has occurred, surcharge liability depends on there being some loss of value or inadequacy of return to the trust, or some improper benefit to the trustee. See § 95, Comment *b*; but also see id., Comment *d*, on the possibility of equitable relief from surcharge. Other possible remedies for breach of trust are considered in id., Comment *c*. This section does not comprehensively address the subject of trustee liability for breach of trust, on which see Chapter 19.

The duties of trustees are not reviewed in this section. What various duties may require of trustees in various circumstances, as well as what conduct may satisfy or violate a given duty, are considered at length elsewhere throughout this Restatement, and particularly in Chapters 14 through 17 of this Part 6.

b. *Definition.* A breach of trust is a violation by a trustee of a fiduciary duty—that is, of any duty the trustee owes, *as trustee*—to the trust beneficiaries or to further the trust's charitable purpose(s). Thus, for example, "breach of trust" does not include a trustee's failure to perform a duty owed *individually*, rather than as trustee, to one who is a trust beneficiary. Nor does it refer to a trustee's violation of a duty to a third party (see Chapter 21 on liability to third parties), except as the trustee's conduct also violates a fiduciary duty to the trust beneficiaries or to further a charitable purpose of the trust.

A breach of trust occurs if the trustee, intentionally or negligently, fails to do what the fiduciary duties of the particular trusteeship require or does what those duties forbid, or if the trustee fails in performing a permissible act to conform to applicable fiduciary standards (see particularly § 86). Even without such personal fault, however, a trustee may commit a breach of trust by conduct (action or inaction) that results from a mistake (see further Comment *c*), typically a mistake regarding the nature or extent of a trustee's duties or powers.

c. *Effect of professional advice.* Questions of breach of trust often turn on the reasonableness of trustee judgments and whether the trustee in question has acted with proper care or caution. See § 77 on the pervasive duty of prudence. In cases of this type, typically involving *exercise* of the powers and performance of the duties of the trusteeship, a trustee's reliance on the advice of financial, legal, and other advisers is a significant factor in determining whether the trustee's conduct was prudent. See, e.g., § 77, Comment *b* (relating a trustee's need for assistance to that trustee's skills and experience) and id., Comment *b(2)* (reliance on legal counsel). Also, cf. § 80, Comments *d–d(2)* and *g* (duties and effects of delegation). Reliance on relevant professional advice does not afford a complete defense to allegations of breach of trust, for that protection should not apply, for example, if the trustee acted unreasonably in following the advice or in procuring it, as might be the case in shopping for advice to support a desired course of conduct. If, however, a trustee has selected an adviser prudently and in good faith, has provided the adviser with relevant information, and has relied on plausible advice on a matter within the adviser's competence, this conduct provides significant evidence of the prudence of the trustee's action or inaction in the matter at issue.

Traditionally, a quite different view has been taken of breach-of-trust questions involving mistakes as to the nature and extent of the trustee's duties and powers. (Contrast, e.g., Comment *b* of Restatement Second, Trusts § 201 *with* id., Comment *c*.) Mistakes of this type occur not only in regard to statutory or common-law rules, but also when a trustee interprets trust provisions as permitting certain action or inaction that a court later determines to be improper. A breach of trust may be found even though the trustee acted reasonably and in good faith, perhaps even in reliance on advice of counsel. Trustees can ordinarily be protected from this risk by obtaining instructions (§ 71) concerning uncertainties of law or interpretation; or the risk may be diminished by modern common-law doctrine or legislation softening at least some aspects of the traditionally strict application of various fiduciary duties. See, e.g., § 76, Comment *f*, on improper application or distribution of trust funds. . . .

d. Additional cross-references. Even when a breach of trust has occurred, a trustee's reasonable reliance on professional advice will be relevant to the possible avoidance of surcharge under § 95, Comment *d* (on equitable relief) or under § 96(1) (on exculpatory clauses).

On the duties (or rights) of trustees and successor trustees, and perhaps the rights of beneficiaries, regarding redress of professional malpractice, see generally § 76, Comment *d* . . . . Also, see § 82, Comment *f*, . . .; cf. § 80, Comment *d(2)* . . . .

§ 94. Standing to Enforce a Trust

(1) A suit against a trustee of a private trust to enjoin or redress a breach of trust or otherwise to enforce the trust may be maintained only by a beneficiary or by a co-trustee, successor trustee, or other person acting on behalf of one or more beneficiaries.

(2) A suit for the enforcement of a charitable trust may be maintained only by the Attorney General or other appropriate public officer or by a co-trustee or successor trustee, by a settlor, or by another person who has a special interest in the enforcement of the trust.

General Comment:

a. Introduction. Considerations of practicality, especially for charitable trusts (see Comment *g*), and the proprietary nature of beneficiaries' interests in private trusts have led to the development of rules regarding *standing*, such as those stated in this section. These rules limit the persons who may maintain suits against trustees for the enforcement of trusts.

If a trust has both private and charitable purposes (see § 27(1), Comment *a*, and § 28, Comment *e*), standing may be based on either Subsection (1) or Subsection (2) of this section.

References in this section and its commentary to suits against trustees include suits against former trustees (or their estates) as appropriate to the context. The reference to "beneficiaries" in Subsection (1) is to persons described in Comment *b*. References to persons "acting on behalf" of beneficiaries of private trusts or having "a special interest" in enforcing charitable trusts include, among others (Comments *c* and *d* and Comments *g–g(3)*), persons upon whom enforcement authority is conferred by trust provision (Comments *d(1)* and *g(2)*).

On the "enforcement" of noncharitable *purpose* (or *honorary*) trusts and of indefinite-beneficiary private trusts, see, respectively, § 47 and § 46(2).

a(1). Scope of section. This section applies to questions of standing to intervene in, as well as to initiate and maintain, proceedings regarding the enforcement of trusts . . . . The rule of this section does not, however, apply to proceedings that do not involve the enforcement of a trust, such as a suit against a trustee to protect a nontrust interest in a parcel of land or other specific asset in which both the plaintiff and the trustee hold undivided or successive interests (see § 2, Comment *c*) or to set aside a trust based on, for example, incapacity, fraud, or undue influence (see §§ 11 and 12).

The rule of this section does not prevent a court, on its own motion in the course of a trust proceeding (such as a trustee's accounting), from compelling the performance of the trustee's duties under the trust. Nor does the rule prevent a trustee who has committed a breach of trust from maintaining a suit against a beneficiary (Chapter 20) or third party (Chapter 22), such as the recipient of an improper distribution or transfer.

Comment on Subsection (1):

b. *"Beneficiaries."* A suit to enforce a private trust ordinarily . . . may be maintained by any beneficiary whose rights are or may be adversely affected by the matter(s) at issue. The beneficiaries of a trust include any person who holds a beneficial interest, present or future, vested or contingent. See generally § 48.

This includes a person who is eligible to receive a discretionary distribution (§ 50) or who holds a reversionary interest by operation of law, as well as one who has succeeded to a beneficial interest by assignment, inheritance, or otherwise. The holder of a power of revocation or withdrawal (§ 74) is a beneficiary; so is the donee of a special or general power of appointment, as is an expressed or implied (§ 46, Comment *c*) taker in default of appointment. See § 48, Comment *a*. Persons who might incidentally benefit from the performance of the trust are not beneficiaries (id.; compare, however, id., Comment *b*).

A person who holds a power to control or right to advise a trustee for the power holder's own benefit (see § 75, Comment *c*) is a beneficiary of the trust. See § 48, Comment *c*. The power holder has standing to enforce the trustee's duties regarding the beneficial power (§ 75, Comments *b* and *b(1)*) but not with regard to aspects of administration that do not affect the power holder's rights or authority. (On analogous *fiduciary* powers, see Comment *d(1)*.)

c. *Co-trustees or successor trustees.* If a trust has several trustees, one or more of them can maintain a suit against one or more others to compel them to perform their duties under the trust or to enjoin them from committing or compel them to redress a breach of trust. On the duty of a co-trustee to bring such a suit, see § 81. (That a trustee who has participated in a breach of trust may be prevented by the court from maintaining a suit against the other trustee-participants, because of a conflict of interest, even though the suit is on behalf of the beneficiaries, compare § 107, Comments *c(2)* and *d*.)

If a trustee who commits a breach of trust is thereafter removed or otherwise ceases to serve as trustee, a successor trustee can maintain a suit against the former trustee (or that trustee's personal representative) to redress the breach of trust. On the successor's duty to bring such a suit, see § 76, Comment *d*.

If a trustee who commits a breach of trust is not removed but continues to serve as trustee, a beneficiary may bring suit to redress the breach or, if preferable, a trustee ad litem may be appointed for that purpose. (See § 37, Comment *g*, ...)

d. *Others acting on behalf of beneficiaries.* If a beneficiary is under an incapacity, suit may be brought against a trustee on behalf of that beneficiary by a personal fiduciary (conservator, natural or legally appointed guardian, or the like, or an agent so empowered under a durable power of attorney). Although the trustee in bankruptcy of a bankrupt beneficiary normally succeeds to the beneficiary's interest in a trust and thereby becomes a "beneficiary" (Comment *b*), a creditor holding a lien on a beneficiary's interest is not a beneficiary but nevertheless has the right, and standing, to maintain a suit on behalf of the beneficiary for the purpose of protecting the lien.

d(1). Fiduciary power reserved or granted by settlor. By the terms of a trust, the settlor may reserve or confer upon others the power to enforce the trust. The holder of such a power has standing, on behalf of the beneficiaries, to bring suit against the trustee, although the power does not prevent a beneficiary from acting on his or her own behalf.

Similarly, the terms of a trust may reserve to the settlor or confer upon others a fiduciary power (contrast *beneficial* powers in Comment *b*) to control or advise the trustee (§ 75, especially id., Comments *c–c(2)*) or to amend the trust (§ 64(2), Comment *d*). Such a power enables the holder to sue on behalf of the beneficiaries, but only to enforce the trustee's duties (§ 75, Comments *b, b(1),* and *e*) with regard to that power.

The character and breadth of authority sometimes reserved or granted by trust provision to one or more persons designated, for example, as "trust protector(s)" . . ., are so diverse and so subject to issues of interpretation as to preclude ready generalization about the nature and extent of a designated person's standing to enforce the trust. The principles, however, are analogous to those applicable to powers to enforce, direct, advise, or amend described in the preceding paragraphs and in Comment *b*.

d(2). Settlor, as such, lacks standing. Neither the settlor of a private trust nor the personal representative or successors in interest of the settlor can, *as such*, maintain a suit against the trustee to enjoin or redress a breach of trust or otherwise to enforce the trust, absent contrary legislation. This does not, however, preclude settlor-standing based on a retained beneficial power or interest (including by resulting trust) under Comment *b*, based on serving as trustee under Comment *c*, or based on a retained fiduciary role or power under Comment *d(1)*. Nor does it mean that a settlor cannot obtain standing to enforce a trust on behalf of incapacitated, unascertained, or unborn beneficiaries who are not otherwise adequately represented, by acting as "next friend" or otherwise by initiating suit with an accompanying petition for appointment as guardian ad litem.

Comment on Subsection (2):

e. Attorney General. Because the community is interested in the enforcement of charitable trusts, a suit to enforce a charitable trust can be maintained by the Attorney General of the state in which the charitable trust is to be administered. In some states, the local district or county attorney, or other public official, can maintain such a suit; as appropriate, references here to the "Attorney General" include such officials.

A suit also may be brought by the Attorney General on the relation of a third person, a "relator," who is liable for the costs that the state would otherwise be required to bear. The Attorney General, however, cannot be compelled to sue (or to allow suit) by the relator; and the Attorney General may exercise control over the conduct of the suit, and may terminate the suit and the authorization granted to the relator.

The Attorney General's standing to enforce charitable trusts (with or without a relator) is not exclusive. When, however, suit to enforce a charitable trust is brought under Comments *f–g(3)* by a person other than the Attorney General, the Attorney General must be joined as a party.

f. *Co-trustee or successor trustee.* A suit for the enforcement of a charitable trust can be maintained by one or more of several trustees against one or more of the other trustees. If a trustee who has committed a breach of trust is thereafter removed or otherwise ceases to serve as trustee, a successor trustee can maintain a suit against that former trustee to redress the breach of trust. Similarly, if a sole trustee who has committed a breach of trust nevertheless continues to serve as trustee, a trustee ad litem (see Comment *c*) may be appointed to sue for redress.

On the duty of a co-trustee or successor trustee to bring such a suit, see, respectively, § 81(2), Comment *d*, and § 76, Comment *d*.

Trustee standing is not dependent on authorization, or subject to control, by the Attorney General. (Contrast the role of "relator" under Comment *e*.)

g. *Person having a special interest.* A charitable trust need not have definite beneficiaries as required for the validity of private trusts. (Contrast § 28, Comment *a*, with §§ 44–46.) A suit to enforce a charitable trust cannot be maintained by persons who have no special interest in its enforcement. The mere fact that, as members of the public, they may be said to benefit from the performance of the trust is not a sufficient ground to entitle them to sue; that degree of public interest is to be represented by the Attorney General. Furthermore, the mere fact that a person is a possible recipient of benefits under a charitable trust is not sufficient, without more, to entitle that person to maintain a suit for enforcement of the trust.

A person who has a "special interest" in the performance of a charitable trust, however, can maintain a suit against the trustee to enforce the trust. The special-interest concept is not limited to rights or potential rights to receive benefits under a charitable trust, although the nature of a person's special interest may affect the extent of the person's standing—that is, the types of trustee misconduct the person may maintain a suit to enjoin or redress (see below).

The special-interest concept and its application involve a balancing of policy concerns and objectives. The special-interest requirement provides a safeguard for charitable resources and trustees by limiting the risk, and frequency, of potentially costly, unwarranted litigation; but the recognition of special-interest standing, in appropriate situations, is justified by society's interest in honoring reasonable expectations of settlors and the donor public and in enhancing enforcement of charitable trusts, in light of the limitations (of information and resources, plus other responsibilities and influences) inherent in Attorney General enforcement. . . . .

Special-interest standing, unlike the role of a "relator" (Comment *e*), is not dependent on the approval or subject to the control of the Attorney General.

g(1). Special interest in charitable benefits. Charitable trusts are often designed so that a particular charitable institution or purpose is to receive benefits from the trust or so that one or more identifiable individuals will become entitled to benefits under the terms of the trust. Thus, if the terms of a charitable trust require that its income be paid periodically to a particular incorporated church, hospital, school, or the like, the corporation can maintain a suit against the trustee (with notice to the Attorney General) for enforcement of the trust. If the trust is to benefit an unincorporated charitable association, suit can be maintained in the name of the association ordinarily (cf. § 43, Comment *d*) by the appropriate officer. Similarly, if the purpose of a charitable trust is to pay the salary of the pastor of a particular church, the pastor has special-interest standing (as does the church) to enforce the trust. In addition, a charitable institution that is designated in the trust terms to receive benefits upon particular circumstances has standing to enforce the trust so that the institution can protect (or assert) its interest under the trust, including under § 67, Comment *b*, in what would otherwise be a cy pres situation.

If a charitable trust is created to benefit the members of a described group of persons that is reasonably limited (though "indefinite" in the sense of § 28, Comment *a(1)*), one or more members of that group may be allowed to maintain a suit, on behalf of its members generally, against the trustee for enforcement of the trust. Thus, the purpose of a charitable trust to contribute to the costs of medical care for "needy residents" of a specified small town ordinarily can be enforced by any reasonably qualified member of the community. So, too, if a college is trustee of a trust the terms of which direct that its income be used to provide graduate-study scholarships each year to selected students graduating from the college, based on prescribed procedures and criteria, the trust purpose may be enforced by one or more of the current students who might reasonably expect to meet the criteria. The special-interest standing of members of a group described in this paragraph, however, would ordinarily be limited to suing to compel adherence to the trust's designated charitable purpose(s)—that is, to enjoin or redress breach of trust by diversion of funds to another purpose—a matter of common concern to all members of the potential-recipient group. Standing based on a special interest of this type ordinarily would not be granted, for example, with regard to matters of ongoing management (absent flagrant trustee misconduct that is tantamount to disregard or constructive abandonment of the settlor's purpose). . . . .

In recent years, stimulated by tax incentives, many property owners have granted conservation easements to governmental entities or other nonprofit organizations to be held (usually perpetually) for environmental, recreational, or other purposes that are "beneficial to the community" (§ 28, Comments *k* and *l*). Owners of adjoining land have special-interest standing to enforce adherence to the easement's charitable purpose, as in many circumstances do others (such as nearby or downstream landowners) who benefit significantly more than the public in general.

g(2). Private beneficial interests; and powers reserved or granted by settlor. If an otherwise charitable trust has one or more noncharitable beneficiaries, such as potential takers by gift over or resulting trust, those beneficiaries have standing to protect or assert their interests in the trust. . . . .

The terms of a charitable trust may reserve to the settlor or confer upon others power to enforce the trust, power to control or advise the trustee, or even power to modify the terms of the trust. Express powers of these types give the power holder a special interest in enforcing the charitable trust, and therefore standing, essentially . . . to the same extent that similar powers provide standing to sue trustees of private trusts under Comment *d(1)*.

g(3). Standing of settlor, as such. The settlor of a charitable trust has a special interest in the performance of the trust's charitable purpose(s). . . . . Accordingly, even without a retained property interest or power (Comment *g(2)*), the settlor has standing to enforce a charitable trust, subject to three qualifications.

First, if a nonprofit organization receives a restricted gift or devise that applicable law treats as a charitable trust (see . . . also § 28, Comment *a*), special-interest standing entitles the settlor to maintain a suit against the trustee-organization only to enforce the restriction—that is, to restrain the trustee from diverting funds from the specified charitable purpose without a grant of cy pres, and to compel restitution for any such breach of trust. (This qualification reflects a balancing of the concerns and objectives described in Comment *g*, third paragraph; see also Comment *g(1)*, end of second paragraph.) Second, when numerous donors contribute to the funding of a trust, only a settlor who is a major contributor relative to the trust's total funding has the required special interest; the safeguards and advantages mentioned in the next-to-last paragraph of Comment *g* would be insufficient to justify recognition of special-interest standing for all contributors to a fund-raising campaign. Finally, absent contrary provision or agreement, settlor standing is "personal," although exercisable by an incapacitated settlor's personal fiduciary (see Comment *d*) or by a deceased settlor's personal representative during a reasonable period of estate administration. . . . .

§ 95. Nature of Beneficiaries' Remedies

With limited exceptions, the remedies of trust beneficiaries are equitable in character and enforceable against trustees in a court exercising equity powers.

Comment:

a. General principles; scope of section. The remedies of, or on behalf of, trust beneficiaries are, with limited exceptions (below), equitable in nature (typically, for example, without jury trial) and granted against trustees by courts of chancery or other courts exercising equity powers. Even a trustee's express agreement to perform the duties of the trusteeship does not make those duties enforceable in an action at law.

A beneficiary is not prevented from pursuing an equitable remedy against a trustee merely because under common-law principles, or perhaps an occasional statute, the beneficiary is allowed to bring an action at law against the trustee for the same cause. The possibility of a remedy at law is not further dealt with in this Restatement, except to note that traditional principles allow a beneficiary to proceed against a trustee at law to enforce a right to a chattel or money if the trustee has violated an immediate, unconditional duty to transfer the chattel or pay the money to the beneficiary. (These situations are unlike a suit in equity to compel a trustee to restore misappropriated money, or a misappropriated chattel, that is to remain an asset of the trust.)

That the beneficiaries may affirm a transaction that constitutes a breach of trust, with the trustee accountable for any profits accruing to the trust as a result of the breach transaction, see § 100, Comment *a(1)*. Cf. § 97. (This ordinarily neither relieves the trustee of a duty thereafter to administer the trust properly, nor prevents beneficiaries from seeking other remedies for fiduciary misconduct under Comment *c*, below.)

b. Surcharge liability for breach of trust. If a breach of trust causes a loss, including any failure to realize income, capital gain, or appreciation that would have resulted from proper administration, the beneficiaries are entitled to restitution and may have the trustee surcharged for the amount necessary to compensate fully for the consequences of the breach. See § **100**. Alternatively, the trustee is subject to such liability as may be necessary to prevent the trustee from benefiting individually from the breach of trust. Id., Comment *c*.

c. *Other remedies*. In surcharging a trustee for a breach of trust under Comment *b*, or if no surcharge is involved because the improper transaction was affirmed or caused no loss, a court may impose one or more other remedies, as appropriate to the circumstances, for the trustee's misconduct.

These possible additional or alternative remedies include: ordering the trustee to account (cf. § 83); instructing the trustee as may be necessary regarding the terms of the trust or the powers and duties of the trusteeship (§ 71), including perhaps directing the trustee to administer the trust accordingly; enjoining the trustee to take or refrain from taking certain action(s) or otherwise to avoid committing a breach of trust (see, e.g., § 87 on abuse of discretion); setting aside an improper action of the trustee and, if necessary, compelling the trustee to recover property improperly distributed to beneficiaries (see, e.g., § 50 and § 104) or improperly transferred to third parties (§ 107); denying or reducing the trustee's compensation (see § 38, Comment *c(1)* . . .); removing the trustee (§ 37, Comments *b–f(1)*) and, if necessary or conducive to sound administration of the trust, appointing an additional trustee or a successor co-trustee (id., Comment *g*, and § 34, Comments *d* and *e*); appointing a temporary trustee (or a receiver or other special fiduciary) to take possession of the trust property and administer the trust, or a trustee ad litem to make certain decisions and perhaps to handle certain transactions (§ 37, Comment *g*, and see § 78, Comment *c(1)*, . . .); issuing such other orders or taking such other action as may be appropriate to the circumstances and in the interest of sound administration of the trust.

Court orders of most of the foregoing types are not limited to the present breach-of-trust context but may well be appropriate to other situations in which changes in trusteeship would, for other reasons, promote sound administration of a trust or in which clarification appears necessary. See, e.g., § 71 (on instructions), § 37, Comments *d, e*, and *g* (on diverse grounds for removing or adding trustees), § 78, Comment *c(1)* (on trustees ad litem), and § 83, Comments *b* and *b(1)* (on accountings).

d. *Equitable power to excuse trustee from liability*. The mere fact that a trustee has acted reasonably and in good faith may not be sufficient to prevent the trustee from being held liable for breach of trust. See § 93. If, however, the court concludes that, in the circumstances, it would be unfair or unduly harsh to require the trustee to pay, or pay in full, the liability that would normally result from a breach of trust, the court has equitable authority to excuse the trustee in whole or in part from having to pay that liability. Ordinarily, such relief would be based on a finding that the trustee had made a conscientious effort to understand and comply with applicable fiduciary standards and the duties of the trusteeship.

Illustrative of special circumstances that might justify equitable relief are: the judicial overruling of precedent, on which the particular trustee reasonably relied, concerning a relevant fiduciary duty or the construction of certain trust language; and a determination of fiduciary liability in a matter in which the trustee's conduct reasonably reflected typical fiduciary practice or a widely held view of the applicable law. Comparably excusable in some circumstances might be all or part of a trustee's liability for a breach of trust resulting from some aspect of delegating, or monitoring a delegation, to an agent (§ 80, Comments *d–g*) or co-trustee (§ 81, Comments *c(1)* and *e*), or perhaps resulting from a trustee's purchase of trust property, out of apparent necessity, to further the interests of the beneficiaries (which, nevertheless, would be a breach of the duty of loyalty under § 78; see id., Comment *b* . . .).

In determining whether and to what extent to grant a trustee relief from surcharge, it would be appropriate for the court to consider all circumstances of the breach and of the trustee, such as: what is reasonable to expect of the particular trustee (§ 77, Comment *b*, and id., Subsection (3) and Comment *e*); the sincerity of the trustee's efforts to understand and perform the responsibilities in question; and whether the trustee reasonably relied on guidance from legal or other advisers (compare § 93, Comment *c*), including whether the trustee was aware of the availability (in an appropriate situation) of court instruction (§ 71) and, if so, the reasons for the trustee's decision not to seek instruction.

§ 96. Exculpatory and No-Contest Clauses

(1) A provision in the terms of a trust that relieves a trustee of liability for breach of trust, and that was not included in the instrument as a result of the trustee's abuse of a fiduciary or confidential relationship, is enforceable except to the extent that it purports to relieve the trustee

(a) of liability for a breach of trust committed in bad faith or with indifference to the fiduciary duties of the trustee, the terms or purposes of the trust, or the interests of the beneficiaries, or

(b) of accountability for profits derived from a breach of trust.

(2) A no-contest clause shall not be enforced to the extent that doing so would interfere with the enforcement or proper administration of the trust.

General Comment:

a. Scope and cross-references. This section deals with two commonly used types of trust provisions that are either designed to protect trustees from liability for breaches of trust ("exculpatory clauses") or that trustees might assert as having the effect of insulating them from litigation over trust administration ("no-contest clauses"). This section describes the limits the law imposes on the effect that may be given to these clauses. These limits and the underlying policies . . . of the rules stated in this section apply as well to document provisions that might seek to circumvent these rules by wording or form different from typical exculpatory or no-contest clauses but designed to have similar effect . . . .

The no-contest clause is normally used to deter challenges to the *validity* of various types of donative instruments and their provisions, thus generally serving purposes other than inhibiting litigation to enforce a trust created by the instrument. The subject is therefore comprehensively dealt with in Restatement Third, Property (Wills and Other Donative Transfers) § 8.5. The present section considers only narrower matters affecting the enforcement and administration of trusts. See Subsection (2) and Comment *e* of this section; also cf. § 29, Comment *m*.

Subsection (1) and Comments *b–d* recognize the general validity of exculpatory clauses but limit their effect. Exculpatory clauses are to be distinguished from trust provisions that modify a trustee's powers and duties; modifications may affect the question of whether certain conduct by the trustee *constitutes* a breach of trust, whereas an exculpatory clause may eliminate or limit the trustee's *liability* when a breach of trust does occur.

Comment on Subsection (1):

b. Construction of exculpatory provisions. Except as stated in Comments *c* and *d,* the terms of the trust can relieve the trustee of liability for breaches of trust. However, these exculpatory provisions are strictly construed; the trustee is relieved of liability only to the extent the provision clearly so provides.

Furthermore, despite similarities of language in various exculpatory clauses, the intent to be attributed to the settlor and the effect to be given to the particular clause may depend on the circumstances of the document's preparation and execution or on the settlor's expectations about the circumstances to which the clause might apply. Thus, the appropriate standard for exemption from liability may depend on expectations about performance, as well as about the skills and facilities, of the trustee contemplated by the settlor, and perhaps on particular risks or concerns that (even if unexpressed) may have prompted the inclusion of the clause. A clause that apparently was designed, for example, for the settlor's spouse as trustee may be differently applied, or even found inapplicable, to a professional trustee who succeeds the spouse.

c. Effect limited by public policy. Notwithstanding the breadth of language in a trust provision relieving a trustee from liability for breach of trust, for reasons of policy trust fiduciary law imposes limitations on the types and degree of misconduct for which the trustee can be excused from liability. Hence, an exculpatory clause cannot excuse a trustee for a breach of trust committed in bad faith. Nor can the trustee be excused for a breach committed with indifference to the interests of the beneficiaries or to the terms and purposes of the trust—that is, committed without reasonable effort to understand and conform to applicable fiduciary duties. In some situations, courts have, not inappropriately, sought to distinguish between simple and gross negligence, while authorities in analogous contexts have emphasized fiduciaries' sustained inattention to their duty of care. It is not possible to state with precision and uniform applicability the permissible limits of exculpatory relief, especially recognizing that it is appropriate in this regard to take account of what may be reasonable to expect of a particular trustee. . . . .

d. Clause improperly included in terms of trust. If the terms of the trust were drafted by the trustee, or if the exculpatory clause was caused to be included in the trust by the trustee, the clause is presumptively unenforceable. Cf. § 78(3) and id., Comments *g* and *h.* The presumption is rebuttable, and the clause will be given effect if the trustee proves that the exculpatory provision is fair under the circumstances (including, when applicable, the fiduciary risks to be assumed) and that the existence, contents, and effect of the clause were adequately communicated to or otherwise understood by the settlor. Thus, if a father asks his daughter, a lawyer, to draw a will under which she is to act as trustee, and she includes an exculpatory clause in the will and the father is aware of its existence, nature, and effect when he executes his will, the exculpatory provision is effective.

In determining whether an exculpatory clause was included in the trust instrument as a result of an abuse of a fiduciary or confidential relationship, the following factors (as well as other relevant factors) may be considered: whether the instrument was drawn by the trustee or another acting wholly or in part on behalf of the trustee; whether the trustee prior to or at the time of the trust's creation had been in a fiduciary relationship to the settlor, such as by serving as the settlor's conservator or as the settlor's lawyer in providing the trust instrument or relevant part(s) of it; whether the settlor received competent, independent advice regarding the provisions of the instrument; whether the settlor was made aware of the exculpatory provision and was, with whatever guidance may have been provided, able to understand and make a judgment concerning the clause; and the extent and reasonableness of the provision.

In any event, an exculpatory clause is unenforceable if it is found, by presumption or otherwise, to be the product of undue influence or other improper conduct on the part of the trustee. Furthermore, the terms of a trust are subject to reformation (see § 62) if clear and convincing evidence establishes that the inclusion or content of an exculpatory clause was the result of a mistake.

Comment on Subsection (2):

e. Undermining enforcement or proper administration of trust. In most jurisdictions, no-contest (or "anti-contest" or, somewhat inaptly, "*in terrorem*") clauses are valid and generally enforceable, although subject to various statutory or common-law limitations. See, e.g., Restatement Third, Property (Wills and Other Donative Transfers) § 8.5, which states: "A provision in a donative document purporting to rescind a donative transfer to, or a fiduciary appointment of, any person who institutes a proceeding challenging the validity of all or part of the donative document is enforceable unless probable cause existed for instituting the proceeding." See also id., Comments *b* and *c*. That such clauses are "construed narrowly, consistent with their terms," and on other matters, see id., Comments *d–i*; . . . .

The rule of Subsection (2) provides only that an otherwise enforceable no-contest clause is unenforceable insofar as doing so would inhibit beneficiaries' enforcement of their rights under a trust (whether created by the will or other instrument) or would otherwise undermine the effective, proper administration of the trust. Suits to enforce the duties of trustees, or to determine the proper meaning or effect of the terms of a trust or to enforce those terms, normally have the effect of seeking to ascertain and implement settlor intentions and trust provisions under the instrument—rather than constituting a "contest" or challenge to the instrument or its provisions.

Accordingly, a no-contest clause ordinarily . . . is unenforceable to prevent or punish: a beneficiary's petition for instructions (§ 71, even though, for example, it seeks an interpretation contrary to the trustee's interpretation. . . .); a demand for or challenge to a trustee's accounting (§ 83); a suit to enjoin or redress a breach of trust (§ 95); a petition for removal of a trustee for unfitness or for repeated or serious breach of trust (§ 37); a suit alleging that a trustee's particular exercise of discretion or even "absolute" discretion constituted an abuse of discretion (§ 87); or the like. Similarly, a beneficiary's allegation that a trustee's misconduct exceeded the standard of misconduct permissibly protected by an exculpatory clause (Comments *b* and *c*) is not a contest of that provision of the instrument. See generally § 27(2) and § 27, Comment *b*, ... See also Restatement Third, Property (Wills and Other Donative Transfers) § 8.5, Comment *d*, on suits to construe, reform, or modify.

The rule of this Subsection (2) does not prevent enforcement of a no-contest clause insofar as it would, absent probable cause, exact forfeiture: (a) for a beneficiary's challenge to the validity of a trust or trust provision on grounds of incapacity (§ 11), lack of due execution (§§ 17–23), or forgery, fraud, undue influence, or other wrongful procurement (§ 12); or (b) for a beneficiary's claim either (i) as a creditor or (ii) as the owner of property that the settlor intended to include in the trust, provided, in either case, that the no-contest clause is clearly intended to apply to such a claim.

§ 97. Effect of Beneficiary Consent, Ratification, or Release

A beneficiary who consented to or ratified, or released the trustee from liability for, an act or omission that constitutes a breach of trust cannot hold the trustee liable for that breach, provided:

(a) the beneficiary, at the time of consenting to or ratifying the breach or granting the release, had the capacity to do so or was bound in doing so by the act of or representation by another; and

(b) the beneficiary (or the beneficiary's representative), at the time of the consent, ratification, or release, was aware of the beneficiary's rights and of all material facts and implications that the trustee knew or should have known relating to the matter; and

(c) the consent, ratification, or release was not induced by improper conduct of the trustee.

Comment:

a. Scope of section; cross-references. This section does not deal with trust modification based on the consent of all beneficiaries (on which see § 65) or on the exercise of express powers of modification, whether retained by a settlor (see § 63) or granted to others (see § 64). Nor does this section deal with beneficiary liability for participation in a breach of trust or receipt of improper benefits (see § 104, Comments *f* and *g(3)*, and also id., Comment *g(1)*, on indemnification agreements), or comprehensively (but see briefly Comment *c(2)* below) with the acts of settlors of revocable trusts (see § 74(1)) or donees of presently exercisable general powers of appointment (see § 74(2)).

The rule of this section applies to beneficiaries whose interests are subject to spendthrift restraints. (Cf. § 58, Comment *d(1)*, and (on releases) Comment *c*; also cf. § 65, Comment *e*, and (on modification) id., Comment *f*.) And the rule may be applied, but only as stated in Comments *c(2)* and *d*, to beneficiaries who are under legal incapacity or to unborn or unidentified beneficiaries. (The holder of a legally competent beneficiary's power of attorney can act for the beneficiary in these matters to the extent so empowered by law or the terms of the agency.)

The assignee of a beneficiary's interest is a "beneficiary" (§ 48, Comment *a*, and cf. § 94, Comment *b*) whose actions are subject to the rule of this section.

b. Overview: consent, ratification, and release. A beneficiary's "consent" may be given before or at the time of the trustee's act or omission. The rule of this section applies even if the consent involved self-dealing or other adverse interest on the part of the trustee, and regardless of whether the trustee's act or omission was requested by the beneficiary or the beneficiary's consent was sought by the trustee; and it applies regardless of whether the beneficiary and trustee merely recognized that the propriety of the contemplated act or omission was uncertain or actually knew that it would constitute a breach of trust.

A "ratification" or "release" occurs when a beneficiary subsequently, with knowledge of the breach, affirms a trustee's improper conduct or agrees to discharge the trustee from liability for the misconduct.

Consent or ratification ordinarily requires more than mere failure of the beneficiary to object to conduct that the beneficiary was aware would or did constitute a breach of trust (but cf. § 98 on laches); the consent or ratification is normally expressly communicated to the trustee, orally or by delivery of a writing, although the consent or ratification may be implied by the beneficiary's conduct in some circumstances. . . . . A release is typically contractual, thus subject to principles of contract law, but occasionally is donative in character . . . .

c. Effects of beneficiary's consent, ratification, or release. The consent, ratification, or release by one or more of the beneficiaries of a trust ordinarily (but see Comments *c(2)* and *d*) does not preclude other beneficiaries of the trust—that is, nonconsenting present or future beneficiaries—from holding the trustee liable for a breach of trust. Nor does consent or ratification by one or more of the beneficiaries ordinarily constitute a modification or amendment of the trust or otherwise alter the powers and duties of the trustee. (But see, e.g., § 65 on consent of *all* possible beneficiaries.)

A consenting beneficiary who retracts his or her consent *prior* to the trustee's improper act or omission is not precluded from holding the trustee liable for the breach of trust. Although a retraction after a breach prevents the consenting beneficiary from holding the trustee liable for that breach, the retraction does enable the beneficiary to hold the trustee liable for thereafter continuing the improper conduct. Similarly, a ratification may be limited or terminated to allow the beneficiary to sue the T, for example, for subsequent retention of an improper investment. (Absent express withdrawal or termination of a beneficiary's consent or ratification, however, that beneficiary is presumptively prevented from suing the trustee for continued holding of the same property under essentially the same circumstances. Cf. Comment *c(3)*.) On the other hand, a mere release from liability for prior misconduct does not implicitly prevent the beneficiary from suing for a continued violation of the trustee's duties, such as by further retention of an improper investment.

c(1). Nonconsenting beneficiaries generally unaffected. Except as stated in Comment *c(2)* or Comment *d* (especially regarding virtual representation), the consent to or ratification of a breach of trust, or the granting of a release, by one or more of the beneficiaries does not preclude other beneficiaries of the trust from holding the trustee liable for the breach, insofar as their interests are affected. . . . .

c(2). Act by holder of ownership-equivalent power. For purposes of this section, as elsewhere (see, e.g., § 94, Comment *b*), the owner of a power of revocation, withdrawal, or appointment under a trust is a "beneficiary" of the trust. See generally § 48, Comment *a*. To the extent that a trust is subject to revocation or to a presently exercisable general power of appointment (including certain powers of withdrawal) the settlor or the donee of the power has the equitable equivalent of ownership of the trust property. See § 74, Comment *a*. As a result of such a power, the rights of the other beneficiaries are exercisable by and subject to the control of the settlor (§ 74(1)(b)) or donee (§ 74(2)), so that the settlor or donee can consent to or ratify a breach of trust or release the trustee from liability from the breach. The settlor or donee thereby acts on behalf of and binds all present and future beneficiaries whose interests are subject to the power. See § 74, Comments *d* and *g*; also see id., Comments *a(2)* (required capacity of settlor or donee) and *h* (power over portion of trust).

Under some circumstances, donees of powers of appointment that are nongeneral or not presently exercisable may represent certain beneficiaries. See generally Comment *d*.

c(3). Effect on subsequent administration. Except as stated in § 65 or in § 74 (see especially id., Comment *i*), beneficiary consent to or ratification of, or release of the trustee from liability for, fiduciary misconduct does not modify the terms of the trust or alter the trustee's powers and duties. In such cases, not only is the trustee's misconduct a breach of trust for which *nonassenting* beneficiaries may hold the trustee liable should a loss result, but those beneficiaries also may enjoin the trustee's continuation or repetition of the misconduct and seek other remedies (§ 95, Comment *c*) for the breach of trust.

Even a beneficiary who has consented to or ratified the trustee's misconduct can terminate that approval and, in any event, can hold the trustee liable for subsequent misconduct that involves a new breach of trust, such as the trustee's failure to dispose of an improper but ratified investment that *later* becomes imprudent or otherwise improper because of a change of circumstances.

If a beneficiary who has consented to a contemplated breach of trust assigns his or her interest to another, and the trustee commits the breach after the assignment, the transferee-beneficiary is not precluded from holding the trustee liable for the breach unless the trustee was unaware of the assignment at the time of committing the breach.

Comment on Clauses (a)–(c):

d. Required capacity or representation of beneficiary. In order for a beneficiary personally to consent to or ratify a breach of trust, or to release the trustee from liability for the breach, the beneficiary must have legal capacity to do so. Rather than acting personally, however, a beneficiary who is a minor or is otherwise legally incapacitated may be represented by a personal fiduciary (such as a guardian, conservator, or agent acting under a durable power of attorney) who is empowered by law or by the terms of the appointive instrument or court order to grant such a consent, ratification, or release on behalf of the beneficiary. Furthermore, absent such a personal fiduciary, one or more of the other beneficiaries of the trust may represent and bind legally incapacitated, and even unascertainable and afterborn, beneficiaries in appropriate circumstances under the doctrine of virtual representation. . . . .

In addition, the rights of beneficiaries can be exercised, thus binding the beneficiaries (legally competent or incapacitated, unascertainable or unborn) by the act of a holder of an ownership-equivalent power, as indicated in Comment *c(2)*. See also § 74, especially Comments *d* and *g*.

e. Requirement of fully informed consent, ratification, or release. A beneficiary's consent, ratification, or release does not preclude the beneficiary from holding the trustee liable for harm resulting from a violation of the trustee's fiduciary duties unless at the time of acting the beneficiary understood: (i) that the trustee's act or omission would or might be, or was or might have been, a breach of trust; (ii) the relevant information about, and the implications of, the act or omission in question; and (iii) the beneficiary's right to prevent or remedy trustee misconduct (see §§ 95 and 100).

It is not necessary that the trustee inform the beneficiary of all the details of which the trustee has knowledge; but, because of the strict fiduciary relationship between trustee and beneficiary, a trustee who would rely on a beneficiary's consent, ratification, or release normally has the burden of showing that the beneficiary (or his or her representative) was sufficiently informed to understand the character of the act or omission and was in a position to reach an informed opinion on the advisability of consenting, ratifying, or granting a release. If, however, the trustee is led by the beneficiary reasonably to believe that the beneficiary is aware of the relevant information and rights, and the trustee acts in reliance on that belief, the beneficiary cannot hold the trustee liable even though the beneficiary was in fact insufficiently informed.

Illustration:

9. S leaves her residuary estate to T in trust for L for life, remainder to R or R's issue. T asks L if he is agreeable to having some of the trust funds invested in the shares of X Company, which T believes to be a particularly good investment. L consents to the investment but does not realize that the amount of the investment contemplated by T would leave the trust portfolio imprudently underdiversified, a matter that T did not discuss with L. Should harm result from the underdiversification, L will not be precluded from maintaining a suit against T for breach of trust (§ 90(b)).

f. *Improper conduct of trustee.* A beneficiary's consent to or ratification of a breach of trust, or release of the trustee from liability for the breach, does not preclude the beneficiary from holding the trustee liable for the breach if the beneficiary's act was induced by fraud, duress, or undue influence by the trustee, or if the trustee induced the consent, ratification, or release by abusing the fiduciary relationship. Fiduciary abuse may result if the trustee brings unwarranted pressure to bear on the beneficiary, for example, by threatening to withhold a distribution to which the beneficiary is entitled unless the beneficiary executes a release. An abuse may also result if a trustee procures a release from liability, or procures a beneficiary's approval of a transaction in which the trustee's personal interest is adverse to that of the beneficiary, and the release or transaction involves a bargain that is not substantively fair and reasonable. . . . .

In matters considered here and in Comment *e*, it will often be significant to consider whether and to what extent the beneficiary had competent advice or had experience in and understanding of matters relevant to the trustee's conduct.

§ 98. Laches and Statutes of Limitations

A beneficiary may not maintain a suit against a trustee for breach of trust if the beneficiary is barred from doing so by the doctrine of laches or by a statutory period of limitation.

Comment:

a. *Scope of section.* This section does not consider the preclusive effect of prior court decrees upon beneficiaries' suits against trustees. See, however, § 71, Comment *b*, . . . (on judicial instructions), and § 83, Comment *c*, . . . (on court accountings). Nor does it consider the possibility of a trustee's personal discharge in bankruptcy and the exception for certain violations of fiduciary duty. . . . . Also, with laches, compare and contrast implied ratification, which is considered in § 97, Comment *b*, ...

The doctrine of laches evolved in equity in English and American jurisdictions during times in which statutes of limitations did not apply to equitable causes of action. The doctrine ordinarily remains applicable today along with modern statutes of limitations that either specify time limits for suits to enforce trusts (express, resulting, or constructive) or contain a catch-all provision that is held to encompass the enforcement of trusts. (Either laches or the statute may bar suit even though the other does not.) This section deals with both of these rather different means of discouraging excessive delay in the bringing of suits against trustees.

a(1). Effect of bar. Although laches or a statute of limitations bars a beneficiary from recovering damages for a particular breach of trust, the bar ordinarily does not preclude the beneficiary from otherwise enforcing the trust. If, however, the trustee has repudiated the trust, either expressly or by conduct inconsistent with its existence, and the beneficiary with knowledge or reason to know of the repudiation fails to bring suit within a reasonable time or a time prescribed by statute, the beneficiary may be barred from enforcing the trust. Thus, for example, if an alleged trustee disputes the existence of a trust, laches or a statute of limitations may bar one who claims to be a beneficiary from asserting rights under the alleged trust.

On situations in which laches or a statute of limitations bars a claim by one or more beneficiaries but not others, compare § 97, Comment *c(1)* . . . .

a(2). Charitable trusts: immunity of attorneys general. In the enforcement of charitable trusts, under the so-called "public-rights principle," attorneys general (or other appropriate public officials) are subject neither to statutes of limitations, unless a statute otherwise provides, nor to the doctrine of laches, except as the court concludes that, in the particular case, the period of the Attorney General's unexcused (cf. Comment *b(1)*) delay has been so unreasonably long and circumstances have so changed (cf. Comment *c(2)*) that it would be inequitable to surcharge the trustee for the particular breach of trust. Even in such an exceptional situation the bar does not preclude the Attorney General from otherwise enforcing the trust (see Comment *a(1)*), such as by suit to remedy other misconduct by the trustee or to compel adherence to the specified purpose(s) of the trust. . . . .

b. Laches. The often-stated policy that suits should be brought without unreasonable delay is based on a general assumption that the passage of time increases the difficulty (i) of a trustee's defense against allegations of misconduct and (ii) of a court's attempt to ascertain truth. But the reality and extent of these difficulties vary from case to case, depending on such matters as the continued availability of records and witnesses, the reliability of recollections about events and conditions, and the like. Thus, more is involved than mere lapse of time.

A determination of whether a trust beneficiary is precluded by laches from holding a trustee liable for a breach of trust inevitably depends on the facts and circumstances and ultimately on whether the court concludes that the beneficiary has so delayed bringing suit against the trustee that it would be inequitable to allow the suit to proceed. In making this determination, the court will consider among others the following factors: (1) the nature of the alleged breach of trust; (2) the length of the delay after the beneficiary learned or should have learned of the alleged misconduct; (3) the reasons for the beneficiary's delay in bringing suit; and (4) the nature and effect (especially on the trustee's defense) of changed circumstances during the delay.

b(1). Excuses for delay. Laches does not result from the passage of time while a beneficiary neither knew nor had reason to know of the trustee's alleged misconduct. Nor will the bar of laches apply as long as the beneficiary is under a legal incapacity. In either of these situations, however, laches may apply if suit is not brought within a reasonable time after the incapacity is removed and after the beneficiary learns or should have learned of the alleged breach of trust. Although laches may apply to a future-interest beneficiary who is harmed by a trustee's misconduct and knows or should know of that misconduct, the deferral and uncertainties of the beneficiary's eventual enjoyment (compared, for example, to the cost of protecting the interest) are relevant in determining whether or to what extent a delay in bringing suit was reasonable.

A trustee's concealment of misconduct, or of the trust or the beneficiary's interest in it, excuses a beneficiary's failure to learn of the existence or effect of a breach of trust, as may the trustee's disregard of duties under §§ 82 and 83 to report, account, or provide information to the beneficiary. In addition, if a beneficiary complained of a breach of trust and was assured by the trustee of corrective action, the beneficiary is excused from a delay that reasonably resulted from reliance on that assurance.

b(2). Delay prejudicial to trustee. A trustee may show that the opportunity of defending a breach-of-trust suit is prejudiced by the period of delay in any of several ways. Frequently the prejudice is shown by evidence of the death or incapacity of (or perhaps the inability to locate) important witnesses, or even by the death or disability of the trustee. And, in any event, recollection of distant events and understanding of context may be vague and uncertain. Or the difficulty may be attributable to the innocent loss or destruction of material documents. Furthermore, fairness may be affected by changed position of the trustee, potentially including loss of rights against third persons.

c. Statutes of limitations. Although subject to potential due-process requirements . . ., these statutes prescribe specific time limits within which beneficiaries must bring suits against trustees. Limitations on the time allowed vary considerably from state to state, and have varied from time to time, as do the events and circumstances that trigger or prevent the running of a statutory period and the specifics of protections for legally incapacitated beneficiaries. Also relevant to beneficiaries and to the personal representatives of deceased trustees are provisions of probate codes prescribing time limits for the filing of claims against decedents' estates. (Statutes of this type are beyond the scope of this Restatement.)

Increasingly, modern trust codes, especially the growing number that include a version of Uniform Trust Code § 1005, allow a relatively short period for bringing suit against a trustee who has presented a report to the beneficiary adequately disclosing the potential existence of a claim for breach of trust. On the requirement of adequate disclosure, cf. § 83, Comment *c*. Statutes of this type are usually accompanied by a provision allowing a substantially longer limitation period for most other situations, plus language or a separate provision for continued recognition of the doctrine of laches.

UTC § 1005 (Limitation of Action Against Trustee) provides: "(a) A beneficiary may not commence a proceeding against a trustee for breach of trust more than one year after the date the beneficiary or a representative of the beneficiary was sent a report that adequately disclosed the existence of a potential claim for breach of trust and informed the beneficiary of the time allowed for commencing a proceeding." Subsection (b) explains that disclosure is adequate "if it provides sufficient information so that the beneficiary or representative knows of the potential claim or should have inquired into its existence." Subsection 1005(c) adds: "If subsection (a) does not apply, a judicial proceeding by a beneficiary against a trustee for breach of trust must be commenced within five years after the first to occur of: (1) the removal, resignation, or death of the trustee; (2) the termination of the beneficiary's interest in the trust; or (3) the termination of the trust." . . . .

The various statutes of limitations in the various states, or some elements of these statutes, may operate without regard to the beneficiary's awareness of the breach of trust and generally delineate rather carefully any other "excuses" for delay, with no showing required of a delay's prejudicial effect on the trustee. Thus, the statutes are generally designed to operate free of the balancing, nuances, and many of the qualifications of the doctrine of laches.

CHAPTER 19

TRUSTEE LIABILITY TO BENEFICIARIES

Introductory Note: Section 99 recognizes that a trustee is not liable for a loss to the trust unless the loss is caused by a breach of trust. Whether or not a breach of trust has occurred, however (as noted in both § 99(b) and § 100, Comment *a(1)*), a trustee is accountable to the trust and its beneficiaries for any profits that arise from administration of the trust.

Section 100 and its commentary (especially Comments *b–b(2)*) adapt to the present context the principle on loss determination and trustee liability that was adopted in § 205 (also see §§ 208–211) of the preliminary (1992) volume entitled Restatement Third, Trusts (Prudent Investor Rule). A supplemental part of that volume revised a number of "Other Sections Affecting or Affected by the Prudent Investor Rule." (The Rule itself, preliminarily §§ 227–229, is now Chapter 17, §§ 90–92, of this Restatement.) Revised §§ 205 and 208–211 departed significantly from the counterpart provisions (§§ 205–211) of Restatement Second, Trusts. The present § 100 restates the 1992 principle, which has become known as a "total-return" (or "lost-profits" or "lost-appreciation") measure of loss and damages for breach of trust—that is, for determining whether and in what amount the breach has caused a "loss," and thus measuring the trustee's liability, by reference to what the results "would have been if the portion of the trust affected by the breach *had been properly administered*." (Emphasis added.)

The counterpart language of Restatement Second, Trusts § 205(c) (referring to "any profit which would have accrued to the trust estate *if there had been no breach*") might have appeared to call for results like those now called for by the principle stated in 1992—in fact, Uniform Trust Code § 1002(a)(1) (2000) uses similar language ("*had the breach not occurred*") avowedly to adopt the 1992 liability principle (see comment to id. § 1002). (Emphasis added.) Nevertheless, the associated commentary and sections (especially § 207) of Restatement Second, Trusts, as well as then-prevailing case law, called for *interest* on losses rather than total-return damages, as aptly illustrated by language in Restatement Second, Trusts § 209(1): "If the trustee fails to sell trust property which it is his duty to sell [because, e.g., the trust so directs or diversification so requires], the beneficiary can charge him with the amount which he would have received [by timely sale] . . ., *with interest thereon*" to the time of delayed sale or, if unsold, to the time of the accounting. (Emphasis added.) . . . .

Section 101 examines the question of when, in determining trustee liability, it might be permissible to offset profits against losses resulting from a trustee's acts of misconduct. Section 102 states rules governing contribution between or among trustees who are jointly and severally liable for a breach of trust.

§ 99. Absence of Breach of Trust

Absent a breach of trust, a trustee

(a) is not liable for a loss or depreciation in the value of trust property or a failure to make a profit greater than actually generated, but

(b) is accountable for any profit arising from the administration of the trust.

Comment:

a. Scope of section; cross-references. This section addresses the absence of trustee liability when there has been no breach of trust. ("Breach of trust" is defined in § 93). On a trustee's liability when there has been a breach of trust, see § 100.

A trustee who is not liable under this section because there has been no breach of trust may nevertheless be subject to removal (see § 37, especially Comment *e*) or other remedies to improve the administration of the trust (see § 95, Comment *c*).

Other cross-references are contained in the Comments below.

b. No liability for loss, depreciation, or low return. Absent a breach of trust, the trustee is not a guarantor of the safety or value of trust property or of the success of the trust's investment program.

This principle means that the trustee is not liable for a loss of trust property or a depreciation in its value if there is no breach of trust. If, for example, the trustee exercises reasonable care and skill to preserve trust property (including insuring as prudence may require) and does not otherwise commit a breach of trust, the trustee is not liable for a loss resulting from theft, damage, or destruction of a trust asset. Nor is the trustee liable for making or retaining an investment that declines in value where there is no breach of trust.

Similarly, a failure to make a profit, or a profit greater than that actually generated, does not subject the trustee to liability in the absence of a breach of trust. Thus, if the trustee was authorized but not required to make or retain a particular investment that subsequently appreciated more than the investment(s) acquired instead, the trustee is not liable for the difference if the trustee's decisions and conduct were prudent and otherwise conformed to fiduciary standards. And if the total return from the trust's investments is negative or less than that of allegedly "comparable" trusts, the trustee is not liable for the investment program's alleged underperformance unless the trustee has committed a breach of trust. Cf. § 77, Comment *a* ("The test of prudence is one of conduct not of performance. . . . Investment performance or other results . . . become relevant, however, when a breach of trust is found and the measure of liability is in issue").

c. Accountability for profit. When the administration of a trust produces a profit, whether there has or has not been a breach of trust, the trustee is accountable for the profit, including any income, realized gains, and unrealized appreciation in the value of trust property. This accountability reflects the fundamental principle that value generated by the trust estate and trust activities belongs to the trust, not to the trustee personally, and is to be held or applied for trust purposes. . . . .

On the trustee's duties to provide information to beneficiaries, to maintain records, and to provide reports or accountings, see §§ 82 and 83.

§ 100. Liability of Trustee for Breach of Trust

A trustee who commits a breach of trust is chargeable with

(a) the amount required to restore the values of the trust estate and trust distributions to what they would have been if the portion of the trust affected by the breach had been properly administered; or

(b) the amount of any benefit to the trustee personally as a result of the breach.

General Comment:

a. Introduction; cross-references. This section addresses the measure of a trustee's personal liability for a breach of trust. ("Breach of trust" is defined in § 93; the word "chargeable" is used in the initial phrase of the black letter to recognize that the beneficiaries may fail or decide not to sue the trustee for the breach in question. See Comment *a(1).*) When circumstances permit recovery alternatively under Clause (a) or Clause (b), recovery is to be based on the alternative that is more beneficial to the trust and its beneficiaries, unless all affected beneficiaries are sui juris and agree on the other alternative. . . . .

The primary objectives of the rule of this section, if suit is brought against a trustee and if that suit is successful, are (i) to make the trust and its beneficiaries whole, usually by restoring the trust estate and trust distributions to what they would have been if the portion of the trust affected by the breach had been properly administered (Clause (a)) and (ii) to ensure that the trustee does not personally benefit from the breach (Clause (b)).

The goal of making the trust and beneficiaries whole is not always taken literally, however, either as a floor or as a ceiling. For example, an award of attorney fees and other costs incurred by the trust or the beneficiaries in remedying the breach is not automatic but a matter of judicial discretion (see Comment *b(2)*; cf. § 88, Comment *d*). Also see Comment *d* on the possibility, in some jurisdictions, of adding punitive damages.

a(1). Beneficiaries' right to affirm or refrain from taking action. Beneficiary awareness or suspicion that a trustee has committed a breach of trust may arise in the context of an accounting or report submitted (or not submitted), or from information provided (or not provided), by the trustee. On the trustee's duty to provide information to beneficiaries, see § 82; and on the duty to maintain records and provide reports, see § 83.

If beneficiaries know or suspect that the trustee has committed a breach of trust, they are entitled, collectively (with proper representation as necessary) or individually, to ratify the transaction or simply take no action regarding the trustee's possible misconduct. On the effect of laches and statutes of limitations on beneficiaries who refrain from acting, see § 98. On the potentially preclusive effect of court accountings, see § 83, Comment *c*, . . . ; and on the effect of judicial instructions, see § 71, Comment *b*, ... On the requirements and effects of beneficiary ratification and release, see generally § 97; that ratification or release by some beneficiaries ordinarily does not preclude suit by other beneficiaries, see id., Comment *c(1)*.

In all of the above circumstances, the trustee is accountable for any profit accruing to the trust as a result of the breach (see § 83, especially Comment *b*).

The beneficiaries' decision to accept (or to hold the trustee liable for) the results of a breach ordinarily does not modify the trustee's duties or relieve the trustee of the duty thereafter properly to administer the trust (requiring, for example, that the trustee dispose of an improper investment and reinvest the proceeds). See § 97, Comment *c(3)*.

a(2). Form of recovery from trustee. If suit for breach of trust is successfully brought against the trustee, recovery may take the form of a money judgment or (if feasible) specific restitution. On the latter, see Restatement Third, Restitution and Unjust Enrichment §§ 54–61, especially § 55 (constructive trust) and § 58 (following property into its product and against transferees). The form of the recovery should, to the extent practicable, reflect the preferences and best interests of the beneficiaries.

Ordinarily, the trustee (or a successor) receives the amount of a recovery and retains it or distributes it, in whole or in part, as appropriate to the terms and circumstances of the trust. The court, however, may allocate some or all of the surcharged amount directly to one or more of the beneficiaries to the extent the court has the information necessary to do so. Thus, ordinarily, if it is clear, for example, that a specific beneficiary is entitled to all of the trust income (but see adjustment power in § 111), any recovery for lost income belongs to that beneficiary, to be paid either directly pursuant to court order or by distribution by the trustee. By way of contrast, if the trust is wholly discretionary as to distributions, the trustee (or successor) should determine and make any appropriate distributions to the beneficiaries.

a(3). Additional cross-references. Various obstacles that might limit or preclude suit against a trustee for breach of trust are examined in §§ 96–98. The power of the court, pursuant to its equitable authority or statute, to excuse the trustee in whole or in part from liability for a breach of trust is considered in § 95, Comment *d*, ...

In addition to or instead of liability, a trustee who commits a breach of trust may, in appropriate circumstances, be subject to removal (see § 37, especially Comment *e*) or other remedies to respond to the trustee's misconduct or to improve the administration of the trust (see § 95, Comment *c*).

The possibility of offsetting profits against losses from a trustee's misconduct is considered in § 101. The rules governing contribution from another trustee are discussed in § 102. Additional cross-references are contained in the Comments below.

References to "return" in this section (and elsewhere in this Restatement) refer to "total return," meaning capital gain and appreciation as well as income. See, e.g., § 90, Comment *e*.

Comment on Liability of Trustee Under Clause (a):

b. Measure of trustee liability. Ordinarily (but compare, e.g., Comment *b(2)*, second paragraph), the liability of a trustee who is sued and found to have committed a breach of trust is the amount required to restore the values of the trust estate and its distributions to what they would have been if the affected portion of the trust estate had been properly administered. This amount to be restored is generally referred to as the "loss" throughout the commentary to this section.

b(1). Determining amount of loss. If a breach of trust causes a loss, including any failure to realize income, capital gain, or appreciation that would have resulted from proper administration of the trust, the trustee is liable for the amount necessary to compensate fully for the breach.

Occasionally a situation arises that offers an essentially objective means of ascertaining the loss for which a trustee is liable under Clause (a). For example, if the trustee failed to retain (or to acquire) certain property as specifically required by the terms of the trust, whether and in what amount the trust suffered a loss can be determined by ascertaining the specified property's value and earnings as of the time of surcharge and comparing that with the results of the trustee's investment of the sale proceeds (or of the funds that would have been needed to purchase the property as directed). . . . . Also, on other potential remedies, see Comment *a(2)*.

If the breach of trust involved accepting too low a price in an otherwise proper sale of trust property, the trustee's liability would be the amount by which the sale price was inadequate, plus (or minus) a projected total return on that amount to the time of surcharge. In this situation, the return projection probably . . . can be based simply on the return received on the trustee's investment of the actual proceeds of the sale. (If the only breach was in selling the property for too little, the trustee is not chargeable with the amount of any subsequent increase in that property's value.)

Illustrative of more difficult "loss" determinations is the determination of the recovery from a trustee for imprudent or otherwise improper investments. The recovery in such a case ordinarily would be the difference between (1) the value of those investments and their income and other product at the time of surcharge and (2) the amount of funds expended in making the improper investments, increased (or decreased) by a projected amount of total return (or negative total return) that would have accrued to the trust and its beneficiaries if the funds had been properly invested. (A return projection for "properly invested" funds should reflect the standards of prudent investment in § 90(a), and should not rely on hindsight (cf. § 77, Comment *a*) in selecting a benchmark (below) for hypothetical performance.)

Depending on the type of trustee and the nature of the breach involved, the availability of relevant data, and other facts and circumstances of the case, the projected returns on indefinite hypothetical investments during the surcharge period may appropriately be based, inter alia, on: the return experience (positive or negative) for other investments, or suitable portions of other investments, of the trust in question; average return rates of portfolios, or suitable parts of portfolios, of a representative selection of other trusts having comparable objectives and circumstances; or return rates of one or more suitable common trust funds, or suitable index mutual funds or market indexes (with such adjustments as may be appropriate). . . . .

In some situations, especially involving breaches of short duration, or relatively minor or complicated details of loss measurement, it may be appropriate simply to use compound interest rather than total-return projections in determining the amount of loss to be recovered from a trustee.

b(2). Attorney fees and other costs. The "make whole" objective (see Comment *a*) of recovery from a trustee under Clause (a) may include, in an appropriate case, the attorney fees and other litigation costs of a successful plaintiff—that is, a co-trustee or successor trustee, or a beneficiary who qualifies for reimbursement from the trust under § 88, Comment *d*. This element of recovery, however, is a matter of judicial discretion and not a routine part of trustee liability for breach of trust (see id.). Among the facts and circumstances courts consider in exercising their judgment in these matters are the nature and extent of trustee misconduct in committing the breach, the conduct of the trustee in presenting the accounting or defending the surcharge action, and the significance of imposing costs on the trustee as a deterrent to misconduct.

A trustee's payment of a beneficiary's costs is especially significant and appropriate with regard to violations of fiduciary duty that are unlikely to cause losses of the types considered in Comment *b(1)*, such as a trustee's improper refusal to provide information requested by a beneficiary (see § 82(1)). (For other remedial actions that might serve a similar purpose in breach-of-trust cases of this type, see § 91, Comment *c*.)

Comment on Liability of Trustee Under Clause (b):

c. Liability to prevent personal benefit to trustee. A trustee who commits a breach of trust normally is not allowed to benefit individually from the breach, and the trustee is subject to liability to eliminate any such benefit. (The term "benefit" used here and in Clause (b) is comprehensive; thus, if a trustee misappropriates trust funds and invests them, the trustee's "benefit" includes the amount misappropriated as well as any profit from the investment.) Unless the beneficiaries choose to affirm the breach transaction or otherwise allow it to stand (see Comment *a(1)*) or they achieve a greater recovery under Clause (a) (see Comments *b–b(2)*), the trustee's improper benefit is eliminated by a decision of the beneficiaries (or on their behalf) to set aside the transaction or act constituting the breach of trust.

For example, if a trustee breaches the duty of loyalty by selling trust property to the trustee individually (or to certain of the trustee's family members defined in § 78, Comment *e*), even in good faith at a fair price (see "no further inquiry" principle, § 78, Comment *d*), and if the property thereafter appreciates, the beneficiaries may avoid the sale in order to eliminate the trustee's profit. The trust thus restores the purchase price and its return (positive or negative) to the trustee (these funds remaining subject to a lien to secure any unpaid surcharge) and recovers instead the value of the property at the time of the decree, or (if feasible) the property itself, plus the earnings from the property or its proceeds. (On the potential liability of a family-member buyer to the trust, see §§ 107–108.)

Conversely, if the trustee breaches the duty of loyalty in *purchasing* an asset for the trust from the trustee individually or from a family member, the beneficiaries may compel the trustee to restore the purchase price, plus an appropriate return on it, with the trustee (or family member) thereby becoming entitled to the asset and any return received by the trust from that asset (subject to a lien for any unpaid surcharge).

Also, if the trustee is a real-estate broker and receives a commission for handling (through the firm of which the trustee is a member) a purchase or sale of land for the trust, and the beneficiaries affirm the purchase or sale (also cf. § 78, Comment *c(5)*), the trustee commits a breach of trust by retaining the commission rather than accounting for it to the trust. The trustee is liable for the amount of the commission, plus an appropriate return on that amount to the time of surcharge.

In each of the foregoing examples, avoidance of the transaction, or recovery of an improper profit, eliminates the trustee's benefit from the breach. The trustee may also be liable for fees and other costs incurred in recovering that benefit. See Comment *b(2)*.

Additional General Comment:

d. *Punitive damages.* Ordinarily, a recovery under this section would not be supplemented by an additional award of exemplary damages. The rule stated in Clause (a) of this section is restorative (see Comment *a*), not punitive. On the distinction between restitution and punishment, see Restatement Third, Restitution and Unjust Enrichment § 49, Comment *a*, and id. § 51, Comment *a*.

In the egregious case, however, punitive damages are permissible under the laws of many jurisdictions. This is especially so if the trustee has acted maliciously, in bad faith, or in a fraudulent, particularly reckless, or self-serving manner. Among the facts and circumstances that are relevant when punitive damages are being considered in such jurisdictions are the nature and extent of the trustee's wrongdoing, the trustee's conduct in presenting an accounting or defending a surcharge action, and the extent to which punitive damages are important in order to punish the trustee, to recognize the harm to the beneficiaries, and to deter similar misconduct.

e. *Loss: causation requirement.* A trustee who commits a breach of trust is liable for a loss resulting from the breach. A question may arise, therefore, as to the causal connection between the breach of trust and the loss. If a trustee commits the breach and a loss is incurred, the trustee ordinarily is not chargeable with the amount of the loss if the same loss would have occurred in the absence of a breach of trust. However, special rules govern a breach of the duty to earmark (§ 84) and a breach of the duty of loyalty (§ 78).

If a trustee has committed a breach of trust in failing to earmark trust property (see especially Comment *d* to § 84), the trustee ordinarily is not liable for a loss that is shown not to have resulted from the breach. A special prophylactic rule applies, however, if the trustee's failure to earmark the property presents a danger that the trustee might claim that the property is a personal asset if it increases in value and that it is a trust asset if its value declines. In such a case, the trustee is liable for the loss even without proof of causation or that the trustee had this purpose in mind, as long as the failure to earmark puts the trustee in a realistic position to make such a claim. On the other hand, if the trustee can show that there is no realistic danger that such a claim could successfully be made, the failure to earmark does not render the trustee liable for a loss resulting from the otherwise proper investment. See, however, § 95, Comment *c*, on other remedies the beneficiaries might pursue; and also see Comment *b(2)* to this section.

An analogous prophylactic rule governs a breach of the duty of loyalty. For example, if the trustee purchases, for the trust, property owned by the trustee individually (or by a family member described in § 78, Comment *e*) and the property subsequently loses value, it is immaterial that the trustee could properly have purchased identical property for the same price from a third person. In order to deter breaches of the duty of loyalty, under the "no further inquiry" principle (id., Comment *d*, and for the reasons explained in id., Comment *b*), the trustee is chargeable with the loss.

f. *Burden of proof.* When a plaintiff brings suit against a trustee for breach of trust, the plaintiff generally bears the burden of proof. This general rule, however, is moderated in order to take account of the trustee's duties of disclosure (§ 82) and of recordkeeping and reporting (§ 83) as well as the trustee's superior (often, unique) access to information about the trust and its activities, and also to encourage the trustee's compliance with applicable fiduciary duties.

Furthermore, there are examples in trust fiduciary law where the normal burden of proof (resting on the plaintiff to prove all elements of the cause of action) does not obtain. For example, the "no further inquiry" principle (see § 78, Comment *b*) operates to relieve the plaintiff of proving that the transaction was affected by a conflict between the trustee's fiduciary and personal interests. Similarly, an exculpatory clause drafted (or caused to be included in the trust instrument) by the trustee is presumptively unenforceable, with the trustee having the burden of rebutting the presumption (see § 96, Comment *d*). And once a plaintiff shows a loss associated with an inadequately diversified trust portfolio, the plaintiff need not negate, but the trustee has the burden to establish, the existence of an exception to the normal duty to diversify (see § 90(b) and id., Comment *g*).

Also, in matters of causation (Comment *e*), when a beneficiary has succeeded in proving that the trustee has committed a breach of trust and that a related loss has occurred, the burden shifts to the trustee to prove that the loss would have occurred in the absence of the breach.

The trustee also bears an analogous burden of proving each item in an accounting or report, if challenged by a beneficiary, with doubts about the accuracy and completeness of the trustee's records being resolved against the trustee (see § 83, especially Comments *a* and *b*). . . .

§ 101. Offsetting Profit Against Loss

The amount of a trustee's liability for breach of trust may not be reduced by a profit resulting from other misconduct unless the acts of misconduct causing the loss and the profit constitute a single breach.

Comment:

a. Scope, effect, and rationale of section. If a trustee is liable for a loss caused by a breach of trust, the amount of the liability is not reduced by a profit resulting from actions of the trustee that do not involve a breach of trust. The rule of this section applies only where the trust estate has experienced a profit as well as a loss from *improper* administration.

If it is determined under the rule of this section that profit and loss are to be offset (see Comment *c*), the trust and its beneficiaries are entitled, as the case may be, either to hold the trustee accountable for the net profit or to charge the trustee with the net loss.

The rule of this section balances fairness to the trustee and regard for the interests and entitlements of the beneficiaries. Whether or not there is a breach of trust, the profits for which the trustee is accountable belong to the trust and its beneficiaries (see § 99, Comment *c*). Moreover, the law is well settled that profits arising from *proper* administration do not reduce a trustee's liability for breach of trust; it would be ironic to permit a profit from *improper* administration to be offset against the trustee's liability. Indeed, a rule that always allowed such a profit to offset a loss would tend to place undue emphasis on the timing of accountings and reports, and even on whether profitable conduct was a breach of trust, and would tend to encourage multiple breaches of trust. For example, a trustee whose misconduct has caused a loss might take improper risks in pursuit of offsetting profit.

Notwithstanding these concerns, in circumstances in which it is appropriate to treat the misconduct as a single breach, it would be unduly harsh to hold a trustee liable for the loss without taking into account a related profit.

b. *Meaning of "loss" and "profit" from breach.* The trust's loss from a breach of trust is the amount necessary to restore the values of the trust estate and trust distributions to what those values would have been if the affected portion of the trust had been properly administered (see § 100, Comment *c*). The trust's profit from a breach of trust is the amount by which the values of the trust estate and trust distributions exceed what those values would have been had the affected portion of the trust been properly administered.

c. *Determining whether multiple acts of misconduct should be considered to constitute a single breach.* No bright-line rule can be offered to determine whether misconduct resulting in a profit and misconduct resulting in a loss should be treated as constituting a single breach. The following are illustrative of factors to be weighed to determine whether the misconduct should be considered to be a single breach for purposes of this section:

(1) Whether the improper acts are the result of a single strategy or policy, a single decision or judgment, or a single set of interrelated decisions;

(2) The amount of time between the instances of misconduct and whether the trustee was aware of the earlier misconduct and its resulting loss or profit;

(3) Whether the trustee intended to commit a breach of trust or knew the misconduct was a breach of trust; and

(4) Whether the profit and loss can be offset without inequitable consequences, for example to beneficiaries having different beneficial interests in the trust.

Although factor (1) is likely to be of particular significance, no definite rules can be stated with respect to the relative weight to be given to various factors; and no single factor or combination of factors is necessarily determinative of whether offset is appropriate.

In the Illustrations that follow, the meaning of "profit" and "loss" is as defined in Comment *b*.

Illustrations:

1. T received $500,000 in trust. T decided to invest the funds entirely in the common stock of two or three "successful" companies. Soon thereafter, acting in good faith but in violation of her duty with respect to diversification (§ 90(b)), T implemented the decision by investing the funds in the shares of two corporations. By the time of T's first accounting, one of the investments had produced a substantial profit and the other a substantial loss. Because T's conduct is the result of a single misjudgment, made in good faith, the conduct is properly treated as a single breach of trust. T is either accountable for the net profit or chargeable with the net loss resulting from these investments.

2. The same facts as in Illustration 1, except that a substantial profit resulted from both stock investments and that T also received Blackacre in trust, authorizing but not requiring her to retain it. In response to an offer from a real-estate developer, T sold Blackacre in good faith but for a price under its fair market value, as T would have known had she exercised reasonable care (§ 77(2)). T is chargeable with

the full loss that resulted from this breach of her duty to act with prudence (§ 77, Comment *b*), no offset being allowable for the profit resulting from the unrelated breach involving the stock investments.

3. T is trustee for L for life, remainder to R or R's issue. Erroneously believing that certain property would be a prudent investment for this trust portfolio, T purchased that property and soon thereafter sold it for a profit; under the same erroneous belief, T immediately reinvested the proceeds in similarly unsuitable property, later selling it at a loss. The misconduct causing the profit and the misconduct causing the loss are the result of a single misjudgment, made in good faith, about the suitability of this kind of investment for the trust portfolio, and therefore are properly treated as a single breach. T is accountable for the net profit or chargeable with the net loss.

4. T received $200,000 in Treasury securities in trust primarily for the educational and other needs of B, the trust to terminate, with distribution to B, when B reaches age 24. The terms of the trust direct T to retain the inception assets. Erroneously (thus, for example, with no grounds for deviation under § 66) believing that the law required the portfolio to be diversified, T liquidated some of the Treasury securities and used the proceeds to purchase shares of two mutual funds. Upon learning that the change in investments was a breach of trust, T redeemed the shares of one fund at a loss and of the second fund at a profit. The misconduct causing the loss and the misconduct causing the profit are properly treated as a single breach. B may hold T accountable only for the net profit or chargeable only with the net loss.

5. T received in trust the stock of X Co. and Y Co., neither of which was appropriate for the trust and its circumstances. X stock was performing extraordinarily well; Y stock was declining in value. Despite thereafter discovering that retention of these stocks was a breach of trust, T decided to retain them, rationalizing that the Y stock might recover, and that in any event the gain from X stock would likely outweigh a loss from Y stock. When the value of X stock began to level off, T sold both stocks, realizing a profit on X stock and a loss on Y stock. Because T intentionally committed the breaches, hoping that a profit from one would outweigh a loss from the other, the misconduct causing the profit and the misconduct causing the loss are not treated as a single breach. The beneficiaries are entitled to the full profit from X stock and to charge T for the full loss from Y stock.

§ 102. Liability of Multiple Trustees: Contribution

(1) Except as otherwise provided in this section, if two or more trustees are liable for a breach of trust, they are jointly and severally liable, with contribution rights and obligations between or among them reflecting their respective degrees of fault.

(2) A trustee who committed a breach in bad faith is not entitled to contribution unless the trustee or trustees from whom contribution is sought also acted in bad faith.

(3) A trustee who benefited personally from the breach is not entitled to contribution to the extent of that benefit.

General Comment:

a. Scope of section; cross-references. This section describes that aspect of the law of contribution resting on principles of trust law applicable to trustees who are jointly and severally liable for a breach of trust (see definition of "breach of trust" in § 93). Cf. Restatement Third, Restitution and Unjust Enrichment § 23 and id., Comment *a*. A beneficiary (or other plaintiff, such as a successor trustee or co-trustee) may compel complete redress of the breach by any one or more of the trustees who are jointly and severally liable. The allocation of ultimate liability between or among those trustees is determined by the contribution rules of this section.

It is important to distinguish the joint and several liability of co-trustees who participate in the same breach of trust from the separate liability of a successor trustee (see § 85, Comment *d*, and § 86) or co-trustee (see § 81, Comment *e*) who improperly neglects to seek redress. To the extent that failure to obtain redress is a breach of trust (see § 76, Comment *d*, and § 81, Comment *e*), it is distinct from the original breach, and the liability of the successor trustee or co-trustee in such a case is only for the harm caused by that failure. Neither joint and several liability nor the combination of these distinct breaches may result in collections by the trust of duplicative amounts.

On the effect of the terms of the trust on the existence or degree of trustee fault, see § 81, Comment *b*. Cf. Restatement Third, Restitution and Unjust Enrichment § 23, Comment *a* (on contractual provisions governing contribution). . . . .

Comment on Subsection (1):

b. Amount and manner of contribution. If a trustee has a right or duty of contribution under this section, the amount of the contribution is based on the trustees' respective degrees of fault (see Comments *b(1)-b(3)*). On the effect of a trustee's insolvency, see Comment *c*. . . . .

b(1). Substantially equally at fault. If the trustees are substantially equally at fault, each is entitled to equal contribution from the other(s). Thus, if two co-trustees participate in a breach of trust and are substantially equally at fault, one who makes good the breach is entitled to be reimbursed by the other for one-half of the liability. If three co-trustees participate in a breach of trust and are substantially equally at fault, one who makes good the breach is entitled to reimbursement from each of the others for one-third (thereby achieving a total contribution of two-thirds) of the liability.

b(2). Fault so disproportionate as to prevent contribution. If the fault between or among trustees is sufficiently disproportionate, a trustee who is significantly more at fault is not entitled to contribution, and the trustee(s) significantly less at fault are entitled to a full indemnity.

Whether the fault *is* sufficiently disproportionate to prevent contribution (or merit indemnity) depends on the facts and circumstances. Among the factors to be considered are the following: (1) Did one trustee mislead the other(s) into joining in the breach? (2) Did one trustee commit the breach intentionally (on the distinction between intentional and bad-faith breaches, see Comment *d*), while the other(s) did so by simple negligence? (3) Did one trustee, having greater experience or expertise, essentially control the actions of the other(s), such as where a trustee without business experience regularly relied on the judgment of the experienced trustee? (4) Did one trustee act essentially alone while the joint and several liability of the other(s) resulted merely from a failure to exercise reasonable care to prevent the breach or from improper delegation or monitoring? See generally § 81 and id., Comments *b–e*.

Illustration:

1. S devised her estate to T Co. and her brother B as trustees for her minor children. B is well acquainted with the beneficiaries and their needs but has little experience in financial matters and no experience in trust administration. Relying on T Co.'s reputation and expertise, B neglected to keep informed and to participate in or monitor the investment decisions of T Co. (cf. § 81, Comments *c* and *c(1)*). Imprudent investments by T Co. caused a loss to the trust estate. The degrees of fault of T Co. and B are sufficiently disproportionate that T Co. is not entitled to contribution from B. If B made good the loss or any part of it, he is entitled to full indemnity from T Co.

b(3). Fault neither substantially equal nor so disproportionate as to prevent contribution. If the fault of the trustees who are liable for a breach of trust is not substantially equal (Comment *b(1)*), but not so disproportionate as to prevent contribution (Comment *b(2)*), the trustees' contribution obligations are proportionate to their respective degrees of fault. Thus, if two trustees participate in a breach of trust and the one who has made good the breach is determined to be 75 percent at fault (considering factors generally similar to those described in Comment *b(2)*), that trustee is entitled to contribution from the other for 25 percent of the liability.

Illustration:

2. T1 and T2 are jointly and severally liable for a breach of trust. T1 made good the full $300,000 loss. It is determined that T2's degree of fault is double that of T1. T1 is entitled to contribution from T2 in the amount of $200,000.

c. Insolvency. To the extent that contribution cannot be obtained from an insolvent trustee, the other trustees with contribution rights and obligations share the insolvent trustee's liability, equally if they are substantially equally at fault (Comment *b(1)*) or proportionately if not (Comments *b(2)* and *b(3)*). For example, if three co-trustees are substantially equally at fault for participating in a breach of trust, the one who has made good the breach would ordinarily be entitled to equal contribution from each of the other two. If it is determined in an insolvency proceeding, however, that one of the two trustees from whom contribution is sought can pay only part or none of that obligation, then the two solvent trustees bear the uncollectable contribution liability equally.

Comment on Subsection (2):

d. Trustee acting in bad faith. A trustee who commits a breach of trust in bad faith is generally not entitled to contribution from another trustee who participated in the breach. There is an exception to this general rule, however. If a trustee from whom contribution is sought *also* acted in bad faith, contribution is required, with contribution rights and liabilities determined in accordance with Subsection (1). A bad-faith trustee may not hide behind another's unclean hands.

For purposes of Subsection (2) and this Comment, bad faith includes fraud, embezzlement, and other misconduct involving a dishonest motive or conscious disregard for the interests of the beneficiaries or the purposes of the trust. Intentional participation in a known breach of trust, however, does not necessarily entail bad faith. Thus, if trustees join in what they know to be a breach of trust, even one involving self-dealing, they do not act in bad faith if their objective is to advance the interests of the beneficiaries.

Comment on Subsection (3):

e. *Benefit received by trustee.* A trustee who receives a benefit from a breach of trust is not entitled to contribution from the other trustee(s) to the extent of the benefit received. The other(s) are entitled to exoneration to the same extent.

Illustration:

3. Co-trustees A and B purchased, for the trust, property owned by B, a breach of the duty of loyalty (see § 78, Comment *d*). The purchase price exceeded the property's fair market value by $50,000, resulting in a pecuniary benefit to B and a corresponding loss to the trust estate. As between A and B, B is liable for the full $50,000, with no contribution from A; and any of the loss made good by A would entitle A to indemnification from B.

CHAPTER 20

BENEFICIARY LIABILITY

Introductory Note: This chapter reflects generally well-established principles of beneficiary liability and limitations thereon. Section 103 concerns the potential personal liability of a trust beneficiary to a third party for an obligation incurred by the trustee in the course of trust administration. Section 104 addresses the potential personal liability of a beneficiary to the trust—that is, to the trustee in a representative capacity.

§ 103. Liability of Beneficiary to Third Party for Trust Obligation

A beneficiary is not personally liable to a third party for an obligation incurred by the trustee in the administration of the trust except:

(a) to the extent the beneficiary is personally liable to the trust under § 104; or

(b) as provided by other law, such as the law of contract, tort, or unjust enrichment.

Comment:

a. Scope of section. This section addresses the potential personal liability of a beneficiary to a third party for an obligation incurred by a trustee in the course of trust administration. This personal liability differs from the normal impairment of a beneficiary's interest in the trust by satisfaction of a third-party claim from the trust estate.

This section does not address the occasional circumstance of a trustee acting *also* as the beneficiary's agent. The topic of a principal's liability for an obligation incurred by an agent is considered in the Restatement Third, Agency, Chapters 6 and 7.

b. General rule. As a general rule, a beneficiary is not subject to personal liability to a third party for an obligation incurred by the trustee in the course of trust administration. Thus, a beneficiary ordinarily is not personally liable on a contract entered into, or for a tort committed by, the trustee or an agent of the trustee. Similarly, if a third party has a claim against the trustee based on the trustee's ownership of trust property, the third party ordinarily is not entitled to enforce the claim against a beneficiary personally.

c. Exceptions. Exceptions to the general no-personal-liability rule of this section apply (1) to the extent a beneficiary is personally liable to the trust under § 104 or (2) as provided by other law.

c(1). Beneficiary liable to trust. A beneficiary is personally liable to a third party for an obligation incurred by the trustee in the administration of the trust to the extent the beneficiary is personally liable to the trust under § 104. In such a case, the beneficiary's liability to the trust is a trust asset, which may be reached by the third party. For example, if the trustee contracts with a third party, and the third party is entitled to satisfaction from the trust property, and the beneficiary is liable to the trust under § 104 (a liability based, for instance, on unjust enrichment under id., Comment *g(3)*), the beneficiary is liable to the third party to the extent of the beneficiary's liability to the trust.

c(2). Beneficiary liable to third party under other law. A beneficiary is personally liable to a third party for an obligation incurred by the trustee in the administration of the trust to the extent provided by other law, such as the law of contract, tort, or unjust enrichment. For example, if a beneficiary agrees to indemnify a third party in the event of the trustee's nonperformance, and the trustee fails to perform, the beneficiary is liable to the third party to the extent provided by the law of contract. Similarly, if a beneficiary makes a fraudulent representation to a third party, inducing the third party to do business with the trustee and resulting in loss to the third party, the beneficiary is liable to the third party to the extent provided by the law of tort.

§ 104. Liability of Beneficiary to Trust

(1) A beneficiary is not personally liable to the trust except to the extent:

(a) of a loan or advance to the beneficiary from the trust;

(b) of the beneficiary's debt to the settlor that has been placed in the trust, unless the settlor manifested a contrary intention;

(c) the trust suffered a loss resulting from a breach of trust in which the beneficiary participated; or

(d) provided by other law, such as the law of contract, tort, or unjust enrichment.

(2) If a beneficiary is personally liable to the trust, the trust is entitled to a charge against the beneficiary's interest in the trust to secure the payment of the liability.

General Comment:

a. Scope of section. This section concerns the potential personal liability of a beneficiary to the trust (that is, to the trustee in a representative capacity; cf. Introductory Note to Chapter 21).

This section does not address the personal liability of a beneficiary to a trustee individually (that is, not in the trustee's representative capacity); in such a case, the trustee is in the same position as any other creditor of the beneficiary, there being no security interest in the beneficiary's interest in the trust except as effectively granted by the beneficiary (on the validity and effect of spendthrift restraints, see §§ 58 and 59).

Comment on Subsection (1):

b. General rule. As a general rule, a beneficiary is not personally liable to the trust for matters connected with trust administration. Subsection (1) of this section articulates this general rule.

c. Exceptions. Subsection (1) also articulates the exceptions to the general rule. A beneficiary is personally liable to the trust to the extent provided in Clauses (a)-(d) of Subsection (1) (see Comments *d–g*). If a beneficiary is personally liable to the trust, then the trust is entitled, as stated in Subsection (2), to a charge on the beneficiary's interest in the trust to secure the payment of the beneficiary's liability (see Comment *h*).

d. Loan or advance of trust property (Clause (a)). If the trustee makes a loan or advance of trust property to a beneficiary, the beneficiary ordinarily is personally liable to the trust for the unrepaid amount of the loan or advance. The nature and extent of the obligation, however, may be affected by the terms of the trust (see, e.g., § 50, Comment *d(6)*, and the final paragraph of id., Comment *f*, on a loan or advance as a permissible form of discretionary distribution).

e. Beneficiary's debt to settlor (Clause (b)). Unless the settlor manifested a contrary intention . . ., if a beneficiary owes a debt to a settlor and the debt has been placed in trust (commonly by the residuary clause of the settlor's will), the beneficiary ordinarily is personally liable to the trust for the unrepaid debt. The running of a statute of limitations might bar recovery from the beneficiary personally, however, leaving the debt enforceable only as an advancement or charge against the beneficiary's interest.

f. Loss resulting from breach of trust in which beneficiary participated (Clause (c)). A beneficiary owes a duty to the other beneficiaries not to participate in a breach of trust. If a beneficiary participates in a breach of trust, causing a loss to the trust (see the definition of "loss" in § 100, Comment *b*), the beneficiary is personally liable to the trust for all or part of the loss, as appropriate. (Cf. § 102, on contribution and indemnity.)

Certainly, the beneficiary participates in a breach of trust if the beneficiary performs, or joins in performing, an act the beneficiary knows is a breach. Otherwise, the question of what conduct of the beneficiary constitutes participation in a breach of trust is a question of degree. For example, a beneficiary has participated in a breach of trust if the beneficiary induced the misconduct knowing that it would or might be a breach of trust. However, mere knowledge of, or consent to, the breach, without more, is insufficient to constitute participation (though the beneficiary may be liable under the law of unjust enrichment for any resulting benefit received; also cf. § 97, barring suit by consenting beneficiary).

g. Liability to trust under other law (Clause (d)). In many instances, the personal liability of a beneficiary to the trust arises under other, perhaps overlapping, law, such as the law of contract, tort, or unjust enrichment.

g(1). Contract. A beneficiary may incur personal liability to the trust by contract. A common example of such a contract is an indemnification agreement by which the beneficiary agrees to reimburse the trust for a loss resulting from a risky course of action, and also perhaps to exonerate the trustee from liability if the conduct turns out to be a breach of trust. (Cf. § 97, on beneficiary consent, ratification, or release.) The nature of the fiduciary relation exposes such an agreement to special scrutiny (see § 78(3), and id., Comment *g*).

g(2). Tort. A beneficiary may incur personal liability to the trust under the law of tort. For example, if a beneficiary misappropriates trust property, causing a loss to the trust, the beneficiary is liable to the trust for the resulting loss. (On the definition of "loss," see § 100, Comment *b*.)

g(3). Unjust enrichment. A beneficiary may incur personal liability to the trust under various applications of the law of unjust enrichment. For example, if a beneficiary receives trust property to which the beneficiary is not entitled (whether or not (e.g., § 76, Comment *f*) resulting from a breach of trust, and without regard to whether the beneficiary knew the distribution was improper), the beneficiary is liable to the trust for the improper distribution, except to the extent that a defense to restitution applies. On defenses to restitution, see Restatement Third, Restitution and Unjust Enrichment §§ 62–70.

Comment on Subsection (2):

h. Charge on beneficiary's interest. If a beneficiary is personally liable to the trust, the trust is entitled, as stated in Subsection (2), to a charge against the beneficiary's interest in the trust to secure the payment of the liability. This rule applies even though the beneficiary's interest is subject to a spendthrift restraint (see § 59, Comment *a(2)*).

CHAPTER 21

LIABILITY OF TRUST OR TRUSTEE TO THIRD PARTY

Introductory Note: This chapter states now-prevalent doctrine in the United States reflecting common-law and statutory concepts as they have evolved since the Second Restatement of Trusts. Id. § 268, Comment *a*, succinctly stated the traditional approach to trustee liability to third parties:

> [A] person to whom a trustee had incurred a liability in the administration of the trust . . . could obtain a judgment against the trustee personally and obtain satisfaction out of the trustee's individual property, and the trustee could then obtain reimbursement from the trust estate, provided that the liability was properly incurred by the trustee and that he had committed no breach of trust.

Under this traditional approach, which may still apply in a few American jurisdictions and generally elsewhere in the common-law world, a trustee is personally liable on any contract made by the trustee, even if the trustee acted properly. Similarly, the trustee is personally liable for torts committed by the trustee or the trustee's agents or employees, without regard to whether the trustee is personally at fault. A trustee is entitled to indemnification from the trust estate if the trustee acted properly.

Commentators have long criticized the traditional approach as unfair to trustees whenever the trust estate is insufficient to provide full indemnity, and perhaps to third parties if the trustee's own assets are insufficient to satisfy all of the trustee's debts .... Reacting to these concerns, most American states . . . no longer follow the traditional rules. Under the modern approach adopted in this chapter, third parties may proceed against a trustee in the trustee's fiduciary ("representative") capacity whether or not the trustee is also personally liable, with the trustee shielded from personal liability insofar as the trustee acted properly.

The approach in §§ 105 and 106 recognizes modern reality rather than traditional concepts. Technically, the trust is still not generally recognized as a legal "entity," but it is generally for federal tax purposes, and in practice trustees act on behalf of their trusts and are sued as trust representatives. Indeed, in this chapter and elsewhere in this country, the trust is *treated* as an entity to such an extent that it is no longer inappropriate to refer to claims against or liabilities of a "trust" (as in the title and content of this chapter) and to the liability or debt of a beneficiary to a "trust" (as in Chapter 20), or to refer to and treat trusts, in law and in practice, as if they were entities in numerous other contexts. See particularly § 2, Comment *a* (second paragraph) .... See also Internal Revenue Code Subchapter J, as well as discussion throughout M. Carr Ferguson, James J. Freeland & Mark L. Ascher, Federal Income Taxation of Estates, Trusts, and Beneficiaries (3d ed. 1998 and supplements thereto).

§ 105. Claim Against Trust

A third party may assert a claim against a trust for a liability incurred in trust administration by proceeding against the trustee in the trustee's representative capacity, whether or not the trustee is personally liable (§ 106).

Comment:

a. Scope of section; cross-references. This section and § 106 address the liability of a trustee to a third party for obligations incurred in the administration of a trust. This section states a rule that is both procedural and substantive: claims against a trust may be asserted by proceeding against the trustee in a representative capacity. . . . . Section 106 states a related substantive rule: in appropriate circumstances, the trustee is insulated from personal liability.

This section does not preclude a third party from proceeding against a trustee in both the trustee's individual and representative capacities; in fact, this is frequently done (see Comment *c*).

On the possibility of beneficiary liability to third parties, see § 103. Nothing in this section creates a right in a third party to enforce a trust. See generally § 48, Comment *a*, and § 94.

b. Background; general rule. In administering trusts, trustees frequently incur liabilities to third parties. These liabilities may arise from a trustee's ownership or control of trust property or from contracts made, or torts committed, by the trustee or the trustee's agents (see § 80) or employees (on respondeat superior, see Restatement Third, Agency § 2.04). Historically, the trustee was sued personally by third parties and was personally liable for all liabilities incurred in the course of trust administration, with the trustee receiving indemnity from the trust to the extent the trustee acted properly and the trust estate was sufficient. The modern approach, reflected in this section and § 106, as well as in widespread legislation . . ., is to authorize suit against the trustee in the trustee's representative capacity (often also in an individual capacity, see Comment *c*) and to excuse the trustee from personal liability to the extent the trustee acted properly.

c. Suit against trustee in representative capacity. The rule stated in this section provides that a third party may sue a trust by bringing a proceeding against the trustee in the trustee's representative capacity. Claims appropriately asserted against the trust are for obligations allegedly arising from the trustee's administration of the trust. Thus, a third party may sue a trustee in the trustee's representative capacity on a contract entered into, or for a tort committed, by the trustee (or the trustee's agent or employee) in the course of trust administration. Similarly, a third party may sue a trustee in the trustee's representative capacity on claims, including claims for unjust enrichment, arising from the trustee's ownership or control of trust property. In each of these situations, the alleged liability arises in the trustee's representative capacity.

The rule stated in this section does not insulate a trustee from also being sued in an individual capacity (see Comment *a* and § 106). Plaintiffs may sue trustees in both individual and representative capacities, it frequently being unclear at the outset of litigation whether the facts will give rise to representative or individual liability. Questions of personal liability, fiduciary authority, and trustee fault are often best resolved in the same litigation. A third party may not, however, use individual and representative causes of action to recover duplicative amounts.

§ 106. Personal Liability of Trustee; Limitations

A trustee is personally liable:

(1) on a contract entered into in the course of trust administration only if:

(a) in so doing, the trustee committed a breach of trust; or

(b) the trustee's representative capacity was undisclosed and unknown to the third party; or

(c) the contract so provides;

(2) for a tort committed in the course of trust administration, or for an obligation arising from the trustee's ownership or control of trust property, only if the trustee is personally at fault.

Comment:

a. Scope of section; cross-references. This section and § 105 address the liability of a trustee to a third party for obligations incurred in the administration of the trust. Section 105 provides that claims against a trust may be asserted by proceeding against the trustee in a representative capacity. This section states a related substantive rule: the trustee is insulated from personal liability except in specified circumstances in which the trustee is personally at fault.

For background, see § 105, Comment *b*, and for additional cross-references, see id., Comment *a*.

b. Limitation on personal liability of trustee. The rule stated in this section provides that a trustee is personally liable for obligations arising in the course of trust administration only if the trustee, in some manner, has acted improperly in administering the trust, or has agreed to be liable.

b(1). Contract. A trustee is personally liable on a contract entered into in the trustee's representative capacity only if: the terms of the contract so provide; or the trustee's representative capacity was not disclosed or known to the third party; or the trustee, in entering into the contract, acted improperly either (i) by exceeding the scope of the trustee's authority (see, on the extent of a trustee's powers, § 70(a) and § 85, especially id., Comment *c(1)*) or (ii) by violating a fiduciary duty of the trustee in exercising an authorized power (see §§ 70(b) and 86).

Thus, unless otherwise provided in the contract, a trustee who properly enters into a contract with a third party and discloses that the trustee is acting in a representative capacity is not personally liable on the contract (there being no justifiable reliance on the trustee's personal credit). On the other hand, if the trustee's representative capacity is undisclosed and unknown to the third party, the trustee is personally liable on the contract though entitled to indemnity from the trust estate if the contract is otherwise proper. In this latter case, however, the trustee runs the risk that the trust might not have sufficient assets to provide full indemnification.

b(2). Tort. A trustee is personally liable for a tort committed in the course of trust administration only if the trustee is personally at fault. Thus, a trustee is not personally liable for a tort committed by the trustee's agent or employee where there is no personal fault on the part of the trustee. On liability of the trust (that is, the trustee in a representative capacity), however, see § 105, and id., Comment *b*; see also § 80, Comment *g*.

b(3). Obligation arising from ownership or control of trust property. A trustee is not personally liable for an obligation arising from the trustee's ownership or control of trust property provided the trustee is not personally at fault. For example, in the absence of the trustee's personal fault, the trustee is not liable individually for personal injuries occurring, or taxes imposed, on trust property, or for the expense of remedying the toxic or hazardous condition of trust property . . . .

CHAPTER 22

THIRD-PARTY LIABILITY TO TRUST

Introductory Note: This chapter addresses matters of third-party liability to a trust. Section 107 deals with the authority of a trustee (including a trustee ad litem), and the exceptional right of a beneficiary, to bring an action against a third party on behalf of the trust. Section 108 describes limitations on third-party liability to a trust.

§ 107. Proceeding Against a Third Party

(1) A trustee may maintain a proceeding against a third party on behalf of the trust and its beneficiaries.

(2) A beneficiary may maintain a proceeding related to the trust or its property against a third party only if:

> **(a) the beneficiary is in possession, or entitled to immediate distribution, of the trust property involved; or**
>
> **(b) the trustee is unable, unavailable, unsuitable, or improperly failing to protect the beneficiary's interest.**

(3) In appropriate circumstances, a trustee ad litem may be appointed to consider and, if appropriate, to maintain a proceeding against a third party on behalf of the trust and its beneficiaries.

General Comment:

a. Scope of section. This section addresses the authority of a trustee (including a trustee ad litem, see Comment *d*) or the right of a beneficiary to bring an action against a third party on behalf of the trust and its beneficiaries.

The rule of this section applies whenever third-party liability is alleged. Third-party liability may arise not only from trust law (e.g., from participation in a breach of trust) but also from other bodies of law, such as when a third party breaches a contract with a trustee or tortiously takes trust property or interferes with its use.

Limitations on third-party liability are considered in § 108.

Comment on Subsection (1):

b. General rule. As holder of the title to trust property (including choses in action), and as the representative of the trust and its beneficiaries, the trustee is normally the appropriate person to bring (and to decide whether to bring) an action against a third party on behalf of the trust. Except as provided in Subsection (2), a beneficiary has no standing to sue a third party on behalf of the trust.

b(1). Wrongdoing trustee: no estoppel. A trustee is not estopped from suing a third party, even if a loss or potential loss to the trust or an improper benefit to the third party is attributable to the trustee's misconduct. For example, an action to recover trust property transferred in breach of trust may be maintained against a third party by the very trustee who made the improper transfer. This is because, in suing the third party, the trustee acts not individually but in a representative capacity on behalf of the beneficiaries.

Comment on Subsection (2):

c. Beneficiary standing. Because the trustee is ordinarily the appropriate person to bring (and to decide whether to bring) an action against a third party on behalf of the trust, a beneficiary may maintain a proceeding relating to the trust or its property against a third party only in the following limited circumstances: (1) the beneficiary is in possession, or entitled to immediate distribution, of the trust property involved (Comment *c(1)*); or (2) the trustee is unable or unavailable, or improperly refuses or fails, or is not well suited to protect the beneficiaries' interests (Comment *c(2)*).

c(1). Possession of or right to trust property. A beneficiary may maintain a proceeding related to the trust or its property if the beneficiary is in possession of the trust property involved or is entitled to receive immediate distribution of it. For example, a beneficiary who, under the terms of the trust, is in possession of land held in the trust estate may bring an action of trespass against a third party who has wrongfully entered or damaged the land. Similarly, on termination of the trust or otherwise under its terms, a beneficiary who is entitled to immediate distribution of, for example, personal property may bring an action against a third party who has damaged that property or interfered with its delivery to the beneficiary.

c(2). Derivative action: trustee unavailable, etc. It bears repeating that the trustee, and not a beneficiary, is ordinarily the only proper person to bring (and to decide whether to bring) an action on behalf of the trust against a third party. The trustee may well decide, and rightly, not (or not yet) to bring an action. There are circumstances, however, when it is necessary for a beneficiary to act. If, for example, the beneficiary can show that the trustee is improperly refusing or neglecting to bring an action, or if the trustee is unavailable or unable to act, the protection of the trust estate may depend on the initiative of a beneficiary (including by seeking appointment of a trustee ad litem, see Comment *d*). Similarly, evidence that the trustee and the third party are committing or have committed a breach of trust may justify action by a beneficiary, as may a showing that the trustee is unsuitable to protect the beneficiaries because of the trustee's conflicting interests (see § 78, Comment *e*).

Comment on Subsection (3):

d. Trustee ad litem. Although a trustee is ordinarily the proper person to bring (and to decide whether to bring) a proceeding on behalf of a trust (Comment *b*), a court on its own motion or on application by a beneficiary, or even on application by the trustee . . ., may appoint a trustee ad litem . . . to act in the matter if the trustee is unable, failing or delaying, or not to be relied upon to bring a proceeding, for example because the trustee has a significant conflict of interests. The trustee ad litem's duties begin with independently evaluating whether the proceeding in question should be brought against the third party.

The appointment of a trustee ad litem is particularly useful in circumstances in which it may be unnecessary or premature, or the need for action too urgent, to remove and replace the trustee, even temporarily with respect to other aspects of administration, and in which the court finds it to be in the best interests of the beneficiaries and appropriate to the trust purposes to assure independent and disinterested decisions regarding the prosecution of the proceeding in question.

Additional General Comment:

e. Entitlement to recovery. A cause of action that may be brought on behalf of the trust is itself a trust asset, and any recovery ordinarily belongs to the trust estate, regardless of who prosecuted the action. Ordinarily, the trustee (or a successor) then either retains or distributes the amount recovered, in whole or in part, as appropriate to the terms and circumstances of the trust, although the court may allocate some or all of the amount recovered to one or more of the beneficiaries, to the extent the court has the information necessary to do so. (See § 100, Comment *a(2)*.)

f. Options for recovery where more than one potential defendant. Judicial economy is probably best served if a wrongdoing trustee and the third-party participant in that wrongdoing are joined in one action, but this is not a prerequisite to recovery on behalf of the trust. Thus, for example, the beneficiaries or one acting on their behalf may simply pursue the third party. The trust may not, however, use action(s) against multiple defendants to recover duplicative amounts.

§ 108. Limitation on Third-Party Liability

(1) A third party is protected from liability in dealing with or assisting a trustee who is committing a breach of trust if the third party does so without knowledge or reason to know that the trustee is acting improperly.

(2) A third party who acquires an interest in trust property through a breach of trust is entitled to retain or enforce the interest to the extent the third party is protected as a bona fide purchaser.

(3) In dealing with a trustee, a third party need not:

(a) inquire into the extent of the trustee's powers or the propriety of their exercise; or

(b) ensure that assets transferred to the trustee are properly applied to trust purposes.

General Comment:

a. Scope of section; cross-references. This section describes limitations on third-party liability. For a discussion of the occasions of third-party liability to a trust, see § 107, Comment *a*.

The limitations in Subsection (1) apply to third parties who assist or deal with a trustee without knowledge or reason to know that the trustee's conduct is improper, and Subsection (2) applies to third-party transferees protected as bona fide purchasers. Subsection (3) limits the responsibilities of a third party in dealing with a trustee.

Comment on Subsection (1):

b. Assisting trustee who is committing breach of trust. A third party dealing with or otherwise assisting a trustee who is committing a breach of trust, without knowledge or reason to know that the trustee's conduct is improper, is protected from liability as if the trustee's conduct were proper. For example, a bank is not liable for permitting a trustee to have access to the trust's safe-deposit box if the bank did not know or have reason to know that the trustee would misappropriate the box's contents.

Similarly, a third party who assists a former trustee without knowledge or reason to know that the trusteeship has terminated is protected from liability as if the former trustee were still a trustee.

Comment on Subsection (2):

c. *Bona fide purchase.* A third party who acquires an interest in trust property through a breach of trust is entitled to retain or enforce the interest to the extent the third party is protected as a bona fide purchaser. Thus, for example, one who purchases from a trustee a painting that the trustee was directed to retain in trust is entitled, free of trust, to keep the painting (or to obtain it through an action for specific performance) to the extent that the doctrine of bona fide purchase so provides. The doctrine applies to third-party transactions with a trustee (or with an agent, employee, or previous transferee of the trustee) to the same extent as it applies to transactions in other contexts.

The doctrine of bona fide purchase and the definition of a "bona fide purchaser" are addressed in other Restatements and in commercial law. See, e.g., Restatement Third, Restitution and Unjust Enrichment § 66 (purchaser-for-value rule, including discussion of good faith in id., Comment *d*), § 67 (creditor-as-"purchaser" issue), § 68 (defining value), and § 69 (defining notice, including knowledge and reason to know). . . . . See also Restatement Second, Contracts § 342 (successive assignees from the same assignor).

Restatement Third, Restitution and Unjust Enrichment § 66, Comment *f*, states: "The requirement that the purchaser complete the acquisition of legal title as a condition of protection has long been relaxed in favor of a purchaser who has acquired an indefeasible *right* to legal title . . ." (emphasis in original).

Comment on Subsection (3):

d. *No duty to inquire into trustee powers or application of assets.* A third party, in dealing with a trustee, need not inquire into the extent of the trustee's powers or the propriety of their exercise, nor is the third party responsible to see that assets transferred to the trustee will be properly applied to trust purposes. Knowledge of and compliance with the powers and duties of the trusteeship are responsibilities of the trustee, whose fiduciary obligations are enforceable by the beneficiaries. In modern law, third parties are ordinarily (Comment *b*) entitled to assume proper conduct by trustees with whom they deal. See generally §§ 70(a) and 85 (extent of trustee powers) and §§ 70(b) and 86 (trustee duties in exercising powers).

CHAPTER 23

ACCOUNTING FOR PRINCIPAL AND INCOME

Introductory Note: Fundamental change in prevailing principal-and-income accounting rules became inevitable with the widespread adoption of the Uniform Prudent Investor Act, which was promulgated in 1994 to offer a ready means of codifying the Restatement Third of Trusts investment principles. See generally Chapter 17, §§ 90–92 [originally §§ 227–229 in the 1992 Prudent Investor volume]. The "prudent investor rule" encourages trustees to invest for optimal total return (i.e., to make a reasonable effort to achieve the highest total return that is suitable to the trust's purposes and the circumstances of the trust and its beneficiaries, especially risk tolerance). See generally § 90. Yet, under many circumstances, the combination of traditional rules of principal-and-income accounting and the trustee's duty of impartiality, especially the element of income productivity (see § 79(2)), constrains the ability of trustees to invest for suitable total return.

Commentators recognized that, collectively, all beneficiaries of a trust would be expected to benefit if the investment and distribution functions were separated, so that the trustee could invest for an optimal total return and then make distribution decisions that would be reasonably appropriate to the terms and purposes of the trust and to the diverse present and future interests of the beneficiaries (i.e., decisions that would satisfy the § 79 duty of impartiality). . . . .

Legislatures responded. Forty-five states and the District of Columbia have now (2011) adopted all or portions of the 1997 Uniform Principal and Income Act, with its adjustment power (id. § 104) and the stated goal of harmonizing principal-and-income accounting with prudent investing. The Prefatory Note to the Uniform Act observes: "Revision is needed . . . to provide a means for implementing the transition to an investment regime based on [prudent investor] principles . . ., especially the principle of investing for total return rather than a certain level of 'income' as traditionally perceived in terms of interest, dividends, and rents." To serve essentially the same objective, 30 states now (2011) have some form of unitrust-conversion statute, usually as an alternative accompanying the adjustment power.

If trust "income" could affect the distribution rights of a beneficiary or the expenditures for a charitable purpose, § 109 requires the trustee to determine a tentative amount of income under § 110 (which this chapter refers to as "§ 110 income"). If the amount of § 110 income is inappropriately low or high in light of the duty of impartiality (as defined in § 79, Comment *b*), § 111 generally requires the trustee (to the extent empowered) to exercise an adjustment power (under Comment *b(1)* or *b(2)* of § 111) or a statutory election to convert the income right to a unitrust interest (§ 111, Comment *c*). See § 79, Comment *i*, regarding the power of equitable adjustment.

Section 111, Comment *a*, recognizes that a trustee who has a duty to achieve a level of income productivity that is "reasonably appropriate to the purposes of the trust and to the diverse present and future interests of its beneficiaries" (§ 79(2)) must satisfy that duty, one way or another. Therefore, if under governing law and the circumstances and purposes of the trust, the trustee does not reasonably expect to be able to adjust § 110 income or to make a unitrust election, then the trustee has a duty to pursue an investment strategy that is reasonably expected to yield an appropriate amount of § 110 income to satisfy the requirements of § 79(2).

This chapter does not include a comprehensive system of principal-and-income accounting. Every state plus the District of Columbia now has a statutory principal-and-income regime that provides detailed trust-accounting rules. Most of these statutes are based on the 1997 Uniform Principal and Income Act. . . . .

Although much of the discussion in this chapter refers to the income rights of beneficiaries, the rules and commentary apply as well to expenditures for charitable purposes based on trust income, except as superseded by statute (see § 109, Comment *b*, . . .).

Cross-references. On the trustee's duty of prudence, see § 77, and cf. § 86; on the duty of loyalty, see § 78; and on the duty to comply with trust terms and applicable law, see § 76, and cf. § 87 on the effects of trustee "discretion" in the exercise of powers. On the duty to maintain records and to furnish information to beneficiaries, see, respectively, § 83 and § 82. On the nature of the duty of impartiality, see § 79, and on the associated duty of income productivity, see § 79(2) and § 90, Comment *i*. With equitable adjustment, compare § 66 (equitable deviation).

§ 109. Duty to Account for Principal and Income

If the income of the accounting period could at any time affect the distribution rights of or expenditure requirements for a trust beneficiary or purpose, the trustee has a duty to account for principal and income in accordance with § 110; and, if the duty of impartiality is not then satisfied, the trustee has a duty to comply with § 111.

Comment:

a. *Scope and cross-references.* The duty to account for principal and income under this section applies to trusts described in Comment *b*. Sections 110 and 111 prescribe how that duty is to be implemented.

A trustee's compliance with this section will result in a determination of "§ 110 income" (i.e., trust-accounting income determined without adjustment or conversion under § 111). If the amount of this § 110 income is inappropriately low or high in light of the trustee's duty of impartiality (as defined in § 79, Comment *b*), § 111 generally requires the trustee (to the extent authorized) to exercise an adjustment power (under Comment *b(1)* or *b(2)* of § 111) or a statutory election to convert the income right to a unitrust interest (§ 111, Comment *c*).

Satisfying the duty of impartiality may not be as simple as to comply with § 110 and then, if necessary, to take appropriate action under § 111. In some situations, the trustee may not be authorized or willing (see § 111, Comment *b(1)*) to take action under § 111. In anticipation of such situations, the trustee has a duty (§ 79(2)) to *invest* with a goal of yielding a suitable amount of § 110 income. See generally § 111.

A trustee may need to maintain principal-and-income records for reasons other than compliance with this section. For example, trust-accounting income can be important in calculating distributable net income, which is fundamental in determining who is accountable for trust income for federal income-tax purposes, or for comparable reasons under state tax law. Also, a trustee who adjusts income or elects a unitrust conversion under § 111 must calculate § 110 income so that affected beneficiaries can determine the impact of the adjustment or conversion on their interests. See § 82.

b. *Trusts affected by "income" entitlements.* A prime example of where § 109 will apply is a trust to pay net income to B, remainder to others. See § 79(2). The income right may be of uncertain duration (e.g., B's lifetime) or of fixed duration (a stated or ascertainable term of years), or some combination of these (e.g., until B attains a specified age or sooner dies). The added fact that B may also receive principal in the trustee's discretion does not eliminate the duty because B has an unqualified right that is determined by trust-accounting income.

There will be many trusts to which § 109 does not apply. A prime example is a purely discretionary trust established by H to pay "such amounts of income or principal or both as the trustee determines appropriate to my wife, W, during her lifetime, remainder to my issue." Discretionary distribution rights (see § 50) that, with or without standards (e.g., "support") to guide the trustee, do not distinguish between income and principal sources are not subject to § 109. The result would be different, however, and § 109 would apply, if W's benefits had been limited to discretionary amounts of the trust's net income. See generally § 79, Comment *f*.

Illustrations:

1. W creates a trust to pay "such amounts of income or principal or both as T determines appropriate to any one or more of a group consisting of H and our issue, with remainder on H's death to our issue." Although this is a trust for successive beneficiaries, § 109 does not apply because its terms draw no distinction between distributions from income and from principal.

2. S's will leaves $500,000 to T in trust for the benefit of S's infant grandchild, G, with T to pay to or for the benefit of G "such amounts as necessary to provide for G's comfortable support and education until G reaches age 30," and then to distribute the trust estate to G; if G dies before that time, the trust is to terminate, with the trust estate to go to G's issue, if any, and if not, to others. No distinction being drawn between principal and income, the trust is not subject to § 109.

3. The same facts as in Illustration 2, except that the trust terms provide that G becomes entitled to all of the current income each year once she reaches the age of 21, and that upon reaching age 25 she is also to receive accumulated income (i.e., undistributed income from the initial period) in equal shares annually until termination of the trust when she reaches age 30. T not only is subject to § 109 after G reaches the age of 21 and is entitled to the current income, but in these facts T must also so account for income in the earlier period because of G's right (albeit conditional) to periodic distributions of accumulated income upon reaching the age of 25.

Section 109 does not apply to pure annuity trusts (e.g., a trust that provides solely for annual distributions in fixed-dollar amounts to L for life, with remainder thereafter to others) or to pure unitrusts the original terms of which provide solely for distributions to L in amounts equal to a fixed percent of the trust estate's value each year, with remainder to others at L's death. Section 109 would apply, however, if the terms of an annuity trust or unitrust include an income "ceiling" (i.e., limiting distributions to income) or "floor" (i.e., requiring distributions to be no less than income). See § 79, Comment *f*.

Section 109 also may apply to "split-interest" trusts for charitable and private purposes in succession, in either order. For example, a trust may provide for periodic distributions to an individual for life or a term of years with remainder to charity, or to charity for a period with remainder to family members. Although for tax reasons the lead interest in a split-interest trust is ordinarily a form of annuity or unitrust interest, in some such trusts the current distributions may come only from income (i.e., are subject to an income "ceiling"), so that § 109 would apply. . . . .

Illustrations:

4. S transfers land to T in trust, retaining the right to annual distributions for life in amounts equal to five percent of the trust estate valued annually. At S's death, the trust estate is to go outright to a named charity. (Such charitable remainder unitrusts ("CRUTs") are commonly used as one means of complying with I.R.C. § 664.) Because accounting for trust income would not affect any beneficial interest in the trust, § 109 does not apply.

5. The same facts as in Illustration 4, except that S includes a provision that limits the amount of any yearly distribution to the lesser of trust income and the five percent unitrust amount. (A likely reason for including such an income "ceiling" in this net-income charitable remainder unitrust, or "NICRUT," is to avoid forcing the trustee to sell the land or borrow money in order to make a required distribution to S.) Because the amount of trust income may affect S's distribution entitlements, § 109 applies.

The duty under § 109 may apply to a purely charitable trust not only when there are different charitable purposes in succession (e.g., a trust to pay its income to Charity A for 20 years and then to distribute its principal to Charity B), but also in a trust for a single charitable purpose in perpetuity (see § 79, Comment *h*).

Illustration:

6. S transfers property to T in trust, with instructions that T use only trust income to support a specifically described charitable activity in perpetuity. Section 109 applies because trust income limits the amount T may properly expend in any accounting period.

§ 110. Determining Principal and Income

Except as provided in § 111, a trustee fulfills the § 109 duty to account for principal and income by applying the terms of the trust and governing law, without adjustment, to the transactions and circumstances of the trust.

Comment:

a. In general. Every state has enacted principal-and-income accounting legislation that, absent contrary terms of the trust, trustees are to follow when determining the amount of "§ 110 income"—that is, the trust's net income determined without adjustment between the principal and income accounts, and without a unitrust election, all as discussed in § 111.

Principal-and-income accounting statutes and associated judicial precedents are default rules that may be preempted by the terms of a trust (Comment *b*). As elsewhere in this Part 6 (see Introductory Note to Part 6, preceding Chapter 14), the phrase "terms of the trust" refers to the settlor's intention "with respect to the trust provisions" manifested "in a manner that admits of its proof in judicial proceedings" (§ 4), as reformed (§ 62) or as modified by court decree (§§ 66, 67), by the settlor or others so empowered (§§ 63, 64, and cf. § 74), or by consent of all beneficiaries (§ 65).

The interaction of and potential conflict between trust terms and fiduciary law, and related limits on the power of a settlor, are considered generally in § 76, Comment *b(1)*, as well as in specific contexts elsewhere (e.g., §§ 77–84, 87, 90–92, and 96; and cf. § 50, Comment *c*). Although the principles there discussed do not limit the power of a settlor to direct specific departures from the default law of principal-and-income accounting (see Comment *b*), they do generally apply to discretionary powers (see Comments *c–c(3)*). For discussion of the limits of settlor power to modify fiduciary law, see § 78, Comment *c(2)*, § 87, Comment *d*, § 96, Comments *c* and *e* . . . .

a(1). Terms of trust or statute unclear. The meaning of a trust provision or statute may be unclear about, or the statute may fail to address, the proper accounting for a particular transaction or situation, with no precedent governing the matter and no statutory or instrument-granted discretionary power (Comment *c*) to resolve it. In these circumstances, the trustee may apply to the court for instructions (§ 71), as may especially be justified when the accounting issue is a recurring one, when its resolution will have a substantial impact on one or more of the beneficiaries, or when the rights of beneficiaries will be difficult to adjust if an initial accounting by the trustee is erroneous. It would normally be proper, however, for the trustee in circumstances of uncertainty to proceed without instruction to account in a manner that appears reasonable and fair to the affected beneficiaries and that seeks to reflect the terms and purposes of the trust and any relevant policies discernible from the jurisdiction's default law. On the trustee's duty in such cases to provide information or reports to beneficiaries, see §§ 82 and 83 and, on adequacy of disclosure, see § 83, Comment *c*.

In deciding how to proceed in a case of this type, the parties should be aware that the situation differs from one in which discretionary authority has been conferred upon the trustee to decide the accounting issue involved (Comment *c*). In the former situation, the proper interpretation of the trust or statute is ultimately a matter for the court, not the trustee, to decide, and without the deference to which a trustee's decision would be entitled with respect to an accounting matter over which the trustee holds an instrument-granted discretionary power—that is, in which a court is to substitute its judgment for the trustee's judgment only if the latter involved an abuse of discretion (see Comment *c(3)*, and, more generally, § 87).

b. Specific direction in terms of trust. If a trust provision instructs the trustee to account for a certain situation in a particular way, the trustee has a duty to follow the direction even though it conflicts with an otherwise-applicable statute or controlling precedent. . . . .

c. Discretion granted by terms of trust. Trust terms often confer discretionary powers on trustees with respect to matters of principal and income, perhaps in language that provides little guidance regarding the intended nature and scope of the authority or about any specific objective(s) the power is intended to serve. Issues sometimes arise concerning trustee conduct in allocating receipts or disbursements, or in other trust-accounting matters, and whether a particular action exceeds or otherwise constitutes an abuse of the trustee's authority. In such cases, the extent of a trustee's discretion under a provision of this type is a matter of interpretation. See generally § 87 on abuse of discretion; and compare § 50 (on discretionary power over distributions) and §§ 91, Comments *f–g(2)*, and 92, Comments *d–d(2)* (on grants of discretion in investment matters).

Some instruments grant discretionary powers that are limited to specified issues of principal-and-income accounting (Comment *c(1)*), and others confer broader authority to make decisions about principal-and-income issues more generally (Comment *c(2)*). Neither of these types of discretionary powers is the equivalent of a power to invade principal or accumulate income (cf. § 50), nor is the broader form of instrument-granted power normally interpreted as authority to make an overall adjustment between principal and income accounts of the type described in § 111 (see especially id., Comments *b–b(2)*). The trustee's exercise of discretion under either type of discretionary power is reviewable for abuse. See Comment *c(3)*.

c(1). Discretion granted for specific accounting matters. When the terms of a trust limit the scope of a discretionary power to specified trust-accounting issues (e.g., determining whether to allocate capital gains to income or principal, or whether to establish reserves for depreciation when the trust estate includes depreciating assets), the normal construction is that the settlor intended that the trustee exercise discretion in the specified matter(s) to accomplish the purposes of the trust, even though an otherwise-applicable statute calls for a different accounting treatment.

Illustration:

2. T is trustee of a trust to pay income to L for life, remainder to R. A provision of the trust specifically grants T the discretionary power to determine whether and to what extent stock dividends are to be allocated to income or principal; an otherwise-applicable statute provides that stock dividends are allocable to principal. Subject to review for abuse of discretion (Comment *c(3)*), T can properly allocate one or more stock dividends to income.

c(2). Discretion granted for accounting matters generally. When a grant of discretionary power is expressed in terms of principal-and-income accounting generally (even if subject to certain specified exceptions), it is readily inferred that the trustee is authorized to exercise discretion to resolve accounting uncertainties when statutory or decisional law fails to provide a clear answer. It is less clear whether and to what extent such a provision grants the trustee discretion to account for principal and income in a manner that is inconsistent with the otherwise-applicable rules. Normal construction for a provision of this type—particularly useful when "adjustment" or "conversion" under § 111 may not be available or desired—allows the exercise of discretion if the trustee reaches a reasonable judgment that the otherwise-applicable rule would produce, in the particular circumstances, a result that would be inequitable to one or more beneficiaries or detrimental to the accomplishment of a purpose of the trust. Again, however, the question is ultimately one of interpretation.

Illustration:

5. T is trustee of a trust to pay income to L for life, remainder to settlor's issue. An applicable statute provides that the trustee is to allocate to principal 90 percent of certain receipts from a private or commercial annuity, individual retirement account, or pension plan (e.g., 1997 Uniform Principal and Income Act § 409), but a trust provision authorizes T "to exercise its discretion in matters of principal-and-income accounting." T has received and will continue to receive distributions from settlor's pension plan. T can properly exercise its general discretionary power to deviate in a reasonable manner from the statutory rule if an allocation of 90 percent of these receipts to principal would produce a result that is inequitable to L or detrimental to the accomplishment of a purpose of the trust.

c(3). Discretion must not be abused. Whether an instrument limits a discretionary power to one or more specified types of accounting issues (Comment *c(1)*) or confers discretion with regard to principal-and-income accounting generally (Comment *c(2)*), the trustee is subject to the fiduciary duties and remedies that apply to the exercise of discretionary powers in general. See § 87. This is so even though the provision granting the power describes it in terms such as "absolute" or "sole and uncontrolled" discretion (id., Comment *d*, on extended discretion).

A court will interfere with a trustee's exercise, or nonexercise, of a discretionary trust-accounting power only to prevent abuse of discretion. Thus, judicial intervention is not warranted merely because the court would have exercised the discretion differently, but is appropriate only if the trustee's conduct was unreasonable, based on a misinterpretation of the terms of the trust, or otherwise inconsistent with the trustee's fiduciary duties (see, e.g., §§ 76–78, and especially § 79 on the duty of impartiality).

Further on what constitutes an abuse of discretion, see § 87, Comments *b–d*, and on the meaning of impartiality among successive beneficiaries, see § 79, Comments *b*, *c*, and *g*.

If there is uncertainty about the scope of a discretionary power or about other aspects of a trustee's trust-accounting duties, the trustee (or a beneficiary) may petition the court for instructions under § 71. One advantage of a grant of discretionary authority in principal-and-income matters, however, is that when default rules are unclear, or possibly unsatisfactory, the trustee ordinarily may make an initial determination without first obtaining instructions.

d. Relationship to § 111. Whether by following the default rules of principal-and-income accounting, complying with accounting directions in the terms of the trust, or exercising discretionary accounting authority, or some combination of these, the trustee of a trust described in § 109 has a duty to determine the amount of § 110 income before applying § 111, or despite having made a unitrust election.

§ 111. Duty to Distribute to Income Beneficiaries Amounts Appropriate to Duty of Impartiality

If trust income as determined under § 110 does not satisfy the trustee's duty of impartiality (as defined in § 79, Comment *b*), the trustee has a duty under this Section

(a) to exercise a statutory adjustment power or a statutory unitrust election, except as the trustee's authority or duty is limited by the statute, or

(b) to make an equitable adjustment, except as preempted or precluded by statute, or as limited by the terms, objectives, or circumstances of the trust.

Comment:

a. Rationale and cautionary note. A trustee has both a duty to invest prudently (§ 90) and a duty to act impartially (§ 79) in administering the trust. These duties, however, may conflict if the trust's level of income productivity affects the rights of any beneficiary. See Introductory Note to this chapter.

It is normally advantageous to beneficiaries collectively and therefore prudent for the trustee to seek a total return that is optimal in light of the trust's purposes and circumstances, especially the risk tolerance of the trust and its beneficiaries. But a significant aspect of the duty of impartiality in many trusts is the requirement (§ 79(2)) of suitable income productivity. The ideal way of reconciling these potentially conflicting responsibilities (see Introductory Note and § 79, Comment *i*) is to invest for optimal total return and, if necessary, to adjust principal and income (Comments *b–b(2)*) or to make a unitrust election (Comment *c*) in order to achieve an appropriate level of income productivity.

This section describes the accounting-related "tools" (Comments *b–c*) that are generally available to trustees for accomplishing the second step of this process. If a trustee expects not to be authorized, or is unwilling (see Comment *b(1)*), to use these tools, the trustee has a duty (§ 79(2)) to *invest* with a goal of producing a suitable amount of § 110 income.

On the inapplicability of this section to many trusts, see § 109, Comment *b*, ...

b. Power to adjust. When the trustee determines that § 110 income for the period is higher or lower than appropriate for the trust (see Comment *e* and § 79, Comments *b* and *g*; . . .), the trustee generally has the power and a duty to make an "adjustment" that increases or reduces the § 110 income, with an equal but opposite adjustment to the principal account. The power to adjust may be statutory (Comment *b(1)*) or based in common law (Comment *b(2)*), or it might be expressly conferred by the terms of the trust.

On the duty not to abuse authority under this section, see Comment *e*.

b(1). Statutory adjustment power; duty to exercise. Legislation in nearly all states grants an adjustment power to trustees under prescribed conditions that sometimes significantly limit the availability of the power . . ., and, except as expressly negated in some statutes (id.), imposes a duty on the trustee to exercise that power if necessary to satisfy the trustee's duty of impartiality.

Specifically, §§ 103 and 104 of the 1997 Uniform Principal and Income Act, which are the model for virtually all adjustment-power legislation, mandate that the trustee determine a tentative, pre-adjustment amount of income based on governing law and the terms of the trust, and that the trustee, if so empowered, adjust that tentative amount whenever necessary to achieve an appropriate (impartial) level of productivity. This is consistent with the present chapter; see Introductory Note and § 109, Comment *a*.

On the range of (and factors affecting) reasonable fiduciary judgment in such matters, see Comments *d–e*. On the trustee's duty to review the investment strategy and distribution plan periodically, see Comment *d* . . . .

b(2). Equitable adjustment. If the investment strategy pursued by a trustee fails to achieve a suitable level of productivity (§ 79, Comments *b* and *g*), the trustee who lacks a statutory power may nevertheless have a duty to adjust the entitlements of the beneficiaries to comply with the duty of impartiality (see § 79, Comment *i*). The trustee has a common-law power to do so—that is, a power of equitable adjustment—unless the power is prohibited by the terms of the trust or is preempted or precluded by statute. As a matter of preemption, for example, the common-law power normally is superseded by the enactment of a statutory adjustment power or a unitrust-conversion statute; or language in a traditional principal-and-income act might be interpreted as precluding equitable adjustment in this context.

In any event, a trustee is empowered to make an equitable adjustment only in a manner that is consistent with, and does not jeopardize, the purposes of the trust. For example, an adjustment that would pose a risk of adverse tax consequences . . . would ordinarily be impermissible without the assurance of a private revenue ruling. Cf. § 62, Comment *c*, and Restatement Third, Property (Wills and Other Donative Transfers) § 12.2.

c. Unitrust conversion. Many states have enacted statutes that permit a trustee to elect to convert an income right into a unitrust interest. A trustee who so elects will determine a beneficiary's income entitlements by applying, rather than the rules of principal-and-income accounting, a fixed percentage (the unitrust rate) to what typically is a rolling average of the trust estate's value for each of the past few years (usually three), thereby producing a proxy for trust income. Although the details of unitrust-conversion statutes vary somewhat . . ., most states allow the trustee to choose a unitrust rate ranging from three to five percent.

Several statutes authorize only the unitrust election, while many unitrust statutes also allow the trustee to use the adjustment power as an alternative (Comment *b(1)*). A trustee who has only the unitrust-conversion election has a duty (unless the statute states otherwise) to exercise that option when it is or can be expected to be needed to comply with the duty of impartiality (§ 79) and to facilitate prudent investing (§ 90 and see also § 77).

Whether the unitrust election is more desirable than periodic adjustments to § 110 income involves an exercise of fiduciary judgment. Except as limited by the terms of a statute, a trustee who has made a unitrust election should review that decision from time to time, and may, as warranted . . ., change the unitrust rate or terminate the election and rely on the adjustment power. . . . .

d. Determining and effectuating suitable level of productivity. For generations, long before adoption of the "tools" described in this section, trustees of trusts with income beneficiaries have routinely (if sometimes almost subconsciously) determined what would be an appropriate income-productivity target for the trust, and have invested the trust estate with an objective of achieving that goal. This section does not fundamentally change a trustee's duty to determine an appropriate level of income productivity for the trust. See generally § 79(2) and § 79, Comment *g*. Although modern principles of trust management generally free investment planning from the inhibitions traditionally imposed by rules of principal-and-income accounting, a trustee's distribution and investment decisions remain interrelated, with a special challenge often presented by trusts of modest size relative to the settlor's objectives. (This, incidentally, is also true of wholly discretionary trusts, despite § 109, Comment *b*.) This Comment and its Illustrations assume a trust that calls for "income" or "net income" to be distributed currently (id.).

Determining a suitable distribution or income level for such a trust is necessarily an inexact process, beginning with risk-return projections upon which a trustee's judgment about an optimal investment strategy is based (see generally § 90, Comments *e*, *e(1)*, and *g*). Impartiality analysis (see § 79, Comments *b* and *g*) then involves the further exercise of fiduciary judgment, seeking to balance competing interests and objectives based on any settlor preferences and priorities that may be discernible, by interpretation or inference, from the terms, purposes, and circumstances of the trust and from the nature of the beneficial interests. An "impartial" outcome in many situations will be one that properly reflects the settlor's intention that a particular purpose or the interests of a particular beneficiary (e.g., a surviving spouse) be given priority over others. All that can be expected of the trustee in these matters of judgment is to act reasonably, with competent advice as needed (§ 77, Comment *b*), in light of the purposes and circumstances of the trust and the trustee's fiduciary duties (§§ 76–79). See Comment *e*.

With an optimal-return investment strategy for the trust in mind, and an impartiality analysis that reveals no purpose or settlor preference that would favor one beneficiary or set of beneficiaries over another, the trustee has a duty to identify and implement a distribution level that is as high as the trustee reasonably believes will be sustainable. A "sustainable" distribution level is one that can reasonably be expected, over time, to preserve the inflation-adjusted value of the trust estate not only for the remainder beneficiaries, but also for the current beneficiary by maintaining the purchasing power of future distributions.

In some cases, however, a trustee's impartiality analysis will reveal that *less* than a maximum sustainable distribution level is appropriate to provide an impartial level of distributions suitable to the trust's objectives. In such circumstances, the trustee and beneficiaries can reasonably expect the real (inflation-adjusted) value of the trust estate to increase over time.

The more difficult "modest-trust" problem arises when an abstractly suitable distribution level (based, for example, on a primary purpose of enabling a life beneficiary to maintain an accustomed standard of living) *exceeds* a sustainable level. In such a case a serious "principal-depletion" risk arises, not only endangering the remainder interests but also increasing the risk that the trust estate could be exhausted during an income beneficiary's lifetime. Prudence may require that the settlor's objective and the beneficiary's expectations be scaled back. The trustee might instead consider investing for a total return higher than would otherwise be appropriate, based on "the purposes, terms, distribution requirements, and other circumstances of the trust" (§ 90), but prudence requires that the trustee take particular account of the risk-tolerance issue inherent in this alternative. . . . .

On the trustee's duty to inform beneficiaries, see § 82(1)(c), especially regarding the modest-trust problem and contemplated solutions.

The trustee has a duty periodically to review the distribution plan, considering any relevant changes in the circumstances of the trust and its beneficiaries, and to modify the targeted level of productivity as warranted. A modification may be warranted if the trustee concludes that the previous judgment was simply mistaken or if the circumstances of the beneficiaries or of the trust have changed significantly, perhaps because trusts often pass through various phases of purpose and emphasis, with different distribution requirements from one period of administration to another. A trust's distribution objectives may change, for example, if the income beneficiary retires, encounters major problems of uninsured illness, or enters a costly period of higher education. However, trustees should commit to a process and not make changes in investment or distribution objectives simply because trust investment performance for a given year exceeds or falls short of initial expectations. Volatility in investment performance is inevitable, especially with regard to the principal element of total return. Trust purposes, however, usually require that the trustee emphasize a stable level of income distributions (productivity).

The amount and stability of distributions to an income beneficiary tend to be fundamentally important considerations, as does the *long-term* preservation of the principal's purchasing power. Such considerations generally conflict, especially in the short term, but in the longer term protecting the real value of trust principal also protects the purchasing power of the income beneficiary's future distribution stream. See § 90, Comment *e(1)*. . . .

Illustrations:

1. T is the trustee of a trust to pay income to L for life, remainder to R or R's issue. T has authority to exercise an adjustment power (Comments *b–b(2)*). T properly determines that an appropriate long-term goal for the trust includes periodic distributions to L in maximum sustainable amounts (i.e., the highest amounts a prudent trustee could distribute periodically while reasonably expecting, over time, to maintain the purchasing power of the trust estate and the periodic distributions), and that this goal can be achieved by distributing monthly amounts to L that, in annual total, will be within the range of 3.7 to 4 percent of the trust estate's value as of the beginning of the year. (It would not be objectionable had T selected a specific rate (e.g., 3.8 percent) within this range . . . .) Rather than investing with a goal of achieving a 3.7 to 4 percent yield of § 110 income (cf. Illustration 3), T properly invests for an optimal total return (not expecting to yield the targeted level of productivity), and later adjusts the § 110 income to an amount within the 3.7 to 4 percent range. During the course of the year, T will make monthly distributions reflecting the targeted level, and make a final adjustment at the end of the year if necessary to achieve an appropriate level of productivity. The process results in corresponding adjustments to the principal account. Thus, if the trust's net total return for a year is 10 percent, after T has paid L the targeted amount, the trust's principal will have increased by the year's return reduced by the distributions (assuming no additional distributions under other provisions of the trust). If, instead, the total return for a year is negative one percent, the principal account will be reduced by one percent plus the total of the distributions to L.

2. Same trust as in Illustration 1, except that T has a statutory power to convert L's income right to a unitrust interest with a statutory rate range of three to five percent, and properly, based on T's impartiality analysis, selects a unitrust rate of 3.8 percent of the trust estate, valued as prescribed in the statute. T has a duty to invest for an optimal total return and to make appropriate distributions to L periodically in accordance with the unitrust formula.

3. Same trust as in Illustration 1, except that T has no authority to adjust income or to make a unitrust election. T has a duty to adopt a prudent investment strategy that is reasonably designed to yield a suitable amount of § 110 income (which may be below the 3.7 to 4.0 percent range in Illustration 1 because T in Illustration 3, rather than investing for an optimal total return, must invest with an objective of yielding an appropriate level of income).

In Illustration 3, if instead T had common-law authority to make an equitable adjustment (Comment *b(2)*), then, as in Illustration 1, T would have a duty to invest for an optimal total return and to make distributions to L within the 3.7 to 4 percent range. . . . .

e. Resolving uncertainty; abuse of discretion; cross-references. If there is reasonable doubt about whether a trustee has authority to make adjustments or a unitrust election, or about impartiality of distributions to an income beneficiary, the trustee or a beneficiary may petition the appropriate court, in a proceeding for instructions (§ 71), accounting (§ 83), or perhaps even equitable deviation (§ 66), for an order directing, authorizing, or preventing certain conduct, or even future conduct in similar circumstances. Cf. § 79, Comment *i*, ... Also, an informal arrangement, with properly informed consent by some or all beneficiaries (§ 97 and § 65), may facilitate administration and allow the trustee to proceed with a degree of comfort in matters of doubt.

A trustee's exercise or nonexercise of an adjustment power or unitrust election is subject to judicial review to assure compliance with the duty stated in the black letter of this section. Matters that are within the trustee's fiduciary judgment (see § 87, Comment *a*), such as establishing an optimal total-return strategy (§ 90) or a suitably impartial level of distributions (or perhaps § 110 income) for an income beneficiary (Comment *d*), are subject to judicial review for abuse of discretion (§ 87). In the absence of a finding of abuse, the court will not substitute its judgment for that of the trustee. On what constitutes an abuse of discretion, and on the range of (and factors affecting) reasonable fiduciary judgment in such matters, see § 87, Comments *b–d*; cf. § 86. Also cf. § 50, Comment *f* (and Illustration[ ] 9 . . .), on inferences that might be drawn from the relationships of beneficiaries to the settlor, and relationships among the beneficiaries, in making distributions among multiple discretionary beneficiaries.

On a trustee's duty to provide beneficiaries with information needed for the protection of their interests, see § 82 (but see id., Comment *e*, and § 83, Comment *d*). This duty suggests that trustees should maintain principal-and-income records that show not only § 110 income (§ 110, Comment *d*) but also the methodology used in impartiality analyses affecting adjustments or unitrust elections.

INDEX

References are to sections and comments

INDEX

INDEX

INDEX

INDEX